REFERENCE

S0-AXO-304

NOTABLE
TWENTIETH-CENTURY
SCIENTISTS

NOTABLE
TWENTIETH-CENTURY
SCIENTISTS

VOLUME 1   A-E

Emily J. McMurray, Editor

Jane Kelly Kosek and Roger M. Valade III, Associate Editors

*Ref
925
NOT
5/96*

 **Gale Research Inc.**

An International Thomson Publishing Company

I(T)P

NEW YORK • LONDON • BONN • BOSTON • DETROIT • MADRID
MELBOURNE • MEXICO CITY • PARIS • SINGAPORE • TOKYO
TORONTO • WASHINGTON • ALBANY NY • BELMONT CA • CINCINNATI OH

Editor
Emily J. McMurray

Production Editor
Donna Olendorf

Associate Editors
Joanna Brod
Pamela S. Dear
Kathleen J. Edgar
Marie Ellavich
David M. Galens
Jeff Hill
Denise E. Kasinec
Thomas F. McMahon
Jane Kelly Kosek
Mark F. Mikula
Mary L. Onorato
Scot Peacock
Terrie M. Rooney
Deborah A. Stanley
Aarti Dhawan Stephens
Brandon Trenz
Roger M. Valade III
Polly A. Vedder
Thomas Wiloch

Assistant Editors
John Jorgenson
Margaret Mazurkiewicz
Geri J. Speace
Linda Tidrick
Kathleen Wilson

Senior Editor
James G. Lesniak

Picture Permissions Supervisor
Margaret A. Chamberlain

Picture Permissions Assistant
Susan Brohman

Front Matter Design
Paul Lewon

Art Director
Cynthia Baldwin

Cover Design
Mark Howell

Library of Congress Cataloging-in-Publication Data

Notable twentieth century scientists / Emily J. McMurray, editor.
   p. cm.
   Includes bibliographical references and index
   ISBN 0-8103-9181-3 (set)
   1. Scientists—Biography—Dictionaries. 2. Engineers-
-Biography—Dictionaries. I. McMurray, Emily J., 1959-
Q141.N73 1995
509.2′2—dc20
[B]
              94-5263
              CIP

10 9 8 7 6 5 4 3 2

Contents

Introduction vii

Advisory Board xi

Contributors xii

Photo Credits xiii

Entry List xv

Chronology xxiii

Author Listings

    Volume 1: A-E 1

    Volume 2: F-K 607

    Volume 3: L-R 1153

    Volume 4: S-Z 1749

Selected Biographical Sources 2307

Field of Specialization Index 2309

Gender Index 2325

Nationality/Ethnicity Index 2333

Subject Index 2345

Introduction

Over the past several years, Gale Research Inc. has received numerous requests from librarians for a source providing biographies of scientists. *Notable Twentieth-Century Scientists* has been designed specifically to fill that niche. The four-volume set provides students, educators, librarians, researchers, and general readers with an affordable and comprehensive source of biographical information on approximately 1,300 scientists active in this century in all of the natural, physical, and applied sciences, including the traditionally studied subjects of astronomy, biology, botany, chemistry, earth science, mathematics, medicine, physics, technology, and zoology, as well as the more recently established and as yet sparsely covered fields of computer science, ecology, engineering, and environmental science. International in scope, *Notable Twentieth-Century Scientists* coverage ranges from the well-known scientific giants of the early century to contemporary scientists working at the cutting edge of discovery and knowledge.

Superior Coverage of Women, Minority and Non-Western Scientists

Addressing the growing interest in and demand for biographical information on women, minority and non-Western scientists, *Notable Twentieth-Century Scientists* also seeks to bring to light the achievements of more than 225 women scientists, almost 150 Asian American, African American, Hispanic American, and Native American scientists, and nearly 75 scientists from countries outside North America and Western Europe. The scarcity of published information on scientists representing these groups became evident during the compilation of this volume; as a result, information for many of the sketches on these listees has been obtained through telephone interviews and correspondence with the scientists themselves or with their universities, companies, laboratories, or families.

Though we have made every attempt to include key figures, we make no claim to having isolated the "most notable" women, minority, or non-Western scientists—an impossible goal. We are pleased that the majority of the biographies we wanted to feature are included; however, time constraints, space limitations, and research and interview availability prevented us from listing more scientists deserving of inclusion. Our hope is that in presenting these entries, we are providing a basis for future research on the lives and contributions of these important and historically marginalized segments of the scientific community.

Inclusion Criteria

A preliminary list of scientists was compiled from a wide variety of sources, including established reference works such as the *Dictionary of Scientific Biography*, history of science indexes, science periodicals, awards lists, and suggestions from organizations and associations. The advisory board, made up of librarians, academics, and individuals from scientific associations, evaluated the names and made suggestions for inclusion. Final selection of names to include was made by the editors on the basis of the following criteria:

- Discoveries, inventions, overall contributions, influence, and/or impact on scientific progress in the twentieth century
- Receipt of a major science award; all Nobel Prize winners in Physics, Chemistry, and Physiology or Medicine are found here, as are selected recipients of numerous other awards, including the Fields Medal (mathematics), Albert Lasker awards (medicine), the Tyler Prize (environmental science), the National Medal of Science, and the National Medal of Technology
- Involvement or influence in education, organizational leadership, or public policy
- Familiarity to the general public
- Notable "first" achievements, including degrees earned, positions held, or organizations founded; several listees involved in the first space flights are also included

Entries Provide Easy Access to Information

Entries are arranged alphabetically by surname. The typical *Notable Twentieth-Century Scientists* entry provides the following information:

- **Entry head**—offers an at-a-glance information: name, birth/death dates, nationality and primary field(s) of specialization.

- **Biographical essay**—ranges from 400 to 2500 words and provides basic biographical information [including date and place of birth, parents names and occupations, name(s) of spouse(s) and children, educational background and degrees earned, career positions, awards and honors earned] and scientific endeavors and achievements explained in prose accessible to high school students and readers without a scientific background. Intratextual headings within the essays highlight the significant events in the listee's life and career, allowing readers to find information they seek quickly and easily. In addition, **bold-faced** names in entries direct readers to entries on scientists' colleagues, predecessors, or contemporaries also found in *Notable Twentieth-Century Scientists*.

- **Selected Writings** by the Scientist section—lists representative publications, including important papers, textbooks, research works, autobiographies, lectures, etc.

- **Sources** section—provides citations of biographies, interviews, periodicals, obituaries, and other sources about the listee for readers seeking additional information.

Indexes Provide Numerous Points of Access

In addition to the complete list of scientists found at the beginning of each volume, readers seeking the names of additional individuals of a given country, heritage, gender, or profession can consult the following indexes at the end of volume 4 for additional listings:

- **Field of Specialization Index**—groups listees according to the scientific fields to which they have contributed
- **Gender Index**—provides lists of the women and men covered
- **Nationality/Ethnicity Index**—arranges listees by country of birth and/or citizenship and/or ethnic heritage
- Comprehensive **Subject Index**—provides volume and page references for scientists and scientific terms used in the text. Includes cross references.

Photos

Individuals in *Notable Twentieth-Century Scientists* come to life in the 394 photos of the scientists.

Acknowledgments

The editors would like to thank, in addition to the advisory board, the following individuals for their assistance with various aspects of the production of *Notable Twentieth-Century Scientists*: Bruce Seely, Secretary of the Society for the History of Technology and Professor at Michigan Technological University, Houghton, Michigan for his assistance in identifying notable engineers; Nancy Anderson, librarian at University of Illinois at Urbana Champaign Mathematics Library for assistance with mathematicians; Arthur Norberg, former director of the Charles Babbage Institute Center for the History of Information Processing at the University of Minnesota, Minneapolis, for assistance with computer scientists; and Kathleen Prestwidge for much assistance in identifying and providing information about minority and women scientists. Special acknowledgment is also due to Jim Kamp and Roger Valade for their technical assistance and to Denise Kasinec for her administrative assistance in the preparation of these volumes.

Advisory Board

Contributors

Russell Aiuto, Ethan E. Allen, Julie Anderson, Olga K. Anderson, Denise Adams Arnold, Nancy E. Bard, Dorothy Barnhouse, Jeffery Bass, Matthew A. Bille, Maurice Bleifeld, Michael Boersma, Barbara A. Branca, Hovey Brock, Valerie Brown, Leonard C. Bruno, Raymond E. Bullock, Marjorie Burgess, Gerard J. Buskes, Joseph Cain, Jill Carpenter, Dennis W. Cheek, Kim A. Cheek, Tom Chen, Miyoko Chu, Jane Stewart Cook, Kelly Otter Cooper, G. Scott Crawford, Tom Crawford, Karin Deck, Margaret DiCanio, Mindi Dickstein, Rowan L. Dordick, John Henry Dreyfuss, Thomas Drucker, Kala Dwarakanath, Marianne Fedunkiw, Martin R. Feldman, Eliseo Fernandez, George A. Ferrance, Jerome P. Ferrance, William T. Fletcher, David N. Ford, Karyn Hede George, Chris Hables Gray, Loretta Hall, Betsy Hanson, Robert M. Hawthorne, Jr., Elizabeth Henry, T. A. Heppenheimer, Frank Hertle, J. D. Hunley, Roger Jaffe, Jessica Jahiel, Jeanne Spriter James, J. Sydney Jones, D. George Joseph, Mark J. Kaiser, Lee Katterman, Sandra Katzman, Janet Kieffer Kelley, Evelyn B. Kelly, Karen S. Kelly, James Klockow, Susan E. Kolmer, Geeta Kothari, Jennifer Kramer, Marc Kusinitz, Roger D. Launius, Penelope Lawbaugh, Benedict A. Leerburger, Jeanne M. Lesinski, Linda Lewin, John E. Little, Pamela O. Long, C. D. Lord, Laura Mangan-Grenier, Gail B. C. Marsella, Liz Marshall, Renee D. Mastrocco, Patricia M. McAdams, William M. McBride, Mike McClure, Avril McDonald, Christopher McGrail, Kimberlyn McGrail, Donald J. McGraw, William J. McPeak, Carla Mecoli-Kamp, Leslie Mertz, Robert Messer, Philip Metcalfe, Fei Fei Wang Metzler, George A. Milite, Carol L. Moberg, Sally M. Moite, Patrick Moore, Paula M. Morin, M. C. Nagel, Margo Nash, Laura Newman, David E. Newton, F. C. Nicholson, Joan Oleck, Donna Olshansky, Nicholas Pease, Daniel Pendick, David Petechuk, Tom K. Phares, Devera Pine, Karl Preuss, Rayma Prince, Barbara J. Proujan, Amy M. Punke, Lewis Pyenson, Susan Sheets Pyenson, Jeff Raines, Mary Raum, Leslie Reinherz, Jordan P. Richman, Vita Richman, Francis Rogers, Terrie M. Romano, Daniel Rooney, Shari Rudavsky, Kathy Sammis, Karen Sands, Neeraja Sankaran, Joel Schwarz, Philip Duhan Segal, Alan R. Shepherd, Joel Simon, Michael Sims, Julian A. Smith, Linda Wasmer Smith, Lawrence Souder, Dorothy Spencer, John Spizzirri, David Sprinkle, Darwin H. Stapleton, Sharon F. Suer, Maureen L. Tan, Peter H. Taylor, Melinda Jardon Thach, Sebastian Thaler, R. F. Trimble, Cynthia Washam, Wallace Mack White, C. A. Williams, Katherine Williams, Nicholas S. Williamson, Philip K. Wilson, Rodolfo A. Windhausen, Karen Wilhelm, Karen Withem, Alexandra Witze, Cathleen M. Zucco.

Photo Credits

Photographs appearing in *Notable Twentieth-Century Scientists* were received from the following sources:

AP/Wide World Photos: **pp. 1, 31, 36, 38, 45, 48, 75, 98, 108, 112, 129, 150, 166, 169, 172, 174, 186, 192, 195, 198, 202, 203, 207, 211, 219, 221, 231, 234, 241, 278, 285, 295, 297, 299, 310, 313, 315, 321, 322, 326, 331, 341, 344, 348, 358, 373, 377, 388, 390, 397, 401, 402, 414, 417, 424, 434, 437, 441, 456, 476, 481, 484, 496, 503, 507, 516, 518, 529, 539, 541, 544, 550, 556, 565, 568, 573, 597, 613, 624, 628, 649, 657, 660, 668, 671, 675, 685, 702, 707, 709, 713, 722, 725, 744, 746, 756, 761, 763, 768, 771, 774, 778, 803, 806, 833, 835, 842, 853, 855, 877, 885, 890, 900, 932, 939, 949, 951, 959, 970, 986, 990, 1023, 1045, 1057, 1060, 1062, 1084, 1090, 1125, 1134, 1137, 1160, 1163, 1172, 1184, 1185, 1188, 1191, 1202, 1203, 1206, 1211, 1216, 1219, 1234, 1236, 1240, 1246, 1253, 1261, 1271, 1281, 1284, 1313, 1339, 1346, 1354, 1357, 1386, 1392, 1405, 1410, 1414, 1420, 1429, 1436, 1444, 1455, 1465, 1475, 1483, 1493, 1499, 1507, 1513, 1516, 1525, 1536, 1549, 1568, 1573, 1591, 1600, 1618, 1643, 1654, 1666, 1678, 1680, 1683, 1714, 1720, 1724, 1733, 1741, 1751, 1762, 1767, 1777, 1781, 1800, 1802, 1803, 1808, 1818, 1832, 1849, 1865, 1877, 1891, 1894, 1898, 1908, 1917, 1961, 1970, 1975, 2005, 2016, 2029, 2034, 2039, 2041, 2049, 2064, 2072, 2101, 2106, 2112, 2122, 2125, 2128, 2153, 2158, 2161, 2168, 2170, 2176, 2200, 2208, 2227, 2236, 2245, 2266, 2273, 2302, 2305;** The Bettmann Archive: **pp. 12, 426, 739, 925, 1037;** Courtesy of Keiiti Aki: **p. 14;** UPI/Bettmann: **pp. 58, 511, 546, 583, 751, 945, 1003, 1016;** Courtesy of Francisco Jose Ayala: **p. 80;** UPI/Bettmann Newsphotos: **pp. 83;** Archive Photos: **pp. 102, 523, 1040, 1210, 1769, 1990, 2132, 2276;** Courtesy of George Keith Batchelor: **pp. 124;** Photograph by Ingbert Gruttner, Courtesy of Arnold Beckman: **pp. 131;** Courtesy of Robert Arbuckle Berner: **p. 160;** Courtesy of Yvonne Brill: **p. 255;** Courtesy of Lester Brown: **p. 266;** Courtesy of Glenn W. Burton: **p. 283;** Courtesy of John R. Cairns: **p. 291;** The Granger Collection, New York: **pp. 304, 469, 652, 655, 1050, 1086, 1168, 1480, 1588, 1754, 1796, 2019, 2054;** New York University Medical Center Archives: **p. 355;** Courtesy of Stanley N. Cohen: **p. 379;** Courtesy of Rita R. Colwell: **p. 386;** Courtesy of Francisco Dallmeier: **p. 445;** Courtesy of Michael Ellis DeBakey: **p. 466;** Courtesy of Dennis Jack: **p. 489;** Courtesy of Nance K. Dicciani: **p. 495;** Courtesy of Theodor O. Diener: **p. 499;** Courtesy of Edsgar Dijkstra: **p. 501;** Archive/DPA: **pp. 513, 839, 1958;** Courtesy of Mildred Dresselhaus: **p. 521;** Courtesy of Cecile Hoover Edwards: **p. 559;** Courtesy of Helen T. Edwards: **p. 561;** Courtesy of the estate of Philo T. Farnsworth: **p. 609;** Courtesy of Lloyd Ferguson: **p. 622;** Courtesy of Solomon Fuller: **p. 710;** Courtesy of William Gates: **p. 733;** Courtesy of Adele Jean Goldberg: **p. 781;** Courtesy of Mary L. Good: **p. 796;** © Michael K. Nichols/Magnum Photos: **p. 798;** Courtesy of Govindjee: **p. 809;** Courtesy of Evelyn Granville: **p. 812;** Photograph by Washington University Photographic Services, Courtesy of Viktor Hamburger: **p. 851;** Courtesy of Wesley L. Harris, Sr.: **p. 868;** Courtesy of William Hewlett: **p. 918;** Photograph by Bradford Bachrach, Courtesy of Gladys Hobhy: **p. 935;** Archive/Express Newspapers: **pp. 937, 961;** Courtesy of Phillip G. Hubbard: **p. 967;** Courtesy of Russell Hulse: **p. 978;** Courtesy of Keiichi Itakura: **p. 998;** Courtesy of Frank B. Jewett: **p. 1021;** Courtesy of Barbara Crawford Johnson: **p. 1026;** Courtesy of Marvin M. Johnson: **p. 1032;** Courtesy of Harold S. Johnston: **p. 1036;** Courtesy of Yuet Wai Kan: **p. 1056;** Courtesy of Motoo Kimura: **p. 1097;** Courtesy of Georges Köhler: **p. 1117;** Courtesy of Thomas E. Kurtz: **p. 1147;** Courtesy of Raymond Kurzweil: **p. 1149;** Mary Evans Picture Library: **pp. 1178, 1462, 1637, 1829, 2027, 2119, 2138, 2250;** The Granger Collection: **p. 1197, 1640, 1737;** Courtesy of Susan E. Leeman: **p. 1213;** Courtesy of Carroll Leevy: **p. 1214;** © Leonard Freed/Magnum Photos: **p. 1222;** Courtesy of Aldo Leopold: **p. 1226;** Courtesy of Julian H. Lewis: **p. 1239;** Courtesy of Irene D. Long: **p. 1270;** © Dennis Stock/Magnum Photos: **p. 1277;** Courtesy of Stanford University Visual Services: **p. 1350;** Courtesy of Evangelia Micheli-Tzanakou: **p. 1370;** Courtesy of Elizabeth and James Miller: **p. 1376;** Courtesy of Stanley L. Miller: **p. 1379;** Courtesy of Beatrice Mintz: **p. 1394;** Courtesy of Russell Mittermeier: **p. 1397;** Courtesy of Robert N. Noyce: **p. 1491;** Courtesy of NASA: **p. 1497;** Courtesy of David Packard: **p. 1523;** Courtesy of Jennie Patrick: **p. 1535;** Brown Brothers, Sterling, Pa.: **pp. 1542, 1708, 1871, 1998,**

Entry List

A

Abelson, Philip Hauge
Adams, Roger
Adams, Walter Sydney
Adamson, Joy
Adrian, Edgar Douglas
Ahlfors, Lars V.
Aiken, Howard
Aki, Keiiti
Alcala, Jose
Alcorn, George Edward
Alder, Kurt
Aleksandrov, Pavel S.
Alexander, Archie Alphonso
Alexander, Hattie
Alexanderson, Ernst F. W.
Alfvén, Hannes Olof Gösta
Alikhanov, Abram Isaakovich
Allen, Jr., William E.
Altman, Sidney
Alvarez, Luis
Alvariño, Angeles
Amdahl, Gene M.
Ames, Bruce N.
Ammann, Othmar Hermann
Anders, Edward
Andersen, Dorothy
Anderson, Carl David
Anderson, Gloria L.
Anderson, Philip Warren
Anderson, W. French
Anfinsen, Christian Boehmer
Appleton, Edward
Arber, Agnes
Arber, Werner
Armstrong, Edwin Howard
Armstrong, Neil
Arrhenius, Svante August
Artin, Emil
Astbury, William
Aston, Francis W.
Atanasoff, John
Atiyah, Michael Francis
Auerbach, Charlotte
Avery, Oswald Theodore
Axelrod, Julius
Ayala, Francisco J.

Ayrton, Hertha

B

Baade, Walter
Bachrach, Howard L.
Backus, John
Baeyer, Johann Friedrich Wilhelm
    Adolf von
Baez, Albert V.
Bailey, Florence Merriam
Baird, John Logie
Baker, Alan
Baker, Sara Josephine
Baltimore, David
Banach, Stefan
Banks, Harvey Washington
Banting, Frederick G.
Bárány, Robert
Barber, Jr., Jesse B.
Bardeen, John
Barkla, Charles Glover
Barnard, Christiaan Neethling
Barnes, William Harry
Barr, Murray Llewellyn
Bartlett, Neil
Barton, Derek H. R.
Bascom, Florence
Basov, Nikolai
Batchelor, George
Bateson, William
Bayliss, William Maddock
Beadle, George Wells
Beckman, Arnold
Becquerel, Antoine-Henri
Bednorz, J. Georg
Begay, Fred
Behring, Emil von
Békésy, Georg von
Bell, Gordon
Bell Burnell, Jocelyn Susan
Beltrán, Enrique
Benacerraf, Baruj
Benzer, Seymour
Berg, Paul
Berger, Hans
Bergius, Friedrich

Bergström, Sune Karl
Berkowitz, Joan B.
Bernays, Paul
Berner, Robert A.
Bernstein, Dorothy Lewis
Berry, Leonidas Harris
Bers, Lipman
Best, Charles Herbert
Bethe, Hans
Bhabha, Homi Jehangir
Binnig, Gerd
Birkhoff, George David
Bishop, Alfred A.
Bishop, J. Michael
Bishop, Katharine Scott
Bjerknes, Jacob
Bjerknes, Vilhelm
Black, Davidson
Black, James
Blackburn, Elizabeth H.
Blackett, Patrick Maynard Stuart
Blackwell, David
Bloch, Felix
Bloch, Konrad
Blodgett, Katharine Burr
Bloembergen, Nicolaas
Bluford, Guion S.
Blumberg, Baruch Samuel
Bohr, Aage
Bohr, Niels
Bolin, Bert
Bondi, Hermann
Booker, Walter M.
Bordet, Jules
Borel, Émile
Borlaug, Norman
Born, Max
Bosch, Karl
Bose, Satyendranath
Bothe, Walther
Bott, Raoul
Bovet, Daniel
Bowie, William
Boyer, Herbert W.
Boykin, Otis
Brady, St. Elmo
Bragg, William Henry
Bragg, William Lawrence

Branson, Herman
Brattain, Walter Houser
Braun, Karl Ferdinand
Breit, Gregory
Brenner, Sydney
Bressani, Ricardo
Bridgman, Percy Williams
Brill, Yvonne Claeys
Bronk, Detlev Wulf
Brønsted, Johannes Nicolaus
Brooks, Ronald E.
Brouwer, Luitzen Egbertus Jan
Brown, Herbert C.
Brown, Lester R.
Brown, Michael S.
Brown, Rachel Fuller
Browne, Marjorie Lee
Bucher, Walter Herman
Buchner, Eduard
Bullard, Edward
Bundy, Robert F.
Burbidge, E. Margaret
Burbidge, Geoffrey
Burnet, Frank Macfarlane
Burton, Glenn W.
Bush, Vannevar
Butenandt, Adolf

Cairns, Jr., John
Calderón, Alberto P.
Caldicott, Helen
Callender, Clive O.
Calvin, Melvin
Cambra, Jessie G.
Canady, Alexa I.
Cannon, Annie Jump
Cantor, Georg
Cardona, Manuel
Cardozo, W. Warrick
Cardús, David
Carlson, Chester
Carothers, Wallace Hume
Carrel, Alexis
Carrier, Willis
Carruthers, George R.
Carson, Benjamin S.
Carson, Rachel
Carver, George Washington
Castro, George
Cech, Thomas R.
Chadwick, James
Chain, Ernst Boris
Chamberlain, Owen
Chamberlin, Thomas Chrowder
Chance, Britton
Chandrasekhar, Subrahmanyan
Chang, Min-Chueh
Chargaff, Erwin

Charpak, Georges
Chaudhari, Praveen
Cherenkov, Pavel A.
Chestnut, Harold
Chew, Geoffrey Foucar
Child, Charles Manning
Chinn, May Edward
Cho, Alfred Y.
Chu, Paul Ching-Wu
Church, Alonzo
Clarke, Edith
Claude, Albert
Claude, Georges
Clay, Jacob
Clay-Jolles, Tettje Clasina
Cloud, Preston
Cobb, Jewel Plummer
Cobb, William Montague
Cockcroft, John D.
Cohen, Paul
Cohen, Stanley
Cohen, Stanley N.
Cohn, Mildred
Cohn, Zanvil
Colmenares, Margarita
Colwell, Rita R.
Commoner, Barry
Compton, Arthur Holly
Conway, Lynn Ann
Conwell, Esther Marly
Cooke, Lloyd M.
Coolidge, William D.
Cooper, Leon
Corey, Elias James
Cori, Carl Ferdinand
Cori, Gerty T.
Cormack, Allan M.
Cornforth, John
Coulomb, Jean
Courant, Richard
Cournand, André F.
Cousteau, Jacques
Cowings, Patricia S.
Cox, Elbert Frank
Cox, Geraldine V.
Cox, Gertrude Mary
Cram, Donald J.
Cray, Seymour
Crick, Francis
Cronin, James W.
Crosby, Elizabeth Caroline
Crosthwait Jr., David Nelson
Curie, Marie
Curie, Pierre

Dale, Henry Hallett
Dalén, Nils
Dallmeier, Francisco

Dalrymple, G. Brent
Daly, Marie M.
Daly, Reginald Aldworth
Dam, Henrik
Daniels, Walter T.
Dantzig, George Bernard
Darden, Christine
Dart, Raymond A.
Dausset, Jean
Davis, Margaret B.
Davis, Marguerite
Davis, Jr., Raymond
Davisson, Clinton
DeBakey, Michael Ellis
de Broglie, Louis Victor
Debye, Peter
de Duvé, Christian
de Forest, Lee
de Gennes, Pierre-Gilles
Dehmelt, Hans
Deisenhofer, Johann
Delbrück, Max
Deligné, Pierre
Dennis, Jack B.
de Sitter, Willem
d'Hérelle, Félix
Diaz, Henry F.
Dicciani, Nance K.
Diels, Otto
Diener, Theodor Otto
Dijkstra, Edsger W.
Dirac, Paul
Djerassi, Carl
Dobzhansky, Theodosius
Doisy, Edward A.
Dole, Vincent P.
Domagk, Gerhard
Donaldson, Simon
Douglas, Donald W.
Draper, Charles Stark
Dresselhaus, Mildred S.
Drew, Charles R.
Drucker, Daniel Charles
Dubois, Eugène
Dubos, René
Dulbecco, Renato
Durand, William F.
Durrell, Gerald
du Vigneaud, Vincent
Dyson, Freeman J.

Earle, Sylvia A.
Eccles, John C.
Eckert, J. Presper
Eddington, Arthur Stanley
Edelman, Gerald M.
Edgerton, Harold
Edinger, Tilly

Edison, Thomas Alva
Edwards, Cecile Hoover
Edwards, Helen T.
Ehrenfest, Paul
Ehrenfest-Afanaseva, Tatiana
Ehrlich, Paul
Ehrlich, Paul R.
Eigen, Manfred
Eijkman, Christiaan
Einstein, Albert
Einthoven, Willem
Eisner, Thomas
Eldredge, Niles
Elion, Gertrude Belle
El-Sayed, Mostafa Amr
Elton, Charles
Emerson, Gladys Anderson
Enders, John F.
Engler, Adolph Gustav Heinrich
Enskog, David
Erlanger, Joseph
Ernst, Richard R.
Esaki, Leo
Esau, Katherine
Estrin, Thelma
Euler, Ulf von
Euler-Chelpin, Hans von
Evans, Alice
Evans, James C.

Faber, Sandra M.
Farnsworth, Philo T.
Farquhar, Marilyn G.
Farr, Wanda K.
Fauci, Anthony S.
Favaloro, René Geronimo
Fedoroff, Nina V.
Feigenbaum, Edward A.
Feigenbaum, Mitchell
Fell, Honor Bridget
Ferguson, Lloyd N.
Fermi, Enrico
Fersman, Aleksandr Evgenievich
Feynman, Richard P.
Fibiger, Johannes
Fieser, Louis
Fieser, Mary Peters
Fischer, Edmond H.
Fischer, Emil
Fischer, Ernst Otto
Fischer, Hans
Fisher, Elizabeth F.
Fisher, Ronald A.
Fitch, Val Logsdon
Fitzroy, Nancy D.
Fleming, Alexander
Fleming, John Ambrose
Flexner, Simon

Florey, Howard Walter
Flory, Paul
Flügge-Lotz, Irmgard
Fokker, Anthony H. G.
Forbush, Scott Ellsworth
Ford, Henry
Forrester, Jay W.
Forssmann, Werner
Fossey, Dian
Fowler, William A.
Fox, Sidney W.
Fraenkel, Abraham Adolf
Fraenkel-Conrat, Heinz
Franck, James
Frank, Il'ya
Franklin, Rosalind Elsie
Fraser-Reid, Bertram Oliver
Fréchet, Maurice
Freedman, Michael H.
Frenkel, Yakov Ilyich
Friedman, Jerome
Friedmann, Aleksandr A.
Friend, Charlotte
Frisch, Karl von
Frisch, Otto Robert
Fujita, Tetsuya Theodore
Fukui, Kenichi
Fuller, Solomon

Gabor, Dennis
Gadgil, Madhav
Gadgil, Sulochana
Gagarin, Yuri A.
Gajdusek, D. Carleton
Gallo, Robert C.
Gamow, George
Gardner, Julia Anna
Garrod, Archibald
Gasser, Herbert Spencer
Gates, Bill
Gates, Jr., Sylvester James
Gaviola, Enrique
Gayle, Helene Doris
Geiger, Hans
Geiringer, Hilda
Geller, Margaret Joan
Gell-Mann, Murray
Ghiorso, Albert
Giacconi, Riccardo
Giaever, Ivar
Giauque, William F.
Gibbs, William Francis
Giblett, Eloise R.
Gilbert, Walter
Gilbreth, Frank
Gilbreth, Lillian
Glaser, Donald
Glashow, Sheldon Lee

Glenn, Jr., John H.
Goddard, Robert H.
Gödel, Kurt Friedrich
Goeppert-Mayer, Maria
Goethals, George W.
Gold, Thomas
Goldberg, Adele
Goldmark, Peter Carl
Goldring, Winifred
Goldschmidt, Richard B.
Goldschmidt, Victor
Goldstein, Avram
Goldstein, Joseph L.
Golgi, Camillo
Good, Mary L.
Goodall, Jane
Goudsmit, Samuel A.
Gould, Stephen Jay
Gourdine, Meredith Charles
Gourneau, Dwight
Govindjee
Granit, Ragnar Arthur
Granville, Evelyn Boyd
Greatbatch, Wilson
Greenewalt, Crawford H.
Griffith, Frederick
Grignard, François Auguste Victor
Gross, Carol
Grothendieck, Alexander
Groves, Leslie Richard
Guillaume, Charles-Edouard
Guillemin, Roger
Gullstrand, Allvar
Gutenberg, Beno
Guth, Alan
Gutierrez, Orlando A.

Haagen-Smit, A. J.
Haber, Fritz
Hadamard, Jacques
Hahn, Otto
Haldane, John Burdon Sanderson
Hale, George Ellery
Hall, Lloyd Augustus
Hamburger, Viktor
Hamilton, Alice
Hanafusa, Hidesaburo
Hannah, Marc R.
Hansen, James
Harden, Arthur
Hardy, Alister C.
Hardy, Godfrey Harold
Hardy, Harriet
Harmon, E'lise F.
Harris, Cyril
Harris, Wesley L.
Hartline, Haldan Keffer
Hassel, Odd

Hauptman, Herbert A.
Hausdorff, Felix
Hawking, Stephen
Hawkins, W. Lincoln
Haworth, Walter
Hay, Elizabeth D.
Hazen, Elizabeth Lee
Healy, Bernadine
Heimlich, Henry Jay
Heinkel, Ernst
Heisenberg, Werner Karl
Hench, Philip Showalter
Henderson, Cornelius Langston
Henry, John Edward
Henry, Warren Elliott
Herschbach, Dudley R.
Hershey, Alfred Day
Hertz, Gustav
Hertzsprung, Ejnar
Herzberg, Gerhard
Herzenberg, Caroline L.
Hess, Harry Hammond
Hess, Victor
Hess, Walter Rudolf
Hevesy, Georg von
Hewish, Antony
Hewlett, William
Heymans, Corneille Jean-François
Heyrovský, Jaroslav
Hicks, Beatrice
Hilbert, David
Hill, Archibald V.
Hill, Henry A.
Hinshelwood, Cyril N.
Hinton, William Augustus
Hitchings, George H.
Hobby, Gladys Lounsbury
Hodgkin, Alan Lloyd
Hodgkin, Dorothy Crowfoot
Hoffmann, Roald
Hofstadter, Robert
Hogg, Helen Sawyer
Holley, Robert William
Holmes, Arthur
Hopkins, Frederick Gowland
Hopper, Grace
Horn, Michael Hastings
Horstmann, Dorothy Millicent
Houdry, Eugene
Hounsfield, Godfrey
Houssay, Bernardo
Hoyle, Fred
Hrdlička, Aleš
Huang, Alice Shih-hou
Hubbard, Philip G.
Hubbert, M. King
Hubble, Edwin
Hubel, David H.
Huber, Robert
Huggins, Charles B.
Hulse, Russell A.
Humason, Milton L.

Hunsaker, Jerome C.
Hutchinson, G. Evelyn
Huxley, Andrew Fielding
Huxley, Julian
Hyde, Ida H.
Hyman, Libbie Henrietta

Imes, Elmer Samuel
Ioffe, Abram F.
Isaacs, Alick
Itakura, Keiichi
Iverson, F. Kenneth

Jackson, Shirley Ann
Jacob, François
Jansky, Karl
Janzen, Dan
Jarvik, Robert K.
Jason, Robert S.
Jeffreys, Harold
Jeffries, Zay
Jemison, Mae C.
Jensen, J. Hans D.
Jerne, Niels K.
Jewett, Frank Baldwin
Jobs, Steven
Johannsen, Wilhelm Ludvig
Johnson, Barbara Crawford
Johnson, Clarence L.
Johnson, Jr., John B.
Johnson, Joseph Lealand
Johnson, Katherine Coleman
  Goble
Johnson, Marvin M.
Johnson, Virginia E.
Johnston, Harold S.
Joliot-Curie, Frédéric
Joliot-Curie, Irène
Jones, Fred
Jones, Mary Ellen
Josephson, Brian D.
Julian, Percy Lavon
Juran, Joseph M.
Just, Ernest Everett

Kamerlingh Onnes, Heike
Kan, Yuet Wai
Kapitsa, Pyotr
Kapitza, Pyotor Leonidovich
  See Kapitsa, Pyotr
Karle, Isabella
Karle, Jerome

Karlin, Samuel
Karrer, Paul
Kastler, Alfred
Kates, Robert W.
Kato, Tosio
Katz, Bernard
Katz, Donald L.
Kay, Alan C.
Keith, Arthur
Kelsey, Frances Oldham
Kemeny, John G.
Kendall, Edward C.
Kendall, Henry W.
Kendrew, John
Kettering, Charles Franklin
Kettlewell, Bernard
Khorana, Har Gobind
Khush, Gurdev S.
Kilburn, Thomas M.
Kilby, Jack St. Clair
Kimura, Motoo
Kinoshita, Toichiro
Kinsey, Alfred
Kirouac, Conrad
  See Marie-Victorin, Frère
Kishimoto, Tadamitsu
Kistiakowsky, George B.
Kittrell, Flemmie Pansy
Klug, Aaron
Knopf, Eleanora Bliss
Knudsen, William Claire
Knuth, Donald E.
Koch, Robert
Kocher, Theodor
Kodaira, Kunihiko
Kohler, Georges
Kolff, Willem Johan
Kolmogorov, Andrey Nikolayevich
Kolthoff, Izaak Maurits
Konishi, Masakazu
Kornberg, Arthur
Korolyov, Sergei
Kossel, Albrecht
Kountz, Samuel L.
Krebs, Edwin G.
Krebs, Hans Adolf
Krim, Mathilde
Krogh, August
Kuhlmann-Wilsdorf, Doris
Kuhn, Richard
Kuiper, Gerard Peter
Kurchatov, Igor
Kurtz, Thomas Eugene
Kurzweil, Raymond
Kusch, Polycarp

Ladd-Franklin, Christine
Lamb, Jr., Willis E.
Lancaster, Cleo

Lancefield, Rebecca Craighill
Land, Edwin H.
Landau, Lev Davidovich
Landsberg, Helmut E.
Landsteiner, Karl
Langevin, Paul
Langmuir, Irving
Latimer, Lewis H.
Lattes, C. M. G.
Laub, Jakob Johann
Laue, Max von
Lauterbur, Paul C.
Laveran, Alphonse
Lawless, Theodore K.
Lawrence, Ernest Orlando
Leakey, Louis
Leakey, Mary
Leakey, Richard E.
Leavitt, Henrietta
Le Beau, Désirée
Lebesgue, Henri
Le Cadet, Georges
Leder, Philip
Lederberg, Joshua
Lederman, Leon Max
Lee, Raphael C.
Lee, Tsung-Dao
Lee, Yuan T.
Leeman, Susan E.
Leevy, Carroll
Leffall, Jr., LaSalle D.
Lehmann, Inge
Lehn, Jean-Marie
Leloir, Luis F.
Lemaître, Georges
Lenard, Philipp E. A. von
Leopold, Aldo
Leopold, Estella Bergere
Leopold, Luna
Lester, Jr., William Alexander
Levi-Civita, Tullio
Levi-Montalcini, Rita
Lewis, Gilbert Newton
Lewis, Julian Herman
Lewis, Warren K.
Li, Ching Chun
Li, Choh Hao
Libby, Willard F.
Liepmann, Hans Wolfgang
Lillie, Frank Rattray
Lim, Robert K. S.
Lin, Chia-Chiao
Lipmann, Fritz
Lippmann, Gabriel
Lipscomb, Jr., William Nunn
Little, Arthur D.
Lizhi, Fang
Lloyd, Ruth Smith
Loeb, Jacques
Loewi, Otto
Logan, Myra A.
London, Fritz

Long, Irene D.
Lonsdale, Kathleen
Lord Rayleigh
    See Strutt, John William
Lorentz, Hendrik Antoon
Lorenz, Edward N.
Lorenz, Konrad
Lovelock, James E.
Luria, Salvador Edward
Lwoff, André
Lynen, Feodor
Lynk, Miles Vandahurst

M

Maathai, Wangari
MacArthur, Robert H.
Macdonald, Eleanor Josephine
MacDonald, Gordon
MacGill, Elsie Gregory
Mac Lane, Saunders
MacLeod, Colin Munro
Macleod, John James Rickard
Maillart, Robert
Maiman, Theodore
Maloney, Arnold Hamilton
Mandelbrot, Benoit B.
Mandel'shtam, Leonid Isaakovich
Manton, Sidnie Milana
Marchbanks, Jr., Vance H.
Marconi, Guglielmo
Marcus, Rudolph A.
Margulis, Gregori Aleksandrovitch
Margulis, Lynn
Marie-Victorin, Frère
Markov, Andrei Andreevich
Martin, A. J. P.
Massevitch, Alla G.
Massey, Walter E.
Massie, Samuel P.
Masters, William Howell
Matthews, Alva T.
Matuyama, Motonori
Mauchly, John William
Maunder, Annie Russell
Maury, Antonia
Maury, Carlotta Joaquina
Maynard Smith, John
Mayr, Ernst
McAfee, Walter S.
McCarthy, John
McCarty, Maclyn
McClintock, Barbara
McCollum, Elmer Verner
McConnell, Harden
McMillan, Edwin M.
Medawar, Peter Brian
Meitner, Lise
Mendenhall, Dorothy Reed
Merrifield, R. Bruce

Meselson, Matthew
Metchnikoff, Élie
Meyerhof, Otto
Michel, Hartmut
Micheli-Tzanakou, Evangelia
Michelson, Albert
Midgley, Jr., Thomas
Miller, Elizabeth C. and James A.
Miller, Stanley Lloyd
Millikan, Robert A.
Milne, Edward Arthur
Milnor, John
Milstein, César
Minkowski, Hermann
Minkowski, Rudolph
Minot, George Richards
Minsky, Marvin
Mintz, Beatrice
Mitchell, Peter D.
Mittermeier, Russell
Mohorovičić, Andrija
Moissan, Henri
Molina, Mario
Moniz, Egas
Monod, Jacques Lucien
Montagnier, Luc
Moore, Charlotte E.
Moore, Raymond Cecil
Moore, Ruth
Moore, Stanford
Morawetz, Cathleen Synge
Morgan, Arthur E.
Morgan, Garrett A.
Morgan, Thomas Hunt
Mori, Shigefumi
Morley, Edward Williams
Morrison, Philip
Moseley, Henry Gwyn Jeffreys
Mössbauer, Rudolf
Mott, Nevill Francis
Mottelson, Ben R.
Moulton, Forest Ray
Muller, Hermann Joseph
Müller, K. Alex
Müller, Paul
Mulliken, Robert S.
Mullis, Kary
Munk, Walter
Murphy, William P.
Murray, Joseph E.

N

Nabrit, Samuel Milton
Nagata, Takesi
Nambu, Yoichiro
Nathans, Daniel
Natta, Giulio
Neal, Homer Alfred
Néel, Louis

Neher, Erwin
Nernst, Walther
Neufeld, Elizabeth F.
Newell, Allen
Newell, Norman Dennis
Nice, Margaret Morse
Nichols, Roberta J.
Nicolle, Charles J. H.
Nier, Alfred O. C.
Nirenberg, Marshall Warren
Nishizawa, Jun-ichi
Nishizuka, Yasutomi
Noble, G. K.
Noddack, Ida Tacke
Noether, Emmy
Noguchi, Hideyo
Nomura, Masayasu
Norrish, Ronald G. W.
Northrop, John Howard
Novikov, Sergei
Noyce, Robert

Oberth, Hermann
Ocampo, Adriana C.
Ochoa, Ellen
Ochoa, Severo
Odum, Eugene Pleasants
Odum, Howard T.
Ogilvie, Ida H.
Olden, Kenneth
Oldham, Richard Dixon
Onnes, Heike Kamerlingh
    See Kamerlingh Onnes, Heike
Onsager, Lars
Oort, Jan Hendrik
Oparin, Aleksandr Ivanovich
Oppenheimer, J. Robert
Osborn, Mary J.
Osterbrock, Donald E.
Ostwald, Friedrich Wilhelm

Packard, David
Palade, George
Panajiotatou, Angeliki
Panofsky, Wolfgang K. H.
Papanicolaou, George
Pardue, Mary Lou
Parker, Charles Stewart
Parsons, John T.
Patrick, Jennie R.
Patrick, Ruth
Patterson, Claire
Patterson, Frederick Douglass
Paul, Wolfgang

Pauli, Wolfgang
Pauling, Linus
Pavlov, Ivan Petrovich
Payne-Gaposchkin, Cecilia
Peano, Giuseppe
Pearson, Karl
Peden, Irene Carswell
Pedersen, Charles John
Pellier, Laurence Delisle
Pennington, Mary Engle
Penrose, Roger
Penzias, Arno
Perey, Marguerite
Perrin, Jean Baptiste
Pert, Candace B.
Perutz, Max
Péter, Rózsa
Petermann, Mary Locke
Peterson, Edith R.
Piasecki, Frank
Piccard, Auguste
Pimentel, David
Pinchot, Gifford
Pincus, Gregory Goodwin
Planck, Max
Pogue, William Reid
Poincaré, Jules Henri
Poindexter, Hildrus A.
Polanyi, John C.
Polubarinova-Kochina, Pelageya
    Yakovlevna
Pólya, George
Ponnamperuma, Cyril
Porter, George
Porter, Rodney
Poulsen, Valdemar
Pound, Robert
Powell, Cecil Frank
Powless, David
Prandtl, Ludwig
Pregl, Fritz
Prelog, Vladimir
Pressman, Ada I.
Prichard, Diana García
Prigogine, Ilya
Prokhorov, Aleksandr
Punnett, R. C.
Purcell, Edward Mills

Qöyawayma, Alfred H.
Quarterman, Lloyd Albert
Quimby, Edith H.
Quinland, William Samuel

Rabi, I. I.

Rainwater, James
Ramalingaswami, Vulimiri
Raman, C. V.
Ramanujan, S. I.
Ramart-Lucas, Pauline
Ramey, Estelle R.
Ramón y Cajal, Santiago
Ramsay, William
Ramsey, Frank Plumpton
Ramsey, Norman Foster
Randoin, Lucie
Rao, C. N. R.
Ratner, Sarah
Ray, Dixy Lee
Rayleigh, Lord
    See Strutt, John William
Reber, Grote
Reddy, Raj
Reed, Walter
Rees, Mina S.
Reichmanis, Elsa
Reichstein, Tadeus
Reid, Lonnie
Reines, Frederick
Revelle, Roger
Richards, Jr., Dickinson Woodruff
Richards, Ellen Swallow
Richards, Theodore William
Richardson, Lewis Fry
Richardson, Owen W.
Richet, Charles Robert
Richter, Burton
Richter, Charles F.
Rickover, Hyman G.
Ride, Sally
Rigas, Harriett B.
Risi, Joseph
Ritchie, Dennis
Robbins, Frederick
Roberts, Lawrence
Roberts, Richard J.
Robinson, Julia
Robinson, Robert
Rock, John
Rockwell, Mabel M.
Roelofs, Wendell L.
Rogers, Marguerite M.
Rohrer, Heinrich
Roman, Nancy Grace
Romer, Alfred Sherwood
Romero, Juan Carlos
Röntgen, Wilhelm Conrad
Ross, Mary G.
Ross, Ronald
Rossby, Carl-Gustaf
Rothschild, Miriam
Rous, Peyton
Rowland, F. Sherwood
Rowley, Janet D.
Rubbia, Carlo
Rubin, Vera Cooper
Runcorn, S. K.

Ruska, Ernst
Russell, Bertrand
Russell, Elizabeth Shull
Russell, Frederick Stratten
Russell, Henry Norris
Russell, Loris Shano
Rutherford, Ernest
Ružička, Leopold
Ryle, Martin

S

Sabatier, Paul
Sabin, Albert
Sabin, Florence Rena
Sagan, Carl
Sager, Ruth
Sakharov, Andrei
Sakmann, Bert
Salam, Abdus
Salk, Jonas
Samuelsson, Bengt
Sanchez, David A.
Sanchez, Pedro A.
Sandage, Allan R.
Sanger, Frederick
Satcher, David
Schaller, George
Schally, Andrew V.
Scharff Goldhaber, Gertrude
Scharrer, Berta
Schawlow, Arthur L.
Schneider, Stephen H.
Schou, Mogens
Schrieffer, J. Robert
Schrödinger, Erwin
Schultes, Richard Evans
Schwartz, Melvin
Schwinger, Julian
Seaborg, Glenn T.
Segrè, Emilio
Seibert, Florence B.
Seitz, Frederick
Semenov, Nikolai N.
Serre, Jean-Pierre
Shannon, Claude
Shapiro, Irwin
Shapley, Harlow
Sharp, Phillip A.
Sharp, Robert Phillip
Shaw, Mary
Sheldrake, Rupert
Shepard, Jr., Alan B.
Sherrington, Charles Scott
Shockley, Dolores Cooper
Shockley, William
Shoemaker, Eugene M.
Shokalsky, Yuly Mikhaylovich
Shtokman, Vladimir Borisovich
Shurney, Robert E.

Siegbahn, Kai M.
Siegbahn, Karl M. G.
Sikorsky, Igor I.
Simon, Dorothy Martin
Simon, Herbert A.
Simpson, George Gaylord
Singer, I. M.
Singer, Maxine
Sioui, Richard H.
Sitterly, Charlotte Moore
     See Moore, Charlotte E.
Skoog, Folke Karl
Slater, John Clarke
Slipher, Vesto M.
Slye, Maud
Smale, Stephen
Smith, Hamilton O.
Smith, Michael
Snell, George Davis
Soddy, Frederick
Solberg, Halvor
Solomon, Susan
Sommerfeld, Arnold
Sommerville, Duncan McLaren
     Young
Sorensen, Charles E.
Sørensen, Søren Peter Lauritz
Spaeth, Mary
Sparling, Rebecca H.
Spedding, Frank Harold
Spemann, Hans
Sperry, Elmer
Sperry, Roger W.
Spitzer, Jr., Lyman
Stahl, Franklin W.
Stanley, Wendell Meredith
Stark, Johannes
Starling, Ernest H.
Starr, Chauncey
Starzl, Thomas
Staudinger, Hermann
Stefanik, Milan Ratislav
Stein, William Howard
Steinberger, Jack
Steinman, David B.
Steinmetz, Charles P.
Steptoe, Patrick
Stern, Otto
Stevens, Nettie Maria
Stever, H. Guyford
Steward, Frederick Campion
Stewart, Thomas Dale
Stibitz, George R.
Stock, Alfred
Stoll, Alice M.
Stommel, Henry
Størmer, Fredrik
Strassmann, Fritz
Straus, Jr., William Levi
Strutt, John William
Strutt, Robert
Stubbe, JoAnne

Sturtevant, A. H.
Sumner, James B.
Suomi, Verner E.
Sutherland, Earl
Sutherland, Ivan
Sutton, Walter Stanborough
Svedberg, Theodor
Swaminathan, M. S.
Synge, Richard
Szent-Györgyi, Albert
Szilard, Leo

T

Tamm, Igor
Tan Jiazhen
Tapia, Richard A.
Tarski, Alfred
Tatum, Edward Lawrie
Taube, Henry
Taussig, Helen Brooke
Taylor, Frederick Winslow
Taylor, Jr., Joseph H.
Taylor, Moddie
Taylor, Richard E.
Taylor, Stuart
Telkes, Maria
Teller, Edward
Temin, Howard
Tereshkova, Valentina
Terman, Frederick
Terzaghi, Karl
Tesla, Nikola
Tesoro, Giuliana Cavaglieri
Tharp, Marie
Theiler, Max
Theorell, Axel Hugo Teodor
Thom, René Frédéric
Thomas, E. Donnall
Thomas, Martha Jane Bergin
Thompson, D'Arcy Wentworth
Thompson, Kenneth
Thomson, George Paget
Thomson, J. J.
Thurston, William
Tien, Ping King
Tildon, J. Tyson
Timoshenko, Stephen P.
Tinbergen, Nikolaas
Ting, Samuel C. C.
Tiselius, Arne
Tizard, Henry
Todd, Alexander
Tombaugh, Clyde W.
Tomonaga, Sin-Itiro
Tonegawa, Susumu
Townes, Charles H.
Trotter, Mildred
Trump, John G.
Tsao, George T.

Tsiolkovsky, Konstantin
Tsui, Daniel Chee
Tswett, Mikhail
Turing, Alan
Turner, Charles Henry
Tuve, Merle A.

Uhlenbeck, George
Uhlenbeck, Karen
Urey, Harold
Uyeda, Seiya

Vallois, Henri-Victor
Van Allen, James
Van de Graaff, Robert J.
van der Meer, Simon
van der Waals, Johannes Diderik
van der Wal, Laurel
Vane, John R.
van Straten, Florence W.
Van Vleck, John
Varmus, Harold E.
Vassy, Arlette
Veksler, V. I.
Vernadsky, Vladímir Ivanovich
Virtanen, Artturi Ilmari
Vollenweider, Richard
Volterra, Vito
von Braun, Wernher
von Kármán, Theodore
von Klitzing, Klaus
von Mises, Richard
von Neumann, John
Voûte, Joan George Erardus
    Gijsbert
Vries, Hugo de

Waelsch, Salome
Wagner-Jauregg, Julius
Waksman, Selman
Wald, George
Wallach, Otto
Walton, Ernest
Wang, An
Wang, James C.
Wankel, Felix
Warburg, Otto
Washington, Warren M.
Watkins, Jr., Levi
Watson, James D.
Watson-Watt, Robert
Weber-van Bosse, Anne Antoinette

Weertman, Julia
Wegener, Alfred
Weidenreich, Franz
Weil, André
Weinberg, Robert A.
Weinberg, Steven
Weinberg, Wilhelm
Weizsäcker, Carl F. Von
Weller, Thomas
Went, Frits
Werner, Alfred
West, Harold Dadford
Wetherill, George West
Wexler, Nancy
Weyl, Hermann
Wheeler, John Archibald
Whinnery, John R.
Whipple, Fred Lawrence
Whipple, George Hoyt
White, Augustus
White, Gilbert Fowler
Whitehead, Alfred North
Whittaker, Robert Harding
Whittle, Frank
Wickenden, William E.
Widnall, Sheila E.
Wiechert, Emil
Wieland, Heinrich
Wien, Wilhelm
Wiener, Alexander
Wiener, Norbert
Wiesel, Torsten
Wigglesworth, Vincent
Wigner, Eugene Paul
Wiles, Andrew J.
Wilkes, Maurice
Wilkins, Jr., J. Ernest
Wilkins, Maurice Hugh Frederick
Wilkinson, Geoffrey
Williams, Anna W.
Williams, Daniel Hale
Williams, Frederic C.
Williams, O. S.
Williamson, James S.
Willstätter, Richard
Wilson, C. T. R.
Wilson, Edmund Beecher
Wilson, Edward O.
Wilson, J. Tuzo
Wilson, Kenneth G.
Wilson, Robert R.
Wilson, Robert Woodrow
Windaus, Adolf
Wirth, Niklaus
Witkin, Evelyn Maisel
Witten, Edward
Wittig, Georg
Wolman, Abel
Wood, Harland G.
Woodland, Joseph
Woodward, Robert B.
Woodwell, George M.

Wozniak, Stephen
Wright, Almroth Edward
Wright, Jane Cooke
Wright, Louis Tompkins
Wright, Sewall
Wright, Wilbur and Orville
Wu, Chien-Shiung
Wu, Y. C. L. Susan

Xie Xide

Yalow, Rosalyn Sussman
Yang, Chen Ning
Yau, Shing-Tung
Young, Grace Chisholm
Young, J. Z.
Yukawa, Hideki

Zadeh, Lotfi Asker
Zeeman, E. C.
Zeeman, Pieter
Zel'dovich, Yakov Borisovich
Zen, E-an
Zernike, Frits
Ziegler, Karl
Zinder, Norton
Zinsser, Hans
Zsigmondy, Richard
Zuse, Konrad
Zworykin, Vladimir

Chronology of Scientific Advancement

1895 Scottish physicist *C. T. R. Wilson* invents the cloud chamber

French physicist *Jean Baptiste Perrin* confirms the nature of cathode rays

1896 American agricultural chemist *George Washington Carver* begins work at the Tuskegee Institute

1897 English physicist *J. J. Thomson* discovers the electron

1898 Polish-born French radiation chemist *Marie Curie* and French physicist *Pierre Curie* discover polonium and radium

1900 German physicist *Max Planck* develops Planck's Constant

1901 Austrian American immunologist *Karl Landsteiner* discovers A, B, and O blood types

German geneticist *Wilhelm Weinberg* outlines the "difference method" in his first important paper on heredity

1902 English geneticist *William Bateson* translates Austrian botanist Gregor Mendel's work

1903 Polish-born French radiation chemist *Marie Curie* becomes the first woman to be awarded the Nobel Prize

German chemist *Otto Diels* isolates molecular structure of cholesterol

1904 English electrical engineer *John Ambrose Fleming* develops the Fleming Valve

Russian physiologist *Ivan Petrovich Pavlov* receives the Nobel Prize for digestion research

1905 German-born American physicist *Albert Einstein* publishes the theory of relativity

German chemist *Fritz Haber* publishes *Thermodynamics of Technical Gas Reactions*

German chemist *Walther Nernst*'s research leads to the Third Law of Thermodynamics

1906 Danish physical chemist *Johannes Nicolaus Brønsted* publishes his first paper on affinity

English neurophysiologist *Charles Scott Sherrington* publishes *The Integrative Action of the Nervous System*

1907 Prussian-born American physicist *Albert Michelson* becomes the first American to receive the Nobel Prize for physics

1908 American astrophysicist *George Ellery Hale* discovers magnetic fields in sunspots

1909 German bacteriologist and immunologist *Paul Ehrlich* discovers a cure for syphilis

American engineer and inventor *Charles Franklin Kettering* successfully tests the first prototype of the electric automobile starter

1910 English American mathematician *Alfred North Whitehead* and English mathematician and philosopher *Bertrand Russell* publish the first volume of *Principia Mathematica*

American engineer and inventor *Lee De Forest* attempts the first live broadcast of radio

New Zealand-born English physicist *Ernest Rutherford* postulates the modern concept of the atom

1911 English mathematician *Godfrey Harold Hardy* begins his collaboration with J. E. Littlewood

Polish-born French radiation chemist *Marie Curie* becomes the first scientist to win a second Nobel Prize

1912 Danish physicist *Niels Bohr* develops a new theory of atomic structure

Austrian physicist *Victor Hess* discovers cosmic rays

English biochemist *Frederick Gowland Hopkins* publishes a groundbreaking work illustrating the nutritional importance of vitamins

German physicist *Max von Laue* discovers X-ray diffraction

Austrian physicist *Lise Meitner* becomes the first woman professor in Germany

German meteorologist and geophysicist *Alfred Wegener* proposes the theory of continental drift

1913 German bacteriologist and immunologist *Paul Ehrlich* gives an address explaining the future of chemotherapy

English physicist *Henry Gwyn Jeffreys Moseley* discovers atomic number

French physicist *Jean Baptiste Perrin* verifies German-born American physicist *Albert Einstein*'s calculations of Brownian Motion

American astronomer and astrophysicist *Henry Norris Russell* publishes Hertzsprung-Russell diagram

Russian-born American aeronautical engineer *Igor I. Sikorsky* designs *Ilya Mourometz* bomber

German chemist *Richard Willstätter* and Arthur Stoll publish their first studies of chlorophyll

American geneticist *A. H. Sturtevant* develops gene mapping

1916 American chemist and physicist *Irving Langmuir* receives a patent for an energy-efficient, longer-lasting tungsten filament light bulb

American geneticist and embryologist *Thomas Hunt Morgan* publishes *A Critique of the Theory of Evolution*

German theoretical physicist *Arnold Sommerfeld* reworks Danish physicist *Niels Bohr*'s atomic theory

American anatomist *Florence Rena Sabin* publishes *The Origin and Development of the Lymphatic System*

1918 Danish physical chemist *Johannes Nicolaus Brønsted* publishes his thirteenth paper on affinity

1919 New Zealand-born English physicist *Ernest Rutherford* determines that alpha particles can split atoms

1920 American astronomer *Harlow Shapley* convinces the scientific community that the Milky Way is much larger than originally thought and the Earth's solar system is not its center

1921 Canadian physiologist *Frederick G. Banting* and Canadian physiologist *Charles Herbert Best* discover insulin

1923 Danish physical chemist *Johannes Nicolaus Brønsted* redefines acids and bases

English astronomer *Arthur Stanley Eddington* publishes *Mathematical Theory of Relativity*

American astronomer *Edwin Hubble* confirms the existence of galaxies outside the Milky Way

American physicist *Robert A. Millikan* begins his study of cosmic rays

1924 French theoretical physicist *Louis Victor de Broglie* publishes findings on wave mechanics

English astronomer *Arthur Stanley Eddington* determines the mass-luminosity law

1925 German-born American physicist *James Franck* and German physicist *Gustav Hertz* prove Danish physicist *Niels Bohr*'s theory of the quantum atom

Italian-born American physicist *Enrico Fermi* publishes a paper explaining Austro-Hungarian-born Swiss physicist *Wolfgang Pauli*'s exclusion principle

English statistician and geneticist *Ronald A. Fisher* publishes *Statistical Methods for Research Workers*

1926 German-born English physicist *Max Born* explains the wave function

American physicist and rocket pioneer *Robert H. Goddard* launches the first liquid-propellant rocket

American geneticist *Hermann Joseph Muller* confirms that X rays greatly increase the mutation rate in *Drosophila*

Austrian physicist *Erwin Schrödinger* publishes his wave equation

1927 American physicist *Arthur Holly Compton* receives the Nobel Prize for X-ray research

English physiologist *Henry Hallett Dale* identifies the chemical mediator involved in the transmission of nerve impulses

German chemist *Otto Diels* develops a successful dehydrogenating process

German physicist *Werner Karl Heisenberg* develops the Uncertainty Principle

Belgian astronomer *Georges Lemaître* formulates the big bang theory

Hungarian American mathematical physicist *Eugene Paul Wigner* develops the law of the conservation of parity

American astronomer *Edwin Hubble* puts together the theory of the expanding universe, or Hubble's Law

1928 German chemist *Otto Diels* and German chemist *Kurt Alder* develop the Diels-Alder Reaction

Scottish bacteriologist *Alexander Fleming* discovers penicillin

Austro-Hungarian-born German physicist *Hermann Oberth* publishes a book explaining the basic principles of space flight

Indian physicist *C. V. Raman* discovers the Raman Effect

1929 American physicist *Robert Van de Graaff* constructs the first working model of his particle accelerator

Danish astronomer *Ejnar Hertzsprung* receives the Gold Medal Award for calculating the first intergalactic distance

Norwegian American chemist *Lars Onsager* develops the Law of Reciprocal Relations

German-born American mathematician *Hermann Weyl* develops a mathematical theory for the neutrino

Russian-born American physicist and engineer *Vladimir Zworykin* files his first patent for color television

1930 English statistician and geneticist *Ronald A. Fisher* publishes *The Genetical Theory of Natural Selection*

Austrian-born American mathematician *Kurt Friedrich Gödel* proves the incompleteness theorem

Austro-Hungarian-born Swiss physicist *Wolfgang Pauli* proposes the existence of the neutrino

1931 American engineer *Vannevar Bush* develops the differential analyzer with colleagues

American chemist *Wallace Hume Carothers* founds the synthetic rubber manufacturing industry with his research

South African-born American virologist *Max Theiler*'s research leads to the production of the first yellow-fever vaccine

German biochemist *Otto Warburg* establishes the Kaiser Wilhelm Institute for Cell Physiology

1932 English atomic physicist *John Cockcroft* and Irish experimental physicist *Ernest Walton* split the atom

American physicist *Carl David Anderson* discovers the positron

English-born Indian physiologist and geneticist *John Burdon Sanderson Haldane* publishes *The Causes of Evolution*

American physicist *Ernest Orlando Lawrence* develops the cyclotron and disintegrates a lithium nucleus

1933 Canadian-born American biologist and bacteriologist *Oswald Theodore Avery* identifies DNA as the basis of heredity

English physicist *Paul Adrien Maurice Dirac* wins the Nobel Prize for his work on the wave equation

Italian-born American physicist *Enrico Fermi* proposes his beta decay theory

German inventor *Felix Wankel* successfully operates the first internal combustion, rotary engine

1934 French nuclear physicist *Frédéric Joliot-Curie* and French chemist and physicist *Irène Joliot-Curie* discover artificial radioactivity

American inventor *Edwin H. Land* develops a commercial method to polarize light

New Zealand-born English physicist *Ernest Rutherford* achieves the first fusion reaction

American chemist and physicist *Harold Urey* receives the Nobel Prize in chemistry for his discovery of deuterium, or heavy hydrogen

1935 American seismologist *Charles F. Richter* and German American seismologist *Beno Gutenberg* develop the Richter(-Gutenberg) Scale

English physicist *James Chadwick* receives the Nobel Prize for the discovery of the neutron

1936 German experimental physicist *Hans Geiger* perfects the Geiger-Mueller Counter

Russian biochemist *Aleksandr Ivanovich Oparin* publishes his origin of life theory

English mathematician *Alan Turing* publishes a paper detailing a machine that would serve as a model for the first working computer

1937 Russian-born American biologist *Theodosius Dobzhansky* writes *Genetics and the Origin of Species*

Australian English pathologist *Howard Walter Florey* discovers the growth potential of polymeric chains

German-born English biochemist *Hans Adolf Krebs* identifies the workings of the Krebs Cycle

Hungarian American biochemist and molecular biologist *Albert Szent-Gyorgyi* receives the Nobel Prize for isolating vitamin C

1938 German chemist *Otto Hahn*, Austrian physicist *Lise Meitner*, and German chemist *Fritz Strassmann* discover nuclear fission

American physicist *Carl David Anderson* discovers the meson

1939 Swiss-born American physicist *Felix Bloch* measures the neutron's magnetic movement

American chemist *Wallace Hume Carothers* founds the synthetic fiber industry with his research

French-born American microbiologist and ecologist *René Dubos* discovers tyrothricin

American chemist *Linus Pauling* develops the theory of complimentarity

Russian-born American aeronautical engineer *Igor I. Sikorsky* flies the first single-rotor helicopter

1940 American physicist and inventor *Chester Carlson* receives a patent for his photocopying method

English experimental physicist *George Paget Thomson* forms the Maud Committee

1941

German-born English biochemist *Ernst Boris Chain* and Australian English pathologist *Howard Walter Florey* isolate penicillin

German-born American physicist *Hans Bethe* develops the Bethe Coupler

American biochemist *Fritz Lipmann* publishes "Metabolic Generation and Utilization of Phosphate Bond Energy"

1942

Hungarian American physicist and biophysicist *Leo Szilard* and Italian-born American physicist *Enrico Fermi* set up the first nuclear chain reaction

German-born American biologist *Ernst Mayr* proposes the theory of geographic speciation

American physicist *J. Robert Oppenheimer* becomes the director of the Manhattan Project

1943

German-born American molecular biologist *Max Delbrück* and Italian-born American molecular biologist *Salvador Edward Luria* publish a milestone paper regarded as the beginning of bacterial genetics

English physicist *James Chadwick* leads the British contingent of the Manhattan Project

French oceanographer *Jacques-Yves Cousteau* patents the Aqualung

Italian-born American molecular biologist *Salvador Edward Luria* devises the fluctuation test

1944

German American rocket engineer *Wernher Von Braun* fires the first fully operational V-2 rocket

Austrian-born American biochemist *Erwin Chargaff* discovers the genetic role of DNA

American nuclear chemist *Glenn T. Seaborg* successfully isolates large amounts of plutonium and develops the actinide concept

American paleontologist *George Gaylord Simpson* publishes *Tempo and Mode in Evolution*

Russian-born American microbiologist *Selman Waksman* develops streptomycin

1945

English physicist *James Chadwick* witnesses the first atomic bomb test

American biochemist *Fritz Lipmann* discovers coenzyme A

Hungarian American mathematician *Johann Von Neumann* publishes a report containing the first written description of the stored-program concept

American chemist *Linus Pauling* determines the cause of sickle-cell anemia

Austrian physicist *Erwin Schrödinger* publishes *What Is Life?*

1946

American geneticist *Joshua Lederberg* and American biochemist *Edward Lawrie Tatum* show that bacteria may reproduce sexually

English zoologist *Julian Huxley* becomes the first director-general of UNESCO

1947

French oceanographer *Jacques-Yves Cousteau* breaks the free diving record using his Aqualung

Hungarian-born English physicist *Dennis Gabor* discovers holography

American inventor *Edwin H. Land* demonstrates the first instant camera

American mathematician *Norbert Wiener* creates the study of cybernetics

1948

American physicist *John Bardeen* develops the transistor

American chemist *Melvin Calvin* begins research on photosynthesis

Russian-born American physicist *George Gamow* publishes "Alpha-Beta-Gamma" paper

American zoologist and sex researcher *Alfred Kinsey* publishes *Sexual Behavior in the Human Male*

American biochemist *Wendell Meredith Stanley*

receives Presidential Certificate of Merit for developing an influenza vaccine

Swedish chemist *Arne Tiselius* receives the Nobel Prize for research in electrophoresis

1949 Hungarian-born American physicist *Edward Teller* begins developing the hydrogen bomb

American astronomer *Fred Lawrence Whipple* suggests the "dirty snowball" comet model

1950 American geneticist *Barbara McClintock* publishes the discovery of genetic transposition

1951 American chemist *Katharine Burr Blodgett* receives the Garvan Medal for women chemists

American biologist *Gregory Goodwin Pincus* begins work on the antifertility steroid the "pill"

Dutch-born English zoologist and ethologist *Nikolaas Tinbergen* publishes *The Study of Instinct*

1952 German-born American astronomer *Walter Baade* presents new measurements of the universe

French-born American microbiologist and ecologist *René Dubos* publishes a book linking tuberculosis with certain environmental conditions

American microbiologist *Alfred Day Hershey* conducts the "Blender Experiment" to demonstrate that DNA is the genetic material of life

Italian-born American molecular biologist *Salvador Edward Luria* discovers the phenomenon known as restriction and modification

American microbiologist *Jonas Salk* develops the first polio vaccine

English chemist *Alexander Todd* establishes the structure of flavin adenine dinucleotide (FAD)

1953 Russian theoretical physicist *Andrei Sakharov* and Russian physicist *Igor Tamm* develop the first Soviet hydrogen bomb

English molecular biologist *Francis Crick* and American molecular biologist *James D. Watson* develop the Watson-Crick model of DNA

English molecular biologist *Rosalind Elsie Franklin* provides evidence of DNA's double-helical structure

American physicist *Murray Gell-Mann* publishes a paper explaining the strangeness principle

American zoologist and sex researcher *Alfred Kinsey* publishes *Sexual Behavior in the Human Female*

French microbiologist *André Lwoff* proposes that "inducible lysogenic bacteria" can test cancerous and noncancerous cell activity

English biologist *Peter Brian Medawar* proves acquired immunological tolerance

American chemist *Stanley Lloyd Miller* publishes "A Production of Amino Acids under Possible Primitive Earth Conditions"

Austrian-born English crystallographer and biochemist *Max Perutz* develops method of isomorphous replacement

1955 English chemist *Alexander Todd* and English chemist and crystallographer *Dorothy Crowfoot Hodgkin* determine the structure of vitamin B12

American biochemist *Sidney W. Fox* begins identifying properties of microspheres

American microbiologist *Jonas Salk*'s polio vaccine pronounced safe and ninety-percent effective

English biochemist *Frederick Sanger* determines the total structure of the insulin molecule

1956 American biochemist *Stanley Cohen* extracts NGF from a mouse tumor

American experimental physicist *Leon Max Lederman* helps discover the "long-lived neutral kaon"

1957 American biochemist *Arthur Kornberg* and Spanish biochemist *Severo Ochoa* use DNA polymerase to synthesize DNA molecules

1958   American physicist *James Van Allen* discovers Van Allen radiation belts

American geneticist *George Wells Beadle* receives the Nobel Prize for the One Gene, One Enzyme Theory

American population biologist *Paul R. Ehrlich* makes his first statement regarding the problem of overpopulation

German physicist *Rudolf Mössbauer* discovers recoilless gamma ray release

1959   American computer scientist *Grace Hopper* develops the COBOL computer language

German physicist *Rudolf Mössbauer* uses the Mössbauer Effect to test the theory of relativity

1960   English physicist and biochemist *John Kendrew* and Austrian-born English crystallographer and biochemist *Max Perutz* formulate the first three-dimensional structure of the protein myoglobin

American Chemist *Willard F. Libby* receives the Nobel Prize for his development of radiocarbon dating

Russian-born American virologist *Albert Sabin*'s oral polio vaccine is approved for manufacture in the United States

1961   French biologists *François Jacob* and *Jacques Monod* discover messenger ribonucleic acid (mRNA)

American chemist *Melvin Calvin* receives the Nobel Prize in his chemistry for research on photosynthesis

American biochemist *Marshall Warren Nirenberg* cracks the genetic code

1962   American marine biologist *Rachel Carson* publishes *Silent Spring*

Russian theoretical physicist *Lev Davidovich Landau* receives the Nobel Prize for his research into theories of condensed matter

Hungarian-born American physicist *Edward Teller* becomes the first advocate of an "active defense system" to shoot down enemy missiles

New Zealand-born English biophysicist *Maurice Hugh Frederick Wilkins* shows the helical structure of RNA

1963   German American physicist *Maria Goeppert-Mayer* becomes the first woman to receive the Nobel Prize for theoretical physics

American chemist *Linus Pauling* becomes the only person to receive two unshared Nobel Prizes

1964   American psychobiologist *Roger W. Sperry* publishes the findings of his split-brain studies

1965   American geneticist *A. H. Sturtevant* publishes *The History of Genetics*

1967   English astrophysicist *Antony Hewish* and Irish astronomer *Jocelyn Susan Bell Burnell* discover pulsars

South African heart surgeon *Christiaan Neethling Barnard* performs the first human heart transplant

American primatologist *Dian Fossey* establishes a permanent research camp in Rwanda

1968   American physicist *Luis Alvarez* wins the Nobel Prize for his bubble chamber work

1969   American astronaut *Neil Armstrong* becomes the first man to walk on the moon

1970   Indian-born American biochemist *Har Gobind Khorana* synthesizes the first artificial DNA

American biologist *Lynn Margulis* publishes *Origins of Life*

1971   English ethologist *Jane Goodall* publishes *In the Shadow of Man*

1972   American evolutionary biologist *Stephen Jay Gould* and American paleontologist *Niles*

Eldredge introduce the concept of punctuated equilibrium

American physicist *John Bardeen* develops the BCS theory of superconductivity

American inventor *Edwin H. Land* reveals the first instant color camera

1973 American radio engineer *Karl Jansky* receives the honor of having the Jansky unit adopted as the unit of measure of radiowave intensity

Austrian zoologist and ethologist *Konrad Lorenz* receives the Nobel Prize for his behavioral research

American biochemist and geneticist *Maxine Singer* warns the public of gene-splicing risks

1974 English astrophysicist *Antony Hewish* receives the first Nobel Prize awarded to an astrophysicist

1975 French oceanographer *Jacques-Yves Cousteau* sees his Cousteau Society membership reach 120,000

American zoologist *Edward O. Wilson* publishes *Sociobiology: The New Synthesis*

1976 American computer engineer *Seymour Cray* introduces the CRAY-1 supercomputer

1977 Russian-born Belgian chemist *Ilya Prigogine* receives the Nobel Prize in chemistry for his work on nonequilibrium thermodynamics

1980 American biochemist *Paul Berg* receives the Nobel Prize for the biochemistry of nucleic acids

1981 American virologist *Robert C. Gallo* develops a blood test for the AIDS virus and discovers human T-cell leukemia virus

1982 American astronaut and physicist *Sally Ride* becomes the first American woman in space

1983 Indian-born American astrophysicist and applied mathematician *Subrahmanyan Chandrasekhar* receives the Nobel Prize for research on aged stars

American primatologist *Dian Fossey* publishes *Gorillas in the Mist*

French virologist *Luc Montagnier* discovers the human immunodeficiency virus (HIV)

American astronomer and exobiologist *Carl Sagan* publishes an article with others suggesting the possibility of a "nuclear winter"

1986 American physicist *Richard P. Feynman* explains why the space shuttle *Challenger* exploded

1987 Chinese American physicist *Paul Ching-Wu Chu* leads a team that discovers a method for higher temperature superconductivity

1987 American molecular biologist *Walter Gilbert* begins the human genome project to map DNA

1988 English theoretical physicist *Stephen Hawking* publishes *A Brief History of Time: From the Big Bang to Black Holes*

English pharmacologist *James Black* receives the Nobel Prize for his heart and ulcer medication work

1989 German-born American physicist *Hans Dehmelt* and German physicist *Wolfgang Paul* share the Nobel Prize for devising ion traps

1990 American physicists *Jerome Friedman, Henry W. Kendall,* and *Richard E. Taylor* are awarded the Nobel Prize for confirming the existence of quarks

American surgeon *Joseph E. Murray* receives the Nobel Prize for performing the first human kidney transplant

1991 German physician and cell physiologist *Bert Sakmann* and German biophysicist *Erwin Neher*

are awarded the Nobel Prize for inventing the patch clamp technique

 1993 English biochemist *Richard J. Roberts* and American biologist *Phillip A. Sharp* share the Nobel Prize for their research on DNA structure

American astrophysicists *Russell A. Hulse* and *Joseph H. Taylor, Jr.* receive the Nobel Prize for their work on binary pulsars

NOTABLE
TWENTIETH-CENTURY
SCIENTISTS

Philip Hauge Abelson
1913-
American nuclear physicist

As an acclaimed nuclear physicist, biochemist, microbiologist, physiologist and geologist, Philip Hauge Abelson ranks among the most versatile scientists of his day. His achievements include discovering the element neptunium and designing the blueprint for nuclear submarines. Not content to excel solely in the sciences, Abelson is also an accomplished writer and editor of distinguished scientific periodicals. In 1993, at age 80, he was working as science advisor and deputy editor for the American Association for the Advancement of Science. "I will continue to do things, partly because I can write," Abelson said during an interview with contributor Cynthia Washam. "I will find a way of remaining active."

Abelson was born April 27, 1913, in Tacoma, Washington. His father, Ole Andrew Abelson, was a civil engineer, while his mother, Ellen (Hauge) Abelson, was a homemaker and among the few women of her day to attend college. Abelson learned the value of education at age fourteen when his father arranged for him to work as a surveyor at a construction camp, directing laborers installing steel pipes. The young surveyor quickly realized that the only way to communicate with the steel workers was to adopt their language and was soon exchanging curses with the best of them. "The seven months spent at the construction camp as a surveyor was a maturing experience," Abelson related in an article for the *Annual Review of Earth Planet Science*. "It made me appreciate the potential value of a college education."

In 1930, Abelson enrolled in the chemical engineering program at Washington State College (now Washington State University). Although working as a surveyor through college to help pay for tuition, Abelson managed to take a heavy course load and earn his bachelor's degree in chemistry in three years. He took graduate courses in physics and was fortunate to receive a teaching assistantship in 1933 during the Great Depression. Two years later, Abelson was awarded a master's degree in physics from Washington State University. One of his graduate assignments was to read an article describing the cyclotron—an accelerator which propels charged particles using an alternating electric field in a constant magnetic field.

Philip Hauge Abelson

It was invented in 1929 by American physicist **Ernest Orlando Lawrence** at the University of California at Berkeley, placing the institution in the forefront of nuclear physics. Captivated by the article and determined to become part of the work it described, Abelson secured a teaching assistantship in physics at Berkeley.

Discovers Neptunium

After obtaining his doctoral degree in nuclear physics from the University of California at Berkeley in 1939, Abelson joined the Carnegie Institution of Washington. There he studied the products generated from the activation of uranium by neutrons and became intrigued by a particular unidentified element. Collaborating with **Edwin M. McMillan** of the Lawrence Radiation Laboratory at Berkeley, the two scientists discovered that the product was a new chemical element, classifying it as radioactive element 93. It was later named neptunium. More than 50 years later—in which he has been part of a multitude of landmark achievements—Abelson still regarded the discovery as the greatest moment in his career. "A good many very bright and competent people had access to the same information I did," he told Washam. "Because I re-read something in the literature and thought about it, it occurred to me that this required a different approach. Getting that connection led me to the discovery."

During World War II, Abelson became a physicist on the staff of the Naval Research Laboratory in Washington, DC. His work there was connected with the Manhattan Project, code name for the most secret scientific U.S. operation of World War II, in which the objective was to create an atomic bomb. Abelson, along with John I. Hoover, developed the liquid thermal diffusion process for separating uranium isotopes—groups of chemically identical atoms of the same element and atomic number with differing atomic mass. Abelson and Hoover were credited with decreasing the time needed to develop the bomb by eight days. For his wartime contributions, Abelson was in 1945 awarded the Navy Distinguished Civilian Service Medal, the first of many important awards he would receive during his career. After the war, Abelson remained at the lab until 1946, designing the blueprint for a nuclear-powered submarine that could cruise underwater for months without surfacing. His design would serve as the model for the U.S. Navy's nuclear submarines.

In 1946, Abelson returned to the Carnegie Institution as chair of biophysics in the Department of Terrestrial Magnetism. He and his colleagues used newly developed radioactive isotopes to tag chemical elements in order to observe their behavior in microorganisms. The results of their study were published in 1955 by the Carnegie Institution as "Studies of Biosynthesis in *Escherichia coli.*" Escherichia is a bacterium of the rod-like species *bacillus,* found in the intestinal tract of mammals as well as in soil and in aquatic habitats, and is known to cause bacterial dysentery. The book became a reference work on what is commonly referred to as "E. coli" bacteria, and has remained in wide use for over four decades, particularly since E. coli was determined the key microorganism for genetic engineering.

In 1953, Abelson became the director of the Geophysical Laboratory at the Carnegie Institution. There, he sought to determine whether amino acids—essential building blocks of proteins—were preserved in fossils. He discovered that the life-span of amino acids is strongly affected by temperature and that they can at low temperatures survive as long as hundreds of millions of years. Abelson's study results, published in the Carnegie Institution's annual report and in *Scientific American,* generated considerable interest among the branch of biochemists involved in paleontology—the study of fossil remains from previous geological eras. During the 1960s, the Geophysical Laboratory grew into a premier research center for organic geochemistry—the study of the chemical configuration of both terrestrial and extraterrestrial

solid matter. There, scientists examined if ancient life forms employed the same biosynthetic processes—in which living organisms generate chemical compounds—as those of today, and if life exists elsewhere in the solar system.

In 1959, Abelson was honored with induction into the National Academy of Sciences, where he chose to be listed in the geology division. Over the years, he was also awarded honorary doctoral degrees from several universities, including Yale University in 1964, Southern Methodist University in 1969, Tufts University in 1976, Duke University in 1981, and the University of Pittsburgh in 1982. The University of Puget Sound awarded Abelson an honorary doctorate degree in humane letters in 1968.

While serving as director of the Geophysical Laboratory, Abelson consistently participated in research. He also edited the manuscripts for a book the institution produced annually. Editing stimulated Abelson, and when he was asked to become coeditor of the *Journal of Geophysical Research* in 1958, he readily accepted. Within a few years, he and coeditor James Peoples had expanded the annual journal page count from eight hundred to six thousand.

Appointed Editor of *Science*

So strong was Abelson's reputation that in 1962 he was offered the position of editor at *Science,* the highly-respected weekly forum for American scientists. Unwilling to give up his research, Abelson arranged it so he could edit the magazine while remaining at the Geophysical Laboratory. Abelson's first mission as editor was to make the magazine more engaging and current. He began by cutting the time between article submission and publication from about three months to as little as nine days. To bring readers the latest science news, he recruited scouts of scientific news at several leading schools and research centers. Abelson's most memorable contribution to *Science* was his thoughtful, often controversial editorials. Never afraid to ruffle feathers, Abelson frequently used his forum to attack popular institutions and fellow scientists. One of his prime targets was the space program. He wrote in a February 12, 1965, editorial that "in looking for life on Mars we could establish ourselves the reputation of being the greatest Simple Simons of all time," and on March 17, 1967, his editorial claimed that "manned missions have contributed little scientifically. The unmanned missions have had a cost-effectiveness for scientific achievements perhaps one hundred times that of the manned flights." Addressing the spiraling cost of health care, Abelson warned in an editorial on May 14, 1976, that the 118.5 billion dollars that the nation spent that year on medical care could not buy better health. Instead, he advised Americans to abandon their sedentary lifestyles, poor diets, and smoking habits.

In spite of the critical tone of many of Abelson's editorials, his outlook was essentially optimistic. A January 9, 1976, editorial commemorating the Bicentennial year challenged political leaders to adopt the optimism and forward thinking of Benjamin Franklin and Thomas Jefferson: "This country has turned its back on optimism and is becoming a nation of pessimists." "Pessimism," he continued, "is a kind of sickness that debilitates the individual and the country. One would not advocate that we become a nation of Panglosses. However, enough of pessimism. It leads nowhere but to paralysis and decay." A collection of one hundred of Abelson's editorials was published by the American Association for the Advancement of Science in 1985 as *Enough of Pessimism.*

In 1971, Abelson became president of the Carnegie Institution. He continued as editor of *Science,* but was unable to maintain his involvement in research. Seeking to replace the stimulation research had offered, Abelson served on the visiting committees of universities and on the advisory council of the Jet Propulsion Laboratory. His scientific curiosity led him to automobile manufacturing plants in the United States and Japan, research laboratories in Japan and China, and the Alaska pipeline during its final construction phase.

Abelson stepped down from his editing post at *Science* in 1984 with more than 450 editorials to his credit. He remained with the magazine as deputy editor for engineering and applied science and with the American Association for the Advancement of Science as a science advisor. Throughout the 1970s and 1980s, Abelson continued receiving awards for his numerous achievements. In 1970, Carnegie-Mellon University gave him its Mellon Award, and in 1972 he received the Kalinga Prize from the United Nations Educational, Scientific, and Cultural Organization.

In 1974, Abelson gave three lectures at the University of Washington, which were collected in a book titled *Energy for Tomorrow.* In his lectures, Abelson discussed the energy shortage, proposed ways to increase the energy supply, and recommended a program for conserving energy. In 1984, the National Science Foundation honored Abelson with its Distinguished Public Service Award. Three years later, he received the President's National Medal of Science from the National Academy of Science, who also awarded Abelson the Public Welfare Medal in 1992. Abelson returned to research in 1985, when he accepted a two-year post as a natural science fellow at the Washington-based think tank, Resources for the Future, where his work centered around reviewing and recommending public policy on toxic chemicals.

Outside of the working environment, Abelson lives by the common sense philosophy he often promoted in his editorials. He runs three to four miles most mornings. On his eightieth birthday, he ran five. His hobbies include playing bridge, reading, and tending his tomato garden. Even at his home in Washington, DC, science is a part of Abelson's life. He and his wife, retired physician and professor of medicine Neva (Martin) Abelson, enjoy keeping each other current on new developments in their respective fields. They were married December 30, 1936, while Abelson was a graduate student at Berkeley, and have one daughter, Ellen (Abelson) Cherniavsky.

SELECTED WRITINGS BY ABELSON:

Books

(With Richard B. Roberts and others) *Studies of Biosynthesis in Escherichia Coli,* Carnegie Institution, 1955.
Energy for Tomorrow, University of Washington Press, 1975.
Food: Politics, Economics, Nutrition, and Research, Academic Press, 1976.
Electronics: The Continuing Revolution, American Association for the Advancement of Science, 1977.
Energy Two: Use, Conservation, and Supply, American Association for the Advancement of Science, 1978.
Health Care: Regulation, Economics, Ethics, Practice, American Association for the Advancement of Science, 1978.
Enough of Pessimism, American Association for the Advancement of Science, 1985.

Periodicals

"Adventures in Lifelong Learning," *Annual Review of Earth Planet Science,* 1992, pp. 1–17.
"The High Cost of Exaggerating Health Risks," *The Public Perspective,* July/August, 1993, pp. 3–7.

SOURCES:

Books

Current Biography, H. W. Wilson, 1965.

Periodicals

New York Review of Books, February 19, 1976.

Other

Abelson, Philip Hague, interview with Cynthia Washam conducted July 30, 1993.

—*Sketch by Cynthia Washam*

Roger Adams
1889-1971
American chemist

Roger Adams was a member of the chemistry department at the University of Illinois from 1916 to 1954 and headed the department for the last twenty-eight years of that period. Some of his most important work involved the elucidation of complex organic structures such as tetrahydrocannabinol (from marijuana), chaulmoogric acid (used in the treatment of leprosy), and gossypol (a toxic agent found in cottonseed oil). He is probably best known, however, for inventing a method for the preparation of platinum in a form usable in catalysis, a substance now known as Adams's catalyst. Throughout his career, Adams was also very active in the administrative aspects of science. Many of his students assumed positions of leadership in the chemical industry, and Adams is credited with having contributed significantly to the rapid development of chemistry in the United States.

Roger Adams was born in Boston on January 2, 1889. He was the youngest of four children born to Austin Winslow Adams and the former Lydia Curtis. He attended the Boston and Cambridge Latin schools and then, at the age of sixteen, entered Harvard University. In spite of his solid precollege training, Adams apparently "did not take college seriously" until he was a junior at Harvard, according to biographer Nelson J. Leonard in a 1969 retrospective on Adams in the *Journal of the American Chemical Society*. From that point forward, he became intent on his chemical education, earning in quick order his A.B. in 1909, his A.M. in 1910, and his Ph.D. in 1912.

For his postdoctoral studies, Adams traveled to Europe where he studied with **Otto Diels** at the University of Berlin and with **Richard Willstätter** at the Kaiser Wilhelm Institute in Dahlem. He began a second postdoctoral year at Harvard in 1913 under C. L. Jackson and was also soon asked to teach an introductory course in organic chemistry at the college. Adams continued to teach and do research at Harvard until 1916.

Begins Long Career at Illinois

In 1916, W. A. Noyes, chairman of the chemistry department at the University of Illinois, offered Adams a position as assistant professor of chemistry. Adams accepted and over the next four decades was promoted successively to professor in 1919, to head of the department in 1926, to research professor in 1954, and finally to professor emeritus in 1957. During his long academic career at the University of Illinois, Adams was awarded honorary doctorates from ten universities and twenty-four medals and awards from organizations around the world. Among these were the Willard Gibbs Medal of the Chicago Section of the American Chemical Society (ACS) in 1936, the Elliott Cresson Medal of the Franklin Institute in 1944, the Davy Medal of the Royal Society in 1945, the Priestly Medal of the ACS in 1946, the Medal for Merit of the U.S. government in 1948, the Gold Medal of the American Institute of Chemists in 1964, and the National Medal of Science in 1964.

Adams's tenure at Illinois coincided with a growing demand in the chemical industry for academically trained doctorate holders. Convinced of the interdependence of universities and industry, Adams set about strengthening links between the two spheres by training graduates specifically to go into the field. His department's ability to supply quality industrial chemists in bulk reinforced the demand for them, and Adams therefore garnered much of the credit for the growth of chemistry in the United States.

Shortly before moving from Harvard to Illinois, Adams was married on August 29, 1918, to Lucile Wheeler. The Adamses later had one daughter, Lucile, who later married William E. Ranz, a chemical engineer at the University of Minnesota.

Laboratory Accident Leads to Discovery of New Catalyst

Adams studied three major subjects during his career as a researcher: catalysis, stereochemistry, and structural analysis. Perhaps his best-known discovery, Adams's catalyst, came about as the result of an accident in a University of Illinois laboratory. During a student experiment, a mixture of chloroplatinic acid, formaldehyde, and alkali was spilled on a laboratory desk. Hoping to salvage the materials, Adams gave directions by which the mixture should be treated and the reactants should be recovered.

When these directions were carried out, the platinum was regenerated in a new form, brown platinum oxide. Treatment of the oxide with hydrogen gas resulted in the formation of a very finely divided platinum metal. Adams discovered that in this form the platinum was an extraordinarily efficient catalyst in the conversion of unsaturated organic compounds to their saturated (that is, consisting of molecules that have only single bonds) counterparts, a process with many important industrial applications. For nearly a half century thereafter, Adams's catalyst continued to be one of the most valuable intermediates for a number of industrial preparations.

During the 1920s and 1930s, Adams focused his research on stereochemistry, a study of the properties and behaviors of molecules determined by their three-dimensional structures. In particular, he investigated the ways in which free rotation around a single bond can be blocked and how this kind of restriction affects the properties of a molecule.

Adams was also successful in elucidating the structures of a number of complex organic molecules. In the 1930s, for example, he was asked by the U.S. Narcotics Bureau to study the components of marijuana. Adams was able to separate out and determine the molecular composition of cannabinol, cannabidol, tetrahydrocannabinol, and other related compounds found in marijuana. As an unexpected side effect of this research, Adams found that the bureau's standard test for marijuana actually identified a harmless substance that occurs in conjunction with the marijuana itself.

In later research, Adams found the structure of gossypol, a toxic compound that occurs in cottonseed oil and had long limited the uses of that material. This work allowed the development of a procedure for removing gossypol from cottonseed, vastly increasing the uses of that important substance. Adams also determined the structures of chaulmoogric and hydrocarpic acids, components of the chaulmoogra oil that had been used for centuries in the treatment of leprosy, and of necic acid and its derivatives, responsible for cirrhosis of the liver in cattle, sheep, and horses. Beyond his many research interests, Adams was actively involved in a wide variety of political and professional activities throughout his life. In the mid–1930s, for example, he served on President Franklin D. Roosevelt's short-lived Science Advisory Board. From 1941 to 1946 he was a member of the National Defense Research Committee. During the last year of that term, he served as science advisor to Lieutenant General Lucius D. Clay, U.S. deputy military governor in the American occupation zone of Germany. In 1947 Adams was the leader of a scientific advisory committee whose job it was to recommend to General Douglas MacArthur the most effective methods for democratizing Japanese science.

Adams's first major professional position was as chair of the organic division of the American Chemical Society in 1920. He later served on the board of directors of the ACS (from 1930 to 1935 and from 1940 to 1950), as president of the organization (1935) and as chair of the ACS board (from 1944 to 1950). He was also president of the American Association for the Advancement of Science in 1950, a member of its executive committee from 1941 to 1946 and from 1948 to 1952, and chair of the board of directors in 1951. Adams died at his home in Urbana, Illinois, on July 6, 1971.

SELECTED WRITINGS BY ADAMS:

Books

(With J. R. Johnson) *Elementary Laboratory Experiments in Organic Chemistry,* Macmillan, 5th edition, 1963.

Periodicals

"Bacteriological Action of Certain Organic Acids toward *Mycobacterium leprae* and Other Acid-Fast Bacteria," *Journal of Pharmacology and Experimental Therapy,* Volume 45, 1932, pp. 121–162.
"Marijuana," *Harvey Lectures,* Volume 37, pp. 168–197.
"Universities and Industry in Science," *Industrial and Engineering Chemistry,* Volume 46, 1954, pp. 506–510.

SOURCES:

Books

Dictionary of Scientific Biography, Volume 15, Supplement 1, Scribner, 1975, pp. 1–3.

Periodicals

Leonard, Nelson J., "Roger Adams," *Journal of the American Chemical Society,* January 2, 1969, pp. a-d.

—*Sketch by David E. Newton*

Walter Sydney Adams
1876-1956
American astronomer

Walter Sydney Adams was a pioneering astronomer who served as acting director and then director of the Mount Wilson Observatory for more than thirty years. At Mount Wilson and earlier at the Yerkes Observatory, Adams participated in the revolution that took astronomy from its reliance on visual observation to a newer focus that brought laboratory methods to the study of the sun and stars. By using the stars' own spectra, Adams helped categorize stars and determine their motions. Perhaps his greatest accomplishment was developing a new method of measuring the distances to stars.

Adams was born on December 20, 1876, at Kessab, near Antioch, in northern Syria, where his parents, Lucien Harper and Dora Francis Adams, were missionaries of the American Board of Commissioners for Foreign Missions. During their years in Syria, Adams and his siblings were taught by their mother. Adams absorbed knowledge of history and the classics from his father's library and from missionary trips through the history-rich countryside, where Alexander the Great and the Crusaders once campaigned. The constellations above yielded Adams's first lessons in astronomy. The family returned to Derry, New Hampshire, in 1885, when Adams was eight years old.

Chooses a Career in Science

Adams received a baccalaureate degree from Dartmouth College in 1898, graduating with the highest honors. He enjoyed studying Latin and Greek, but at the advice of spectroscopist Edwin Frost, his astronomy teacher, he chose scientific studies at the University of Chicago for his graduate work. He also began working with Frost at the Yerkes Observatory at Williams Bay, Wisconsin, where Frost had been hired by observatory founder and director **George Ellery Hale** to head the stellar spectroscopy department. Adams did his first research at the University on the polar compression, or distortion, of Jupiter, publishing his first scientific paper in 1898. At Yerkes, he studied the radial velocities of stars—their speeds approaching or retreating from Earth—with Frost. Adams completed his master's degree in 1900, studied for a year at the University of Munich, and returned to Yerkes in 1901 as an assistant.

In early 1904, Adams traveled with Hale to set up an observing station on Mount Wilson, near Pasadena, California. The Mount Wilson Observatory was established on December 20, 1904, with Hale as director and Adams as a staff member. Adams, accustomed to the hills of Syria and New Hampshire, delighted in the ruggedness of the early days at Mount Wilson, which at that time could only be reached on foot or by mule or donkey.

At Mount Wilson, Adams and Hale determined that the temperatures of sunspots were cooler and their gases denser than the rest of the sun. Studies of spectra, the colored lines and bands produced by viewing a star's light through a spectroscope, yielded methods of classifying stars and determining their velocities. Analyses of these velocities greatly advanced scientific knowledge of the behavior of stars and galaxies. As Alfred H. Joy wrote in *Biographical Memoirs of the National Academy of Sciences*, "The completion of these great programs of stellar velocity and luminosity with the resulting distances of the stars constitutes an enduring memorial to the untiring industry and devotion of Dr. Adams."

Combines Observatory Administration with Research

Adams became assistant director of Mount Wilson in 1913. He succeeded Hale as director in 1923 and held that post until his retirement in 1946. He continued a heavy research schedule in addition to his administrative duties and became known for both his work in cataloguing stars and his contribution to the development of new instruments. In 1914, Adams and Arnold Kohlschütter discovered that they could determine the intrinsic brightness of many stars by looking at the intensity of particular lines in their photographed spectra. They found that the intensity of the spectral lines yielded a new method of measuring the distances of stars. This method, known as spectroscopic parallax, led to the acquisition of knowledge about the structure of the galaxy and the nature of dwarf and giant stars. His work with such stars inspired interest in 1915 in Sirius B, a faint companion to Sirius, which he had identified as a white dwarf star. In 1925, Adams made a spectrogram of the smaller companion body, noting a shift in the spectral lines toward the red end of the spectrum, confirming English astronomer **Arthur Stanley Eddington**'s prediction that Sirius B was dense enough to produce a redshift and thus supporting American physicist **Albert Einstein**'s general theory of relativity.

Adams also studied pulsing stars called Cepheid variables, binary stars, and novae. In 1932, he helped determine that Venus's atmosphere contains carbon dioxide and, two years later, found that Mars's atmosphere contains little oxygen. Toward the end of his career, he looked at the spectral lines of interstellar gases, which blended in among the lines of stellar spectra, and determined some velocities that gave clues to the motions caused by the galaxy's rotation.

In 1910, Adams married Lillian M. Wickham, who died in 1920. Two years later, he married Adeline L. Miller, with whom he had two sons, Edmund and John. His long research career, during which he published more than 270 papers, continued for ten years after his retirement from Mount Wilson. He received a number of awards, including the National Academy of Sciences's Draper Medal in 1918, and served in many scientific organizations, presiding over the American Astronomical Society from 1931 to 1934 and serving as vice president of the International Astronomical Union from 1935 to 1948. Adams was interested in politics and education and served for forty years on Pasadena's Library Board. He enjoyed detective stories as well as golf, bridge, and tennis. Adams suffered a stroke in the spring of 1956 and died on May 11 at his home in Pasadena, California.

SELECTED WRITINGS BY ADAMS:

Periodicals

"The Relativity Displacement of the Spectral Lines in the Companion of Sirius," *Proceedings of the National Academy of Sciences,* Volume 2, 1925, pp. 382–387.
"The Past Twenty Years of Physical Astronomy," *Science,* June 29, 1928, pp. 637–645.

SOURCES:

Books

Biographical Memoirs of the National Academy of Sciences, Columbia University Press, 1958, pp. 1–31.
Dictionary of Scientific Biography, Scribner, 1970, pp. 54–58.

Periodicals

Merrill, Paul W., "Walter S. Adams, Observer of Sun and Stars," *Science,* July 13, 1956, p. 67.
Shapely, Harlow, "A Master of Stellar Spectra," *Sky & Telescope,* July, 1956, p. 401.

—*Sketch by Julie Anderson*

Joy Adamson
1910-1980
Austrian naturalist

J oy Adamson gained global acclaim for her book *Born Free: A Lioness of Two Worlds* (1960), which led to a 1964 film version and an American television series. In an interview with Roy Newquist, Adamson observed that the enormous sales of *Born Free* "proves the hunger of people to return . . . to a world of genuine proportion, a world in which our balance and basic values have not been destroyed. All this shows how important it is to preserve the animal life we have left." Both naturalist and artist, Adamson

produced approximately 400 painting of wildflowers, 80 renditions of coral fish, and 570 studies of African tribes. For illustrating seven books on the flora of East Africa, she received the Gold Grenfall medal of the Royal Horticultural Society in 1947.

Christened Friederike Viktoria Gessner, Adamson was born on January 20, 1910, in Troppau, Silesia (now Opava in the Czech Republic). Her parents were Viktor Gessner, an architect, urban planner, and civil servant, and Traute (Greipel) Gessner, whose family were wealthy paper manufacturers. Her parents divorced when Adamson was twelve. At Vienna schools, Adamson pursued studies in music, metalwork, woodsculpting, art history, dressmaking, and design, and then began preparations for a medical career. In 1935, Adamson married the Austrian businessman Viktor von Klarwill.

Immigrates to Africa

In 1937, Adamson traveled to Kenya to explore the prospect of establishing residence in East Africa. Her marriage to Von Klarwill ended in divorce at this time, with Adamson remaining in Africa. In 1938, Adamson married Peter Bally, a botanist with the Nairobi Museum, whom she had met on her voyage. It was Bally who renamed Adamson "Joy." The couple spent their honeymoon on a scientific expedition to the Chyullu mountains, on the border of Kenya and Tanzania. A meticulous painter of flowers himself, Bally encouraged Adamson to paint the plants he collected. Adamson gradually expanded her range of subjects to include tribal life (providing valuable anthropological records), landscapes, and animals. Adamson and Bally were divorced in 1942. In 1943, she married George Adamson, a warden with Kenya's Game Department. Adamson continued her work painting flowers during these years, and contributed botanical samples to Kew Garden in England.

In 1956, George Adamson shot a lioness that attacked him when he inadvertently approached her cubs. He brought the lioness's three cubs home to Adamson, who had already raised many animals. Despite her protests, the chief game warden insisted that the three cubs would require too much care. On his orders, two cubs were sent to the Rotterdam Zoo. The departure of the two cubs focused Adamson's attention on the fate of young animals that were orphaned or wounded in the wild. She began a national animal orphanage that, after more than half a century, continues to operate in Nairobi.

The smallest of the cubs, Elsa, remained with the Adamsons. Adamson indicated to Roy Newquist that she developed an "utterly genuine and simple and natural" relationship with this lion, who "could understand my thoughts and act according to them. . . . I know that she was not merely responding [to] my mood or from physical signals. Elsa opened, for me, so many completely new and staggering insights into animal psychology." From the outset, nonetheless, Adamson was resolved not to turn Elsa into a pet, and she accepted an offer from the warden of the Maasai Mara Reserve to provide Elsa with a permanent home. The attempt, however, failed. Born in the high altitudes and dry climate of northern Kenya, Elsa fell ill in the hotter and lusher conditions 350 miles to the south. Moreover, George Adamson could find no way to persuade local prides to accept her.

The district commissioner at Meru in Northern Tanzania, close to where Elsa was born, subsequently offered to provide sanctuary for the lion. At two and a half years, Elsa was old enough to fend for herself, join a pride, and mate, but her upbringing had not given her the necessary skills. George Adamson help provide Elsa with training, and looked for ways to integrate her with local prides. When it was clear that Elsa had mated, the Adamsons left Elsa on her own. After the birth of her cubs, Elsa disappeared for six weeks. After this period, Elsa paid the Adamsons the first of many visits with her cubs. When Elsa was five, she died of a tick infection, and a local lioness drove the cubs out of the territory. After a long search, George Adamson found the cubs and transported them to the Serengeti National Park, where they were set free. Adamson told the cubs' story in her best-selling books *Living Free* and *Forever Free;* a film version was released in 1971.

Establishes Wildlife Preservation Fund

Adamson's books, films, and lectures, as noted in the January 5, 1985, *New York Times,* "brought a new awareness of relations between man and animal to millions of people." Exploiting this awareness, Adamson established the Elsa Wild Animal Appeal fund in the United Kingdom in 1961, in the United States in 1969, and in Canada in 1971. Adamson donated most of the proceeds from her books and films to this wildlife conservation fund. In addition, she was a pioneer in efforts to protect endangered species by boycotting products made from fur and other animal parts. Increasingly preferring wild animals to people, Adamson began living by herself in 1971, at a lakeside estate outside of Nairobi.

During these years, Adamson achieved a unique success in raising a cheetah, about whom she wrote two books, *The Spotted Sphinx* and *Pippa's Challenge.* Surprisingly little was known about cheetahs when Adamson began her studies. In 1976, Adamson embarked on her last major enterprise. She was given a leopard cub, which she named Penny. Fundamentally solitary and secretive, Penny nevertheless brought Adamson to see her cubs when they were only a few days old. The story of finding a habitat and reintro-

ducing Penny to the wild is described in Adamson's *Queen of Shaba.*

In addition to her Gold Grenfall medal, Adamson received many awards for her wildlife preservation work, including an award of merit from Czechoslovakia in 1970, the Joseph Wood Krutch medal of the United States Humane Society in 1971, and the Austrian Cross of Honor for Art and Science in 1977. Adamson's paintings were exhibited at the National Museum in Nairobi, the Tyron Galleries in Nairobi and London, the Fort Jesus Museum in Mombasa, the Indian Tea Center in London, and the Natural History Museum in Los Angeles. Adamson was a member of the Nanyuki and the Nairobi clubs in Kenya. On January 3, 1980, at age seventy, Adamson was murdered by a Turkana servant she had dismissed. On August 20, 1989, at age eighty-three, George Adamson was shot while driving to the rescue of a German woman being attacked by Somali thieves. Adrian House, in *The Great Safari: The Lives of George and Joy Adamson,* described the Adamsons as prophets of the green movement, who stimulated concern for animals and for the planet that humans and animals share.

SELECTED WRITINGS BY ADAMSON:

Books

Born Free: A Lioness of Two Worlds, Pantheon, 1960.
Living Free, Harcourt, 1961.
Forever Free, Harcourt, 1962.
The Spotted Sphinx, Harcourt, 1969.
Pippa's Challenge, Harcourt, 1972.
The Searching Spirit: An Autobiography, Collins Harvill, 1978, Harcourt, 1979.
Queen of Shaba: The Story of an African Leopard, Harcourt, 1980.

Illustrator

Arthur J. Jex-Blake, editor, *Gardening in East Africa,* Longmans, second edition, 1939, fourth edition, 1957.
Muriel Jex-Blake, *Some Wildflowers of Kenya,* Longmans, 1948.
Flores des spermatophytes, Parc National du Congo belge, 1955.
W. J. Eggeling, *Indigenous Trees of the Uganda Protectorate,* Government Printer (Entebbe), 1957.
Ivan R. Dale and Percy J. Greenway, *Kenya Trees and Shrubs,* Hatchards, 1961.

SOURCES:

Books

Adamson, George, *My Pride and Joy,* Collins Harvill, 1986.
House, Adrian, *The Great Safari: The Lives of George and Joy Adamson,* William Morrow, 1993.
Major Twentieth Century Writers, Gale, 1991.
Newquist, Roy, *Counterpoint,* Rand McNally, 1964.

Periodicals

Newsweek, January 21, 1980.
New York Times, January 5, 1980.

—*Sketch by Margaret DiCanio*

Edgar Douglas Adrian
1889-1977
English neurophysiologist

Lord Edgar Douglas Adrian, noted Cambridge University physiologist, won renown for his research on the functions of the brain and the nervous system. With Sir **Charles Scott Sherrington**, he received the Nobel Prize in physiology or medicine in 1932 in recognition of his work on the role of neurons in the stimulation of muscles and sense organs. Adrian's research also made possible the development of electroencephalography, or the measurement of electrical activity in the brain.

Born in London on November 30, 1889, Adrian was the son of Flora Lavinia Barton and Alfred Douglas Adrian. His father was legal counsel to the Local Government Board in London and saw to it that his son had a good education. Adrian attended London's Westminster School and in 1908 won a science scholarship which opened the doors of Cambridge University's Trinity College to him. Besides taking courses in other natural sciences, he studied physiology under the direction of the physiologist Keith Lucas. Lucas was researching the reactions of muscles and nerves to electrical stimulation. When Adrian joined in this pursuit, he set his course for a lifelong career investigating the nervous system. He graduated from Trinity College in 1911 with first-class honors in five subjects.

Develops New Understanding of the Nervous System

His work in neurophysiology with Lucas led Adrian into the analysis of the functioning of neurons (nerve cells) in the stimulation of muscles and sense organs. The physiologist Sherrington had already made discoveries in this field, which Adrian was to advance further. His early research with Lucas resulted in his election as a fellow of Trinity College in 1913. Adrian earned his bachelor of medicine degree in 1915 at St. Bartholomew's in London and was able to pursue his interest in the nervous system when he served in the British Army during World War I. He was assigned to the treatment of nerve injuries and disorders of servicemen at the Hospital for Nervous Diseases. The effect of shell shock was a particular area of study. The young doctor's efforts to get assigned to a post in France were unsuccessful, however.

Adrian's career took an unexpected turn when Lucas died in an airplane crash during the war and Adrian was appointed to take charge of his laboratory in 1919, the same year he received his doctor of medicine degree. In the laboratory, he resumed his work on nerve impulses and began using advanced electrical techniques. He was able to amplify by 5,000 times the impulses in a single nerve fiber and single end organ in a frog's muscle. Adrian published his first observations on these nerve stimuli experiments in 1926 and came forth with definitive conclusions in 1928. Impulses that led to the sensation of pain were of particular interest to Adrian, and he directed his attention to a study of the brain. He found that the regions of the brain leading to a particular sense organ varied between species of animals. In pigs, which use their snouts to explore their environment, for instance, almost the entire region of the cortex dedicated to touch is taken up with nerve endings of the fibers that lead to the snout. In humans, a large area is taken up with the endings of fibers leading to the hands. Adrian's work cast new light on the nature of the nervous impulse, the action of the neuron and the physical nature of sensation. Today's understanding of the human nervous system is to an important extent informed by Adrian's findings.

In 1929, Adrian was elected Foulerton Professor of the Royal Society. He made a trip to New York, where he worked with **Detlev Wulf Bronk** on converting electrical impulses to sound. Returning to Cambridge, he continued his investigations of how sensory impulses reach the brain. One of his aims was to develop a practical method of reading the brain's electrical wave patterns. His work laid the foundation for the development of clinical electroencephalography, which could accomplish such brain analysis. The electroencephalogram (EEG) made it possible to study such conditions as epilepsy and brain tumors.

Wins the Nobel Prize

It was announced on October 27, 1932, that Adrian and Sherrington were to share the Nobel Prize in physiology or medicine. The news was greeted enthusiastically throughout the scientific world and hailed particularly by the British press. Adrian was named professor of physiology at Cambridge in 1937 and was appointed to the Medical Research Council in 1939. From 1951 to 1965, he held the post of master of Trinity College and from 1957 to 1959 was also vice chancellor of Cambridge University. During these later years, he also served terms as president of the Royal Society, president of the British Association for the Advancement of Science, and president of the Royal Society of Medicine. He served on committees of the World Health Organization and, in 1962, was elected a trustee of Rockefeller University in New York.

Among the many awards received for his research achievements were the Royal Medal (1934), the British Order of Merit (1942), the Copley Medal from the Royal Society (1946), the Albert Gold Medal of the Royal Society of the Arts (1953), the Harben Medal (1955), the French Legion of Honor (1956), the Medal for Distinguished Merit of the British Medical Association (1958) and the Jephcott Medal of the Royal Society of Medicine (1963). In 1955, he was knighted First Baron Adrian of Cambridge. Adrian did not confine his activities to the laboratory or lecture hall. He and his wife enjoyed mountain climbing. He also enjoyed fencing, sailing and fast bicycle riding. He took a strong interest in the arts, particularly painting. The exhibit of eighty of his works in Cambridge marked the high point of his hobby. When he retired from Trinity in 1965, he continued to live in the college's Neville's Court almost until his death on August 4, 1977.

SELECTED WRITINGS BY ADRIAN:

Books

The Basis of Sensation: The Action of the Sense Organs, Christophers, 1928.
The Mechanism of Nervous Action, University of Pennsylvania Press, 1932.
The Physical Basis of Perception, Clarendon Press, 1947.

Periodicals

(With Yngve Zotterman) "The Impulses Produced by Sensory Nerve Endings," *Journal of Physiology,* Volume 62, 1926.
(With Detlev W. Bronk) "The Discharge of Impulses in Motor Nerve Fibres," *Journal of Physiology,* Volume 66, 1928.

"The Activity of the Nervous System in the Caterpillar," *Journal of Physiology,* Volume 70, 1930.
(With Bryan Harold Cabot Matthews), "The Interpretation of Potential Waves in the Cortex" *Journal of Physiology,* Volume 81, 1934, pp. 440–471.

SOURCES:

Books

Fox, Daniel M., Marcia Meldrum, and Ira Rezak, editors, *Nobel Laureates in Medicine or Physiology,* Garland, 1990.
Magill, Frank N., editor, *Nobel Prize Winners, Physiology or Medicine,* Volume 1, *1901–1944,* Salem Press, 1991.

—*Sketch by Tom K. Phares*

Lars V. Ahlfors
1907-
Finnish-born American mathematician

Lars V. Ahlfors is a mathematician whose major area of research has been in complex analysis. In 1936 he was one of the first to receive a Fields Medal. Often considered the equivalent of the Nobel Prize, the Fields Medal is given every four years to a mathematician under the age of forty who has achieved important results in his or her work. Ahlfors received this award for his work on Riemann surfaces, which are schematic devices for mapping the relation between complex numbers according to an analytic function. Ahlfors's results led to new developments in the field of meromorphic functions (functions that are analytic everywhere in a region except for a finite number of poles); the methods he developed to obtain these results created an entirely new field of analysis.

Lars Valerian Ahlfors was born on April 18, 1907 in Helsingfors, Finland. His mother, Sievä Helander Ahlfors, died giving birth to him. His father, Axel Ahlfors, was a mechanical engineering professor at the Polytechnical Institute. Even as a child, Ahlfors was interested in mathematics; his high school did not offer calculus courses, but Ahlfors taught himself by reading his father's engineering books.

He did not have access to mathematical books until he began his studies in 1924 at the University of

Helsingfors, where he was taught by Ernst Lindelöf and Rolf Nevanlinna. Lindelöf worked in complex analysis and was known as the father of mathematics in Finland—mostly because, in the 1920s, all Finnish mathematicians were his students. Ahlfors received his degree in the spring of 1928, and he also began his graduate work that year. Although there were no official graduate courses in mathematics at the university, Lindelöf supervised students' advanced readings.

Proposes Geometric Interpretation of Nevalinna Theory

Ahlfors took his first official graduate course in mathematics in the fall of 1928, when he accompanied Nevanlinna to Zürich. The class Nevanlinna taught was on contemporary function theory. Topics included the major parts of Nevanlinna's theory of meromorphic functions and Denjoy's conjecture on the number of asymptotic values of an entire function, as well as Carleman's partial proof of it. During his study of this subject, Ahlfors proved the full Denjoy conjecture after he discovered a new approach based on conformal mapping. A conformal map is a function in which, if two curves intersect at an angle, then the images of the curves in the map will also intersect at the same angle.

When the course ended, Ahlfors travelled to Paris, where he continued his work for three months before returning to Finland. His research there led to a geometric interpretation of the Nevanlinna theory, which he would publish in 1935. Although this interpretation was also discovered independently in Japan, it was the beginning of Ahlfors's concentration on meromorphic functions.

When he returned to Finland, Ahlfors was given the position of lecturer at Åbo Academy, a Swedish-language university. He also began work on his thesis, the subject of which was conformal mapping and entire functions. He had finished his thesis by the spring of 1930, and received his Ph.D. in 1932. Ahlfors was named a fellow of the Rockefeller Institute in 1932, which allowed him to live and do research in Paris for a year. In July of 1933, he married Erna Lehnert; they would have three daughters. He returned to the University of Helsingfors that same year as an adjunct professor and taught there until the fall of 1935, when he began a three-year assignment as assistant professor at Harvard University.

Receives Fields Medal

For his research in Riemann surfaces of inverse functions in terms of covering surfaces, Ahlfors was awarded the Fields Medal by the International Congress of Mathematicians in 1936. Ahlfors was

attending the ceremony in Oslo, but he learned only hours before it began that he had been chosen as the recipient. In the talk about Ahlfors's work he gave to the congress, German mathematician Constantin Carathéodory specifically noted the contribution of Ahlfors's paper, "On the Theory of Covering Surfaces," which explained the methods Ahlfors had developed in his work on Riemann surfaces. Carathéodory pointed out that these methods were also the start of a new branch of analysis, which he termed "metrical topology."

In the spring of 1938, Ahlfors left the United States and returned to Finland to take a position as a professor at the University of Helsinki. World War II soon spread to Finland, however, and the university closed because there were not enough students. Although his family was evacuated to Sweden, Ahlfors stayed in Helsinki. He was not called for military duty because of a physical condition, but he participated in the military's communications setup.

In the summer of 1944, the University of Zürich offered Ahlfors a professorship, and he accepted the position. After an arduous journey from Sweden to Switzerland because of the war, he began teaching in the summer of 1945. He was not happy there, however, so when Harvard University asked him to return he gladly accepted. He began teaching there in the fall of 1946 and became a naturalized United States citizen in 1952. In 1953, Ahlfors's book *Complex Analysis* was published. It is still widely used as a basic text in graduate courses. Ahlfors remained at Harvard until his retirement as professor emeritus in 1977.

SELECTED WRITINGS BY AHLFORS:

Books

Complex Analysis, McGraw-Hill, 1953.
(With L. Sario) *Riemann Surfaces,* Princeton University Press, 1960.
Lectures on Quasiconformal Mappings, D. Van Nostrand Company, 1966.
Conformal Invariants, McGraw-Hill, 1973.
Lars Valerian Ahlfors: Collected Papers, Volume I: 1929–1955, Volume II: 1956–1979, Birkhäuser, 1982.

—*Sketch by Laura Mangan-Grenier*

Howard Aiken
1900-1973
American computer scientist and inventor

Howard Aiken

A noted physicist and Harvard professor, Howard Aiken designed and built the Mark I calculator in the late 1930s and early 1940s. The first large-scale digital calculator, the Mark I provided the impetus for larger and more advanced computing machines. Aiken's later conceptions, the Mark II, Mark III, and Mark IV, each surpassed its previous model in terms of speed and calculating capacity.

Howard Hathaway Aiken was born on March 8, 1900, in Hoboken, New Jersey, and was raised in Indianapolis, Indiana. Because of his family's limited resources, he had to go to work after completing the eighth grade. He worked twelve-hour shifts at night, seven days a week, as a switchboard operator for the Indianapolis Light and Heat Company. During the day he attended Arsenal Technical High School. When the school superintendent learned of his round-the-clock work and study schedule, he arranged a series of special tests that enabled Aiken to graduate early. In 1919 Aiken entered the University of Wisconsin at Madison and worked part-time for Madison's gas company while he attended classes. He received his bachelor of science degree in 1923 and upon graduation was immediately promoted to chief engineer of the gas company. Over the next twelve years he became a professor at the University of Miami and later went into business for himself. By 1935, however, he had decided that he wanted to return to school to work on his Ph.D. He began his graduate studies at the University of Chicago before going on to Harvard. He received a master's degree in physics in 1937 and was made an instructor. He wrote his dissertation while he was teaching and received his doctorate in 1939.

Proposes Design for First Modern Computer

As a graduate student in physics, Aiken completed a great deal of work requiring many hours of long and tedious calculations; it was at that time that he began to think seriously about improving calculating machines to reduce the time needed for figuring large numerical sequences. In 1937, while at Harvard, Aiken wrote a 22-page memorandum proposing the initial design for his computer. His idea was to build a computer from existing hardware with electromagnetic components controlled by coded sequences of instructions, and one that would operate automatically after a particular process had been developed. Aiken proposed that the punched-card calculators then in use (which could carry out only one arithmetic operation at a time) could be modified to become fully automated and to carry out a wide range of arithmetic and mathematical functions. His original design was inspired by a description of a more powerful calculator in the work of English mathematician Charles Babbage, who devoted nearly forty years to developing a calculating machine.

Although Aiken was by then an instructor at Harvard (and was to become an associate professor of applied mathematics in 1941 and a full professor in 1946), the university offered little support for his initial idea. He therefore turned to private industry for assistance. Although his first attempt to muster corporate support was turned down by the Monroe Calculating Machine Company, its chief engineer, G. C. Chase, approved of Aiken's proposal and suggested he contact Theodore Brown, a professor at the Harvard Business School; Brown, in turn, put Aiken in touch with IBM. Aiken's idea impressed IBM enough that the company agreed to back the construction of his Mark I. In 1939 IBM President Thomas Watson, Sr., signed a contract that stated that IBM would build the computer under Aiken's supervision and with additional financial backing from the U.S. Navy. At the time IBM only manufactured office machines, but its management wanted to encourage research in new and promising areas and was eager to establish a connection with Harvard. During that same year, Aiken became a school officer of the Naval Warfare School at Yorktown, and when the Mark I contract was worked out he was made officer in charge of the U.S. Navy Computing Project. The Navy agreed to support Aiken's computer because the Mark I offered a great deal of potential for expediting the complex mathematical calculations involved in aiming long-range guns onboard ship. The Mark I provided a solution to the problem by calculating gun trajectories in a matter of minutes.

Builds Mark I-IV

With a grant from IBM and a Navy contract, Aiken and a team headed by IBM's Clair D. Lake began work at IBM's laboratories in Endicott, New York. Aiken's machine was electromechanical—mechanical parts, electrically controlled—and used ordinary telephone relays that enabled electrical currents to be switched on or off. The computer consisted of thousands of relays and other components, all assembled in a 51-foot-long and 8-foot-high stainless steel and glass frame that was completed in 1943 and installed at Harvard a year later. The heart of this huge machine was formed by 72 rotating registers, each of which could store a positive or negative 23-digit number. The telephone relays established communication between the registers. Instructions and data input were entered into the computer by means of continuous strips of IBM punch-card paper. Output was printed by two electrical typewriters hooked up to the machine. The Mark I did not resemble modern computers, either in appearance or in principles of operation. The machine had no keyboard, for instance, but was operated with approximately 1,400 rotary switches that had to be adjusted to set up a run. Seemingly clumsy by today's computer standards, the Mark I nevertheless was a powerful improvement over its predecessors in terms of the speed at which it performed a host of complex mathematical calculations. Many scientists and engineers were eager for time on the machine, underscoring the project's success and giving added impetus for continued work on improved models. However, a dispute developed with IBM over credit for the computer, and subsequently the company withdrew support for all further efforts. A more powerful model was soon undertaken under pressure from competition from ENIAC, the much faster computer then being built at Columbia University.

Mark I was to have three successors, Mark II through IV. It was with the Mark III that Aiken began building electronic machines. Aiken had a conservative outlook with respect to electronic engineering and sacrificed the speed associated with electronic technology for the dependability of mechanics; only after World War II did he begin to feel comfortable using electronic hardware. In 1949 Aiken finished the Mark III with the incorporation of electronic components. Data and instructions were stored on magnetic drums with a capacity of 4,350 sixteen-bit words and roughly 4,000 instructions. With Aiken's continued concern

for reliability over speed, he called his Mark III "the slowest all-electronic machine in the world," as quoted by David Ritchie in *The Computer Pioneers: The Making of the Modern Computer.* The Mark III's final version, however, was not completely electronic; it still contained about 2,000 mechanical relays in addition to its electronic components. The Mark IV followed on the heels of the Mark III and was considerably faster.

Aiken contributed to the early computing years by demonstrating that a large, calculating computer could not only be built but could also provide the scientific world with high-powered, speedy mathematical solutions to a plethora of problems. Aiken remained at Harvard until 1961, when he moved to Fort Lauderdale, Florida. He went on to help the University of Miami set up a computer science program and a computing center and became Distinguished Professor of Information there. At the same time he founded a New York-based consulting firm, Howard Aiken Industries Incorporated. Aiken disliked the idea of patents and was known for sharing his work with others. He died on March 14, 1973.

SOURCES:

Books

Augarten, Stan, *Bit by Bit,* Ticknor & Fields, 1984.

Fang, Irving E., *The Computer Story,* Rada Press, 1988.

Moreau, R., *The Computer Comes of Age,* MIT Press, 1984.

Ritchie, David, *The Computer Pioneers: The Making of the Modern Computer,* Simon and Schuster, 1986.

Slater, Robert, *Portraits in Silicon,* MIT Press, 1987. Stine, Harry G., *The Untold Story of the Computer Revolution: Bits, Bytes, Bauds, and Brains,* Arbor House, 1985.

Wulforst, Harry, *Breakthrough to the Computer Age,* Charles Scribner's Sons, 1982.

—Sketch by Dorothy Spencer

Keiiti Aki
1930-
Japanese-born American seismologist

Keiiti Aki

Keiiti Aki is one of the world's foremost earthquake experts. His contributions to the science of seismology, or the study of earthquakes, have been many and varied, both at the theoretical level and in practical applications. His discoveries have helped scientists to better anticipate earthquakes and to control casualties from seismic events. He has also pursued research in the propagation of seismic waves, discovery of geothermal energy sources, and analysis of the earth's crustal structure.

Aki was born in Yokohama, Japan, on March 3, 1930, the son of Koichi and Humiko (Kojima) Aki. He was educated at the University of Tokyo, where he earned a bachelor's degree in 1952 and a doctorate in geophysics in 1958. That same year he came to the United States as a Fulbright resident fellow in geophysics at the California Institute of Technology (Cal Tech), where he remained for two years before returning to Japan. At the Earthquake Research Institute at the University of Tokyo he was first a research fellow in seismology from 1960 to 1962, and then an associate professor from 1963 to 1965. He returned briefly to Cal Tech for the academic year 1962–63 as a visiting associate professor of geophysics. Aki came to the United States permanently in 1966, when he joined the geophysics faculty at the Massachusetts Institute of Technology (MIT). He became a U.S. citizen in 1976 and remained at MIT until 1984. In 1956 Aki married Haruko Uyeda, the sister of geophysicist and tectonics expert **Seiya Uyeda**. The couple has two sons.

Aki's single most important contribution was his introduction, in 1966, of a new method of measuring the size of an earthquake. Called the seismic moment, it is calculated using three types of ways to study earthquakes: geodetic, geologic, and seismic observations. It is a refinement over the less precise Richter scale. Aki considers his most original contribution to his field, however, to be his concept of coda waves. These are named after the musical term *coda,* which is the section that brings a musical piece to a close. An earthquake generates several kinds of waves that radiate outward from the epicenter in all directions. When these waves have dissipated, the earth near the epicenter continues to vibrate, and these remaining vibrations (the "tail" of the waves, or very ends) are called coda waves. The amplitude of the coda waves remains consistent throughout similar geological structures and decays at a uniform rate. Analysis of coda waves reveals information about the source of

the earthquake and the geology of the places where the recording instruments are located.

In the 1970s, Aki developed an idea that is now called seismic tomography. It is similar to medical tomography in that it provides a means for scientists to create three-dimensional models of the interior of the earth, much as physicians can do with the human body. More recently, Aki formulated quantitative models to explain the "harmonic tremor" that accompanies volcanic eruptions, and a technique called the Aki-Larner method, which calculates seismic motion in layered earth media with irregular interfaces. He has also applied fractal geometry to investigations of fault systems.

Aki has served as an adviser to many scientific organizations, including the Los Alamos National Laboratory, the Nuclear Regulatory Commission, and the U.S. Geological Survey. He has also acted as an advisor to the United Nations. In 1984 he became the W. M. Keck Foundation Professor of Geological Sciences at the University of Southern California in Los Angeles.

Aki's book *Quantitative Seismology* became a standard textbook for advanced seismology students. He has edited numerous other books ranging in subject matter from the process of mountain development to the seismology of volcanoes. He is a member of the National Academy of Sciences, the American Geophysical Union, and other scientific organizations, and is an honorary member of a number of international societies, such as the Royal Astronomical Society and the Seismological Society of Japan. In 1987 Aki became the tenth medalist of the Seismological Society of America, and in 1993 he was honored by the University of Southern California for the creativity of his research. He became director of the Southern California Earthquake Center in 1991.

SELECTED WRITINGS BY AKI:

Books

(With Paul Richards) *Quantitative Seismology: Theory and Methods,* Volumes 1 and 2, W. H. Freeman, 1980.

(With A. Miyashiro and A. M. Celeal Sengor), editors, *Orogeny,* Wiley, 1982.

(With W. D. Stuart), editors, *Intermediate-Term Earthquake Prediction,* Birkhäuser, 1988.

Periodicals

"Generation and Propagation of G Waves from the Niigata Earthquake of June 16, 1964, Part 1. A Statistical Analysis," *Bulletin of the Earthquake Research Institute,* Volume 44, 1966, pp. 73–88.

"Generation and Propagation of G Waves from the Niigata Earthquake of June 16, 1964, Part 2. Estimation of Earthquake Moment, Released Energy, and Stress-Strain Drop from the G Wave Spectrum," *Bulletin of the Earthquake Research Institute,* Volume 44, 1966, pp. 73–88.

"Analysis of the Seismic Coda of Local Earthquakes as Scattered Waves," *Journal of Geophysical Research,* Volume 74, 1969, pp. 6215–6231.

(With W. H. K. Lee) "Determination of Three-Dimensional Velocity Anomalies under a Seismic Array using First P Arrival Times from Local Earthquakes. 1. A Homogeneous Initial Model," *Journal of Geophysical Research,* Volume 81, 1976, pp. 4381–4399.

SOURCES:

Keiiti, Ali, letter to C. A. Williams dated November 5, 1992.

—*Sketch by C. A. Williams*

Jose Alcala
1940-
Puerto Rican American anatomist

Much of what is known about the membranes of cells that make up the lens of the human eye was discovered by Jose Alcala, a Puerto Rican-American professor of anatomy who developed laboratory methods to study the histology of this ocular tissue. Alcala's work helped to explain the development of cataracts, a condition in which the lens of the eye becomes cloudy. Alcala has also helped other researchers to develop animal models of cataracts in order to study this condition. Jose Ramon Alcala was born on May 1, 1940, in Ponce, Puerto Rico. His father, Jose Antonio Alcala, a civil engineer, died when his son was eight-years-old. His mother, Aurea Estela Ruiz, a registered nurse, remarried the following year. Alcala's stepfather was a U.S. Army sergeant who took his new family to back to Fort Leonard Wood, Missouri, where he was stationed. After graduating from Waynesville High School, Alcala returned briefly to Puerto Rico to work but soon traveled back to Missouri to earn money for college. He graduated from the University of Missouri, Columbia, in 1964, the same day he married Susan E. Vesper. He received his M.S. in zoology from the University of Missouri in 1966.

For his master's thesis, he studied the uterus masculinus (remnant of the embryonic uterus) in male tree shrews. He demonstrated that the structure developed into a secondary sexual gland in conjunction with the prostate gland and the seminal vesicles. Because this structure is present in some species of tree shrews and not in others, Alcala proposed, some species should be reclassified. For his doctoral research at the University of Illinois Medical Center in Chicago he studied the immunological characteristics of tubulin, a protein in the brain that is a component of nerve axons and dendrites.

After receiving his doctorate in 1972, Alcala joined the faculty at Wayne State University School of Medicine in Detroit, Michigan, as assistant professor of anatomy. He was promoted to full professor in 1987 and held a joint appointment as associate professor of ophthalmology from 1986–88. In addition, Alcala was Wayne State's academic director of the post-baccalaureate program for disadvantaged students for many years. In 1990 he was named director of the gross anatomy programs of the School of Medicine. He was also supervisor of the body bequest program and a member of the anatomy board of the state of Michigan.

During the 1970s Alcala analyzed the structure of the fiber cell membranes of the eye's lens. He developed a technique for isolating these membranes in cows and chickens as well as laboratory tests for studying their protein and lipid composition. He later modified this technique and used it to analyze human lens fiber plasma membranes. This led to a better understanding of the aging of the human lens and the process of cataract formation.

Alcala's work also contributed to an understanding of the lens fiber gap juncture, an area in which adjacent cell membranes are separated by a narrow cleft. He also explained that the difference between the physiological functioning of the lens gap and the gap junctions of other organs is due to the presence of a lipid called sphingomyelin. His later studies examined the breakdown of protein in the lens fiber plasma membranes and helped to clarify the development of cataract.

Alcala returned to Puerto Rico in 1992 to become chair of the anatomy department at the Ponce School of Medicine, in Ponce, where he continued his studies of lens proteins. He is supervisor of the school's body donation program and a member of the state anatomy board of the Commonwealth of Puerto Rico. Alcala is a member of the New York Academy of Sciences, the American Association of Clinical Anatomists, the Association for Research in Vision and Ophthalmology, the International Society for Eye Research, and the American Association of Anatomists.

SELECTED WRITINGS BY ALCALA:

Periodicals

(With C. H. Conaway) "The Gross and Microscopic Anatomy of the Uterus Masculinus of Tree Shrews," *Folia Primatologica,* Volume 9, 1968, pp. 216–245.
(With J. Valentine and H. Maisel) "Human Lens Fiber Cell Plasma Membranes. I. Isolation, Polypeptide Composition and Changes Associated with Ageing," *Experimental Eye Research,* Volume 30, 1980, pp. 659–677.
(With D. Putt and H. Maisel) "Limited Proteolysis of Gap Junction Protein Is Intrinsic in Mammalian Lens Fiber-Cell Plasma Membranes," *Biochemical and Biophysical Research Communications,* Volume 147, 1987, pp. 846–853.
(With W. Harries) "Crosslinkage of MP26 Membrane Domains and Its Effect on the Limited Proteolysis of MP26," *Investigative Ophthalmology and Visual Science* (Supplement), Volume 33, 1992, p. 866.

—Sketch by Marc Kusinitz

George Edward Alcorn
1940-
American physicist

George Edward Alcorn is responsible for a number of inventions now widely used in the semiconductor industry. He is perhaps best known for inventing an imaging X-ray spectrometer which uses the thermomigration of aluminum, an achievement which earned him the 1984 Inventor of the Year Award from the National Aeronautics and Space Administration (NASA) and the Goddard Space Flight Center. Alcorn has worked in industry and government, as well as academics, and he is currently chief of the Office of Commercial Programs for the Goddard Space Flight Center.

Alcorn was born on March 22, 1940, to George and Arletta Dixon Alcorn. His father was an auto mechanic who sacrificed so Alcorn and his brother could get an education. Alcorn attended Occidental College in Pasadena, California, where he maintained an excellent academic record while earning eight letters in baseball and football. Alcorn graduated with a B.A. in physics in 1962, and in 1963 he completed a master's degree in nuclear physics from Howard University. During the summers of 1962 and 1963, Alcorn worked as a research engineer for the Space Division of North American Rockwell, computing trajectories and orbital mechanics for missiles. A NASA grant supported Alcorn's research on negative ion formation during the summers of 1965 and 1966. In 1967 he earned his doctorate from Howard University in atomic and molecular physics. After earning his Ph.D., Alcorn spent twelve years in industry. He was senior scientist at Philco-Ford, senior physicist at Perker-Elmer, and advisory engineer at IBM Corporation. In 1973, Alcorn was chosen to be IBM Visiting Professor in Electrical Engineering at Howard University, and he has held positions at that university ever since, rising to the rank of full professor. Alcorn is also a full professor in the department of electrical engineering at the University of the District of Columbia, where he has taught courses ranging from advanced engineering mathematics to microelectronics.

Alcorn left IBM in 1978 as a Second Plateau Inventor to join NASA. While at NASA, Alcorn invented an imaging X-ray spectrometer using thermomigration of aluminum, for which he earned a patent in 1984, and two years later he devised an improved method of fabrication using laser drilling. His work on imaging X-ray spectrometers earned him the 1984 NASA/GSFC Inventor of the Year Award. During this period he also served as deputy project manager for advanced development, and in this position he was responsible for developing new technologies required for the space station Freedom. Alcorn served as manager for advanced programs at NASA/GSFC from 1990 to 1992, and his primary duties concerned the managing of technology programs and evaluating technologies which were required by GSFC. He also managed the GSFC Evolution Program, concerned with ensuring that over its thirty-year mission the space station develops properly while incorporating new capabilities. Since 1992, Alcorn has served as chief of Goddard's Office of Commercial Programs supervising programs for technology transfer, small business innovation research, and the commercial use of space programs.

Alcorn holds over twenty-five patents. He is a recognized pioneer in the fabrication of plasma semiconductor devices, and his patent "Process for Controlling the Slope of a Via Hole" was an important contribution to the process of plasma etching. This procedure is now used by many semiconductor manufacturing companies. Alcorn was one of the first scientists to present a computer-modeling solution of wet etched and plasma etched structures, and he has received several cash prizes for his inventions of plasma-processing techniques.

Alcorn has been extensively involved in community service. In 1984, he was awarded a NASA-EEO medal for his contributions in recruiting minority and women scientists and engineers and his assistance to minority businesses in establishing research programs. He is a founder of Saturday Academy, which is a weekend honors program designed to supplement and extend math-science training for inner-city students in grades six to eight. Alcorn also works with the Meyerhoff Foundation, whose goal is to encourage and support African American males interested in pursuing doctorates in science and engineering. Alcorn married Marie DaVillier in 1969; they have one son, born in 1979. Alcorn's younger brother Charles is a research physicist at IBM.

SELECTED WRITINGS BY ALCORN:

Periodicals

(With J. Feeley and T. Lyman) "Aluminum-Copper-Silicon Subetch Process," *IBM Technical Disclosure Bulletin,* Volume 19, 1976, p. 981.

(With F. H. De La Moneda and H. N. Kotecha) "Stepped-Oxide CCD With Asymmetrical Oxide Geometry," *IBM Technical Disclosure Bulletin,* Volume 24, 1981, pp. 1383–1387.

(With K. A. Kost and F. E. Marshall) "X-ray Spectrometer by Aluminum Thermomigration," *International Electron Devices Meeting, Proceedings,* 1982, pp. 312–314.

SOURCES:

Periodicals

"Space Station Freedom," *Journal of the NTA,* fall, 1988, p. 22.

Other

Alcorn, George E., interview with Mark J. Kaiser conducted February 24, 1994.

—*Sketch by Mark J. Kaiser*

Kurt Alder
1902-1958
German chemist

Kurt Alder was recognized for his contribution to synthetic organic chemistry, especially for the reaction which has been called the diene reaction, or the Diels-Alder reaction, after Alder and his mentor-colleague, Otto Diels. This reaction, discovered in 1928, was so useful in the synthesis of every type of organic compound that Diels and Alder were awarded the Nobel Prize in chemistry in 1950 for their development of the method. It was Alder who explored the reaction deeply, and wrote many papers on the nature of the reactants and products, including the stereochemistry, or geometric consequences, of the reaction.

Alder was born on July 10, 1902, in Königshütte, Germany. His father, Joseph Alder, was a schoolteacher in the nearby town of Kattowitz. Kurt attended the local schools, but at the end of World War I, the region in which the Alders lived became part of Poland, and Joseph Alder moved his family to Kiel in order to retain their German citizenship. Kurt Alder completed his secondary education in Berlin, and enrolled in the University of Berlin in 1922. He began to study chemistry at Berlin, but transferred to the Christian Albrecht University (now University of Kiel) and worked under **Otto Diels**, professor of organic chemistry and director of the chemical institute. Alder obtained his Ph.D. in 1926, and remained at the university as Diels's assistant. Diels and Alder collaborated in their research at Kiel for a decade. Alder was promoted to reader in organic chemistry in 1930 and extraordinary professor in 1934. The direct interaction between the two chemists ended in 1936 when Alder accepted an appointment as director of scientific research at the Bayer Werke laboratory at

Leverkusen, a branch of I. G. Farbenindustrie. This position gave Alder direct experience with industrial chemistry, and his expertise was directed to the development of synthetic rubber, which was a goal of organic chemists in every nation at that time. Alder left Bayer in 1940 and returned to academic life. He was appointed to the chair of experimental chemistry and chemical technology at the University of Cologne, and he was also director of the university's Chemistry Institute. He served as Dean of the Faculty of Philosophy in 1949 and 1950. He remained at Cologne until his death on June 20, 1958.

Receives Nobel Prize for Discovery of New Synthetic Method

The diene synthesis is one of a few methods which has proven to be so useful to organic chemists that their development led to Nobel Prizes for the chemists who discovered them. The diene synthesis requires two components, the diene and the dienophile. The diene contains four atoms, in which the first and second are joined by a double bond, as are the third and fourth: 1=2-3=4. The greatest number of dienes have carbon as the numbered atoms, but nitrogen, oxygen, or sulfur may be substituted for a carbon atom. The dienophile contains a double bond: 5=6. Again, the atoms are usually carbon, but may be other elements. When the diene and dienophile react, a ring containing the six atoms is formed, with new single bonds between all the atoms except 2 and 3, which is joined by a double bond. In general, all of the new bonds are formed in one step, in what is termed a concerted reaction. Because six-membered rings are found in many natural products, the diene synthesis has been used successfully in the syntheses of such complex molecules as reserpine, morphine, and many steroids. Commercial products have been synthesized with the reaction, including the insecticides dieldrin and aldrin (named for the chemists) and chlordane. Alder and his students carried out extensive investigations on the geometry of the ring formation, and discovered regularities which allowed the geometry to be predicted with certainty.

In the course of his research at Bayer Werke, Alder found that the reaction between butadiene, a diene, and styrene, a dienophile, gave a normal diene reaction under certain experimental conditions. However, by allowing the reaction to take place in the presence of peroxides, a polymer—a molecule consisting of similar or identical small molecules linked together—was formed, which was the synthetic rubber known as "Buna S." This was developed commercially in Germany in the 1930s, and was ultimately important during World War II, when supplies of natural rubber were curtailed.

Alder discovered another reaction in 1943, which has been named the ene reaction. This is also a concerted reaction, and Alder recognized its essential similarity to the diene synthesis. In the ene reaction, one reactant contains three atoms, with a double bond between atoms 1 and 2, and a hydrogen atom attached to atom 3: 1=2-3-H. The other reactant contains a double bond: 4=5. In the product, the hydrogen atom moves from atom 3 to atom 4, atom 1 joins atom 5, and a double bond forms between atoms 2 and 3: H-4-5-1-2=3. Alder called this type of reaction a substituting addition. The ene reaction also has found widespread use in synthesis. The mechanism of the diene reaction and the ene reaction was a matter of great interest for many years, for Alder and others. The theoretical foundation was not completely established until 1965, when **Robert B. Woodward** (Nobel Prize, 1965) and **Roald Hoffmann** (Nobel Prize, 1981) showed that these concerted reactions were governed by rules determined by quantum mechanics. The Diels-Alder reaction is one of many known "cycloaddition reactions" in which rings are formed from open-chain compounds, and the Woodward-Hoffmann rules accurately predict the course of these reactions.

Alder never married, and his greatest interests were his science, his colleagues, and students. He was committed to world peace and joined other Nobel laureates in 1955 in an appeal to governments to end war. His failing health limited his activities, and he died in Cologne at the early age of fifty-five.

SELECTED WRITINGS BY ALDER:

Books

"Diene Synthesis and Related Reaction Types," in *Nobelstiftelsen: Nobel Lectures: Chemistry, 1942–1962,* Elsevier, 1964, pp. 267–303.

SOURCES:

Books

Carruthers, W., *Some Modern Methods of Organic Synthesis,* third edition, Cambridge, 1986, pp. 184–262.

—*Sketch by Martin R. Feldman*

Pavel S. Aleksandrov
1896-1982
Russian mathematician

Pavel S. Aleksandrov laid the foundation for the field of mathematics known as topology. In addition to writing the first comprehensive textbook on the subject, Aleksandrov introduced several basic concepts of topology and its offshoots, homology and cohomology, which blend topology and algebra. His important work in defining and exploring bicompact (compact or locally compact) spaces laid the groundwork for research done by other mathematicians in these fields.

The youngest of the six children of Sergei Aleksandrovich Aleksandrov and Tsezariia Akimovna Zdanovskaia, Pavel Sergeevich Aleksandrov was born in Bogorodsk, Russia, on May 7, 1896. A year later the family moved to Smolensk, where Aleksandrov's father became head doctor in the state hospital. Although educated mainly in public schools, Aleksandrov learned German and French from his mother, who was skilled in languages.

In grammar school Aleksandrov developed an interest in mathematics under the guidance of Aleksandr Eiges, his arithmetic teacher. Aleksandrov entered the University of Moscow in 1913 as a mathematics student, and achieved early success when he proved the importance of Borel sets after hearing a lecture by Nikolai Nikolaevich Luzin in 1914. Aleksandrov graduated in 1917 and planned to continue his studies. However, after failing to reach similar results on his next project—**Georg Cantor**'s continuum hypothesis (since acknowledged unsolvable; that is, it can be neither proved nor disproved)—Aleksandrov dropped out of the mathematical community and formed a theater group in Chernigov, a city situated seventy-seven miles north of Kiev, in the Ukraine. Besides participating in the theater group, he lectured publicly on various topics in literature and mathematics. He also was involved in political support of the new Soviet government, for which he was jailed briefly in 1919 by counterrevolutionaries.

Key Friendship Leads to Lifelong Career

Later that same year, Aleksandrov suffered a lengthy illness, during which he decided to return to Moscow and mathematics. To help himself catch up, he enlisted the help of another young graduate student, Pavel Samuilovich Uryson. The two immediately became close friends and colleagues. After a brief, unsuccessful marriage in 1921 to his former teacher's sister, Ekaterina Romanovna Eiges, Alek-

sandrov joined some fellow graduate students in renting a summer cottage. There, he and Uryson began their study of the new field of topology, the branch of mathematics that deals with properties of figures related directly to their shape and invariant under continuous transformation (that is, without cutting or tearing). In topology, often called rubber-sheet geometry, a cylinder and a sphere are equivalent, because one can be shaped (or transformed) into the other. A doughnut, however, is not equivalent to a sphere, because it cannot be shaped or stretched into a sphere. No textbooks were available on the subject, only articles by **Maurice Fréchet**, **Felix Hausdorff**, and a few others. Nonetheless, from these articles, Uryson and Aleksandrov came up with their first major topological discovery: the theorem of metrization. Metrization is the process of deriving a specific measurement for the abstract concept of a topological space. In order to do this, Aleksandrov and Uryson first had to develop definitions of topological spaces. They initially defined a *bicompact* space (now known as compact and locally compact spaces), whose property is that for any collection of open sets (or groups of elements) that contains it (the interior of a sphere is an example of an open set). There is a subset of the collection with a finite number of elements that also contains it. Prior to their work, the concept of space was too abstract to be applicable to other mathematical fields; Aleksandrov and Uryson's research led to the acceptance of topology as a valid field of mathematical study.

With this result, the pair rose to fame within the mathematical community, gaining the approval of such notable scholars as **Emmy Noether**, **Richard Courant**, and **David Hilbert**. In 1924 Uryson and Aleksandrov went to Holland and visited with **Luitzen Egbertus Jan Brouwer**, who suggested that they publish their studies on topology. Aleksandrov and Uryson went on to the seaside in France for a spell of work and relaxation that ended tragically when Uryson drowned while swimming. In the aftermath of his friend's death, Aleksandrov lost himself in his work, conducting a seminar on topology that he and Uryson had begun organizing in 1924, and spending 1925 to 1926 working with Brouwer in an attempt to get his research into a form suitable for publication. During this time he further developed his theories of topology and compact space, with an eye to applying topology to the investigation of complex problems.

Defines New Mathematical Field of Cohomology

In 1927 Aleksandrov left Europe for a year to continue his work with a new friend and colleague, Heinz Hopf, at Princeton. Aleksandrov had met Hopf during the summer of 1926 in Göttingen, which along with Paris was considered to be the mathematical hub of Europe. It was in Göttingen in 1923 that Aleksandrov and Uryson first presented their results outside the U.S.S.R., and it was Aleksandrov's preferred summer residence until 1932. There he worked with others, including Noether, who gave the topological work of Aleksandrov and Hopf its algebraic bent. This may have led to Aleksandrov's growing interest in homology, the offshoot of topology incorporating algebra. Homology had first been developed by the French mathematician **Jules Henri Poincaré**, but only for certain types of topological spaces. In 1928 Aleksandrov made a major step in expanding the field when he was able to generalize homology to other topological spaces.

In 1934 Aleksandrov at last received his doctorate from the University of Moscow. The next year, he would issue his most famous work. After much difficult research, the first volume of Aleksandrov and Hopf's still-classic work *Topologie* was published (the remaining two volumes would not be published until after World War II, though they were completed sooner). In the tome they outlined, often for the first time, many basic concepts of this branch of mathematics. They also introduced the definition of cohomology, which is the "dual" theory, or mirror image, of homology. Cohomologists consider the same topics as homologists, but from a different vantage point, providing different results. The publication achieved, Aleksandrov settled in a small town outside of Moscow with his friend and colleague **Andrey Nikolayevich Kolmogorov**. They stayed together here, teaching at the University of Moscow, for the rest of their lives.

Always concerned with the younger generation of mathematicians, Aleksandrov in later years crafted ground-breaking textbooks in the fields of topology, homology, and group theory, which studies the properties of certain kinds of sets. He guided his students—noted mathematicians such as A. Kuros, L. Pontriagin, and A. Tikhonov—to great heights. He also led the mathematical community in Moscow, presiding over that city's mathematical society for more than thirty years. In 1979 Aleksandrov wrote his autobiography. He died three years later in Moscow on November 16, 1982.

SELECTED WRITINGS BY ALEKSANDROV:

Books

(With Heinz Hopf) *Topologie I,* Springer-Verlag, 1935.
Combinatorial Topology, three volumes, Graylock Press, 1956–60.
An Introduction to the Theory of Groups, Hafner, 1959.

Periodicals

"Pages from an Autobiography," *Russian Mathematical Surveys,* Volume 34, number 6, 1979, pp. 267–302 and Volume 35, number 3, 1980, pp. 315–358.

SOURCES:

Books

Boyer, C., and Volume Merzbach, *A History of Mathematics,* second edition, Wiley, 1989.
Brown, Ronald, *Elements of Modern Topology,* McGraw-Hill, 1968.
Dictionary of Scientific Biography, Volume 17, Scribner's, 1990, pp. 11–15.
Fang, J., *Mathematicians from Antiquity to Today,* Volume 1, Paideia Press, 1972, p. 156.
Temple, George, *100 Years of Mathematics,* Springer-Verlag, 1981.

Periodicals

Arkhangelskii, A. V., and others, "Pavel Sergeevich Aleksandrov (On His 80th Birthday)", *Russian Mathematical Surveys,* Volume 31, number 5, 1976, pp. 1–13.

—*Sketch by Karen Sands*

Archie Alphonso Alexander
1888-1958
American civil engineer

Archie Alphonso Alexander was an African American civil engineer who built tunnels, bridges, freeways, airfields, railroad trestles, viaducts, and power plants. Alexander maintained a successful engineering firm for over thirty-five years. He was also a Republican who was active in politics, and he was appointed Governor of the Virgin Islands in 1954 by President Dwight D. Eisenhower. Alexander was born in Ottumwa, Iowa, on May 14, 1888. His father was a janitor, who later moved the family to a farm outside Des Moines. The oldest son of a large family, Alexander worked his way through high school and graduated in 1905. After working a few years, he enrolled in the College of Engineering at the University of Iowa in 1908. Although discouraged by officials from pursuing an academic degree because of his race, Alexander persevered and graduated in 1912 with a B.S. in civil engineering. He maintained an excellent scholastic record, and became such an effective tackle for the university football team that he was known as "Alexander the Great" during his years in college. In 1913, Alexander married Audria Linzey; they moved into a house which Alexander had designed and built himself. The couple would have one child, a son.

After graduating from college, Alexander worked for two years as a design engineer for the Marsh Engineering Company, a bridge-building firm. In 1914, while still only twenty-six years old, he formed his own firm, A. A. Alexander, Inc., with a fellow employee from the Marsh Company, George Higbee. The firm secured contracts to build concrete and steel bridges and sewer systems; they were quite successful by the spring of 1925, when Higbee died in an accident while supervising the construction of a bridge. In that same year, Alexander received an honorary civil engineering degree from his alma mater and was awarded the "Laurel Wreath," given to the member of Kappa Alpha Psi Fraternity who had the greatest accomplishment during that year. In 1928 Alexander was cited as the second most successful Negro in business, and the NAACP awarded him the Spingarn Medal, given annually for the "highest achievement of an American Negro."

In 1929 Alexander joined a fellow classmate from the University of Iowa named M. A. Repass to form the firm Alexander and Repass. The new company built a concrete tunnel, as well as a heating plant and a power house, for the University of Iowa. While much of their work was in Iowa, the firm also built the Tidal Basin Bridge and K Street Freeway in Washington, DC. They were also responsible for a sewage-disposal plant in Grand Rapids, Michigan, a civilian airfield at Tuskegee, Alabama, a power plant in Columbus, Nebraska, and railroad bridges in Iowa and Missouri. Howard University bestowed an honorary doctorate in civil engineering on Alexander in 1946, and at the centennial celebration of the University of Iowa in 1947, he was named one of its outstanding alumni and "one of the first hundred citizens of merit."

In April of 1954, President Eisenhower appointed Alexander the Governor of the Virgin Islands, but ill health forced him to resign the post in August of 1955. He died at his home in Des Moines in 1958. Ralph W. Bullock, writing in *In Spite of Handicaps,* said of Alexander: "When he was a lad he read that Abraham Lincoln said that if one will only prepare himself for his life's work, his opportunity will come some day, and ... this has been the guiding principle of his life. Unquestionably, he ... made good under it."

SOURCES:

Books

Blacks in Science and Medicine, Hemisphere Publishing, 1990, p. 14.
Bullock, Ralph W., *In Spite of Handicaps,* [New York], 1927, pp. 79–84.
Negro Almanac, 5th edition, Gale, 1989.
Toppin, Edgar A., *Biographical History of Blacks,* David McKay, 1971, pp. 246–247.

Periodicals

Ebony, September, 1949, p. 16.
New York Times, February 14, 1954, p. 34.
Time, April 19, 1954, p. 38.

—*Sketch by Mark J. Kaiser*

Hattie Alexander
1901-1968
American microbiologist and pediatrician

Hattie Alexander, a dedicated pediatrician, medical educator, and researcher in microbiology, won international recognition for deriving a serum to combat influenzal meningitis, a common disease that previously had been nearly always fatal to infants and young children. Alexander subsequently investigated microbiological genetics and the processes whereby bacteria, through genetic mutation, acquire resistance to antibiotics. In 1964, as president of the American Pediatric Society, she became one of the first women to head a national medical association.

Hattie Elizabeth Alexander was born on April 5, 1901, in Baltimore, Maryland. She was the second of eight children born to Elsie May (Townsend) Alexander and William Bain Alexander, a merchant. Alexander attended Baltimore schools and then enrolled in Goucher College in Baltimore on a partial scholarship. There, she excelled at sports but was an average student in her course work, which included bacteriology and physiology. Alexander graduated from Goucher with an A.B. degree in 1923. For the next three years she worked as a bacteriologist for the U.S. Public Health Service laboratory in Washington, D.C., and at a branch laboratory of the Maryland Public Health Service. Impressed with her research experience, Johns Hopkins University in Baltimore admitted her to their medical program. Alexander performed exceptionally at Johns Hopkins, earning her M.D. in 1930.

As an intern at the Harriet Lane Home of Johns Hopkins Hospital from 1930 to 1931, Alexander became interested in influenzal meningitis. The source of the disease was *Hemophilus influenzae,* a bacteria that causes inflammation of the meninges, the membranes surrounding the brain and spinal cord. In 1931, Alexander began a second internship at the Babies Hospital of the Columbia-Presbyterian

Medical Center in New York City. There, she witnessed first-hand the futility of medical efforts to save babies who had contracted influenzal meningitis.

Beginning in 1933, with her medical training complete, Alexander held a series of pediatric, teaching, and research positions at the Babies Hospital, the Vanderbilt Clinic of the Columbia-Presbyterian Medical Center, and Columbia University's College of Physicians and Surgeons. She was appointed an adjunct assistant pediatrician in 1933 and an assistant attending pediatrician in 1938 by the Babies Hospital, and held parallel posts at the Vanderbilt Clinic; she would be promoted to attending pediatrician at the Babies Hospital and the Vanderbilt Clinic in 1951. At Columbia, she held a fellowship in children's diseases from 1932 to 1934 and became an assistant in children's diseases in 1933 and an instructor in children's diseases in 1935. Known as a gifted teacher who disliked lecturing but excelled at clinical instruction, she rose steadily through the teaching ranks, becoming associate professor in 1948 and full professor in 1958 and retiring as professor emeritus in 1966.

Develops Anti-Influenzal Rabbit Serum

Alexander's early research focussed on deriving a serum (the liquid component of blood, in which antibodies are contained) that would be effective against influenzal meningitis. Serums derived from animals that have been exposed to a specific disease-producing bacterium often contain antibodies against the disease and can be developed for use in immunizing humans against it. Alexander knew that attempts to develop an anti-influenzal serum from horses had been unsuccessful. The Rockefeller Institute in New York City, however, had been able to prepare a rabbit serum for the treatment of pneumonia, another bacterial disease. Alexander therefore experimented with rabbit serums, and by 1939 was able to announce the development of a rabbit serum effective in curing infants of influenzal meningitis.

In the early 1940s, Alexander experimented with the use of drugs in combination with rabbit serum in the treatment of influenzal meningitis. Within the next two years, she saw infant deaths due to the disease drop by eighty percent. With improvements in diagnosis and the standardization of treatment, the mortality rate fell still further in later years. In recognition of her research on influenzal meningitis, Alexander received the E. Mead Johnson Award for research in pediatrics from the American Academy of Pediatrics in 1942 and the Elizabeth Blackwell Award from the New York Infirmary in 1956, and in 1961, she became the first woman recipient of the Oscar B. Hunter Memorial Award of the American Therapeutic Society.

Researches Microbiological Genetics

Alexander's research in supplementary drug treatment for influenzal meningitis led her to the study of antibiotics (antibacterial substances generally produced by a bacterium or a fungus). As was evident from the cultures of influenza bacilli utilized in Alexander's research, antibiotics do not provide a permanent defense against bacteria. Alexander was among the first to recognize that it was through genetic mutation that bacteria are able to develop resistance to antibiotics, and she became a pioneer in research on DNA, the nucleic substance that bears an organism's genetic blueprint. By 1950, due to lab work conducted in association with Grace Leidy, Alexander was able to alter the genetic code of *Hemophilus influenzae* by manipulating its DNA. Alexander subsequently extended this line of research to other bacteria and to viruses.

In addition to her hospital service, research, and teaching duties, Alexander also served on the influenza commission under the United States Secretary of War from 1941 to 1945, served as consultant to the New York City Department of Health from 1958 to 1960, and joined the medical board of the Presbyterian Hospital of the Columbia-Presbyterian Medical Center in 1959. After chairing the governing council of the American Pediatric Society from 1956 to 1957 and serving as vice president from 1959 to 1960, she became president of the society in 1964.

In addition to her affiliation with the American Pediatric Society, Alexander was a member of several other pediatric associations as well as the Society for Experimental Biology and Medicine, the American Association for the Advancement of Science, the New York Academy of Medicine, and other professional and scientific bodies. During her career she published some 150 papers as well as chapters in textbooks on microbiology and pediatrics and delivered many honorary lectures at medical and academic institutions. Alexander lived with her companion, Dr. Elizabeth Ufford, in Port Washington, N.Y. In her spare time, Alexander enjoyed music, boating, travel, and growing exotic flowers. She died from cancer on June 24, 1968, at the age of 67.

SELECTED WRITINGS BY ALEXANDER:

Periodicals

(With Grace Leidy) "Experimental Investigations as a Basis for Treatment of Type-B Hemophilus Influenzae Meningitis in Infants and Children," *Journal of Pediatrics,* December, 1943, pp. 640–655.

(With Michael Heidelberger and Leidy) "The Protective or Curative Element in Type B H. Influenzae Rabbit Serum," *Yale Journal of Biology and Medicine,* May, 1944, pp. 425–434.

"A Broad Horizon" (1965 Presidential Address of the American Pediatric Society), *Journal of Pediatrics,* November, 1965 (Supplement), pp. 993–999.
(With Leidy and Iris Jaffee) "Genetic Modifiers of the Phenotypic Level of Deoxyribonucleic Acid-Conferred Novobiocin Resistance in Haemophilus," *Journal of Bacteriology,* November, 1966, pp. 1464–1468.

SOURCES:

Books

Notable American Women: The Modern Period, Belknap, 1980, pp. 10–11.

Periodicals

New York Times, June 25, 1968, p. 41.
Rustin, McIntosh, "Hattie Alexander," *Pediatrics,* Volume 42, 1968, p. 554.

—*Sketch by Miyoko Chu*

Ernst F. W. Alexanderson
1878-1975

Swedish-born American engineer and inventor

Ernst F. W. Alexanderson was a Swedish American engineer and inventor who is best remembered for masterminding the first live radio broadcast and for helping to develop color television. He also invented the first electronic amplifier and the amplidyne; in all, Alexanderson held 322 patents for his inventions. His most important work was carried out while he was an engineer at General Electric, and his association with that company lasted 46 years. He was also the first-ever chief engineer of the Radio Corporation of America.

Ernst Frederik Werner Alexanderson was born on January 25, 1878, in Uppsala, Sweden. His father, Aron M. Alexanderson, taught classical languages at the University of Uppsala and was later chair of classical languages at the University of Lund. Alexanderson's mother was the former Amelie von Heidenstam. The young Alexanderson was educated at Lund High School and later at the University of Lund between 1896 and 1897. He continued his studies at the Royal Institute of Technology in Stockholm, graduating with a degree in mechanical and electrical

engineering in 1900. Alexanderson proceeded to study overseas at the Royal Technical Institute in Berlin under the instruction of Adolf K. H. Slaby, the inventor of a primitive form of radio communication.

Alexanderson was keen to put his knowledge to practical use. America, which seemed at that time to be the fountainhead of many important technological advancements, beckoned. He decided to seek his fortune there. Alexanderson arrived in New York in 1901 and immediately went to work as a draftsman for the C. & C. Electrical Company in New Jersey. Alexanderson sought out and was quickly befriended by the esteemed engineers **Thomas Edison** and **Charles Steinmetz**. In 1904, after passing General Electric's engineering exams, he became a member of that company's engineering staff.

Alexanderson's big break came when he was commissioned by Reginald Fessenden, a wealthy pioneering ham radio operator, to build a radio alternator that could produce alternate, high frequency currents. These currents would be used to generate a continuous, dependable wave for radio transmission and thus enable a broadcast of more complexity. On Christmas Eve of 1906, Alexanderson's invention was used to broadcast the first radio show which featured singing and conversation. Two years later, on the advice of his father, who predicted that Europe would be riven by war, Alexanderson became a U.S. citizen. The following year he married Edith B. Lewin on February 20. She died in 1912. He married Gertrude Robart on March 30, 1914.

Refines Alternator into Essential Radio Component

Alexanderson continued to improve his alternator, which, soon after, helped give rise to regular radio communication. **Guglielmo Marconi**, the Italian engineer and inventor, visited Alexanderson in 1915 and bought one of his 50-foot alternators for the Trans-Atlantic Marconi Center in New Jersey. Using a 200-foot Alexanderson alternator, Marconi broadcast radio transmissions during World War I which were heard all over Europe. Within a few years, Alexanderson's alternators were to be found in numerous countries. In 1916, the engineer made another important contribution to radio broadcasting when he unveiled his tuned radio frequency receiver, which allowed for selective tuning. It quickly became an integral part of radio broadcasting.

Alexanderson's alternator played an important part in history when President Woodrow Wilson used it to broadcast his 1918 ultimatum to Germany, ending the war. Afterwards, the Marconi company sought to buy exclusive world rights to the alternator, but was rebuffed by the U.S. government. Wishing to keep control of the invention within American hands, the government set up the Radio Corporation of America (RCA) in 1919, with Alexanderson as its head engineer. Concurrently, Alexanderson continued to work for General Electric.

In 1919, he made history with yet another of his inventions when his multiple-tuned antenna, antistatic receiver, and magnetic amplifier were used to transmit the first two-way radio conversation. This great event took place 900 miles out to sea, between the Trans-Atlantic Marconi Company station at New Brunswick and the steamship *George Washington,* with President Wilson on board as a witness. The magnetic amplifier was outmoded by another Alexanderson invention, the electronic modulator, which used vacuum tubes to help generate high frequency transmitters of great power.

In 1923, Alexanderson became a direct beneficiary of his own ingenuity when his son Verner was kidnapped. A janitor at the lakeside resort in upstate New York heard an appeal for help over broadcast over the radio—a phenomenon which Alexanderson helped to engineer—and recognized the six-year-old boy from the description given. He contacted the police and the boy was returned to his parents unharmed.

In 1924, Alexanderson retired his RCA position to concentrate on his work for GE, although he remained a consulting engineer for RCA until 1932. Also in 1924, Alexanderson scored another first when he transmitted the first facsimile message across the Atlantic to his father in Sweden. Alexanderson's inventions were not restricted to radio, however. He also made enormous contributions to the development of television. In 1927, he received the first TV program at his home in Schenectady, New York, on a set of his own design. The following year, on January 13, he gave the first public demonstration of television using high frequency neon lamps and a perforated scanning disk.

Alexanderson also helped to create the amplidyne, a direct current generator. By the use of compensating coils and a short circuit across two of its brushes, the amplidyne uses a small power input to precisely control a large power output. Its system of amplification and control was designed for use in steel mills, was later adapted to the firing of antiaircraft guns during World War II, and proved to have hundreds of other applications. Alexanderson also held patents for his inventions of telephone relays, radiant energy guided systems for aircraft, electric ship propulsion, automatic steering, motors and power transmission systems, railway electrification systems, as well as inventions in the fields of radio and television.

Alexanderson retired from General Electric in January 1948, although he remained a consultant engineer to the company. That year, his second wife died. He married Thyra Oxehufwud the following year in June. In all, Dr. Alexanderson had four children, Amelie, Edith, Gertrude, and Verner. In 1952, while continuing to work as a consultant to GE, he became a consultant to his erstwhile employer, RCA, with whom he cooperated on the development of color television. He invented a color television receiver which could also receive black and white television programs.

Ernst Alexanderson's enormous contribution to technology was acknowledged more than once. Some of the honors and awards he received during his long life are: The Gold Medal of the Institute of Radio Engineers in 1919, the Order of the Polonia Restituta in 1924, the John Ericcson Medal in 1928, the Edison Medal of the American Institute of Electrical Engineers in 1944, the Cedergren Medal of the Royal Institute of Technology of Sweden in 1945, the Valdemar Poulsen Gold Medal and the Royal Danish Medal, both in 1946. He received honorary degrees from Union College, Schenectady, New York in 1926, and the University of Uppsala in 1938. He was a fellow of the Institute of Radio Engineers, a member and president of the Institute of Radio Engineers, and a member of the Swedish Royal Academy and Sigma Xi. In his spare time, Dr. Alexanderson enjoyed sailing, and was elected the first commodore of the Lake George Yacht Club in New York. Alexanderson died on May 14, 1975, in Schenectady. He was 97 years old.

SOURCES:

Periodicals

Krebs, Albin, "Dr. Ernst Alexanderson, Radio Pioneer, Dies at 97," *New York Times,* May 15, 1975, pp. 46.
New York Times, January 25, 1945, pp. 13; February 12, 1955, p. 22.
Popular Science, July, 1942, p. 89.

—Sketch by Avril McDonald

Hannes Olof Gösta Alfvén
1908-
Swedish American physicist

Hannes Olof Gösta Alfvén has made a number of important discoveries in the fields of plasma physics, space physics, and astrophysics, and has been called the father of the science of magnetohydrodynamics (MHD), a field of study whose applications are as diverse as the properties of stars and the production of fusion power by artificial means. In 1970, he was awarded the Nobel Prize with **Louis Néel** in physics for his achievements in MHD and their practical uses in plasma physics. MHD deals with the behavior of electrically conducting gases and liquids as they interact with magnetic fields. The first space scientist to receive the Nobel, Alfvén's discoveries grew out of his research in sunspots.

Hannes Olof Gösta Alfvén was born in Norrkoeping, Sweden, on May 30, 1908. His parents, Johannes Alfvén and Anna-Clara (Romanus) Alfvén, were both physicians. After completing elementary and secondary school in Norrkoeping, Alfvén enrolled at the University of Uppsala and received his Ph.D. in physics in 1934. He became a lecturer in physics at Uppsala, and three years later was appointed research physicist at the Nobel Institute of Physics. In 1940, he became a member of the faculty at the Royal Institute of Technology in Stockholm where he held successively the titles of professor of the theory of electricity from 1940 to 1945, professor of electronics from 1945 to 1963, and professor of plasma physics from 1963 to 1967. In 1935, Alfvén was married to the former Kerstin Maria Erikson. They have five children.

Sunspot Research Leads to Magnetohydrodynamics

Alfvén's primary research interest has long been the application of physical principles to astronomical phenomena. In the early 1940s, he began a study of sunspots that would continue for many years. One of the consequences of his research was his discovery of hydromagnetic waves (named Alfvén waves in his honor), which challenged some long-held and widely-accepted physical concepts, including James Clerk Maxwell's electromagnetic theory. Traditionally, electromagnetic waves were believed to be incapable of penetrating a conductor to any significant degree. For example, light (a form of electromagnetic radiation) is almost perfectly reflected by a conductor such as copper or silver metal.

During his study of sunspots, however, Alfvén came to a very different conclusion. He hypothesized that electromagnetic waves were very good conductors, able to extend through the highly ionized solar gas. In 1942, he published a detailed and elegant demonstration of his theory, although his observations were largely ignored and even rejected by the vast majority of his colleagues. His biographer, A. J. Dessler, explains that Alfvén's theory of hydromagnetic waves was not taken seriously until six years later when he presented his ideas in a lecture at the University of Chicago. **Enrico Fermi** is said to have nodded in approval after Alfvén had delivered his paper, remarking, "Of course." Dessler claims that on the next day, "the entire world of physics said, 'Oh, of course' also."

That bit of recognition did not push Alfvén to the forefront of the physics community, however. He continued to work for the most part in private, publishing a relatively small number of papers on his discoveries. Out of that work, however, grew an important new field of physics now known as magnetohydrodynamics (MHD).

Discoveries in Plasma Physics Applied to Fusion Research

An important aspect of Alfvén's work in MHD has been his study of plasma, sometimes referred to as the fourth state of matter. A gas-like mixture of electrons and positively-charged ions, plasma exists only at very high temperatures, such as those encountered in stars. At such extreme temperatures, atoms and molecules are completely ionized. Most of Alfvén's early research on plasma was based on studies of sunspots, magnetic storms, and other stellar phenomena. One of his most important discoveries in this area came in the 1930s when he proposed the concept of magnetic field lines that become "frozen" within a plasma. He showed that under certain circumstances in which a plasma moves, the magnetic field associated with it moves as well. The primary goal of Alfvén's work with plasma and MHD has been to better understand the origin of the universe, which he believes was formed from plasma. By studying properties of primordial plasma through exploration of asteroids, for example, Alfvén felt more could be learned about how stars, planets, and other astronomical bodies were formed. As a result, he has been a strong supporter of space research programs, such as those carried out by the U.S. National Aeronautics and Space Administration. Such programs, he believes, provide an invaluable way of testing theoretical concepts like those he has developed.

Although Alfvén's own research has centered on outer space, many of his discoveries have had important practical applications. For example, developing fusion power plants that can supply energy on a commercial basis depends on the ability to produce and contain very hot masses of material within which fusion reactions can occur. At the high temperatures inside a fusion reactor, these materials exist in the form of plasma, inviting the many important applications of Alfvén's discoveries.

Alfvén left Sweden in 1967 to accept an appointment as professor of physics at the University of California at San Diego. His decision to leave his native country was supposedly based on disagreements with the Swedish government over certain policies, particularly those involving education and nuclear power. For instance, although he had originally been a strong supporter of the construction of nuclear power plants, he later developed concerns about the environmental risks posed by such plants. He argued against the increasing dependence on nuclear power in Sweden, and eventually decided that all applications of nuclear power—both peaceful and military—were dangerous. He became active in the anti-nuclear movement of the 1970s and 1980s. In addition to his Nobel Prize, Alfvén received the Gold Medal of the Royal Astronomical Society in 1967, the Lomonosov Gold Medal of the Soviet Academy of Sciences in 1971, the Franklin Medal of the Franklin Institute in 1971, and the Bowie Gold Medal in 1987.

SELECTED WRITINGS BY ALFVÉN:

Books

Cosmical Electrodynamics, Clarendon Press, 1950, 2nd edition (with Carl-Gunne Faelthammar), 1963.
On the Origin of the Solar System, Clarendon Press, 1954.
Worlds-Antiworlds: Antimatter in Cosmology, W. H. Freeman, 1966.
(Under pseudonym Olof Johanneson) *Sagan om den stora datamaskinen* (novel), translation by Naomi Wallford published as *The Tale of the Big Computer,* Coward-McMann, 1968, translation published in England as *The Great Computer: A Vision,* Gollancz, 1968.
(With wife, Kerstin Alfven) *Living on the Third Planet,* W. H. Freeman, 1972.
(With Gustav Arrhenius) *Structure and Evolutionary History of the Solar System,* D. Reidel, 1975.

SOURCES:

Books

Contemporary Authors, Volumes 29–32, 1st revision, Gale, 1978.
McGraw-Hill Modern Scientists and Engineers, Volume 1, McGraw-Hill, 1980, pp. 10–12.

Periodicals

Dessler, A. J., "Nobel Prizes: 1970 Awards Honor Three in Physics and Chemistry," *Science,* November 6, 1970, pp. 604–606.

—*Sketch by David E. Newton*

Abram Isaakovich Alikhanov
1904-1970
Russian physicist

Abram Isaakovich Alikhanov was a Russian theoretical physicist, who worked closely with his brother, Artem Isaakovich Alikhanian, researching particle physics and cosmic rays. He is best remembered for his contributions in the 1930s to the discovery of pair emission by excited nuclei, the formulation of the relationship between beta spectra and atomic numbers, the proof of momentum conservation during pair annihilation, and the discovery of unstable mesons. Following World War II, Alikhanov constructed the first nuclear reactor in the former Soviet Union and subsequently devoted his research to the refinement of nuclear reactors.

Born Abram Isaakovich Alikhanian in Elisavetpol (now Kirovabad, Azerbaijan) on March 4, 1904, Alikhanov russified his name in adulthood. His father was a railway engineer; his mother was a homemaker. The family moved to Aleksandropol (now Gyumri, Armenia) in 1912. There Alikhanov began his education, later transferring to a commercial school in Tiflis (now Tbilisi, Georgia), from which he graduated in 1921. That year, he began his higher education at the Georgian Polytechnical Institute but quickly moved to Petrograd (now St. Petersburg, Russia), where he attended Petrograd Polytechnical Institute.

While still a student at the Polytechnical Institute, Alikhanov began work at the Physical-Technical Institute. In his first project there he used X rays to penetrate aluminum heated to 550–600° C, discovering that the structure of that substance remained unchanged by this degree of heat. In later experiments at the institute, Alikhanov investigated the nature of X rays themselves. He completed his studies at the Petrograd Polytechnical Institute in 1930.

In 1932 the Physical-Technical Institute initiated a nuclear physics program to which Alikhanov turned his attention, subsequently assuming directorship of its laboratory for positron physics. Positrons are positively charged elementary particles found in cosmic ray showers and result from what is called "pair production," the production of an electron and a positron from a photon. Alikhanov and his team researched pair production and the resultant positron spectrum, particularly focusing on the ways in which gamma radiation released during the process and the atomic number of the irradiated material effect the spectrum. Working with Alikhanian and a student, M. S. Kozodaev, Alikhanov developed a method for observing positrons using a magnetic spectrometer and two Geiger-Müller counters making coincidence counts. This technique became known as Alikhanov-Kozodaev spectrometry and was later used to investigate the beta decay of artificially radioactive nucleides. Beta decay is a type of radioactive deterioration in which the identity of a nucleus is changed but not its mass. Alikhanov-Kozodaev spectrometry was also used to elucidate how the atomic number of the source of radiation effects aspects of the beta spectrum.

In the late 1930s, Alikhanov and his colleagues at the Physical-Technical Institute researched neutrinos. Massless, uncharged elementary particles often emitted during radioactive decay, neutrinos are associated with two forms, the electron and the muon—a very light elementary particle, created at the top of the earth's atmosphere by the collision of protons and air molecules. Alikhanov's work in this regard was interrupted by the outbreak of the Second World War, as was a planned trip to the Pamir Mountains of Tadzhikistan to observe cosmic rays—streams of atomic nuclei that penetrate the earth's atmosphere. An expedition was eventually conducted in the Armenian Mountains in 1942, and Alikhanov was able to demonstrate that cosmic rays contain beams of fast moving protons but mistakenly concluded that the rays have "varitrons," or particles with a broad range of masses. During this period, Alikhanov worked closely with **Pyotr Kapitsa**, who built instruments used in the cosmic ray observations.

Contributes to Soviet Efforts to Develop Nuclear Energy

In 1942 Alikhanov became involved in the Soviet effort to develop nuclear energy, and he led research into the use of deuterium oxide (also known as "heavy water") in operating nuclear power stations. In 1944 he helped **Igor Kurchatov** design and construct the first Soviet cyclotron—a particle accelerator that drives protons in circles at great speed by the force of a magnetic field. The following year he set up the Institute of Theoretical and Experimental Physics, which became a research center for the use of heavy water as a moderator and coolant in nuclear reactors. Until virtually the end of his life, Alikhanov was the institute's director. In 1949 the institute became the first laboratory to build and operate a heavy water reactor.

After the war he returned to the study of particles. He was responsible for the construction of a high energy proton accelerator at the institute, and an even more powerful one at Serpukhov. He ended his career engaged in the study of mesons—unstable, strongly interacting nuclear particles that have a mass between that of an electron and a proton. In 1954 in recognition of his services to Soviet science, Alikhanov was made a Hero of Socialist Labor. He had received the Stalin Prize in 1941 and 1948 and was a

fellow of the U.S.S.R. Academy of Sciences. Married twice, Alikhanov had three children. In 1968 ill health forced his retirement. He died on December 8, 1970.

SELECTED WRITINGS BY ALIKHANOV:

Books

Cosmic Rays: Recent Problems in Science and Technology, [Moscow], 1949.
Recent Research on Beta-Disintegration, translated by William E. Jones, [New York], 1963.

Periodicals

(With Artem I. Alikhanian and L. A. Artsimovich) "The Conservation of Momentum Law in Positron Annihilation," *Doklady Akademii nauk SSSR,* Volume 1, number 7, 1936, p. 275.
"Pair Creation under Gamma-Ray Influence," *Izvestiia Akademii nauk SSSR, seriia fizicheskaia,* Volume 33, numbers 1–2, 1938, p. 33.
"The Spectrum Mode of RaE Near the Upper Bound and the Mass of the Neutrino," *Doklady Akademii nauk SSSR,* Volume 19, number 5, 1938, p. 375.
"New Data on the Nature of Cosmic Rays," *Uspekhi fizicheskikh nauk,* Volume 27, number 1, 1945, p. 22.
(With Volume V. Vladimirskii, P. A. Petrov, and P. I. Khristenko) "The Heavy-Water Energy Reactor with Gas Cooling," *Atomnaia energiia,* Volume 1, 1956, p. 5.

SOURCES:

Books

Dictionary of Scientific Biography, Volume 17, supplement 2, edited by Frederic L. Holmes, Scribner, 1981, pp. 15–16.
Gasparin, B. G., A. P. Grinber, and Volume J. Frenkel, *A. I. Alikhanov in the Physical-Technical Institute,* [Leningrad], 1986.

Periodicals

Aleksandrov, A. P., et al., "In Memory of A. I. Alikhanov," *Uspekhi fizicheskikh nauk,* Volume 112, number 3, 1974, pp. 725–27.
"Positive Electrons from Lead Ejected by Gamma Rays," *Nature,* Volume 133, 1934, p. 581.

—Sketch by Avril McDonald

William E. Allen, Jr.
1903-1981
American physician

As a radiologist, researcher, professor, and philanthropist, William E. Allen, Jr. was a significant influence in the field of radiology during its development in the 1930s. He focused his skills on shaping radiology as a science and as a profession and on increasing access to education and scientific careers for other African Americans.

William Edward Allen, Jr. was born August 14, 1903, just eight years after the X ray was discovered. The son of Marian and William Allen, a Pensacola, Florida building contractor, he attended Howard University and earned his B.S. degree in 1927 and his M.D. in 1930. By the time he completed his residency at City Hospital No. 2 in St. Louis, he had organized one of the nation's first approved training schools for black X-ray technicians at St. Mary's Infirmary. In 1935, one year after the American Board of Radiology examinations were established, he became the first African American certified X-ray technician. By the late 1930s Allen had established one of the first approved residencies in radiology for minorities. He also became a founding member of the National Medical Association's Commission on X-Ray and Radium.

Several months before the United States entered World War II, Allen volunteered for active military service. However, since there was no place in the segregated military for a black radiologist, he accepted assignment as a battalion surgeon. When a military hospital staffed by black medical officers was established at Ft. Huachuca, Arizona, Allen became its chief of X-ray service. He provided elementary radiology training for medical officers headed for hospitals in most of the war's theaters. He also established the first and only black Women's Army Corps school for X-ray technologists. In 1945 he was elected to fellowship in the American College of Radiology.

Returning to Homer G. Phillips Hospital in St. Louis after the war, Allen immediately established yet another school for X-ray technologists, which eventually gained international recognition. For the first two years after the war, he served as consultant on radiology to the U.S. Secretary of War. In 1949 the National Medical Association (NMA) radiology section was born, and Allen served as its first chairman. Long active with the NMA, he was elected vice-president of the organization in the early 1960s.

As radiology developed from a chiefly diagnostic tool in its early years to having treatment applications for tumors and cancer, Allen's career followed the emerging fields of radiology and radiation oncology. His later research focused on nuclear medicine and radiation therapy in prostate tumors and carcinoma of the cervix. In addition to his research and writings, Allen taught for many years at St. Louis University Medical School and gained the rank of emeritus professor at the Washington University School of Medicine.

In addition to founding several training schools, he developed scholarships for students from Haiti, Nigeria, Liberia, and South Africa to study radiology. Through his efforts more than two dozen men and women became X-ray technologists; five became diagnostic radiologists. He also spearheaded efforts that brought West Africa its first cobalt treatment unit.

The American College of Radiology presented Allen with a gold medal in 1974. Homer G. Phillips Hospital, Howard University, the St. Louis chapter of the NAACP, the American Cancer Society, and the National Medical Association all presented him their highest awards for service. In 1978 the American Board of Radiologists inaugurated a series of annual lectures in his honor. On December 31, 1981, Allen succumbed to stomach cancer at the age of 78. He was survived by his wife Para Lee Batts Allen, a former head nurse at Homer G. Phillips Hospital.

SELECTED WRITINGS BY ALLEN:

Periodicals

"Malignancy of the Esophagus with Bronchial Fistula," *Radiology,* March, 1934, p. 366.
"Transverse Fracture of the Sacrum," *American Journal of Roentgenology,* 1934, Volume 31, p. 676.
With Vaughn C. Payne, and Reginald Jackson, "Scout Film of the Abdomen in Appendicitis," *Journal of the National Medical Association,* 1949, Volume 41, p. 119.

SOURCES:

Periodicals

Alexander, Leslie L., "Section on Radiology Celebrates Thirtieth Year," *Journal of the National Medical Association,* 1980, Volume 72, p. 277.
Evens, Ronald G., "In Memoriam: William E. Allen, Jr., M.D.," *Radiology,* 1982, Volume 143, p. 575.

Other

Pamphlet on History I, edited by John W. Coleman, National Medical Association Section on Radiology.

—Sketch by Penelope Lawbaugh

Sidney Altman
1939-

Canadian American molecular biologist

In the early 1980s, Sidney Altman discovered that ribonucleic acid (RNA) molecules can act as enzymes. This disclosure, independently and concurrently made by **Thomas R. Cech** of the University of Colorado, broadened our understanding of the origins of life. Before this discovery, it was believed that all enzymes were made of protein and that primitive cells, therefore, used proteins to catalyze biochemical processes. Now it appears that RNA may have acted as a catalyst. Altman and Cech's work has not only had a "conceptual influence on basic natural sciences," according to the Royal Swedish Academy of Sciences, but in addition, "the discovery of catalytic RNA will probably provide a new tool for gene technology, with potential to create a new defense against viral infections." As a result of their findings, Altman and Cech were jointly awarded the 1989 Nobel Prize for chemistry.

Altman was born in Montreal, Quebec, on May 8, 1939, the second son of Victor Altman, an immigrant grocer, and Ray Arlin, who before her marriage worked in a textile mill. He attended West Hill High School in Montreal and the Massachusetts Institute of Technology, from which he graduated with a bachelor of science in physics in 1960. Between 1960 and 1962, he was a teaching assistant in the Department of Physics at Columbia University, while he waited for a suitable position in a lab. Around this time, Altman switched from physics to the newly emerging interdisciplinary field of molecular biology. He moved to the University of Colorado in Boulder in late 1962 to work as a research assistant under Leonard S. Lerman. He was mainly preoccupied with studying the replication of the T4 bacteriophage, a substance that infects bacterial cells in much the same way as a virus infects human cells. Altman received his Ph.D. in biophysics in 1967.

After graduation, Altman briefly worked as a research assistant in molecular biology at Vanderbilt University before winning a grant from the Damon Runyon Memorial Foundation for Cancer Research. This permitted him to work as a research fellow in molecular biology at Harvard University. From 1967 to 1969, working under the biochemist **Matthew Meselson**, he continued his research into the genetic structure of the T4 bacteriophage. His receipt of the Anna Fuller Foundation Fellowship in 1969 enabled him to transfer to the Medical Research Council Laboratory of Molecular Biology in Cambridge, England, to work with molecular biologists **Sydney Brenner** and **Francis Crick**. The latter, in partnership with **James D. Watson**, discovered DNA's double-helix structure in 1954.

Discovers Complexities in DNA Production

It was clear to scientists that genetic information is carried by DNA (deoxyribonucleic acid) into a cell's nucleus. In the cytoplasm (the substance inside the cell wall, surrounding the nucleus), the genetic code is copied into RNA. It is then converted into proteins, which are built of chains of amino acids. Altman originally intended to study the three-dimensional structure of transfer RNA (tRNA), which is a small component of RNA that transfers amino acids onto a growing polypeptide chain as proteins are made. Much of the breakthrough work in this area had already been accomplished, however, so Altman decided to switch his attention to the transcription of tRNA from DNA. He found that the DNA from which tRNA is produced is not directly copied into tRNA but first undergoes an intermediary stage when it becomes a long strand of what is called "precursor RNA." This is composed of a strand of tRNA with additional genetic sequences at each end which are somehow later removed before it becomes tRNA.

While still working at the Medical Research Council in Cambridge, Altman studied the tRNA genes of the Escherichia coli (E. coli) bacterium, to which he added toxic chemicals. Subsequent mutations in the tRNA enabled him to isolate precursor tRNA from bacterial cells. Altman discovered that the additional sequences at each end of the strand of precursor tRNA were removed by something in the cells of the bacteria, probably an enzyme. The scientists found that the enzyme, named ribonuclease P (RNase P), would only cut off the extra sequences at a precise point.

When he returned the United States in 1971, Altman joined Yale University's biology department as an assistant professor. In 1972, he married Ann Korner. They have a son, Daniel, and a daughter, Leah. Altman was promoted to associate professor in 1975. In 1978, he published the results of an experiment carried out by one of his graduate students, Benjamin Stark. It demonstrated that RNase P was at least partially composed of RNA, which meant that RNA itself played an integral part in the activity of the enzyme. This finding was highly unorthodox, as it was then presumed that enzymes are made of protein, not nucleic acids.

Proves RNA is a Catalyst

In 1980, Altman attained a full professorship of biology at Yale. The following year, Cech at the University of Colorado published independent results similar to Altman's. Cech discovered that the precursor RNA from the protozoan *Tetrahymena* were reduced to their final size as tRNA without the assistance of protein, and suggested that the precursor RNA catalyzed this itself. His findings lent weight to Altman's. Cech's use of the word "catalyst" to describe the action of the RNA was questioned, however, because rather than just speeding up a reaction, it used itself up in the process.

Three years later, by which time Altman had become chairman of Yale's biology department, his colleague, Cecilia Guerrier-Takada, was testing the catalytic activity of RNase P. She discovered catalysis even in the control experiments that used the RNA subunit of RNase P (the M1 RNA) but which contained no protein. Altman was able to prove that the M1 RNA demonstrated all the classical properties of a catalyst, especially as, unlike that studied by Cech, it remained unchanged by the reaction. This removed the last shadow of a doubt that RNA could act as an enzyme.

In 1984, Altman became a naturalized American, but retained his Canadian citizenship. From 1985 until 1989, as the dean of Yale College, Altman established a greater role for scientific education in all of Yale's curriculums. In 1989 he and Cech jointly received the Nobel Prize for chemistry for their discovery of RNA's catalytic ability. Their work put an end to the conundrum regarding proteins and nucleic acids which had long mystified scientists. They had been unable to discover which came first in the development of life, proteins or nucleic acids. Proteins catalyze biological reactions, whereas nucleic acids, such as RNA, transport the genetic codes that create the proteins. Altman and Cech proved that nucleic acids were the building blocks of life, acting as both codes and enzymes.

High hopes exist for the practical applications of their discovery, which was described by the Nobel Academy as one of "the two most important and outstanding discoveries in the biological sciences in the past 40 years," the other being Crick and Watson's discovery of DNA's double helix structure. If RNA enzymes are able to cut additional sequences of tRNA from a strand of precursor tRNA, doctors could possibly use RNA enzymes to cut infectious RNA from the genetic system of a person with an infectious viral disease. Research into this field is ongoing and, if fruitful, could contain the key to curing viral infections such as cancer and AIDS.

In addition to receiving the Nobel Prize, Altman was honored with the Rosentiel Award for Basic Biomedical Research in 1989. He is a member of the National Academy of Sciences and the American Society of Biological Chemists, of the Genetics Society of America, and is a fellow of the American Association for the Advancement of Science. He holds honorary degrees from the Université de Montréal, York University in Toronto, Connecticut Uni-

versity, McGill University, the University of Colorado, and the University of British Columbia. In 1991, he was selected to present the DeVane lecture series at Yale on the topic "Understanding Life in the Laboratory."

Altman has held a number of other part-time positions in addition to his full-time academic positions, including associate editor of *Cell* from 1983 to 1987, member of the Board of Directors of the Damon Runyon-Walter Winchell Fund for Cancer Research, member of the Board of Governors of the Weizmann Institute of Science, member of the Scientific Advisory Board of Bio-Méga, Inc., and Special Consultant to the Pathogenesis Corporation in Seattle.

SELECTED WRITINGS BY ALTMAN:

Books

Transfer RNA, edited by Altman, MIT Press, 1978.

Periodicals

(With M. Meselson) "A T4-Induced Endonuclease which Attacks T4 DNA," Proceedings of the National Academy of Science, 1970, p. 716.

(With H. D. Robertson) "RNA Precursor Molecules and Ribonucleases in *E. coli.*" *Molecular and Cellular Biochemistry,* 1973, pp. 83–93.

"Biosynthesis of Transfer RNA in *Escherichia Coli,*" *Cell,* 1975, pp. 21–29.

(With G. McCorkle) "Large Deletion Mutants of *Escherichia coli* tRNA1Tyr," *Journal of Molecular Biology,* 1982, pp. 83–103.

(With C. Guerrier-Takada) "Catalytic Activity of an RNA Molecule Prepared by Transcription *in vitro,*" *Science,* 1984, pp. 285–286.

"Ribonuclease P: An Enzyme with a Catalytic RNA Subunit," *Advanced Enzymology,* 1989, pp. 1–36.

"Enzymatic Cleavage of RNA by RNA," (Nobel lecture), *Angewandte Chemie,* 1990, pp. 749–758.

"Ribonuclease P: Postscript," *Journal of Biological Chemistry,* 1990, pp. 20,053–20,056.

(With C. Guerrier-Takada) "Reconstitution of Enzymatic Activity from Fragments of M1 RNA," *Proceedings of the National Academy of Science,* 1992, pp. 1266–70.

SOURCES:

Books

Nobel Prize Winners, 1987–1991 Supplement, H. W. Wilson, 1987.

Periodicals

Bishop, Jerry E., "Nobel Prize in Chemistry Cites Discovery that Spawned New Genetic Engineering," *Wall Street Journal,* October 13, 1989, p. B2.

Broad, William J., "5 Win the Nobel Prizes in Chemistry and Physics," *New York Times,* October 13, 1989.

Oliwenstein, Lori, "All the Way with RNA," *Discover,* January, 1993, p. 69.

Scientific American, December, 1989.

U.S. News & World Report, October 23, 1989, p. 20.

Waldrop, M. Mitchell, "Catalytic RNA Wins Chemistry Nobel," *Science,* October 20, 1989, p. 325.

Washington Post, October 13, 1989.

Yale Weekly Bulletin and Calendar, October 16–23, 1989.

—*Sketch by Avril McDonald*

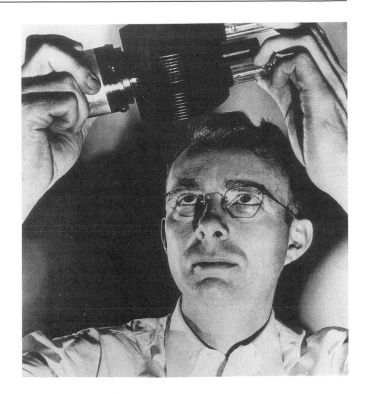

Luis Alvarez

Luis Alvarez
1911-1988
American physicist

Luis Alvarez's scientific contributions to the military during World War II included the development of a narrow beam radar system that allows airplanes to land in inclement weather. He was also involved in the Manhattan Project to develop the world's first nuclear weapons. One of Alvarez's more controversial theories involved the possibility of a massive collision of a meteorite with the earth 65 million years ago, an event that Alvarez believed may account for the disappearance of the dinosaurs. Among the many honors that Alvarez received was the 1968 Nobel Prize for physics for his development of giant bubble chambers used to detect a variety of subatomic particles.

Luis Walter Alvarez was born in San Francisco, California, on June 13, 1911. His father, Dr. Walter Clement Alvarez, was a medical researcher at the University of California at San Francisco and also maintained a private practice. Luis' mother was the former Harriet Skidmore Smythe. His grandfather Alvarez was born in Spain but ran away to Cuba, and later made a fortune in Los Angeles real estate before moving to Hawaii and then to San Francisco. Luis' mother's family, originally from Ireland, established a missionary school in Foochow, China. Alvarez's parents met while studying at the University of California at Berkeley.

Alvarez attended grammar school in San Francisco and enrolled in the city's Polytechnic High School, where he avidly studied science. When his father accepted a position at the prestigious Mayo Clinic, the family moved to Rochester, Minnesota. Alvarez reported in his autobiography *Alvarez: Adventures of a Physicist,* that his science classes at Rochester High School were "adequately taught [but] not very interesting." Dr. Alvarez noticed his son's growing interest in physics and hired one of the Mayo Clinic's machinists to give Luis private lessons on weekends. Alvarez enrolled at the University of Chicago in 1928 and planned to major in chemistry. He was especially interested in organic chemistry, but soon came to despise the mandatory chemistry laboratories. Alvarez "discovered" physics in his junior year and enrolled in a laboratory course, "Advanced Experimental Physics: Light" about which he later wrote in his autobiography: "It was love at first sight." He changed his major to physics and received his B.S. in 1932. Alvarez stayed at Chicago for his graduate work and his assigned advisor was Nobel Laureate **Arthur Compton**, whom Alvarez considered "the ideal graduate advisor for me" because he visited Alvarez's laboratory only once during his graduate career and "usually had no idea how I was spending my time."

Alvarez earned his bachelor's, master's, and doctoral degrees at the University of Chicago before joining the faculty at the University of California at Berkeley, where he remained until retiring in 1978. His doctoral dissertation concerned the diffraction of light, a topic considered relatively trivial, but his other graduate work proved to be more useful. In one series of experiments, for example, he and some colleagues discovered the "east-west effect" of cosmic rays, which explained that the number of cosmic rays reaching the earth's atmosphere differed depending on the direction from which they came. The east-west effect was evidence that cosmic rays consist of some kind of positively charged particles. A few days after passing his oral examinations for the Ph.D. degree, Alvarez married Geraldine Smithwick, a senior at the University of Chicago, with whom he later had two children, Walter and Jean. Less than a month after their wedding the Alvarezes moved to Berkeley, California, where Luis became a research scientist with Nobel Prize-winning physicist **Ernest Orlando Lawrence**, and initiated an association with the University of California that was to continue for forty-two years.

Alvarez soon earned the title "prize wild idea man" from his colleagues because of his involvement in such a wide variety of research activities. Within his first year at Berkeley, he discovered the process of K-electron capture, in which some atomic nuclei decay by absorbing one of the electrons in its first orbital (part of the nuclear shell). Alvarez and a student, Jake Wiens, also developed a mercury vapor lamp consisting of the artificial isotope mercury–198. The wavelength of the light emitted by the lamp was adopted as an official standard of length by the U.S. Bureau of Standards. In his research with Nobel Prize-winning physicist **Felix Bloch**, Alvarez developed a method for producing a beam of slow moving neutrons, a method that was used to determine the magnetic moment of neutrons (the extent to which they affect a magnetic field). Just after the outbreak of World War II in Europe, Alvarez discovered tritium, a radioactive isotope (a variant atom containing a different number of protons) of hydrogen.

World War II Research Leads to Atomic Bomb

World War II interrupted Alvarez's work at Berkeley. In 1940 he began research for the military at Massachusetts Institute of Technology's (MIT's) radiation laboratory on radar (radio detecting and ranging) systems. Over the next three years, he was involved in the development of three new types of radar systems. The first made use of a very narrow radar beam to allow a ground-based controller to direct the "blind" landing of an airplane. The second system, code-named "Eagle," was a method for locating and bombing objects on the ground when they could not be seen by a pilot. The third invention became known as the microwave early-warning sys-

tem, a mechanism for collecting images of aircraft movement in overcast skies.

In 1943, Alvarez left MIT to join the Manhattan Project research team working in Los Alamos, New Mexico. His primary accomplishment with the team was developing the detonating device used for the first plutonium bomb. Alvarez flew in the B–29 bomber that observed the first test of an atomic device at Alamogordo, south of Los Alamos. Three weeks later, Alvarez was aboard another B–29 following the bomber "Enola Gay" as it dropped the first atomic bomb on Hiroshima, Japan. Like most scientists associated with the Manhattan Project, Alvarez was stunned and horrified by the destructiveness of the weapon he had helped to create. Nonetheless, he never expressed any doubts or hesitation about the decision to use the bombs, since they brought a swift end to the war. Alvarez became one of a small number of scientists who felt strongly that the United States should continue its nuclear weapons development after the war and develop a fusion (hydrogen) bomb as soon as possible.

After the war, Alvarez returned to Berkeley where he had been promoted to full professor. Determining that the future of nuclear physics lay in high energy research, he focused his research on powerful particle accelerators—devices that accelerate electrons and protons to high velocity. His first project was to design and construct a linear accelerator for use with protons. Although his machine was similar in some ways to the electron accelerators that had been available for many years, the proton machine posed a number of new problems. By 1947, however, Alvarez had solved those problems and his forty-foot-long proton accelerator began operation.

Particle Accelerator Research Results in Nobel Prize

Over the next decade, the science of particle physics (the study of atomic components) developed rapidly at Berkeley. An important factor in that progress was the construction of the 184-inch synchrocyclotron at the university's radiation laboratory. The synchrocyclotron was a modified circular particle accelerator capable of achieving much greater velocities than any other type of accelerator. The science of particle physics involves two fundamental problems: creation of particles to be studied in some type of accelerator and detection and identification of those particles. After 1950, Alvarez's interests shifted from the first to the second of these problems, particle detection, because of a chance meeting in 1953 with University of Michigan physicist **Donald Glaser**. Glaser had recently invented the bubble chamber, a device that detects particles as they pass through a container of superheated fluid. As the particles move through the liquid, they form ions that act as nuclei on which the superheated material can begin to boil, thereby forming a track of tiny bubbles that shows the path taken by the particles. In talking with Glaser, Alvarez realized that the bubble chamber could be refined and improved to track the dozens of new particles then being produced in Berkeley's giant synchrocyclotron. Among these particles were some with very short lifetimes known as resonance states.

Improving Glaser's original bubble chamber involved a number of changes. First, Alvarez decided that liquid hydrogen would be a more sensitive material to use than the diethyl ether employed by Glaser. In addition, he realized that sophisticated equipment would be needed to respond to and record the resonance states that often lasted no more than a billionth of a second. The equipment he developed included relay systems that transmitted messages at high speeds and computer programs that could sort out significant from insignificant events and then analyze the former. Finally, Alvarez aimed at constructing larger and larger bubble chambers to record a greater number of events. Over a period of about five years, Alvarez's chambers grew from a simple one inch glass tube to his most ambitious instrument, a seventy-two inch chamber that was first put into use in 1959. With these devices, Alvarez eventually discovered dozens of new elementary particles, including the unusual resonance states.

The significance of Alvarez's work with bubble chambers was recognized in 1968 when he was awarded the Nobel Prize for physics. At the awards ceremony in Stockholm, the Swedish Academy of Science's Sten von Friesen told Alvarez that, because of his work with the bubble chamber, "entirely new possibilities for research into high-energy physics present themselves. . . . Practically all the discoveries that have been made in this important field [of particle physics] have been possible only through the use of methods developed by Professor Alvarez." Alvarez attended the Nobel ceremonies with his second wife, Janet Landis, whom he married in 1958. Largely as a result of their war-related separation, Alvarez and his first wife had divorced. With Janet, Alvarez had two more children, Donald and Helen.

Did an Asteroid Kill the Dinosaurs?

Advancing years failed to reduce Alvarez's curiosity on a wide range of topics. In 1965 he was in charge of a joint Egyptian-American expedition whose goal was to search for hidden chambers in the pyramid of King Kefren at Giza. The team aimed high energy muons (subatomic particles produced by cosmic rays) at the pyramid to look for regions of low density which would indicate possible chambers. However, none were found. Alvarez shared the last major scientific achievement with his son Walter, who was then a professor of geology at Berkeley. In

1980, the Alvarezes accidentally discovered a band of sedimentary rock in Italy that contained an unusually high level of the rare metal iridium. Dating techniques set the age of the layer at about 65 million years. The Alvarezes hypothesized that the iridium came from an asteroid that struck the earth, thereby sending huge volumes of smoke and dust (including the iridium) into the earth's atmosphere. They suggested that the cloud produced by the asteroid's impact covered the planet for an extended period of time, blocked out sunlight, and caused the widespread death of plant life on earth's surface. The loss of plant life in turn, they theorized, brought about the extinction of dinosaurs who fed on the plants. While the theory has found favor among many scientists and has been confirmed to some extent by additional findings, it is still the subject of debate.

Alvarez's hobbies included flying, golf, music, and inventing. He made his last flight in his Cessna 310 in 1984, almost exactly 50 years after he first learned to fly. In 1963 he assisted the Warren Commission in the investigation of President John F. Kennedy's assassination. Among his inventions were a system for color television and an electronic indoor golf-training device developed for President Eisenhower. In all, he held 22 patents for his inventions. Alvarez died of cancer in Berkeley, on September 1, 1988.

SELECTED WRITINGS BY ALVAREZ:

Books

Alvarez: Adventures of a Physicist (autobiography), Basic Books, 1987.

SOURCES:

Books

A Biographical Encyclopedia of Scientists, Volume 1, Facts on File, 1981.
Current Biography 1947, H. W. Wilson, 1947, pp. 9–10.
Current Biography 1988, H. W. Wilson, 1988, p. 88.
McGraw-Hill Modern Scientists and Engineers, Volume 1, McGraw-Hill, 1980, pp. 12–13.
Nobel Lectures in Physics, 1963–1970, Elsevier, 1972, pp. 291–292.
Nobel Prize Winners, H. W. Wilson, 1987, p. 12–14.
Weber, Robert L., *Pioneers of Science: Nobel Prize Winners in Physics,* American Institute of Physics, 1980, pp. 212–214.

—*Sketch by David E. Newton*

Angeles Alvariño
1916-
Spanish-born American marine biologist

For more than four decades, fishery research biologist and marine scientist Angeles Alvariño has made an immense contribution to knowledge about the ecology and geographic distribution of marine zooplankton (small drifting animal life in the ocean) and other marine organisms. During the course of her work, Alvariño discovered twenty-two new ocean species.

Alvariño was born on October 3, 1916 in El Ferrol, Spain, to Antonio Alvariño Grimaldos and Maria del Carmen González Diaz-Saavedra de Alvariño. An intelligent, curious child, Alvariño often enjoyed her physician-father's library, especially his volumes on natural history. She aspired to become a physician herself, but her father discouraged such a choice. He did not want her to experience, as he had, the pain associated with patients whose suffering could not be alleviated.

Alvariño studied a wide range of courses in physical and natural sciences, social science, and humanities during her undergraduate years at the Lycée. After passing final examinations and completing two dissertations for baccalaureate degrees in both science and letters, she graduated *summa cum laude* in 1933 from the University of Santiago de Compostela, Spain. During the next year, Alvariño's desire to study medicine persisted, but her father's viewpoint remained unchanged. Therefore, she entered the University of Madrid in 1934 to study natural sciences. Her studies were interrupted when the university closed from 1936 to 1939 as a result of the Spanish Civil War.

In 1940 Alvariño married Sir Eugenio Leira Manso, Captain of the Spanish Royal Navy and Knight of the Royal and Military Order of Saint Hermenegild. Alvariño continued her studies at the University of Madrid and in 1941 was awarded a master's degree in natural sciences. From 1941 to 1948, she taught biology, zoology, botany, and geology at various colleges in El Ferrol.

In order to do active research, Alvariño left teaching in 1948 to become a research biologist with the Spanish Department of Sea Fisheries in Madrid. In spite of a ban against women, she began to conduct research and study oceanography at the Spanish Institute of Oceanography in Madrid. The quality of her work persuaded officials to admit her as a student researcher in 1950. Academic work at the University of Madrid led in 1951 to a doctoral certificate in experimental psychology, chemistry, and plant ecology.

Studies Aquatic Life Forms

Alvariño's success in a competitive examination resulted in an appointment as a marine biologist-oceanographer with the Spanish Institute of Oceanography in 1952. In 1953 a British Council Fellowship enabled her to work on zooplankton at the Marine Biological Laboratory in Plymouth, England. At the Plymouth lab, she met English marine biologist **Frederick Stratten Russell**, an expert on jellyfish, who directed her attention to chaetognaths (arrow-worms), hydromedusae (jellyfish), and siphonophores (small, free-swimming water organisms). In the 1950s, these animals had received such little study that Alvariño designed and made plankton nets, which she provided to captains of Spanish fishing vessels and research ships so they could collect zooplankton samples for her research.

In 1956, Alvariño was granted a Fulbright Fellowship, allowing her to conduct research in Massachusetts at the Woods Hole Oceanographic Institute. Impressed by her work, Mary Sears, president of the first U.S. Oceanographic Congress, recommended Alvariño to Dr. Roger Revelle, the director of the Scripps Institute of Oceanography at La Jolla, California. He offered Alvariño a position as a biologist and she accepted. Alvariño's years of research at Scripps produced a significant body of knowledge about chaetognaths, siphonophores, and hydromedusae. Her Scripps research also contributed toward completion of work toward her doctoral degree at the University of Madrid (now known as the University Complutense), which awarded her a doctor of sciences degree in 1967, *summa cum laude.*

To further expand her research opportunities, Alvariño in 1970 accepted a position as a fisheries biologist with the Southwest Fisheries Science Center (SWFSC) in La Jolla, a division of the newly-formed National Marine Fisheries Service. There she continued research on predatory chaetognaths, siphonophores, and hydromedusae and their relationship to larval fish survival.

Although officially retired in 1987, Alvariño continues her work, adding to the body of knowledge about zooplankton. She has shed light on how zooplankton relate to the dynamics of the oceanic environment and about which ones are "indicator species," those species associated with specific currents or concentrations of other aquatic life, including spawning fish and their eggs and larvae.

On July 25, 1993, Alvariño was awarded the Great Silver Medal of Galicia by King Juan Carlos I and Queen Sophia of Spain. She participated in numerous expeditions aboard research vessels of several countries, and was the first woman to serve as a scientist aboard a British research vessel.

Alvariño and her husband live in La Jolla. Their only child, Angeles Leira-Alvariño, is an architect and city planner. In addition to her first love, marine science, Alvariño enjoys classical music, literature, and art.

SELECTED WRITINGS BY ALVARIÑO:

Books

Atlantic Chaetognatha, Distribution and Essential Notes of Systematics, Travaux Spanish Institute of Oceanography, 1969.

Siphonophores of the Pacific; with a Revision of the World Distribution, University of California Press, 1971.

"Chaetognatha. Oogenesis, Ovopostion, and Oosorption," in *Reproductive Biology of Invertebrates,* Volume 1, edited by K. G. and R. G. Adiyodi, pp. 585–610, Wiley & Sons, 1983.

"Chaetognatha. Spermatogenesis and Sperm Function," in *Reproductive Biology of Invertebrates,* Volume 2, edited by K. G. and R. G. Adiyodi, pp. 531–544, Wiley & Sons, 1983.

"Fertilization, Development and Parental Care in Chaetognatha," in *Reproductive Biology of Invertebrates,* Volume 4, edited by K. G. and R. G. Adiyody, pp. 255–282, Oxford & IBH Publishing, 1990.

"Sexual Differentiation and Behavior in Chaetognatha. Hermaphroditi," in *Reproductive Biology of Invertebrates,* Volume 5, edited by K. G. and R. G. Adiyody, pp. 424–470, Oxford & IBH Publishing, 1992.

Periodicals

"The Relation Between the Distribution of Zooplankton Predators and *Engraulis Mordax* (Anchovy) Larvae," *California Cooperative Oceanic Fisheries Investigations Reports,* 1980, pp. 150–60.

"The Depth Distribution, Relative Abundance and Structure of the Population of the Chaetognatha *Sagitta Scrippsae* Alvariño 1962, in the California Current off California and Baja California," *Anales del Instituto de Ciencias del Mar y Limnologia,* Universidad Nacional Autonoma de Mexico, 1983, pp. 47–84.

"Abundance of Zooplankton Species, Females and Males, Eggs and Larvae of Holoplanktonic Species. Zooplankton Assemblages and Changes in Zooplankton Communities Related to *Engraulis mordax* Spawning and Survival of the Larvae," *Mem. III Encontro Brasileiro de Plancton,* 1989, pp. 63–149.

SOURCES:

Alvariño, Angeles, interviews conducted by Susan Smith and Connie Blair of the Southwest Fisheries Science Center Public Information staff.

—*Sketch by Margaret DiCanio*

Gene M. Amdahl
1922-
American computer designer

Gene M. Amdahl revolutionized business computing, first by developing the IBM System/360 series and later by founding his own companies, including the Amdahl Corporation and Trilogy Ltd., to compete with IBM through the production of "clone" computers and the ongoing development of cutting edge technology in mainframe systems.

Amdahl was born November 16, 1922, in Flandreau, South Dakota. The son of Anton E. Amdahl, a farmer, and Inga Brendsel Amdahl, he was the second youngest of five children. He spent his high school years first at a local school and then at a boarding school. Farm chores left him little time for other activities, although he did play some football (suffering a few broken ribs in the process). He entered South Dakota State College in 1941, but his academic career was interrupted by World War II. From the middle of 1943 to 1944 he taught physics for the U.S. Army, and then from 1944 to mid–1946 he taught electronics for the Navy. He returned to South Dakota State after the war and graduated in 1948 with a B.S. in engineering physics. Amdahl went on to study theoretical physics at the University of Wisconsin, receiving his Ph.D. in 1952. His doctoral thesis was a description of how to build a computer he had designed—a machine which is now known as the Wisconsin Integrally Synchronized Computer, or WISC for short.

Begins Career in Computer Industry

Amdahl joined IBM in June of 1952. His first assignment was in Poughkeepsie, New York, where he worked on the Defense Calculator, the IBM 701. He later helped design the IBM 704, a more powerful machine and the first computer to use a programming language (Fortran) other than the strings of zeros and ones used internally. Amdahl was the first planner in the development of the IBM 709, the successor to the IBM 704. In 1955, IBM began the development of its

Gene M. Amdahl

first supercomputer, the IBM 7030, also known by its code name, STRETCH. It was to be twice as powerful as existing computers and would be the first large computer to use disk drives. But Amdahl was not offered a leading role in this project, and he consequently left IBM in December of 1955.

Amdahl's first departure from IBM was not permanent. He joined Ramo-Woodridge, a new venture in Los Angeles, where he served as a group head until the summer of 1956. He then moved to a Ford Motors subsidiary, Aeronautics, in Newport Beach, California, to become a manager of systems design. He returned to IBM in the fall of 1960, working first in Yorktown and then in Poughkeepsie again, where he started development of the System/360 series. The new system consisted of a series of computers with a common architecture; the components of the system used the same internal instructions and organized their data in the same way. This approach gave IBM's customers the ability to move easily from small machines to larger and more powerful ones as their businesses changed and their computing needs grew. The System/360 machines were the force behind IBM's domination of the computer marketplace for two decades.

Amdahl's work kept him on the east coast until 1965, when he was made an IBM Fellow and allowed to work on whatever projects he wanted for five years. He returned to California during this period and founded the IBM Advanced Computing Laboratory

in Menlo Park. In 1970, Amdahl made his second and final departure from IBM. A dispute had arisen between him and top executives over the way the company priced its large systems. The pricing strategy was based on performance rather than on cost; it kept the price of information processing constant across IBM's line of products but it discouraged the construction of very large computers. Management believed that the market for these computers was not large enough to cover the costs of designing and building them. It was these large computers that most interested Amdahl, both as a technical challenge and a business opportunity.

Founds the Amdahl Corporation

Amdahl founded the Amdahl Corporation in October of 1970 and went directly into competition with his former employer. The machines he planned and built were plug-compatible, which meant that IBM customers could replace their IBM with an Amdahl computer without having to change their software or peripheral devices. Amdahl targeted his initial machine, the 470 V/6, at IBM's System/370, which was the successor to the System/360. The System/370 used an architecture based on the System/360 so customers could transfer their applications from one to the other. Amdahl took advantage of the compatibility feature of these IBM machines, while building a computer that was four times as powerful at one-quarter the size. And he was able to offer his 470 V/6 at the same price as the IBM System/370: $3.5 million. It was a triumph for Amdahl, both financially and technically, and the 470 V/6 was a great success, especially as it became operational in a relatively short time for a machine of this size—a little more than four years. Amdahl taught the computer industry that companies could make money by building IBM clones.

One of the major advances in computer engineering was made by Amdahl during this period; in 1971, he announced the development of the first high-performance large-scale integration (LSI) chip. LSI chips, unlike the simple integrated circuits that preceded them, could do complete jobs rather than single functions. Each LSI contained a small silicon chip holding 100 electronic circuits. At the time, IBM was using LSI technology only in the area of memory, not for computer logic circuits, and it was this technology that enabled the 470 V/6 to be smaller and still more powerful than System/370 computers. Amdahl placed the central processor logic for the 470 V/6 on a panel three feet by six feet, as compared to the usual size of six feet by twenty-four feet.

During the first two years the Amdahl corporation produced the 470 V/6, over fifty of the new computers were delivered. When IBM cut its prices in 1977, Amdahl responded with cuts of his own; sales were three times those of the comparable period in 1976, and the company saw a seven-fold gain in net profits. The computer wars had begun. In March of 1977, IBM announced the 3033, a new, more powerful computer which was to be two times as fast as its predecessor, for two-thirds the price. In response, Amdahl lowered the price of the V/6 and then brought out the V/7, a machine which was faster by a third than the 3033 and did not cost much more. But for businesses needing large mainframe systems, the cost of keeping pace with the rapidly changing technology was prohibitive. Eventually, consumers of these systems adopted a new strategy: leasing. The practice of leasing machines and the continuing, relentless competition of IBM cut into Amdahl's profits and in the second quarter of 1979 the Amdahl Corporation only broke even. To raise cash, Amdahl sold a large percentage of his stock to Fujitsu, thereby losing control of the company that bore his name.

Leads Challenges to IBM in the Mainframe Market

In 1980, Amdahl founded a second company, Trilogy, Ltd., whose goal was to challenge IBM's dominance of the high end of the mainframe market. Trilogy raised $230 million in it first four years, more money than any other new company in Silicon Valley, and Amdahl promised to revolutionize the industry. He planned to develop a computer at once more powerful and less expensive than the largest machines then being produced by either IBM or the Amdahl Corporation. The crux of his plan was a new technology called wafer-scale integration. With this approach, circuits could be etched onto 2.5 inch square silicon wafers; twenty such wafers could replace up to 2,000 separate chips.

Applying the new technology, however, proved more of a challenge than Amdahl and the Trilogy planners had expected. A twenty-wafer central processing unit was designed without a full understanding of the characteristics of these wafers. As a result, some of the circuitry handling essential arithmetic functions was divided among individual wafers, resulting in a level of power and speed that was considerably lower than initial design specifications. The target date for delivering the new computer had originally been 1984, but by the spring of 1985 the date had to be pushed back to 1987. In the summer of 1985, the effort was abandoned altogether, although Amdahl still envisioned producing the wafer-scale chip. Trilogy's failure lost its investors $230 million, and the venture seemed to prove the old adage that haste makes waste. In their rush to put out a new mainframe, Trilogy's developers overlooked or tried to shortcut the technical problems that destroyed the project in the end.

Amdahl tried to save Trilogy in 1985 by merging it with Elxsi, another Silicon Valley company that was bringing out a new computer. In the winter of 1986, Amdahl made a breakthrough at Elxsi; he was able to use new technological developments to link the Elxsi machine with the VAX minicomputer made by the Digital Equipment Corporation (DEC). The Elxsi machine allowed VAX users to increase their computing power at a reasonable price, but this was not enough to sustain the company. Amdahl left Elxsi in 1988 and formed Andor Systems in Cupertino, California.

Andor took its name from the "and" and the "or" computer logic circuits. Amdahl's vision for his new company was again to challenge IBM, this time at the lower end of the mainframe market. He planned to use very large-scale integrated circuit (VLSI) technology to reduce the size of his machine. He also believed he could simplify and accelerate the design process by using a high-level programming language to describe the computer. When complete, the program would generate the details, thus eliminating the necessity for chips to be designed on a circuit-by-circuit basis. The new machines would be much smaller than their IBM counterparts, with one result being the generation of less heat and a consequent reduction in cooling costs.

Misfortune and competition from IBM forced Andor to curtail its plans and expectations. The Andor effort was delayed for two years when the company received bad chips from a supplier, while IBM introduced the AS/400 system, which did very well in the market segment Andor was targeting. By 1990 Andor was in trouble, and Amdahl changed his original design into a machine that would do data backup and provide disaster recovery for mainframe systems. As 1991 came to a close, however, Andor had produced only a few of the machines and the future of the company was in doubt. This was the same year that the Amdahl Corporation had sales of close to $2 billion. But by 1993 Andor had sold systems to Lufthansa, the Italian Interbank Clearing House, and AT&T.

Amdahl's brilliance as a scientist and entrepreneur has been recognized many times. In 1973, he received the Distinguished Alumnus award from his alma mater, South Dakota State College. In 1976, he was awarded the Data Processing Management Association's Computer Science Man of the Year Award. In 1976, he was honored with the W. Wallace McDowell Award for his contributions to the computer industry. Amdahl was recognized with the Michelson-Morley award presented by Case Western Reserve University in 1977, and in 1983 he received the Harry Goode Memorial award for his work on high-performance computers. Amdahl is credited with over twenty computer patents, including one for the design of the IBM System/360.

He married Marian Quissell June 23, 1946, and they had three children, two daughters and a son, Carlton, who is also a computer designer and was a partner with his father in the founding of Trilogy. Amdahl resides with his wife in California.

SOURCES:

Books

Encyclopedia of Computer Science, Van Nostrand Reinhold, 1993, pp. 517.
Slater, Robert, *Portraits in Silicon,* MIT Press, 1987.

Other

Amdahl, Gene M., telephone interview with Frank Hertle conducted December 15, 1993.

—*Sketch by Frank Hertle*

Bruce N. Ames

Bruce N. Ames
1928-
American biochemist and molecular biologist

Bruce N. Ames is a professor of biochemistry and molecular biology at the University of California at Berkeley. He is best known for the development of a test that has been used as an indicator of the carcinogenicity (cancer-causing potential) of chemicals. Known as the Ames test, it measures the rate of mutation in bacteria after the introduction of a test substance. His research led to a greater appreciation of the role of genetic mutation in cancer and facilitated the testing of suspected cancer-causing chemicals. He also developed a data base of chemicals that cause cancer in animals, listing their degree of virulence. Ames has been involved in numerous controversies involving scientific and environmental policies relevant to cancer prevention. In the 1970s he vociferously advocated strict government control of synthetic chemicals. In the 1980s, however, the discovery that many natural substances were also mutagenic (causing gene mutation), and thus possibly cancer causing, led him to reverse his original position.

Bruce Nathan Ames was born on December 16, 1928, in New York City, the son of Dr. Maurice U. and Dorothy Andres Ames. His father taught high school science and then became assistant superintendent of schools. Ames himself graduated from the

Bronx High School of Science in 1946. He received a B.A. in biochemistry from Cornell University in 1950 and a Ph.D. in the same field from the California Institute of Technology in 1953. He recalled in *Omni* that although he "was never terribly good at getting A's," he "was always good at problem solving." He worked at the National Institutes of Health, primarily in the National Institute of Arthritis and Metabolic Diseases, from 1953 to 1967. In 1968 he moved to the Department of Biochemistry and Molecular Biology at the University of California at Berkeley as a full professor. He was Chairman of the Department from 1984 to 1989. In addition, he became Director of the National Institute of Environmental Health Science at the University in 1979. In 1960 he married Dr. Giovanna Ferro-Luzzi, a biochemist who is also on the faculty at Berkeley. They have two children, Sofia and Matteo.

Develops the Ames Test

In the 1960s and early 1970s, Ames developed a test that measured the degree to which synthetic chemicals cause gene mutation (a change in the deoxyribonucleic acid, or DNA, the molecule that carries genetic information). He began by deliberately mutating a *Salmonella* bacterium. The changed bacterium could not produce an amino acid called histidine that normal bacteria produce and that they need to survive. The next step was to add just enough histidine to allow the bacteria to live, and to add, as well, the synthetic chemical being tested. If the added chemical caused genetic mutation, the abnormal gene of the *Salmonella* bacteria would mutate and again be able to produce histidine. When this happened, the added chemical was marked as a suspected carcinogen,since cancer is associated with somatic cell mutation, that is to say, mutation of any cells with the exception of germ cells.

Over eighty percent of organic chemicals known to cause cancer in humans tested positive as mutagens in the test developed by Ames and his colleagues. This result gave support to the theory that somatic mutation causes cancer and helped to validate the use of the test for initial identification of mutagens when considering synthetic chemicals for industrial and commercial use. In addition to these practical results, the research of Ames and a colleague, H. J. Whitfield, Jr., led to important advances in understanding the biochemistry of mutagenesis. Beyond his work in genetic toxicology, Ames made important discoveries in molecular biology including ground-breaking studies on the regulation of the histidine operon (the gene or locus of the gene that controls histidine) and the role of transfer ribonucleic acid (RNA) in that regulation.

In the 1980s Ames set up a data base of animal cancer test results with colleague Lois Swirsky Gold of Lawrence Berkeley Laboratory. The data base can be used to determine whether a chemical has tested positive as a carcinogen and gives the degree of its virulence. From these data, Ames developed a value measuring the carcinogenic danger of a chemical to humans. HERP (daily Human Exposure dose/Rodent Potency dose) is the value determined by comparing the daily dose of a chemical that will cause cancer in half a group of test animals with the estimated daily dose to which humans are normally exposed. The result is a percentage that suggests the degree of carcinogenicity of a chemical for humans.

Advocates Regulatory Policies

In the 1970s Ames was a conspicuous advocate of particular regulatory and environmental public policies that relate to the cancer-causing potential of synthetic substances. In the 1970s he believed that even trace amounts of mutagenic chemicals could cause a mutation (and thus possibly cancer). He found that *tris* phosphate, the chemical that was used as a flame retardant on children's pajamas, was a mutagen in the Ames test; he was instrumental in getting it banned. Similarly, he found that some hair dyes contained mutagens. His advocacy led to governmental regulations that forced manufacturers to reformulate their products. In his position on the regulation of synthetic chemicals, he was a natural ally of environmentalists.

However, in the early 1980s he reversed his position, arguing that there is no scientific evidence that most synthetic chemicals cause human cancers in the small doses that humans absorb them and that, in the absence of such evidence, they should not be controlled. This about-face was partly a result of a growing body of knowledge concerning the mutagenic properties of numerous chemicals found in nature. Ames began arguing against the existing large public expenditures for pollution control and the regulation of synthetic chemicals, noting that cancer might just as plausibly be caused by the chemicals in plants. His arguments were based primarily on three factors: his view that more scientific evidence should be required before controls are implemented; his attitude toward the setting of priorities, which he believed should be centered on basic research rather than regulation; and finally his belief that the large public expenditures incurred by the regulatory process hurt American economic competitiveness.

Ames and his colleague Gold have also argued that the use of bioassays (animal tests) of chemicals to predict their carcinogenic potential in humans should be abandoned. In a typical bioassay, rats are given a "maximum tolerated dosage" (MTD) of a particular chemical daily for a period of time (such as a year). The maximum tolerated dosage is as much as the animal can be given without immediately becoming ill or dying. At the end of the time period, the number of animals that have developed cancers is tabulated as an indicator of the cancer causing potential of the chemical being tested. Ames suggested that it is often the large dosage itself, rather than the nature of the particular chemical, that induces the rat cancers. He argued that, since humans are not normally exposed to such large doses, the assays were not valid for predicting human cancers.

Ames's views have some support both within and outside scientific communities. However, he also has numerous critics among scientists and others. Critics note that pollution control involves issues that include but also go beyond cancer (such as acid rain). They suggest that Ames has not offered a substitute for animal assays (the Ames test has not proved to be such a substitute), and that neither he nor they have a good idea of what goes on at low dosages. They say he has an over-simplified view of the regulatory process, which is based on a consideration of animal assays but also on other factors. It has also been argued that the discovery that natural chemicals have a high mutagenic rate just as synthetic chemicals do should not lead to the assumption that synthetic chemicals pose less risk than was previously supposed. Such an assumption places too much emphasis on mutagenic rate as a sole indicator of carcinogenicity, ignoring the complex, multi-stage developmental process of the disease.

Yet the disagreements between Ames and his critics are based on several points of commonality—that cancer is a complex multi-stage process that is not fully understood; that there is no perfect test or group of tests that can fully predict the potential carcinogenicity of many substances in humans; and that public regulatory and environmental policies must be made and carried out in spite of this deficiency of knowledge. As for Ames, he has described his public policy activism as a hobby, and has noted that his recent scientific work includes studies in the biochemistry of aging.

Elected to the National Academy of Sciences in 1972, Ames has received many awards, including the Eli Lilly Award of the American Chemical Society (1964), the Mott Prize of the General Motors Cancer Research Foundation (1983), and the Gold Medal of the American Institute of Chemists (1991). He is the author or coauthor of more than 250 scientific articles.

SELECTED WRITINGS BY AMES:

Periodicals

(With Lois Swirsky Gold) "Too Many Rodent Carcinogens: Mitogenesis Increases Mutagenesis," *Science,* August 31, 1990, pp. 970–971.

SOURCES:

Periodicals

Edelson, Edward, "The Man Who Upset the Apple Cart," *Popular Science,* February, 1990, pp. 64–68.
Marx, Jean, "Animal Carcinogen Testing Challenged," *Science,* November 9, 1990, pp. 743–745.
Moseley, Bill, "Interview: Bruce Ames," *Omni,* February, 1991, pp. 75–106.
Weinstein, I. Bernard, "Mitogenesis Is Only One Factor in Carcinogenesis," *Science,* January 25, 1991, pp. 387–388.

—*Sketch by Pamela O. Long*

Othmar Hermann Ammann
1879-1965
Swiss-born American civil engineer

Othmar Hermann Ammann, besides being the designer of two of the four longest bridges in the United States, is important for having led the movement that placed the esthetics of public works projects on an equal level with their functionality and cost. Two of his bridges, the George Washington Bridge crossing the Hudson River and the Golden Gate Bridge spanning the mouth of the San Francisco Bay, are widely regarded as both engineering and artistic masterpieces.

Ammann was born in the small village of Schaffhausen in Switzerland, on March 29, 1879, the son of Emanuel and Emilie Ammann. From early childhood he was fascinated by the 400 foot-long wooden bridge that spanned the Rhine River in Schaffhausen. Deciding that his career would be in bridge building, he studied civil engineering at the Swiss Federal Polytechnic Institute in Zurich. In 1904, after working in Germany for two years, Ammann realized that if he wanted to build bridges that he should go where they were still being built. Thus, he emigrated to the United States.

Ammann designed railroad bridges for Joseph Mayer in New York City and then moved on to the Pennsylvania Steel Company, where he worked on the detailed plans for the actual fabrication of bridges. In 1907, while working for the steel company, he was appointed to the board investigating the collapse of the Quebec River Bridge. The bridge collapsed during the final stages of its construction, killing seventy-five steel workers, and making it the worst disaster in North American construction history. The twenty-eight-year-old Ammann was the author of the final report on the disaster. His report, widely read in the profession, thrust him to the forefront of American bridge design. Ammann then took a position as the chief assistant of Gustav Lindenthal, the leading bridge designer of the period, in 1910. He worked with Lindenthal on New York's Hell Gate railroad bridge, the largest arch bridge ever built. In 1914, Ammann was forced to give up his position and return to Switzerland, to serve in the Swiss Army. Arriving again in the United States, he continued with his former position until 1924, when he was appointed chief engineer of the New York Port Authority.

Builds the World's Largest Bridge

As the chief engineer for the port authority, Ammann drew the plans for what was to be the world's longest bridge, the George Washington

Bridge, which stretches across the Hudson River, connecting New York and New Jersey. With a span length of 3500 feet (for suspension bridges, the span is measured from tower to tower), the George Washington Bridge was literally twice as long as the previous record holder. While with the port authority, Ammann also designed the Triborough Bridge, the Bronx-Whitestone Bridge, the Goethals Bridge and the Outerbridge Crossing, between Staten Island and New Jersey. In addition, he was one of the chief consultants for the design of the bridge that was to eclipse the George Washington Bridge's title as the world's longest, the Golden Gate Bridge. Amman's influence on the Golden Gate Bridge can be seen in the graceful portal arches (the portal arches are the holes in the towers through which traffic passes) of the Art Deco masterpiece.

In 1946, at the age of 67, Ammann and his partner Charles Whitney, founded the firm of Ammann and Whitney. By 1964, with Ammann still actively in charge of the company, the staff of Ammann and Whitney had grown to almost 500, with offices in Washington, Philadelphia, Paris, Athens, Teheran, Lahore and Addis Ababa. Ammann's last great bridge, which he designed at the age of 83 and which would win back the title of world's longest from the Golden Gate Bridge, was the Verrazano Narrows Bridge, a structure that crosses the mouth of New York Harbor. The span of the Verrazano Narrows Bridge is 4260 feet. Its towers are 690 feet high and the wires in its suspension cables are long enough to encircle the earth at the equator fifty-five times. At $350,000,000, it is also the most expensive bridge ever built.

Ammann died within a year of the completion of the Verrazano Narrows bridge. He had received numerous honors in his lifetime, including honorary degrees from Yale and New York University and the National Medal of Science in 1964. His legacy to the world amounts to much more than a list of honors and a number of very large bridges, however. Ammann believed, and proved to the world by example, that money spent on making our public structures beautiful was money well spent. As Ammann told the *New York Times* in 1934, "Although I believe that the art of engineering is one of the activities of modern civilization which contribute greatly to the benefit of humanity, nevertheless I recognize its shortcomings. I am a lover of fine art and I advocate its application to our engineering works of today. After all, art is an expression of our intellectual and moral life. We cannot urge too strongly the importance of the architectural or esthetic side of our planning of public works. ... It is perfectly possible to apply art to our public engineering problems. It is not necessary to conceive these structures as cold creations of scientific formula or as crude creations to perform utilitarian functions."

SOURCES:

Books

Gies, Joseph, *Bridges and Men,* Doubleday, 1963.
Plowden, David, *Bridges: The Spans of North America,* Viking Press, 1974.
Steinman, David B., and Sara R. Watson, *Bridges and Their Builders,* Dover, 1941.

Periodicals

Woolf, S. J., "A Master Bridge Builder Looks Ahead," *New York Time,* April 15, 1934, p. 7, 19.

—*Sketch by Jeff Raines*

Edward Anders
1926-
Latvian-born American cosmochemist

Edward Anders studied bits of meteorites gathered from all over the world and samples of rocks taken from the surface of the moon, applying principles of chemistry in order to advance the understanding of the early history of the solar system. During a prolific career, he helped further the knowledge of the nature and origin of organic matter and diamonds in meteorites, the amounts of elements in the solar system, the abundance of volatile elements such as hydrogen and helium in planets, and the connection between meteorites and asteroids. With his collaborators, he studied the grains of interstellar dust, which give clues to the nuclear and chemical processes of stars and to the evolution of the solar system.

Anders was born on June 21, 1926, in Libau, Latvia. He fled his home country during World War II and in 1946 began three years of study at the University of Munich. He was prohibited from entering the United States for two years but finally arrived in his adopted country in 1949. He received a master's degree from Columbia University in 1951 and followed with a doctorate in 1954, studying with the radiochemist J. M. Miller. Anders spent a year as a chemistry instructor at the University of Illinois at Urbana before accepting positions in 1955 both with the chemistry department at the University of Chicago and at the Enrico Fermi Institute. He also became a naturalized citizen that year. Anders accepted several visiting professorships during the 1960s and became a consultant to the National Aeronautics and

Space Administration (NASA). He was appointed the Horace B. Horton Professor of Physical Sciences in 1973 and retired in 1991.

Focuses Career on Cosmochemistry

After his studies in radiochemistry, Anders switched his sights to cosmochemistry—the study of the chemical makeup of and changes in the universe—and focused in particular on meteorites. In 1956 **Harold Clayton Urey** of the University of Chicago had proposed that the tiny diamonds found in some meteorites had formed under high pressure, the kind created by gravitational forces inside a large object in space, and suggested that most meteorites originated in bodies as large as the moon. Anders found flaws in this theory. He traveled to Sedona, Arizona, in 1959 to visit H. H. Nininger, who had advanced the theory that diamonds found in the Canyon Diablo meteorite were formed by the shock of the two-million-ton meteorite striking the Earth, not by the gravitational pressures of a large body. Anders, with Michael E. Lipschutz, examined the samples and demonstrated, by studying the telltale physical patterns imprinted in the meteorite fragments, that the shock of impact had indeed created the diamonds. A year later, another group of scientists found a modification of silica called coesite, which forms only under high pressure, in the sandstone under the crater, supporting the idea that a shock wave had been present at the meteorite site. In 1965 Anders wrote in *Scientific American* that "the intellectual climate became almost balmy" with the news that Stanford Research Institute's Paul S. DeCarli and University of Chicago's John C. Jamieson had converted graphite to diamond by exposing it to a shock wave generated by an explosive charge. Anders, along with R. A. Fish and G. G. Goles, went on to show that heat from a source such as an extinct, radioactive isotope of aluminum, not just the forces associated with a large body, could cause materials to melt and change phases.

Anders also contributed to knowledge about the origins of meteorites and the history of the solar system. He won the American Association for the Advancement of Science's senior award, the Newcomb Cleveland Prize, for establishing that meteorites originate from asteroids, not moon-sized bodies. "Meteorites," he told a contributor to the *Saturday Evening Post* in 1962, "are the most ancient relics of the solar system. They are the raw material of which the earth, its mountains and its living creatures are the final products." In 1964 Anders wrote an influential review of the origins of meteorites. He and John Larimer studied the behavior of elements in the solar nebula, learning of the inorganic chemistry of meteorites and planets. And Anders contributed to the emerging notion that meteorites were some of the pieces left over after the solar nebula condensed out

of a part of the gas-dust cloud making up the early Milky Way, forming large pieces that eventually coalesced into planets. He also studied samples of moon rocks and soil beginning with the *Apollo 11* mission in 1969, and with colleagues including R. Ganapathy, J. Hertogen, and J. W. Morgan, established that the moon was bombarded first by large meteorites and later by smaller micrometeorites.

During the same period, Anders also studied the origin of organic matter in meteorites, demonstrating through experiments conducted with Martin Studier and Ryoichi Hayatsu that this organic material could be made in the solar nebula from carbon monoxide, hydrogen, helium, and ammonia when meteoritic iron was present. The process was a form of the Fischer-Tropsch reaction used to make gasoline during World War II in Germany (the Fischer-Tropsch process is a method of obtaining hydrocarbons through the use of a catalyst). Anders and F. W. Fitch had debunked a claim in the early 1960s that the organic matter found in meteorites came from extraterrestrial life, concluding in one case that meteorite fragments had been doctored.

Studies Interstellar Grains in Meteorites

As far back as 1970, Anders and his colleagues also looked for pristine interstellar grains of material created by stars and locked into meteorites, studies that Anders continued even after his retirement in 1991. These grains, with their unusual ratios of isotopes (groups of chemically identical atoms of the same element and atomic number with differing atomic mass), hold information about nuclear and chemical processes in stars. With R. S. Lewis, B. Srinivasan, and L. Alaerts, Anders studied noble gases formed before the solar system, including xenon carried in meteoritic diamonds, and found new ways to separate the unusual isotopes they found. Anders published papers on the abundances of elements in the solar system in 1982 with M. Ebihara and in 1989 with N. Grevesse and wrote several reviews of interstellar grains, tiny pieces from other stars, in primitive meteorites. His studies contributed to the theory that all elements heavier than helium were made by stars, a process called nucleosynthesis.

Anders married Joan Fleming on November 12, 1955. They had two children, George and Nancy. Among the honors Anders has received for his work are the National Academy of Sciences's J. Lawrence Smith Medal in 1971, NASA's Medal of Exceptional Scientific Achievement in 1973, the Meteoritical Society's Frederick C. Leonard Medal in 1974, and the American Astronomical Society's Kuiper Prize in 1991. He is a member of the National Academy of Sciences, an associate of the Royal Astronomical Society, and a fellow of the American Association for the Advancement of Science, the Academy of Arts and Sciences, the American Geophysical Union, and the Meteoritical Society.

SELECTED WRITINGS BY ANDERS:

Periodicals

(With Michael E. Lipschutz) "On the Mechanism of Diamond Formation," *Science,* December 29, 1961, pp. 2095–2099.

(With Frank W. Fitch) "Search for Organized Elements in Carbonaceous Chondrites," *Science,* December 28, 1962, pp. 1392–1399.

"Diamonds in Meteorites," *Scientific American,* October, 1965, pp. 26–36.

(With N. Grevesse) "Abundances of the Elements: Meteoritic and Solar," *Acta Geochimica et Cosmochimica,* Volume 53, 1989, pp. 197–214.

(With Ernst Zinner) "Interstellar Grains in Primitive Meteorites: Diamond, Silicon Carbide, and Graphite," *Meteoritics,* September, 1993.

SOURCES:

Books

Modern Scientists and Engineers, McGraw-Hill, 1980, pp. 16–17.

Periodicals

"AAS Division Awards Given to Researchers," *Physics Today,* February, 1992, pp. 117–118.

"Four Major AAAS Awards Presented at Association's New York Meeting," *Science,* December 30, 1960, p. 1938.

Jacobsen, Sally, "Edward Anders on Meteorites and the Moon," *Bulletin of the Atomic Scientists,* December, 1972, pp. 32–38.

"People on the Way Up," *Saturday Evening Post,* June 23, 1962, p. 22.

Sobel, Dava, "Diamonds in Space," *Omni,* September, 1987, p. 31.

—Sketch by Julie Anderson

Dorothy Andersen
1901-1963
American physician and pathologist

Dorothy Andersen was the first medical researcher to recognize the disorder known as cystic fibrosis. She devoted much of her life to the further study of this disease, as well as to study of congenital defects of the heart. During World War II, Anderson was asked to develop a training program in cardiac embryology and anatomy for surgeons learning techniques of open-heart surgery.

Dorothy Hansine Andersen was born on May 15, 1901, in Asheville, North Carolina. She was the only child of Hans Peter Andersen and the former Mary Louise Mason. Hans Peter Andersen was a native of Denmark and was employed by the Young Men's Christian Association (YMCA) in Asheville. Andersen's mother was a descendent of Benning Wentworth, for whom the town of Bennington, Vermont, was named.

Andersen was forced to take responsibility for her own upbringing early in life. Her father died when she was thirteen years old, leaving behind an invalid wife dependent on her daughter's care. They moved to Saint Johnsbury, Vermont, where Mary Andersen died in 1920. Her death left young Dorothy "with not a single close relative," according to biographer Libby Machol in *Notable American Women.*

Plans a Career in Medicine

Andersen put herself through Saint Johnsbury Academy and Mount Holyoke College before enrolling in the Johns Hopkins School of Medicine, from which she received her M.D. in 1926. While still a medical student, Andersen published in the journal *Contributions to Embryology* two scientific papers dealing with the reproductive system of the female pig. After graduating from Johns Hopkins, Andersen accepted a one-year position teaching anatomy at the Rochester School of Medicine. She then did her internship in surgery at the Strong Memorial Hospital in Rochester, New York. For medical students an internship is normally followed by a residency, which ultimately leads to certification as a physician. Andersen found, however, that she was unable to find a hospital that would allow her to do a residency in surgery or to work as a pathologist, her other major interest. The reason for this slight, according to Machol, was that Andersen was a woman.

Denied the opportunity to have a medical practice, Andersen turned instead to medical research. She took a job as research assistant in pathology at

Columbia University's College of Physicians and Surgeons that allowed her to begin a doctoral program in endocrinology, the study of glands. She completed the course in 1935 and was granted the degree of doctor of medical science by Columbia University. From 1930 to 1935 Andersen also served as an instructor in pathology at the Columbia Medical School. Andersen later accepted an appointment as a pathologist at Babies Hospital of the Columbia-Presbyterian Medical Center in New York City, where she stayed for more than twenty years, eventually becoming chief of pathology in 1952. By 1958 she had become a full professor at the College of Physicians and Surgeons.

Research Focuses on Cardiology and Cystic Fibrosis

Andersen's research interests fell into two major categories. The first of these involved a long and careful study of congenital (existing from birth) heart problems based on the examination of infants who had died of cardiac conditions. She began that study during her first year at Babies Hospital and was still publishing her findings on the subject in the late 1950s. Andersen's experience with cardiac problems was put to use during World War II when she was asked to teach courses for physicians who wanted to learn how to conduct open-heart surgery.

The second area of research, for which Andersen is probably best known, evolved out of her discovery in 1935 of cystic fibrosis. That discovery came about during the postmortem examination of a child who had supposedly died of celiac disease, a nutritional disorder. According to Machol, "her researcher's sixth sense alerted, Dr. Andersen searched for similar cases in the autopsy files and in the literature." Eventually she realized that she had found a disease that had never been described in the medical literature, to which she gave the name cystic fibrosis. Cystic fibrosis is a congenital disease of the mucous glands and pancreatic enzymes that results in abnormal digestion and difficulty in breathing; it is believed to affect approximately one in fifteen hundred people. Over the next twenty-six years, Andersen was successful in developing diagnostic tests for cystic fibrosis but less successful in her efforts to treat and cure the disease.

Andersen died of lung cancer in New York City on March 3, 1963. A contributing factor may well have been her smoking habits. As Machol has written: "Ashes from the cigarette that usually dangled from the corner of her mouth were virtually a part of her costume." Among the honors Andersen received were the Mead Johnson Award for Pediatric Research in 1938, the Borden Award for Research in Nutrition from the American Academy of Pediatrics in 1948, the Elizabeth Blackwell Citation for Women in Medi-

cine from the New York Infirmary in 1954, a citation for outstanding performance from Mount Holyoke College in 1952, and, posthumously, the distinguished service medal of the Columbia-Presbyterian Medical Center.

SELECTED WRITINGS BY ANDERSEN:

Periodicals

(With F. R. Bailey) "Acute Interstitial Myocarditis," *American Heart Journal,* Volume 6, number 3, February, 1931, pp. 2–12.
(With E. F. Doob) "Leomyosarcoma of the Duodenum," *Archives of Pathology,* Volume 16, December, 1933, pp. 795–802.

SOURCES:

Books

Sicherman, Barbara, and Carol Hurd Green, editors, *Notable American Women, the Modern Period: A Biographical Dictionary,* Belknap Press, 1980, pp. 18–20.

Periodicals

"Andersen, Dorothy Hansine," *Journal of the American Medical Association,* May 25, 1963, p. 150.
Damrosch, Douglas S., "Dorothy Hansine Andersen," *Journal of Pediatrics,* October, 1964, pp. 477–479.

—Sketch by David E. Newton

Carl David Anderson
1905-1991
American physicist

Carl David Anderson discovered two of the elementary particles of matter—the positron ("positive electron") and the meson, also known as muon (identical to the negatively charged electron in almost every aspect except mass). His discoveries dramatically expanded physicists' understanding of the nature and structure of the atom and confirmed theoretical predictions about the existence of such subatomic particles. Anderson's experimental identi-

Carl David Anderson

fication of the positron earned him a Nobel Prize in 1936.

Anderson was born on September 3, 1905, in New York City, New York, the only son of Swedish immigrants from farming families. His mother was Emma Adolfina (Ajaxson) Anderson. His father, also named Carl David Anderson, came to the United States in 1896. When Anderson was a boy, the family moved to Los Angeles, where the father was just able to support the family by managing small restaurants. Anderson attended the Los Angeles Polytechnic High School. He had ambitions to be a track star—a high jumper—but his future career interest was more accurately indicated by his membership in Polytech's science club. After high school graduation in 1924, Anderson could not afford to live away from home and pursue his studies, so he commuted to the California Institute of Technology (Caltech) in nearby Pasadena. Although financial necessity dictated his choice of school, it was a happy one, as Anderson remained at Caltech for his entire career. Originally, he intended to study electrical engineering, but in his sophomore year he chose physics as his major. His outstanding undergraduate work brought him tuition grants and a prize of a trip to Europe. He earned his bachelor's degree in physics and engineering in 1927, after just three years of study, and became a member of the honor society Sigma Xi in recognition of original scientific work he had done.

Continuing his studies at Caltech in physics and mathematics, Anderson was Coffin research fellow from 1927 to 1928 and a teaching fellow in physics from 1928 to 1930. One of his graduate courses was physicist **J. Robert Oppenheimer**'s first course in quantum mechanics, which the professor persuaded Anderson to stick with after everyone else had dropped out. Anderson agreed even though the course focused on theoretical physics, while he preferred experimental work. His graduate research concentrated on X rays and electrons; his doctoral thesis dealt with the space distribution of photoelectrons (electron exposed to radiation) scattered from various gases by X rays. After receiving his Ph.D. magna cum laude in 1930, Anderson stayed at Caltech as a research fellow in physics. In 1933 he joined Caltech's faculty as an assistant professor of physics; in 1937 he became an associate professor and in 1939, a full professor.

Launches Study of Cosmic Rays

While Anderson was a graduate student, his research director was physicist Robert A. Millikan, whose scientific reputation (he had won the 1923 Nobel Prize in physics for successfully measuring the charge of an electron) and fund-raising talent had helped to make Caltech a premier research institute. Millikan was at the time interested in measuring energies of cosmic rays (very penetrating radiation from outer space). Soon after Anderson received his doctorate, Millikan asked him to stay at Caltech and help him develop a type of cloud chamber that could make the cosmic ray measurements. Anderson agreed to Millikan's request and, as it turned out, this was the work that won Anderson his Nobel Prize.

The cloud chamber was developed by Scottish physicist **C. T. R. Wilson** in the early 1900s as a means of detecting charged particles. Particles with an electric charge pass through a cloud of moist air inside the chamber, ionizing (charging) gas molecules along their path. Water vapor condenses on the ionized molecules, and the hail of these water droplets can be photographed through a glass cover on one side of the chamber. Particle types can be identified by their characteristic trails. The cloud chamber is positioned between the poles of a electromagnet, which causes positively and negatively charged particles to curve in different directions within the chamber. In order to study cosmic rays, Anderson and Millikan designed a cloud chamber with an extremely powerful electromagnet capable of deflecting the high-energy cosmic particles. Millikan then left his assistant in charge of the project. Anderson's task was to photograph clouds hoping to capture shots of particles jolted into action by a cosmic ray. The particles' curvature trails would yield a measurement of their energy. As so often happens in science, the experiment yielded a unexpected result.

Discovers Subatomic Particle

Anderson made and studied a thousand photographs, at 15-second intervals day and night, during 1930 and 1931. He noticed that some photographs showed paths of particles curving in opposite directions. The negatively charged particles were electrons; the particles curving away from them must be positively charged. At the time, only two elementary particles were known to exist—the electron and the positively charged proton. Continuing his experiments to prove that the mysterious particles were protons, Anderson instead found that the particles seemed to have a mass comparable to the electron, much less than that of the proton. His suggestion to Millikan that he had found either positively charged electrons or a new, previously unknown particle resulted in what Anderson described later as "frequent and at times somewhat heated discussions" between the two physicists, with Millikan holding out for the particles' identity as protons (*American Journal of Physics*). Anderson then inserted a lead plate across the middle of the cloud chamber—which would lessen the particles' energy and therefore clarify the direction of the particles' motion. This resulted on August 2, 1932, in a very clear photograph of an upwardly moving positively charged particle that measurements showed to have a mass consistent with an electron. Additional photographs confirmed the finding, a difficult feat as subsequent investigations showed that these particles have a average life of just a few billionths of a second. Anderson concluded, and Millikan concurred, that he had found a new particle, which he called the positron, or positive electron. At Millikan's urging, Anderson announced his discovery in a letter to *Science* on September 9, 1932.

The existence of the positron (and other antiparticles, with opposite charges from existing known particles) had been predicted by **Paul Dirac** in 1928. Still, other researchers had ignored the diverging tracks that caught Anderson's attention. And, as Anderson stated in the *American Journal of Physics,* "The discovery of the positron was wholly accidental," although, he added, if a researcher had taken "the Dirac theory at face value he could have discovered the positron in a single afternoon." (Anderson himself had not been familiar with Dirac's theory at the time of his experiments.) While the discovery confirmed the existence of antimatter, the positron's existence was not greeted enthusiastically by Anderson's fellow physicists, because it seemed to complicate rather than clarify attempts to understand atomic structure. As a reporter in the *New York Times* noted, "Dr. Anderson's positron was a bomb. When it exploded it burst all conceptions of the atom's constitution apart." By the spring of 1933, however, experimenters at Great Britain's Cavendish Laboratory had confirmed the existence of positrons. Also in 1933, Anderson and Seth Neddermeyer, his student

and then colleague, succeeded in producing positrons in the laboratory by directing powerful gamma rays from thorium C" (a radioactive substance) at atomic nuclei. Further investigations by Anderson and others of electron-positron interactions provided proof of Albert Einstein's famous formula relating energy and mass. Anderson and other researchers found that positrons and electrons annihilate one another, creating gamma rays (transforming mass into energy), and that gamma rays could combine to convert into an electron-positron pair (changing energy into mass). Anderson also made contributions to science concerning the energy spectrum of cosmic rays and the energy loss experienced by the rays as they pass through matter.

Discovers Second Previously Unknown Particle

As Anderson and Neddermeyer continued their experiments with cosmic rays, using the same cloud chamber in which the positron was discovered, they began to suspect the existence of yet another new elementary particle. They painstakingly tracked it down over a period of act four years, taking thousands of cloud-chamber photographs in Pasadena, in Panama, and at the top of Pike's Peak in Colorado. The new particle was charged, so it had to be either an electron (negative), positron (positive), or a proton (positive). But it was far more penetrating than allowed by current atomic theory, and its mass seemed to be somewhere between that of the electron and the proton. Anderson hinted at the existence of the new particle in a paper he presented to the International Conference on Physics in London in 1934, and mentioned it again at the end of his Nobel Prize lecture in 1936. Finally, in 1938 he announced the existence of the mesotron (soon shortened to meson), which could carry either a positive or negative electric charge and has an average life span of two-millionths of a second.

As Anderson pointed out in the *American Journal of Physics,* this discovery—unlike that of the positron—was not accidental but rather was the result of a "series of careful, systematic investigations." As with the positron, however, the existence of the meson had been predicted by a theoretical physicist, in this case **Hideki Yukawa** of Japan, in 1935, although Yukawa's theory was little known. Also like the positron, the positive identification of the meson was not welcomed by physicists because it too complicated understanding of subatomic structure. On this point, Anderson wryly commented in a 1948 Sigma Xi address (reprinted in the Smithsonian Institution's annual report of 1949), "Apparently the Creator does not favor a world of too great simplicity." In 1947 physicists **Cecil Frank Powell** and Giuseppe P. S. Occhialini found a meson somewhat heavier than Anderson's, which was identified as the particle predicted by Yukawa. Anderson's meson, which he has called "an oddball particle," was renamed muon, an example cited by Anderson in his Sigma Xi address of the great difficulties faced by physicists who must name new discoveries or concepts before they have accumulated a full set of knowledge about them.

At the age of 31 in 1936, Anderson became one of the youngest Nobel laureates ever, recognized, as the Nobel presenter told him, for "utilizing ingenious devices" to find "one of the buildingstones of the universe" (*Physics* [Nobel Lectures, 1922–1941]). He shared the Nobel Prize in physics with Austrian physicist **Victor Hess**, who discovered cosmic radiation and thus provided the foundation for the investigations of Anderson's career. During World War II, Anderson worked on rocket research for the Office of Scientific Research and Development and the National Defense Research Committee. He was offered the directorship of the Manhattan Project, the government effort to develop the atomic bomb, but turned it down. In 1947, after the war, Anderson took his cloud chamber up in a Navy plane to photograph cosmic ray energy in the stratosphere and captured the disintegration of a meson on film.

At the time Anderson won his Nobel prize, a journalist in the *New York Times* described him as "shy and retiring," while an interviewer for *Scientific American* concluded that Anderson's "very approachable manner brands him as one of the more human scientists." In 1946, Anderson married Lorraine Elvira Bergman; they had two sons, Marshall (who became a mathematician and computer analyst) and David (who became an engineer). Anderson served as chairman of Caltech's division of physics, mathematics, and astronomy from 1962 to 1970. He maintained his research and teaching activities, focusing on cosmic radiation and elementary particles, until his retirement in 1976 with the title professor emeritus. He published many of his findings in Science and The Physical Review. Anderson died at his home in San Marino, California, near Pasadena on January 11,1991, at the age of 85 of undisclosed causes. He had earned many honorary degrees and awards, including medals from the American Institute of the City of New York, the Franklin Institute, and the American Society of Swedish Engineers. His memberships included the National Academy of Science and the American Academy of Arts and Sciences.

SELECTED WRITINGS BY ANDERSON:

Books

"New Facts about the Nucleus of the Atom," *Annual Report of the Board of Regents of the Smithsonian Institution,* U.S. Government Printing Office, 1935, pp. 235–47.

"The Elementary Particles of Physics," *Annual Report of the Board of Regents of the Smithsonian Institution,* U.S. Government Printing Office, 1949, pp. 203–12.

Periodicals

"The Positron," *Nature,* March, 1934, pp. 313–16.
"Early Work on the Positron and Muon," *American Journal of Physics,* December, 1961, pp. 825–30.

SOURCES:

Books

Davis, Nuel Pharr, *Lawrence and Oppenheimer,* Simon & Schuster, 1968.
Heathcote, Niels H. de V., *Nobel Prize Winners in Physics 1901–1950,* Henry Schuman, 1953.
Kevles, Daniel J., *The Physicists: The History of a Scientific Community in Modern America,* Harvard University Press, 1987.
Magill, Frank N., *The Nobel Prize Winners: Physics,* Volume 1: *(1901–1937),* Salem Press, 1989.
Nobelstiftelsen, *Physics* (Nobel lectures, 1922–1941), Elsevier, 1965.
Segre, Emilio, *From X-Rays to Quarks,* University of California, 1980.
Weaver, Jefferson Hane, *The World of Physics,* Simon & Schuster, 1987.

Periodicals

Los Angeles Times Sunday Magazine, December 27, 1936, p. 9.
New York Times, November 14, 1936, p. 18; November 15, 1936, Sec. 2, p. 4; November 29, 1936, Sec. 2, p. 2; January 12, 1991, p. 13.
Scientific American, August, 1935, pp. 70–72; March, 1937, p. 147; July, 1938, pp. 20–22.

—*Sketch by Kathy Sammis*

Gloria L. Anderson
1938-
American chemist

Gloria L. Anderson is a distinguished chemist, educator, and college administrator. Her scientific research has involved industrial, medical and military applications of fluorine–19 chemistry. As an

Gloria L. Anderson

educator, she has served as the Callaway professor of chemistry, chair of the chemistry department, and dean of academic affairs at Morris Brown College in Atlanta. Anderson, in addition, has been a board member and vice-chair of the Corporation for Public Broadcasting, for which she has lectured nationally on issues related to minorities and women in mass media and public television.

Anderson was born in Altheimer, Arkansas, on November 5, 1938, the daughter of Charley Long and Elsie Lee Foggie. She enrolled at the Arkansas Agricultural, Mechanical and Normal College (now the University of Arkansas at Pine Bluff), where she was awarded a Rockefeller Scholarship from 1956 to 1958. Anderson received her B.S. degree summa cum laude in 1958. She married Leonard Sinclair Anderson on June 4, 1960; they have one son, Gerald. In 1961, Anderson was awarded her M.S. degree from Atlanta University. For the next year, she worked as a chemistry instructor at South Carolina State College in Orangeburg. From 1962 to 1964, she held an instructorship at Morehouse College in Atlanta, then went on to take a position as a teaching and research assistant at the University of Chicago, where she received her doctorate in organic chemistry in 1968.

Researches Fluorine–19 Chemistry

Anderson's dissertation and aspects of her subsequent research have related to fluorine–19 chemistry. (The '19' following fluorine refers to a particular isotope of fluorine that, like other elements with odd numbered masses, has magnetic properties.) Fluorine–19 chemistry became an important field of research shortly before World War II when many commercial uses for fluorine compounds were discovered. Much of Anderson's research has involved nuclear magnetic resonance (NMR) spectroscopy, a method of investigating organic compounds by analyzing the nucleic responses of molecules subjected to radio-frequency radiation within a slowly changing magnetic field. NMR spectroscopy, which has been widely exploited for chemistry, biochemistry, biophysics, and solid-state physics research, enables extremely sophisticated analysis of the molecular structures and interactions of various materials. The small size, low reactivity, and high sensitivity of fluorine–19 make it particularly suited for NMR spectroscopy. Since the late 1960s, fluorine NMR spectroscopy has been applied to a range of biochemical problems, including the study of the human metabolism and the formulation of new pharmaceuticals.

Anderson joined the faculty of Morris Brown College in Atlanta in 1968 as associate professor and chair of the chemistry department. From 1973 to 1984, Anderson was the Fuller E. Callaway professor of chemistry at Morris Brown, and continued her service as the chemistry department chair. Anderson left the chemistry department to serve as dean of academic affairs at Morris Brown for the years 1984–89. In 1990, Anderson resumed her post as the Callaway professor of chemistry. In 1976, Anderson was recognized as an Outstanding Teacher at Morris Brown, and received a Scroll of Honor award from the National Association of Negro Business and Professional Women. In 1983, she received a Teacher of the Year award and was voted into the Faculty/Staff Hall of Fame at Morris Brown. In 1987, she received an Alumni All-Star Excellence Award in Education from the University of Arkansas at Pine Bluff.

In addition to her work at Morris Brown, Anderson has conducted research through a number of independent and government facilities. Beginning in 1971 she continued her investigations of fluorine–19 chemistry—first in association with the Atlanta University Center Research Committee, then under the National Institutes of Health, the National Science Foundation, and the Office of Naval Research. She also conducted research on amantadines (a drug used to prevent viral infection) under the Minority Biomedical Support Program of the National Institutes of Health. She held a faculty industrial research fellowship with the National Science Foundation in 1981, and with the Air Force Office of Scientific Research in 1984. In 1985, Anderson investigated the synthesis of potential antiviral drugs as a United Negro Fund Distinguished Scholar. In that same year, she conducted research on the synthesis of solid rocket propellants under the Air Force Office of Scientific Research. Since 1990, she has been affiliated with BioSPECS of The Hague, Netherlands, as a research consultant.

In 1972, Anderson was appointed to a six-year term on the board of the Corporation for Public Broadcasting (CPB). At the CPB, Anderson chaired committees on Minority Training, Minorities and Women, and Human Resources Development; she was vice-chair of the CPB board from 1977–79. She is a member of the American Institute of Chemists, the American Chemical Society, the National Institute of Science, the National Science Teachers Association, the Association of Computers in Mathematics and Science Teaching, the Georgia Academy of Science, and the Atlanta University Science Research Institute, among other scientific and professional bodies. She has served as a proposal review panel member, contract reviewer, or field reader for the Department of Health, Education and Welfare's Office of Education, the National Science Foundation's Women in Science Program, the Nation Cancer Institute, the Department of Education, and the National Institute of Drug Abuse.

SELECTED WRITINGS BY ANDERSON:

Periodicals

(With L. M. Stock) "^{19}F Chemical Shifts for Bicyclic Fluorides," *Journal of the American Chemical Society,* Volume 90, 1968, p. 212.

(With L. M. Stock) "^{19}F Chemical Shifts for Bicyclic and Aromatic Molecules," *Journal of the American Chemical Society,* Volume 91, 1969, p. 6804.

(With R. C. Parish and L. M. Stock) "Transmission of Substituent Effects, Acid Dissociation Constants of 10-Substituted–9-Anthroic Acids," *Journal of the American Chemical Society,* Volume 93, 1971, p. 6984.

(With Issifu I. Harruna) "Synthesis of Triflate and Chloride Salts of Alkyl *N, N*-Bis (2, 2, 2-Tri-Fluoroethyl) Amines," *Synthetic Communications,* Volume 17, 1987, pp. 111–114.

(With Winifred A. Burks and Issifu I. Harruna) "Novel Synthesis of 3-Fluoro–1-Aminoadamantane," *Synthetic Communications,* Volume 18, 1988, pp. 1967–1974.

(With Betty J. Randolph and Issifu I. Harruna) "Novel Synthesis of Some 1-N-(3-Fluoroadamantyl) Ureas," *Synthetic Communications,* Volume 19, 1989, pp. 1955–1963.

SOURCES:

Periodicals

"Atlanta's Best and Brightest Scientists," *Atlanta Magazine,* April, 1983.

New York Times, December 1, 1973, p. 39.

—*Sketch by M. C. Nagel*

Philip Warren Anderson
1923-
American physicist

The 1977 Nobel Prize in physics that Philip Warren Anderson shared with **Nevill Francis Mott** and **John Van Vleck** was given not so much for one specific discovery but for his contributions over a number of years to the study of magnetism and disordered states. In fact, Anderson's interests have extended well beyond those areas and have included work on the broadening of line spectra, electron tunneling, and superconductivity.

Philip Warren Anderson was born in Indianapolis, Indiana, on December 13, 1923, but he grew up in Urbana, Illinois. Anderson came into a family that boasted a number of teachers, including his own father, Harry Warren Anderson, who was a professor of plant pathology at the University of Illinois. Anderson's mother, the former Elsie Osborne, was herself the daughter of another teacher, a professor of mathematics. Anderson graduated from University High School in Urbana in 1940 and was then awarded a scholarship to Harvard University. He graduated from Harvard with a B.S., summa cum laude, in 1943.

World War II prevented Anderson from beginning his graduate studies immediately. Instead he accepted a job at the Naval Research Laboratory in Washington, D.C., where he worked on the design of radio and radar antennae. At the war's conclusion, Anderson returned to Harvard to begin his graduate studies in physics. His doctoral advisor there was the physicist John Hasbrouck Van Vleck, later to share a Nobel Prize with Anderson.

Anderson's graduate studies focused on the problem of line spectrum broadening. The term *line spectrum* suggests a spectrum in which electron transitions within an atom result in the formation of clear, distinct lines. In fact, that type of event is often not the case. Interactions among atoms and among molecules often cause slight variations in the emission of energy from an atom, variations that result in a "smearing" of lines. Anderson found that modern quantum theory, which posits that energy exists in discrete units, provided a means for developing a quantitative explanation of the broadening effect. For this line of research, Anderson was awarded his M.S.

degree in 1947 and then his Ph.D. in 1949 from Harvard.

Works on Magnetic Effects and Superconductivity

Anderson's first job after graduation was with the Bell Telephone Research Laboratories in Murray Hill, New Jersey. Perhaps the most exciting work then taking place at the Bell Labs focused on solid-state physics, especially the research on superconductivity (the tendency of a material to lose all resistance to the flow of an electrical current, usually at temperatures close to absolute zero). Anderson, however, was at first involved in studies on magnetism. Once again, he used the techniques of quantum mechanics to show how the properties of individual atoms and electrons could be used to explain magnetic properties on a macroscopic scale. This work was one of the fields singled out by the Nobel Prize committee in its award of the 1977 physics prize to Anderson.

The atmosphere at Bell was such, however, that Anderson could hardly have avoided some contact with studies on superconductivity, particularly with reference to its occurrence in semiconductors (materials that are neither good insulators nor good conductors). In 1964, for example, he designed and carried out an experiment that demonstrated the existence of electron tunneling in semiconductors with AC currents. He also examined the effects of impurities in semiconductors, as predicted by quantum theory.

Mott Leads Anderson to the Problem of Disordered States

During the academic year 1953–54, Anderson was a visiting professor at the University of Tokyo. At a conference on theoretical physics held in Kyoto during the year, Anderson made the acquaintance of Nevill Mott (later, Sir Nevill Mott), an English physicist with interests similar to Anderson's. Mott suggested that Anderson visit him at his own laboratories at Cambridge University. The two eventually worked out a plan whereby Anderson could spend half of each year at Cambridge and half at the Bell Laboratories.

The topic to which Anderson and Mott devoted much of their attention was the behavior of electrons in amorphous solids. Traditionally, physicists had done most of their research on ordered solids, that is, crystals in which ions and electrons occupy relatively clearly defined positions. The mathematics of such systems, while not always simple, was at least easier than for systems in which ions and electrons are more randomly distributed through a material.

In 1958 anderson published a paper, "Absence of Diffusion in Certain Random Lattices," in which he announced a new theory of disordered solids. The behavior of electrons in such solids as well as the properties of the solid itself can best be understand, he said, by acknowledging that electrons are often "tied" to specific locations within the solid and are not free to move throughout it. This phenomenon has become known as Anderson localization and has made it possible to design materials with very specific and desirable properties. The use of relatively inexpensive amorphous silicon in place of the more expensive pure silicon in semiconductors is one example of the practical applications of Anderson's discovery. The analysis of disordered solids was the second basis for the Nobel Prize committee's decision to award the 1977 physics prize to Anderson.

Anderson commuted to Mott's laboratory from 1967 to 1975 and then abandoned that practice in order to become consulting director at Bell Labs and Joseph Henry Professor of Physics at Princeton University. He held his Bell post until his retirement in 1984, although he continued to teach at Princeton. Retirement did not mean an end to Anderson's research work, however. Indeed, one of his most important accomplishments was the development of a new theory of superconductivity, announced in 1987, in which he was able to explain the recent discovery of high-temperature superconducting materials.

Anderson was married in 1947 to Joyce Gothwaite. The couple has one daughter. In addition to the Nobel Prize, Anderson has been awarded the Oliver E. Buckley Prize of the American Physical Society (1964), the Dannie Heineman Prize of the Göttingen Academy of Sciences (1975), the Guthrie Medal of the London Institute of Physics (1978), and the National Medal of Science (1982).

SELECTED WRITINGS BY ANDERSON:

Books

Concepts in Solids, W. A. Benjamin, 1963.
Basic Notions of Condensed Matter Physics, Benjamin/Cummings, 1984.

Periodicals

"The Limits of Validity of the Van Vleck-Weisskopf Line Shape Formula," *Physical Review,* Volume 76, 1949, p. 471.
"An Approximate Quantum Theory of the Antiferromagnetic Ground State," *Physical Review,* Volume 86, 1952, pp. 694–701.
"New Method in the Theory of Superconductivity," *Physical Review,* Volume 110, 1958, pp. 985–86.

SOURCES:

Books

Magill, Frank N., editor, *The Nobel Prize Winners: Physics,* Volume 3, 1968-1988, Salem Press, 1989, pp. 1133–1142.

McGraw-Hill Modern Men of Science, Volume 1, McGraw, 1984, pp. 11–12.

Wasson, Tyler, editor, *Nobel Prize Winners,* H. W. Wilson, 1987, pp. 20–22.

Periodicals

Cohen, Marvin, and L. M. Falicov, "The 1977 Nobel Prize in Physics," *Science,* November 18, 1977, pp. XX.

Lubkin, Gloria, "Physicists Share in Nobel Prizes in Three Disciplines," *Physics Today,* December 1977, pp. 77–78.

—*Sketch by David E. Newton*

W. French Anderson
1936-
American biochemist and geneticist

The age of gene therapy—the treatment of disease by genetic engineering—began on September 14, 1990, when a four-year-old girl suffering from a hereditary immune deficiency was transfused with her own white blood cells that had been mixed with the gene needed to cure her. The doctor in charge of the treatment, W. French Anderson, had labored long and hard not only in the laboratory to make this therapy a reality but in the halls of government as well, working his clinical approach or protocol through a myriad of bureaucratic and scientific review boards. Gene therapy, like all revolutionary procedures, had as many detractors as supporters: the specter of genetic designing hovers over the field. But Anderson had insisted to the committees that he was concerned with curing the sick, not creating test-tube super humans. The test—the first ever approved gene therapy—was allowed to proceed as scheduled. It was the pinnacle of achievement for a man who had spent his career researching human biochemical genetics, hematology, and the synthesis of hemoglobin and proteins.

William French Anderson was born in Tulsa, Oklahoma, on December 31, 1936. His father was an engineer and his mother a journalist, and Anderson grew up preferring books to sports. He was something of a child prodigy with grade-school and high-school test scores going off the charts. By the age of fourteen, he was already reading college-level medical texts and studying astronomy. Even as a child, Anderson showed a determination to overcome any obstacle. A stutterer, he decided that a good way to cure his stammer would be to join a debating team. This crude form of homeopathy worked. In 1953, he applied for early entrance to Harvard University, writing on his application that he wanted to gain knowledge of disease at the molecular level. That same year, **James Watson** and **Francis Crick** unlocked the structure of DNA (deoxyribonucleic acid—the carrier of genetic information).

Anderson was a natural mathematician, publishing a paper in 1956 that demonstrated how to perform higher arithmetic with Roman numerals, a concept thought unworkable because such numerals do not have place values like Arabic numerals do. But he soon gave up on a mathematical career, opting instead for one in medicine, doing original research even as an undergraduate. A course in DNA and genetics taught by James Watson set Anderson on the track of genetic therapy. Graduating magna cum laude from Harvard in 1958, he went to Cambridge University in England to study under Francis Crick, working on research that led to the discovery of the underlying structure of the genetic code: its organization in triplets. It was while at Cambridge that Anderson also met his future wife, Kathryn, who was studying medicine. He graduated with honors from Cambridge in 1960, earning his M.A., and returned to Harvard University's medical school where he received his M.D. magna cum laude in 1963. He then interned in pediatric medicine at Boston's Children's Hospital Medical Center.

Joins Research Team at NIH

In 1965 Anderson joined the staff of the National Institutes of Health at Bethesda, Maryland. There he initially worked with **Marshall Warren Nirenberg**, who broke the genetic code, and whose name in genetics ranks with those of Watson and Crick. Anderson soon proved his own worth at NIH in research that led to synthesizing hemoglobin, the oxygen-carrying pigment in red blood cells, as well as discovering how cells initiate protein synthesis. Blood research was his focus for many years, and he became well known for his work in thalassemia, a hereditary and fatal form of anemia, pioneering the use of iron chelators or organic reagents which absorb excess iron in the body, thus prolonging the lives of the victims of this disease. He also conducted important research in sickle-cell anemia. Meanwhile, he worked his way up the ladder of promotion at NIH. By 1977 he had become the director of the molecular hematology laboratory at the National Heart, Lung, and Blood

Institute, as well as a research fellow at the American Cancer Society.

Once gene-splicing techniques had been developed in the 1970s, Anderson turned his attention back to his original goal: dealing with disease on the molecular level—gene therapy. (Gene splicing refers to the process of recombining, or engineering, specific fragments of DNA, usually from more than one species of organism.) In particular, Anderson sought ways in which engineered genes could be transferred into cells. One of his developments was a microscopic needle used for injection of genes directly into cells, but this technique was too limited. For gene therapy to be effective, a wide spectrum of cells had to be reached, Anderson knew. Other researchers around the world were looking at this same problem, and some—including Richard Mulligan of the Whitehead Institute for Biomedical Research in Cambridge, Massachusetts—thought they had come up with a solution. The vector, or agent to transport genetic material into the cell, they hit on was a form of virus. These simple organisms function by getting into cells and taking over the genetic works. Most viruses, like those of the cold or smallpox, simply kill the cells off; but one strain, the retrovirus, actually tricks the cell's DNA into reproducing the virus's genetic material over and over again. Mulligan and others saw how these retroviruses—acquired immune deficiency syndrome (AIDS) is caused by a retrovirus—could be used as a Trojan horse for genes they wanted to insert into cells. By the early 1980s, techniques had been perfected for stripping the viruses of their harmful genetic material and for inserting cloned genes in their stead. The retroviral vector had come into existence.

ADA Deficiency Inaugurates Gene Therapy

Anderson, meanwhile, was hoping to use these new technologies to tackle thalassemia, but because of its complexity—several genes are responsible for the disease—he finally had to give up on it as a pioneer case in gene therapy. Other researchers hit on another hereditary disease of the more than four thousand that plague humans: adenosine deaminase (ADA) deficiency. ADA is an enzyme vital to the functioning of the immune system, and in rare cases a single gene responsible for its creation is missing. Here was a more workable disease on which researchers could focus. By 1984 John Hutton of the University of Cincinnati had managed to clone the ADA gene and shared his research with Anderson at the NIH. Two parts of the puzzle were in place now: the vector and the gene. They needed to discover what type of cells in which to insert the gene.

Logically, the stem cells of the bone marrow—those that manufacture blood cells and have a long lifespan—would be the place to begin, using bone marrow transplant surgery to implant genetically altered retroviruses. But as these stem cells occur only once in 100,000 bone marrow cells, the probability of reaching them was considered too low. Instead, Anderson decided to use a white blood cell called the T cell. A crucial step in perfecting the procedure was a 1988 trial in which Anderson, in collaboration with Steven A. Rosenberg of the National Cancer Institute, managed successfully to put genetically tagged cells into terminal cancer patients. Tracing the progress of these earmarked cells, the scientists could see that in fact such cells would reproduce once in the body. Still, there were political hurdles to jump, and it took until September 14, 1990, to clear them all. On that day Anderson, in collaboration with R. Michael Blaese and Kenneth W. Culver, treated a young ADA patient with T cells withdrawn from her own body, which had been "infected" with a genetically engineered virus, and then cultured in the laboratory. The initial transfusion replaced more than one billion of these genetically altered cells—with the ADA manufacturing gene in place—and further treatments and tests indicated that the cells were reproducing in the patient's body, creating ADA. Gene therapy, in fact, appeared to work.

From this initial trial, the number of ongoing and planned gene therapy protocols has mushroomed worldwide, including experimental treatments for melanoma, cystic fibrosis, cardiovascular disease, high cholesterol, and AIDS. In 1991 Anderson also took research out of federal laboratories, helping to found Genetic Therapy, a Maryland-based company that works closely with NIH to provide genetically engineered vectors to hospitals and universities. In 1992 Anderson moved his laboratory to the University of Southern California's Kenneth J. Norris Jr. Comprehensive Cancer Center so his wife could accept the position of surgeon-in-chief at the Children's Hospital of Los Angeles.

Anderson has been widely acknowledged for his work, receiving the Scientific Achievement Award for Biological Sciences from the Washington Academy of Sciences in 1971; the Thomas B. Cooley Award for Scientific Achievement in 1977; and the Mary Ann Liebert Biotherapeutic Award in 1991, among others. He and his wife have no children: they opted early in their marriage for career over family life. In his spare time, Anderson practices Korean marshal arts—tae kwon do—in which he has a fourth-degree black belt.

SELECTED WRITINGS BY ANDERSON:

Periodicals

(With J. M. Gilbert) "Cell-free Hemoglobin Synthesis. II. Characteristics of the Transfer of Ribonucleic Acid-dependent Assay System," *Journal of Biological Chemistry,* May 10, 1970, pp. 2342–2349.

"Cell-free Synthesis of Globin Chains: An Overview," *Annals of the New York Academy of Sciences,* November 29, 1974, pp. 142–155.

(With A. B. Deisseroth and others) "A New Technique for Mapping the Human Hemoglobin Genes," *Cytogenics and Cell Genetics,* Volume 16, 1976, pp. 367-371.

"Gene Therapy," *Journal of the American Medical Association,* December 11, 1981, pp. 2737-2739.

"Prospects for Human Gene Therapy," *Science,* October 26, 1984, pp. 401–409.

(With K. W. Culver and others) "Correction of ADA Deficiency in Human T Lymphocytes Using Retroviral-Mediated Gene Transfer," *Transplantation Proceedings,* February 23, 1991, pp. 170–171.

"Human Gene Therapy," *Science,* May 8, 1992, pp. 808-813.

SOURCES:

Books

Kimbrell, Andrew, *The Human Body Shop,* HarperCollins, 1993.

Periodicals

Beardsley, Tim, "Profile: Gene Doctor," *Scientific American,* August, 1990, p. 33.

Culliton, Barbara J., "Gene Therapy Begins," *Science,* September 21, 1990, p. 1372.

Glick, Daniel, "A Genetic Road Map," *Newsweek,* October 2, 1989, p. 46.

Henig, Robin Marantz, "Dr. Anderson's Gene Machine," *New York Times Magazine,* March 31, 1991, pp. 31–34.

Herman, Robin, "Gene Therapy Pioneer, Surgeon Wife Leave D.C.," *Washington Post,* June 30, 1992, p. WH8.

"Interview: W. French Anderson," *Omni,* July, 1991, pp. 62–66.

Lehrman, Sally, "Risky Alliance on Medicine's Cutting Edge," *Washington Post,* August 26, 1991, p. WB1.

Maugh, Thomas H., "Pioneer Gene Therapist, Noted Surgeon to Join USC," *Los Angeles Times,* July 25, 1992, p. B3.

Miller, Susan Katz, "Genetic Privacy Makes Strange Bedfellows," *Science,* September 21, 1990, p. 1368.

Thompson, Larry, "Human Gene Therapy Debuts at NIH," *Washington Post,* September 15, 1990, p. A1.

Thompson, Larry, "Medicine's 4-Year-Old Pioneer," *Washington Post,* September 25, 1990, p. WH8.

—*Sketch by J. Sydney Jones*

Christian Boehmer Anfinsen
1916-
American biochemist

Biochemist Christian Boehmer Anfinsen is best known for establishing that the structure of an enzyme is intimately related to its function. This discovery was a major contribution to the scientific understanding of the nature of enzymes. For this achievement, Anfinsen shared the 1972 Nobel Prize for Chemistry with the research team of **Stanford Moore** and **William Howard Stein**.

Anfinsen was born on March 26, 1916, in Monessen, Pennsylvania, a town located just outside of Pittsburgh. He was the child of Christian Anfinsen, an engineer and emigrant from Norway, and Sophie Rasmussen, who was also of Norwegian heritage. Anfinsen earned his B.A. from Swarthmore College in 1937. Subsequently, he attended the University of Pennsylvania, earning an M.S. in organic chemistry in 1939. After earning his master's degree, Anfinsen received a fellowship from the American Scandinavian Foundation to spend a year at the Carlsberg Laboratory in Copenhagen, Denmark. Upon his return in 1940, he entered Harvard University's Ph.D. program in biochemistry. His doctoral dissertation involved work with enzymes; he described various methodologies for discerning the enzymes present in the retina of the eye, and he earned his Ph.D in 1943.

After earning his Ph.D., Anfinsen began teaching at Harvard Medical School in their department of biological chemistry. From 1944 to 1946 he worked in the United States Office of Scientific Research and Development. He then worked in the biochemical division of the Medical Nobel Institute in Sweden under Hugo Theorell as an American Cancer Society senior fellow from 1947 to 1948. Harvard University promoted him to associate professor upon his return, but in 1950 he accepted a position as head of the National Institutes of Health's (NIH) National Heart Institute Laboratory of Cellular Physiology. He served in this position until 1962. Anfinsen returned to teaching at Harvard Medical School in 1962, but he returned to NIH a year later. This time he was named director of the Laboratory of Chemical Biology at the National Institute of Arthritis, Metabolism, and Digestive Diseases. He held this position until 1981; he spent a year at the Weizmann Institute of science and then in 1982 accepted an appointment as professor of biology at Johns Hopkins University.

Anfinsen began his research concerning the structure and function of enzymes in the mid–1940s. Enzymes are a type of protein; specifically, they are what drive the many chemical reactions in the human body. All proteins are made up of smaller components called peptide chains, which are amino acids linked together. Amino acids are, in turn, a certain class of organic compounds. The enzymes take on a globular, three-dimensional form as the amino acid chain folds over. The unfolded chain form of an enzyme is called the primary structure. Once the chain folds over, it is said to be in the tertiary structure. From one set of amino acids for one particular enzyme there are 100 different possible ways in which these amino acids can link together. (Only certain amino acids can "fit" next to other amino acids.) However, only one configuration will result in an active enzyme. In general, Anfinsen's research concerned finding out how a particular set of amino acids knows to configure in a way that results in the active form of the enzyme.

Anfinsen chose to study the enzyme ribonuclease (RNase), which contains 124 amino acids and is responsible for breaking down the ribonucleic acid (RNA) found in food. This reaction enables the body to recycle the resultant smaller pieces. He felt that by determining how a particular enzyme assumes its particular active configuration, the structure and function of enzymes could be better understood. He reasoned that he could determine how an enzyme protein is built and when the enzyme becomes functional by observing it adding one amino acid at a time. He utilized techniques developed by Cambridge University's **Frederick Sanger** to conduct this research. Another research team headed by Stanford Moore and William Howard Stein was working simultaneously on the same enzyme as Anfinsen, ribonuclease; in 1960, using ribonuclease, Moore and Stein were the first to determine the exact amino acid sequence of an enzyme. However, Anfinsen remained more concerned with how the enzyme forms into its active configuration.

Anfinsen eventually changed his methodology of research during an opportunity to study abroad. While at the NIH, Anfinsen took yet another leave of absence when a Rockefeller Public Service Award allowed him to spend 1954 to 1955 at the Carlsberg Laboratory studying under the physical chemist Kai Linderstrøm-Lang. Anfinsen had been studying ribonuclease by building it up; Linderstrøm-Lang convinced him to start with the whole molecule and study it by stripping it down piece by piece. Anfinsen began with the whole ribonuclease molecule and then successively broke the various bonds of the molecule. The process is called denaturing the protein or, in other words, causing it to lose its functional capacity. By breaking certain key bonds, other bonds formed between the amino acids resulting in a random, inactive form of ribonuclease. By 1962 Anfinsen had confirmed that when this inactive form is placed into an environment that mimics the environment in which ribonuclease normally appears in the body, that

inactive form would slowly revert to the active configurationon its own and thus regain its enzymatic activity. This discovery revealed the important fact that all the information for the assembly of the three-dimensional, active enzyme form was within the protein's own sequence of amino acids.

Receives Nobel Prize for Enzyme Research

For uncovering the connection between the primary and tertiary structure of enzymes, Anfinsen received half of the 1972 Nobel Prize for Chemistry. Moore and Stein and were awarded the other half. In addition to his numerous journal articles on protein structure, enzyme function, and related matters, in 1959 Anfinsen published a book entitled *The Molecular Basis of Evolution.* After receiving the Nobel Prize, Anfinsen began focusing his research on the protein interferon, known for its key role as part of the body's immunity against both viruses and cancer. He has succeeded in isolating and characterizing this important human protein.

Anfinsen's other honors received after winning the Nobel Prize include being the recipient of seven honorary degrees from universities including Georgetown University and New York Medical College. Anfinsen is a member of the National Academy of Sciences, the American Society of Biological Chemists, and the Royal Danish Academy. He married Florence Bernice Kenenger in 1941, and together they had three children before divorcing in 1978. In 1979, Anfinsen was married for a second time, to Libby Esther Schulman Ely. Outside the professional world, his interests include sailing and music.

SELECTED WRITINGS BY ANFINSEN:

Books

The Molecular Basis of Evolution, Wiley, 1959.

SOURCES:

Books

Wasson, Tyler, editor, *Nobel Prize Winners,* H. W. Wilson, 1987, pp. 24–26.

Periodicals

"Nobel Prize Winners in Physics, Chemistry," *New York Times,* October 21, 1972, p. 14.
Richards, Frederic M., "The 1972 Nobel Prize for Chemistry," *Science,* November 3, 1972, pp. 492–493.

—Sketch by Carla Mecoli-Kamp

Edward Appleton
1892-1965
English physicist

The existence and location of an ionized reflecting layer in the Earth's atmosphere was identified by Edward Appleton, whose research responded to the first long distance radio messages transmitted across the Atlantic Ocean. After **Guglielmo Marconi** made his successful transmission in 1901, two physicists, Oliver Heaviside and Arthur E. Kennelly postulated the existence of an ionized band in the atmosphere. More than twenty years later, Appleton, then Wheatstone Professor of Physics at King's College at the University of London verified that hypothesis and later discovered two more layers, one of which is now named in his honor. For his work on atmospheric structure, Appleton was awarded the 1947 Nobel Prize in physics.

Edward Victor Appleton was born in Bradford, Yorkshire, England, on September 6, 1892. His parents were Peter and Mary (Wilcock) Appleton. Appleton attended Barkerend Elementary School from 1899 to 1903 and Hanson Secondary School from 1903 to 1911. He gave evidence of a brilliant future at an early age, passing the entrance examination at the University of London with first class honors at the minimum age permitted of 16. Two years later he won a scholarship at St. John's College, Cambridge, from which he graduated, again, with honors in physics in 1913. Upon graduation, Appleton continued his studies in crystallography under **William Henry Bragg**, but his work was interrupted by the outbreak of World War I. In August of 1914, he enlisted in the British infantry and eventually rose to the rank of captain in the Royal Engineers. After his discharge, Appleton returned to Cambridge and became first a fellow at St. John's College and later demonstrator in physics at the Cavendish Laboratories. His major area of interest was vacuum tubes, a topic he first learned about during the war. Some years later, he was to publish a monograph on this research, *Thermionic Vacuum Tubes*.

Atmospheric Studies Lead to the Discovery of the Ionosphere

In 1924, at the age of 32, Appleton was appointed Wheatstone Professor of Physics at King's College at the University of London. The first major research topic to which he turned his attention was the propagation of radio signals. While serving his country, he had become aware of the problem that radio signals have—a tendency to fade out at various times of the day. That same year, assisted by graduate student Miles Barnett, he designed and carried out a series of experiments to elucidate the mechanism by which radio waves are transmitted in the atmosphere.

Appleton and Barnett were able to convince the British Broadcasting Corporation (BBC) to allow them to use the network's radio signals outside of regular broadcasting hours. They varied the frequency of the BBC signal on a regular basis, looking for points at which interference occurred between direct waves from the ground and reflected waves from the atmosphere. Their results indicated the existence of a reflecting layer in the atmosphere approximately 100 kilometers (60 miles) above the Earth's surface. The layer corresponded to a region that had been predicted more than twenty years earlier by Britain's Oliver Heaviside and American physicist A. E. Kennelly. That region was later named the Heaviside-Kennelly, or "E," layer. It is now known to be the lower boundary of the ionosphere.

Appleton continued his research on the atmosphere throughout his life. In 1926, he discovered a second reflecting layer above the E-layer, established as the F- or Appleton-layer. He calculated the lower boundary of this region to be about 230 kilometers (150 miles) above the Earth's surface. The discovery of these reflecting bands in the ionosphere made possible later developments in radio, shortwave, and radar technologies. Appleton's research also led him to discover a number of important characteristics of the reflecting layers. In 1927, for example, his observations of a solar eclipse convinced him that the existence of such layers are the consequence of solar radiation bombarding the Earth's atmosphere.

Investigative studies on the atmosphere brought Appleton a number of honors. He was elected a fellow of the Royal Society in 1927, was knighted in 1941, and received the Nobel Prize in physics in 1947 for "his work on the physical properties of the upper atmosphere, and especially for the discovery of the so-called Appleton layer." In addition, he was awarded many honorary doctorates, including those from the universities of Aberdeen, Glasgow, London, Oxford, and Cambridge.

Appointed to Posts at Cambridge, the DSIR, and Edinburgh

In 1936, Appleton succeeded to the Jacksonian Chair of Natural Philosophy at Cambridge, left vacant two years earlier by the retirement of **Charles Thomson Rees Wilson**. He brought with him most of his research staff from King's College, began the construction of a new field laboratory for atmospheric research, and initiated an active program for the study of ionized gases at the Cavendish Laboratories at Cambridge.

Appleton remained at Cambridge for only three years, however, before accepting an appointment as secretary of the Department of Scientific and Industrial Research (DSIR). In that post, he rapidly converted the DSIR from a civilian research agency to one making preparations for the war then looming on the horizon in Europe. Included among the DSIR's later military activities was Great Britain's first research on nuclear weapons. At the war's conclusion, Appleton returned to academia, becoming Principal and Vice-Chancellor of the University of Edinburgh, where he remained until his death on April 21, 1965.

Appleton married Jessie Longson in 1916, with whom he had two daughters, Marjery and Rosalind. Lady Appleton died in 1964 from a stroke suffered three years earlier. A month before he died, Appleton was married for a second time, to Mrs. Helen Allison, his secretary of more than 13 years. His biographer in *Biographical Memoirs of Fellows of the Royal Society,* J. A. Ratcliffe, says that Appleton was known for many admirable qualities, among which were "his wide humanity, his ability as a public speaker, and his continuing dedication to his scientific researches."

SELECTED WRITINGS BY APPLETON:

Books

(With W. J. G. Beynon) *The Application of Ionospheric Data to Radio Communications,* 1931, H. M. Stationary Off. (London), 1948.
Thermionic Vacuum Tubes, E. P. Dutton, 1933.
(With W. J. G. Beynon) *Science and the Nation,* Edinburgh University Press, 1957.

Periodicals

"Local Reflection of Wireless Waves from the Upper Atmosphere," *Nature,* Volume 115, 1925, p. 333.
"Equivalent Heights of the Atmospheric Ionized Regions in England and America," *Nature,* Volume 123, 1929, p. 445.

SOURCES:

Books

A Biographical Dictionary of Scientists, Wiley, 1974, pp. 14–15.
A Biographical Encyclopedia of Scientists, Facts on File, Volume 1, 1981, p. 23.
Biographical Memoirs of Fellows of the Royal Society, Volume 12, Royal Society (London), 1966, pp. 1–21.
Dictionary of Scientific Biography, Volume 1, Scribner, 1975, pp. 195–196.

Heathcote, Niels H. de V., *Nobel Prize Winners in Physics, 1901–1950,* Henry Schuman, 1953, pp. 431–437.
McGraw-Hill Modern Scientists and Engineers, Volume 1, McGraw-Hill, 1980, pp. 24–25.
Nobel Prize Winners, H. W. Wilson, 1987, pp. 29–30.
Weber, Robert L., *Pioneers of Science: Nobel Prize Winners in Physics,* American Institute of Physics, 1980, pp. 129–130.

—*Sketch by David E. Newton*

Agnes Arber
1879-1960
English botanist

Agnes Arber was a botanist who incorporated her artistic and philosophical interests into her scientific studies. She is perhaps best known for her beautifully illustrated publications, which included seven books and dozens of papers. In addition to conducting important research on the morphology of plants, through her later philosophical works, Arber brought an insight into the ways scientists think.

Arber was born in 1879 in London, England, the eldest child of Henry Robert Robertson and Agnes Lucy Turner. According to H. Hamshaw Thomas in *Biographical Memoirs of Fellows of the Royal Society,* "At an early age her mother inspired her with an interest in plants and her father gave her regular drawing lessons from the age of three until she went to school. This early training developed her powers of observation, and laid the foundation of the skill and artistry which later formed such a notable feature of her books and papers."

Arber's interest in botany continued to grow during her schooling in northern London and throughout her college education at University College in London and Newnham College, Cambridge. Arber's work received a great boost when she left Newnham and became research assistant to Ethel Sargant in her private laboratory. Sargant particularly influenced Arber's interest in comparative plant anatomy. From 1903 to 1908, she was a Quain Student in Biology at University College. During this period, she published several papers on plant morphology and anatomy.

First Book Becomes a Standard

In 1908, Arber became a fellow of the Linnean Society of London. A year later, she married E. A.

Newell Arber, a noted palaeobotanist at Cambridge University, and returned to Cambridge where she continued her research at the Balfour Laboratory. By 1912, she published her first book, *Herbals, Their Origin and Evolution,* which traced two centuries— from 1470 to 1670—of materials printed about plants. This book became a standard work. "It is a charming and fascinating book, abundantly illustrated, about the early history of study of plants and the men who worked at it," Thomas wrote in *Nature.* Arber published a revised second edition in 1938.

Arber continued her research and her writing, publishing *Water Plants: A Study of Aquatic Angiosperms* in 1920 and *Monocotyledons: A Morphological Study* in 1925. In 1927, Arber moved her research to a private laboratory in her home, where she continued her scientific work and began to foster her interest in philosophy. In 1934, she published a book about one group of monocots (a type of seed-bearing, flowering plant), *The Gramineae: A Study of Cereal, Bamboo, and Grass.* It was followed by *The Natural Philosophy of Plant Form* in 1950. Considered by some to be her most important book, *The Natural Philosophy of Plant Form* investigates the type of logic used to categorize plants and the history of this type of thought. She approached a similar topic in *The Mind and the Eye, a Study of the Biologist's Standpoint,* a 1954 work in which Arber attempts to explain the mental processes of a scientist as he or she explains information that has been observed about a particular subject. Arber also wrote *The Manifold and the One* in 1957.

Her work did not go unnoticed. In 1946, she became the third woman and the first female botanist to be elected to the Fellowship of the Royal Society. She received the Gold Medal of the Linnean Society in 1948 and was appointed a corresponding member of the Botanical Society of America. Agnes Arber died in Cambridge, England, on March 22, 1960, at the age of 82. She and her husband, who died in 1918, had one child, a daughter. Writing in *Biographical Memoirs of Fellows of the Royal Society,* Thomas stated that Arber was a major contributor to "a distinct period in the development of botany in England, a period in which comparative anatomy and morphology were regarded as the center points of investigation." Thomas concluded that "the careful investigation of plant structure by Mrs. Arber and her contemporaries made a lasting contribution to botanical knowledge which is not likely to be superseded."

SELECTED WRITINGS BY ARBER:

Books

Herbals: Their Origin and Evolution, Cambridge University Press, 1912.

Monocotyledons: A Morphological Study, Cambridge University Press, 1925.
The Natural Philosophy of Plant Form, Cambridge University Press, 1950.
The Mind and the Eye: A Study of the Biologist's Standpoint, Cambridge University Press, 1954.

SOURCES:

Books

Biographical Memoirs of Fellows of the Royal Society, Royal Society (London), Volume 6, 1960.

Periodicals

Nature, June 11, 1960, pp. 847–848.
Phytomorphology, 1960, pp. 261–263.

—*Sketch by Leslie Mertz*

Werner Arber
1929-
Swiss molecular biologist

Werner Arber's discovery of an enzyme that could cleave long strands of deoxyribonucleic acid (DNA) led to a revolution in genetics research, providing the foundation that led to techniques to separate and reassemble basic genetic material. Gene splicing, as it was called, proved invaluable for DNA sequencing and gene mapping, which focuses on genetic organization. The most controversial outcome of this research, however, was the eventual manipulation of DNA structures by geneticists, first in test tubes and then *in vivo,* or within a living organism. Arber received the 1978 Nobel Prize in physiology or medicine for his research on gene splicing, sharing the prize with United States scientists **Hamilton O. Smith** and **Daniel Nathans**, who had also played an essential role in the development of gene splicing. A devoted family man, Werner eschewed politics but was well aware of the implications of genetic manipulation and warned his fellow scientists that such genetic research should be used carefully. As a result, Arber conducted studies and participated in symposia on how to prevent the unintentional release of a genetically altered virus into the environment.

Werner Arber was born in Gränichen, Switzerland, on June 3, 1929. Educated in the Swiss public

Werner Arber

United States, Arber also took the opportunity to visit several colleagues who were studying bacteriophages.

Formulates Restriction-Modification Theory

Arber returned to Switzerland to join the faculty at the University of Geneva in 1960. With support from the Swiss National Science Foundation, he embarked on studies of the molecular basis of bacteriophage restriction. Working with one of his graduate students, Daisy Dussoix, Arber found in 1962 that restriction was host-controlled and involved changes in the phage's DNA. In effect, the DNA of the invading phages is cut into component parts, although some phages survived the operation. This discovery set in motion a series of studies that jump-started genetics to become the new frontier in biomedical research.

Arber himself formulated a hypothesis presupposing that an endonuclease enzyme in the host severs the DNA of invading phages into component parts, while a methylase enzyme modifies the DNA of the host to make it invulnerable to its own endonuclease enzyme. Although he had yet to discover such an enzyme, Arber hypothesized that an endonuclease recognizes specific sequences of nucleotides, a fundamental building block of DNA and RNA, and cuts the DNA of the invading phages at the specific locations of these nucleotides. Arber called this two-enzyme theory a restriction-modification system. The theory received initial confirmation when Arber, with the biophysicist Urs Kühnlein, isolated phage mutants that were inert to restriction and modification by mutation at specific nucleotide recognition sites. This discovery directly correlated Kühnlein's observation of DNA methylation with host-controlled modification in phages.

In 1965 Arber was appointed extraordinary professor of molecular genetics at the University of Geneva. He continued his research on restriction-modification and discovered, in 1968, the restriction endonuclease of *Escherichia coli* B, a common gut bacterium widely used in genetic studies. (At the same time **Matthew Meselson** and Robert Yuan identified the endonuclease from *Escherichia coli* K.) Although Arber's enzyme recognized specific nucleotide sequences, it cut the DNA at random spots and would later be known as a Type I restriction endonuclease. Since these Type I endonucleases severed the DNA at areas away from the recognition sites, they were unsuitable for studies of gene splicing. The second part of Arber's theory—that the endonuclease cut the invader's DNA at *specific* sites—was confirmed by the microbial geneticist Hamilton Smith and his colleagues, K. W. Wilcox and Thomas J. Kelley. Working at Johns Hopkins University, they identified what eventually came to be known as Type II, or specific, endonuclease. Daniel Nathans, also at Johns

school system, he entered the Federal Institute of Technology in Zurich in 1949, where he focused on the natural sciences. Arber soon became exposed to experimental research and embarked on studies to isolate and characterize the radioactive isotope of chlorine. After graduation in 1953, he entered the University of Geneva as a graduate student, received an appointment as a research assistant in a laboratory, and studied biophysics. Werner became interested in bacterial viruses (bacteriophages) through the biophysicist Jean J. Weigle's studies of variations in these viruses, which aimed to show that a specific bacteriophage will only infect a specific host. Another biophysicist, **Salvador Edward Luria**, showed that when phages infect a different strain of bacteria, a few survive to plate efficiently with the new host strain. Most of the phages die out, and the surviving phages are no longer capable of infecting an earlier host. The phenomenon was first called host-induced variation and is now commonly known as host-controlled restriction-modification.

During his graduate studies, Arber assisted biophysicists at Geneva in developing high-level magnification techniques in electron microscopy to study bacteriophages. He completed his dissertation on deficiencies of a mutant strain of bacteriophage lambda and received his Ph.D. in 1958. Arber then went to the University of Southern California for further study and to refine his laboratory techniques in genetics and bacteriophage research. While in the

Hopkins, was a cancer researcher who first identified eleven cleaved fragments of a simian (monkey or ape) virus and eventually deduced the order in which individual fragments were replicated, showing that they began at a specific site and went in both directions around a circle, stopping approximately 180 degrees from where they started. Nathans and colleagues went on to isolate messenger RNA (mRNA), a type of RNA that is complementary to the protein-encoding segments of the host strand of DNA and communicates genetic information to proteins. They then began to map transcription sites (the origin and direction of each mRNA transcript during infection) by looking at different stages of infection and testing the RNA's ability to hybridize to the various "restriction fragments" due to their nucleotide sequences. This pioneering research led to a barrage of genetic studies aimed at mapping genetic codes, culminating in the international human genome project, which geneticists began in the late 1980s to develop a comprehensive road map of the human genetic system. Over the years, geneticists built upon the work of Arber, Smith, and Nathans to develop techniques to produce enough of a particular gene to study and then to artificially alter DNA through the transfer or insertion of genetic material.

Arber eventually became dissatisfied with what he perceived to be academic politics and the dearth of students devoting themselves to research careers at the University of Geneva. He left the university in 1970 and spent a year at the University of California at Berkeley as a visiting professor in the Department of Molecular Biology. Upon returning to Switzerland, he took an appointment as ordinary professor of molecular biology at the University of Basel and was reserved extensive modern facilities in the Biozentrum research institute, which was then under construction.

Wins Nobel Prize

In 1978, Arber, Smith, and Nathans won the Nobel Prize for physiology or medicine, Arber being noted for his research showing that the host can alter DNA to prevent invasion by phages and other foreign genes through methylation (combining DNA with two carbons and three hydrogens), which cleaves the DNA. The cumulative efforts of these three scientists were an example of the growing emphasis on interdisciplinary communication and cooperation in scientific research as new discoveries in genetics were made simultaneously at many institutions throughout the world.

Arber's subsequent research has focused on genetic systems and their diversification. With the confirmation in the 1970s of **Barbara McClintock**'s theories of transposable genes that could "jump" to different strands of DNA during the early stages of

meiosis (the process of cell division), Arber and other geneticists began to experiment with gene transplantation. Arber has theorized that genetic exchange through transposition may account for the diverse bacterial genetic codes that occur during evolution.

Formulates Guidelines for Genetic Engineering

Investigations into recombinant DNA technology, however, also had controversial aspects. Studies of combining eukaryotic DNA (that is, DNA from an organism consisting of more than one cell) with bacterial or viral DNA in a molecule raised concerns about producing pathogens (a micro-organism that can carry disease), especially since these pathogens could be cloned by copying the DNA molecules. Arber participated in discussions that led to a set of guidelines developed by the National Institutes of Health to conduct recombinant DNA research safely. As Arber points out in his introductory paper for the proceedings of the symposium, *Genetic Manipulation: Impact on Man and Society,* the initial risk was faced by the experimenters themselves, who were in direct contact with potential pathogens. What concerned the public, however, was the possibility of potential pathogens being accidentally introduced into the environment. Arber called for a realistic evaluation of the risks, saying that the guidelines had been designed to reduce the risks to a minimum.

Because of these precautions, geneticists have avoided serious mishaps and developed remarkable recombinant DNA studies, including a promising biomedical application known as gene therapy. Gene therapy begins with the splicing of DNA segments from various origins into a vector DNA molecule. Vectors act as "molecular delivery trucks," carrying genes to targeted cell types or organ systems, and are carefully chosen for their ability to colonize certain cell types and tissues in the body and become an inheritable trait. In gene therapy, disease-causing genes (specific nucleotide sequences) are replaced with normal sequences or additional genetic material is inserted to change the genes. This genetic material, for example, could carry a gene that expresses an inhibitor of a certain protein or hormone that causes a disease, such as arthritis. Investigators have also focused on gene therapies for cancer.

Arber married his wife, Antonia, in 1965. They have two daughters. Outside of his scientific pursuits, Arber has devoted his time to his family, who strongly support his scientific efforts.

SELECTED WRITINGS BY ARBER:

Books

(Editor, with others) "The Natural Mechanisms of Microbial Evolution," in *Genetic Manipulation: Impact on Man and Society,* Cambridge University Press, 1984.

Periodicals

"Host-Controlled Modification of Bacteriophage," *Annual Review of Microbiology,* Volume 19, 1968, pp. 365–378.

"DNA Modification and Restriction," *Progress in Nucleic Acid Research in Molecular Biology,* Volume 14, 1974, pp. 1–37.

SOURCES:

Periodicals

"The 1978 Nobel Prize in Physiology or Medicine," *Science,* Volume 202, 1978, pp. 1069–1071.

—*Sketch by David Petechuk*

Edwin Howard Armstrong
1890-1954
American inventor and electrical engineer

Edwin Howard Armstrong was one of the last of a breed of scientists who worked independently of major corporations. His work in early radio principles and later in more sophisticated uses of radio was directly responsible for the many ways radio waves are used today and for the popularity of high-fidelity (hi-fi) sound. Armstrong began inventing during the earliest days of radio, when he found a way to amplify sound and to transmit continuous waves, and his subsequent work during World War II has had implications for military radar and space travel. Although protracted legal proceedings frustrated his attempts to secure patent rights to several of his inventions, he is remembered as the father of regeneration and superregeneration, and as the inventor of the superheterodyne and frequency modulation (FM) broadcasting. From these inventions proceeded many important applications that are vital today.

Born on December 18, 1890, Armstrong enjoyed a privileged and sheltered life, first in New York City, then in Yonkers. His mother, Emily Smith Armstrong, taught in the New York public schools until Armstrong was born. His father, John Armstrong, was initially a salesman for Oxford University Press and later rose to become a vice-president. In the senior Armstrong's travels, notably to London, he picked up books for his young son. Memorable among them were *The Boy's Book of Inventions: Stories of the*

Wonders of Modern Science and *The Adventures of Inventors and Engineers: True Incidents and Personal Experiences;* read when Armstrong was thirteen and fourteen, these books helped to shape his ambition.

Among the young Armstrong's interests was the game of tennis, which he mastered with zeal. He also developed a passion for heights and speed, and loved machines, especially trains. However, electronics, and radio in particular, was his life's focus. Early on, neighborhood children routinely brought him their broken toys to fix. Later he developed an interest in automobiles. But his greatest hobby was the wireless station he set up in his third-floor bedroom. There he transmitted to and received signals from other youths all over Yonkers, some of whom remained lifelong friends. He also experimented with and built many circuits in his bedroom, always seeking to understand precisely how each circuit worked and why. Through his uncle, Frank Smith, Armstrong met Charles Underhill, the inventor of an early version of the teletype. For the next two years, Underhill was Armstrong's mentor and thoroughly explained to him the work of physicists Michael Faraday, James Clerk Maxwell, and Heinrich Hertz, and clarified to him the principles of electromagnetic waves. Armstrong pursued his interest in radio following his graduation from Yonkers High School in 1909, enrolling in Columbia University's School of Mines, Engineering, and Chemistry and receiving his bachelor of science degree in 1913.

Investigates Vacuum Tube Circuit and Discovers Feedback

While Armstrong was at Columbia, the audion—a vacuum tube circuit invented by **Lee de Forest**—was one of the primary components used in wireless telegraphs to detect incoming electromagnetic signals. Since the functionality of the audion was not understood with absolute certainty, the quality of the audions often varied. In 1911 Armstrong decided to investigate how the audion worked, with the help of John Morecroft and Columbia's laboratory equipment. Whereas de Forest believed the audion to work as a function of which gas he used to manufacture it, Armstrong soon discovered that the audion moved electrons in a steady, oscillating current. Armstrong theorized that if he fed the current back over the grid plate many times a second (since electrons move at the speed of light), he could amplify the signal. The challenge was to build such a circuit.

On the evening of September 22, 1912, Armstrong achieved his goal. Calling his discovery the principle of feedback, or "regeneration,"his new circuit allowed instantaneous amplification of even the weakest signals. Tinkering more with his invention, Armstrong noted that the circuit's clear tones would change to hissing ones at the point of maximum amplification. Careful investigation of this phenomenon revealed that, near maximum amplification, the circuit was transmitting its own signal. With some modification, Armstrong was able to make his circuit transmit continuous waves. Instead of the very large machines employed at that time to generate continuous waves, Armstrong's small vacuum tube circuit could do the same job much better. This ushered in the type of radio transmission and reception used even today.

Armstrong confided to a close friend what he had accomplished, and then asked his father for money to take out a patent that December. The elder Armstrong refused to help until Armstrong graduated. So on January 31, 1913, Armstrong sketched his new circuit in order to have it notarized but waited until October 29th of that year to make his patent application. The patent issued on October 6, 1914. On December 18, 1913, Armstrong applied for a second patent that used his circuit to transmit continuous, oscillating waves. This was the basic circuit of the modern radio transmitter.

After graduating from Columbia in June of 1913, Armstrong stayed on as an assistant at Columbia University, where he taught Navy classes in wireless for six hundred dollars a year. The position allowed him free use of Columbia's laboratories for further exploration into the nature of radio. He was able to license his circuit to the Telefunken and American Marconi companies, as well as to others, for royalties which lasted up until the start of World War I. In the fall of 1915 Armstrong also procured an assistantship at the Marcellus Hartley Laboratory. It was the closest he ever came to working for a corporation.

Wartime Research Results in Precision Radio Tuning

In 1917, Armstrong became a captain in the U.S. Army Signal Corps. Stationed in Paris, his assignment was to install and test radio sets in airplanes. Germany was rumored to be transmitting messages at very high frequencies, and Armstrong was assigned to work on detecting such transmissions. This assignment led directly to his invention of the superheterodyne, a device that detects incoming signals of one frequency, generates a signal of a second frequency, and produces a third frequency that retains all of the characteristics of the initial, incoming signal—including tones, voices, and modulation. The third signal can be made to be within the range of human hearing. The superheterodyne became the basis for all precision radio tuning. Patents were filed in France in December of 1918, and in the United States in February of 1919.

Armstrong was promoted to major early in 1919; it was a title by which he referred to himself for the rest of his life. Later in 1919, while he was still stationed in Paris, he learned he had been awarded the Institute of Radio Engineers' Medal of Honor. This was the organization's highest award, and to Armstrong, the most significant he ever received. Armstrong's stay in Paris after the war was cut short, however, by the news that Lee de Forest was suing him over regeneration. In a protracted legal battle that lasted nearly twenty years, de Forest gained the patent rights to regeneration from Armstrong as a result of two appearances in front of the Supreme Court—though most scientists in the industry believed that Armstrong was the true inventor of the idea. Armstrong was so humiliated by his loss at court that he attempted, unsuccessfully, to return his medal to the Institute of Radio Engineers. Before the Supreme Court handed down its ruling in 1934, Westinghouse, in 1920, had purchased Armstrong's regeneration and superheterodyne patents for $335,000.

In 1921 Armstrong happened on the principle of superregeneration. With regeneration, a signal could be amplified 20,000 times before the circuit "howled." By adding a squelching circuit to the original, amplification was boosted to 100,000 times the original signal. Because the purchase of patent rights by Westinghouse had meant serious competition to RCA, David Sarnoff, then vice-president and general manager of RCA, moved aggressively to strike a deal with Armstrong. Sarnoff's secretary was Marion MacInnis, and over the spring and summer of 1923 Armstrong courted her. They married on December 1, 1923. Also in 1923 Armstrong, along with Harry Houck, patented a simpler form of the superheterodyne circuit. It allowed tuning to be accomplished using only three knobs.

Frequency Modulation Becomes a Reality

Frequency modulation (FM) had been experimented with since the days of **Guglielmo Marconi** with unsatisfactory results, while amplitude modulation (AM) broadcasting continued to suffer problems, most noticeably producing static, tinny tones, and interruptions caused by spurious radiation in the atmosphere. When Armstrong put his talents to the task of frequency modulation, he accepted the theory that the only way to get a favorable signal-to-noise ratio and to reduce the static was to use as narrow a carrier band as possible. Extensive experiments, however, proved frustrating.

In the meantime, mathematician John R. Carson had theorized that broadcasting by frequency modulation could never be achieved. Needing no stronger incentive, Armstrong started over by throwing out the idea of using a narrow-band carrier signal. What he did invent was not frequency modulation but a system that made frequency modulation workable. Static was nearly eliminated, and for the first time true high-fidelity sound (the highly accurate reproduction of a sound effect) was possible. During this time Armstrong received an honorary degree from Columbia University in 1929, and eventually became a professor there.

Armstrong covered his invention with a range of patents issued on December 26, 1933, then approached RCA in 1934, since he had agreed to give RCA the right of first refusal for any new inventions. David Sarnoff, now RCA's president and a close friend of Armstrong's, showed interest, but would not commit to the new technology, most probably because he believed the advent of television would make radio a passing fad. On November 19, 1934, Armstrong demonstrated yet another useful application of FM—multiplexing, the sending of multiple signals on just one carrier, which his system had made practical. For five years, however, RCA took no action. By 1939, impatient with RCA's and with what he saw as the rest of the industry's intransigence, Armstrong inaugurated broadcasting from his own station, W2XMN, in Alpine, New Jersey, on July 18, 1939. Although FM worked very well, the industry still remained skeptical.

Before the United States entered World War II, Armstrong received the Franklin Medal in January of 1941 from the Franklin Institute. During the war, he provided service to the government—initially for free (as his patriotism dictated), and later for pay, as financial concerns forced him to work on government contract. His superregeneration circuit had military application in the Identify, Friend or Foe (IFF) system, whereby radar could tell which planes were friendly and which were not. FM also was used to relay signals, as first demonstrated on January 5, 1940. It worked well and fast.

Of Armstrong's work in World War II on "Project Diana" for the government, this much is known: he studied extending the range of radar by continuous wave FM, as FM broadcasting was not limited to line-of-sight transmissions as was AM. It was after the war that this came to fruition in a dramatic demonstration at Fort Evans, New Jersey. There, on January 10, 1946, Armstrong bounced a signal off of the moon and back to Earth. This proved that, unlike AM waves, FM could penetrate the ionosphere, opening up the possibilities of communicating with spacecraft, measuring distances in space, and mapping heavenly bodies topographically. In 1947 Armstrong further proved the advantages of FM broadcasting by bouncing signals off of the ionosphere from his station in Alpine, New Jersey, to a mobile receiving station in Alabama. This work had direct application to the development of military early warning defense systems and domestic microwave relay stations.

After the war Armstrong continued to battle RCA and the rest of the industry over their use of his FM system of broadcasting, for which he was receiving no royalties. Then the Federal Communications Commission (FCC) decided to move FM broadcasting from the 42–50 megacycle range (one megacycle equals one million cycles) to between 88 and 108 megacycles, where it remains today. This was disastrous for FM broadcasting, as it suddenly rendered all transmitting and receiving equipment obsolete. Indeed, very little equipment was capable of operating at those frequencies initially. On July 22, 1948, Armstrong filed suit against RCA and NBC, primarily for failure to pay royalties. In a complex series of legal maneuvers, RCA managed to drag the pretrial phase on until all but one of Armstrong's patents had expired.

In March of 1953 Armstrong patented with John Bose his system of multiplexing. It would be his last patent. As a result of his never-ending legal wrangling with RCA and his sense of betrayal by David Sarnoff, Armstrong became very despondent. On January 31, 1954, he penned a note to his wife and jumped from his thirteenth-story window to his death. Marion Armstrong later won all suits filed on behalf of her husband's estate after his death, including the one with RCA.

SELECTED WRITINGS BY ARMSTRONG:

Periodicals

"Theory of Tuned Circuits," *Proceedings of the Radio Club of America,* May-December, 1913.

"A New Method of Receiving Weak Signals for Short Waves," *Proceedings of the Radio Club of America,* December, 1919.

"The Regenerative Circuit," *Electrical Journal,* Volume 18, Number 4, 1921, pp. 153–154.

"The Super-Regenerative Circuit," *Proceedings of the Radio Club of America,* June, 1922.

"The Super-Heterodyne: Its Origin, Development, and Some Recent Improvements," *Proceedings of the Institute of Radio Engineers,* October, 1924, pp. 539–552.

"Evolution of Frequency Modulation," *Electrical Engineering,* December, 1940, pp. 485–488.

"Frequency Modulation and Its Future Uses," *Annals of the Academy of Political and Social Science,* January, 1941, pp. 153–159.

"Some Recent Developments in the Multiplexed Transmission of Frequency Modulated Broadcast Signals," *Proceedings of the Radio Club of America,* October, 1953.

SOURCES:

Books

Archer, Gleason L., *History of Radio,* American Historical Society, 1938.

Barnouw, Erik, *A Tower in Babel: A History of Broadcasting in the United States to 1933,* Oxford University Press, 1966.

Chase, Francis, Jr., *Sound and Fury: An Informal History of Broadcasting,* Harper & Row, 1942.

Erickson, Don V., *Armstrong's Fight for FM Broadcasting: One Man vs Big Business and Bureaucracy,* University of Alabama Press, 1973.

Lessing, Lawrence P., *Man of High Fidelity: Edwin Howard Armstrong, A Biography,* Lippincott, 1956.

Lewis, Tom, *Empire of the Air: The Men Who Made Radio,* HarperCollins, 1991.

Licthy, Lawrence W., and Malachi C. Topping, *A Source Book on the History of Radio and Television,* Hastings House, 1975.

—*Sketch by Susan E. Kolmer*

Neil Armstrong
1930-
American engineer and astronaut

Neil Armstrong was the first human being to stand on the Moon. This former test pilot's lunar stroll on July 20, 1969, marked the pinnacle of the most ambitious engineering project ever undertaken. Armstrong went on to pursue a career in aerospace teaching, research, and business.

Born August 5, 1930, Neil Alden Armstrong was fascinated by flying ever since he had his first airplane ride when he was a six-year-old boy in Ohio. He was the son of Stephen Armstrong, an auditor who moved his family several times during Armstrong's childhood. When Neil was thirteen, Stephen and his wife, the former Viola Louise Engel, along with Neil and his younger brother and sister, settled in the town of Wapakoneta. Armstrong earned his pilot's license before his driver's license, and at sixteen was not only flying airplanes but experimenting with a wind tunnel he had built in his basement. He worked a variety of jobs to pay for his flying lessons and also played in a jazz band, pursuing the musical interest that remained a hobby throughout his life. Armstrong earned a navy scholarship to Purdue University, which he entered in 1947. His schooling was interrupted when the navy called him to active duty. Armstrong soon qualified as a navy pilot, and he was flying combat missions in Korea at the age of twenty. He flew twenty-eight missions, earning three air medals.

Tests X–15 Rocket Plane

When the war was over, Armstrong left the navy and returned to Purdue. In 1955 he earned his bachelor's in aerospace engineering. In January, 1956, he married fellow Purdue student Janet Shearon. By then, Armstrong was a test pilot for the National Advisory Committee for Aeronautics, the forerunner of the National Aeronautics and Space Administration (NASA). At NACA's facility at Edwards Air Force Base in California, Armstrong flew a variety of aircraft under development. He and Janet also started their family, adding son Eric in 1957 and daughter Karen in 1959. (Karen died three years later of a brain tumor.) In 1960, Armstrong made his first of seven trips to the fringes of space in the X–15 rocket plane. The X–15, a sleek craft airlaunched from a B–52 bomber and landed on Edwards's famous dry lake bed, gathered data about high-speed flight and atmospheric reentry that influenced many future designs, including the space shuttle.

When the astronaut program was first announced, Armstrong discounted it, believing that the winged X–15 design and not the *Mercury* capsule was the better approach to space. After **John Glenn** made the first U.S. orbital flight in 1962, Armstrong changed his mind and applied for NASA's astronaut corps. He was accepted into the second group of astronauts, becoming the first civilian to be chosen. The Armstrongs relocated to Houston, where their second son, Mark, was born in 1963. In March, 1966, after serving as a backup for the *Gemini-Titan 5* mission, Armstrong made his first spaceflight as commander of *Gemini-Titan 8.* On this mission, Armstrong's capsule achieved the first docking between spacecraft in orbit. After docking the Gemini spacecraft to the Agena target vehicle, however, the combined vehicles began to tumble uncontrollably. Armstrong and co-astronaut David Scott disengaged the *Agena* and found the problem was a thruster on their capsule that was firing continuously. They had to shut down the flight control system to stop it, an action that forced the two astronauts to abort their flight.

Commands First Lunar Landing Mission

Armstrong moved on to the moon-bound *Apollo* program. He was instrumental in adding a system that, in the event of a failure of the *Saturn 5* booster's guidance system, would allow the astronauts to fly the enormous vehicle manually. Armstrong was on the backup crew for *Apollo 8,* and in January, 1969, was selected to command *Apollo 11.* The crew included lunar module pilot Edwin "Buzz" Aldrin Jr. and command module pilot Michael Collins. Armstrong carried with him a piece of fabric and a fragment of a propeller from American aviators **Wilbur and Orville Wrights'** first airplane.

On July 20, 1969, the spider-shaped lunar module *Eagle* carried Armstrong and Aldrin toward the Sea of Tranquility. The preselected landing area turned out to be much rougher than thought, and Armstrong was forced to guide the *Eagle* over the terrain until he found a vacant site. The two men finally brought their craft to a soft landing with approximately thirty seconds' worth of fuel remaining. "The Eagle has landed," Armstrong reported. Almost seven hours later, he climbed down the ladder and took the epochal first step on the moon. Television viewers around the world watched as the astronaut in his bulky white suit uttered the words, "That's one small step for a man, one giant leap for mankind." (Viewers did not hear the word "a"; Armstrong later explained that his voice-operated microphone, which "can lose you a syllable," failed to transmit the word.)

Joined by Aldrin, Armstrong spent nearly three hours walking on the moon. The astronauts deployed experiments, gathered samples, and planted an American flag. They also left a mission patch and medals commemorating American and Russian space explorers who had died in the line of duty, along with a plaque reading, "Here men from the planet Earth first set foot upon the Moon. We came in peace for all mankind." Then the three men took their command module *Columbia* safely back to Earth. After eighteen days of quarantine to control any lunar microorganisms, Armstrong and the others traveled around the world for parades and speeches. The mission brought honors including the Presidential Medal of Freedom, the Harmon International Aviation Trophy, the Royal Geographic Society's Hubbard Gold Medal, and other accolades from a total of seventeen nations. Armstrong became a Fellow of the Society of Experimental Test Pilots, the American Astronautical Society, and the American Institute of Aeronautics and Astronautics.

That was Armstrong's final space mission. He moved to NASA's Office of Advanced Research and Technology, where he served as deputy associate administrator for aeronautics. One of his major priorities in this position was to further research into controlling high-performance aircraft by computer. In 1970, he earned his master's degree in aerospace engineering from the University of Southern California.

A quiet man who valued his privacy, Armstrong rejected most opportunities to profit from his fame. He left NASA in 1971 and moved his family back to Ohio to accept a position at the University of Cincinnati. There he spent seven years engaged in teaching and research as a professor of aerospace engineering. He took special interest in the application of space technology to challenges on Earth such as improving medical devices and providing data on the environment. In 1978, Armstrong was one of the first six recipients of the Congressional Space Medal of Honor, created to recognize astronauts whose "exceptionally meritorious efforts" had contributed to "the welfare of the Nation and mankind."

Armstrong was also a member of the board of directors of Gates Learjet Corporation, and in 1979 he piloted that company's new business jet to five world-altitude and time-to-climb records for that class of aircraft. Other boards Armstrong served on included those of USX Corporation and United Airlines. In between his business ventures and such hobbies as fishing and sailplaning, he also found time to be chair of the board of trustees of the Cincinnati Museum of Natural History.

Armstrong did accept two further government appointments. In 1984, he was named to the National Commission on Space, which two years later completed a report outlining an ambitious future for American space programs. (The commission's recommendations were embraced by then president Ronald Reagan, but went largely unfunded.) Also in 1986, Armstrong was named deputy chair of the Rogers Commission to investigate the explosion of the space shuttle *Challenger*. The commission's work resulted in major changes in NASA's management structure and safety practices.

From 1980 to 1982, Armstrong was chair of the Board of Cardwell International. In 1982, he moved on to take a similar post with Computing Technologies for Aviation. CTA provided software for flight scheduling and support activities, allowing corporate jet operators to maximize the efficient use of their aircraft. Although the company was based in Charlottesville, Virginia, Armstrong maintained his residence at his farm near Lebanon, Ohio. He stepped down as head of CTA in 1993.

SELECTED WRITINGS BY ARMSTRONG:

Books

(With Michael Collins and others) *First on the Moon,* Little, Brown, 1970.
(With Luis Alvarez and others) *Pioneering the Space Frontier: The Report of the National Commission on Space,* Bantam, 1986.

SOURCES:

Books

Aldrin, Buzz, and Malcolm McConnell, *Men From Earth,* Bantam, 1989.

Periodicals

Plimpton, George, "Neil Armstrong's Famous
    First Words," *Esquire,* December, 1983, pp.
    113–119.

Other

Fulk, Dale, marketing manager, CTA, interview
    with Matthew A. Bille conducted February 17,
    1994.
Gregory, Jim, press release, Gates Learjet Corpo-
    ration, February 21, 1979.
Kuettner, Al, press release, University of Cincin-
    nati, August 3, 1976.

—*Sketch by Matthew A. Bille*

Svante August Arrhenius
1859-1927
Swedish chemist

Svante August Arrhenius was awarded the 1903
Nobel Prize in chemistry for his research on the
theory of electrolytic dissociation, a theory that had
won the lowest possible passing grade for his Ph.D.
two decades earlier. Arrhenius's work with chemistry
was often closely tied to the science of physics, so
much so that the Nobel committee was not sure in
which of the two fields to make the 1903 award. In
fact, Arrhenius is regarded as one of the founders of
physical chemistry—the field of science in which
physical laws are used to explain chemical phenomena. In the last decades of his life, Arrhenius became
interested in theories of the origin of life on Earth,
arguing that life had arrived on our planet by means
of spores blown through space from other inhabited
worlds. He was also one of the first scientists to study
the heat-trapping ability of carbon dioxide in the
atmosphere in a phenomenon now known as the
greenhouse effect.

Arrhenius was born on February 19, 1859, in Vik
(also known as Wik or Wijk), in the district of
Kalmar, Sweden. His mother was the former Carolina
Thunberg, and his father was Svante Gustaf Arrhenius, a land surveyor and overseer at the castle of Vik
on Lake Målar, near Uppsala. Arrhenius's uncle,
Johan, was a well-known botanist and agricultural
writer who had also served as secretary of the Swedish
Agricultural Academy.

Young Svante gave evidence of his intellectual
brilliance at an early age. He taught himself to read by
the age of three and learned to do arithmetic by
watching his father keep books for the estate of which
he was in charge. Arrhenius began school at the age of
eight, when he entered the fifth-grade class at the
Cathedral School in Uppsala. After graduating in
1876, Arrhenius enrolled at the University of Uppsala.

At Uppsala, Arrhenius concentrated on mathematics, chemistry, and physics and passed the candidate's examination for the bachelor's degree in 1878.
He then began a graduate program in physics at
Uppsala, but left after three years of study. He was
said to be dissatisfied with his physics advisor, Tobias
Thalén, and felt no more enthusiasm for the only
advisor available in chemistry, Per Theodor Cleve. As
a result, he obtained permission to do his doctoral
research in absentia with the physicist Eric Edlund at
the Physical Institute of the Swedish Academy of
Sciences in Stockholm.

Solves the Problem of Electrical Conductivity in Solutions

The topic Arrhenius selected for his dissertation
was the electrical conductivity of solutions. The
problem was of some interest to scientists because of
the fact that while neither pure water nor dry salts
conduct an electrical current, a solution made by
dissolving salts in water does. A number of other
phenomena related to solutions were also puzzling.
For example, a given amount of sodium chloride
causes twice the lowering in freezing point of a
solution as does a comparable amount of sugar, while
other salts, such as barium chloride and aluminum
chloride, cause a freezing point depression of three or
four times as much as that of a sugar solution.

In 1884 Arrhenius submitted his thesis on this
topic. In the thesis he hypothesized that when salts are
added to water, they break apart into charged particles now known as ions. What was then thought of as
a molecule of sodium chloride, for example, would
dissociate into a charged sodium atom (a sodium ion)
and a charged chlorine atom (a chloride ion). The
doctoral committee that heard Arrhenius's presentation in Uppsala was totally unimpressed by his ideas.
Among the objections raised was the question of how
electrically charged particles could exist in water. In
the end, the committee granted Arrhenius his Ph.D.,
but with a score so low that he did not qualify for a
university teaching position.

Convinced that he was correct, Arrhenius had his
thesis printed and sent it to a number of physical
chemists on the continent, including Rudolf Clausius,
Jacobus van't Hoff, and **Wilhelm Ostwald**. These
men formed the nucleus of a group of researchers
working on problems that overlapped chemistry and
physics, developing a new discipline that would
ultimately be known as physical chemistry. From this

group, Arrhenius received a much more encouraging response than he had received from his doctoral committee. In fact, Ostwald came to Uppsala in August 1884 to meet Arrhenius and to offer him a job at Ostwald's Polytechnikum in Riga. Arrhenius was flattered by the offer and made plans to leave for Riga, but eventually declined for two reasons. First, his father was gravely ill (he died in 1885), and second, the University of Uppsala decided at the last moment to offer him a lectureship in physical chemistry.

Work Recognized with Nobel Prize

Arrhenius remained at Uppsala only briefly, however, as he was offered a travel grant from the Swedish Academy of Sciences in 1886. The grant allowed him to spend the next two years visiting major scientific laboratories in Europe, working with Ostwald in Riga, Friedrich Kohlrausch in Würzburg, Ludwig Boltzmann in Graz, and van't Hoff in Amsterdam. After his return to Sweden, Arrhenius rejected an offer from the University of Giessen, Germany, in 1891 in order to take a teaching job at the Technical University in Stockholm. Four years later he was promoted to professor of physics there. In 1903, during his tenure at the Technical University, Arrhenius was awarded the Nobel Prize in chemistry for his work on the dissociation of electrolytes.

Arrhenius remained at the Technical University until 1905 when, declining an offer from the University of Berlin, he became director of the physical chemistry division of the Nobel Institute of the Swedish Academy of Sciences in Stockholm. He continued his association with the Nobel Institute until his death in Stockholm on October 2, 1927.

Although he was always be remembered best for his work on dissociation, Arrhenius was a man of diverse interests. In the first decade of the twentieth century, for example, he became especially interested in the application of physical and chemical laws to biological phenomena. In 1908 Arrhenius published a book entitled *Worlds in the Making* in which he theorized about the transmission of life forms from planet to planet in the universe by means of spores.

Arrhenius's name has also surfaced in recent years because of the work he did in the late 1890s on the greenhouse effect. He theorized that carbon dioxide in the atmosphere has the ability to trap heat radiated from the Earth's surface, causing a warming of the atmosphere. Changes over time in the concentration of carbon dioxide in the atmosphere would then, he suggested, explain major climatic variations such as the glacial periods. In its broadest outlines, the Arrhenius theory sounds similar to current speculations about climate changes resulting from global warming.

Arrhenius was married twice, the first time in 1894 to Sofia Rudbeck, his pupil and assistant at the Institute of Technology. That marriage ended in 1896 after the birth of one son, Olev Wilhelm. Nine years later Arrhenius was married to Maria Johansson, with whom he had two daughters, Ester and Anna-Lisa, and one son, Sven. Among the honors accorded Arrhenius in addition to the Nobel Prize were the Davy Medal of the Royal Society (1902), the first Willard Gibbs Medal of the Chicago section of the American Chemical Society (1911), and the Faraday Medal of the British Chemical Society (1914).

SELECTED WRITINGS BY ARRHENIUS:

Books

Textbook of Electrochemistry, Longmans, Green, 1902.
Immunochemistry, Macmillan, 1907.
Worlds in the Making: The Evolution of the Universe, Harper, 1908.
Theories of Solutions, Yale University Press, 1912.
Quantitative Laws in Biological Chemistry, G. Bell, 1915.
The Destinies of the Stars, Putnam, 1918.
Chemistry in Modern Life, Van Nostrand, 1925.

Periodicals

"On the Influence of Carbonic Acid in the Air upon the Temperature of the Ground," *Philosophical Magazine,* Volume 41, 1896, Series 5, pp. 237–276.
"Zur Physik des Vulkanismus," *Geologiska förenigens i Stockholm förhandlingar,* Volume 22, Number 5, 1901, p. 26.
"Electrolytic Dissociation," *Journal of the American Chemical Society,* Volume 34, 1912, pp. 353–364.

SOURCES:

Books

A Biographical Dictionary of Scientists: Chemistry, edited by Trevor Williams, Wiley, 1974, pp. 9–10.
Dictionary of Scientific Biography, Volume 1, Scribner, 1975, pp. 296–302.
Fleck, George, "Svante Arrhenius," *Nobel Laureates in Chemistry: 1901–1992,* edited by Laylin K. James, American Chemical Society and the Chemical Heritage Foundation, 1993, pp. 15–22.

Jaffe, Bernard, *Crucibles: The Great Chemists, Their Lives and Achievements,* Tudor, 1930, pp. 219–241.

Nobel Prize Winners, edited by Tyler Wasson, H. W. Wilson, 1987, pp. 34–35.

Oesper, Ralph, "Svante Arrhenius," *Great Chemists,* edited by Eduard Farber, Interscience, 1961, pp. 1095–1109.

—*Sketch by David E. Newton*

Emil Artin
1898-1962
Austrian mathematician

Emil Artin, a leading theorist in modern algebra and one of the most influential mathematicians of the twentieth century, is a best known for his reformulation of the Galois theory, development of class field theory, and introduction of braid theory. One of his main goals was the clarification of mathematical theories so that people could understand and appreciate the beauty of mathematics; starting with a vision of the whole, he would break down a complex theory into simple steps that could then be understood and applied. A brilliant and dedicated educator, he served for forty years at various universities in Germany and the U.S., and mentored many students who became prominent mathematicians. The University of Clermont-Ferrand in France paid special tribute to Artin in 1962 by awarding him an honorary doctorate on the 300th anniversary of French philosopher and mathematician Blaise Pascal's death.

Artin was born on March 3, 1898, in Vienna, Austria to Emil Artin, an art dealer, and Emma Laura-Artin, an opera singer. The deep appreciation for art and music Artin gained from his parents was evident in his ability to play the flute, harpsichord, and clavichord. His father died when Artin was still a child. When his mother remarried, the family moved to Bohemia, now a region within the Czech Republic. Except for one year of study in France, Artin completed high school in Bohemia, passing his high school examination in the summer of 1916.

Artin completed one semester of study in mathematics and chemistry at the University of Vienna before being drafted into the Austrian army for World War I. In 1919, after the war, Artin continued his education at the University of Leipzig in Germany. His closest friends were students in the other sciences, who gave him the nickname "Ma," short for mathematician. Artin completed his doctorate under Gustav Herglotz in 1921. In his dissertation, Artin formulated an analogue of the Riemann hypothesis (named after the nineteenth-century German mathematician Georg Bernhard Riemann, the hypothesis relates to the zeta function and prime numbers); the theories Artin posed in his dissertation were later verified by French mathematician **André Weil**.

Artin spent 1922 at the University of Göttingen in Germany, where he collaborated with the German mathematicians **David Hilbert** and **Emmy Noether**. He became a part of what is known as the Noether school, which played an important role in unifying what were then classified as the three branches of algebra: the theory of numbers, linear algebra, and permutation groups. The study of permutation groups (the internal permutations of a fixed group of objects) had been initiated in the nineteenth century by the work of the French mathematician Évariste Galois on the roots of polynomials. Aiming for clarity, Artin was able to reformulate Galois's fundamental theory, the core of field theory in relation to algebraic solutions, and prove it through representation theory (which involves the mapping of a mathematical system onto a more concrete system). Artin's formulation has become the standard way to present the Galois theory in algebra texts.

Organizes Hamburg Mathematics Seminar

In 1923, Artin moved to the University of Hamburg where, in addition to mathematics, he lectured on mechanics and the theory of relativity. Along with the German mathematician Erich Hecke and Austrian mathematician Wilhelm Blaschke, Artin organized the Mathematical Seminar of the University of Hamburg. Several other prominent mathematicians, including the Netherlands' B. L. Van der Waerden and France's Claude Chevalley, came to Hamburg to work with this group. Artin stayed in Hamburg for fourteen productive years, during which he published twenty-two papers. Among his most notable accomplishments during this period was developing the "Artin reciprocity theorem," the fundamental theorem of class field theory, which relates to the extension of mathematical fields. Artin's theorem generalized all the reciprocity laws since the work of the German mathematician Karl Friedrich Gauss in the previous century. Artin subsequently collaborated with Otto Schreier to develop the theory of formally real fields, one of the first successes for the new abstract algebra created by the Göttingen school.

Artin's interest in biology led him to introduce the theory of braids (an aspect of the study of knots, the points where curves intersect themselves in two- or three-dimensional space) in a 1926 paper. This and subsequent papers earned him the title, "father of the braid theory"—a popular field that has applications to the structure of DNA. Artin also extended to new applications the Scottish-American mathematician Joseph Wedderburn's theorem involving rings (sets defined as the area between two concentric circles). Artin supervised eleven doctoral students in Hamburg, including Max Zorn and Hans Zassenhaus, who were themselves to become famous mathematicians.

Immigrates to the U.S.

In 1929, Artin married one of his students, Natalie Jasny (known as Natasha); they had three children, Karin, Michael and Thomas. The 1920s had been a distinguished era for mathematics at Göttingen, but the 1930s saw the rise of the Nazi regime and the resulting exodus of scholars from the University. Although Artin was not Jewish, his wife and many of his close associates were. Artin himself was committed to ideas of personal freedom and deplored physical violence. In 1937, the Artin family chose to emigrate to the U.S. to escape the brutality of German society under the Nazi regime. He held a position lecturing at the University of Notre Dame in Indiana for one year, and then joined the faculty of the University of Indiana at Bloomington. In 1944, while at Bloomington, Artin published a paper on the special class of rings with minimum conditions that are now known as Artin rings. In 1946, Artin moved to Princeton University in New Jersey, where he was to remain until 1958. Artin continued his research in algebraic number theory and geometrical aspects of algebra, writing papers on the theory of rings, finite groups, and braids.

During his years at Indiana and Princeton, Artin supervised twenty doctoral students. One of his more famous students from this period was the American mathematician John T. Tate, who co-authored the crowning book of Artin's career, *Class Field Theory*, and who was to marry Artin's daughter. (Tate also collaborated with Artin's son Michael, who himself became a mathematician.) Another student of Artin's was the French-American mathematician Serge Lang, who has authored many books in algebra.

Artin collaborated well, as he was full of original ideas and generous enough to communicate them to others at their inception. During these years, instead of publishing papers, Artin often preferred to give his best ideas to his students to work on, and frequently made conjectures that other mathematicians were then left to prove. In these and other ways, Artin established himself as a great teacher of mathematics. Teaching was very important to him, and he analyzed several different methods whereby mathematics could be learned, including visual, acoustic and kinematic. He was certain that a method based on kinematics (a branch of dynamics) in the classroom was best. That is, he would give an energetic, forceful lecture that emphasized motivation and succeeded first and foremost in interesting the students in the material. Artin explored the craft of teaching in the classroom, through many elementary and advanced mathematics textbooks, and in preparing his doctoral students.

Returns to Germany

In 1956, Artin returned to Germany for a sabbatical year as Gauss Professor of Mathematics in Göttingen and then Hamburg. After an additional year at Princeton, Artin returned to Hamburg permanently in 1958. At this time, he collaborated with Hel Braun in algebraic topology (the use of algebraic methods to investigate the properties of certain figures that remain unaffected by forms of distortion) as well as devoting efforts to the modernization of high school mathematics in developing countries. In addition to his passion for mathematics, Artin read widely in biology, astronomy, mechanics, music and Buddhism. Artin died of a heart attack on December 20, 1962, at the age of sixty-four.

SELECTED WRITINGS BY ARTIN:

Books

(With John T. Tate) *Class Field Theory,* Princeton University Press, 1961.
Collected Papers of Emil Artin, edited by Tate and Serge Lang, Addison-Wesley, 1965.

SOURCES:

Books

Dictionary of Scientific Biography, Scribner, New York, 1970.

Periodicals

Brauer, R., "Emil Artin," *Bulletin of the American Mathematical Society,* Volume 73, 1967, pp. 25–43.
Zassenhaus, Hans, "Emil Artin, His Life and his Work," *Notre Dame Journal of Formal Logic,* January, 1964, pp. 1–9.

—Sketch by Karin Deck

William Astbury
1898-1961
English chemist and molecular biologist

William Astbury's standing in the history of science lies primarily with his work in the structure of organic fibers (e.g., wool). He is also an early figure of importance in the race to discover the structure of deoxyribonucleic acid (DNA), the genetic material, and therefore a founder of molecular biology. His work as an applied scientist, slowly decoding the nature of molecular structure of virtually the largest organic materials, fibrous and globular proteins, was valuable to both science and industry.

Born on February 25, 1898, at Longton, England, later to be incorporated into Stoke-on-Trent, William Thomas Astbury was the son of a potter, though he, like his brother, the physicist N. F. Astbury, had the fortune of an excellent collegiate education. Having won a scholarship to Jesus College, Cambridge University in 1916, he began the study of mathematics and physics. Only two years into his work, Astbury was drafted into the Royal Army Medical Corps X-ray unit. That introduction in World War I to the use of X-ray methods in human war injuries later became the central tool in his life-long study of organic structure.

Works in Crystallography

Upon returning to Cambridge, Astbury added chemistry and mineralogy to his interests. It was under the mineralogist A. Hutchinson that Astbury discovered crystallography, and he spent the rest of his career studying how X rays could be applied to crystallographic problems. After graduation in 1921, he joined the crystallographic group at University College, London, headed by **William Henry Bragg**. Two years later, Bragg's laboratory moved to the Royal Institution and Astbury went with it. In 1928, Astbury was appointed a lecturer in textile physics at the University of Leeds. During his years with Bragg, he had begun his investigation into the structure of wool, and within two years of his arrival at Leeds, he had explained how wool can stretch and fold. The protein that is wool, keratin, was the subject of his first book, *Fundamentals of Fibre Structure*. Explaining the molecular structure of keratin secured his reputation in science and became a springboard for much of his later research.

Bragg had recommended him to Leeds and it turned out to be a happy relationship; Astbury remained at the University of Leeds moving up the professional ladder from lecturer to reader (1937) to honorary reader (1945) and, finally, to the first occupancy of the then new Chair of Biomolecular Structures (from 1945 until his death). Astbury had been successful in Bragg's laboratory even before his departure for Leeds, however. With **Kathleen Lonsdale**, Astbury produced the first table of space groups. These groups define the internal symmetry of crystals, whether inorganic (e.g., table salt) or organic (e.g., keratin). Astbury and Lonsdale's work remains central in crystallography.

Unfortunately, part of the detail of how Astbury believed keratin to be structured turned out to be wrong. The brilliant chemist and (later) two-time Nobelist, **Linus Pauling**, replaced much of the Astbury model for keratin's structure with his notion of the alpha helix and beta-pleated sheet configurations for large proteins. Pauling's explanation has endured, but the groundwork laid by Astbury had been crucial to the movement forward in large molecule crystallography. Another major feature of Astbury's career is his work in globular protein structure. Wool, hair, and fingernails are made up of a long, fibrous protein (keratin) that is mostly inert, but globular proteins include the active proteins such as enzymes and others, such as hemoglobin—carrier of blood-bound oxygen. Astbury showed that such globular proteins were three-dimensional, folded chains that could be denatured (unfolded) and, in some examples, renatured (refolded to their original shapes). This was a significant discovery.

Spots DNA's Helical Molecule in Laboratory

In the 1930's, Astbury discovered what was a major feature of DNA in one of the X-ray pictures taken in his laboratory, the famous 3.4 Angstrom spot (an X-ray dense repeating shadow indicating a helical molecule of a certain size). The X-ray picture of the 3.4 Angstrom spot was published jointly by Astbury and doctoral student Florence Bell, the individual who actually made the picture. Astbury was the living expert on fibrous materials and as such was the most informed about their complex structure, and he grasped the importance of DNA as a molecule that might be able to transmit hereditary information. That was the more remarkable because **Oswald Theodore Avery**, **Colin Munro MacLeod** and **Maclyn McCarty** had not yet published their seminal paper (of 1944) showing that DNA surely was the genetic material.

Astbury's Leeds laboratory had been, for a number of years, supported by generous funding from the Rockefeller Foundation of New York; no similar resources were at that time available in the United Kingdom. In this well-financed situation, expensive X-ray studies were possible. Even with that, X-ray pictures taken by **Rosalind Elsie Franklin** in 1952–53 at King's College, London, proved better and were then used by **James Watson** and **Francis Crick** as they defined the structure of DNA. The Leeds pictures made by Bell, Astbury, and others were inferior to those of Franklin due to a number of technical reasons. Even so, by 1951, excellent pictures emanated from Astbury's laboratory and Mansel Davies, a student of Astbury's who has written on this critical period, has argued that Astbury had all that was necessary in front of him to solve the structure of DNA. The only suggestion Davies could make for why Astbury did not move forward was due to his individualistic personality. Astbury had, in another situation said: "I am not prepared to be anybody's lackey." Davies argued that since Astbury realized how close Watson and Crick were in the early 1950s, he (Astbury) would not preempt their work, but would, rather, follow his own investigations on other topics. Nevertheless, the discovery of the 3.4 Angstrom spot provided essential grist for the Watson-Crick mill and what some have called the greatest biological discovery of the 20th century. Six years before Watson and Crick, Astbury even proposed a model for the structure of DNA. His model, however, was far from correct (not even helical). For his lifetime of creative research, Astbury was elected a Fellow of the Royal Society. Author of two books and over 100 articles, Astbury remains a figure of considerable stature in his several specialties.

SELECTED WRITINGS BY ASTBURY:

Books

Fundamentals of Fibre Structure, London, 1933.
Textile Fibres under the X-Rays, London, 1940.

Periodicals

"Protein and Virus Studies in Relation to the Problem of the Gene," *Proceedings of the 7th International Congress of Genetics,* Cambridge, 1941.
"X-Ray Studies of Nucleic Acids," *Symposium of the Society for Experimental Biology,* Volume 1, 1947, pp. 66–76.

SOURCES:

Books

Biographical Memoirs of Fellows of the Royal Society, Royal Society (London), Volume 9, 1963, pp. 1–35.
Davies, Mansel, "W. T. Astbury, Rosie Franklin and DNA: A Memoir," *Annals of Science,* Volume 47, 1990, pp. 607–618.

—Sketch by Donald J. McGraw

Francis W. Aston
1877-1945
English chemist and physicist

Francis W. Aston was an English chemist and physicist whose motto—"Make more, more, and yet more measurements"—summed up the hard work and dedication he brought to a lifetime of achievement. Among his most important contributions were detailed observations of atomic phenomena with a mass spectrograph that he built himself. This device allowed him to articulate the theory that the atomic weight of each element is a whole number, but that most elements have isotopes (atoms of the same element with the same number of protons in their nucleus, but different numbers of neutrons). For these insights he received the 1922 Nobel Prize in chemistry. From evidence he gathered in the 1920s, Aston went on to note that the weights of atoms vary minutely from whole numbers in proportion to the density of their nuclei.

Francis William Aston was born on September 1, 1877, in Harborne, Birmingham, England, the third of seven children. His parents were William Aston, farmer and metal merchant, and Fanny Charlotte Hollis Aston, the daughter of a gunmaker. From an early age Aston showed great scientific curiosity, performing experiments in his makeshift laboratory on the family farm. In 1893 he graduated from high school at the top of his class in math and science. While at Mason College (which became the University of Birmingham), he worked with P. F. Frankland in organic chemistry and optics, issuing a paper in 1901 on his results. Lacking scholarship money for continued studies, he went to work for a brewing company as resident chemist in the early 1900s. He also performed experiments in electricity with sophisticated devices he built at home.

For this work he was awarded a scholarship in 1903 to the new University of Birmingham. There he discovered a phenomenon, now called the Aston space, that appears in electrical currents passed through gases at low pressures. In 1910, working with **Joseph John Thomson** both at Cambridge University and the Royal Institution in London, he began experiments on the gas neon. When his work was interrupted by World War I, Aston returned to Cambridge. In 1919 he became a fellow of Trinity College, Cambridge, where he stayed for the rest of his life. That same year he managed to perfect the mass spectrograph. In this instrument, a beam of neon atoms directed onto a photographic plate angled away from the flow of atoms created a distinctive pattern when the heavier atoms deflected farther down the plate than the lighter atoms. Taking the average of these deflections, Aston was able to calculate the proportion of heavier to lighter atoms in the element neon. From this information Aston deduced that most elements are mixtures of isotopes and that the weights of atoms are always whole numbers (the whole number rule). He posited that isotopic constituents accounted for the fractional weights observed for some atoms.

Not one to rest on his 1922 Nobel Prize laurels, Aston built larger and even more accurate spectrographs. From a new round of observations taken with one of these instruments in 1927, Aston measured fractional deviations from the whole number rule. He discovered that the tighter the packing of the particles in an atomic nucleus, the greater a fraction of its mass became converted to energy devoted to keeping the nucleus together. He incorporated these "packing fractions" into calculations from which physicists and chemists have derived essential information about the abundance and stability of the elements.

Politically conservative, Aston preferred working alone to collaborating with colleagues. He never married, preferring to keep busy with outdoor sports, traveling by sea and becoming an accomplished photographer and amateur musician. He also loved animals. Aston acquired some financial skills, leaving behind a large estate to Trinity College and various scientific enterprises. He held many honorary degrees and received, in addition to the Nobel Prize, awards such as the 1938 Royal Medal of the Royal Society, of which he was a member, and the 1941 Duddell Medal and Prize of the Institute of Physics. He died on November 20, 1945, in Cambridge.

SELECTED WRITINGS BY ASTON:

Books

Isotopes, E. Arnold, 1922.
Mass Spectra and Isotopes, Longmans, Green, 1933.

Periodicals

"Experiments on the Length of the Cathode Dark Space," *Proceedings of the Royal Society of London,* Volume 79A, 1907, pp. 80–95.
"The Possibility of Separating Isotopes," *London, Edinburgh and Dublin Philosophical Magazine,* Volume 37, 1919, pp. 523–534.
"A New Mass-spectrograph," *Proceedings of the Royal Society of London,* Volume 115A, 1927, pp. 487–514.

SOURCES:

Books

Dictionary of Scientific Biography, Volume 1, Scribner's, 1970, pp. 320–322.

—*Sketch by Hovey Brock*

John Atanasoff
1903-
American physicist

John Atanasoff is a pioneer in the field of computer science. In the late 1930s, while teaching at Iowa State University, he designed and built an electronic computing machine with one of his graduate students, Clifford Berry. The Atanasoff-Berry Computer (ABC) was probably the first machine to use vacuum tubes to perform its calculations. Although he abandoned his work on the ABC to do war work during World War II, Atanasoff became involved with computers again in 1971 when a suit was filed by Sperry Rand, which held the patent of the Electronic Numerical Integrator and Computer (ENIAC) built during the War, against Honeywell.

John Vincent Atanasoff was born on October 4, 1903, in Hamilton, New York, the son of Ivan (John) Atanasoff, a Bulgarian immigrant engineer who worked in a phosphate mine, and an American mother who taught. Atanasoff became interested in calculating devices at an early age—he began studying his father's slide rule when he was only nine and read technical books on mathematics, physics, and chemistry. He decided to be a theoretical physicist while in high school and went on to the University of Florida, obtaining a degree in electrical engineering. He then received a graduate assistantship at Iowa State College (now Iowa State University) and received a master's degree in mathematics, with a minor in physics, in 1929. He transferred to the University of Wisconsin to complete his doctoral work, receiving his Ph.D. in 1930, and then returned to Iowa State to teach both physics and mathematics.

Constructs a Calculating Machine

Atanasoff's interest in building a calculating machine arose from his need to solve partial differential equations without doing the number crunching by hand, a very slow method. He decided that his machine would have to use base two, in which the only two digits are zero and one, a convention that may be represented electronically in a number of different ways. In particular, the machine that Atanasoff and Berry built did arithmetic electronically, using vacuum tubes to perform the arithmetic operations and capacitors to store the numbers. Numbers were input with punched cards. The primary innovation was that numbers in the computer were digital and not analog in nature. The difference between an analog computer—several working versions of which existed at the time—and a digital one is that an analog machine stores its data in terms of position, such as the exact degree of rotation of a numbered wheel, but a digital computer stores its data as a series of binary digits, the zeros and ones of base two. Atanasoff claims to have originated the term "analog" in this application.

The ABC was never expanded or used other than as a calculator. Although Atanasoff and Berry had plans to create a larger machine using the ABC as a building block, those plans were set aside for the War and were never resumed. During the War, Atanasoff worked at the Naval Ordnance Laboratory in Maryland. His only connection with computers at this time occurred when the Navy needed a computer and asked Atanasoff to construct it. Eventually, however, the Navy gave up on the project. Atanasoff then left the computer field. In 1952, he started a firm of his own, Ordnance Engineering Corp., in Frederick, Maryland, and, four years later, sold it to Aerojet General Corp., becoming the firm's vice president and manager of its Atlantic division. Atanasoff left Aerojet in 1961 to become a consultant in package handling automation. He founded another company, Cybernetics, Inc., which his son oversaw.

Wins Sperry Rand-Honeywell Suit

Sperry Rand's 1971 suit alleged that Honeywell had violated the ENIAC patent by not paying Sperry Rand royalties. Honeywell filed a counter-suit charging, among other things, that the inventors of the ENIAC machine were not the inventors of the electronic computer but that Atanasoff was, a fact that would render the ENIAC patent invalid. The judge handed down his decision on October 19, 1973, finding for Honeywell and also specifically ruling that Atanasoff was the inventor of the electronic computer.

This decision touched off a great deal of controversy. Many people believe that Atanasoff did not really invent the computer but that he was responsible for designing and building a number of early computer components (such as a memory drum). It is recognized that Atanasoff did make significant contributions to the development of the electronic computer even though he never built a general-purpose computing machine. For his efforts, Atanasoff re-

ceived Bulgaria's highest award. He now lives with his second wife on a farm near Monrovia, Maryland, for which he has designed a number of interesting devices, such as a hot-air recirculating system that conserves heat.

SOURCES:

Books

Shurkin, James, *Engines of the Mind: A History of the Computer,* Norton, 1984.
Slater, Robert, *Portraits in Silicon,* MIT Press, 1987

—Sketch by Alan R. Shepherd

Michael Francis Atiyah
1929-
English mathematician

Michael Francis Atiyah was awarded the Fields Medal in 1966 for his work in the field of topology. Atiyah is also one of the pioneers of a fundamental new way of looking at the structure of matter known as string theory, which proposes that the fundamental building blocks of matter are lengths rather than points. In 1990 Atiyah was elected president of the Royal Society of London.

Atiyah was born in London on April 22, 1929. His father was Edward Selim Atiyah, originally from Lebanon, and his mother was the former Jean Levens, an English citizen. Atiyah was educated in Egypt, where his father was a broadcaster for the British Broadcasting Company. After completing his secondary education at Victoria College in Egypt, Atiyah enrolled at Manchester Grammar School, a preparatory school in England. At the end of a year, he was accepted as a mathematics student at Trinity College, Cambridge.

Holds a Number of Academic Posts

During his years at Trinity, Atiyah was first a research student and then a research fellow in mathematics. He earned his doctorate in 1955 and was then offered an appointment as a fellow at the Institute for Advanced Studies in Princeton, New Jersey. Over the next two decades, Atiyah held a variety of positions on both sides of the Atlantic, as professor of mathematics at Cambridge University, 1957–61, and at the Institute for Advanced Studies, 1969–72, and as visiting lecturer at Harvard University, 1962–63. From 1963 to 1969 Atiyah was Savilian Professor of Geometry at Oxford University and a fellow of Oxford's New College. After his last assignment at the Institute for Advanced Studies, he returned to Oxford as Royal Society Research Professor and as a fellow of St. Catherine's College. He held the Oxford posts until 1990, when he was elected president of what is arguably the most prestigious scientific association in the world, the Royal Society. In the same year, he was elected to a second post of significant influence, mastership of Trinity College. Trinity is, according to author Glyn Jones in *New Scientist,* "this pre-eminent mathematicians' college."

Atiyah's major field of interest in mathematics has been in the field of topology. Topology is the study of objects whose properties do not change under continuous deformation, that is, stretching and bending. It is sometimes referred to as "rubber-sheet geometry." Because the principles of topology apply to such a wide variety of conditions, it has proved to be the one field that may be able to tie together many other seemingly unrelated fields of mathematics.

Begins Research on String Theory

During the 1970s Atiyah became interested in a new topic, a field of research known as string theory. Physicists have traditionally constructed theories about the nature of matter based on the assumption that the fundamental particles of matter can be thought of as discrete, dimensionless points. String theory adopts a radically new assumption, that the fundamental units of matter do have a dimension, length, and can be thought of as stringlike objects. This approach to the study of matter has evolved out of mathematical theories than out of experimental observations. As a result, string theory tends to be both more complex and less easily interpreted in physical terms than have been traditional theories of matter. For example, one consequence of string theories is that matter has to be thought of in terms of many (often, more than a dozen) dimensions. For most scientists, it is not clear what it means to speak about objects in, say, fourteen dimensions. It is hardly surprising, therefore, that string theory has been received with something less than an enthusiastic response from many physicists. Yet it has become, in the words of writer William Bown in the *New Scientist,* "the most influential theory [of matter] in the 1980s."

For his work in topology and string theory Atiyah has garnered a number of awards and honors. In addition to the 1966 Fields Medal, the highest honor in mathematics, he has received the Royal Medal, 1968, and the Copley Medal, 1988, of the Royal Society, the De Morgan Medal of the London Mathematical Society, 1980, the Feltrinelli Prize of the Accademia Nazionale dei Lincei, 1981, and the King Faisal International Prize for Science, 1987. He has been awarded honorary doctorates from some twenty universities, including those of Bonn, Dublin, Chicago, Helsinki, Rutgers, and Montreal. He was also knighted by Queen Elizabeth II.

Atiyah is a universalist in more ways than one. In addition to his skills as a researcher, he is a highly respected teacher. Indeed, a colleague, Claude LeBrun, wrote in a 1991 review of one of Atiyah's books that he is "one of the great mathematical teachers of our time." Atiyah has long been involved in the professional and administrative aspects of mathematics and science as well. He served as president of the London Mathematical Society from 1974 to 1976 and as president of the Mathematical Association in 1981. For a five-year period from 1984 to 1989 he was also a member of the British government's Science and Engineering Research Council. Atiyah was married to Lily Brown in 1955. The couple have three sons.

SELECTED WRITINGS BY ATIYAH:

Books

K-Theory, W. A. Benjamin, 1966.
Collected Works, 5 volumes, Oxford University Press, 1988.
Geometry and Dynamics of Magnetic Monopoles, Princeton University Press, 1988.
The Geometry and Physics of Knots, Cambridge University Press, 1990.

SOURCES:

Periodicals

Jones, Glyn, "Topologist at the Top," *New Scientist,* January 19, 1991, pp. 42–45.
LeBrun, Claude, "Review of *Michael Atiyah: Collected Works,*" *American Scientist,* May-June, 1991, p. 283.
Stasheff, Jim, "Review of *The Geometry and Physics of Knots,*" *American Scientist,* November-December, 1991, pp. 568–569.

—*Sketch by David E. Newton*

Charlotte Auerbach
1899-
German geneticist

Charlotte Auerbach is a German-born geneticist best known for her work on chemical mutagenesis, that is, the use of chemicals to induce genetic mutations in living things. Notable among her research efforts are her study of mutagens and other genes on the fruit-fly, or *Drosophila*. While her work was part of an ongoing research effort to discover the nature of genetic mutation, Auerbach made important contributions to the study of mutagenesis and was highly decorated for her efforts.

Auerbach was born in Krefeld, Germany, on May 14, 1899, to a scientifically inclined German-Jewish family. Her own father was a chemist and one of her uncles a physicist. Her grandfather, an anatomist, identified the Auerbach's plexus in the human intestine. After being educated in Germany, Auerbach had to flee Germany in 1933 with the rise of nazism. She went to Scotland and joined the Institute of Animal Genetics in Edinburgh, where she obtained her Ph.D. in 1935. She remained here throughout her career except for several sabbaticals taken in the United States and Japan.

Begins Studies on Mutagenesis

In 1938 Auerbach became familiar with the research of **Hermann Joseph Muller**, an American geneticist who spent a year at the Institute of Animal Genetics. In 1927 Muller had shown how X rays could be used to induce mutations in the fruit fly *Drosophila melanogaster.* Mutations are changes or breakage in parts of the chromosomes, the cell organelles that contain deoxyribonucleic acid (DNA), the source of genetic information and inheritance. Mutations spontaneously occur in nature, giving rise to different characteristics. However, when an organism is exposed to a mutagenic agent, the mutation rate increases dramatically. Many mutations can be lethal for the organism.

At the University of Edinburgh, Auerbach was asked to research the effects of mustard gas on *Drosophila.* Mustard gas, a compound used in chemical warfare during World War I and then outlawed, appeared to have pharmacological effects similar to X rays, so it was thought that its mutagenic effects might be similar. To this end, Auerbach designed and executed many experiments, the results of which were more dramatic than expected. Although other mutagens were being discovered in Germany, Switzerland, and the Soviet Union at about the same time, Auerbach's research on chemical mutagenesis was conducted with greater depth. Rarely hypothesizing, and carefully progressing from one conclusion to another, Auerbach discovered the relationship between chromosome breakage and gene mutation by experimenting on fruit flies. She noted how chemical mutagens have a slower action than the immediate effect of X rays. Auerbach also conducted experiments using yeast-one-celled fungi-to try to explain replication of unstable genes. She also used yeast in experiments to study how one-strand lesions in DNA are changed into two-strand mutations.

While visiting the United States at one time, Auerbach visited the national laboratory in Oak Ridge, Tennessee. There she began experimenting on the bread mold *Neurospora;* she wished to show that spontaneous mutations can happen without DNA replication. Her work on fungi also focused on the analysis of mutagen specificity-that is, the selective action of certain mutagens on certain genes. This line of research on the metabolic and physiological influence on the action of mutagens was carried out by her successor, B. J. Kilbey.

During the early 1950s, when DNA was discovered as the compound that carries the genetic code, Auerbach was able to explain how chemical mutagenesis is a process that occurs in many steps, the first of which is a chemical change in DNA. Because of her expertise on the effects of chemical mutagens, Auerbach has been involved in the detection and analysis of environmental mutagens. She served as a member of a government committee, honorary president of the second International Congress on Environmental Mutagen Research, and acted as sponsor and advisor to the European Economic Community Program.

For her outstanding work, Auerbach won several honorary degrees from such institutions as the universities of Leiden, Cambridge, and Dublin. She received the Keith Medal from the Royal Society of Edinburgh in 1947 and the Darwin Medal from the Royal Society of London in 1977. The University of Edinburgh awarded her a D.Sc. in 1947, and in 1967 gave her a personal chair. Other honors received by Auerbach include election to the Genetical Society of Japan in 1966, the Danish Academy of Science in 1968, and an appointment as foreign associate of the U.S. National Academy of Sciences in 1970. She has also won awards of the Environmental Mutagen Society of the United States (1972) and Europe (1974).

SELECTED WRITINGS BY AUERBACH:

Books

Genetics in the Atomic Age, illustrated by I. G. Auerbach, Oliver and Boyd, 1956.

The Science of Genetics, illustrated by I. G. Auerbach, Harper, 1962.

—*Sketch by Barbara A. Branca*

Oswald Theodore Avery
1877(?)-1955
Canadian-born American biologist and bacteriologist

Oswald Theodore Avery

Oswald Theodore Avery was one of the founding fathers of immunochemistry (the study of the chemical aspects of immunology) and a major contributor to the scientific evolution of microbiology. His studies of the pneumococcus virus (causing acute pneumonia) led to further classification of the virus into many distinct types and the eventual identification of the chemical differences among various pneumococci viral strains. His work on capsular polysaccharides and their role in determining immunological specificity and virulence in pneumococci led directly to the development of diagnostic tests to demonstrate circulating antibody. These studies also contributed to the development of therapeutic sera used to treat the pneumonia virus. Among his most original contributions to immunology was the identification of complex carbohydratesas playing an important role in many immunological processes. Avery's greatest impact on science, however, was his discovery that deoxyribonucleic acid (DNA)) is the molecular basis for passing on genetic information in biological self-replication. This discovery forced geneticists of that time to reevaluate their emphasis on the protein as the major means of transmitting hereditary information. This new focus on DNA led to **James Watson** and **Francis Crick**'s model of DNA in 1952 and an eventual revolution in understanding the mechanisms of heredity at the molecular level.

Avery was born on October 21, 1877 (one source says 1887), in Halifax, Nova Scotia, to Joseph Francis and Elizabeth Crowdy Avery. His father was a native of England and a clergyman in the Baptist church, with which Avery was to maintain a lifelong affiliation. In 1887 the Avery family immigrated to the United States and settled in New York City, where Avery was to spend nearly sixty-one years of his life. A private man, he guarded his personal life, even from his colleagues, and seldom spoke of his past. He believed that research should be the primary basis of evaluation for a scientific life, extending his disregard for personal matters to the point that he once refused to include details of a colleague's personal life in an obituary. Avery's argument was that knowledge of matters outside of the laboratory have no bearing on the understanding of a scientist's accomplishments. As a result, Avery, who never married, managed to keep his own personal affairs out of the public eye.

Avery graduated with a B.A. degree from Colgate University in 1900 and received his M.D. degree from Columbia University's College of Physicians and Surgeons in 1904. He then went into the clinical practice of general surgery for three years but soon turned to research and became associate director of the bacteriology division at the Hoagland Laboratory in Brooklyn. Although his time at the laboratory enabled him to study species of bacteria and their relationship to infectious diseases and was a precursor to his interest in immunology, much of his work was spent carrying out what he considered to be routine investigations. Eventually, Rufus Cole, director of the Rockefeller Institute hospital, became acquainted with Avery's research, which included work of general bacteriological interest, such as determining the optimum and limiting hydrogen-ion concentration for pneumococcus growth, developing a simple and rapid method for differentiating human and bovine streptococcus hemolyticus, and studying bacterial nutrition. Impressed with Avery's analytical capabilities, Cole asked Avery to join the institute hospital in 1913. Avery spent the remainder of his career there.

Research Focuses on Pneumonia Virus

At the institute, Avery teamed up with A. Raymond Dochez in the study of the pneumococci (pneumonia) viruses, an area that was to take up a large part of his research efforts over the next several decades. Although Dochez eventually was to leave the institute, he and Avery maintained a lifelong scientific collaboration. During their early time together at the Rockefeller Institute, the two scientists further classified types of pneumococci found in patients and carriers, an effort which led to a better understanding of pneumococcus lung infection and of the causes, incidence, and distribution of lobar pneumonia. During the course of these immunological classification studies, Avery and Dochez discovered specific soluble substances of pneumococcus during growth in a cultured medium. Their subsequent identification of these substances in the blood and urine of lobar pneumonia patients showed that the substances were the result of a true metabolic process and not merely a result of disintegration during cell death.

Avery was convinced that the soluble specific substances present in pneumococci were somehow related to the immunological specificity of bacteria. In 1922, working with Michael Heidelberger and others at Rockefeller, Avery began to focus his studies on the chemical nature of these substances and eventually identified polysaccharides (complex carbohydrates) as the soluble specific substances of pneumococcus. As a result, Avery and colleagues were the first to show that carbohydrates were involved in immune reactions. His laboratory at Rockefeller went on to demonstrate that these substances, which come from the cell wall (specifically the capsular envelopes of the bacteria), can be differentiated into several different serological types by virtue of the various chemical compositions depending on the type of pneumococcus. For example, the polysaccharide in type 1 pneumococci is nitrogen-containing and partly composed of galacturonic acid. Both types 2 and 3 pneumococci contain nitrogen-free carbohydrates as their soluble substances, but the carbohydrates in type 2 are made up mainly of glucose and those of type 3 are composed of aldobionic acid units. Avery and Heidelberger went on to show that these various chemical substances account for bacterial specificity. This work opened up a new era in biochemical research, particularly in establishing the immunologic identity of the cell.

In addition to clarifying and systemizing efforts in bacteriology and immunology, Avery's work laid the foundation for modern immunological investigations in the area of antigens (parts of proteins and carbohydrates) as essential molecular markers that stimulate and, in large part, determine the success of immunological responses. Avery and his colleagues had found that specific anti-infection antibodies worked by neutralizing the bacterial capsular polysac-

charide's ability to interfere with phagocytosis (the production of immune cells that recognize and attack foreign material). Eventually, Avery's discoveries led scientists to develop immunizations that worked by preventing an antigenic response from the capsular material. Avery also oversaw studies that showed similar immunological responses in *Klebsiella pneumonia* and *Hemophilus influenza*. These studies resulted in highly specific diagnostic tests and preparation of immunizing antigens and therapeutic sera. The culmination of Avery's work in this area was a paper he coauthored with **Colin Munro MacLeod** and **Maclyn McCarty** in 1944 entitled "Studies on the Chemical Nature of the Substance Inducing Transformation of Pneumococcal Types. Induction of Transformation by a Desoxyribonucleic Fraction Isolated from Pneumococcus Type III." In their article, which appeared in the *Journal of Experimental Medicine,* the scientists provided conclusive data that DNA is the molecular basis for transmitting genetic information in biological self-replication.

Identifies DNA as the Basis of Heredity

In 1931 Avery's focus turned to "transformation" in bacteria, building on the studies of microbiologist **Frederick Griffith** showing that viruses could transfer virulence. In 1928, Griffith first showed that heat-killed virulent pneumococci could make a nonvirulent strain become virulent (produce disease). In 1932 Griffith stunned the scientific world when he announced that he had manipulated immunological specificity in pneumococci. At the time, Avery was on leave suffering from Grave's disease. He initially denounced Griffith's claim and cited inadequate experimental controls. But in 1931, after returning to work, Avery began to study transmissible hereditary changes in immunological specificity, which were confirmed by several scientists. His subsequent investigations produced one of the great milestones in biology.

In 1933 Avery's associate, James Alloway, had isolated a crude solution of the transforming agent. Immediately, the laboratory's focus turned on purifying this material. Working with type 3 capsulated pneumococcus, Avery eventually succeeded in isolating a highly purified solution of the transforming agent that could pass on the capsular polysaccharides' hereditary information to noncapsulated strains. As a result, the noncapsulated strains could now produce capsular polysaccharides, a trait continued in following generations. The substance responsible for the transfer of genetic information was DNA. These studies also were the first to alter hereditary material for treatment purposes.

Avery, however, remained cautious about the implications of the discovery, suspecting that yet another chemical component of DNA could be responsible for the phenomenon. But further work by McCarty and Moses Kunitz confirmed the findings. While some scientists, such as **Peter Brian Medawar**, hailed Avery's discovery as the first step out of the "dark ages" of genetics, others refused to give up the long-held notion that the protein was the basis of physical inheritance. The subsequent modeling of the DNA molecule by James Watson and Francis Crick led to an understanding of how DNA replicates, and demonstration of DNA's presence in all animals produced clear evidence of its essential role in heredity.

Avery also continued to work on other antigenic aspects of carbohydrates and the immune system. He was the first to create antibody-based treatments that were successful in protecting laboratory animals from infection, essentially by removing the protective capsular coat of the virulent cell. Collaborating with Dochez, he immunologically classified hemolytic (destructive to blood cells) streptococcus and identified many of the specific antigens at work. These efforts revealed that hemolytic streptococcus had many serological types. Eventually hemolytic streptococcus was identified as the infectious agent in scarlet and acute rheumatic fever and hemorrhagic nephritis (kidney disease). Avery's work was the foundation for the eventual discovery of effective antibiotics for hemolytic streptococcus.

Despite the fact that Avery guarded his personal life, some information is known about his interests outside of science. A musician, he played cornet with the New York Conservatory of Music Orchestra and organized his own band. He also painted water colors. An independent Republican, he was a commissioned captain in the U.S. Army Medical Corps during World War I, assigned to the Institute for Medical Research. He served on various advisory committees during World War II, including the U.S. Army Board for the Study and Control of Epidemic Disease.

A highly reserved individual, Avery preferred to be remembered by his scientific accomplishments. He was fondly remembered by many of his colleagues and former students and clearly recognized for his efforts in helping to solve the puzzle of heredity. His honors were many, including several honorary degrees, the Paul Ehrlich Gold Medal, and the Copley Medal of the Royal Society of London. He also was a member of the National Academy of Sciences and foreign member of the Royal Society of London. He continued to conduct research in laboratories at the Rockefeller Institute Hospital for several years after his retirement. Eventually, he moved to Nashville, Tennessee, in 1947. He died there on February 20, 1955.

SELECTED WRITINGS BY AVERY:

Periodicals

(With A. R. Dochez) "Varieties of Pneumococcus and Their Relation to Lobar Pneumonia," *Journal of Experimental Medicine,* Volume 21, 1915, p. 114.

"Determination of Types of Pneumococcus in Lobar Pneumonia: A Rapid Cultural Method," *Journal of the American Medical Association,* Volume 70, 1918, p. 17.

(With M. Heidelberger) "The Specific Soluble Substance of Pneumococcus," *Proceedings of the Society of Experimental Biology and Medicine,* Volume 20, 1923, p. 435.

"The Role of Specific Carbohydrates in Pneumococcus Infection and Immunity," *Annals of Internal Medicine,* Volume 6, 1932, p. 1.

(With Colin Munro MacLeod and Maclyn McCarty) "Studies on the Chemical Nature of the Substance Inducing Transformation of Pneumococcal Types. Induction of Transformation by a Desoxyribonucleic Fraction Isolated from Pneumococcus Type III," *Journal of Experimental Medicine,* Volume 79, 1944, p. 137.

SOURCES:

Books

Biographical Memoirs of Fellows of the Royal Society, Royal Society (London), Volume 2, 1956, pp. 34–47.

Dochez, A. R., "Oswald Theodore Avery," *Biographical Memoirs,* Volume 32, National Academy of Sciences, 1958, pp. 31–48.

Gillispie, Charles Coulston, editor, *Dictionary of Scientific Biography,* Volume 1, Scribner's, 1970, pp. 342–343.

Magner, Lois N. *A History of the Life Sciences,* Marcel Dekker, 1979, pp. 452–454.

McGraw-Hill Modern Men of Science, McGraw Hill, 1966, pp. 15–17.

—*Sketch by David Petechuk*

Julius Axelrod
1912-
American biochemist and pharmacologist

Julius Axelrod is a biochemist and pharmacologist whose discoveries relating to the role of neuro-transmitters in the sympathetic nervous system earned him the Nobel Prize in physiology or medicine in 1970, together with **Ulf von Euler** of Sweden and Sir **Bernard Katz** of Great Britain. As Axelrod himself has said, he was a late starter as a distin-guished scientist, due to both the humble circum-stances of his birth and his coming of age in the Great Depression of the 1930s. He only began real scientific research in 1946, and earned his Ph.D. in 1955. From then on he compensated for lost time and became the first chief of the pharmacology section of the National Institute of Mental Health, a branch of the prestigious National Institutes of Health.

Axelrod was born on May 30, 1912, in a tene-ment house in New York City, the son of Isadore Axelrod, a maker of flower baskets for merchants and grocers, and Molly Leichtling Axelrod. His parents had immigrated to the United States from Polish Galicia in the early years of the century, met and married in New York, and settled in the heavily Jewish area of the Lower East Side of Manhattan. Julius Axelrod attended public elementary and high schools near his home but later recalled that he got his real education in the neighborhood public library, reading voraciously through several books a week, everything from pulp novels to Upton Sinclair and Leo Tolstoy. He studied for a year at New York University, but when his money ran out he trans-ferred to the tuition-free City College of New York, from which he graduated in 1933 with majors in biology and chemistry. He later claimed that he did most of his studying on the long subway rides between his home and the uptown Manhattan campus of City College.

Rejected for Medical School, Axelrod Pursues Research Career

Axelrod applied to several medical schools but was not admitted to any. It has been widely reported, in the *New York Times,* for example, that he failed to get into medical school because of quotas for Jewish applicants. It was difficult to find any work in New York in the depths of the Depression, and Axelrod was fortunate to find employment in 1933 as a laboratory assistant at the New York University Medical School at $25 per month. In 1935 he took a position as chemist at the Laboratory of Industrial Hygiene, a nonprofit organization set up by the New York City Department of Public Health to test vitamin supplements added to foods. He married Sally Taub on August 30, 1938, and they eventually had two sons, Paul Mark and Alfred Nathan. Axelrod took night courses and received an M.A. in chemistry from New York University in 1941. In the early 1940s he lost the sight of one eye in a laboratory accident.

Axelrod later speculated that he might have remained at the Laboratory of Industrial Hygiene for the rest of his working life. The work, he said, was moderately interesting, and the pay adequate. How-ever, in 1946, quite by chance, he received the opportunity to do some real scientific research and found it exciting. The laboratory received a small grant to study the problem of why some persons taking large quantities of acetanilide, a non-aspirin pain-relieving drug, developed methemoglobinemia, the failure of hemoglobin to bind oxygen for delivery throughout the body. Axelrod, who had little experi-ence in such work, consulted Dr. Bernard B. Brodie of Goldwater Memorial Hospital of New York. Brodie was intrigued with the problem and worked closely with Axelrod in finding its solution. He also found Axelrod a place among the research staff at New York University. The two men soon discovered that the body metabolizes acetanilide into a substance with an analgesic effect, and another substance that causes methemoglobinemia. They recommended that the beneficial metabolic product be administered directly, without the use of acetanilide. Related analgesics were investigated in the same manner.

In 1949, Axelrod, Brodie, and several other researchers at Goldwater Hospital were invited to join the National Heart Institute of the National Institutes of Health in Bethesda, Maryland. There Axelrod studied the physiology of caffeine absorption and then turned to the sympathomimetic amines, drugs which mimic the actions of the body's sympathetic nervous system in stimulating the body to prepare for strenu-ous activity. He studied such compounds as amphet-amine, mescaline, and ephedrine and discovered a new group of enzymes which allowed these drugs to metabolize in the body. By the mid 1950s, Axelrod decided that he needed a doctorate to advance in his career at the National Institutes of Health. He took a year off to prepare for comprehensive examinations at George Washington University in the District of Columbia, submitted research work he had already done to satisfy the thesis requirements, and received a Ph.D. in pharmacology in 1955, at the age of forty-three. He was then offered the opportunity to create a section in pharmacology within the Laboratory of Clinical Sciences at the National Institute of Mental Health, another branch of the National Institutes of Health. He became chief of the section in pharmacol-ogy and held that position until his retirement in 1984.

Receives Nobel Prize for Research on Neurotransmitters

In 1957 Axelrod began the research which eventually led to the Nobel Prize. He and his colleagues and students studied the manner in which neurotransmitters, the chemicals which transmit signals from one nerve ending to another across the very small spaces between them, operate in the human body. In the 1940s the Swedish scientist Ulf von Euler had discovered that noradrenaline, or norepinephrine, was the neurotransmitter of the sympathetic nervous system. Axelrod was concerned with the way in which noradrenaline was rapidly deactivated in order to make way for the transmission of later nerve signals. He discovered that this was accomplished in two basic ways. First, he found a new enzyme, which he named catechol-O-methyltransferase (COMT), which was essential to the metabolism, and hence the deactivation, of noradrenaline. Second, through a series of experiments on cats, he determined that noradrenaline was reabsorbed by the nerves and stored to be reused later. These seemingly esoteric discoveries in fact had enormous implications for medical science. Axelrod demonstrated that psychoactive drugs such as antidepressants, amphetamines, and cocaine achieved their effects by inhibiting the normal deactivation or reabsorption of noradrenaline and other neurotransmitters, thus prolonging their impact upon the nervous system or the brain. His experiments also pointed the way to many new discoveries in the rapidly growing field of neurobiological research and the chemical treatment of mental and neurological diseases. The 1978 Nobel Prize in physiology or medicine, shared with Ulf von Euler and Bernard Katz, crowned his achievements in this area.

In his later years, Axelrod has worked in many areas of biochemical and pharmacological research, notably in the study of hormones. Especially important to the advancement of medical science was his development of many new experimental techniques which could be widely applied in the work of other researchers. He also had a great impact through his training of and assistance to a long line of visiting researchers and postdoctoral students at the National Institutes of Health. He continued his own research at the National Institute of Mental Health following his formal retirement in 1984. Early in 1993 Axelrod had the unusual experience of having his own life saved through a scientific discovery he had made many years before. At the age of eighty, he suffered a massive heart attack. The cardiologists at Georgetown University Medical Center soon determined that several of his coronary arteries were almost completely blocked by blood clots and that he must have immediate triple coronary-artery bypass surgery. The complication was that his blood pressure had fallen so dangerously low that he might not survive the operation. The solution to this crisis was to inject a synthetic form of noradrenaline to stimulate the contractions of his heart and thus raise his blood pressure to a more acceptable level. Axelrod survived the operation and within two months was back at work and attending conferences in foreign countries.

SELECTED WRITINGS BY AXELROD:

Periodicals

"Neurotransmitters," *Scientific American,* June, 1974, pp. 59–71.
"An Unexpected Life in Research," *Annual Review of Pharmacology and Toxicology,* 1988, pp. 1–23.

SOURCES:

Periodicals

"Neurobiology: On the Research Frontier," *Science News,* October 24, 1970, p. 331.
Newsweek, October 26, 1970, p. 83.
New York Times, October 16, 1970, pp. 1, 27.
Stevens, Carol, "The Man Who Saved Himself," *Washingtonian,* June, 1993.
Udenfriend, Sidney, "Nobel Prize: Three Share 1970 Award for Medical Research," *Science,* October 23, 1970, pp. 422–423.

—Sketch by John E. Little

Francisco J. Ayala
1934-
Spanish-born American evolutionary geneticist

Well into the age of genetic engineering and cloning, the Darwinian debate continues, and few other scientists have done such concentrated work in elucidating the mechanism of evolution—and thus shedding light on that debate—as Francisco J. Ayala. He has made vital contributions to the modern theory of evolution, both by theory and experiment, examining the rates and patterns of molecular evolution, the causes of genetic polymorphism (the ability of two or more distinct forms of an organism to coexist in the same interbreeding population) or gene mutation (changes in the hereditary material) in one species, the importance of natural selection versus random selec-

Francisco J. Ayala

tion, as well as the role that reproductive isolation and environment play on population growth. Additionally, Ayala has been a major voice in the philosophical and ethical issues related to the study of human evolution.

Francisco Jose Ayala was born in Madrid, Spain, on March 12, 1934, the son of a businessman, Francisco Ayala, and of Soledad (Pereda) Ayala. His early education was attained in the city of his birth, and in 1955 he graduated with a B.S. from the University of Madrid. Six years later, after studies at the University of Salamanca, Ayala came to the United States to study at Columbia University in New York. He earned his M.A. there in 1963 and his Ph.D. in genetics the next year. Following graduation, Ayala remained on the east coast, in and around New York, first as a research associate at Rockefeller University (1964–1965), and then as an assistant professor both at Providence College, Providence Rhode Island (1965–1967), and at Rockefeller University (1967–1971). During these years Ayala worked on an experimental model to relate the amount of genetic polymorphism to the rate of evolutionary change, using principally the *Drosophila,* or various species of the fruit fly as the control subject. His resulting publications established a new understanding of the mechanics of adaptation in evolution. It was also during the late 1960s that Ayala met his future wife, Mary Henderson. They were married on May 27, 1968 and have two children. Ayala became a naturalized United States citizen in 1971.

Continues Research at University of California

It was also in 1971 that Ayala accepted a post as assistant professor of genetics at the University of California at Davis, and was made full professor three years later. He remained at Davis until 1987, when he became a distinguished professor of biological science at the University of California at Irvine. His work since the late 1960s has been focussed in three primary areas: the process of geographic speciation or divergence of species; the study of adaptive significance of genetic variation in various populations; and the process of molecular evolution. In the first of these, Ayala and his researchers studied three groups of species from various parts of the world and were able—by using molecular techniques—to ascertain how much genetic change occurred during the several stages of speciation. In studying adaptive significance, Ayala and his colleagues have been able to demonstrate how environmental factors such as food supply, density of population, and temperature affect the selection of genetic variants. Finally, in the field of molecular evolution, Ayala's studies of DNA cloning have broken new ground and challenged old models of evolutionary change.

Ayala's research in the 1980s with various disease-causing protozoa has also had direct impact on medicine. Various parasitic protozoa affect millions of people worldwide, and Ayala discovered that many of these organisms have a clonal—reproduce by cloning—rather than a sexual population structure. This discovery was vital to the production of vaccines that fight such organisms.

For his work in genetics and evolution, Ayala has been honored with many awards: the Medal of the College of France, 1979; the W. E. Key Award from the American Genetics Association, 1985; and the Scientific Freedom and Responsibility Award of the American Association for the Advancement of Science, 1987, among others. A fellow of scientific societies around the world and the holder of numerous honorary doctorates, Ayala is also an eloquent spokesperson in the debate between evolution and creationism, and has published widely on the humanistic aspects of science.

SELECTED WRITINGS BY AYALA:

Books

(Editor with T. Dobzhansky) *Studies in the Philosophy of Biology,* University of California, 1974.
(Editor) *Molecular Evolution,* Sinauer, 1976.
(With T. Dobzhansky and others) *Evolution,* W. H. Freeman, 1977.

(With J. W. Valentine) *Evolving: The Theory and Process of Organic Evolution,* Benjamin/Cummings, 1979.

(With J. A. Kiger) *Modern Genetics,* Benjamin/Cummings, 1980, 2nd edition, 1984.

Periodicals

"Evolution of Fitness. I.," *Genetics,* Volume 53, 1966, pp. 883–95.

"Experimental Invalidation of the Principle of Competitive Exclusion," *Nature,* Volume 224, 1969, pp. 1076–79.

"Competition Between Species: Frequency Dependence," *Science,* Volume 171, 1971, pp. 820–24.

(With M. E. Gilpin) "Adaptive Foci in Protein Evolution," *Nature,* Volume 253, 1975, pp. 725–26.

"Nothing in Biology Makes Sense Except in the Light of Evolution," *Journal of Heredity,* Volume 68, 1977, pp. 3–10.

(With E. J. Bruce) "Humans and Apes Are Genetically Very Similar," *Nature,* Volume 276, 1978, pp. 264–65.

(With L. D. Mueller) "Dynamics of Single-Species Population Growth," *Ecology,* Volume 62, 1981, pp. 1148–54.

"Genetic Polymorphism," *Experientia,* Volume 39, 1983. pp. 813–23.

(With G. L. Stebbins) "The Evolution of Darwinism," *Scientific American,* Volume 253, 1985, pp. 315–20.

(With others) "Natural Selection vs. Random Drift," *Genetics,* Volume 111, 1985, pp. 517–54.

"Evolution and Creation: One Missed Opportunity," *BioScience,* Volume 37, 1987, p. 450.

(With others) "A Clonal Theory of Parasitic Protozoa," *Proceedings of the National Academy of Science, U.S.A.,* Volume 87, 1990, pp. 214–18.

SOURCES:

Books

Contemporary Authors, Volume 85–88, Gale, 1980, p. 30.

Other

Personal information provided by Francisco J. Ayala, 1993.

—*Sketch by J. Sydney Jones*

Hertha Ayrton
1854-1923
English physicist

Hertha Ayrton's contributions to science in the early-twentieth century included research on areas as diverse as electrical engineering and wave formation. Her inventions included the Ayrton Fan that dispelled poison gases from the trenches in World War I and refinements to early model film projectors. A leading expert on electric arc lamps, she wrote *The Electric Arc,* which became a standard textbook in the field. She became the first woman elected to the Institution of Electrical Engineers and was involved in the suffrage and peace movements.

Hertha Ayrton was born Phoebe Sarah Marks in Portsea, England, the third of Alice Moss Marks' and Levi Marks' five children. Her father was a clock maker and jeweler. After his death in 1861, Alice Marks supported the family by selling her needlework. In spite of the family's limited finances, young Sarah attended the school her aunt ran in London. When she became a teenager, Sarah changed her name to Hertha as an expression of her independence, and, although she remained proud of her Jewish heritage, also regarded herself as an agnostic.

At the age of sixteen Ayrton left school to become a governess in order to help support her family. In 1873 she met Barbara Bodichon, a philanthropist who supported women's causes and had helped found Girton College at Cambridge. With Bodichon's financial assistance, Ayrton entered Girton in 1874 after passing the Cambridge University Examination for Women with honors in mathematics and English. She exhibited an aptitude for science by inventing the sphygmograph, a device that charts pulse beats, before discovering that a similar machine had already been developed. Although her studies were interrupted by illness, Ayrton passed her Cambridge baccalaureate honors examinations in 1881 but did not receive a degree because Cambridge did not offer degrees to women at that time.

Following her graduation, Ayrton taught high school mathematics and later became a private tutor. In 1884 Ayrton invented and patented her line divider, an instrument that could immediately divide a line into any given number of equal parts. This inspired her to launch a career in science, and she enrolled in Finsbury Technical College in London, again with Bodichon's financial assistance. At Finsbury, she worked with W. E. Ayrton, a professor of physics and a pioneer in electrical engineering whom she had first met while she was a teacher. Ayrton was a widower who strongly supported women's rights.

The couple married in 1885; their only child, Barbara Bodichon Ayrton, was born in 1892. In 1893 Ayrton took over her husband's electric arc experiments while he was lecturing in Chicago. Electric arc lamps, which were widely used for lighting at the time, were much in need of improvement: they hissed, hummed, and burned unsteadily. Her experiments solved many of these problems, and she published the results in a series of articles for *The Electrician* in 1895 and 1896. Her conclusions regarding humming arcs led to later discoveries concerning the musical arc—an important step in the development of radio. She also presented several papers on the arc to the British Association, and in 1899 she was invited to read her paper on the cause of the hissing arc to the Institution of Electrical Engineers. She became a recognized authority on the arc and with support from the organization's president was the first woman elected to membership in the Institution of Electrical Engineers. In 1902 Ayrton published a compilation of her findings, *The Electric Arc,* which became the standard text in the field.

By 1901 her husband's health was deteriorating, and they moved to the seaside town of Margate where Ayrton became interested in the action of the ocean's waves and the formation of sand ripples. Her writing on the topic proved noteworthy to the scientific community, and although she had been refused admittance to the Royal Society in 1902, two years later she became the first woman to read her own paper before the group. In 1906 the Society awarded Ayrton its Hughes Medal for her work on the electric arc and sand ripples. The following several years she spent working with the British Admiralty on standardizing types and sizes of carbon for searchlights, and later research involved air currents. In 1912 she developed improved lamp house designs for movie projectors, and during World War I she invented the Ayrton Fan to drive poison gas out of the trenches. She became a founding member of the National Union of Scientific Workers in 1920.

After the war Ayrton continued her research on the fan principles and became active in the suffrage movement, participating in many demonstrations along with her daughter. For a time during these years, Ayrton also provided a home for the ailing **Marie Curie**, whom she had known since 1903. Ayrton died in North Lancing, Sussex, on August 27, 1923.

SELECTED WRITINGS BY AYRTON:

Books

The Electric Arc, [London], 1902.

SOURCES:

Books

Abir-Am, Pnina G., and Dorinda Outram, editors, *Uneasy Careers and Intimate Lives: Woman in Science 1789–1979,* Rutgers University Press, 1989, pp. 115–123.
Dictionary of Scientific Biography, Volume 17, supplement II, Scribner's, 1990, pp. 40–42.
Ogilvie, Marilyn Bailey, *Women in Science: Antiquity through the Nineteenth Century,* MIT Press, 1986, pp. 32–34.

Periodicals

Armstrong, Henry E., "Mrs. Hertha Ayrton," *Nature,* December 1, 1923, pp. 800–801.
Mather, T., "Mrs. Hertha Ayrton," *Nature,* December 29, 1923, p. 939.
Trotter, A.P., "Mrs. Ayrton's Work on the Electric Arc," *Nature,* January 12, 1924, pp. 48–49.

—*Sketch by Kathy Sammis*

B

Walter Baade
1893-1960
German-born American astronomer

W alter Baade's discoveries in astronomy were monumental in their scope. After he discovered that two distinct types of stars existed, he was able to establish a new "yardstick" for the distances of Cepheid variable, or light pulsating, stars. This led to a major reappraisal of the size and age of the universe. Baade also suggested a mechanism for the formation of neutron stars before the existence of such objects had been confirmed. He was responsible for motivating the construction of radio telescopes, devices that use sound to locate celestial bodies, and linking strong radio sources with visual galaxies.

Wilhelm Heinrich Walter Baade (pronounced "Bah-duh"), the son of school teacher Konrad Baade and Charlotte Wulfhorst Baade, was born on March 24, 1893, in Schröttinghausen, Westphalia, Germany. He attended the Friedrichs-Gymnasium (secondary school) from 1903 to 1912. Baade's parents intended for him to study theology as a career and eventually become a Protestant minister. Like many theology students, Baade's eyes were on the heavens, but only when looking through a telescope. Deciding that astronomy offered him more than theology, Baade entered the University of Münster in 1912 and, the following year, went to the University of Göttingen where he served as mathematician Felix Klein's assistant from 1913 to 1919.

Because of persistent trouble from a dislocated hip suffered during birth, Baade was exempt from military service during World War I. He was required, however, to spend eight hours a day performing war work at an installation which tested model airplanes. After receiving his Ph.D. in July of 1919, Baade became an assistant to Richard Schorr at the observatory of the University of Hamburg in Bergedorf.

A meeting in 1920 with American astronomer **Harlow Shapley**, from California's Mount Wilson Observatory, inspired Baade to embark on his own research. He began making discoveries at Bergedorf. In 1920 he discovered a minor planet (known as an asteroid) that turned out to have the most distant orbit of any asteroid known until that time, traveling nearly as far as the orbit of Saturn, the sixth planet from the sun. This remarkable asteroid was dubbed

Walter Baade

"944 Hidalgo" (asteroids receive a number as well as a name). His methodical observations of the sky led to the discovery of a comet two years later: Comet 1922c Baade (comets are identified by the year in which they are discovered; the letter "c" indicates Comet Baade was the third comet discovered in 1922). Coincidentally, Baade would discover another remarkable asteroid in 1948, one that had the closest orbit to the sun. Identified as 1566 Icarus after the mythological character who built wings and flew too close to the sun, the asteroid comes as close as 29 million kilometers (18 million miles) to the sun. That's closer than Mercury, the planet nearest the sun. (Most asteroids, which Baade, tongue-in-cheek, called "vermin in the sky," orbit the sun between the arcs of Mars and Jupiter.)

His meeting with Shapley interested Baade in the study of pulsating variable stars within distant globular star clusters. The relatively small size of the telescope at Bergedorf was a handicap for Baade; its mirror had a diameter of only one meter (39.4 inches) and the proximity of Hamburg, with its haze and light pollution, contributed to the poor visibility. Nonetheless, Baade began observing the clusters and, in 1926,

83

offered a suggestion to prove that the surface of the pulsating stars physically rises and falls.

Happiness and Disappointment

The results of his work won Baade a Rockefeller fellowship, which provided him with the funds to attain his dream of visiting the big telescopes in California. He returned to Bergedorf in 1927 and was promoted to observer, but he became disappointed when his request that the telescope be moved to a better location was ignored. Rejecting the offer of a job at Jena, which had worse observing conditions than Bergedorf, he became a Privatdozent (private tutor) in 1928. In 1929 Baade married Hanni Bohlmann, a calculator at the Hamburg Observatory, and later romantically named a new asteroid "Muschi," which was her nickname.

The opportunity of a lifetime presented itself to Baade in 1931: an invitation to join the staff at the Mount Wilson Observatory. He accepted the post instantly, quit his position in Hamburg, and headed to California. It was a dream come true, for the best telescopes in the world were now at his disposal. Although the skies were clearer than those to which he was accustomed, the city of Los Angeles, with its light pollution and smog, presented some problems. This, however, was a small price for Baade to pay in exchange for the chance to study distant galaxies with **Edwin Hubble** and examine supernovas with Fritz Zwicky.

In his work with Zwicky, Baade hypothesized about the mechanisms leading up to and following a supernova explosion in space. Baade and Zwicky believed that a supernova results when a massive star collapses upon itself. Most stars produce light and energy by turning hydrogen atoms into helium atoms, a process called nuclear fusion. Once a large star had depleted the hydrogen at its core, Baade and Zwicky speculated, the core of the star would contract under its tremendous gravitation since the outward push of radiation pressure caused by the fusion had ceased. This would raise the temperature of the core and permit helium atoms to begin fusing into carbon atoms, releasing energy and halting the contraction of the core. In very large stars, this process would repeat itself several times until iron atoms were being produced within the core. Once the core was composed of iron, no more fusion could take place, and under tremendous gravitational pressure, the star's center would collapse, releasing the gravitational energy that held it in place, as well as most of the star's mass. This released energy would combine with many of the star's particles and carry them at high speeds away from the star, resulting in the bright light that characterizes a supernova. Particles without a positive or negative charge would not couple with energy and would thus be left behind, creating a new star comprised entirely of neutral particles, or neutrons. Baade and Zwicky explained that in this manner a supernova would create a neutron star.

Dark Days, Darker Nights

When the United States entered World War II in 1941, Baade, because of his German ancestry, found himself classified as an "enemy alien." He had applied for American citizenship but the papers had been lost. He was scornful of bureaucracy and never bothered to complete the process. Because of his status, Baade was prohibited from engaging in war work, which other astronomers were required to do, and that meant he could concentrate on his purely scientific investigations. Then, because of the fear of a Japanese invasion along the West coast, a blackout was imposed; the sky over Los Angeles was very dark.

At Baade's disposal were the 1.5-meter (60-inch) and 2.5-meter (100-inch) telescopes and, in the darkened skies, they afforded him an unparalleled view of the cosmos. Up to this point, individual stars within the spiral arms of galaxies had been seen by Hubble but not those within the bright, glowing core. Using the larger telescope, Baade was able to photograph individual stars within the center of the Andromeda Galaxy and its two companion galaxies. Baade noticed a difference between the stars in the spiral arms, whose blue color indicated that they were hot and relatively young, and the stars in the core, whose red color defined them as older, cooler stars. Baade classified the younger blue stars as Population I and the older red stars as Population II (also known as Type I and Type II).

In 1948, Baade was also able to identify over three hundred Cepheid variable stars in the Andromeda Galaxy with the 5-meter (200-inch) telescope on Mt. Palomar near San Diego, California. Cepheid variable stars brighten and dim at a regular rate. In 1904 American astronomer **Henrietta Leavitt** discovered that the longer a Cepheid's period (or length of pulsation) the brighter the star's luminosity. Her findings were incorporated by astronomer **Ejnar Hertzsprung** into a period-luminosity curve, which enabled astronomers to determine a star's distance from the earth and further, to use these calculations to estimate distances to other objects in the universe. Baade's observations of Cepheid stars, which he found in both Population I and Population II, showed that Hertzsprung's period-luminosity curve was valid only for estimating the distance to Population II stars. Yet the generally accepted measurements of distances to stars, other galaxies, and the size of the universe, were based on observations of Population I stars. Thus, Baade determined that many current estimates of cosmic distances were incorrect.

Presents New Measurements of the Universe

Baade used his data to establish a new period-luminosity curve. He presented the results at the meeting of the International Astronomical Union in Rome in 1952, showing that many currently accepted measurements of the universe had to be revised. The distances to all the galaxies, the size of the universe, and, more importantly, the age of the universe, were double what had been believed. The distance to the Andromeda Galaxy was not eight hundred thousand light-years, as Hubble had calculated; it was closer to two million light-years.

The concept of an older universe had enormous ramifications. First of all, it introduced complications to the "Steady-State" theory of the origin of the universe. The theory, suggested in 1948 by **Thomas Gold** and Hermann Bondi, and popularized by English astronomer **Fred Hoyle**, held that the universe was perpetual; that there was no beginning and would be no end. Steady-State was at odds with **George Gamow**'s "big bang" theory, which proposes that the universe was born out of a cosmic explosion and has continually expanded over time. An older universe meant there had been more time for the expansion to have occurred, and this concept fit in nicely with the big bang theory.

Although proponents of steady-state were unhappy with Baade's assertions, geologists were delighted. In a big-band universe, the size of the cosmos is correlated with the time elapsed since its creation, so Baade's findings meant that the earth had more time to evolve, and was therefore older than previously believed. Geologists had been certain the crust of the earth was at least three billion years old, but using the smaller cosmic measurements, as defined by Hubble, the age of the earth had been limited to only two billion years.

The idea of a larger universe gave scientists and the public alike pause; in a vaster universe, the other galaxies had to be much farther away, hence they had to be much larger and brighter than realized in order to be seen. Astronomers began to view the cosmos in much larger terms. Gone was the picture of individual galaxies sprinkled randomly across the heavens. Now, clusters and super-clusters of galaxies were envisioned. Our Milky Way Galaxy was no longer arrogantly considered a huge object amid smaller satellite galaxies. The shock of realization must have been very similar to that which the sixteenth-century astronomer Nicholas Copernicus unleashed when he proposed the earth was not the center of the solar system, and what Shapley caused when he showed the sun was not at the center of the Milky Way.

"Tuning in" on the Sky

As one might expect, astronomy became a very hot topic following Baade's announcement. The re-sults spurred the construction of bigger and better radio-telescopes that could "see" farther than their optical cousins and detect strong sources of outer-space radiation that were believed to be part of the Milky Way. Baade and his associate, **Rudolph Minkowski**, initiated a survey to identify the strong radio sources visually. Baade and Minkowski identified radio sources Cygnus A and Perseus A, which had been thought to be located within the Milky Way, as distant galaxies actually located far outside our galaxy. Baade identified another galaxy, known as M–87 and identified with radio source Virgo A, which showed a peculiar, strongly polarized jet of light extending from it. The object is now considered to be a quasar (a celestial object, possibly a massive black hole at the center of a distant galaxy that discharges great quantities of energy). His study of the polarization of the Crab Nebula revealed its magnetic field and the synchrotron radiation (radiation emitted by highly charged particles that are accelerated by a magnetic field) of the exploded star that created it.

In 1958 Baade retired and gave a series of lectures at Harvard which were published after his death as *Evolution of Stars and Galaxies* in 1963. He followed his lectures with a trip to Australia, where the 1.9-meter (74-inch) telescope at Mt. Stromlo provided an excellent view of the southern hemisphere's sky, and he returned to University of Göttingen to accept a position as Gauss professor. Perhaps ill-advisedly, he had an operation for his congenital hip problem which required six months' bed rest for recuperation. This may have contributed to his death, due to respiratory failure, on June 25, 1960.

Baade did not like publishing his papers. In some cases he was dissatisfied with the work; he also found writing to be a tedious job and preferred to be active in research. A tribute was bestowed by Fred Hoyle who, as quoted in the *Dictionary of Scientific Biography,* remarked of the few papers Baade had written: "Almost every one of Baade's papers turned out to have far-reaching consequences." In spite of Baade's great advances in astronomy, he received very few honors. The Gold Medal of Great Britain's Royal Astronomical Society was bestowed *in absentia* in 1954 for his investigations of galactic and extragalactic objects, and he received the Bruce Medal from the Astronomical Society of the Pacific in 1955. Baade was, however, perhaps happier performing research and revising concepts about the universe than receiving awards.

SELECTED WRITINGS BY BAADE:

Books

Evolution of Stars and Galaxies, edited by Cecilia Payne-Gaposhkin from tape recordings of Baade's Harvard lectures, [Cambridge, MA], 1963.

Periodicals

(With Rudolph Minkowski) "Spectrophotometric Investigations of Some O- and B-type Stars Connected with the Orion Nebula," *Astrophysical Journal,* Volume 86, 1937, pp. 119–22, 123–35.

(With Edwin Hubble) "New Stellar Systems in Sculptor and Fornax," *Publications of the Astronomical Society of the Pacific,* Volume 51, 1938, pp. 40–44.

(With Fritz Zwicky) "The Crab Nebula," *Astrophysical Journal,* Volume 88, 1938, pp. 411–21.

"A Program of Extragalactic Research for the 200-inch Hale Telescope," *Publications of the Astronomical Society of the Pacific,* Volume 60, 1948, pp. 230–34.

(With Lyman Spitzer, Jr.) "Stellar Populations and Collisions of Galaxies," *Astrophysical Journal,* Volume 113, 1950, pp. 413–18.

(With Minkowski) "On the Identification of Radio Sources," *Astrophysical Journal,* Volume 119, 1954, pp. 215–31.

"Polarization in the Jet of Messier 87," *Astrophysical Journal,* Volume 123, 1956, pp. 550–51.

Other

"Bahnbestimmung des spektroskopischen Doppelsterns β Lyrae nach Spectrogrammen von Prof. Hartmann," lecture at Göttingen, August 3, 1921.

SOURCES:

Books

Abbott, David, *Biographical Dictionary of Scientists, Astronomers,* Peter Bedrick Books, 1984.

Abell, George, David Morrison, and Sidney Wolfe, *Exploration of the Universe,* sixth edition, Holt, 1991.

Gillispie, Charles Coulston, editor, *Dictionary of Scientific Biography,* Scribner, 1971.

Modern Men of Science, McGraw-Hill, 1966.

—*Sketch by Raymond E. Bullock*

Howard L. Bachrach
1920-
American biochemist and molecular biologist

Howard L. Bachrach has been awarded more than two dozen honors, including the National Medal of Science in 1983, for his pioneering research in the molecular biology of viruses. After earning a bachelor's degree in chemistry from the University of Minnesota in 1942, he chose to specialize in organic chemistry and biochemistry and received his Ph.D. in these fields in 1949. Bachrach spent the war years doing research on the development of chemical explosives and then was sent by the U.S. Department of Agriculture (USDA) to Denmark to learn more about foot-and-mouth disease (FMD). In 1953, Bachrach accepted an appointment as head of biochemical research at the USDA's Plum Island Animal Disease Center, an affiliation he maintained for the next four decades. During the 1970s, he developed a method for producing FMD vaccine by means of recombinant DNA (genetic engineering) techniques.

Bachrach was born on May 21, 1920, in Faribault, Minnesota. His parents were Elizabeth P. and Harry Bachrach, the owner of a clothing store for men and boys. Bachrach attended Faribault High School, from which he graduated as salutatorian in 1938. That fall, he entered the University of Minnesota, to major in chemistry. He graduated with a B.S. *cum laude* in that field four years later, having also been inducted into the Phi Lambda Upsilon national honorary fraternity in chemistry and the Gamma Alpha honorary fraternity in science. After graduation, Bachrach worked briefly for the Joseph E. Seagram Company before joining the war effort with the Office of Scientific Research and Development at the Carnegie Institute of Technology. His first work there involved research on chemical explosives. He was later assigned to a problem closer to his own field, being asked to study the chemical changes that take place as bread becomes stale. This research had been requested by the Quartermaster Corp of the U.S. Army in its attempt to find ways of preserving food for longer periods of time.

Begins Pioneering Work on Hog Cholera

At war's end, Bachrach returned to the University of Minnesota, where he undertook a doctoral program in biochemistry. He completed that program in 1949 and received his Ph.D. His doctoral thesis involved a study of the virus that causes cholera in hogs, a disease that cost the swine industry millions of dollars in losses each year. Bachrach was able to demonstrate that hog cholera is produced not only by the virus itself, but also by a soluble protein that it produces.

Bachrach's background in viral immunology made him a logical candidate for important research then going on in connection with FMD. Prior to the 1930s, this disease had caused enormous losses in the U.S. livestock industry. It had been brought under control, however, and no cases had been reported in this country since 1929. During the 1940s, however, the disease had reappeared in Mexico and was spreading rapidly. The USDA became concerned about the possible spread of the disease into the United States and had begun a crash program to find ways of protecting the U.S. livestock industry against its reappearance here.

As part of that program, the USDA invited Bachrach to spend a year in Denmark studying at the USDA's European Commission on Foot-and-Mouth Disease laboratories. That experience provided him with invaluable knowledge about the FMD virus and about viral immunology in general.

Having completed his year in Denmark, Bachrach accepted an appointment at the University of California's Virus Laboratory in Berkeley, where he worked with Nobel Laureate biochemist **Wendell Meredith Stanley**. At Berkeley, Bachrach's major accomplishment was the first purification of the poliomyelitis virus. He was also able to obtain the first pictures of the virus using the university's electron microscope.

Begins a Forty-Year Affiliation with the USDA

At the conclusion of his three years at the Virus Laboratory, in 1953, Bachrach was offered an appointment as head of the Chemical and Physical Investigations Section of the USDA's Plum Island Animal Disease Center in Greenport, New York. There he continued his efforts to develop a vaccine for FMD. Among the many discoveries he made during his four decades at Plum Island was that certain portions of the virus known as capsid proteins are able to produce an immune response in an organism even though the proteins themselves are not infectious. Working with scientists at the Genentech Corporation, he was able to incorporate these proteins into carrier molecules by means of gene splicing techniques. The resulting product was the first effective vaccine for use in humans or other animals produced by genetic engineering techniques.

The techniques developed by Bachrach hold promise for the development of other types of viral vaccines. One line of research, for example, involves the search for a human immunodeficiency virus (HIV) vaccine, one that involves the incorporation by gene splicing of a capsid protein from the virus into a carrier molecule.

In 1961 Bachrach became chief scientist at Plum Island, besides continuing in his post as the head of biochemical research. Twenty years later, Bachrach ended his most intensive duties at Plum Island but maintained his relationship with the research center. Although officially retired, he continues his research on viral diseases there. From 1981 on he has also been particularly active as a consultant to a number of organizations, including the Walter Reed Army Institute for Research, the Office of Technology Assessment, the National Research Council, the National Cancer Institute, and the Texas A&M University Institute of Biosciences and Technology.

Bachrach was awarded the National Medal of Science in 1983 for his work in molecular virology and his role in developing gene-splicing techniques. He has also been awarded a USDA Certificate of Merit (1960), a U.S. Presidential Citation (1965), the AAAS-Newcomb Cleveland Prize (1982), the USDA Distinguished Service Award (1982), and the Alexander von Humboldt Award (1983). He was elected to the National Academy of Sciences in 1982 and to the USDA's Agricultural Research Service's Science Hall of Fame in 1987.

Bachrach was married to Shirley Faye Lichterman on June 13, 1943. They had two children, Eve Elizabeth, an attorney, and Harrison Jay, a physician. Bachrach lists his hobbies as golf, walking, gardening, photography, and his family.

SELECTED WRITINGS BY BACHRACH:

Periodicals

(With C. E. Schwerdt) "Purification Studies on Lansing Poliomyelitis Virus II: Analytical Electron Microscopic Identification of the Infectious Particle in Preparation of High Specific Infectivity," *Journal of Immunology,* 72, 1954, pp. 30–38.

(With D. M. Moore, P. D. McKercher, and J. Polatnick) "Immune and Antibody Responses to an Isolated Capsid Protein of Foot-and-Mouth Disease Virus," *Journal of Immunology,* 115, 1975, pp. 1636–1641.

(With D. G. Kleid and others) "Cloned Viral Protein Vaccine for Foot-and-Mouth Disease: Responses in Cattle and Swine," *Science,* 214, 1981, pp. 1125–1129.

SOURCES:

Poppensiek, George C., letter to Norman Hackerman, January 10, 1989.

—Sketch by David E. Newton

John Backus
1924-

American computer scientist

Winner of the 1993 Charles Stark Draper Prize, a prestigious engineering award, the 1977 Association for Computing Machinery's (ACM) Turing Award, and the 1975 National Medal of Science, John Backus headed a pioneering group of IBM engineers, who in the 1950s developed FORTRAN, the first widely used programming language. FORTRAN, which gave programmers the freedom from the tedious task of writing out instructions as strings of 1s and 0s, is the precursor of nearly all contemporary computer languages.

Backus was born in Philadelphia, Pennsylvania, in 1924, and grew up in Wilmington, Delaware. Planning to major in chemical engineering, he enrolled in the University of Virginia in 1942, but was thrown out after one semester for cutting classes. He was drafted into the army in early 1943, where he first served in an antiaircraft program. From September 1943 until March of 1944 he studied engineering at the University of Pittsburgh as part of the army's specialized training. This was followed by six months of premedical training in a hospital in Atlantic City, New Jersey, and an additional six months at Flower and Fifth Avenue Medical School in New York City. By May of 1946 Backus had left behind both the army and his interest in a medical career.

Remaining in New York City he entered the Radio Television Institute, a training school for radio and television repairmen. It was here that he developed an interest in mathematics and began taking courses in math at Columbia University. He earned a bachelor of arts degree in 1949, and the following year he received a master's degree, also from Columbia, and also in mathematics. Upon graduation, he went directly to work for IBM even though he knew very little about computers. One of the very few programmers in the computer industry in the early 1950s, Backus soon earned a reputation as a trailblazer in the field.

Develops and Promotes the Use of FORTRAN

In 1952 he led the group of IBM researchers who produced the Speedcoding system for the IBM 701 computer. The following year Backus, while a project manager, wrote a memo to his boss, Cuthbert Hurd, outlining the need for a general-purpose, high-level computer programming language. The programming language was called FORTRAN (an acronym for formula translator) and was designed to perform mathematical, scientific, and engineering computa-tions on the IBM 704 computer. More importantly, FORTRAN was developed to serve as a translator between the human user and the computer brain, which at that time could only think in zeroes and ones. In the 1950s computers were somewhat rare and prohibitively expensive, also, three-quarters of the cost of running a computer was given to debugging and programming; FORTRAN was created to address these problems.

In an interview in 1978 Backus noted: "In the early 1950s, because of the lack of high-level languages, the cost of programming was at least equal to that of the equipment, and this held back the development of computers." To overcome this difficulty, Backus and his team of fellow researchers at IBM, pursued the idea of developing languages that were easy to use and efficient translators. Although the odds against success in developing such a program were great, Backus was able to convince the IBM directors that it was possible. The language proved to be a useful tool for IBM, helpful in promoting its computers. In addition, FORTRAN, despite being written for one IBM computer, was quickly adopted to be used with other systems, and continues to be used today.

The FORTRAN compiler (a compiler is a computer program designed to translate high-level language statements into a form that can directly activate the computer hardware), considered to be the forerunner of all modern compilers, was the first to have the power and scope to perform the complicated computing tasks that had previously been done by handwritten machine-code programs. With its innovative capabilities, FORTRAN quickly became the most important innovation in the history of programming languages. People using FORTRAN were able to deal with computers without knowing the internal workings of the machine and its assembly languages.

In 1954 IBM published the first version of the language, FORTRAN I. Although there were bugs in this original version, by 1955 Backus, in collaboration with R.A. Nelson and I. Ziller, began work on correcting them. Several changes were made in the original language enabling FORTRAN to evolve along lines that were suggested by the experience gained with its usage. During the late 1950s there were two opposing views on programming languages. A mainly American group contended that only specialized languages could meet the needs of users; at the same time, a European group of scientists expressed the concern that this view led to too many programming languages. Dr. F. Bauer of the University of Munich, Germany, initiated the movement to define a multipurpose language that would be completely independent of specific computers, and in which any algorithm could be clearly stated. Bauer approached the American Association of Computing Machinery (ACM) who, in turn, formed a committee to cooperate with the Europeans. In the spring of 1958 a meeting was held in Zurich, Switzerland, and the committee later published a report defining an International Algebraic Language, later called AL-GOL.

Joins International Computer Programming and Design Team

Backus, who was part of the American group that met in Zurich, moved his research to IBM's Watson Research Center in Yorktown Heights, New York, to become part of the international programming and design team that created ALGOL. Although ALGOL never gained widespread use commercially, it had an important influence on three other widely used programming languages: Pascal, C, and Alda. In 1978 Backus, still working on ways to improve computer languages, wrote a paper suggesting that they should be restructured. "Programming languages appear to be in trouble," he wrote, "conventional languages create unnecessary confusion in the way we think about programs." By the early 1980s he had become an IBM Fellow, which enabled him to devote his time to his own research projects, including advancing mathematical theories of programming. "The complacent acceptance most of us give to these enormous, weak languages has puzzled and disturbed me for a long time," he said, "I have tried to analyze some of the basic defects of conventional languages and show that those defects cannot be resolved unless we discover a new kind of language framework."

Backus has spent the last ten years pursuing his search for a more efficient programming language. Designed with great care and attention to logic, his "functional" language is constructed from ones already defined, thereby eliminating the programmer's need to spell out every instruction in minute detail. "Our goal is to produce a functional language ... so that you can run functional programs on personal computers," he has explained, describing his language. He retired from IBM in 1991 after forty-one years with the company. He lives in San Francisco where he continues to work on programming research and to keep an eye on his functional programming language, which is still gaining in popularity.

SOURCES:

Books

Moreau, R., *The Computer Comes of Age,* MIT Press, 1984.

Slater, Robert, *Portraits in Silicon,* MIT Press, 1987.

Periodicals

"In the Beginning," *Datamation,* September, 1982, pp. 51–52.

Pauly, David with Gerald C. Lubenow, "IBM's Mavericks in the Lab," *Newsweek,* January 10, 1983, p. 58.

Peterson, Ivars, "Computer Languages: In Search of a Better Bug Finder," *Science News,* Volume 124, September 24, 1983, pp. 202–203.

—Sketch by Dorothy Spencer

Johann Friedrich Wilhelm Adolf von Baeyer
1835-1917
German chemist

Johann Friedrich Wilhelm Adolf von Baeyer was a German organic chemist best known for synthesizing a wide variety of important compounds, including barbituric acid and indigo. Additionally, Baeyer also conducted research on phthalein dyes, concentrating his later research efforts to expanded knowledge of synthetic compounds and to develop a theory explaining the stability of five- and six-carbon rings. For his accomplishments in compound synthesis, Baeyer was awarded the 1905 Nobel Prize in chemistry.

Baeyer was born in Berlin on October 31, 1835. His father, Johann Jacob Baeyer, was an officer in the Prussian army who also conducted geodetic surveys for the Prussian government, and his mother, Eugenie Hitzig, was the daughter of a prominent authority on criminal law and historian of literature. Baeyer developed an interest in science at an early age, and chemistry was the subject that intrigued him most. In his autobiography, *Erinnerungen aus meinem Leben,* he reports that he carried out his first chemical experiments at the age of nine and, three years later, discovered a previously unknown double carbonate of copper and sodium. At age thirteen, Baeyer performed his first experiments with indigo, the compound that later made him famous.

Baeyer attended the Friedrich Wilhelm Gymnasium in Berlin, where he assisted his science teacher with chemistry lectures. Upon his graduation in 1853, Baeyer entered the University of Berlin, intending to major in mathematics and physics. Two years later he left the university for a year of military service and then decided to continue his college education. By now Baeyer was committed to a program in chemistry and elected to attend the University of Heidelberg as Berlin had no chemistry laboratories. Heidelberg's chemistry department was headed by Robert Bunsen, a brilliant scholar responsible for developing such things as the electric cell and the Bunsen burner. Bunsen, however, had little interest in organic chemistry, the field that had become Baeyer's passion. As a result, Baeyer soon found himself gravitating toward the laboratories of Friedrich Kekulé, a German chemist known for his work on organic compounds. At this time Kekulé was a privatdozent at Heidelberg and one of the few organic chemists of the time. Although his collaboration with Kekulé was interesting and productive, Baeyer returned to Berlin in 1858 to complete his doctoral work on the compound known as cacodylic (arsenic methyl chloride).

Baeyer Synthesizes Barbituric Acid and Indigo

After receiving his degree, Baeyer returned to work with Kekulé, who had by now accepted a call to the University of Ghent. Two years later, in 1860, Baeyer returned to Berlin and took a position at the Berlin Institute of Technology. Although his salary was very low, he had a large, relatively well-equipped laboratory in which to work and he remained at the institute for twelve years. It was during this time that he made most of his important discoveries, the first of which was developing a derivative of uric acid, in 1863. Barbituric acid is the parent compound of a group of drugs known as the *barbiturates,* which have a number of medical applications.

It was also at this time that Baeyer began his classic research on the dye indigo. For centuries the beautiful blue dye had been obtained from the plant of the same name, but its extraction was a costly process. By 1866 Baeyer had found a method for determining the approximate structural formula of indigo and then, four years later, first produced the compound synthetically in his laboratory. Baeyer continued to work on indigo for another two decades, finally announcing an even more precise formula for the compound in 1883.

Baeyer's years at the Berlin Institute of Technology were marked by a number of other important discoveries. In 1871, for example, he first reported on the structures of the dyes phenolphthalein and fluorescein. One of his students, Karl Graebe, determined the structure of another important dye, alizarin, by means of a technique outlined by Baeyer and after Baeyer had ordered him to do the experiment. In 1872 Baeyer was called to be professor of chemistry at the University of Strasbourg, the first significant academic appointment in his career. His most notable accomplishment at Strasbourg was the development of methods for preparing condensation products from the reaction between phenol and formaldehyde. Three decades later, Leo Baekeland would adapt Baeyer's

method in the synthesis of a phenol-formaldehyde resin known as bakelite, one of the world's first commercial plastics.

Success and Recognition Come to Baeyer at Munich

Baeyer reached the pinnacle of his career in 1875 when he was appointed professor of organic chemistry at the University of Munich. In the forty years he held this post, Baeyer wielded enormous influence on his profession, largely through the students he trained but also as a result of his continued research. His most important achievement during this period was the theory of strain that he developed to explain the structure of ring compounds. Extending Kekulé's work on the tetrahedral bonding of the carbon atom, Baeyer concluded that five- and six-membered rings are dynamically more stable than are rings with greater or lesser numbers of atoms, thus accounting for the much larger number of compounds of the former type.

Baeyer continued to perform most of his academic duties into his eightieth year. He then retired to his country house near Lake Starnberg, where he died on August 20, 1917. He had been married in 1868 to Lida Bendemann, and the couple had three children: Eugenie, Hans, and Otto. In addition to the 1905 Nobel Prize in chemistry, the honors accorded Baeyer included the Liebig Medal of the Congress of Berlin Chemists and the Davy Medal of the Royal Society. In 1885, King Ludwig II of Bavaria made Baeyer a member of the nobility, allowing him to add the honorific "von" to his name.

SELECTED WRITINGS BY BAEYER:

Books

Gesammelte Werke, Fr. Vieweg und Sohn, 1905.
Erinnerungen aus meinem Leben, Braunschweig, 1905.

SOURCES:

Books

Gillispie, Charles Coulson, editor, *Dictionary of Scientific Biography,* Volume 1, Scribner, 1975, pp. 389–391.
Schmorl, Karl, *Adolf von Baeyer,* Wissenschaftliche Verlagsgesellschaft, 1952.
Steinmüller, Frank, "Adolf von Baeyer," Laylin K. James, editor, *Nobel Laureates in Chemistry, 1901–1992,* American Chemical Society and the Chemical Heritage Foundation, 1993, pp. 30–34.

Willstätter, Richard, "Adolf Baeyer," Eduard Farber, editor, *Great Chemists,* Interscience, 1961, pp. 734–47.

—*Sketch by David E. Newton*

Albert V. Baez
1912-
Mexican-born American physicist

Albert V. Baez conducted pioneering work with X rays that laid important foundations for the newly developing science of X-ray imaging optics and had important applications to X-ray optics many years later. He went on to become an outstanding and highly effective promoter of science education worldwide.

Albert Vinicio Baez was born in Puebla, Mexico, on November 15, 1912, the son of Alberto Baez, a Methodist minister, and Thalia Baez. He grew up in Brooklyn, New York, where his mother was a social worker for the YWCA. He earned his B.A. in mathematics and physics from Drew University in 1933 and his M.A. in mathematics from Syracuse University in 1935, then taught physics and mathematics at Morris Junior College, Drew, and Wagner College. In 1936 Baez married Joan C. Bridge; they had three daughters: Pauline, Joan (who would become a well-known folk singer), and Mimi. Baez became a naturalized U.S. citizen in 1938. During World War II, Baez went to Stanford University to teach a physics course for the U.S. Army and stayed on, teaching and conducting graduate research under Paul Kirkpatrick. In a speech on "The Early Days of X-Ray Optics," Baez recalled earning thirty-five cents an hour for scavenging through the physics machine shop debris for materials with which to build laboratory equipment. Kirkpatrick and Baez built the first X-ray microscope, which used mirrors to produce the first focused X rays; they coined the term "X-ray optics" for Baez's dissertation, for which he received a Ph.D. in 1950.

From 1950 to 1956 Baez was professor of physics at the University of Redlands in California, with a year's leave from 1951 to 1952 to teach physics at the University of Baghdad in Iraq. At Redlands, Baez attempted to make an X-ray hologram using an X-ray source with a very small focal spot, but the X rays could not be focused finely enough. In 1960 Baez worked at the Smithsonian Astrophysical Observatory in Cambridge, Massachusetts, developing a single Fresnel zone plate (a flat device for focusing radiation using concentric circular elements) that could focus X rays and modifying the X-ray microscope principle by using nested arrays of curved mirrors, a concept that was later incorporated in the plans for an X-ray telescope intended for use in space in the 1990s.

The launch of the Russian satellite *Sputnik* in 1957 focused attention in the United States on the teaching of science, and Baez increasingly devoted himself to these efforts. From 1958 to 1960 he was the studio physicist for the first films produced by the newly formed Physical Science Study Committee, aimed at improving the teaching of high school physics. This led to an invitation from UNESCO to be its first director of the Division of Science Teaching in Paris. From 1961 to 1967 Baez oversaw programs that helped developing nations design science and math curricula adapted to their cultures and individual conditions and also promoted innovative methods for teaching science. From 1967 to 1974 Baez produced nearly one hundred educational physics films for the Encyclopaedia Britannica Educational Corporation.

During his career Baez was also associated as a teacher or researcher with Harvey Mudd College, England's Open University, the University of Maryland, Harvard University, the University of California's Lawrence Hall of Science, the Algerian Institute of Electricity and Electronics, and the National Polytechnic Institute of Mexico. At Harvard, Baez was a member of the summer school faculty and honorary research associate from 1967 to 1971. Both Drew and Open University awarded him honorary doctoral degrees. He also chaired and acted as consultant to a number of bodies concerned with science education. Toward the end of the 1970s, Baez entered into what he has called a "peripatetic" retirement. He was drawn into the environmental movement after becoming chairman (from 1979 to 1983, and later chairman emeritus) of the Commission on Education of the International Union for Conservation of Nature and Natural Resources. In 1986 he became president of Vivamos Mejor ("Let Us Live Better")/USA, an organization that sponsors improvements in health, housing, and nutrition and environmentally beneficial technologies in Latin America. He went on to worldwide lecturing on topics such as holography, the physics of music, and science education. In 1991 he and Kirkpatrick were awarded the Dennis Gabor Award of the International Society for Optical Engineering in recognition of their pioneering contributions to the development of X-ray imaging microscopes and telescopes.

SELECTED WRITINGS BY BAEZ:

Books

The New College Physics: A Spiral Approach, W. H. Freeman, 1967.

Innovation in Science Education—World-Wide,
    UNESCO, 1976.
(Editor with John Smyth and Gary Knamiller)
    *The Environment and Science and Technology
    Education,* Pergamon, 1987.
(With wife, Joan Baez, Sr.) *A Year in Baghdad,*
    John Daniel & Co., 1988.

SOURCES:

Periodicals

"American Association of Physics Teachers: Dis-
    tinguished Service Citations for 1978," *Ameri-
    can Journal of Physics,* March, 1980, p. 179.

Other

Baez, A. V., "The Early Days of X-Ray Optics:
    New Light—New Knowledge" (speech), Ad-
    vanced Light Source Annual User's Associa-
    tion, 1993.
"Paul Kirkpatrick and Albert V. Baez Share the
    1991 Dennis Gabor Award," news release, In-
    ternational Society for Optical Engineering,
    October 16, 1991.

                                    —Sketch by Kathy Sammis

Florence Merriam Bailey
1863-1948
American ornithologist

A prominent ornithologist, Florence Merriam Bailey wrote numerous works for a wide range of
people interested in birding. In addition to publishing
technical guides for specialists in the field, Bailey was
able to pique the interest of young people and novices
through her informative and entertaining books.

The last of four children, Florence Augusta
Merriam was born to Clinton Levi Merriam and
Caroline Hart Merriam on August 8, 1863, in Locust
Grove, a New York village in Lewis County. Mer-
riam's mother was the daughter of County Judge Levi
Hart. Her father, a merchant banker, retired about the
time Merriam was born.

Merriam's love of nature was inspired by the
natural setting of her family's home in the foothills of
the Adirondack Mountains. It was also nurtured by
her father and by her brother, Clinton, a physician

and a naturalist, who eventually became the chief of
the U.S. Biological Survey.

Because she planned to be a writer, Merriam
attended the newly-opened Smith College in Northampton, Massachusetts, for four years as a special
student. Although she left in 1886 without a degree,
Smith awarded her one in 1921. While at Smith,
Merriam led nature groups into the countryside,
founded one of the nation's first Audubon societies,
and wrote articles on birds for *Audubon Magazine.*

The Audubon articles became the core of her first
book, *Birds through an Opera Glass* (1889), which was
part of a series for young people. The first book's
entertaining style, enhanced by close observation and
enthusiasm for the subjects, became Merriam's hall-
mark.

In addition to her love of nature, Merriam was
also interested in people. During the summer of 1891
she worked a month at a Chicago school for working
girls, and that same winter she worked in a working
girl's club in New York City. Her social service was
curtailed when she contracted tuberculosis, an illness
that prompted Merriam to travel west in 1893 in
search of a better climate in which to recover.

Life in a small Utah town led to Merriam's *My
Summer in a Mormon Village* (1894), a description of
everyday Mormon life. From Utah, Merriam traveled
to Palo Alto, California, where she attended Stanford
University for six months. In the spring of 1894, she
visited Twin Oaks, an area of California, to take notes
on birds, and then moved on to observe in the
mountains of Arizona.

Her trip west had a profound influence on her
career. *A Birding on a Bronco* (1896), her first big
western bird book, written for beginners in ornithology, became one of the first popular American bird
guides. Merriam's *Handbook of the Birds of the
Western United States* (1902) complimented Frank
Chapman's *Handbook of Birds of Eastern North
America* (1895). The handbook became a standard
reference book—informative, succinct, technical, and
filled with illustrations of the area's hundreds of
species.

Birds of New Mexico (1928), originally intended
for inclusion in a Biological Survey report, became in
Merriam's hands a comprehensive book for general
use. It won her the Brewster Medal of the American
Ornithologist's Union in 1931—she was the first
woman to be thus honored. Two years later she
received an honorary LL.D. from the University of
New Mexico.

Both the handbook and the New Mexico volumes
contain substantial contributions by biologist Vernon
Bailey, who later became the chief naturalist of the
U.S. Biological Survey. Merriam met Vernon at her
brother's home in Washington, D.C., and married

him on December 16, 1899. Shortly after their marriage, Vernon began a series of biological field trips to New Mexico, often accompanied by Florence. Over the years, each contributed to the other's books. Her New Mexico book and his *Mammals of New Mexico* (1931) are considered classics on western natural history.

Although Florence looked delicate, her arduous travels testified to her stamina and unflagging spirit. From one end of the country to the other, the Baileys journeyed by railroad, wagon, pack train, or on foot. Although the couple remained childless, Florence aimed to transmit her love of birds to young people. The subtitle of her fourth book, *Birds of Village and Field: A Bird Book for Beginners,* suggests that she had youngsters in mind.

When the Baileys were not away on a field trip, their home in Washington, D.C., was a gathering place for amateur and professional naturalists, young and old. Florence tirelessly promoted the Audubon Society of Washington, D.C., which she helped to found in 1887. She also directed and taught the society's program for teachers of nature studies.

The last major work of Florence Merriam Bailey, *Among the Birds in the Grand Canyon National Park* (1939), was published by the National Park Service just four years before her husband's death and nearly ten years before her own death on September 22, 1948, of myocardial degeneration. She is buried on the grounds of her childhood home in Locust Grove, New York.

In addition to Bailey's books, a tribute to her work in the West lives on in a resident of the higher mountains of southern California. A form of a chickadee, *Parus gambeli baileyae,* was named for her in 1908.

SELECTED WRITINGS BY BAILEY:

Books

Birds through an Opera Glass, Houghton, 1889.
My Summer in a Mormon Village, Houghton, 1894.
A-Birding on a Bronco, Houghton, 1896.
Birds of Village and Field: A Bird Book for Beginners, Houghton, 1898.
Handbook of Birds of Western United States, Houghton, 1902.
Birds of New Mexico, New Mexico Department of Game and Fish, 1928.
Among Birds in the Grand Canyon Country, National Park Service, 1939.

SOURCES:

Books

Oehser, Paul H., "Bailey, Florence Augusta Merriam," *Notable American Women: A Biographical Dictionary,* edited by Edward James, Belknap Press, 1971.
Welker, Robert H., "Bailey, Florence Augusta Merriam," *Dictionary of American Biography,* Supplement Four, 1946–1950, edited by John Garraty and Edward James, Scribner, 1974.

—Sketch by Margaret DiCanio

John Logie Baird
1888-1946
English electrical engineer

Although the transmission of visual images had been an object of speculation for many years, John Logie Baird was the first person to assemble a television that actually worked. In 1923, he created an apparatus that transmitted a picture, and with successive, improved versions of this invention, he achieved many "firsts" in the early years of television. His system, however, was mechanical rather than electronic, and Baird had the misfortune of seeing his system superseded by a vastly superior one developed around the cathode-ray tube only a few years after his own breakthrough.

Baird was born on August 13, 1888, in Helensburgh, Scotland, the youngest of four children. His mother was Jessie Morrison Inglis Baird and his father was Reverend John Baird, the minister of a parish church in Helensburgh. Baird showed an early interest in invention and experimentation; he studied electrical engineering at the Royal Technical College in Glasgow and later at the University of Glasgow. In the final year of work toward a bachelor of science degree his studies were interrupted by the beginning of World War I. Rejected as physically unfit for military service, he spent the war years as an engineer with the Clyde Valley Electrical Power Company.

In 1919 Baird left that organization to set up his own company for the manufacture of socks. He sold the firm a year later and went to the island of Trinidad in the Caribbean, where he established a factory to produce jam and chutney. He sold this as well, and in 1921 he founded a soap-making company in London, which he also sold in 1922. He had a small amount of profit from his business ventures, and in the autumn of that year he moved from London to Hastings, a seacoast town in Sussex, to devote himself to the invention of a successful means of transmitting visual signals by wire or wireless.

The basis of all television transmission is the scanning of an object by a beam of light in a series of lines moving from top to bottom and from left to right. Each part of the object, as the light passes over it, produces light signals that are then converted into electrical impulses that are strong or weak, depending on whether that part of the object is light or dark. These electrical impulses are then transmitted through wires, or through the air by means of radio waves, to a receiver. The receiver reconverts the electrical impulses into light signals in the same order and strength as those originally taken from the object. The human eye sees these signals as a complete picture of the object because the scanning is done so rapidly; the eye cannot react swiftly enough to see that the picture is being constantly built up line by line.

In 1894 the German inventor Paul Nipkow had patented what came to be called the Nipkow disc: a disc in which a number of small holes were cut in a spiral arrangement. Nipkow had invented the device to provide a mechanical means by which both the scanning of the transmitter and the reassembling of the picture by the receiver could be accomplished, provided that the rapidly rotating discs in both pieces of apparatus were properly synchronized. It was his theory that a powerful beam of light could be focused on the disc in the transmitter, and the spiral holes in the whirling disc would form the necessary lines of light to scan the object. The light signals could then be collected by a light-sensitive photoelectric cell that would create the electrical impulses for transmission. The disc in the receiver would reverse the process and the resulting lines of light would appear on a small screen before the viewer. Before Baird, however, this was all largely theoretical. Up to the 1920s, neither Nipkow himself nor anyone else had been able to make the apparatus work well enough to transmit an actual picture.

Develops Method to Transmit Images

Baird's great contribution was to take the Nipkow disc and the other components of the system and put them together in such a way that a picture could actually be transmitted and received. His first transmitter and receiver were made out of cardboard discs and other odds and ends. With this very crude apparatus he succeeded in early 1923 in transmitting over a distance of a few feet the first very blurred television picture: a cross and a human hand. In July, 1923, Baird and a business associate applied for a patent on his system, which was granted in May, 1924.

At about this time Baird moved his tiny laboratory from Hastings to London, where he worked to improve his apparatus so that it could show detailed images such as the features of a human face. He also began demonstrations for news reporters and even showed his system to the public at Selfridge's, a department store in London, in March, 1925. His most important early demonstration was on January 26, 1926, for a group of scientists who were members of the British Royal Institution. This event was widely reported by the press in both Great Britain and the United States, and Baird and several associates soon formed the Baird Television Development Company to exploit his invention.

During the next few years Baird and his colleagues achieved a series of "firsts" in television. They built the first television transmission station in London in 1926. In November and December of that year, Baird demonstrated a new system he called "noctovision," which substituted infrared rays for visible light in the scanning process, thus making it possible to transmit images scanned even in total darkness. In May, 1927, spurred on by an American success in televising across the 200 miles between Washington, D.C., and New York, Baird transmitted a visual picture across 438 miles of telephone lines between London and Glasgow. In February, 1928, Baird succeeded in transmitting a picture by wireless across the Atlantic Ocean from London to New York; a few weeks later, he sent an image to an ocean liner in the middle of the Atlantic. In June of 1928, he transmitted the first television pictures taken outdoors in daylight, and in early July he sent out the first color television image.

Baird and his business associates also carried out a very successful publicity campaign for his television system. In 1929, under pressure from the British post office department and members of Parliament, the British Broadcasting Company allowed Baird to use its facilities for a series of experimental television broadcasts to that small portion of the general public who had television receiving sets. This arrangement continued, with various modifications, through 1934. During this period Baird and his company made other striking achievements, such as the first broadcast of the famous English horse race, the Derby, on June 3, 1931. Encouraged by his successes, Baird married Mary Albu, a concert pianist, in 1931; they eventually had a son and a daughter.

Cathode-Ray Tube Makes His System Obsolete

By 1934, however, the period of Baird's supremacy in television was almost over. Though much improved over its simple beginnings, his mechanical system remained a cumbersome and unreliable apparatus, prone to frequent breakdowns and producing at best a very mediocre, low-definition picture. The basic element for a superior system of television, the cathode-ray tube, had been invented in Germany in 1897. Several scientists since then had suggested that television scanning might best be done by a moving beam of electrons or cathode rays operating within such a tube. The problems of developing an all-electronic system of television around the cathode-ray tube were very complex; nevertheless, teams of scientists and technicians working for the large Marconi-EMI Company in Great Britain and the even larger Radio Corporation of America in the United States were rapidly solving them in the 1930s.

Baird's dilemma was partly an economic one: his small company was composed largely of working engineers and publicists, and it simply could not compete with the financial resources of the major business concerns and the large research and development staffs they were able to support. Also, the entirely electronic, high-definition television system developed by the big companies was simply a much better product. In early 1935, the British Broadcasting Company agreed to a test period in which Baird's system and that developed by Marconi-EMI would broadcast alternately to determine which was best. The result, despite frantic efforts by the Baird company to improve its system, was an almost unanimous verdict in favor of Marconi-EMI. In February 1937, the BBC announced that it was dropping the Baird apparatus and would continue its television broadcasting with the Marconi-EMI system only. Baird accomplished little in the years of life that were left to him. He died in Bexhill, Sussex, on June 14, 1946, at the age of fifty-seven.

SOURCES:

Books

Abramson, Albert, *The History of Television*, McFarland & Co., 1987.
Briggs, Asa, *The Golden Age of Wireless*, Oxford University Press, 1965, pp. 519–609.
The Dictionary of National Biography, 1941–1950, Oxford University Press, 1959, pp. 39–40.
Exwood, Maurice, *John Logie Baird: 50 Years of Television*, Institution of Electronic and Radio Engineers, 1976.
Norman, Bruce, *Here's Looking at You: The Story of British Television, 1908–1939*, British Broadcasting Corporation and the Royal Television Society, 1984, pp. 24–141.

—*Sketch by John E. Little*

Alan Baker
1939-
English mathematician

Alan Baker is an English mathematician whose work on number theory was honored in 1970 with a Fields Medal, which is often considered to be the equivalent of the Nobel Prize. Baker won the award for his work on transcendental numbers, or non-algebraic numbers—specifically, for extending the Gelfond-Schneider theorem and applying the results to the theory of diophantine equations. Baker's work was also applied in the solution of several of German mathematician Karl Friedrich Gauss's classical problems and in the improvement of French mathematician Joseph Liouville's approximation of algebraic numbers by rationals. It created new areas of research in elliptic and Abelian functions, and the techniques Baker developed to obtain his results have become the foundation for methods used in number theory today.

Baker was born in London on August 19, 1939. His mathematical studies began in 1958 when he entered University College, London. He received his B.S. in 1961 and went on to do graduate work at Trinity College, Cambridge, where he was awarded his Ph.D. in 1964. Both institutions had strong schools in number theory, which probably influenced Baker's choice of a research field. He was named a research fellow at Trinity College from 1964 to 1968 and then served as director of studies in mathematics from 1968 to 1974. He became a professor of pure mathematics at Cambridge University in 1974, and has remained there since.

Obtains Results in Work on Transcendental Numbers

It was at Trinity College that Baker achieved the important results in his work with transcendental numbers. Transcendental numbers are numbers that cannot be expressed as the root of a rational integral (polynomial) equation with rational coefficients, and the study of them developed from the work of several mathematicians in the nineteenth and twentieth centuries. In 1844, Joseph Liouville proved the existence of transcendental numbers based on continuous fractions. His theories were advanced in 1900 when German mathematician **David Hilbert** posed his famous seventh problem, which asked whether an exponential number was transcendental when the exponent was not rational. A. O. Gelfond and T. Schneider both independently solved this problem in 1934. Their result was known as the Gelfond-Schneider theorem. At this time, some mathematicians believed this theorem would have an impact on many areas of mathematics if it were extended. No one was able to extend it, however, until 1966, when Baker obtained results on linear forms in the logarithms of algebraic numbers. From this, he generalized the Gelfond-Schneider theorem and generated previously unidentified transcendental numbers.

In 1967, Baker applied the results from his work on transcendental numbers to the theory of diophantine equations. This area of mathematics deals with the search for integer solutions to equations that have more than one independent variable and integer coefficients. Diophantine equations, named for the Greek mathematician Diophantus, have been studied for over 1,000 years, but until the beginning of the twentieth century the discipline consisted only of isolated problems and ad hoc methods. A. Thue was the first to obtain any general results. In 1909, he proved that only a finite number of solutions exists for a certain class of diophantine equations. C. L. Siegel and British mathematician Klaus Friedrich Roth then extended this theorem to more general classes of diophantine equations, but their methods did not allow them to obtain all solutions. Baker considered Thue's equation and proved an effective bound B for the solutions, which meant that each unknown in the solution was less than or equal to B and that B could be determined. This result made it possible to determine all the solutions (or the nonexistence of them) for a large class of equations and, therefore, provided the first effective theorem in the study of diophantine equations.

In 1970, the International Congress of Mathematicians awarded Baker the Fields Medal in Nice. In his report to the congress on Baker's work, published in *Actes du congrès international des mathématiciens 1970,* Paul Turán spoke of the significance of the results, crediting Baker for showing that two different approaches to mathematics could "live in peaceful coexistence." Baker's methods, he said, had shown "that beside the worthy tendency to start a theory in order to solve a problem it pays also to attack specific difficult problems directly," and "that a direct solution of a deep problem develops itself quite naturally into a healthy theory and gets into early and fruitful contact with other significant problems of mathematics." Baker also gave a talk to the congress, entitled "Effective Methods in the Theory of Numbers."

Baker won the Adams Prize in 1972 for his essay "Transcendental Number Theory," which was published as a book with the same title in 1975. He was elected a fellow of the Royal Society in 1973. In 1978, Baker was appointed the first Turán Lecturer of Hungary's János Bolyai Mathematical Society. Two years later, he was elected a foreign fellow of the Indian National Science Academy. He has held many visiting professorships at European and American institutions, including Stanford University.

SELECTED WRITINGS BY BAKER:

Books

Transcendental Number Theory, Cambridge University Press, 1975.

Periodicals

"Linear Forms in the Logarithms of Algebraic Numbers," *Mathematica,* Volume 13, 1966, pp. 204–216.

SOURCES:

Books

Modern Scientists and Engineers, Volume 1, McGraw-Hill, 1980, pp. 42–43.
Turán, Paul, "On the Work of Alan Baker," *Actes du congrès international des mathématiciens 1970,* Gauthier-Villars, 1971, pp. 3–5.

—Sketch by Laura Mangan-Grenier

Sara Josephine Baker
1873-1945
American physician

Sara Josephine Baker was a pioneer in the field of public health and active in the women's movement. She was the first woman to receive a doctorate in public health. As chief of the newly created division of child hygiene, she reduced New York City's infant mortality rate to the lowest of all major cities worldwide. From 1922 to 1924 she represented the United States on the health committee of the League of Nations.

Born on November 15, 1873, in Poughkeepsie, New York, Sara Josephine Baker was the daughter of affluent parents. Her Quaker father, Orlando Daniel Mosser Baker, was a studious lawyer, and her mother was one of the first women to attend Vassar College. It was her Quaker Aunt Abby who stimulated her intellectually and instilled in her the courage to be a nonconformist. This background influenced her decision to enter medicine and establish innovative programs in preventive health, particularly in obstetrics and pediatrics.

At the age of sixteen, Baker lost both her father and her brother in a typhoid epidemic. Devastated, she abandoned plans for attending Vassar and decided to go directly to New York Women's Medical College. She was determined to become a doctor and to help support her mother and sister. After four years of intensive study, Baker graduated in 1898, second in a class of eighteen. She interned at New England Hospital for Women and Children in Boston in an outpatient clinic serving residents of the city's worst slums. Later she moved to New York City with her roommate and fellow intern, where they set up a practice near Central Park West. Unable to make ends meet, Baker took a job as a medical inspector for the city department of health. She examined sick children in schools and worked toward controlling the spread of contagious disease.

In 1902, under the direction of Walter Benzel, Baker was given the job of searching for sick infants in the Hell's Kitchen area of New York and trying to save some of the fifteen hundred dying each week of dysentery. In 1908 the New York City department of health established a division of child hygiene, with Baker as its chief. She was the first woman in the United States to hold an executive position in a health department. There she shaped policy regarding progressive health reform and made preventive medicine and health education the responsibility of government. Her program saved the lives of countless infants, and she revolutionized pediatric health care across the United States and in other nations as well.

One of Baker's projects was setting up "milk stations" throughout the city, where nurses examined babies, dispensed low-cost, high-quality milk, and scheduled checkups. In 1911 fifteen milk stations prevented more than one thousand deaths, and the next year forty more stations were opened. Another of Baker's programs was the training and licensing of midwives. Many immigrant women were used to midwifery and were reluctant to allow their babies to be delivered by male doctors; but midwives were often unqualified, and the cost in terms of infant mortality was high. Baker instituted a mandatory licensing program with results so successful that she was able to demonstrate that rates of infection for home deliveries were lower than those for hospitals. Baker also set up a program to train young girls in the care of babies, since many girls were put in charge of their younger siblings while their mothers worked. Through the Little Mothers' League, nurses instructed schoolgirls in feeding, exercising, dressing, and general care of infants.

An even more significant method of reducing infant mortality rates was Baker's establishment of a foster care system to provide orphaned babies a better environment than that available in institutions. Her efforts helped reduce death rates from one-half to one-third of infants born in a year. Baker also introduced the concept of prenatal care to prevent infant mortality during and just after childbirth.

Among Baker's other accomplishments were the organization and streamlining of the recordkeeping system for health departments, which was adopted nationwide, and the school inspections system. She opened specialized clinics and instituted parent training by public health nurses. In 1912 she established the Federal Children's Bureau and planned to create a division of child hygiene in every state. Besides being a leader in the medical field, Baker was in the forefront of the fledgling women's movement. In 1915 she was invited by officials at the New York University (NYU) Medical School to lecture on child hygiene for a new course leading to a degree of doctor of public health. Since she did not have an actual degree in the field of public health herself, she offered to teach in return for the opportunity to earn the diploma. Dean William Park turned down her request on the grounds that the medical school did not admit women, and Baker refused the appointment. Park searched in vain for a year for another instructor, finally giving up and admitting Baker and other women to the program. Baker's reception by some of the male students was invariably hostile, but she continued teaching at NYU for fifteen years. Along with five other women, Baker founded the College Equal Suffrage League and marched in the first annual Fifth Avenue Suffrage Parade.

During her term serving as U.S. representative on the health committee of the League of Nations from 1922 to 1924, Baker was also appointed consulting director in maternity and child hygiene of the U.S. Children's Bureau. During her retirement years she participated on more than twenty-five committees to further children's health. She also served a term as president of the American Medical Women's Association.

Baker died of cancer on February 22, 1945, in New York City. Her work laid the foundation for preventive health procedures that saved the lives of hundreds of thousands of babies—an improvement in mortality rates from 1 in 6 in 1907 to 1 in 20 by 1943.

SELECTED WRITINGS BY BAKER:

Books

Fighting for Life, Krieger, 1939.

SOURCES:

Books

Peavy, Linda, and Ursula Smith, *Women Who Changed Things,* Scribner's, 1983, pp. 1–22.

Morantz-Sanchez, Regina Markell, *Sympathy and Science: Women Physicians in American Medicine,* Oxford University Press, 1985.

Morantz, Regina Markell, Cynthia Stodola Pomerleau, and Carol Fenichel, editors, *In Her Own Words: Oral Histories of Women Physicians,* Yale University Press, 1982, p. 30.

—*Sketch by Linda Lewin*

David Baltimore
1938-
American microbiologist

David Baltimore won the Nobel Prize in physiology or medicine in 1975. He shared the award with the virologist **Renato Dulbecco** and the oncologist **Howard Temin** for the ground-breaking discovery that genetic information doesn't just travel from DNA (deoxyribonucleic acid, which contains genetic information) to RNA (ribonucleic acid, which communicates DNA information to proteins), although that concept had been at the heart of modern genetic theory. Rather, Temin and Baltimore independently discovered that some viruses could replicate their RNA into the DNA of healthy cells, causing tumors. This process is known as reverse transcription and is catalyzed by the enzyme reverse transcriptase. Its implications had a great effect on the study of cancer and the role of viruses in causing the disease. Born March 7, 1938, in New York City to Richard Baltimore and Gertrude Lipschitz, David was a gifted student of science. While still in high school he attended a prestigious summer program for talented students of science at the Jackson Laboratory in Bar Harbor, Maine, where the focus was mammalian genetics. It was there that Baltimore decided to pursue a career in the research sciences and first met his future colleague, Howard Temin, also a student at the time.

Baltimore attended Swarthmore College in Pennsylvania and graduated in 1960 with high honors in chemistry. He started graduate work at the Massachusetts Institute of Technology (M.I.T.) but transferred after one year to the Rockefeller Institute, now called Rockefeller University, in New York. There he studied with Richard M. Franklin, who was a molecular biophysicist specializing in RNA viruses. Baltimore earned his Ph.D. in 1964 and returned to M.I.T. for a postdoctoral fellowship the following year.

David Baltimore

Baltimore was interested in a specific group of RNA viruses, the picornaviruses, which include mengovirus and poliovirus, that do not have DNA but nevertheless seemed to reproduce in cells of complex organisms that carry their genetic information in DNA. Since 1964, Temin had been suggesting that RNA viruses could replicate themselves in DNA, but the scientific community disbelieved and even ridiculed him. Baltimore, however, persisted in looking for RNA or DNA enzymes in the genetic material of poliovirus to solve this riddle.

He continued his research in this area as a fellow at the Albert Einstein College of Medicine in the Bronx (1964–65) and as a research associate at the Salk Institute in California (1965–68). At the Salk Institute he met Renato Dulbecco, who had developed innovative techniques for examining animal viruses in the laboratory. He also met **Alice Shih-hou Huang**, a postdoctoral fellow studying vesicular stomatitis virus.

Discovers Reverse Transcriptase

In 1968, Baltimore returned with Huang to Boston, where they were married. They have one daughter. Baltimore became an associate professor of microbiology at M.I.T. and continued to focus his research on poliovirus. By 1970, however, a number of scientists had suggested that all RNA viruses might not be alike. Baltimore's focus on poliovirus therefore might not reveal clues to the behavior of other viruses. Baltimore began to classify RNA viruses according to their varying replication strategies. It was during his work on this project that he discovered an enzyme that enabled an RNA virus to replicate its single strand of RNA and thus become compatible with the double-stranded DNA in a sample of Rauscher murine leukemia virus. The enzyme was later called reverse transcriptase.

Meanwhile, Temin had independently demonstrated the same thing, using a sample of Rous sarcoma virus. In 1970, both scientists made the initial announcements of reverse transcription within days of each other, at separate conferences. One month later they published an article detailing their findings in the journal *Nature*. The excitement of their news was instantaneous. Many scientists jumped to the conclusion that reverse transcription held the key to a cure for cancer. But Baltimore and Temin were more reserved in their response. They knew that their work did not establish a direct link between viruses and cancer. Their discovery did, however, quickly become a key to the study of cancer. Baltimore immediately began to be recognized for his achievement. In 1972 he was promoted to full professor at M.I.T. and in 1973 he was awarded a lifetime research professorship by the American Cancer Society.

While continuing to study reverse transcriptase, Baltimore and his colleagues at M.I.T. partially synthesized a mammalian hemoglobin gene. Other teams around the country were performing similar experiments at the same time, which raised the specter of genetic engineering. As a prominent figure in the scientific community, Baltimore became outspoken about the risks of genetic engineering. He was concerned that modern science—and biology in particular—might be misused. In 1975, he initiated a conference in which scientists attempted to design a self-regulatory system regarding experiments with recombinant DNA. In 1976, the National Institutes of Health established a committee to oversee federally funded experiments in the field of genetic engineering. After winning the Nobel Prize in 1975, Baltimore continued to be honored for his work. He was elected to the National Academy of Sciences and the American Academy of Arts and Sciences in 1974. In 1983 he became the director of the Whitehead Institute for Biomedical Research, where he remained until 1990. In that position, he made significant advances in the field of immunology and synthetic vaccine research. In 1990 he became President of Rockefeller University.

Implicated in Controversy over Falsified Data

Baltimore's career took a sudden turn in 1989 when it was revealed that the conclusions of a 1986 paper he had coauthored while still at M.I.T. were based on falsified data. A young scientist, Margaret O'Toole, confronted Thereza Imanishi-Kari, also a coauthor of the article and a supervising scientist in the M.I.T. lab, with suspicions of misconduct. Imanishi-Kari denied any wrongdoing. Baltimore stood by Imanishi-Kari, and O'Toole was subsequently demoted, later claiming that her career had been ruined because she had spoken out against her superiors.

The matter was taken up by a House subcommittee and the Office of Scientific Integrity, which eventually lent credence to O'Toole's suspicions. Baltimore retracted the article but it was too late. Though he was cleared of any wrongdoing and though Imanishi-Kari was not prosecuted, Baltimore's name had been attached to a major breach of scientific ethics. That Baltimore had earlier taken such a strong stand on the ethics of bioengineering was a particular irony not lost on the scientific community. In 1991, under pressure from the faculty, Baltimore resigned as President of Rockefeller University, though he remains a professor there and continues to do research.

SELECTED WRITINGS BY BALTIMORE:

Periodicals

"Viral RNA-Dependent DNA Polymerase," *Nature,* 226, 1970, pp. 1211–1213.
"RNA-Directed DNA Synthesis and RNA Tumor Viruses," *Advances in Virus Research,* 17, 1972, pp. 51–94.

SOURCES:

Periodicals

Beardsley, Tim, "A Troubled Homecoming," *Scientific American,* 226, 1992, pp. 33–35.
Eckhart, Walter, "The 1975 Nobel Prize for Physiology or Medicine," *Science,* 190, 1975, pp. 650, 712, 714.
Marwick, Charles, "Possible Scientific Fraud Questions Prompt Debate Over Which Federal Office(s) Should Investigate," *Journal of the American Medical Association,* 265, 1991, pp. 2309–2312.

—Sketch by Dorothy Barnhouse

Stefan Banach
1892-1945
Polish mathematician

In spite of his somewhat fragmented education (he never completed a formal doctoral program), Stefan Banach made important contributions to a number of fields of mathematics, including the theory of orthogonal series, topology, the theory of measure and integration, set theory, and the theory of linear spaces of an infinite number of dimensions. He is probably best remembered, however, for his work on functional analysis.

Stefan Banach was born on March 30, 1892, in Kraków, Poland. His father was named Greczek, a railway official from peasant background. He and Stefan's mother (whose name has been lost) abandoned their young child to a laundress almost immediately after his birth. The child took on his foster mother's surname of Banach, but almost nothing else is known about his early childhood. Banach apparently developed an interest in mathematics at an early age and taught himself the fundamentals of the subject. By the age of fifteen he was supporting himself as a private teacher of mathematics. He also taught himself enough French to master Tannery's text on the theory of functions, *Introduction à la théorie des fonctions*. Banach attended lectures on mathematics at Jagellon University on an irregular basis before entering the Lwów Institute of Technology in the Ukraine in 1910. He did not, however, graduate from the institute.

In 1914, with the outbreak of World War I, Banach returned to Kraków. Two years later, a chance event was to change his life. While sitting on a park bench in Kraków talking with a friend about mathematics, he was overhead by the mathematician H. Steinhaus. Steinhaus later wrote that he was "so struck by the words 'the Lebesque integral'" that he heard from the two that he came closer and introduced himself to the young men. As the group talked, the conversation turned to a problem on the congruence of a Fourier series on which Steinhaus had been working. "I was greatly surprised," Steinhaus went on to say, "when, after a few days, Banach brought me a negative answer with a reservation which resulted from his ignorance of [a technical point about which he did not know]." Banach and Steinhaus were later to collaborate on a number of mathematical studies.

Banach's natural gift for mathematics soon became more widely known, and at the conclusion of the war he was offered a position as mathematical assistant at the Lwów Institute of Technology by Antoni Łomnicki. For the first time in his life Banach had some degree of financial security and he married. Beginning in 1919, Banach was assigned to lecture on mathematics and mechanics. In the same year, he was awarded his doctoral degree although he had not completed the full program of courses expected for that degree.

Publishes Historic Paper on Integral Equations

The primary basis for Banach's degree was the paper he had written on integral equations, which had been published in *Fundamenta mathematicae* in 1922 as "Sur les opérations dans les ensembles abstraits et leur application aux équations intégrales." At about the same time he was made an instructor at the institute; in 1927 he was promoted to full professor. From 1939 to 1941 Banach also served as dean of the faculty at the institute.

The mathematical work for which Banach is best known is his book *Théorie des opérations linéaires,* which appeared in 1932 as the first volume in the Mathematical Monographs series, published in Warsaw. In this book, Banach developed a general theory for working with linear operations that proved to be a landmark in the field. Prior to this work, a number of individual, discrete methods had been developed for solving specific problems. But there was no comprehensive theory that could be applied to a great variety of problems. In his book, Banach introduced the concept of normed linear spaces, now known as Banach spaces, which, Steinhaus later wrote, can be used "to solve in a general way many problems which formerly called for special treatment and considerable ingenuity."

Banach's significance in the history of mathematics goes beyond his own research. He was also an effective teacher whose influence was spread throughout Europe and the United States by a number of brilliant students. In addition, he wrote an important popular textbook, *Differential and Integral Calculus* (1929–30) and was founder with Steinhaus of the journal *Studia mathematica.*

World War II was a personal disaster for Banach. After the German army occupied the city of Lwów, he was forced to work in a German laboratory studying infectious diseases. His job there was to feed the lice used in experiments. As degrading as this work was, Banach was able to continue teaching in underground schools and carry on his own research. By the time the war ended, however, his health had so badly deteriorated that he lived only a few more months. Banach died in Lwów on August 31, 1945. Among the honors accorded him during his lifetime were election as corresponding member of the Polish Academy of Sciences and of the Kiev Academy of Sciences. He also received the Prize of the City of Lwów in 1930 and the Prize of the Polish Academy in 1939. Upon his death, the city of Warsaw renamed one of its streets in his honor.

SELECTED WRITINGS BY BANACH:

Books

Differential and Integral Calculus, Ossolineum, 1929, and Ksiaznica-Atlas, 1930.
Théorie des opérations linéaires, Z subwencji Funduszu kultury narodowej, 1932.
Mechanika w zakresie szkol akademickich, Czytelnik, 1938.

Periodicals

"Sur le problème de la mesure," *Fundamenta mathematicae,* Volume 4, 1923, pp. 7–33.

SOURCES:

Books

Dictionary of Scientific Biography, Volume 1, Scribner's, 1975, pp. 427–428.

Periodicals

Steinhaus, H., "Stefan Banach," *Studia mathematica,* special series, Volume 1, 1963, pp. 7–15.
Ulam, S., "Stefan Banach, 1892–1945," *Bulletin of the American Mathematical Society,* Volume 52, 1946, pp. 600–603.

—*Sketch by David E. Newton*

Harvey Washington Banks
1923-1979
American astronomer and astrophysicist

Harvey Washington Banks was the first African American to earn a Ph.D. in astronomy from Georgetown University. After working and teaching in the areas of solar and planetary astronomy, he moved to the Howard University Department of Physics and Astronomy, where he was teaching at the time of his death.

The son of Harvey Banks Sr. and Nettie Lee Jackson Banks, Dr. Banks was born in Atlantic City, New Jersey, on February 7, 1923. After his family moved to Washington, D.C., Banks attended Dunbar High School and later Howard University in that city. He received his B.S. and master's degrees in physics from that university in 1946 and 1947 respectively and became a research associate in physics at Howard in 1948.

In 1952, Banks entered the private sector as an electronic engineer at National Electronics Inc. Two years later he returned to education and accepted a physics and mathematics teaching position in the D.C. public school system. In 1956, Banks became a research assistant and student at Georgetown University in Washington, D.C., until 1961, when he was awarded a Ph.D. in astronomy. He lectured and taught at Georgetown University, American University, and Delaware State College during the years 1963 to 1968, after which he became an assistant professor in mathematics and astronomy at Howard on September 1, 1969. He became an associate professor in physics and astronomy one year later and remained in that position at Howard until his death.

Banks's dissertation was titled "The First Spectrum of Titanium from 6000 to 3000 Angstroms," and throughout his career he was concerned with planetary spectroscopy or the study of the nature of light emitted from distant sources. He also worked on the determination of orbits and celestial mechanics and was interested in geodetic determinations (involving a mathematical method of measuring the shortest line between two points on earth by using objects or points in outer space) from observations of solar eclipses and satellites. Banks also oversaw the Beltsville project outside of Washington, D.C., which involved the construction of an observatory and other facilities for the teaching of astrophysics. He served as coordinator of the Astronomy and Space Seminar for the National Science Teacher's Association.

Banks was a member of the American Astronomical Society, the Optical Society, the Washington Academy of Science, the New York Academy of Science, the Washington Philosophical Society, and the Spectrographic Society, as well as Sigma Xi, Sigma Pi Sigma, and Beta Kappa. When he died, he left his wife, the former Ernestine Boykin, and four children (Harvey III, Deborah, Dwann, and Darryle).

—*Sketch by Leonard C. Bruno*

Frederick G. Banting
1891-1941
Canadian physiologist

Frederick G. Banting

Frederick Grant Banting was a Canadian physician who discovered insulin with the collaboration of **Charles H. Best**, **John James Rickard Macleod**, and James Bertram Collip. Insulin is a hormone that is secreted by the pancreas, and that regulates the level of sugar in the blood. The discovery of insulin led to a treatment for diabetes, a disease which at the time meant death within a few years for those who developed it. For his contribution to this work, Banting shared the 1923 Nobel Prize in physiology or medicine with Macleod, the physiologist in whose laboratory the insulin research was carried out. It was the first Nobel Prize to be awarded to a Canadian.

Banting was born November 14, 1891 near Alliston, Ontario, about 40 miles north of Toronto. He was the youngest of five children of William Thompson Banting, a farmer whose parents had emigrated to Canada from Ireland, and Margaret Grant Banting, the daughter of a miller and the first Canadian of European descent to be born in Alliston. Banting attended local schools, where he was a serious, but average, student, excelling in sports. Following his father's wishes, Banting entered Victoria College of the University of Toronto to prepare for the Methodist ministry. After a year, however, he switched to medicine, and he began medical courses in the fall of 1912. The university accelerated his course of study with the outbreak of World War I. Banting completed his degree in December 1916 and was dispatched to England shortly thereafter, as a lieutenant in the Canadian Army Medical Corps. He was assigned to an orthopedic hospital at Ramsgate. There he gained experience in surgery under the direction of Clarence L. Starr. Later he was sent to France, and in September 1918 Banting's right forearm was severely wounded by shrapnel near Haynscourt, in the Cambrai sector. In 1919 the British Government awarded him the Military Cross for valorous conduct in action.

Banting returned to Toronto after his injury healed and worked as an intern for a year at the Hospital for Sick Children under his wartime mentor Clarence Starr, who was surgeon-in-chief. In 1920 Banting set up his own surgical practice in London, Ontario. He chose London because his fiancée, Edith Roach, was working there as a teacher. The couple had become engaged before Banting went off to war, but they never married. Banting's practice got off to a slow start. In the first month after he posted office hours only one patient visited. To make ends meet,

Banting sought an appointment as a demonstrator in surgery and anatomy at the University of Western Ontario, a job which took up only a few hours a week of his time. He also got his first taste of medical research there, working in the laboratory of neurophysiologist Frederick R. Miller.

Insomnia Leads to Breakthrough in Diabetic Research

To prepare for a lecture to his students on the pancreas in October 1920, Banting was reading up on how the body metabolizes carbohydrates, including sugar. The pancreas was known to secrete digestive enzymes and thus to play a role in the metabolism of sugar. Thirty years earlier the researchers Oscar von Mering and Joseph Minkowski had found that when they surgically removed the pancreas of a dog, the animal developed diabetes. Among the first symptoms were frequent urination and high levels of sugar in the urine, the same symptoms as in human diabetes. But in the intervening years, no one had clarified just how the pancreas prevented diabetes. On October 30, 1920, reading himself to sleep with the November issue of the journal *Surgery, Gynecology, and Obstetrics,* Banting noted the lead article, titled "The Relation of the Islets of Langerhans to Diabetes, With Special Reference to Cases of Pancreatic Lithiasis." This article gave Banting an idea for an experiment that would reveal the role of the pancreas in diabetes.

The article described an autopsy where the main duct of the pancreas was found to be blocked by a stone. The pancreas itself had wasted away, except for certain groups of cells known as the islets of Langerhans. Banting suspected that these islet cells held the key to understanding diabetes. As he later recalled in his Cameron Lecture in Edinburgh in 1928, he was unable to sleep. So at 2:00 a.m. he jotted down notes for an experiment: "Tie off pancreas ducts of dogs. Wait six or eight weeks. Remove and extract."

The next day Banting mentioned his idea to Miller. Miller suggested he talk to J. J. R. Macleod at the University of Toronto, a world-renowned expert on carbohydrate metabolism. Early in November 1920, Banting met with Macleod to propose his idea and to ask Macleod to be his sponsor by providing his laboratory. The elder scientist was not impressed. In fact, Macleod told Banting, other researchers had already spent years in unsuccessful attempts to find the role of pancreatic extracts in diabetes. Although scientists had previously tied off the pancreatic ducts of dogs and observed the organ atrophy, it seemed that no one had tried to prepare an extract. Banting wanted to do this and administer the extract to dogs that had been made diabetic by the removal of the pancreas. This idea intrigued Macleod. After six months of persuasion, Banting finally convinced Macleod to help him. In mid-May of 1921, Banting shut down his practice, which he considered an utter failure, resigned his university position, and moved to Toronto to begin his experiments. Macleod had agreed to provide him for eight weeks with a laboratory, ten dogs, and an assistant who knew how to perform chemical analysis of blood and urine. That assistant was 22-year-old Charles H. Best, who had just finished his undergraduate degree in physiology and biochemistry.

Begins Work With Pancreatic Extract

Banting and Best set about performing surgery on the dogs, tying off the pancreatic ducts in some and removing the pancreas from others, to render them diabetic. Macleod supervised the research for a month and then left the pair to themselves while he went to his home in Scotland for vacation. Banting and Best spent several weeks working out technical surgical problems. In their first attempts, they tied off the pancreatic ducts of the dogs with catgut, which disintegrated, leaving the ducts open and the pancreas healthy. They solved this problem by switching to silk. Banting also developed a method for removing the pancreas in one procedure, whereas previously it had been done in two operations. Finally on July 30, both a diabetic dog and a dog whose pancreatic ducts had been tied were ready.

Banting removed the shriveled pancreas from the dog whose ducts had been tied. He and Best prepared an extract from it by chopping the pancreas into small pieces, grinding it in a chilled mortar with salt water, and filtering the mixture through cheesecloth. A blood sample from the diabetic dog showed its blood sugar level to be 0.2. Banting and Best injected some of their extract into the dog. An hour later its blood sugar level had dropped to 0.12. After another injection it registered 0.11. This dog died the next day, presumably from an infection. But Banting and Best were encouraged by the result and tested their extract on more diabetic dogs. They called the extract "isletin."

During the following months Banting and Best performed additional experiments to confirm and explain their results. They also looked for a more practical way of obtaining their extract than by performing risky duct-tying surgery on dogs and then waiting seven weeks for the pancreas to atrophy. They also wanted a procedure that would provide larger quantities of the substance. First they tried a technique of forcing the pancreas to secrete all of its digestive enzymes except "isletin." This, however, still required surgery. Then Banting recalled that the pancreases of fetal animals contain more islet cells than those of adults. He prepared an extract using pancreases from fetal calves obtained from a local slaughterhouse. It worked, and this new method provided the researchers with a steady supply of the hormone.

In the meantime, Macleod returned from his holiday. He was pleased with Banting's progress, but suggested that still more experiments be done. Banting, who had been working without a salary, threatened to quit unless Macleod gave him a job and more help in the lab. Macleod eventually granted this, enlisting J. B. Collip, a Ph.D. biochemist and an expert on blood chemistry, to obtain a purified version of the pancreatic extract. But combined with Macleod's initial doubts about Banting, the confrontation had driven a rift in their relationship that never healed.

By January 1922, the researchers felt ready to test insulin, a name suggested by Macleod, on a human diabetic. Banting and Best initially injected each other with the extract to be sure it would not cause harm. Their first patient was 14-year-old Leonard Thompson. He had suffered from diabetes for two years. As was typical for child diabetics, his weight was down to 65 pounds. Without treatment he would soon slip into a coma and die. The boy's blood sugar level did fall after insulin injections, but the researchers stopped the trial because impurities in the extract seemed to cause complications. Twelve days later, however, they started treatment again, with a more pure and potent extract. The boy's blood sugar dropped, and so did the level of sugar in his urine. The researchers reported in the *Journal of the Canadian Medical Association* in 1922 that "the boy became brighter, more active, looked better and said he felt stronger." The first human test of insulin was a success: Leonard Thompson lived another 13 years, dying of pneumonia following a motorcycle accident. Combined with a regulated diet, insulin soon became the standard treatment for diabetes. The University of Toronto contracted with Eli Lilly and Company to scale up production of the drug.

Insulin Discoverers Awarded Nobel Prize

In 1923 the Nobel Prize in physiology or medicine was awarded to Banting and Macleod. Banting split his half of the money with Best and was furious that Macleod could claim credit for the discovery. In Banting's view, the idea that started the experiments had been his alone, and the crucial scientific work had been done while Macleod was on vacation. The Nobel Committee, however, wished to acknowledge Macleod's role in directing the research, which also required the collaboration of Best and Collip to carry through. Macleod, for his part, split his share of the award with Collip. The Nobel Prize was followed by numerous additional accolades for Banting. The Canadian parliament awarded him an annuity in 1923. The same year the University of Toronto established a Banting and Best Chair of Medical Research, with Banting its first recipient. This grew into the Banting and Best Department of Medical Research, which Banting headed for the rest of his life. In 1930 the University of Toronto honored him by naming a new medical building the Banting Institute. In 1934 King George V, who was a diabetic, made Banting a knight commander of the British Empire. Banting was elected a fellow of the Royal Society of London in 1935.

Banting achieved fame for the discovery of insulin. He did not, however, contribute much to its refinement and use, perhaps because of his feud with Macleod. Instead, he turned his attention to a range of medical problems far removed from diabetes. He contributed to cancer research, studying a type of tumor caused by a virus, known as Rous sarcoma. He studied the physiological problems associated with insufficient secretion of the suprarenal gland, for which he attempted to develop an extract, and he did research on silicosis. He also became involved in the Canadian government's support of medical research as chairman of the Medical Research Committee of the National Research Council, and chairman of the Associate Committee on Aviation Medical Research. In the latter position, he did research on the physiological effects of flying at high altitudes.

Banting married Marion Robertson in 1924. They had one son. The marriage was unhappy almost from the start, however, and the couple divorced in 1932 after a long separation. During the 1920s Banting began to nurture a long-standing interest in art. He collected paintings by Canadian artists and joined the Arts and Letters Club in Toronto. Eventually he began painting himself, under the tutelage of his friend A. Y. Jackson, a well-known landscape artist. Beginning in 1927 Banting and Jackson made trips to northeastern Quebec, Ellesmere Island, and other northern reaches of Canada to sketch and paint.

In 1939 Banting married Henrietta Ball, a technician in his department at the University of Toronto. That same year he volunteered for military service when Canada entered World War II. He was soon promoted to the rank of major, and spent much of the next two years shuttling between Canada and England as a liaison between authorities on wartime medicine in the two countries. He had embarked on such a mission on February 21, 1941, when the airplane carrying him crashed in Newfoundland and he was killed.

SELECTED WRITINGS BY BANTING:

Periodicals

(With Charles H. Best) "The Internal Secretion of the Pancreas," *Journal of Laboratory and Clinical Medicine,* Volume 7, no. 5, 1922, pp. 256–271.
(With Best, J. B. Collip, W. R. Campbell, and A. A. Fletcher) "Pancreatic Extracts in Diabetes," *Journal of the Canadian Medical Association,* 12, 1922, pp. 141–146.
"Early Work on Insulin," *Science,* 85, 1937, pp. 594–596.

SOURCES:

Books

Bliss, Michael, *The Discovery of Insulin,* University of Chicago Press, 1982.
Harris, Seale, *Banting's Miracle,* J. B. Lippincott, 1946.
Stevenson, Lloyd, *Sir Frederick Banting,* Toronto, 1946.

—Sketch by Betsy Hanson

Robert Bárány
1876-1936
Austrian Swedish physician

Robert Bárány made significant contributions to our understanding of the vestibular apparatus, part of the inner ear that plays an important role in maintaining balance. He devised ingenious tests to diagnose inner-ear disease, and he investigated the relationship between the vestibular and nervous systems. Because of his ground-breaking research in this area, he is credited with creating a new field of study, otoneurology. Bárány's achievements were recognized in 1914 with the Nobel Prize in physiology or medicine.

Bárány was born on April 22, 1876, in Rohonc (near Vienna), Austria-Hungary (now Austria), the eldest of six children. His father, Ignaz Bárány, was a bank official. His mother, Marie Hock Bárány, was the daughter of a well-known Prague scientist, and it was her intellectual influence that predominated in the family. When Bárány was young, he contracted tuberculosis of the bones, which left him with a permanent stiffness in his knee but which also first awakened his interest in medicine.

Develops Tests for Inner Ear Disease

Always a top student, Bárány began attending medical school at the University of Vienna in 1894. In 1900 he received a doctor of medicine degree. He then spent two years studying internal medicine, neurology, and psychiatry at clinics in Frankfurt, Heidelberg, and Freiburg. Next, he returned to Vienna, where he received hospital surgical training. Finally, in 1903, he accepted a post at the Ear Clinic, also in Vienna, which was then directed by Adam Politzer. Bárány's association with Politzer, a leading figure in the history of otology (the study of the ear and its diseases), proved to be highly fruitful.

It was the chance observation that clinic patients often became dizzy after having their ears irrigated that led Bárány to develop one test that still bears his name. The Bárány caloric test involves stimulating each of a patient's inner ears separately by syringing one with hot liquid and the other with cold. Normally, this results in rapid, involuntary movements of the eyeballs, termed nystagmus. Bárány demonstrated that the direction of the nystagmus is determined by the temperature of the water and the position of the head. He also showed that the absence or delay of nystagmus indicates a problem with the balance structures of the ear. The test was an eminently practical technique for diagnosis, since it could easily be performed at a patient's bedside.

Another diagnostic procedure introduced by Bárány was the chair test. The patient is turned in a rotating chair with a specially designed headrest that inclines the head slightly forward. Once again, any deviation from the normal pattern of nystagmus afterward indicates a problem. Yet another of Bárány's inventions during this period was the noise box, a much-used device that effectively isolates the hearing performance of one ear by creating a masking noise in the other.

World War I Interrupts Research

Unfortunately, this phase of great productivity was to be interrupted by the start of World War I. Bárány, who was of Jewish descent, was dispatched by the army to the fortress of Przemysl on the border between Poland and Russia, where he served as a medical officer. While there, Bárány continued to study the connection between the vestibular apparatus and the nervous system. He also developed an improved surgical technique for dealing with fresh bullet wounds to the brain.

However, in April 1915, the Russians occupied Przemysl, and Bárány was transported along with other prisoners by cattle car to Merv in central Asia. Conditions there were unsanitary and difficult, and Bárány came down with malaria. Still, he was relatively fortunate: the medical commander in Merv knew him by reputation and placed him in charge of otolaryngology (the medical specialty concerned with the ear, nose and throat) for both Russian natives and Austrian prisoners. The Russians were grateful patients. After Bárány had successfully treated the local mayor and his family, he became a daily dinner guest in their home.

It was while he was still a prisoner of war that Bárány received the news that he had won the Nobel Prize. Thanks to the personal intervention of Prince Carl of Sweden, Bárány was released in 1916. He returned to Vienna that same year, but was bitterly disappointed by the reception he received from colleagues there. They claimed he had inadequately cited their own contributions to his work. These accusations were investigated by the Nobel Prize Committee, which found them groundless. Nevertheless, the attacks prompted Bárány to accept a post as professor at the University of Uppsala in Sweden in 1917, where he remained for the rest of his life. Eventually, he rose to the position of chairman of the department of ear, nose, and throat medicine there.

While at Uppsala, Bárány studied the role of the part of the brain called the cerebellum in controlling body movement. He had previously devised another test for disturbances in cerebellar function, known as the pointing test, in which the patient points at a fixed object with the eyes alternately open and closed.

Consistent errors while the eyes are closed indicates a brain lesion.

Bárány also developed a surgical technique for treating chronic sinusitis. For this, he was awarded the Jubilee Medal of the Swedish Society of Medicine in 1925. Among his numerous other awards were the Belgian Academy of Sciences Prize, the ERB Medal from the German Neurological Society, and the Guyot Prize from the University of Groningen in the Netherlands. He also received honorary degrees from several universities, including the University of Stockholm. Austria issued a stamp in his honor in 1976, to commemorate the 100th anniversary of his birth.

Bárány was described as a quiet and solitary man, fanatically devoted to his work. Yet at home, he also enjoyed music and played the piano well; he particularly liked the music of composer Robert Schumann. And despite having had a stiff knee since childhood, he was an avid mountain hiker and tennis player.

Bárány married Ida Felicitas Berger in 1909. They had three children, all of whom went on to become physicians or medical scientists. Their elder son, Ernst, became a professor of pharmacology in Uppsala; their second son, Franz, became a professor of internal medicine in Stockholm; and their daughter, Ingrid, became a psychiatrist in Cambridge, Massachusetts.

Bárány's last years were marred by a series of strokes, which resulted in partial paralysis. He was aware of an international meeting that was organized to celebrate his sixtieth birthday, but, sadly, he died in Uppsala only a few days before the occasion on April 8, 1936. Yet his memory has been kept alive with the Bárány medal, first awarded by the University of Uppsala in 1948, honoring deserving scientists for investigations of the vestibular system. In addition, the Bárány Society was established in 1960 to conduct international symposia on vestibular research.

SELECTED WRITINGS BY BÁRÁNY:

Books

"Some New Methods for Functional Testing of the Vestibular Apparatus and the Cerebellum," in *Nobel Lectures, Including Presentation Speeches and Laureates' Biographies: Physiology or Medicine. 1901–1921,* Elsevier, 1967, pp. 500–513.

Periodicals

"Bárány's *History of Vestibular Physiology:* Translation and Commentary," *Annals of Otology, Rhinology & Laryngology,* March-April 1984, supplement 110, pp. 1–16.

SOURCES:

Periodicals

Diamant, Herman, "The Nobel Prize Award to Robert Bárány—A Controversial Decision?," *Acta Otolaryngol,* 1984, supplement 406, pp. 1–4.

Holmgren, Gunnar, "Robert Bárány," *Annals of Otology, Rhinology and Laryngology,* 1936, pp. 593–595.

Nylen, C. O., "Robert Bárány," *Archives of Otolaryngology,* September, 1965, pp. 316–319.

Shampo, Marc A. and Robert A. Kyle, "Robert Bárány," *Journal of the American Medical Association,* May 16, 1980, p. 1914.

—*Sketch by Linda Wasmer Smith*

Jesse B. Barber, Jr.
1924-
American neurosurgeon

Jesse B. Barber, Jr. was the first African American to be certified by the American Board of Neurosurgery and became the third black American to practice neurosurgery in the United States. Throughout his career, Barber has made significant contributions to his profession, his school, and his city, holding various positions of importance, including director of the Howard University Medical Stroke Project. He also served as the chief of Neurosurgery at Howard and became the university's first professor of social medicine.

Jesse Belmary Barber, Jr. was born on June 22, 1924 in Chattanooga, Tennessee to the former Mae Fortune and Jesse, Sr., who was a Presbyterian minister and an educator. Although he admired his father deeply and aspired to be a preacher like him, Barber's excellent academic performance led him to begin taking pre-engineering courses. However, after being ranked first in a pre-medical examination, Barber moved toward medicine. After first attending Swift Memorial Junior College and then Hampton Institute and Yale University, Barber received his B.A. from Lincoln University. He was then accepted at the Howard University Medical College where he received his M.D. in 1948.

Barber's practicing career began at Freedman's Hospital where he was an intern and a resident general surgeon from 1948 to 1954. In 1956 he became an instructor of surgery and pathology at Howard, moving two years later to serve as a resident at the McGill University Montreal Neurological Institute. In 1961, however, Barber returned to Howard University to become chief of the division of neurosurgery as well as professor of surgery. He founded the university's Medical Stroke Project in 1968, and in 1983 he became Howard's first professor of social medicine, a field of study which he pioneered.

In addition to his professional contributions, Barber has been a leader as well as a member of many organizations. He was president of both the National Medical Association (1977–1978) and the Washington Academy of Neurosurgery (1973–1974). He also is a member of the National Advisory Committee of the Epilepsy Foundation of America, the Executive Committee for Strokes of the American Heart Association, Kappa Pi and Alpha Omega Alpha. Among the many honors and awards he has received are the Howard University Alumni Federation Award for Meritorious Professional and Community Service (1970), the William Alonzo Warfield Award (1974), the YMCA Century Award (1974), the Distinguished Service Award of the National Medical Association (1974), and the Distinguished Service Award of the Howard University Department of Surgery (1979).

Barber achieved notoriety in 1973 as the neurosurgeon chosen by Hamaas Abdul Khaalis, leader of the Hanafi sect of the Black Muslims, to operate on his wife who had been shot in the head several times during an attack by an opposing sect. Barber also made headlines with his surgical skills when he successfully attempted an extremely rare and difficult transposition of the spinal cord operating procedure in the early 1970s. He performed this operation on a teenager whose scoliosis or curvature of the spine was becoming so severe that it was paralyzing him. Barber literally took the cord out of the spine, straightened it, and reinserted it, resulting in a marked improvement in the boy's paralysis.

Barber attributes his "social medicine perspective," an ideal that has guided his actions throughout his medical career, to the values instilled in him by his missionary parents. He is most proud of his education-oriented efforts, having guided scores of Howard University students toward the field of neurological study. In 1993, he was the facilitator of new exhibit at Howard University that focused on African American neurosurgeons.

Barber married the former Constance Bolling and has four children, Clifton, Jesse III, Charles, and Joye. Retired from active practice, Barber now lives in Washington, DC.

SOURCES:

Books

Sammons, Vivian O., *Blacks in Science and Medicine,* Hemisphere Publishing, 1990, p. 19.

Other

Barber, Jesse B., Jr., interview with Leonard C. Bruno conducted January 18, 1994.

　　　　　　　　　—Sketch by Leonard C. Bruno

John Bardeen
1908-1991
American physicist

John Bardeen has the unique distinction of being the first—and so far only—person to have won two Nobel Prizes in physics. The first, shared with **Walter Brattain** and **William Shockley**, came in 1956 for his role in the discovery of the transistor. Only a few months after receiving this award, Bardeen completed another research project that would lead to his second Nobel Prize in 1972, this one for his part in the development of the BCS theory of superconductivity, named for its three inventors, Bardeen, **Leon Cooper**, and **J. Robert Schrieffer**, who shared the Nobel Prize. The BCS theory accounts for the tendency of certain materials to lose all electrical resistance when they are cooled to temperatures close to absolute zero. The theory not only accounted for all known superconductivity phenomena, but also suggested an extensive agenda of new research on the topic.

John Bardeen was born in Madison, Wisconsin, on May 23, 1908. His father was Charles Russell Bardeen, a professor of anatomy and Dean of the Medical School at the University of Wisconsin. His mother was Althea Harmer Bardeen, an artist and teacher. John had two younger brothers, Thomas and William, and a sister, Helen. When John was twelve, his mother died; his father was later remarried to Ruth Hames and had another daughter with her. John's parents encouraged his intellectual development while he was still young. They introduced him to logical word problems in mathematics, for example, before he even entered school.

Bardeen attended Madison public schools through the third grade before transferring to the University High School, skipping three grades and

John Bardeen

entering as a seventh grader. It was there that he had his first course in general science and discovered his interest in the subject. Nonetheless, mathematics was his first love. He was allowed to take algebra when he was only ten years old, and at the end of each school year, he was named outstanding student in the class. Bardeen later transferred to Madison Central High School, from which he graduated in 1923.

When he enrolled at the University of Wisconsin, Bardeen decided to major in electrical engineering with minors in mathematics and physics. He was awarded his bachelor's degree in 1928 and stayed on to complete his master of science degree in electrical engineering a year later. For his master's degree, he carried out research on the radiation emitted by antennas and on problems of applied geophysics.

Upon graduation from Wisconsin, Bardeen accepted a research job at the Gulf Research and Development Corporation in Pittsburgh. His work there put him in the forefront of a new and growing field of physics, geophysics. He worked with Leo J. Peters on the development of new methods for locating deposits of petroleum. Although the work was interesting and well paid ($3,000 per year in the midst of the Depression), Bardeen concluded that he wanted a different kind of life. He had heard about the establishment of the new Institute for Advanced Studies at Princeton University and hoped to have an opportunity to work with some of the great scientists associated with the Institute. He decided, therefore, to

apply for the doctoral program in mathematics at Princeton, where the Institute was to be housed. He was accepted and was assigned the great **Eugene Paul Wigner** as his advisor. That assignment was propitious, as Wigner was one of the world's leading authorities on the application of quantum mechanics to solid-state physics. It was not long before Bardeen, too, became deeply involved in this subject. For his doctoral research, Bardeen chose to study the forces that act on electrons in metals. In the midst of that research, he left Princeton to accept an appointment as a Junior Fellow at Harvard University in 1935, an appointment that lasted officially until 1938. At Harvard, Bardeen worked with **Percy Bridgman**, the world's leading authority on high pressure physics, and with **John Van Vleck**, who was to win the 1977 Nobel Prize for his research on the electronic structure of magnetic and disordered systems. Bardeen eventually completed his dissertation at Princeton and was awarded a Ph.D. in mathematics and physics in 1936.

Bardeen's first academic appointment was as assistant professor of physics at the University of Minnesota in 1938. While at Minnesota, he continued to study the behavior of electrons in metals; in 1939, he published a paper on this topic with his former advisor, Van Vleck. When World War II began, Bardeen left Minnesota to take a job as physicist at the Naval Ordnance Laboratory in Washington, D.C. His work there dealt with the magnetic fields of ships as they move through salt waters.

Develops Transistor

When World War II ended, Bardeen took a job at the Bell Telephone Laboratories at Murray Hill, New Jersey. One reason for this move was that Bardeen felt that he could no longer support his family on the salary of an academic. He had married Jane Maxwell on July 18, 1938, and by 1945 they had three children, James Maxwell, William Allen, and Elizabeth Ann.

The move to Bell Labs was an extremely fortunate one for Bardeen. He was assigned to work there with Brattain and Shockley, who had been studying the properties of semiconductors for many years. The impetus for this research was the general dissatisfaction among physicists with the fundamental problems posed by existing electronic systems. Those systems depended on vacuum tubes, which were bulky, fragile, and huge consumers of electrical power. Brattain and Shockley, among others, were convinced that the solution to this problem lay in the use of semiconductors, materials that conduct an electrical current better than do insulators like rubber and plastics, but not nearly as well as conductors such as copper and silver.

Shockley had developed an idea for using semiconductors as amplifiers as early as 1939, but his work had been interrupted by the war. When Bardeen arrived at Bell Labs in 1945, Shockley had had no success in producing a model of his idea that actually worked. As Bardeen began to think about this problem, it occurred to him that the atoms on the surface of the semiconductor might be acting as a barrier to incoming electrical signals, preventing the material from behaving as Shockley had expected.

This idea led to a new approach to Shockley's work, one in which he, Bardeen, and Brattain began to study the fundamental properties of semiconductors. By 1948, enormous progress had been made, and Bardeen and Brattain had constructed the first working model of Shockley's concept, the transistor. In the transistor (short for "transfer resistor"), a semiconductor is placed between two wires, which serve as electrical contacts for the current. For their work, the three Bell scientists were jointly awarded the 1956 Nobel Prize in physics. Shockley's part of the prize was given for his fundamental theoretical work, while Bardeen and Brattain were honored for their accomplishment in producing a working model of Shockley's theory.

The invention of the transistor revolutionized electronics. It also brought honors and awards to Bardeen, as well as to Brattain and Shockley. Among these were the Stuart and Ballantine Medal of the Franklin Institute (1952), the John Scott Medal of the city of Philadelphia (1955), the Oliver E. Buckley Solid-State Physics Prize of the American Physical Society (1954), and the Fritz London Award (1962), as well as election to the National Academy of Sciences in 1954.

Conducts Revolutionary Research in Superconductivity

The collaboration among Bardeen, Brattain, and Shockley came to an end in 1951, when Bardeen accepted an appointment as Professor of Electrical Engineering and Physics at the University of Illinois. Once settled at Illinois, Bardeen turned to the problem of superconductivity, which he had been interested in as a graduate student at Princeton but had set aside because of World War II. The phenomenon of superconductivity had first been described by the Dutch physicist **Heike Kamerlingh-Onnes** in 1911. Kamerlingh-Onnes had reported that some metals lose all resistance to the flow of electrical current, becoming "superconductive," as they are cooled to temperatures close to absolute zero. The heightened conductivity derives from a free flow of electrons in the metal. Scientists were intrigued by this phenomenon for both theoretical and practical reasons. An understanding of superconductivity could potentially revolutionize the electronics industry. Every device

that operates by means of an electric current wastes a huge amount of energy in overcoming electrical resistance. If superconducting materials could be used in those devices, virtually no energy would be lost to resistance. The practical problem posed by Kamerlingh-Onnes's discovery was the low temperature required for superconductivity. In the intervening half century, scientists had been singularly unsuccessful in improving on his work. By the 1950s, the highest temperature at which superconductivity had been observed was still only about 20 degrees Kelvin, 20 degrees above absolute zero.

As his coworkers on the problem of superconductivity Bardeen selected a postdoctoral associate at Illinois, Leon Cooper, and a graduate student, J. Robert Schrieffer. One of their first breakthroughs on the problem came in 1956, when Cooper showed that an electron moving through a crystal causes a slight deformation of the crystal and, in the process, attracts a second electron to itself. Eventually, electrons throughout the crystal become joined to each other in pairs (now known as "Cooper pairs"). The difficulty lay in showing how Cooper pairs could be used to explain the free flow of *all* valence electrons in a superconductor. That problem required a sophisticated mathematical analysis, which Schrieffer set out to perform. While Bardeen was at Stockholm to receive his first Nobel Prize, Schrieffer found an answer to the problem. The theory that eventually evolved from Cooper pairs and Schrieffer's mathematical analysis is now known as the BCS theory of superconductivity, in honor of its three creators, Bardeen, Cooper, and Schrieffer. Often described as one of the most important developments in theoretical physics since quantum theory, it brought the 1972 Nobel Prize for physics to its three codiscoverers.

Superconductivity promises to revolutionize technology in much the way transistors did. For example, research is now being conducted on the development of maglev railway trains. The term *maglev* is shorthand for *mag*netic *lev*itation, a phenomenon that occurs when one object (such as a rail car) is suspended above another object (such as a track) by the repulsive force of magnetic fields. Long a dream of inventors, maglev trains have only recently become a realistic possibility with the development of powerful, low-cost magnets made from superconducting materials.

In 1959, Bardeen moved to the Center for Advanced Study at the University of Illinois, where he continued to carry out research on solid-state physics and low-temperature phenomena. He retired officially in 1975 and was designated professor of physics emeritus. Bardeen spent his leisure time in golfing, swimming, and traveling. He died in Boston on January 30, 1991, as the result of heart failure following surgery that had revealed the presence of lung cancer.

SELECTED WRITINGS BY BARDEEN:

Books

Understanding Superconductivity, Plenum, 1964.
(With Behram Kurçunoğlu) *Impact of Basic Technology,* Plenum, 1973.

Periodicals

"Research Leading to the Point-Contact Transistor," *Science,* Volume 126, 1957.
"Theory of Superconductivity," *Physical Review,* Volume 108, 1957.
"To a Solid State," *Science,* November, 1984.

SOURCES:

Books

National Geographic Society, Special Publications Division, *Those Inventive Americans,* National Geographic Society, 1971, pp. 208–217.
Nobel Prize Winners, H. W. Wilson, 1987, p. 55–59.
Weber, Robert L., *Pioneers of Science: Nobel Prize Winners in Physics,* American Institute of Physics, 1980, pp. 159–160.

Periodicals

Burtch, Robert L., "Interview with a Nobel Laureate," *Science and Children,* November-December, 1990, pp. 14–17.
"A Few Uncommon Engineers," *IEEE Spectrum,* November, 1988, p. 59.

—*Sketch by David E. Newton*

Charles Glover Barkla
1877-1944
English physicist

Charles Glover Barkla's fame as a physicist rests on his study of X rays, a field in which he made a number of important discoveries. That research began while Barkla was still a graduate student at King's College in the early 1900s. It resulted in the production of more than seventy scientific papers on the characteristics of X rays. Among Barkla's most important findings were the discovery that the scattering of X rays is dependent on the molecular weight of gases through which they pass, that X rays are polarized like other forms of electromagnetic radiation, and that secondary radiation produced by the absorption of X rays consists of two types, later referred to as K radiation and L radiation. The first of these discoveries was intimately related to **Henry Gwyn Jeffreys Moseley**'s eventual discovery of the concept of atomic number and resulted in Barkla's being awarded the 1917 Nobel Prize for physics. After 1916, Barkla became obsessed with the search for a third type of secondary radiation that he called the "J phenomenon." In this search, he gradually withdrew from the larger community of physicists, citing only his own research and rejecting many of the fundamental new concepts of modern physics, such as quantum theory, then being put forward.

Charles Glover Barkla was born on June 27, 1877, in Widnes, Lancashire, England. His mother was the former Sarah Glover, daughter of a watchmaker, and his father was John Martin Barkla, secretary of the Atlas Chemical Company. Young Charles was educated at Liverpool Institute, from which he graduated in 1895. He then entered University College, Liverpool, where he majored in physics and mathematics. Barkla studied experimental physics under Oliver Lodge, for whom he occasionally substituted as lecturer. He eventually earned his B.Sc. degree with first class honors in 1898 and his M.Sc. a year later.

In 1899, Barkla was awarded an 1851 Exhibition Scholarship that allowed him to do graduate work at Trinity College, Cambridge, where he studied with George Stokes and **J. J. Thomson**. After eighteen months, however, he transferred to King's College in order to become a member of the famous chapel choir there. Barkla had an excellent voice (said to be either baritone or bass according to various biographers) which drew crowds for his solo performances.

Barkla decided not to continue a professional career in music, however, and instead accepted an appointment as Oliver Lodge Fellow at the University of Liverpool in 1902. At Liverpool he continued in earnest his research on X rays originally begun during his last year at Cambridge. The topic of that research was secondary radiation produced when X rays pass through a material.

Makes Many Discoveries about Secondary Radiation

In his original studies, **Wilhelm Conrad Röntgen**, the discoverer of X rays, had observed the phenomenon of secondary radiation, or the radiation produced when a substance is exposed to primary radiation. However, he failed to continue his research on it. Barkla picked up this line of study in 1902, and made a number of critical discoveries. In the first place, he found that secondary radiation is absorbed by a material essentially to the same extent that primary radiation is absorbed. This conclusion provided important support for the hypothesis that X rays are a form of electromagnetic radiation.

In his next series of experiments, Barkla exposed a variety of different materials to X-radiation. He found that the intensity of secondary radiation produced in each case was related to the density (and, hence, the molecular weight) of each gas. The logical conclusion from this finding was that the number of particles in the atom of each material is responsible for the differences in the way the radiation is scattered. In his article "Secondary Radiation from Gases Subject to X-Rays" in *Philosophy Magazine,* he pointed out that "[these results give] further support to the theory that the atoms of different substances are different systems of similar corpuscles, the number of which in the atom is proportional to its atomic weight." This conclusion, first published in 1903, presaged Moseley's own hypothesis, announced a decade later, of the concept of atomic number.

Continued observations of secondary radiation uncovered additional findings. In 1904, for example, Barkla demonstrated that secondary radiation is polarized, an additional piece of evidence supporting the electromagnetic character of X rays. He also found that secondary radiation consisted of two distinct types, originally called "A" and "B," but later renamed "K" and "L." Subsequent investigations revealed that these two forms of radiation are produced by electron transitions occurring in the lower energy levels of an atom.

Barkla's success in working with X rays led to his rapid advancement in academic circles. After receiving his D.Sc. from Liverpool in 1904, he was appointed demonstrator and assistant lecturer in physics in 1905 and, two years later, assumed the duties of lecturer in advanced electricity in a post created for him at Liverpool. In 1909 he accepted an appointment as Wheatstone Professor of Physics at King's College, London, and then moved to the University of Edinburgh in 1913 as professor of natural philosophy. He remained at Edinburgh until his death on October 23, 1944. The crowning recognition of his research career was the award of the 1917 Nobel Prize for physics. Barkla was also elected a fellow of the Royal Society in 1912.

Although there was never a dispute about Barkla's talent as an experimentalist, serious doubts surrounded his abilities as a theoretical physicist. By the late 1910s, for example, Barkla had begun to fall behind the rapid revolution taking place in physics, rejecting discoveries and new concepts such as the Compton effect and quantum theory. Instead, he committed himself to finding a third type of secondary radiation, the so-called "J phenomenon." That

pursuit, however, became a wild goose chase with no useful discoveries resulting from it.

Barkla was married to the former Mary Esther Cowell in 1907. They had three sons and one daughter, all of whom eventually graduated from Edinburgh. Barkla's youngest son, Michael, was killed in a flying accident in North Africa in August 1943, while serving as a surgeon in the Royal Air Force. This tragic loss was generally believed to have contributed to Barkla's own death only a year later.

SELECTED WRITINGS BY BARKLA:

Books

Radiation and Matter, Telegraph Printing Works, 1920.

Periodicals

"Secondary Radiation from Gases Subject to X-Rays," *Philosophical Magazine,* 6th Series, Volume 5, 1903, pp. 685–698.
"Secondary Roentgen Radiation," *Philosophical Magazine,* 6th Series, Volume 11, 1906, pp. 812–828.
(With Charles A. Sadler) "Secondary X-Rays and the Atomic Weight of Nickel," *Philosophical Magazine,* 6th Series, Volume 14, 1907, pp. 408–422.

SOURCES:

Books

A Biographical Dictionary of Scientists, Wiley, 1974, p. 35.
Dictionary of Scientific Biography, Volume 1, Scribner's, 1975, pp. 456–459.
Heathcote, Niels H. de V., *Nobel Prize Winners in Physics, 1901–1950,* Henry Schuman, 1953, pp. 141–150.
Nobel Prize Winners, H. W. Wilson, 1987, pp. 59–61.
Obituary Notices of Fellows of the Royal Society, Volume 5, Royal Society (London), 1947, pp. 341–366.
Weber, Robert L., *Pioneers of Science: Nobel Prize Winners in Physics,* American Institute of Physics, 1980, pp. 56–57.

Periodicals

Stephenson, Reginald, "The Scientific Career of Charles Glover Barkla," *American Journal of Physics,* February 1967, pp. 141–152.

—*Sketch by David E. Newton*

Christiaan Neethling Barnard
1922-
South African heart surgeon

Christiaan Neethling Barnard

Christiaan Neethling Barnard rose to international prominence when he performed the world's first human heart transplant at Groote Schuur Hospital in Cape Town, South Africa, on December 3, 1967. In the years preceding this daring operation he had introduced open heart surgery and kidney transplantation to South Africa. Barnard is also known for discovering in the early 1950s that the fatal birth defect called intestinal atresia—a gap in the small intestine—is caused by an inadequate supply of blood to the fetus during pregnancy; in addition, Barnard developed a surgical procedure to correct the defect. He devoted his research in the early 1960s to correcting congenital heart malformations in children. He also designed an artificial heart valve for use in surgery. Barnard spent all of his 25-year career as a surgeon at Groote Schuur Hospital.

Barnard was born on November 8, 1922, in Beaufort West, South Africa, the fourth of five sons of Adam Hendrik Barnard and Maria Elisabeth de Swart Barnard, both of whom were Afrikaaner missionaries. His father, a reverend in the Dutch Reformed Church, preached to a non-white congregation; his mother had been a school teacher before marriage. Barnard attended a local high school and went on to the University of Cape Town where he received his preliminary medical degree in 1946. He served as an intern at Groote Schuur Hospital in Cape Town in 1947 and then spent two years in general practice in Ceres, South Africa. Barnard returned to Cape Town in 1950, becoming Senior Resident Medical Officer at City Hospital. There he developed his research skills while working on treatments for children with tuberculosis. After writing a thesis on his tuberculosis work, Barnard was awarded his M.D. in 1953 by the University of Cape Town.

Begins Career in Surgery

Barnard became a resident surgeon at Groote Schuur Hospital the same year. He also began an ambitious after-hours research project to develop techniques of open heart surgery, using dogs as research subjects. In order to operate successfully, he needed to find a way to safely slow down the animals' body processes by lowering their temperatures. He achieved this by running cold water through a balloon inserted into a dog's stomach. This technique was later used during surgery on humans. Barnard also turned to the technique in his experiments to determine the cause of intestinal atresia, a deadly birth defect in which babies are born with a gap in the bowel. By operating on pregnant dogs to induce the defect in their puppies, Barnard found the cause to be an insufficient blood supply to the developing fetus. He then created a way to successfully repair the incompletely formed intestine with surgery.

In 1956, traveling on a Charles Adams Memorial Scholarship, Barnard joined Dr. Owen Wangensteen and his pioneering team of researchers in cardiothoracic surgery at the University of Minnesota in Minneapolis. There he collaborated in research to make and test an artificial heart valve. During this time Barnard came to regard Wangensteen as both a mentor and a father-figure. In 1958, the University of Minnesota awarded Barnard the Ph.D. in surgery. Wangensteen bestowed Barnard with an additional reward; he arranged for Barnard to bring a heart-lung machine back to South Africa. This piece of equipment, only a few of which existed at the time, oxygenates a patient's blood and pumps it through the body during open heart surgery. With the machine, Barnard was able to perform heart surgery at home in South Africa; it would later make possible his most famous operation.

On his return to Groote Schuur Hospital, Barnard focused on developing surgical techniques to correct congenital heart defects, such as transposition of the great vessels, and to replace diseased or malformed heart valves with prostheses. Aided by his younger brother Marius, also a heart surgeon, Barnard began experimenting with heart transplantation in dogs. Before a human heart transplant could be attempted, however, the problem of preventing the patient's immune system from attacking a foreign organ had to be solved. Other researchers interested in kidney transplantation were working to control this immune rejection with drugs. Barnard later wrote in his autobiography *One Life,* "The kidney had become a stepping stone to the heart. Its transplant would be a run-through for a heart transfer." With future heart transplants in mind, in 1966 Barnard attended a training course in kidney transplantation at the Medical College of Virginia in Richmond. In October 1967, back home in Cape Town, he organized the surgical team that performed the first kidney transplant in South Africa.

Achieves First Human Heart Transplant

Barnard felt ready at this point to attempt a heart transplant. With their kidney transplant experience, his 20-person surgical team was well-versed in the steps necessary for successful organ transplantation: selecting a donor, typing the blood and tissue of donor and recipient for compatibility, caring for both patients before surgery, coordinating the operations, and controlling organ rejection with drugs that suppress the immune system. The opportunity for Barnard to try his heart transplant technique on a human arrived when 55-year-old Louis Washkansky was hospitalized at Groote Schuur in November 1967. Washkansky, a Lithuanian emigrant to Cape Town and a grocer by trade, had suffered a series of heart attacks over the previous seven years. His heart was failing, and cardiologists at the hospital expected him to die within a few weeks. Barnard obtained Washkansky's consent to try heart transplant surgery and then put his surgical team on 24-hour alert for a suitable heart donor. On December 2, that donor, a 25-year-old bank clerk who had been struck by a car, was carried into the hospital. Her brain was dead, no longer able to control vital functions such as breathing and maintaining blood pressure, but her heart was still beating. The donor, a woman named Denise Darvall, was kept alive by a respirator while the surgeons prepared for the operation. Barnard performed the transplant early the next morning. Washkansky recovered well enough to sit up in bed and eat steak and eggs. But 18 days after his surgery he died of double pneumonia. His immune system, suppressed with drugs and radiation so that it would not attack his new heart, had been unable to fight the infection.

Barnard followed a transplant procedure that does not require removing all of a dying patient's diseased heart. Rather, he cut away only the bottom portion of the heart, leaving in place the tops of the upper chambers and the blood vessels connected to them, as well as the patch of nerve cells that regulates the heart beat. The matching bottom of the donor's heart was then stitched in place. Although Barnard had practiced the procedure on dogs, credit for developing it goes to Norman E. Shumway of Stanford University in California. Shumway had performed the first successful heart transplant in a dog in 1958 and had been working to improve the technique and his understanding of how to suppress the immune system. Indeed, many surgeons had anticipated that Shumway would be the first to use his technique in a human heart transplant. Physicians at many medical centers, however, had been practicing heart transplants on dogs and were poised to perform operations on humans. Within a year of Barnard's groundbreaking effort, more than 100 heart transplants had been performed around the world.

Heart transplant surgery opened a host of ethical questions, which were widely discussed in forums such as newspapers and magazines. Many people expressed concern about a scenario in which a doctor would have to decide to give up hope of resuscitating a potential organ donor and declare the person medically dead in order to transplant body parts. In such a case, particularly if the potential donor were being kept alive by elaborate medical equipment, would the death of a potential donor be hastened in order to have the healthiest organs possible available for transplant? In the first human heart transplant operation, Barnard disconnected the donor's respirator and waited for her heart to stop beating before removing it, even though doing so might damage the heart. "I did not want to touch this girl until she was conventionally dead," Barnard wrote in *One Life.* "Brain death had already been established, but I felt we could not put a knife into her until she was truly a cadaver."

The initial enthusiasm for heart transplant surgery faded quickly, not over ethical quandaries, but because heart recipients continued to succumb to infection. Amid criticism that he had rushed too hastily into a risky procedure, however, Barnard continued to perform and perfect the transplant procedure, as did Shumway and a few other surgeons. As the operation became more routine, more patients survived longer. In 1974 he performed the first double heart transplant. By 1983, 63 successful heart transplants had been done at Groote Schuur under Barnard's direction.

Barnard served as head of cardiac research and surgery at Groote Schuur Hospital in Cape Town until chronic arthritis in his hands forced him to retire from surgical practice in 1983. Since 1985 he has been senior consultant and scientist in residence at the Oklahoma Heart Center, an organ transplant center, at Baptist Medical Center in Oklahoma City, Oklahoma.

Remains in Public Eye after Medical Career

As the world's first heart transplant surgeon, Barnard was thrust into the public eye, appearing on television and being interviewed in magazines. After his surgical successes, however, Barnard's flamboyant private life helped him maintain celebrity status. His reported womanizing, including an affair with Italian film star Gina Lollobrigida, made gossip-column headlines. In 1970 he divorced Aletta Gertruida Louw, the woman he met while an undergraduate and married in 1948, in order to marry Barbara M. Zoeller, a 19-year-old fashion model and steel heiress from Johannesburg. The couple kept up a jet-setting reputation; Barnard opened a chain of Italian restaurants, which served dinners on plates embellished with his signature, while his wife ran a boutique. The couple divorced in 1982. In 1987, Barnard married Karin Setzkorn. Barnard has a son and a daughter by his first wife, two sons from his second marriage, and one son from the third.

In the mid–1980s Barnard again became embroiled in scandal, this time by endorsing an anti-wrinkle skin cream called Glycel, thereby lending it dubious scientific credibility. He also served on the scientific board of La Clinique La Prairie, an alpine spa where clients received injections of fetal sheep cells, purportedly to ward off the effects of aging.

Barnard is the author of numerous books, including an autobiography, a tract condoning euthanasia and suicide, an analysis of South African apartheid, and several ghost-written novels. In his retirement he maintains an interest in fishing, flying, farming, and ornithology. He is also the author of numerous medical articles and a text on the surgery of common congenital heart malformations. He has been presented with many honorary doctorates, foreign orders, and awards, including the Dag Hammarskjold International Prize and Peace Prize, the Kennedy Foundation Award, and the Milan International Prize for Science.

SELECTED WRITINGS BY BARNARD:

Books

(With Velva Schrire) *Surgery of Common Congenital Cardiac Malformations,* Harper & Row, 1968.
(With Curtis Bill Pepper) *One Life,* Macmillan, 1969.
South Africa: Sharp Dissection, Books in Focus, 1977.
Good Life/Good Death: A Doctor's Case for Euthanasia and Suicide, Prentice-Hall, 1980.

SOURCES:

Periodicals

"Christiaan Barnard Retires to the Farm," *Newsweek,* September 5, 1983, p. 9.

"The Hasty Hearts?," *Newsweek,* January 22, 1968, pp. 60–61.
"The Heart: Miracle in Cape Town," *Newsweek,* December 18, 1967, pp. 86–90.

—*Sketch by Betsy Hanson*

William Harry Barnes
1887-1945
American otolaryngologist, surgeon, and inventor

Dr. William Harry Barnes was a distinguished ear, nose, and throat specialist who invented an instrument to facilitate reaching the pituitary gland surgically. He was Chief Otolaryngologist at Frederick Douglass Hospital in Philadelphia, and, as a diplomate of the American Board of Otolaryngology, he was the first black to become a board-certified specialist. Barnes was active in the National Medical Association, an organization of black doctors, dentists, and pharmacists, and served as its 37th president from 1935 to 1936.

Barnes was born on April 4, 1887, in Philadelphia, Pennsylvania, and spent nearly his entire life in that city. He grew up in a poor neighborhood, and his parents worked at menial jobs to support him and his two sisters. During high school he walked ten miles a day to school and work because he couldn't afford the trolley. His family and friends ridiculed his idea of becoming a doctor, but they were not aware of his fierce determination to rise out of poverty and to pursue a career as a professional.

After graduating from Philadelphia's Central High School in 1908, Barnes spent the summer preparing for the University of Pennsylvania Medical School scholarship exam. He won the scholarship, becoming the first black to do so. He received his M.D. in 1912 and interned at Douglass and Mercy Hospitals the following year, with a specialty in ear, nose, and throat. Douglass Hospital appointed him assistant otolaryngologist in 1913. In 1918 he served in the U.S. Public Health Service as an acting assistant surgeon.

In 1921, having completed seven years of clinical experience, Barnes returned to the University of Pennsylvania to do postgraduate work in ear, nose, and throat treatment and surgery. He desired further advanced training but couldn't find it in the United States, so he went to France in 1924 to study at the University of Paris and the University of Bordeaux.

Later, in the United States, the renowned Dr. Chevalier Jackson of Philadelphia also served as Barnes's mentor, teaching him to use the bronchoscope, a device used for inspecting the bronchial tubes. The first black to master bronchoscopy, Barnes set up a department of bronchoscopy at Mercy Hospital. In 1931 he accepted a teaching position in bronchoscopy at Howard University Medical School in Washington, D.C.

Barnes was an innovator in his field. His invention of the hypophyscope, an instrument used to visualize the pituitary gland through the sphenoid sinus, made him famous. His accomplishments included other innovative operative techniques as well as a streamlined, efficient medical record system. Barnes was very active in the National Medical Association, for which he presented papers and gave demonstrations. One such demonstration showed the speedy and bloodless technique of his ten-minute tonsillectomy. He became the president of the association in 1935. Barnes was also one of the founders of the Society for the Promotion of Negro Specialists in Medicine. Among his other affiliations were the American Medical Association and the American Laryngological Association. Locally, he served as president of the Philadelphia Academy of Medicine and Allied Sciences for three years.

Barnes was married to Mattie E. Thomas in 1912. The couple had five sons: W. Harry Barnes, Jr., a mortician; Lloyd T. Barnes, an internist; Ralph W. Barnes, an industrial designer; Leroy T. Barnes, a radiologist; and Carl L. Barnes. In 1938 Barnes began to suffer from hypertension, and in 1943, he incurred a spinal injury with paraplegia. He later died of bronchial pneumonia on January 15, 1945, at the age of 58. His obituary in the March 1945 *Journal of the National Medical Association* paid tribute to him as a nationally recognized ear, nose, and throat specialist whose "ability as a diagnostician and surgeon was equalled by few, and surpassed by none."

SELECTED WRITINGS BY BARNES:

Periodicals

"A Simplified Method of Removing Naso-Pharyngeal Fibromas," *Eye, Ear, Nose, and Throat Monthly,* November 1924.
"An Improved Hypophyscope," *Laryngos,* 1927, pp. 379–380.

SOURCES:

Books

Dictionary of American Medical Biography, Greenwood Press, 1984, pp. 37–38.

Sammons, Vivian Ovelton, *Blacks in Science and Medicine,* Hemisphere Publishing, 1990, pp. 20–21.

Periodicals

Cobb, W. Montague, "William Harry Barnes, 1887–1945," *Journal of the National Medical Association,* January 1955, pp. 64–66.
"In Memoriam, W. Harry Barnes, A Tribute," *Journal of the National Medical Association,* March 1945, p. 72.
Venable, H. Phillip, "Pseudo-Tumor Cerebri," *Journal of the National Medical Association,* November 1970, pp. 435–436.

—*Sketch by Linda Lewin*

Murray Llewellyn Barr
1908-
Canadian anatomist and geneticist

Murray Llewellyn Barr helped create a new field of genetic research with a chance finding in 1949. He discovered a structure present only in the cells of females, known as the sex chromatin or Barr body, which provided physicians with a new diagnostic tool. The discovery of the sex chromatin inspired further research into human cytogenetics, a discipline which approaches questions of heredity through both genetics and cytology, the study of cells. Barr's findings especially influenced investigations into chromosomal defects as causes of developmental abnormalities; several disorders, including Down's syndrome, were soon linked to chromosomal errors. Since some of these disorders are marked by retarded mental development, Barr's work has also led to great advances in understanding the causes of mental retardation.

Barr was born in Belmont, Ontario, on June 20, 1908, the son of William Llewellyn Barr and Margaret McLellan Barr. His father was a farmer, originally from Northern Ireland, and his mother was a homemaker. As a youngster, Barr attended schools in Belmont and nearby London, Ontario. In 1926, he entered the University of Western Ontario with a scholarship in French but turned his attention to science and medicine, receiving his B.A. in 1930 and his M.D. in 1933. Several years later, in 1938, Barr would also earn an M.Sc. from Western. Barr served his medical internship at Hamot Hospital in Erie, Pennsylvania, from 1933 to 1934.

Returning to Ontario, Barr was in general practice in London from 1934 to 1936. On July 5, 1934, he married Ruth Vivian King, with whom he would eventually raise four children. He left general practice in 1936 to serve as an instructor in the department of anatomy at the University of Western Ontario. This marked the beginning of his long career at this institution, broken only by military service during World War II when he served as a medical officer with the Royal Canadian Air Force. Barr returned to Western in 1945 as an associate professor; he then served as professor from 1949 to 1973, when he retired. The head of the department of microscopic anatomy from 1953 to 1964, Barr became chairman of the department of anatomy from 1964 to 1967.

Discovers Sex Chromatin by Accident

Barr's serendipitous discovery in the field of genetics was made while conducting an experiment on the physiology of nerve cells. In the course of the experiment, Barr and Ewart G. Bertram, a graduate student, noticed that some of the nerve cells contained a mass of chromatin in their nuclei. Chromatin is the substance of which chromosomes are made. By reviewing their notes, the two men realized that the mass of chromatin was present in the nerve cells of female cats but not in male cats. That such a sex difference existed in the tissue cells was an unexpected and almost unbelievable discovery at the time. The mass of chromatin came to be called the sex chromatin or Barr body. Further research showed that it was present in tissues other than the nerve cells and that sex chromatin existed in the cells of most mammals, including humans. Barr and Bertram published the results of their experiments in *Nature* in 1949.

Barr's discovery of the sex chromatin offered physicians a way to determine a person's sex from their cells, and for patients with developmental defects of the reproductive system this promised to be an important diagnostic tool. Until this discovery, no simple test existed for determining the basic sex of a hermaphrodite. Although it was known that females and males had different sets of sex chromosomes (females XX and males XY), examining the sex chromosomes directly was very difficult in the early 1950s. It would be a few more years before chromosomal analysis, known as karyotyping, became sophisticated enough for clinical use, and in the meantime the sex chromatin test proved to be immensely useful. At first, the sex chromatin test was done on small skin biopsies. Barr and a colleague, Keith Moore, soon devised an easier way to gather cells. By scraping the lining of a patient's mouth, also known as the buccal cavity, cells could be collected for testing. The buccal smear test made obtaining a diagnosis even simpler.

Establishes Association Between Sex Chromatin and Several Disorders

For scientists, Barr's discovery raised fascinating new questions about the relationship between the sex chromatin and the sex chromosomes. It seemed obvious that the sex chromatin had something to do with the X chromosomes, but it would take ten years and several crucial scientific advances to determine the precise nature of this correspondence. Barr continued his research by conducting buccal smear tests on large numbers of patients. He and his associates quickly found that abnormalities in the presence of the sex chromatin corresponded with several known disorders. Most men tested negative for sex chromatin, while men who tested positive typically suffered from Klinefelter's syndrome, which is marked by sterility and mental retardation. The cells of most women contain sex chromatin, but those without it showed symptoms of Turner's syndrome, marked by sterility and short height.

Barr's work during the 1950s fostered an extremely fruitful period in the history of genetics, when one discovery often led quickly to another. As karyotyping improved, new discoveries related to human chromosomes were made. In 1956, Jo Hin Tjio and Albert Levan declared the chromosome count in human beings to be forty-six, and not forty-eight as previously believed. In 1959, Jerome Lejeune identified the cause of Down's syndrome as an extra chromosome; he showed that Down's syndrome patients carry a total of forty-seven chromosomes.

With these discoveries, it now seemed quite likely that abnormalities in the sex-chromosome complex were not only associated with such disorders as Klinefelter's syndrome and Turner's syndrome but actually responsible for them. Indeed, Charles Ford and his associates showed that Turner's syndrome is marked by an XO sex-chromosome complex, with O standing for the lack of a second sex chromosome. Patricia Jacobs and her group discovered that Klinefelter's syndrome is indicated by an additional one or more X chromosomes: XXY or even XXXY. For the first time, the genetic origins of these disorders were understood. In 1961, S. Ohno determined that in normal women, one of the two X chromosomes in the body cells was very concentrated and genetically inactive. It was this chromosome that Barr had recognized and named the sex chromatin in 1949. Although the buccal smear test persisted as a useful way to test large populations quickly for any suspected abnormalities, karyotyping continued to improve. It eventually replaced the buccal smear test altogether.

People with Down's syndrome or Klinefelter's syndrome suffer varying degrees of mental retardation. Although Barr never set out to elucidate the causes of mental retardation, his research accomplished great strides in this direction. In 1962, Barr and four other scientists, including Jo Hin Tjio and Jerome Lejeune, received the first awards given by the Joseph P. Kennedy Jr. Foundation for work in combatting mental retardation; the awards were personally presented by President John F. Kennedy.

Other important awards that Barr received include the Flavelle Medal of the Royal Society of Canada in 1959 and the Gairdner Foundation Award of Merit in 1963. He was a fellow of the Royal Society of Canada and the Royal Society of London. Barr was also honored by the University of Western Ontario with a series of annual lectures, and the first Murray L. Barr lecture was given in 1993.

SELECTED WRITINGS BY BARR:

Books

The Human Nervous System: An Anatomical Viewpoint, Harper, 1972.

A Century of Medicine at Western: A Centennial History of the Faculty of Medicine, University of Western Ontario, University of Western Ontario, 1977.

(With Keith Moore and Ewart G. Bertram) *Study Guide and Review Manual of the Human Nervous System,* Saunders, 1979.

SOURCES:

Books

Hsu, T.C., "Sex and the Single Chromosome," *Human and Mammalian Cytogenetics: An Historical Perspective,* Springer-Verlag, 1979.

Proceedings and Transactions of the Royal Society of Canada, Volume 53, Royal Society of Canada, 1959, pp. 48–49.

Periodicals

New York Times, December 7, 1962, p. 1; December 12, 1962, p. 6.

—*Sketch by Liz Marshall*

Neil Bartlett

1932-

English American chemist

Neil Bartlett has been called "the foremost fluorine chemist in the world" by a colleague, as reported in *Chemical and Engineering News.* In 1962 he used his skill with that highly active reagent to produce the first-ever compound of a noble gas.

Bartlett's success forced a reexamination of basic valence theory, which proposes that the number of free electrons in an atom is the prime factor in determining that atom's bonding behavior.

Bartlett was born September 15, 1932, in Newcastle-upon-Tyne, England, the middle sibling in a family of three children. His father, Norman Bartlett, was a shipwright, a trade plied by the Bartletts for over a century. His mother was Anne Vock Bartlett. After attending Heaton Grammar School from 1944 to 1951, Bartlett entered King's College of the University of Durham, where he received his bachelor of science degree in 1954 and his doctorate in 1958. In 1957 he married Christina Isabel Cross. They have four children: Jeremy, Jane, Christopher, and Robin.

Following graduation, Bartlett taught at the Duke's School, then emigrated to Canada when he was appointed a lecturer in chemistry at the University of British Columbia in Vancouver in 1958. By 1964 he had worked his way up to full professor of chemistry. In 1966 Bartlett was named professor of chemistry at Princeton University; simultaneously, he became a member of the research staff at Bell Telephone Laboratories. In 1969 he joined the faculty of the University of California at Berkeley as a professor of chemistry and faculty senior scientist at the Lawrence Berkeley Laboratory.

Begins Work with Fluorines

While at the University of British Columbia, Bartlett began studying the factors that limit the combining capacity, or oxidation states, of various elements. He concentrated on the noble metals, such as gold and platinum, because they offered a range of oxidation states. He was particularly interested in the relationship of the geometry of the molecules to their valence, or outer shell electron configurations.

As part of this work, Bartlett was using fluorines, the most powerful oxidizing agents (electron acceptors) of the known elements, and reacting them with the noble metals. Treating platinum or platinum compounds with fluorine, Bartlett produced a highly reactive red solid, which was thought to be platinum oxyfluoride. After devising special techniques to study the solid, Bartlett and D. H. Lohmann determined that it was a actually a salt, dioxygenyl hexafluoroplatinate, and the first compound to contain both positively and negatively charged ions. This discovery paved the way for what *Chemical and Engineering News* called "one of the most important developments in inorganic chemistry in modern times": Bartlett's creation of a compound of a noble gas.

Since the discovery of argon and helium in 1894 by Sir **William Ramsay** and Lord John Rayleigh, the noble gases—which also included neon, krypton, and xenon—had proved remarkably inert. Valence theory offered an explanation. Atoms are brought together by the electrons orbiting their nuclei. These orbits, or shells, can hold only a certain number of electrons. For example, oxygen's outermost shell can hold eight electrons, but the atom itself has only six in the outer shell. Oxygen atoms seek to fill their outer ring by joining with atoms that can provide two electrons. Hydrogen atoms have only one electron each, so two hydrogen atoms are a perfect complement to an oxygen atom.

The outer shell of electrons in a noble gas atom, however, is already full. Helium, for instance, has two electrons—its maximum—orbiting its nucleus; the other noble gases have eight. Because the outer shell is complete, a noble gas atom does not need to share electrons with any other atoms. Thus, valence theory reasoned, the noble gases are completely inert. In 1933 **Linus Pauling** surmised that xenon, the heaviest stable noble gas, might react with a very active compound, perhaps a fluorine. A number of experiments to create a compound with xenon failed. Attempts continued for years without success.

But in 1962 Bartlett succeeded, using platinum hexafluoride to oxidize (remove electrons from) xenon. Since his discovery, scientists have become aware of the limitations of simple valence theory. Noble gas compounds have been the subject of a new field of study, and other researchers, building on Bartlett's work, have prepared new compounds of xenon and two other noble gases, radon and krypton. While he is best known for his work with noble gases, Bartlett's other research includes preparing new synthetic metals from graphite or graphite-like boron nitride; synthesizing salts containing perfluoroaromatic cations; preparing new binary fluorides, and discovering, with B. Žemva and his co-workers, a new method of synthesizing thermodynamically unstable high oxidation state fluorides.

The author of more than one hundred scientific papers, Bartlett has received numerous accolades from his peers in recognition of his work. Besides honorary degrees from universities in the United States, Canada, and Europe, he was awarded the Corday-Morgan Medal and Prize of the Chemical Society, London. In 1965 he received both the Research Corporation Prize and the Steacie Prize in Natural Sciences (with **John C. Polanyi**). Bartlett received the Dannie-Heineman Prize from Göttingen Academy in Germany in 1971, and in 1976, the Robert A. Welch Award. In 1988 he received the Prix Moissan (with George Cady) in Paris, and in 1992 was recognized with the Bonner Chemiepreis from Friedrich-Wilhelms University of Bonn, Germany.

SELECTED WRITINGS BY BARTLETT:

Books

(With F. O. Sladky) "The Chemistry of Krypton, Xenon, and Radon," in *Comprehensive Organic Chemistry*, Volume 1, 1973.

(With B. W. McQuillan) "Graphite Chemistry," in *Intercalation Chemistry*, edited by M. Stanley Whittingham and Allan J. Jacobson, Academic Press, 1982, pp. 19–53.

Periodicals

"A Novel Graphite-Like Material of Composition BC3 and Nitrogen-Carbon Graphites" (with J. Kouvetakis, R. B. Kaner, and M. L. Sattler), *Journal of the Chemical Society, Chemical Communications*, 1986, p. 1758.

"The Spontaneous Oxidation of Xenon to Xe(II) by Cationic Ag(II) in Anhydrous Hydrogen Fluoride Solutions" (with B. Žemva and others), *Journal of the American Chemical Society*, Volume 112, 1990, p. 4846.

SOURCES:

Periodicals

"A.C.S. 1992 Award Winners," *Chemical and Engineering News*, October 7, 1991, p. 48.

Other

Bartlett, Neil, telephone interview with F. C. Nicholson for *NTCS*, September 27, 1993.

—Sketch by F. C. Nicholson

Derek H. R. Barton
1918-
English chemist

Derek H. R. Barton has had a long and distinguished career in several universities in different countries in the field of natural products chemistry. He was active in structure determination, synthesis, and biosynthesis of a number of complex molecules, and had a special interest in the invention of new and useful chemical reactions. However, he is known most for his brilliant understanding of the importance of geometry in the behavior of organic compounds. He shared the Nobel Prize in 1969 with **Odd Hassel**, a Norwegian physical chemist, "for developing and applying the principles of conformation in chemistry," that is, how the shapes of molecules determine their physical and chemical properties.

Derek Harold Richard Barton was born in Gravesend, Kent, England, on September 8, 1918. His grandfather and father were carpenters, and his father, William Thomas Barton, owned a successful lumberyard. Derek was able to attend a good private school, but was forced to leave at seventeen without a degree because of his father's sudden death. He helped his mother, Maude Lukes Barton, in the lumber business for two years, then enrolled in Gillingham Technical College. After a year at the college, he entered Imperial College, University of London, a center of science in England. He could not afford to live in London, and commuted two hours each way. At Imperial College, he received his B.Sc. with first-class honors in 1940, and then his Ph.D. in 1942. He did his graduate thesis work on the synthesis of vinyl chloride (the starting compound for vinyl plastics) under the supervision of two eminent organic chemists, I. M. Heilbron and E. R. H. Jones. After completion of his Ph.D., Barton remained at Imperial College to work on the formulation of secret inks for military intelligence, and in 1944 left to work on the synthesis of organic phosphorous compounds for a company in Birmingham. After a year in the chemical industry, Barton returned to Imperial College as a junior lecturer in inorganic chemistry. He taught inorganic and physical chemistry for four years until a position in organic chemistry became available.

When Barton returned to Imperial College, he began research on the structures of complex organic compounds, including triterpenoids and steroids. He correlated structures with a physical property of the molecule, molecular rotation, and was able to assign structures based on a simple physical measurement. During his work with these complex molecules, he became aware of the work of Odd Hassel, who had determined the precise geometry of cyclohexane, a compound that is a ring of six carbon atoms, with each carbon bonded to two hydrogen atoms. Cyclohexane is a structural unit commonly found in steroids and triterpenoids, and Barton extended Hassel's structure to the complex molecules. He designed a set of models that accurately represented the actual geometry of steroids, and had them built in 1948. These models provided Barton with an understanding of the three-dimensional geometry (stereochemistry) of these molecules, which was unknown to other chemists at the time.

Wins Nobel Prize for Work on Conformational Analysis

Barton's work on steroids had come to the attention of **Louis Fieser**, a professor of organic chemistry at Harvard University, and an eminent authority on steroids. Fieser invited Barton to Harvard as a visiting lecturer, replacing **Robert B. Woodward** for his sabbatical year. Barton arrived at Harvard in 1949, at a time of intense interest in the chemistry of steroids because their spectacular use in medicine (cortisone therapy) had just been announced. During a seminar lecture by Fieser, in which he discussed unsolved problems in the chemistry of steroids, Barton realized that the results could be explained by the precise shapes of the molecules, which he knew from his models. He formulated a four-page paper and submitted it to the Swiss journal *Experientia,* which had a modest readership. This paper provided a stimulus for countless investigations in practical and theoretical chemistry, and was the basis for Barton's Nobel Prize in 1969. Barton's description of the influence of molecular geometry on chemistry is called conformational analysis; the principles are readily understood, and are introduced early in undergraduate organic chemistry textbooks. But conformational analysis is also a powerful tool in solving complex biochemical problems, such as enzyme catalysis and pharmacological studies. Although Barton's contribution to the field was seminal, he left its development to others. He used the principles of conformational analysis to understand the chemistry of the molecules in which he was interested, but his primary concern was always the molecules themselves.

Another of his major interests was one-electron oxidation of organic compounds, which he exploited to explain how complex molecules like morphine are produced in the opium poppy (biosynthesis). Key intermediates in one-electron oxidation are reactive species called free radicals, and Barton vigorously explored the use of free-radical chemistry in synthesis. Free radicals may be formed in chemical reactions, or by using energy to rupture chemical bonds. The latter method may involve energy from ultraviolet light, and the radicals are thereby generated photochemically. Barton was able to use photochemical reactions effectively in syntheses, and the "Barton reaction" was invented in 1958 to synthesize the steroid aldosterone, a hormone that regulates electrolyte balance in the body. At the time, the world supply of aldosterone was only several milligrams, and Barton's synthesis yielded sixty grams of the hormone by a simple procedure. Barton devoted many of his studies to the invention, rather than the discovery, of new reactions. He and his coworkers contributed many new reagents and procedures that accomplish otherwise difficult chemical transformations.

Barton's great command of all areas of chemistry let him see connections between what appear to be unrelated facts; he called this ability "gap jumping." For example, his knowledge of chemical physics and steroid chemistry led to the development of conformational analysis. From an early age, he developed the habit of closely reading the literature, and was associated with many other outstanding chemists throughout his career who kept him informed of the latest discoveries. His routine brought him to the laboratory daily to check on the progress of his students and associates, and even in his seventies, his workday lasted from three or four in the morning until seven in the evening.

Barton was married to Jeanne Kate Wilkins, and had a son, William Godfrey Lukes Barton. The marriage ended in divorce, and Barton married Christiane Cognet. Barton has held several positions in academic institutions, and was also associated with companies in the chemical and pharmaceutical industries. After his return to England from Harvard in 1950, he accepted a position as reader in organic chemistry at Birkbeck College, University of London, in which all classes were held in the evening. He was promoted to professor at Birkbeck College in 1953 and left in 1955 to become Regius Professor at the University of Glasgow. After two years, he returned to Imperial College in London as professor of organic chemistry, and he remained for twenty years.

In 1977, at the age of fifty-nine, Barton was appointed director of research of the Centre National de la Recherche Scientifique (CNRS) at the Institut de Chimie des Substances Naturelles (ICSN) at Gif-sur-Yvette in France. A year later, he retired from Imperial College. He had an excellent command of the French language, and his French wife was delighted to return home. At the ICSN, Barton continued his work in inventing reactions, producing a series of "Gif" reagents, named for the site of the ICSN. After eight years, Barton retired again, and this time accepted a Distinguished Professorship at Texas A&M University in College Station. He continued to pursue chemical research at his usual active pace in his newly adopted country. Barton had previously visited the United States many times to give lectures and courses, and he spent several summers at the Research Institute for Medicine and Chemistry (RIMAC) in Cambridge, Massachusetts. It was at RIMAC that the Barton reaction for the synthesis of aldosterone was invented. He has been recognized for his achievements by chemical societies and universities of many nations, and is among the most noted organic chemists of the twentieth century.

SELECTED WRITINGS BY BARTON:

Books

"The Principles of Conformational Analysis," Nobelstiftelsen: *Nobel Lectures: Chemistry, 1963–1970,* Elsevier, 1972, pp. 295–313.
Some Recollections of Gap Jumping, American Chemical Society, 1991.
(With S. I. Parekh) *Half a Century of Radical Chemistry,* Cambridge, 1993.

Periodicals

"The Conformation of the Steroid Nucleus," *Experientia,* Volume 6, 1950, pp. 316–319, reprinted in *Topics in Stereochemistry,* Volume 6, 1972, pp. 1–10.

SOURCES:

Books

Bezoari, Massimo D., "Derek H. R. Barton," *The Nobel Prize Winners: Chemistry,* edited by F. N. Magill, Volume 3, Salem Press, 1990, pp. 841–850.
Feldman, Martin R., "Derek Harold Richard Barton," *Nobel Laureates in Chemistry, 1901–1992,* edited by L. K. James, American Chemical Society, 1993, pp. 507–513.

—*Sketch by Martin R. Feldman*

Florence Bascom
1862-1945
American geologist

Florence Bascom was a pioneer in expanding scientific career opportunities for women. She was the first woman to receive a Ph.D. in geology from an American university, the first female to receive a Ph.D. of any kind from the Johns Hopkins University (1893), and the first woman to join the United States Geological Survey as an assistant geologist (1896). She began teaching at Bryn Mawr College in 1895, turning one course into a full major in less than a decade. Bascom was a widely known (her students came from all over the world) and respected geologist whose work mapping the crystalline rock formations in the Pennsylvania, New Jersey, and Maryland region became the basis for many later studies of the area.

Bascom was born on July 14, 1862, in Williamstown, Massachusetts, home of prestigious Williams College, where her father, Dr. John Bascom was professor of oratory and rhetoric. Both Professor Bascom and his wife Emma (Curtiss) Bascom actively supported women's rights issues and held strong avocational interests in the natural sciences. In 1874, John Bascom accepted the presidency of the University of Wisconsin, and his family left Williamstown. Florence Bascom was less than fifteen years old when she graduated high school in Madison, Wisconsin. She then obtained, in 1882, two degrees—a Bachelor of Arts and a Bachelor of Letters—from the university of which her father was president. Two years later she earned a Bachelor of Science degree, and in 1887 completed a Master of Arts in geology.

Roland D. Irving and Charles R. Van Hise were Bascom's mentors at the University of Wisconsin. Both were eminent geologists, and it was under their tutelage that Bascom learned the techniques of an emerging field of geology—the analysis of thin, translucent rock sections using microscopes and polarized light. These methods had only recently been developed in Germany, and there existed no textbook from which to learn them. Instead, Bascom studied directly from the original research papers, written in German.

As president of the University of Wisconsin, John Bascom was instrumental in instituting coeducation. Conversely, Florence Bascom faced immense obstacles in applying for a doctoral program. She hoped to study with George H. Williams, a professor at the Johns Hopkins University renowned for his use of microscopic geological techniques. The Johns Hopkins, however, had not yet allowed a woman to officially complete a degree program. Bascom applied for admission to the Geology Department at the university in September of 1890. Seven months later, the executive committee concluded that Bascom could attend without being officially enrolled as a student, and charged only for her laboratory fees. During classes, Bascom's seat was located in the corner of the classroom—and hidden behind a screen. Undaunted, Bascom applied formally to the doctoral program in 1892. She was accepted secretly. By intrepidly completing difficult and often solitary field work, Bascom produced a dissertation that a writer in *American Mineralogist* later described as "brilliant." For this, Bascom earned in 1893 the first Ph.D. in geology ever awarded to a woman by an American university.

After receiving her Ph.D., Bascom taught for two years at Ohio State University. In 1895, she accepted an invitation to join the faculty of Bryn Mawr College in Pennsylvania as a Reader in Geology. She was hired to teach a single course, and the college had no plans to create a new department of geology. Because of her success, however, within a few years the single course grew into an entire major. Bascom was granted full professorship in 1906. Bascom's specialty was petrology, the study of how present-day rocks were formed. Much of her research focused on the mid-Atlantic Piedmont region, and she wrote approximately forty publications.

Bascom retired from Bryn Mawr in 1928. She had been editor of *The American Geologist*, a Fellow of the Geological Society of America (1894), and vice-president of that organization (1930). Through her research and teaching, Bascom left an important scientific legacy. In 1937, a total of eleven women were Fellows of the Geological Society of America; eight of them were Bryn Mawr College graduates. Never married, Bascom lived after retirement in her farmhouse atop Hoosac Mountain in northwestern Massachusetts. For several winters, she traveled to Washington, D.C., to complete work for the United States Geological Survey. Despite being shy, concise, and serious-minded, Bascom maintained close ties to her academic family of students and colleagues. She died of cerebral hemorrhage in Williamstown, Massachusetts, on June 18, 1945, and was buried next to her family in a small Williams College cemetery. According to former student Eleanora Bliss Knopf writing in *American Mineralogist*, Bascom's death left "to her colleagues, her students, and her friends the inspiring memory of a scholarly and brilliant mind combined with a forceful and vigorous personality."

SELECTED WRITINGS BY BASCOM:

Periodicals

"The New Geology," *Journal of the National Institute of Social Sciences*, January, 1917.

SOURCES:

Books

Arnold, Lois Barber, *Four Lives in Sciences*, Schocken Books, 1984.
Smith, Isabel F., *The Stone Lady: A Memoir of Florence Bascom*, Bryn Mawr College, 1981.

Periodicals

American Mineralogist, Volume 31, 1946, pp. 168–172.
Bryn Mawr Alumnae Bulletin, November, 1945, pp. 12–13; spring, 1965, pp. 11–14.
Science, September, 1945, pp. 320–321.
University of Wisconsin Department of Geology and Geophysics Alumni Newsletter, 1991, pp. 61–63.

—*Sketch by Peter H. Taylor*

Nikolai Basov
1922-
Russian physicist

Nikolai Basov is one of the inventors of the laser and its technical predecessor, the maser. Lasers have become one of the most widely used of all twentieth-century inventions. They find diverse applications from delicate surgery to the cutting of steel, astronomical research, and even popular entertainment. Working with theoretical concepts first developed by **Albert Einstein** four decades earlier, Basov found ways of amplifying a beam of incoming electromagnetic radiation until it becomes a discrete, intense, monochromatic and amplified version of itself, a source of high-intensity radiation. For this discovery, Basov shared the 1964 Nobel Prize for physics with his teacher **Aleksandr Prokhorov** and **Charles Townes**, an American who made the same discovery independently.

Nikolai Gennadiyevich Basov was born on December 14, 1922, in the small village of Usman, outside the city of Voronezh, Russia. His mother was the former Zinaida Andreyevna Molchanova, and his father, Gennady Fedorovich Basov, was a professor at the Voronezh Forest Institute. Basov attended local schools in Voronezh and then in 1941 was drafted into the Soviet army. He was trained as a medical assistant and served on the Western front until his discharge in December of 1945.

As a civilian, Basov entered the Moscow Engineering and Physics Institute (also referred to as the Moscow Institute of Physical Engineers or the Moscow Institute of Engineering Physics), where he studied theoretical and experimental physics. Five years later, he was awarded his candidate's degree, comparable to a master's degree in Western universities. While still at the Moscow Institute, he became a laboratory assistant at the P. N. Lebedev Physical Institute of the Academy of Sciences of the U.S.S.R. In 1956, he was awarded his doctorate in physico-mathematical sciences. After receiving his degree, Basov remained at the Lebedev Institute, eventually becoming deputy director and director of the laboratory. In 1963, Basov also became professor of physics at his alma mater, the Moscow Engineering and Physics Institute, a post he still holds. In that same year, he founded the Laboratory of Quantum Radio Physics at the Lebedev Institute and became its director. Since 1967, he has also been editor of the prestigious Soviet science magazine *Priroda* (*Nature*) and the more specialized *Soviet Journal of Quantum Electronics*.

Designs the First Maser

During the early 1950s, a number of physicists had begun to consider the possibility of developing a device that amplifies a given electromagnetic wave, that is, a device that increases the strength of an incoming wave while preserving its original phase. Such a device had been made possible by theoretical research carried out by Albert Einstein around 1917. According to classical physics, electrons are capable of absorbing discrete amounts of energy that cause them to jump from lower energy levels to higher energy levels. When they do so, they remain in the higher energy level only instantaneously before re-emitting the absorbed energy and returning to their ground state.

Einstein re-studied this problem from the standpoint of quantum mechanics and made an intriguing discovery. He found that in the presence of specific types of radiation, an electron already present in a higher energy level could jump to a lower energy level, emitting energy as it did so. Since this change is contrary to classical laws of physics, it was designated as a "stimulated emission" of energy.

Research in the 1950s was aimed at translating this theoretical concept into a practical device. The most difficult challenge was to find a way of promoting electrons from lower to higher energy levels where they could be stimulated by an external source of radiation. That problem was solved independently and almost simultaneously by Charles H. Townes in the United States and by Basov and Prokhorov in Russia. In 1952, the two Russian scientists read a paper before the All-Union (Soviet Union) Conference on Radio Spectroscopy in which they described a "molecular generator." The "molecular generator" was identical with an amplification device that became better known as a maser (for *m*icrowave *a*mplification by *s*timulated *e*mission of *r*adiation).

Continued Research Earns Honors

Over the next three decades, Basov continued and expanded his research on the amplification of electromagnetic radiation. In 1955, he and Prokhorov suggested a more elegant method of promoting electrons, called the three-level technique, since electrons are maintained at three different energy levels within an atom. Basov also examined the possibility of using semiconductors in the manufacture of masers and lasers and, in 1968, was able to initiate a thermonuclear fusion reaction by means of an especially powerful laser. Basov's accomplishments have earned him a number of honors, most notably the Nobel Prize for physics in 1964, the Lenin Prize in 1959 and 1964, and gold medals from the Czechoslovakian Academy of Sciences, the Italian Physical Society, and the Slovak Academy of Sciences. He was married to Kseniya Tikhonova Nasarova on July 18, 1950, with whom he has two sons, Gennadiy and Dmitriy. He reports that his favorite leisure time activities are skiing and photography.

SELECTED WRITINGS BY BASOV:

Books

Lasers and Their Applications, translated by Albin Tybulewicz, Consultants Bureau, Volume 7, 1976, p. 223.

Superconductivity, translated by G. D. Archard, Volume 9, Consultants Bureau, 1977, p. 168.

High-Power Lasers and Laser Plasmas, translated by J. George Adashko, Volume 8, Consultants Bureau, 1978, p. 241.

Pulsed Neutron Research, Volume 7, Consultants Bureau, 1979, p. 104.

Periodicals

(With A. M. Prokhorov) "Theory of the Molecular Generator and the Molecular Power Amplifier," *Zh. Eksp. Teor. Fiz,* Volume 30, 1950, pp. 560–563.

SOURCES:

Books

A Biographical Encyclopedia of Scientists, Facts on File, Volume 1, 1981, pp. 52–53.

Great Soviet Encyclopedia, Volume 3, Macmillan, 1979, p. 58.

McGraw-Hill Modern Scientists and Engineers, Volume 10, McGraw-Hill, 1980, pp. 60–61.

Nobel Prize Winners, H. W. Wilson, 1987, pp. 62–64.

Turkevich, John, *Soviet Men of Science,* Van Nostrand, 1963, pp. 40–41.

Weber, Robert L., *Pioneers of Science: Nobel Prize Winners in Physics,* American Institute of Physics, 1980, pp. 197–198.

Periodicals

Gordon, J. P., "Research on Maser-Laser Principle Wins Nobel Prize in Physics," *Science,* November 13, 1964, pp. 897–899.

"Nobel Prize Winners," *Science News,* November 7, 1964, p. 295.

—*Sketch by David E. Newton*

George Batchelor
1920-
Australian-born English applied mathematician

George Batchelor, a mathematician at Cambridge University for over forty years, has played a predominant role in advancing the understanding of several difficult areas of fluid mechanics, especially areas associated with the dynamical properties of media with random structure. The first half of his research career was devoted mainly to problems of turbulent flow fluids, centering on the fundamental problem of flow energy of turbulence from large to small length scales. At the same time, Batchelor was active in strengthening the field of fluid dynamics and its applications as an academic discipline. He founded the department of applied mathematics and theoretical physics at Cambridge, serving as its head from 1959 to 1983, and made it a center of excellence, particularly in fluid mechanics. He also founded the *Journal of Fluid Mechanics* and has headed its editorial board since 1956.

George Keith Batchelor was born on March 8, 1920, in Melbourne, Australia, the son of George Conybere and Ivy Constance (Berneye) Batchelor. His father was an electrician and, later, a bookseller, who gave him the help and encouragement he needed to climb the educational ladder. In 1937, Batchelor entered the University of Melbourne, where he studied mathematics and physics, earning a B.Sc. degree in 1940 and an M.Sc. degree in 1941. He then joined the war effort, working on problems in aeronautics under the Commonwealth Council for Scientific and Industrial Research, also in Melbourne. This work introduced him to fluid mechanics and, in particular, the problem of turbulence.

Contributes Strongly to Studies of Turbulence

Turbulence in fluids is of enormous practical significance. It is responsible for drag on airplanes, mixing and dispersion processes, the generation of noise, and many other effects. It also intrigues physicists because it resists fundamental understanding. In principle, the basic equations of fluid dynamics, known as the Navier-Stokes equations, can be solved for the physical quantities representing a fluid flow. Unfortunately, such solutions rarely offer broadbrush views of fluid behavior, but rather present the details of every turbulent eddy and fluctuation, down to the smallest sizes. This is somewhat like trying to learn about a gas by taking account of every individual molecule. During the 1930s, Geoffrey Taylor of Great Britain took the lead in using statistical methods to yield some understanding of turbulence. He

George Batchelor

dealt particularly with the cascade, a hierarchy of eddies of different sizes that appear in turbulent flows. Large eddies receive energy from the bulk flow, passing it down to successively smaller ones. The smallest eddies carry little energy, but dissipate the energy they receive, turning it into heat. Inspired by Taylor's work, Batchelor wrote to him in 1944 and won his permission to study with him for a Ph.D. at Cambridge University. Batchelor entered Cambridge in 1945, receiving his degree in 1948, and a research fellowship at Trinity College in 1947.

Batchelor paid particular attention to work by Russian mathematician **Andrey Kolmogorov**, who argued in 1941 that the small-scale, or energy-dissipating eddies, have a simple, universal character which is independent of the source of the energy of the turbulence. This work was little known outside the Soviet Union, but Batchelor made it a point of departure for his own. He also made other original contributions, showing particularly how turbulence in an electrically-conducting gas or liquid could generate a magnetic field. This represented an early and important contribution to the nascent field of magneto-hydrodynamics and shed light on the origin of the earth's magnetic field, which is believed to arise from convection in the molten iron compounds within the inner core. In his 1953 work, *The Theory of Homogeneous Turbulence,* Batchelor applied Taylor's mathematical methods to Kolmogorov's insights, and added much that was his own. It went on to gain the status of a scientific classic.

Batchelor made a further contribution to his field with the 1967 text for students, *An Introduction to Fluid Dynamics,* in which he tried to convey the modern, physical understanding of the dynamics of real fluids as distinct from the idealized, frictionless fluids treated in classical texts. He describes the book as a product of his teaching at Cambridge, requiring several years of work and being more difficult to write than his previous book, although it repaid his efforts by gaining wide influence. It has been translated into four languages and serves as a standard reference and text in a number of countries.

Begins to Tinker with Mechanics of Dispersions

By the late sixties, Batchelor felt he had contributed as much to turbulence as he was ever likely to do and decided to make a major change in his primary research field. When writing his text book, he was struck by the potential for useful research on the effective transport properties of a fluid in which small particles are dispersed. **Albert Einstein** had published virtually the only paper on this topic in 1906, in which he calculated the effective viscosity of a dispersion of spherical particles of very small concentration. Einstein, however, neglected the all-important effect of hydrodynamic interaction of the particles, and Batchelor foresaw a need for work which would be a novel mix of hydrodynamics and colloid science, with probability-theory methods like those used in turbulence. Batchelor made many contributions to this new field of mechanics of dispersions.

In 1944, Batchelor married Wilma Maud Ritz, with whom he had three daughters, Adrienne, Clare and Bryony. He remains active in research, and has acknowledged his debt to his mentor, Geoffrey Taylor, by editing his scientific papers. Published during Taylor's lifetime, they fill four volumes. He also raised money for the endowment of a G. I. Taylor Professorship of Fluid Mechanics at Cambridge. Honored in 1957 with election as a Fellow of the Royal Society, he received its Royal Medal in 1988, following approval of the Queen. A foreign member of six national academies, Batchelor was awarded the Timoshenko Medal of the American Society of Mechanical Engineers in 1988, and holds an honorary doctorate of science from five foreign universities.

SELECTED WRITINGS BY BATCHELOR:

Books

The Theory of Homogeneous Turbulence, Cambridge University Press, 1953.
An Introduction to Fluid Dynamics, Cambridge University Press, 1967.

SOURCES:

Books

McGraw-Hill Modern Scientists and Engineers,
    Volume 1, McGraw, 1980.

—*Sketch by T. A. Heppenheimer*

William Bateson
1861-1926
English geneticist

William Bateson was an English biologist whose most important contribution to the history of science was probably his translation of Austrian botanist Gregor Mendel's *Laws of Heredity* into English in 1902. Mendel's work had recently been discovered in an obscure journal, and the translation Bateson wrote was extremely popular; it sold out immediately and launched a series of scientific investigations and debates. Bateson himself was a central researcher and a respected authority in the field for the first two decades of the twentieth century. He coined the term "genetics" in 1906 and in 1908 was appointed to the first chair in genetics at Cambridge University. Bateson is distinguished not so much for originating as inaugurating the modern science of genetics, but he did raise important questions about the relationship between evolution and genetics which are still being addressed today.

Bateson was born in Whitby, Yorkshire, England, on August 8, 1861. He was the son of William Henry and Anna Aiken Bateson. His father was a classicist who had served as master of St. John's College, Cambridge, in 1857; Bateson grew up in Cambridge and lived in this town for most of his life. As a child he was sent to Rugby School, where he was not considered a serious student, despite being raised in an academic household. After entering Cambridge University, however, he discovered zoology and morphology. At Cambridge, he was influenced greatly by A. Sedwick and W. F. R. Weldon. He is said to have very much surprised his school teachers by his distinguished efforts at the university. He performed brilliantly as a science student, receiving his B.S. in 1883 with first-class honors.

Challenges the Doctrine of Natural Selection

After graduating from Cambridge, Bateson spent two years in the United States, where he did research on the marine organism *Balanoglossus*. Besides gill slits, the *Balanoglossus* had suggestions of a notochord and a dorsal nerve chord. Bateson identified the animal as a primitive chordate, hypothesizing that chordates might be offshoots of primitive echinoderms, a theory which has come to be widely accepted. W. K. Brooks at John Hopkins University was highly influential in Bateson's development during this period, and while in the United States Bateson became convinced that there were flaws in Charles Darwin's natural selection hypothesis.

According to the theory of natural selection, the environment favors certain changes in species and not others; Darwinian theory proposed a relatively smooth progression, with evolution being the accumulation of many small changes. But in the history of evolution there is evidence of a number of changes which are actually quite large; variations can occur suddenly and completely in individual organisms or entire species. Bateson did not believe that the interrelation between species and their environment could account for all these changes, and he set out to find another way of explaining them.

When he returned to Cambridge in 1885 as a fellow at St. John's College, Bateson began searching for a new approach to evolutionary studies through the laws of heredity. He traveled to Russia and Egypt to look for parallels between local variations of aquatic species and local conditions; he was unable to find such a correlation and developed a hypothesis that variation is discontinuous and not related to environment. He conducted a series of breeding experiments to prove this theory. The results of his efforts were set down in his first major article, "Materials for the Study of Variation," which was published in 1894. His theories were not only ignored by the academic community, but they actually seemed to have harmed his career. He received no regular teaching appointments at the Cambridge University during this period.

Translates Mendel's Work

With his interests divided between mathematics and botany, Gregor Mendel had proved that seven inherited characteristics of the pea plant could be predicted to fall within certain patterns of distribution. The characteristics would separate independently, then recombine in hybrid progeny. These results led Mendel to the conclusion that certain particles or factors within one generation were responsible for the characteristics of the succeeding ones. Mendel correctly determined that for every characteristic there was a pair of factors: one was passed to the next generation from the maternal parent, while the other was passed along from the paternal parent. Although the results of Mendel's pioneering investigation had been published in 1866, they had been largely ignored for many years. Bateson, however, realized the relevance his work on heredity had to the questions he was raising about variation.

Bateson read about Mendel's research in May 1900, and he published an English translation in 1902. Mendel's research lent much credibility to the work Bateson had done in the previous decade, and he suddenly rose to prominence within the academic community. He embarked on some ambitious research projects, extending Mendel's laws to include animals as well as plants. He was widely considered the authority in this discipline, and he reinterpreted much contemporary research into Mendelian terms.

Bateson established the application of Mendel's work to hereditary in animals through an investigation he conducted with L. Cuénot. Their research concentrated on the inheritance of comb shape in fowl, and they established that the trait occurred in the ratio that Mendel had stated, as well as in other ratios that Bateson attributed to gene interaction. Bateson conducted another investigation with pea plants, which indicated that the characteristics which passed from one generation to the next were not inherited independently—a finding contrary to the central point of Mendel's laws. Because the seven characteristics Mendel had selected were always independently inherited, it had been assumed that there were separate factors for every characteristic. But Bateson's work established that certain characteristics were actually governed by more than one gene. His investigation raised many questions about the nature of chromosomes and genes that would later be explained by the theory of gene linkage—the tendency of certain genes to link and move as one because their location on a chromosome is so close.

Bateson viewed the phenomena of variation and heredity as manifestations of the same fundamental law. He coined the term genetics, to refer to the study of heredity and variation, using this term in 1906 in an address to the Third Conference on Hybridization and Plant Breeding. Bateson became the first professor of genetics in England when he was appointed to teach this subject at Cambridge University in 1908. In 1910 he founded the *Journal of Genetics* with **R. C. Punnett**, and he left Cambridge to become director of the John Innes Horticultural Institution in London.

Bateson's tenure as the spokesman for the science of genetics did not last long. He parted company with the scientific community over the nature of chromosomes. From the time of the rediscovery of Mendel's work, chromosomes were considered to be a possible agent of heredity within the nucleus of the cell. Even during the early days of research, many biologists leaned toward such a hypothesis. Yet Bateson rejected the idea that inheritance was determined by the chemical processes in a material entity such as a chromosome. He argued that inheritance must be controlled by forces that were more abstract, and he proposed a theory of heredity which he claimed was not materialistic. In 1910 an American biologist, **Thomas Hunt Morgan**, explained the relationship between genes and chromosomes with research centered on the fruit fly, *Drosophila melanogaster*. The gene was no longer considered an abstract unit as Bateson still believed but was an integral part of the chromosome. The hypothesis that the chromosome was a collection of factors made sense to the majority of geneticists. They shifted their support to Morgan and away from Bateson. His articles were published more infrequently in research journals, and he had fewer followers. Bateson was elected to the Royal Society in 1894. He was awarded the Darwin Medal in 1904, and in 1914 he was elected president of the British Association for the Advancement of Science. He won the Royal Medal from the Royal Society in 1920, and he served as a trustee of the British Museum from 1922 to 1926. He died in London on February 8, 1926. His portrait, by W. A. Foster, hangs in the National Portrait Gallery.

SELECTED WRITINGS BY BATESON:

Books

Materials for the Study of Variation Treated with Especial Regard to Discontinuity in the Origin of Species, [London], 1894.

Mendel's Principles of Heredity: A Defense, Cambridge University Press, 1902.

Problems of Genetics, Yale University Press, 1913.

William Bateson, F.R.S., Naturalist: His Essays and Addresses, edited by B. Bateson, Cambridge University Press, 1918.

Scientific Papers of William Bateson, edited by R. Punnett, Cambridge University Press, 1928.

SOURCES:

Books

Bronowski, J., *The Ascent of Man,* Little, Brown (Boston), 1973.

Bynum, W. F., E. J. Browne, and R. Porter, editors, *Dictionary of the History of Science,* Princeton University Press, 1981.

Gillespie, C. C., editor, *Dictionary of Scientific Biography,* Scribner's, 1970.

Moore, R., editor, *Evolution,* Time-Life Books, 1962.

—Sketch by Patricia M. McAdams

William Maddock Bayliss
1860-1924
English physiologist

The name William Maddock Bayliss is inevitably linked with that of **Ernest Starling** for the duo's collaborative scientific research on the digestive, nervous, and vascular systems. Their 1902 investigations into the trigger mechanism for the release of pancreatic digestive juices led to the discovery of an entirely new class of chemical messengers which they called hormones. Additionally, Bayliss's pioneering work with enzymes and the innervation of the heart and intestines made important contributions to the understanding of physiology. In 1914, Bayliss authored *Principles of General Physiology,* a basic physiology textbook that is still considered a landmark in biological literature. His long and distinguished career won for him the Copley Medal of the Royal Society, the Baly Medal of the Royal College of Physicians, and, in 1922, a knighthood.

William Maddock Bayliss was born on May 2, 1860, in the town of Wednesbury, Staffordshire, England. His father, Moses Bayliss, who was a wealthy iron manufacturer, and his mother, Jan Maddock, lived in the affluent industrial midlands between Birmingham and Wolverhampton. Bayliss attended a local private school and entered his father's firm for a short time after graduation. However, finding that he was more interested in science than manufacturing, Bayliss decided to study medicine, and was apprenticed to a local physician for training.

Embarks on Career at University College, London

In 1880 the family moved to a prosperous home on four acres of parkland in Hampstead, London, where Bayliss entered University College to study physiology and anatomy. However, after pursuing a degree in medicine, Bayliss decided instead to devote his life to a study of the then-emerging science of physiology—a branch of biology that analyzes bodily functions. At University College, he was influenced by both John Burdon-Sanderson in physiology and Ray Lankester in zoology. In 1885 Bayliss's studies took him to Wadham College in Oxford where, in 1888, he took a first-class degree in physiology, then returned to University College as a teaching and research assistant. He remained at University College for the rest of his life, becoming assistant professor in 1903 and, from 1912 to his death, professor of general physiology, a chair created specifically for him.

In 1890 Bayliss met E. H. Starling, a fellow physiologist, and the pair began a long professional collaboration and personal friendship; within three years Bayliss married Starling's sister, Gertrude. Following the death of Bayliss's father in 1895, the couple moved into the Hampstead home and raised one daughter and three sons, the youngest of whom, Leonard, also went on to become a physiologist. Bayliss was left financially secure by his father, and the family entertained a good deal at the Hampstead home where Bayliss, a lover of music, often played the violin. In addition, Bayliss was an experienced photographer, and his pictures were published as illustrations for his professional books and papers.

Bayliss and Starling collaborated first on a project in electrophysiology, charting the electrical changes of the mammalian heart. Using a new instrument called a capillary electrometer, the researchers studied the hearts of mammals to observe cardiac cycles. Next they turned to the vascular system, recording nerve-controlled dilation and contraction of blood vessels. This work resulted in the development of an improved device for measuring blood pressure called a hemopiezometer. Yet another area of interest for Bayliss and Starling was intestinal movements. This study led to a description of the peristaltic wave—a function of the intestines which contracts and relaxes to propel the contents of the intestines forward during the process of digestion. At about this same time, 1892, Bayliss followed an independent line of study into the physiology of the depressor nerve, leading to a general examination of vasomotor reactions (nerves which dilate or constrict blood vessels) and their coordination.

Study of Pancreatic Secretion Leads to Hormone Discovery

By far the best known achievement of Bayliss and Starling was the discovery, in 1902, of hormones. Following up on the work of the famous Russian physiologist **Ivan Petrovich Pavlov**, who had shown that pancreatic secretions were created by a stimulation of the vagus nerve, Bayliss and Starling experimented with dogs whose nerves to the upper intestine had been severed. At the time, the only known means to excite glands to secretion was the action of secretory nerves. However, when the researchers introduced dilute hydrochloric acid (HCL) into the dog's duodenum—the first part of the small intestine which connects to the stomach—they discovered that pancreatic digestive juices were still secreted, and concluded that communication with the pancreas could only be through the bloodstream. In a further experiment in which dilute HCL was injected into the jugular vein of an anesthetized dog, they found a chemical substance activated in the epithelial cells, or the tissue covering the surface or lining of the duodenum. They called this chemical substance "secretin," because, when it was released into the bloodstream, it came into contact with the pancreas and stimulated it to secrete a digestive juice into the intestine. Starling went on to coin the term "hormone"—from the Greek *horman,* "to set in motion." This discovery proved that a hormone secreted by one internal organ could have a direct effect on another internal organ.

After 1903, Bayliss and Starling collaborated for one more paper, this one on enzyme action, studying the activation of the enzyme trypsin in pancreatic digestive juice. Bayliss then worked on his own to demonstrate how trypsin was formed in the small intestine. He measured the time required for a trypsin solution to digest specific amounts of proteins and established, in the course of the studies, that enzymes acted as catalysts. He proved, further, that much of the enzymes' effect came from being in a colloidal or emulsion state (substances that do not dissolve when dispersed). This latter conclusion prompted Bayliss to continue with a general study of colloids in the properties of membranes and in surface action.

Bayliss applied physical chemistry to physiological problems. One of Bayliss's findings during World War I was that the intravenous use of a gum saline solution to replace lost blood was effective in treating soldiers in danger of wound shock. The use of these saline injections prevented the onset of surgical shock by maintaining an equal colloidal osmotic pressure in the blood circulation. It was a practice that saved many lives.

Bayliss's book *Principles of General Physiology,* which appeared in 1914, secured his lasting reputation. It was a landmark publication in a fledgling science. Bayliss was honored for his work from many quarters. In 1903 he was elected a fellow of the prestigious Royal Society and served on its council for three years. He was awarded honorary degrees from such universities as Aberdeen, Oxford, and St. Andrews, and was a member of the Royal Academy of Belgium and the Royal Danish Academy of Science. Bayliss died on August 27, 1924, following an illness of some months.

SELECTED WRITINGS BY BAYLISS:

Books

The Nature of Enzyme Action, Longmans, Green, 1908.
Principles of General Physiology, Longmans, Green, 1914.
Intravenous Injection in Wound Shock, Longmans, Green, 1918.

Periodicals

(With E. H. Starling) "On Some Points in the Innervation of the Mammalian Heart," *Journal of Physiology,* Volume 13, 1892, pp. 407–418.

"On the Physiology of the Depressor Nerve," *Journal of Physiology,* Volume 14, 1893, pp. 303–325.
(With Starling) "The Movements and Innervation of the Small Intestine," *Journal of Physiology,* Volume 24, 1899, pp. 99–143.
(With Starling) "The Mechanism of Pancreatic Secretion," *Journal of Physiology,* Volume 28, 1902, pp. 325–353.
"The Kinetics of Tryptic Action," *Archives des sciences biologiques,* Volume 11, 1904, pp. 261–296.
"The Osmotic Pressure of Congo Red and of Some Other Dyes," *Proceedings of the Royal Society,* Volume 81B, 1909, pp. 269–286.

SOURCES:

Books

Bayliss, L. E., "William Maddock Bayliss (1860–1924)," *Perspectives in Biology and Medicine,Volume 4,* University of Chicago Press, 1961, pp. 460–479.

—*Sketch by J. Sydney Jones*

George Wells Beadle
1903-1989
American geneticist

Early in his professional life, George Wells Beadle worked in the laboratory of **Thomas Hunt Morgan**, the geneticist who helped to revolutionize what we know about genetics—the inheritance of characteristics by the deoxyribonucleic acid (DNA) found in the chromosomes of cells. Beadle's innovative research on such diverse living things as corn, fruit flies, and bread mold helped to demystify the activities of genes, making it possible to reduce the inheritance of a particular characteristic to a series of steps needed for the manufacture of biochemicals, notably enzymes. For his work on the "one gene-one enzyme" concept, he shared the Nobel Prize for Physiology or Medicine with **Edward Lawrie Tatum** and **Joshua Lederberg** in 1958.

Beadle was born in Wahoo, Nebraska, on October 22, 1903, to Chauncey Elmer and Hattie Albro Beadle. He probably would have worked on the family farm if not for a high school science teacher

George Wells Beadle

Stanford University in California, where he remained from 1937 to 1946. As a professor of biology there, he began working with a red bread mold, *Neurospora crassa.* He would work with neurospora for seventeen years. In 1941 he began collaborating with Edward Tatum, and their work eventually won them—with Joshua Lederberg, who later worked with Tatum at Yale—the Nobel Prize.

Neurospora crassa, once the bane of bakers, became a boon for geneticists Beadle and Tatum. Not only does the mold have a short life cycle and grow on a basic sugar medium, but it reproduces both sexually and asexually. Also, the final cell division that produces its reproductive cells, known as ascospores, leaves them in a linear arrangement along the pod-like ascus (spore case), making the trail of inherited characteristics very clear to follow.

Taking a hint from fellow geneticist **Hermann Joseph Muller,** who in the mid–1920s had shown that the rate of mutation increases with exposure to X rays, Beadle and Tatum grew thousand of cultures of molds in which they had induced mutations. The wild strain of the mold can grow on a medium containing very few nutrients. With just some sugar sprinkled with a little biotin (a growth vitamin) and inorganic salts, a wild-type mold can synthesize all the proteins it needs to live. A mold with a mutation, however, loses the ability to make a particular compound it needs to grow, such as a specific amino acid (amino acids are the building blocks of proteins such as those used to construct DNA). Beadle expected that a missing amino acid would have to be supplied to the mold, but found to his surprise the mold was sometimes able to convert a similar compound to the necessary amino acid. Through a process of trial and error, Beadle was able to deduce the sequence of chemical steps involved in the work of conversion.

Once Beadle had pieced together the pathways of chemical production, his ideas could be applied to other molds. One immediate application was to use his techniques to mass-produce the antibiotic penicillin. Penicillin and other antibiotics are derived from compounds produced naturally by certain molds, which use them as a defense against invading bacterial cells.

Beadle also crossed two different mutant strains of mold and found that the resulting hybrid could produce a particular amino acid that neither parent strain could produce alone. This was because one mutant lacked genetic coding for a certain enzyme (a protein that can encourage or inhibit chemical reactions), causing a breakdown in the chemical synthesis along one spot in the sequence, while the other mutant lacked different coding for an enzyme from another spot along the sequence. When crossed, the resulting mold could produce the missing amino acid because it had inherited both genetic patterns, one

who advised him to go on to college. At the College of Agriculture at the University of Nebraska, Beadle gained an interest in genetics, especially that of corn. He received his undergraduate degree in biology in 1926, then left for Cornell University in New York where he earned his doctorate in genetics. During this time Beadle married Marion Cecile Hill. They would have one son, David.

In 1931 Beadle went to work in the genetics laboratory of Thomas Hunt Morgan at the California Institute of Technology (Caltech) in Pasadena, California. Morgan had pioneered genetics work on the fruit fly, *Drosophila melanogaster.* As Beadle studied inherited characteristics such as eye color, he began to think that genes might influence heredity by chemical means. When he left California for Paris in 1935, he continued this line of work with Boris Ephrussi at the Institut de Biologie Physico-Chimique. Carefully transplanting eye buds from the larvae of one type of mutant fruit fly to larvae of another, Beadle showed that eye color in the insects is not a quirk of nature but the result of a long chain of chemical reactions. For all the relative ease of working with fruit flies, however, Beadle sought a simpler organism and a simpler set of chemical reactions to study.

One Gene, One Enzyme

Several years later, Beadle found what he was looking for. When he returned from Paris in 1936 he briefly taught genetics at Harvard and then went on to from each parent. Beadle concluded that specific genes (sequences of protein groups in DNA serving as functional units of inheritance) controlled each step in the sequence. Each gene held the information for the manufacture of a single enzyme, a concept that became known as "one gene, one enzyme."

Extended to other plants and animals, Beadle's theory could be used to explain all of genetic inheritance in terms of chemical reactions. Different genes control the different stages of chemical reactions. For example, cells must be able to produce the pigment that gives an animal's eyes their color. The production of pigment might occur in several steps, with enzymes used to hasten each chemical reaction. If the gene for any one of the enzymes is missing, the cells cannot produce the pigment.

The one gene-one enzyme concept caused a breakthrough in genetic research during the 1940s by shifting the study of genetics away from physical characteristics of organisms to the production of biochemicals. On the heels of this line of research, the compound deoxyribonucleic acid (DNA) was analyzed, and the mechanism of the genetic code was pieced together in the early 1950s. Beadle and Tatum parted ways when Tatum left for Yale University in 1945. Using the same mutation induction techniques on bacteria, Tatum worked along with Joshua Lederberg to show how genetic information can be transferred from one bacterium to another.

From Recognition with a Nobel Prize to the Corn Wars

Beadle became professor and chairman of the division of biology at Caltech in 1946 and stayed on until 1961. For his work in genetics he won the Lasker Award of the American Public Health Association in 1950. He and his first wife divorced, and he then married Muriel Barnett in 1953. With his second wife he wrote several books on genetics for a general audience. Recognition for years of work came in 1958 when Beadle, Tatum and Lederberg won the Nobel Prize. In that same year Beadle won the Albert Einstein Commemorative Award in Science, and in the following year he received the National Award from the American Cancer Society.

In the 1960s Beadle renewed his interest in the genetics of corn. He became a player in the "corn wars," a debate among geneticists and archaeologists over the domestication of corn or maize in the Americas. Beadle contended that modern corn comes from a Mexican wild grass rather than a now-extinct species of maize. Beadle drew his conclusion from the corn remains that show that domestication occurred at the time of the Mayans and Aztecs.

In 1961 Beadle left California for Chicago, Illinois, where he became the sixth chancellor of the University of Chicago. He remained there until he retired in 1968. By then he had accumulated over thirty honorary degrees from many universities around the country and been awarded memberships into several prestigious academic societies. For their work in popularizing genetics, he and his wife Muriel won the Edison Award in 1967. In the late 1960s Beadle became director of the American Medical Association's Institute for Biomedical Research. He died on June 9, 1989, in Pomona, California, at age eighty-five from complications of Alzheimer's disease.

SELECTED WRITINGS BY BEADLE:

Books

(With A. H. Sturtevant) *An Introduction to Genetics,* W. B. Saunders, 1939.
(With others) *The Place of Genetics in Modern Biology,* Massachusetts Institute of Technology, 1959.
(With wife, Muriel Beadle) *The Language of Life: An Introduction to the Science of Genetics,* Doubleday, 1966.

Periodicals

(With R. A. Emerson and A. C. Fraser) "A Summary of Linkage Studies in Maize," *Cornell University Agricultural Experimental Station Memo,* number 180, 1935.
(With L. Tatum) "Genetic Control of Biochemical Reactions in Neurospora," *Proceedings of the National Academy of Sciences,* Volume 27, 1941, pp. 499–506.
"Genetics and Metabolism in Neurospora," *Physiological Review,* Volume 25, 1945, pp. 643–663.

SOURCES:

Books

The Annual Obituary, 1989, St. James Press, 1990, pp. 336–339.

—*Sketch by Barbara A. Branca*

Arnold Beckman
1900-
American inventor and chemist

Arnold Beckman

Arnold Beckman is a chemist, inventor, and industrialist. His most important inventions include the pH meter, a device for measuring the acidity of solutions, and the spectrophotometer, which analyzes biochemical material. Founder of Beckman Instruments, a world leader in the production and development of scientific and medical instrumentation, he has shared his fortune philanthropically through the establishment of research, education, and medical treatment facilities around the United States.

Arnold Orville Beckman was born on April 10, 1900, in Cullom, Illinois, the first of two children to George W. and Elizabeth Ellen Jewkes Beckman. As a small boy Beckman spent countless hours watching his father, a blacksmith, pounding iron bars against his anvil. He also devoted time to practicing the piano, eventually developing enough skill to bring himself an income as a musician. Neither blacksmithing nor music, however, had the profound influence on young Beckman that a single book was to have. At the age of nine, in the attic of his home, he came upon an aging volume of Steele's "Series in the Natural Sciences" (circa 1893). It was a fourteen-week study in chemistry and contained descriptions of experiments that could be carried out with simple household chemicals. In his mother's kitchen Beckman experimented with red cabbage juice, lemons, baking soda, and vinegar. His interest in chemistry was so strong that for his tenth birthday his father built him a laboratory shed, complete with shelves for his numerous bottles of chemicals.

When Beckman was eleven, his mother died. His father remarried, and Beckman and his younger sister moved to Normal, Illinois, with their new stepmother and two stepbrothers. Normal, Illinois, was a college town, and for Beckman this afforded a special opportunity. Since he had mastered so much chemistry by the time he entered high school, he was allowed to take courses at Illinois Normal Teacher's College. By the time he finished high school, he had completed two and half years of college chemistry courses. In his spare time Beckman played the piano in movie theaters, helping to finance his education and contribute to his family's income.

In 1918, the summer after high school, Beckman enlisted in the Marines. World War I was winding to a close and his military career was short. Perhaps the most important outcome of his service was that he met Mabel S. Meinzer. A quirk of fate brought them together at a Thanksgiving Day dinner the Red Cross held for soldiers coming home from war. There were two dinner sittings planned that day and Beckman was assigned to eat at the first one. Fewer soldiers showed up than were expected for the second sitting and the military commander, not wanting to disappoint the hardworking Red Cross volunteers, requested that Beckman attend both meals. Had he not gone to the second dinner he would not have been introduced to Mabel. The couple married in 1925, spending sixty-four years with one another until Mabel's death in 1989. Together they had two children, a son Arnold, and a daughter, Patricia.

Beckman enrolled in college after the war, and in 1922 he graduated with a bachelor's degree in chemical engineering from the University of Illinois. He continued his studies at the California Institute of Technology (Caltech), receiving his master's degree in physical chemistry in 1923. He went to work briefly at the New York research laboratory of the American Telephone and Telegraph Company (AT&T), studying vacuum tube technology. In 1925 he returned to California and began his doctoral studies. He received his Ph.D. in photochemistry in 1928 from Caltech, and was offered a position on the chemistry faculty there, which he held from 1928 until 1939.

In 1934 an old college friend from the University of Illinois, Glen Joseph appeared in Beckman's chemistry laboratory. Joseph worked for the California Fruit Growers Exchange and, remembering that his friend was a chemist, he sought his help. Fruit growers were hoping to find a way to accurately analyze the degree of acidity of citrus juices. The tartness of bottled juice sold under the same label varied considerably, and producers wanted to be able to deliver a more consistent product to the public. They were limited, though, by technology. Getting an accurate reading of acidity requires measuring the electrical properties of the substance, but in the early 1930s the only measuring devices available were delicate and their results unreliable. To solve Joseph's problem, Beckman called on his research experience at AT&T during the mid–1920s. Using a vacuum tube sensitive to electrical currents but also sturdy, he built his first "acidimeter" or pH meter. Soon after Joseph had received his pH meter, he asked for another one—his colleagues were constantly borrowing his. By the end of the year Beckman had sold eighty-seven of the devices, grossing over eleven thousand dollars. For a college chemistry professor in the 1930s this was a small fortune.

In 1935 Beckman started a company, Beckman Instruments, and began mass production of the pH meter. By 1939 his business was demanding so much of his time that he reluctantly left his teaching post at the Caltech. A year later he introduced a quartz photoelectric spectrophotometer, whose precision to within 99.9 percent accuracy (compared with the 25 percent accuracy of existing technology) revolutionized the chemical analysis of biological assays. And Beckman's machine worked in minutes, rather than weeks. In 1940 he also introduced the Beckman Helipot, a volume control device that was to become a critical component of World War II radar equipment. In only a few decades, Beckman Instruments grew to become one of the nation's largest supplier's of scientific and medical instrumentation. Beckman Instrument products are found today in pharmaceutical companies, hospitals, and scientific laboratories worldwide.

Beckman's contributions to the development of scientific analytical instrumentation have won him considerable recognition and honor. In 1987 he was inducted into the National Inventors Hall of Fame. He was awarded the Presidential Citizens' Medal of Technology for outstanding contributions to the United States through technology in 1988, and in 1989 he received the National Medal of Science from George Bush.

Contributes Fortune to Science Education and Research

The wealth Beckman acquired because of his industrial success has enabled him to contribute philanthropically to his interests. In particular, science education and research have benefited from his generosity. During the 1980s, through the Arnold and Mabel Beckman Foundation, over $175 million was awarded for the advancement of education and scientific research worldwide. In Irvine, California, Beckman's hometown, he founded the Beckman Laser Institute and Medical Clinic as well as the Beckman Center, western headquarters for the National Academy of Sciences. He established research institutes and scientific laboratories at the University of Illinois, the University of California at San Francisco, Stanford University, and the Scripps Clinic. He built a center for the management of technology at Pepperdine University in Malibu, California, and a research and education facility at Cold Spring Harbor Laboratory on Long Island, New York. He gave most generously to Caltech, where several buildings and institutes bear his and Mabel's name. In 1990 he received the Spirit of Philanthropy Award from Orange County in California.

Though Beckman left Caltech early in his career to devote more time to his company matters, he retained close ties to his alma mater. In 1953 he was elected to serve on its board of trustees and, from 1964 till 1974, he was the board's chair. He served on boards at more than half a dozen other universities and was a director of Security Pacific National Bank, the Southern California Edison Company, Continental Airlines, SCM, and the Stanford Research Institute. During the course of his career he has been awarded nine honorary degrees. He holds fourteen patents for scientific instruments. He helped found the Instrument Society of America, which in 1960 honored him by establishing a technical achievement award in his name. Beckman has maintained an interest in good government and, in 1956, he became the president of the Los Angeles Chamber of Commerce. In 1967 he presided over the California Chamber of Commerce. He helped found the Lincoln Club of Orange County, California, an organization devoted to promoting good government. He served as chair from its inception in 1962 until 1978, when he was elected chair emeritus.

SELECTED WRITINGS BY BECKMAN:

Periodicals

(With H. H. Cary) "A Quartz Photoelectric Spectrophotometer," *Journal of the Optical Society of America,* Volume 31, 1941, pp. 682–689.

(With E. W. Malloy) "Modern Radiation-Detection Instruments for Health Protection," *Mechanical Engineering,* Volume 71, 1949, pp. 649–652.

"A Businessman's View on the Failure of Education," *U.S. News & World Report,* November 30, 1956, pp. 83–86, 89.

"Instruments and Progress in Chemistry," *Chemist,* July-August, 1987, pp. 6–8, 16–19.

SOURCES:

Books

Stephens, Harrison, *Golden Past, Golden Future: The First Fifty Years of Beckman Instruments, Inc.,* Claremont University Center Press, 1985.

—*Sketch by Leslie Reinherz*

Antoine-Henri Becquerel
1852-1908
French physicist

Antoine-Henri Becquerel's landmark research on X rays and his discovery of radiation laid the foundation for many scientific advances of the early twentieth century. X rays were discovered in 1895 by the German physicist **Wilhelm Conrad Röntgen**, and in one of the most serendipitous events in science history, Becquerel discovered that the uranium he was studying gave off radiation similar to X rays. Becquerel's student, **Marie Curie**, later named this phenomenon radioactivity. His later research on radioactive materials found that at least some of the radiation produced by unstable materials consisted of electrons. For these discoveries, Becquerel shared the 1903 Nobel Prize in physics with Marie and **Pierre Curie**. Becquerel's other notable research included the effects of magnetism on light and the properties of luminescence.

Becquerel was born in Paris on December 15, 1852. His grandfather, Antoine-César Becquerel, had fought at the Battle of Waterloo in 1815 and later earned a considerable reputation as a physicist. He made important contributions to the study of electrochemistry, meteorology, and agriculture. Antoine-Henri's father was Alexandre-Edmond Becquerel, who also made a name for himself in science. His research included studies on photography, heat, the conductivity of hot gases, and luminescence.

Becquerel's early education took place at the Lycée Louis-le-Grand from which he graduated in 1872. He then enrolled at the Ecole Polytechnique, and two years later he moved on to the Ecole des Ponts et Chaussées. It appears that there was never any question about the direction of Becquerel's career, as he concentrated on scientific subjects throughout his schooling. In 1877 he was awarded his engineering degree and accepted an appointment as an *ingénieur* with the National Administration of Bridges and Highways.

Earliest Research Deals with Magneto-Optics

During his years at the Ecole des Ponts et Chaussées, Becquerel became particularly interested in English physicist Michael Faraday's research on the effects of magnetism on light. Faraday had discovered in 1845 that a plane-polarized beam of light (one that contains light waves that vibrate to a specific pattern) experiences a rotation of planes when it passes through a magnetic field; this phenomenon was called the Faraday effect. Becquerel developed a formula to explain the relationship between this rotation and the refraction the beam of light undergoes when it passes through a substance. He published this result in his first scientific paper in 1875, although he later discovered that his initial results were incorrect in some respects.

Although the Faraday effect had been observed in solids and liquids, Becquerel attempted to replicate the Faraday effect in gases. He found that gases (except for oxygen) also have the same ability to rotate a beam of polarized light as do solids and liquids. Becquerel remained interested in problems of magneto-optics for years, and returned to the field with renewed enthusiasm in 1897 after Dutch physicist **Pieter Zeeman**'s discovery of the Zeeman effect, whereby spectral lines exposed to strong magnetic fields split, provided new impetus for research.

In 1874 Becquerel had married Lucie-Zoé-Marie Jamin, daughter of J.-C. Jamin, a professor of physics at the University of Paris. She died four years later in March of 1878, shortly after the birth of their only child, Jean. Jean later became a physicist himself, inheriting the chair of physics held by his father, grandfather, and great-grandfather before him. Two months prior to Lucie's death, Becquerel's grandfather died. At that point, his son and grandson each moved up one step, Alexandre-Edmond to professor of physics at the Musée d'Histoire Naturelle, and Antoine-Henri to his assistant. From that point on, Becquerel's professional life was associated with the Musée, the Polytechnique, and the Ponts et Chaussées.

In the period between receiving his engineering degree and discovering radioactivity, Becquerel pursued a variety of research interests. In following up his work on Faraday's magneto-optics, for example, he became interested in the effect of the earth's magnetic field on the atmosphere. His research determined how the earth's magnetic field affected carbon disulfide. He proposed to the International Congress on Electric Units that his results be used as the standard of electrical current strength. Becquerel also studied the magnetic properties of a number of materials and published detailed information on nickel, cobalt, and ozone in 1879. He also reported the surprising discovery that nickel-plated iron becomes magnetic when heated to redness.

Becomes Interested in the Study of Luminescence

In the early 1880s Becquerel began research on a topic his father had been working on for many years—luminescence, or the emission of light from unheated substances. In particular, he made a detailed study of the spectra produced by luminescent materials and examined the way in which light is absorbed by various crystals. Becquerel was especially interested in the effect that polarization had on luminescence. For this work Becquerel was awarded his doctoral degree by the University of Paris in 1888, and he was once again seen as an active researcher after years of increasing administrative responsibility.

When his father died in 1891, Becquerel was appointed to succeed him as professor of physics at the museum and at the conservatory. The same year he was asked to replace the ailing Alfred Potier at the Ecole Polytechnique. Finally, in 1894 he was appointed chief engineer at the Ecole des Ponts et Chaussées. Becquerel married his second wife, Louise-Désirée Lorieux, the daughter of a mine inspector, in 1890; the couple had no children.

Study of Luminescence Leads to Discovery of Radioactivity

The period of quiescence in Becquerel's research career came to an end in 1895 with the announcement of Röntgen's discovery of X rays. The aspect of the discovery that caught Becquerel's attention was that X rays appeared to be associated with a luminescent spot on the side of the cathode-ray tube used in Röntgen's experiment. Given his own background and interest in luminescence, Becquerel wondered whether the production of X rays might always be associated with luminescence.

To test this hypothesis Becquerel wrapped photographic plates in thick layers of black paper and placed a known luminescent material, potassium uranyl sulfate, on top of them. When this assemblage was then placed in sunlight, Becquerel found that the photographic plates were exposed. He concluded that sunlight had caused the uranium salt to luminesce, thereby giving off X rays. The X rays then penetrated the black paper and exposed the photographic plate. He announced these results at meeting of the Academy of Sciences on February 24, 1896.

Through an unusual set of circumstances the following week, Becquerel discovered radioactivity. He began work on February 26th as usual by wrapping his photographic plates in black paper and taping a piece of potassium uranyl sulfate to the packet. Since it was not sunny enough to conduct his experiment, however, Becquerel set his materials aside in a dark drawer. He repeated the procedure the next day as well, and again a lack of sunshine prompted him to store his materials in the same drawer. On March 1st Becquerel decided to develop the photographic plates that he had been prepared and set aside. It is not clear why he did this since, according to his hypothesis, little or no exposure would be expected. Lack of sunlight had meant that no luminescence could have occurred; hence, no X rays could have been emitted.

Surprisingly, Becquerel found that the plates had been exposed as completely as if they had been set in the sun. Some form of radiation—but clearly not X rays—had been emitted from the uranium salt and exposed the plates. A day later, according to Oliver Lodge in the *Journal of the Chemical Society,* Becquerel reported his findings to the academy, pointing out: "It thus appears that the phenomenon cannot be attributed to luminous radiation emitted by reason of phosphorescence, since, at the end of one-hundredth of a second, phosphorescence becomes so feeble as to become imperceptible."

With the discovery of this new radiation Becquerel's research gained a new focus. His advances prompted his graduate student Marie Curie to undertake an intensive study of radiation for her own doctoral thesis. Curie later suggested the name radioactivity for Becquerel's discovery, a phenomenon that had until that time been referred to as Becquerel's rays.

Becquerel's own research continued to produce useful results. In May of 1896, for example, he found uranium metal to be many times more radioactive than the compounds of uranium he had been using and began to use it as a source of radioactivity. In 1900 he also found that at least part of the radiation emitted by uranium consists of electrons, particles that were discovered only three years earlier by **Joseph John Thomson**. For his part in the discovery of radioactivity, Becquerel shared the 1903 Nobel Prize in physics with Curie and her husband Pierre.

Honors continued to come to Becquerel in the last decade of his life. On December 31, 1906, he was elected vice president of the French Academy of Sciences, and two years later he become president of the organization. On June 19, 1908, he was elected one of the two permanent secretaries of the academy, a post he held for less than two months before his death on August 25, 1908, at Le Croisic, in Brittany. Among his other honors and awards were the Rumford Medal of the Royal Society in 1900, the Helmholtz Medal of the Royal Academy of Sciences of Berlin in 1901, and the Barnard Medal of the U.S. National Academy of Sciences in 1905.

SELECTED WRITINGS BY BECQUEREL:

Periodicals

"Emission de radiations nouvelles par l'uranium métallique," *Comptes rendus de l'Académie des Sciences, Paris,* Volume 122, 1896, pp. 1086–1088.

"Sur les radiations émises par phosphorescence," *Comptes rendus de l'Académie des Sciences, Paris,* Volume 122, 1896, pp. 420–421.

"Sur les radiations invisibles émises par les corps phosphorescents," *Comptes rendus de l'Académie des Sciences, Paris,* Volume 122, 1896, pp. 501–503.

"Recherches sur une propriété nouvelle de la matière: Activité radiante spontanée ou radioactivité de la matière," *Mémoires de l'Académie des Sciences, Paris,* Volume 46, 1903.

SOURCES:

Books

Magill, Frank N., editor, *The Nobel Prize Winners: Physics,* Volume 1, 1901–1937, Salem Press, 1989, pp. 55–63.

Ranc, Albert, *Henri Becquerel et la découverte de la radioactivité,* Editions de la Liberté, 1946.

Zaban Jones, Bessie, editor, *The Golden Age of Science,* Simon & Schuster, 1966, pp. 581–598.

Periodicals

Lodge, Sir Oliver, "Becquerel Memorial Lecture," *Journal of the Chemical Society,* Volume 101, 1912, pp. 2005–2042.

—*Sketch by David E. Newton*

J. Georg Bednorz
1950-
German physicist

German-born physicist J. Georg Bednorz, now a Swiss resident, has a particular genius for finding solutions to problems of equipment and technique in physics research. He is the discoverer, with Swiss physicist **K. Alex Müller**, of ceramic substances that become superconducting, or allow electrical current to flow without resistance, at temperatures higher than possible with any previous superconductors. The discovery promises to lead to a host of new superconduction applications. Bednorz was only thirty-seven and had had his Ph.D. only four years when he shared the 1987 Nobel Prize in Physics with Müller for the research on superconductivity. He has also won a number of other prizes for his work.

Johannes Georg Bednorz was born on May 16, 1950, in Nevenkirchen in what was then West Germany. He graduated from the University of Münster in 1976 and received his doctorate from the Swiss Federal Institute of Technology in Zurich in 1982. That year he went to work at the IBM Zurich Research Laboratory and met Müller, who invited him to participate in his study of superconductors—generally metals and alloys, whose electrical resistance becomes virtually nonexistent at temperatures close to absolute zero. Bednorz's own interest in the applications of superconductivity, especially in connection with the design of high-speed trains, made the project particularly appealing to him. Superconducting levitation would reduce power requirements in rail transportation: if a magnet is placed on a superconducting surface, it will float above it when the temperature of the surface is lowered.

Discovers Superconducting Ceramics

Scientists have long sought materials that were superconductive at as high a temperature as possible to provide for the most effective electrical conduction for ordinary and practical use. After World War II, superconductors were put to many practical uses. Among these was the operation of large electromagnets, but they only worked at very low temperatures. Finding new materials would open up huge possibilities in reducing power requirements and preventing power losses in overhead power transmissions.

All of the metallic elements and many alloys had been studied, but superconductivity could not be found at a temperature higher than 23 degrees Kelvin (23 degrees above absolute zero). Superconductivity was only possible when materials were cooled by expensive liquid helium. If materials could be made superconductive at the temperature of liquid nitrogen, 77 degrees Kelvin, superconductivity would be more practical, since liquid nitrogen is relatively inexpensive, safe, and easy to make. In 1983, Bednorz and Müller began testing ceramic substances made of mixtures of metallic oxides in the hope that they would serve as superconductors at higher temperatures. Bednorz was largely responsible for making and testing the oxides. On January 27, 1986, the researchers found that a barium-lanthanum-copper oxide became superconductive at 35 degrees Kelvin (−238 degrees Celsius), more than 10 degrees Kelvin above the highest temperature for previous superconductors.

Many scientists were skeptical about the results until teams from the University of Tokyo, the University of Houston, and Bell Laboratories confirmed them. In 1987 researchers at the University of Houston, working with similar ceramics, announced their discovery of superconductors effective at 90 degrees Kelvin, above the boiling point of liquid nitrogen. The same year President Ronald Reagan announced an initiative to develop superconductivity. Scientists around the world rushed to study ceramics and superconductivity in the liquid nitrogen temperature range.

The Nobel Prize committee took note of the excitement when they awarded Bednorz and Müller the physics prize, stating that the discovery had generated "an explosive development in which hundreds of laboratories the world over" were taking part. Still, the speed with which the award was given—only two years after the discovery was made—generated some surprise. Prize winners often wait much longer to be recognized.

Despite Bednorz's and Müller's discovery, no theoretical explanation for the behavior of the ceramic substances has yet been made. Nor did their ceramic materials immediately lend themselves to technological applications, since they are not easily made into wire. The Japanese have gone farthest in the field: the Nippon Steel Company developed a "melt-processing" technique to produce a superconducting wire out of the ceramics. Room-temperature superconductivity has yet to be achieved.

SELECTED WRITINGS BY BEDNORZ:

Periodicals

"Possible High T_c Superconductivity in the Ba-La-Cu-O System," *Zeitschrift für Physik B,* Volume 64, 1986, pp. 189–93.
"The Discovery of a Class of High Temperature Superconductors," *Science,* Volume 237, 1987, pp. 1133–39.
"The Discovery of Superconductivity at High Temperature," *Recherche,* January, 1988, pp. 52–60.

SOURCES:

Books

Nobel Prize Winners: Physics, Volume 3, Salem Press, 1988, pp. 1336–48.

Periodicals

Science, Volume 238, 1987, pp. 481–82.

—Sketch by Margo Nash

Fred Begay
1932-
American physicist

Fred Begay is a Native American physicist who has performed research in the area of high energy gamma ray, solar wind, and neutron physics. A staff member of the laser fusion division at Los Alamos Scientific Laboratory since 1972, Begay has investigated plasma physics in exploding wire systems as well as various theoretical and experimental issues in thermonuclear fusion.

Begay was born on the Ute Mountain Indian Reservation in Towaoc, Colorado in about 1932. His mother was Navajo and Ute and his stepfather was Navajo and Piute. Because the Navajo language is not written, Begay's name is actually an Americanized extraction from his native language. Begay's parents were nomadic, and some of his earliest memories are of hunting barefoot and sleeping in the open with his four brothers and sisters. Gathering enough food to survive and staying warm were primary day-to-day concerns as his family roamed the desert and mountain regions of the Southwest. When Begay was about ten years old, his parents sent him to a U.S. government-run boarding school in Ignacio, Colorado, where he was given the last name of "Young" and the estimated birthdate of July 2, 1932 for record-keeping purposes. He was taught to speak English, but after ten years he graduated with only an elementary ability to read or write the language.

One of Begay's primary reasons for continuing his education was to understand nature. In a 1979 television interview for *Nova* he explained, "A scientist looks at the world like a child always wondering what it is made out of. What are the pieces of the pieces of the pieces?" At the age of 23, Begay enrolled in the University of New Mexico and studied intensely to improve his ability to read and write English. He worked part time to support himself in school and switched majors from engineering to physics. A restless student, he would often disappear for days at a time to return to the reservation for purification ceremonies and other rituals. In 1961 Begay graduated from the University of New Mexico with a B.S. in physics and mathematics, received a M.S. degree in physics in 1963, and was awarded a doctorate in physics in 1972. Begay's Ph.D. is especially noteworthy because of the fact that he never attended high school—the government school was, in essence, a trade school.

Begay worked as a research physicist at the Air Force Weapons Lab at Kirtland Air Force Base, New Mexico, from 1963 to 1965, and later worked for

NASA designing satellite experiments and high energy gamma ray and neutron detector systems for research on the sun. Begay conducted research in high energy neutron physics at the University of New Mexico from 1965 to 1971, and was a staff member in X-ray spectroscopy from 1971 to 1972. Since that time Begay has worked at Los Alamos National Laboratories in laser physics and fusion research. In 1979 Begay was the subject of a television biography for *Nova* titled "The Long Walk of Fred Young," produced by the British Broadcasting Corporation (BBC). In addition to his work at Los Alamos, Begay taught at Stanford in 1975 and spent a sabbatical at the University of Maryland during the academic year 1987–88.

For more than twenty-five years Begay has devoted his principal efforts to understanding plasma physics. His research seeks to harness the power of nuclear fusion, considered a cleaner, safer power source than standard fission reactors. Begay has investigated the use of lasers to confine and ignite fuel pellets in a fusion reactor. Other research interests include general relativity, mathematical physics, and quantum theory. A prolific reader, Begay also devotes time to maintaining Navajo/Ute language and traditions. He married a Navajo woman in 1952 and has seven children: Fred, Jr., Joyce, William, Janet, Teresa, Christina, and Caroline.

SOURCES:

"The Long Walk of Fred Young," *Nova* (television program), number 602, produced by BBC-TV, Journal Graphics, 1979.
Begay, Fred, interview and correspondence with Geri J. Speace, May 17, 1994.

—*Sketch by Mark J. Kaiser*

Emil von Behring
1854-1917
German bacteriologist

Emil von Behring was one of the founders of the science of immunology. His discovery of the diphtheria and tetanus antitoxins paved the way for the prevention of these diseases through the use of immunization. It also opened the door for the specific treatment of such diseases with the injection of immune serum. Behring's stature as a seminal figure in modern medicine was recognized in 1901 when he received the first Nobel Prize in physiology or medicine.

Emil Adolf von Behring was born on March 15, 1854, in Hansdorf, West Prussia (now Germany). He was the eldest son of August Georg Behring, a schoolmaster with thirteen children, and his second wife, Augustine Zech Behring. Although his father planned for him to become a minister, young Behring had an inclination toward medicine. The family's meager circumstances seemed to put this goal out of his reach, however. Then one of Behring's teachers, recognizing great promise, arranged for his admission to the Army Medical College in Berlin, where he was able to obtain a free medical education in exchange for future military service. He received his doctor of medicine degree in 1878, and two years later he passed the state examination that allowed him to practice.

Discovers Diphtheria and Tetanus Antitoxins

The army promptly sent Behring to Posen (now Poznan, Poland), then to Bonn in 1887, and finally back to Berlin in 1888. His first published papers, which date from this period, dealt with the use of iodoform as an antiseptic. After completing his military service in 1889, Behring became an assistant at the Institute of Hygiene in Berlin, joining a brilliant team of researchers headed by **Robert Koch**, a leading light in the new science of bacteriology.

It was while working in Koch's laboratory that Behring began his pioneering investigations of diphtheria and tetanus. Both of these diseases are caused by bacilli (bacteria) that do not spread widely through the body, but produce generalized symptoms by excreting toxins. Diphtheria, nicknamed the "strangling angel" because of the way it obstructs breathing, was a terrible killer of children in the late nineteenth century. Its toxin had first been detected by others in 1888. Tetanus, likewise, was fatal more often than not. In 1889, the tetanus bacillus was cultivated in its pure state for the first time by Shibasaburo Kitasato, another gifted member of Koch's team.

The next year, Behring and Kitasato jointly published their classic paper, "Ueber das Zustandekommen der Diphtherie-Immunität und der Tetanus-Immunität bei Thieren" ("The Mechanism of Immunity in Animals to Diphtheria and Tetanus"). One week later, Behring alone published another paper dealing with immunity against diphtheria and outlining five ways in which it could be achieved. These reports announced that injections of toxin from diphtheria or tetanus bacilli led animals to produce in their blood substances capable of neutralizing the disease poison.

Behring and Kitasato dubbed these substances antitoxins. Furthermore, injections of blood serum from an animal that had been given a chance to develop antitoxins to tetanus or diphtheria could confer immunity to the disease on other animals, and even cure animals that were already sick.

The news created a sensation. Several papers confirming and amplifying these results, including some by Behring himself, appeared in rapid succession. In 1893, Behring described a group of human diphtheria patients who were treated with antitoxin. That same year, he was given the title of professor. However, Behring's diphtheria antitoxin did not yield consistent results. It was the bacteriologist **Paul Ehrlich**, another of the talented associates in Koch's lab, who was chiefly responsible for standardizing the antitoxin, thus making it practical for widespread therapeutic use. Working together, Ehrlich and Behring also showed that high-quality antitoxin could be obtained from horses, as well as from the sheep used previously, opening the way for large-scale production of the antitoxin.

Develops Tuberculosis Vaccine for Cattle

In 1894, Behring accepted a position as professor at the University of Halle. A year later, he was named a professor and director of the Institute of Hygiene at the University of Marburg. Thereafter he focused much of his attention on the problem of immunization against tuberculosis. His assumption, unfounded as it turned out, was that different forms of the disease in humans and in cattle were closely related. He tried immunizing calves with a weakened strain of the human tuberculosis bacillus, but the results were disappointing. Although his bovine vaccine was widely used for a time in Germany, Russia, Sweden, and the United States, it was found that the cattle excreted dangerous microorganisms afterward. Nevertheless, Behring's basic idea of using a bacillus from one species to benefit another influenced the development of later vaccines.

Behring did not entirely abandon his work on diphtheria during this period. In 1913, he announced the development of a toxin-antitoxin mixture that resulted in longer-lasting immunity than did antitoxin serum alone. This approach was a forerunner of modern methods of preventing, rather than just treating, the disease. Today children are routinely and effectively vaccinated against diphtheria and tetanus.

However, the first great drop in diphtheria mortality was due to the antitoxin therapy introduced earlier by Behring, and it is for this contribution that he is primarily remembered. The fall in the diphtheria death rate around the turn of the century was one of the sharpest ever recorded for any treatment. In Germany alone, an estimated 45,000 lives per year were saved. It is no wonder, then, that Behring

received the 1901 Nobel Prize "for his work on serum therapy, especially its application against diphtheria, by which he ... opened a new road in the domain of medical science and thereby placed in the hands of the physician a victorious weapon against illness and deaths." Behring was also elevated to the status of nobility and shared a sizable cash prize from the Paris Academy of Medicine with Émile Roux, the French bacteriologist who was one of the men who had the diphtheria toxin in 1888. In addition, Behring was granted honorary memberships in societies in Italy, Turkey, France, Hungary, and Russia.

There were other, financial rewards as well. From 1901 onward, ill health prevented Behring from giving regular lectures, so he devoted himself to research. A commercial firm in which he had a financial interest built a well-equipped laboratory for his use in Marburg, Germany. Then, in 1914, Behring established his own company to manufacture serums and vaccines. The profits from this venture allowed him to keep a large estate at Marburg, on which he grazed cattle used in experiments. This house was a gathering place of society. Behring also owned a vacation home on the island of Capri in the Mediterranean.

In 1896 Behring married 18-year-old Else Spinola, daughter of the director of a Berlin hospital. They had seven children. Yet despite all outward appearances of personal and professional success, Behring was subject to frequent bouts of serious depression, some of which required sanatorium treatment. In addition, a fractured thigh led to a condition that increasingly impaired his mobility. He was already in a weakened state when he contracted pneumonia in 1917. His body was unable to withstand the added strain, and he died on March 31 in Marburg, Germany.

SELECTED WRITINGS BY BEHRING:

Books

(With Shibasaburo Kitasato) "The Mechanism of Immunity in Animals to Diphtheria and Tetanus," *Milestones in Microbiology,* American Society for Microbiology, 1961, pp. 138–40.
"Studies on the Mechanism of Immunity to Diphtheria in Animals," *Milestones in Microbiology,* American Society for Microbiology, 1961, pp. 141–44.
"Serum Therapy in Therapeutics and Medical Science," in *Nobel Lectures Including Presentation Speeches and Laureates' Biographies: Physiology or Medicine,* 1901–1921, Elsevier, 1967, pp. 6–18.

SOURCES:

Books

deKruif, Paul, *Microbe Hunters,* Harcourt, 1926, pp. 169–189.
Parish, H. J., *A History of Immunization,* E. and S. Livingstone, 1965, pp. 92–95, 118–127, 141–143, 166–168.

Periodicals

Grundbacher, F. J., "Behring's Discovery of Diphtheria and Tetanus Antitoxins," *Immunology Today,* May, 1992, pp. 188–190.
MacNalty, Arthur S., "Emil von Behring," *British Medical Journal,* March 20, 1954, pp. 668–670.

—Sketch by Linda Wasmer Smith

Georg von Békésy
1899-1972
Hungarian American physicist

Georg von Békésy was educated as a physicist, but is best known for his research on the physics of hearing. He was awarded the 1961 Nobel Prize for medicine or physiology for his research on the physical mechanism of hearing, particularly with regard to the changes that take place within the cochlea. His discoveries have been important in the development of surgical procedures and prosthetic devices for the treatment of hearing disorders.

Békésy was born on June 3, 1899, in Budapest, Hungary. His father was Alexander von Békésy, a member of the Hungarian diplomatic service, and his mother was the former Paula Mazaly. As his father was assigned to a variety of diplomatic posts, Georg grew up in a number of cities, including Munich, Constantinople (now Istanbul), and Zürich, as well as his native Budapest. He entered the University of Bern in 1916, where he concentrated in chemistry. Békésy remained at Bern until 1920. After serving briefly in the military, he enrolled at the University of Budapest and was awarded a Ph.D. in physics for his thesis on fluid dynamics in 1923.

Intrigued as a boy by gypsy music, Békésy maintained a lifelong interest in the study of sound. His first job as a communications engineer with the Hungarian Post Office, beginning in 1923, allowed Békésy to begin a serious investigation into the physics of sound, as the postal service was also responsible for the nation's telephone system. As he began to deal with the practical problems of telephone systems, Békésy realized that it would be helpful to better understand the precise physical mechanism by which sound travels through the human ear. By the 1920s, anatomists had a reasonably thorough understanding of the physical structure of the human ear, but physiologists were still disputing the physical process by which sound stimulates the inner ear and causes the brain to detect differences in pitch.

Carries Out Experiments on the Physics of Hearing

Békésy conducted research on the physics of hearing throughout his tenure with the Hungarian Postal Service from 1923 to 1946. During that period, he also worked as a consultant in the central laboratories of Siemens and Halske in Berlin (1926–27) and was employed by the University of Budapest as lecturer (1932–34), special professor (1939–40), and full professor (1940–46). In 1946–47, he spent a year as research professor at the Karolinska Institute in Stockholm. Throughout this time, Békésy designed and carried out an extensive series of experiments intended to determine exactly what happens to sounds that enter the ear. In some of these experiments, he performed very delicate surgery on the inner ear itself. In order to do so, he had to design and build very small tools with which to operate on the less-than-fingernail-sized cochlea. He is reputed, for example, to have designed and built a pair of scissors with blades measuring less than a hundredth of an inch long. Using these tools and various combinations of mirrors, Békésy was able to observe changes that occurred within the cochlea as it received sounds.

In 1947, Békésy accepted an appointment as senior research fellow at Harvard University's Psycho-Acoustic Laboratory, where he had built and carried out experiments using a model cochlea. Békésy's model cochlea consisted of a water-filled plastic tube thirty centimeters long. He stimulated one end of the tube with a sound and then placed his forearm along the length of the tube. He found that the sound wave was noticeable at only one particular point on his forearm, and that he could vary that point by changing pitch. From his many experiments, Békésy concluded that sound moves as a traveling wave across the cochlea by way of the basilar membrane. Based on its frequency, a wave produces a maximum vibration at one particular point along the membrane—waves of a higher pitch reach their peak nearer the base of the cochlea than those of a lower pitch. As the wave peaks along the membrane, adjacent cells along the organ of Corti are stimulated, and an auditory message is sent to the brain. It is by this mechanism, then, that the brain is able to determine the pitch of the sound that it is "hearing."

In 1961, Békésy became the first physicist to receive the Nobel Prize for medicine or physiology. He left Harvard in 1966 for the University of Hawaii, where he became professor of sensory sciences. As this title suggests, his interests broadened from the physics of sound to the relationship among all senses, especially sound, taste, and touch.

Among his many honors are the Denker Prize in Otology (1931), the Leibnitz Medal of the German Academy of Sciences (1937), the Howard Crosby Warren Medal of the Society of Experimental Psychologists (1955), and the Gold Medals of the American Otological Society (1957) and the Acoustical Society of America (1961). Békésy died in Honolulu, Hawaii, on June 13, 1972.

SELECTED WRITINGS BY BÉKÉSY:

Books

Experiments in Hearing, translated by Ernest G. Weaver, McGraw, 1960.
Sensory Inhibition, Princeton University Press, 1967.

SOURCES:

Books

McGraw-Hill Modern Scientists and Engineers, Volume X, McGraw-Hill, 1980, p. 72.
Stevens, S. S., Fred Warshofsky, and others, *Sound and Hearing,* Time-Life Books, 1970, pp. 54–56.

Periodicals

"Nobel Prize for Physiology: Dr. Georg von Békésy," *Nature,* December 2, 1961, p. 800.

—*Sketch by David E. Newton*

Gordon Bell
1934-
American computer scientist

Computer designer and computer science scholar Gordon Bell performed ground-breaking work in computer design for Digital Equipment Corporation (DEC), during the 1960s and 1970s, a period of dramatic changes in the design of computers. During this time, computers evolved from machines filling entire rooms and selling for millions of dollars to continually smaller and less expensive models, making computer technology accessible to a whole new market of smaller businesses. Bell has remained an innovator at the forefront of his field throughout his career.

Chester Gordon Bell was born August 19, 1934, in Kirksville, Missouri, the son of Roy Chester and Lola Dolph Gordon Bell. At age six, Bell began working for his father, who ran an electrical contracting and appliance business, and was soon repairing appliances and even wiring houses. This early interest in electronics eventually led Bell to the Massachusetts Institute of Technology (MIT), where he earned a B.S. in 1956 and an M.S. in 1957, both in electrical engineering. Upon completing his work at MIT, Bell travelled to Australia as a Fulbright scholar to study at the University of New South Wales. While there, Bell taught the first graduate course on computer design offered at the university. He also teamed up with another Fulbright scholar at the university, Gwendolyn Kay Druyer, whom he married upon returning to the United States in 1959. She would eventually be named director of the Boston Computer Museum.

Returning to MIT, Bell worked as an engineer in the Speech Communication Lab, but left the institution in 1960 to work for DEC. That year DEC introduced the PDP–1, which was one of the first computers to take advantage of transistor technology. At 250 pounds, the PDP–1 was one quarter the weight of other computers on the market and its price was significantly lower than larger computers. Bell arrived at DEC in time to help finish the design and the software library of the PDP–1. He was then architect of the PDP–4, which DEC released in 1962, a machine smaller and less expensive than the PDP–1. In 1963, Bell played an essential role in the development of the PDP–5, which under his direction became the smallest computer to date. This machine was designed for the Atomic Energy Commission to use in gathering nuclear reactor data. The following year, Bell headed the development of software and hardware design of the PDP–6, which was DEC's first large computer able to perform multiple tasks simultanously. In 1965, DEC released the PDP–8, the first successfully mass-produced minicomputer. About the size of a small refrigerator, the computer was built using integrated circuits, making it far less expensive to produce, and was sold at about half the cost of many competitive machines. Bell was instrumental in the development of this machine, which was a major success for DEC.

Bell gave up his position at DEC in 1966 to become an associate professor of computer science at Carnegie-Mellon University in Pittsburgh, Pennsylvania. While at Carnegie-Mellon, he continued his work in computer design and maintained his relationship with DEC. Bell was primary architect of the PDP–11, a minicomputer DEC released in 1970. The machine was used by the Chicago Police Department, allowing operators of the 911 emergency number to quickly identify the address and phone number of callers.

Heads Development of VAX Computer

In 1972, Bell left Carnegie-Mellon and returned to DEC as vice-president in charge of engineering. Three years later, Bell and his team of engineers had designed the VAX–11, which was based on the PDP–11. The VAX–11 provided significantly more working memory than its predecessors, making it possible to create and run larger programs. In 1978, Bell defined a plan that would enable the VAX to be used throughout an organization. The plan, known as "the VAX strategy," connected personal work stations to a departmental minicomputer. The departmental computers were in turn connected to larger computers via a network. With the help of the "VAX strategy," sales of VAX computers skyrocketed, accounting for nearly all of DEC's revenues by the mid 1980s.

Assists in Establishing a Joint Venture of American Computer Companies

In 1982, Bell participated in the formation of the Microelectronics and Computer Technology Corporation, a joint venture involving a number of American computer companies. The corporation was formed as a cooperative response to Japanese gains in the computer market. In 1983, Bell left DEC to form Encore Computer with two partners. Bell's role in the new company was computer design. In 1986, upon completing his design responsibilities for Encore, Bell again moved on, eventually traveling to Washington, D.C., to become an assistant director of the National Science Foundation, in which his focus was on computer science. He later became chief scientist at Stardent Computer of Concord, Massachusetts. In addition to Bell's interest in computer design, he has also worked with computer art. Bell and his wife have two children: Brigham Roy and Laura Louise.

SELECTED WRITINGS BY BELL:

Books

(With Allen Newell) *Computer Structures,* McGraw, 1971.
(With J. Grason and Allen Newell) *Designing Computers and Digital Systems,* Digital Press, 1972.

(With Mudge and John E. McNamara) *Computer Engineering,* Digital Press, 1978.
(With Daniel Paul Siewiorek and Allen Newell) *Computer Structures,* McGraw, 1982.
(With John E. McNamara) *High-Tech Ventures: The Guide for Entrepreneurial Success,* Addison-Wesley, 1991.

SOURCES:

Books

Slater, Robert, *Portraits in Silicon,* MIT Press, 1987, pp. 207–215.

Periodicals

"Computers in the 21st Century," *The Futurist,* March/April, 1992, pp. 51–52.
Kenner, Hugh, "Tales from the Venture Woods," *Byte,* October, 1991, pp. 330–331.

—Sketch by Dan Rooney

Jocelyn Susan Bell Burnell
1943-
Irish astronomer

Jocelyn Susan Bell Burnell is the astronomer who discovered stars which release regular bursts of radio waves, known as pulsars, while working under **Antony Hewish** at Cambridge University. Hewish was awarded the Nobel Prize in 1974 for this discovery, though Bell Burnell was not included in the citation. She has been Senior Research Fellow at the Royal Observatory in Edinburgh, Scotland, since 1982, and following the discovery of pulsars her work has concentrated on gamma-ray and infrared astronomy, as well as millimeter wave astronomy.

Bell Burnell was born in Belfast, Northern Ireland, on July 15, 1943. Her father was an architect who designed the Armagh Observatory, an astronomical observatory which was close to their home, and her early interest in astronomy was encouraged by the observatory staff. Bell Burnell attended the Mount School in York and then the University of Glasgow in Scotland, where she earned her B.S. degree in 1965. That same year, she began work on her Ph.D. under Hewish at Cambridge.

Discovers Pulsars While Looking for Quasars

Bell Burnell chose to do her doctoral work on recently discovered quasars—star formations the size of galaxies that are so distant from Earth that they appear to be single stars. She worked in radio astronomy, as opposed to optical astronomy, and she spent her first two years as a graduate student building a special radio telescope designed by Hewish to pick up and record rapid variations in radio signals. Radio telescopes have an advantage over visible-light telescopes in that they can pick up radiation in the form of long wavelength radio waves from objects in deep space that cannot be seen using an optical telescope.

In 1964 astronomers had discovered that the radio signals given off by sources in spaces were not always steady, just as light from stars (visible wavelengths of radiation) appears to twinkle. This twinkling of radio signals, called scintillation, could be used to calculate the size of radio source, if it were known how much the signal varied as its radio waves passed through the wispy gas between planets. The radio telescope which Hewish had designed was able to record time variations in the strength of radio sources. The telescope had over two thousand separate receivers spread out over four acres. It was constantly receiving and recording signals onto rolls of paper, producing some 400 feet of charts every week. Once the telescope was operating in July of 1967, it was Bell Burnell's job to make sense out of the signals recorded by the instrument.

The month after the receivers were in place, in August of 1967, Bell Burnell noticed some curious variations in signals which had been recorded at about midnight the night before. They came from the direction opposite the sun, between the stars Vega and Altair. This seemed odd, because strong changes in signals from quasars occur as a result of the solar wind and thus are usually weak during the night. This source gave off short bursts of energy, lasting less than one hundredth of a second and occurring very rapidly, though at precise intervals.

Bell Burnell approached Hewish with the problem, and he thought there was a problem with the equipment. If it was not a problem with the new telescope, he believed it was a ham radio, car ignition, or some other local radio wave or electrical transmission causing interference. No one realized at the time that stars could emit radio waves that began and ended so quickly, and there was a good reason why they believed stars could not do such a thing: A star giving off a signal that rapid would have to be very, very small, and if it were that small it could not possibly have enough energy to travel so far. Hewish had her check out the instruments many more times to eliminate any possible source of interference.

No interference or problems with the telescope were found. The scintillating star continued to wink at her through the radio telescope, and the signals grew earlier and earlier each night, just as stars appear to do. After a month of precise observation, Bell Burnell was able to establish that the signals continued and remained fixed with respect to the stars—which meant they were coming from somewhere other than the earth or the sun. By November, Bell Burnell measured some strong signals. The rapid set of pulses occurred regularly every 1.3373013 seconds and lasted for only 0.016 of a second.

This extraordinary regularity was perhaps the most compelling aspect of these signals. The research team felt obliged, at least initially, to consider the possibility that the source of the signals was a beacon from some extraterrestrial civilization. Initially, the source of the signals was jokingly named LGM 1, for Little Green Men 1. Hewish wanted to be sure that LGM 1 was not an anomaly, and searching through miles and miles of charts recorded in previous months, Bell Burnell found three other sources with similar signals. Soon other members of the team found other sources of these signals. Hewish named the sources "pulsating stars," and the term was soon contracted to pulsars, because they pulsated at regular intervals. He announced the discovery on February 9, 1968. Some British tabloid newspapers distorted the nature of the discovery and claimed scientists had made contact with alien civilizations.

The pulsars were named for the observatories where they were found: CP for the Cambridge Pulsar, HP for Harvard, and so on, followed by four numbers that indicated their location in the sky. The biggest theoretical problem with all of these signals was the short duration of the burst and their rapid repetition. Calculations based on what was known about the radio emissions from other stars continued to indicate a source which, by astronomical standards, was extremely small. The pulsars had to be less than ten miles in radius, when the radius of an average star is hundreds of thousands of miles. Furthermore, a star like our sun could not turn on and off in less than two seconds. Hewish initially speculated that they were either white-dwarf stars or perhaps even neutron stars —stars that had been predicted but never seen.

It was an astrophysicist named **Thomas Gold** who solved this problem. Working across the Atlantic at Cornell University in New York, Gold hypothesized that the pulsars must be neutron stars that resulted from the explosion of a supernova. The existence of neutron stars had been predicted by Russian theorist and Nobel Prize winner **Lev Davidovich Landau**. When a star is dying, the outer parts explode, causing a bright light known to astronomers as a supernova. But what happens to its inner core is a compression: Rather than exploding, it implodes. The star's inner mass squeezes so tightly together that it actually overcomes the forces that hold atoms together. It pulls the electrons right into the nuclei, and the electrons and protons of the matter join, forming neutrons. Furthermore, all of this mass close to the center of the imploded star causes it to spin very fast.

Neutron stars would be very small in diameter, but incredibly dense with matter, 1015 times the density of water. (The one Bell Burnell found could only be about ten miles in diameter.) Gold argued that the LGM signals were from neutron stars; these stars would be small, very dense spheres spinning rapidly, which would cause an intense magnetic field. Ionized atomic particles rotating within the field would create a narrow beam of radiation that would turn around rapidly, and the radio waves would appear through the radio telescope as a beam similar to a lighthouse beacon flashing periodically in our direction.

Gold's theory was almost completely ignored at first, and this interpretation of the Bell Burnell's data obviously needed some support. The support came late in 1968 when two other astronomers, David Staelin and Edward Reifenstein at the National Radio Astronomy Observatory at Green Bank, West Virginia, found a pulsar which they named NP 0532. It was located right at the center of the Crab Nebula, the remains of an exploded supernova. The scientific community acknowledged that pulsars were indeed neutron stars.

After the discovery of pulsars and the completion of her doctorate, Bell Burnell accepted a position at the University of Southampton and began working on gamma-ray astronomy. Like radio astronomy, gamma-ray astronomy involves detecting signals from space. The difference is the length of the waves involved: Along the radio spectrum, radio signals have the longest wavelengths and gamma rays have the shortest. The visible spectrum, the light used in an optical telescope, lies somewhere in between these extremes. From 1974 to 1982 Bell Burnell worked at the Mullard Space Science Laboratory in X-ray astronomy using signals from the British satellite Ariel V. Along the spectrum, X rays are longer in wavelength than gamma rays, but still shorter than the visible spectrum. In 1982 Bell Burnell was appointed Senior Research fellow at the Royal Observatory in Edinburgh, Scotland. Her research there has continued in detecting and analyzing spectra that come from different parts of the sky using a variety of techniques, including optical astronomy, infrared astronomy, and millimeter wave astronomy.

Bell Burnell was awarded the Michelson Medal from the Franklin Institute in Philadelphia in 1973. She won the J. Robert Oppenheimer Memorial Prize in 1978, the Beatrice M. Tinsley Prize from the American Astronomical Society in 1987, and the Herschel Medal from the Royal Astronomical Society in 1989. She is a member of the Royal Astronomical Society and the International Astronomical Union. In 1968 she was married; she has one child.

SOURCES:

Books

Branley, Franklyn M., *Black Holes, White Dwarves, and Supernovas,* Crowell, 1976, pp. 78–82.

Fisher, David E., *The Origin and Evolution of Our Own Particular Universe,* Atheneum, 1988, pp. 94–99.

Halperin, Paul, *Cosmic Wormholes: The Search for Interstellar Shortcuts,* Dutton, 1992, pp. 45–48.

Shipman, Harry L., *Black Holes, Quasars, and the Universe,* Houghton Mifflin, 1976, pp. 51–53.

World of Scientific Discovery, Gale, 1994, p. 72–73.

—Sketch by Barbara A. Branca

Enrique Beltrán
1903-
Mexican biologist

Enrique Beltrán was Mexico's first professionally trained biologist. He is an authority on single-celled organisms and united the different disciplines of zoology, agriculture and public health in his work. His importance derives not only from his work as a research scientist, however, but also from his administrative efforts in a wide variety of fields. He was largely responsible for the establishment of biology as a science in its own right in Mexico. Later in his career, Beltrán became interested in conservation and served as Mexico's first secretary of forests and game for several years. His work in the history of science led to the creation of the Mexican Society for the History of Science and Technology.

Beltrán was the grandson of a French colonel who had been sent to Mexico with the expeditionary force of Napoleon III. His father, an official in the Mexican navy who had diplomas in both civil engineering and law, was part of the group that constructed the corvette "Zaragoza," a Mexican training ship, in France. From the time of his youth, Beltrán was familiar with the literature of both France and Mexico. He formed the notion of a biological vocation from Luis Murillo's *Animales de México,* featuring chromolithographic illustrations, as well as from books by Paul Bert, Henri Milne Edwards, and Georges Cuvier.

Becomes Mexico's First Professional Biologist

In the second decade of the twentieth century, professional biology as such did not exist in Mexico. Biologists and naturalists all held positions unrelated to their discipline. Upon graduating from secondary school, Beltrán went to the National University of Mexico, which had just been reorganized following the Mexican revolution. There he matriculated in the Facultad de Altos Estudios, the university faculty where students could prepare for a career in science. He took basic courses with botanist Guillermo Gándara and zoologist Agustín Reza (by training as a surgeon), and he was assistant to the botanist Ezequiel Chávez. In 1921, as Chávez's assistant, eighteen-year-old Beltrán gave the first biology lectures in the faculty. (In 1902 Alfonso L. Herrera, a parasitologist, had given the first biology lectures in Mexico at the teacher's college in the capital.) Beltrán's wages were four pesos per day. Then he studied advanced biology with parasitologist Herrera and also with Carlos Reiche.

In 1923, under Herrera, Beltrán began to work on a thesis dealing with protozoans in Lake Xochimilco. Single-celled animals thereafter became the focus of Beltrán's scientific research, allowing him to move freely among specialists in zoology, agriculture, and public health. Beltrán's thesis was completed in 1925 under extreme conditions, for at the end of 1924 the government had suspended the faculty's budget and then changed its name to the more conventional Facultad de Filosofía y Letras en la Especialidad de Ciencias Naturales. Near the close of 1926, Beltrán graduated from the faculty with the diploma Profesor Académico en Ciencias Naturales. The diploma was the Mexican equivalent of a doctorate.

Having received certification as Mexico's first trained biologist, Beltrán began teaching in a succession of posts in the capital. (Mexico's system of higher education resembled that of France in its multiplicity of independent schools for advanced study and in the academic practice of holding down teaching assignments at a number of schools at once.) Beltrán directed the Marine Biological Station at Veracruz until it was suppressed in 1927, but by then he had attracted the attention of administrators in both the educational and agricultural ministries, each of which funded schools of science. In 1931 he received a part-time professorship for biology at the Escuela Nacional Preparatoria. However, the Mexican political climate induced him to spend 1932 at Columbia University, where he worked as a Guggenheim fellow with the senior protozoologist Gary Nathan Calkins. His research netted him a Ph.D. there. Beltrán returned to Mexico in 1933, where for the next twenty years he trained students and carried out research in a succession of posts, notably a chair in the faculty of sciences at the national capital. In 1936 he entered the Mexican National Academy of Medicine—an unusual honor for someone who was not a physician, and from 1937 to 1939 he served as the head of secondary instruction in Mexico.

Promotes Study of Life Sciences

Between 1939 and 1952 Beltrán served as head of the Department of Protozoology of the Institute for Tropical Health and Disease. His output in the 1940s alone was remarkable—127 papers and 10 books. In the following year, he founded the independent Mexican Institute of Renewable Resources, and over the next decades he focused his efforts on guiding its fortunes. His organizing ability led to his appointment in 1958 as head of the new ministry of state (*subsecretaría*) of forests and game. In the 1960s he revived a longstanding interest in history of science to organize an series of colloquia and publications leading to the creation in 1964 of the Mexican Society for the History of Science and Technology; he was the society's first president.

Enrique Beltrán occupies a unique position in twentieth-century Mexico. For the life sciences, he is the *bucinator*—the trumpeting herald—the value of whose patronage may be measured in the work of scores of talented colleagues.

SELECTED WRITINGS BY BELTRÁN:

Books

Medio siglo de ciencia mexicana, 1900–1950, Secretaria de Educación Pública (Mexico), 1952.
Medio siglo de recuerdos de un biólogo mexicano, Sociedad Mexicana de Historia Natural, 1977.
Contribución de México a la biologia, [Mexico City], 1982.

Periodicals

"*Curriculum vitae* de Enrique Beltrán," followed by "Bibliografía de Enrique Beltrán (1924–1949)" and "Veinticinco años de ciencias biológicas en México," *Revista de la Sociedad Mexicana de Historia Natural,* Volume 10, 1949, pp. 5–26.
"Cómo y cuándo me interesé en la historia de la ciencia," *Quipu,* Volume 2, number 2, 1985, pp. 319–328.

SOURCES:

Books

Villa Salas, Avelino B., editor, *Homenaje al Dr. Enrique Beltrán,* Academia Nacional de Ciencias Forestales (Mexico), 1980.

—*Sketch by Lewis Pyenson*

Baruj Benacerraf
1920-
Venezuelan-born American pathologist and immunochemist

Baruj Benacerraf is a Venezuelan-born immunologist whose major contribution to modern immunology was the discovery of the immune-response gene (Ir), which triggers the body's war on disease. For his work linking Ir genes to the major histocompatibility complex or supergene, which controls the nature and vigor of the body's immune response, Benacerraf was awarded the 1980 Nobel Prize in physiology or medicine, which he shared with two other immunologists.

Benacerraf was born on October 29, 1920, in Caracas, Venezuela, to Henriette Lasry and Abraham Benacerraf. His father was a Sephardic Jew who had emigrated from North Africa to Venezuela, working his way to wealth and prominence as a financier and textile importer. When Benacerraf was five, the family moved to France where Benacerraf attended the Lycée Janson and received a classic French education in pre-World War II Paris. In 1938, fearing the outbreak of war in Europe, the family returned to Venezuela; Benacerraf was sent to the United States to follow in his father's footsteps, enrolling as a student in the Textile Engineering School of the Philadelphia Museum of Art. To his family's regret, he left after only two weeks and entered Columbia University to pursue a career in science and medicine.

He graduated in 1942 but was rejected by twenty-five medical schools, including Columbia, Harvard, and Yale, due to his Jewish background and Venezuelan nationality. Eventually, he was accepted by the Medical College of Virginia in Richmond and became a naturalized citizen. In 1943 he married Annette Dreyfus, niece of Nobel laureate **Jacques Lucien Monod** and descendent of Captain Alfred Dreyfus of Devil's Island fame. They had one child, a daughter, Beryl, who would later become a medical radiologist.

Begins Work in Immunology

Benacerraf interned at Queens General Hospital in New York and then spent two years in the U.S. Army Medical Corps. He was nearly thirty before he began his training in experimental immunology as an unpaid research fellow at the Neurological Institute of Columbia University. The director of the institute, Elvin Kabat, was a pioneer in immunology.

Immunochemistry in the 1950s was an esoteric backwater of biology awaiting the development of powerful electron microscopes, DNA modeling, and a commitment of massive government funding. Only the most general principles of immunity were understood: that proteins called antibodies were manufactured by the body to fight off substances called antigens produced by invading bacteria, viruses, and environmental pollutants. How antibodies were made, by which cells, and how the body distinguished self from nonself were still mysteries.

At Columbia, under Kabat's stern tutelage, Benacerraf learned the importance of precise measurement in immunological research and the value of critical thinking based on firm, empirical evidence. His first experiments dealt with the nature of hypersensitivity, the body's allergic reaction to the overproduction of antibodies. As a child Benacerraf had suffered from bronchial asthma, and his later research would focus on the relationship between allergic diseases and immunological response. In 1949 he moved to Paris to work at the Broussais Hospital with Bernard Halpern, the discoverer of antihistamines. In Paris, Benacerraf studied the action of phagocytes, the cellular scavengers responsible for cleaning the body of diseased cells and foreign contaminants. With Guido Biozzi, an Italian immunologist, Benacerraf developed the equations that describe the amount of particulate matter phagocytes can remove from the liver and spleen.

Due to a heart attack that had crippled his father, Benacerraf was forced to devote considerable time each year to overseeing his family's financial interests in Venezuela. Trips to South America sometimes lasted as long as six months and dealt with such unscientific matters as accounting, high finance, and personnel management. Not until 1956, when he received his first paid appointment as assistant professor of pathology at the New York University School of Medicine, was Benacerraf able to devote his full attention to research and shake the suspicion that he was only a dilettante in science. Later he would come to see that his years of business experience gave him a distinct advantage as an administrator of university departments and government agencies.

In retrospect, Benacerraf came to view the late 1950s and early 1960s as the golden age of his career. His family's finances had been successfully transferred to the United States; he spent only one day a week managing the Colonial Trust Company from its headquarters at Rockefeller Center. At New York University he received a well-equipped laboratory, ample funding, and the support of enthusiastic and innovative colleagues.

Discovers the Immune Response Gene

With **Gerald M. Edelman** of Rockefeller University, Benacerraf undertook a series of experiments on antibody structure that eventually led Edelman to the 1972 Nobel Prize and Benacerraf to the discovery of a completely unknown gene. Seeking to produce identical immunization in a group of guinea pigs, Benacerraf discovered by accident that when guinea pigs were injected with the same foreign substance, some made antibodies and others did not. By breeding the "responders" with the "nonresponders," Benacerraf isolated a gene that appeared to control immune response. He called the gene Ir (for immune response) and traced it to a hitherto unmapped region of the MHC, or major histocompatibility complex, an intricate and ancient supergene located within a specific chromosome.

Scientists were busily mapping the MHC in a variety of mammals and soon 30 Ir genes were identified for the mouse, guinea pig, rat, and rhesus monkey. It was only a matter of time before researchers began mapping the supergene in humans. By then a great deal more was known about the immune response at the cellular level. T-cells (from the thymus) apparently triggered the response and performed a variety of functions. "Killer" T-cells moved to neutralize and destroy the invader; "helper" T-cells joined with B-cells (from bone marrow) to help manufacture antibodies; and finally "suppressor" T-cells slowed and stopped the attack after the enemy had been destroyed. Benacerraf's work had broad medical implications and shed light on why some individuals were more susceptible than others to diseases such as multiple sclerosis and rheumatoid arthritis. His research in the chemistry of suppressor T-cells opened the possibility of controlling the immune response and treating so-called autoimmune diseases, where the body mistakenly mounts an attack against its own tissues.

In 1968 Benacerraf left New York University to become chief of the laboratory of immunology at the National Institute of Allergy and Infectious Diseases in Bethesda, Maryland. Two years later he was appointed chairman of the Department of Pathology at Harvard Medical School and Fabyan Professor of Comparative Pathology. In July 1980 he became president and chief executive officer of the Dana Farber Cancer Institute in Boston.

In October of 1980 it was announced that he would share the 1980 Nobel Prize in physiology or medicine with immunologists **Jean Dausset** and

George Snell for their joint elucidation of how the immune response was controlled by the MHC supergene. What had begun as an arcane branch of biology had led in barely twenty-five years to a series of genetic discoveries of vital importance to medicine, cancer research, virology, and developmental biology.

Benacerraf is the author of more than five hundred scientific papers, a fellow of the American Academy of Arts and Sciences, and a member of the National Academy of Sciences. He has also been an associate editor of several periodicals, including *American Journal of Pathology, Laboratory Investigation,* and *Journal of Immunology and Immunogenetics.*

A gregarious, cultured man, he has enjoyed a life of rich professional contacts. At home on three continents, he is intimately acquainted with the disparate worlds of immunochemistry, international banking, and classical music. Professionally, he cultivates a skeptical, even pessimistic frame of mind. Well versed in the anecdotal history of science, he believes that accident and error play a far greater role in scientific discovery than historians like to admit.

SELECTED WRITINGS BY BENACERRAF:

Books

(With David H. Katz) *Immunological Tolerance: Mechanisms and Potential Therapeutic Applications,* Academic Press, 1974.

Immunogenetics and Immunodeficiency, University Park Press, 1975.

(With Katz) *The ROLE of Products of the Histocompatibility Gene Complex in Immune Response,* Academic Press, 1976.

(With Emil R. Unanue) *Textbook of Immunology,* Williams & Wilkins, 1979.

Periodicals

"Lecture for the Nobel Prize for Physiology or Medicine, 1980: The Roll of MHC Gene Products in Immune Regulation and Its Relevance to Alloreactivity," *Scandinavian Journal of Immunology,* April 1, 1992, pp. 373–396.

"Reminiscences," *Immunological Reviews,* July, 1985, pp. 7–27.

SOURCES:

Books

Fox, Daniel M., et. al., editors, *Nobel Laureates in Medicine or Physiology: A Biographical Dictionary,* Garland, 1990, pp. 39–41.

McGraw-Hill Modern Scientists and Engineers, Volume 1, McGraw-Hill, 1980, pp. 75–76.

Magill, Frank N., editor, *The Nobel Prize Winners: Physiology or Medicine,* Volume 3, Salem Press, 1991, pp. 1341–1347.

Periodicals

Grey, Howard M., Alessandro Sette, and Søren Buus, "How T-Cells See Antigens," *Scientific American,* November, 1989, pp. 56–64.

Jaret, Peter, "Our Immune System: The Wars Within," *National Geographic,* June, 1986, pp. 702–734.

Marx, Jean L., "1980 Nobel Prize in Physiology or Medicine," *Science,* November, 1980, pp. 621–623.

—*Sketch by Philip Metcalfe*

Seymour Benzer
1921-
American geneticist

In an extraordinarily varied career, one that embraced several scientific disciplines, Seymour Benzer contributed greatly to the understanding of the structure and function of genes. His early work revealed that while a single gene had clear beginning and end points, it could also be split into many smaller parts. These parts were capable of recombining and creating a new, mutated gene. Later in his career, Benzer worked with fruit fly mutations to study how genes influenced the development of the nervous system and how this influence, in turn, produced behavior. His pioneering experiments created a new area of research, known as molecular neurogenetics. This field, which unites genetics, neuroscience, and molecular biology, offers a new approach for the study of human genetic diseases.

Seymour Benzer was born on October 15, 1921, in New York City, to Mayer Benzer and Eva Naidorf. He was the third of four children, and the only son. In 1942, Benzer received his B.A. in physics from Brooklyn College. He then went to Purdue University where he received his M.S. in 1943 and his Ph.D. in physics in 1947. As a graduate student he worked under the direction of Karl Lark-Horovitz in a group that was developing germanium semiconductor devices to be used for radar. Out of the group's research on crystal detectors came a number of other discoveries that helped set the stage for the development of the transistor. Despite these early successes as a physicist, Benzer was willing to leave physics in order to follow his intellectual curiosity wherever it might lead him. After reading a book titled *What Is Life?*, written in 1945 by physicist **Erwin Schrödinger**, Benzer's imagination was kindled by the possibilities of applying concepts borrowed from physics to biological problems. By bringing physics and biology together, scientists were able to theorize about the structure of the gene in new and fruitful ways. Benzer was particularly interested in Schrödinger's conjecture that the gene had the structure of an aperiodic crystal. He was also intrigued by the way biologist **Max Delbrück** described mutations as transitions between stable energy states. Benzer's desire to work on these problems prompted him to take a year's leave of absence from Purdue (where he was then an assistant professor) in order to immerse himself in the study of biology. The proposed one-year leave actually lasted for four years. It was the first time in his career, but not the last, that Benzer would apprentice himself to scientists in other fields and attach himself to their laboratories in order to add to his own experience and knowledge.

After leaving Purdue, Benzer spent one year at Oak Ridge National Laboratory, two years at the California Institute of Technology with future Nobel laureate Max Delbrück, and one year as a Fulbright scholar at the Pasteur Institute in Paris, working with **François Jacob** and **Jacques Lucien Monod** in the laboratory of **André Lwoff**. (Jacob, Monod, and Lwoff shared the 1965 Nobel Prize for physiology or medicine.) Benzer also spent a summer with Cornelius van Niel at Pacific Grove. In these renowned laboratories, Benzer met scientists who inspired his study of molecular biology.

Upon his return to Purdue in 1952, Benzer was named an assistant professor of biophysics. With his training in physics and biology, Benzer was well-equipped to study the nature of the gene. He was working at a very exciting time for anyone interested in better understanding deoxyribonucleic acid (DNA) and the genetic code. **Alfred Day Hershey**, in 1952, demonstrated that the genetic code was carried by DNA. **James Watson** and **Francis Crick** announced their discovery of the double helix structure of DNA in 1953. These discoveries of the 1950s laid the groundwork for the biotechnology explosion of the 1980s.

From Physicist to Geneticist

When Benzer began his genetics research, there were several theories concerning the structure of genes. Some scientists pictured genes as being like beads on a string; they could be rearranged, but the genes themselves did not change. Benzer believed otherwise. He wished to demonstrate that the internal parts of the gene itself were subject to rearrangement and recombination. By working with a virus that infects bacteria, known as bacteriophage T4, he devised a system by which the internal structure of a bacteriophage gene could be elucidated. To do this, he used two bacteriophage T4 mutants whose genes were identical except for one important difference. Benzer identified mutants that had lost their ability to multiply when placed on a specific strain of the bacteria *E.coli.* He then combined them with mutants that had mutated in different parts of the same gene. If the genes could not recombine, then the phage gene would fail to multiply and be unable to destroy the *E.coli.* If they could recombine—as Benzer believed they could—then they would thrive and destroy the *E. coli.* A clear area in the dish of bacteria demonstrated to Benzer that the phage genes had recombined. This discovery that genes could separate into smaller units that were capable of recombining was made in 1954. Benzer named these smaller units "cistrons."

Benzer and his associates also studied how genes undergo mutation. His lab demonstrated that spontaneous mutations occur at different points within the gene, some points being "hot spots" of mutation. They also showed that mutations could be artificially induced with chemicals that altered the DNA. From 1957–58, Benzer went to the Cavendish Laboratory of the University of Cambridge where he worked with Francis Crick and **Sydney Brenner** to better understand the molecular basis of mutation.

Upon returning to Purdue, Benzer began studying transfer RNA, an important component in the chain of command by which a gene produces a protein. His work made significant contributions to the understanding of the action of transfer RNA. Benzer and his associates also showed that there were considerable differences in the properties of transfer RNA from one species to another and that mistakes in the transfer RNA may be responsible for failures to construct the proper protein. The possibility for these mistakes offers physical evidence for the so-called degeneracy in the genetic code. In recognition of the excellence of his work, Benzer was named Stuart Distinguished Professor of Biology at Purdue in 1961.

In the mid–1960s, Benzer's intellectual curiosity once again led him in a new direction. What was the link between genes and behavior? Were aberrations in the genes responsible for behavioral disorders? Did the brain and nervous system fail to respond appropriately because of the lack of a crucial protein? And was that protein missing because of a flaw in the genetic code? Asking these questions steered Benzer toward the study of behavioral biology and neuroscience.

In 1965, Benzer again left Purdue and attached himself to the psychobiology laboratory of **Roger W.**

Sperry at the California Institute of Technology (Caltech). (Sperry received the Nobel Prize for medicine or physiology in 1981). In 1967, Benzer elected to remain at Caltech as professor of biology. Eight years later, in 1975, he was named the James Griffin Boswell Professor of Neuroscience. Here in California, Benzer brought together disciplines that traditionally had little to do with each other—molecular biology, behavioral biology, genetics, and neuroscience—and in doing so created a new and fruitful field, molecular neurogenetics.

Tackles Genetic Basis of Behavior

To study the relationship between genes and behavior, Benzer chose to work with the fruit fly, *Drosophila.* Much was already known about its genetic structure, and large populations of genetically identical flies made it possible for scientists to design meaningful experiments. Benzer wished to study how single gene mutations affect the normal behavior of the fruit flies. To study this correspondence, he began identifying mutant flies—those flies with deviant behavior—and separating them from normal flies. The mutant flies were then collected and bred in a separate group. To increase the number of mutants in the population, the flies were treated with mutagens, chemicals that will cause genetic damage through changes in DNA.

To identify the flies with atypical behavior (and, thus, mutated genes), Benzer and his associates observed them carefully. In some cases, the special equipment had to be built to test for unusual behavior, such as an apparatus designed to test the flies' response to light. Normal flies moved toward the light. The flies that did not do this were identified as mutants and tested further to determine whether their abnormal behavior was due to poor eyesight, sluggishness, or a preference to move away from the light. In another experiment, designed to identify aberrant learning behavior, Benzer's team gave the flies tiny electric shocks when they approached a specific odor. Normal flies learned to avoid the odor associated with the shock. A mutant fly was unable to remember, and was dubbed "dunce." Other mutant behaviors that Benzer identified included: defective mobility, stress sensitivity, and deviations from ordinary sexual courtship activities or the daily 24-hour activity cycle (circadian rhythm).

Identifying deviant behavior, and the gene mutation that corresponds to it, is but the first step in understanding how genes govern behavior. What proteins, what nerve membrane channels, what organs play a role in the complex cascade of events that lead from gene to behavior? To better answer these questions, Benzer's laboratory worked closely with the *Drosophila* eye. By studying fly mutants with a certain kind of defect in the photoreceptor cells of their eyes,

Benzer was able to begin to trace the path from gene to protein product to defect. This demonstration of the feasibility of this research has prompted many other laboratories to investigate eye development in *Drosophila*. Indeed, in labs around the world, many of them filled with his former students and colleagues, are continuing and extending Benzer's study of the molecular neurogenetics of *Drosophila*.

Fly Research May Lead to Further Understanding of Human Diseases

The work of Benzer and his associates laid the foundation for an improved understanding of the nervous system, both at the cellular level and at the behavioral level. While the genetic basis of such complex behaviors as memory and learning is largely unknown, Benzer's work with fruit fly neurogenetics may offer insight into human genes and behavior. Several of the fruit fly genes under examination have closely related counterparts in the human cell. The fly mutants with defective visual responses, for instance, may offer new approaches for studying human disease. The genetic defect of this mutant is similar to one that has been linked to retinitis pigmentosa, an untreatable eye disease in humans that often leads to blindness. Benzer's team has received a grant from the National Eye Institute to further study such genes. In the same fashion, a mutant fly strain with a degenerative brain disorder may help shed light on the study of Alzheimer's disease. Observing flies that fail to function on a normal, daily 24-hour cycle may offer clues to better understanding human situations in which circadian rhythms are disrupted, perhaps elucidating the problems associated with night shift work and jet-air travel.

Benzer married Dorothy Vlosky on January 10, 1942. They had two daughters, Barbara Ann and Martha Jane. Dorothy Benzer died in 1978. On May 11, 1980, Benzer married Carol A. Miller, a neuropathologist at the University of Southern California. Miller and Benzer worked together to identify possible similarities between the human and fly nervous systems. For his contributions to genetics, particularly molecular neurogenetics, Benzer received much acclaim. His major awards included: the Craford Prize (1993), the Bristol-Myers Squibb Award for Distinguished Achievement in Neuroscience Research (1992), the Wolf Foundation Prize in Medicine (1991), the National Medal of Science (1983), the Lasker Award (1971), and the Gairdner Award of Merit (1964). He was elected to the National Academy of Sciences, the American Academy of Arts and Sciences, the American Philosophical Society, the Royal Society (London) and the Indian Academy of Sciences.

SOURCES:

Books

McGraw-Hill Modern Scientists and Engineers, McGraw-Hill, 1980, pp. 77–80.

—*Sketch by Liz Marshall*

Paul Berg
1926-
American biochemist

Paul Berg made one of the most fundamental technical contributions to the field of genetics in the twentieth century: he developed a technique for splicing together deoxyribonucleic acid (DNA)—the substance that carries the genetic information in living cells and viruses from generation to generation—from different types of organisms. His achievement gave scientists a priceless tool for studying the structure of viral chromosomes and the biochemical basis of human genetic diseases. It also let researchers turn simple organisms into chemical factories that churn out valuable medical drugs. In 1980 he was awarded the Nobel Prize in chemistry for pioneering this procedure, now referred to as recombinant DNA technology.

Today, the commercial application of Berg's work underlies a large and growing industry dedicated to manufacturing drugs and other chemicals. Moreover, the ability to recombine pieces of DNA and transfer them into cells is the basis of an important new medical approach to treating diseases by a technique called gene therapy.

Berg was born in Brooklyn, New York, on June 30, 1926, one of three sons of Harry Berg, a clothing manufacturer, and Sarah Brodsky, a homemaker. He attended public schools, including Abraham Lincoln High School, from which he graduated in 1943. In a 1980 interview reported in the *New York Times,* Berg credited a "Mrs. Wolf," the woman who ran a science club after school, with inspiring him to become a researcher. He graduated from high school with a keen interest in microbiology and entered Pennsylvania State University, where he received a degree in biochemistry in 1948.

Before entering graduate school, Berg served in the United States Navy from 1943 to 1946. On September 13, 1947, he married Mildred Levy and they had one son, John Alexander. After completing

Paul Berg

his duty in the navy, Berg continued his study of biochemistry at Western Reserve University (now Case Western Reserve University) in Cleveland, Ohio, where he was a National Institutes of Health fellow from 1950 to 1952 and received his doctorate degree in 1952. He did postdoctoral training as an American Cancer Society research fellow, working with **Herman Kalckar** at the Institute of Cytophysiology in Copenhagen, Denmark, from 1952 to 1953. From 1953 to 1954 he worked with biochemist **Arthur Kornberg** at Washington University in St. Louis, Missouri, and held the position of scholar in cancer research from 1954 to 1957.

He became an assistant professor of microbiology at the University of Washington School of Medicine in 1956, where he taught and did research until 1959. Berg left St. Louis that year to accept the position of professor of biochemistry at Stanford University School of Medicine. Berg's background in biochemistry and microbiology shaped his research interests during graduate school and beyond, steering him first into studies of the molecular mechanisms underlying intracellular protein synthesis.

Experiments with Genetic Engineering

During the 1950s Berg tackled the problem of how amino acids, the building blocks of proteins, are linked together according to the template carried by a form of RNA (ribonucleic acid, the "decoded" form of DNA) called messenger RNA (mRNA). A current

theory, unknown to Berg at the time, held that the amino acids did not directly interact with RNA but were linked together in a chain by special molecules called joiners, or adapters. In 1956 Berg demonstrated just such a molecule, which was specific to the amino acid methionine. Each amino acid has its own such joiners, which are now called transfer RNA (tRNA).

This discovery helped to stoke Berg's interest in the structure and function of genes, and fueled his ambition to combine genetic material from different species in order to study how these individual units of heredity worked. Berg reasoned that by recombining a gene from one species with the genes of another, he would be able to isolate and study the transferred gene in the absence of confounding interactions with its natural, neighboring genes in the original organism.

In the late 1960s, while at Stanford, he began studying genes of the monkey tumor virus SV40 as a model for understanding how mammalian genes work. By the 1970s, he had mapped out where on the DNA the various viral genes occurred, identified the specific sequences of nucleotides in the genes, and discovered how the SV40 genes affect the DNA of host organisms they infect. It was this work with SV40 genes that led directly to the development of recombinant DNA technology. While studying how genes controlled the production of specific proteins, Berg also was trying to understand how normal cells seemed spontaneously to become cancerous. He hypothesized that cells turned cancerous because of some unknown interaction between genes and cellular biochemistry.

In order to study these issues, he decided to combine the DNA of SV40, which was known to cause cancer in some animals, into the common intestinal bacterium *Escherichia coli*. He thought it might be possible to smuggle the SV40 DNA into the bacterium by inserting it into the DNA of a type of virus, called a bacteriophage, that naturally infects E. coli.

A DNA molecule is composed of subunits called nucleotides, each containing a sugar, a phosphate group, and one of four nitrogenous bases. Structurally, DNA resembles a twisted ladder, or helix. Two long chains of alternating sugar and phosphate groups twist about each other, forming the sides of the ladder. A base attaches to each sugar, and hydrogen bonding between the bases—the rungs of the ladder—connects the two strands. The order or sequence of the bases determines the genetic code; and because bases match up in a complementary way, the sequence on one strand determines the sequence on the other.

Berg began his experiment by cutting the SV40 DNA into pieces using so-called restriction enzymes, which had been discovered several years before by other researchers. These enzymes let him choose the exact sites to cut each strand of the double helix. Then, using another type of enzyme called terminal transferase, he added one base at a time to one side of the double-stranded molecule. Thus, he formed a chain that extended out from the double-stranded portion. Berg performed the same biochemical operation on the phage DNA, except he changed the sequence of bases in the reconstructed phage DNA so it would be complementary to—and therefore readily bind to—the reconstructed SV40 section of DNA extending from the double-stranded portion. Such complementary extended portions of DNA that bind to each other to make recombinant DNA molecules are called "sticky ends."

This new and powerful technique offered the means to put genes into rapidly multiplying cells, such as bacteria, which would then use the genes to make the corresponding protein. In effect, scientists would be able to make enormous amounts of particular genes they wanted to study, or use simple organisms like bacteria to grow large amounts of valuable substances like human growth hormone, antibiotics, and insulin. Researchers also recognized that genetic engineering, as the technique was quickly dubbed, could be used to alter soil bacteria to give them the ability to "fix" nitrogen from the air, thus reducing the need for artificial fertilizers.

Questions the Ethics of Recombinant DNA Technology

Berg had planned to inject the monkey virus SV40-bacteriophage DNA hybrid molecule into *E. coli*. But he realized the potential danger of inserting a mammalian tumor gene into a bacterium that exists universally in the environment. Should the bacterium acquire and spread to other *E. coli* dangerous, pathogenic characteristics that threatened humans or other species, the results might be catastrophic. In his own case, he feared that adding the tumor-causing SV40 DNA into such a common bacterium would be equivalent to planting a ticking cancer time bomb in humans who might subsequently become infected by altered bacteria that escaped from the lab. Rather than continue his ground-breaking experiment, Berg voluntarily halted his work at this point, concerned that the tools of genetic engineering might be leading researchers to perform extremely dangerous experiments.

In addition to this unusual voluntary deferral of his own research, Berg led a group of ten of his colleagues from around the country in composing and signing a letter explaining their collective concerns. Published in the July 26, 1974, issue of the journal *Science*, the letter became known as the "Berg letter." It listed a series of recommendations supported by the Committee on Recombinant DNA Molecules Assembly of Life Sciences (of which Berg was chairman) of the National Academy of Sciences.

The Berg letter warned, "There is serious concern that some of these artificial recombinant DNA molecules could prove biologically hazardous." It cited as an example the fact that *E. coli* can exchange genetic material with other types of bacteria, some of which cause disease in humans. "Thus, new DNA elements introduced into *E. coli* might possibly become widely disseminated among human, bacterial, plant, or animal populations with unpredictable effects." The letter also noted certain recombinant DNA experiments that should not be conducted, such as recombining genes for antibiotic resistance or bacterial toxins into bacterial strains that did not at present carry them; linking all or segments of DNA from cancer-causing or other animal viruses into plasmids or other viral DNAs that could spread the DNA to other bacteria, animals or humans, "and thus possibly increase the incidence of cancer or other disease."

The letter also called for an international meeting of scientists from around the world "to further discuss appropriate ways to deal with the potential biohazards of recombinant DNA molecules." That meeting was held in Pacific Grove, California, on February 27, 1975, at Asilomar and brought together a hundred scientists from sixteen countries. For four days, Berg and his fellow scientists struggled to find a way to safely balance the potential hazards and inestimable benefits of the emerging field of genetic engineering. They agreed to collaborate on developing safeguards to prevent genetically engineered organisms designed only for laboratory study from being able to survive in humans. And they drew up professional standards to govern research in the new technology, which, though backed only by the force of moral persuasion, represented the convictions of many of the leading scientists in the field. These standards served as a blueprint for subsequent federal regulations, which were first published by the National Institutes of Health in June 1976. Today, many of the original regulations have been relaxed or eliminated, except in the cases of recombinant organisms that include extensive DNA regions from very pathogenic organisms. Berg continues to study genetic recombinants in mammalian cells and gene therapy. He is also doing research in molecular biology of HIV-1.

Nobel Prize Awarded for the Biochemistry of Nucleic Acids

The Nobel Award announcement by the Royal Swedish Academy of Sciences cited Berg "for his fundamental studies of the biochemistry of nucleic acids with particular regard to recombinant DNA." But Berg's legacy also includes his principled actions in the name of responsible scientific inquiry.

Berg was named the Sam, Lula and Jack Willson Professor of Biochemistry at Stanford in 1970, and was chairman of the Department of Biochemistry there from 1969 to 1974. He was also director of the Beckman Center for Molecular and Genetic Medicine (1985), senior postdoctoral fellow of the National Science Foundation (1961–68), and nonresident fellow of the Salk Institute (1973–83). He was elected to the advisory board of the Jane Coffin Childs Foundation of Medical Research, serving from 1970–80. Other appointments include the chair of the scientific advisory committee of the Whitehead Institute (1984–90) and of the national advisory committee of the Human Genome Project (1990). He was editor of *Biochemistry and Biophysical Research Communications* (1959–68), and a trustee of Rockefeller University (1990–92). He is a member of the international advisory board, Basel Institute of Immunology.

Berg received many awards in addition to the Nobel Prize, among them the American Chemical Society's Eli Lilly Prize in biochemistry (1959); the V. D. Mattia Award of the Roche Institute of Molecular Biology (1972); the Albert Lasker Basic Medical Research Award (1980); and the National Medal of Science (1983). He is a fellow of the American Academy of Arts and Sciences, and a foreign member of the Japanese Biochemistry Society and the Académie des Sciences, France.

SELECTED WRITINGS BY BERG:

Books

(With Maxine Singer) *Genes and Genomes: A Changing Perspective,* University Science Books, 1991.
(With Maxine Singer) *Dealing with Genes,* University Science Books, 1992.
(With Maxine Singer) *Genes and Genomes: Volume II,* University Science Books, in press.

Periodicals

(With D. A. Jackson and R. H. Symons) "A Biochemical Method for Inserting New Genetic Information into SV40 DNA: Circular SV40 DNA Molecules Containing Lambda Phage Genes and the Galactose Operon of *E. coli,*" *Proceedings of the National Academy of Sciences,* Volume 69, 1972, pp. 2904–2909.
(With others) *Science,* July 26, 1974, p. 303.
(With S. P. Goff) "Construction of Hybrid Viruses Containing SV40 and Lambda Phage DNA Segments and Their Propagation in Cultured Monkey Cells," *Cell,* Volume 9, 1976, pp. 695–705.

SOURCES:

Books

Antebi, Elizabeth, and David Fishlock, *Biotechnology: Strategies for Life,* MIT Press, 1986.
Magill, Frank N., editor, *The Nobel Prize Winners: Chemistry,* Volume 3: *1969–1989,* Salem Press 1990, pp. 1027–1034.
Wade, Nick, *The Ultimate Experiment,* Walker, 1977.
Watson, James, *Recombinant DNA,* W. H. Freeman, 1983.

Periodicals

New York Times, February 2, 1975, p. A1; October 15, 1980, p. A1.

—*Sketch by Marc Kusinitz*

Hans Berger
1873-1941
German psychiatrist and neurologist

Hans Berger was a professor of psychiatry and director of the Jena Psychiatric University Clinic from 1919 until his forced retirement in 1938. But it is his research into the correlation of brain activity and consciousness for which he is remembered. This research led him by a long and frustrating path to the discovery of the electroencephalogram (EEG) of man. The EEG is a graphic representation of electrical waves measured repeatedly between two points of the skull, and though Berger himself did not develop its full potential as a diagnostic tool, the EEG has since come to be invaluable in diagnosing and treating such neurological disorders as epilepsy and brain tumors.

Born on May 21, 1873 in the small northern Bavarian town of Neuses near Coburg, Germany, Berger was the son of Paul Friedrich Berger, a physician, and of Anna Rückert, daughter of a German poet who was well known for his studies in oriental philosophy. In his life and work, Berger combined both sides of this intellectual inheritance, determining early on to become a scientist-philosopher. Berger graduated with honors from the Gymnasium in Coburg and then enrolled at the University of Berlin as an astronomy student in 1892. The next year he volunteered for military service in the German army, and it was as a result of a near fatal accident he had in the army that he set his course to uncover the link between the brain and consciousness. The very day of his accident, Berger's sister informed their parents that she knew Berger had had an accident, so Berger's father sent an urgent telegram to see if his son was all right. This seemed to Berger to be a pure case of telepathic communication with his sister, and he became convinced that he could find the objective proof of such a psychic power.

Released from the army in 1893, Berger began studying medicine, finally earning his doctorate of medicine at Jena in 1897 and becoming a junior staff member at the Psychiatric Clinic of the University of Jena where he would remain until 1938. In 1901 he became Privatdozent, or lecturer at the university and also published his first investigations on the functioning of the brain, recording the change of size as modified by the circulation of blood. He accomplished this by studying brain pulsation in the skull defect of a patient who had undergone a trepanation or surgery through the skull. On the staff of a medical clinic, Berger had access to a wide variety of patients who were willing to participate in his experiments. He continued a variety of experiments searching for some objective, measurable results of psychic or conscious conditions. These included investigations of the influence of heartbeat, vascular measurements, and position of the head on pulsations of the brain, as well as the effects of medications such as caffeine, morphine, camphor, and cocaine on brain activity. As early as 1902 he hit upon recording the electrical activity of the cerebral cortex of a dog in an attempt to measure psychic activity, but by 1910 he had given up on these experiments because they provided such scant results. During these same years, Berger also pursued another line of inquiry: the changes of temperature of the cerebral cortex as measured by introducing minute and precise thermometers into the brains of patients who had undergone cerebral puncture, then a new and popular diagnostic procedure. Searching for the elusive psychic energy (P-energie), these experiments also seemed to lead to a dead end.

Focusses Once Again on Electrical Activity of Brain

Berger served on the western front during the First World War, in a military hospital at Rethel. He came back to a Germany on the brink of revolution. The director of the psychiatric clinic at Jena resigned and returned to his native Switzerland, and Berger was appointed the new director. For the next several years administrative duties deterred Berger's further researches into the correlation between brain and psyche, but in his few private moments he started once again to focus on measuring the electrical activity of the brain. He became known to his colleagues as a punctual and rather strict director, and few of them knew of his researches. His day was

strictly defined by the clock of duty, and it was only from 5:00 to 8:00 P.M. that he found time to continue his experiments. As a result of the war, there was a surplus of patients at the clinic with skull defects whose pulsating brain was protected by only a few millimeters of tissue. These patients made excellent subjects for his experiments with electrode stimulation of the brain, specifically of the motor cortex. Berger measured the time between stimulus and corresponding touch sensations in the extremities of his subjects. But soon he hit on a new idea: searching for currents or brain waves in these same patients. Employing rather crude instruments, such as the Edelmann string galvanometer used to record electrocardiograms, he made his first successful EEG on July 6, 1924, when he observed small movements on the galvanometer on a young patient named Zedel. Berger continued these experiments for five more years before publishing his results, using not only patients with skull imperfections or trepanations, but also patients with intact skulls. With this latter group he placed one electrode at the front and another at the back of the skull. In 1929 he published his results in the prestigious *Archiv für Psychiatrie und Nervenkrankheiten*. Entitled "Über das Elektrenkephalogramm des Menschen," it was the first of fourteen such articles published between 1929 and 1938 on the results of his experiments with the EEG. His 1929 article not only shows that regular electrical current oscillations can be recorded from the scalp of humans, but also that these oscillations are not due to blood flow, electrical properties of the skin or any of several other possibilities. His third paper definitely proves the cerebral origin of the waves, yet Berger's findings were largely ignored by the scientific community, and it was not until 1934 when other researches, chief among them neurophysiologist **Edgar Douglas Adrian** and B. C. H. Matthews, finally drew attention to what Berger himself long knew as a certainty: the electrical activity of the brain could be measured.

Becomes Increasingly Isolated in Nazi Germany

Berger led a relatively happy domestic life, married in 1911 to a young technical assistant at the clinic, Baroness Ursula von Bulow. They had four children: Klaus, Ruth, Ilse and Rosemarie. Berger continued his studies on the EEG, always balancing research with his administrative duties, installing his increasingly elaborate set of instruments in a tiny annex just off his office. But despite growing international recognition for his achievements, he was largely ignored in Germany. Part of the reason for this was his antipathy for the Nazis and their distrust of him. In 1938, following an International Congress of Psychology in Paris in which he found himself to be something of an international celebrity, he was greeted in Germany by humiliation: his forced retirement. His laboratory was dismantled and he moved to the small town of Bad Blankenburg in Thuringia to live out his days. He could no longer pursue his researches, and on June 1, 1941, following a long depression which he had misdiagnosed as a cardiac condition, Berger took his own life.

In the final analysis, Berger's work on the human electroencephalogram must be viewed as a means to an end. At the back of his mind always was the search for the secret of man's psychophysical nature; of the connection between brain and psyche. Thus his interest in the EEG was towards that end, not in the use of it as a diagnostic tool for which it has become known.

SELECTED WRITINGS BY BERGER:

Books

Zur Lehre von der Blutzirkulation in der Schädenhöhle des Menschen, Gustav Fischer, 1901.
Über die körperlichen Äuserrungen psychischer Zustände, 2 volumes, Gustav Fischer, 1904 -1907.
Untersuchungen über die Temperatur des Gehirns, Gustav Fischer, 1910.
Psychophysiologie in 12 Vorlesungen, Gustav Fischer, 1921.
Über die Lokalisation im Grosshirn, Gustav Fischer, 1927.
Psyche, Gustav Fischer, 1940.

Periodicals

"Über das Elektrenkephalogramm des Menschen," *Archiv für Psychiatrie und Nervenkrankheiten,* Volume 87, 1929, pp. 527–570; Volume 94, 1931, pp. 16–60; Volume 97, 1932, 6–26; Volume 98, 1932, pp. 231–254; Volume 99, 1933, pp. 555–574; Volume 100, 1933, pp. 301–320; Volume 101, 1934, pp. 452–469; Volume 102, 1934, pp. 538–557; Volume 103, 1935, pp. 444–454; Volume 104, 1936, pp. 678–689; Volume 106, 1937, pp. 176–187, 577–584; Volume 108, 1938, pp. 407–431.

SOURCES:

Books

A Biographical Dictionary of Scientists, John Wiley & Sons, 1982, p. 48.
Dictionary of Scientific Biography, Scribners, 1970, pp. 1–2.
Grosse Nervenärzte, Georg Thieme Verlag, 1970, pp. 1–6.

Periodicals

Fischgold, H., "Hans Berger und seine Zeit," *Beitrage zur Neurochirurgie,* 14, 1967, pp. 7–11.
Gloor, P., "Hans Berger and the Discovery of the Electroencephalogram," *Electroencephalography and Clinical Neurophysiology, Supplement,* 28, 1969, pp. 1–36.
Klapetek, J., "Errinerung an Hans Berger," *Deutsche Medizinische Wochenschrift,* October 10, 1969, pp. 2123–2126.

—*Sketch by J. Sydney Jones*

Friedrich Bergius
1884-1949
German chemist

Friedrich Bergius was an organic chemist who, as research director of the Goldschmidt Company in Essen, Germany, was able to develop two hydrogenation processes that were widely used in industry. These high-pressure methods enabled both Germany and England to have sufficient supplies of motor fuel during World War II. Bergius also developed high-pressure methods for breaking wood down into edible products, a process that was called "food from wood." For his work with these methods, Bergius was awarded the 1931 Nobel Prize in chemistry.

Friedrich Karl Rudolf Bergius was born October 11, 1884, in Goldschmieden, Germany (now part of Poland). His father, Heinrich Bergius, was the head of a local chemical factory and his mother, Marie Haase Bergius, was the daughter of a classics professor. Both of Bergius's parents valued education, and at a young age Bergius observed the chemical processes in his father's factory. In addition, his father sent him to study metallurgy at a factory in the Ruhr valley, an area known for its heavy industry.

Bergius began his formal training in chemistry at the University of Breslau in 1903 under Albert Ladenburg and Richard Abegg. He conducted some doctoral research under Arthur Hantzsch at the University of Leipzig and completed his research under Abegg on concentrated sulfuric acid as a solvent. He was awarded his doctorate from the University of Breslau in 1907.

For several years after receiving his doctorate, Bergius worked with **Walther Nernst** in Berlin and **Fritz Haber** in Karlsruhe to develop a way of making ammonia from hydrogen and atmospheric nitrogen.

By 1909 Bergius was working with Ernest Bodenstein at his chemical laboratory in Hanover. Under Bodenstein, Bergius used pressure as high as 300 atmospheres (one atmosphere equals 14.7 pounds per square inch) to study the breakdown of calcium peroxides. It was during these apprentice years that Bergius developed leakproof high-pressure apparatus that enabled him to extend his research into other areas. In order to advance his research in more than one area, Bergius established his own laboratory in Hanover. He used high-pressure techniques to transform heavy oils and oil residues into lighter oils. This procedure boosted gasoline output, of great interest at the time since the automobile was becoming the preferred form of transportation. In 1913 he was granted a patent for the manufacture of liquid hydrocarbons (compounds containing carbon and hydrogen) from coal. During this time Bergius was also teaching physical and industrial chemistry at a university in Hanover.

In addition to his position as research director for the Goldschmidt Company in Essen from 1914 to 1945, Bergius was instrumental in the construction of a plant at Rheinau to facilitate the development of coal-hydrogenation processes on a large scale. When the demand for gasoline decreased after World War I, however, this project was neglected until 1921. After selling his patent rights to German and foreign companies, Bergius was able to develop new equipment to process the coal hydrogenation. Previously, equipment had only been able to use high-pressure methods with gases.

Although he was able to improve the process of coal hydrogenation in numerous ways during the years between 1922 and 1925, it never became economically feasible. In 1926 he sold his patents to Badische Anilin-und Sodafabrik (BASF), a large German chemical company, which later joined other German chemical companies to form I. G. Farben. Farben expanded hydrogenation research, improved Bergius's processes, and increased the yield of gasoline from coal. Two years later Farben built a plant to produce oil from coal.

Another of Bergius's research projects was to produce sugar from wood and convert it into alcohol, yeast, and dextrose. He hoped to do this by using concentrated hydrochloric acid and water to promote the breakdown of wood cellulose. This work proved valuable to Germany during World War II, because it furnished a great deal of the carbohydrate material that was needed during food shortages.

Both of Bergius's lifetime interests, the hydrogenation of coal into gasoline and the hydrogenation of wood into food products, became widely used commercially and industrially. In 1931 he shared the Nobel Prize in chemistry with **Karl Bosch**, who had continued Bergius's work after he sold his patents to BASF. During the presentation of the award at the Royal Swedish Academy of Sciences, the presenter called Bergius's high-pressure methods an extraordinary improvement in the field of chemical technology.

Through the 1930s and the 1940s, Bergius continued his research on the hydrolysis (the breakdown of a substance using water) of wood. The plant he established in Rheinau in 1943 provided basic products that Germany needed during World War II. After the war, Bergius left Germany and lived briefly in Austria. For a time he lived in Madrid, where he founded a company at the invitation of the Spanish government. From 1946 to 1949 he was a technical research adviser to the government of Argentina in its ministry of industries. He died in Buenos Aires on March 30, 1949.

Bergius was married to Ottilie Krazert, and the couple had two sons and one daughter. Besides the Nobel Prize, Bergius was awarded the Liebig Medal of the German Chemical Society and received honorary degrees from the University of Heidelberg and the University of Hanover. He also contributed many articles to newspapers and to scientific and technical magazines and was a member of the American Chemical Society and the Verein Deutscher Chemiker.

SELECTED WRITINGS BY BERGIUS:

Books

Die Anwendung Hoher Drucke bei Chemischen Vorgangen und Eine Nachbildung des Entstehungsprozesses der Steinkohle, Knapp, 1913.
"Die Herstellung von Zucker aus Holz und ähnlichen Naturstoffen," *Ergebnisse der angewandten physikalischen Chemie,* Volume 1, 1931.
"Chemische Reaktionen unter hohem Druck," *Les prix Nobel en 1931,* 1933.

Periodicals

"Die Verflussigung der Kohle," *Zeitschrift des Vereins Deutscher Ingenieure,* Volume 69, 1926.
"Gewinnung von Alkohol and Glucose aus Holz," *Chemical Age* Volume 29, 1933, pp. 481–83.

—*Sketch by Jordan Richman*

Sune Karl Bergström
1916-
Swedish biochemist

Sune Karl Bergström is best known for his research on prostaglandins. These substances, which were first discovered in the prostate gland and seminal vesicles, were found by Bergström and his colleagues to affect circulation, smooth muscle tissue, and general metabolism in ways that can be medically beneficial. Certain prostaglandins, for example, lower blood pressure, while others prevent the formation of ulcers on the stomach lining. For his research, Bergström shared the 1982 Nobel Prize in medicine or physiology with **John R. Vane** and **Bengt Samuelsson**.

Sune Bergström was born in Stockholm on January 10, 1916, to Sverker and Wera (Wistrand) Bergström. Upon completion of high school he went to work at the Karolinska Institute as an assistant to the biochemist Erik Jorpes. The young Bergström was assigned to do research on the biochemistry of fats and steroids. Jorpes was impressed enough with his assistant to sponsor a year-long research fellowship for Bergström in 1938 at the University of London. While there, Bergström focused his research on bile acid, a steroid produced by the liver which aids in the digestion of cholesterol and similar substances.

Bergström had planned to continue his research in Edinburgh the following year thanks to a British Council fellowship, but the fellowship was canceled after World War II broke out. He did, however, receive a Swedish-American Fellowship in 1940, which allowed him to study for two years at Columbia University and to conduct research at the Squibb Institute for Medical Research in New Jersey. At Squibb, Bergström researched the steroid cholesterol, particularly its reaction to chemical combination with oxygen at room temperature, a process called auto-oxidation.

Bergström returned to Sweden in 1942, receiving doctorates in medicine and biochemistry from the Karolinska Institute two years later. He was appointed assistant in the biochemistry department of Karolinska's Medical Nobel Institute. While there, he continued experiments with auto-oxidation, working with linoleic acid, which is found in some vegetable oils. He discovered a particular enzyme was responsible for the oxidation of linoleic acid, and helped attempt to purify the enzyme while working with biochemist **Hugo Theorell**.

While attending a meeting of Karolinska's Physiological Society in 1945, Bergström met the physiologist Ulf von Euler. Von Euler, who was better known as the discoverer of the hormone norepinephrine, had been doing research on prostaglandins. Scientists had observed in the 1930s that seminal fluid used in artificial insemination stimulated contraction and subsequent relaxation in the smooth muscles of the uterus. Von Euler isolated a substance from the seminal fluid of sheep and found it had the same effect in relaxing the smooth muscle of blood vessels. Impressed with Bergström's work on enzyme purification, von Euler gave him some of the extract for further purification.

Begins Pioneering Work on Prostaglandins

Bergström began initial experiments but put his work on hold when in 1946 he was named a research fellow at the University of Basel. Returning from Switzerland in 1947, he was appointed professor of physiological chemistry at the University of Lund. His first task was to help revitalize the university's research facilities, which had fallen into disuse during the war. Afterwards, he resumed his research on prostaglandins, assisted by graduate students such as Bengt Samuelsson. Working with new large supplies of sheep seminal fluid, Bergström and his colleagues were able to isolate and purify two prostaglandins by 1957. Bergström was appointed professor of chemistry at Karolinska a year later, and brought his research on prostaglandins and his collaboration with Samuelsson with him. By 1962, six prostaglandins, identified as A through F, had been identified.

Bergström and Samuelsson then worked on determining how prostaglandins are formed. They discovered that prostaglandins are formed from common fatty acids, and further identified specific functions performed by each prostaglandin. Over the next few years, Bergström and Samuelsson surmised that certain prostaglandins could be used to treat high blood pressure, blocked arteries, and other circulatory problems by relaxing muscle tissue. These prostaglandins were also shown to prevent ulceration of the stomach lining and to protect against side effects of such drugs as aspirin, long known to irritate the stomach lining. Other prostaglandins could be used to raise blood pressure or stimulate uterine muscle by their contracting effect.

Bergström remained at Karolinska, serving as dean of its medical school from 1963 to 1966 and as rector of the institute from 1969 to 1977. He was chairman of the Nobel Foundation's Board of Directors from 1975 to 1987, and from 1977 to 1982 he served as chairman of the World Health Organization's Advisory Committee on Medical Research. He retired from teaching in 1981, choosing to devote his full time to research at Karolinska.

A modest, reserved man, Bergström's reaction upon learning of his Nobel award was gratitude—first, that his colleagues appreciated his efforts, and second, that his former student Samuelsson had also been named. The book *Nobel Prize Winners* reports him as saying that there is "no greater satisfaction than seeing your students successful." His connection with the Nobel Foundation had led some to wonder whether he might be passed over for a prize of his own. But the *New York Times,* reporting on the 1982 awards, noted that "it was only a matter of time, most scientists agree, before Dr. Bergström's research would be honored by the foundation he directs—for the work was too important to be ignored through any concern over apparent conflicts of interest."

The scientist married the former Maj Gernandt in Sweden in 1943; the couple has one son. Bergström's memberships include the Royal Swedish Academy of Science (he served as its president from 1983 to 1985), the American Philosophical Society, and the American Academy of Arts and Sciences. Other awards given to Bergström besides the Nobel include the Albert Lasker Award in 1977, Oslo University's Anders Jahre Prize in Medicine in 1970, and Columbia's Louisa Gross Horwitz Prize in 1975.

SELECTED WRITINGS BY BERGSTRÖM:

Books

(With Bengt Samuelsson) *Prostaglandins,* Interscience, 1967.
(With John Vane) *Prostacyclin,* Raven Press, 1979.
Holman, R. T., editor, *Progress in Lipid Research,* Volume 20, Pergamon Press, 1982, pp. 7–12.

SOURCES:

Books

Wasson, Tyler, editor, *Nobel Prize Winners,* H. W. Wilson, 1987, pp. 91–93.

Periodicals

New York Times, October 12, 1982, p. C3.
Science, November 19, 1982.

—*Sketch by George A. Milite*

Joan B. Berkowitz
1931-
American physical chemist

Joan B. Berkowitz is a physical chemist who has worked in a number of different research areas throughout her career, including the thermodynamics of inorganic systems, the electrochemistry of flames, oxidation studies of refractory metals and alloys, inorganic coating technology, and high-temperature vaporization. Berkowitz has specialized in the area of environmental management since 1972, when she contributed to the U.S. Environmental Protection Agency's first report to Congress on hazardous waste. Berkowitz was the first woman president of the Electrochemical Society, and in 1983 she received the Achievement Award of the Society of Women Engineers for her pioneering contributions in the field of hazardous-waste management. Berkowitz is currently managing director of Farkas, Berkowitz, and Company, an environmental consulting agency based in Washington, D.C., which focuses on the evaluation of waste treatment and disposal, as well as remediation technologies and market-potential assessment.

Berkowitz was born in Brooklyn, New York, on March 13, 1931. Her father, Morris Berkowitz, worked as a salesman for the Englander Mattress Company and struggled to support his family during the Great Depression. Although her mother, Rose Gerber Berkowitz, did not work, she had been influenced by the women's suffrage movement and the extension of the vote; her interest in women's rights played a major role in Berkowitz's own life decisions. At the age of twelve, Berkowitz knew she would always earn a living and she saw the best opportunities for herself in science. She attend Swarthmore College on a scholarship and received a B.A. degree in chemistry in 1952. She wanted to follow her high-school boyfriend Arthur Mattuck to Princeton, where he was studying mathematics, but the chemistry department there did not then admit women. She was accepted at the University of Illinois at Urbana, however, and she completed her Ph.D. in physical chemistry in 1955 with both theoretical and experimental research on electrolytes (nonmetallic substances which conduct electricity).

Berkowitz accepted a postdoctoral position at Yale University from 1955 to 1957, and on September 1, 1959, she married Mattuck, who had obtained a professorship at the Massachusetts Institute of Technology. Berkowitz then began her long consulting career with Arthur D. Little, Inc. Here, she worked on studies of high-temperature oxidation, which was part of the research involved in the space program; compounds that could withstand the reentry temperatures of the upper atmosphere were important for rocket design and manned flights into space. Berkowitz worked mainly with the transition metals (those elements lying roughly in the middle of the periodic table), and in particular molybdenum, tungsten, and zirconium, and investigated the properties of alloys (which are mixtures of pure elements) for their strength and hardness at extremely high temperatures. With this work, Berkowitz developed a patent for manufacturing reusable molds for iron and steel castings from molybdenum and tungsten—a patent which was eventually used to make space vehicles.

Berkowitz served as adjunct professor in the department of chemistry at Boston University from 1963 to 1968, teaching undergraduate courses in physical chemistry. Her work on high-temperature oxidation led to her investigations in hazardous-waste disposal. In 1975 Berkowitz headed a team that evaluated various physical, chemical, and biological techniques in the treatment of hazardous wastes and produced a two-volume report which still serves as an important reference work in the field of hazardous-waste treatment.

Berkowitz participated in the senior executive program of the Sloan School of Management at the Massachusetts Institute of Technology in 1979, and the following year became vice president of A. D. Little. Divorced in 1977, she moved to Washington, D.C., in 1986, where she first served as chief executive officer at Risk Science International. In 1989, along with Allen Farkas, she formed the firm of Farkas, Berkowitz, and Company, which specializes in management consulting on environmental projects and hazardous-waste management.

SELECTED WRITINGS BY BERKOWITZ:

Books

(Editor) *Physical, Chemical and Biological Treatment Techniques for Industrial Wastes,* 2 volumes, U.S. National Technical Information Services, 1976.

Periodicals

"Outlook for the Industry," *The Environmental Forum,* Volume 1, 1992, p. 19.
(With A. L. Farkas) "Commercializing Innovative Cleanup Technologies," *Environmental Science Technology,* Volume 26, 1992, p. 247.

SOURCES:

Books

Rose, R. K., and L. Grinstein, editors, *Women in Physics and Chemistry,* Greenwood Press, 1993.

Periodicals

"Candidates for E.C.S. Officer for 1979," *Journal of the Electrochemical Society,* Volume 125, 1978, pp. 396c–398c.

Other

Berkowitz, Joan B., interview conducted by Mark J. Kaiser, January 30, 1994.

—Sketch by Mark J. Kaiser

Paul Bernays
1888-1977
English-born Swiss mathematician

Paul Bernays secured his reputation with a classic treatise on mathematical logic, the *Foundations of Mathematics,* and through his refinement and consolidation of set theory into the von Neumann-Bernays system. Bernays was a platonic mathematician—one who thought of the world of mathematics as separate from the world of material reality. Although Bernays's concept of mathematics as a mental product meant that no system could be designated as right or wrong, he believed that there were truths within the mathematical realm that allowed for a system to remain consistent and logical within itself.

Paul Isaac Bernays was born in London on October 17, 1888, to Julius Bernays, a Swiss businessman from a prominent Jewish family, and Sara Bernays. Shortly after his birth, the family moved to Paris and then to Berlin, where Bernays studied from 1895 to 1907. While studying engineering at the Technische Hochschule (Technical High School) in Charlottenburg, Germany, he developed an interest in pure mathematics. This led him to transfer to the University of Berlin where he studied for four semesters under a distinguished faculty that included philosopher Ernst Cassirer and physicist Max Planck. Bernays then attended the University of Göttingen where physicist **Max Born** and mathematician **David Hilbert** were among his professors. In 1912 Bernays received his doctorate degree from Göttingen under Hilbert.

In 1912 Bernays completed his postdoctoral thesis on modular elliptic functions at the University of Zurich in Switzerland under the German mathematician Ernst Zermelo. Bernays remained at Zurich until 1917 when he was invited by Hilbert to return to Göttingen to assist with a program on the foundations of mathematics. Bernays completed a second postdoctoral thesis at Göttingen in 1918 on propositional logic. In addition to serving as assistant to Hilbert, he gave lectures at Göttingen until the Nazi party's rise to power in 1933 when Bernays's right to lecture was withdrawn because of his Jewish background.

Publishes *Foundations of Mathematics* and *Axiomatic Set Theory*

Bernays escaped to Zurich in 1934, eventually teaching at the Eidgenossische Technische Hochschule. In 1935 and 1936 he participated in the Institute for Advanced Study at Princeton University in New Jersey. Bernays published the first volume of his work on mathematical logic, *Foundations of Mathematics,* in 1934; the second volume was published in 1939. Research for this work was a collaborative effort between Bernays and Hilbert, but Bernays wrote both volumes singlehandedly. In this book Bernays and Hilbert created the mathematical discipline of proof theory, in which the correctness of a mathematical statement or theorem is demonstrated in terms of accepted axioms. E. Specker, a colleague of Bernays at the Eidgenossische Technische Hochschule, remarked in *Logic Colloquium '78* that the *Foundations of Mathematics* is unique because "it does not reduce mathematics to logic, or logic to mathematics—both are developed at the same time."

Over the years Bernays published a series of articles in the *Journal of Symbolic Logic* that was published collectively as *Axiomatic Set Theory* in 1958. Axiomatic set theory applies proof theory to set theory, the study of the properties and relationships of sets. Thus, axiomatic set theory involves the presentation of set theory in terms of fundamental axioms and logical rules of inference, rather than as a formalization of tabulated or intuitive knowledge. Classical set theory was largely established by Zermelo at the turn of the century and improved by the German mathematician **Abraham Fraenkel** in the 1920s. The Zermelo-Fraenkel (ZF) system was defined exclusively in terms of sets, but it could not address transfinite sets (for example, the set consisting of all possible sets). In the late 1920s the axioms of Hungarian mathematician **John von Neumann** accomplished many tasks previously left unsolved by the Zermelo-Fraenkel system. However, von Neumann's system was expressed in symbolic logic and was defined in terms of function rather than set, and it was less practical in both pure and applied mathematics.

Bernays's contribution to set theory both improved and simplified von Neumann's system. Bernays introduced a distinction between "sets" and "classes" to set theory. He did not view "classes" as mathematical objects in the normal sense. As G. H. Muller characterizes Bernays's distinction in *Mathe-*

matical Intelligencer, a set is a collection of elements or members, a "multitude forming a proper thing." A class is a collection of objects that can be manipulated or extended, a "predicate regarded only with respect to its extension." For each set there was a corresponding class, but for each class there need not be a corresponding set. This idea created two axiomatic systems, one for sets and one for classes. The sets in the von Neumann-Bernays system operate similarly to those in the Zermelo-Fraenkel system, and thus a new system was created to allow for the construction of classes.

After World War II Bernays became Extraordinary Professor at the Eidgenossische Technische Hochschule. He also served as visiting professor at the University of Pennsylvania and at Princeton, where he was again a member of the Institute for Advanced Study in 1959–60. Bernays served as the president of the International Academy of the Philosophy of Science, as honorary chair of the German Society for Mathematical Logic and Foundation Research in the Exact Sciences, and as a corresponding member of the Academy of Science of Brussels and of Norway. He also served on the editorial boards of several journals, including *Dialectica, Journal of Symbolic Logic,* and *Archiv fur mathematische Logik und Grundlangenforschung.* Bernays received an honorary doctorate from the University of Munich in 1976 for his contributions to proof and set theory. Although he remained based in Zurich until his death from heart disease in 1977, Göttingen was always more of a home for Bernays. Bernays, who never married, lived most of his life with his mother and two sisters.

SELECTED WRITINGS BY BERNAYS:

Books

(With D. Hilbert) *Foundations of Mathematics,* 2 volumes, 1934–39.
Axiomatic Set Theory, North-Holland, 1958.
Abhandlungen zur Philosophie der Mathematik, Wissenschaftliche Buchgemeinschaft, Darmstadt, 1976.
Sets and Classes, North-Holland, 1976.

SOURCES:

Books

Dictionary of Scientific Biography Supplement, Scribners, 1970.
Specker, E., "Paul Bernays," *Logic Colloquium '78,* North-Holland, 1979, pp. 381–389.

Periodicals

Muller, G. H., "Paul J. Bernays," *Mathematical Intelligencer,* 1978/1979, number 1, pp. 27–28.

—*Sketch by Fei Fei Wang Metzler*

Robert A. Berner
1935-
American geochemist

Robert A. Berner

Robert A. Berner's research in sedimentary geochemistry led to the application of mathematical models to describe the physical, chemical, and biological changes that occur in ocean sediment. Berner, a professor of geology and geophysics at Yale University, also developed a theoretical approach to explain larger geochemical cycles, which led to the creation of a model for assessing atmospheric carbon dioxide levels and the greenhouse effect over geological time. A prolific researcher, Berner has written many scientific journal articles and is one of the most frequently quoted earth scientists in the *Science Citation Index.*

Robert Arbuckle Berner was born in Erie, Pennsylvania, on November 25, 1935, to Paul Nau Berner and Priscilla (Arbuckle) Berner. As a young man Berner decided to become a scientist because of his propensity for logical thinking. "Science forces you to seek the truth and see both sides of an argument," he told Patricia McAdams. Berner began his academic studies at the University of Michigan where he earned his B.S. in 1957 and his M.S. a year later. He then went to Harvard University and earned his Ph.D. in geology in 1962. He married fellow geology graduate student Elizabeth Marshall Kay on August 29, 1959; they have three children—John Marshall, Susan Elizabeth, and James Clark.

Begins Career as Geologist

Berner began his professional career at the Scripps Institute of Oceanography in San Diego, where he won a fellowship in oceanography after graduating from Harvard. In 1963 he was appointed assistant professor at the University of Chicago, and two years later he became an associate professor of geology and geophysics at Yale University. Since 1968 Berner has also served as associate editor or editor of the *American Journal of Science.* He was promoted to full professor at Yale in 1971, and in 1987 he became the Alan M. Bateman Professor of geology and geophysics.

Principles of Chemical Sedimentology, which Berner published in 1971, reflects the interest that has fueled much of his research. Berner sees the application of chemical thermodynamics and kinetics as a valuable tool in unveiling the secrets of sediments and sedimentary rocks. Thus, Berner's is an unconventional approach to sedimentology (the chemical study of sediments rather than the study of chemical sediments). Berner identifies his goal in *Principles of Chemical Sedimentology* as illustrating "how the basic principles of physical chemistry can be applied to the solution of sedimentological problems." Berner's *Early Diagenesis,* published in 1980, is a study of the processes over geological time whereby sedimentary materials are converted into rock through chemical reactions or compaction. Because of the frequency with which *Early Diagenesis* has been quoted, it was declared a Science Citation Classic by the Institute for Scientific Information.

Models the Geochemical Carbon Cycle

Berner observes in *Scientific American* that "the familiar biological carbon cycle—in which atmospheric carbon is taken up by plants, transformed through photosynthesis into organic material and then recovered form this material by respiration and bacterial decomposition—is only one component of a much larger cycle: the geochemical carbon cycle."

Berner has studied an aspect of this geochemical carbon cycle that is analogous to the transfer of carbon between plants, animals, and their habitats—the "transfer of carbon between sedimentary rocks at or near the earth's surface and the atmosphere, biosphere and oceans." Carbon dioxide is vital to both these aspects of the geochemical carbon cycle, as carbon is primarily stored as carbon dioxide in the atmosphere. Berner's research has contributed to the "BLAG" model (named after Berner and his associates Antonio L. Lasaga and Robert M. Garrels) for assessing the changes in atmospheric levels of carbon dioxide throughout the earth's geological eras. First published in 1983 and subsequently refined, the BLAG model quantifies factors such as degassing (whereby carbon dioxide is released from beneath the earth), carbonate and silicate rock weathering, carbonate formation in oceans, and the rate at which organic matter is deposited on and buried in the earth that enable scientists to assess the climactic conditions of the planet's previous geological eras.

Berner's research on atmospheric carbon dioxide levels includes the study of the greenhouse effect, whereby carbon dioxide and other gases trap excessive levels of radiated heat within the earth's atmosphere, leading to a gradual increase in global temperatures. Since the nineteenth-century industrial revolution, this phenomenon has increased primarily because of the burning of fossil fuels such as coal, oil, and natural gas, and also because of deforestation. Berner reports in *Scientific American* that "slow natural fluctuations of atmospheric carbon dioxide over time scales of millions of years may rival or even exceed the much faster changes that are predicted to arise from human activities." Thus, the study of the carbon cycle is essential to an objective evaluation of the greenhouse effect within larger geological processes. In 1986 Berner published the textbook *The Global Water Cycle: Geochemistry and Environment* which he co-authored with his wife Elizabeth, who is also a geochemist. *The Global Water Cycle* reviews the properties of water, marine environments, and water/energy cycles, and includes a discussion of the greenhouse effect. Berner's research has since focused on Iceland where he is investigating how volcanic rock is broken down by weathering and by the plant-life that gradually takes root on it.

Berner is enthusiastic about every aspect of his work as a geochemist. He enjoys the travelling associated with his research and likes to help students learn to think creatively for themselves. "I'm very proud of the twenty or so graduate students that have received Ph.D.s working with me. I've learned as much from them as they have from me," he told McAdams. Berner served as president of the Geochemical Society in 1983, and he is also a member of the National Academy of Sciences, the American Academy of Arts and Sciences, the Geological Society of America, and the Mineral Society. He has chaired the Geochemical Cycles Panel for the National Research Council and served on the National Committee on Geochemistry, the National Science Foundation Advisory Committees on Earth Sciences and Ocean Sciences, and the National Research Council Committee on Oceanic Carbon. He has received numerous awards, including an honorary doctorate from the Université Aix-Marseille III in France in 1991 and Canada's Huntsman Medal in Oceanography in 1993. His hobbies include Latin American music, tennis, and swimming.

SELECTED WRITINGS BY BERNER:

Books

Principles of Chemical Sedimentology, McGraw, 1971.
Early Diagenesis: A Theoretical Approach, Princeton University Press, 1980.
(With Elizabeth Kay Berner) *The Global Water Cycle: Geochemistry and Environment,* Prentice-Hall, 1987.

Periodicals

(With Eric J. Barron) "Comments on the BLAG Model: Factors Affecting Atmospheric CO_2 and Temperature over the Past 100 Million Years," *American Journal of Science,* December, 1984, pp. 1183–1192.
"Models for Carbon and Sulfur Cycles and Atmospheric Oxygen: Application to Paleozoic Geologic History," *American Journal of Science,* March, 1987, pp. 177–196.
(With Gary P. Landis) "Gas Bubbles in Fossil Amber as Possible Indicators of the Major Gas Composition of Ancient Air," *Science,* March 18, 1988, pp. 717–724.
(With Antonio C. Lasaga) "Modeling the Geochemical Carbon Cycle," *Scientific American,* March, 1989, pp. 74–81.
(With Donald E. Canfield) "A New Model for Atmospheric Oxygen over Phanerozoic Time," *American Journal of Science,* April, 1989, pp. 333–361.
"Paleozoic Atmospheric CO_2: Importance of Solar Radiation and Plant Evolution," *Science,* July 2, 1993, pp. 68–70.

SOURCES:

Berner, Robert Arbuckle, interview with Patricia M. McAdams conducted September 24, 1993.

—*Sketch by Patricia M. McAdams*

Dorothy Lewis Bernstein
1914-
American mathematician

Dorothy Lewis Bernstein is a distinguished mathematician and educator in the fields of applied mathematics, statistics, and computer programming. Her research focused on the Laplace transform, a mathematical function named after the French mathematician Pierre-Simon Laplace. The Laplace transform is used in the solution of partial differential equations (equations that contain the partial derivatives of functions of two or more variables) and has been widely applied in the twentieth century in conjunction with operational calculus. Bernstein was a pioneer in incorporating applied mathematics and computer science into the undergraduate mathematics curriculum. In 1979, she became the first woman president of the Mathematical Association of America, a national association concerned with college mathematics. Bernstein was born in Chicago on April 11, 1914, to Jacob and Tillie Bernstein, who were Russian immigrants. The family lived in Milwaukee during Bernstein's youth. In 1930, Bernstein began her studies at the University of Wisconsin at Madison. During her junior and senior years, she studied mathematics under an independent curriculum. In 1934, based on an oral examination and her thesis on the complex roots of polynomials (mathematical expressions containing certain algebraic terms), she received both a bachelor's (summa cum laude) and a master's degree in mathematics.

After another year at Madison as a teaching fellow, Bernstein received a scholarship to the doctoral program in mathematics at Brown University in Rhode Island. As Ann Moskol indicates in *Women of Mathematics,* Bernstein's experiences at Brown reflect various forms of discrimination. Bernstein's graduate teaching was restricted to only three female students. When she sought advice on finding a teaching position, the graduate school dean advised her not to apply in the South because she was Jewish or in the West because of her gender. Bernstein underwent an unusually arduous doctoral examination, which her advisor later acknowledged was due to her gender and to her midwestern university credentials.

Nonetheless, Bernstein independently secured a teaching position at Mount Holyoke College in Massachusetts. Bernstein taught at Mount Holyoke from 1937 to 1940, completing her doctorate from Brown in 1939 with a thesis related to the Laplace transform. In 1941, Bernstein returned to Madison as an instructor. In the summer of 1942, she was a research associate at the University of California at Berkeley under the Polish mathematician and statistician Jerzy Neyman. In 1943, Bernstein took an instructorship at the University of Rochester in New York, where she became an assistant professor in 1946.

Studies Computer Applications of Mathematics

At Rochester, Bernstein's research was directed toward exploiting the computational potential of digital computers (their ability to perform complex mathematical operations on large amounts of data at high speeds) in solving partial differential equations. This research, intended for military application and conducted in affiliation with the Office of Naval Research, led to the publication of Bernstein's *Existence Theorems in Partial Differential Equations* in 1950. In 1951, Bernstein was a member of the Institute for Advanced Study in Princeton, New Jersey. Bernstein became an associate professor at Rochester in 1951, and a full professor in 1957. From 1957 to 1958, she was a visiting professor at the University of California in Los Angeles.

In 1959, Bernstein assumed a professorship at Goucher College in Baltimore, Maryland, where she chaired the mathematics department from 1960 to 1970 and directed the computer center from 1961 to 1967. She served on the board of governors of the Mathematical Association of America, the professional association with which she was most closely involved, from 1965 to 1968. As a department administrator at Goucher, Bernstein brought applied mathematics and the emerging field of computer science into the undergraduate mathematics curriculum, and integrated computer programming into her own courses in statistics. Moskol notes that Bernstein "believed that applied mathematics not only made material more relevant to students, but it also motivated them to understand the axioms and theorems of pure mathematics, which could then be used in applied problems." Bernstein's practical vein was further indicated by the internship program she established for Goucher's math majors.

During her tenure at Goucher, Bernstein was also involved through the National Science Foundation in promoting computer programming instruction and the use of computers in advanced mathematics courses at area high schools. She helped establish the Maryland Association for Educational Use of Computers in 1972 and served on its governing board from 1972 to 1975. Bernstein was vice-president of the Mathematical Association of America from 1972 to 1974 and president from 1979 to 1981. She also served on the Joint Projects Committee and the Joint Committee on Women of the Mathematical Association of America, the American Mathematical Society, and the Society of Industrial and Applied Mathematics, and on the editorial board of the *Two Year College Mathematics Journal.* Bernstein retired from Goucher College in 1979.

SELECTED WRITINGS BY BERNSTEIN:

Books

Existence Theorems in Partial Differential Equations, Princeton University Press, 1950.

Periodicals

"The Double Laplace Integral," *Duke Mathematical Journal,* Volume 8, 1941, pp. 460–496.
(With Geraldine A. Coon) "Some Properties of the Double Laplace Transformation," *Transactions of the American Mathematical Society,* Volume 74, 1953, pp. 135–70.
(With Coon) "Some General Formulas for Double Laplace Transformations," *Proceedings of the American Mathematical Society,* Volume 14, 1963, pp. 52–59.
(With Coon) "On the Zeros of a Class of Exponential Polynomials," *Journal of Mathematical Analysis and Applications,* Volume 11, 1965, pp. 205–212.
"The Role of Applications in Pure Mathematics," *American Mathematical Monthly,* Volume 86, 1979, pp. 245–253.
"Women Mathematicians before 1950," *Association for Women in Mathematics Newsletter,* July-August, 1979, pp. 9–11.

SOURCES:

Books

Moskol, Ann, "Dorothy Lewis Bernstein," in *Women of Mathematics,* edited by Louise S. Grinstein and Paul J. Campbell, Greenwood, 1987, pp. 17–20.

Periodicals

Coon, Geraldine A., "Coon on Bernstein," *Goucher Quarterly,* fall, 1979, pp. 16–17.

—*Sketch by Nicholas Pease*

Leonidas Harris Berry
1902-

American physician

As a leading physician and educator, Leonidas Harris Berry was an active force in the Chicago-area medical community for more than forty years. The first African American internist at Cook County Hospital and the first black doctor at Michael Reese Hospital and Medical Center, Berry was an inspiration to minority medical students throughout his long career. In 1955 Berry invented the gastrobiopsyscope, a first-of-its-kind instrument for exploring the digestive tract, now part of the medical collection at the Smithsonian Institution. In 1993 a scholarship fund was established at Rush Medical College in Berry's name.

Berry was born on July 20, 1902, in Woodsdale, North Carolina, to Lewellyn and Beulah Anne Harris Berry. He received a B.S. degree from Wilberforce University in Ohio in 1924. At the University of Chicago, he earned a second B.S. in 1925 and an M.D. in 1930. The University of Illinois awarded him an M.S. in pathology in 1933. After an internship at Freedmen's Hospital in Washington, he served a residency in internal medicine and gastroenterology, then joined the medical staff at Cook County Hospital in Chicago. Following his residency, he joined the medical staff of Provident Hospital in 1935, founded the division of gastroenterology, and served thirty-four years as its chairperson. For eight of those years, 1966 to 1974, Berry also was chief of Cook County Hospital's gastrointestinal endoscopy service. He taught at the University of Illinois Medical School from 1950 to 1957, then at the Cook County Graduate School of Medicine until 1967. In 1955 he invented the direct-vision gastrobiopsyscope, the first instrument for viewing the inside of the digestive tract.

Long active in medical and civic affairs from the local to the international level, Berry organized and coordinated clinics for medical counseling on narcotics for the Illinois Department of Health, helped found the Council on Medical Careers, served as chairperson of the health committee for the Chicago Commission on Human Relations, and organized Flying Black Medics in Chicago and Cairo, Illinois. At the national level he served from 1966 to 1968 on the U.S. Department of Health, Education, and Welfare's first national advisory council on regional medical programs in heart disease, cancer, and stroke. Sponsored by the U.S. Department of State, he traveled to East Africa, West Africa, Japan, Korea, the Philippines, and France as a foreign cultural exchange lecturer in 1965, 1966, and 1970.

Berry also served as senior author and editor of the textbook *Gastrointestinal Panendoscopy,* published in 1974, and contributed various articles to medical publications and books. He conducted research on racial, sociological, and pathological aspects of tuberculosis, on gastroscopy techniques, gastrobiopsy instrumentation, therapy for chronic gastritis and peptic ulcer, gastric cancer, and narcotic rehabilitation. In 1977 he was the recipient of the Rudolph Schindler Award. Berry wrote a personal chronicle entitled *I Wouldn't Take Nothin' for My Journey: Two*

Centuries of an Afro-American Minister, published in 1981.

In 1937 Berry married Opheila Flannagan Harrison, with whom he had a daughter, Judith Berry Griffin. After the marriage ended, he wed Emma Ford Willis in 1959. For his energy, dedication, and achievement in the medical profession, Berry received two honorary doctorate degrees and many other awards and honors. Chief among these are the first Clinical Achievement Award from the American College of Gastroenterology; professional achievement and distinguished service awards from the Cook County Physicians Association; and the Marshall Bynum Service Award from the Chicago branch of the NAACP. The Leonidas Berry Society for Digestive Diseases was organized in his honor in 1983. In 1993 graduates and members of the staff of Rush Medical College established a fund in Berry's name to provide scholarships to promising minority students, and kicked off a fund-raising campaign on the occasion of his ninety-first birthday.

SELECTED WRITINGS BY BERRY:

Books

Gastrointestinal Panendoscopy, Thomas, 1974.
I Wouldn't Take Nothin' for My Journey: Two Centuries of an Afro-American Minister, Johnson, 1981.

Periodicals

"The Continuing Task of Medicine in a Great Democratic Society," *Journal of the National Medical Association,* Volume 57, 1965, pp. 412–415.
"How Important Is Endoscopic Premedication?," *Gastrointestinal Endoscopy,* Volume 51, 1969, pp. 170–171.

SOURCES:

Periodicals

Carwell, Hattie, "Blacks in Science," *Exposition,* 1977, p. 30.
"Rush Medical College Sets up Scholarship Fund for Minorities in Honor of Dr. Leonidas Berry," *Jet,* December 13, 1993.

—*Sketch by Penelope Lawbaugh*

Lipman Bers
1914-
Latvian American mathematician

Lipman Bers has had a long and prolific career as a mathematician which has covered nearly all aspects of the field of analysis, or theoretical calculus. His work in the mathematical aspects of gas dynamics, partial differential equations, and complex function theory has redefined several applied mathematical fields. The American Mathematical Society recognized his achievements in 1974 when they awarded him the Steele Prize. A leader in the mathematical community, Bers has also used his position to speak out for human rights and equality.

Born in Riga, Latvia on May 22, 1914, his youth was less than ideal. His parents, Isaac A. Bers and Bertha Weinberg Bers, separated when Bers was still very young, and he spent much time being shuttled back and forth between his father, who was an engineer, and his mother, who was studying to be a psychoanalyst in Berlin. While in Berlin, the eleven-year-old Bers was told by a teacher that he was destined to be a mathematician. Bers did not believe him, and it was only in high school, after discovering that he had unknowingly duplicated the results of the mathematician Kamke, that he withdrew his application to engineering school.

Bers entered the University of Zurich in 1932 to study mathematics, but for economic reasons he was only able to stay in Switzerland for one term. He returned home and entered the University of Latvia. The mathematics department there was poor, however, and Bers devoted much of his time to underground political activities. He became involved in the socialist youth and anti-fascist movements, which made it dangerous for him to stay in Latvia after the coup by the fascists in 1934. Bers escaped to Czechoslovakia, where he completed his schooling at the University of Prague. His dissertation adviser, Karl Löwner (later known as Charles Loewner) was an important mentor, and Bers would have an opportunity to help him in the future.

Escapes from Nazis and Finds Refuge in America

By 1938, the shadow of Hitler and the Nazis had fallen across Czechoslovakia. It was clear that the country would not be a haven for Bers, who was Jewish, for long; his mother had already left Latvia for America. Bers married Mary Kagan in 1938, and they tried to emigrate to the United States. However, conditions all over Europe had worsened, and the pair could only get as far as France, where they spent a tense time waiting and wondering, as war broke out and France seemed about to fall. Their first child, a daughter, was born during this period; their son, however, would be born in America. After the fall of Paris, Eleanor Roosevelt convinced her husband to issue special visas for European intellectuals who wished to escape the Nazi regime. In an interview with the *College Mathematics Journal,* Bers has said, "I literally owe my life to Mrs. Roosevelt." He and his wife reached the United States in December of 1940.

But the country was still in an economic depression at that time and jobs were scarce. Bers could only manage to find a poorly paid summer research appointment at Brown University. The couple had to live with Bers's mother, who was in New York City practicing psychoanalysis. But the need for applied mathematicians increased when America entered World War II, and in 1942 Bers was appointed research director at Brown.

Career Unites Theoretical and Applied Mathematics

The war work Bers did at Brown was largely concerned with gas laws and fluid dynamics, as well as applications of partial differential equations to these fields. His research during this time not only furthered the American war effort, it laid the foundation for his later insistence on the importance of applied as well as theoretical mathematics. Bers also had the pleasure of welcoming his former mentor, Charles Loewner, to Brown. R. G. D. Richardson, Brown's graduate dean, had rescued Loewner from a position at the University of Louisville where he had a heavy teaching load, including remedial classes. Bers and Loewner would continue to work together for many years at various institutions.

After the war, Bers accepted an assistant professorship at Syracuse University, where he remained from 1945 to 1951. Many excellent mathematicians were there, including Loewner and Paul Erdös, and Bers found the atmosphere stimulating. He also did research at the prestigious Institute for Advanced Study at Princeton University between 1949 and 1951. During this time, Bers began to publish his first major research papers, which dealt with partial differential equations, analytic functions, and the mapping of "minimal" surfaces (so called because a minimal surface generally defines the smallest area spanned by a curve).

In 1951 Bers moved to New York University, where he gained a full professorship in 1953. During 1953 he also published the first of a series of important papers on his theory of pseudoanalytic functions and their applications, which he termed quasi-conformal mappings. This theory involved a series of exceptions to classical analytic functions, whose applications are called conformal mappings. Conformal mappings display a smooth curvature when graphed, but the pseudoanalytic functions described by Bers had irregularities—breaks or changes of direction—that necessitated new rules and a new terminology.

Before Bers did his research on pseudoanalytic functions, engineers and other applied mathematicians had been forced to utilize the classical framework when confronted by these exceptions in practical situations, and often their results were imperfect. Bers's quasi-conformal mappings were more readily suited to practical problems. But his theories were not simply practical; they also dealt with the more abstract topological concept of Riemann surfaces, providing connections between the fields of topology and differential equations.

In the late 1960s, Bers published a textbook, *Calculus,* which was a standard for many years. His continuing interest in topology, however, led his research in new directions, and he began the study of Kleinian groups. Kleinian groups are an algebraic method for describing rotations and motions of objects. Bers lectured on this subject at a 1974 meeting of the American Mathematical Society, where he was presented with the Steele Prize.

Also during 1974, *Contributions to Analysis* was published in honor of Bers's sixtieth birthday, written by his colleagues and former students. In the dedication, the editors commented not only on Bers's mathematical achievements, but also on his activism in support of human rights and his love of literature and the theatre. The members of the American Mathematical Society showed their appreciation by electing him president from 1975 to 1977. One of Bers's most important contributions to the field of mathematics has been his encouragement of women students, and the Association of Women in Mathematics has honored him by holding a symposium on his teaching.

In 1988, Bers retired from teaching at the City University of New York, where he had been visiting professor since 1984. However, he has continued to give lectures and seminars on various subjects, from Kleinian groups to his experience with the Nazi regime.

SELECTED WRITINGS BY BERS:

Books

Theory of Pseudoanalytic Functions, New York University Press, 1952.
Introduction to Several Complex Variables, Courant Institute of Mathematical Sciences, 1964.
Calculus, Holt, Rinehart and Winston, 1969.
(Editor with Irwin Kra, and contributor) *A Crash Course on Kleinian Groups,* Springer-Verlag, 1974.

SOURCES:

Books

Ahlfors, L., I. Kra, B. Maskit, and L. Nirenberg, editors, *Contributions to Analysis: A Collection of Papers Dedicated to Lipman Bers,* Academic Press, 1974.

Furtmuller, L., and M. Pinl, *Mathematicians Under Hitler,* Secker and Warberg, 1973.

Periodicals

Albers, D. J., and C. Reid, "An Interview with Lipman Bers," *College Mathematics Journal,* September, 1987, pp. 266–290.

—*Sketch by Karen Sands*

Charles Herbert Best

Charles Herbert Best
1899-1978
Canadian physiologist

Charles Herbert Best was most renowned as co-discoverer of insulin with **Frederick G. Banting**. Insulin, which is a hormone secreted by the pancreas, regulates the level of sugar in the blood. Its discovery in 1921 led to its use as a treatment for diabetes, which until that time had led swiftly to emaciation, coma, and death. Later in his career, Best assisted in the establishment of associations of diabetics to promote support groups and educational programs for their members. He also did important research on the nutrient choline and the blood anticoagulant heparin.

Best was born on February 27, 1899, in West Pembroke, Maine, a town near the border of the Canadian province of New Brunswick. His parents were Canadian citizens, both originally from Nova Scotia. Best was a direct descendant of Major William Best, who in 1749 was one of the founders of Halifax, Nova Scotia. Best's father, Herbert Huestes Best, was a country doctor whose practice straddled the U.S.-Canadian border. As a teenager, Best often accompanied his father on his rounds in a horse-drawn buggy. Best's mother was Luella Fisher Best.

After finishing high school, Best entered the University of Toronto in a liberal arts program. When World War I interrupted his education, he served as a sergeant in a regiment of the Canadian Tank Corps. He returned to Toronto in 1919 after the war to complete his education, but switched his course of study to physiology and biochemistry in preparation for a medical degree. Best played professional baseball in order to finance his education. He received his B.A. in 1921. In May of 1921, Best's physiology professor, **John James Rickard Macleod**, introduced him to Frederick Grant Banting, a 29-year-old orthopedic surgeon from London, Ontario. Best had worked as a research assistant for Macleod and planned to begin studying for master's degree under him in the fall. Banting would be using Macleod's lab during the intervening summer to do experiments to find out the function of the pancreas in preventing diabetes, and he needed an assistant to help with analyses of blood chemistry. Another of Macleod's students was also interested in the job, so he and Best flipped a coin. Best won. On May 17, 1921, the day after he completed his examinations for his undergraduate degree, Best began working with Banting. It was a collaboration that would set the course of his career.

Discovers Treatment for Diabetes

Experiments done 30 years earlier had shown that when a dog's pancreas was removed by surgery the animal developed the symptoms of diabetes: it would grow insatiably thirsty, begin excreting large amounts of sugar in its urine, and then become listless, go into a coma, and die. Banting's idea was that the pancreas must secrete something in addition to its digestive enzymes in order to prevent this process. He was convinced that the crucial substance would be found in groups of cells on the pancreas called the islets of Langerhans. These cells could be isolated by tying off a dog's pancreatic ducts; the rest of the pancreas would atrophy after several weeks, but the islets of Langerhans would remain intact. An extract could then be made from the cells and injected into a diabetic dog. If Banting's idea was right, such an extract would relieve the symptoms of diabetes.

The way he originally planned the work, Banting would do the surgery, removing the pancreas from some dogs to make them diabetic and tying off the pancreatic ducts in others to isolate the islet cells. Best would do blood and urine tests on the dogs. As the research progressed, however, Best learned to do some surgery too. Best, for his part, had a personal interest in diabetes. His father's sister, who had lived with the Best family in West Pembroke, had died in a diabetic coma in 1918.

Banting and Best had expected to spend only eight weeks on their study. But it was July 30 before they were ready to prepare the extract. On that day, Banting removed the shriveled pancreas from a dog whose ducts had been tied. He and Best prepared an extract from it by chopping the pancreas into small pieces, grinding it in a chilled mortar with salt water, and filtering the mixture through cheesecloth. A blood sample from the diabetic dog showed its blood sugar level to be 0.2. Banting and Best injected some of their extract into the dog. An hour later its blood sugar level had dropped to 0.12. After another injection it registered 0.11. This dog died the next day, presumably from an infection. But Banting and Best were encouraged by the result and tested their extract on more diabetic dogs. They called the extract "isletin."

During the following months Banting and Best performed additional experiments to confirm and explain their results. With an injection of their extract they could revive a diabetic dog from its coma and prevent its imminent death. They found ways of obtaining the extract more easily and in larger quantities from the pancreases of fetal calves obtained from a local slaughterhouse. Macleod, who had been vacationing at his home in Scotland during the summer, returned in September and made suggestions for further studies. He also hired James Bertram Collip, a Ph.D. biochemist, to help purify the active component of the extract. Best continued with the work, but also began his M.A. program at the University of Toronto. That fall Banting and Best wrote their first paper describing the experiments with dogs, titled "The Internal Secretion of the Pancreas." It was accepted for publication in the February 1922 issue of the *Journal of Laboratory and Clinical Medicine.*

By the time the paper was published, however, Banting and Best had already treated a human diabetes patient with the extract. They had also begun to call their extract by the now familiar name of insulin, at the suggestion of Macleod. The word "insulin" is based on the Latin word for island. The first patient to receive insulin was 14-year-old Leonard Thompson, who was so weak after two years of suffering from diabetes that he had been admitted to Toronto General Hospital. Thompson's weight was down to 65 pounds, and his doctors expected him to live for only a few more weeks. Before administering insulin to the boy, Banting and Best performed a perfunctory clinical trial: they injected each other with their extract. Since there seemed to be no side effects other than soreness around the injection, in January 1922 they went ahead and treated the boy. After an initial problem with impurities in the insulin was solved, his condition began to improve. He regained his energy and put on weight. Thompson lived another 11 years, dying in 1935 from pneumonia contracted after a motorcycle accident. This success, a literal pulling back of a diabetic child from the brink of the grave, was repeated again and again in the next months, as insulin became a standard treatment for diabetes.

Nobel Committee Leaves Best Out

The 1923 Nobel Prize in physiology and medicine for that year was awarded to Banting and Macleod for the discovery of insulin. Banting was furious. In his opinion, Macleod had done little more than provide laboratory space, whereas Best had shared the work of research. Best was in Boston the day the news arrived, giving an address to medical students at Harvard. Banting immediately sent Best a telegram stating that he would share both the credit for the discovery and the Nobel Prize cash award with Best. Macleod, who considered the work a collaboration, divided his portion of the prize with Collip.

Best continued his studies, receiving his M.A. in 1922 and his M.D. in 1925, while also working on a commercial process for producing insulin. At the same time he received the M.D., Best was also awarded the Ellen Mickle Fellowhip for highest standing in the medical course. During the years Best was doing insulin research he had been courting Margaret Mahon, writing her love letters that also included details about the experiments on dogs. She was so well versed in the work that she helped Banting and Best write their first paper about it. Best married Margaret Mahon in 1924, and later they had two sons. In 1926 the couple sailed to England, where Best spent two years doing postgraduate research in the laboratory of Sir Henry Dale in London. This research led Best to the discovery of histaminase, an anti-allergic enzyme. He received his doctorate from the University of London in 1928.

Before the degree was awarded, however, Best had returned to the University of Toronto in 1927 to head the department of physiological hygiene, a post he held until 1941. In 1929, when Macleod retired, Best was also made chair of the department of physiology. He was just 30 years old at the time. He remained in that position until 1965.

Best's study of insulin led him to a related avenue of research. He had noticed that the laboratory dogs whose pancreases had been removed to render them diabetic developed fatty livers, similar to cirrhosis of the liver in alcoholics. Best and his colleagues found that feeding such dogs lecithin prevented this change in the liver. In the 1930s they isolated choline as the active nutritional component of lecithin, a component found in the cells of many plants and animals, and did studies on the role of choline in metabolism. In the 1930s Best also became interested in heparin, which had just been discovered. He recognized that heparin could be an important anticoagulant drug for preventing blood clotting and went to work purifying it for human use. With the outbreak of World War II, Best continued his research interest in blood. He established the Canadian project for supplying dried blood serum to the wounded overseas and personally worked collecting blood from volunteers. This project was a predecessor to the blood transfusion service of the Red Cross. In 1941 Best was appointed director of the medical research unit of the Canadian Navy. In this capacity he coordinated studies to find ways to enhance night vision and to remedy motion sickness.

A Friend to Diabetics

In 1941, Frederick Banting was killed in a airplane crash en route to a wartime mission. After Banting's death, Best took over his directorship of the Banting and Best department of medical research at the University of Toronto. Best also worked to organize associations of diabetics that provided support groups and educational programs for their members, including summer camps for diabetic children. He was president of the American Diabetes Association from 1948 to 1949 and remained honorary president thereafter. He was also honorary president of the International Diabetes Foundation. In 1953 the University of Toronto named a new building for medical research the Best Institute. The same year, Best became the first president of the International Union of Physiological Sciences.

Best retired from the University of Toronto in 1965. In 1966 friends of Best purchased Best's parents' clapboard house in West Pembroke, Maine and gave it to the American Diabetes Association. Later the home was proposed to the U.S. National Trust for Historic Preservation as a cultural landmark and turned into a museum. Best spent his retirement

years traveling around the world with his wife, who was a historian and a botanist, visiting friends and colleagues.

Best received scores of medals, awards, and honorary degrees and was praised by the Pope, the Queen of England, and other heads of state. He wrote numerous scientific articles, and was co-author of a widely used physiology textbook. In March of 1978 one of Best's sons died of a heart attack. Hours after hearing the news, Best himself collapsed from a ruptured blood vessel in his abdomen. He died several days later, on March 31, 1978, at Toronto General Hospital.

SELECTED WRITINGS BY BEST:

Books

(With N. B. Taylor) *The Physiological Basis of Medical Practice,* Williams and Wilkins, 1966.
Selected Papers of Charles H. Best, Toronto, 1963.

Periodicals

(With Frederick G. Banting) "The Internal Secretion of the Pancreas," *Journal of Laboratory and Clinical Medicine,* Volume 7, February 1922, pp. 256–271.
"The Discovery of Insulin," *Proceedings of the American Diabetes Association,* Volume 6, 1946, pp. 85–93.
"The History of Insulin," *Diabetes,* Volume 2, number 6, 1962, pp. 495–503.

SOURCES:

Books

Bliss, Michael, *The Discovery of Insulin,* University of Chicago, 1982.

—*Sketch by Betsy Hanson*

Hans Bethe
1906-
German-born American physicist

Hans Bethe is one of the premier physicists of the twentieth century, and one of only a very small number whose understanding and contributions span nearly all of the subfields of physics. His achieve-

Hans Bethe

ments range widely through science, his most well-known achievement being a theory that accounts for the energy production of stars. He also contributed to theories regarding quantum mechanics, fundamental particles, nuclear reactors, nuclear weapons, and astrophysics, and has been active for many years in the scientific community's efforts to limit the spread of nuclear weapons.

Hans Albrecht Bethe was born in Strasbourg (then part of Germany) on July 2, 1906. He was the only child of Albrecht Theodore Julius Bethe, a *privatdocent* (unsalaried lecturer) in physiology at the University of Strasbourg, and Anna Kuhn, the daughter of a professor. Bethe showed an early precocity in mathematics. He recalls walking with his mother at age five and noting to her that it was strange that a zero at the end of a number means a lot, while one at the beginning means nothing. At seven he learned about exponents and filled a book with the powers of two and three. The family moved to Kiel in 1912 when Bethe's father became chair of the physiology department at the University of Kiel. In 1915 Albrecht Bethe was invited to start a department of physiology at the University of Frankfurt, and the family moved again.

The period between the two world wars was a time of severe inflation for the German economy. While in Frankfurt, Bethe's father was paid twice a week to keep up with the continuing devaluation of the German mark. Bethe's excellent grasp of numbers

earned him the responsibility of collecting his father's salary in the morning and spending it on food for the family before the new value of the mark was calculated in the afternoon and prices increased dramatically. This early preoccupation with money undoubtedly contributed to Bethe's lifelong amateur fascination with economics. Due to his frail health, Bethe did not attend school until the family went to Frankfurt. In Kiel he went to a tutor several times a week with several other children. In Frankfurt he entered the Goethe Gymnasium. His father recognized his son's talent in mathematics but did not want him to get too far ahead of his peers. In fact, when Bethe wanted to borrow his father's trigonometry and calculus books, he had to do so secretly. He excelled in his academic subjects, but did poorly at physical education. In his last few years in the Gymnasium, he took some elective physics courses and found the subject stimulating.

First Exposure to Quantum Mechanics

Bethe entered the University of Frankfurt in 1924, continuing to live at home during that time. In 1926 he went to the University of Munich, where he spent two and a half years. He earned his Ph.D. in theoretical physics under **Arnold Sommerfeld** in 1928. While a graduate student, Bethe became interested in quantum mechanics, the new theory of interactions between matter and radiation. In 1927 he wrote a paper on electron diffraction by crystals, using quantum mechanics to explain how electrons behave like waves. After his graduation Bethe returned to the University of Frankfurt as an instructor. One year later he went to the Technical College of Stuttgart to work with Paul Ewald. Bethe was welcomed into the Ewald family, and was often invited over for dinner and Sunday walks. In 1929 Bethe was appointed a *privatdocent* at the University of Munich but spent much of the next three years outside Germany. A Rockefeller Foundation fellowship allowed him the opportunity to go to Cambridge University. He also spent some time working in Rome with **Enrico Fermi**, a physicist who had earned worldwide respect for his scientific contributions and who already, at age thirty, was a full professor.

Bethe went to the University of Tübingen in 1932 as an assistant professor but lost that job one year later when Hitler came to power. Like others of Jewish ancestry, Bethe was summarily dismissed. During his time at Tübingen he had many fruitful discussions with **Hans Geiger**, a professor of theoretical physics and the inventor of the Geiger counter. Geiger regularly attended Bethe's classes on quantum mechanics and in turn explained his own work to Bethe. To Bethe's sorrow, however, once he was dismissed, Geiger withdrew his friendship. In contrast, Arnold Sommerfeld spent much of the summer of 1933 searching for jobs for Bethe and other Jewish academics.

Leaves Germany for the United States

Bethe spent the years 1933–35 at the Universities of Manchester and Bristol in England as a postdoctoral refugee scientist. Then in 1935 he was invited to Cornell University in Ithaca, New York, as an assistant professor. He recounts in Jeremy Bernstein's *Hans Bethe, Prophet of Energy,* "I met a physicist who had been there. He said, 'Don't go to that place. It is a terrible place. It is so straitlaced that you have to go to church every Sunday. You won't like it at all.' I accepted anyway, and was offered a salary of three thousand dollars a year. I considered myself immensely rich." Bethe became a full professor at Cornell in 1937, and with the exception of a hiatus during World War II, has remained there. At Cornell Bethe found his colleagues eager but not very knowledgeable. He devoted much time to explaining theoretical physics to the physics faculty who were mainly experimentalists. In 1936 he worked on a series of articles with American physicists Robert F. Bacher and M. Stanely Livingston, and his old mentor, Arnold Sommerfeld, which summarized the current knowledge in nuclear physics. These articles were so seminal in their description and presentation that they were considered essential reading for two generations of graduate students in physics.

In 1938 Bethe attended a meeting on astrophysics in Washington, D.C., convened by **Edward Teller** and **George Gamow**. It was here that Bethe began to consider the question of the mechanism whereby the Sun and other stars get their energy. Many had already concluded that the necessary reactions must be thermonuclear, but no one had been able to determine the reactions that could account for the observed data. In characteristic fashion, Bethe solved the problem in six weeks. He proposed two different mechanisms by which different types of stars released their massive amounts of energy. One of these, which had already been suggested independently by **Carl Friedrich von Weizsäcker** of Germany, begins with the fusion of two protons and proceeds through a series of steps to ultimately result in a helium nucleus and two excess protons that are released to repeat the process (a proton-proton reaction). The other process for more massive stars, derived solely by Bethe, involves a series of six steps that begins with carbon 12 and finishes with one carbon 12 atom and one atom of helium 4. Energy is released as a consequence of each of the six steps in the process. Generally considered to be Bethe's greatest achievement, the end product was published as one page in *Physical Review* in 1939. Polish-born scientist and author Jacob Bronowski noted in *The Ascent of Man:* "Hans Bethe's explanation is as vivid to me as my own wedding day, and the subsequent steps that followed

as the birth of my own children. Because what was revealed in the years that followed (and finally sealed in what I suppose to be the definitive analysis in 1957) is that in all the stars there are going on processes which build up the atoms one by one into more and more complex structures."

Bethe is also well known throughout the world of science for another famous paper he coauthored with Ralph Alpher and George Gamow. Bethe was added at the suggestion of Gamow to make the sequence of authors' names resemble alpha, beta, and gamma, the first three letters of the Greek alphabet. This paper dealt with the early history of the universe and presented a mathematical case for what is now termed the Big Bang. As **Stephen Hawking**, who occupies Newton's chair at Cambridge University, explains in *A Brief History of Time,* "In this paper they made the remarkable prediction that radiation (in the form of photons) from the very hot early stages of the universe should still be around today, but with its temperature reduced to only a few degrees above absolute zero (–273° C). It was this radiation that [American physicist Arno] Penzias and [American physicist Robert] Wilson found in 1965."

On September 14, 1939, Bethe married Rose Ewald, the daughter of his former mentor Paul Ewald, in New Rochelle, New York. She had emigrated to the United States and was a student at Smith College. That same year his mother emigrated to the United States, as life became increasingly more difficult for Jews in Nazi Germany.

Contributes to the War Effort

Like many others Bethe was convinced of the inevitability of the participation of the United States in World War II. He wished to help the war effort, but prior to his naturalization in 1941 was not permitted to do any classified research. He did work for a time with Edward Teller on shock waves that would later prove particularly useful on the atomic bomb project. After receiving a security clearance in 1941, Bethe worked on the development of radar at the Massachusetts Institute of Technology (MIT). While working on this project, he developed a device used to measure an increase in electromagnetic waves, now known as a Bethe coupler.

Bethe renewed his acquaintance with **Robert Oppenheimer**, who later became the director of the Manhattan Project, at an American Physical Society meeting in Seattle in 1941. The two had met briefly in Germany in 1929. In 1942 Bethe had become aware of the work of Enrico Fermi and Edward Teller in Chicago on a graphite nuclear reactor. At that point Teller was already looking past the atomic bomb to the more powerful hydrogen bomb. Despite his wife Rose's reservations, Bethe accepted Oppenheimer's invitation to join the Manhattan Project at its Los

Alamos, New Mexico, facilities as director of the theoretical physics division. Rose was placed in charge of housing for all those working on the project. Bethe believed the threat of the Germans producing such a device was real and had to be countered by an American device. The project required him to pull together his knowledge of nuclear physics, shock waves, and electromagnetic theory to explain in advance how the atomic bomb would work and with what effect. This extended to mathematically tackling serious questions such as whether the entire atmosphere would explode when the bomb was detonated.

It was a relatively young group of scientists who gathered at Los Alamos. Bethe was thirty-seven at the time and Oppenheimer was thirty-nine. In fact the average age of those working on the project was twenty-seven. One outgrowth of the work there was Bethe's collaboration with **Richard P. Feynman**, a young physicist whom Bethe considered the brightest individual with whom he had ever worked, to devise a formula to calculate the efficiency of a nuclear weapon. Known as the Bethe-Feynman formula, it is still used today. Richard Feynman, recalling those days in his autobiography, *Surely You're Joking, Mr. Feynman!*, wrote of Bethe's mathematical abilities: "I had a lot of fun trying to do arithmetic fast, by tricks, with Hans. It was very rare that I'd see something he didn't see and beat him to the answer, and he'd laugh his hearty laugh when I'd get one. He was nearly always able to get the answer [mentally] to any problem within a percent. It was easy for him—every number was near something he knew."

Bethe left Los Alamos in 1946 to return to Cornell over the objections of Teller. Teller for some time had considered the Russians as great a threat as the Germans and wanted the Manhattan Project to continue to work on the hydrogen bomb. Bethe, however, longed to return to teaching physics and dealing with theoretical questions in physics that did not have military applications.

Crusades for Peace

After the war Bethe was active in the disarmament movement. He advocated civilian control of atomic energy in this country and international control of atomic energy worldwide. Along with other scientists, such as Oppenheimer and **Leo Szilard**, he tried to educate the public about the severe destruction caused by nuclear weaponry. Bethe had a chance to return to Los Alamos in 1949, but was deterred by his wife's arguments and Los Alamos scientist and author Victor F. Weisskopf's description of the destructive capabilities of the H-bomb. He was active at the Geneva test ban discussion in 1958. From 1956 to 1959 he served on the President's Science Advisory Committee.

Not surprisingly, Bethe's research after the war demonstrated his breadth of knowledge. In 1947 **W. E. Lamb** and R. C. Retherford measured a tiny shift in the energy levels of the electron in a hydrogen atom, now known as the Lamb shift. Previous theoretical methods were unable to account for the shift, but in 1947 Bethe was able to produce the first theoretical calculation of the Lamb shift. During the late 1940s and 1950s Bethe served as a consultant to several laboratories that were developing nuclear reactors. He was also involved in work with lasers, rockets, and astrophysics.

Bethe was awarded the Nobel Prize in physics in 1967 with commendation "for his contributions to the theory of nuclear reactions, especially his discoveries concerning the energy production in stars." In his presentation speech Oskar Klein of the Royal Swedish Academy of Sciences remarked that several of Bethe's discoveries were individually worthy of the Nobel Prize. Bethe's other awards include the Presidential Medal of Merit (1946), the Henry Draper Medal of the National Academy of Sciences (1947), the Max Planck Medal of the German Physical Society (1955), the Enrico Fermi Award (1961), the National Medal of Science (1976), and the Vannevar Bush Award (1985).

Retired from Cornell as an emeritus professor since 1975, Bethe still maintains an office there and remains busy lecturing, consulting, and keeping up with correspondence. In earlier years he enjoyed skiing and mountain climbing, and remains interested in economics as he has been for much of his life. The Bethes have two children, a son Henry and a daughter Monica.

SELECTED WRITINGS BY BETHE:

Books

Elementary Nuclear Theory, Wiley, 1947.
(With E. E. Salpeter) *Quantum Mechanics of One- and Two-Electron Atoms,* Plenum, 1957.
American Energy Choices Before the Year 2000, Lexington Books, 1978.

Periodicals

"Energy Production in Stars," *Physical Review,* Volume 55, 1939, p. 434.
"Supernovae," *Physics Today,* Volume 43, Number 9, 1990, pp. 24–27.
(With R. A. Alpher and G. Gamow) "The Origin of Chemical Elements," *Physical Review,* Volume 73, 1948, pp. 803–804.

SOURCES:

Books

Bernstein, Jeremy, *Hans Bethe: Prophet of Energy,* Basic Books, 1980.

Bronowski, Jacob, *The Ascent of Man,* Little, Brown, 1974.

Feynman, Richard, *Surely You're Joking, Mr. Feynman!,* Norton, 1985.

Hawking, Stephen W., *A Brief History of Time: From the Big Bang to Black Holes,* Bantam, 1988.

McGraw-Hill Modern Scientists and Engineers, Volume 1, McGraw-Hill, 1980.

Weintraub, P., editor, *The Omni Interviews,* Omni Magazine, 1984.

—*Sketch by Dennis W. Cheek and Kim A. Cheek*

Homi Jehangir Bhabha

Homi Jehangir Bhabha
1909-1966
Indian physicist

Homi Jehangir Bhabha was an Indian physicist who is primarily noted for his contributions to the development of science in his native country. He founded and was chairman of the Tata Institute of Fundamental Research (TIFR) in Bombay and held other important posts, including chairman of the Indian Atomic Energy Commission, governor of the International Atomic Energy Agency, secretary of the Department of Atomic Energy, and director of the Trombay establishment, India's leading research and development center into atomic energy, which he also helped to establish. One of Bhabha's most important scientific contributions was his observation that the lifetimes of fast, unstable cosmic ray particles are increased by the time-dilation effect (that is unstable particles decay more slowly than identical stationary particles) that follows as a result of **Albert Einstein's** special theory of relativity. Bhabha was a vocal champion of international cooperation in finding peaceful uses for nuclear energy. His support for nuclear energy in providing electricity led to the construction of India's first nuclear reactors.

Bhabha was born in Bombay on October 30, 1909, into the privileged Parsi caste. His early education was at the Cathedral and John Connon High School. Later, he attended Elphinstone College and the Royal Institute of Science in Bombay, receiving a degree in mechanical engineering in 1930.

Bhabha won a Rouse Ball Traveling Studentship in mathematics and enrolled in Gonville and Caius College in Cambridge, England. He received a Ph.D. in 1935 and remained at Cambridge's Cavendish Laboratory until 1939. That year, while he was visiting India, World War II began in Europe, and he was unable to return to England. He accepted a position as special reader in theoretical physics at the Indian Institute of Science in Bangalore and became professor in the Cosmic Ray Institute in 1942. He stayed there until 1945, despite offers of chairs in physics from the University of Allahabad and the Indian Association for the Cultivation of Science. His belief was that those positions would not provide him with the opportunity to develop a school of physics that would be outstanding. He was seized with the idea of setting up just such an institution, and, to this end in August, 1943 he wrote to the wealthy Tata family to ask for funding. In his view at the time the scientific talent in India for developing science was greater than the funds available to support scientists and scientific development. On April 14, 1944, the trustees of Sir Dorab Tata Trust agreed to help Bhabha establish his proposed Institute provided government support could also be secured.

Establishes Tata Institute of Fundamental Research

In 1945 Bhabha realized a dream when the TIFR opened in Bombay, with Bhabha as its director. Soon after, research began into the variation of the vertical intensities of the total and penetrating part of cosmic rays using lead absorbers 10 centimeters thick. Bhabha and his team carried out experiments at a range of different latitudes in India, using a Geiger counter and nuclear emulsions. During 1944 and 1945, Bhabha also undertook a series of flights in U.S. Air Force planes from Bangalore during which he measured the intensity of the penetrating component of cosmic rays to an altitude of 40,000 feet.

Bhabha was a enthusiastic exponent of India's developing a nuclear-powered electrical system. His influence led to the establishment of the Indian Atomic Energy Commission. Bhabha strongly believed in the value of nuclear energy for peaceful ends and forged working partnerships with nuclear physicists from other countries. As a result of this work, he was made a governor of the International Atomic Energy Agency. Bhabha served as president of the First International Conference on the Peaceful Uses of Atomic energy, held in Geneva in 1955. There, he addressed the conference on the subject of nuclear fusion, which led to calls for the declassification of thermonuclear research. A member of many distinguished bodies and a fellow of the Royal Society of London, Bhabha was made an honorary fellow of Gonville and Caius College, Cambridge University, in 1957. Outside his work, Bhabha was a keen artist. He died in 1966 en route to Austria, when the Air India plane on which he was traveling crashed in the French Alps.

SOURCES:

Books

Essays on Particles and Fields, edited by R. R. Daniel and B. V. Sreekantan, Indian Academy of Sciences, 1989.

Periodicals

Greenstein, George. "A Gentleman of the Old School: Homi Bhabha and the Development of Science in India," *American Scholar,* summer, 1992, pp. 409–19.
Obituary, *The Times,* January 25, 1966, p. 10.

—*Sketch by Avril McDonald*

Gerd Binnig
1947-
German physicist

Along with his research colleague **Heinrich Rohrer**, Gerd Binnig invented the first microscope that opened the individual atom to view. The Royal Swedish Academy of Sciences found this scanning tunneling microscope (STM) so important that it awarded the device's inventors half of the 1986 Nobel Prize in physics just five years after the first successful test of the STM. The academy declared that even though development of the STM was in its infancy, it was already clear that "entirely new fields are opening up for the study of the structure of matter." Binnig was only thirty-nine years old when he received the honor.

Binnig was born in Frankfurt am Main, then West Germany, on July 20, 1947, the son of Ruth Bracke Binnig, a drafter, and Karl Franz Binnig, a machine engineer. Binnig pursued interests in both physics and music-classical and rock-and earned both a diploma and a Ph.D. in physics from Johann Wolfgang Goethe University in Frankfurt. Immediately after receiving his doctorate for work on superconductivity in 1978, Binnig joined the staff of the research laboratory operated by International Business Machines (IBM) in Zurich, Switzerland, and began his collaboration with Rohrer on the development of the STM.

Binnig and Rohrer Examine Surfaces

Rohrer had been at the IBM lab since 1963 and also had a background in superconductivity. Together Binnig and Rohrer became interested in exploring the characteristics of the surface of materials. This was a challenging proposition: the atomic structure of the surface of a solid differs from the atomic structure of the solid's interior in that atoms on the surface can interact only with atoms at, on, and immediately below the surface, making surface structures frustratingly complex. In the words of physicist **Wolfgang Pauli**, quoted by Binnig and Rohrer in the introduction to their description of the STM in *Scientific American* (August 1985), "The surface was invented by the devil."

To accomplish their goal, Binnig and Rohrer turned to a phenomenon of quantum mechanics known as tunneling. Quantum mechanics had earlier revealed that the wavelike nature of electrons permits them to escape the surface boundary of a solid—they "smear out" beyond the surface and form an electron cloud around the solid. Electrons can "tunnel" through touching and overlapping clouds between two

Gerd Binnig

surfaces. **Ivar Giaever** of General Electric verified this experimentally in 1960. Binnig had investigated tunneling in superconductors during his graduate studies. Now he and Rohrer decided to make electrons tunnel through a vacuum from a sample solid surface to a sharp, needlelike probe. This proved surprisingly easy to accomplish: as the needle tip approaches within a nanometer (one billionth of a meter) of the sample, their electron clouds touch and a tunneling current starts to flow. The probe's tip follows this current at a constant height above the surface atoms, producing a three-dimensional map of the solid's surface, atom by atom.

In order to insulate their microscope against the serious problem of distorting vibration and noise, Binnig and Rohrer made a series of technical advances that included the creation of a probe tip consisting of a single atom. The colleagues and their research team soon demonstrated practical uses of the STM, revealing the surface structure of crystals, observing chemical interactions, and scanning the surface of DNA (deoxyribonucleic acid) chains. Using the STM, Binnig became the first person to observe a virus escape from a living cell. The tremendous importance of the STM lies in its many applications—for basic research in chemistry, physics, and biology and for applied research in semiconductor physics, microelectronics, metallurgy, and bioengineering. On winning the Nobel Prize for his development of the STM, Binnig was quoted in the *New York Times* as having mixed emotions: "It was beautiful and terrible at the same time"-beautiful because it signaled a great success but terrible because it concluded "an exciting story of discovery."

Develops Atomic Force Microscope

However, Binnig had continued the "exciting story" while he was on leave at Stanford University in California in 1985. Freed from his constant work on the STM, Binnig had time to contemplate using the atomic force between atoms, rather than tunneling current, to move the scanning tip over a solid's surface. Binnig shared his ideas with Christoph Gerber of IBM Zurich and Calvin Quate of Stanford, and soon they had produced a prototype of a new type of scanner, the atomic force microscope (AFM), which started a new field of microscopy. The AFM made it possible for the first time to image materials that are not electrically conductive.

Binnig became group leader at IBM's Zurich lab in 1984, and also an IBM Fellow. He was visiting professor at Stanford from 1986 to 1988. In 1969 he married Lore Wagler, a fellow student, who became a psychologist. They had a daughter in 1984 and a son, born in the United States, in 1986. Binnig is interested in a number of outdoor pursuits including sailing, golf, tennis, soccer, and skiing, and he has maintained his involvement in music as a composer, player of various instruments, and singer. He was the author of a popular German book on human creativity and chaos titled *Aus dem Nichts* (*Out of Nothing*), which argued that creativity arises from disordered thoughts. He and Rohrer shared a number of prestigious international awards for their pioneering research in microscopy.

SELECTED WRITINGS BY BINNIG:

Periodicals

(With Heinrich Rohrer) "The Scanning Tunneling Microscope," *Scientific American*, August, 1985, pp. 50–56.
(With C. F. Quate and C. Gerber) "Atomic Force Microscope," *Physical Review Letters*, Volume 56, 1986, pp. 930–933.
(With Rohrer) "Scanning Tunneling Microscopy: From Birth to Adolescence," *Review of Modern Physics*, Volume 59, Number 3, 1987.

SOURCES:

Books

Guntherodt, H. J., and R. Wiesendanger, editors, *Scanning Tunnelling Microscopy*, Springer-Verlag, 1992.

Hansma, Paul K., *Tunneling Spectroscopy: Capabilities, Applications, and New Techniques,* Plenum, 1982.
Nobel Prize Winners: Physics, Volume 3, Salem Press, 1989.
Nobel Prize Winners, H. W. Wilson, 1987.

Periodicals

Business Week, November 3, 1986, pp. 134–136.
Fortune, October 13, 1986, p. 54.
Lancet, September 5, 1992, pp. 600–601.
New Scientist, February 1, 1992, p. 53.
New York Times, October 16, 1986, pp. A1, B18.
Physics Today, January, 1987, p. 17–21, S–70.
Rugar, Daniel, and Paul Hansma, "Atomic Force Microscopy," *Physics Today,* October, 1990, pp. 23–29.
Science, November 14, 1986, pp. 821–822.
Science News, October 25, 1986, pp. 262–263.
Wickramasinghe, H. Kumar, "Scanned-Probe Microscopes," *Scientific American,* October, 1989, pp. 98–105.

—*Sketch by Kathy Sammis*

George David Birkhoff
1884-1944
American mathematician

George David Birkhoff's contributions as a theoretical mathematician, a teacher, and a member of the international scientific community rank him as one of the foremost mathematicians of the twentieth century. He made extensive contributions to the area of differential equations and continued the work of the great French mathematician **Jules Henri Poincaré** on celestial mechanics. He is considered the founder of the modern theory of dynamical systems.

Born in Overisel, Michigan, on March 21, 1884, Birkhoff was the eldest of six children born to David Birkhoff, a physician, and Jane Gertrude Droppers. When Birkhoff was two years old, his family moved to Chicago, where he spent most of his childhood. From 1896 to 1902 Birkhoff studied at the Lewis Institute (now the Illinois Institute of Technology). Following a year at the University of Chicago as an undergraduate, Birkhoff transferred to Harvard University in 1903. In 1904, while still an undergraduate, he wrote his first mathematics paper, on number theory. He earned a bachelor's degree at Harvard in 1905 and a master's degree in 1906. Returning to the University of Chicago for his doctorate, Birkhoff wrote a dissertation on differential equations under the guidance of Eliakim Hastings Moore. He was awarded a doctorate *summa cum laude* in 1907.

Leaves His Mark through His Students

Birkhoff taught mathematics at the University of Wisconsin from 1907 to 1909, when he took a position as assistant professor at Princeton University. He joined the faculty of Harvard University in 1912, teaching there until his death in 1944. Birkhoff, though not a great lecturer, was an inspiring teacher. Many of the influential American mathematicians of the mid-twentieth century, including Marston Morse and Marshall Stone, studied with Birkhoff at the doctoral or post-doctoral level. Six of his former students went on to become members of the National Academy of Sciences. From 1935 to 1939 Birkhoff also served as Dean of the Faculty of Arts and Science at Harvard.

The single most important influence on Birkhoff's mathematical research was that of Poincaré. The two never met, but Birkhoff studied Poincaré's work and adopted some of the problems in differential equations and celestial mechanics Poincaré left behind at his death in 1912. In 1913 Birkhoff first attracted international attention by proving a geometrical theorem that Poincaré had proposed but not proved in his last published paper. Birkhoff's accomplishment marked a special advance in solving the problem of three bodies. The three-body problem of celestial mechanics concerns trajectories and orbits of bodies moving in systems in such a way that each body affects the motion of the others.

Advances Understanding of Dynamical Systems

From Poincaré's theorem, Birkhoff went on to consider the entire field of dynamical systems and made contributions that have become fundamental to this branch of mathematics. In his book *Dynamical Systems* (1927), Birkhoff wrote that "the final aim of the theory of motions of a dynamical system must be directed towards the qualitative determination of all possible types of motions and the interrelation of these motions." Using ideas developed by Poincaré, Birkhoff laid the foundations for the topological theory of dynamical systems by defining and classifying possible types of dynamic motions. Another signal achievement came in 1931, when Birkhoff offered further proof of the so-called ergodic theorem, which demonstrates the conditions needed for the behavior of a large dynamical system, such as a container of a gas, to reach equilibrium. This problem had baffled scientists for more than fifty years.

Birkhoff's journal articles and books reflect the breadth of his talent and the diversity of his interests.

Among his published works is a basic geometry text that for many years formed the basis of high-school geometry curricula. Birkhoff also wrote extensively about the theory of relativity and quantum mechanics. Although his ideas in this field are not widely accepted, the mathematical tools that he developed for his approach play an important role in modern relativity theory. Birkhoff's other work encompasses number theory and point-set theory and the famous four-color problem, which is concerned with the possibility of coloring any map using only four colors. In 1933, his life-long passion for art, music, and poetry led him to write *Aesthetic Measure,* in which he attempted to create a general mathematical theory of the fine arts, starting out from the Pythagorean notion that beauty is mathematical in nature. He later extended the theory to ethics. Birkhoff was also the editor of several mathematical journals, including the *Annals of Mathematics, Transactions of the American Mathematical Society,* and the *American Journal of Mathematics.*

Recognized Worldwide for Mathematical Achievements

During his lifetime, Birkhoff received many honors and honorary degrees from universities worldwide. Among others, he was awarded the Querini-Stampalia prize of the Royal Institute of Science, Letters and Arts, Venice (1918); the Bôcher prize of the American Mathematical Society (1923) for his research in dynamics; the annual prize of the American Association for the Advancement of Science (1926); and the biennial prize of the Pontifical Academy of Sciences (1933) for his research on systems of differential equations. Birkhoff was elected to membership in the National Academy of Sciences (1918), the American Philosophical Society, and the American Academy of Arts and Sciences. He was made an officer of the French Legion of Honor in 1936, and was an honorary member of the Edinburgh Mathematical Society, the London Mathematical Society, the Peruvian Philosophic Society, and the Scientific Society of Argentina.

Birkhoff was fluent in French, the language of his famous mathematical predecessor, Poincaré, and presented several of his fundamental papers in that language. He traveled widely, promoting his belief in international fellowship among scientists. Because of his preeminence in research, he was able to represent mathematics in international scientific circles, and he played an important role in the creation of the mathematical institutes at Göttingen and Paris after World War I.

Birkhoff married Margaret Elizabeth Grafius of Chicago on September 2, 1908, and they had three children: Barbara, Garrett, and Rodney. Garrett went on to become a professor of mathematics at Harvard.

Birkhoff died of a heart attack on November 12, 1944, in Cambridge, Massachusetts.

SELECTED WRITINGS BY BIRKHOFF:

Books

Relativity and Modern Physics, Harvard University Press, 1923.
Dynamical Systems, American Mathematical Society, 1927.
(With Ralph Beatley) *Basic Geometry,* Scott Foresman, 1941.
Collected Mathematical Papers, 3 volumes, American Mathematical Society, 1950.
"Mathematics of Aesthetics," *The World of Mathematics,* Volume 4, Simon and Schuster, 1956, pp. 2185–2195.
"A Mathematical Approach to Ethics," *The World of Mathematics,* Volume 4, Simon and Schuster, 1956, pp. 2198–2208.

SOURCES:

Books

Diner, S., D. Fargue, and G. Lochak, editors, *Dynamical Systems: A Renewal of Mechanism,* World Scientific, 1986.
Fang, J., *Mathematics From Antiquity to Today,* Volume 1, Paideia Press, 1972, pp. 212–213.
Newman, James R., *The World of Mathematics,* Volume 4, Simon and Schuster, 1956, pp. 2182–2208.
Turner, R., editor, *Thinkers of the Twentieth Century,* St. James Press, 1987, pp. 79–81.

—*Sketch by Maureen L. Tan*

Alfred A. Bishop
1924-
American chemical and nuclear engineer

Alfred A. Bishop is a nuclear engineer whose career with Westinghouse Corporation focused on the development of safety devices for nuclear reactors. In addition to writings in the field of heat transfer and fluid mechanics, Bishop holds a patent for a flow distributor for a nuclear reactor core.

Bishop was born in Philadelphia on May 10, 1924. After a stint in the U.S. Army from 1943 to 1946, during which he won three battle stars, Bishop entered the University of Pennsylvania, where he obtained his B.S. degree in 1950. In 1965, he earned his M.S. in chemical engineering at the University of Pittsburgh. In 1974, at the age of 50, he obtained his Ph.D. in mechanical engineering from Carnegie Mellon University. After working as a chemical engineer for the Naval Experimental Station in Philadelphia from 1950 to 1951, Bishop spent three years with the Fisher & Porter Company as an engineer and manager before taking an engineering position with the Westinghouse Corporation. An engineer with Westinghouse from 1956 to 1965, he served as manager of reactor safety, thermal and hydraulic design and development from 1965 to 1970. In 1970, Bishop became a consulting engineer with Westinghouse, and in 1974 became a partner in BB Nuclear Energy Consultants as well. He also taught at the University of Pittsburgh beginning in 1970, serving as the director of the university's nuclear engineering program from 1974 to 1980.

Bishop's contributions to nuclear engineering focus on the problem of heat control in a nuclear reactor core. The nuclear power industry depends on the heat generated by controlled nuclear chain reactions. By applying that heat to a suitable absorbing material (most often water, but sometimes gases or liquid metals like sodium), steam can be produced to run the turbines that generate electricity. The core of a nuclear reactor, where the fission reactions take place, must have the coolant material flowing through it to absorb the heat evenly. The engineering requirements of such a system are very high; it must be leak-tight, stable under conditions of high radioactivity, with special monitoring instrumentation and valves for redistributing the flow to avoid hot spots. Bishop was granted a patent for a flow distributor, a device to regulate water flow for cooling purposes, for a nuclear reactor core.

Bishop won a DuPont Research Award in 1971, and a National Science Foundation Award in 1975. He holds memberships in several professional societies, including the American Society of Chemical Engineers and the American Society of Mechanical Engineers, and served on the board of directors of the Pennsylvania Youth Centers and the United Fund.

SOURCES:

Books

Blacks in Science and Medicine, Hemisphere Publishing, 1990.

Taylor, Julius H., *The Negro in Science,* Morgan State College Press, 1955.

—*Sketch by Gail B. C. Marsella*

J. Michael Bishop
1936-
American molecular biologist

For work in cancer research, J. Michael Bishop shared the 1989 Nobel Prize in physiology or medicine with **Harold Varmus**. He and Varmus found that cancer genes (oncogenes) could be derived from normal cell genes which had not been inherently cancer-causing, as was previously thought; they stopped normal functioning and became cancerous under certain conditions. In presenting the Nobel Prize, Erling Norrby of the Karolinska Institute praised them for their discovery of "the cellular origin of retroviral oncogenes," and claimed they had "set in motion an avalanche of research on factors that govern the normal growth of cells."

John Michael Bishop was born February 22, 1936, to John and Carrie Grey Bishop. The family, which included another son and daughter, lived in York, Pennsylvania, where John Bishop was a Lutheran minister. Bishop's early schooling was almost entirely devoid of science, and even when he entered Gettysburg College in 1953 as a premedical student, he had no firm plans for a career. He graduated with a chemistry degree in 1957 and went to Harvard Medical School but took several detours while he was there, first to work in the pathology department of the Massachusetts General Hospital and later to work with the virologist Elmer Pfefferkorn. He obtained his medical degree in 1962 and spent the required amount of time as an intern and resident at Massachusetts General, but his interest had finally focused on investigating the molecular biology of viruses. He worked for three years at the National Institutes of Health as a postdoctoral fellow, learning to do fundamental research. After a year of study in Germany with Gebhard Koch, Bishop took a teaching position in 1968 at the University of California at San Francisco. He was eventually appointed professor in the department of microbiology and immunology, as well as the director of the G. W. Hooper Research Foundation of the University of California Medical Center.

Research on Cancer Genes Leads to Nobel Prize

A cancer cell's principal characteristic is unregulated growth and multiplication. Carcinogenesis is a particularly difficult field to study because there appear to be many factors contributing to it (genetics and environment being only two), and also because a cell is an intricate structure with hundreds of different chemical reactions and enzymes controlling and affecting each other. Bishop studied the genetic component of cancer, and of this subject he has written in an article in *Science:* "Genetic damage remains undetected in the great majority of human tumors. We may have to invent new ways to search for this damage, and we must remain open to the possibility that we will not always find it because it is not always there."

Many theories of cancer causation already existed when Bishop began his investigations, and new discoveries relevant to the field were made frequently. Robert Huebner and George Todaro had postulated that cancer genes (oncogenes) might lay hidden in cells, the result of viral infection many generations ago, waiting for particular environmental stresses to set them off. **Peyton Rous** had identified a sarcoma virus that caused tumors in chickens. G. Steven Martin found an oncogene, named *src,* on the Rous sarcoma virus. **Howard Temin** identified the sarcoma virus discovered by Rous as a retrovirus—one that could somehow copy its own RNA information into the DNA of the host cell (which is reverse of the usual process of DNA to RNA reproduction). Temin also participated in David Baltimore's discovery of the enzyme called reverse transcriptase which accomplished that copying.

Bishop, Varmus, and their colleagues Deborah Spector and Dominique Stehelin conducted a search for *src* oncogenes in different species and found *src*-like genes just about everywhere, apparently as Huebner and Todaro had predicted. They were astonished to find, however, that these genes were not inherently oncogenes but functioned as a regular part of the cellular machinery, performing work for the cell until their normal functioning was somehow changed. Bishop and his colleagues called these genes proto-oncogenes. Retroviruses apparently picked up these normal cellular genes and instigated changes that caused them to become cancerous, although retroviruses were only one possible cause of the transformation; some chemical carcinogens may also convert proto-oncogenes to oncogenes. In a review in *Science,* Bishop uses an analogy to describe proto-oncogenes, though he warns that the analogy is oversimplified: "The proliferation of cells is governed by an elaborate circuitry that reaches from the surface of the cell to the nucleus. The products of proto-oncogenes may represent some of the junction boxes in that circuitry. . . . What we now know of oncogenes allows us to view their actions as 'short circuits' at the corresponding junction boxes."

For this discovery Bishop and Varmus received the 1989 Nobel Prize. Controversy erupted when Stehelin demanded a share of the prize for the work

he had done with the two laureates, but the awarding committee remained firm. Stehelin, as well as Spector, had contributed important experiments, but the committee believed that the fundamental intellectual creativity belonged to Bishop and Varmus.

A strong proponent of basic research, in 1993 Bishop coauthored a paper in *Science* which sharply criticized the government's role in the field. The article mentioned "inadequate funding . . . , flawed governmental oversight of science, confusion about the goals of federally supported research, and deficiencies in science education," and offered a set of guidelines for solving these problems.

Bishop married Kathryn Ione Putnam in 1959; they have two sons. Among his other honors, Bishop won the Gairdner Foundation International Award and the Armand Hammer Cancer Prize in 1984, the American Cancer Society National Medal of Honor in 1985, and the American College of Physicians Award in 1987. He is known as an outstanding teacher and outspoken individual, with a great fondness for music.

SELECTED WRITINGS BY BISHOP:

Periodicals

"DNA Related to the Transforming Gene(s) of Avian Sarcoma Viruses Is Present in Normal Avian DNA," *Nature,* Volume 260, March, 1976, pp. 170–173.

"Oncogenes," *Scientific American,* Volume 246, March, 1982, pp. 80–91.

"The Molecular Genetics of Cancer," *Science,* Volume 235, January, 1987, pp. 305–311.

(With Marc Kirschner and Harold Varmus) "Science and the New Administration," *Science,* Volume 259, January, 1993, pp. 444–445.

SOURCES:

Periodicals

Marx, J. L., "Cancer Gene Research Wins Medicine Nobel," *Science,* Volume 246, October, 1989, pp. 326–327.

—*Sketch by Gail B. C. Marsella*

Katharine Scott Bishop
1889-1975
American physician

Katharine Scott Bishop was one of the few women to pursue medical research in the early twentieth century. She worked with anatomist Herbert McLean Evans to identify vitamin E and its function in reproduction. She was also a practicing anesthesiologist and teacher. Bishop's career in medicine spanned a time when few women received full credit for their professional work.

Bishop was born on June 23, 1889, in New York City, New York. The daughter of Walter and Katherine Emma Scott, Bishop attended the Somerville, Massachusetts Latin School before enrolling at Wellesley College. After graduating from Wellesley in 1910, she took premedical courses at Radcliffe College. She received her medical degree from Johns Hopkins Medical School in 1915.

Bishop taught histology at the University of California Medical School from 1915 to 1923. During that time she also worked with Herbert McLean Evans. In 1922 Bishop and Evans were codiscoverers of vitamin E. They proved its existence by identifying its deficiency in laboratory rats. Initially calling it "substance X," known to be related to fat-soluble vitamin A, they observed that depriving rats of the substance disturbed their ability to reproduce. Pure vitamin E was isolated by Evans and others in 1935. The same year she codiscovered vitamin E, Bishop married Tyndall Bishop, an attorney. The couple had two daughters, Edith and Katherine.

From 1924 to 1929 Bishop worked as a histopathologist at the George William Hooper Institute of Medical Research in San Francisco, California, publishing several papers on histology and physiology. Bishop was a member of the American Association of Anatomists, the Association for the Advancement of Science, and the Society for Experimental Biology and Medicine. During the 1930s she took time off from her career to raise her daughters, and studied public health for two years at the University of California Medical School. When her husband became an invalid, Bishop supported her family by practicing anesthesiology and general medicine privately, later joining the anesthesiology staff at St. Luke's Hospital in San Francisco. Tyndall Bishop died in 1938. In 1940 Bishop began practicing at Alta Bates Hospital in Berkeley, where she remained until her retirement in 1953. She died on September 20, 1975, in Berkeley, California.

SELECTED WRITINGS BY BISHOP:

Periodicals

(With Herbert Evans) "Existence of a Hitherto-Unknown Dietary Factor Essential for Reproduction," *Journal of the American Medical Association,* Volume 81, 1923, pp. 889–892.

SOURCES:

Books

Apple, Rima D., editor, *Women, Health and Medicine in America: A Historical Handbook,* Garland, 1990.
Rossiter, Margaret, *Women Scientists in America: Struggles and Strategies to 1940,* Johns Hopkins University Press, 1982.

—*Sketch by Valerie Brown*

Jacob Bjerknes
1897-1975
Norwegian meteorologist

Jacob Bjerknes was one of the seminal figures of in the field of meteorology and possessed a gift for the simplification of complex atmospheric dynamics. He developed the classic northern hemisphere extratropical cyclone model , which showed how cyclones crossing the ocean could lose power before resurging as intense storm systems. With associates, he also formulated a body of thought on weather fronts. He did early research on upper atmospheric waves and on the interactive dynamics of the atmosphere and oceans. His contributions to modern meteorology garnered him, among many other awards, the Royal Meteorological Society Symons Memorial Medal in 1940, the AGU Bowie Medal in 1945, the Norwegian Royal Order of St. Olav in 1947, the American Meteorological Society Rossby Medal in 1960, and the U.S. National Medal of Science in 1966.

Jacob Aall Bonnevie Bjerknes was born in Stockholm, Sweden, on November 2, 1897. He was the son of the important Norwegian theoretical physicist and geophysicist **Vilhelm Bjerknes** and Honoria Bonnevie. His father's groundwork in dynamic meteorological theory and weather forecasting inspired his own collaboration and life's work in the atmospheric sciences. After attending the University of Kristiania (now Oslo) from 1914 to 1916, Bjerknes followed his friend **Halvor Solberg** to the University of Leipzig, where his father was chair of a newly formed geophysical institute. The team in Leipzig carried out research into the practical applications of the elder Bjerknes' recent formulations of dynamic meteorology.

Resolves Extratropical Cyclone and Polar Front Theories

Reflecting German interest in predicting weather for army ground and air planning, the neutral Norwegians were studying storm movements. Jacob Bjerknes was investigating the physical characteristics of what was called the "squall line," the boundary along which shower clouds develop and precipitate. The squall line is characterized by a steep temperature gradient. From surface data plots of atmospheric wind and precipitation patterns, he found that weather develops along those lines where wind fields converge. An analysis of the development and movement of these lines, Bjerknes realized, would provide a basis for predicting associated weather patterns.

The prediction of significant weather was a practical goal of the elder Bjerknes' theories of atmospheric movement and general circulation. Jacob Bjerknes' discovery provided the initial validation of viable forecasting techniques, and his father decided to capitalize of Jacob's discovery. Since war conditions were increasingly complicating the Norwegians' research, Vilhelm Bjerknes accepted an offer to found a new geophysical institute at Bergen on the west coast of Norway. By February of 1918, research at Bergen, using surface analysis and mathematical methods, was geared to forecasting storm and rainfall associated with the squall line. Through such research Bjerknes deepened his understanding of convergence and airmass characteristics, concluding that such converging winds result in low pressure centers which develop along the squall line.

The cyclonic (characterized by counterclockwise winds and upward motion) low pressure system that followed such weather development, and the squall line as well, had been defined as separate phenomena into the later nineteenth century. Bjerknes' analysis revealed that the cyclone and convergence line displayed such a close relationship that they should be understood as all part of one integrated weather system. In effect, Bjerknes had discovered a dynamically integrated and cyclical atmospheric system potentially more useful as a means of forecasting a progression to weather change than all previous observational and theoretical results. Thus the basic extratropical cyclone model was born, a model that would undergo modifications as the Bergen meteorologists researched the variability of local atmospheric characteristics and created a total three-dimensional

view of the atmosphere in analyzing vertical airmass changes.

The first published study of these results was Bjerknes' classic article "On the Structure of Moving Cyclones," which appeared in 1919. The research at Bergen was already complemented by an experimental weather service operational by the middle of 1918. The Norwegian government recognized the value of the Bergen meteorologists when the country lost access to weather forecasts from other parts of Europe. In July of 1919, therefore, the West Norwegian Weather Bureau began operation with Vilhelm Bjerknes as head and the twenty-year-old Jacob as chief.

After mid–1918 the Bjerkneses and Solberg began a preliminary campaign of worldwide dissemination of the Bergen theory and practice, which was essentially the inception of meteorology as an applied scientific means of systematic analysis and prognostication of atmospheric change. Other important contributors, particularly the Swedes **Carl-Gustaf Rossby** and Tor Bergeron, joined them. Jacob Bjerknes and Halvor Solberg formed a traveling and research team, going to Sweden both to promote the Bergen meteorology and to continue study of the squall line discontinuity. Solberg found that, as the structure of an old squall line dissipates, a new wave often develops to the rear. From this Bjerknes and Solberg theorized that the tumultuous dynamics of the squall line and its following airmass can generate a small "family" of cyclones. Bergeron's three-dimensional analysis of the squall line revealed that over time the line can be lifted or "occluded" and squeezed or "secluded" into dissipation, a modification of the original cyclone model which Bjerknes initially resisted.

The Bergen group as a whole studied the temperature gradient along the discontinuity of the squall line, realizing that its relatively regular extent was hemisphere-wide and likening it to a "battle line." By late 1919, they took the basic term "front" from World War I terminology to name the now familiar "polar front." The two basic convergence lines of the cyclone model were also relabeled. The forward "steering line," which moves along a cold airmass, became the "warm front," leading a "warm sector," a progressively squeezed warm airmass drawn into the circulation. The following squall line became the "cold front," which leads the colder airmass from the north. The last wave of the cold front cyclone family tended to precipitate the southerly "outbreak" of polar air. By 1922, when Bjerknes and Solberg's "The Life Cycle of Cyclones and the Polar Front Theory of Atmospheric Circulation" appeared in print, the Bergen meteorology had reached a mature stage.

Moves to the United States

For his work on the cyclone/polar front model, Bjerknes received a Ph.D. in 1924 from the University of Kristiania. A respite from his usual work came in 1926 when he served as a meteorologist in Iceland in support of Roald Amundsen's polar dirigible flight. In 1928 he married Hedvig Borthen; they eventually had two children. He continued as the superintendent of the weather service at Bergen until 1931, when he became professor of meteorology at the Geophysical Institute of Bergen. From 1932, his research centered on the analysis of upper tropospheric wave development and on further development of the three-dimensional structure of the cyclone with atmospheric balloon sounding data. By 1937 he resolved his systematic research of pressure tendency, or local pressure change of the atmosphere, integrating it with the existing mathematics of cyclone development.

By 1939, with the escalation of World War II in the north, he and his wife contemplated the possibility of emigrating. Bjerknes had spent a year as visiting lecturer at the Massachusetts Institute of Technology (MIT) between 1933 and 1934. Carl-Gustaf Arvid Rossby had been a professor there since 1928 and was engaged in integrating the Bergen approach with work done in the United States. Another Norwegian associate, Jörgen Holmboe, one of Vilhelm Bjerknes' student/collaborators, had also come to MIT, lecturing from 1936 to 1940 on dynamic meteorology. In 1939 Bjerknes was invited to the United States for a lecture tour, a fortuitous offer as Norway was overrun by the Germans in April of 1940, shortly after his departure. The University of California at Los Angeles (UCLA) asked him to start a meteorology annex to the physics department that same year. The rapid advance of aeronautics technology and the worldwide extent of the war made weather forecasting one of the prime arenas of applied science at the time. Under Bjerknes' direction, UCLA became an important training center for military forecasters, and, at the war's end, the new department of synoptic meteorology was the foremost in the United States.

Bjerknes' role in the Bergen legacy continued when he and Jörgen Holmboe returned to the problem of surface pressure tendency theory, which resulted in their joint "On the Theory of Cyclones" (1944). The final formulation of the theory of cyclone development integrates the upper and lower atmospheric relationship. The first of Bjerknes' Ph.D.'s, Jule Gregory Charney, used these results for the first computer-aided weather prediction, carried out at the Princeton Center of Advanced Study. These two- and three-level atmospheric models simulating Bjerknes' theory of cyclogenesis provided a first accurate computer-aided weather forecast in 1950.

Bjerknes' wartime consulting duties led to affiliations with meteorological offices in several countries, including the U.S. Weather Bureau. As a result, Bjerknes turned to global atmospheric general circulation research and was one of the first to see the importance of photographic data from rockets and later from weather satellites. His later research (beginning in 1959) focused on the interrelation of the atmosphere and oceans and demonstrated the physical response of global wind systems to the variable heat supply of equatorial belt oceans. This work contributed to the explanation of the annual variability of world climates and the ocean warming effect referred to as "El Niño." Bjerknes was emeritus professor at UCLA from 1965 until his death in Los Angeles, California, on July 7, 1975, from complications due to a heart attack.

SELECTED WRITINGS BY BJERKNES:

Books

(With Volume Bjerknes, H. Solberg, and T. Bergeron) *Physikalische Hydrodynamik mit Anwendung auf die dynamische Meteorologie,* [Berlin], 1933.

(With C. L. Godske, T. Bergeron, and R. C. Bundgaard) *Dynamic Meteorology and Weather Forecasting,* American Meteorological Society/Carnegie Institution, 1957.

Periodicals

"On the Structure of Moving Cyclones," *Geofysiske Publikasjoner,* Volume 1, number 2, 1919.

(With H. Solberg) "The Life Cycle of Cyclones and the Polar Front Theory of Atmospheric Circulation," *Geofysiske Publikasjoner,* Volume 3, number 1, 1922.

(With J. Holmboe) "On the Theory of Cyclones," *Journal of Meteorology,* Volume 1, numbers 1 and 2, 1944.

SOURCES:

Books

Byers, Horace R., *General Meteorology,* McGraw Hill, 1959.

Holmboe, Jörgen, George E. Forsythe and William Gustin, *Dynamic Meteorology,* Wiley, 1945.

Wurtele, Morton G., editor, *Selected Papers of Jacob Aall Bonnevie Bjerknes,* Western Periodicals Co., 1975.

Other

Bjerknes, Hedvig Borthen, interview with William J. McPeak, conducted October 30, 1993.

—Sketch by William J. McPeak

Vilhelm Bjerknes
1862-1951
Norwegian physicist and geophysicist

Vilhelm Bjerknes established the foundations of modern atmospheric dynamic meteorology as an exact science by integrating the fundamental theories of hydrodynamics and thermodynamics in descriptions of atmospheric motion. To advance his dynamic approach, commonly known as the Bergen school of meteorology, he formulated an agenda of weather analysis and forecasting and founded the Geophysical Institute and Weather Service of Bergen, Norway. For his important contributions to physics and geophysics, Bjerknes was awarded many honors and was inducted as a foreign member of the Royal Society of London and the National Academy of Science.

Vilhelm Frimann Koren Bjerknes was born on March 14, 1862, to Carl Anton Bjerknes and Aletta Koren at Kristiania (now Oslo), Norway. His father, educated as a mining engineer, became a well-regarded teacher of physics, who turned to research in hydrodynamic forces on bodies in frictionless fluids, also investigating possible analogies in electrodynamic phenomena. The younger Bjerknes began collaborating with his father at an early age and maintained an interest in his father's research problems for the rest of his life. Beginning his formal studies in mathematics and physics at the University of Kristiania in 1880, Vilhelm focused his research on hydrodynamics until 1887, when he decided to set an independent course as he moved on to complete his M.S. degree, which he received in 1888. His understanding of the need for creative and intellectual independence in scientific research would later make Bjerknes an ideal collaborative partner for younger scientists.

After receiving his degree, Bjerknes went to Paris on a state fellowship. He became acquainted with Heinrich Hertz's studies in electrical wave diffusion while taking **Jules Henri Poincaré**'s university lectures in electrodynamics. In 1890 he went to Bonn, attending the university for two years as assistant and first collaborator to Heinrich Hertz himself. Research done by Bjerknes at that time resulted in important contributions to resonance and oscillatory circuit theory. His resonance curve experiments also contributed to verification of Hertz's theory and experiments. Bjerknes then returned to Norway and school, focusing on electrodynamics, and completed his Ph.D. in 1892. After obtaining a lectureship at Stockholm's School of Engineering in 1893, he secured a position as professor of applied mechanics and mathematical physics at the University of Stock-

holm in 1895. He married Honoria Bonnevie the same year. Their son, **Jacob Bjerknes**, who was to become a famous meteorologist in his own right and one of his father's important collaborators, was born in 1897. While at Stockholm, Bjerknes discontinued active research in electrodynamics in favor of returning to his father's hydrodynamic studies. He published an overview of the work in hydrodynamics in *Vorlesungen über hydrodynamische Fernkräfte* (1900–1902).

Lays Foundations of a New Meteorology

In returning to hydrodynamics, Bjerknes sought to avoid the pitfalls of his father's theoretical isolation. By 1898 he had integrated his own mechanical research with a general analysis of the two primitive circulation theorems of absolute motion that had been derived by British mathematician and physicist William Thomson Kelvin and German physicist Hermann Helmholtz. The theorems concerned velocities of circulation and the conservation of a circular vortex, which describes the remarkable stability of vortex motion. Bjerknes applied his modification of these theorems to nature's largest fluid systems, the atmosphere and the ocean, and formulated the theory of "physical hydrodynamics." Bjerknes' physical hydrodynamics differs from classical hydrodynamics in that it incorporates thermodynamic laws into classical fluid mechanics. The sun's heat is converted to motion in the atmosphere. In addition, the friction of atmospheric motion itself generates heat, which is again converted to motion. Bjerknes realized that atmospheric motion therefore can be properly understood and predicted only in a framework that integrates hydrodynamics and thermodynamics.

Since atmospheric motion creates weather patterns, Bjerknes' work held great promise for meteorological forecasting. Although observation of the progression of weather systems, understood as cyclonic low pressure phenomena, had already become important as a means of weather forecasting, predictions were not very reliable, particularly in the longer term. Bjerknes's theory offered a rigorously defined general atmospheric dynamics that promised to enable meteorologists to forecast weather accurately even in the longer term, based on a systematic and detailed, three-dimensional analysis of atmospheric conditions.

Bjerknes grasped the importance of firm economic support for the research and its practical consequences for weather forecasting. He visited the United States in 1905 to present his program in lectures at MIT and to seek funding. He was rewarded with a research associateship at the Carnegie Institute in Washington, D.C., and an annual stipend from the Carnegie Foundation. (Bjerknes was to receive the stipend until 1941.) Soliciting the world meteorological community at large in regard to his intensive analysis and forecasting techniques, he began a campaign of lecturing after 1909, also calling for awareness of the analytical importance of upper-air wind observations with the relatively new pilot balloon and theodolite tracking technique. Bjerknes moved to the University of Kristiania as professor of applied mechanics and mathematical physics in 1907. His most significant collaborations began shortly afterwards. With his new assistant Johann Wilhelm Sandström, he wrote the first volume of *Dynamic Meteorology and Hydrography* (dealing with the static state of the atmosphere and fluids) in 1910. The second volume, dealing with the kinematic or massless movement of the atmosphere and fluids, was published the next year in collaboration with his new assistants Theodor Hesselberg and Olav M. Devik. The final volume was written entirely by Bjerknes' collaborators and was not published until 1951. Other collaborators followed. Fellow Norwegian and later noted polymathic geophysicist Harald Ulrik Sverdrup was among them, arriving in 1911.

In 1912 Bjerknes' geophysical work was made more visible with his acceptance of a professorship of geophysics at the University of Leipzig in Germany. He also became chair of its new geophysical institute, and soon brought Hesselberg, Sverdrup, Halvor Solberg, and his son, Jacob Bjerknes, to work with him. Several years later, however, World War I made research conditions increasingly difficult at Leipzig. Therefore, when his friend zoologist and arctic explorer Fridtjof Nansen presented Bjerknes with the opportunity to found his own geophysical institute at the new University of Bergen in 1917, the scientist accepted. The move to Bergen initiated the most productive period of Bjerknes's career.

Founds the Geophysical Institute and Weather Service of Bergen

Initially, the new geophysical institute was housed in the Bergen Museum's Meteorological Observatory in rather cramped quarters. Nevertheless, Bjerknes started a multi-faceted program of research in the dynamic theory of atmospheric movement, systematic daily observation of the basic meteorological conditions, intensive calculation of predictions and graphic representation of meteorological change, and timely weather forecasts. The need for an intensive synoptic method became clear at the end of the war, when Norway lost access to lower European weather reports and the Bergen program became indispensable. The Norwegian government set up a dense weather observation network in response, based on Bjerknes' persuasive practical applications.

By July 26, 1918, with the study of new analytical techniques still in progress, the experimental Western Bergen Weather Service, manned by the Bjerkneses and Solberg, was issuing detailed reports for the benefit of the government and military. The center for their work had been moved to the attic of a large home donated to Bjerknes for use as headquarters for the meteorology division of the Bergen Geophysical Institute. Eventually, the public utility of the weather service was realized in more sophisticated local forecasts made available to fishermen, farmers, and the budding commercial aviation industry.

Continued airmass research by Bjerknes's team resulted in the theory of motion in cyclone systems (cyclones are winds moving counterclockwise and upwards), the polar front theory, and the more complex upper front theory. Bjerknes continued to publish prolifically. His most comprehensive work, *On the Dynamics of the Circular Vortex with Applications to the Atmosphere and to Atmospheric Vortex and Wave Motion,* appeared in 1921, and *Physical Hydrodynamics,* written with his son, Solberg, and Bergeron, came out in 1933. Bjerknes's many enthusiastic collaborators disseminated the Bergen meteorological approach when they later fanned out to many different countries in the West, particularly the United States.

In 1926 Bjerknes left the Geophysical Institute of Bergen in the hands of Sverdrup, his son, and other scientists he had trained, to accept a position as professor of mechanics and mathematical physics at the University of Oslo. He began teaching theoretical physics and planned a series of textbooks on the subject. The first of these, on vector analysis and kinematics, was published in 1929. He also returned to his father's "hydromagnetic" theories with meteorologist Einar Høiland for the projected second textbook in the series, but he was unable to solve a number of difficulties in his father's theories. At the same time, he remained a forceful spokesman for modern meteorology as both a practical and theoretical science, even after his retirement from the University of Oslo in 1932. Bjerknes died of heart failure at Oslo on April 9, 1951.

SELECTED WRITINGS BY BJERKNES:

Books

(With J. W. Sandström, Th. Hesselberg, and O. Devik) *Dynamic Meteorology and Hydrography,* 2 volumes, [Washington, D. C.], 1910–11.

On the Dynamics of the Circular Vortex with Applications to the Atmosphere and to Atmospheric Vortex and Wave Motion, [Kristiania], 1921.

(With J. Bjerknes, H. Solberg, and T. Bergeron) *Physikalische Hydrodynamik mit Anwendung auf die dynamische Meteorologie,* [Berlin], 1933.

SOURCES:

Books

Friedman, Robert Marc, *Appropriating the Weather: Vilhelm Bjerknes and the Construction of a Modern Meteorology,* Cornell University Press, 1989.

Gillispie, Charles Coulston, editor, *Dictionary of Scientific Biography,* Volume 15, Supplement I, Scribner's, 1978, pp. 167–69.

Shaw, Napier, *Manual of Meteorology,* part 4, Cambridge University Press, 1919, pp. 102–03.

Other

Bjerknes, Hedvig Borthen, interview with William J. McPeak, including recollections of Vilhelm Bjerknes, conducted on October 30, 1993.

—*Sketch by William J. McPeak*

Davidson Black
1884-1934
Canadian physician and paleoanthropologist

Davidson Black was an anatomist who became intrigued with discovering the origins of humanity. He spent much of his career in China, where in 1927 he deduced that fossil teeth found in caves at Zhoukoudian (formerly Cho-k'ou-tien) came from a previously undiscovered species of early man that he named *Sinanthropus pekinensis,* or Peking Man. Several years later, Black noted similarities between the teeth and other fossil remains including skull fragments recovered at Zhoukoudian and the Java man fossils found in 1894 in Indonesia. Both sets of fossils have subsequently been classified as being members of the same extinct hominid species, *Homo erectus.*

Black, the second of two sons, was born on July 25, 1884, in Toronto to Davidson Black, a lawyer, and Margaret Bowes Delamere. Two years after his birth, Black's mother was forced to find a government office position when the elder Davidson Black, then serving as a Queen's counsel in Toronto, died suddenly at age forty-nine of a heart attack. As a young boy Black was interested in natural history and graduated from his high school as the top student. In 1903 he was accepted into the University of Toronto and entered the school of medicine. Almost immediately

he was attracted to anatomy. Black completed his medical studies and earned his M.D. before the end of the decade.

Black intended to practice medicine, but one of his professors convinced him that he should return to the university and broaden his education. So Black worked toward a bachelor of arts degree, which he received in 1909 at the University of Toronto. That summer he accepted a position as a lecturer at what is today Case Western Reserve University in Cleveland. With that decision, the Canadian-born Black was destined to do virtually all of his scientific work outside Canada, with the exception of spending several summers with the Geological Survey of Canada. His work with the survey gave him a firm foundation in geology that later proved valuable in China.

Archaeologist Fires Black's Imagination

In 1913 he was appointed an assistant professor of anatomy at Case Western, and became engaged to and then married Adena Nevitt, the daughter of a physician affiliated with the Northwest Mounted Police. The following year Black took a leave of absence to study in Europe. There he took a short course in advanced anatomy and neurology at Manchester University taught by Graflon Elliot Smith, a British archaeologist who was then trying to reconstruct the skull of Piltdown Man, the seeming "missing link" between apes and humans. The skull is now remembered as a notorious archaeological hoax. Smith fired Black's imagination about paleoanthropology and also taught Black how make casts of fossils, a skill in which Black became an expert. In 1915, the book *Climate and Evolution* by fellow Canadian William Diller Matthew pointed Black toward China and Asia, where Black decided he wanted to search for humanity's origins.

World War I delayed Black, who in 1917 became a captain in the Canadian Army Medical Corps. In 1918 an old college friend, E. V. Cowdry, was appointed head of the anatomy department of Peking Union Medical College in China, which was founded and being funded by the Rockefeller Foundation. Cowdry asked Black to join him as a professor of neurology and embryology. Black agreed, and he and his wife left for China in the summer of 1919. Although he was primarily occupied with setting up a laboratory and teaching at the hospital, Black found time to go on his first field expedition in 1920 to eastern Mongolia. When Cowdry resigned in 1921, Black became the head of the anatomy department and almost immediately became interested in developing an anthropological museum at the college.

Several hominid molars were discovered in a cave about twenty-five miles from Beijing (then Peking) in 1923. Discovery of the teeth was announced in 1926, and after examining them, Black applied for and received funding from the Rockefeller Foundation to mount a large-scale archaeological dig at Zhoukoudian in the spring of 1927. That October, a well-preserved left lower molar was uncovered. After studying the new tooth and the earlier finds, Black deduced that they were from an early human ancestor that he named Peking Man. A number of other teeth and fragments of at least two jaws were found in 1928, and in 1929 a well-preserved, nearly complete skull of an adolescent was dug out of one of the caves at Zhoukoudian in expeditions organized and headed by Black. Using the casting skills he learned in England, Black made copies of the Peking Man skull and other fossils for study by other scientists outside China. This is fortunate, because the skulls and many other fossils dug up at Zhoukoudian subsequently disappeared in the chaos that followed in China with the Japanese invasion during World War II and the intermittent Chinese civil war that preceded and followed it.

Hunt for Early Ancestors Continues

Continued funding from the Rockefeller Foundation enabled Black to establish the Cenozoic Research Laboratory at Peking Union Medical College in 1929 to continue his search for human ancestors. That year Black also delivered a paper on Java and visited Trinil, the site where in 1894 the Dutch physician Eugène Dubois had found the teeth and brain pan of Java man, or *Pithecanthropus erectus*. In 1930 Black was named an honorary fellow of the Royal Anthropological Institute in England and an honorary member of the National Academy of Sciences. Membership in the Royal Society of London followed.

The caves at Zhoukoudian continued to yield fossils from 1930 to 1932, including crudely chipped stone artifacts uncovered in 1931 that were smudged with traces of carbon, indicating humans were using fire at least 500,000 years ago. A year later, Black embarked on a long journey to search for other traces of early humans and to study geography in India, Afghanistan, Persia, Iraq, Palestine, and Egypt before visiting Canada and then returning to China. Black suffered a minor heart attack in the fall of 1933, but recovered and continued working at Peking Union Medical College. On March 15, 1934, he suffered a second and fatal heart attack, however, leaving a wife and two young sons.

SOURCES:

Books

Asimov's Chronology of Science and Discovery, Harper, 1989, pp. 5, 498.

Hood, Dora, *Davidson Black: A Biography,* University of Toronto Press, 1964.

—*Sketch by Joel Schwarz*

James Black
1924-
English pharmacologist

Sir James Black was one of the founders of a revolution in the way pharmaceutical companies search for medicines. He developed a method of discovering and evaluating new medicines by studying the basic biological mechanisms that underlie disease. His approach led to new, more effective treatments for heart ailments, including heart attack, and to the first successful drug to treat ulcers. For his pioneering efforts, Black shared the 1988 Nobel Prize for physiology or medicine with **George H. Hitchings** and **Gertrude Belle Elion** of Burroughs Wellcome Co. in the United States.

James Whyte Black was born on June 14, 1924, in Uddingston, Scotland, to a working-class family. His father was a Scottish coal miner who worked his way up to mining engineer. Black was the youngest of four sons. One of his older brothers studied medicine and Black soon followed in his footsteps. At age fifteen, he won a residential scholarship to St. Andrew's University, where he received his medical degree in 1946. He remained as an assistant lecturer from 1946 to 1947 before traveling to Malaysia to serve as a senior lecturer in physiology at the University of Malaya from 1947 to 1950. He returned to Scotland in 1950 and lectured in physiology at Glasgow Veterinary School until 1958. During this time he began research on the mechanism of increase in gastric secretions caused by the body's production of histamine. This research formed the basis for his later work on blocking histamine receptors (chemical groups in plasma membrane or cell interior that have an affinity for a specific chemical or compound, in this case histamine) to reduce gastric secretions. During his time in Glasgow, Black also became familiar with the alpha and beta adrenergic receptors, which are responsible for regulating heart beat.

Develops Treatment for Angina Pectoris

Black joined Imperial Chemical Industries in 1958. There he sought better ways of treating angina pectoris, a painful disease caused by insufficient oxygenation of the heart. The painful episodes suf-

James Black

fered by angina patients are caused by increased heart rate, which increases the heart's requirement for oxygen. Black's research led him to theorize that a drug that would neutralize the effects of the hormones adrenaline and noradrenaline, which mediate heart rate, would relieve the symptoms of angina.

The existence of receptors for these hormones had been understood since 1948, when the biochemist Raymond P. Ahlquist first described their action. Black developed a chemically similar but nonfunctional version of the active hormones that would block one of these receptors, the beta receptor. His first studies were with analogs of isoprenaline, a compound similar to noradrenaline. One of these analogs, known as propanolol or the trade name Inderol, had the desired effect. It constricted heart muscle, stopping angina attacks.

In 1964 Black joined the British subsidiary of Smith Kline & French Laboratories. There he worked on new approaches to treating intestinal ulcers. Black knew from his earlier studies that histamine stimulated the secretion of excess acid that causes ulcers. The antihistamines in use at that time inhibited muscle contractions but not acid secretion. Black attacked the problem using the same strategy that worked in the development of the angina treatment—he sought a chemical that would inhibit histamine receptors, blocking the action of the hormone. Many thousands of compounds were tested. Finally in 1972 a partial histamine receptor antagonist was found, guanylhista-

mine. Unfortunately, it had serious side effects and clinical tests were halted in 1974. After further modification to the chemical structure, Black's group introduced cimetidine, now known as Tagamet (registered trademark), a successful ulcer drug.

Black himself left Smith Kline in 1973. He spent four years as head of the department of pharmacology at University College in London. Then in 1978 he returned to industry, accepting a post as director of therapeutic research at the Wellcome Research Laboratories in Kent. He remained there until 1984, when the lure of academia led him to King's College of Medicine and Dentistry, where he remains today.

Recognized with Nobel Prize

In 1988 Black was honored with the Nobel Prize in physiology or medicine, an award he shared with George Hitchings and Gertrude Elion, pharmaceutical researchers from Burroughs Wellcome in the United States. It is unusual for the prize to go to pharmacologists, and the award was a recognition of a truly outstanding contribution to medicine.

Black's success in designing new medicines may be attributed in part to the rational method he employed. Instead of randomly searching for chemicals with a physiological effect, he sought to understand the underlying biological processes and designed drugs that mimic life processes. To test his drugs, he designed "bioassays" that tested how well his drugs would work in the body.

Black is a shy man who does not like to publicize his personal life. He is said to enjoy reading beyond his scientific subjects, music, and the arts. He was married for many years; his wife, Hilary, died in 1987. The couple had one daughter, Stephanie. Black has received several awards and honorary degrees for his work. He was elected to the Royal Society of London in 1976 and received its Mullard Award in 1978. He received the Albert Lasker Clinical Medicine Award in 1976 and was elected a foreign associate of the U.S. National Academy of Sciences in 1991. He was knighted in 1981.

SELECTED WRITINGS BY BLACK:

Periodicals

"Drugs from Emasculated Hormones: The Principle of Syntopic Antagonism," *Science,* Volume 245, August 4, 1989, pp. 486–493.

SOURCES:

Books

Frank N. Magill, editor, *The Nobel Prize Winners: Physiology or Medicine,* Salem Press, 1991, pp. 1529–1537.

Periodicals

"The 'Pharmaceutical Toolmaker's' Rational Approach to Drug Design: An Appreciation of Sir James Black" in *Trends in Pharmacological Sciences,* December, 1988, pp. 435–437.

　　　　　　　—*Sketch by Karyn Hede George*

Elizabeth H. Blackburn
1948-

Australian-born American molecular biologist

Elizabeth H. Blackburn is a molecular biologist and biochemist who conducted ground-breaking research on deoxyribonucleic acid (DNA) and cell division that has provided a new line of inquiry into the chemical bases of life. Her discovery of a key enzyme, telomerase, which is necessary for chromosomes to make copies of themselves before cell division, has been applied to the study of chromosome behavior and of certain diseases, such as fungal infections and cancer. Widely recognized as one of the top researchers in her field, Blackburn is the first woman to head the Department of Microbiology and Immunology at the University of California, San Francisco.

Elizabeth Helen Blackburn was born in Hobart, Australia, on November 26, 1948. Her interest in medicine and biology was influenced early on by her parents, Harold Blackburn and Marcia (Jack), both of whom were physicians. Blackburn graduated from the University of Melbourne with a B.S. degree in 1970 and with a M.S. degree in 1971. She then attended Cambridge University in England, where she obtained a Ph.D. in molecular biology in 1975. Following her graduation, Blackburn came to the United States, drawn by both professional and personal reasons. At that time, Blackburn recognized that some of the most exciting opportunities and advances in her chosen field of molecular biology were being made in the U.S., which also had more physical and financial resources dedicated to science than most other countries. But Blackburn had another incentive to come to the U.S. While attending Cambridge, she had met her husband-to-be, John Sedat, an American postdoctoral researcher in biology. They married in 1975 and have one son, Benjamin.

Embarks on Pioneering Research of Chromosomes

In the U.S., Blackburn was awarded a fellowship in biology at Yale University, where she worked with Joseph Gall, who was conducting investigations into the functional aspects of chromosomes, especially their replication, expression, and structure. It was at Yale that Blackburn began her work with telomeres, which help chromosomes to remain stable and whole, thereby ensuring completion of the DNA replication cycle. In 1978, Blackburn accepted a position as an assistant professor at the University of California, Berkeley, where she was to make her ground-breaking discoveries concerning chromosomes and DNA.

Chromosomes are thread-like structures that occur in the cell nucleus and carry thousands of genes. Both chromosomes and genes are made of deoxyribonucleic acid, or DNA. A long molecule composed of two chains of nucleotides containing the sugar deoxyribose, DNA is the hereditary material in all organisms— except for some viruses. Blackburn was studying the telomeric DNA sequences and chromosomal structures in eukaryotes (one of two types of cells with a well-defined nucleus containing rod-like chromosomes) when she observed that the chromosomes appeared to shrink and grow in length. Intrigued, Blackburn set out to solve this biological riddle.

Without telomeres, daughter cells have shortened versions of the parent cells' chromosomes, and will eventually die. Blackburn found that, in order to survive, cells had developed a process to replace lost telomeres. Specifically, Blackburn discovered a key novel enzyme, telomerase, which is necessary for chromosomes to make complete copies of themselves before cell division. Telomerase is an unusual enzyme in that it contains ribonucleic acid, or RNA, which is involved in protein synthesis in all organisms and serves as the hereditary material in a few viruses. By first studying the single-celled protozoan, *Tetrahymena,* Blackburn removed its telomerase and found that the DNA progressively shortened until it died. She discovered that telomerase makes DNA from an RNA template. Known as a specialized type of reverse transcriptase enzyme, telomerase adds DNA onto the end of the *Tetrahymena* chromosome to preserve the chromosome, thus preventing eventual cell death due to broken chromosome ends, as well as ensuring the completion of cell division.

Blackburn has used her discoveries to make artificial chromosomes for studying chromosome behavior and telomere synthesis. Such studies on the RNA of telomerase could provide information on how some of the earliest forms of life evolved. A more speculative area of her continuing work has focused on whether further research into the role of telomerase in chromosome survival may be used to devise new therapies to fight fungal diseases and to provide new information on how cancerous cells divide. Based on her observations of the action of telomerase in *Tetrahymena,* Blackburn has conducted studies on whether drugs that block enzymes with similar structures will also work against telomerase in other organisms. This line of research focuses on determining whether fungi and other pathogens, as well as cancer cells, could be prevented from dividing by interfering with their telomere functions.

After 12 years at Berkeley, Blackburn joined the University of California, San Francisco, in 1990 as a professor of microbiology and immunology. In July 1993, she became the first woman chair of the University's Department of Microbiology and Immunology. Blackburn has obtained worldwide eminence in the field of molecular biology and was elected as a foreign associate to the National Academy of Sciences, one of the highest honors that can be accorded to a scientist in the United States. She has also won the National Academy of Sciences Award in Molecular Biology and is a fellow of the Royal Society, an independent organization in the United Kingdom.

SELECTED WRITINGS BY BLACKBURN:

Periodicals

(With Carol W. Greider) "Identification of a Specific Telomere Terminal Transferase Activity in *Tetrahymena* Extracts," *Cell,* Volume 43, 1985, pp. 405–413.

(With Guo-Liang Yu, John D. Bradley, and Laura D. Attardi) "*In vivo* Alteration of Telomere Sequences and Senescence Caused by Mutated *Tetrahymena* Telomerase RNAs," *Nature,* Volume 344, 1990, pp. 126–132.

SOURCES:

Blackburn, Elizabeth H., interview with David Petechuk conducted in 1993.

—*Sketch by David Petechuk*

Patrick Maynard Stuart Blackett
1897-1974
English physicist

Patrick Maynard Stuart Blackett was an English physicist with wide-ranging scientific and personal interests. He is best known for his improvements to the Wilson cloud chamber leading to important discoveries about fundamental particles

and cosmic rays. His contributions to the study of magnetism helped confirm continental drift theory. Throughout his career he was admired as an ingenious experimenter. Blackett was involved in British military defense strategies during World War II, but remained an outspoken critic of Western nuclear policies to the end of his life. For his work with the Wilson cloud chamber, Blackett was awarded the 1948 Nobel Prize in physics.

Blackett was born in London, England, on November 18, 1897, to Arthur Stuart and Caroline Frances Maynard Blackett. His grandfather had been Anglican vicar of Croydon, Surrey, and his father was a stockbroker. As a child he developed a strong interest in nature, especially birds. Intending a naval career, Blackett attended Osborne Royal Naval College and Dartmouth Royal College. He began active naval duty when World War I broke out in 1914.

After the war, while still in the navy, he studied for six months at Magdalene College, Cambridge. This experience, coupled with his sense that the navy was unlikely to pursue technological innovations, convinced him to pursue a scientific career. He left the service, graduating from Cambridge with a B.A. in physics in 1921. In 1924 Blackett married Costanza Bayon, with whom he had a daughter, Giovanna, and a son, Nicholas.

Cambridge's Cavendish Laboratory under **Ernest Rutherford**'s direction was one of the world's foremost centers of theoretical physics after World War I. When Blackett received a fellowship to continue studying there, Rutherford put him to work with the Wilson cloud chamber. A cloud chamber is a device which makes it possible to track the movements of fundamental particles. It consists of a transparent cylinder filled with supersaturated water vapor. The cylinder is set between the poles of an electromagnet. When charged particles are fired into it, the water vapor condenses on the resulting ions and creates trails which can be photographed.

Blackett made improvements to a cloud chamber he inherited from a previous student, and by 1924 was able to confirm Rutherford's prediction that one element could be transmuted into another artificially. By filling the cloud chamber with nitrogen gas and water vapor and bombarding the mixture with alpha particles (helium atoms), Blackett produced a hydrogen atom and an oxygen isotope.

In 1932 Blackett began a productive collaboration studying cosmic rays with the Italian physicist Giuseppe P. S. Occhialini. Cosmic rays were known to reach earth from extraterrestrial sources, but their exact composition was unclear. At the time, very few fundamental particles were postulated, and cosmic rays were thought to be high-energy photons, or light quanta.

Discovery of the Positron

Blackett and Occhialini further modified the cloud chamber by combining it with two Geiger counters so that they could obtain more continuous photographs of the particle tracks. After three years and many thousands of photographs, they were able to confirm the existence of the first antimatter particle, the positron, which had been predicted by **Carl Anderson**. The American physicist **Robert A. Millikan** had thought this positively charged particle was a proton, but Blackett and Occhialini showed that the particle had the same mass as an electron, and that positrons occurred in "showers" paired with equal numbers of electrons. Blackett also noted a curious high energy component of cosmic rays later found to be the meson.

In 1937 Blackett replaced W. L. Bragg at the University of Manchester and began to build a strong research facility there. With the onset of World War II, he was tapped by the British government to assist in defense measures. He served on the Tizard Committee from 1935 to 1936, and became Director of Naval Operational Research, where he made statistical analyses of the predicted results of differing military strategies.

Blackett, however, opposed Britain's efforts to develop its own nuclear weapons, and, though he supported the American bomb project, he was highly critical of Allied nuclear policy during and after the war. He decried the bombing of German civilians and the use of atomic bombs at Hiroshima and Nagasaki. In 1948 his book *Military and Political Consequences of Atomic Energy* appeared (published in America as *Fear, War and the Bomb*). That same year he was also awarded the Nobel Prize, but public hostility to his political views in the paranoid climate of the early Cold War overshadowed the acclaim accompanying the prize. Blackett did not return to public service until the election of a Labor government in 1964.

In the late 1940s, Blackett became interested in magnetism and the rotation of massive bodies. The idea that all rotating bodies generate magnetism had been discussed for many years, and if confirmed would have been a major new physical theory. Based on his study of existing observations of the magnetism of the sun, the Earth, and some stars, Blackett thought the hypothesis was plausible. In order to test it, he devised a magnetometer that was ten thousand times more sensitive than any previous such instrument. Ultimately Blackett decided the theory was incorrect, but his interest in geological magnetism continued. He investigated the history of changes in the earth's magnetic field and came to support the theory of continental drift, which postulates that the earth's continents are made of crustal plates that slowly move atop a layer of molten rock (magma). His magnetometer proved to be very useful in the study of the magnetic fields of small rocks, which eventually helped to confirm continental drift.

In 1965 Blackett became president of the Royal Society, which under his leadership became international in focus. Though he was happy to be welcomed back into the public mainstream, Blackett continued making his political views known, describing himself as a Fabian Socialist and advocating a closer solidarity between scientists and the working class. He also devoted several years to studying scientific, political, and economic conditions in India. Blackett's last academic post was at London's Imperial College of Science and Technology from 1953 to 1965. During his career he received numerous awards in addition to the Nobel Prize, including twenty honorary degrees. In 1969 he was made a life peer, Baron Blackett of Chelsea. Blackett died on July 13, 1974, in London.

SELECTED WRITINGS BY BLACKETT:

Books

The Atom and the Charter, Fabian/Gollancz (London), 1946.
Military and Political Consequences of Atomic Energy, Turnstile Press (London), 1948, published in the U.S. as *Fear, War, and the Bomb: Military and Political Consequences of Atomic Energy,* Whittlesey House (New York), 1949.

Periodicals

"Cosmic Rays: The 30th Kelvin Lecture," *Journal of the Institution of Electrical Engineers,* Volume 85, 1939.
"The Magnetic Field of Massive Rotating Bodies," *Philosophical Magazine,* Volume 40, 1949.

SOURCES:

Books

Browne, Laurie M., and Lillian Haddeson, editors, *The Birth of Particle Physics,* Cambridge University Press, 1983.
Lovell, Bernard, *P. M. S. Blackett: A Biographical Memoir,* The Royal Society, 1976.
Nobel Prize Winners, H. W. Wilson, 1987.
Nobel Prize Winners: Physics, Volume 2, Salem Press, 1989.
Snow, C. P., *The Physicists: A Generation that Changed the World,* Little, Brown, 1981.

Periodicals

Bromberg, Joan, "The Concept of Particle Creation before and after Quantum Mechanics," *Historical Studies in the Physical Sciences,* number 7, 1976, pp. 161–191.

New York Times, July 14, 1974.

—*Sketch by Valerie Brown*

David Blackwell
1919-
American mathematician

David Blackwell is a theoretical statistician noted for the rigor and clarity of his work. Blackwell's career has been dedicated to exploring and teaching topics in set theory and probability theory, and he has made important contributions to Bayesian statistical analysis (a method of incorporating observation into the estimate of probability), dynamic programming (the theory of multistage decision processes), game theory (the analysis of decision-making in situations of conflict or competition), and information theory (the application of probability to the storage and transmission of information). In 1979, Blackwell was awarded the von Neumann Prize by the Operations Research Society of America and the Institute of Management Science. In 1986, he received the R. A. Fisher Award from the Committee of Presidents of Statistical Societies, the most prestigious award in the field of statistics.

David Harold Blackwell was born in Centralia, Illinois, on April 24, 1919 to Grover Blackwell, a hostler for the Illinois Central Railroad, and Mabel (Johnson) Blackwell. Although two of the city's elementary schools were racially segregated, Blackwell attended one that was integrated. Blackwell was intrigued with games like checkers, and wondered about such questions as whether the first player could always win. His interest in mathematical topics increased in high school. The mathematics club advisor would challenge members with problems from the *School Science and Mathematics* journal and submit their solutions; Blackwell was identified three times in the magazine as having solved a problem, and one of his solutions was published.

After graduating from high school at the age of sixteen, Blackwell entered the University of Illinois in 1935. Through a family friend, he was assured of a job teaching elementary school upon graduation. However, he enjoyed his mathematics courses so much that he never got around to taking the education courses that were required for teacher certification. After his freshman year at the University of Illinois, Blackwell became concerned because his father was borrowing money to send him to college, and support-

ed himself with jobs such as washing dishes, waiting tables, and cleaning entomology lab equipment. Nonetheless, by taking summer courses and proficiency exams, Blackwell graduated in 1938, after only three years of enrollment.

Blackwell stayed at Illinois to earn a master's degree, shifting his aspirations to teaching at the high school or perhaps college level. As he noted in an interview with Donald J. Albers in *Mathematical People:* "During my first year of graduate work I knew that I could understand mathematics. . . . But whether I could do anything original I didn't know." Blackwell completed his master's degree in 1939, and received a fellowship from the university to work toward a doctorate. His dissertation, under American mathematician Joe Doob, was on Markov chains (in which the probability of each "state" in a sequence of events depends exclusively on what occurs in the preceding state; named after the Russian mathematician **Andrei Markov**). This research led to his first publications in 1942 and 1945. After receiving his Ph.D. in 1941, Blackwell was a Rosenwald Fellow for a year at the Institute for Advanced Study in Princeton. At the Institute, he became acquainted with the Hungarian mathematician **John von Neumann**, whose work provided the basis for game theory. In 1942, Blackwell launched a job search by writing to each of the 105 black colleges in the country, simply assuming that his role would be teaching at a black institution. The Polish Jewish mathematician Jerzy Neyman did interview Blackwell for a position at the University of California at Berkeley, where Neyman chaired the mathematics department. Neyman's support for hiring Blackwell, however, would not prevail until over a decade had passed. Southern University in Baton Rouge, Louisiana was the first of three schools to offer Blackwell a position, and he taught there for the 1942–1943 academic year. The following year, he was an instructor at Clark College in Atlanta. In 1944, Blackwell joined the faculty of Howard University in Washington, D.C., the most prestigious black institution of higher learning in the country. In this same year, Blackwell married Ann Madison; they have three sons and five daughters.

The focus of Blackwell's research shifted to statistics in 1945, when he heard the mathematician Abe Girshick lecture on sequential analysis (the analysis of an experiment that does not have a fixed number of trials, such that the analysis can respond to provisional outcomes). He was intrigued by the presentation, and later contacted Girshick with what he thought was a counterexample to a theorem presented in the lecture. That contact resulted in an enduring friendship and fruitful collaboration. Blackwell's first statistical paper, "On an Equation of Wald," appeared in 1946. A year later, Blackwell published what is perhaps his most significant contribution to modern statistics, "Conditional Expectation and Unbiased Sequential Estimation." In this paper, he helped establish what is now known as the Rao-Blackwell theorem, which relates to the sufficient statistic (whereby, in the study of the distribution of a population, a characteristic of the entire population can be determined if the distribution of a sample population is known). Blackwell was promoted to full professor at Howard in 1947, and served as head of the mathematics department until 1954.

Explores Problems in Game Theory

During the summers of 1948 to 1950, Blackwell developed an interest in game theory while working at the RAND Corporation headquarters in Santa Monica, California. In game theory, game-like situations are devised in which opposing "players" are assigned specific objectives (which can partially but not fully coincide) and capabilities. The decision-making options of these players are then statistically analyzed. Blackwell and a few colleagues, including Girshick, became interested in the theory of duels, a form of two-player zero-sum game. In zero-sum games, the players are assigned no common objectives, so the gain of one player involves an equivalent loss for the other. In the theory of duels, the initial condition concerns two players who advance toward each other, each holding a gun with one bullet. If one fires and misses, that player is required to continue walking toward the opponent. The problem is how a dueler should decide the optimal time to shoot. After developing the theory of that situation, Blackwell proposed and investigated the more challenging case where each gun was silent, such that a dueler doesn't know whether the opponent has fired unless that dueler has been hit.

The "conflict" situation in Blackwell's duelling game suggests the Cold War context within which game theory was developed. The RAND corporation, principally funded by the Air Force, was formed in the wake of World War II as a nonprofit consortium of scientists investigating problems with implications for military strategy and technology. Although Blackwell's own work remained at the theoretical level, his involvement with game theory began when an economist at RAND consulted him about determining funding recommendations for the Air Force in relation to the probability of war within a given period. The RAND corporation's fifteenth anniversary monograph describes game theory's utility for policy analysis in "the way it focuses attention on conflict with a live, dynamic, intelligent, and reacting opponent" and for tactical applications such the timing of missile fire, radar detection, and inspection for arms control.

Blackwell and Girshick subsequently coauthored *Theory of Games and Statistical Decisions*, first published in 1954. In the same year, Blackwell accepted a professorship in statistics at Berkeley, serving as chair of the department from 1956 to 1961. An important contribution of this period was applying game theory to topology (a branch of mathematics concerned with the properties of geometrical configurations that remain unaltered by certain forms of deformation) by finding a game theory proof for the Kuratowski Reduction Theorem (named after the Polish mathematician Kazimierz Kuratowski). During the 1973–1975 academic years, Blackwell directed the University of California Study Center for the United Kingdom and Ireland. In 1974, he gave the prestigious Rouse Ball Lecture at the University of Cambridge.

Blackwell was less interested in doing systematic research than in exploring problems that interested him personally. "I guess that's the way scholars *should* work," Blackwell commented in an interview with Morris H. Degroot in *A Century of Mathematics in America.* "Don't worry about the overall importance of the problem; work on it if it looks interesting. I think there's probably a sufficient correlation between interest and importance." Indeed, in addition to the military strategy context of game theory, Blackwell's work has found application in a variety of fields, including economics and accounting. Moreover, Blackwell's enthusiasm for mathematical knowledge was contagious, and he was a compelling and effective teacher. In his interview with Albers, Blackwell responded to a question about what made teaching fun: "Why do you want to share something beautiful with somebody else? It's because of the pleasure he will get, and in transmitting it you appreciate its beauty all over again."

Blackwell has been president of the Institute of Mathematical Statistics (1955) and the International Association for Statistics in the Physical Sciences, and is a member of the American Statistical Association, the National Academy of Sciences (the first black mathematician to be elected), and the American Academy of Arts and Sciences. He has also served on the Committee on National Statistics and the Mathematical Sciences Education Board. Blackwell, who retired from Berkeley in 1989, has been awarded honorary degrees by Howard, Harvard, and the National University of Lesotho, among other institutions.

SELECTED WRITINGS BY BLACKWELL:

Books

(With M. A. Girshick) *Theory of Games and Statistical Decisions,* Wiley, 1954.
Basic Statistics, McGraw-Hill, 1970.

Periodicals

"On An Equation of Wald," *Annual of Mathematical Statistics,* Volume 17, 1946, pp. 84–87.

"Conditional Expectation and Unbiased Sequential Estimation," *Annual of Mathematical Statistics,* Volume 18, 1947, pp. 105–110.

(With Ken Arrow and Abe Girshick) "Bayes and Minimax Solutions of Sequential Decision Problems, *Econometrica,* Volume 17, 1949, pp. 213–244.

"On Multi-Component Attrition Games," *Naval Research Logistics Quarterly,* Volume 1, 1954, pp. 210–216.

"An Analogue of the Minimax Theorem for Vector Payoffs," *Pacific Journal of Mathematics,* Volume 6, 1956, pp. 1–8.

"Infinite Games and Analytic Sets," *Proceedings of the National Academy of Science,* Volume 58, 1967, pp. 1836–1837.

SOURCES:

Books

A Century of Mathematics in America, Part III, American Mathematical Society, 1989, pp. 589–615 (reprinted from *Statistical Science,* February, 1986, pp. 40–53).

Mathematical People, Contemporary Books, 1985, pp. 18–32.

The Rand Corporation: The First Fifteen Years, Rand, 1963.

Other

Blackwell, David, interview with Loretta Hall conducted January 14, 1994.

—*Sketch by Loretta Hall*

Felix Bloch
1905-1983
Swiss-born American physicist

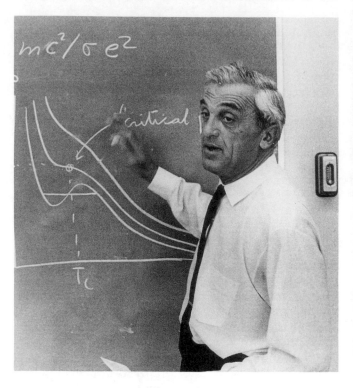

Felix Bloch

Felix Bloch made many important contributions to twentieth-century solid-state physics, including several theorems and laws named for him. He is best known for his development of nuclear magnetic resonance techniques, which allowed highly precise measurements of the magnetism of atomic nuclei and became a powerful tool in both physics and chemistry to analyze large molecules. Bloch was awarded a share of the 1952 Nobel Prize for his work in this field. Bloch was born in Zurich, Switzerland, on October 23, 1905, the son of Agnes Mayer Bloch and Gustav Bloch, a wholesale grain dealer. Bloch's early interest in mathematics and astronomy prompted his family to enroll the boy in an engineering course at the Federal Institute of Technology in Zurich in 1924. His first year's introductory course in physics revealed to Bloch what his true career would be. After completing his studies in the Division of Mathematics and Physics at the Institute in 1927, Bloch studied at the University of Leipzig in Germany under Professor **Werner Karl Heisenberg**, who was engaged in ground-breaking research in quantum mechanics. Bloch earned his Ph.D. in physics from Leipzig in 1928 with a dissertation on the quantum mechanics of electronics in crystals.

Leaves Hitler's Germany for the U.S.

Returning to Zurich, Bloch worked as a research assistant from 1928 to 1929. A Lorentz Fund fellowship allowed him to do research in 1930 at the University of Utrecht in the Netherlands, and later that year he returned to Leipzig to do more work with Heisenberg. An Oersted Fund fellowship took him to the University of Copenhagen in 1931, where he worked with **Niels Bohr**, director of the university's Institute for Theoretical Physics. From 1932 to 1933

Bloch once again returned to the University of Leipzig, where he was a lecturer in theoretical physics. After Adolf Hitler came to power, Bloch, who was Jewish, left Germany, lecturing at Paris's Institut **Henri Poincaré** and working with **Enrico Fermi** in Rome on a Rockefeller Fellowship. In 1934, Bloch accepted an invitation to join the faculty of Stanford University in the United States as an assistant professor of physics. He became a full professor in 1936 and remained at Stanford in that capacity, with a few leaves of absence, until his retirement in 1971, when he became professor emeritus.

European refugees like Bloch were a boon to physics in the United States, as many of them—again, like Bloch—were theorists who added valuable insight to the discoveries of U.S. experimental physicists. Practicing physics in the United States, in turn, was advantageous to Bloch and his fellow refugees because they could attain professorship, accumulate graduate students, and secure research money and facilities with much greater ease in the U.S. than they could in Europe.

Even before he came to the United States at the age of twenty-eight, Bloch had made significant contributions to theoretical physics. His concept of the conduction of electrons in metals, presented in his Ph.D. thesis, became the foundation of the theory of solids. In 1928 he developed the Bloch-Fouquet theorem, which specifies the form of wave functions for electrons in a crystal. (Fouquet was a mathematician who solved an identical abstract math problem many years earlier.) Functions that satisfy the conditions of the theorem are called Bloch functions by physicists, who use them in theoretically probing the nature of metals. Bloch also derived the Bloch-Grüneisen relationship in 1928, which gives a theoretical explanation for Eduard Grüneisen's law about the temperature dependence of the electric conductivity of metals. The Bloch T 3/2 law describes how magnetization in ferromagnetic material is dependent upon temperature, Bloch walls are the transition region between parts of a ferromagnetic crystal that are magnetized with different orientations, and the Bloch theorem eliminates some of the possible explanations for superconductivity. In 1932 Bloch developed the Bethe-Bloch expression, extending the work of Bohr and **Hans Bethe** on the slowing down of charged particles in matter. He also advanced the quantum theory of the electromagnetic field and, once in the United States, worked with Nordsieck to resolve the infrared problem in quantum electrodynamics. Bloch began contributing to scientific publications in 1927, while still a student.

Searches for Neutron's Magnetism

Soon after arriving at Stanford, Bloch's interest was drawn to the neutron, a nuclear particle that had been discovered in 1932 by **James Chadwick**. **Otto Stern**'s experiments in 1933 suggested that the neutron had a magnetic moment (magnetic strength). As he explained in his Nobel Prize address, Bloch was fascinated by the idea that an elementary particle with no electrical charge could have a magnetic moment. **Paul Dirac** had explained that the electron's magnetic moment resulted from its charge. Clearly, Bloch explained in his Nobel address, "the magnetic moment of the neutron would have an entirely different origin," and he set out to discover it. First, he needed direct experimental proof that the neutron's magnetic moment actually existed. He predicted in 1936 that the proof could be obtained by observing the scattering of slow neutrons in iron and that magnetic scattering of the neutrons would produce polarized neutron beams. These predictions were confirmed in 1937 by experimenters at Columbia University.

The next step was to measure the neutron's magnetic moment accurately. In 1939—the same year he became a naturalized American citizen—Bloch moved from theoretical to experimental physics and achieved that goal, working with **Luis Alvarez** and the cyclotron at the University of California at Berkeley. As Bloch described in his Nobel address, the two physicists passed a polarized neutron beam through an area with a weak, oscillating magnetic field superimposed on a strong, constant magnetic field. Bloch's experiments were halted by World War II, when he took a leave of absence from Stanford. He joined the Manhattan Project in 1941, whose goal was to produce an atomic bomb, and he worked on that goal at Los Alamos in New Mexico from 1942 to 1944, studying uranium isotopes. In 1944 he joined the Harvard University Radio Research Laboratory, where he was an associate group leader in counter-radar research.

The knowledge Bloch acquired of radio techniques at Harvard proved invaluable when he returned to his nuclear magnetic moment research at Stanford in 1945. **I. I. Rabi** had developed a technique in the 1930s for measuring nuclear magnetic moments through resonance, that is, by exciting atomic nuclei with electromagnetic waves and then measuring the frequencies of the signals the vibrating nuclei emit. Rabi's technique, however, worked only with rays of molecules, was not particularly precise, and vaporized the sample being studied. Working with William W. Hansen and Martin Packard, Bloch used the basic principle of magnetic resonance—the reorientation of nuclei after being excited—to develop a new method of "nuclear induction." In Bloch's technique, small containers of the material being studied (for Bloch, it was the hydrogen nuclei in water solutions) are placed in a strong electromagnetic field. A much weaker electromagnetic field controlled by radio frequencies then excites the nuclei. The nuclei, induced to spin by the electromagnetism, act like tiny radio transmitters, giving off signals detected by a receiver. These signals make it possible to measure the nuclear magnetic moment of an individual nucleus very precisely and provide a great deal of very accurate and valuable information about the nuclear particles emitting them. Precise measurements of magnetic moment and angle of momentum of individual nuclei made possible by Bloch's nuclear induction technique provided new knowledge about nuclear structure and behavior. Observations of changes in the frequency of the nuclear signals depending on the strength of the magnetic field aided the design of much improved magnetometers, especially useful in measuring the earth's magnetic field. Nuclear induction also provided new knowledge about the interaction of nuclear particles and about isotopes. Because magnetic moment is affected by surrounding charged electrons, and because each atom has a characteristic nuclear frequency, nuclear induction also yielded information about the atomic and molecular structure of solids, gases, and liquids—all without destroying the subject material, as Rabi's method had.

Work Recognized with Nobel Prize

Bloch announced his discovery in two papers published in *Physical Review* in 1946. The first, a paper titled "Nuclear Induction," described the theory of his technique and the second, written with Hansen and Packard and titled "The Nuclear Induction Experiment," described the mechanics of the experiment itself. At about the same time, **Edward Mills Purcell** of Harvard University and his colleagues H. C. Torrey and **Robert Pound** published the nearly identical results of their totally independent work with protons in paraffin. Purcell and his group called their technique "nuclear magnetic resonance absorption." Bloch and Purcell soon saw that their work, although it initially appeared different, was based on the same principle. The two men shared the 1952 Nobel Prize in physics for, in the words of the Nobel committee, their "development of high precision methods in the field of nuclear magnetism and the discoveries which were made through the use of these methods." Although the two had not worked together, Bloch described Purcell at the time as his "good friend" and a "distinguished scientist" and commented in the *New York Times* that he was very happy to be sharing the award with his colleague. "NMR," as Bloch's and Purcell's method came to be known, has become an invaluable tool of physics and analytic chemistry, revealing information about the molecular structure of complex compounds. The fact that NMR is nondestructive later led to its use as a sophisticated diagnostic tool in medicine. NMR scanners were developed that could produce images of human tissue that were both safer (because they did not use X rays) and more advanced that those produced by CAT scanners.

Bloch's prominence as a physicist was recognized by his election to the National Academy of Sciences in 1948. In April 1954 he was unanimously chosen to serve as the first director-general of CERN, the Conseil Européen de la Recherche Nucléaire (European Council of Nuclear Research) in Geneva, a twelve-nation project for research into peacetime uses of atomic energy. Again he left Stanford on a leave of absence, returning after 1955 to continue his research on nuclear and molecular structure and uses of NMR. He also worked with the theory of superconductivity.

Bloch married Lore C. Misch in Las Vegas in 1940. His wife was a professor's daughter and fellow German-born physicist who had immigrated to the United States a few years after Bloch. She had been working as a research associate at the Massachusetts Institute of Technology when the two met in New York at a professional society function. They had three sons, George, Daniel, and Frank, and a daughter, Ruth. In addition to his research, Bloch published many articles in professional journals, especially *Physical Review,* and he enjoyed piano playing, skiing, and mountain climbing. He held an endowed chair as Max H. Stein Professor of Physics at Stanford from 1961 until his retirement in 1971. He was also a fellow of the American Academy of Arts and Sciences and the American Physical Society. After retiring, Bloch returned to his birthplace of Zurich, where he died of a heart attack on September 10, 1983, at the age of seventy-seven.

SELECTED WRITINGS BY BLOCH:

Periodicals

"The Magnetic Moment of the Neutron," *Annual of the Institut Henri Poincaré,* Volume 8, 1938, pp. 63–78.

"Nuclear Induction," *Physical Review,* Volume 70, 1946, pp. 460–474.

(With W. W. Hansen and Martin Packard) "The Nuclear Induction Experiment," *Physical Review,* Volume 70, 1946.

"The Principle of Nuclear Induction" (Nobel address), *Science,* Volume 118, 1953, pp. 425–430.

"Dynamical Theory of Nuclear Induction, II," *Physical Review,* Volume 102, 1956, pp. 104–135.

SOURCES:

Books

Chodorow, Marvin, editor, *Felix Bloch and Twentieth-Century Physics,* William Marsh Rice University Press, 1980.

Kevles, Daniel J., *The Physicists: The History of a Scientific Community in Modern America,* Harvard University Press, 1987.

Magill, Frank N., *The Nobel Prize Winners: Physics,* Volume 1, 1901–1937, Salem Press, 1989.

Walecka, John Dirk, *Fundamentals of Statistical Mechanics, Manuscript and Notes of Felix Bloch,* Stanford University Press, 1989.

Periodicals

New York Times, November 7, 1952, pp. 1, 21; September 12, 1983, p. D13.

—*Sketch by Kathy Sammis*

Konrad Bloch

Konrad Bloch
1912-
German-born American biochemist

Konrad Bloch's investigations of the complex processes by which animal cells produce cholesterol have helped to increase our understanding of the biochemistry of living organisms. His research established the vital importance of cholesterol in animal cells and helped lay the groundwork for further research into treatment of various common diseases. For his contributions to the study of the metabolism of cholesterol, he was awarded the 1964 Nobel prize for Physiology or Medicine.

Konrad Emil Bloch was born on January 21, 1912 in the German town of Neisse (now Nysa, Poland) to Frederich (Fritz) D. Bloch and Hedwig Bloch. Sources list his mother's maiden name variously as Steiner, Steimer, or Striemer. After receiving his early education in local schools, Bloch attended the Technische Hochschule (technical university) in Munich from 1930 to 1934, studying chemistry and chemical engineering. He earned the equivalent of a B.S. in chemical engineering in 1934, the year after Adolf Hitler became chancellor of Germany. As Bloch was Jewish, he moved to Switzerland after graduating and lived there until 1936.

While in Switzerland, he conducted his first published biochemical research. He worked at the Swiss Research Institute in Davos, where he performed experiments involving the biochemistry of phospholipids in tubercle bacilli, the bacteria that causes tuberculosis.

In 1936, Bloch emigrated from Switzerland to the United States; he would become a naturalized citizen in 1944. With financial help provided by the Wallerstein Foundation, he earned his Ph.D. in biochemistry in 1938 at the College of Physicians and Surgeons at Columbia University, and then joined the Columbia faculty. Bloch also accepted a position at Columbia on a research team led by Rudolf Schoenheimer. With his associate David Rittenberg, Schoenheimer had developed a method of using radioisotopes (radioactive forms of atoms) as tracers to chart the path of particular molecules in cells and living organisms. This method was especially useful in studying the biochemistry of cholesterol.

Cholesterol, which is found in all animal cells, contains 27 carbon atoms in each molecule. It plays an essential role in the cell's functioning; it stabilizes cell membrane structures and is the biochemical "parent" of cortisone and some sex hormones. It is both ingested in the diet and manufactured by liver and intestinal cells. Before Bloch's research, scientists knew little about cholesterol, although there was speculation about a connection between the amount of cholesterol and other fats in the diet and arteriosclerosis (a buildup of cholesterol and lipid deposits inside the arteries).

While on Schoenheimer's research team, Bloch learned about the use of radioisotopes. He also developed, as he put it, a "lasting interest in intermediary metabolism and the problems of biosynthesis." Intermediary metabolism is the study of the biochemical breakdown of glucose and fat molecules and the creation of energy within the cell, which in turn fuels other biochemical processes within the cell.

Conducts Research on Cholesterol

After Schoenheimer died in 1941, Rittenberg and Bloch continued to conduct research on the biosynthesis of cholesterol. In experiments with rats, they "tagged" acetic acid, a 2-carbon compound, with radioactive carbon and hydrogen isotopes. From their research, they learned that acetate is a major component of cholesterol. This was the beginning of Bloch's work in an area that was to occupy him for many years—the investigation of the complex pattern of steps in the biosynthesis of cholesterol.

Bloch stayed at Columbia until 1946, when he moved to the University of Chicago to take a position as assistant professor of biochemistry. He stayed at Chicago until 1953, becoming an associate professor in 1948 and a full professor in 1950. After a year as a Guggenheim Fellow at the Institute of Organic Chemistry in Zurich, Switzerland, he returned to the United States in 1954 to take a position as Higgins Professor of Biochemistry in the Department of Chemistry at Harvard University. Throughout this period he continued his research into the origin of all 27 carbon atoms in the cholesterol molecule. Using a mutated form of bread mold fungus, Bloch and his associates grew the fungus on a culture that contained acetate marked with radioisotopes. They eventually discovered that the two-carbon molecule of acetate is the origin of all carbon atoms in cholesterol. Bloch's research explained the significance of acetic acid as a building block of cholesterol, and showed that cholesterol is an essential component of all body cells. In fact, Bloch discovered that all steroid-related substances in the human body are derived from cholesterol.

The transformation of acetate into cholesterol takes 36 separate steps. One of those steps involves the conversion of acetate molecules into squalene, a hydrocarbon found plentifully in the livers of sharks. Bloch's research plans involved injecting radioactive acetic acid into dogfish, a type of shark, removing squalene from their livers, and determining if squalene played an intermediate role in the biosynthesis of cholesterol. Accordingly, Bloch traveled to Bermuda to obtain live dogfish from marine biologists. Unfortunately, the dogfish died in captivity, so Bloch returned to Chicago empty-handed. Undaunted, he injected radioactive acetate into rats' livers, and was able to obtain squalene from this source instead. Working with Robert G. Langdon, Bloch succeeded in showing that squalene is one of the steps in the biosynthetic conversion of acetate into cholesterol.

Bloch and his colleagues discovered many of the other steps in the process of converting acetate into cholesterol. **Feodor Lynen**, a scientist at the University of Munich with whom he shared the Nobel Prize, had discovered that the chemically active form of acetate is acetyl coenzyme A. Other researchers, including Bloch, found that acetyl coenzyme A is converted to mevalonic acid. Both Lynen and Bloch, while conducting research separately, discovered that mevalonic acid is converted into chemically active isoprene, a type of hydrocarbon. This in turn is transformed into squalene, squalene is converted into anosterol, and then, eventually, cholesterol is produced.

Awarded Nobel Prize for Cholesterol Research

In 1964, Bloch and his colleague Feodor Lynen, who had independently performed related research, were awarded the Nobel Prize for Physiology or Medicine "for their discoveries concerning the mechanisms and regulation of cholesterol and fatty acid metabolism." In presenting the award, Swedish biochemist **Sune Bergström** commented, "The importance of the work of Bloch and Lynen lies in the fact that we now know the reactions that have to be studied in relation to inherited and other factors. We can now predict that through further research in this field ... we can expect to be able to do individual specific therapy against the diseases that in the developed countries are the most common cause of death." The same year, Block was honored with the Fritzsche Award from the American Chemical Society and the Distinguished Service Award from the University of Chicago School of Medicine. He also received the Centennial Science Award from the University of Notre Dame in Indiana and the Cardano Medal from the Lombardy Academy of Sciences the following year.

Bloch continued to conduct research into the biosynthesis of cholesterol and other substances, including glutathione, a substance used in protein metabolism. He also studied the metabolism of olefinic fatty acids. His research determined that these compounds are synthesized in two different ways: one comes into play only in aerobic organisms and requires molecular oxygen, while the other method is used only by anaerobic organisms. Bloch's findings from this research directed him toward the area of comparative and evolutionary biochemistry.

Bloch's work is significant because it contributed to creating "an outline for the chemistry of life," as E.P. Kennedy and F.M. Westheimer of Harvard wrote in *Science.* Moreover, his contributions to an understanding of the biosynthesis of cholesterol have contributed to efforts to comprehend the human body's regulation of cholesterol levels in blood and tissue. His work was recognized by several awards other than those mentioned above, including a medal from the Societe de Chimie Biologique in 1958 and the William Lloyd Evans Award from Ohio State University in 1968.

Bloch served as an editor of the *Journal of Biological Chemistry,* chaired the section on metabolism and research of the National Research Council's Committee on Growth, and was a member of the biochemistry study section of the United States Public Health Service. Bloch has also been a member of several scientific societies, including the National Academy of Sciences, to which he was elected in 1956, the American Academy of Arts and Sciences, and the American Society of Biological Chemists, in addition to the American Philosophical Society.

Bloch and his wife, the former Lore Teutsch, met in Munich and married in the United States in 1941. They have two children, Peter and Susan. Bloch is known for his extreme modesty; when he was awarded the Nobel Prize, the *New York Times* reported that he refused to have his picture taken in front of a sign that read, "Hooray for Dr. Bloch!" He enjoys skiing and tennis, as well as music.

SELECTED WRITINGS BY BLOCH:

Books

Lipide Metabolism, Wiley, 1960.

Periodicals

(With B. Berg and D. Rittenberg) "Biological Conversion of Cholesterol to Cholic Acid," *Journal of Biological Chemistry,* Volume 149, 1943, pp. 511–17.
(With Rittenberg), "The Utilization of AcOH for Fatty Acid Synthesis," *Journal of Biological Chemistry,* Volume 154, 1944, pp. 311–12.
(With R. G. Langdon) "Biosynthesis of Squalene," *Journal of Biological Chemistry,* Volume 200, 1953, pp. 129–34.

SOURCES:

Books

Modern Men of Science, McGraw-Hill, 1966, pp. 46–47.
Nobel Prize Winners, H.W. Wilson Company, 1987, p. 104.

Periodicals

Kennedy, E.P. and F. H. Westheimer, "Nobel Laureates: Bloch and Lynen Win Prize in Medicine and Physiology," *Science,* October 23, 1964, pp. 504–506.
New York Times, October 16, 1964, pp. 1 and 3.

—*Sketch by Donna Olshansky*

Katharine Burr Blodgett
1898-1979
American chemist

Katharine Burr Blodgett, the first woman to become a General Electric (GE) scientist, made several significant contributions to the field of industrial chemistry. The inventor of invisible, or non-reflecting, glass, Blodgett spent nearly all of her professional life working in the Schenectady, New York, GE plant. Although Blodgett's name has little household recognition, some of the techniques in surface chemistry that she and her supervisor and mentor **Irving Langmuir** developed are still used in laboratories; in addition, Blodgett's invisible glass is used extensively in camera and optical equipment today.

Blodgett was born on January 10, 1898 in Schenectady, New York, the town in which she spent most of her life. Her parents had moved to Schenectady earlier in the decade from their native New England when Blodgett's father, George Bedington Blodgett, became the head of the patent department at the GE plant opening up in town. Blodgett never knew her father, who died a few weeks before she was born. Left widowed with two small children, Blodgett's mother, Katharine Buchanan Burr, decided to move back east to New York City; three years later, she moved the family to France so that her children would be bilingual. After a few years of French schooling, Blodgett spent a year at an American school in Saranac Lake, New York, followed by travel in Germany. While in her mid-teens, Blodgett returned with her family to New York City where she attended the now-defunct Rayson School. Blodgett later won a scholarship to the all-women's Bryn Mawr College, where she excelled at mathematics and physics.

After college, Blodgett decided that a career in scientific research would allow her to further pursue both of these academic interests. During Christmas vacation of her senior year, she traveled to upstate New York to explore employment opportunities at the Schenectady GE plant. Some of George Blodgett's former colleagues in Schenectady introduced his daughter to research chemist Irving Langmuir. After conducting to a tour of his laboratory, Langmuir told

Katharine Burr Blodgett

eighteen-year-old Blodgett that she would need to broaden her scientific education before coming to work for him.

Hired As First Woman Researcher at General Electric

Taking Langmuir's advice, Blodgett enrolled in the University of Chicago in 1918 to pursue master's degree in science. Since she knew that a job awaited her in industrial research, Blodgett picked a related thesis subject: the chemical structure of gas masks. Upon graduating, Blodgett returned to GE, where Langmuir hired her as his assistant (the first female research scientist the company had ever employed). At the time, Langmuir—who had worked on vacuum pumps and light bulbs early in his GE career—had turned his attention to studying current flow under restricted conditions. Blodgett soon started working with Langmuir on these studies; between 1918 and 1924, the two scientists wrote several papers about their work. Blodgett's collaboration with the 1932 Nobel winner lasted until Langmuir's death in 1957.

Blodgett soon realized that she would need a doctoral degree if she wanted to further her career at GE. Six years after Blodgett started working for him, Langmuir arranged for his associate to pursue doctoral studies in physics at the Cavendish Laboratory at England's Cambridge University. Blodgett needed her mentor's help to gain admission to Cavendish because laboratory administrators hesitated to give one of

their few open spots to a woman. With Langmuir's endorsement, however, Blodgett was able to persuade the Cambridge physicists—including Nobel winner **Ernest Rutherford**—to allow her entrance. In 1926, Blodgett became the first woman to receive a doctorate in physics from Cambridge University.

When Blodgett returned to Schenectady, Langmuir encouraged her to embellish some of his earlier discoveries. First, he set her to work on perfecting tungsten filaments in electric lamps (the work for which he had received a patent in 1916). Langmuir later asked his protege to concentrate her studies on surface chemistry. In his own long-standing research on the subject, Langmuir had discovered that oily substances formed a one-molecule thin film when spread on water. By floating a waxed thread in front of stearic acid molecules, the scientist showed that this layer was created by the molecules' active ends resting on the water's surface. Blodgett decided to see what would happen if she dipped a metal plate into the molecules; attracted to the metal, a layer of molecules formed similar to that on the water. As she inserted the plate into the solution again and again, Blodgett noticed that additional layers—all one molecule—formed on top of one another. As the layers formed, different colors appeared on the surface, colors which could be used to gauge how many layers thick the coating was. Because this measurement was always constant, Blodgett realized she could use the plate as a primitive gauge for measuring the thickness of film within one micro-inch.

Not long after Blodgett's discovery, GE started marketing a more sophisticated version of her color gauge for use in scientific laboratories. The gauge was comprised of a sealed glass tube that contained a six-inch strip on which successive layers of molecules had formed. To measure the thickness of film few millionths of an inch thick, the user need only compare the color of film with the molecular grades. The gauge could measure the thickness of a transparent or semi-transparent substances within one to twenty millionths of an inch as effectively as much more expensive optical instruments, a very effective device for physicists, chemists, and metallurgists.

Work Leads to Development of Invisible Glass

Blodgett continued working in the field of surface chemistry. Within five years, she had found another practical application that stemmed from Langmuir's original studies: non-reflecting, or invisible, glass. Blodgett discovered that coating sheets of ordinary glass with exactly forty-four layers of one-molecule thick transparent liquid soap rendered the glass invisible. This overall layer of soap—four-millionths of an inch thick and one quarter the wave length of white light—neutralized the light rays coming from the bottom of the glass with those coming from the top so that no light was reflected. Since the transparent soap coating blocked only about one percent of the light coming in, invisible glass was perfect for use in optical equipment—such as cameras and telescopes—in which multiple reflecting lenses could affect performance.

Blodgett did not hold sole credit for creating invisible glass. Two days after she announced her discovery, two physicists at the Massachusetts Institute of Technology (MIT) publicized that they had found another method of manufacturing non-reflecting glass using calcium fluoride condensed in a vacuum. Both groups of scientists, however, were concerned that their coatings were not hard and permanent enough for industrial use. Using some Blodgett's insights, the MIT scientists eventually found a more appropriate method of producing invisible glass. Today, the fruits of Blodgett's discovery can be found in almost all lenses used in cameras and other optical equipment, as well as automobile windows, showcases, eyeglasses, picture frames, and submarine periscopes.

During World War II, GE moved away from studies such as the one that lead to invisible glass in favor of tackling problems with more direct military applications. Following suit, Blodgett temporarily shelved her glass research, but did not move far from the field of surface chemistry. Her wartime experiments lead to breakthroughs involving plane wing deicing; she also designed a smoke screen that saved numerous lives during various military campaigns.

Receives Garvan Medal for Women Chemists

When the war ended, Blodgett continued doing research that had military ramifications. In 1947, for example, she worked with the Army Signal Corps, putting her thin film knowledge to use by developing an instrument that could be placed in weather balloons to measure humidity in the upper atmosphere. As Blodgett worked, plaudits for her research continued to pour in. Along with receiving numerous honorary degrees, Blodgett won the 1945 Annual Achievement Award from the American Association of University Women for her research in surface chemistry. In 1951, she accepted the Francis P. Garvan Medal from the American Chemical Society; that same year, Blodgett also had the distinction of being the only scientist honored in Boston's First Assembly of American Women in Achievement. To top off the year, Schenectady decided to honor its own by celebrating Katharine Blodgett Day.

Blodgett spent all of her adult life in the home she bought overlooking her birthplace. She was active in civil affairs in her beloved Schenectady, serving as treasurer of the Travelers Aid Society. Blodgett summered in a camp at Lake George in upstate New York, where she could pursue her love of gardening.

She also enjoyed amateur astronomy, collecting antiques, and playing bridge with her friends. Blodgett died at her home on October 12, 1979, at the age of eighty-one.

SOURCES:

Books

Golemba, Beverly, *Lesser Known Women: A Biographical Dictionary,* Lynne Rienner, 1992.
O'Neill, Lois Decker, editor, *Women's Book of World Records and Achievements,* Anchor Press, 1979.
Rothe, Anne, and Evelyn Lohr, editors, *Current Biography,* H. W. Wilson, 1952, pp. 55–57.
Yost, Edna, *American Women of Science,* Frederick A. Stokes, 1943.

Periodicals

Clark, Alfred E., "Katharine Burr Blodgett, 81, Developer of Nonreflecting Glass," *New York Times,* October 19, 1979, p. 24.
McLaughlin, Kathleen, "Creator of 'Invisible Glass' Woman of Many Interests," *New York Times,* September 24, 1939, section 2, p. 4.

—Sketch by Shari Rudavsky

Nicolaas Bloembergen
1920-
Dutch-born American physicist

Overcoming the academic hardships imposed by the Nazi occupation in his native Netherlands, Nicolaas Bloembergen went on to conduct important work in the study of nuclear magnetic resonance (NMR), the study of the absorption or emission of energy by an atomic nucleus subjected to a strong magnetic field, during his graduate studies at Harvard University. Together with **Edward Mills Purcell** and **Robert Pound**, Bloembergen eventually coauthored one of the most cited papers on the subject, now known as "BPP" for its authors' initials. As a result of his work with NMR, Bloembergen was drawn to research on continuously-operating solid-state masers and their applications. In 1981, he was awarded a share of the Nobel Prize in physics for an extension of this work, the use of lasers for spectroscopic analysis of materials. In later years, Bloembergen turned his attention to another aspect of laser research, the field of nonlinear optics, a modern theory of the interaction between electromagnetic radiation and matter.

Nicolaas Bloembergen was born in Dordrecht, Netherlands, on March 11, 1920. His father was Auke Bloembergen, a chemical engineer, and his mother was the former Sophia Maria Quint, who had taught French before she was married. Young Nicolaas attended elementary school in Bilthoven, where his family had moved, and high school in Utrecht, the next largest town to Bilthoven. In 1938, Bloembergen graduated from high school and entered the University of Utrecht. He claims to have decided on a physics major because "it was the most difficult and challenging subject" for him.

The late 1930s were a difficult time to be starting a college education in northern Europe. World War II had just begun and by 1940 the Netherlands had fallen to invading German armies. Many universities were closed or their operations were restricted. Still, Bloembergen was able to complete his education at Utrecht, earning a Phil. Cand. (the equivalent of a B.A.) in 1941 and a Phil. Drs. (the equivalent of an M.A.) in 1943.

He remained in the Netherlands for the next two years, teaching himself quantum physics while evading the Nazis. By the war's end in 1945, however, he had decided to come to the United Sates and continue his graduate studies. He was accepted at Harvard University and was assigned to work with Purcell, one of the discoverers of nuclear magnetic resonance techniques. Bloembergen soon became engaged with NMR studies and, in 1948, coauthored "Relaxation Effects in Nuclear Magnetic Absorption" (BPP) with Purcell and Pound.

By the time BPP appeared in print, Bloembergen had returned to the Netherlands as a graduate student at the University of Leiden. He submitted much of the BPP research as part of his doctoral thesis, for which he was awarded his Ph.D. in 1948. He then returned to the United States and Harvard where he was successively a junior fellow in the Society of Fellows (1949–1951), professor of applied physics (1951–1957), Gordon McKay Associate Professor of Physics (1957—), Rumford Professor of Physics (1974–1980), and finally Gerhard Gade University Professor (1980—).

Applies NMR Principles to Laser Technology

One of the most exciting research topics of the 1950s was maser and laser technology. It was therefore no surprise that Bloembergen soon began to find ways in which his NMR research experience could be put to use in the design of masers and lasers. One of the first problems with which he dealt involved the development of a continuous beam laser.

The first masers built by **Nikolai G. Basov** and **Aleksandr Prokhorov** in Russia and by **Charles H. Townes** in the United States had a common disadvantage. They could all produce intense, monochromatic beams of microwave radiation, but they all had to rest briefly after the emission of a beam before a second pulse could be produced. The recovery period was needed in order to pump electrons from lower to higher energy levels in an atom, levels from which they could then be released to produce the next emission of radiation.

Bloembergen suggested a variation in maser design that would overcome this disadvantage. According to this scheme, electrons are distributed in three energy levels in an atom, each one higher than the next. In the first stage of this design, electrons fall from the highest level to the middle level and emit radiation. They then fall immediately from the middle to the lowest level, producing without pause another burst of radiation. Bloembergen's first working model of this three-stage maser consisted of a solid crystal of cobalt potassium cyanide in contrast to the gaseous masers originally designed by Basov, Prokhorov, and Townes.

Research Leads to New Theory of Nonlinear Optics

Over the next three decades, Bloembergen developed a number of applications of laser spectroscopy, beams that are directed at a material in order to study its properties. The beam excites electrons in the atoms and molecules of which the material is composed. Radiation re-emitted when electrons return to lower energy levels can then be studied to understand the structural characteristics of the material.

The use of laser spectroscopy demanded, however, an entirely new theoretical analysis of the way electromagnetic radiation interacts with matter. Traditionally, these interactions were thought to have a relatively straightforward relationship, with an increase of intensity of radiation having a linear change in effect. Bloembergen had found, though, that such effects are actually more complex than described by classical theory. His research has resulted in the development of a new approach to analyzing these interactions, an approach known as nonlinear optics. His success in this field was recognized in 1979 when he was awarded the Frederic Ives Medal of the American Optical Society.

In addition to the Ives Medal, Bloembergen has received a number of other honors including the Buckley Prize of the American Physical Society in 1958, the Ballantine Medal of the Franklin Institute in 1961, the U.S. National Medal of Science in 1974, the Lorentz Medal of the Royal Dutch Academy of Sciences in 1978, and the 1981 Nobel Prize in physics, shared with **Arthur L. Schawlow** and **Kai M. Siegbahn**.

Bloembergen was married to Huberta D. Brink, a native of Indonesia whom he met in the Netherlands in 1948. The Bloembergens have two daughters, Antonia and Juliana, and a son, Brink. Bloembergen, who became a U.S. citizen in 1958, lists hiking, skiing, and tennis among his hobbies.

SELECTED WRITINGS BY BLOEMBERGEN:

Books

Nuclear Magnetic Relaxation, M. Nijhoff, 1948.
Nonlinear Optics, Benjamin, 1965.

Periodicals

"Relaxation Effects in Nuclear Magnetic Absorption," *Physical Review,* Volume 73, 1948, pp. 679–712.
"Proposal for a New-Type Solid-State Maser," *Physical Review,* Volume 104, 1956, pp. 324–327.

SOURCES:

Books

McGraw-Hill Modern Scientists and Engineers, Volume 10, McGraw-Hill, 1980, pp. 107–108.
Nobel Prize Winners, H. W. Wilson, 1987, pp. 106–108.
Weber, Robert L., *Pioneers of Science: Nobel Prize Winners in Physics,* American Institute of Physics, 1980, pp. 273–274.

Periodicals

"Frederic Ives Medalist for 1979," *Journal of the Optical Society of America,* December, 1980, pp. 1423–1428.
"Nobel Physics Prize for Bloembergen, Schawlow, and Siegbahn," *Physics Today,* December, 1981, pp. 17–20.
Stoicheff, Boris P., "The 1981 Nobel Prize in Physics," *Science,* November 6, 1981, pp. 629–633.

—Sketch by David E. Newton

Guion S. Bluford
1942-
American engineer and astronaut

Guion S. Bluford, the first African American astronaut to fly in space, participated in four shuttle missions. An aerospace engineer and Air Force pilot, Bluford performed a variety of experiments in life sciences, materials research, and other disciplines during his shuttle flights. In recognition for his service as an astronaut, he was awarded the NASA Exceptional Service Medal, the 1991 Black Engineer of the Year Award, and eleven honorary doctorates.

Guion S. Bluford, Jr., was born in Philadelphia, Pennsylvania, on November 22, 1942, the oldest of three sons. His father, Guion S. Bluford, Sr., was a mechanical engineer and inventor and his mother, Lolita Harriet (Brice) Bluford, was a special education teacher. Devout Christian Scientists, Bluford's parents encouraged him to study, to be determined, and to have faith in himself as well as God. Bluford developed an early interest in aviation, earning a reputation as the best model airplane builder in his neighborhood. By the time he entered high school, he had already decided he wanted a military career and an engineering degree. Graduating in 1960, Bluford enrolled at Pennsylvania State University, where he concentrated on engineering studies and joined the Air Force Reserve Officer Training Corps. Bluford also volunteered for ROTC flight training, in large part because he felt having hands-on experience as a pilot would make him a better engineer.

Flying and Research Lead to Astronaut Program

Bluford graduated in 1964 with a bachelor's degree in aerospace engineering. That same year he married Linda Tull, an accountant, with whom he would have two sons, Guion Stewart III and James Trevor Bluford. Second Lieutenant Bluford then entered air force flight training at Williams Air Force Base in Arizona, moving on to advanced training in the F-4C Phantom fighter-bomber a year later. In 1967, Bluford's 557th Tactical Fighter Squadron was sent to Vietnam, where he flew 144 combat missions. After his tour Bluford served as an instructor pilot, logging thirteen hundred hours as an instructor in the supersonic T-38 trainer at Sheppard Air Force Base in Texas. He also served as an executive support officer in the same unit until he applied and was accepted to the Air Force Institute of Technology (AFIT) at Wright-Patterson Air Force Base in Ohio. There he earned his master's degree in 1974 and went to work as a staff development engineer at the Air Force Flight Dynamics Laboratory. Serving in the

Guion S. Bluford

aeromechanics division as deputy for advanced concepts, he later became chief of the aerodynamics and airframe branch. In 1978, Bluford received his doctorate from AFIT in aerospace engineering with a minor in laser physics. Bluford considered his dissertation, "A Numerical Solution of Supersonic and Hypersonic Viscous Flow Fields Around Thin Planar Delta Wings," to be his most important contribution to engineering.

Holding the rank of major, Bluford applied for mission specialist astronaut training at the Lyndon B. Johnson Space Center and was among the thirty-five astronaut candidates selected in January, 1978. Group 8, as NASA called Bluford and his classmates, included two other black men and the first women chosen for American space flight.

Becomes First African American in Space

Publicity over the selection of Bluford and the other minority candidates was intense, and when he was selected to fly the eighth space shuttle mission in April, 1982, the attention increased even more dramatically. Aware of his place in history, Bluford did not dwell on it publicly and played down his role as the first black U.S. astronaut in space (while Bluford was to be the first African American, a black Cuban had flown earlier as a "guest cosmonaut" in a Soviet spacecraft). Bluford coped with the spotlight by focusing on what he saw as most important: doing a good job and accomplishing the work of the mission.

Bluford's first flight, on the shuttle *Challenger,* began on August 30, 1983, with a spectacular nighttime takeoff. On that mission Bluford ejected the main payload, a multipurpose satellite for India called INSAT–1B. He also operated the Continuous Flow Electrophoresis System, studying ways to isolate proteins from living cells in a weightless environment for medical research. The successful flight resulted in numerous honors for Bluford, including the Ebony Black Achievement Award and an NAACP Image Award. Accepting speaking engagements across the country, he encouraged young people to be dedicated and persevering in pursuit of their dreams.

Bluford flew for the second time in October, 1985, as part of the largest crew ever to fly in space. He and seven other astronauts—again aboard the *Challenger*—spent a week in orbit. This was the twenty-second shuttle flight, designated STS 61-A. The crew's main task was to operate the German-built Spacelab module, which filled most of the cargo bay with pressurized workspace, in effect turning the shuttle into a short-duration space station. There were seventy-six experiments on the agenda, encompassing the fields of materials solidification, life science, fluid physics, medicine, and navigation. After that flight, Bluford became the Astronaut Office's specialist on all issues involving Spacelab missions and space shuttle pallet experiments.

Bluford returned to space on April 28, 1991. This time, he rode the orbiter *Discovery* on the first dedicated military shuttle mission. Bluford and his crewmates operated a variety of Strategic Defense Initiative experiments on ballistic missile tracking. They also studied the environment of orbital space and of the Earth below, and launched a classified experimental satellite. Bluford's fourth and final spaceflight, lasting from December 2 to December 9, 1992, was another military mission, which deployed a classified satellite payload and also performed a variety of experiments for the Defense Department and NASA. Subsequently, Bluford served as lead astronaut of the Space Station Operations Group, specializing in defining and presenting the astronauts' point of view on all aspects of space station design and operation.

Bluford left NASA and the Air Force in July, 1993, having logged 688 hours in space in addition to 5,200 hours in jet aircraft. He then became the vice president and general manager of Engineering Services Division of NYMA, Inc., in Greenbelt, Maryland. In this position, Bluford directs engineers, scientists, and technicians who provide engineering support to NASA's Lewis Research Center. Their research encompasses aircraft propulsion, aircraft structures, and space experiments.

SOURCES:

Books

Furniss, Tim, *Space Shuttle Log,* Jane's, 1986.
Hawthorne, Douglas B., *Men and Women of Space,* Univelt, 1992.

Periodicals

Ebony, March, 1979, pp. 54–62.
Leavy, Walter, "A Historic Step Into Outer Space," *Ebony,* November, 1983, pp. 162–70.

Other

Bluford, Guion S., Jr., interview with Matthew A. Bille conducted January 25, 1994.
Bluford, Guion S., Jr., curriculum vitae, June, 1993.

—*Sketch by Matthew A. Bille*

Baruch Samuel Blumberg

Baruch Samuel Blumberg
1925-

American research physician

When Baruch Samuel Blumberg was notified on October 14, 1976 that he was a co-winner of the Nobel Prize for physiology or medicine, he made a humorous and low-key comment to the *New York Times:* "I'm especially pleased that someone from Philadelphia won. It's appropriate in the Bicentennial year and makes up in part for the Phillies not making it to the World Series." But there was nothing low-key about the research Blumberg had done to win the prize. In 1963 he had discovered a protein in the blood of Australian Aborigines, the so-called Australia antigen, which he determined to be part of the hepatitis B virus. This discovery has led to the introduction of blood screening programs as well as a successful vaccine against this disease, which has a mortality rate of up to 15 per cent.

Blumberg was born on July 28, 1925, in New York City, one of three children of Meyer Blumberg, a lawyer, and Ida Simonoff. After graduating in 1943 from Far Rockaway High School in Far Rockaway, New York, Blumberg enlisted in the Navy. He was assigned to study physics at Union College in Schenectady, where he earned a B.S. in 1946, and then enrolled at Columbia University graduate school in physics and mathematics. But Blumberg had become more and more interested in medical and biochemical

matters, and partly at his father's urging he entered Columbia's College of Physicians and Surgeons in 1947. Four years later he earned his M.D. and completed his internship and residency at Bellevue and Presbyterian hospitals in New York. It was during this period that he met Jean Liebesman, another medical student, whom he married in 1954; they would have four children. Blumberg won a fellowship to Balliol College, Oxford University, in 1955, working toward a Ph.D. in biochemistry. His specific field of interest was hyaluronic acid, one of the major constituents of connective tissue, synovial fluid and the vitreous humor of the eyes. By 1957 he had earned his doctorate and was also hard at work on research which would later win him the Nobel Prize.

Seeks Clues to Variation in Disease Susceptibility

As a medical student working in Surinam (then Dutch Guiana), South America, Blumberg had become interested in the manner in which various ethnic groups respond to disease and infection. He began to ask himself a very simple question: why do some people get sick while others do not? It was this question that increasingly guided his work, even while at Oxford. Epidemiologists had already speculated that an answer to this question might lie in the blood, and more specifically in the variations of genetically reproduced proteins in the blood. To study such polymorphisms would necessitate a large variety of blood samples from around the world. Blumberg, on his return from England, took the perfect job for such research as chief of the geographic medicine and genetics section of the National Institutes of Health (NIH). From 1957 to 1964, his travels took him from Alaska, to Africa, the Pacific, South America, Europe and Australia. Often he journeyed to remote areas accompanied only by his blood drawing and testing equipment. It was during this time as well that Blumberg became interested in anthropology.

Soon Blumberg and former Balliol colleague Anthony C. Allison were studying blood samples from patients who had received multiple transfusions, such as hemophiliacs, focusing on the antigen/antibody connection. An antigen is the substance that causes the body to produce a chemical defense, or antibody, against a foreign substance. Their reasoning was that people who had received numerous transfusions might prove to be excellent test cases, producing antibodies other than those they had inherited. The serum of such patients would therefore provide a wide variety of antibody responses once they were tested against other serum samples. Blumberg hypothesized that antibodies created in the serum of hemophiliacs and other transfusion donors would react with unknown antigens in the homogeneous serum of donors from disparate geographic areas.

In 1963, the serum of a New York hemophiliac reacted with that of an Australian Aborigine, and Blumberg labeled the detected antigen the Australia antigen, Au. Initially he and other researchers thought Au, an antigen rare in North America but prevalent in Asia and Africa, might be an indicator of leukemia, because it appeared in many patients suffering from that disease. Later research dealt with groups of patients with Down's syndrome, who also show a high incidence of the antigen.

In 1964 Blumberg left NIH for the Institute of Cancer Research of the Fox Chase Cancer Center in Philadelphia, where he accepted the position of associate director of clinical research. He continued his researches on the Australia antigen, and in 1966 he discovered the link between Au and hepatitis B. A Down's patient who had previously tested negative for Au suddenly tested positive, and soon developed hepatitis, as did another with a sudden positive test for the antigen. Researchers in Japan and New York began a long series of controlled experiments which finally established the connection between hepatitis B and Au. That same year, the Australia antigen was identified as part of the B virus itself and was renamed HBsAg (hepatitis B virus antigen).

Heralds New Era in Hepatitis Research

The first practical result of Blumberg's discovery of HBsAg was a blood test which he and others developed to detect and screen out hepatitis B carriers — of which there are approximately one hundred

million worldwide, and perhaps one million in the United States — from blood donors, thereby securing a safe blood supply. As early as 1969, such screening was underway at blood banks worldwide. After the American Association of Blood Banks ordered all of its members to use the hepatitis test in 1971, the incidence of hepatitis after transfusions dropped by 25 per cent. In the 1970s, Blumberg, along with Irving Millman, developed a vaccine from the sera of patients with HBsAg which prevents hepatitis B infection. Since becoming commercially available in 1982, it has been widely and successfully used, especially among high-risk professionals such as healthcare workers. Another spin-off from Blumberg's work is research indicating that chronic infection with hepatitis B virus may be a precursor of cancer of the liver, the most common form of cancer in males in parts of Asia, India and Africa. The discovery of a vaccine against the disease may therefore reduce the risk of primary liver cancer. Mass vaccinations of newborns have been undertaken in some Asian and African nations to that effect.

Blumberg shared the Nobel Prize for physiology or medicine in 1976 with Dr. D. Carleton Gajdusek of the National Institute for Neurological Diseases, "for their discoveries concerning new mechanisms for the origin and dissemination of infectious diseases." They shared the $160,000 stipend equally. This is only one of a plethora of awards and honors Blumberg has won. Others include the Eppger Prize from the University of Freiburg (1973), the Distinguished Achievement Award in Modern Medicine (1975), the Gairdner Foundation International Award (1975), the Governor's Award in the Sciences from the Commonwealth of Pennsylvania (1988), and the Gold Medal Award from the Canadian Liver Foundation (1990).

In 1977 Blumberg became a professor of medicine and anthropology at the University of Pennsylvania; soon thereafter he was named vice president of population oncology at the Fox Chase Institute in Philadelphia. He has continued his researches in antigen systems as well as his studies in a wide range of other fields, including virology, physics, history, anthropology and philosophy. With the advent of the AIDS epidemic, Blumberg's antigen/antibody research has taken on new importance. After a long and distinguished career at Fox Chase, Blumberg returned to Oxford as master of Balliol College, becoming, at 64, the first scientist and first American ever to hold that prestigious chair.

Blumberg, known to friends, family and colleagues as Barry, is an avid movie-goer and reader. He also plays squash and enjoys running, hiking, swimming, and canoeing, in addition to his hobbies of carpentry and photography.

SELECTED WRITINGS BY BLUMBERG:

Books

(Editor) *Conference on Genetic Polymorphisms and Geographic Variations in Diseases. Proceedings,* Grune, 1962.
Primary Hepatocellular Carcinoma and Hepatitis B Virus, [Chicago], 1982.
(With Irving Millman and Toby Eisenstein) *Hepatitis B,* Plenum, 1984.

Periodicals

"A New Antigen in Leukemia Sera," *Journal of the American Medical Association,* Volume 191, 1965, pp. 541–46.
"Relation of Australia Antigen to Virus of Hepatitis," *Bulletin of Pathology,* Volume 10, 1969, p. 164.
"Hepatitis B Virus and the Carrier Problem," *Social Research,* autumn, 1988, pp. 401–12.

SOURCES:

Books

Fox, Daniel M., and others, editor, *Nobel Laureates in Medicine or Physiology,* Garland Publishing, 1990, pp. 56–59.
McGraw-Hill Modern Scientists and Engineers, McGraw-Hill, 1980, pp. 108–10.

Periodicals

Melnick, Joseph L., "The 1976 Nobel Prize in Physiology or Medicine," *Science,* November 26, 1976, pp. 927–28.
New York Times, October 15, 1976, p. 13.

—*Sketch by J. Sydney Jones*

Aage Bohr
1922-
Danish physicist

Aage Bohr followed his father, the eminent physicist **Niels Bohr**, into the field of theoretical physics. Bohr's father was director of the Institute for Theoretical Physics in Copenhagen and instrumental in the development of the Manhattan Project (the U.S. secret program to build the atom bomb during World War II), which the younger Bohr also contributed to as his father's secretary and lab assistant. In the late 1940s and 1950s, Aage Bohr conducted his own research on the structure of the atomic nucleus. With his collaborators, **James Rainwater** and **Ben R. Mottelson**, Bohr developed the collective model of nuclear matter. For their work, the three scientists were awarded the Nobel Prize in physics in 1975.

Aage Neils Bohr was born in Copenhagen on June 19, 1922, the fourth son of Margrethe Nørlund Bohr and Niels Bohr. His early education took place at the Sortedam Gymnasium, as well as informally at his father's Institute for Theoretical Physics, where he met many of the world's leading names in physics. Bohr's physics education was interrupted by the invasion of Denmark by German forces in 1940. The Jewish Bohr family was forced to flee their country to neutral Sweden, and later England, before coming to the United States. The younger Bohr accompanied his father to the United States in 1943, serving as his secretary and lab assistant at the Los Alamos Scientific Laboratory in New Mexico. After World War II, the family returned to Denmark, where Bohr resumed his education at the University of Copenhagen. He received his M.S. degree from the University of Copenhagen in 1946 and his Ph.D. in 1954. He was married in 1950 to Marietta Bettina Soffer. They had two sons and one daughter.

Synthesis Provides a New Atomic Model

During his graduate studies, Bohr accepted a research position at the Institute for Theoretical Physics, but returned to the United States in 1949, where he conducted research at Columbia University on the hyperfine structure of deuterium ("heavy hydrogen") and began working with James Rainwater on the structure of the atomic nucleus. Working together at Columbia to understand the basic makeup of the atomic nucleus, Bohr and Rainwater came to the conclusion that a new model was needed to adequately explain the structural and functional properties of the nucleus. The two model theories previously put forth directly contradicted each other, and over the years the soundness of both had been challenged. One of those models, the liquid-drop model, was developed by Bohr's father in 1936. This model proposed that protons and neutrons (the nucleons) are held together by nuclear forces comparable to the way molecules attract each other in a drop of water. The second and opposing model, the shell model, held that the nucleons move in concentric orbits, or shells, in much the same manner electron shells do in an atom. The shell model, put forth by **Maria Goeppert-Mayer** and **J. Hans D. Jensen** in 1949, also posited that the sum of the forces of the nucleons resulted in a spherical "force field." Later experiments challenged this theory by showing that in cases where the outermost shell was incomplete, the charge distribution around the nucleus was nonspherical. Rainwater's contribution to the existing body of research was to suggest that interactions between particles in an incomplete outer shell and those deep within the nucleus might cause the nucleus to become distorted.

Bohr expanded this research in a collaboration with Benjamin Mottelson when he returned to the Institute for Theoretical Physics in Copenhagen in 1950. Acting on Rainwater's hypothesis, Bohr, working with Mottelson, created a new model for describing nuclear structure. This model, called the collective model, was a synthesis of the liquid and shell models. The new model showed that the surface of the nucleus does indeed act like a liquid drop, but that the shell structure is subject to centrifugal distortions that account for some nuclei being spherical and some oblong. According to H. Feshbach, writing on the 1975 Nobel Prize in physics in *Science,* "It was the resolution of these apparently irreconcilable results . . . that led to the generation of a unified picture of the nucleus which provides a basis for the understanding of the low lying [low energy or ground] states of all nuclei, one of the great achievements of modern physics."

The trio of Bohr, Mottelson, and Rainwater received the 1975 Nobel Prize in physics for what the Royal Swedish Academy of Sciences described as the "discovery of the connection between collective motion and particle motion in the atomic nucleus and the development of the theory of the structure of the atomic nucleus based on this connection," as reported in a *New York Times* article. Speaking to the Nobel audience more than twenty years after this research was conducted, Bohr noted that the results of the research had influenced a variety of scientific fields "ranging from celestial mechanics to the spectra of elementary particles," as quoted in *Nobel Prize Winners.* This statement typified Bohr's scientific vision. Throughout his career, he advocated cooperative scientific research on an international level. Feshback noted in his *Science* article that following their Nobel Prize-winning work on atomic structure, "Bohr and Mottleson acted as an intellectual center orchestrating in a very direct way the experimental programs at many of the nuclear laboratories throughout the world, both with regard to their direction and to the interpretation of the results obtained."

At the time of his father's death in 1962, Bohr had assumed the directorship at the Institute for Theoretical Physics, then renamed the Niels Bohr Institute. He remained there in this administrative capacity until 1970, when his desire to resume active research caused him to relinquish the post. He returned to the administrative side of his field when he became director of the Nordic Institute for Theoretical Atomic Physics (Nordita) in 1975. Bohr continued to do theoretical research until his retirement

from Nordita in 1981. Bohr's first wife died in 1978; he married Bente Meyer Scharff in 1981.

In addition to the Nobel Prize, Bohr has received many other honors from his peers during his career. They include the Dannie Heineman Prize in 1960, the Pope Pius XI Medal in 1963, the Atoms for Peace Award in 1969, the Ørsted Medal in 1970, the Rutherford Medal in 1972, the John Price Wetherill Medal in 1974, and the Ole Rømer Medal in 1976. He has been a member of six academies of science throughout Europe, the National Academy of Science in the United States, and has held membership in many other professional associations. He has received honorary degrees from the Universities of Oslo, Heidelberg, Trondheim, Manchester, and Uppsala.

SELECTED WRITINGS BY BOHR:

Books

Rotational States of Atomic Nuclei, Munksgaard, 1954.
(With Benjamin Mottelson) *Collective and Individual-Particle Aspects of Nuclear Structure,* Munksgaard, 1957.
(With Benjamin Mottleson) *Nuclear Structure,* 2 volumes, W. A. Benjamin, 1969–1975.

Periodicals

"On the Quantization of Angular Momenta in Heavy Nuclei," *Physical Review,* Volume 81, January 1, 1951, pp. 134–138.
"Nuclear Magnetic Moments and Atomic Hyperfine Structure," *Physical Review,* Volume 81, February 1, 1951, pp. 331–335.

SOURCES:

Books

Wasson, Tyler, editor, *Nobel Prize Winners,* H. W. Wilson, 1987, pp. 110–111.

Periodicals

Feshbach, H. "The 1975 Nobel Prize for Physics," *Science,* November 28, 1975, pp. 868–870.
Sullivan, Walter, "Three Physicists Unravel Mystery," *New York Times,* October 18, 1975, p. 15.
Webster, Bayard, "Sketches of the Nobel Physicists," *New York Times,* October 18, 1975, p. 15.

—Sketch by Jane Stewart Cook

Niels Bohr
1885-1962
Danish physicist

Niels Bohr

Niels Bohr received the Nobel Prize in physics in 1922 for the quantum mechanical model of the atom that he had developed a decade earlier, the most significant step forward in scientific understanding of atomic structure since English physicist John Dalton first proposed the modern atomic theory in 1803. Bohr founded the Institute for Theoretical Physics at the University of Copenhagen in 1920, an Institute later renamed for him. For well over half a century, the Institute was a powerful force in the shaping of atomic theory. It was an essential stopover for all young physicists who made the tour of Europe's center of theoretical physics in the mid-twentieth century. Also during the 1920s, Bohr thought and wrote about some of the fundamental issues raised by modern quantum theory. He developed two basic concepts, the principles of complementarity and correspondence, that he said must direct all future work in physics. In the 1930s, Bohr became interested in problems of the atomic nucleus and contributed to the development of the liquid-drop model of the nucleus, a model used in the explanation of nuclear fission.

Niels Henrik David Bohr was born on October 7, 1885, in Copenhagen, Denmark. He was the second of three children born to Christian and Ellen Adler Bohr. Bohr's early upbringing was enriched by a nurturing and supportive home atmosphere. His mother had come from a wealthy Jewish family involved in banking, government, and public service. Her father, D. B. Adler, had founded the Commercial Bank of Copenhagen and the Jutland Provincial Credit Association. Bohr's father was a professor of physiology at the University of Copenhagen. His closest friends met every Friday night to discuss events, so that, as a young boy, Bohr "learned much from listening to these conversations," according to J. Rud Nielsen in *Physics Today.*

Bohr became interested in science at an early age. His biographer, Ruth Moore, has written in her book *Niels Bohr: The Man, His Science, and the World They Changed* that as a child he "was already fixing the family clocks and anything else that needed repair." Bohr received his primary and secondary education at the Gammelholm School in Copenhagen. He did well in his studies, although he was apparently overshadowed by the work of his younger brother Harald, who later became a mathematician. Both brothers were also excellent soccer players.

On his graduation from high school in 1903, Bohr entered the University of Copenhagen, where he majored in physics. He soon distinguished himself with a brilliant research project on the surface tension of water as evidenced in a vibrating jet stream. For this work he was awarded a gold medal by the Royal Danish Academy of Science in 1907. In the same year, he was awarded his bachelor of science degree, to be followed two years later by a master of science degree. Bohr then stayed on at Copenhagen to work on his doctorate, which he gained in 1911. He thesis dealt with the electron theory of metals and confirmed the fact that classical physical principles were sufficiently accurate to describe the qualitative properties of metals but failed when applied to quantitative properties. Probably the main result of this research was to convince Bohr that classical electromagnetism could not satisfactorily describe atomic phenomena. The stage had been set for Bohr's attack on the most fundamental questions of atomic theory.

Bohr decided that the logical place to continue his research was at the Cavendish Laboratory at Cambridge University. The director of the laboratory at the time was English physicist **J. J. Thomson**, discoverer of the electron. Only a few months after arriving in England in 1911, however, Bohr discovered that Thomson had moved on to other topics and was not especially interested in Bohr's thesis or ideas. Fortunately, however, Bohr met English physicist **Ernest Rutherford**, then at the University of Manchester, and received a much more enthusiastic response. As a result, he moved to Manchester in 1912 and spent the remaining three months of his time in England working on Rutherford's nuclear model of the atom.

On July 24, 1912, Bohr boarded ship for his return to Copenhagen and a job as assistant professor of physics at the University of Copenhagen. Also waiting for him was his bride-to-be Margrethe Nørlund, whom he married on August 1. The couple later had four sons: Hans, Erik, **Aage**, and Ernest. Two other sons, one named Christian, died young. Aage earned a share of the 1975 Nobel Prize in physics for his work on the structure of the atomic nucleus.

Develops a New Theory of Atomic Structure

The field of atomic physics was going through a difficult phase in 1912. Rutherford had only recently discovered the atomic nucleus, which had created a profound problem for theorists. The existence of the nucleus meant that electrons must be circling it in orbits somewhat similar to those traveled by planets in their motion around the sun. According to classical laws of electrodynamics, however, an electrically charged particle would continuously radiate energy as it traveled in such an orbit around the nucleus. Over time, the electron would spiral ever closer to the nucleus and eventually collide with it. Although electrons clearly *must* be orbiting the nucleus, they could *not* be doing so according to classical laws.

Bohr arrived at a solution to this dilemma in a somewhat roundabout fashion. He began by considering the question of atomic spectra. For more than a century, scientists had known that the heating of an element produces a characteristic line spectrum; that is, the specific pattern of lines produced is unique for each specific element. Although a great deal of research had been done on spectral lines, no one had thought very deeply about what their relationship might be with atoms, the building blocks of elements.

When Bohr began to attack this question, he decided to pursue a line of research begun by the German physicist Johann Balmer in the 1880s. Balmer had found that the lines in the hydrogen spectrum could be represented by a relatively simple mathematical formula relating the frequency of a particular line to two integers whose significance Balmer could not explain. It was clear that the formula gave very precise values for line frequencies that corresponded well with those observed in experiments.

When Bohr's attention was first attracted to this formula, he realized at once that he had the solution to the problem of electron orbits. The solution that Bohr worked out was both simple and elegant. In a brash display of hypothesizing, Bohr declared that

certain orbits existed within an atom in which an electron could travel *without* radiating energy; that is, classical laws of physics were suspended within these orbits. The two integers in the Balmer formula, Bohr said, referred to orbit numbers of the "permitted" orbits, and the frequency of spectral lines corresponded to the energy released when an electron moved from one orbit to another.

Bohr's hypothesis was brash because he had essentially no theoretical basis for predicting the existence of "allowed" orbits. To be sure, German physicist **Max Planck**'s quantum hypothesis of a decade earlier had provided some hint that Bohr's "quantification of space" might make sense, but the fundamental argument for accepting the hypothesis was simply that it worked. When his model was used to calculate a variety of atomic characteristics, it did so correctly. Although the hypothesis failed when applied to detailed features of atomic spectra, it worked well enough to earn the praise of many colleagues.

Offered a Post at Manchester

Bohr published his theory of the "planetary atom" in 1913. That paper included a section that provided an interesting and decisive addendum to his basic hypothesis. One of the apparent failures of the Bohr hypothesis was its seeming inability to predict a set of spectral lines known as the Pickering series, lines for which the two integers in the Balmer formula required half-integral values. According to Bohr, of course, no "half-orbits" could exist that would explain these values. Bohr's solution to this problem was to suggest that the Pickering series did not apply to hydrogen at all, but to helium atoms that had lost an electron. He rewrote the Balmer formula to reflect this condition.

Within a short period of time spectroscopists in England had studied samples of helium carefully purged of hydrogen and found Bohr's hypothesis to be correct. Although a number of physicists were still debating Bohr's theory, at least one—Rutherford—was convinced that the young Danish physicist was a highly promising researcher. He offered Bohr a post as lecturer in physics at Manchester, a job that Bohr eagerly accepted and held from 1914 to 1916. He then returned to the University of Copenhagen, where a chair of theoretical physics had been created specifically for him. Within a few years he was to become involved in the planning for and construction of the University of Copenhagen's new Institute for Theoretical Physics, of which he was to serve as director for the next four decades.

In many ways, Bohr's atomic theory marked a sharp break between classical physics and a revolutionary new approach to natural phenomena made necessary by quantum theory and relativity. He was very much concerned about how scientists could and should now view the physical world, particularly in view of the conflicts that arose between classical and modern laws and principles. During the 1920s and 1930s, Bohr wrote extensively about this issue, proposing along the way two concepts that he considered to be fundamental to the "new physics." The first was the principle of complementarity that says, in effect, that there may be more than one true and accurate way to view natural phenomena. The best example of this situation is the wave-particle duality discovered in the 1930s, when particles were found to have wavelike characteristics and waves to have particle-like properties. Bohr argued that the two parts of a duality may appear to be inconsistent or even in conflict and that one can use only one viewpoint at a time, but he pointed out that both are necessary to obtain a complete view of particles and waves.

The second principle, the correspondence principle, was intended to show how the laws of classical physics could be preserved in light of the new quantum physics. We may know that quantum mechanics and relativity are essential to an understanding of phenomena on the atomic scale, Bohr said, but any conclusion drawn from these principles must not conflict with observations of the real world that can be made on a macroscopic scale. That is, the conclusions drawn from theoretical studies must correspond to the world described by the laws of classical physics.

Turns to Problems of Electron Configuration and the Atomic Nucleus

In the decade following the publication of his atomic theory, Bohr continued to work on the application of that theory to atoms with more than one electron. The original theory had dealt only with the simplest of all atoms, hydrogen, but it was clearly of some interest to see how that theory could be extended to higher elements. In March, 1922, Bohr published a summary of his conclusions in a paper entitled "The Structure of the Atoms and the Physical and Chemical Properties of the Elements." Eight months later, Bohr learned that he had been awarded the Nobel Prize in physics for his theory of atomic structure, by that time universally accepted among physicists.

During the 1930s, Bohr turned to a new but related, topic: the composition of the atomic nucleus. By 1934, scientists had found that the nucleus consists of two kinds of particles, protons and neutrons, but they had relatively little idea how those particles are arranged within the nucleus and what its general shape was. Bohr theorized that the nucleus could be compared to a liquid drop. The forces that operate between protons and neutrons could be compared in some ways, he said, to the forces that operate between the molecules that make up a drop of liquid. In this

respect, the nucleus is no more static than a droplet of water. Instead, Bohr suggested, the nucleus should be considered to be constantly oscillating and changing shape in response to its internal forces. The greatest success of the Bohr liquid-drop model was its later ability to explain the process of nuclear fission discovered by German chemist **Otto Hahn**, German chemist **Fritz Strassmann**, and Austrian physicist **Lise Meitner** in 1938. It is somewhat ironic that the Nobel Prize won by Bohr's son Aage in 1975 was given for the latter's elucidation of his father's nuclear model (to which many other scientists had also contributed).

Escapes from Copenhagen during World War II

Bohr continued to work at his Institute during the early years of World War II, devoting considerable effort to helping his colleagues escape from the dangers of Nazi Germany. When he received word in September, 1943, that his own life was in danger, Bohr decided that he and his family would have to leave Denmark. The Bohrs were smuggled out of the country to Sweden aboard a fishing boat and then, a month later, flown to England in the empty bomb bay of a Mosquito bomber. The Bohrs then made their way to the United States, where both Bohr and his son became engaged in work on the Manhattan Project to build the world's first atomic bombs.

After the War, Bohr, like many other Manhattan Project researchers, became active in efforts to keep control of atomic weapons out of the hands of the military and under close civilian supervision. For his long-term efforts on behalf of the peaceful uses of atomic energy, Bohr received the first Atoms for Peace Award given by the Ford Foundation in 1957. Meanwhile, Bohr had returned to his Institute for Theoretical Physics and become involved in the creation of the European Center for Nuclear Research (CERN). He also took part in the founding of the Nordic Institute for Theoretical Atomic Physics (Nordita) in Copenhagen. Nordita was formed to further cooperation among and provide support for physicists from Norway, Sweden, Finland, Denmark, and Iceland.

Bohr reached the mandatory retirement age of seventy in 1955 and was required to leave his position as professor of physics at the University of Copenhagen. He continued to serve as director of the Institute for Theoretical Physics until his death in Copenhagen on November 18, 1962.

Bohr was held in enormous respect and esteem by his colleagues in the scientific community. American physicist **Albert Einstein**, for example, credited him with having a "rare blend of boldness and caution; seldom has anyone possessed such an intuitive grasp of hidden things combined with such a strong critical sense." Among the many awards Bohr received were the Max Planck Medal of the German Physical Society in 1930, the Hughes (1921) and Copley (1938) medals of the Royal Society, the Franklin Medal of the Franklin Institute in 1926, and the Faraday Medal of the Chemical Society of London in 1930. He was elected to more than twenty scientific academies around the world and was awarded honorary doctorates by a dozen universities, including Cambridge, Oxford, Manchester, Edinburgh, the Sorbonne, Harvard, and Princeton.

SELECTED WRITINGS BY BOHR:

Books

The Theory of Spectra and Atomic Constitution, Cambridge University Press, 1922.
Atomic Theory and the Description of Nature, Cambridge University Press, 1934.
The Unity of Knowledge, Doubleday, 1955.
Atomic Physics and Human Knowledge, Wiley, 1958.
Essays, 1958–1962, on Atomic Physics and Human Knowledge, Interscience, 1963.
On the Constitution of Atoms and Molecules, Munksgaard, 1963.
Collected Works, 4 volumes, North-Holland, 1972–77.

Periodicals

"On the Constitution of Atoms and Molecules," *Philosophical Magazine,* Volume 25, 1913, pp. 1–25, 476–502, 857–875.
"On the Quantum Theory of Radiation and the Structure of the Atom," *Philosophical Magazine,* Volume 30, 1915, pp. 394–415.
"On the Selection Principle of the Quantum Theory," *Philosophical Magazine,* Volume 43, 1922, pp. 1112–1116.
"Can Quantum-Mechanical Description of Reality Be Considered Complete?," *Physical Review,* Volume 48, 1935, pp. 696–702.
(With J. A. Wheeler) "The Mechanism of Nuclear Fission," *Physical Review,* Volume 56, 1939, pp. 426–450.

SOURCES:

Books

Biographical Memoirs of Fellows of the Royal Society, Volume 9, Royal Society (London), 1963, pp. 37–49.
Dictionary of Scientific Biography, Volume 2, Scribner, 1975, pp. 239–254.
French, A. P., and P. J. Kennedy, *Niels Bohr: A Centenary Volume,* Harvard University Press, 1985.
Moore, Ruth, *Niels Bohr: The Man, His Science, and the World They Changed,* Knopf, 1966.
Pais, Abraham, *Niels Bohr: His Life and Work,* North-Holland, 1967.
Pauli, Wolfgang, editor, *Niels Bohr and the Development of Physics,* Pergamon Press, 1955.
Rozental, Stefan, editor, *Niels Bohr: His Life and Work as Seen by His Friends and Colleagues,* North-Holland, 1967.

Periodicals

"Niels Bohr Memorial Session," *Physics Today,* October, 1963, pp. 21–64.

—*Sketch by David E. Newton*

Bert Bolin
1925-
Swedish meteorologist

Bert Bolin, professor of meteorology at the University of Stockholm and editor of the international scientific journal *Tellus,* was a contributor to the early development of numerical weather forecasting and to research in the chemistry of the atmosphere. Acknowledged as one of the world's leading experts on meteorology, Bolin has stimulated concern over global air pollution, particularly the presence of carbon dioxide in the atmosphere, and was among the first to focus international attention on the existence of acid rain. He served as scientific advisor to the prime minister's office in Sweden from 1986 until 1991. Among his honors and awards are the International Meteorological Organization (IMO) prize in 1981, the Rossby medal from the American Meteorological Society in 1984, the Tyler Prize from the University of Southern California in 1988, the Celcius medal from the Royal Society of Sciences in 1988, and the Rossby medal from the Swedish Geophysical Society in 1993.

Bert Richard Bolin was born in Nyköping, Sweden, on May 15, 1925, to Richard Johannes Bolin and Karen Johansson Bolin, who were school teachers. Bolin began making regular weather observations at an early age—encouraged by his father's interest in meteorology—and by the time he was fourteen, Bolin had progressed to keeping records of outdoor temperatures and drawing data curves with the statistics. In

Bert Bolin

1943, Bolin decided to become a professional meteorologist. His father introduced him to the deputy director of Sweden's weather bureau, Anders Ångström, who employed the young Bolin as an assistant. The next year, Bolin began taking classes at the University of Uppsala and received a bachelor of science degree in 1946.

After enrolling in graduate studies at the University of Stockholm, Bolin interrupted his program in 1947 to serve in the military, a factor which was to prove crucial for his career development. The military assigned Bolin to the weather service in Stockholm, and authorized attendance at lectures given by **Carl-Gustaf Rossby** at the University of Stockholm. Rossby soon became a friend and mentor to Bolin, influencing him to join the research efforts in developing numerical methods for weather forecasting. Numerical forecasting begins with a set of initial weather conditions and develops predictions about disturbances in the atmosphere using numerical solutions to equations about hydrodynamics (the motion of fluids).

Following the completion of his master's degree in 1949 (one source says 1950), Bolin studied on a one-year fellowship from the Swedish-American Foundation at the University of Chicago and the Institute for Advanced Study at Princeton University. According to Henning Rodhe, writing on Bolin's scientific career in *Tellus,* Bolin's Ph.D. thesis focused on "the interaction between wind and pressure fields

and its application to numerical weather prediction." Subsequent research included atmospheric chemistry and pollutants in the atmosphere. Bolin was awarded his doctorate from the University of Stockholm in 1956 and was appointed to succeed Rossby (after Rossby's sudden death in 1957) as director of that university's International Meteorological Institute (IMI). At the age of thirty-two, Bolin became the director of a program that consisted of several established scientists. He wrote in a letter Margaret DiCanio that "I still only had a position as an assistant at the university, since Rossby occupied a personal chair. Not until 1961 was I appointed to the position as full professor of meteorology at the University of Stockholm." It was a position he was to hold for the next thirty years.

Organizes International Cooperative Research

Besides taking over as Institute director in 1957, Bolin also became secretary for the Swedish International Geophysical Year (IGY), a period from July, 1957, through December, 1958, devoted to international cooperation on exploration of geophysics. During a six-month stay in the United States, Bolin secured American support to launch weather research rockets from a military range in Swedish Lapland, research encouraged by the Swedish Council for Natural Sciences. Scientists mounted four campaigns from 1961 to 1964 to explore the nature of noctilucent clouds—high altitude clouds that are especially visible at twilight—at a height of 80 kilometers (50 miles). Following the first meteorological satellite launched by the United States in 1960, American President John F. Kennedy set the stage for international cooperation in satellite meteorology in a speech to the United Nations (UN). Bolin, asked to organize the scientific efforts to foster cooperation, proposed the formation of a new Committee of the Atmospheric Sciences (GAS). In 1964, he became GAS's first chairperson, the same year he became scientific director of the European Space Research Organization (ESRO). Bolin spent 1965 through 1967 working for ESRO in Paris.

In the mid–1960s, Bolin became deeply involved in the creation of the Global Atmospheric Research Program (GARP) aimed at a better understanding of global weather systems. The bulk of his work during the 1960s and 1970s focused on the carbon cycle as concerns about pollution of the atmosphere grew. At IMI, fellow meteorologist Svante Oden analyzed data gathered since the mid–1950s on rain chemistry. He discovered that the pH balance of rain was gradually decreasing. As a result of increasing emissions of sulfur into the atmosphere, rain was becoming systematically more acidic. For a UN-sponsored international conference on the environment scheduled in Stockholm in 1972, Bolin suggested that Sweden present a case study of acid rain across national boundaries. The Swedish National Committee agreed and appointed Bolin to chair the evaluation committee. Bolin's committee report led to widespread interest in acidification of rain in industrialized countries and promoted increased research on atmospheric chemistry, particularly in the United States. Bolin was a member of the committee selected by the U.S. National Academy of Sciences in 1979 to assess existing knowledge about the impact on climate of carbon dioxide emissions introduced into the atmosphere by humans. The committee's final report confirmed the plausibility of a future human-induced climate change. In 1982, Bolin proposed an additional assessment that included chemical and biological factors and the impact that climate change would bring to the environment. The result was a five-hundred-fifty page report, *The Greenhouse Effect, Climate Change, and Ecosystems,* endorsed by twenty-nine countries in October, 1985. The report served as a basis for a subsequent report entitled "Our Common Future," discussed in the UN General Assembly in 1987. In 1988, to promote assessment of climate change, the UN and the World Meteorological Organization formed a joint Intergovernmental Panel on Climate Change (IPCC), which was chaired by Bolin. IPCC's first report to the UN in mid–1990 inspired the General Assembly to begin negotiations for an agreement between nations on environmental issues. This, in turn, led to planning for the UN Conference on Environment and Development, popularly known as the Second Earth Summit, held in Rio de Janeiro, Brazil, in June, 1992.

Bolin married Ulla Karin Irene Frykstrand on June 7, 1952, and the couple has three children: Dan, Karina, and Göran. Bolin sings in a choir and participates in international folk-dancing, cross-country skiing, and mountain hiking.

SELECTED WRITINGS BY BOLIN:

Books

"The Fate of Fossil Fuel Carbon Dioxide in the Oceans," in *Marine Science,* edited by N. R. Anderson and A. Malahoff, Plenum Press, 1977, pp. 81–95.
(Editor, with others) *The Global Carbon Cycle,* SCOPE 13, Wiley, 1979.
(Editor with R. B. Cook) *The Major Biogeochemical Cycles and Their Interactions,* SCOPE 21, Wiley, 1983.
(Editor, with others) *The Greenhouse Effect, Climate Change, and Ecosystems,* SCOPE 29, Wiley, 1986.

Periodicals

"On the Exchange of Carbon Dioxide between the Atmosphere and the Sea," *Tellus,* December 3, 1960, pp. 274–81.

Other

"Climate Changes and Their Effects on the Biosphere," World Meteorological Organization [Geneva] Lecture, 1979.
Keynote address at the White House Conference on Science and Economics Research Related to Global Change, April 17–18, [Washington, DC], 1990.

SOURCES:

Periodicals

"IMO Prize Awarded to Bert Bolin," *American Meteorological Society Bulletin,* July-December, 1981, pp. 1490–91.
Rodhe, Henning, "Bert Bolin and His Scientific Career," *Tellus,* 1991, pp. 3–7.

Other

Bolin, B., letter to Margaret DiCanio, October 5, 1993.

—*Sketch by Margaret DiCanio*

Hermann Bondi
1919-
Austrian-born English mathematician and cosmologist

Trained as a mathematician, Hermann Bondi is best known for his work in the field of astronomy. In the late 1940s, Bondi collaborated with English astronomers **Fred Hoyle** and **Thomas Gold** to refine the "steady-state" theory of cosmology, which asserts that the universe had no beginning and will have no end, and is constantly regenerating itself. Although later research largely discredited the Bondi-Gold-Hoyle theory, their hypothesis has served as a valuable impetus to the subsequent research of many other cosmologists. Since the late 1950s, Bondi has grown increasingly interested and involved in the administrative and political aspects of science and technology, serving in a number of important governmental space and energy agencies.

Bondi was born in Vienna, Austria, on November 1, 1919, to Samuel Bondi and the former Helene Hirsch. He received his primary and secondary education in Vienna, graduating from the Real Gymnasium. He then traveled to England for his college education, earning a B.A. in 1940 and an M.A. in 1944, both from Trinity College in Cambridge. Bondi was made a fellow of Trinity College in 1943 and held this appointment the first time until 1949, and then again from 1952 to 1954. During the period from 1948 to 1954, he also lectured on mathematics at Cambridge University.

Devises Steady-State Theory of Cosmology

Bondi's most important scientific work, completed shortly after the end of World War II, involved the development of a steady-state theory of cosmology with astronomers Gold and Hoyle, and the publication of hotly debated articles and books on the subject. The science of cosmology deals with one of the oldest and most fundamental questions of astronomy: How did the universe originate? In the past half century, two major theories have been dominant. One, the "Big Bang" theory, assumes that at some point in history all matter in the universe was created out of energy within the smallest fraction of a second. The force of that explosion is taken to be the force that continues to drive all matter in the universe in its relentless outward expansion.

The "Steady-State" theory, to which Bondi was a major contributor, assumes that the universe had no beginning and will have no end because it is in a constant state of being. The trio's assumption was that matter is constantly being created from energy everywhere in the universe, thus keeping up with its continuing outward expansion, and maintaining a "steady state." Bondi outlined the major features of this concept in his 1952 book, *Cosmology*.

For a period of two decades, the steady-state theory received serious consideration from many astronomers. Gradually, however, evidence against it became so strong that it was largely abandoned by scholars. Still, as the commentator on the steady-state theory in *Great Events from History II* observes, Bondi's work "had been useful to stimulate science and to fire the imaginations of many."

Bondi Becomes an Administrator of Science

In 1954 Bondi left Cambridge to accept a position as professor of applied mathematics at King's College, London, a post he held for thirty years. After a dozen years in London, Bondi took a leave of absence in 1967 to become director-general of the European Space Research Organization (ESRO) in Paris, France. His job at ESRO was to coordinate the multinational agency's efforts to design, build, and launch space satellites.

When his tour of duty with ESRO ended in 1971, Bondi returned to England and was appointed Chief Scientific Advisor to the Ministry of Defence. His responsibilities in that post were to provide a purely scientific and technological assessment of various weapons systems as well as other needs of the British military. In 1977 Bondi moved to the British Department of Energy, where he held the title of chief scientist. Over the next half decade, he became very much interested in the nation's energy needs and in the technology that might become available to meet those needs. In connection with this phase of his career, Bondi also served on the Offshore Energy Board, the Advisory Council on Research and Development for Fuel and Power, and the Natural Environment Research Council.

In 1947 Bondi married Christine Mary Stockman, with whom he had five children. In recognition of his contributions to science and government, he has been given honorary doctorates by the universities of Sussex, Bath, Surrey, York, Southampton, Salford, Birmingham, and St. Andrews. He has been a visiting scholar at both Cornell University, from 1951 to 1960, and at the Harvard College Observatory in 1953. He was knighted by Queen Elizabeth in 1959 and made a fellow of the Royal Society in the same year.

SELECTED WRITINGS BY BONDI:

Books

Cosmology, 1952.
The Universe at Large, Anchor Books, 1961.
Relativity and Common Sense, 1964.
Assumption and Myth in Physical Theory, 1967.

SOURCES:

Books

The Blue Book, Leaders of the English-Speaking World, 1973–74, St. James Press, 1973, p. 145.
Great Events from History II, Science and Technology Series, Volume 3, 1931–1952, Salem Press, 1991, pp. 1320–1324.

Periodicals

"Prof. Sir Hermann Bondi," *Electronics and Power,* December, 1978, pp. 859–861.

—*Sketch by David E. Newton*

Walter M. Booker
1907-1988
American biologist and pharmacologist

Walter M. Booker was a biologist, physiologist, and pharmacologist who served for twenty years as the chairman of the Department of Pharmacology of the College of Medicine at Howard University, Washington, D. C. As the author of over one hundred scientific papers, Booker studied liver damage in trauma, the effects of anesthesia, and gastrointestinal physiology. He was very active even after his retirement, focusing on such important issues as drug abuse and addiction.

Walter Monroe Booker was born in Little Rock, Arkansas on November 4, 1907. A 1928 graduate of Morehouse College in Atlanta, Georgia, where he obtained a B. A. degree, he received a master's degree from the University of Iowa in 1932, and a doctorate in physiology and chemistry from the University of Chicago in 1943. During those years, he also taught biology and chemistry at Leland College in Louisiana and at Prairie View College. After receiving his Ph.D., he accepted a teaching position at Howard University in 1943, and became an associate professor in 1948, He was appointed Chairman, Department of Pharmacology of the College of Medicine, Howard University in 1954. Booker remained in that position until 1973 when he retired as a full professor.

Booker had done a great deal of research on the heart's response to drugs, and participated in conferences on the subject in nearly a dozen nations. Besides running the pharmacology department at Howard University, Booker was a consultant to the Walter Reed Army Research Institute where he taught during the 1960s and 1970s. He was a consultant to the National Institute on Drug Abuse and the Department of Health, Education and Welfare. His specialization proved useful to the Washington Heart Association, and he was a representative of the American Society for Pharmacology and Experimental Therapeutics to the National Research Council.

Among the many groups to which he belonged were the American College of Clinical Pharmacology and the American Physiological Society. He was a fellow of the American College of Cardiology and a charter member of Sigma Xi, an honorary scientific society. As a senior Fulbright scholar, he studied at the Heymans Institute in Ghent, Belgium during 1957 and 1958.

When he died of cardiac arrest on August 29, 1988, at Howard University Hospital, he was survived by a son, Walter Jr., a daughter, Marjorie Courm, and four grandchildren. His wife, the former Thomye Collins, died in 1986.

SOURCES:

Periodicals

Journal of Negro History, Volume 35, 1950, p. 145.
Washington Post, September 1, 1988, C6.

—*Sketch by Leonard C. Bruno*

Jules Bordet
1870-1961
Belgian physician, bacteriologist, and immunologist

Jules Bordet was an important pioneer in the field of immunology. It was his research that made clear the exact manner by which serums and antiserums act to destroy bacteria and foreign blood cells in the body, thus explaining how human and animal bodies defend themselves against the invasion of foreign elements. Bordet was also responsible for developing complement fixation tests, which made possible the early detection of many disease-causing bacteria in human and animal blood. For his various discoveries in the field of biology Bordet was awarded the Nobel Prize in medicine for 1919.

Jules Jean Baptiste Vincent Bordet was born on June 13, 1870, in Soignies, Belgium, a small town situated twenty-three miles southwest of Brussels. He was the second son of Charles Bordet, a schoolteacher, and Célestine Vandenabeele Bordet. The family moved to Brussels in 1874, when his father received an appointment to the École Moyenne, a primary school. Jules and his older brother Charles attended this school and then received their secondary education at the Athénée Royal of Brussels. It was at this time that Bordet became interested in chemistry and began working in a small laboratory which he constructed at home. He entered the medical program at the Free University of Brussels at the age of sixteen, receiving his doctorate of medicine in 1892. Bordet began his research career while still in medical school, and in 1892 he published a paper on the adaptation of viruses to vaccinated organisms in the *Annales de l'Institut Pasteur* of Paris. For this work, the Belgian government awarded him a scholarship to the Pasteur Institute, and from 1894 to 1901 he stayed in Paris at the laboratory of the Ukrainian-born scientist **Élie Metchnikoff**. In 1899 Bordet married Marthe Levoz; they eventually had two daughters and a son, Paul, who also became a medical scientist.

Discoveries in Immunology Lead to Nobel Prize

During his seven years at the Pasteur Institute, Bordet made most of the basic discoveries that led to his Nobel Prize of 1919. Soon after his arrival at the Institute, he began work on a problem in immunology. In 1894 Richard Pfeiffer, a German scientist, had discovered that when cholera bacteria was injected into the peritoneum of a guinea pig immunized against the infection, the pig would rapidly die. This bacteriolysis, Bordet discovered, did not occur when the bacteria was injected into a non-immunized guinea pig, but did so when the same animal received the antiserum from an immunized animal. Moreover, the bacteriolysis did not take place when the bacteria and the antiserum were mixed in a test tube unless fresh antiserum was used. However, when Bordet heated the antiserum to 55 degrees centigrade, it lost its power to kill bacteria. Finding that he could restore the bacteriolytic power of the antiserum if he added a little fresh serum from a non-immunized animal, Bordet concluded that the bacteria-killing phenomenon was due to the combined action of two distinct substances: an antibody in the antiserum, which specifically acted against a particular kind of bacterium; and a non-specific substance, sensitive to heat, found in all animal serums, which Bordet called "alexine" (later named "complement").

In a series of experiments conducted later, Bordet also learned that injecting red blood cells from one animal species (rabbit cells in the initial experiments) into another species (guinea pigs) caused the serum of the second species to quickly destroy the red cells of the first. And although the serum lost its power to kill the red cells when heated to 55 degrees centigrade, its potency was restored when alexine (or complement) was added. It became apparent to Bordet that hemolytic (red cell destroying) serums acted exactly as bacteriolytic serums; thus, he had uncovered the basic mechanism by which animal bodies defend or immunize themselves against the invasion of foreign elements. Eventually, Bordet and his colleagues found a way to implement their discoveries. They determined that alexine was bound or fixed to red blood cells or to bacteria during the immunizing process. When red cells were added to a normal serum mixed with a specific form of bacteria in a test tube, the bacteria remained active while the red cells were destroyed through the fixation of alexine. However, when serum containing the antibody specific to the bacteria was destroyed, the alexine and the solution separated into a layer of clear serum overlaying the intact red cells. Hence, it was possible to visually determine the presence of bacteria in a patient's blood serum. This process became known as a complement fixation test. Bordet and his associates applied these findings to various other infections, like typhoid fever, carbuncle, and hog cholera. August von Wasserman eventually used a form of the test (later known as the Wasserman test) to determine the presence of syphilis bacteria in the human blood.

Continues Research and Pens a Classic Text

Already famous by the age of thirty-one, Bordet accepted the directorship of the newly created Antirabies and Bacteriological Institute in Brussels in 1901; two years later, the organization was renamed the Pasteur Institute of Brussels. From 1901, Bordet was obliged to divide his time between his research and the administration of the Institute. In 1907 he also began teaching following his appointment as professor of bacteriology in the faculty of medicine at the Free University of Brussels, a position which he held until 1935. Despite his other activities, he continued his research in immunology and bacteriology. In 1906 Bordet and Octave Gengou succeeded in isolating the bacillus that causes whooping cough in children and later developed a vaccine against the disease. Between 1901 and 1920, Bordet conducted important studies on the coagulation of blood. When research became impossible because of the German occupation of Belgium during World War I, Bordet devoted himself to the writing of *Traité de l'immunité dans les maladies infectieuses* (1920), a classic book in the field of immunology. He was in the United States to raise money for new medical facilities for the war-damaged Free University of Brussels when he received word that he had been awarded the Nobel Prize. After 1920, he became interested in bacteriophage, the family of viruses which kill many types of bacteria, publishing several articles on the subject. In 1940 Bordet retired from the directorship of the Pasteur Institute of Brussels and was succeeded by his son, Paul. Bordet himself continued to take an active interest in the work of the Institute despite his failing eyesight and a second German occupation of Belgium during World War II. Many scientists, friends, and former students gathered in a celebration of his eightieth birthday at the great hall of the Free University of Brussels in 1950. He died in Brussels on April 6, 1961.

SELECTED WRITINGS BY BORDET:

Books

Studies in Immunity, collected and translated by Frederick P. Gay, J. Wiley, 1909.

Traité de l'immunité dans les maladies infectieuses, Masson, 1920.

SOURCES:

Books

De Kruif, Paul, *Men Against Death,* Harcourt, 1932, pp. 229–48.
Silverstein, Arthur M., *A History of Immunology,* Academic Press, 1989.

Periodicals

Beumer, J., "Jules Bordet, 1870–1961," *Journal of General Microbiology,* 1962, pp. 1–13.

—*Sketch by John E. Little*

Émile Borel
1871-1956
French mathematician

Émile Borel was one of the most powerful mathematicians of the twentieth century. He displayed great virtuosity in working in a number of different areas of mathematics, particularly complex numbers and functions, but in addition served visibly as a representative of the mathematical community to the general public. He brought the influence of the mathematical spirit to bear, thanks to his popular writings and to his participation in academic and national politics. His views on mathematics and how it should be supported affected French national policy on mathematics for many years after his death.

Émile Félix-Édouard-Justin Borel was born in Saint-Affrique in the Aveyron district of France, the son of Protestant pastor Honoré Borel and Émilie Teissié-Solier, the daughter of a successful merchant. He had two older sisters, but rapidly impressed the neighborhood with his intelligence. Born on the 7th of January in 1871, he entered a France still in disarray after the setbacks of the Franco-Prussian war. His original education was at the hands of his father, from which he passed at the age of eleven to the lycée at Montauban, the nearest cathedral town. His merits were recognized quickly enough that he was sent to Paris to study at some of the leading preparatory schools for the university. His efforts were crowned by admission to the École Normale Supérieure, an institution that was at the summit of French scientific

education and with which he was to be associated throughout the rest of his career.

Academically Borel made rapid progress through the next few years. He was welcome in the family circle of the eminent geometry specialist Gaston Darboux and married mathematician Paul Appell's daughter Marguerite in 1901. Although they had no children, they adopted one of Borel's nephews, Fernand, who was later killed during the First World War. After Borel graduated first in his class at the École Normale, he was offered a teaching position at the university at Lille, exceptionally early since he had not finished his doctoral thesis. He took his doctorate in 1894 and returned a couple of years later to the École Normale. Despite his busy schedule of research and publication, Borel always took his responsibilities at the École Normale seriously, paying attention both to his own teaching and to the curriculum. The École Normale rewarded his work by instituting a special chair in the theory of functions, of which Borel was the first occupant.

Borel started his career of research by publishing three brief articles at the age of 18. From there he went to a life in which writing always played a large part, as witnessed by his over 300 papers and books. In addition to his research articles, the dedicated teacher also devoted effort to the re-creation of French textbooks in mathematics. His activities as a writer were supplemented by his editing one of the best known series of expositions, known as the Borel collection. The first of these, written when he was still only 27, *Leçons sur la théorie des fonctions* (*Lessons on the Theory of Functions*), went through several editions and rapidly acquired the status of a classic, for it laid the foundation for the field of measure theory. The French publishing house of Gauthier-Villars owed its preeminence in mathematics to the work that Borel did on behalf of this series.

Borel's earliest mathematical work was already distinguished by its variety, but two of the areas in which his contributions attracted attention were the study of complex functions and of the topology, or properties of geometric configuration, of real numbers. Functions serve as a type of formula in which different numbers, known as variables, are plugged into a mathematical expression for a resulting value. Just as there are functions of real numbers that give out real numbers as values, so there are functions of complex numbers—numbers that include the imaginary unit i, the square root of -1—that give out complex numbers as values. There was a clear geometric significance attached to the existence of certain objects from calculus for real functions, but the geometry of curves representing functions of complex numbers was more complicated. Borel was able to use the information that complex functions had derivatives—the limits of rates of change as the function's variable approaches zero—to prove what is known as

Picard's theorem, concerning the number of possible values that a complex function can take. The theorem and the methods used to prove it are fundamental to the study of complex functions.

Borel's important results were not limited to complex functions, however. It might seem easy to talk about the area of a region in two dimensions, but as the region gets more complicated, it becomes harder to define exactly what is meant by area. Borel extended older ideas and results about areas to more general kinds of regions, including those defined by an infinite sequence of operations. Such regions or sets are said to be "Borel-measurable," and the more general notion of area introduced by Borel (called "measure" from the French "mesure") became the basis of the field called "measure theory." Although the most general notion of area that was taken up by the next generation of mathematicians came from Borel's younger colleague, Frenchman **Henri Lebesgue**, Borel influenced Lebesgue's work in many ways, including personal encouragement.

In his thesis, Borel articulated another idea that is now identified with his name. The idea of compactness has been a central one in twentieth-century mathematics and comes out of topology. The term is not easy to summarize, but perhaps the simplest way to consider compactness is that it describes the extent to which even an infinite set can have some of the simpler characteristics of a finite set. Borel showed that the set of real numbers includes the property that every closed interval (such as the real numbers between 1 and 2, inclusive) is compact, at least for collections of basic sets of certain size. This theorem is known as the Heine-Borel theorem—a somewhat misleading name, as German mathematician Eduard Heine observed but never articulated the significance of the idea.

One way of getting a perspective on Borel's central role in French mathematics from early in his career is to look at a debate about the role of the infinite that took place in the year 1905. As a result of the publication of a proof involving a controversial axiom in set theory called the axiom of choice (which allowed for an infinite number of choices from a set), Borel published an article expressing distrust of the general principle involved. There was a rapid exchange of letters between leading French mathematicians including Lebesgue, not all of whom agreed with Borel's restrictions. Nevertheless, the entire discussion was centered about Borel, who kept it going by forwarding letters he had received to those who might have more to say on the issue. There are many ways of describing the philosophy of mathematics that crystallized out of this discussion, and the views of Borel had been influenced by those of **Jules Henri Poincaré** of the previous generation, but Borel's role in raising the issue and trying to reach a modicum of agreement testifies to his central position.

Moves into Applications and Politics

Borel's interests had never been restricted entirely to mathematics. In 1906 he took the money that he had received for the Petit Prix d'Ormoy and used it to start a journal entitled *La revue du mois* (*Monthly Review*) that dealt with issues of general interest. Both he and his wife worked on the editing with success in the quality of the articles and the range of subscribers. It only ceased publication in 1920 as a result of the darker economic climate created by World War I.

The war also had the effect of moving Borel's interests in the direction of applied mathematics. Among the long-term consequences was a stream of publications in probability, which had become a standard subject in the mathematical curriculum. The original notions of finite probability had been developed in the seventeenth century, and the progress of calculus shortly thereafter allowed for the generalization of probabilistic notions to the real numbers as well. As in his work on measure, Borel was able to extend the notions of probability to more complicated sets of events. Some of his work in probability was fundamental to the new field called game theory, including his observation that there were situations where random behavior had its advantages. In addition to his strictly mathematical work on the subject, Borel wrote for a popular audience to make the subject of probability more widely accessible.

As an indication of the width of Borel's scientific interests, he wrote a volume in 1922 on **Albert Einstein**'s theory of relativity that was subsequently translated into English as *Space and Time.* The discussion proceeds almost entirely without equations, since Borel's concern once again was to make the subject comprehensible to the widest audience. The discussion includes both the special and general theories of relativity and is characterized by many references to familiar objects to remove the sense of strangeness. Although Borel did not contribute to the mathematical details of Einstein's theories, he took it as a public responsibility of the mathematical community to help make science comprehensible.

His sense of public responsibility extended to the political sphere as well. Although he remained a resident of Paris, he was elected mayor of Saint-Affrique, perhaps partly as a tribute to his scientific standing. He represented the area as a member of the Chamber of Deputies from 1924 to 1936 under the banner of the Radical-Socialist party, although it was neither radical nor socialist as those terms are customarily used. He also served as Minister of the Navy in 1925, but his most lasting accomplishments in the political arena concerned the funding of mathematical and scientific research. The Centre National de la Recherche Scientifique (CNRS) received funding under his aegis and has continued to be essential for the support of research in France. He helped plan the

Institut Henri Poincaré and served as its director for many years, from its founding in 1928 until his death, thereby paying tribute to one of the great influences on his own approach to mathematics.

Borel was elected to the Academy of Sciences in 1921, rather later than one might have expected and perhaps out of a distrust of his political involvement. He served as president of the Academy in 1934, another expression of his stature in the wider scientific community, and received the gold medal of the CNRS on its first being awarded. He was decorated for his work during World War I, and again for having stood up to the German Gestapo during World War II. He had left his chair at the École Normale and had taken up a position at the Sorbonne (the University of Paris) instead, as his memories of the generation of French mathematicians dead on the battlefields of World War I were too painful in the familiar surroundings. He retired from the Sorbonne but remained mathematically active for the rest of his life, including regular attendance at international congresses. Part of the reason for his success in accomplishing so much was that he welcomed those who had something constructive to say and chose not to waste time on formalities and empty words. As a lecturer he was impressive, thanks to his tall, dignified manner and his air of distinction. His death on the 3rd of February in 1956, hastened by a fall on board ship returning from a conference in Brazil, was met with a sense of great loss by colleagues and pupils, but the heritage he left in his mathematics and in his writing testifies to a strong belief in the mathematician's obligation to serve the community at large.

SELECTED WRITINGS BY BOREL:

Books

Leçons sur la théorie des fonctions, Gauthier-Villars, 1898.
Éléments de la théorie des probabilités, Hermann, 1909.
Le hasard, Alcan, 1914.
L'espace et le temps, Alcan, 1922.
La politique républicaine, [Paris], 1924.
Les probabiliités et la vie, [Paris], 1943.
Les nombres inaccessibles, Gauthier-Villars, 1951.
L'imaginaire et le réel en mathématiques et en physique, Albin Michel, 1952.
Émile Borel: Philosophe et homme d'action, Gauthier-Villars, 1967.
Oeuvres de Émile Borel, 4 volumes, CNRS, 1972.

SOURCES:

Books

Dictionary of Scientific Biography, Scribner, 1970–1978, Volume 2, pp. 302–305.

Moore, Gregory H., *Zermelo's Axiom of Choice,* Springer-Verlag, 1982.

—*Sketch by Thomas Drucker*

Norman Borlaug
1914-
American plant pathologist and geneticist

Norman Borlaug began his career as a plant pathologist and became a force in international politics through a stint as a consultant in agronomy (the science of raising crops) to the Mexican government. Through the work he performed in Mexico, he created a system of plant breeding and crop management that was then exported to countries throughout the world to create what was dubbed the Green Revolution. Borlaug's unique combination of technical innovation, idealism, energy, and impatience with bureaucratic inefficiency took whole countries from starvation to self-sufficiency in the space of a few years. Some countries even became net exporters. Borlaug was aware, however, that his innovations were no final answer to the world's population explosion but had only bought humankind time to deal with this essential ecological problem. In 1970 Borlaug became the first agricultural scientist, and the fifteenth American—after Martin Luther King in 1964—to win the Nobel Peace Prize for his service to humanity.

Norman Ernest Borlaug was born on March 25, 1914, to Henry O. and Clara Vaala Borlaug, Norwegian immigrants who owned a fifty-six-acre farm near Cresco, Iowa. With his two sisters, Borlaug grew up on his family's farm. Cresco and its surroundings had a large, hard-working Norwegian population whose lifestyles reflected experiences with hunger and privation that led them to emigrate to the New World. The importance of careful planning and hard work in order to survive came home to Borlaug at an early age. In Cresco he attended the grade school and high school, where he was the captain of the football team. Harry Shroeder, a teacher of agriculture at Cresco High School, recalled that Borlaug showed considerable interest in crop and soil management. Shroeder rewarded his interest by supplying Borlaug with supplementary teaching on different aspects of agriculture.

In 1932 Borlaug graduated from high school, and instead of becoming a farmer entered the University of Minnesota to satisfy his grandfather's insistence

Norman Borlaug

that he should go to college. Borlaug worked his way through college to earn a bachelor of science in forestry in 1937. During his freshman year, he attended a lecture by the head of the plant pathology department, Elvin Charles Stakman, an authority on crop research. Stakman's lecture had such an impact on Borlaug that he determined to study plant pathology under the professor's direction. At Stakman's urging, Borlaug stayed on at the University for postgraduate study. Earning money as a forester working part-time, he completed his M.S. in 1939 and his Ph.D. in 1942 in the field of plant pathology. In his doctoral thesis, he discussed a fungal rot endemic to the flax plant. After graduating from college, Borlaug married Margaret G. Gibson on September 24, 1937. They had two children, a daughter, Norma Jean (Borlaug) Rhoda, and a son, William Gibson Borlaug.

Before Borlaug left graduate school, widespread use of chemical pesticides had begun. **Paul Müller** had already developed dichlorodiphenyltrichloroethane (DDT) in 1939. During World War II, the United States government made extensive use of DDT, especially in the military, and pushed hard to put agriculture on an industrial footing with the development of new chemicals to control plant diseases and insects. In 1942 Borlaug went to E. I. du Pont de Nemours and Company in Wilmington, Delaware, to apply his expertise in plant pathology to draw conclusions about the effects these new chemicals had on plants and their diseases. He stayed with du Pont for

two years, researching ways to counteract chemically the fungus and bacteria that attack plants.

Joins Team as Agricultural Consultant to Mexico

In 1944, worried by a succession of crop failures in wheat, the Mexican Ministry of Agriculture asked the Rockefeller Foundation to send a team of agricultural scientists to share the technological advances the United States had made in agronomy with the Mexican people. The Rockefeller Foundation named George Harrar, a plant pathologist and future head of the foundation, as leader of this group and left it up to him to gather the scientists he wanted. Harrar chose Edward Wellhouse, a corn breeder picked for his expertise in Mexico's major grain crop, William Colwell, an agronomist, and Borlaug, who was appointed director of the Cooperative Wheat Research and Production Program in Mexico.

Apart from some modernization in Sonora in the northwest, most wheat production in Mexico had not changed since the conquering Spaniards had established the crop in the sixteenth century. The fields were prepared with wooden ploughs pulled by draft animals and the harvesting and winnowing (separating the grain from the husk) were done by hand. Borlaug recalled that there was only one scientist in Mexico available to conduct wheat-breeding experiments, and he was so busy with other duties that he could only contribute a fraction of his time. There existed no government programs for soil management or disease and insect control.

At first Borlaug sought to improve the variety of wheat commonly grown. This breed was tall and thin-stemmed, an adaptation to centuries of competition with weeds for sunlight. Together with Mexican agricultural scientists, Borlaug's team of researchers began breeding this species of wheat to develop a high-yield, disease-resistant strain that would thrive in the wide range of growing conditions that Mexico offered. Borlaug strove for results and showed that it was possible to speed up crop production by harvesting two generations of this new wheat every year, one in Sonora, close to sea level, and the other in the mountains near Mexico City.

Wheat production improved so dramatically that by 1948, instead of importing half its wheat to feed its people as before, Mexico had become self-sufficient. However, problems surfaced with the strain of wheat that Borlaug had developed. In the 1950s, wheat yields stagnated. Considerable losses were incurred as the heads on the plants, enlarged by the use of fertilizer and irrigation, grew too heavy for the thin stalks to support, causing the plants to fall over or "lodge." Borlaug realized that he would have to breed a wheat plant with a shorter, thicker stem to support the larger heads. In 1954 he and his assistants created a hybrid strain using the improved Mexican grain and a Japanese dwarf variety called Gaines that was perfected by Orville A. Vogel of Washington State University.

Exports the Green Revolution to the World

Not only did Borlaug's Mexican-Gaines hybrid prove effective at preventing lodging, but it actually used fertilizer more efficiently by concentrating the growth in the head rather than the stalk. This latest strain was twice as productive as Borlaug's improvement and ten times as productive as the original Mexican strain. In 1961 Mexican farmers began growing the new dwarf hybrid. By the late 1950s the International Center for Maize and Wheat Improvement, Borlaug's research team, began expanding its activities to other countries. He visited Pakistan in 1959 and India in 1963. His experiences in both countries drove him to point out that even the best grain varieties would be of no use when bureaucratic inertia stood in the way. In other words, the way a nation fed its population was as much a political issue as an agricultural one.

Borlaug was not shy in articulating what resources a nation had to supply for his agrarian reforms to succeed: a stable governing body with the political will to enact his proposals; the ability to provide the chemicals and machinery necessary to modern agriculture; an economy structured to reward greater agricultural productivity; and, of greatest importance, a commitment to training young scientists in agronomy. Without this brain trust, there would be no ongoing improvement of crop strains to counteract new diseases or pests.

As noted in *Nobel Prize Winners,* Borlaug became so weary of red tape that he remarked on the subject, "One of the greatest threats to mankind today is that the world may be choked by an explosively pervading but well-camouflaged bureaucracy." His desire to see results quickly led him to inaugurate his Green Revolution programs in the mid–1960s. His aim was to double wheat yields in the host country in the first year of his agricultural improvements. The purpose here was twofold: one, to greatly reduce the country's reliance on imports for food for a quick economic boost, and, two, to break through the skepticism of the country's officials. Borlaug's programs ultimately benefited countries in Latin America, the Middle East, and Asia.

In the 1960s, scientists at the International Rice Research Institute in the Philippines succeeded in breeding strains of dwarf rice using techniques similar to those Borlaug used to develop dwarf wheat in Mexico. These new rice strains allowed the Green Revolution to spread to Southeast Asia, a region of the world where the staple grain is not wheat but rice.

Accepts the 1970 Peace Prize for His Agricultural Reforms

In 1970 Borlaug accepted the Nobel Peace Prize for starting the Green Revolution, which allowed a greater measure of peace and prosperity throughout the less-developed world. In his Nobel Prize speech, he made it very clear that an adequate food supply, although essential to a stable world order, was only a first step and that there was much left to be done. He identified population growth as the biggest problem facing humanity, saying, "Since man is potentially a rational being, I am confident that within the next two decades he will recognize the self-destructive course he steers along the road of irresponsible population growth and will adjust the growth rate to levels which will permit a decent standard of living for all mankind."

Environmentalists in the 1970s began to criticize Borlaug's techniques on the grounds that they relied on polluting industrial products such as fertilizers and insecticides. Borlaug found these accusations missed the point he had made in his Nobel Prize speech, which was that the greatest danger to the environment came not from industrialization but from the population explosion. Having an ample food supply actually helped countries to break the cycle of poverty and starvation that led to overpopulation. While admitting that even after the Green Revolution problems of distribution remained, he asserted that these difficulties were an improvement over the ones caused by famine.

In 1979 Borlaug retired from the International Center for Maize and Wheat Improvement in Mexico City but maintained his position as associate director of the Rockefeller Foundation. In this capacity he continued cooperating with the Mexican Ministry of Agriculture in research projects. He became Distinguished Professor of International Agriculture at Texas A & M University in 1984.

After receiving his Nobel Peace Prize, Borlaug gave the benefit of his expertise to the Renewable Resources Foundation, the United States Citizen's Commission of Science, Law, and Food Supply, the Commission on Critical Choices for America, and the Foundation for Population Studies in Mexico. He coauthored several books and wrote over seventy articles. Throughout his career, he received awards and honors from governments of Mexico, Pakistan, and the United States among others as well as scientific and agricultural societies the world over.

SELECTED WRITINGS BY BORLAUG:

Books

(With R. Glen Anderson and Haldore Hanson) *Wheat in the Third World,* Westview, 1982.

(With Paul F. Bente, Jr.) *Land Use, Food, Energy, and Recreation,* University of Colorado Press, 1983.

SOURCES:

Books

Current Biography Yearbook, H. W. Wilson, 1971, pp. 50–52.

Wasson, Tyler, editor, *Nobel Prize Winners: An H. W. Wilson Biographical Dictionary,* H. W. Wilson, 1987, pp. 118–121.

Periodicals

Critchfield, Richard, "Bring the Green Revolution to Africa," *New York Times,* September 14, 1992, p. A19.

"Crop Genetics International Corp.," *Wall Street Journal,* January 12, 1990, p. B6.

—*Sketch by Hovey Brock*

Max Born

Max Born
1882-1970
German-born English physicist

Max Born's early scientific research involved a study of the dynamics of crystal lattices, a topic to which he returned from time to time throughout his life. The theories he developed eventually came to form the basis of modern solid-state physics. Born is perhaps better known for his role in establishing and clarifying a number of fundamental concepts in modern quantum theory. In the early 1920s, he collaborated with two of his students, German physicist **Werner Heisenberg** and Pascual Jordan, in the development of matrix mechanics, one of the two fundamental mathematical systems for working with the new concepts of quantum theory. He later attacked the problem of finding a physical interpretation for the mathematical formulations that had been developed to describe the wave-particle character of matter. It was primarily for these contributions that Born shared the 1954 Nobel Prize in physics with German physicist **Walther Bothe**.

Born was born on December 11, 1882, in Breslau, then capital of the Prussian province of Silesia, and later re-named Wroclaw when ceded to Poland after World War I. His father was Gustav Born, an eminent embryologist and professor of anatomy at the University of Breslau, and his mother was the former Margarete Kaufmann, daughter of a successful textile merchant. Born's mother died when he was four years old; in 1890, his father married Bertha Lipstein. Born's home life was a strong factor in his early educational development. His mother was particularly fond of music, which may explain Born's own lifelong love of music. Born's father introduced him to a number of important scientific figures of the time, including German bacteriologist **Paul Ehrlich** and German physician Albert Neisser.

Studies Wide Range of Subjects and Frustrates His Teachers

Born attended the Kaiser Wilhelm Gymnasium in Breslau and then, in 1901, enrolled at the University of Breslau and spent the summer semesters of 1902 and 1903 studying in Heidelberg and Zürich. He studied a wide range of subjects, including chemistry, physics, zoology, philosophy, logic, mathematics, and astronomy, finding the last two of particular interest. In 1904, he enrolled at the University of Göttingen, which housed three of the most brilliant German mathematicians of the day, **David Hilbert**, Felix Klein, and **Hermann Minkowski**. Born quickly impressed his teachers with his own brilliance and was invited to become Hilbert's special assistant. Born also seemed to have a knack for frustrating his prestigious instructors. On one occasion, Klein based the topic for a university competition on a paper Born had written on the elasticity of wires and tapes. Born at first refused to enter because he was more interested at the time in learning about Minkowski's work on relativity, but he eventually relented and his paper won him both the competition and, in 1907, a Ph.D. in physics.

After receiving his doctorate, Born began his year of compulsory military service with the German army, but was discharged early because of a severe asthmatic condition. His army experience apparently engendered in Born an anti-military feeling that was to remain with him for the rest of his life. He then left for Cambridge University, where he spent six months studying with English physicist **J. J. Thomson** and English mathematician Joseph Larmor in order to learn about electrons.

Returning to Breslau in 1908, Born first became familiar with American physicist **Albert Einstein's** papers on the special theory of relativity, which had been published three years earlier. Combining Minkowski's mathematical approach to relativity with the theory put forth by Einstein, Born developed a more accurate method of calculating an electron's electromagnetic mass. Intrigued by Born's work, Minkowski invited him back to Göttingen to work on relativity. That collaboration lasted only a few weeks, however, as a result of Minkowski's unexpected death following an operation for appendicitis.

Born remained at Göttingen and was eventually appointed Privatdozent under Woldemar Voigt. During this period, Born carried out a study of the heat capacity of solids, particularly crystals, with Hungarian aerodynamicist **Theodore von Kármán**, resulting in the Born-Kármán theory of specific heats. During his tenure at Göttingen, Born met Hedwig Ehrenberg, the daughter of a professor of law at the University. They married on August 2, 1913, and had three children, Irene, Margaret, and Gustav, who would later become head of the department of pharmacology at Cambridge University.

Moves to Berlin, Joins the War Effort

Two events at the outset of World War I almost simultaneously changed Born's life. In 1915, he was offered a post as extraordinary (assistant) professor at the University of Berlin so that he might relieve German physicist **Max Planck** of his lecturing duties. At the same time, Born was inducted into the Germany army. Through a stroke of good fortune, he was able to get an assignment in Berlin, allowing him to form and maintain a connection with the University while carrying out his military obligations in the army's ordinance testing division. While not particularly productive for Born, his years in Berlin seemed especially enjoyable for him. Part of Berlin's appeal at the time had been the opportunity it gave Born to

work with such notable scientists as Planck and Einstein, with whom he would form a lifelong friendship. Born, a talented pianist, also shared with Einstein a love of music and was known to have accompanied Einstein, a violinist, in chamber music.

In 1919, Born moved once again, this time to the University of Frankfurt-on-the-Main. He had been asked by German physicist **Max von Laue**, then professor of physics at Frankfurt, to exchange teaching positions so that von Laue could work with Planck in Berlin. At Frankfurt, Born carried out a series of experiments on the mean free path of gas molecules with his assistant, Elisabeth Bormann.

Born Returns to Göttingen

Born's reputation at Göttingen had not dimmed during his absence and when Dutch American chemical physicist **Peter Debye** left as director of the University's Physical Institute in 1921, the post was offered to Born. He accepted and spent perhaps the most productive period of his life during his twelve years at Göttingen. Born had initially planned to continue his earlier research on the thermodynamics of crystal lattices but soon became interested in a new topic, one that had been suggested by Danish physicist **Niels Bohr**, architect of modern atomic theory. Bohr had elucidated in 1922 his "correspondence principle," suggesting that a new quantum theory could be developed by finding its transitory relationship to classical physics. Challenged by Bohr's ideas, Born set out to derive a new formulation of physical laws using, according to his own terminology, a "quantum mechanics."

The real breakthrough in this effort came in 1925, when one of Born's assistants, Heisenberg, showed him a paper he had written on this general topic. Heisenberg had begun with the premise that only observable quantities should be used in the development of theoretical principles. With this assumption, Heisenberg had derived a new mathematical approach for dealing with such principles. When Born read Heisenberg's paper, he realized that the mathematical system described there was essentially the same as that of matrix algebra. Since Heisenberg had gone on vacation after giving Born his paper, Born asked another of his students, Jordan, to assist him in developing and refining Heisenberg's paper. Ultimately, a series of three papers—the original by Heisenberg, a collaborative effort by Born and Jordan building on the Heisenberg paper, and a final paper coauthored by all three—was published. These three papers outlined the fundamentals of what was later to become known as matrix mechanics.

Only a year later, an entirely different approach to the treatment of quantum physics was proposed by Austrian physicist **Erwin Schrödinger**, an approach that became known as wave mechanics. Eventually,

Schrödinger was able to demonstrate that these two mathematical formulations—matrix mechanics and wave mechanics—are entirely consistent with each other. The most familiar portion of the Heisenberg-Born-Jordan matrix theory is the equation relating the position (q) and momentum (p) of a particle. Born himself regarded this accomplishment as the most significant of his career and had the equation, $pq - qp = h/2\pi i$, engraved on his tombstone.

Explains the Wave Function

For most physicists, Schrödinger's wave mechanics were easier to use and understand than matrix mechanics. Wave mechanics rather quickly gained acceptance, therefore, and became the tool used to interpret particle phenomena. The one troubling problem, however, was that Schrödinger's wave mechanics was an entirely mathematical analysis of particle behavior based on a few fundamental properties of matter. The wave equation produced by this analysis was an elegant and obviously useful way of analyzing particle properties, but it had no apparent physical meaning. Physicists wondered, in particular, how they were to interpret the wave function, Ψ, that constituted the heart of wave mechanics.

In the summer of 1926, Born proposed a solution for this dilemma. He suggested that the square of the wave function, Ψ^2, should be understood as the probability of finding a particle at any particular point along the wave. Thus, if one thinks of the particle as being carried along on the wave, the square of the amplitude of the wave at any particular point is equal to the likelihood of finding the particle at that location. For this work, as well as for his earlier studies on quantum mechanics, Born shared the 1954 Nobel Prize in physics with Bothe.

Immigrates to Great Britain

One of the early laws passed by German leader Adolf Hitler's regime was the "Gesetz zür Wiederherstellung des Berufsbeamtentums," requiring the removal of Jews from civil service. As a result, Born was fired from his post at Göttingen on April 25, 1933, after which he traveled to the Italian Tyrol. In June, he was invited by English physicist **Patrick Maynard Stuart Blackett** to take up a Stokes Lectureship at Cambridge University, where he worked on problems of nonlinear electrodynamics and wrote two immensely popular books, *Atomic Physics* and *The Restless Universe*. When his fellowship at Cambridge expired in 1936, Born traveled to Bangalore, India, where he visited physicist and Nobel laureate **C. V. Raman**. He then returned to Great Britain and became Tait Professor of Natural Philosophy at the University of Edinburgh. Born's tenure at Edinburgh was spent primarily in the supervision of graduate students, and he produced relatively little new research of his own.

Born retired in 1953 at the age of 70; he returned to Germany and built a home at Bad Pyrmont, a small town near Göttingen. The German government returned the personal property that had been confiscated from him in 1933 and restored the pension that had been denied him by the Nazis. In the last decade of his life, Born became especially active in writing and speaking about the social responsibilities of scientists. In July, 1955, for example, he was one of the signers of the Mainau Declaration, condemning the development of atomic weapons. In addition to the Nobel Prize, Born was awarded the Max Planck Medal of the German Physical Society in 1948, and was a member of many scientific academies throughout the world. Born was elected a member of the Royal Society in 1939 and received its Hughes Medal in 1950. He was also awarded the Macdougall-Brisbane Prize of the Royal Society of Edinburgh in 1945. Born died in Göttingen on January 5, 1970.

SELECTED WRITINGS BY BORN:

Books

Dynamik der Kristallgitter, Teubner, 1915.
The Constitution of Matter, translated by E. W. Blair and T. S. Wheeler, Methuen, 1923.
Einstein's Theory of Relativity, translated by H. L. Brose, Methuen, 1924.
Mechanics of the Atom, translated by J. W. Fisher, Bell, 1927.
Atomic Physics, translated by J. Dougall, Blackie, 1935.
The Restless Universe, translated by W. M. Deans, Blackie, 1935.
Physics and Politics, Oliver and Boyd, 1962.
My Life and Views, Scribner, 1968.
The Born-Einstein Letters, translated by I. Born, Macmillan, 1971.

SOURCES:

Books

Biographical Memoirs of Fellows of the Royal Society, Volume 17, Royal Society (London), 1971, pp. 17–52.
A Biographical Encyclopedia of Scientists, Volume 1, Facts on File, 1981, p. 94.
Gillispie, Charles Coulson, editor, *Dictionary of Scientific Biography,* Volume 15, Scribner, 1975, pp. 39–44.
McGraw-Hill Modern Scientists and Engineers, Volume 1, McGraw-Hill, 1980, pp. 118–19.

Wasson, Tyler, editor, *Nobel Prize Winners,* H. W. Wilson, 1987, pp. 121–23.
Weber, Robert L., *Pioneers of Science: Nobel Prize Winners in Physics,* American Institute of Physics, 1980, pp. 150–52.

—Sketch by David E. Newton

Karl Bosch
1874-1940
German chemist

Karl Bosch, a German chemist, engineer, and industry leader, developed a commercial process for converting gaseous hydrogen and nitrogen into ammonia, an important component in the production of fertilizers and explosives. In addition, methods that he helped develop to synthesize gasoline, methanol, and hydrogen had a profound influence on the chemical industry. In 1931, Bosch and **Friedrich Bergius** shared the Nobel Prize in chemistry for their pioneering work in chemical high-pressure methods.

Bosch was born in Cologne, Germany, on August 27, 1874, the eldest child of Karl and Paula Bosch. The elder Bosch sold gas and plumbing supplies and prospered as a businessman and entrepreneur. Young Bosch, who showed an interest in and talent for science and technology, was prompted by his father to study metallurgy. In 1894, Bosch enrolled at the Technical University in Charlottenburg, Germany. He studied metallurgy and mechanical engineering, and acquired practical machine-shop experience. But he was disappointed with the semi-empirical methods used in his technical classes, and in 1896 he decided to enter the University of Leipzig to study chemistry. Two short years later, after submitting a dissertation on the study of carbon compounds, he received his doctorate.

Discovers Inexpensive Method to Produce Synthetic Ammonia

In 1899, Bosch went to work as a chemist for the Badische Anilin- und Sodafabrik (BASF) at Ludwigshafen am Rhein. BASF was a company specializing in making coal tar dyes. Bosch's first assignment was to find an inexpensive method of producing indigo, a dark blue dye important in dyeing cotton.

At the beginning of the twentieth century, Germany was importing a half million tons of Chilean sodium nitrate every year for use in producing fertilizers and explosives. Because ammonia, a scarce natural resource, can be used to produce sodium nitrate, many investigators had sought a simple way of using electricity to produce ammonia from hydrogen and nitrogen. The existing method was costly, however, because Germany lacked a plentiful and inexpensive source of hydroelectric power. In 1904, **Fritz Haber** found that large quantities of ammonia could be produced by combining hydrogen and nitrogen at high pressures and temperatures and using osmium and uranium as catalysts.

In 1909, under Bosch's leadership, BASF acquired from Haber the patent rights for the ammonia process. Bosch realized that for the Haber process to be commercially feasible he would need huge quantities of hydrogen and nitrogen, an effective cheap catalyst, and equipment able to withstand extreme pressures and temperatures. He devised a method of separating large quantities of hydrogen from a mixture of hydrogen and carbon monoxide. Nitrogen was obtained in pure form by collecting fractions of liquid air. More than 20,000 experiments were necessary to find a suitable catalyst to replace Haber's expensive uranium and osmium. But Bosch's greatest challenge was to construct a reaction chamber that could withstand temperatures of 500 degrees Celsius and pressures that would easily rupture most vessels. Haber had used a steel chamber that had become brittle and dangerously unstable because the hydrogen used in the process caused the steel to lose its carbon content. Bosch cleverly substituted a double-walled chamber. The inside chamber was made of soft steel and could leak hydrogen. The outer chamber was fortified with heavy-duty carbon steel. By forcing a cold mixture of hydrogen and nitrogen gas at 200 atmospheres into the space between the inner and outer chambers, Bosch was able to equalize the pressure on the inner chamber while keeping the outer chamber cool. In 1911, only two years after acquiring the Haber process, BASF began producing commercial quantities of ammonia at a plant near Oppau. During World War I, BASF expanded its production facilities, and by 1918 Germany was producing more than 200,000 tons of synthetic ammonia annually.

From Chemist to Chairman of the Board

In 1919 Bosch became the managing director of BASF. Nonetheless, he remained active in the laboratory, and four years later he succeeded in developing a commercial method for preparing methyl alcohol by combining carbon monoxide and hydrogen at high pressures. In 1925, faced with increasing competition from dye industries in Britain and America, BASF merged with six other German chemical firms to become I. G. Farben, and Bosch was appointed its president. The same year, Friedrich Bergius sold BASF his rights to a method of making gasoline from coal dust and hydrogen. Although Bosch succeeded in applying his technical skills to the Bergius method, the process never became profitable. However, for their work in large scale chemical synthesis, Bosch and Bergius shared the 1931 Nobel Prize in chemistry. Four years later Bosch became chairman of the I.G. Farben board of directors.

In addition to his work on ammonia and gasoline, Bosch studied catalytic methods, phase relationships, photochemistry, and polymers. He influenced the design of large-scale chemical reactors, compressors, and monitoring devices. He published articles on chemical reactions and received many awards, including the Liebig Medal of the German Chemical Society and the Carl Lueg Memorial Medal of the Association of German Metallurgists. As a tribute to his intellect and leadership abilities he was elected in 1937 to Germany's highest scientific position, president of the Kaiser Wilhelm Institute (later renamed the Max Planck Society). Ironically, while Bosch had helped Germany become independent from Chilean sodium nitrate and assured his country a steady supply of ammonia for the weapons industry, he openly opposed Hitler and the Nazi regime.

Bosch married Else Schilbach in 1902; they had two children, a son and a daughter. Committed to education and life-long learning, Bosch relaxed by collecting butterflies, beetles, plants, and minerals. He also enjoyed stargazing from his private observatory near Heidelberg. He died in 1940 in Heidelberg after a long illness.

SELECTED WRITINGS BY BOSCH:

Periodicals

"Verfahren zur Herstellung von Ammoniak aus seinen Elementen mit Hilfe von Katalysatoren," *Chemisches Zentralblatt,* 1913, p. 195.
"Entwicklung der chemischen Hockdrucktechnik bei dem Aufbau der neuen Ammoniakindustrie," *Les Prix Nobel en 1931,* [Stockholm], 1933.
"Probleme grosstechnischer Hydrierunqs-Verfahren," *Chemische Fabrik,* Volume 7, 1934, pp. 1–10.

SOURCES:

Books

Nobel Prize Winners, H. W. Wilson, 1987, pp. 123–125.

Periodicals

Holdermann, K., "Karl Bosch, 1874–1940," *Chemische Berichte,* Volume 90, 1957, xix-xxxix.

—Sketch by Mike McClure

Satyendranath Bose
1894-1974
Indian physicist

Satyendranath Bose was a physicist whose derivation of **Max Planck**'s black body radiation law—a fundamental law of quantum theory that is concerned with the concept of energy transfer associated with light, X rays, and other radiations—verified **Albert Einstein**'s concept of photons and played a major role in the development of quantum statistics and theoretical physics. Einstein used his influence to have Bose's groundbreaking paper published while building upon it to develop a system of quantum statistical mechanics known as Bose-Einstein statistics. As a result of Bose's contribution to the field, bosons—certain subatomic particles of finite mass studied in quantum physics using the Bose-Einstein statistical approach—were named after him.

Although Bose published a relatively low number of original papers throughout his scientific career, his interests in physics and mathematics were wide ranging and included statistical mechanics, electromagnetics, X-ray crystallography, and the unified field theory. Still, Bose failed to develop the worldwide reputation enjoyed by Einstein, who readily acknowledged Bose's contribution as the major step in the development of quantum statistical mechanics. Within India, Bose was highly regarded for both his scientific and political accomplishments, being among a group of pioneering nationalist scientists and intellectuals who helped spur colonial India's independence movement from Great Britain.

Born in Calcutta, India, on January 1, 1894, Bose was the son of Surendranath Bose, an accountant who would eventually found the East India Chemical and Pharmaceutical Works, and Amodini Raichaudhuri. His education began in the English-language schools set up by the British during their colonial reign over India, but he was soon transferred by his father to a Bengali-language school during the resurgence of Bengali nationalism in 1907 (Bengal is a region in the northeast section of the Indian peninsula). After graduation from secondary school, Bose attended

Presidency College in Calcutta, where he studied under noted Indian physicist Jagadischandra Bose (no relation). In 1915 Bose continued his postgraduate studies at the university and finished first in his class with an M.Sc. degree in mathematics. Two years later he became a lecturer in the physics department at the University of Calcutta's college of science, which was established in 1914 and was the first Indian college to offer advanced science studies.

Bose's interest and natural gifts in mathematics soon became evident with the publication of two papers he coauthored with Meghnad Saha on the equation of state. In 1919 they coedited one of the first anthologies in English of Einstein's scientific papers on relativity. Then, in the next year, Bose published his first paper on quantum statistics in the *Philosophical Magazine.*

Bose Lays Foundation for Quantum Statistics

In 1921, Bose accepted a position as a reader, or professor, at the University of Dacca, a newly established university in East Bengal. At Dacca, Bose focused his attention on the statistics of photons, a quantum of electromagnetic energy that has no charge or mass but carries energy such as light and X rays in both wave and particle form. In an interview with American physicist William A. Blanpied for the *American Journal of Physics,* Bose commented that he "spent many sleepless nights" contemplating Planck's law. Finally, according to Bose, a new theory for quantum mathematics dawned on him while he was lecturing in class one day. By 1923, he had written and submitted a paper on his new theory to *Philosophical Magazine,* but it was rejected.

Bose was persistent, however, and sent the article to Einstein along with a letter requesting his assistance. Einstein, who in 1905 had first tried to prove that electromagnetic radiation had an atomic structure made up of a measurable, or quantum, amount of electromagnetic energy, was impressed with Bose's theory. Essentially, Bose had succeeded in substantiating Einstein's proposal where Einstein himself and others had failed. With Einstein's endorsement and translation into German, Bose's paper, "Planck's Law and the Hypothesis of Light Quanta," was published in *Zeitschrift Für Physik* in 1924.

Bose's paper focused on how to derive Planck's black body radiation law, in which the black body is a theoretical ideal body that absorbs all radiation and reflects none. Planck's equation describes the spectral energy distribution from such a body. Einstein's 1905 paper questioned Planck's assumption that his law could be applied *ad hoc* to unquestionable classical electrodynamics laws (electrodynamics is a discipline within physics concerned with the inter-relatedness of electric and other currents and magnets). In Einstein's thermodynamic approach, the quantum structure of

electromagnetic radiation could be viewed the same as an ordinary gas and its atomic structure. Without reference to classical electrodynamics, Bose used a phase-space approach that treated radiation as an ideal gas to show that Einstein's model and Planck's law were consistent. Bose's paper both vindicated Einstein's theory and pointed the way for future developments in electrodynamics.

Unfortunately, Bose concentrated on the mathematical implications of his work and was not as quick to see the far-reaching ramifications it had in the field of physics, especially in the areas of electrodynamics and quantum gases. As a result, he failed to gain the international renown of such famous physicists as Planck and Einstein, who, building on Bose's work, developed the foundation for the Bose-Einstein statistics. This statistical approach to quantum physics was the first of two approaches to determine the distribution of certain subatomic particles among the various possible energy values. Depending on the approach used, the particles that adhere to these mathematical laws are known as bosons—named after Bose—or fermions, named after the developer of the second approach, **Enrico Fermi**.

Although Einstein's endorsement and further support led to Bose leaving India for two years to study in Germany and France, Bose's dream of working with Einstein never materialized; in fact, the two scientists had only one brief personal meeting. In 1926, Bose returned to Dacca and became a professor of physics. Dedicated to his teaching duties, Bose's production of scientific papers was, by many standards, meager, amounting to only twenty-six original papers focusing on mathematical statistics, electromagnetic properties of the ionosphere, X-ray crystallography, thermoluminescence, and the unified field theory.

Bose was appointed in 1945 as the Khaira Professor of Physics at Calcutta University. In 1956, he became vice-chancellor of Visva-Bharati University, which was established by Rabindranath Tagore, who had won the Nobel Prize in poetry. He was then appointed a national professor by the Indian government in 1959.

Bose married Ushabala Ghosh in 1914; the couple had two sons and five daughters. Devotedly nationalistic during the days of British rule, Bose abhorred the fact that some people thought he was German. He remained dedicated to his country and particularly to the Bengali cultural renaissance. He was among a core group of Indian intellectuals who assisted with India's political emergence, primarily by instilling pride in the intellectual capabilities of the populace. The founder of the Science Association of Bengali in 1948, which helped popularize science in his native language, Bose also served in the Indian parliament from 1952 to 1958 and as president of the

National Institute of Sciences of India. He received India's Padma Vibhushan award from the government in 1954, and, in 1958, was elected to the Royal Society. Fluent in Bengali, Sanskrit, English, and French, Bose loved poetry.

Bose died on February 4, 1974, in Calcutta. Jagadish Sharma, who studied physics under Bose, commented in Bose's obituary in *Physics Today* that the scientist's remarkable rise to "the highest echelons of science" must be placed in the context of an India that was ruled by Great Britain. Such an environment was not conducive to fostering the native Indian intellect, Sharma noted, evidenced by the "very few Indian scientists of international reputation." Sharma also added that Bose's kindness was endearing to all and that he "was liberal with his pocketbook whenever the situation demanded."

SELECTED WRITINGS BY BOSE:

Periodicals

(With Meghnad N. Saha) "On the Influence of the Finite Volume of Molecules on the Equation of State," *Philosophical Magazine,* Volume 36, 1918.

"Plancks Gesetz und Lichtquanten Hyhpothesis" (title means, "Planck's Law and the Hypothesis of Light Quanta"), *Zeitschrift Für Physik,* Volume 26, 1924, pp.

SOURCES:

Books

A Biographical Encyclopedia of Scientists, Facts On File, 1981, p. 95

Blanpied, William A., *Dictionary of Scientific Biography,* Scribner, 1978, p. 325

Periodicals

Blanpied, William A., "Satyendranath Bose: Co-Founder of Quantum Statistics," *American Journal of Physics,* Volume 40, 1972, pp. 1212–1220

Sharma, Jagadish, "Satyendra Nath Bose," *Physics Today,* April, 1974, pp. 129–131

—*Sketch by David Petechuk*

Walther Bothe
1891-1957
German physicist

Walther Bothe was a prominent German physicist during the "Golden Age of Physics," circa 1900–1930. He was one of the few graduate students to study with physicist **Max Planck** in Berlin and began his professional career with **Hans Geiger**, inventor of the Geiger counter. During the 1920s he developed the coincidence counting technique for tracking the collisions between electrons and electromagnetic quanta, for which he was awarded the Nobel Prize in 1954. Bothe also contributed many ideas to nuclear reaction theory.

Walther Wilhelm Georg Bothe was born in Oranienburg, Germany, on January 8, 1891, the son of Fritz and Charlotte Hartung Bothe. His father was a merchant. At age 23, Bothe received his Ph.D. degree from the University of Berlin. His dissertation concerned the interactions between light and molecules as they related to the reflection, refraction, dispersion, and absorption of light. After graduation he began work at the Physical-Technical Institute under Hans Geiger, the inventor of the Geiger counter.

World War I was just beginning, and Bothe immediately entered the army as a machine gunner. He was soon captured and spent the rest of the war as a Russian prisoner in Siberia, where he managed to study Russian and work on physics. His war experience also resulted in Bothe's meeting Barbara Below of Moscow, whom he married in 1920 and with whom he had two daughters, Elena and Johanna. Barbara died in 1951.

After World War I, Bothe returned to research with Geiger and taught at the University of Berlin. He became interested in quantum theory, which was generally accepted by 1920 but had not yet been confirmed experimentally. The theory suggested that electromagnetic energy, such as light, displays characteristics of particles as well as of waves. The work of **Arthur Holly Compton** in 1923 had shown that electrons could scatter X rays in patterns as if they were particles, and that in the process the X rays would transfer some energy and momentum to the electrons, which would recoil from their atoms. This phenomenon became known as the Compton effect.

Establishes Coincidence Counting Technique

After Compton's discoveries, **Niels Bohr** and others had hypothesized that the electron's recoil would bear a statistical relationship, not a direct relationship, to a wave quantum, and that the energy and momentum of the participating objects would be conserved in the sum of many collisions rather than at the level of each interaction. In 1924 Bothe and Geiger tested this hypothesis using two of Geiger's particle counters, one to detect the recoil of electrons from hydrogen atoms, and the other to track the scattering of X-ray quanta. They found that the recoil and scattering events occurred together much more often than could be explained by chance, and concluded that each scatter event corresponded with a specific electron recoil. This showed that energy and momentum were conserved in each interaction, and that the laws of classical physics applied at the subatomic level. It was this work that earned Bothe his share of the 1954 Nobel Prize with **Max Born**. The technique became known as coincidence counting and turned out to be useful in the study of nuclear reactions and cosmic rays.

During the 1930s life became difficult for German physicists as the National Socialists gained power under Adolf Hitler. Nazi ideology associated theoretical physics, especially **Albert Einstein**'s, with Jewish intellectualism. At least eleven Nobel laureates in physics left the country before the end of World War II. As one of those who stayed, Bothe was faced with the decline of physics education and a slowing of research momentum. He opposed National Socialism and was disliked by the Nazis because he continued to support the theory of relativity. In 1932 Bothe was chosen to replace the Nazi favorite **Philipp E. A. von Lenard** at the University of Heidelberg. But Bothe stayed only two years in the Reich-dominated department before transferring to the Kaiser Wilhelm Institute (later the Max Planck Institute). Bothe continued teaching and research, convinced that staying involved in the educational system would be a form of resistance to National Socialism. In the late 1920s Bothe's study of radioactivity laid the groundwork for **James Chadwick**'s later discovery of the neutron, and in 1929 he used the coincidence counting method to detect cosmic rays. At the Max Planck Institute for Medical Research, Bothe supervised construction of Germany's first cyclotron, a circular particle accelerator, completed in 1943.

During the war, Bothe worked with **Werner Karl Heisenberg** on Germany's efforts to develop an atom bomb. Early experiments had used the isotope uranium 235 as an explosive, but plutonium worked as well and was easier to isolate from uranium 238, a more common form of uranium. Plutonium 239 is created by bombarding common uranium with neutrons until it absorbs some of them. Like the Americans, the Germans had to develop a reactor in order to acquire a large enough supply of plutonium, and the reactor required a substance that could moderate the speed of the neutrons. At the time, the choice for this medium lay between heavy water (deuterium oxide) and graphite. The former was difficult to obtain, whereas the latter was relatively plentiful.

Between 1940 and 1941, Bothe measured graphite's ability to absorb neutrons and concluded that graphite would be inferior to heavy water. His calculations were wrong, but no one detected the error at the time. As a result, the Germans chose to rely on heavy water, while the Americans, who had made more accurate measurements, chose graphite. Thus the German bomb project, already slowed by the Nazis' inability to make long-range research commitments, fell far behind the American effort. Some people have speculated that Bothe's error was intentional, since he was known as an especially careful experimenter. He himself never accounted for it.

After World War II, Bothe continued work at the Max Planck Institute and the University of Heidelberg. Besides his scientific gifts, he was a talented painter with oils and watercolors, as well as an accomplished pianist, enjoying the works of J. S. Bach and Beethoven. In later years he suffered from a serious circulatory ailment which required the amputation of one of his legs. His illness prevented him from receiving the Nobel Prize in person. Bothe died in Heidelberg on February 8, 1957.

SELECTED WRITINGS BY BOTHE:

Periodicals

(With Hans Geiger) "Ein Weg zur Experimentellen Nachprufung der Theorie von Bohr, Kramers, und Slater," (title means "A Way to Experimentally Test the Theory of Bohr, Kramers, and Slater"), *Zeitschrift für Physik,* Volume 26, 1925.
(With Werner Kolhorsten) "Das Wesen der Hohenstrahlung," (title means "The Nature of Cosmic Rays"), *Zeitschrift für Physik,* Volume 56, 1929.

SOURCES:

Books

Beyerchen, Alan D., *Scientists Under Hitler: Politics and the Physics Community in the Third Reich,* Yale University Press, 1977.
Nobel Lectures: Physics, 1942–1962, Nobel Foundation, 1964.
Nobel Prize Winners, H. W. Wilson, 1987.
The Nobel Prizewinners: Physics, Volume 2, Salem Press, 1989.

—Sketch by Valerie Brown

Raoul Bott
1923-
Hungarian American mathematician

Raoul Bott is a research mathematician who has made important contributions to the fields of geometry and topology. His major discovery, known as the Bott periodicity theorem, opened up new directions in topological research and earned him the Veblen Prize in 1964. The American Mathematical Society recognized the importance of Bott's career contributions by awarding him the Steele Career Prize in 1990 for his work in topology and algebraic geometry.

Bott was born September 24, 1923, to Rudolph and Margit Kovacs Bott, in Budapest, Hungary. He lost both his parents to cancer when he was still a young child, and he was adopted by Oskar Pfeffer. Pfeffer was a businessman who never went to college, but he placed a high value on education. The young Bott was greatly influenced by this, and after he and Pfeffer immigrated to America, Bott entered McGill University in Toronto. His degree program was not in mathematics but in electrical engineering; he received his bachelor's degree in 1945 and a master's degree in 1946, also in engineering. The only other field he considered at the time was music, but he did not feel gifted enough. In fact, in an interview with Karen Sands, Bott said: "The reason it took me so long to decide on math was because I did not feel gifted there, either."

A brief stint in the Canadian Army convinced Bott that he did not want a career in engineering. He returned to McGill and applied to a master's program in mathematics. He was frustrated, however, by the prerequisites for this degree; McGill officials required a B.A. rather than a B.S., and he would have had to earn another undergraduate degree before even beginning graduate study. Lloyd Williams, a professor at McGill and mentor to Bott, suggested he try the newly formed graduate program in mathematics at the Carnegie Institute of Technology. Bott hitchhiked to Pittsburgh in April, 1947, but once there he again ran into difficulty. At Carnegie, his lack of mathematical foundation meant that the master's degree program would require three years of study. The sympathetic director of the program, John Lighton Synge, pointed out that the requirements for a doctorate in mathematics were more flexible, requiring a time commitment of only two years. Accordingly, Bott entered this program in 1947.

His dissertation adviser at Carnegie, Richard J. Duffin, encouraged Bott to study mathematics in his own way, so Bott brought an unsolved problem from engineering to serve as the subject of his dissertation. Together, Bott and Duffin worked out a theorem (which bears their names) in which a two-point network can be synthesized without the use of ideal transformers. To reach this conclusion, Bott and Duffin used the theory of positive real functions, an important part of the field of analysis, and their work has led to more realistic models of electrical systems.

After receiving his doctoral degree from Carnegie in 1949, Bott was appointed to a research position at the prestigious Institute for Advanced Study (IAS) at Princeton. Because of his interest in analysis, Bott was delighted to be able to study Morse theory from its inventor, Marston Morse, who was at the IAS at the time. Whereas most of analysis is primarily concerned with the minimum and maximum values of functions, Morse theory uses topology to look at the entire function, making it part of a discipline called global analysis. The interweaving of analysis and topology would interest Bott throughout his career.

Periodicity Theorem Leads to Veblen Prize

In 1951, Bott left the IAS for an instructorship at the University of Michigan. While he was there, he completed his most important research, his work on the periodicity theorem. Bott applied what he had learned about Morse theory to Lie groups—topological groups which can be given a certain analytic structure—and he determined that certain rings found within Lie groups are isomorphic. Rings are sets whose elements can be combined using addition and multiplication but not division. To say that two rings are isomorphic means that the members of the sets share a one-to-one correspondence and therefore are interchangeable. The periodicity theorem which Bott developed showed to the surprise of many that even as the rings become more complicated, the isomorphisms do not. His theory has applications not only for topology and functional analysis, but for theoretical physics as well.

Harvard University offered Bott a position as professor in 1959; he accepted and has spent most of his career there, becoming William Gaspar Graustein professor of mathematics in 1977. In 1963 the English mathematician **Michael Atiyah** visited Harvard, and he and Bott collaborated to apply Bott's periodicity theorem in terms of K-theory, which studies chains of rings. They were successful, and in 1964 the American Mathematical Society awarded Bott the Veblen Prize for his work in periodicity.

That same year, Atiyah and Bott met again at a conference in Woods Hole, Massachusetts, where they decided to work together for a second time. Their goal was to apply **Luitzen Brouwer**'s idea of a fixed-point formula to sheaf theory, which is the study of all the planes which go through a certain point. Atiyah and Bott, with Lars Gårding, would again work together in

1970, this time on the applications of algebraic geometry to certain classes of differential equations relating to the path of light through crystals. Bott's work on the periodicity theorem also led to an important collaboration with Shiing-Shen Chern, in which they further studied the vector bundles Bott had defined earlier. This work produced Bott-Chern forms, a redefinition of the vector bundles in terms of differential geometry to allow a broader use.

In 1987, Bott was awarded the National Medal of Science for his career accomplishments. The American Mathematical Society also acknowledged his work in 1990 with the Steele Career Prize. While others have recognized his mathematical achievements, Raoul Bott values above all his opportunities to teach and to collaborate with other mathematicians. His career goal, he commented to interviewer Karen Sands, has been to "further the cause of mathematics in any way possible." Bott has been married to Phyllis Aikman Bott since 1947. They have four children.

SELECTED WRITINGS BY BOTT:

Books

Lectures on K(X), Benjamin, 1969.
"Some Recollections from 30 Years Ago," *Constructive Approaches to Mathematical Models,* edited by C. Volume Coffman and G. J. Fix, Academic Press, 1979, pp. 33–40.
"The Topological Constraints on Analysis," *A Century of Mathematics in America: Part Two,* edited by P. Duren, American Mathematical Society, 1988, pp. 527–542.

Periodicals

"The Stable Homotopy of the Classical Groups," *Annals of Mathematics (2),* Volume 70, 1959, pp. 313–337.
(With Michael F. Atiyah) "On the Periodicity Theorem for Complex Vector Bundles," *Acta Mathematica,* Volume 112, 1964, pp. 229–247.
(With Shiing-Shen Chern) "Hermitian Vector Bundles and the Equidistribution of the Zeroes of Their Holomorphic Sections," *Acta Mathematica,* Volume 114, 1965, pp. 71–112.
(With M. F. Atiyah and L. Gårding) "Lacunas for Hyperbolic Differential Operators with Constant Coefficients I, II," *Acta Mathematica,* Volume 125, 1970, pp. 109–189, and Volume 131, 1973, pp. 145–206.

SOURCES:

Periodicals

"1990 Steele Prizes," *Notices of the American Mathematical Society,* September, 1990, pp. 805–807.

Other

Bott, Raoul, interview with Karen Sands conducted December 13, 1993.

—*Sketch by Karen Sands*

Daniel Bovet
1907-1992
Swiss-born Italian pharmacologist

Daniel Bovet had the distinction of making basic contributions in at least three distinct areas of pharmacology, the science of drugs. His research made possible the commercial development of sulfa drugs, antihistamines, and muscle relaxants. For his accomplishments in pharmacology he was awarded the Nobel Prize in physiology or medicine in 1957.

Bovet was born on March 23, 1907, in Neuchatel, Switzerland, the only son among the four children of Pierre Bovet and Amy Babut Bovet. Pierre Bovet was a professor of experimental education at the University of Geneva and the founder of the Institut J. J. Rousseau. His son later recalled in *Time* that he and his sisters were "guinea pigs" for testing his father's educational theories. Daniel Bovet received his primary and secondary school education in Neuchatel, then studied biology at the University of Geneva, from which he received his *license* in 1927. He did his graduate study in physiology and zoology at the same institution and earned his doctor of science degree in 1929.

Bovet went to Paris in 1929 to become an assistant in the Laboratory of Therapeutic Chemistry at the Pasteur Institute, working under the direction of Ernest Fourneau. In his 1965 article "Role of the Scientist in Modern Society," Bovet declared that being Fourneau's "pupil and collaborator . . . for nearly twenty years . . . was the greatest good fortune of my life." Bovet succeeded Fourneau as director of the Laboratory of Therapeutic Chemistry in 1939. It was there that he met Filomena Nitti, a fellow researcher and the daughter of Francesco Saverio Nitti, a former prime minister of Italy who had been driven into exile to Paris following Benito Mussolini's rise to power. Bovet and Filomena Bovet-Nitti, wife and collaborator (as she thereafter identified herself), were married in 1938 and she became his collaborator in nearly all of his research, as well as the coauthor of many of his scientific books and articles. They had two daughters and one son, Danièle Bovet, who

Daniel Bovet

became a professor of information science at the University of Rome.

Researches Sulfa Drugs and Antihistamines

In the early 1930s, the German scientist **Gerhard Domagk** discovered that Prontosil, a dye product, effectively combated streptococcal infections. Prontosil was a complex chemical, however, and expensive to produce. Bovet and his colleagues at the Pasteur Institute reasoned that the therapeutic action of the substance was probably due to some part of the drug's molecule that was only released when the molecule broke down in the body. After months of work and many experiments, they discovered that the active therapeutic agent was sulfanilamide. This product was much cheaper to produce than Prontosil and was soon being manufactured in quantity, becoming the first of the so-called "wonder drugs." Over the next several years Bovet and his associates went on to synthesize many other sulfanamide derivatives that together formed the group of sulfa drugs that were to save millions of lives during World War II and afterward. Domagk was awarded the Nobel Prize in physiology or medicine in 1939 for his discovery of the therapeutic action of Prontosil, but it was the work of Bovet and his team that had made sulfa drugs a practical reality.

In 1937 Bovet turned his attention to histamine, a hormone that occurs naturally in all body tissues. When an irritant is introduced, an overproduction of free histamine can occur in some localized area of the body. The free histamine in turn causes swelling or an allergic reaction that often leads to severe discomfort, damage to body tissues, or—in extreme cases—to fatal shock. Bovet was struck by the fact that there was no natural product in the human body that would counteract the negative effects of free histamine; he believed that what was needed was an artificial substance which would block them. Bovet and his assistants soon synthesized the first antihistamine, although it had too many problems to be a viable commercial product. Between 1937 and 1941, Bovet and others performed some three thousand experiments to find a practical substitute. Eventually several were developed, including Bovet's own discovery, pyrilamine. These were the first of the many antihistamines now used in modern medicine.

Shifts Focus to Muscle Relaxants and Mental Illness

In 1947 Bovet and his family left Paris for Rome, where he was to organize and direct the Laboratory of Therapeutic Chemistry at the Istituto Superiore di Sanità. He also became an Italian citizen. It was about this time that he began to study the muscle relaxant properties of curare, the poison certain South American Indians had long used on their arrows. A chemically pure form of curare had been produced earlier and was used to relax body muscles before surgery, thus allowing the surgeon to use much smaller doses of potentially dangerous anesthetics. However, the effects of the curare itself were very unpredictable, and it was also expensive. Bovet set himself the task of finding a synthetic form of the drug that would have the advantages of predictability and low cost. During eight years of work he produced over four hundred synthetic forms of curare, including gallamine and succinylcholine, the latter becoming widely used. During his research on curare, Bovet spent some time with the Indians of South America to learn how they produced and used the drug. He later remarked humorously that he had done so out of a spirit of adventure; curare was only the pretext.

Bovet left Rome in 1964 to become professor of pharmacology at the University of Sassari on the Italian island of Sardinia. He returned to Rome as director of the Laboratory of Psychobiology and Psychopharmacology of the Italian national research council in 1969. He became professor of psychobiology at the University of Rome in 1971 and remained there as an honorary professor following his retirement in 1982. The positions in Rome reflected still another shift in the focus of his research, indicating an interest in the complex area of mental illness and its treatment through the use of chemicals.

As early as 1957, *Time* had reported Bovet's belief that the key to mental illness lay in chemistry.

His studies centered on the effect of various chemical compounds on the central nervous system of the human body. While his work did not produce the kind of dramatic practical breakthroughs that he had achieved in sulfa drugs, antihistamines, and muscle relaxants, he did contribute much important basic research to this field.

Frequently collaborating with his wife, Bovet produced several books and over four hundred articles in the course of his professional life. Before 1947 most of his writings were in French; afterward many appeared in Italian and some in English. However, even this large output does not fully reveal the breadth of his intellectual interests. He was concerned with the impact of scientific discovery on political, social, and economic affairs and with the equally strong impact of those affairs on science. He illustrated this in "Role of the Scientist in Modern Society." "Unfortunately, in our century," he wrote, "two-thirds of the global population are illiterate and walk barefooted, ten to fifteen per cent suffer from hunger, thirty-three per cent to forty per cent do not have an adequate diet, seventy per cent are not provided with sufficient water supply, and eighty per cent lack adequate hygienic conveniences. Even the best drugs are ineffective for people living in very poor hygienic conditions." Science, he concluded, could not solve all of the world's problems. Personally, Bovet was a humble, enthusiastic man who singlemindedly pursued his quest for scientific progress without personal gain in mind. As *Time* noted when he received the Nobel Prize in 1957, Bovet had never taken out a patent in his own name and never made any money from his scientific discoveries. He was the recipient of numerous international awards in addition to the Nobel Prize. He died of cancer in Rome on April 8, 1992.

SELECTED WRITINGS BY BOVET:

Books

(With F. Bovet-Nitti) *Structure et activité pharmacodynamique des médicaments du système nerveux végétatif: adrénaline, acétylcholine, histamine et leurs antagonistes,* S. Karger, 1948.
(Edited, with F. Bovet-Nitti and G. B. Marini-Bettòlo) *Curare and Curare-like Agents,* Elsevier, 1959.
(With Richard H. Blum and James Moore) *Controlling Drugs,* Jossey-Bass, 1974.
Une chimie qui guérit: Histoire de la découverte des sulfamides, Editions Payot, 1988.

Periodicals

"Role of the Scientist in Modern Society," *Perspectives in Biology and Medicine,* summer, 1965, pp. 533–545.

SOURCES:

Books

Magill, Frank N., editor, *The Nobel Prize Winners: Physiology or Medicine,* Volume 2, Salem Press, 1991, pp. 741–748.

Periodicals

New York Times, April 11, 1992, p. 33.
Time, November 4, 1957, p. 41.

—*Sketch by John E. Little*

William Bowie
1872-1940
American geologist

Although William Bowie may be remembered more among geologists for his theories on abnormalities in geologic formations, his lasting impact on nonscientists comes from his improvement in cartography. Bowie, who worked with the U.S. Coast and Geodetic Survey for more than forty years, participated in many national projects, the results of which are still applicable today. Throughout his career, he published more than 400 scientific articles, detailing his geological studies and arguing for improved mapping services. He also strived to lay the groundwork for an international, as well as national, geophysics community, serving as the president of two international organizations.

Bowie was born on May 6, 1872, at Grassland, his family's estate in Anne Arundel County, Maryland. The Bowie family traced their lineage back to English ancestors, many of whom had been knighted. William's father, Thomas John Bowie, served as a Deputy Provost Marshal in Maryland during the Civil War, and later as a representative in the Maryland legislature. Thomas's wife, Susanna Anderson, had a lineage to match his own, and her family was also well known in Maryland for its service to the state. Bowie was one of three sons; his brother Edward grew up to become a prominent meteorologist, and his brother John became keeper of the family estate. William attended the local public schools before enrolling at St. Johns College in Annapolis, Maryland. He transferred to Connecticut's Trinity College, from which he received a Bachelor of Science degree in 1893. Shortly after receiving his civil engineering degree from Lehigh University in 1895, Bowie joined the

United States Coast and Geodetic Survey as a junior officer. Within a few years, he was leading survey teams in collecting triangulation and base-line measurements across the United States, as well as the Philippines, Puerto Rico, and Alaska.

On June 28, 1899, he married Elizabeth Taylor Wattles, who hailed from an old Alexandria, Virginia family. The young couple had two sons: William, who died soon after birth, and Clagett, who later became an aeronautical engineer and designer. Bowie earned a master's degree from Trinity College in 1907 and, within two years, was appointed inspector of Geodetic Work and chief of the Survey's Computing Section, renamed the Division of Geodesy in 1915. When he took office, the Survey had completed 10,000 miles of triangulation and 30,000 miles of leveling. In the twenty-seven years that Bowie presided over this division, those numbers increased to 68,000 and 261,000 respectively. During his first years in office, he sought to improve the Survey's instruments, suggesting that the bronze circles in theodolites, a surveying tool used to measure angles, be replaced with more reliable silver ones. He devised his own field version of the base tape-stretcher, which later served as the standard model for those made in the Survey's instrument shop.

Makes Overtures to International Geological Community

Bowie did not limit his efforts to the Survey. From 1912 to 1917, he offered a summer course in geodetic surveying and practical astronomy at a Columbia University surveying camp near Litchfield, Connecticut. He also turned his attention to projects far beyond American geologic boundaries. After just four years as head of the Geodesic Survey, Bowie began one of his many efforts to unite international concerns in geology, spearheading a project to standardize Canadian, U.S., and Mexican survey methods. Accepting the North American Datum in 1913, the three countries agreed to engage in standardized triangulation studies. While World War I interrupted more grandiose plans for the creation of an international community of geophysicists, Bowie's appetite for international collaboration had already been whetted at a meeting of the International Geodetic Association in Hamburg, Germany, in 1912. Although the association attempted to carry on during the war under the moniker of Reduced Geodetic Association (an alliance of seven neutral countries, including the United States), when the war ended, so did the International Geodetic Association.

During World War I, Bowie was commissioned as a major in the Corps of Engineers and assigned to the Mapping Division of the Office of the Chief of Engineers, an assignment that could not have suited him better. Towards the end of the war, Bowie began his campaign to improve the process by which government workers produced national maps. He argued that standardizing the maps and eliminating unnecessary duplications could save expenditure of public funds. In 1919, these efforts came to fruition in the form of a Board of Surveys and Maps, of which he was naturally named chair. Similarly, he persuaded the American Society of Civil Engineers to create a Division of Surveying and Mapping. Again, with Bowie as chair, this division studied the economic benefits associated with the utilization of accurate maps. He gained another academic accolade as well that year, when he received his Doctor of Science degree from Trinity.

Studies the Theory of Isostasy

After the war, Bowie turned once more to international organization. In 1919, he joined a group of international delegates to create the International Union of Geodesy and Geophysics. Its section of geodesy, of which Bowie served as president from 1919 to 1933, remained a vestige of the defunct International Geodetic Association. That same year, he also accepted the chair of the American Geophysical Union's geodesy section, a post which he held for a comparatively short four years, and served as the union's general secretary from 1929 to 1932. But none of these activities detracted from his scientific endeavors. Since 1912, Bowie had been exploring the theory of isostasy, the concept that, under the effect of gravity, the rocks of the earth's crust displace the denser rock materials beneath them, and thus literally float in equilibrium. Drawing on the work of the American civil engineer J. F. Hayford, Bowie led the Survey in studies of how gravity anomalies show that some parts of the crust are out of this equilibrium. Bowie turned his attention to mountains, speculating that mountains arose from the underlayer of the earth when parts of the earth's crust became either lightened by erosion or overloaded by sediment deposited on them. To restore equilibrium, sub-crustal rock flows beneath the light crustal rock and forces it upward to form mountains. Bowie embellished Hayford's work by creating tables to determine how much the subcrust compensated for the loss of the light rock, the first time that isostasy had been mathematically evaluated.

In 1922 Bowie received an additional Doctor of Science degree from Lehigh, and was elected to the National Academy of Sciences in 1927. That same year, he summarized his geological theories in his book *Isostasy*. Bowie expanded upon his earlier work by speculating that the earth's crust demonstrated the same isostatic equilibrium under water that it did on the surface. He arranged for the U.S. government to collaborate with the Dutch scientist F. A. Vening Meinesz, an expert on measuring gravity in the ocean areas. The two nations sponsored joint sea expeditions in 1928 and 1931–1932 to calculate gravity levels underwater. From 1933 to 1936, Bowie served as president of the International Union of Geodesy and Geophysics, which created a medal in his name and honored him as its first recipient in 1939. After a brief illness, Bowie died on August 28, 1940, in Washington, D.C. He was buried in Arlington National Cemetery.

SELECTED WRITINGS BY BOWIE:

Books

Isostasy, Dutton, 1927.
The Objectives of the Pan American Institute of Geography and History, D. F. Tacubaya (Mexico), 1937.

Periodicals

"The Function of Geodesy in Surveying," *The Military Engineer,* Volume 16, No. 36, 1924, pp. 140–143.
"Shaping the Earth," *Journal of the Washington Academy of Sciences,* Volume 21, No. 6, 1931.

Herbert W. Boyer

SOURCES:

Books

Dictionary of Scientific Biography, edited by Charles Gillespie, Scribner, 1970.

Periodicals

Heck, N. H., "Memorial to William Bowie," *Proceedings of the Geological Society of America,* Volume 40, June, 1941, pp. 163–66.
Heiskanen, W., "William Bowie as an Isostasist and as a Man," *Transactions of the American Geophysical Union,* 30, 1949, pp. 629–635.

—Sketch by Shari Rudavsky

Herbert W. Boyer
1936-
American biochemist

Herbert W. Boyer has long been one of the leaders in both the science and the business of biotechnology, the engineering of genetic material. It was Boyer, in collaboration with the Stanford bio-

chemist **Stanley Cohen**, who first cloned, or artificially constructed, new and functional deoxyribonucleic acid (DNA) from two separate gene sources. Following the work of **Paul Berg**, who had developed the technique of gene splicing, in 1973 Boyer and Cohen managed to take genes from two bacteria, recombine them, and insert them in another cell which divided itself and reproduced the new genetic material. It was the dawn of a new biological age, one full of potential and fraught with ethical problems.

Herbert Wayne Boyer was born on July 10, 1936, in Pittsburgh, Pennsylvania; his father was a coal miner and railroad worker. He grew up in the nearby town of Derry and attended both grammar and high school there, where he showed more of an aptitude for football than for science. But his football coach was also his science teacher, and Boyer soon became interested in that subject. In 1954 he entered St. Vincent College in Latrobe, Pennsylvania, a Benedictine liberal arts school, where he embarked on premedical studies. He soon abandoned medicine, however, when he discovered the field of DNA research. **James Watson** and **Francis Crick** had made their ground-breaking discovery of the double-helix structure of DNA in 1953, and scientists were racing to map human genes. Boyer was fascinated; he soon dubbed his pet cats Watson and Crick. Boyer graduated from St. Vincent in 1958.

Concentrates on Restriction Enzymes of Bacteria

In 1958, Boyer married a young woman from Latrobe, Grace Boyer, and entered the University of

Pittsburgh as a graduate student in bacterial genetics. He earned his Ph.D. in bacteriology in 1963, and he went on to Yale for three years as a postdoctoral fellow, studying enzymology and protein chemistry. It was here that he began to focus more and more on restriction enzymes, proteins which are designed to cut up and destroy foreign DNA invading the cell. In 1966 he was appointed assistant professor at the University of California at San Francisco.

At the University of California, Boyer was given a laboratory where he could continue his research on restriction enzymes, specifically those of the bacterium *Escherichia coli* (*E. coli*). This one-celled bacterium has long been a favorite for laboratory study because of its simple structure and because it rapidly reproduces and is comparatively easy to culture. Within ten hours of inception, a single cell of *E. coli* will multiply into over a billion daughter cells. Along with another young biochemist, Howard Goodman, Boyer isolated certain of the restriction enzymes in *E. coli,* and he began to see that they could be used as chemical scissors to cut the DNA molecule at certain points. One such enzyme, *Eco*RI, always cut the same genetic phrase along the DNA molecule. Not only did it cut the DNA, but it did so in such a way that it left two flaps or "sticky ends"; these ends made it possible to bind other cut pieces of DNA if they were inserted into the incised section. *Eco*RI was, Boyer began to see, a revolutionary biochemical tool, which could be used not only for cutting DNA but for pasting it as well.

At this time, during the early 1970s, scientists at both Stanford and Harvard were researching gene splicing and recombining. At Stanford, Paul Berg had managed to splice genes or segments of the DNA molecule of one virus—SV40, a simian virus—into another virus to be used as a transporter or "vector." He had stopped short, however, at then inserting such recombined or recombinant DNA into the *E. coli*, for fear that his viral vector might somehow escape his laboratory and then become established in the human intestine. But Berg's work had pointed the way for others. Two floors below Berg's lab at Stanford, Stanley Cohen was at work isolating genetic material from *E. coli*. But Cohen was not concerned with the one round chromosome of the bacterium which contains most of *E. coli*'s genetic material—nearly 4,000 genes. Rather he was isolating small rings of genetic material separate from the chromosome known as plasmids. Using detergents, Cohen could isolate these plasmids and their DNA molecule more easily than it was possible to do with the chromosome itself.

Participates in the Invention of Gene Technology

Cohen heard Boyer describing the action of his *Eco* RI enzyme at a conference in Hawaii, and, in a meeting that is now legendary, the two talked over a sandwich at a delicatessen and agreed to work together. Combining their technologies, they saw how they could splice genes from two bacteria and insert them in a third which could then be replicated billions of times. In San Francisco, Boyer and Cohen worked out the basics of genetic engineering. Boyer's restrictive enzyme would cut segments of DNA along Cohen's plasmids. The segments could then be inserted or spliced in the cut segments of different plasmid rings using the enzyme ligase—whose function is the opposite of a restriction enzyme—to secure the splice. This hybrid plasmid or vector could then be inserted into *E. coli* where it would replicate itself, creating a new, genetically engineered organism. Cohen called the resulting organism a chimera after the mythical Greek monster—part goat, part serpent, and part lion—but they are more commonly referred to as clones.

Boyer and Cohen first published their results in 1973, and they followed it up with work involving gene splicing and cloning of the African clawed toad, again employing *E. coli* as the replicating organism. Boyer soon saw the commercial potential of the process he helped pioneer. By splicing in segments of higher organisms—the genetic material responsible for the creation of proteins or hormones, for instance—one could make the bacteria into factories, producing these various materials as they replicated themselves. It was this sort of thinking that created the biotechnology business; Boyer invested 500 hundred dollars with the young venture capitalist Robert Swanson and became one of the first in the field, cofounding the company Genentech in 1976.

That same year, Boyer became a full professor of biochemistry at the University of California in San Francisco and an investigator at the Howard Hughes Medical Institute. He continued his research as well as his job as vice president of Genentech, contracting his own university laboratory for results in many instances. Genentech began producing somatostatin, a brain hormone, in 1977; they were manufacturing insulin by the next year and a growth hormone the year after, and by 1980 they were manufacturing interferon, a protein which acts as an antiviral within the cell. Following the initial, difficult years of research and a 1980 Supreme Court ruling which made it legal to patent life forms, Boyer's company went public. With the public offering of Genentech, Boyer became a millionaire many times over, and he began to draw criticism from the academic community for possible conflicts of interest. He was also stung by criticism of the new gene technology and its ethics. Many laypersons and scientists alike argued that the new technology was like playing god, and some believed that the manufacture and sale of body parts was a new form of slavery. Boyer withdrew from the public eye as a result of such criticism; he resigned from the vice presidency of Genentech and began to work for them as a consultant, though retaining his stock shares. He returned to his laboratory work and began new research in methylation patterns of DNA —places that show how vital proteins of the cell such as restriction enzymes actually work with the double helix. In collaboration with a team from the University of Pittsburgh, Boyer helped discover how the restriction enzyme, *Eco* RI, actually interacts on the atomic level with DNA.

Boyer has been widely honored for his research. Among other awards, he has won the V. D. Mattia Award in 1977, the Albert and Mary Lasker Medical Research Award in 1980, the Moet Hennessy-Louis Vuitton Prize in 1988, and the National Medal of Science in 1990. He was elected a member of the National Academy of Sciences in 1985 and is a fellow of American Academy of Arts and Sciences and the American Society of Microbiology. Boyer and his wife have two children.

SELECTED WRITINGS BY BOYER:

Periodicals

(With D. Roulland-Dussoix) "The Escherichia coli B Restriction Endonuclease," *Biochimica et Biophysica Acta,* November 19, 1969, pp. 219–229.

(With S. N. Cohen, et al.) "Construction of Biologically Functional Bacterial Plasmids in Vitro," *Proceedings of the National Academy of Sciences of the United States of America,* November, 1973, pp. 3240–3244.

(With K. Itakura, et al.) "Expression in Escherichia coli of a Chemically Synthesized Gene for the Hormone Somatostatin," *Science,* December 9, 1977, pp. 1056–1063.

(With S. N. Cohen) "Process for Producing Biologically Functional Molecular Chimeras," *Biotechnology* (reprint of 1979 article), Volume 24, 1992, pp. 546–555.

(With J. M. Rosenberg, et al.) "The Structure and Function of the Eco RI restriction Endonuclease," *Gene Amplification and Analysis,* Volume 1, 1981, pp. 131–164.

(With M. C. Needels, et al.) "Determinants of Eco RI Endonuclease Sequence Discrimination," *Proceedings of the National Academy of Sciences of the United States of America,* May, 1989, pp. 3579–3583.

SOURCES:

Books

Hall, Stephen S., *Invisible Frontiers: The Race to Synthesize a Human Gene,* Atlantic Monthly Press, 1987.

Periodicals

Bass, Alison B., "Managing for Success: The Genentech Story," *Technology Review,* May/June, 1985, pp. 28–29.

Boly, William, "The Gene Merchants," *California,* September, 1982, pp. 76–79.

Golden, Frederic, "Shaping Life in the Lab," *Time,* March 9, 1981, pp. 50–59.

Hopson, Janet L., "Recombinant Lab for DNA and My 95 Days in It," *Smithsonian,* June, 1977, pp. 54–63.

—*Sketch by J. Sydney Jones*

Otis Boykin
1920-1982
American electronics engineer and inventor

Otis Boykin was an inventor of some twenty-six electronic devices widely used today in computers and guided missiles. Perhaps most noteworthy of his inventions, though, was a regulating unit for the first heart pacemaker.

Otis Frank Boykin was born in Dallas, Texas, on August 29, 1920, to Walter Benjamin and Sarah Boykin. The young Boykin's academic career started in 1938 at Fisk University in Nashville, Tennessee. Boykin's first job after graduating in 1941 was with Majestic Radio & TV Corporation in Chicago. Although he had become a foreman, he left Majestic Radio in 1944 to take a position as a research engineer with P. J. Nilsen Research Labs of Oak Park, Illinois. He stayed at Nilsen Labs for five years before leaving to found his own company, Boykin-Fruth, Inc.; at the same time, he attended the Illinois Institute of Technology. In 1949 Boykin became chief chemist for ceramics and plastics at Radio Industries in Chicago; he remained there just two years, after which time he took a position as a senior research engineer at C. T. S. Corporation in Elkhorn, Indiana. Boykin left C. T. S. in 1964 to work as an electronics consultant for several American and European firms, three of them in Paris.

Many of the devices Boykin invented and patented became components in computers and guided missiles. He invented, for example, a type of resistor that became common in radios, computers, and television sets. He also invented a chemical air filter, a burglar-proof cash register, and a thick-film resistor for use in computers. Most notable of Boykin's inventions was probably the electronic device he built for regulating the pacemaker; first invented by Paul Zoll and perfected in 1960 by **Wilson Greatbatch**, the pacemaker is a device that uses electrical pulses to maintain the regular beating of the heart.

Boykin's inventiveness and his many patents won him the Cultural Science Achievement Award from the Old Pros Unlimited Club. Boykin's professional memberships included the American Association for the Advancement of the Sciences, the International Society for Hybrid Micro-electronics, and the Chicago Physics Club. Boykin died of heart failure in Chicago in 1982; he was 61.

SOURCES:

Books

Ploski, Harry A. and Williams, James, editors, *The Negro Almanac: A Reference Work on the African American,* 5th ed., Gale, 1989, p. 1080.
Sammons, Vivian Ovelton, editor, *Blacks in Science and Medicine,* Hemisphere, 1990, p. 34.
Van Sertima, Ivan, editor, *Blacks in Science: Ancient and Modern,* Transaction Books, 1984, p. 226.

Periodicals

Jet, April 12, 1982, p. 13.

—*Sketch by Karl Preuss*

St. Elmo Brady
1884-1966
American chemist

St. Elmo Brady was the first African American to receive the Ph.D. degree in chemistry. He taught general and organic chemistry to a great number of scientists and health professionals at four historically black colleges in a long and distinguished career. Primarily a teacher, he followed the example of **George Washington Carver** and carried out research on plants native to the southern United States, searching for useful chemical products.

Brady was born in Louisville, Kentucky, in 1884. He attended elementary and high school there and graduated from high school with honors. He began Fisk University in Nashville, Tennessee in 1904, where he studied under Thomas W. Talley, one of the early teachers of modern chemistry in black colleges. When he graduated from Fisk in 1908, he accepted a position at Tuskegee Institute (now Tuskegee University) in Alabama. At Tuskegee he became the friend of educator and Tuskegee founder Booker T. Washington and agricultural researcher George Washington Carver and learned from them the value of working for the advancement of others.

He took leave from Tuskegee in 1913 to attend the graduate program in chemistry at the University of Illinois. At the time, no African American had earned a doctorate in chemistry, and few had advanced degrees in any academic field. He received the M.A. degree in 1914 and was given a graduate fellowship which enabled him to continue his study towards the Ph.D. His research director was Clarence G. Derick, who was exploring the effect of structure on the strength of organic acids. Brady added to the knowledge of this subject, studying the effect of the divalent oxygen atom, which played an important role in the development of theoretical organic chemistry later in the century. At Illinois, Brady was the first African American admitted to Phi Lambda Upsilon, the chemistry honor society (1914), and was one of the first inducted into Sigma Xi, the science honor society (1915). Derick left Illinois in 1916 for the rapidly expanding chemical industry, and Brady, who received the Ph. D. in 1916, returned to Tuskegee. Brady realized, as quoted by Samuel P. Massie in the *Boule Journal,* that his work in a modern research laboratory could not be reproduced in a "school in the heat of Alabama, where I wouldn't even have a Bunsen burner," but his spirit of service led him back to Tuskegee where he was appointed head of the division of science.

In 1920, Brady accepted an offer to be professor and head of the chemistry department at Howard University in Washington, DC. He remained at Howard for seven years, building the undergraduate program in chemistry, but left when he had the opportunity to return to his alma mater, Fisk University, to head the chemistry department there. Brady spent the major part of his career at Fisk, retiring in 1952 after 25 years in the chemistry department. He taught general and organic chemistry to hundreds of students, and published his research on the chemical constituents of magnolia seeds and castor beans. He supervised the construction of the first modern chemistry building at a black college, which was eventually named after him and his teacher, Thomas Talley. He was also able to begin a graduate program in chemistry, which was the first in a black college. In conjunction with the graduate program, Brady established the Thomas W. Talley lecture series, which brought outstanding chemists to Fisk. He established, in conjunction with faculty from the University of Illinois, a summer program in infrared spectroscopy at Fisk which was open to faculty members of all colleges and universities. Because of limited opportunities for employment for educated black women in Nashville, Brady's wife, Myrtle, had lived and worked in Washington while he traveled often between Washington and Nashville. They had one son, a physician, who died very young, and two granddaughters. When Brady retired from Fisk, he moved to Washington. In his retirement, Brady was asked to assist the development of the chemistry department at Tougaloo College, a small college in Mississippi, and he was eager to help design their new science building and obtain new faculty members. St. Elmo Brady died in Washington on Christmas Day, 1966, at the age of 82.

SOURCES:

Books

Sammons, Vivian O., "St. Elmo Brady," in *Blacks in Science and Medicine,* Hemisphere, 1990, p. 35.

Periodicals

Crisis, August 1916, p. 190–91.
Massie, Samuel P., "St. Elmo Brady, A Pioneer," *Boule Journal* (Sigma Pi Phi Fraternity publication), Fall 1979, p. 12.

—*Sketch by Martin R. Feldman*

William Henry Bragg
1862-1942
English physicist and mathematician

Sir William Henry Bragg was a noted English physicist, mathematician, and teacher whose reputation rests on his pioneering work on the determination of crystal structure by the use of X-ray diffraction. For this achievement, he was awarded the 1915 Nobel Prize for physics with his eldest son, **William Lawrence Bragg**. Bragg's work advanced understanding of the way atoms bond together to form molecules, and resulted in practical repercussions throughout industry. He is also noted for his efforts to win physics a popular audience, particularly through his acclaimed Christmas lectures for the Royal Society.

Bragg was born in Cumberland, England, to Robert John Bragg, a former Merchant Marines

officer, and Mary Wood, a vicar's daughter. After the death of his mother when he was only seven years of age, Bragg went to live with his uncle, a pharmacist, and attended school at Market Harborough in Leicestershire. After six years there, Bragg completed his early schooling at King William's College on the Isle of Man. After winning a partial scholarship to Trinity College, Cambridge, Bragg studied pure maths under Dr. E. J. Routh. In his last year, he also attended lectures at the Cavendish Laboratory given by its chair, **J. J. Thomson**, and Lord Rayleigh, the esteemed English physicist.

In 1885, Bragg accepted a professorship in mathematics and physics at the University of Adelaide, Australia. He arrived in 1886 and immediately adapted to the country's easy-going pace and outdoor life. He wrote that "going to Australia, to a new work and an assured position, the people I met there, the sunshine, the fruit and flowers, was a marvellous change for me. I know that I had been lucky enough in England, but I am not ungrateful when I say that going to Australia was like sunshine and fresh invigorating air." In 1889 Bragg married Gwendoline Todd, the daughter of Charles Todd, government astronomer and postmaster general. The Braggs had three children, two boys and a girl. Their eldest son, Lawrence, was to prove as gifted and pioneering a physicist as his father.

Bragg's lifelong interest in education was sparked in Adelaide, where he found his students to be of a low caliber. This set him wondering what could be wrong with the educational system that it had produced such a poor quality student and how it could be ameliorated. He wrote what would be his first of many dissertations on the subject in 1888. Perhaps surprisingly, Bragg published no important research studies while in Adelaide. For one thing, his laboratory was simply not equipped for the task. In fact, he was driven to apprentice himself to a company of equipment manufacturers in the town to learn how to make his own laboratory supplies. The other explanation was Bragg's lack of technical training and his isolation from the throes of the exciting new developments unfolding in the field at that time. He wrote in 1927, looking back: "Perhaps it may seem wrong that a professor of mathematics and physics should be so long content with the ordinary round of teaching and management, but there may be some explanation in the fact that I had no laboratory training nor had I come into contact with research. I had indeed never studied physics as now understood."

Nonetheless, Bragg was far from idle. He closely followed developments in England and continental Europe and carried out what basic experiments his inadequate equipment would permit. A trip home to England via Egypt and Italy in 1897 allowed Bragg to meet with his peers and catch up on all the exciting advances that had been made, especially at Cambridge, in his absence.

Upon his return to Adelaide, he continued his usual schedule of lecturing, both to his students and to the public. His speeches on subjects such as radium, the electron, and X rays did much to increase the public understanding of the new scientific and technological developments.

Speech Leads to Interest in Experimental Physics

It was through his work as a teacher and administrator at the University of Adelaide that Bragg chanced upon the subject that was to ignite his interest in experimental physics and start him on the path of fame. Asked to deliver the presidential address to the mathematical and physical section of the Australasian Association for the Advancement of Science, Bragg decided to review the latest developments in physics, concentrating largely on radioactivity. As he prepared for his speech, he reviewed the recent work of Madame **Marie Curie** in France, and was suddenly seized by an explanation for her results which had hitherto not been proposed. Curie had shown that when a radium atom breaks into two parts, the smaller part, which is an atom of helium, otherwise known as an alpha particle, is released into the air as alpha radiation. Bragg was intrigued as to how the alpha particles managed to travel straight through the air when clearly their way was blocked by atoms of air. He concluded that they must pass through the air atoms, which meant that at the moment the alpha particles met the air atoms they occupied the same space. The alpha particles would collide with the air atoms and scatter only if the protons of the two atoms met: a chance of about one in a million. Bragg confirmed his suspicions in an experiment in which he passed alpha particles straight through an inch of air. This proved that the atom is not a solid body and that two atoms can occupy the same space.

Between 1904 and 1908, Bragg continued his experiments on the passage through matter of the beta, and gamma, and especially alpha rays emitted from radioactive substances. He discerned that alpha rays have a definite range, velocity, and ability to produce ionization in gases, that is, to change their atomic configuration by the addition or subtraction of one or more electrons. It was this ionizing effect that, Bragg deduced, caused the loss of energy of an alpha ray as it sped through the air. He concluded that at a certain distance from the point of the alpha ray's departure, the ionizing effect would stop. Exactly where would depend on the speed at which the alpha ray was traveling and the nature of the substance through which it passed, a distance Bragg referred to as its range. He discovered that alpha rays with different velocities, and thus different ranges, exist,

each corresponding to a different kind of radioactivity in its source. As a result of these findings, it became possible to identify different radioactive substances by the measurement of their alpha rays. Bragg was able to show, for instance, that helium atoms of four different ranges were expelled from a preparation of radium, confirming the existence of the four different radioactive substances, identified by English physicist **Ernest Rutherford**, who won the Nobel Prize in chemistry in 1908. Bragg lost no time in conveying his results to Rutherford himself, who encouraged him to publish them in one of the British journals. As a result, in 1907, his papers appeared in *The Philosophical Magazine* and *The Philosophical Transactions of the Royal Society*.

Bragg's important findings were the spur he needed to begin the research that would occupy him the rest of his life. He began publishing papers every few months, was elected a fellow of the Royal Society of London, and in 1908 was appointed to the Cavendish Professorship of Physics at the University of Leeds. The position represented a major change from the free and easy life in Adelaide and it took Bragg some years to fit in. During his first years in Leeds, the research that had brought him there ground to a halt and Bragg was more miserable than ever before in his life. Only his friendship with Rutherford helped to sustain him during this difficult period. One particular source of irritation to Bragg was an ongoing feud with Professor **Charles Glover Barkla** concerning the nature of X rays. Many angry letters were exchanged between them in the pages of *Nature,* with Barkla propounding his wave theory of X rays and Bragg clinging to the corpuscular, or particle, theory that he had formed in Adelaide. Actually, both men were right: X rays are both waves and particles. They had formed their different views, however, by studying different aspects of X rays.

Shares Nobel Prize with Son

Bragg's spirits were raised in 1911 and 1912 with the discovery of X-ray diffraction by crystals, or the bending of the rays as they pass through the crystal. He immediately grasped its significance and realized that he could no longer deny the wave-like properties of X rays. He understood that a theory was necessary that could account for both its wave and corpuscular properties.

During the next two years, Bragg worked with his son Lawrence on the study of crystal structure by means of X rays, using the X-ray spectrometer he had designed in 1913. Together, they worked out a method to determine the atomic structure of a number of crystals using X rays and were thus able to account for their behavior and properties.

Their findings were jointly published in 1915 in *X-rays and Crystal Structure,* a study which led to much greater understanding of the nature of solid bodies. As Bragg said in one of his Christmas lectures, popular talks at the Royal Institution given in simple language on physics: "We are now able to look ten thousand times deeper into the structure of the matter that makes up our universe than when we had to depend on the microscope alone." For their findings, Bragg and his son shared the Nobel Prize in physics in 1915. The mathematical equation derived from their discovery, called Bragg's Law, is now used to study the molecular structure of complex substances.

Bragg's research using X rays to gain a greater understanding of crystal structure took a back seat during the First World War as Bragg served his government through his work for the Admiralty. During this time, he invented the hydrophone, a device to detect submarines. In 1916, he was made resident director of research at the Naval Experiment Station at Hawkcraig, with a staff of two physicists and a mechanic. For his work for the Royal Admiralty, Bragg was knighted in 1920.

By 1919, Bragg was finally able to take up the Quain Professorship of Physics at the University College, London, that he had been offered in 1915, and began building the college's reputation as a research establishment. In 1923, Bragg became director of the Royal Institute of Great Britain, and moved most of his research team there to its Davy-Faraday lab. As a result of Bragg's leadership, the lab gained a worldwide reputation for excellence, especially for its work surrounding crystal structure. There, Bragg and his son continued their analyses of organic crystals, work that has been of fundamental importance in the development of molecular biology. At the Royal Institute, Bragg was also responsible for the spread of his methodology to other fields, such as work on the structures of organic molecules.

During his lifetime, Bragg was honored with countless awards and a total of sixteen honorary doctorates by universities in Britain and overseas. In 1916, he was presented with the Rumford Medal by the Royal Society of London, and with the Copley Medal in 1930. Bragg was named president of the Royal Society in 1935.

Bragg is remembered not only as a great physicist but also as a gifted teacher who was able to communicate the complexities of physics in a clear and dynamic manner. His annual Christmas lectures at the Royal Institute, originally geared toward children, made Bragg a household name and succeeded in communicating the complexities of physics to the general public. He also published no fewer than 237 books and research papers. He believed that science should not offer solutions to the conundrum of our existence, but gather knowledge to increase our understanding of the physical world. Bragg was a family man, devoted to the relationships in his life as well as to his work. It is not surprising, then, that after his death from old age on March 12, 1942, at the age of eighty, he was remembered in the obituary notices of the Fellows of the Royal Society as "a gentle man."

SELECTED WRITINGS BY BRAGG:

Books

(With son, William Lawrence Bragg) *X-rays and Crystal Structure,* Bell & Sons (London), 1915, 4th edition, 1924.
Concerning the Nature of Things: Six Lectures Delivered at the Royal Institution, Bell & Sons, 1924, Harper & Brothers, 1925.
Creative Knowledge, Harper & Brothers, 1927. *The Universe of Light,* Macmillan, 1933.
The World of Sound: Six Lectures Delivered at the Royal Institution, Bell & Sons, 1933.
(Editor with W. L. Bragg) *The Crystalline State,* four volumes, Bell & Sons, 1933–1953.

Periodicals

"X-rays and Crystals," in *Nature,* Volume 90, October 24, 1912, p. 219.
"The Reflection of X-rays by Crystals," in *Proceedings of the Royal Society of London,* Volume 88A, June, 1913, pp. 428–438.

SOURCES:

Books

Bridges, T. C. and H. Hessell Tiltman, *Master Minds of Modern Science,* Books for Libraries Press, 1969, pp. 37–47.
Caroe, G. M., *William Henry Bragg: Man and Scientist,* Cambridge University Press, 1979.
Dictionary of Scientific Biography, Volume 2, Scribner, 1972, pp. 397.
Robert L. Weber, *Pioneers of Science: Nobel Prize Winners in Physics,* Institute of Physics, 1980.
Trevor I. Williams, editor, *A Biographical Dictionary of Scientists,* 3rd edition, Halsted Press, 1982.

Periodicals

da C. Andrade, E. N. "William Henry Bragg 1869–1942," in *Obituary Notices of Fellows of the Royal Society of London,* Volume 4, 1943, pp. 277–300.
Bragg, Sir Lawrence and G. M. Caroe, "Sir William Bragg, F.R.S.," in *Notes and Records of the Royal Society of London,* Volume 16, 1961, pp. 169–182.

"William Henry Bragg and the New Crystallography," *Nature,* Volume 195, July 28, 1962, pp. 320–325.

—Sketch by Avril McDonald

William Lawrence Bragg

William Lawrence Bragg
1890-1971
Australian English physicist

William Lawrence Bragg shared a remarkable two-year collaboration with his father and fellow physicist, **William Henry Bragg**, during which they founded the new science of X-ray crystallography. The methods developed by this father-son team made it possible to explore the atomic structure of matter very precisely and in great detail. The Braggs shared the 1915 Nobel Prize in physics for their work.

Bragg was born in Adelaide, Australia. His father was professor of physics and mathematics at the University of Adelaide; his mother, Gwendoline Todd Bragg, was the daughter of Sir Charles Todd, South Australia's postmaster general and government astronomer. Bragg had a brother one year younger than he, Robert, who was killed at Gallipoli in Turkey during World War I, and a sister, Gwendolen, seventeen years his junior. The children's parents were a contrast; Gwendolen later wrote in the biography *William Henry Bragg* that their father wanted his children to be absolutely free and avoided advising them on what they should do, whereas their mother "always knew exactly what one ought to do, and said so." Foreshadowing the field of the Braggs' future work, Bragg's father built a primitive X-ray machine within weeks after **Wilhelm Conrad Röntgen**'s 1896 announcement of his discovery of the rays. Soon thereafter, five-year-old W. L. fell from his tricycle and broke his elbow. Professor Bragg used his device to reveal the location and extent of the injury. This was the first recorded use of X rays for medical diagnosis in Australia.

As a child, Bragg was solitary, being academically ahead of boys his age and poor at sports because, as he explained it, he wasn't aggressive or self-confident enough. His sister quoted him as telling her, "You and I find *things* easier than people." He expressed his interest in natural sciences by collecting shells; a new cuttlefish species he discovered, *Sepia braggii,* was named after him. With his brother, he enjoyed creating mechanical devices out of discarded scraps,

and a chemistry master aroused his interest in scientific experimentation.

A gifted scholar, Bragg attended St. Peter's College (a secondary school) in Adelaide and entered the University of Adelaide in 1905 at the age of fifteen. His father was beginning to experiment with X rays at the university at that time, and W. H. often talked to his son about his results. "I lived in an inspiring scientific atmosphere," Bragg wrote of those years in a chapter he contributed to *Fifty Years of X-Ray Diffraction* entitled "Personal Reminiscences." He graduated in 1908, after just three years, with first-class honors in mathematics. In January 1909 the family left Australia for England, where W. H. Bragg had accepted a professorship at the University of Leeds. W. L. enrolled at Trinity College, Cambridge, where he began by studying mathematics. At the end of his first year, taking an exam while sick in bed with pneumonia, he won a major scholarship. Then, following his father's suggestion, he switched his concentration to physics. Again he graduated with first-class honors, this time in natural sciences, in 1912. He stayed at Cambridge, doing research under **J. J. Thomson** at the Cavendish Laboratory, and began his very fruitful collaboration with his father in the fall of 1912.

Enters Father-Son Collaboration

Earlier that year, **Max von Laue** had discovered the diffraction of X rays in crystals: X rays passing through crystals are bent, producing distinct patterns. At the time, physicists were engaged in a lively debate about the nature of X rays: Were they particles or waves? Bragg's father had a deep interest in X rays and favored the particle theory. He was excited by Laue's discovery, even though the diffraction patterns could be explained only if X rays were waves, and he thought further investigation of the new phenomenon might provide the missing evidence to support either the wave or the particle theory, or even a new theory incorporating both wave and particle properties. W. L. Bragg, too, was excited by Laue's discovery, especially as it related to the structure of crystals.

During the summer holiday of 1912, father and son talked often about Laue's discovery, and when W. L. returned to Cambridge that fall, he launched into a series of experiments using X-ray diffraction. He concluded that Laue's wave interpretation was correct, but that his explanation of diffraction was unnecessarily complex. W. L. suggested that since atoms are arranged in a regular way in crystals, the diffraction patterns might be caused by X rays reflecting off the planes of atoms within the crystals. He developed an equation relating angles of rays, wavelength, and perpendicular distance between atomic planes, which became known as Bragg's law, with the glancing angle of the X rays called Bragg's angle. Both Braggs saw the great implications of W. L.'s idea: the reflected patterns of the X rays would reveal the previously hidden arrangement of the atoms within the crystals. The Braggs plunged into investigations of crystals, with W. L. first analyzing sodium chloride (table salt) and potassium chloride (a crystalline salt used as a fertilizer), though they were hampered by inadequate equipment. Bragg's father solved this problem in 1913 by his invention of the X-ray spectrometer, a device that measured X-ray angles and intensities precisely and allowed for analysis of complex crystals. The elder Bragg used the spectrometer to continue his studies of radiation, while W. L. used it to pursue his interest in analyzing the structure of crystals.

W. L. Bragg published his first suggestion about the wave nature of X rays as shown by Laue's discovery in November 1912. W. L. and his father published their first joint paper early in 1913 in the *Proceedings of the Royal Society,* which established the basic principles of the new science of crystal analysis by X-ray diffraction. W. L. followed this a few months later with his own paper on the structure of sodium chloride, which he showed was not made up of molecules, as had been thought, but rather of ions (charged atoms) of sodium and chloride. This finding became very important in the analysis of solutions, as it was the first distinction made between compounds that consist of ions and those made up of molecules. In July 1913 the Braggs published a joint paper on the structure of diamond, and W. L.

published another paper in November describing more crystal structure discoveries. By 1914 the Braggs had set the standards for X-ray crystallography. They had also transformed crystallography from its role as a secondary, if interesting, branch of science to its new position as a fundamental branch of modern physics with applications to many other sciences. In "Personal Reminiscences" W. L. said of this period of collaboration with his father, "We had a thrilling time together in an intense exploitation of the new fields of research."

The Braggs were recognized for their groundbreaking achievements in exploring the arrangements of atoms by the 1915 Nobel Prize in physics, awarded—in the Nobel Committee's words—"for their contributions to the study of crystal structure by means of X rays." W. L. was only twenty-five years old, the youngest Nobel laureate ever. But the "thrilling time" of collaboration had ended abruptly with the outbreak of World War I in August 1914. Bragg volunteered for service and found himself assigned to a horse artillery battery among "hunting men." After a year, he was sent to France to adapt the new method of locating enemy guns by sound, called sound ranging, for use by the British forces. He later recalled that it was while setting up a sound-ranging base in Belgium that he learned of his Nobel Prize. The parish priest in whose house he was lodged broke out a bottle of wine to celebrate. After the war, Bragg returned to Cambridge as a lecturer.

Develops New Field of Science

In 1919 Bragg was named to succeed **Ernest Rutherford** as professor of physics at the University of Manchester. The first years were difficult, as Bragg was inexperienced and he had to handle classes full of war veterans. Gradually, however, he built up a fine research facility, concentrating on improving methods of using X rays to determine crystal structure. He published a list of atomic sizes and measured absolute intensities of X-ray reflections. He then turned to the silicate family of minerals, whose complex structure had proved elusive. This work, completed around 1930, was of fundamental importance to the science of mineralogy. In 1927 Bragg spent four months at the Massachusetts Institute of Technology as a visiting professor, lecturing on X-ray diffraction and crystal structure. During the 1930s Bragg oversaw and encouraged investigations into metals and metal alloys, which provided new basic knowledge about the chemistry of metals, and he encouraged the application of these X-ray diffraction techniques to industrial firms in northern England, where the university was located.

In 1938 Bragg left Manchester to became director of the National Physical Laboratory. But a year later Rutherford died, and Bragg was invited to take his place as professor of physics at the Cavendish Laboratory at Cambridge. During World War II, Bragg remained at Cambridge (except for eight months in Canada as scientific liaison), advising the British navy on methods of underwater detection of submarines and assisting with further development of sound ranging. After the war had ended, Bragg organized an international meeting of crystallographers in London, which resulted in the formation of the International Union of Crystallography; he was named its first president in 1948. He also secured funds from British industries to help establish *Acta Crystallographica,* a scientific journal first published in 1948 and devoted to the new crystallography.

Although in his later years Bragg was more involved with administration than with hands-on, day-to-day scientific research, he continued to have a powerful influence on the development of X-ray analysis. He organized and found resources to support the very challenging work of **Max Perutz**, later joined by **John C. Kendrew**, in investigating globular proteins, molecular structures that contain many thousands of atoms. This work dramatically culminated in the structural analysis of hemoglobin by Perutz and Kendrew and of DNA (deoxyribonucleic acid, the molecule that carries the genetic formula) by **Francis Crick**, **James Watson**, and **Maurice Wilkins**.

In 1954 Bragg became director of the Davy-Faraday Research Laboratory as well as professor of chemistry at London's Royal Institution. He revitalized the laboratory with much-needed infusions of research funds from sources such as the Rockefeller Foundation, the National Institutes of Health, and industrial firms, and by pooling resources with the Cavendish Laboratory. He was actively interested in the Royal Institution's long-standing tradition of sponsoring public lectures on science to nonscientific audiences, and he took particular pleasure in developing a program to bring the excitement of science to schoolchildren. Bragg himself was a popular lecturer owing to his ability to explain complex scientific concepts in clear, simple terms, and he gave a series of scientific talks on television. In the 1960s, at the government's request, he created a series of elementary science lectures to provide civil servants with basic scientific knowledge.

After his retirement in 1966, Bragg continued lecturing, especially to young people, and writing. He completed a definitive book on the history of his field, *The Development of X-Ray Analysis,* only a week before he died on July 1, 1971. In 1921 Bragg had married Alice Hopkinson, the daughter of a doctor. Mrs. Bragg was mayor of Cambridge in 1945, and served on a number of public bodies. The couple had four children, two sons and two daughters. Bragg was knighted in 1941 and was named a Companion of Honour in 1967. He received many awards and honorary doctorates and was a member of numerous scientific academies around the world. His contributions to science were immense, touching as they did on a number of fields in addition to physics, including chemistry, metallurgy, mineralogy, and molecular biology. These contributions came both from Bragg's own direct research and from his notably energetic, effective, and committed organization and leadership of the research efforts of others. In *William Henry Bragg,* Bragg's sister summed up the lives of both W. H. and W. L. Bragg in these words: "To each, science was an art, research an adventure, and life an experimental journey which they lived with enthusiasm."

SELECTED WRITINGS BY BRAGG:

Books

(With W. H. Bragg) *X-Rays and Crystal Structure,* G. Bell & Sons, 1915.

The Crystalline State, 4 volumes, G. Bell & Sons, 1933–65.

(With W. H. Bragg) *Atomic Structure of Minerals,* Oxford University Press, 1937.

"Forty Years of Crystal Physics," in *Background to Modern Science,* Joseph Needham and Walter Pagel, editors, Macmillan, 1938, pp. 77–89.

"Personal Reminiscences," in *Fifty Years of X-Ray Diffraction,* P. P. Ewald, editor, International Union of Crystallography, 1962, pp. 531–539.

The Development of X-Ray Analysis, D. C. Phillips and H. Lipson, editors, Bell (London), 1975.

Periodicals

"Manchester Days," *Acta Crystallographica,* Volume 26A, 1960, pp. 171–196.

"The Development of X-Ray Analysis," *Proceedings of the Royal Society,* Volume 262A, 1961, pp. 145–158.

"Reminiscences of Fifty Years of Research," *Proceedings of the Royal Institution of Great Britain,* Volume 41, 1966, pp. 92–100.

SOURCES:

Books

Biographical Memoirs of Fellows of the Royal Society, Volume 25, 1975, pp. 75–143.

Caroe, G. M. *William Henry Bragg 1862–1942: Man and Scientist,* Cambridge University Press, 1978.

Dictionary of Scientific Biography, Volume 25, Scribner, 1978, pp. 61–64.

Ewald, P. P., editor, *Fifty Years of X-Ray Diffraction,* International Union of Crystallography, 1962.

Heathcote, Niels H. de V., *Nobel Prize Winners in Physics 1901–1950,* Henry Schuman, 1953.

Magill, Frank N., *The Nobel Prize Winners: Physics,* Volume 1 (1901–1937), Salem Press, 1989.

Periodicals

Lipson, Henry S., et al., "Dedicated to Sir Lawrence Bragg on His Eightieth Birthday," *Acta Crystallographica,* Volume 26A, special issue, March 31, 1970, pp. 171–188.

Phillips, David, "William Lawrence Bragg, 31 March 1890–1 July 1971."

—*Sketch by Kathy Sammis*

Herman Branson

1914-

American physicist

Herman Branson was one of few African Americans to direct graduate research in physics. He collaborated with chemist **Linus Pauling** on defining the structure of proteins, which was a significant contribution to the fields of biochemistry and biology. As head of the physics department at Howard University and president of Central State University and Lincoln University, Branson has been devoted to the development of black scientists and other scholars.

Herman Russell Branson was born August 14, 1914, in the small town of Pocahontas, Virginia, and he received his early education there. His family moved to Washington, D.C., and Branson graduated as valedictorian in 1932 from segregated Dunbar High School, which was famous for its outstanding faculty and curriculum. He attended the University of Pittsburgh for two years, then transferred to Virginia State College in Petersburg. He graduated *summa cum laude* in 1936, and received a fellowship to study physics in the graduate program at the University of Cincinnati. His dissertation included a practical section, on measuring X-ray intensity, and a theoretical section, on the quantization of mass. Branson was the first African American to obtain a Ph. D. in a physical science at the University of Cincinnati when he graduated in 1939. He left for New Orleans, Louisi-

ana, to teach mathematics and physics at Dillard University for two years, then accepted an appointment as assistant professor of physics and chemistry at Howard University in Washington, D.C., in 1941. He was named professor in 1944, and served as head of the Physics Department from 1941 to 1968.

At Howard University, Branson was able to obtain research grants and develop an undergraduate major in physics as well as a graduate program, both of which were rare in black colleges. In the 1940's, physics courses at those colleges were for the most part service courses for premedical students and other science majors, but Branson was able to expand the department at Howard, and to offer an accredited physics major. Later, he added graduate courses and provided research opportunities at the University and at nearby government laboratories in Washington. Branson's own research at Howard was varied. He investigated biological reaction kinetics using isotopic labeling (isotopes are species of an element having identical atomic numbers, but varying masses), and he studied mass spectral fragmentation on an instrument he acquired for Howard. In the 1948–49 academic year, he received a National Research Council Senior Fellowship to travel to the California Institute of Technology, where he worked with Linus Pauling. His research led to one of Pauling and Robert B. Corey's first papers on the helical structure of proteins, which had a profound effect on the development of molecular biology and biochemistry, and to the understanding of diseases like sickle cell anemia, which are the result of aberrant protein structure.

Branson was always involved in the educational and economic improvement of African Americans, and he believed that the nation's demand for scientists would provide great opportunities for them. In World War II, he directed a program in physics in the Engineering, Science and Management War Training Program at Howard, to provide science education for civilians in the war effort. It was one of the few programs of its kind in physics at a black college. He was also involved in programs for increasing the number of African Americans enrolled in science courses in high school, and in the health professions. He served on many boards which gave scholarship aid and research grants, as well as in other civic and professional organizations.

In 1968, Branson accepted an offer from Central State University, in Wilberforce, Ohio, to serve as its president, and after two years, left to become president of Lincoln University, near Philadelphia, Pennsylvania. Lincoln University was the first college for black students in the United States, founded for the training of ministers. The appointment of Branson as president indicated that the University hoped to improve its science curriculum, and increase its prestige. Branson served as president until his retirement in 1985, at the age of 71. He returned to Howard at that time, and supervised a program which recruited bright high school students into science careers. Branson has received many awards and honors, including honorary degrees from institutions such as Brandeix University, Western Michigan University, Shaw College at Detroit, Virginia State University, Drexel University, University of Cincinnati, and Lincoln University. In 1939, Branson married Corolynne Gray of Cincinnati, Ohio, at the end of his graduate studies. The couple has one son, Herman Edward, and one daughter, Corolynne Gertrude, both physicians.

SELECTED WRITINGS BY BRANSON:

Periodicals

(With Linus Pauling and Robert B. Corey) "Structure of Proteins: Two Hydrogen-Bonded Helical Configurations of the Polypeptide Chain," *Proceedings of the National Academy of Sciences of the U. S.,* Volume 37, 1951, pp. 205–211.

—*Sketch by Martin R. Feldman*

Walter Houser Brattain
1902-1987
American physicist

A small semiconducting device capable of great amplification, the transistor invented by Walter Houser Brattain and colleagues **John Bardeen** and **William Shockley** revolutionized many aspects of modern society, especially systems of communication. In recognition of this work, Brattain, Bardeen, and Shockley were jointly awarded the 1956 Nobel Prize in physics.

Brattain was born in Amoy, China, on February 10, 1902. He was the eldest of five children born to Ross R. Brattain and Ottilie Houser Brattain. At the time of Walter's birth, his father was employed as a teacher in a school for Chinese boys. While Walter was still a young child, his family returned to the United States and settled in Washington state, where both of his parents' families had been pioneers. Brattain spent his childhood on a cattle ranch near the small town of Tonasket, where he attended public schools. He later told the editors of *Those Inventive Americans* that he loved the out-of-doors, but was not

very fond of farming. "Following three horses and a harrow in the dust was what made a physicist out of me," he said.

With no desire to stay on the family ranch, Brattain entered Whitman College in Walla Walla, Washington, in 1920, earning his B.S. degree in physics four years later. During his senior year he was elected to the national honorary fraternity Phi Beta Kappa and the national scientific society, Sigma Xi. He moved on to the University of Oregon to complete his master's degree in physics in 1926 and then to the University of Minnesota for his Ph.D. in 1929. While completing his doctorate, Brattain took a job in the radio section of the National Bureau of Standards (NBS). It was "the only non-teaching job I was offered. I was a very green Ph.D. [in fact, he had not yet received the degree], and I didn't feel qualified to teach," he added in *Those Inventive Americans.*

Shockley's Arrival at Bell Labs Initiates Semiconductor Studies

Shortly after receiving his Ph.D., Brattain was offered a job at the Bell Telephone Laboratories in Murray Hill, New Jersey, one of the major corporate research centers in the United States. During his first few years at the Bell Labs, Brattain was engaged in a variety of projects, including research on infrared radiation, frequency standards, and magnetic phenomena. In 1936, however, his work focused in a new direction upon the arrival at Bell Labs of William Shockley.

Shockley had been working on finding a substitute for the bulky three-vacuum-tube core that made up the modern radio. He knew that a special type of material known as a semiconductor had been used in early radios as a rectifier, a device that changes alternating current to direct current. Semiconductors are material that conduct an electric current better than a nonconductor, but not as well as a conductor. Speculating that other kinds of semiconductors might also be suitable as amplifiers, Shockley designed a number of arrangements containing semiconductors that he though might work. Brattain's job was to build and test each of these arrangements; he found that none of them worked as Shockley had hoped and predicted.

After a half dozen years of research, these trials were interrupted by World War II. Brattain and Shockley were both assigned to work at Columbia University on devices for the magnetic detection of submarines. After twenty-two months of wartime research, Brattain and Shockley returned to Bell Labs, where they were joined by a new partner, John Bardeen. Like Shockley, Bardeen was primarily a theorist. He studied the work being done on semiconductors in the Bell Labs and concluded that earlier failures might be explained by an accumulation of electrons on the surface of the semiconductors. Based on this suggestion, an accelerated program for the detailed study of semiconductor surfaces was initiated.

First Transistor Announced

Late in 1947, important progress in the development of Shockley's semiconductor amplifier had been made. Brattain and Bardeen constructed a device consisting of a germanium crystal with two closely spaced (0.005 cm apart) gold contacts on one side and a third terminal on the opposite side. When an electrical signal was fed into one side of the crystal, it was emitted on the opposite side with an amplification of 18. The success of this invention was announced publicly in July of 1948, but the news received very little interest. It was buried on page 46 of the *New York Times,* for example, with no mention of its enormous potential.

Brattain, Bardeen, and Shockley also realized that the new device, now called a transistor (for *trans*fer re*sistor*), could be greatly improved. Soon Shockley suggested modifying the transistor design so that it contained a p-type semiconductor (electron-deficient) on one side and an n-type semiconductor (electron surplus) on the other side. By 1950, Brattain had built and successfully tested such a device. For their invention of the transistor, Brattain, Bardeen, and Shockley were jointly awarded the 1956 Nobel Prize in physics.

Brattain continued to study the properties of semiconductors at Bell Labs until he reached mandatory retirement age of sixty-five in 1967. He then returned to Washington state and Whitman College to teach physics to non-majors and to carry out research on the physical properties of living cell surfaces. He retired from Whitman in 1972 and remained in Washington state until his death in Seattle on October 13, 1987.

Brattain was married on July 5, 1935, to the former Keren Gilmore, a physical chemist. They had one son, William Gilmore. After his first wife died in April of 1957, he was married a second time, to Emma Jane Kirsch Miller, on May 10, 1958. Among Brattain's honors were the Ballantine Medal of the Franklin Institute in 1952, the John Scott Award of the city of Philadelphia in 1955, and election to the National Inventors Hall of Fame in 1974.

SELECTED WRITINGS BY BRATTAIN:

Periodicals

(With John Bardeen) "The Transistor: A Semi-Conductor Triode," *Physical Review,* Volume 74, 1948, pp. 230–231.

(With John Bardeen) "Nature of the Forward Current in Germanium Point Contacts," *Physical Review,* Volume 74, 1948, pp. 231–232.
"Surface Properties of Semiconductors," *Science,* Volume 126, 1957, pp. 151–153.

SOURCES:

Books

National Geographic Society, Special Publications Division, *Those Inventive Americans,* National Geographic Society, 1971, pp. 208–217.

—Sketch by David E. Newton

Karl Ferdinand Braun
1850-1918
German physicist

Karl Ferdinand Braun was a theoretical physicist whose research into the behavior of electricity led him to produce several ground-breaking applications. The most important of these was his modification of the cathode-ray tube to create the oscilloscope, a device which displays a fluctuating electrical quantity and that, with improvements, is still used in electronics today. Braun's research into the conductivity of minerals helped others to create electronic components made out of crystals, early precursors of solid-state circuitry. His interest in radio waves led him to redesign Italian inventor **Guglielmo Marconi**'s radio-transmitting system, thereby greatly increasing its range beyond the original twelve-mile limit. For this work he shared with Marconi the 1909 Nobel Prize in physics.

On June 6, 1850, Braun was born at Fulda, in the electorate of Hesse-Kassel, which became part of Prussia in 1866. His parents were Konrad Braun, a clerk in the court system, and Franziska Göhring Braun, the daughter of Konrad's superior in the civil service. Braun began his education at the *gymnasium* in his hometown. From there he went to the Universities of Marburg and subsequently Berlin, where he completed his doctorate in 1872. The subject of his thesis paper concerned the vibrations of elastic rods and strings. Aside from this topic and a theoretical investigation from a thermodynamic standpoint into the impact of pressure on the solubility of solids (1887), his work centered almost entirely on electricity. After receiving his Ph.D., he assisted German physicist Georg Quincke at Würzburg for two years, followed by two years as a lecturer at the St. Thomas *gymnasium* in Leipzig. In 1874 Braun published a paper outlining the fruits of his research into mineral metal sulfides. These crystals, he discovered, only conducted electrical currents in one direction. This was an important contribution to electrical research for systematizing the measurement of conductivity, a key property of matter. A practical application of Braun's findings came about in the early twentieth century with the advent of radio receivers made out of crystal components.

Returning to the university at Marburg in 1876, he became professor extraordinary of theoretical physics. In 1880 he went to Strasbourg in Alsace, which at that time belonged to Germany, to take a similar position at the university there. Braun continued moving, occupying a post as professor of physics at the Technical High School at Karlsruhe in 1883. In 1885 he went to Tübingen to help establish the new Physical Institute. That year he married Amelie Bühler, who in time would bear two sons and two daughters. Braun returned to Strasbourg in 1895, this time as physics professor and director of the Physical Institute. He occupied this position until his death despite being offered the prestigious position of the physics chair at Leipzig, which was empty in 1899.

Develops the Oscilloscope

Braun published a paper on the Braun tube, or first oscilloscope, in 1897. As the name suggests, this device gave a picture of the oscillations of high-frequency alternating currents. In order to study them, Braun applied an alternating electromagnetic current to the fixed beam in the early cathode-ray tube. Instead of a fixed spot of green fluorescence, what appeared on the screen of the cathode-ray tube was a linear wave pattern made by the current's fluctuations. The design of the oscilloscope provided the basis for developing all the video screens that function with cathode-ray tubes. Updated versions of the original Braun tube became essential tools in electrical research and technology.

Shares the 1909 Nobel Prize with Marconi

In 1896 Marconi took out a patent on his radio transmitter, which had a broadcasting range of only eight to twelve miles. Braun was aware of Marconi's work and was intrigued by the limits of the transmitter's reach. It seemed clear to Braun that the range could be increased simply by raising the transmitter's electrical power. His research, aided by the oscilloscope he had just perfected, revealed that there was a an upper limit to the efficiency of a particular component, the Hertz oscillator, in the antenna system of the transmitter. When power was increased

in the Hertz oscillator, the gap over which the electrical current sparked became wider—Braun soon discovered that expanding the gap beyond a certain point actually reduced the transmitter's output.

Braun set about designing an antenna circuit without sparks. First he separated the antenna from the transmitter circuit. Then the power from the transmitter was conveyed to the antenna magnetically using condensers, huge wire coils that converted the electricity into magnetic fields. In this way, the antenna obtained increased power from the transmitter indirectly without running into the problems caused by the Hertz oscillator. As a result, the range of radio expanded beyond the original twelve-mile limit. The practice of isolating the antenna from the transmitter circuit has been implemented in all subsequent transmission technologies for radio, television, and other wireless media. Braun also redesigned the radio receiver so that it, too, operated with condensers. He received a patent for these improvements in 1899. Because his work on Marconi's transmitter made radio practical for telecommunications, he shared with Marconi the 1909 Nobel Prize in physics for the invention of "wireless telegraphy."

Braun's interest in radio also resulted in unidirectional broadcasting antennas and the use of radio waves as beacons for boats at sea. In 1914 he came to the United States in order to testify in a patent litigation concerning radio broadcasting. Because of ill health and delays in the lawsuit he was detained in America until the United States entered the war against Germany. Braun was then prevented from returning to Strasbourg by the American government on the grounds that he was an enemy alien. Before the war ended, Braun died on April 20, 1918, in a Brooklyn hospital.

SOURCES:

Books

Heathcote, Niels H. de V., *Nobel Prize Winners in Physics, 1901–1950*, Schuman, 1953, pp. 81–86.
Kurylo, Friedrich, and Charles Susskind, *Ferdinand Braun: A Life of the Nobel Prize Winner and Inventor of the Cathode-Ray Oscilloscope*, MIT Press, 1981.

—*Sketch by Hovey Brock*

Gregory Breit
1899-1981
Russian-born American physicist

Gregory Breit distinguished himself in both theoretical and experimental physics. In 1925, he launched the study of the upper atmosphere by probing the ionosphere with radio waves. He went on to build one of the first particle accelerators, and later disclosed the nuclear force as a fundamental force in physics. His studies with Eugene Wigner led to a better understanding of fission and earned Breit a role in the early development of the atomic bomb during the Manhattan Project. In 1968, President Johnson presented him with the National Medal of Science, the nation's highest scientific award.

Breit was born on July 14, 1899, in Nikolayev, Ukraine. His parents, Alfred and Alexandra (Smirnova) Breit, emigrated to America in 1915. He took his education at Johns Hopkins University in Baltimore, earning his B.A., M.A. and Ph.D. degrees in electrical engineering between 1918 and 1921. Winning a National Research Council fellowship, he departed for the University of Leyden in the Netherlands in 1921 to work in physics. His mentors included **Paul Ehrenfest**, a leading theorist, and **Heike Kammerlingh Onnes**, an experimentalist who had won the Nobel Prize. Breit continued his fellowship at Harvard, where he published his first works on quantum theory. In 1923, he took an assistant professorship at the University of Minnesota, where he taught some of the first graduate courses in quantum physics to be offered in the United States.

Probes the Ionosphere with Radio Waves

In 1924, Breit moved to the department of terrestrial magnetism at the Carnegie Institution in Washington, where the director, L. A. Bauer, hoped that studies of the earth's magnetism might shed light on fundamental physics. Transatlantic radio was already a reality, and the physicists Arthur Kennelly and Oliver Heaviside had proposed that radio signals, unlike light waves, could traverse the Earth's curvature because they were being reflected off an electrically-charged region in the upper atmosphere. In 1925, Breit and his colleague, **Merle Tuve**, transmitted a series of pulsated radio waves to probe that region. By analyzing the echoes picked up by a receiver located thirteen miles away, they were able to determine the height and density of this upper layer, thus offering the first proof of Heaviside's ionosphere. This work marked the beginning of the study of the upper atmosphere; it also represented a key step toward the invention of radar.

Pursues Fundamental Studies of Atomic Nuclei

Physicists such as **Ernest Rutherford** had made key discoveries in nuclear science by bombarding the atoms of many of the lighter elements with energetic particles emitted from radioactive materials. After 1925, an important direction for research lay in improving the process by which such bombardments were produced. Again, Breit and Tuve worked together in constructing a multi-section, high-voltage accelerating tube, the first proton accelerator built in the United States.

Breit left Washington in 1929 to teach physics at the University of New York. By 1934, he had joined the physics staff of the University of Wisconsin, where he continued his work on particle acceleration and reactions. Working with Hungarian physicist **Eugene Wigner**, Breit was able to determine that the forces acting upon the protons and neutrons in an atom's nucleus work on a short-range level and do not rely on the electrical charge of the particles. Hence, this interaction had to feature a new force, which, in time, would be called the strong force. Like gravity, it is one of the four fundamental forces of nature. Further collaboration between the two physicists introduced the Breit-Wigner formula, which explains the absorption of neutrons and the subsequent decay of the nucleus as a result of certain nuclear reactions. This advanced the science of nuclear fission in the development of weapons and medical imaging.

Directs Studies of the Atomic Bomb

On the eve of World War II, nuclear physicists became aware that their research might lead to atomic weapons. In April of 1940, Breit raised the issue of security, urging his colleagues to withhold publication of articles concerning nuclear physics, particularly on the topic of uranium fission, until after the war. Between 1940 and 1941, Breit worked in the Naval Ordnance Laboratory at the Washington Naval Yard, where his background in electrical engineering again served him well. There, he developed the magnetic extrapolator, which demagnetized the steel hull of a ship to protect it from German magnetic mines. With his invention, the same process that once took a month, now took only a day. By 1942, Breit had joined the Metallurgical Laboratory at the University of Chicago, which then served as the Manhattan Project's principal research center. He took on the task of coordinating research on the Fast Neutron Project, geared toward the manufacture of a uranium bomb, subcontracting studies to twenty other universities.

But Breit's excessive concern with secrecy soon led him to resign. In *The Making of the Atomic Bomb,* the historian Richard Rhodes cites a memo Breit wrote in May of 1942: "One of the men coaxed my secretary to give him some official reports out of my safe while I was away on a trip . . . I have heard him advocate the principle that all parts of the work are so closely interrelated that it is desirable to discuss them as a whole." He was speaking of **Enrico Fermi**, who was leading the development of the first nuclear reactor. Breit was replaced as project leader by **J. Robert Oppenheimer**. In 1942, he took a management post at the Applied Physics Laboratory of Johns Hopkins University, where he worked on the proximity fuse, used to detonate guided weapons within close range of a given target. A year later, he became head physicist and a member of the scientific advisory committee for the Aberdeen Proving Ground's Ballistic Research Laboratory. Then, in 1947 he took a professorship at Yale University. But his contributions to nuclear-weapons studies were not finished.

The prospect of a hydrogen bomb, after 1950, raised a horrifying possibility: that such a weapon might touch off an uncontrolled chain reaction in the Earth's oceans or atmosphere. **Edward Teller**, a principal leader in H-bomb studies, arranged for Breit to carry out calculations looking into this possibility. Breit reported that such a disaster appeared unlikely, but proposed experimental tests that could set the matter to rest. Teller later credited Breit's work as a key element in the first detonation of an H-bomb in November of 1952.

Breit married Marjorie MacDill in 1927, and adopted a stepson, Ralph Wyckoff. His wife had grown up on a farm near Lake Seneca in upstate New York, and Breit himself loved the outdoors. He particularly enjoyed rowing. He published some six papers a year for more than forty years. In 1958, Breit became Yale's first Donner Professor of Physics, retiring in 1968 to teach at the State University of New York at Buffalo. In 1973, well into his seventies, he retired to Salem, Oregon, where Wyckoff had made his home. Breit died there of cancer, on September 13, 1981.

SOURCES:

Books

Bromley, D. Allan and Vernon W. Hughes, editors, *Facets of Physics*, Academic Press, 1970.

Periodicals

Hull, McAllister H., Jr., "Gregory Breit," *Physics Today*, October, 1983, pp. 102–04.

—*Sketch by T. A. Heppenheimer*

Sydney Brenner
1927-
South African-born English geneticist and molecular biologist

Sydney Brenner is a geneticist and molecular biologist who has worked in the laboratories of Cambridge University since 1957. Recognized as one of the founders of molecular biology, Brenner played an integral part in the discovery and understanding of the triplet genetic code of DNA. He was also a member of the first scientific team to introduce messenger RNA, helping to explain the mechanism by which genetic information is transferred from DNA to the production of proteins and enzymes. In later years, Brenner conducted a massive, award-winning research project, diagramming the nervous system of a particular species of worm and attempting to map its entire genome.

Brenner was born in Germiston, South Africa, on January 13, 1927. His parents were neither British nor South African—Morris Brenner was a Lithuanian exile who worked as a cobbler, and Lena Blacher Brenner was a Russian immigrant. Sydney Brenner grew up in his native town, attending Germiston High School. At the age of fifteen, he won an academic scholarship to the University of the Witwatersrand in Johannesburg, where he earned a master's degree in medical biology in 1947. In 1951 Brenner received his bachelor's degree in medicine, the qualifying degree for practicing physicians in Britain and many of its colonies. The South African university system offered no Ph.D. degrees and could offer him no further education, so he embarked on independent research. He studied chromosomes, cell structure, and staining techniques, built his own centrifuge, and laid the foundation for his interest in molecular biology.

Frustrated by his lack of resources and eager to pursue his interest in molecular biology, Brenner decided to seek education elsewhere, and was encouraged by colleagues to contact **Cyril Hinshelwood**, professor of physical chemistry at Oxford University. In 1952 Hinshelwood accepted Brenner as a doctoral candidate and put him to work studying a bacteriophage, a virus that had become the organism of choice for studying molecular biology in living systems. Brenner's change of location was an important boost to his career; while at Oxford he met **Seymour Benzer**, with whom Brenner collaborated on important research into gene mapping, sequencing, mutations and colinearity. He also met and exchanged ideas with **James Watson** and **Francis Crick**, the Cambridge duo who published the first paper elucidating the structure of DNA, or deoxyribonucleic acid, the basic genetic molecule. Brenner and Crick were to become the two most important figures in determining the general nature of the genetic code.

Brenner earned his Ph.D. from Oxford in 1954, while still involved in breakthrough research in molecular biology. His colleagues tried to find a job for him in England, but he accepted a position as lecturer in physiology at the University of the Witwatersrand and returned to South Africa in 1955. Brenner immediately set up a laboratory in Johannesburg to continue his phage research, but missed the resources he had enjoyed while in England. Enduring almost three years of isolation, Brenner maintained contact with his colleagues by mail. Distracted by the tense political situation in South Africa, Brenner, as quoted in Horace Judson's *The Eighth Day of Creation,* wrote, "It is worse here than I ever imagined in my most terrible nightmares."

Appointed to Cambridge Staff

In January 1957 Brenner was appointed to the staff of the Medical Research Council's Laboratory of Molecular Biology at Cambridge, and he and his family were able to settle in England permanently. Brenner immediately attended to theoretical research on the characteristics of the genetic code that he had begun in Johannesburg, despite the chaotic atmosphere. At the time, the world's foremost geneticists and molecular biologists were debating about the manner in which the sequences of DNA's four nucleotide bases were interpreted by an organism. The structure of a DNA molecule is a long, two-stranded chain that resembles a twisted ladder. The sides of the ladder are formed by alternating phosphate and sugar groups. The nucleotide bases adenine, guanine, thymine, and cytosine—or A, G, T, and C—form the rungs, a single base anchored to a sugar on one side of the ladder and linked by hydrogen bonds to a base similarly anchored on the other side. Adenine bonds only with thymine and guanine only with cytosine, and this complementarity is what makes it possible to replicate DNA. Most believed that the bases down the rungs of the ladder were read three at a time, in triplets such as ACG, CAA, and so forth. These triplets were also called codons, a term coined by Brenner. Each codon represented an amino acid, and the amino acids were strung together to construct a protein. The problem was understanding how the body knew where to start reading; for example, the sequence AACCGGTT could be read in several sets of three-letter sequences. If the code were overlapping, it could be read AAC, ACC, CCG, and so forth.

Brenner's contribution was his simple theoretical proof that the base triplets must be read one after another and could not overlap. He demonstrated that an overlapping code would put serious restrictions on the possible sequences of amino acids. For example, in an overlapping code the triplet AAA, coding for a particular amino acid, could only be followed by an amino acid coded by a triplet beginning with AA—AAT, AAA, AAG, or AAC. After exploring the amino acid sequences present in naturally occurring proteins, Brenner concluded that the sequences were not subject to these restrictions, eliminating the possibility of an overlapping code. In 1961 Brenner, in collaboration with Francis Crick and others, confirmed his theory with bacteriophage research, demonstrating that the construction of a bacteriophage's protein coat could be halted by a single "nonsense" mutation in the organism's genetic code, and the length of the coat when the transcription stopped corresponded to the location of the mutation. Interestingly, Brenner's original proof was written before scientists had even determined the universal genetic code, although it opened the door for sequencing research.

Also in 1961, working with Crick, **François Jacob**, and **Matthew Meselson**, Brenner made his best-known contribution to molecular biology, the discovery of the messenger RNA (mRNA). Biologists knew that the DNA, which is located in the nucleus of the cell, contains a code that controlled the production of protein. They also knew that protein is produced in structures called ribosomes in the cell cytoplasm, but did not know how the DNA's message is transmitted to, or received by, the ribosomes. RNA had been found within the ribosomes, but did not seem to relate to the DNA in an interesting way. Brenner's team, through original research and also by clever interpretation of the work of others, discovered a different type of RNA, mRNA, which was constructed in the nucleus as a template for a specific gene, and was then transported to the ribosomes for transcription. The RNA found within the ribosomes, rRNA, was only involved in the construction of proteins, not the coding of them. The ribosomes were like protein factories, following the instructions delivered to them by the messenger RNA. This was a landmark discovery in genetics and cell biology for which Brenner earned several honors, including the Albert Lasker Medical Research Award in 1971, one of America's most prestigious scientific awards.

Turns to the Worm

In 1963 Brenner set out to expand the scope of his research. For most of his career, he had concentrated on the most fundamental chemical processes of life, and now he wanted to explore how those processes governed development and regulation within a living organism. He chose the nematode *Caenorhabditis elegans,* a worm no more than a millimeter long. As reported in *Science,* Brenner had initially told colleagues, "I would like to tame a small metazoan," expecting that the simple worm would be understood after a small bit of research. As it turned out, the nematode project was to span three decades, involve almost one hundred laboratories and countless researchers, make *C. elegans* one of the world's most studied and best understood organisms, and become one of the most important research projects in the history of genetics.

Brenner's nematode was an ideal subject because it was transparent, allowing scientists to observe every cell in its body, and had a life cycle of only three days. Brenner and his assistants observed thousands of *C. elegans* through every stage of development, gathering enough data to actually trace the lineage of each of its 959 somatic cells from a single zygote. Brenner's team also mapped the worm's entire nervous system by examining electron micrographs and producing a wiring diagram that showed all the connections among all of the 309 neurons. This breakthrough research led Brenner to new discoveries concerning sex determination, brain chemistry, and programmed cell death. Brenner also investigated the genome of the nematode, a project that eventually led to another milestone, a physical map of virtually the entire genetic content of *C. elegans*. This physical map enabled researchers to find a specific gene not by initiating hundreds of painstaking experiments, but by reaching into the freezer and pulling out the part of the DNA that they desired. In fact, Brenner's team was able to distribute copies of the physical map, handing out the worm's entire genome on a postcard-size piece of filter paper.

Brenner's ultimate objective was to understand development and behavior in genetic terms. He originally sought a chemical relationship that would explain how the simple molecular mechanisms he had previously studied might control the process of development. As his research progressed, however, he discovered that development was not a logical, program-driven process—it involved a complex network of organizational principles. For example, Brenner would say that the simple mechanics of the genetic code can explain how to make insulin, but cannot explain how to make a hand or a foot. The instructions for making complex body parts are not explicitly coded; they are embedded in higher organizational principles. Brenner's worm project was his attempt to understand the next level in the hierarchy of development. What he and his assistants have learned from *C. elegans* may have broad implications about the limits and difficulties of understanding behavior through gene sequencing. The Human Genome Project, for instance, is an effort to sequence the entire human DNA. James Watson has pointed to Brenner's worm experiments as a model for the project.

Brenner's research has earned him worldwide admiration. He has received numerous international awards, including the 1970 Gregor Mendel Medal from the German Academy of Sciences, the prestigious Kyoto Prize from Japan, as well as honors from France, Switzerland, Israel, and the United States. He has been awarded honorary degrees from several institutions, including Oxford and the University of Chicago, and has taught at Princeton, Harvard, and Glasgow Universities. Brenner is known for his aggressiveness, intelligence, flamboyance, and wit. His tendency to engage in remarkably ambitious projects such as the nematode project, as well as his ability to derive landmark discoveries from them, led *Nature* to claim that Brenner is "alternatively molecular biology's favorite son and *enfant terrible*."

While still in Johannesburg in 1952, Brenner married May Woolf Balkind. He has two daughters, one son, and one stepson. In 1986 the Medical Research Council at Cambridge set up a new molecular genetics unit, and appointed Brenner to a lifelong term as its head. Research at the new unit is centered on Brenner's previous work on *C. elegans* and the mapping and evolution of genes.

SELECTED WRITINGS BY BRENNER:

Periodicals

(With F. Jacob and M. Meselson) "An Unstable Intermediate Carrying Information from Genes to Ribosomes for Protein Synthesis," *Nature,* May 13, 1961, pp. 576–581.

(With F. H. C. Crick, Leslie Barnett, and R. J. Watts-Tobin) "General Nature of the Genetic Code for Proteins," *Nature,* December 30, 1961, pp. 1227–1232.

SOURCES:

Books

Judson, Horace Freeland, *The Eighth Day of Creation,* Simon & Schuster, 1979.

Periodicals

Herman, Robert K., "Genes Make Worms Behave," *Nature,* July 22, 1993, pp. 282–283.

Lewin, Roger, "Why Is Development So Illogical?," *Science,* June 22, 1984, pp. 1327–1329.

Rennsberger, Boyce, "4 Scientists Win Lasker Awards," *New York Times,* November 10, 1971, p. 22.

Roberts, Leslie, "The Worm Project," *Science,* June 15, 1990, pp. 1310–1313.

—Sketch by G. Scott Crawford

Ricardo Bressani
1926-
Guatemalan biochemist

Ricardo Bressani is a prominent Central American food scientist who has contributed significantly to the knowledge of human nutrition and food production. Long associated with the Institute of Nutrition of Central America and Panama (INCAP), Bressani has focused his chief efforts toward increasing the availability of high quality foods for humans. His contributions include improving production of high nutrition foods; investigating the composition and nutritional value of basic foods such as maize, sorghum rice, beans, and amaranth; studying the effects of food processing on nutritional value; evaluating food storage techniques; and analyzing the efficient biological utilization of foods.

Ricardo Bressani Castignoli was born on September 28, 1926, in Guatemala City, Guatemala, to Primina (Castignoli), a homemaker, and César Bressani, a farmer. He obtained a B.S. degree from the University of Dayton (Ohio) in 1948. In 1951 he was awarded a master's degree from Iowa State University and began directing the food analysis laboratories at INCAP. Then two years old, INCAP had assessed the nutritional status of Central America, finding widespread malnutrition and a heavy reliance by Central Americans on cereals and legume grains. This first, brief association with INCAP stimulated Bressani's interest in the serious nutrition problems of populations in Central America.

In 1952 Bressani enrolled in Purdue University in Indiana, where he was a graduate research assistant at the Biochemical Research Institute and where he obtained his Ph.D. in 1956. He then returned to Guatemala to head INCAP's agricultural and food sciences division, a position that he held for 32 years. During this time, from 1963 to 1964, he was a visiting professor in the Department of Food Science at Rutgers State University in New Jersey; and in 1967 he was a visiting lecturer in the food science and nutrition department at the Massachusetts Institute of Technology. Other positions he has held for INCAP include that of research coordinator from 1983 to 1988; research advisor in food science and agriculture from 1988 to 1992; and consultant in food science, agriculture and nutrition beginning in 1993.

Identifies Nutritive Value of Natural Resources in Central America

Bressani conducted important studies regarding the nutritional value of resources already in abundance in Central America, such as Brazil nuts, rubber tree seeds and jicara seeds, caulote, jack beans, African palm, corozo, and buckwheat. These studies resulted from his concern that these resources held food value yet would vanish from the area because populations were ignorant of their nutritional value. The grain and vegetable amaranth, for instance, cultivated by Aztec, Mayan, and Inca civilizations, was rediscovered and converted into highly nutritional flour. In addition, Bressani's research on legumes not indigenous to Central America nor normally consumed by its populations—such as the jack bean and the cowpea—spurred agricultural production of some high-yield as well as highly nutritional beans. For instance, he obtained a protein isolate from the jack bean, uncovering it as a valuable food resource. The Central American Cooperative Program for the Improvement of Food Crops (PCCMCA) honored Bressani and his staff for their outstanding work in cereal and legume research.

As early as 1956, in Bressani's Ph.D. dissertation, he expressed concern about the nutritional problems of people whose diets consisted mainly of corn and beans. He conducted research into the effects of soil fertilization with minor elements on the yield and protein value of cereals and legumes. According to his dissertation, he was convinced that "in order to produce a corn of a high nutritive value, the ratio of germ to whole grain must be increased, or else the relative quantities of proteins other than zein should be increased in the endosperm." Eight years later at Purdue, scientist Edwin T. Mertz successfully isolated the Opaque–2 gene, the chemical-nutritive qualities of which follow the postulations in Bressani's dissertation. Subsequently, such organizations as INCAP, ICTA (Guatemala), and CIMMYT (Mexico) developed a superior maize called NUTRICTA. It was ready for agricultural production in October 1983.

Bressani has made numerous other contributions to nutrition and agriculture in Central America and has published over 450 articles in scientific journals. He is married to Alicia Herman, and they have seven children. He enjoys farming, horseback riding, reading, and photography.

SELECTED WRITINGS BY BRESSANI:

Books

Maize in Human Nutrition, F.A.O, 1992.
Nutritional Value and Use in Human Feeding of Some Authochtonous Underexploited Crops of Middle America, F.A.O., 1994.

SOURCES:

Bressani, Ricardo, correspondence with Janet Kieffer Kelley, February 28, 1994.

—Sketch by Janet Kieffer Kelley

Percy Williams Bridgman
1882-1961
American physicist

Percy Williams Bridgman was an experimental physicist whose principal focus was on developing apparatus for producing high pressures and on measuring the effects of high pressures on materials. His work in high-pressure physics won him the Nobel Prize in 1946. The results of his work continued to have implications for such diverse fields as solid-state physics, geophysics, and cosmology.

As an academic concerned with doing experiments rather than constructing theories, Bridgman made a number of discoveries that had profitable applications. His work on the electrical and thermal conductivity of metals became important to industrial metallurgists. The refrigeration industry was intrigued when Bridgman's high-pressure experiments produced "hot ice," a form of water that was solid at eighty degrees centigrade (the normal melting point of water is zero degrees centigrade). Hot ice turned out to be of no practical value, but other entrepreneurs speculated that a similar process might produce artificial diamonds. Bridgman felt that such a process was possible but not practical and did not pursue it in earnest. Later, though, in 1955, much of his work on high-pressure physics became the basis of the development of synthetic diamonds by General Electric.

A Scientific Puritan

Percy Bridgman was born on April 21, 1882, in Cambridge, Massachusetts. His father, Raymond Landon Bridgman, was a writer and journalist as well as a devout Protestant. His mother was Mary Ann Maria Williams. Both came from established New England families. Bridgman entered Harvard in 1900. He graduated in 1904 and remained at Harvard to earn his M.A. in 1905 and his Ph.D. in 1908. He joined the Harvard physics department as a research fellow in 1908 and became an instructor in 1910, a full professor in 1919, Hollis Professor in 1926, and Higgins Professor in 1950. He retired from Harvard in 1954.

Bridgman was known to be shy but tenaciously principled. He had absorbed his father's Protestant values of honesty and hard work to such an extent that one biographer, Maila Walter, called him "a scientific puritan." However, in spite of his upbringing, from an early age he steadfastly rejected religion in any form, although later he did not object to his wife's religious practices or his children's participation in Sunday school. He viewed religion as another form of absolutism and as such an impediment to human progress. So strong were his convictions about religion that in 1948 he declined to participate in a conference on science, philosophy, and religion because the word "religion" appeared in its title.

Bridgman conducted his work by collecting data through measurement and then progressing toward theories. But most of his effort went toward the former. Bridgman took great pride in making things work. He paid scrupulous attention to the details of his experimental apparatus. For example, when nothing of the quality he needed was commercially available, he bored his own pipes for one of his high-pressure experiments. Bridgman did not avoid theorizing, but he preferred the laboratory, where his work was guided more by motor and visual operations than by abstract concepts. Although Bridgman spent his life in academia, he did not consider himself a good lecturer. He worked hard at his presentations, but he often expressed frustration over his apparent inability to communicate well with his students. As a result he much preferred the laboratory to the lecture hall. Nevertheless, Bridgman had considerable impact on many of his students, who included **John C. Slater** and **J. Robert Oppenheimer**.

Putting the Pressure On

Bridgman is best known for his experiments to fashion apparatus strong enough to produce higher and higher pressures. In his early work he attained pressures of up to 6,000 kg/cm², which was twice the limit set by nineteenth-century French experimenters. In 1909 he pushed his equipment to the point of collapse at 7,000 kg/cm², twice that attained by any other experimenter at the time. Through a combination of meticulous craftsmanship and innovative metallurgical techniques Bridgman soon was able to reach pressures of up to 20,000 kg/cm². In his forty years of research in high-pressure physics, Bridgman eventually attained pressures of up to 500,000 kg/cm².

Bridgman entered his field of study, high-pressure physics, by accident. In the course of working on his doctorate at Harvard, he stumbled on a form of packing that allowed him to construct an assembly capable of pressures higher than ever attained before. The pressures he could create were limited only by the strength of the metal parts of his equipment. Years later, discussing this discovery in his textbook *The Physics of High Pressure*, he recalled, "The whole high-pressure field opened up at once before me like a vision of the promised land."

As Bridgman developed equipment capable of producing higher pressures, he needed gauges to measure them. Bridgman knew, in fact, that these new pressures were of no use to science unless they could be measured accurately. Bridgman had worked with pressure gauges since his student days at Harvard, where they were the subject of his Ph.D. dissertation,

"Mercury Resistance as a Pressure Gauge." From this dissertation Bridgman in 1909 wrote three papers, the second of which described the construction of a scale that correlated the electrical resistance of mercury with pressure. The gauges he developed could measure pressures up to 7,000 kg/cm^2, at which point the steel used in their construction began to weaken. In 1911 Bridgman developed another pressure gauge, using manganin, an alloy of copper, manganese, and nickel. This gauge could measure pressures up to 13,000 kg/cm^2 and was more accurate than the earlier mercury-based gauge because it had a more linear (direct) response between pressure and electrical resistance.

Caught in a Revolution

Bridgman felt he was too busy doing experiments and writing up results for publication to enter the discussions over relativity, which **Albert Einstein** had introduced at the time. But in 1914 the death of a colleague at Harvard forced Bridgman to teach a course in advanced electrodynamics, a field that had just been revolutionized by Einstein's work. As a classically trained physicist, Bridgman lacked the background to teach this new material, so he was forced to study it himself. What he learned disturbed him and altered his view of physics.

For Bridgman and most other physicists of his generation, Einstein's relativity rendered obsolete their Newtonian beliefs in absolutes like time and space. Bridgman was so troubled by this development that in 1927 he wrote *The Logic of Modern Physics,* in which he confessed his despair over the disarray in the foundations of physics that resulted from relativity. His struggles to reconcile the classical physics of his own training with the revolutionary physics that emerged during his career were protracted and arduous.

Bridgman was able to regain some measure of equanimity when he extracted from Einstein's work a way for physicists to interpret the world by maintaining contact with experience and not by searching for ideals like absolute time. Bridgman called this approach to physics operationalism. It was a method that scientists could use to distinguish what is physically real from what is not. Operationalism required scientists to define things with respect to how their physical qualities are measured. For Bridgman operationalism implied that knowledge was not possible without some human presence.

No sooner had Bridgman regained his balance after the assault by relativity than he was tripped up by another revolutionary idea, quantum mechanics. Bridgman felt in particular the effects of **Werner Heisenberg**'s uncertainty principle, which states that it is impossible to know both the exact position and the exact momentum of a particle. This principle forced Bridgman to concede that beyond a certain point in nature science has no place. Operationalism did nothing to resolve this dilemma, but as it turned out, the discussions of quantum mechanics were indebted to operationalism for their vocabulary.

Even though Bridgman felt he had made peace with relativity, many aspects of it bothered him until his death. In fact, he wrote *A Sophisticate's Primer of Relativity* as a critical examination of special relativity late in his life, by which time the theory had gained general acceptance. In his *Primer* Bridgman spelled out his criticisms of Einstein's theory. For example, he felt that light was no more than the illumination of things, not, as relativity said, something that traveled. Bridgman doubted the constancy of the speed of light, and he searched without success for ways to verify through experiments Einstein's notions about light.

Champion of the Individual

Bridgman was fiercely individualistic. He valued individual freedom not only in the context of science but also in the broadest areas of life. He believed that society existed for the sake of the individual, not the individual for society. On that basis Bridgman espoused the principle that society should interfere as little as possible with the activities of the individual, a practice that makes the fewest assumptions and creates the fewest expectations. On the other hand, Bridgman felt that the individual must not take more from society than he gives, and, in fact, he should give a bit more just for good measure.

Bridgman believed that science could liberate people and protect their freedom because it is a practice based on intellectual integrity. This practice can help humankind to ignore false gods and subdue base urges and emotions. Science can do this, Bridgman believed, because it rests not on authority but on fact.

As an individualist, Bridgman bristled under any show of authority. During World War I he refused to get caught up in the intense patriotism that emerged in the United States. Maila Walter reports that when he found out that a paper of his was going to be edited, he demanded that the byline read "amplified and edited from the manuscript of P. W. Bridgman."

Bridgman objected most to religious authority. He felt that in yielding to the ethical system of some divine will, people avoid responsibility for themselves. Bridgman believed that ethics ought to come not from some absolute authority but from an analysis of all the outcomes of various actions. In an article for *Harper's,* Bridgman wrote that he welcomed the reported decline of religious belief because he saw it as an indication of greater intellectual honesty brought about by the popularization of science.

In the spring of 1961 Bridgman began to suffer from what he thought was a muscular rheumatism. By June he felt worse, and in July he was told that he had a nonoperable cancer in his pelvis. Bridgman believed that his condition would worsen quickly, and he lamented that he would not have enough time to finish the preparation of his complete scientific papers, which Harvard University Press would eventually publish posthumously in 1964. In spite of his pain and despair, Bridgman continued to work until August, finishing *A Sophisticate's Primer of Relativity* and submitting a book review for *Science*. On August 20, 1961, Percy Bridgman died by his own hand at his home in Randolph, New Hampshire. He was survived by his wife, Olive Ware Bridgman, and two children, Jane and Robert.

SELECTED WRITINGS BY BRIDGMAN:

Books

The Logic of Modern Physics, Macmillan, 1927.
The Physics of High Pressure, G. Bell, 1931.
Reflections of a Physicist, Philosophical Library, 1950.
A Sophisticate's Primer of Relativity, Wesleyan University Press, 1962.
Collected Experimental Papers, 7 volumes, Harvard University Press, 1964.

Periodicals

"The Struggle for Intellectual Integrity," *Harper's,* December, 1933.

SOURCES:

Books

Walter, Maila, *Science and Cultural Crisis: An Intellectual Biography of Percy Williams Bridgman,* Stanford University Press, 1990.

—*Sketch by Lawrence Souder*

Yvonne Claeys Brill
1924-
Canadian-born American aerospace engineer

Yvonne Claeys Brill developed new rocket propulsion systems for communications satellites. Her innovative hydrazine resistojet, a single propellant rocket system she developed in the 1970s and for

Yvonne Claeys Brill

which she holds the patent, is still in use today. Brill served with the National Aeronautics and Space Administration's (NASA) space shuttle program office from 1981 to 1983, and she played a role in developing the propulsion system design for the International Maritime Satellite Organization (INMARSAT).

A native of Winnipeg, Canada, Brill was born on December 30, 1924. Her family discouraged her ambition to pursue science but she prevailed, earning her B.S. degree in mathematics at the University of Manitoba in 1945. Unable to find work in Canada, she relocated to Santa Monica, California, where she accepted a position as a mathematician for the Douglas Aircraft Company. At Douglas, Brill initially assisted with studies of aircraft propeller noise. Seeking more challenging work, she began graduate studies in chemistry at the University of Southern California.

At the end of World War II, Brill transferred to Douglas' aerodynamics department, where she remained for a short time before accepting a position as a research analyst with the RAND think tank in Santa Monica. During her association with RAND, a mentor helped her to obtain a promotion to the propellant department. During the day, Brill researched rocket and missile designs and propellant formulas, while continuing to pursue her graduate degree at night. When her association with RAND ended, her work became more theoretical. Dissatisfied, Brill joined Marquardt, a small firm, as a group leader, performing more applied work on super propellants and experimental ramjets.

Moves to East Coast

Brill earned her M.S. degree in chemistry in 1951, the same year she met and married her husband, a research chemist. In 1952 the couple moved to Connecticut, where Brill took a position as a staff engineer with United Aircraft Research Laboratory in East Hartford. During her tenure there, she resumed her study of rocket and ramjet engines and evaluated proposals for new projects. In 1955, Brill joined Wright Aeronautical Division of Curtiss-Wright Corporation where, as a project engineer, she directed corporate development of high energy fuels and studied state-of-the-art turbojet and turbofan engines adapted for advanced aircraft. Following the birth of her first child in 1957, Brill served as a part-time consultant on rocket propellants to FMC Corporation in Princeton. She had two more children before returning to full-time work in 1966.

Contributes to Mars Spacecraft

Brill accepted a position as Senior Engineer with RCA Astro-Electronics (now GE Astro) in 1966, and was named manager of NOVA Propulsion in 1978. She found her work at RCA challenging, and it was here that she made the most significant contributions of her career. She developed a hydrazine/hydrazine resistojet thruster, for which she later received a patent; the thruster was a monumental advance for single propellant rockets and is still used today. In addition, Brill performed preliminary work on the Mars Observer spacecraft, which was launched in 1992. She also tracked launch vehicle performance on the Scout, Delta, Atlas and Titan spacecrafts. In 1970, Brill received RCA's Astro-Electronics Engineering Excellence Award.

Brill left RCA in 1981 to serve as the director of the Solid Rocket Motor program in the Office of Space Flight (Shuttle Program) at NASA, a post she held for two years. Brill later remarked that while she missed the "hands-on work" she had performed at RCA, she found her experience with NASA valuable, having gained greater understanding of the interplay between the space program and federal political and budgetary processes.

Returning to RCA Astro-Electronics in 1983, Brill was disappointed to find that reorganization had changed management philosophy. She found herself simply writing proposals. In 1986, she accepted the position of space segment engineer with INMARSAT in London, where she worked until retiring from that project in 1991. That same year, Brill participated in the creation of two studies commissioned by the National Research Council. She subsequently was employed as a consultant for Telespace, Ltd., in Skillman, New Jersey, while monitoring propulsion system activities for all of the INMARSAT-2 spacecraft—communication satellites which were in orbit in 1994.

Brill's many honors include the 1993 Resnik Challenger Medal for her "innovative concepts for satellite propulsion systems and her breakthrough engineering solutions (which) have designated her as a pioneer in expanding space horizons." She also received the Society of Women Engineers (SWE) Achievement Award in 1986; the Diamond Super Woman Award from *Harper's Bazaar* and DeBeers Corporation; and the American Institute of Aeronautics and Astronautics' (AIAA) National Capitol Section Marvin C. Demler Award for Outstanding Service, 1983, having previously been elected a fellow of the AIAA. She is also a fellow of the SWE, and a member of the National Academy of Engineering, the British Interplanetary Society, and the scientific societies Sigma Xi and Tau Beta Pi. She has authored 40 publications.

SELECTED WRITINGS BY BRILL:

Periodicals

"Going for the Assignments," *Aerospace America,* November, 1984, p. 88.

SOURCES:

Periodicals

Parsons, Susan V., "1993 Resnik Challenger Medal Recipient: Yvonne C. Brill," *SWE,* September/October, 1993, pp. 18–20.
Sharp, Daisy, "When Not Propelling Satellite, Enjoys Cooking and Concerts," *Trenton Advertiser,* December 8, 1968.

—*Sketch by Karen Withem*

Detlev Wulf Bronk
1897-1975
American biophysicist

Detlev Wulf Bronk was an American biophysicist who had an important career as an administrator as well as a researcher. His research career was devoted to studying the neurophysiological activity of the autonomic nervous system—the nervous system responsible for the physiological functions such as breathing and digestion that a person can not willfully control. In addition to this work, Bronk was an influential organizer of American science. Aside from serving as president of the Johns Hopkins University in Baltimore and the Rockefeller Institute for Medical Research in New York City, Bronk also headed the National Research Council, the National Academy of Sciences, and the American Association for the Advancement of Science. From these posts, Bronk played an instrumental role in shaping America's national science policy after World War II.

Born August 13, 1897, in New York City, Bronk was the son of Mitchell Bronk, a Baptist minister, and Cynthia Brewster Bronk. The family's surname reflected their Dutch ancestry. Bronk spent his childhood in New York and New Jersey until 1915, when he enrolled at Swarthmore College in Pennsylvania. When the United States entered World War I in 1917, Bronk enlisted for military service, serving as a pilot in the Naval Aviation Corps. Although he returned to civilian life in 1918, he remained an ensign and kept his pilot's qualification.

In 1920, Bronk received his B.S. degree in electrical engineering from Swarthmore College. After spending an additional year studying physics at the University of Pennsylvania, Bronk left Pennsylvania to study physics at the University of Michigan. In September, 1921, before beginning his graduate studies at Michigan, Bronk married Helen Alexander Ramsey, who had also been a student at Swarthmore. Bronk earned a master's degree in 1922 and a doctoral degree in physics in 1926. His intention was to apply physical and quantitative methods to problems in biological science, and his training in physics and mathematics gave him an extraordinarily broad and versatile background. This interdisciplinary approach to studying biological issues made Bronk a pioneer in the field of biophysics.

Begins Work on Neurophysiology

Bronk returned to Swarthmore after receiving his doctoral degree and served as professor of physiology and the school's Dean of Men. Although he was well liked by students and he enjoyed their company, his teaching and administrative posts at Swarthmore allowed him little time to perform physiological research. He successfully applied for a fellowship from the National Research Council which allowed him to spend a year from 1928 to 1929 in England. During his fellowship, he studied in the laboratory of **Edgar D. Adrian** (later Lord Adrian) at Cambridge University, and at the University of London with **Archibald V. Hill**; Hill had won the 1922 Nobel Prize in Physiology or Medicine, and Adrian would receive the same distinction in 1932.

It was Adrian who introduced Bronk to neurophysiology—a field that allowed Bronk to make use his training in the biological and physical sciences. Adrian's laboratory, like many of the late 1920s, studied the nerve. Consisting of a bundle of fibers, nerves relay sensations (like touch and smell) and instructions concerning motor activity (like moving an arm or a leg) by electrical impulses. The electrical activity of nerve fibers is too faint and too brief to be measured by normal recording devices. Adrian and Bronk successfully collaborated on isolating a single nerve fiber and measuring its electrical activity.

Bronk returned to the United States from England in 1929. He continued the research that he began in Adrian's laboratory at the Eldridge Reeves Johnson Foundation for Medical Physics at the University of Pennsylvania. His work at the foundation helped define, on a national scale, the new field of biophysics—one which integrated biology, chemistry, physics, mathematics, medicine, and other disciplines. He was also director of the Institute of Neurology and professor of biophysics. While serving as director of the Johnson Foundation, Bronk oversaw a laboratory that produced two 1967 Nobel Prize winners—**Ragnar Arthur Granit** and **Haldan Keffer Hartline**. In 1935, Bronk and Herbert Gasser served as representatives to the Physiological Congress in Leningrad; the pair repeated their duties again in Zurich in 1938. During this period, Bronk also served as editor of the influential *Journal of Cellular and Comparative Physiology,* a position he retained until 1951. Except for one year that he spent at Cornell University, Bronk remained director of the Johnson Foundation until 1949. But by 1941, the increasing demands of his administrative duties were making it more difficult for him to pursue his physiological research.

Becomes Policymaker for American Science

After the United States entered World War II in 1941, Bronk contributed to the war effort his experience as a research scientist, administrator, and military officer. He served as Coordinator of Research for the Air-Surgeon's Office of the U.S. Army Air Force, which gave him considerable control over the course of scientific research. When Bronk returned to civilian life in 1945, he turned his attention away from conducting research and focused his energy almost entirely on the organization of American science.

Bronk had been well prepared for the path that his career now followed. The directorship of the Johnson Foundation and his participation in the American Physiological Society gave him a commanding presence among other scientists. In 1946, the Rockefeller Institute for Medical Research elected Bronk to its Board of Scientific Directors. He also served as foreign secretary of the National Academy of Sciences from 1945 to 1950, and as chair of the National Research Council from 1946 to 1950. The late 1940s saw Bronk assume other positions that increased his influence in the making of science policy. In 1949, he resigned as director of the Johnson Foundation and assumed the presidency of Johns Hopkins University, a post he held until 1953. His tenure as president of Johns Hopkins was marked by the addition of new buildings to the university's campus and by attempts to unify an institution that had been divided by the prominence of its medical school.

When Bronk's long-time friend, Herbert Gasser, retired as director of the Rockefeller Institute for Medical Research, Bronk assumed the position in 1953. This year began a period of intense administrative activities for Bronk. Under his leadership, the Rockefeller Institute was converted from a research institute to a graduate university, Rockefeller University. Just as he had done at the Johnson Foundation, Bronk influenced the kind of research being done at Rockefeller University. He presided over an ambitious construction campaign and added a number of new departments; he also directed the growth of interdisciplinary biological research.

While heading Johns Hopkins and Rockefeller Universities, Bronk also held other key national positions. In 1950, he was the president of the American Association for the Advancement of Science, and from 1956 to 1964 he chaired the National Science Board of the National Science Foundation. The pinnacle of his achievements was serving as president of the National Academy of Sciences from 1950 to 1962. Consisting of the most important scientists in the country, the National Academy of Sciences has a key responsibility in shaping science policy in the United States. Bronk retained an even more direct role in this process by being a member of President's Science Advisory Committee from 1956 to 1964, serving under Dwight D. Eisenhower, John F. Kennedy, and Lyndon B. Johnson. From these posts he advocated more funding for nonmilitary scientific research, staunchly defended the importance of maintaining the independence of scientific research, and argued that scientific advances were best made by small groups of researchers.

Bronk's administrative career overshadowed his scientific career. Although he made some important contributions to understanding nerve physiology, these achievements were minor when compared to the enduring legacy of his administrative actions. By advising presidents and by heading every important scientific organization in the United States, he did much to shape the national science policy pursued after World War II. Bronk died on November 17, 1975, after suffering a cerebral hemiplegia. At the time of his death, he had been preparing to attend the anniversary meeting of the Royal Society of London.

SELECTED WRITINGS BY BRONK:

Books

"The Nature of Science and Its Humane Values," in *The Shape of Likelihood: Relevance and the University,* edited by Loren Eisely, Detlev W. Bronk, et al., University of Alabama Press, 1970, pp. 21–40.

Periodicals

(With E. D. Adrian) "The Discharge of Impulses in Motor Nerve Fibers. Part I. Impulses in Single Fibers of the Phrenic Nerve," *Journal of Physiology,* Volume 66, 1928, pp. 88–101.
(With L. K. Ferguson) "The Nervous Control of Intercostal Respiration," *American Journal of Physiology,* Volume 110, 1934–35, pp. 700–707.
"The Role of Scientists in the Furtherance of Science," *Science,* Volume 119, 1954, pp. 223–27.

SOURCES:

Books

Biographical Memoirs, National Academy of Sciences, Volume 50, 1979, pp. 3–87.
Biographical Memoirs of Fellows of the Royal Society, Volume 22, 1976, pp. 1–9.
Holmes, Frederick L., editor, *Dictionary of Scientific Biography,* Volume 17, Scribner, 1990, pp. 111–113.
Year Book of the American Philosophical Society, American Philosophical Society, 1978, pp. 54–66.

—*Sketch by D. George Joseph*

Johannes Nicolaus Brønsted
1879-1947
Danish physical chemist

Johannes Nicolaus Brønsted carried on the tradition of earlier distinguished Danish scientists who made major contributions to the field of chemistry and left a legacy that included a widely used model of how acids and bases work and the establishment of a major research institute. Known among friends for his intellectual curiosity beyond the sciences, Brønsted believed that the lack of logic and clear thinking in politics was the cause of many social problems.

Brønsted was born on February 22, 1879, in the small West Jutland town of Varde. His mother died shortly after he was born, and his father, an engineer, remarried several years later. Young Brønsted was greatly influenced by his father's work with Hedeselskabet, a corporation that reclaimed moors by draining, irrigating, and planting. Until 1891 the family lived at one of the farms of the Society for Cultivation of Heaths. It was here that his love of unspoiled nature flowered, and he developed a lifelong interest in birds. For the rest of his life he worked to protect them from the encroachment of civilization.

When Brønsted was twelve, the family moved to Aarhus, the second largest city in Denmark, where he attended school, excelling in mathematics, and enjoyed the surrounding countryside. He also developed an interest in chemistry after finding an agricultural dictionary in the attic of his house and performed primitive experiments at home. His life in Aarhus came to an end after his father died in 1893, leaving the family in a precarious financial situation. Against the advice of family friends who thought young Johannes should start earning a living, his stepmother insisted on ensuring that he and his sister received a good education; she moved her family to Copenhagen, where Brønsted attended the Metropolitan School. At the school, he met Niels Bjerrum, a student who was to become a lifelong friend and chief rival among Danish chemists whose work brought fame to their country.

In 1897 Brønsted entered the Polytechnic Institute in Copenhagen, where he studied engineering, intending to follow his father's career. Brønsted apparently did not find his studies to be a burden, and he was able to cultivate interests such as philosophy, art, and poetry. He also enjoyed singing and music, becoming a performer in the circle of his family and friends. While at the Polytechnic Institute, he met Charlotte Louise Warberg, a chemical engineer, whom he married in 1903. The couple settled down in the small town of Birkerød. Through his sister-in-law's husband, the painter Johannes Larsen, Brønsted's life became filled with art as well as science; it may have been this influence that led Brønsted to take up painting during World War I.

After earning his engineering degree in 1899, Brønsted switched his studies to chemistry and was awarded his magister scientiarum (M.Sc.) degree in chemistry in 1902. The degree was so rare at the time that Brønsted's friends nicknamed him Magister. He worked for a time in an electrical engineering business until 1905, when he accepted a position as assistant at the University of Copenhagen's chemical laboratory. He earned his doctorate in 1908, presenting as his doctoral thesis the third in a series of papers on measurements of chemical affinities in reactions, in this case between water and sulfuric acid. In all, Bronsted published thirteen monographs on chemical affinity.

Work on Chemical Affinity Clarifies Thermodynamic Principles

The year he obtained his doctorate, Brønsted was appointed professor of chemistry at the University of Copenhagen, a position in which he taught elementary inorganic chemistry to students at the Polytechnic Institute and physical chemistry to chemical engineers and the students of the university. In 1912 he wrote a small textbook on elementary physical chemistry called *Outlines of Physical Chemistry,* which by the 1930s would be outdated and require the addition of his work in thermodynamics. In 1919 he was exempted from teaching inorganic chemistry, which gave him more time for his work. That work extended Danish chemist Julius Thomsen's studies on chemical processes, an important problem in the field of physical chemistry. A major area of research at this time was the measure of affinities: the strengths of acids and the tendency of substances to react with each other.

Formerly, such phenomena were described in vague terms, but in the early twentieth century, chemists were learning to express affinities mathematically and precisely by using the principles of thermodynamics. These principles describe changes in the heat of substances that react with each other, the direction of chemical processes, and the energy absorbed or released in the reactions. Thermodynamics allowed chemists to make predictions of how substances would behave and to describe accurately what happened in observed reactions. Julius Thomsen originally believed that the amount of heat released by chemical processes could be used to measure affinity. Yet by 1900 it was clear that the true measure of affinity was the maximum work the processes produced, not the heat of the reaction. However, there were very few accurate or systematic measurements of affinity before Brønsted set to work.

Brønsted's series of thirteen papers on affinity, which appeared from 1906 to 1918, was a major step in consolidating and explaining thermodynamic principles and a significant contribution to the field of chemical thermodynamics. After 1913 Brønsted's work on thermodynamics included the measurement of specific heat (the number of calories absorbed in raising the temperature of a gram of pure material by one degree centigrade) and the solubility of substances.

Brønsted's continuing interest in thermodynamics also led him to study electrolytes, substances that conduct electricity in solution, including both electromotive force and solubility measurements. At the time, the term electrolyte activity was new and reflected the newly developed concept that electrostatic forces between ions (charged atoms) might be chemically important. Brønsted embarked on several years of study of the properties of ionic solutions, publishing a series of papers on the topic beginning in 1919. In 1921 he published "The Principle of the Specific Interaction of Ions," which states that individual properties of an ion depend mainly on the presence of oppositely charged ions in the same solution.

Brønsted incorporated the use of electrochemical cells into his work. Because the voltage of the electrodes or conductors of these cells is proportional to the concentration of ions involved in reactions at a particular electrode, these cells can measure concentrations of ions. When current flow is produced by the electrochemical reactions, the cell is called a galvanic cell. Brønsted built his own galvanic cells and measured their electromotive force. During World War I, he even built batteries from such cells and used them to light his house in Birkerød.

During the 1920s Brønsted's new interests tumbled one onto another, his solubility studies leading into the field of reaction kinetics, the study of the rate at which chemical reactions occur and the intermediate steps that take place during the reactions. Brønsted's first studies in kinetics measured the effect of salts on acid-base equilibria, the point at which the conversion of an acid to a base equals the reverse reaction. For example, he demonstrated that the concentration of hydrogen ions released by acetic acid (vinegar) increases with the addition of salt, while salt has little effect on hydrogen ions released by ammonium ions.

Redefines Acids and Bases

Brønsted's extensive work with the effect of salt on acid-base equilibria led him to redefine the terms acid and base. According to the original definition, proposed by the Swedish chemist **Svante Arrhenius** in 1887, acids are compounds that dissociate or break up in water to yield hydrogen ions, and bases ionize in water to yield hydroxide ions. The extent to which these reactions occur determines the strength or weakness of the acid or base. Whereas a strong acid produces many hydrogen ions in an aqueous solution, a strong base yields many hydroxide ions, suggesting that certain substances act only as acids, others only as bases.

In 1923 Brønsted published simultaneously with Thomas Lowry in Britain a new theory of acids and bases that distinctly changed the concept of acids and bases. The theory had the advantage of applying to reactions that take place in all solvents, not just water. But more important, it explained that an acid is a substance that tends to release a proton, while a base

tends to take up a proton. Thus any acid in releasing a proton becomes a base, which can take up a proton to become an acid again. And any base can accept a proton, becoming an acid in the process. This concept that all acids and bases can be arranged in conjugate, or corresponding, pairs, broadened the range of substances that were recognized either as acids or bases.

By 1921 Brønsted's work was drawing visiting scientists from the United States and England who crowded into his modest laboratory at the Polytechnic Institute to study under his supervision. The fame these collaborations brought him bore impressive fruit during his 1926–27 visit to the United States, where he was visiting professor at Yale University. While in the United States, he sought funding to build a new physicochemical laboratory in Copenhagen. His efforts were rewarded when the International Education Board agreed to finance a new University Physicochemical Institute, which he helped to design. When the institute opened in 1930, Brønsted not only had ideal working conditions but also a comfortable residence, noted for the charm and hospitality of the Brønsteds, who entertained often.

While his close friends enjoyed his eclectic interests and charming personality, his students and younger colleagues, who were generally more in awe of him, found Brønsted distant. This may have been due in part to the intellectual rigor he demanded during discussion and debate, whether on topics of science, politics, or some other issue. Brønsted was a fervent Danish patriot but traveled widely in Europe. While his early contacts were with German scientists, after World War I his sympathies turned to England, which he visited often, particular for meetings of the Faraday Society. He spoke fluent English, enjoyed the English people and their literature, and the quaint and beautiful English countryside. The German occupation of Denmark during World War II made these visits impossible; but Brønsted contented himself with studying Anglo-European politics of the nineteenth and twentieth centuries and listening to news broadcasts from London.

After the war Brønsted continued to be preoccupied with politics, particularly the question of whether Germany or Denmark should control Schleswig, an area on the southern part of the Denmark's Jutland peninsula. The question had troubled both countries since the nineteenth century, and in 1947, vexed by the old debate, Brønsted took action. He accepted nomination as a candidate for the Danish Parliament, and on October 28 he was elected to that body. Brønsted threw himself into his new endeavor and began to study parliamentary procedure. However, before he could begin his government service, he died on December 17, 1947.

Bronsted was an honorary fellow of the British Chemical Society (1935), and in 1949, the organization hosted a memorial lecture honoring the Danish chemist and patriot. He had also been honored by his British colleagues by being made an honorary member of the Academy of Arts and Sciences in 1929 and an honorary doctor of London University in 1947; in addition he was awarded an honorary degree of doctor of science from the University of London in 1947. He was a member of the Royal Danish Academy of Sciences and Letters beginning in 1914 and belonged to the Danish Academy of Technical Sciences since its establishment in 1937. In 1928 he was awarded the Ørsted Medal.

SELECTED WRITINGS BY BRØNSTED:

Periodicals

(With Volume K. la Mer) "The Activity Coefficients of Ions in Very Dilute Solutions," *Journal of the American Chemical Society,* Volume 46, 1924, p. 555.

"The Acid-Basic Function of Molecules and Its Dependency on the Electric Charge Type," *Journal of Physical Chemistry,* Volume 30, 1926, p. 777.

"On the Activity of Electrolytes," *Transactions of the Faraday Society,* Volume 23, 1927, p. 416.

"The Fundamental Principles of Energetics," *Philosophical Magazine,* Volume 29, 1940, p. 449.

SOURCES:

Books

Dictionary of Scientific Biography, Scribner's, 1972, pp. 498–499.

Abbot, David, editor, *The Biographical Dictionary of Scientists: Chemists,* Peter Bedrick Books, 1984, pp. 22–23.

Periodicals

Bell, R. P., "The Brønsted Memorial Lecture," *Journal of the American Chemical Society,* Part 1, 1950, pp. 409–419.

Bell R. P., "Joannes Nicolaus Brønsted—An English View-Point," *Acta Chemica Scandinavica,* Volume 3, 1949, p. 1201.

Christiansen, J. A., "J. N. Brønsted," *Acta Chemica Scandinavica,* Volume 3, 1949, p. 1187.

Hevesy, G., "A Great Physical Chemist," *Acta Chemica Scandinavica,* Volume 3, 1949, p. 1205.

—*Sketch by Marc Kusinitz*

Ronald E. Brooks
1935-1989
American chemist

R onald E. Brooks led a research unit at General Electric which developed oil-eating microorganisms to clean up environmentally-damaging oil spills in the ocean. His management of the General Electric Research and Development Center's environmental unit in the 1970s and 1980s crossed the scientific and technological boundaries of chemistry, electronics, research physics, engineering and environmental science.

Born in New York City on May 28, 1935, Ronald Elmer Brooks was the son of Elmer, a minister, and Oretha (Beverley) Brooks. Both parents were known for their exhaustive religious and civic activities in the New York City region. During the Korean War era, Brooks served as a second lieutenant in the United States Army. His academic career began shortly afterward, and he graduated with a bachelor's degree in chemistry from the City College of New York in 1958. At the time of his graduation, the field of chemistry had opened new frontiers in the development of research instruments that were utilized in electrochemical analyses. From 1958 to 1960 Brooks worked as an assistant chemist at Burroughs Wellcome Company Research Laboratories in Tuckahoe, New York. He left to complete graduate studies at Brown University, and in 1965 received his Ph.D. in organic chemistry. Brooks' dissertation topic required detailed research in solvolytic rearrangement, the adding of a liquid substance such as water or hydrogen peroxide to a solution to form a new compound. This artificial production of a compound was historically used to make alcohol, ammonia and rubber.

Begins Career with General Electric

The Research and Development Center of General Electric (GE) in Schenectady, New York, employed about 600 nationally-recognized scientists. In 1964 Brooks began his career with GE in the Information Physics Branch as a research chemist. His talents and leadership skills very quickly earned him a promotion as a project manager of the Photocharge Recording Materials Program, a unit studying the composition of organic materials with the aid of advanced measuring instruments. Photocharge recording was, at the time, superior to early twentieth-century inventions such as the spectroscope and to the mid-century developments of vacuum tubes and photoelectric cells.

Brooks also led his research team through studies of photoresist, impactless printing, and photoconduction. These processes required the use of apparati such as chemical etching, photographic and thermoplastic film and electron beam recording to "make pictures" of patterns found in organic compounds. Each pattern of each compound would show different color spectra, diffraction patterns or wavelengths once they were analyzed. Analyses and comparisons could then be made of the content of each compound. As a result of his efforts, Brooks was eventually placed at the helm of the Environmental Technology Program of the Materials Engineering Laboratory.

Wins Landmark Patent for Oil-Digesting Microorganism

In 1969 the first report of the President's Panel for Oil Spills stated that the United States did not have an adequate oil spill technology. A year later, the Marine Science Affairs Committee of the U.S. government reported to Congress that oil pollution was a major source of concern in the marine environment and, in 1971, world oil pollution was estimated to be one million metric tons a year. The problem of water pollution was also discussed within the context of the residuals causing the pollution, the high costs of controlling the pollutants and the difficulty in tracing pollution sources. With these conditions in mind, Brooks was appointed manager of the General Electric Research and Development Center's Environmental Unit. According to GE, Brooks' position involved the development of "innovative technical solutions to . . . national environmental problems."

In 1972, Dr. Ananda M. Chakrabarty, a member of Brooks' research unit, with the consensus of General Electric, applied for a patent on an oil-digesting microorganism. The microbe, within laboratory conditions, was found to metabolize several hydrocarbons that were found in petroleum, and was effective in converting hydrocarbons into carbon dioxide and water which lessened the toxicity of the petroleum. With decreased toxicity, microorganisms that appeared naturally in water systems could eat the petroleum. The advantage of this microbe was that it could degrade crude oil at increased rates and thus quickly counteract the damage caused by an oil spill.

The microbe gained international attention. By 1976, it had been patented in England and the following year it was patented in France, but the U.S. Patent and Trademark Office did not grant rights to General Electric for the discovery until 1981. Originally denied patent rights, in a landmark case the Supreme Court overturned the earlier decision and found that Chakrabarty's microbe could not be denied patent protection merely because it was a living organism. It was the first time a genetically-engineered microorganism was awarded a U.S. patent. Brooks began personal research on microbial PCB degradation in 1982. PCBs (polychlorinated biphe-

nyls) are industrial chemicals used primarily as dielectric fluid in transformers and capacitors. However, Brooks died without seeing the formulation and implementation of his plan to neutralize PCBs.

Brooks was killed at the age of 54 on August 13, 1989, in a motor vehicle accident near his home in Guilderland, New York. His wife Elsa survived the accident and went on to raise their three sons, Hodari, Dahari and Bakari. Along with his scientific accomplishments, Brooks' was known for his association with the Baptist church and for his work with inner city youth. He served as chairman of the deacon board, treasurer, trustee and a Sunday school teacher at his church and founded Project Mercury, a federally funded program that trained minority and disadvantaged students as chemical technicians in Albany, New York. His professional memberships included the American Chemical Society, the Chemical Society of London, the Society of Photographic Scientists and Engineers, and the American Society of Microbiology. Brooks was also a founding member of the National Organization for the Professional Advancement of Black Chemists and Chemical Engineers and served as president of the Capital District Region of the American Chemical Society. John Brown, in the *General Electric R&D Center Post,* said: "Ron was a very kind and caring man. . . . who clearly appreciated his fellow man and whose devotion to his friends and family was obvious to all who knew him."

SELECTED WRITINGS BY BROOKS:

Books

The Solvolytic Rearrangement of Some 1,2-Diphenyl–3,3-Dichloroaziridines, University Microfilms, 1993.

SOURCES:

Periodicals

Brown, John, "Ronald E. Brooks, 1935–1989," *General Electric R & D Center Post,* August 16, 1989, p. 3.
Walker, Jesse H., "GE Chemist Dies," *Newsday,* August 26, 1989.

—*Sketch by Mary Raum*

Luitzen Egbertus Jan Brouwer
1881-1966
Dutch mathematician

The Dutch mathematician Luitzen Egbertus Jan Brouwer made contributions in the fields of topology and logic. He founded the school of thought known as intuitionism, which is based on the notion that the only dependable basis of mathematics consists of proofs that can actually be constructed in the real world. In addition, he developed a fixed-point theorem and demonstrated the connection between two previously distinct fields of topology—point-set topology and combinatorial topology.

Brouwer was born on February 27, 1881, in Overschie, the Netherlands. His parents were Egbert Brouwer and Henderika Poutsma. Brouwer completed high school in the town of Hoorn at the age of fourteen and attended the Haarlem Gymnasium where he satisfied the Greek and Latin requirements needed to enter a Dutch university in 1897.

At the University of Amsterdam Brouwer easily moved through the traditional mathematics curriculum and began some original studies on four-dimensional space that were published by the Royal Academy of Science in 1904. A year later he published his first book, *Leven, Kunst, en Mystiek* (*Life, Art, and Mysticism*), a philosophical treatise in which he considers the role of humans in society. In 1907 Brouwer presented his doctoral thesis and was granted his doctor of science degree by the University of Amsterdam. He began teaching at Amsterdam in 1909 and spent his entire academic career at the university.

Develops the Fundamental Concepts of Intuitionism

His doctoral thesis, "On the Foundations of Mathematics," outlined a field of research that occupied Brouwer on and off for the rest of his life. In the early twentieth century the two primary schools of mathematics were logicism and formalism. Logicism is based on the premise that fundamental concepts in mathematics, such as lines and points, have an existence independent of the human mind. The job of mathematicians is to derive theorems from these concepts. Formalism is less concerned with the nature of fundamental concepts, but insists that those concepts be manipulated according to very strict rules.

Brouwer proposed a third concept of mathematics, later given the name intuitionism (also known as constructivism or finitism). The basic argument of intuitionism, according to Richard von Mises in *World of Mathematics*, is that "the simplest mathematical ideas are implied in the customary lines of thought of everyday life and all sciences make use of them; the mathematician is distinguished by the fact that he is conscious of these ideas, points them out clearly, and completes them. The only source of mathematical knowledge" in intuitionism, von Mises continues, is "the intuition that makes us recognize certain concepts and conclusions as absolutely evident, clear and indubitable."

Brouwer's intuitionist school was not particularly influential when it was first proposed in the 1910s. According to Victor M. Cassidy, in *Thinkers of the Twentieth Century,* "Brouwer made few converts during his lifetime, and Intuitionism has only a tiny number of adherents today."

Makes Contributions in the Field of Topology

The 1910s were a period of intense activity in the field of topology, the mathematical discipline concerned with geometric point sets. In 1912 Brouwer announced perhaps his most famous theorem, the fixed-point theorem, also known as Brouwer's theorem. This theorem stated that during any transformation of all points in a circle or on a sphere, at least one point must remain unchanged. Brouwer was later able to extend this theorem to figures of more than three dimensions.

Brouwer's first appointment at the University of Amsterdam in 1909 was as a tutor. Three years later, he was promoted to professor of mathematics, a position he held for thirty-nine years. In 1951 he retired and was given the title of Professor Emeritus. He died in Blaricum, the Netherlands, on December 2, 1966. Brouwer had been married in 1904 to Reinharda Bernadina Frederica Elisabeth de Holl. She predeceased Brouwer in 1959. The couple had no children.

Brouwer received honorary doctorates from the universities of Oslo (1929) and Cambridge (1955) and was awarded a knighthood in the Order of the Dutch Lion in 1932. He had also been elected to membership in the Royal Dutch Academy of Sciences (1912), the German Academy of Science (1919), the American Philosophical Society (1943), and the Royal Society of London (1948).

SELECTED WRITINGS BY BROUWER:

Books

Leven, Kunst, en Mystiek, [Delft, the Netherlands], 1905.
Over de Grondslagen der Wiskunde, Maas and van Suchtelen, 1907.
Wiskunde, Waarheid, Werkelijkheid, P. N. Noordhoff, 1919.

Collected Works, edited by A. Heyting, American Elsevier, 1975.

Periodicals

"Intuitionism and Formalism," *Bulletin of the American Mathematical Society,* 20, 1913, pp. 81–96.
"Consciousness, Philosophy and Mathematics," *Proceedings of the Tenth International Congress of Philosophy,* I, 1949, pp. 1235–1249.

SOURCES:

Books

Daintith, John, et al., *A Biographical Encyclopedia of Scientists,* Facts on File, Volume 1, 1981, pp. 113–114.
Gillispie, Charles Coulson, editor, *Dictionary of Scientific Biography,* Volume 2, Scribner's, 1975, pp. 512–514.
Mises, Richard von, "Mathematical Postulates and Human Understanding" in *World of Mathematics,* edited by James Newman, Simon & Schuster, 1956.
Turner, Roland, editor, *Thinkers of the Twentieth Century,* St. James Press, 1987, pp. 116–118.

—*Sketch by David E. Newton*

Herbert C. Brown
1912-
American chemist

Herbert C. Brown opened an entirely new field of chemistry for study with his discovery of the organoboranes (an important chemical compound). Much of Brown's career has focused on the investigation of boron reagents, molecules that can temporarily link larger molecules together during a reaction. Because these boron-based molecules are highly active, they can foster chemical reactions that had previously been unachievable; they have become valuable in organic chemistry and in the manufacture of synthetics and pharmaceuticals. A professor at Purdue University, Brown received the 1979 Nobel Prize in chemistry.

Herbert Charles Brown was born in London on May 22, 1912. His parents, Charles Brovarnik and Pearl Gorinstein Brovarnik, were Ukranian Jews who had emigrated to London in 1908. Brown's paternal grandparents had already settled in Chicago and anglicized their surname to Brown; when his family arrived in Chicago in 1914 they followed suit. The only son, Herbert was the second of four children. Charles Brown had been a cabinetmaker in England and worked in the United States as a carpenter. He opened a hardware store in 1920, and the family lived upstairs. After his father died in 1926 of an infection, Herbert dropped out of high school to run the store and support the family. Returning to high school in 1929, he completed two years of work in one year to graduate in 1930.

After the hardware store failed, Brown worked as a shoe salesman and packer of notebook paper and belts, which strengthened his resolve to return to school. In February 1933 he entered Crane Junior College in Chicago. There he met Sarah Baylen, his future wife. The Depression forced Crane, like many other city colleges, to close. Brown worked odd jobs and took classes at Lewis Institute. Both Sarah and Brown attended Wright Junior College in 1934, graduating in 1935. Brown then won a partial scholarship to the University of Chicago. Because the tuition (and the scholarship) amounted to one hundred dollars per semester with no course limit, Brown loaded himself down with course work. Once again, he completed two years of work in one year, working with the noted chemist H. I. Schlesinger to investigate diborane—a rare but excellent reagent that could at the time be produced only in small quantities. In 1936 Brown's graduation gift was a copy of Alfred Stock's *The Hydrides of Boron and Silicon,* prophetically inscribed by his wife "to the future Nobel Prize winner."

Brown intended to find a job in industry after graduation, but his mentor Julius Stieglitz convinced him to go on to graduate school at the university. Again working with Schlesinger, Brown investigated the reactions of diborane with carbonyl compounds (molecules containing a carbon-oxygen double bond), and received his Ph.D. in 1938. Brown and Sarah married while he was in graduate school. Their son, Charles, became a chemist.

Discovers a New Reagent: Sodium Borohydride

Brown remained at the University of Chicago on a one-year postdoctoral fellowship with M. S. Kharasch, one of his mentors; he then became assistant to Schlesinger in his study of the borohydrides. In 1940 the National Defense Research Committee approached the researchers and asked them to search for volatile uranium compounds that could be used to produce the pure uranium needed for the atomic bomb. They used diborane to create uranium borohydride, but the process of preparing diborane was so slow and difficult that they sought a new method. They succeeded in preparing diborane by reacting lithium or sodium hydride with boron trihalides, but by then the war department had obtained what it needed from other sources. Their efforts had not, however, been in vain. Not only did Brown's group discover a new way to create what had been a rare and expensive compound, but they also discovered a new reagent, sodium borohydride, which was to become an important reducing agent, or electron donor, in organic chemistry.

Brown left the University of Chicago in 1943 for a position as assistant professor of chemistry at Wayne (later Wayne State) University in Detroit. Much of his research during his four years at Wayne focused on steric strains, the deviations of the bond angles of a molecule from their norms. He showed that these angles could have as much effect on how a compound reacts as could the constituent atoms' electrical charges.

In 1947 he became a full professor at Purdue University in Indiana. There he experimented with adding diboranes to carbon-carbon double bonds, and accidentally discovered that a process called hydroboration permitted rapid and easy conversion to organoboranes. Subsequent work with these compounds showed them to be of substantial utility in synthetic chemistry, particularly as intermediaries, or temporary links, in the creation of new carbon-carbon bonds. Brown has often compared the investigation of the organoboranes to the discovery of a new continent. As he told Malcolm Brown in the *New York Times,* "I feel that we have uncovered a new continent, just beginning to explore its mountain ranges and valleys. But it will take another generation of chemists to fully explore and apply this new chemistry of boron hydrides and organoboranes."

For his work with boron reagents Brown shared the 1979 Nobel Prize in chemistry with **Georg Wittig** of West Germany. In addition, he has received the Linus Pauling Medal in 1968, the National Medal of Science in 1969, the American Chemical Society's Award in Synthetic Organic Chemistry in 1960, the Chemistry Pioneer Award in 1974, the Priestly Medal in 1981, and the Perkin Medal in 1982.

In the course of his career, Brown has written over seven hundred scientific papers and four books and influenced countless students and colleagues with his thoroughness. In the January 1980 issue of *Science,* James Brewster and Ei-ichi Negishi noted, "Brown has been almost religious in resisting facile conclusions and has thereby succeeded in avoiding erroneous ones. Some of his most significant discoveries and developments have resulted from a dogged, logical pursuit of the kind of everyday chemical puzzle that many would dismiss with a glib rationalization."

SELECTED WRITINGS BY BROWN:

Books

Hydroboration, W. A. Benjamin, 1962.
Boranes in Organic Chemistry, Cornell University Press, 1972.
Organic Syntheses via Boranes, Wiley, 1975.
The Nonclassical Ion Problem, Plenum, 1977.

SOURCES:

Books

H. C. Brown: A Celebration, Purdue University Department of Chemistry, 1980.
Nobel Prize Winners, H. W. Wilson, 1987.
The Nobel Prize Winners: Chemistry, Volume 3, 1969–1989, Salem Press, 1990, pp. 1005–1015.

Periodicals

New York Times, October 16, 1979.
Science, Volume 207, January 4, 1980, pp. 44–46.

—*Sketch by F. C. Nicholson*

Lester R. Brown
1934-
American environmentalist and agricultural economist

A crusader for environmental causes, Lester R. Brown in 1974 founded Worldwatch Institute, a private, non-profit research institute in Washington, D.C., for the study of global environmental and economic issues; today he serves as its president and senior researcher. The institute publishes the annual *State of the World* reports and the Worldwatch Papers, a monograph series. Brown is the author of numerous books and articles, a frequent speaker on environmental issues, and the recipient of several awards, including the 1987 Environmental Prize from the United Nations.

Brown, the oldest of three children, was born on March 28, 1934, in Bridgeton, New Jersey, to Calvin C. and Delia (Smith) Brown, both of whom were tomato farmers. He grew up on a small farm and attended Cumberland County Public Schools. An avid reader, he was particularly fond of biographies of people such as Andrew Jackson, George Washington

Lester R. Brown

with rapid population growth, it received wide attention, including a cover story in the January 6, 1964, issue of *U.S. News and World Report* titled "Why Hunger Is to Be the World's No. 1 Problem." The study also led to Brown's first book, *Man, Land and Food: Looking Ahead at World Food Needs.* In 1962, Brown took a nine-month leave of absence from the USDA to earn a master's degree in public administration from Harvard University.

Brown's expertise earned him the respect of the then-Secretary of Agriculture, Orville L. Freeman, who named him his advisor on foreign agricultural policy in 1964. Together, Brown and Freeman convinced United States officials to demand that India change its food policies before receiving provisions from the United States. This reform prevented untold numbers of people from starving. In 1966, Freeman made Brown administrator of the USDA's International Agricultural Development Service, which conducted projects in about forty countries. Brown left government service in 1969 to help James Grant, now the executive director of UNICEF, form the Overseas Development Council, a private, non-profit institution that analyzes economic and political issues affecting the relationship between the United States and developing countries. At the council, Brown worked as a senior fellow and published four more books.

Carver, and Kit Carson. Brown was an active member of the local 4-H Club and the Future Farmers of America. At fourteen, he and his brother Carl bought a small piece of land and a used tractor and began growing tomatoes. Even after Brown entered Rutgers University in New Brunswick, New Jersey, they continued the farming operation. With a yield of 1.5 million pounds of tomatoes each year, the brothers earned the distinction of being among the top growers on the East Coast. Brown graduated from Rutgers University in 1955 with a bachelor of science degree in agricultural science.

Groundbreaking Study Addresses World Hunger

The year after his graduation from Rutgers, Brown received an opportunity to live and work in a small farming community with villagers in India for six months, thanks to the International Farm Youth Exchange Program of the National 4-H Club Foundation. He had originally intended to become a farmer, but after his experiences overseas he became intrigued by the pervasive problem of Third World hunger. After earning a master's degree in agricultural economics from the University of Maryland in 1959, Brown took up a job as an international agricultural analyst with the Foreign Agricultural Service arm of the United States Department of Agriculture (USDA).

At the USDA, Brown embarked on an intensive study of worldwide agricultural practices. The first study ever to attempt to link the issue of food supply

Launches Research Institute to Study Global Problems

Brown had been nurturing the dream of starting an independent think tank to analyze global environmental issues. In 1973, he had a chance conversation with William Dietel, then the executive vice-president of the Rockefeller Brothers Fund, and learned that Dietel shared many of his own concerns for the environment and supported the idea of a research institute. The following year, with a $500,000 start-up grant from the fund, he founded the Worldwatch Institute, whose goal is "to analyze world conditions and problems such as famine, overpopulation, and scarcity of natural resources" according to an entry in *Contemporary Authors.* The institute conducts research that is global in scope and interdisciplinary in approach. In addition to over one hundred Worldwatch Papers and the annual *State of the World* reports, both of which are translated into several languages, the institute publishes *World Watch,* a bimonthly magazine featuring articles on its research; the Environmental Alert book series; and another annual publication, *Vital Signs: The Trends that Are Shaping Our Future.*

Brown's vision of a better future is a world in which money will be redirected from military spending to finance programs for the improvement of the environment. These would include reforestation, environmental and agricultural research, education, and large-scale birth control and immunization programs in the developing world. "If this Environmental Revolution succeeds, it will rank with the Agricultural and Industrial Revolutions as one of the great economic and social transformations in human history," Brown wrote in an article in the *Unesco Courier*. In his view, development programs cannot ignore the question of environmental degradation.

The Library of Congress has requested Brown's personal papers, and he was named Humanist of the Year by the American Humanist Association in 1991. His numerous awards for environmental involvement include the National Wildlife Federation Special Conservation Award, 1982, and the Gold Medal from the Worldwide Fund for Nature, 1989. From 1986 to 1991 he was a MacArthur Fellow at the John D. and Catherine T. MacArthur Foundation. A sought-after speaker all over the world, he addressed the Nobel Symposium in Stockholm in 1974 and gave the Schumacher Lecture in Bristol, England, in 1991. He has also won several literary awards and holds honorary degrees from fifteen universities. A member of many organizations, Brown serves as an advisor to the Institute for International Economics and the Committee for the National Institutes for the Environment.

Brown does not own a car; he rides his bicycle or walks to work and appointments, an example that is followed by many employees at his institute. He uses a canvas bag to carry groceries. He is divorced and the father of two grown children, Brian and Brenda Ann. Brown runs several times a week and plays football with friends on the weekends.

SELECTED WRITINGS BY BROWN:

Books

Man, Land and Food: Looking Ahead at World Food Needs, United States Department of Agriculture (USDA), 1963.
Increasing World Food Output: Problems and Prospects, USDA, 1965.
Seeds of Change: The Green Revolution and Development in the 1970s, Praeger, 1970.
World without Borders, Vintage, 1972.
(With Erik P. Eckholm) *By Bread Alone,* Praeger, 1974.
The Twenty-ninth Day: Accommodating Human Needs and Numbers to the Earth's Resources, Norton, 1978.
Building a Sustainable Society, Norton, 1981.
(With Christopher Flavin and Sandra Postel) *Saving the Planet,* Norton, 1991.

Periodicals

"The Environmental Crisis: A Humanist Call for Action," *Humanist,* November, 1991, pp. 26–30.
"Launching the Environmental Revolution," *Unesco Courier,* April, 1992, pp. 44–46.
"Worldwatcher's Warning," *World Monitor,* May 18, 1992, pp. 18–20.

SOURCES:

Books

Contemporary Authors, Volume 131, Gale, 1991.

Periodicals

Omni, June, 1992, p. 27.
People, June 11, 1990, pp. 113–116.
"Why Hunger Is to be the World's No. 1 Problem," *U.S. News and World Report,* January 6, 1964, pp. 28–31.

—*Sketch by Kala Dwarakanath*

Michael S. Brown
1941-
American geneticist

Michael S. Brown, a genetics professor and director of the Center for Genetic Diseases at the University of Texas Southwestern Medical School, is one of America's foremost experts on cholesterol metabolism in the human body. In the 1970s, Brown and **Joseph Goldstein** investigated familial hypercholesterolemia, a dangerous inherited disorder which causes elevated levels of cholesterol in the blood. Their research led them to the discovery of a protein in the membranes of a cell, called the LDL receptor, which plays a central role in the body's ability to lower cholesterol levels. For this discovery and their subsequent research on the LDL receptor, Brown and Goldstein shared the 1985 Nobel Prize in physiology or medicine.

Brown was born in New York City on April 13, 1941, to Harvey and Evelyn Katz Brown. He attended the University of Pennsylvania as an undergraduate, receiving his bachelor's degree in 1962. Following his graduation, Brown enrolled in the medical school at the University of Pennsylvania, where he was awarded the Frederick Packard Prize in Internal Medicine for his research. He earned his M.D. in 1966 and served as an intern and a resident at Massachusetts General Hospital in Boston. It was during his residency that he met **Joseph Goldstein**, his future research partner, who was also on the staff at Massachusetts General.

In 1968, Brown was made a clinical associate at the National Institutes of Health (NIH) in Bethesda, Maryland. He was assigned to the biochemistry lab, where he worked with Earl Stadtman, head of the laboratory for the National Heart, Lung, and Blood Institute. While at NIH, Brown focused his research on gastroenterology, particularly on the role of enzymes in digestive chemistry. In 1971, while studying a particular enzyme involved in the production of cholesterol, Brown was offered a position as an assistant professor at the University of Texas Southwestern Medical School in Dallas. He accepted, and Goldstein, who had also served at NIH in Bethesda, joined the Texas Southwestern faculty a year later. At this time the two began a collaboration which was to distinguish them as pioneers in genetics.

In Dallas during the 1970s, Brown and Goldstein examined skin samples from people who suffered from hypercholesterolemia, specifically those rare patients whose condition was homozygous, meaning that they had not just one defective gene but two. In these cases, patients often exhibited extremely high levels of low-density lipoprotein, LDL, even during childhood. LDL carries cholesterol to the cells, and in excessive quantities can clog arteries and encourage heart disease. Brown and Goldstein discovered that the cells of these patients were missing a crucial protein, called a receptor, which binds to LDL and regulates its level in the body. Without the protein, the body can not break down LDL, and it accumulates in the blood. Brown and Goldstein's breakthrough was the discovery and isolation of this LDL receptor protein.

Brown and Goldstein not only identified the LDL receptor, they also located the gene responsible for its production. By sequencing and cloning the gene, they were able to localize the gene mutations responsible for familial hypercholesterolemia, as well as other inherited conditions involving cholesterol metabolism. Their findings also led to possible drug therapies for people with cholesterol disorders. By administering a combination of drugs which would inhibit the liver's ability to synthesize cholesterol, Brown and Goldstein increased their patients' need for cholesterol from outside sources. The patients' bodies subsequently produced more LDL receptors, and their cholesterol levels fell sharply. They also found that a liver transplant can correct genetic deficiencies in the production or expression of LDL receptors. In later research, Brown and Goldstein engineered a mouse which, because of its abnormally

high numbers of LDL receptors, could eat a high-fat diet and yet show no significant rise in LDL.

In a remarkable series of experiments, Brown and Goldstein were ultimately able to define and analyze each step in the path of cholesterol through the body, from production to dissolution. They also demonstrated a mechanism by which a low-fat diet and regular exercise can decrease cholesterol levels. Brown and Goldstein's work had significant implications not only for genetic defects, but also for nutrition and fitness. In addition, the team's research methods contributed to a greater understanding of cell receptors in general, serving as a model for research on over twenty other receptors. In the words of the Nobel Prize committee, as quoted in the *New York Times,* Brown and Goldstein "revolutionized our knowledge about the regulation of cholesterol metabolism and the treatment of diseases caused by abnormally elevated cholesterol levels in the blood."

In addition to the Nobel Prize, Brown has received several honorary degrees and a number of awards for his research, including the Pfizer Award from the American Chemical Society in 1976, the Albert Lasker Medical Research Award in 1985, and the National Medal of Science in 1988. He has been a member of the National Academy of Sciences since 1980. He was appointed Paul J. Thomas Professor of Genetics and director of the Center for Genetic Diseases at the University of Texas Southwestern Medical School, positions he has held since 1977.

Brown balances his scientific and medial careers, and despite his success as a researcher, he still makes rounds at the hospital. He is also well known for his entertaining style of scientific presentations. While still in medical school at Penn, Brown married Alice Lapin on June 21, 1964, and they have two daughters.

SELECTED WRITINGS BY BROWN:

Periodicals

(With Joseph L. Goldstein) "Expression of the Familial Hypercholesterolemia Gene in Heterozygotes: Mechanism for a Dominant Disorder in Man," *Science,* Volume 185, 1974, pp. 61–63.

(With Joseph L. Goldstein) "The LDL Receptor Locus and the Genetics of Familial Hypercholesterolemia," *Annual Review of Genetics,* Volume 13, 1979, pp. 259–289.

(With Joseph L. Goldstein) "The LDL Receptor Locus in Familial Hypercholesterolemia: Multiple Mutations Disrupting the Transport and Processing of a Membrane Receptor," *Cell,* Volume 32, 1983, 941–951.

(With Joseph L. Goldstein, T. C. Sudhof, and D. W. Russell) "The LDL Receptor Gene: A Mosaic of Exons Shared with Different Proteins," *Science,* Volume 228, 1985, pp. 815–822.

SOURCES:

Books

Meant, N. B., *Cholesterol Metabolism, LDL, and the LDL Receptor,* Academic Press, 1990.

Periodicals

"Honors for Seven Achievers," *Time,* October 28, 1985, pp. 85–86.
Motulsky, A. G., "The 1985 Nobel Prize in Physiology or Medicine," *Science,* January 10, 1986, pp. 126–129.
Newmark, Peter, "Cell Cholesterol Wins the Day," *Nature,* October 17, 1985, p. 569.
"Science and the Citizen," *Scientific American,* December, 1985, p. 74
Wilford, John Noble, "Two Americans Win Nobel Medicine Prize," *New York Times,* October 15, 1985, p. 1.

—*Sketch by G. Scott Crawford*

Rachel Fuller Brown
1898-1980
American biochemist

Rachel Fuller Brown, with her associate **Elizabeth Hazen**, developed the first effective antibiotic against fungal disease in humans—the most important biomedical breakthrough since the discovery of penicillin two decades earlier. The antibiotic, called nystatin, has cured sufferers of life-threatening fungal infections, vaginal yeast infections, and athlete's foot. Nystatin earned more than $13 million in royalties during Brown's lifetime, which she and Hazen dedicated to scientific research.

Brown was born in Springfield, Massachusetts, on November 23, 1898, to Annie Fuller and George Hamilton Brown. Her father, a real estate and insurance agent, moved the family to Webster Groves, Missouri, where she attended grammar school. In 1912, her father left the family. Brown and her younger brother returned to Springfield with their mother, who worked to support them. When Brown graduated from high school, a wealthy friend of the family financed her attendance at Mount Holyoke College in Massachusetts.

At Mount Holyoke, Brown was initially a history major, but she discovered chemistry when fulfilling a science requirement. She decided to double-major in history and chemistry, earning her A.B. degree in 1920. She subsequently went to the University of Chicago to complete her M.A. in organic chemistry. For three years, she taught chemistry and physics at the Francis Shimer School near Chicago. With her savings, she returned to the University to complete her Ph.D. in organic chemistry, with a minor in bacteriology. She submitted her thesis in 1926, but there was a delay in arranging her oral examinations. As her funds ran low, Brown took a job as an assistant chemist at the Division of Laboratories and Research of the New York State Department of Health in Albany, New York. Seven years later, when she returned to Chicago for a scientific meeting, Brown arranged to take her oral examinations and was awarded her Ph.D.

Discovers Fungal Antibiotic

Brown's early work at the Department of Health focused on identifying the types of bacteria that caused pneumonia, and in this capacity she helped to develop a pneumonia vaccine still in use today. In 1948, she embarked on the project with Hazen, a leading authority on fungus, that would bring them their greatest acclaim: the discovery of an antibiotic to fight fungal infections. Penicillin had been discovered in 1928, and in the ensuing years antibiotics were increasingly used to fight bacterial illnesses. One side effect, however, was the rapid growth of fungus that could lead to sore mouths or upset stomachs. Other fungal diseases without cures included infections attacking the central nervous system, athlete's foot, and ringworm. Microorganisms called actinomycetes that lived in soil were known to produce antibiotics. Although some killed fungus, they also proved fatal to test mice. Hazen ultimately narrowed the search down to a microorganism taken from soil near a barn on a friend's dairy farm in Virginia, later named streptomyces norsei. Brown's chemical analyses revealed that the microorganism produced two antifungal substances, one of which proved too toxic with test animals to pursue for human medical use. The other, however, seemed to have promise; it wasn't toxic to test animals and attacked both a fungus that invaded the lungs and central nervous system and candidiasis, an infection of the mouth, lungs, and vagina.

Brown purified this second antibiotic into small white crystals, and in 1950 Brown and Hazen announced at a meeting of the National Academy of Sciences that they had found a new antifungal agent. They patented it through the nonprofit Research Corporation, naming it "nystatin" in honor of the New York State Division of Laboratories and Research. The license for the patent was issued to E. R. Squibb and Sons, which developed a safe and effective method of mass production. The product—called Mycostatin—became available in tablet form in 1954 to patients suffering from candidiasis. Nystatin has also proved valuable in agricultural and livestock applications, and has even been used to restore valuable works of art.

In 1951, the Department of Health laboratories promoted Brown to associate biochemist. Brown and Hazen, in continuing their research, discovered two additional antibiotics, phalamycin and capacidin. Brown and Hazen were awarded the 1955 Squibb Award in Chemotherapy. Brown won the Distinguished Service Award of the New York State Department of Health when she retired in 1968, and the Rhoda Benham Award of the Medical Mycological Society of the Americas in 1972. In 1975, Brown and Hazen became the first women to receive the Chemical Pioneer Award from the American Institute of Chemists. In a statement published in the *Chemist* the month of her death, Brown hoped for a future of "equal opportunities and accomplishments for all scientists regardless of sex."

On retirement, Brown maintained an active community life, and became the first female vestry member of her Episcopalian church. By her death on January 14, 1980, she had paid back the wealthy woman who had made it possible for her to attend college. Using the royalties from nystatin, more importantly, she helped designate new funds for scientific research and scholarships.

SELECTED WRITINGS BY BROWN:

Periodicals

"Rachel Fuller Brown, Retired Scientist, New York State Department of Health," *Chemist,* January, 1980, p. 8.

SOURCES:

Books

Baldwin, Richard S., *The Fungus Fighters: Two Women Scientists and Their Discovery,* Cornell University Press, 1981.
Vare, Ethlie Ann and Greg Ptacek, *Mothers of Invention,* Morrow, 1988, pp. 124–126.
Yost, Edna, *Women of Modern Science,* Greenwood, 1959, pp. 64–79.

Periodicals

New York Times, June 29, 1957, p. 22–26; January 16, 1980, p. D19.

—*Sketch by Miyoko Chu*

Marjorie Lee Browne
1914-1979
American mathematician

In 1949 Marjorie Lee Browne, along with **Evelyn Boyd Granville**, was one of the first African American women to receive a Ph.D. degree. By training a topologist (specializing in a branch of mathematics that deals with certain geometric aspects of spaces and shapes), Browne made her greatest contributions in the areas of teaching and university administration. She also provided a leadership role in seeking funding for better educational opportunities; her goals included the strengthening of mathematical preparation for science and mathematics teachers in secondary schools and the increased presence of females and minorities in the mathematical sciences.

Browne was born in Memphis, Tennessee, the second child of Lawrence Johnson Lee, a transportation mail clerk; her stepmother, Lottie Taylor Lee, was a school teacher. As a young woman growing up in Memphis and New Orleans, she was an expert tennis player, a singer, an avid reader—a trait she inherited from her father—and a gifted mathematics student. Browne graduated from LeMoyne High School in Memphis in 1931. In 1935 she received a B.S. degree cum laude in mathematics from Howard University, then earned a M.S. in mathematics in 1939 and a Ph.D. in 1949 from the University of Michigan. She wrote her doctoral dissertation on one-parameter subgroups in certain topological and matrix groups, and her dissertation served as the basis for one of her major publications on the classical groups in 1955.

Browne began her teaching career in 1935 at Gilbert Academy in New Orleans, Louisiana, where she taught physics and mathematics for a year. From 1942 to 1945, she served as an instructor at Wiley College in Marshall, Texas. In 1949, Browne was appointed to the faculty in the department of mathematics at North Carolina Central University (NCCU), where she rose to the rank of professor and became the first chair of the department from 1951 to 1970. She served as a principal investigator, coordinator of the mathematics section, and lecturer for the Summer Institute for Secondary School Science and Mathematics Teachers, a program funded by the first National Science Foundation grant awarded to NCCU in 1957. Browne continued this role until 1970.

Browne was acutely aware of the obstacles which women and minorities faced in pursuing scientific careers. Shortly after receiving her doctorate in 1949 she sought, unsuccessfully, to obtain an instructorship at several major research institutions. After receiving many polite letters of rejection, she decided to remain in the South and resolved that her greatest contributions would be directing programs designed to strengthen the mathematical preparation of secondary school mathematics teachers and to increase the presence of minorities and females in mathematical science careers.

Thus, Browne spent her summers teaching secondary school teachers, and her objective was to insure that the teachers whom she taught would be able to understand and teach their students the so-called "modern math" or "new math." Browne's teaching standards were exacting and her methods were thorough; her demands for excellence and concise, clear ideas contributed greatly to the academic growth and development of her students, and many of her students have made significant contributions in a number of professions. Nine of them have earned doctorates in the mathematical sciences or related disciplines. Browne was also a steady, outspoken critic of racism and the discriminatory practices prevalent among funding agencies relative to minorities and predominantly minority universities and colleges. She was an ardent advocate for the integration of the previously segregated meetings of the national mathematics organizations of which she was a member.

For her work in mathematics education, Browne was awarded the first W. W. Rankin Memorial Award from the North Carolina Council of Teachers of Mathematics in 1974. During her acceptance speech, she described herself as "a pre-sputnik mathematician." She was referring to the purist nature of her advanced mathematical preparation and the practice of many American industries and businesses, prior to the launching of the first Russian satellite in 1957, to allow scientists and mathematicians to pursue research projects that had no immediate real world or job-related applications. The launching of Sputnik had a tremendous impact on mathematics education in the United States. America was viewed as having fallen behind the Russians in space explorations, and as a result there was a shift in emphasis from pure abstract mathematical and scientific research to investigations that were of an applied nature. Browne, however, remained a mathematical purist, and like many great mathematical philosophers of the nineteenth century she viewed mathematics as an intellectual quest, free from the limitations of the physical universe.

Browne was a member of the Woman's Research Society, American Mathematical Society, Mathematical Association of America, and the International Congress of Mathematicians as well as the author of several articles in professional and scholarly journals. In 1960, she received a sixty thousand dollar grant from IBM to establish one of the first electronic digital computer centers at a predominantly minority university, and in 1969, she received the first of seven Shell Foundation Scholarship Grants, awarded to mathematics students for outstanding academic achievements. The director of the first Undergraduate Research Participation Program at NCCU during 1964 and 1965—which was sponsored by the National Science Foundation—Browne was also one of the first African American females to serve on the advisory panel to the National Science Foundation Undergraduate Scientific Equipment Program in 1966, 1967, and 1973. In addition, she served as a Faculty Consultant in Mathematics for the Ford Foundation from 1968 to 1969 at their New York office. Browne was awarded numerous fellowships, including one from the Ford Foundation at Cambridge University in England from 1952 to 1953.

Browne died of an apparent heart attack at her home in Durham, North Carolina, in 1979. At the time of her death, she was preparing a monograph on the development of the real number system from a postulational approach. Browne was a generous humanitarian who believed that no good student should go without an education simply because he or she lacked the financial resources to pay for it. Thus, it was not uncommon for her to assume the financial responsibilities for many able students whose families were unable to provide tuition, books, board, or transportation for them. To continue the philanthropic legacy which she began, four of her former students established the Marjorie Lee Browne Trust Fund at North Carolina Central University in 1979. This fund supports two major activities in the mathematics and computer science department: the Marjorie Lee Browne Memorial Scholarship—which is awarded annually to the student who best exemplifies those traits which Browne sought to instill in young people—and the annual Marjorie Lee Browne Distinguished Alumni Lecture Series.

SELECTED WRITINGS BY BROWNE:

Periodicals

"A Note on the Classical Groups," *American Mathematical Monthly,* August, 1955.

SOURCES:

Periodicals

"$57,500 Granted for High School Teachers Summer Institute at NCC," *Durham Sun,* December 21, 1956.

Other

Personal information supplied to William T. Fletcher by the department of mathematics and computer science of North Carolina Central University, 1994.

—Sketch by William T. Fletcher

Walter Herman Bucher
1889-1965
American geologist

An internationally respected geologist and an influential teacher, Walter Herman Bucher is best known as the author of *The Deformation of the Earth's Crust,* published in 1933. This book explores the origins of what are known as orogenic belts—the areas of folding and fracturing in the earth's crust that create mountain chains. Bucher's work defined the field of structural geology for decades, though most geologists now believe that orogenic belts are better explained by other theories, particularly that of continental drift.

Bucher was born on March 12, 1889, in Akron, Ohio, to Maria (Gebhardt) and Reverend August J. Bucher. His father, a Methodist minister, was assigned in 1895 to a congregation in Germany and young Bucher came to maturity in that country. He studied at the University of Heidelberg as an undergraduate and a graduate student—receiving a Ph.D. in geology in 1911—then returned to Ohio in 1913 to accept a position as an instructor in geology at the University of Cincinnati. Here Bucher began his climb up the academic ladder under the influence of Professor N. M. Fenniman, the chairman of the department. Bucher became assistant professor in 1915, associate professor in 1920, and finally full professor in 1924. He became chairman of the department of geology and geography at the university in 1937, serving in that capacity until 1940. In 1914 Bucher married Hannah E. Schmid, with whom he had four children, two daughters and two sons.

It was during his tenure at the University of Cincinnati that Bucher produced *The Deformation of the Earth's Crust.* The volume was an ambitious effort to confront what W. W. Rubey called, in the *Journal of American Geology,* "the broader problems with which structural geology is concerned." One of these problems is the origin of geologic activity in mountainous regions and the formation of mountain chains. Bucher's work was synthetic as well as analytical, and he made extensive use of the scientific findings of others. Sir **Harold Jeffreys**, for example, had published a theory explaining earthquakes which occur well below the earth's surface. Proposing the existence of a zone one hundred to seven hundred kilometers within the earth—which contracted as the earth cooled—Jeffreys argued that it was the rocks adjusting to these changes in temperatures that caused the earthquakes in this zone. Bucher extended the hypothesis, theorizing that the contractions were of enough force to cause fractures which reached the earth's crust. These fracture lines enabled the escape of heat, water vapor, and volatile substances to the surface.

In addition to contractions at the earth's core, Bucher proposed a second force determining changes in the earth's crust: gravity. He followed Jeffreys's contention that rocks piled high enough would eventually flatten themselves out under their own weight, and he applied this theory to mountain chains. He claimed gravity as the major force involved in his explanation of the structural details found in these regions, and set about constructing a number of models to prove his theory. Plasticine, plexiglas, stitching wax, and even Christmas ornaments were used as materials in his simulations. Applying varying degrees of compression to simulate gravitational force, Bucher saw the models he had constructed experience fracturing; many of the fractures possessed a striking resemblance to the earth's mountain chains.

During 1933, Bucher—along with K. Andree and H. A. Brouwer—also published a two-volume symposium of geological knowledge in German, *Regional Geology of the Earth.* Bucher continued to publish a number of scientific papers, most notably "Volcanic Explosion and Overthrusts" for the American Geophysical Union, and "Cryptovolcanic Structures in the United States" for the Sixteenth International Geological Congress. His international reputation continued to grow, and he was elected to the National Academy of Sciences in 1938.

Bucher left the University of Cincinnati in 1940, accepting a position as full professor of structural geology at Columbia University. He became head of the department in 1950, the same year he gave his presidential address to the American Geophysical Union, which was published in 1951 under the title "Megatectonics and Geophysics by the Union." During his chairmanship at Columbia, Bucher was able to realize a personal dream with the 1951 opening of the Lamont Geological Observatory in Palisades, New Jersey, which was dedicated to exploring the geology of ocean floors.

Bucher published *Geologic Structure and Orogenic History of Venezuela* in 1952, the result of four months of field work there. The published work was accompanied by a tectonic map of the country, and

Bucher retained fond memories of the trip, most notably of his time in the Andes mountains. He stepped down as head of the geology department at Columbia University in 1953, coinciding with the publication of "The Role of Gravity in Orogenesis" in the *Geological Society of America Bulletin.* This was a further development of his hypothesis about the relationship between the contractions at the earth's core and the fracturing of the crust. Bucher retired from Columbia in 1956 and began work as a consultant for the Humble Oil and Refining Company in Houston, Texas, where he was given his own laboratory and staff and was encouraged to pursue his experiments. Bucher was the recipient of the William Bowie Medal from the American Geophysical Union and the Von Buch Medal from the Deutsche Geologische Gesellschaft, both in 1955. Receiving the Penrose Medal of the Geological Society of America in 1960, he was chief delegate to the ninth general assembly of the International Union of Geodesy and Geophysics in Brussels, Belgium, in 1951. Bucher also served as the 1955 American delegate to the International Conference of Scientific Unions in Oslo, Norway.

Bucher died in Houston on February 17, 1965. He had been an enthusiastic teacher who was able to inspire his students. Bucher always attempted to incorporate a broad view into his research, although some critics have decried his hypotheses as mere overview and summaries. Bucher's reliance on radical forces in orogenics is a less popular view among geologists today, but his legacy as an instructor of structural geology and his fully rounded view of the elements of earth sciences remains undiminished.

SELECTED WRITINGS BY BUCHER:

Books

The Deformation of the Earth's Crust, Princeton University Press, 1933.

Periodicals

"Volcanic Explosions and Overthrusts," *Transactions of the American Geophysical Union Fourteenth Annual Meeting,* 1933, pp. 238–242.
"Continental Drift vs. Land Bridges," *Bulletin of the American Museum of Natural History,* Volume 8, 1952, pp. 72–258.
"Geologic Structure and Orogenic History of Venezuela," *Memoirs, Geologic Society of America,* Volume 49, 1952.
"The Role of Gravity in Orogenesis," *The Bulletin of the Geological Society of America,* Volume 67, 1956, pp. 1295–1318.

SOURCES:

Books

Gillespie, Charles, editor, *Dictionary of Scientific Biography,* Volume II, Charles Scribners Sons, 1970.
Green, J., editor, *McGraw-Hill Modern Scientists and Engineers,* Volume I, McGraw-Hill Inc., 1980.

—*Sketch by Christopher McGrail*

Eduard Buchner
1860-1917
German chemist

Eduard Buchner is credited with introducing the field of modern enzyme chemistry. His research put an end to the widely accepted theory that fermentation of sugar to alcohol required the action of living (vital) yeast, which was promoted by such leading scientists as the French chemist Louis Pasteur. His work also discredited the mechanists' view that decomposing yeast cells acted as the catalyst for such change. For his pioneering efforts to scientifically explain the ancient process of fermentation, and for initiating the systematic study of enzymes, Buchner received the Nobel Prize in chemistry in 1907. In addition to being an outstanding chemist, he was a German patriot and soldier.

Eduard Buchner was born in Munich, Germany, May 20, 1860. He was descended from an old and scholarly Bavarian family. His father, Ernst Buchner, was a professor of obstetrics and forensic medicine, and the editor of a medical publication. Buchner's mother was Friederike Martin Buchner. After graduating from the Realgymnasium (high school) in Munich, he served in the field artillery, and later enrolled at Technische Hochschule (Technical College) in Munich, where he studied chemistry. Financial troubles forced him to temporarily leave his studies and work in canneries around Munich. With the help of his older brother, Buchner returned to school in 1884, attending the Bavarian Academy of Sciences in Munich to study under the eminent chemist Adolf von Baeyer.

Becomes Interested in Fermentation

While still a chemistry student at the Academy of Sciences, Buchner began work on the problems of fermentation of sugar to alcohol at the Institute for Plant Physiology. By 1886, he had published his first paper on the subject, disagreeing with Pasteur's opinion that fermentation had to be carried out in an oxygen-free environment. In 1888, Buchner received his doctorate in chemistry from the Academy of Sciences, where he was appointed Baeyer's teaching assistant in 1890, advancing to *Privatdozent,* or lecturer, a year later. Baeyer also acquired the funds for a laboratory that would allow Buchner to continue his work on fermentation.

In 1893, Buchner accepted a position at the University of Kiel, where he was in charge of the analytical chemistry section for three years, while continuing his research on fermentation. Buchner's brother, Hans, was conducting similar research on extracts from bacteria, trying to find medically useful products. His assistant, Martin Hahn, showed Buchner a technique to break down yeast cell walls to extract the cell juices that Buchner required for his research.

In his Nobel address of 1907, translated in part in *Nobel Prize Winners in Chemistry,* Buchner described the extraction process, in which a mixture of *kiesulguhr* (commonly known as diatomite) and black sand is used to reduce the difficulty of grinding the yeast. Buchner attributed a similar technique, in which quartz powder was used, to Marie von Manassein in Vienna, who, he believed, introduced the process in 1872. Buchner further explained that "the initially dust-dry mass . . . becomes dark gray and plastic, like dough. When this thick dough is wrapped in a strong cloth and put into a hydraulic press, a liquid juice seeps out under pressure which is gradually increased to 90 kg./sq. cm. . . . Within a few hours, 500 cu. cm. of liquid can be obtained from 1000 grams of yeast."

Because the clear, yellow fluid pressed from the ground yeast cells readily decomposed, Buchner, his brother, and Hahn added sugar to the syrup as a preservative. To their amazement, gas bubbles soon formed. Fermentation was in progress, yet there were no live, or decomposing, yeast cells in the mixture. Alcohol was being produced by cell-free fermentation; they had made a revolutionary, and controversial, discovery.

Buchner was appointed professor of analytical pharmaceutical chemistry at University of Tübingen in 1896, and published the discovery of cell-free fermentation in the paper, "Alkoholische Gärung ohne Hefezellen" ("Alcoholic Fermentation without Yeast Cells"), the following year. Buchner left Tübingen for the Agricultural College in Berlin, where he was appointed professor of chemistry in 1898.

Work in Berlin Leads to Nobel Prize

Buchner had a greater opportunity for his research in Berlin. Along with his appointment to the College, he was made director of the Institute for the Fermentation Industry. In 1900, he married Lotte Stahl, the daughter of a mathematician at the University of Tübingen. They had two sons and a daughter. Within four years of his arrival in Berlin, Buchner had published fifteen papers on cell-free fermentation. In 1903, the three researchers published a detailed account of their discoveries titled "Die Zymase: Gärung" ("The Zymase: Fermentation"). Buchner named the specific active agent in yeast cell extract "zymase" from the Greek word "zyme," which means yeast or ferment. As his research progressed, Buchner recognized that zymase was one example of an important class of natural substances called enzymes. He described his results in his Nobel address: "The cells of plants and animals appear, with increasing distinctness, as factories where in separate workshops all kinds of products are produced. The foremen in this work are the enzymes."

In 1909, Buchner accepted the position of head of physiological chemistry at the University of Breslau. Two years later, he was pleased to be invited to the University of Würzburg, in a region of Germany where he could also enjoy his hobbies of hunting and climbing. At the outset of World War I in 1914, Buchner volunteered for the army. He saw action as a captain of an ammunition supply unit, and was promoted to major in 1916, just before he returned to the University of Würzburg. Buchner again volunteered for active duty the following year and was sent to Focsani, Rumania, where he died from a shrapnel wound on August 13, 1917.

SELECTED WRITINGS BY BUCHNER:

Books

(With Hans Buchner and Martin Hahn) *Die Zymase-Gärung,* [Munich], 1903.
"Cell-free Fermentation," in *Nobel Lectures Chemistry 1901–1921,* [Amsterdam, London, and New York], 1966.

SOURCES:

Books

Dictionary of Scientific Biography, Volume II, Scribner, pp. 560–563.
Leicester, Henry M., et al., *A Source Book in Chemistry 1400–1900,* Harvard University, 1952, pp. 506–11.

—*Sketch by M. C. Nagel*

Edward Bullard
1907-1980
English geophysicist

English geophysicist Edward Bullard is best known for his theory of continental drift: the idea that at one time in the Earth's history, all the continents of the world were joined together. Bullard, who was knighted by Queen Elizabeth in 1953, also contributed greatly to the study of and theories about earthquakes and the relationship between the Earth's core and magnetic field. Born on September 21, 1907, in Norwich, England, Edward Crisp Bullard was commonly known as Teddy. His family had a long and distinguished history as the brewers of Bullard's Ales, which Bullard's great-grandfather had established. Bullard, the son of Edward John Bullard and Eleanor Howes Crisp, was the only boy in the family; he had three younger sisters.

Bullard began his schooling at the Norwich High School for Girls, which, by all reports, he enjoyed. However, once he enrolled in Norwich Grammar School at age nine, Bullard supposedly became very unhappy and even threatened suicide. He was sent to a psychiatrist, and, as a result, went to Aldeburgh Lodge boarding school. There, he became one of the top students in his class, showing an interest in photography and newspapers. Bullard's worst subjects were spelling and sports.

In September 1921, Bullard enrolled at Repton School. Once again, he was unhappy at school, apparently mainly because he disliked the teaching. His grades suffered, and Bullard began making plans to quit school and work in the family brewery.

Instead, the course of Bullard's life was changed by the arrival of A. W. Barton, a physicist and teacher. Barton had received his Ph.D. at Cambridge, and decided that Bullard, too, was to go to Cambridge. At first, Bullard's father objected to the idea—but he changed his mind when he found out that the degree would count toward an accounting course Bullard had been planning to take before working in the brewery. In 1926, Bullard enrolled at Clare College Cambridge University. He majored in physics, taking courses in natural sciences, physics, chemistry, math and mineralogy. He received his B.A. in 1929. That same year, Bullard became a research student working for his Ph.D. in physics at the Cavendish Laboratory at Cambridge. At the time, physicist **Ernest Rutherford**, a Nobel Prize winner and now considered the founder of atomic physics, directed the lab. In his studies there, Bullard focused primarily on electron scattering. At the end of his studies at Cavendish, in 1931, Bullard married Margaret Ellen Thomas, then a student and later a novelist. They eventually had four daughters.

Choosing Geophysics

At this point, Bullard was faced with the prospect of finding a job as a physicist during the Depression. According to his biography in the *Biographical Memoirs of Fellows of the Royal Society,* Bullard often explained that he chose geophysics out of necessity: A post was open in the newly formed department of geodesy and geophysics at Cambridge, and Bullard accepted it upon Rutherford's advice. According to the Royal Society biography, Rutherford told Bullard, "There are no jobs and there are a lot of people just in front of you. If I were you I would take any job I could get." Sir Gerald Lenox-Conyngham was head of the department at the time.

Bullard completed his Ph.D. in 1932 with a thesis describing the effect of the Earth's magnetic field on gravity measurements. As part of his interest in this area, Bullard traveled to the East African Rift, one of the largest geological structures on the continents. At one point during the expedition, Bullard's car and one shoe were swept away in a stream; he and Margaret attempted to walk to their camp, but were chased up a tree by lions. A rescue party did not arrive until that night. Later in his career, Bullard realized that the conclusions he drew from his research in Africa were wrong. However, his work is still considered important: It demonstrated that geophysical measurements could help uncover the beginnings of the Earth's geological structures.

As a result of his work, Bullard won the Smithson Research Fellowship of the Royal Society beginning in 1936 and continuing until 1943. The fellowship freed him to begin working on many aspects of geophysics, including marine geophysics. Bullard was one of the few scientists of his time interested in rock formations beneath the ocean, an area that was barely explored. In fact, in 1937 Bullard was invited to the United States to pursue work in this area, studying the continental shelf. During his fellowship, he also measured the depths of rock formations under the sea around England, gathering some of his measurements with the help of submarines and others via trawlers chartered by the Royal Society.

At the same time he was studying undersea rock formations, Bullard was interested in the flow of heat in the Earth's interior. His experiments contributed to the areas of seismology, and gravity as well as heat flow. Bullard traveled to South Africa in late 1938 to study this phenomenon, but his work was interrupted by World War II. In 1939, at the age of 32, he became an experimental officer for the Admiralty and began focusing his efforts on detecting mines and preventing submarine attacks.

Bullard remained with the Admiralty until 1945; at the same time, in 1945, he was also appointed Reader in Experimental Geophysics at Cambridge University. According to the Royal Society biography, however, after the war, things at Cambridge were "in a sorry state." Much of the equipment in the geophysics department was either out of date or useless, and there was no money to hire a full-time secretary. These problems, according to the Royal Society biography, were the "final straw[s]" that brought on Bullard's move to the University of Toronto in 1948.

Unfortunately, Bullard regretted the move almost immediately. He spent only one year as professor of physics at the university. Later in his life Bullard was to admit that the year was one of his most productive, according to the Royal Society biography. Among his accomplishments: continued work on heat flow, the use of a recently developed computer, and his first association with Scripps Institution of Oceanography at La Jolla, California.

Bullard resigned his post in Toronto at the end of 1949 and spent his summer at Scripps, studying both heat flow and the Earth's magnetic field. Through a prototype instrument he built, experimenters were able to find areas of increased heat flow in the Pacific ocean. Today we know these are areas where molten rock from the Earth's core pushes up through the ocean floor.

Although offered the director's post at Scripps, Bullard went back to England in 1949 to become the director of the National Physical Laboratory (N.P.L.). In his six years at N.P.L., Bullard published some of his most important papers, according to the Royal Society biography. Bullard designed much of the equipment that he used to measure the flow of heat beneath the sea floor. At one point, when the lab's engineers told him that one of his designs would not work, he proved them wrong by building the instrument himself at home, soldering it on his kitchen stove. During this time, Bullard also worked on the relationship between the Earth's core and its magnetic field: Expanding on the work of other scientists, he showed that the motion of the liquid iron core of the Earth acts as a dynamo, generating electrical currents. This in turns, sets up the Earth's magnetic field.

Knighthood and the Return to Cambridge

In 1953 Bullard was knighted for his efforts at N.P.L. Then, in 1956 he returned to Cambridge—a goal that, according to the Royal Society biography, he had sought since he first left the university. By 1964 Bullard was given a personal chair in the department of geodesy and geophysics: He chose to become professor of geophysics. He was also head of the department for 14 years. Under Bullard, the department became the world's foremost center for the study of geophysics. Around this time, scientists began proposing the idea that the continents moved about the globe—today known as the theory of continental drift. Bullard fit the continents together into one "supercontinent." He also helped set into motion the theory of plate tectonics—the idea that continents ride on huge plates that make up the Earth's crust. In places where the edges of the plates collide, earthquakes are likely. Bullard's ideas in this area have greatly increased our understanding of the mechanisms behind earthquakes. Bullard remained at Cambridge until 1974. During this period he also helped manage his family brewery and was a director of IBM U.K. In addition, he served as chair of a British committee for space research.

After his retirement from Cambridge, Bullard married a second time—to Ursula Curnow—and moved to the United States to become a professor at the University of California at San Diego. For the next six years he lectured at the university, spent three months each year serving as geophysical consultant to the University of Alaska, and worked with the Jet Propulsion Laboratory on solutions to nuclear waste disposal.

He completed his final scientific paper—on changes in the direction of magnetic north since 1570—10 hours before he died of cancer on April 3, 1980. According to his obituary in the *New York Times,* Bullard had worked on the paper as a hobby for 25 years, but called in Dr. Stuart Mallin of the Institute of Geological Sciences in Scotland to help him finish it when he realized he was dying. In an interview with the *New York Times,* Dr. Mallin said, "The doctors said he seemed to be keeping himself alive to finish it."

Bullard wrote hundreds of scientific papers during his lifetime and was the recipient of numerous awards and honors. He was made a Fellow of the Royal Society in 1941. A fracture zone between continental ridges in the South Atlantic—the Bullard Fracture Zone—was named after him.

SELECTED WRITINGS BY BULLARD:

Periodicals

"The Flow of Heat through the Floor of the Atlantic Ocean," *Proceedings of the Royal Society,* A 222, 1954, pp. 408–429.

"Forces and Processes at Work in Ocean Basins," *Oceanography,* number 67, 1961, pp. 39–50.

"Fit of the Continents around the Atlantic," *Science,* Volume 148, 1965, pp. 664.

"Continents on the Move," *Science Digest,* January, 1977, pp. 56–60.

(With S. R. C. Mallin) "The Direction of the Earth's Magnetic Field," *Phil. Trans. of the Royal Society of London,* A 299, 1981, pp. 357–423.

SOURCES:

Books

Biographical Memoirs of Fellows of the Royal Society, Royal Society (London), Volume 33, 1987.

Periodicals

New York Times, April 5, 1980, p. 26.

—*Sketch by Devera Pine*

Robert F. Bundy
1912-
American electrical engineer

Robert F. Bundy worked in an era of important new discoveries in electronics. An African American engineer, his ideas have applied electronic principles to diverse projects, including television, meteorological instrumentation, and hijacking deterrents. His most important contributions include development of the concept behind the travelling-wave tube, the invention of signal generator, and the design of an X-ray system to inspect baggage for the purpose of detecting potential hijackers in airports.

Bundy was born January 7, 1912, in Philadelphia, Pennsylvania, the son of Robert Fleming and Sarah Frances Bundy. He graduated from Central High School, where among other activities he was a member of the astronomy club. He majored in physics at the University of Pennsylvania and remained there after obtaining his degree to do graduate work. During World War II, he headed a research team at the Belmar Radar Laboratories which produced the first radar apparatus transportable by an individual person. He was cited by the U.S. Signal Corps for this achievement. After the war, he worked at Reeves Instrument Laboratories, the Allen B. DuMont Company, and Barkley and Dexter Laboratories; he then took a job with the U.S. Department of Transportation and then with the Federal Aviation Administration.

An enthusiastic inventor, Bundy worked occasionally as a consulting engineer and has filed patent applications on a number of devices. Like other inventors, he has frequently been frustrated by the high cost of filing for patents, and some of his ideas have not been fully developed. (Most patents are funded by corporations, and individuals are at a disadvantage.) While still a graduate student, he anticipated the travelling-wave tube (a microwave electronic tube in which a beam of electrons interacts continuously with a wave that travels along a circuit, used in radar detection devices), which was patented about nine years later by Bell Laboratories. While at the DOT, Bundy worked on the development of the X-ray detection devices now present in all airports to discourage hijacking. The specifications for this project included low levels of radiation and readily available components. Because twenty-two gauge wire is often used in bombs, the X-ray device had to have sufficient optical resolution to be able to detect wire of this size. In addition to his work on various kinds of metal detectors, he has designed an electroluminescent panel and an inductive probe array. He was granted a patent in 1960 for a signal generator, a testing device that puts out an electrical wave of precise frequency. Signal generators are used for diverse purposes, from radio broadcasting to measurement instrumentation. Bundy is a member of the National Technical Association, and he founded the South Jersey Chapter of that organization.

Bundy married Ora L. Mitchell on December 15, 1972. He has four children by a previous marriage: Robert Fleming, Karen, Robin, and Rhoda.

SELECTED WRITINGS BY BUNDY:

Periodicals

"Robert F. Bundy, Engineer-Inventor and Founder of South Jersey Chapter," *National Technical Association Journal,* July, 1979, p. 55.

SOURCES:

Books

"Signal Generator," *McGraw Hill Encyclopedia of Science and Technology,* Volume 16, 1992, p. 416.

—*Sketch by Gail B. C. Marsella*

E. Margaret Burbidge
1919-
English-born American astrophysicist

E. Margaret Burbidge gained recognition for producing the first accurate estimates of galactic masses, for her discoveries concerning quasars, and for her work on the metal content of stars. Burbidge

E. Margaret Burbidge

could use the telescope for her Ph.D. work. "The director had been called to the Admiralty for classified War work," she recalled. "The first assistant had gone in the Army and the mechanic was in the Air Force repairing airplanes. So, in a junior fashion, I was appointed general caretaker and looker-after of everything there." Burbidge's duties included repairing damage to the telescope's dome caused by shrapnel. As the War continued, Burbidge was awarded her Ph.D. in 1943 for her studies of the physics of hot stars.

Her coursework curtailed because of the War, Burbidge returned to the classroom once peace was established. There, in 1947, she met fellow graduate student **Geoffrey Burbidge**, whom she married in April, 1948 (they would later have a daughter). In the late 1940s, Burbidge worked as assistant director and acting director of the Observatory. In 1951, she was invited to Harvard University's Yerkes Observatory on a fellowship with Fulbright funds; her husband travelled with her on an Agassiz fellowship of his own to Harvard. Though the Burbidges liked life in the United States, they were obliged under the terms of their fellowships to return to England, which they did in 1953. Burbidge dove into an analysis of the data she had collected in the U.S. while working at the University of Chicago's telescope in southwest Texas and her husband took a job at Cambridge University's Cavendish Laboratory. It was at Cambridge in 1954 that the Burbidges first teamed up with the English astronomer **Fred Hoyle** and American physicist **William A. Fowler** to study the content of stars.

Works on Metal Content of Stars

Throughout the late 1950s, between Burbidge's stints as a research fellow and associate professor at the University of Chicago and California Institute of Technology, the Cambridge foursome delved into the evolution of stars, continuing the astronomical spectroscopy and analysis of the surface layers of stars Burbidge had engaged in for her doctoral thesis. Together the four looked at star evolution by studying star interiors; they concluded that stars can generate nearly every known metal but that only the lightest elements could have been created during the special conditions—incredible density and heat—of the universe's first moments. Stars can, however, use the metal, created by earlier stars, that exists in the interstellar gas to create increasingly heavier metals. Therefore, the four scientists determined, the metal content of stars and interstellar gas grows as stars build on the metals derived from previous stars.

"It added up to starting with the outside of stars and understanding what you actually observed from the surface of stars, then going on to the study of the interior of stars," Burbidge recalled. "It had been known since 1938 what the nuclear energy source of

also served on the scientific committees that planned and outfitted the Hubble Space Telescope, an instrument designed to provide the clearest snapshots of distant galaxies yet produced. Despite initial difficulties, United States astronauts successfully made repairs to the Hubble Telescope in December, 1993.

Burbidge was born Eleanor Margaret Peachey in Davenport, England, on August 12, 1919, the daughter of Stanley John and Marjorie (Stott) Peachey. Her father was a lecturer in chemistry at the Manchester School of Technology and her mother was a chemistry student there. When Burbidge was only a year and a half old, her father, after obtaining patents in rubber chemistry, set up a laboratory in the London, where the family relocated. There, Burbidge's budding interest in science was encouraged by her parents. "I'd been interested in astronomy but only from the point of view of thinking it would be an amateur interest," Burbidge told Joan Oleck in an interview. "I first got interested in the stars when I was a small child. . . . I had to make do with my father's binoculars."

Later, at the University of London, Burbidge took First Class Honors with her bachelor's degree in science in 1939. In the ensuing years, Burbidge stayed on at the University Observatory for her graduate education. World War II, which was raging across Europe, oddly aided her studies. As Burbidge explained, the lenses of the Observatory's double refracting telescope were buried in its concrete pier for safekeeping against bombing raids, but the twenty-four inch reflector was left intact. At night, Burbidge stars was—so as they use up their hydrogen and convert it to helium, structural changes occur in the stars. [Our work consisted of] understanding those [conversions] and looking at stars of different ages and seeing that the heavy element content of stars was a function of the age of the stars. So, that led to the idea that there must have been production of the elements in the interior of stars. . . .

"We found out a way to produce all of the elements heavier than hydrogen starting with hydrogen, assuming that a first generation of stars was made up of just hydrogen. We actually know now that it was hydrogen and a little bit of helium. How you can get nuclear energy by nuclear reactions that cause our sun to shine—that builds helium out of hydrogen and then a star that is older than our sun or has gone through its life faster than our sun will start further reactions, like building carbon out of helium and so on, through heavier elements. And you can go on getting energy from nuclear reactions up until you build elements as heavy as iron."

Studies Galaxy Rotation and Quasars

During the late 1950s and early 1960s, Burbidge contributed pioneering work to the rotation of galaxies. Burbidge explained: "Galaxies rotate around an axis. Why they don't collapse is because of centrifugal force [which she likens to swinging a stone on a string; if the string is cut, the stone flies off into space]. For our galaxy, the force of gravity holds the material in place and the rotational speed counterbalances this. So a galaxy takes up a structure in which gravitational pull is equated to centrifugal force." Therefore, Burbidge explained, if one wishes to calculate a galaxy's weight and the distribution of its mass, one must measure rotational speed.

In the late 1960s, Burbidge turned her attention to quasars, celestial objects more distant than stars that emit excessive amounts of radiation. By this time, she and her husband were settled in at the University of California at San Diego, having moved there in 1962 (her presidency of the American Astronomical Society from 1976 to 1978 prompted Burbidge to obtain U.S. citizenship). Burbidge became a full professor in 1964 and directed the University's Center for Astrophysics and Space Sciences from 1979 to 1988. Burbidges's work on quasars included measuring their redshifts. When moving objects emit light, the light waves in front of them are closer together than if the object were standing still, a phenomenon evidenced by the light's frequency "shifting" to the blue end of the color spectrum. Conversely, objects moving away have light waves that are farther away from each other, shifting the light toward the red end of the spectrum. (The same phenomenon also occurs with moving objects emitting sound, known as the Doppler effect.) It had been known that all galaxies except those nearest to earth emit redshifted light. "You can measure speed—looking at variations of the elements and measuring their shifts," Burbidge explained. "By a simple relationship you can tell how fast the galaxy is moving away. And this was done for quasars." Burbidge continues her work in spectroscopy and the ultraviolet spectrum of quasars, the latter of which the repaired Hubble Telescope greatly aids.

Burbidge became a professor emeritus in 1990. Over the years she has collected a number of awards, including a National Medal of Science in 1984 and twelve honorary doctoral degrees. She shared the 1959 Warner Prize from the American Astronomical Society with her husband, was elected a fellow of the Royal Society of London in 1964 and the American Academy of Arts and Sciences four years later, was made Abby Rockefeller Mauze Professor of the Massachusetts Institute of Technology in 1968, was elected into the National Academy of Science in 1978, received a Catherine Wolfe Bruce Medal from the Astronomical Society of the Pacific in 1982, and was awarded the Albert Einstein World Award of Science Medal in 1988.

SELECTED WRITINGS BY BURBIDGE:

Books

Lectures on Radio Galaxies and Quasi-Stellar Objects, Tata Institute of Fundamental Research, 1968.

Periodicals

(With Barlow T. A., Cohen R. D., Junkkarinen Volume T. and Womble D. S.), "Extent of Warm Haloes around Medium-Redshift Galaxies," *Astronomy and Space Science,* Volume 157, 1989, pp. 263–269.

SOURCES:

Burbidge, E. Margaret, telephone interview with Joan Oleck conducted on January 20, 1994.

—Sketch by Joan Oleck

Geoffrey Burbidge
1925-
English American astrophysicist

Geoffrey Burbidge is a principal investigator into nucleosynthesis, the creation of elements in space. He studies the manner in which stars synthesize heavy elements and also analyzes the phenomenon of quasars and active galaxies. Burbidge is among a small but provocative group of scientists who are challenging the orthodoxy of the big bang theory of the creation of the universe which states that all matter in the universe was created by a huge explosion.

Geoffrey Burbidge was born on September 24, 1925, in Chipping Norton, England, to Leslie and Eveline Burbidge. He attended Bristol University as a physics student and received his undergraduate degree in 1946. Graduate work commenced at University College, London, shortly thereafter. In 1948, Burbidge married astronomer **Margaret Burbidge**, then Margaret Peachey, whose important influence extended not just into Geoffrey's personal life, but into his professional career as well. Geoffrey, too, ultimately decided to pursue astronomy as his life's work.

Burbidge received his Ph.D. from University College in 1951 before embarking on the typical sequence of post-doctoral fellowships and one-year teaching appointments including an Agassiz Fellowship at Harvard, research fellowships at the University of Chicago and the Cavendish Laboratories, Cambridge, as well as a stint as a Carnegie fellow at Mount Wilson and Palomar Observatories, Caltech. In 1957 he finally landed a position at the University of Chicago as assistant professor in the astronomy department.

A Husband and Wife Astronomy Team Is Created

Burbidge had all the ingredients for a career that would bear much fruit: astronomy expertise, an intensive background in particle physics and a successful collaboration with his astronomer wife. In 1957, Geoffrey and Margaret Burbidge joined astronomers **William A. Fowler** and **Fred Hoyle** to explain the creation of chemical elements in stars. Their work was spurred by the discovery, in 1952, of the relatively new element technetium among the spectral lines (the characteristic pattern of colored lines emitted by each element within a light source) of red giant stars. Technetium is an unstable element that could not possibly have been present at the time of the formation of the giant stars in which it was found. The stars, themselves, must have synthesized the element com-

paratively recently. The Burbidges, Fowler, and Hoyle showed how a massive star lives out its life, synthesizing helium from hydrogen, then carbon, nitrogen and oxygen via the process of nuclear fusion. They further demonstrated how elements heavier than iron, such as iodine, platinum, gold and uranium could be synthesized under the high-energy conditions of a supernova explosion. One of the most important implications of these findings was the realization that the heavier elements, such as carbon, nitrogen and oxygen, which are found in all living organisms, were ultimately forged in the interiors of ancient, long-dead stars. Indeed, all life on Earth is made of "star-stuff."

The Mysterious Quasars Are Explored

Further explorations into even more tantalizing mysteries awaited the Burbidge team. Their research would lead them to ponder the evolution of the entire universe. In 1963, Geoffrey Burbidge became professor of physics at the University of California, San Diego. The work of his wife, a respected observational astronomer, led to Geoffrey's investigation into quasars. First discovered from their intense radio emission and then pinpointed optically, quasars exhibited a curious property; the lines of their spectra were all drastically shifted toward the red end of the spectrum (the range of colors produced by individual elements within a light source). The simplest explanation for the quasar red-shifts was that the quasars were receding from us, flying in directions away from the Earth's line of sight. This motion caused their light to redden due to the Doppler effect which states that light received from objects moving away from us shifts toward the red end of the spectrum. Similar Doppler red-shifting of the light of distant galaxies was the principal evidence presented in the 1920s and 1930s that the universe is expanding. Everything in the universe appears to be moving away from everything else. The quasars displaying huge red-shifts, indicated that they were exceedingly distant from our galaxy at the very "edge" of the observable universe. Because the farther from Earth an object resides in space, and the longer it takes for its light to reach us, the distant quasars represented a kind of "fossil" from the early days of the expanding universe and were studied with great interest. Geoffrey and his wife published one of the first surveys of these mysterious objects in 1967 entitled *Quasi-Stellar Objects*.

The problem with the quasars was that they appeared to be quite small. Yet, for them to be visible at such remote distances meant that the quasars were incredibly energetic and luminous. No one could contrive a suitable explanation or theory that could completely account for the discrepancy between the quasars small size and large energy output. Further research seemed only to compound the mystery. The Burbidges, along with other astronomers, found that seemingly distant quasars were grouped with supposedly nearby, bright galaxies. Other apparent linkages of seemingly distant quasars with less distant objects also appeared in other astronomers' searches. Finally, the possibility was raised by Geoffrey Burbidge, and others, that quasars were not cosmologically distant objects at all, but were smaller, closer objects being energetically ejected from nearby galaxies. This explanation was highly controversial, for it implied that Doppler shifts could not be relied upon as an indicator of the expansion of the universe. For if quasars received their large red-shifts from some other cause than the supposed universal expansion, then perhaps the red-shift observed in distant galaxies was also due to some other cause as well. Under these conditions, there would be no strong basis to assume that the universe was expanding at all and that the big bang ever happened.

Burbidge's alternative explanation for the redshifts of quasars put him at odds with established astronomical acceptance of the big bang theory of the creation of the universe. He was not alone, however, in his reluctance to accept the big bang theory. In his company were other astronomers such as Fred Hoyle and Halton Arp. But rather than present their viewpoint as a complete flouting of the big bang theory, the non-orthodox astronomers have served to focus critical attention on the flaws of the big bang theory in a constructive manner.

Burbidge helped to influence the continued strong health of university-based astronomy programs by serving on the Board of Directors of the Associated Universities for Research in Astronomy (AURA) from 1971–1974. In 1978, Burbidge became Director of Kitt Peak National Observatory, Arizona, which is renowned as one the most productive astronomy facilities in the entire world.

SELECTED WRITINGS BY BURBIDGE:

Books

Quasi-Stellar Objects, W. H. Freeman, 1967.
(Editor with others) *Annual Review of Astronomy and Astrophysics,* Annual Review, 1974—.

SOURCES:

Books

Abbott, David, editor, *The Biographical Dictionary of Scientists: Astronomers,* Peter Bedrick Books, 1984.

—*Sketch by Jeffery Bass*

Frank Macfarlane Burnet
1899-1985
Australian immunologist and virologist

While working at the University of Melbourne's Walter and Eliza Hall Institute for Medical Research in the 1920s, Frank Macfarlane Burnet became interested in the study of viruses and bacteriophages (viruses that attack bacteria). That interest eventually led to two major and related accomplishments. The first of these was the development of a method for cultivating viruses in chicken embryos, an important technological step forward in the science of virology. The second accomplishment was the development of a theory that explains how an organism's body is able to distinguish between its own cells and those of another organism. For this research, Burnet was awarded a share of the 1960 Nobel Prize for physiology or medicine (with **Peter Brian Medawar**).

Burnet was born in Traralgon, Victoria, Australia, on September 3, 1899. His father was Frank Burnet, manager of the local bank in Traralgon, and his mother was the former Hadassah Pollock MacKay. As a child, Burnet developed an interest in nature, particularly in birds, butterflies, and beetles. He carried over that interest when he entered Geelong College in Geelong, Victoria, where he majored in biology and medicine.

In 1917 Burnet continued his education at Ormond College of the University of Melbourne, from which he received his bachelor of science degree in 1922 and then, a year later, his M.D. degree. Burnet then took concurrent positions as resident pathologist at the Royal Melbourne Hospital and as researcher at the University of Melbourne's Hall Institute for Medical Research. In 1926 Burnet received a Beit fellowship that permitted him to spend a year in residence at the Lister Institute of Preventive Medicine in London. The work on viruses and bacteriophages that he carried out at Lister also earned him a Ph.D. from the University of London in 1927. At the conclusion of his studies in England in 1928, Burnet returned to Australia, where he became assistant director of the Hall Institute. He maintained his association with the institute for the next thirty-seven years, becoming director there in 1944. In the same year he was appointed professor of experimental medicine at the University of Melbourne. During his first year back from England, in 1928, Burnet was also married to Edith Linda Druce, a schoolteacher. The Burnets had two daughters, Elizabeth and Deborah, and a son, Ian. When his first wife died in 1973, Burnet was married a second time, to Hazel Jenkin.

Develops Method for Culturing Viruses

Burnet's early research covered a somewhat diverse variety of topics in virology. For example, he worked on the classification of viruses and bacteriophages, on the occurrence of psittacosis in Australian parrots, and on the epidemiology of herpes and poliomyelitis. His first major contribution to virology came, however, during his year as a Rockefeller fellow at London's National Institute for Medical Research from 1932 to 1933. There he developed a method for cultivating viruses in chicken embryos. The Burnet technique was an important breakthrough for virologists since viruses had been notoriously difficult to culture and maintain in the laboratory.

Over time, Burnet's work on viruses and bacteriophages led him to a different, but related, field of research, the vertebrate immune system. The fundamental question he attacked is one that had troubled biologists for years: how an organism's body can tell the difference between "self" and "not-self." An organism's immune system is a crucial part of its internal hardware. It provides a mechanism for fighting off invasions by potentially harmful—and sometimes fatal—foreign organisms (antigens) such as bacteria, viruses, and fungi. The immune system is so efficient that it even recognizes and fights back against harmless invaders such as pollen and dust, resulting in allergic reactions.

Begins Studies of the Immune System

Burnet was attracted to two aspects of the phenomenon of immunity. First, he wondered how an organism's body distinguishes between foreign invaders and components of its own body, the "self" versus "not-self" problem. That distinction is obviously critical, since if the body fails to recognize that difference, it may begin to attack its own cells and actually destroy itself. This phenomenon does in fact occur in relatively rare cases of autoimmune disorders.

The second question on which Burnet worked was how the immune system develops. The question is complicated by the fact that a healthy immune system is normally able to recognize and respond to an apparently endless variety of antigens, producing a specific chemical (antibody) to combat each antigen it encounters. According to one theory, these antibodies are present in an organism's body from birth, prior to birth, or an early age. A second theory suggested that antibodies are produced "on the spot" as they are needed and in response to an attack by an antigen.

For more than two decades, Burnet worked on resolving these questions about the immune system. He eventually developed a complete and coherent explanation of the way the system develops in the embryo and beyond, how it develops the ability to recognize its own cells as distinct from foreign cells, and how it carries with it from the very earliest stages the templates from which antibodies are produced. For this work, Burnet was awarded a share of the 1960 Nobel Prize in physiology or medicine. Among the other honors he received were the Royal Medal and the Copley Medal of the Royal Society (1947 and 1959, respectively) and the Order of Merit in 1958. He was elected a fellow of the Royal Society in 1947 and knighted by King George V in 1951.

Burnet retired from the Hall Institute in 1965, but continued his research activities. His late work was in the area of autoimmune disorders, cancer, and aging. He died of cancer in Melbourne on August 31, 1985. Burnet was a prolific writer, primarily of books on science and medicine, during his lifetime.

SELECTED WRITINGS BY BURNET:

Books

Biological Aspects of Infectious Disease, Cambridge University Press, 1934, 2nd edition published as *Natural History of Infectious Disease,* 1953, 4th edition (with David O. White), 1972.
Production of Antibodies, Macmillan, 1941.
Virus as Organism, Harvard University Press, 1945.
Viruses and Man, Penguin, 1953, 2nd edition, 1955.
Principles of Animal Virology, Academic Press, 1955, 2nd edition, 1960.
Enzyme, Antigen and Virus: A Study of Macromolecular Pattern in Action, Cambridge University Press, 1956.
The Clonal Selection Theory of Acquired Immunity, Cambridge University Press, 1959.
(Editor with W. M. Stanley) *The Viruses: Biochemical, Biological, and Biophysical Properties,* Academic Press, 1959.
The Integrity of the Body: A Discussion of Modern Immunological Ideas, Harvard University Press, 1962.
(With I. R. Mackay) *Auto-Immune Diseases,* Thomas, 1963.
Biology and the Appreciation of Life, Australian Broadcasting Commission, 1966.
Changing Patterns: An Atypical Autobiography, Heinemann, 1968, Elsevier, 1969.
Cellular Immunology, Melbourne University Press, 1969.
Self and Not-Self: Cellular Immunology, Cambridge University Press, 1969.
Immunological Surveillance, Pergamon, 1970.
Dominant Mammal: The Biology of Human Destiny, Heinemann, 1970, St. Martin's, 1972.
Walter and Eliza Hall Institute, 1915–1965, Melbourne University Press, 1971.

Genes, Dreams and Realities, Basic Books, 1971.

Auto-Immunity and Auto-Immune Disease, F. A. Davis, 1972.

Intrinsic Mutagenesis: A Genetic Approach, Wiley, 1974.

Immunology, Aging, and Cancer: Medical Aspects of Mutation and Selection, W. H. Freeman, 1976.

Endurance of Life: The Implications of Genetics for Human Life, Melbourne University Press, 1978.

Credo and Comment: A Scientist Reflects, Melbourne University Press, 1979.

SOURCES:

Books

Norry, R., *Virus Hunter in Australia,* Nelson, 1966.

—*Sketch by David E. Newton*

Glenn W. Burton

Glenn W. Burton
1910-
American plant geneticist

A plant geneticist with the U.S. Department of Agriculture (USDA) for almost sixty years, Glenn W. Burton has been an important figure in forage and turf development, as well as its production and utilization. As he told contributor Patricia McAdams, his efforts have helped "feed the hungry, protect and beautify the environment, and provide recreation for millions." Burton has received a number of national and international awards for his work in agriculture, including the National Medal of Science in 1983.

Glenn Willard Burton was born on May 5, 1910, in Clatonia, Nebraska, the only child of Joseph and Nellie May Rittenburg Burton. In 1915 the family moved to a farm in Bartley, Nebraska, and the experience of working with a team of horses alongside his father formed the basis of Burton's lifelong interest in agriculture. He did his share of the farm work before and after school, and he told McAdams that he learned to do chores quickly and correctly the first time, so he could still do things like play on the basketball team. Burton attended a small high school, which had only four teachers. A motivated student, he

had two compelling goals as a teenager: to become a teacher and to own a farm. Burton attended the University of Nebraska, where he met his tuition payments by working odd jobs and grading agronomy quizzes for thirty-five cents an hour. He graduated with a B.S. in 1932 and then won a graduate assistantship to study agronomy at Rutgers University. At Rutgers, he earned his M.S. in 1933, and his Ph.D. in agronomy in 1936.

When he left graduate school in 1936, Burton began working at the Tifton Experiment Station at the University of Georgia, where he would remain for the rest of his career. Accepting a position in the Division of Forage Crops and Disease, he set up a pioneering research program in grass breeding. The seventh professional staff member on the Coastal Plain Experiment Station, Burton remembers that he had no laboratory in which to work, five acres of unfenced pasture land, and "lots of problems." He fenced in the pasture with the help of an assistant, installed an irrigation system, and built a field house. His primary responsibility was improving the breeds of grasses used by farmers in the South, and he released perhaps his most important hybrid in 1943, coastal bermudagrass. He eventually moved into a leadership position, assuming the role of principal geneticist at the Tifton Experimental Station in the early 1950s.

Burton's primary concentration has been in the area of grass breeding and genetics, but his work has also focused on grass cytology, fertilization and management, grass-seed production, and the revegetation of native ranges. In addition to eight hybrids of bermudagrass, he has also produced hybrids of pangolagrasses, sudangrasses, pearl millets, bahiagrasses and dallis grasses. Burton told McAdams that his most significant contributions to agriculture have been the "innovative plant breeding methods" he developed and "the improved cultivars they produced that better serve man's need for food, forage, recreation, and conservation." He is particularly proud of coastal bermudagrass, because it produces "twice as much hay and pasture as common bermudagrass." His coastal bermudagrass is planted over ten million acres of countryside across the South, and is considered a vital pasture and hay plant. Another example of a superior variety of plant is his pearl millet, which Burton says "doubled food production for people in India, who eat pearl millet grain." Burton has consulted with staff and graduate students in many locations, traveling to a number of foreign countries including the former Soviet Union and the Peoples' Republic of China. Many of Burton's improved forage grasses are now being used in underdeveloped countries.

Burton believes that his work would never have had so much relevance outside the Georgia Coastal Plain Experiment Station were it not for all the time he spent researching and answering questions from local farmers and producers. He has estimated that it has taken about half of his time throughout his years at the USDA to learn how to fertilize and manage the grass varieties he developed so they would grow well on farms. Wayne Hanna writes in *The UGA Coastal Plain Experiment Station: The First 75 Years* that Burton "could always be found in the tall millet fields by looking for an aluminum painted pith helmet moving through the plots." He was always searching for a "better way" to do everything, Hanna says, and was "frequently drawing plans for a thresher, plow, planter, etc. to help get the job done faster and more efficiently. Every idea was tried the day he thought about it (or soon after), and most of them worked."

Burton served as chair of the Division of Agronomy at the University of Georgia from 1950 through 1964. He has also served on a number of committees of the American Society of Agronomy (ASA), and he was chair of the Crops Division in 1952. He served as vice president of ASA in 1961, and president in 1962. In addition to the National Medal of Science, Burton has received many awards. He was the first plant scientist to be inducted into the International Stockman's Hall of Fame, and he was awarded honorary membership in the Grasslands Society of South Africa. Other awards include the USDA Superior Service Award in 1955, the USDA Distinguished Service Award in 1980, and the Georgia Science and Technological Commission's First Citation for Distinguished Service in the Advancement of Science in 1966. Burton was elected to the University of Georgia's Agricultural Alumni Hall of Fame in 1984, and

the Agricultural Research Service Science Hall of Fame in 1987. He received an honorary degree as Doctor of Science from Rutgers in 1955, and the University of Nebraska awarded him another honorary degree in 1962. He has been a member of the National Academy of Sciences since 1975.

On December 16, 1934, Burton married Helen Jeffryes, whom he met at the University of Nebraska. They have five children and eight grandchildren. Burton loves gardening; he remains active in his church and community, and in 1951 he and his family were recognized as "Methodist family of the year." At age eighty-three, Burton still works at the experiment station, arriving early each day as he has for many years.

SELECTED WRITINGS BY BURTON:

Periodicals

(With R. H. Hart) "Curing Coastal Bermudagrass Hay: Effects of Weather, Yield, and Quality of Fresh Herbage on Drying Rates, Yield, and Quality of Cured Hay," *Agronomy Journal,* Volume 59, July-August 1967, p. 367.

(With C. M. Taleoferro, and R. A. Byers) "Effects of Spittlebug Injury on Root Production and Sod Reserves of Coastal Bermudagrass," *Agronomy Journal,* Volume 59, November-December 1967, p. 530.

(With W. G. Monson, E. J. Williams, and J. L. Butler) "Effects of Burning on Soil Temperature and Yield of Coastal Bermudagrass," *Agronomy Journal,* Volume 66, 1974, p. 212.

SOURCES:

Books

Hanna, Wayne, "Glenn Burton," in *The UGA Coastal Plain Experiment Station: The First 75 Years,* edited by Max H. Bass, Lang Printing Company, 1993.

Other

Burton, Glenn W., interview with Patricia M. McAdams, October 11, 1993.

—*Sketch by Patricia M. McAdams*

Vannevar Bush
1890-1974
American engineer

Vannevar Bush

Vannevar Bush's most important contribution to engineering was the differential analyzer, a complex but elegant mechanism capable of solving the intricate and lengthy differential equations that have become increasingly indispensable to modern engineering. During World War II, the differential analyzer was used to solve equations essential to ballistics, acoustics, structures, and atomic physics. In addition to this electronic calculating "machine," Bush published an influential essay about a hypothetical computing machine called Memex. The essay presented a theoretical prototype for the modern day personal computer and helped influence research in such areas as hypertext, multimedia, and artificial intelligence. However, Bush was best known by the public for his government appointment as director of the Office of Scientific Research and Development during World War II. Through this office, Bush coordinated a vast network of industrial and academic research geared toward wartime science, including the early work conducted on the atomic bomb. After the war, Bush successfully lobbied to expand government-supported research, stressing the basic sciences, and to establish the National Academy of Sciences.

Bush was born in Everett, Massachusetts, on March 11, 1890. His grandfather was a whaling captain. His father, Perry Bush, had also tried his hand as a seafarer, but turned to theology and became a minister in the Universalist Church, abandoning his family's traditional Methodist faith. To avoid controversy, Perry Bush moved his wife, Emma Linwood Paine, and family to Chelsea, a suburb across the river from Boston, where he mixed freely with the growing immigrant population, opened his church to people of other faiths, and readily made many "nonsectarian" occasions religious ones. Vannevar attended the Chelsea public schools, spending his summers sailing boats in the Boston harbor and working as a cook on a small fishing boat.

After high school, Bush enrolled in Tufts College, following in the footsteps of his father and two older sisters. Earning his way by tutoring other students, the mathematically-gifted Bush graduated from Tufts in 1913, with B.S. and M.S. degrees. Uncertain of what career to follow, Bush landed a position in the testing department of the General Electric Company and then moved on to the inspecting department of the United States Navy. In 1914, he became an instructor in mathematics at Tufts. But Bush saw that the burgeoning field of engineering would be a more lucrative career and pursued a Ph.D. in engineering, which he received jointly from the Massachusetts Institute of Technology (MIT) and Harvard in 1916, one of the few doctorates jointly awarded by the two schools. Upon receiving his degree, Bush was promoted to assistant professor of electrical engineering at Tufts. On September fifth of that same year, he married Phoebe Davis, also of Chelsea, and a onetime member of his father's church choir. They had two children, Richard Davis and John Hathaway.

The year after Bush graduated, the United States entered World War I. Bush went to New London, Connecticut, to work in a Navy antisubmarine laboratory, where he developed a submarine magnetic detection device that was never used. (He later described his attempt as amateurish, when compared to World War II advances.) However, Bush did gain a valuable first-hand experience in how bureaucracy could stifle science. When Bush coordinated the U.S. research effort during World War II, he centralized authority in his office and had access to the appropriate political leaders in order to avoid the decentralized and often isolated scientific efforts of the First World War.

After World War I, Bush became an associate professor of electrical power transmission at MIT. With the growing importance of engineering in industry, Bush, like many of his colleagues, conducted a lucrative second career as a consultant, primarily with the American Research and Development Corporation (AMRAD), for which he had begun to work in

1916. Although Bush invented many patentable devices, he usually contracted with other firms to develop his inventions into profitable ventures. With Charles G. Smith, Bush invented a gaseous rectifier tube (called the S tube) to replace a cumbersome battery component of the radio, enabling it to be run on residential currents. With his former college roommate and best man, Laurence K. Marshall, he co-founded the Raytheon Corporation, a thermostat and vacuum tube company which, at one point, would become the largest employer in New England.

Bush's academic research focused on applying mathematical equations to analyze electrical power circuits in an effort to solve some of the problems then associated with electricity, such as widespread power failures and blackouts. But Bush's equations were so complex that they either took months of chart and graph -making, or were just plain impossible to solve. As a result, Bush became interested in developing mechanical analysis machines to help engineers in applied mathematics. In the 1920s, Bush and young colleagues at MIT developed the mechanical forerunner of the computer, called the differential analyzer. The first machine was a "breadboard" model made out of available parts, primarily to see if the idea would work. The second, built in 1931, was a mechanical machine composed of several disk integrators, such as a revolving disk and a roller that could be moved at various distances from the center of the disk. Such mechanics allowed the machine to trace solutions to mathematical problems onto drawing boards. The machine soon gained wide popularity among engineers and was used to solve problems in acoustics, atomic physics, geophysics, and quantum mechanics. Shortly before World War II, a completely electrical machine (except for the integrators) was built and named the Rockefeller differential analyzer. It was used for a variety of wartime research, such as calculating ballistic tables and the curvature of radar antennae.

The most advanced calculator of its time, the differential analyzer both accelerated and promoted new areas of research by greatly reducing the time needed to solve complex equations. Although not as precise as later digital machines, the differential analyzer elegantly presented the mathematical concepts in a way that allowed scientists to explore a problem, for example, by changing constants in an equation. The analyzer also had potential as an educational tool, although this aspect was never fully developed because of the cost. In his book *Pieces of the Action,* Bush tells of a young, inexperienced mechanic who was hired as a draftsman at the beginning of the analyzer's development. Through working on the machine, the mechanic essentially learned about differential equations and calculus in mechanical terms. "[A] strange approach," wrote Bush, "and yet he understood it." In an article in

Technology and Culture, Larry Owens called Bush's invention an "elegant, dynamical, mechanical model of the differential equation."

Bush firmly cemented his reputation as one of the founding fathers of the computer age when he published his essay, "As We May Think," in the July, 1945 issue of *Atlantic Monthly.* In the essay, Bush expressed his concern that the staggering exponential growth of scientific knowledge was becoming increasingly difficult for scientists to access readily. "The summation of human experience is being expanded at a prodigious rate," wrote Bush, "and the means we use for threading through the consequent maze to the momentarily important item is the same as was used in the days of square-rigged ships." Bush went on to outline the prototype for the modern personal computer. Called Memex, this theoretical machine greatly influenced later research in such areas as hypertext, multimedia, and information retrieval.

Essentially, Memex would file material by association, and users could retrieve this information by pressing a key that would follow a "trail" of facts. Memex was the prototypical first idea of modern information retrieval through computers. In *Pieces of the Action,* Bush described Memex as a machine "that should be the personal memory and body of knowledge belonging to an individual." He went on to say that it would "emulate [the] mind in its associative linking of items of information, and their retrieval as a result."

Guides Wartime Research Efforts

Through his early business ventures and his administrative duties in academia, Bush became an able administrator. In 1932, he was appointed dean of engineering and vice-president of MIT by the school's president, Karl Compton. Bush and Compton, who shared a belief in the economic benefits of technological innovations, would work many years together both at the university and in government. Although some people at the university were put off by Bush's temper and occasional intolerance in dealings with others, his students were especially loyal to Bush, who was a willing mentor to their research efforts.

Bush's sphere of influence began to branch out from MIT in 1934, when he was appointed to the National Academy of Sciences and worked under Compton on the Science Advisory Board. As a member of the academy, Bush also served as chairman of the National Advisory Committee for Aeronautics, which reported directly to President Franklin D. Roosevelt. Politically conservative, Bush was not enamored with Roosevelt's New Deal efforts to revive the country's economy following the Great Depression. But Bush, along with Compton and friends **Frank Jewett** and James B. Conant, was strongly patriotic in the early days of World War II. They were dedicated to ensuring that, if needed, U.S. wartime technological development would be efficient and productive.

Through his committee work, Bush was becoming more and more familiar with the defense program and how it operated. In the same year he was appointed to the advisory committee, Bush accepted the post as president of the Carnegie Institution of Washington, placing him even closer to the center of political action. In 1940, Bush and colleagues lobbied to create a federal agency to oversee scientific development and keep it out of the hands of politicians. After much lobbying by Bush and his colleagues, Roosevelt established the National Defense Research Committee (NDRC) on June 27, 1940, and appointed Bush its chairman. This civilian organization of scientists and engineers was to develop new weapons for the military as a supplement to the military's own wartime research. Many politicians and military men opposed the NDRC, viewing it as a group of outsiders who had cornered the authority and money for defense research. In *Pieces of the Action,* Bush admitted that this view was accurate and wrote, "it was the only way in which a broad program could be launched rapidly and on an adequate scale." Working with Compton and others, Bush decided that the best approach was to make full use of existing research establishments in universities and corporations. By fostering government-sponsored grants both to large projects and individuals, the NDRC was an early influence in the widespread efforts of government to sponsor research.

Two years later, after the U.S. had entered World War II, Roosevelt created the Office of Scientific Research and Development (OSRD), again largely due to the lobbying efforts of Bush and colleagues, who felt they needed more authority, not only to research new wartime technology, but also to approve its development. The OSRD included the NDRC, the Committee on Medical Research, the Office of Field Service, the Scientific Personnel Office, and a liaison office to help coordinate scientific exchange among the Allies. Under Bush's guidance, the OSRD oversaw the development of microwave radars, antisubmarine devices, amphibious warfare, and the early stages of the atomic bomb. Many medical advances also resulted from OSRD efforts, including antimalarial drugs, blood substitutes, and the large scale production of penicillin. The OSRD achieved much of this success by discarding the one-step-at-a-time approach in favor of a large number of independent teams conducting research from a variety of perspectives. Although Bush conducted no research himself, he forged the OSRD into an exceptionally efficient organization that was able to overcome many obstacles presented by the political and military establishments.

Essentially, Bush understood how power worked in Washington. In an interview with Daniel J. Kevles for the book *The Physicists: The History of a Scientific Community in Modern America,* Bush said: "I knew that you couldn't get anything done in that town unless you organized under the wing of the President." After Roosevelt died, Bush worked under President Harry S. Truman and was among those who advised Truman to use the atomic bomb against the Japanese.

Lobbies for Government Support of Peacetime Research

After the war, Bush continued to work on government committees concerned with fostering scientific research and made many recommendations on how to transfer wartime research to peaceful efforts. Bush was able to form a consensus of opinion among his fellow scientists that resulted in the report "Science, the Endless Frontier," which called for large government support for basic research. As a result of the report, the National Science Foundation was established in 1950 to act, as the report described, as "a new social invention—of government sanction and support but professional guidance and administration."

Although early on Bush described his dealings with President Truman as congenial, their relationship eventually deteriorated, largely over differences about the government's role in controlling scientific research. As a result, his political influence began to wane. Bush, however, was not a man to be cast aside easily. While he had advocated the use of the atomic bomb, he opposed what he saw as the military's tunnel vision in developing the hydrogen bomb, and predicted the resultant arms race and the fear and danger that accompanied the Cold War. Bush and his colleagues were successful in developing the Atomic Energy Commission in 1946, despite a bitter battle among the scientific and political communities over the control of atomic research. Bush also spoke out vociferously against the security investigations of the 1950s, largely spurred on by Senator Joseph McCarthy's infamous hearings which, history shows, unfairly accused many scientists, businessmen, artists, and others of being communists. In particular, Bush came to the defense of **J. Robert Oppenheimer,** who had directed the atomic bomb research and had served a term as chairman of the Atomic Energy Commission's General Advisory Committee. In 1954, Oppenheimer was the focus of a security hearing and ultimately, under the direction of President Dwight D. Eisenhower, had his security clearance for nuclear research suspended. Bush was outraged and believed that Oppenheimer's downfall was largely due to a political power play by those who supported the development of the hydrogen bomb, which, like Bush, Oppenheimer opposed.

Bush stayed at the Carnegie Institution for two decades following the war and helped direct its studies of solar storms and bacterial resistance to antibiotics. His keen acumen, enhanced by his own previous business ventures and his wartime education in the political economy, fostered his success in the private sector, where he would serve as director of American Telephone & Telegraph (AT&T) until 1962, and chairman of the board of directors at Merck from 1957 until 1962. In 1955, Bush retired from the Carnegie Institution and returned to New England. In 1957, he was appointed chairman of the MIT Corporation and became its honorary chairman in 1959.

In addition to his role as an engineer and overseer of scientific research on a national basis, Bush was a prolific and successful author. Writing on science, business, national policy and the lessons of war, Bush's books including *Pieces of the Action, Science Is Not Enough,* and *Modern Arms and Free Man.* Although Bush always thought of himself foremost as an inventor and not as a scientist or statesman, he was, in truth, equally adept at all three. He foresaw the growing complexity of the relationship between science and society, and his efforts had a profound impact on ensuring strong government support for basic research. Bush received many honorary degrees and scientific awards, including the National Medal of Science in 1964 and the Atomic Pioneers Award in 1970. He died from pneumonia after suffering a stroke in 1974.

SELECTED WRITINGS BY BUSH:

Books

Science, the Endless Frontier. A Report to the President, U. S. Government Printing Office, 1945.
Modern Arms and Free Men, Simon & Schuster, 1949.
Science Is Not Enough, Morrow, 1967.
Pieces of the Action, Morrow, 1970.

SOURCES:

Books

Kevles, Daniel J., *The Physicists: The History of a Scientific Community in Modern America,* Knopf, 1987.
Political Profiles: The Eisenhower Years, Facts on File, pp. 85–86.

—Sketch by David Petechuk

Adolf Butenandt
1903-
German biochemist

Adolf Butenandt's groundbreaking research into sex hormones led to the formulation of the compounds estrone and androsterone, hormones involved in the regulation of sexual processes in the body. He has worked on both male and female sex hormones using microanalytical methods developed by the Austrian chemist **Fritz Pregl**. By uncovering the underlying structure of sex hormones, Butenandt opened biochemical study to the relationship of the chemical structure of sex hormones and carcinogenic substances. For his work, Butenandt was awarded the Nobel Prize in chemistry in 1939, an award that he shared with **Leopold Ružička** but was unable to receive until 1949 because the Nazi government did not allow him to accept it.

Adolf Friedrich Johann Butenandt was born in Bremerhaven-Lehe (now Wesermünde), Germany, on March 24, 1903, to Otto Louis Max Butenandt, a businessman, and Wilhelmina Thomfohrde Butenandt. He received his basic education in Bremerhaven at the Oberrealschule, after which he went to the University of Marburg in 1921 to study chemistry and biology. When he continued his studies at the University of Göttingen in 1924, he was inspired to study biochemistry by his professor, **Adolf Windaus**.

Upon completion of his dissertation on a compound used in insecticides, Butenandt was granted a doctorate by the University of Göttingen in 1927. He was also made an assistant at the Institute of Chemistry in Göttingen in 1931. He remained in Göttingen until 1933, when he was appointed professor of organic chemistry at the Danzig Institute of Technology. He remained in Danzig until 1936, rejecting an appointment to Harvard University in 1935. By 1929 Butenandt had isolated a female sex hormone in pure crystalline form. This research was made possible by his association with Walter Schoeller, the director of research for a pharmaceutical firm, Schering Corporation. Schoeller had asked Windaus for help to investigate the female sex hormones and their chemical structures. Windaus recommended his student, Butenandt, for this research. Schoeller provided Butenandt with the necessary hormonal substances needed to carry out the study. Butenandt first called the hormone he isolated folliculin, because it is secreted in the lining of the follicles of the ovary. It was later renamed estrone, however, because it is an estrogen hormone that controls a number of female processes.

In 1931 Butenandt married Erika von Ziegner, his assistant in his early research. They would have two sons, Otfrid and Eckart, and five daughters, Ina, Heide, Anke, Imme, and Maike. Also in 1931, Butenandt was able to confirm the existence of another female sex hormone, estriol, which had been discovered in London by G. F. Merrian. (Another biochemist, the American **Edward A. Doisy**, had also isolated estrone at about this time.) He also isolated and purified in crystalline form the male sex hormone androsterone, which is secreted from the testes. This hormone is related to testosterone, the main male sex hormone. He continued his research with sex hormones, and by 1934 he and his associates had isolated the hormone progesterone. In five years he was able to synthesize progesterone from its cholesterol precursor.

An important aspect of Butenandt's research with sex hormones was the discovery that the exact location of male sex hormone activity is in the nucleus of the carbon atoms. This was a major contribution to the study of human biochemistry; it has made it possible to produce various medical products that alleviate the symptoms of major diseases. Cortisone, a synthetic product closely related to some of the hormones Butenandt researched, has been used in the treatment of arthritis and is one example of the medical applications of hormone research. By 1935 Butenandt completed some significant research on testosterone (the main male sex hormone) that led to his discovery of the chemical sites of biological activities. He found that male and female sex hormones were chemically related by a common sterol nucleus.

Wins Nobel Prize for Chemistry

Butenandt was asked to become director of the Kaiser Wilhelm Society, which oversaw all scientific research in Germany, in 1936. He accepted this position from the physicist **Max Planck**, and the institution now bears Planck's name. The award of the Nobel Prize in chemistry in 1939 was made to Butenandt and Leopold Ružička for their contributions to the study of sex hormones. Because of the intervention of World War II and the objection of the German government, Butenandt was not able to receive his award until 1949.

During the war Butenandt worked on genetic problems relating to eye pigmentation in insects. This research led Butenandt to the one-gene-one enzyme theory that was shared by other researchers. After the war the Kaiser Wilhelm Institute moved to Tübingen; Butenandt became professor of physiological chemis-

try there and continued his research with insects. By 1953 he had isolated the first insect hormone, ecdysone, which stimulates the transformation of a caterpillar into a butterfly. His associate, Peter Karlson, later showed that ecdysone is derived from cholesterol and is also related to sex hormones in mammals.

In 1956 the Kaiser Wilhelm Institute moved again, this time to Munich, and Butenandt became professor of physiological chemistry at the University of Munich. There he studied a substance that is synthesized by female silkworms to attract males. Butenandt continued his association with the Max Planck Society for the Advancement of Science, serving as its president from 1960 until 1972. He retired from his position at the University of Munich in 1971.

Butenandt has received many awards, including the Grand Cross for Federal Services of West Germany and the Adolf von Harnack Medal of the Max Planck Society. He was made a commander of the Legion of Honor of France in 1969. He has received honorary degrees from many universities throughout Europe and holds honorary memberships in scientific societies all over the world. He has published numerous articles in scientific journals and written a number of books.

SELECTED WRITINGS BY BUTENANDT:

Books

Untersuchungen uber das Weiblishe Sexualhormon (Follikel-oder Brunsthomon), Weidmannsche Buchhandlung (Berlin), 1931.
Die Biologische Chemie im Dienste der Volkagesundheit, W. de Gruyter (Berlin), 1941.
Zur Feinstruktur des Tabakmosaik-Virus, W. de Gruyter, 1944.

SOURCES:

Books

Farber, Eduard, *Nobel Prize Winners in Chemistry: 1901–1961,* Abelard-Schuman, 1963, pp. 168–70.
Wasson, Tyler, editor, *Nobel Prize Winners,* H. W. Wilson, 1987, pp. 172–74.

—Sketch by Vita Richman

John Cairns, Jr.
1923-
American limnologist

John Cairns, Jr. is a noted limnologist and environmentalist who has spent his entire career studying how ecosystems respond to stress, primarily to pesticides, industrial wastes, and other pollutants produced by human society. A major part of his research has also focused on the restoration of stressed or affected ecosystems. He is the author of over a thousand publications, including 45 books and more than 460 scientific papers. He has received numerous awards and honors, including being elected in 1993 as foreign member of the Linnean Society of London, which has a membership limit of 50, and a member of the National Academy of Sciences in 1991.

An only child, Cairns was born on May 8, 1923, in Conshohocken, Pennsylvania, to John Cairns, a freight solicitor for a railroad company, and Eunice Fesmire Cairns, a homemaker who had worked as an executive secretary before her son was born. His parents, particularly his mother, placed an extremely high value on education and were determined that he should attend college, even though this was uncommon in the small steel town of Conshohocken, where the family lived.

Cairns entered Pennsylvania State University (Penn State) in 1940. In 1942 military service interrupted his studies, and he joined the U.S. Navy, where he served until 1946. On August 5, 1944, he married Jean Barbara Ogden, whom he had met at Penn State when they both were students there. When he returned from military service, Penn State could not provide accommodation for him and his family which now included a child. He was accepted at Swarthmore College and graduated in 1947 with an A.B. degree in biology. At the recommendation of his advisor at Swarthmore, Robert K. Enders, Cairns went on to receive a M.S. degree from the University of Pennsylvania in 1949 and a Ph.D. in 1953, both in biology.

Enters New Field of Environmental Pollution

In 1948 while still a graduate student at the University of Pennsylvania, Cairns began working at the Academy of Natural Sciences in Philadelphia, as

John Cairns, Jr.

an assistant to the senior curator, **Ruth Patrick**. In the late 1940s and early 1950s, there were no courses offered in environmental pollution; his work at the academy was his introduction to the field. The work involved leading a field crew on studies of rivers both in North America and elsewhere, including the Amazon. He enjoyed the work and spent his time away from the field in laboratories carrying out toxicity tests.

Cairns's master's thesis was based on a study he did for the academy on the effects of pollution on the microbial communities of Conestoga River in Pennsylvania. For his doctoral thesis, however, he changed direction temporarily by doing research on the transfaunation (transfer) of protozoan parasites from one source to another.

He joined the academy as assistant curator, became associate curator, and then curator of limnology. From Dr. Patrick, he learned how to interact with other disciplines and with industry and government. His association with her also taught him how to get extramural funding, which is essential for conducting research in science.

In 1961 Enders invited him to teach a course in comparative limnology at Rocky Mountain Biological Laboratories in Colorado. That experience convinced Cairns that he would enjoy teaching as well as research, particularly working at field stations. In 1966 Cairns decided to make a major career change. He left the Academy of Natural Sciences that year and joined the University of Kansas as professor of zoology. The following year he became associate chairman of the department of zoology. He moved to the Virginia Institute of Technology in 1968 as research professor of zoology. He became director of the University Center for Environmental and Hazardous Materials Studies in 1970 and University Distinguished Professor in 1972. Cairns has also held temporary teaching positions at Temple University in Philadelphia, at the University of Michigan Biological Station, and at the Rocky Mountain Biological Laboratory.

In addition to studying the effects of the pollutional stress on ecosystems—a field now known as "ecotoxicology"—Cairns has spent two-thirds of his career researching methods to heal stressed ecosystems, a field generally known as "restoration ecology". He has also carried out theoretical research on the ways in which freshwater microbial communities—particularly protists and protozoans—are structured and transported, and on their successional processes, that is, how they develop and change. Using this information, he was able to show in the early 1970s how to measure pollutional effects in temperate zone aquatic ecosystems. This is the chief method used for fresh water pollutional studies in the People's Republic of China.

Cairns's career has been marked by extensive publishing. Many of his books have been used as texts for graduate courses and a few have been used for advanced undergraduate courses in Europe. A 1969 article in the journal *American Naturalist* on the relationship of fresh-water protozoan communities to the MacArthur-Wilson equilibrium model, which he coauthored, was the first confirmation of the well-known model.

In many of his writings, Cairns, a concerned environmentalist, cautions against uncontrolled population growth and other factors, which continue to destroy the natural systems. These systems provide a variety of valuable ecological and life support services: the processing of wastes, climate regulation, and maintenance of atmospheric gas balance. According to Cairns, a solution to the depletion of these systems can be found only if members of all the disciplines—wildlife biologists, agronomists, and soil specialists, among others—combine their efforts.

Among his memorable honors are the United Nations Environmental Programme Medal for unique and significant contributions to Environmental Restoration and Sustainability and being elected a Fellow of the American Academy of Arts and Sciences, both in 1988. He was the recipient of Presidential Commendation in 1971 in recognition of his service in the environmental area.

Cairns and his wife have four children, Karen Jean, Stephan Hugh, Duncan Jay, and Heather, and five grandchildren. In his leisure, he fishes, hikes, swims, and folk dances. He remains active in research and publishing.

SELECTED WRITINGS BY CAIRNS:

Books

(Editor with T. Volume Crawford) *Integrated Environmental Management,* Lewis Publishers, Inc., 1991.

Periodicals

(With M. L. Dahlberg, K. L. Dickson, N. Smith, and W. T. Waller) "The Relationship of Fresh-Water Protozoan Communities to the MacArthur-Wilson Equilibrium Model," *American Naturalist,* Volume 103, 1969, pp. 439–54.
"Ecosystem Peril Vs. Perceived Personal Risk," *Chemtech,* February, 1992, pp. 90–93.
"The Zen of Ecological Restoration: Eight Steps on the Path Toward Enlightenment," *Annals of Earth,* Volume 11, number 2, 1993, pp. 13–15.
(With P. Volume McCormick and B. R. Niederlehner) "A Proposed Framework for Developing Indicators of Ecosystem Health," *Hydrobiologia,* Volume 263, 1993, pp. 1–45.

Other

Cairns, John, Jr., interview with Kala Dwarakanath conducted on October 12, 1993.

—*Sketch by Kala Dwarakanath*

Alberto P. Calderón
1920-
Argentine-born American mathematician

Alberto P. Calderón is known for his revolutionary work in the field of mathematics. His influence turned the 1950s trend toward abstract mathematics back to the study of mathematics for practical applications in physics, geometry, calculus, as well many other branches of this field. His award-winning research in the area of integral operators is an example of his impact on contemporary mathematical analysis. Widely considered one of the twentieth-century's foremost mathematicians, Calderón has devoted more than forty-five years to his work, during which time he has created a number of seminal works and ideas.

Alberto Pedro Calderón was born on September 14, 1920, in Mendoza, Argentina, a small town at the foot of the Andes. His father, a descendant of notable nineteenth-century politicians and military officers, was a renowned medical doctor who helped organize the General Central Hospital of Mendoza.

Calderón completed his secondary education in his hometown and in Zug, Switzerland. His interest in mathematics was fueled by Dr. Save Bercovici. After graduating from the School of Engineering of the National University of Buenos Aires in 1947, he studied under Alberto González Domínguez and with the celebrated mathematician Antoni Zygmund, who was working as a visiting professor in Buenos Aires in 1948.

A Rockefeller Foundation fellowship took him to the University of Chicago in Illinois, where he received his Ph.D. in 1950. However, his teaching career actually began in 1948 when he was made an assistant to the chair of electric circuit theory in Buenos Aires. His next stint was as a visiting associate professor at Ohio State University from 1950 to 1953.

Calderón continued his academic pursuits as a member of the Institute for Advanced Study in Princeton from 1954 to 1955. He later worked at the Massachusetts Institute of Technology (MIT) as an associate professor. He returned to the University of Chicago, becoming professor of mathematics from 1959 to 1968, Louis Block professor of mathematics from 1968 to 1972, and chairperson of the mathematics department from 1970 to 1972.

Reverses Mathematic Trends

By that time, Calderón's prestige had been well established in scientific circles, and his research in collaboration with his longtime mentor Zygmund had already been dubbed "The Chicago School of Mathematics," also known today as "the Calderón-Zygmund School of Analysis." The contribution that significantly impacted contemporary mathematics included reversing a predominant trend toward abstract mathematics and turning back to basic questions of real and complex analysis. This work, completed in tandem with Zygmund, came to be known as Calderón-Zygmund Theory of Mathematics.

A landmark in Calderón's scientific career was his 1958 paper titled "Uniqueness of the Cauchy Problem for Partial Differential Equations." Two years later, he used the same method to build a complete theory on hyperbolic partial differential equations. His theory of singular operators, which is used to estimate solutions to geometrical equations, contributed to linking together several different branches of mathematics. It also had practical applications in many areas, including physics and aerodynamic engineering. This theory has dominated contemporary mathematics and has made important inroads in other scientific fields, including quantum physics. Although some authors have tinkered with his theory and changed its name to that of pseudo-differential operators or pseudo-differential calculus, the original idea and basic applications remain credited to Calderón. His extensive work has transformed contemporary mathematical analysis. In addition to his pseudo-differentials work, he also conducted fundamental studies in interpolation theory—the idea that any algebraic problem that has a rational solution is solvable. He was responsible—with R. Arens—for what is considered one of the best theorems in Banach algebras. Calderón also put forth an approach to energy estimates that has been of fundamental importance in dozens of subsequent investigations, and has provided a model for general research in his field.

In the early 1970s, Calderón briefly returned to his home country to serve as visiting lecturer and conduct mathematical Ph.D. dissertation studies at his alma mater, the National University of Buenos Aires. He has continued to encourage mathematics students from Latin America and the United States to pursue their doctoral degrees, in many instances directly sponsoring them. Some of his pupils, in turn, have become reputed mathematicians including Robert T. Seeley.

After his stay in Argentina, Calderón returned to MIT as a professor of mathematics and, in 1975, he became university professor of mathematics, a special position at the University of Chicago, until his retirement in 1985. Between 1989 and 1992 he was a professor emeritus with a post retirement appointment at that same institution. He was awarded the Bôcher Prize for a 1978 paper on the Cauchy integral on Lipschitz curves. In 1989, he shared the Mathematics Prize of the Karl Wolf Foundation of Israel with his American colleague **John W. Milnor**, and has received innumerable other honors around the world. In 1991 U.S. President George Bush granted him the National Medal of Science.

As an author, Calderón has issued more than seventy-five scientific papers on various topics, from real variables to partial differential equations and singular integrals. A number of those papers were written in collaboration with his teacher Antoni Zygmund. Calderón has lectured in major cities the world over.

A member of the American Mathematical Society for more than forty years, Calderón served as a member-at-large of its Council in the mid–1960s and on several of its committees. He has also been an associate editor of various scientific publications, such as the *Duke Mathematical Journal, Journal of Functional Analysis,* and others.

Calderón married Dr. Alexandra Bellow, a well-known mathematician in her own right and a professor at Northwestern University. Their daughter, María Josefina, holds a doctorate in French literature from the University of Chicago and their son, Pablo Alberto, is a mathematician who has studied in Buenos Aires and New York.

SELECTED WRITINGS BY CALDERÓN:

Periodicals

"Uniqueness in the Cauchy Problem for Partial Differential Equations," *American Journal of Mathematics,* Volume 80, 1958, pp. 16–36.
"Lecture Notes on Pseudo-differential Operators and Elliptic Boundary-value Problems," *Instituto Argentino de Matemáticas* [Buenos Aires], 1976.

SOURCES:

Periodicals

Atiyah, M. F. and I. M. Singer, "The Index of Elliptic Operators on Compact Manifolds," *Bulletin of the American Mathematical Society,* Volume 69, 1963, pp. 442–433.
Beals, Richard W., Ronald R. Coifman, and Peter W. Jones, "Alberto Calderón Receives National Medal of Science," *Notices of the American Mathematical Society,* April, 1992.
González Domínguez, Alberto, "Dr. Alberto P. Calderón, Premio Bocher 1979," *Ciencia e Investigación,* November-December, 1978, pp. 221–223.

—*Sketch by Rodolfo A. Windhausen*

Helen Caldicott
1938-
Australian pediatrician and antinuclear activist

Helen Caldicott is a pediatrician and an antinuclear activist, who opposes both nuclear weapons and nuclear power. In the early 1970s she spearheaded an antinuclear movement in her native Australia, which forced an end to French nuclear testing in the South Pacific and managed to stop Australian uranium exports from 1975 to 1982. In the late 1970s and early 1980s, she became a leader in the antinuclear movement in the United States through her role in reviving the organization Physicians for Social Responsibility, which expanded rapidly during her presidency (which ran from 1978 to 1983). She helped found several other organizations which have worked to abolish controlled nuclear fission. Relying on her passionate oratory and intensely personal style, which are grounded in a thorough knowledge of the medical effects of exposure to radiation, she was particularly effective in raising grass-roots support and bringing nuclear issues to the forefront in the 1980s.

Caldicott was born on August 7, 1938, in Melbourne, Australia, the daughter of a factory manager, Philip Broinowski, and an interior designer, Mary Mona Enyd (Coffey) Broinowski. She received a public-school education except for four years spent at Fintona Girls School in Adelaide, a private secondary school. She recalls today that she was strongly affected as an adolescent by reading Nevil Shute's *On the Beach,* a novel about nuclear devastation set in Australia. At the age of 17, she enrolled at the University of Adelaide Medical School, graduating in 1961 with a B.S. in surgery and an M.B. in medicine (the equivalent of an American M.D.).

She moved to Boston with her husband in 1966 for a three-year fellowship in nutrition at Harvard Medical School. Returning to Adelaide in 1969, she accepted a position in the renal unit of Queen Elizabeth Hospital. In the early 1970s at the same hospital, she completed a year's residency and a two-year internship in pediatrics. She also set up a clinic for cystic fibrosis.

Rallies Australian Antinuclear Mass Movement

Both her work with children afflicted with cystic fibrosis, a genetic disorder, and her experience as an expectant mother assuming responsibility for her own children persuaded Caldicott that she had to take a more active role in ensuring a future for human beings. In 1971, she discovered that France had been conducting nuclear tests over its South Pacific colony

Helen Caldicott

of Mururoa for the previous five years and had done so in violation of the International Atmospheric Test Ban Treaty of 1962. Fallout from the tests drifted towards Australia and entered the food chain in various ways. A confidential South Australian government report, for instance, confirmed that higher than normal levels of radiation were present in drinking water in 1971 and in rain in 1972. Caldicott organized opposition at a time when few Australians were aware of either the testing or the radioactive fallout that had resulted. She began by sending a letter of protest to a local newspaper. Subsequently, she made radio and television appearances, commenting on the medical risks of radiation. From her work in pediatrics she was acutely aware that children are more sensitive to the effects of radiation than adults. She always emphasized this fact, appealing to her audience as parents responsible for the well-being of their children. She made public the confidential report (passed on to her by a sympathizer within the state government) describing elevated radiation levels in drinking and rain water. Her speeches began a mass movement against the French tests that had thousands taking part in protest marches and resulted in a boycott of French products. When, in December 1972, the Australian Labor Party swept the Liberal Party out of office, the government undertook legal action against France through the International Court of Justice. Although the court ruled ambiguously, the French government ceased atmospheric testing in the face of widespread organized opposition.

Caldicott was less successful in her attempt to organize against the commercial exploitation of uranium, a relatively rare raw material necessary for most nuclear technology. Australia has rich uranium deposits and exported the material to many different countries. Caldicott got union backing for her proposed export ban by organizing among workers. She recalls today that her emphasis on the fact that radiation exposure causes a deformation of sperm cells (and thus a rise in the rate of birth defects) was her most potent argument. The Australian Council of Trade Unions passed a resolution against the mining, transport, and sale of uranium in 1975. In the same year the government imposed the desired export ban. Under international pressure, however, the ban was lifted in 1982.

Caldicott returned to Boston in 1975, having received an appointment as a fellow in cystic fibrosis at the Children's Hospital Medical Center. Although she and her family went back to Australia for six months in 1976, they returned to the United States in 1977. At that time, she became an associate in medicine at the Children's Hospital Medical Center and an instructor in pediatrics at Harvard Medical School.

Leads Antinuclear Movement in the United States

Physicians for Social Responsibility was a group initially formed in 1962. By 1978, when Caldicott became involved with it, its membership had dwindled and its field of action narrowed significantly. It remained a small group until March 28, 1979, when Pennsylvania's Three Mile Island nuclear reactor came within sixty minutes of a possible meltdown. At once, more than five hundred physicians joined Physicians for Social Responsibility. Thereafter, its membership, budget, and size of paid staff continued to grow impressively. With Caldicott at its head, the group fought the nuclear industry, conducted research on the results of nuclear war, worked politically for nuclear disarmament, and conducted numerous symposia and sponsored countless lectures. Caldicott gave up the practice of medicine in 1980 to devote herself to full-time leadership of the organization. Her gifts as a public speaker had a tremendous impact on a great many audiences. Caldicott consciously espouses a feminine ethic of nurturance, exhorting women to become more aggressive in their role as caretakers of humanity and appealing to men to cultivate the elements of nurturing in their lives. Physicians for Social Responsibility also made a powerful documentary film, *Eight Minutes to Midnight,* which was featured on a tour with Caldicott and was nominated for an Academy Award in 1982. In addition to delivering numerous speeches in church, labor, university, and other settings, she wrote *Nuclear*

Madness: What You Can Do! with Nancy Herrington and Nahum Stiskin. The book provides detailed descriptions of the medical and environmental results of nuclear war as well as political prescriptions for preventing it.

The growth of the organization brought more diverse membership, which, after becoming unwilling to follow Caldicott in her opposition to nuclear power in addition to nuclear weapons, pushed for a more mainstream position. As a result, she resigned as president in 1983, but continued to serve on the board of directors. She also helped found the Medical Campaign Against Nuclear War, the Women's Action for Nuclear Disarmament, the Women's Party for Survival and a number of other organizations concerned with nuclear and other environmental issues. Her second book, *Missile Envy: the Arms Race and Nuclear War,* came out in 1984.

Caldicott's speeches and writings combine detailed medical descriptions with a highly personal and sometimes emotional approach. She describes the devastating physical results of a nuclear detonation in elaborate detail as it would affect particular individuals according to their geographical location. Medical metaphors and analogies illustrate political and environmental problems, while her personal experiences lend force to the narrative. Her own joy in having and raising her children gave her a heightened concern for the future of the earth. Caldicott's witness to this personal experience often makes her successful in convincing audiences that nuclear dangers are not abstract but threaten every individual human life. Although she makes a particularly strong appeal to women, occasionally arguing that women are particularly suited to save the earth from the warmongers and transnational corporations, she also has a strong following among men.

Her books have gained praise but criticism as well, even at times from those who would seem to be her natural allies. Some critics have pointed to superficial documentation and inaccurate statements in overly polemical presentations. She has also been criticized for failing to recognize that her arguments are essentially middle class and do not address the concerns of working-class people. Yet Caldicott has also been praised for bringing awareness of nuclear dangers to center stage and for offering concrete, grass-roots political programs for combatting those dangers.

Returning to Australia, Caldicott ran for a seat in parliament in 1990, losing by a very narrow margin. Since then, she has published a third book, *If you Love This Planet: A Plan to Heal the Earth* (1992), which focuses more broadly on environmental issues than her previous publications. At home in Canberra, she lives by her environmental convictions. As she told reporter Will Nixon, interviewing her for *E Magazine* in 1992, "I've just planted 400 eucalyptus and rain-forest trees on my land. It was like having a baby, the joy it gave me because I'm replenishing the land." She is also experimenting with systems of self-sustaining agriculture.

Caldicott's numerous awards include the Humanist of the Year Award from the American Association of Humanistic Psychology in 1982, and the International Year of Peace Award from the Australian government in 1986. She was one of the nominees for the Nobel Peace Prize in 1985 and holds many honorary degrees. In 1962, she married William Caldicott, a pediatric radiologist, who has worked with her in her campaigns. They have three children, Philip, Penny, and William Jr.

SELECTED WRITINGS BY CALDICOTT:

Books

(With Nancy Herrington and Nahum Stiskin) *Nuclear Madness: What You Can Do!,* Autumn Press, 1978, revised edition, Bantam, 1980.
Missile Envy: The Arms Race and Nuclear War, Morrow, 1984.
If You Love This Planet: A Plan to Heal the Earth, Norton, 1992.

SOURCES:

Books

Browne, Ray B., Glenn J. Browne, and Kevin O. Browne, editors, *Contemporary Heroes and Heroines,* Gale, 1990, pp. 52–55.
McGuinness, Elizabeth Anne, *People Waging Peace: Stories of Americans Striving for Peace and Justice in the World Today,* Alberti Press, 1988.
Ryan, Bryan, editor, *Major Twentieth-Century Writers,* Volume 1, Gale, 1991, pp. 486–488.

Periodicals

Coles, Robert, "The Freeze: Crusade of the Leisure Class," *Harper's,* Volume 270, March, 1985, pp. 21–23.
Dyson, Freeman, "Weapons and Hope, I: Questions," *New Yorker,* Volume 59, February 6, 1984, pp. 52–54 ff.
Nixon, Will, "Helen Caldicott: Practicing Global Preventative Medicine," *E Magazine,* Volume 3, September/October, 1992, pp. 12–15.
Review of *If You Love This Planet, Sierra Club Bulletin,* July/August, 1992, pp. 91–92.

—Sketch by Pamela O. Long

Clive O. Callender
1936-
American surgeon

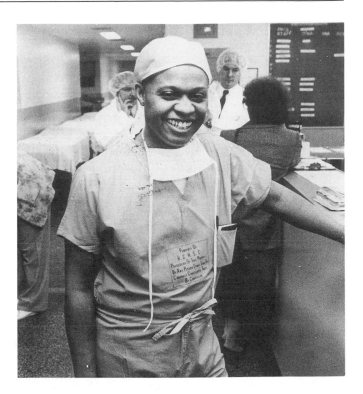

Clive O. Callender

Clive O. Callender has been at the forefront of promoting organ donor programs in the United States and abroad. As the transplant director at Howard University Hospital in Washington, D.C., and as professor of the hospital's department of surgery, Callender is a leading transplant surgeon and spokesperson for health issues pertaining to the African American community.

Clive Orville Callender was born on November 16, 1936, to Joseph Callender and Ida Burke in New York City. He was inspired at an early age to become a missionary doctor after hearing a sermon in his church. Callender graduated from Hunter College in New York in 1959 with degrees in chemistry and physiology and then attended Meharry Medical College in Nashville, Tennessee. In 1963 he graduated first in his class and won the Charles Nelson Gold Medal. He married Fern Irene Marshal in May of 1968, and they eventually had three children: Joseph, Ealena, and Arianne.

During his internship at the University of Cincinnati, Callender became interested in surgery and obtained further training in the specialty as chief resident at Howard University and Freedmen's Hospital. He became an instructor at the university in 1969; the following year he became a medical officer at D.C. General Hospital. Shortly thereafter, his invitation to work as a surgeon at Port Harcourt General Hospital in Nigeria (during the Biafran Civil War) fulfilled his dream of being a missionary doctor.

Upon returning to the United States, Callender became interested in transplant surgery and was granted a two-year National Institutes of Health fellowship and a one-year fellowship at the University of Minnesota to become a transplant specialist. Following this, he formed a transplant center at Howard University. Ten years later in 1983 Callender established another transplant center in the Virgin Islands, which was named in his honor.

Callender became concerned when he detected a resistance among African Americans toward donating organs. His inquiry into the issue uncovered that many felt that needy minorities were less likely to receive an organ transplant than white patients. Some objected to transplants because the procedure violated their religious beliefs about not disturbing the body after death. Others were afraid they would be declared dead prematurely if they had promised an organ.

Callender has travelled throughout the United States, Europe, and the Caribbean on his mission to dispel these misconceptions about organ and tissue transplants. Together with organ donors, recipients, and those waiting for transplants, he has given workshops aimed at increasing the number of minority donors. In addition, he testified before the U.S. Senate in 1983, in a successful attempt to increase government funding for community education on the issue. Callender's efforts have begun to pay off—a 1990 Gallup poll found that 24 percent of African Americans surveyed said they had signed organ donor cards, up from seven percent in 1985.

Callender sees organ transplant awareness as a crucial issue for African Americans because they represent 30 percent of all dialysis patients and because they often fare poorly after the procedure. To prevent a backlash, Callender told *New York Times* writer Paul Delaney that "blacks themselves have to do more," and become more involved in health care issues.

In 1989 Callender was elected to the Hunter College Alumni Hall of Fame. As of 1994, he was the only African American member of the Task Force on Organ Procurement and Transplantation. Since 1979, he has also been the president of the National Capitol Area branch of the National Kidney Foundation.

SELECTED WRITINGS BY CALLENDER:

Periodicals

(With G. M. Dunston) "Organ Donation in Blacks: Once a Dilemma, Now a National Commitment," *Black Health,* 1988, Volume 1, pp. 22–25.

(Contributor) "Special Report: Organ Donation and Blacks, A Critical Frontier," *New England Journal of Medicine,* August 8, 1991.

SOURCES:

Books

Burgess, Marjorie, "Clive O. Callender," *Contemporary Black Biography,* Gale, 1993.

Periodicals

Delaney, Paul, "Fighting Myths in a Bid to Get Blacks to Consider Transplants," *New York Times,* November 6, 1991.

—*Sketch by Linda Lewin*

Melvin Calvin
1911-
American chemist

Melvin Calvin began his academic career with an interest in the practical and physical aspects of chemistry. His greatest accomplishments, however, have been in the interactions between chemistry and the life sciences. In 1961, Calvin was honored with the Nobel Prize in chemistry for his elucidation of the mechanism by which carbon dioxide is incorporated into green plants. In the years that followed, he pursued his interest in some unusual applications of chemistry, such as researching oil-bearing plants for their possible development as alternative energy sources and in the search for other forms of life that may exist in the universe.

Calvin was born in St. Paul, Minnesota, on April 8, 1911, to Elias and Rose Irene (Hervitz) Calvin. Both Calvin's parents had emigrated from Russia in the 1880s: his father from an urban area in northern Russia and his mother from a rural region in southern Russia. Calvin's father had apparently been well-educated before coming to the United States and, in spite of the fact that he ended up as a factory worker, always put a high value on developing intellectual skills.

The Calvins moved to Detroit, Michigan, when Melvin was a young boy so that his father could take a job at the Cadillac factory there. Calvin received both his grade school and high school education in the Detroit Public Schools but his studies made little lasting impact on him. Calvin's only recollection from his high school science classes was a physics teacher telling him that he would never become a scientist because he was too impulsive, because he didn't wait to collect *all* the data needed to solve a problem. Calvin observed that the physics teacher didn't really understand the process of scientific advancement: if one were really to know *all* the data, a computer alone would be all that would be necessary to derive a conclusion.

Calvin's interests in science developed as a result of internal forces. He describes walking home from school with a friend and, in a sudden flash of insight, suddenly understanding the role of atoms as the building blocks of all matter in the universe. For Calvin, that moment was a great thrill because it was his own "personal discovery." By the time he reached high school, Calvin knew that he wanted to become a chemist or, more precisely, a chemical engineer.

The Great Depression Pushes Calvin into Chemical Engineering

Calvin pursued his dream of becoming a chemist after he graduated from high school in 1927. He enrolled at the Michigan College of Mining and Technology (now Michigan Technological University) in Houghton, but had to leave at the end of two years. The first rumblings of the Great Depression were being felt, and Calvin could not afford to stay in school. Instead, he got a job at a brass factory in Detroit where he rapidly became familiar with a number of chemical procedures. The experience convinced him to continue with his plans to major in chemical engineering because "I figured I would always be in demand." He looked closely at the world in which he lived and saw chemical applications everywhere. In a time of economic depression, with his father out of work, it was the possibility of making a living rather than "grand questions about the universe," that, he told Swift, determined his career choice.

In any case, Calvin soon returned to the Michigan College of Mining and completed his bachelor of science degree in 1931. He then entered the doctoral program in chemistry at the University of Minnesota. At Minnesota, he gave evidence of the wide-ranging chemical interests that would be characteristic of his professional career. After pursuing problems in both physical and organic chemistry, he finally settled on a

Melvin Calvin

problem involving the electron affinity of iodine and bromine for his doctoral thesis. Successful completion of that research earned him a Ph.D. degree in 1935.

In the same year, Calvin was awarded a Rockefeller Foundation fellowship allowing him to spend two years of postgraduate study at the University of Manchester, England. At Manchester, Calvin worked under **Michael Polanyi**, professor of physical chemistry. One of Calvin's research assignments involved studying the role of metalloporphyrins—organic molecules from which are derived chlorophyll and hemoglobin—in various catalytic reactions. Such assignments were a modest preview of the research he would undertake three decades later when studying chlorophyll and that compound's role in photosynthesis. According to *Nobel Prize Winners,* Calvin's interest in coordination catalysis remained "paramount" for many years after his work at Manchester, eventually resulting "both in theoretical (the chemistry of metal chelate compounds) and practical (oxygen-carrying synthetic chelate compounds) applications."

Appointment to the University of California at Berkeley

At the conclusion of his two years in Manchester, Calvin accepted an appointment as instructor of chemistry at the University of California at Berkeley. Two important influences at Berkeley were **Gilbert N. Lewis** and G. E. K. Branch, fellow chemists who

spurred Calvin's interests in the structure and behavior of organic molecules.

Calvin's first promotion at Berkeley—to assistant professor—came in 1941, only months before the United States' entry into World War II. Although he continued to teach during the war, Calvin became actively involved in the national war effort, first as an investigator for the National Defense Research Council, and later as a researcher in the Manhattan Project. His most important wartime contribution was the development of a process for obtaining pure oxygen directly from the atmosphere. Variations of that process now have a number of applications, as in machines that provide a continuous supply of oxygen for patients with breathing problems.

After the war, Calvin remained active in national and military organizations. He served as a member of the chemistry advisory committee of the Air Force Office of Scientific Research from 1951 to 1955 and as a delegate to the International Conference on Peaceful Uses of Atomic Energy in Geneva in 1955. In 1942, Calvin was married to Marie Genevieve Jemtegaard, a social worker whose parents were Norwegian immigrants. The Calvins would eventually have two daughters, Elin Bjorna and Karole Rowena, and one son, Noel Morgen.

Calvin was promoted to the position of associate professor in 1945 and to full professor in 1947. In the intervening years, he was also appointed director of the Bioorganic Chemistry Group at the University of California's Lawrence Radiation Laboratory. Calvin pointed out to Swift that this appointment was one of the very few administrative positions he has ever held because "You can't do both jobs [research and administration]." He only agreed to the Lawrence post, he said, in order to insure that he would have "an infrastructure on which I could do my job."

Research on Photosynthesis Brings the Nobel Prize in Chemistry

By 1948, Calvin had begun the research for which he is most famous, the elucidation of the process of photosynthesis. Scientists had known the general outlines of that process since the late eighteenth century, a process with which all beginning science students are familiar. In that process, carbon dioxide and water combine with each other in the presence of sunlight to form complex organic compounds known as carbohydrates. Scientists had also long known that photosynthesis is a far more complex process than is suggested by this simple summarizing statement. They knew that the conversion of carbon dioxide to carbohydrates involves many discrete chemical reactions, some of which were then vaguely known, but most of which were not.

Calvin's foray into the photosynthesis question was not without its problems. The only instruction in biology he had ever received came by way of a course in paleontology at Michigan Tech. Thus, when colleagues in the biology department at Berkeley learned that Calvin was about to take on one of the fundamental problems in biology, they could have been forgiven for some doubts about the successful conclusion of that work. Still, Calvin applied himself to mastering the study of biology for more than a decade, from about 1945 to the late 1950s. Eventually, he was able to convince biologists that he knew what he was talking about when he spoke to them about photosynthesis.

As with most scientific discoveries, unraveling the process of photosynthesis was possible only after the development of certain essential research tools and techniques. In this case, the most important of those tools and techniques were radioactive tracer isotopes and chromatography, the ability to separate the compounds within a solution. The radioactive tracer isotope that Calvin needed—carbon–14—had been available only since 1945. Carbon–14 is an extremely valuable research tool in biological research since, while it behaves in plants and animals in exactly the same way as non-radioactive carbon does, its emission of beta and gamma radiation make it continuously detectable to a researcher.

The design of Calvin's research on photosynthesis was elegantly simple. He maintained a water suspension of the green alga called chlorella in a thin glass flask that could be exposed to light. He then introduced to the flask, under controlled conditions, a certain amount of carbon dioxide consisting of carbon–14. As it carried out its normal life processes, the chlorella incorporated the radioactive carbon–14, converting it to carbohydrate. All Calvin had to in order to study the photosynthesis taking place was to stop the reaction at various points and analyze the compounds present in the chlorella.

The analysis required the use of the second new research tool, chromatography. In paper chromatography—one of many methods available—a mixture of compounds such as that obtained from the chlorella is allowed to diffuse along a strip of paper. Each compound diffuses at its own characteristic rate and can be identified by its position on the strip after a given period of time. The presence of a tracer isotope such as carbon–14 makes the process even simpler. By placing a photographic film in contact with the paper strip, the radioactive isotope "takes its own picture" as a result of the radiation it releases. The film offers a distinct record of the isotope's position on the paper strip.

Probably the greatest technical problem Calvin faced was deciding what compound was represented by each spot on the chromatogram. A decade after

beginning his research, however, he had the answer he was seeking. The first set of reactions and compounds he proposed were not entirely accurate, but he reworked the series of reactions until correct. That set of reactions is now known to all biochemists as the Calvin cycle. It was in recognition of his determination of the cycle of carbon in photosynthesis that Calvin was awarded the 1961 Nobel Prize in chemistry, as well as a number of other honors, including his 1959 election to the Royal Society and receipt of its prestigious Davy Medal five years later.

But receiving the Nobel Prize did not end Calvin's career in chemistry. Shortly after he traced the path of carbon through the photosynthetic process, Calvin did the same for oxygen, this time using a radioactive isotope of that element.

In 1960, Calvin assumed the directorship of the Laboratory of Chemical Biodynamics at Berkeley, a place where many new and exciting types of research were taking place, including studies on brain chemistry, radiation chemistry, solar energy conversion, and the origins of life on Earth. The last of these topics was one in which Calvin had been particularly interested for some time. During the 1950s, a vigorous debate had been going on among scientists as to whether the Earth's primitive atmosphere had consisted exclusively of reducing gases, such as hydrogen, methane, and ammonia, or whether it was an oxidizing atmosphere that also included gases such as carbon dioxide. During this time, Calvin carried out a series of experiments in which a hypothetical primitive atmosphere consisting of hydrogen, carbon dioxide, and water was exposed to intense radiation provided by Berkeley's 60-inch cyclotron. The experiment resulted in the formation of a number of simple organic molecules, such as formaldehyde, formic acid, and glycolic acid. When a similar experiment was later repeated by Calvin's student **Cyril Ponnamperuma**, with nitrogen included this time, simple amino acids—the building blocks of life—were also found among the products.

Calvin's interest in the origins of life on Earth has led him in another direction also: the possibility of life elsewhere in the universe. His own feeling has been that the conditions that led to the formation of life on Earth could hardly have been unique in the universe. Instead, he has argued, "we can assert with some degree of scientific confidence that cellular life as we know it on the surface of the Earth does exist in some millions of other sites in the universe."

During the 1970s, Calvin began research on yet another somewhat unusual application of chemistry, the development of alternative fuels. He discovered that certain members of the rubber tree family produce a sap-like material that can be burned in much the same way as petroleum. He suggested the possibility that such trees could be grown on huge plantations in order to provide an alternative source of energy as our supply of crude oil continues to diminish. With his wife, Calvin eventually established an experimental farm in Northern California to test out this idea.

As Calvin's academic career came to a close, he continued to receive the recognition of his peers in the field of science. In 1978, he was awarded the Priestley Medal of the American Chemical Society (ACS) and the Gold Medal of the American Institute of Chemists. In 1981, Calvin was awarded the Oesper Prize by the ACS. To balance a public life dedicated to science, Calvin has long maintained a number of personal interests, including photography, gardening, politics, and sports.

SELECTED WRITINGS BY CALVIN:

Books

(With G. E. K. Branch) *The Theory of Organic Chemistry,* Prentice-Hall, 1941.
(With A. E. Martell) *Chemistry of the Chelate Compounds,* Prentice-Hall, 1949.
(With others) *Isotopic Carbon,* Wiley, 1949.
(With J. A. Bassham) *The Path of Carbon in Photosynthesis,* Prentice-Hall, 1957.
Chemical Evolution, Oxford University Press, 1961.

SOURCES:

Books

Current Biography 1962, H. W. Wilson, 1962, pp. 68–70.
McGraw-Hill Modern Men of Science, Volume 1, McGraw-Hill, 1984, p. 85.
Nobel Lectures in Chemistry, 1942–1962, Amsterdam, 1964, pp. 645–646.
Nobel Prize Winners, H. W. Wilson, 1987, pp. 176-177.
Swift, David, *SETI Pioneers,* University of Arizona Press, 1990, pp. 116-135.

—*Sketch by David E. Newton*

Jessie G. Cambra
1919-
American engineer

As a pioneering engineer and manager, Jessie G. Cambra's progressive ideas and leadership were vital during the development of California's transportation systems. Cambra broke new ground in both her academic and professional pursuits—besides being was the first female graduate of the University of California, Berkeley, school of engineering, she developed and supervised the first successful highway reconstruction project in California. Cambra was also responsible for the design of the first computerized integrated traffic signal system in a major arterial intersection. The recipient of a 1979 Achievement Award from the National Society of Women Engineers, she was recognized for her outstanding contributions to the planning, design, management and actuation of numerous major public works projects. Cambra progressed from a field engineer to the deputy directorship of public works in a career that spanned thirty years.

Cambra was born in Oakland, California, on September 15, 1919. Her mother, Blanch Prenveille, worked as a bookkeeper, and her father, Andrew Giambroni, was a businessman and banker. Reflecting on her childhood, Cambra commented to writer Mary Raum that "being from a family of five, there was nothing my brothers could do that I couldn't do, so I pursued engineering." Although Cambra had been told that women could not succeed in the field of engineering, she nevertheless applied for and was accepted to the engineering program at the University of California, Berkeley, and in 1942 she became the first woman to graduate with a B.S. degree in civil engineering. Cambra (then Jessie Giambroni) married Manuel S. Cambra on November 6, 1943.

Considering her entrance into the field of engineering, Cambra told Raum, "Had the second world war not occurred when I graduated, I might not have ever entered the field of engineering. There was a great shortage of engineers available to private engineering firms since all the men were in the armed services." Immediately following her graduation from college, Cambra was hired as a field engineer for Bechtel, McCone & Parons of San Francisco, California. Within five months her work on the construction of a major oil refinery for Standard Oil Company earned her a promotion to assistant civil engineer. Early in 1944, Cambra left the private sector and began her public service career in Alameda County, California—an affiliation that lasted until her retirement in 1979. After only one year with the county, she qualified for a promotion to civil engineer. In the same year, 1945, Cambra became the first licensed woman engineer to be registered by examination in California. She joined the East Bay Engineers' Club, an organization for which she was eventually elected president in 1975.

Became Assistant Chief of the Road Department

At the end of World War II, hundreds of technically competent men began to return to the United States. Rivalry for jobs became keen, but Cambra's talents kept her ahead of her challengers. In 1947, she gave birth to her first son and continued to work on the design of roads, road appurtenances, and drainage systems. She was selected to join the American Public Works Association, for which she later became the first woman director. In 1951, when her first son, Joe, was four years old, Cambra attained the title and responsibilities of senior civil engineer and was given charge of several road and bridge construction projects. Within fourteen months, she obtained her sixth promotion in ten years, to supervising civil engineer. Notable among her achievements in this management position were her production of the designs for two major road construction projects and the design for a reinforced concrete bridge.

In 1953, Cambra was appointed principal civil engineer in charge of the engineering division of the Alameda County Road Department. Her work included a variety of road improvement programs and supervision of proposed land development proposals. During her twenty-year stay in this position Cambra was responsible for a number of technological accomplishments, such as the initiation of an in-house computer program that increased the efficiency of engineering analyses and broadened the number of design options available to engineers. Cambra also oversaw many departmental reorganizations and managed her staff in an era of rapid change from manual to computerized innovations in road and transportation services.

Pressured by the conflicting demands of motherhood and her career, Cambra declined two opportunities for advancement after her second son was born in 1957. In 1960, however, she became the first female member of the County Engineers Association of California, serving as its representative to the California transportation commission of the California State Legislature as well as member to several committees.

In 1973, Cambra was appointed assistant chief of the Alameda County Road Department. In this position she acted in place of the deputy director, who was terminally ill. Cambra's leadership skills proved highly successful in what had become an increasingly sensitized public, media, and legislative arena—the San Francisco Bay area was in the midst of rapid population growth, placing a profound strain on the public works of the region.

Officially Named Head of the Road Department

In November, 1974, Cambra was named deputy director of public works and became head of the Alameda-County-Road Department. She worked with a twelve million dollar budget, managed two hundred employees, and organized public works programs for 547 miles of county roads. She oversaw the planning, design, and construction of industrial boulevards, entrance roads to primary service institutions such as universities, concrete reinforced bridges, movable bridges, rehabilitation projects, and signalized intersections. Cambra also initiated and administered the Federal Aid to Urban Highways Program, which required oversight of thirteen city and two mass transportation districts, and served in a public relations capacity with the public and the media.

Throughout her career, Cambra continued her education through extension programs, conventions, and seminars, studying law, real estate, technical writing, computer technology, and engineering design. Before retiring in 1980, Cambra was named the 1977 recipient of the Samuel A. Greeley Award for her outstanding public service in the field of public works. She was recognized in 1978 by the Hayward Boy's Club for her fundraising efforts and was ranked as a top ten engineer by the American Public Works Association. In addition, Tau Beta Pi (the engineering fraternity at the University of California, Berkeley) named her an Outstanding Alumna. Cambra related to Raum that her "major personal and professional contribution to the field was to prove that women were as good as men in the field of engineering."

After thirty-six years with Alameda County, Cambra retired and opened her own office as a consulting engineer. She did estimate work and prepared qualifying plans for public works subcontractors and tract developments. At age seventy-five she remains actively involved in the community, assisting elderly California residents with income tax issues. Commenting to Raum on her notable achievements as an engineer and public servant, Cambra stated, "What I enjoyed most about my work was to see the completed projects in operation and to know I had a small part in its creation."

SOURCES:

Books

Civil Engineering Handbook, McGraw, 1962.
The Engineer in America: A Historical Analogy from Technology and Culture, University of Chicago Press, 1991.
Human Aspects of Man-made Systems, Open University Press, 1977.

Other

Cambra, Jessie G., personal information supplied
to Mary Raum, January, 1994.

—*Sketch by Mary Raum*

Alexa I. Canady
1950-
American neurosurgeon

Alexa I. Canady is the first African American woman to become a neurosurgeon in the United States. Honored with numerous professional and academic awards, she has since held several teaching posts and is the director of neurosurgery at Children's Hospital of Michigan in Detroit.

Alexa Irene Canady was born November 7, 1950, in Lansing, Michigan, to Elizabeth Hortense Golden Canady, an educational administrator, and Clinton Canady, Jr., a dentist. She has three brothers: Clinton III, Alan, and Mark. As the only black girl in her elementary school, Canady experienced racism at an early age. In an interview with Brian Lanker in *I Dream a World: Portraits of Black Women Who Changed the World,* she stated: "During the second grade I did so well on the California reading test that the teacher thought it was inappropriate for me to have done that well. She lied about what scores were mine, and ultimately, she was fired." By the time Canady was in high school in the 1960s, however, she was recognized as a National Achievement Scholar.

While pursuing a mathematics degree at the University of Michigan, Canady attended a minority health careers program and subsequently redirected her studies, receiving a B.S. in 1971 and an M.D. in 1975. As a student, she was elected to Alpha Omega Alpha honorary medical society and received the American Medical Women's Association citation. Canady's internship was spent at the Yale-affiliated New Haven Hospital in 1975–76. After completing the internship, she gained her landmark residency in neurosurgery at the University of Minnesota from 1976 to 1981. Afterward, Children's Hospital in Philadelphia awarded Canady a fellowship in pediatric neurosurgery in 1981–82. Besides treating patients directly, Canady served as an instructor in neurosurgery at the University of Pennsylvania College of Medicine.

In 1982, she moved back to Michigan and took a post in neurosurgery at Henry Ford Hospital in Detroit. The following year, she transferred to pediatric neurosurgery at Children's Hospital of Michigan. She became the assistant director of neurosurgery at Children's Hospital three year's later, and director in 1987. She was named Teacher of the Year there in 1984, the same year she was certified by the American Board of Neurological Surgery. Canady was honored as Woman of the Year by the Detroit chapter of the National Association of Negro Business and Professional Women's Club in 1986 and received the Candace Award from the National Coalition of 100 Black Women in the same year. She began teaching at Wayne State University School of Medicine as a clinical instructor in 1985 and assumed a clinical associate professorship in 1987. Canady married George Davis in June 1988.

SELECTED WRITINGS BY CANADY:

Periodicals

(With J. Donders and B. P. Rourke) "Psychometric Intelligence after Infantile Hydrocephalus: A Critical Review and Reinterpretation," *Childs Nervous System,* May 1990, pp. 148–154.
(With S. Sood, S. Kim, and others) "Useful Components of the Shunt Tap Test for Evaluation of Shunt Malfunction," *Childs Nervous System,* June 1993, pp. 157–162.
(With R. D. Fessler and M. D. Klein) "Ultrasound Abnormalities in Term Infants on ECMO," in *Pediatric Neurosurgery,* July-August, 1993, pp. 202–205.

SOURCES:

Books

Lanker, Brian, *I Dream a World: Portraits of Black Women Who Changed the World,* Stewart, Tabori, 1989, p. 128.
Smith, Jessie Carney, editor, *Notable Black American Women,* Gale, 1992, pp. 155–156.

Periodicals

Ross-Flanigan, Nancy, "Hall of Fame Inductees Followed Their Hearts: Canady Is at Home with Neurosurgery," *Detroit Free Press,* October 17, 1989, p. 1C.

—*Sketch by Linda Lewin*

Annie Jump Cannon
1863-1941
American astronomer

Annie Jump Cannon

Annie Jump Cannon was the best-known American woman astronomer of her time. Educated at Wellesley College, Cannon spent her professional life at the Harvard College Observatory. Her most lasting contribution is the cataloging system she developed that rationally arranges stars by their temperatures and compositions. In her lifetime she classified the spectra of hundreds of thousands of stars, filling ten volumes. In recognition of this achievement, the National Academy of Sciences awarded Cannon the Henry Draper Medal in 1931.

Cannon was born on December 11, 1863, in Dover, Delaware, eldest of the three children of Wilson Lee Cannon, a shipbuilder, farm owner, and state senator, and his second wife, the former Mary Elizabeth Jump. Annie also had four siblings from her father's first marriage. Her mother, who had been educated at a school run by Quakers near Philadelphia, taught Annie the constellations. As a child, Cannon observed the night sky through an attic window, reading her astronomical guidebook by candlelight.

Cannon received her early education at local schools. She graduated from the Wilmington Conference Academy (Methodist) in 1880 and continued her education at Wellesley College in Massachusetts. At Wellesley, she studied with Sarah Frances Whiting, a professor of physics and astronomy. Cannon also delved into spectroscopy, the measurement of the various wavelengths that make up light.

After receiving her bachelor's degree from Wellesley in 1884 Cannon returned to the family home in Dover, where she lived for ten years. Her interest in astronomy persisted, however, and she visited Italy and Spain to observe a solar eclipse. She also pursued her interest in photography. In 1894, following her mother's death, Cannon returned to Wellesley for post-graduate studies. There she worked as a teaching assistant in physics for professor Whiting and participated in experiments to confirm **Wilhelm Conrad Röntgen**'s discovery of X rays. Her interest soon turned to stellar spectroscopy, however, and in 1895 she enrolled at Radcliffe College as a special student in astronomy.

Cataloguing the Stars

In 1896, Cannon became an assistant at the Harvard College Observatory through the support of Edward Pickering, director of the observatory and a leader in the field of spectroscopy. There she began a study of variable stars (stars whose light output varies because of internal fluctuations or because they are eclipsed by another star) and stellar spectra (the distinctive mix of radiation every star emits). She worked for a time at Harvard's astronomical station in Arequipa, Peru, which had been established by Pickering and his brother, William.

Using a hybrid scheme that combined the classification systems developed by **Antonia Maury** and Williamina P. Fleming, Cannon classified 1,122 bright stars whose spectra had been photographed at Arequipa. Cannon's system arranged stars according to the color of the light they emit, which is determined by their temperature. She classified as types O, B, and A the hot, white or blue stars. The type F and G stars, like our own sun, are yellow. Type K stars are orange, and type M, R, N, and S are reddish and therefore relatively cool. This system made possible the easy classification of all stars in relatively few, rationally related categories. In 1910 the astronomical community adopted her new method, known as the "Harvard system." In 1911 Cannon was promoted to curator of astronomical photographs. At this time she began one of the most extensive collections of astronomical data ever achieved by a single observer, the Henry Draper Catalogue of stellar spectra. Published by the Harvard College Observatory in 10 volumes from 1918 to 1924, the catalogue lists the spectral types of 225,300 stars, their positions in the sky, their visual and photographic magnitudes, and includes notes on the eccentricities of particular stars. As soon as Cannon finished this survey, she began enlarging the catalogue to include fainter stars in the Milky Way, the Large Magellanic Cloud, and other selected regions of the cosmos. In all, Cannon classified the spectra of some 400,000 stars in her lifetime.

During the same period Cannon pursued her interest in variable stars. In 1903 she issued a catalogue of the 1,227 variable stars known at the time. Subsequently, she published a second catalogue of variable stars (1907), with precise data and notes on 2,000 stars. In the course of her work, she discovered 300 previously unknown variables and five novae.

Highly esteemed by her colleagues, Cannon was active in professional activities such as the annual meeting of astronomical societies. Astronomers from all over the world visited her at Star Cottage, her home in Cambridge, Massachusetts. She received a number of honorary degrees and awards, including election to the American Philosophical Society (1925). Cannon was the first woman to receive the Henry Draper Gold Medal of the National Academy of Sciences (1931), the first woman to receive an honorary doctoral degree from Oxford University, and the first woman elected to an office of the prestigious American Astronomical Society (treasurer, 1912–1919). In 1929, the National League of Woman Voters listed her as one of the twelve greatest living American women. In 1938 she was appointed William Cranch Bond Astronomer at Harvard University.

Cannon's achievements came at a time in the history of science when the roles for women in astronomy and other male-dominated disciplines were severely limited by prevailing social attitudes and prejudices about women's abilities. Writing about this period, scholars John Lankford and Rickey L. Slavings observe: "Although the field took in large numbers of women, gender dictated who collected data, who reduced it, who analyzed it and who published the results. The assignment of roles reflected the perceptions male astronomers had of females, and those perceptions in turn mirrored the values of American culture."

An incident involving the National Academy of Sciences (NAS) illustrates the extent to which the reward system of science, traditionally held to be based on merit, was influenced by gender. In 1923, two prominent members of the NAS discussed the possibility of electing Cannon to the ranks of the academy, an honor which no women had at that time received. Despite the support of several distinguished fellow astronomers and Cannon's recognized contributions to science, her candidacy received little support, and she was not elected into the academy.

Cannon held her position at Harvard University until her retirement in 1940. She continued observing until shortly before she died in Cambridge on April 13, 1941, at the age of 77.

SELECTED WRITINGS BY CANNON:

Books

Henry Draper Catalogue, in *Annals of the Harvard Observatory,* Volumes 91–99. 1918–1924.

SOURCES:

Books

Rossiter, Margaret W., *Women Scientists in America: Struggles and Strategies to 1940,* Johns Hopkins University Press, 1982.

Periodicals

Lankford, John, and Slavings, Rickey L., "Gender and Science: Women in American Astronomy, 1859–1940," *Physics Today,* March, 1990, pp. 58–65.

New York Times, April 14, 1941, p. 17.

—Sketch by Daniel Pendick

Georg Cantor
1845-1918
Russian-born German mathematician

Georg Cantor, a German mathematician, developed a number of ideas that profoundly influenced twentieth-century mathematics. Among other accomplishments, he introduced the idea of a completed infinity, an innovation that earned him recognition as the founder and creator of set theory. His revolutionary insights, however, were accepted only gradually and not without opposition during his lifetime. The praise for his work was best epitomized by the famous mathematician **David Hilbert**, who said that "Cantor has created a paradise from which no one shall expel us." Besides being the founder of set theory, Cantor also made significant contributions to classical analysis. In addition, he did innovative work on real numbers and was the first to define irrational numbers by sequences of rational numbers.

Georg Ferdinand Ludwig Philipp Cantor was born on March 3, 1845, in St. Petersburg, Russia, the first child of Georg Woldemar Cantor and Maria Böhm. The family moved to Frankfurt, Germany, in 1856 when the father became ill. His father, born in Copenhagen, had moved to St. Petersburg at a young age and had become a successful stockbroker there. His mother came from an artistic family. Cantor's brother Constantin was an accomplished piano player and his sister Sophie had drawing talents. Cantor himself sometimes expressed regret that he had not become a violinist. Of Jewish descent on both sides, Cantor was nevertheless raised in an intensely Christian atmosphere. The breadth and depth of his knowledge of the old masters, theologians, and philosophers was brought about by his religious upbringing and became evident in his more philosophical writings.

At a young age, while still in St. Petersburg, Cantor showed clear signs of mathematical talent. Though he wanted to become a mathematician, his father had charted out an engineering career for him. He attended several schools along the lines of his father's wishes, including the Gymnasium in Wiesbaden and, from 1860, a Technical College in Darmstadt. Cantor finally received parental approval to study mathematics in 1862. He started his studies in the fall of that year in Zurich, but moved to Berlin after one semester. Cantor was a solid student. He spent a summer semester in Göttingen in 1866 and successfully defended a Ph.D. thesis in number theory on December 14, 1867, in Berlin. Cantor then moved to the University of Halle as a *Privatdozent,* becoming an associate there in 1872 and a professor in 1879. He remained at Halle for his entire career.

A friend of his sister's, Vally Guttmann, became his wife in 1874. During their honeymoon in Switzerland, the couple met Richard Dedekind, from then on a friend and mathematical confidant of Cantor's. Georg Cantor and Vally Guttmann had six children.

Discovers Set Theory

When Cantor arrived at Halle, the leading mathematician there was Heinrich Heine, under whose influence Cantor began to study Fourier series. His analysis of the convergence of these trigonometric series eventually led to far-reaching innovations. What started as a slight improvement of a theorem on the uniform convergence of Fourier series contained the first seeds of set theory. Cantor's first paper on set theory proper was published in 1874 under the title *Über eine Eigenschaft des Inbegriffes aller reellen algebraischen Zahlen* and dealt with algebraic numbers. An algebraic number is any real number that is a solution to an equation with integer coefficients. Cantor's paper contained the proof that the set of all algebraic numbers can be put in a one-to-one corre-

spondence with the set of all positive integers. Moreover, Cantor proved that the set of all real numbers cannot be put into a one-to-one correspondence with the positive integers. As he later explained it, the set of positive integers has the same power (called *Mächtigkeit* in German) as the set of algebraic numbers, while the power of the set of real numbers is different from either. The 1874 paper was accepted for publication only after Dedekind's intercession.

The set of all algebraic numbers, containing, for example, the square root of 2, is properly larger than the set of all rational numbers (that is, quotients of integers). In turn, the set of rationals contains infinitely many more elements than the set of positive integers. In spite of that, Cantor showed that the three sets—the rationals, the algebraic numbers, and the positive integers—have the same power. Sets like the algebraic numbers or the rationals are said to be countable, and Cantor furnished proof that this is so. However, he discovered that the set of all real numbers is not countable. Encouraged by these successes, Cantor introduced the notion of equipollency of sets in his next paper, written in 1878. Two sets are equipollent if a one-to-one correspondence exists between them. Where he had previously shown that the set of algebraic numbers is equipollent with the set of positive integers, Cantor then proved that the set of points on any surface such as a plane is equipollent to the set of all real numbers. He finished the 1878 paper with the conjecture that every infinite subset of the set of real numbers is either countable or equipollent to the set of all real numbers. That conjecture became known as the continuum hypothesis. The possibility of a one-to-one correspondence between an infinite set and one of its proper subsets had been observed earlier by scientists such as Galileo and Gottfried Leibniz. The novelty and courage of Cantor's contributions are in his refusal to consider this a contradiction and in using it to define infinite sets of equal power.

Consolidates Set Theory

Cantor's next paper was published in six installments between 1879 and 1884. Where he had previously come to grips with the countable and had realized the gap between the countable and the continuum, his ideas about infinite sets in general had ripened. The paper broaches the idea of a proof of the continuum hypothesis. In 1882, Cantor defined another main concept of set theory, that of well-ordering. In 1883 he wrote that we may assume as a law of thought that every set can be well-ordered. Earlier, in 1878, Cantor had stated, without proof, "If two point-sets M and N are not equipollent then either M will be equipollent to a proper subset of N or N will be equipollent to a subset of N." This principle later became known as the trichotomy of cardinals. However, Cantor was not able to give a solution to the continuum hypothesis or a proof of the trichotomy of cardinals.

In 1884, Cantor had a nervous breakdown; several of such mental crises would follow. He had applied for a professorship in Berlin but was turned down, strongly opposed by Leopold Kronecker, a former teacher of his. In spite of his illness, Cantor remained active. He worked to institute the German Mathematical Society, founded in 1889, and was instrumental in establishing the first International Congress of Mathematicians in 1897 in Zurich. Between 1895 and 1897 Cantor published his last paper, *Beiträge zur Begründung der transfiniten Mengenlehre* ("Contributions to the Foundation of Transfinite Set Theory") in two parts. In these he defined the transfinite numbers that measure the magnitude of infinite sets.

While there was little enthusiasm for his discoveries within his own country of Germany at this time, Cantor's ideas were gaining support in the world mathematical community. The eventual recognition of sets as a notion underlying all of mathematics led to new fields like topology, measure theory, and set theory itself. Developments at the turn of the century reflected the importance of Cantor's work. At the Second International Congress of Mathematicians in Paris in 1900, the continuum hypothesis was first amongst twenty-three problems that Hilbert proposed as central to the development of twentieth-century mathematics. Not much later, in 1904, the mathematician Ernst Zermelo established that every set can be well-ordered, using the so-called axiom of choice. From it followed the trichotomy of cardinals. The earlier controversy between Kronecker and Cantor intensified into a new rage about what was and what was not permitted in mathematics. Much of the debate was later settled by the work of **Kurt Friedrich Gödel** and **Paul Cohen**. The first book on set theory was published in 1906 by William H. Young and **Grace C. Young**. These years also showed the beginnings of the study of topology. In 1911, **L. E. J. Brouwer** proved the topological invariance of dimension, at which Cantor himself had tried his hand earlier. In 1914, Hausdorff published the first book on topology, entitled *Grundzüge der Mengenlehre* ("Principles of Set Theory").

Toward the end of his career Cantor's achievements were recognized with various honors. He became honorary member of the London Mathematical Society (1901) and the Mathematical Society of Kharkov and obtained honorary degrees at several universities abroad. A bust of Cantor was placed at the University of Halle in 1928. Perhaps more fittingly, one special subset of the real numbers that he introduced is now known under his name, the Cantor set. Cantor died on January 6, 1918, at the psychiatric hospital in Halle.

SELECTED WRITINGS BY CANTOR:

Books

Gesammelte Abhandlungen Mathematischen Und Philosophischen Inhalts, edited by Ernst Zermelo and with a biography by Adolf Fraenkel, Georg Olms Verlagsbuchhandlung, 1966.

SOURCES:

Books

Bell, E. T., *Men of Mathematics,* Simon & Schuster, 1986.
Gillispie, Charles Coulson, editor, *Dictionary of Scientific Biography,* Volume III, Scribner, 1971, pp. 52–58.
Itô, Kiyosi, editor, *Encyclopedic Dictionary of Mathematics,* Volume I, MIT Press, 1987, p. 169.
Moore, Gregory, H., *Zermelo's Axiom of Choice, Its Origins, Development, and Influence,* Springer Verlag, 1982.
Noether, Emmy and Jean Cavaillès, *Briefwechsel Cantor-Dedekind,* Hermann, 1937.
Young, Laurence, *Mathematicians and Their Times,* North Holland Publishing Company, 1981.

Periodicals

Stern, Manfred, "Memorial Places of Georg Cantor in Halle," *Mathematical Intelligencer,* Volume 10, 1988, pp. 48–49.

—*Sketch by Gerard J. Buskes*

Manuel Cardona
1934-
Spanish-born American physicist

The elements germanium and silicon are the stuff of Manuel Cardona's research. Those basic substances, which at ordinary temperatures conduct electricity with a potential somewhere between a metal and an insulator, are also at the very heart of the information age; germanium is an important part of the transistor while silicon is used to manufacture the silicon chip of the personal computer. Cardona, employing basic experimental models and investigative tools such as optical spectroscopy, has helped to elucidate the properties of these all-important elements and thus stretch the boundaries of both semiconductor and superconductor research.

Born on September 7, 1934, in Barcelona, Spain, Manuel Cardona showed an early propensity for technology, building and repairing all sorts of electrical equipment. His father, Juan Cardona, was a small-time businessman who barely eked out a living, and his mother, Angela Cardona, was a school teacher. Brought up during the Spanish Civil War, Cardona personally experienced the vicissitudes of that conflict: his father was arrested by Franco for supposed "contacts" with Freemasons. He attended a state high school in Barcelona, and it was there he started focusing on his twin loves, mathematics and physics, encouraged by several excellent teachers. By graduation, he had set his course on a career in science, studying physics at the University of Barcelona from 1950 to 1955. He earned his Licenciado Degree *Summa Cum Laude* and won the Spanish National Prize for the best academic record in the sciences. The following year he went on to do graduate work at Harvard University, researching the effects of light, magnetism, and electricity on germanium and silicon, work which led to his Doctor of Science degree from the University of Madrid in 1958. Further research on dielectric or nonconducting properties of germanium and silicon led to a Ph.D. from Harvard in 1959. That same year, he married Inge Hecht. They have three children: Michael, born in 1959, Angela, born in 1961, and Steven, born in 1964.

From Semiconductors to Superconductors

Cardona joined RCA labs in Switzerland upon graduation from Harvard and then moved to their labs in New Jersey. In 1964 he accepted a position at Brown University as associate professor of physics. In 1966 he became a full professor and remained at Brown until 1971, when he was offered the prestigious directorship of the newly-founded Max Planck Institute of Solid State Research in Stuttgart, Germany, where he has remained ever since. His work during these years included not only spectroscopic analysis of germanium and silicon, but also of materials exhibiting superconductivity. Superconductors are certain metals and alloys that are capable of being almost perfect conductors of electricity at temperatures close to absolute zero. Cardona investigated such materials from 1962 to 1971. Later research at the Max Planck Institute has included a return to superconductivity research, but at high temperatures. He characterizes his research methods as an attempt to extract the maximum amount of information possible from basic experiments. Simplicity is his trademark. Many of his over eight hundred technical papers have become classics in the field, and several of his books are standard texts. In addition to conducting his research

and administrative duties at the Max Planck Institute, Cardona has trained a new generation of solid state physicists as well as serving as editor for several technical journals. A holder of honorary doctorates around the world, Cardona has also been recognized for his research by the 1984 Frank Isakson Prize from the American Physical Society and the 1992 Excellence in Superconductivity Award of the World Congress on Superconductivity. Cardona is a naturalized U.S. citizen.

SELECTED WRITINGS BY CARDONA:

Books

Modulation Spectroscopy, Academic Press, 1965.
(Editor) *Light Scattering in Solids,* Volumes 1–6, Springer Verlag, 1975–91.
(With Peter Y. Yu) *The Physics of Semiconductors,* Springer Verlag, 1994.

Periodicals

(With R. L. Johnson, J. Barth, D. Fuchs, et al.) "Spectroscopic Ellipsometry with Synchrotron Radiation," *Review of Scientific Instruments,* July, 1989, pp. 2209–2212.
(With Z. V. Popovich, E. Richter, D. Strauch, et al.) "Phonons in GAAS/ALAS Superlattices Grown Along the [111] Direction," *Physical Review B-Condensed Matter,* March 15, 1990, pp. 5904–5913.
(With others) "High TC Superconductors—An Introduction and Raman Spectroscopy," *Journal of the Less-Common Metals,* October 15, 1990, pp. 989–993.
(With M. L. Bansal and A. K. Good) "Strongly Dispersive Low Frequency Raman Modes in Germanium," *Solid State Communications,* May, 1991, pp. 579–582.
(With J. Kircher, A. Zibold, H. P. Geserich, et al.) "Dielectric Tensor of YBA2CU4O8—Experiment and Theory," *Physical Review B-Condensed Matter,* August 1, 1993, pp. 3993–4001.

SOURCES:

Cardona, Manuel, interview with J. Sydney Jones, conducted February 8, 1994.

—*Sketch by J. Sydney Jones*

W. Warrick Cardozo
1905-1962
American physician

In 1935, W. Warrick Cardozo was a young pediatrician working at Children's Memorial and Provident hospitals in Chicago under a General Education Board fellowship when, with the aid of a grant from Alpha Pi Alpha fraternity, he began one of the first studies of sickle-cell anemia—a condition in which the majority of red blood cells are crescent-shaped. He found that sickle-cell anemia is inherited. He also established that the disease strikes African Americans almost exclusively, does not cause death among all of the victims of the disease, and that not all persons whose blood contains the sickle cells actually suffer from anemia. These findings arose thirteen years before the nature and characterization of the hemoglobin abnormality that causes sickle-cell anemia was discovered and before the disease became a subject of considerable intensive research.

Born April 6, 1905, in Washington, DC, William Warrick Cardozo was the third generation in his family to attain prominence. His father, Francis L. Cardozo, Jr., was a school principal; his grandfather an educator and politician. William attended Washington public schools, then Hampton Institute in Virginia. At Ohio State University, he received an A.B. degree in 1929 and a M.D. degree four years later. He served his internship at City Hospital in Cleveland, and a residency in pediatrics at Provident Hospital in Chicago.

Cardozo entered private practice in Washington, DC, in 1937, the same year the results of his sickle-cell anemia studies appeared in the Archives of Internal Medicine. He began teaching pediatrics part time at Howard University College of Medicine, where eventually he became a clinical associate professor. He did not stop refining his own learning; in 1942 he sought and gained certification by the American Board of Pediatrics, and in 1948 the American Academy of Pediatrics granted him fellowship. His special interest later turned to children's gastrointestinal disorders.

Despite the demands of a medical practice, Cardozo contributed more than his share of public service. For twenty-four years he served the District of Columbia Board of Health as the school medical inspector. He also served on the Advisory Committee of the District of Columbia Crippled Children's Society. At Howard University College of Medicine, where he taught for many years, he founded Alpha Omega Alpha Honorary Society. On August 11, 1962, Cardozo suffered a fatal heart attack. He was survived by his wife, Julia M. Cardozo, his daughter, Judy, and five sisters.

SELECTED WRITINGS BY CARDOZO:

Periodicals

"Immunologic Studies in Sickle Cell Anemia," *Archives of Internal Medicine,* October, 1937.
(With Katsuji Kato) "Hodgkin's Disease with Terminal Eosinophilia," *Journal of Pediatrics,* February, 1938.
(With Roland B. Scott and others) "Growth and Development of Negro Infants. III. Growth During the First Year of Life," *Journal of Pediatrics,* 1950.

SOURCES:

Books

Dictionary of American Negro Biography, Norton, 1982, p. 90.

Periodicals

Ebony, December, 1948, pp. 19–23.

—*Sketch by Penelope Lawbaugh*

David Cardús
1922-
Spanish-born American physician

A specialist in cardiology and biomathematics, David Cardús is known for his work with mathematical and computer applications for the study of physiological systems, as well as for his research on experimental exercise and respiratory physiology.

Cardús was born August 6, 1922, to Jaume and Ferranda Pascual Cardús of Barcelona, Spain. He received B.A. and B.S. degrees at the University of Montpellier in France in 1942, then attended the University of Barcelona, earning an M.D., magna cum laude, in 1949. He completed his internship at Hospital Clínico, University of Barcelona, and his residency at Sanatorio del Puig d'Olena in Barcelona. In 1953 Cardús accepted a two-year French government research fellowship in cardiology in Paris. He returned to take his diploma in cardiology at the University of Barcelona, then accepted a British research fellowship at the University of Manchester's Royal Infirmary, after which he departed Europe to take up residence in the United States.

In 1957, Cardús joined the Lovelace Foundation in Albuquerque as a research associate. Three years later he began a long association with the Institute for Rehabilitation and Research at Baylor College of Medicine in Houston, where he has served on the medical staff as a professor in the rehabilitation and physiology departments, as director of the biomathematics division, and as head of the exercise and cardiopulmonary laboratories. In addition, he has taught mathematical sciences and statistics at Rice University in Houston for many years and has served as a consultant to the U.S. Public Health Service in the planning of health facilities.

Active in many professional societies, Cardús was president of the International Society for Gravitational Physiology in 1993, and vice chairman of the Gordon Conference on Biomathematics in 1970. His work has been recognized with numerous awards from professional organizations both in the United States and in Spain. In the United States, he received a gold medal from the International Congress of Physical Medicine and Rehabilitation for a 1972 exhibit demonstrating the use of computers and telecommunications in rehabilitation, and first prizes from the International American Congress of Rehabilitative Medicine and the American Urological Association for other exhibits. He also earned an award for science writing from the American Congress of Physical Medicine and Rehabilitation. Honors garnered in Spain include recognition by the Generalitat de Catalunya and the Instituto Catalan de Cooperación Iberoamericana Fundación Bertran. In addition, Cardús has served as chairman of the board of the Institute for Hispanic Culture in Houston and as president of Spanish Professionals in America.

Cardús married Francesca Ribas in 1951, and they have four children. He became a U.S. citizen in 1969.

—Sketch by Penelope Lawbaugh

Chester Carlson
1906-1968
American physicist and inventor

Motivated by a need for a convenient way to reproduce patent drawings, Chester Carlson developed the electrostatic dry-copying process known as xerography. This process made possible the

Chester Carlson

photocopying machine, now an essential piece of office equipment and an invaluable tool in such areas as the preservation of archival materials, the publishing industry, and libraries. After years of neglect, Carlson's idea was developed by others into a product that has revolutionized the workplace all over the world. Yet Carlson remained out of the public spotlight, preferring the distribution of his profits to charitable institutions to the creation of a dynasty for himself.

Chester Floyd Carlson was born on February 8, 1906, in Seattle, Washington, the son of Olaf Adolph Carlson, a barber. His parents were invalids: his father was disabled by arthritis, and both parents suffered from tuberculosis. In an effort to find a climate that might be beneficial to their health, the family moved first to Mexico and then to San Bernardino, California, where they rented a small farm. As a result of his parents' inability to work, Carlson became the sole support of his family from the age of fourteen. His mother's death when Carlson was seventeen left him to care for his father alone. Despite this, he put himself through college—first at Riverside, California, and later at the California Institute of Technology—while working as a janitor and a printer's devil. By 1930, when he received a bachelor of science degree in physics, he had accumulated $1,400 in debts.

Carlson went to work in the patent department of the Bell Telephone Company while he attended law school in the evenings; after he was laid off from that job, he secured a position as a patent lawyer for the P.R. Mallory Company, an electronics firm in New York. Carlson became frustrated by the task of copying patent drawings and descriptions and sought a way to simplify the job. He was aware that experiments had been carried out using chemical or photographic processes to copy documents. Carlson's own experiments involved attempts to print by means of electrostatics, which he had read about in a report of experiments conducted by a Hungarian scientist.

His early experiments were carried out in his apartment in New York City, but after he married his first wife, Linda, he had to move his laboratory out of the house to avoid exposing her to the noxious chemicals—chiefly sulfur—involved in his work; his new laboratory was located in an apartment owned by Linda's mother in Astoria, Queens, Long Island, behind a beauty salon. It was in this apartment that Carlson performed his first successful attempt, in 1937, to transfer writing electrostatically. With the help of engineer and physicist Otto Kornei, a refugee from Nazi Germany, Carlson acquired the engineering background he had lacked.

The experiment devised by Carlson and Kornei used electrostatics to transfer writing from a glass plate to a metal one. The operating principle on which they based their experiments was that photoconducting materials retain a static charge in the dark, but lose it when exposed to light. Writing, with ink, the message "10–22–38, Astoria" on a piece of glass, Carlson created a static charge on a sulfur-coated zinc plate by rubbing it with a cloth. He then projected the glass slide onto the metal plate using a strong light source. When he dusted the plate with a black powder, it statically adhered to the plate where it had not been exposed—that is, to the area corresponding to the message. Pressing a piece of paper on top of the plate completed the transfer of the original message to paper. He named this process "electrophotography"; the term *xerography,* from the Greek for "dry writing," was later coined by a professor of Greek at Ohio State University.

The Machine Nobody Wanted

Carlson was awarded a patent for his photocopying method in 1940, and he followed this with five other patents, all written with the skill he had developed as a patent attorney. For five years he attempted to interest companies in the process—IBM had briefly shown some interest on two occasions—but his idea was rejected by nearly twenty companies, including Eastman Kodak, the A.B. Dick Company, and RCA. The reluctance of companies to take the process seriously was due in part to the poor quality of the images that resulted from the still primitive

device—smudged, on paper damaged by the heat involved in the process.

It was not until 1944 that the Battelle Memorial Institute in Columbus, Ohio, a nonprofit industrial research company, undertook development of the idea. Battelle, however, offered Carlson 25 percent of the profits, increasing to 40 percent if he could reimburse Battelle for its original investment (which had grown to $17,000) within five years. In the meantime, Carlson was to seek a source of financing for additional research; as with his original attempts to find an interested company, however, he was unsuccessful. The emotional and financial strain destroyed Carlson's marriage, and he began suffering from the arthritis that had plagued his father.

An article on electrophotography captured the attention of the Haloid Company of Rochester, New York, and by 1947 Haloid had purchased the commercial rights to the process; later, as Xerox (originally XeroX) Corporation, it would become a world leader in developing and marketing photocopying machines, although it was not until 1958 that it produced its first copying machine suitable for office use. During this period, Carlson remained protective of his methods and would not reveal the formula he had developed for the toner, or black ink, particles; according to John Dessauer in *My Years with Xerox,* the toner remains unpatented to this day in order to keep its components a secret.

Carlson, in the meantime, had married the former Dorris Hudgins. It was around this time that Carlson succeeded in raising enough money to present Battelle with a check for $17,000 and thereby become eligible for a 40 percent share of all profits. Although profits at this time were virtually non-existent, Carlson believed that eventually his invention would meet with the success it deserved. As the technique improved—by, for example, the replacement of hand-applied powders with a mechanical process—the quality of the image improved along with it.

The early machines, such as the Xerox Model A, were slow and cumbersome, although they were an improvement over the "wet" copiers then in use, which involved a two-stage process of exposure and development, and required the user to peel apart the negative and positive images while they were in their wet state and hang them up to dry. They also represented an improvement in convenience over mimeograph machines, with their messy inks and fragile stencils, and carbon paper, which produced a limited number of copies and was difficult to correct. But what made the Model A copier a strong competitor was its potential for saving time, money, and materials in the offset printing industry.

Once it was acknowledged by the industry that the masters generated by xerography could produce up to 20,000 copies without deterioration of image quality, interest spread in the new technique. The Haloid Company sought ways to take advantage of the increasing demand from the industry despite the company's still-limited financial resources. Company executives decided on a plan to lease, rather than sell, machines to other companies. Because of the expense of manufacturing them, the machines would have required an investment beyond the current abilities of the purchaser. Leasing them would make the machines available at a somewhat lower cost, the relatively small immediate cash return being offset by the wide exposure it would allow.

The Spiritual Philanthropist

While Haloid-Xerox continued developing a marketable xerography machine in the early 1950s, Carlson, apparently through the influence of his wife, developed an interest in psychic phenomena and the occult; he also began to voice an interest in promoting international good will and world peace. Dorris Carlson was a Zen Buddhist, and during this period Chet Carlson began studying Zen as well; friends and co-workers often spent evenings in their incense-filled home discussing Buddhism. The Carlsons began holding weekly meditation sessions, and Dorris Carlson became a leader of the local Zen Buddhist community in Rochester, New York.

On September 16, 1959, the Xerox 914 copier was introduced—the culmination of Carlson's research. The machine was called by *Fortune* magazine "the most successful product ever marketed in America," according to the authors of *Xerox: American Samurai.* By the early 1960s, Xerox profits had reached nearly $100 million. The name *Xerox,* although a registered trademark, has become a generic term—even a verb—for xerographic copiers and copying despite Xerox Corporation's insistence that the word always be capitalized.

By 1962 the Xerox machine had made Carlson a millionaire, giving him the financial resources he needed to pursue activities in support of international peace and good will. Carlson had become active in various philanthropic activities. He had become friends with United Nations General Secretary U Thant, and during the last eight years of his life he financed seminars on world peace associated with the U.N. as well as various research projects, including some concerned with psychic phenomena and spiritualism. His will listed numerous universities and other institutions as beneficiaries, and he ultimately left nearly $100 million to philanthropic concerns. Before he died, he gave a block of Xerox stock to Kornei, with whom he had developed the xerographic process in 1938.

Despite his close association with Xerox Corporation, Carlson was never on its payroll. He preferred the role of consultant, which allowed him a degree of independence and let him avoid the machinations and public scrutiny of the corporate world. Carlson remained an extremely shy, private man, but one who maintained the belief that his invention had the potential to change the world. Carlson collapsed from a heart attack while watching a movie in New York City and died on September 19, 1968. He was sixty-two. By the time of his death, the money Carlson had earned on his Xerox stock and royalties totaled more than $200 million, of which he gave away over three quarters.

SOURCES:

Books

Dessauer, John H., *My Years with Xerox: The Billions Nobody Wanted,* Doubleday, 1971.
Jacobson, Gary and John Hillkirk, *Xerox: American Samurai,* Macmillan, 1986.

Periodicals

"Chester F. Carlson Dead at 62; Invented Xerography Process," *New York Times,* September 20, 1968.
"The Invention Nobody Wanted," *Fortune,* July, 1962, p. 155.
"The Man Who Started It All," *Newsweek,* November 8, 1965, p. 77.
Wharton, Don, "Xerox: The Invention that Hit the Jackpot," *Reader's Digest,* March, 1965, pp. 121–124.

—*Sketch by Michael Sims*

Wallace Hume Carothers
1896-1937
American chemist

By the time he was forty, Wallace Hume Carothers had made significant contributions to the field of organic chemistry. Heading a research team at the Du Pont Company in Wilmington, Delaware, Carothers, in the late 1920s and 1930s, framed a general theory for the behavior and synthesis of polymers, huge chainlike molecules that indefinitely repeat the same structure. Two years after Carothers's death, Du Pont began mass production of a polymer he invented—nylon. This and Carothers's other well-known creation, synthetic rubber, laid the foundation for two

Wallace Hume Carothers

industries. In recognition of his services, Du Pont in 1946 named its new laboratory for synthetic fibers research the Carothers Research Laboratory.

Carothers was born on April 27, 1896, in Burlington, Iowa. His father, Ira Hume Carothers, was descended from Scottish farmers and artisans who had settled in Pennsylvania before the American Revolution. Born on an Illinois farm in 1869, Ira Carothers began teaching country school at nineteen. He then went to teach at the Capital City Commercial College in Des Moines, Iowa, where he stayed for forty-five years, eventually becoming vice-president. Hume's mother, Mary Evalina McMullin Carothers of Burlington, Iowa, descended from Scotch-Irish forebears who were mostly farmers and artisans as well. Mary Carothers's family had a strong musical background, which might explain her son's deep appreciation for music. Wallace Hume Carothers, the only scientist in his family, was the eldest of four siblings. One sister, Isobel, was a particular favorite of his. She became a star on the radio as Lu in the musical trio of Clara, Lu, and Em. Her death in 1937 was a loss from which Carothers never recovered.

Carothers began his education in the public schools of Des Moines, Iowa. As a boy he was recognized for his thoroughness in his schoolwork and exhibited an aptitude for experimenting with machines and working with his hands. Graduating from the North High School in 1914, he entered his father's school, the Capital City Commercial College, that fall.

He completed the accountancy curriculum at an accelerated pace, graduating in 1915. In September of the same year, he enrolled at Tarkio College in Missouri to pursue courses in science as well as to assist teaching in the accounting department. From the outset of his college years, Carothers excelled in chemistry and physics.

During World War I, the head of the institution's chemistry department, Arthur M. Pardee, left Tarkio, and the college could not find anyone qualified to fill the position. Carothers, who had taken all the chemistry courses the college had to offer, took over Pardee's duties. Ineligible for military service for health reasons, he served as head of the department all throughout the war. All of the four chemistry majors at Tarkio who studied under Carothers's supervision subsequently obtained doctorates in that field and later testified to his leadership capabilities.

In 1920, after graduating from Tarkio with a bachelor of science degree, Carothers entered the University of Illinois chemistry department, completing his master's degree by the summer of 1921. Arthur Pardee, the former head of the Tarkio chemistry department, had become the head of the chemistry department at the University of South Dakota. He needed someone to teach courses in chemistry and enticed Carothers to take the position for the fall and spring semesters. Carothers accepted Pardee's offer, intending to work just long enough to earn the money to pay for his graduate work.

While teaching, Carothers began to work on some of **Irving Langmuir**'s ideas as they related to organic chemistry. In one of the first papers Carothers published, "The Double Bond" (1924), he described the double bond between atoms, borrowing the notions from physics that Langmuir had developed. Although Carothers enjoyed his contact with the students at South Dakota, it became clear to him that teaching would always remain a distant second to research, which he pursued with prodigious energy and determination. To devote more time to it, he returned to the University of Illinois in 1922 to pursue his Ph.D., which he completed in 1924.

At the University of Illinois, Carothers mastered both organic and inorganic chemistry, and during the years 1923 and 1924 held the Carr fellowship, the chemistry department's highest award. His thesis paper, prepared under the supervision of **Roger Adams**, addressed the reactions undergone by organic compounds known as aldehydes with platinum as a catalyst, or enhancer, of the reactions. After Carothers received his doctorate, the university offered him a position in the chemistry department, which Carothers accepted in the fall of 1924.

Harvard University began a search for an instructor of organic chemistry in 1926 and selected Carothers out of a wide field of applicants. During his first year at Harvard, Carothers taught courses in experimental organic chemistry and structural chemistry, switching his second year to lecturer and lab leader for a course on elementary organic chemistry. He developed a reputation as a researcher with highly original ideas. While at Harvard, Carothers began his experimental investigations into chemical structures of high molecular weight polymers.

Founds Two Industries

In 1928 the Du Pont Company, having learned of Carothers's work with polymers, invited the scientist to become the director of a new research program at their flagship laboratory, the Experimental Station, at Wilmington, Delaware. The program's goal was fundamental research into industrial applications for what was then an emerging field of artificial materials, such as vinyl. Carothers would head an entire team of trained chemists whose duties would be to assist in his research aims. The position was an immense responsibility, but one that offered opportunities on a scale that Harvard could not match. Carothers accepted Du Pont's offer, and in the next nine years he and his team made significant advancements in the field of organic chemistry.

Carothers's creativity, enthusiasm, and capacity to bring out the best in his workers fostered an atmosphere that produced dozens of major contributions to both the theory of polymers and its applications. His initial investigations focused on molecules in the acetylene family, using methods based on discoveries of chemist and botanist Julius Arthur Nieuwland. This line of inquiry produced over twenty papers and patents. Carothers and his colleagues managed to combine vinylacetylene with a chlorine compound to create a polymer with properties like rubber. In 1931 Du Pont started to manufacture this product, which was marketed under the name neoprene.

In what was to prove even more fruitful, a separate area of research dealt with the creation of fibers whose structures resembled natural polymers such as silk and cotton. Carothers began experimenting with reactions among so-called fatty acids that were well understood by organic chemists at that time. What Carothers needed as the basis for his polymer chain was a reaction that would produce long molecules oriented in the same direction. His intuitions on the subject, which, before coming to Du Pont, he had already expressed in a letter to John R. Johnson of Cornell University on February 14, 1928, eventually paid off with the publication of thirty-one papers. With these writings he codified the terminology in the new field of polymers and proposed a general theory to explain the factors that govern their creation. His theories resulted not only in the production of the first synthetic fiber, nylon, in 1939, but

also illuminated how polymers in the natural world operate. New techniques in polymerization proliferated rapidly after Carothers's findings spread through the scientific community.

As Carothers's reputation grew, chemists throughout the world looked to him for advice and guidance. He wrote for and edited scientific journals, among them the *Journal of the American Chemical Society* and *Organic Synthesis*. A frequent speaker at chemists' groups, he made a famous address in 1935 entitled "Polymers and the Theory of Polymerization" to a summer colloquium at John Hopkins. A year later he became the first industrial organic chemist elected to the National Academy of Sciences.

Carothers married Helen Everett Sweetman, an employee of the patent division in Du Pont's chemical division, on February 21, 1936. They had one daughter, Jane, born on November 27, 1937. In spite of success and burgeoning fame, Carothers suffered from periodic bouts of depression that worsened over time, despite the efforts of his friends and colleagues. The death of his favorite sister, Isobel, in January of 1937 plunged Carothers into an emotional slide that proved irreversible. On April 29, 1937, he committed suicide in Philadelphia. His family buried his ashes in Glendale Cemetery in Des Moines, Iowa. Carothers was remembered as a shy man with a generous streak. He disliked publicity but was always ready to help anyone who came to him with a problem or a question. Quiet in a group, he became lively and humorous when talking one-on-one. He took great interest in the world about him, staying well informed on politics, business, and economics. A voracious reader since boyhood, he amassed a great knowledge of literature and philosophy. He enjoyed tennis, although his duties as head researcher at Du Pont eventually forced him to give up playing. Above all he loved music and possessed a talent for singing, a trait he shared with his mother and siblings.

SELECTED WRITINGS BY CAROTHERS:

Books

Collected Papers of Wallace Hume Carothers on High Polymeric Substances, edited by H. Mark Whitby and G. S. Whitby, Inter-Science Publishers, 1940.

Periodicals

"The Double Bond," *Journal of the American Chemical Society,* Volume 46, 1924, pp. 2226–2236.
"Association Polymerization and the Properties of Adipic Anhydride," *Journal of the American Chemical Society,* Volume 52, 1930, pp. 3470–3471.

(With Ira Williams, A. M. Collins, and J. E. Kirby) "Acetylene Polymers and Their Derivatives," *Journal of the American Chemical Society,* Volume 53, 1931, pp. 4203–4225.

SOURCES:

Books

Adams, Roger, "Wallace Hume Carothers, 1896–1937," *Biographical Memoirs,* Volume 19, National Academy of Sciences, 1938, pp. 293–309.
Dictionary of American Biography, Volume 11, Supplement 2, Scribner's, 1958, pp. 96–97.
Dictionary of Scientific Biography, Volume 3, Scribner's, 1971, pp. 85–86.

—*Sketch by Hovey Brock*

Alexis Carrel

Alexis Carrel
1873-1944
French medical scientist

Alexis Carrel was an innovative surgeon whose experiments with the transplantation and repair of body organs led to advances in the field of surgery and the art of tissue culture. An original and creative thinker, Carrel was the first to develop a successful technique for suturing blood vessels together. For his work with blood-vessel suturing and the transplantation of organs in animals, he received the 1912 Nobel Prize in medicine and physiology. Carrel's work with tissue culture also contributed significantly to the understanding of viruses and the preparation of vaccines. A member of the Rockefeller Institute for Medical Research for thirty-three years, Carrel was the first scientist working in the United States to receive the Nobel Prize in medicine and physiology.

Carrel was born on June 28, 1873, in Sainte-Foyles-Lyon, a suburb of Lyons, France. He was the oldest of three children, two boys and a girl, in a Roman Catholic family. His mother, Anne-Marie Ricard, was the daughter of a linen merchant. His father, Alexis Carrel Billiard, was a textile manufacturer. Carrel dropped his baptismal names, Marie Joseph Auguste, and became known as Alexis Carrel upon his father's death when the boy was five years old. As a child, Carrel attended Jesuit schools. Before studying medicine, he earned two baccalaureate degrees, one in letters (1889) and one in science (1890). In 1891, Carrel began medical studies at the University of Lyons. For the next nine years, Carrel gained both academic knowledge and practical experience working in local hospitals. He served one year as an army surgeon with the Alpine Chasseurs, France's mountain troops. He also studied under Leo Testut, a famous anatomist. As an apprentice in Testut's laboratory, Carrel showed great talent at dissection and surgery. In 1900, he received his medical degree but continued on at the University of Lyons teaching medicine and conducting experiments in the hope of eventually receiving a permanent faculty position there.

Early Success with Blood Vessel Sutures

In 1894, the president of France bled to death after being fatally wounded by an assassin in Lyons. If doctors had known how to repair his damaged artery, his life may have been saved, but such surgical repair of blood vessels had never been done successfully. It is said that this tragic event captured Carrel's attention and prompted him to try and find a way to sew severed blood vessels back together. Carrel first taught himself how to sew with a small needle and very fine silk thread. He practiced on paper until he was satisfied with his expertise, then developed steps to reduce the risk of infection and maintain the flow of blood through the repaired vessels. Through his careful choice of materials and long practice at various techniques, Carrel found a way to suture blood vessels. He first published a description of his success in a French medical journal in 1902.

Despite Carrel's growing reputation as a surgeon, he failed to acquire a faculty position at the university. His colleagues seemed indifferent to his research, and Carrel, in turn, was critical of the French medical establishment. The final split between Carrel and his peers came when Carrel wrote a positive account of a miracle he apparently witnessed at Lourdes, a small town famous since 1858 for its Roman Catholic shrine and often visited by religious pilgrims. In his article, Carrel suggested that there may be medical cures that cannot be explained by science alone, and that further investigation into supernatural phenomena such as miracles was required. This conclusion pleased neither the scientists nor the churchmen of the day.

In June, 1904, Carrel left France for the French-speaking city of Montreal, Canada; an encounter with French missionaries who had worked in Canada had sparked Carrel's interest in that country several years earlier. Shortly after his arrival, Carrel accepted an assistantship in physiology from the Hull Physiology Laboratory of the University of Chicago, where he remained from 1904 to 1906. The university provided him with an opportunity to continue the experiments he had begun in France.

Blood transfusion and organ transplantation seemed within reach to Carrel, now that he had mastered the ability to suture blood vessels. In experiments with dogs, he performed successful kidney transplants. His bold investigations began to attract attention not only from other medical scientists but from the public as well. His work was reviewed in both medical journals and popular newspapers such as the *New York Herald*. In the era of Ford, Edison, and the Wright Brothers, the public was easily able to imagine how work in a scientific laboratory could lead to major changes in daily life. Human organ transplantation and other revolutions in surgery did not seem far off.

Begins Lifetime Career at Rockefeller Institute

In 1906, the opportunity to work in a world-class laboratory came to Carrel. The new Rockefeller Institute for Medical Research (now named Rockefeller University) in New York City offered him a position. Devoted entirely to medical research, rather than teaching or patient care, the Rockefeller Institute was the first institution of its kind in the United States. Carrel would remain at the institute until 1939. At the Rockefeller Institute, Carrel continued to improve his methods of blood-vessel surgery. He knew that mastering those techniques would allow for great advances in the treatment of disorders of the circulatory system and wounds. It also made direct

blood transfusions possible at a time when scientists did not know how to prevent blood from clotting. Without this knowledge, blood could not be stored or transported. In the *Journal of the American Medical Association* in 1910, Carrel described connecting an artery from the arm of a father to the leg of an infant in order to treat the infant's intestinal bleeding. Although the experiment was a success, the discovery of anticoagulants soon made such direct transfer unnecessary. For his pioneering efforts, Carrel won the Nobel Prize in 1912.

Carrel's success with tissue cultures through animal experiments led him to wonder whether human tissues and even whole organs, might be kept alive artificially in the laboratory. If so, lab-raised organs might eventually be used as substitutes for diseased parts of the body. The art of keeping cells and tissue alive, and even growing, outside of the body is known as tissue culture. Successfully culturing tissue requires great technical skill. Carrel was particularly interested in perfusion—a procedure of artificially pumping blood through an organ to keep it viable. Carrel's work with tissue culture contributed greatly to the understanding of normal and abnormal cell life. His techniques helped lay the groundwork for the study of viruses and the preparation of vaccines for polio, measles, and other diseases. Carrel's discoveries, in turn, built upon the successes of, among others, Ross G. Harrison, a contemporary anatomist at Yale who worked with frog tissue cultures and transplants.

One of Carrel's experiments in tissue culture became the subject of a sensationalized news story and was viewed as a monstrosity by the public. In 1912, Carrel took tissue from the heart of a chicken embryo to demonstrate that warm-blooded cells could be kept alive in the lab. This tissue, which was inaccurately depicted as a growing, throbbing chicken heart by some newspapers, was kept alive for thirty-four years—outliving Carrel himself—before it was deliberately terminated. The *World Telegram,* a New York newspaper, annually marked the so-called chicken heart's "birthday" each January.

Though working in the United States, Carrel had not bought a house there, and did not become a U.S. citizen. Rather, he spent each summer in France, and on December 26, 1913, Carrel married Anne-Marie Laure (Gourlez de la Motte) de Meyrie, a widow with one son, in a ceremony in Brittany. They had met at Lourdes, where Carrel made an annual pilgrimage each August. Eventually, the couple bought some property on the island of Saint Gildas off the coast of Brittany, and lived in a stone house there. They had no children together.

When World War I began, Carrel was in France. The French government called him to service with the army, assigning him to run a special hospital near the front lines for the study and prompt treatment of severely infected wounds. There, Madame Carrel, his wife of less than one year and a trained surgical nurse, assisted him. In collaboration with biochemist Henry D. Dakin, Carrel developed an elaborate method of cleansing deep wounds to prevent infection. The method was especially effective in preventing gangrene, and was credited with saving thousands of lives and limbs. The Carrel-Dakin method, however, was too complicated for widespread use, and has since been replaced by the use of antibiotic drugs.

After an honorable discharge in 1919, Carrel returned to the Rockefeller Institute in New York City. He resumed his work in tissue culture, and began an investigation into the causes of cancer. In one experiment, he built a huge mouse colony to test his theories about the relationship between nutrition and cancer. But the experiment produced inconclusive results, and the Institute ceased funding it after 1933. Nevertheless, Carrel's tissue culture research was successful enough to earn him the Nordhoff-Jung Cancer Prize in 1931 for his contribution to the study of malignant tumors.

Artificial Heart Collaboration with Charles A. Lindbergh

In the early 1930s, Carrel returned again to the challenge of keeping organs alive outside the body. With the engineering expertise of aviator Charles A. Lindbergh, Carrel designed a special sterilizing glass pump that could be used to circulate nutrient fluid around large organs kept in the lab. This perfusion pump, a so-called artificial heart, was germ-free and was successful in keeping animal organs alive for several days or weeks, but this was not considered long enough for practical application in surgery. Still, the experiment laid the groundwork for future developments in heart-lung machines and other devices. To describe the use of the perfusion pump, Carrel and Lindbergh jointly published *The Culture of Organs* in 1938. Lindbergh was a frequent sight at the Rockefeller Institute for several years, and the Lindberghs and the Carrels became close friends socially. They appear together on the July 1, 1935, cover of *Time* magazine with their "mechanical heart."

Carrel's mystical bent, publicly revealed after his visit to Lourdes as a young man, was displayed again in 1935. That year Carrel published *Man, the Unknown,* a work written upon the recommendation of a loose-knit group of intellectuals that he often dined with at the Century Club. In *Man, the Unknown,* Carrel posed highly philosophical questions about mankind, and theorized that mankind could reach perfection through selective reproduction and the leadership of an intellectual aristocracy. The book, a worldwide best-seller and translated into nineteen languages, brought Carrel international attention.

Carrel's speculations about the need for a council of superior individuals to guide the future of mankind was seen by many as anti-democratic. Others thought that it was inappropriate for a renowned scientist to lecture on fields outside his own.

Unfortunately, one of those who disliked Carrel's habit of discussing issues outside the realm of medicine was the new director of the Rockefeller Institute. **Herbert S. Gasser** had replaced Carrel's friend and mentor, **Simon Flexner**, in 1935. Suddenly Carrel found himself approaching the mandatory age of retirement with a director who had no desire to bend the rules and keep him aboard. On July 1, 1939, Carrel retired. His laboratories and the Division of Experimental Surgery were closed.

Carrel's retirement coincided with the beginning of World War II in September, 1939. Carrel and his wife were in France at the time and Carrel immediately approached the French Ministry of Public Health and offered to organize a field laboratory, much like the one he had run during World War I. When the government was slow to respond, Carrel grew frustrated. In May, 1940, he returned to New York alone. As his steamship was crossing the Atlantic, Hitler invaded France.

Creates New Scientific Institute in Occupied Paris

Carrel made the difficult return to war-torn Europe as soon as he was able, arriving in France via Spain in February, 1941. Paris was under the control of the Vichy government, a puppet administration installed by the German military command. Although Carrel declined to serve as director of public health in the Vichy government, he stayed in Paris to direct the Foundation for the Study of Human Problems. The Foundation, supported by the Vichy government and the German military command, brought young scientists, physicians, lawyers, and engineers together to study economics, political science, and nutrition. When the Allied forces reoccupied France in August, 1944, the newly restored French government immediately suspended Carrel from his directorship of the Foundation and accused him of collaborating with the Germans. Mercifully, perhaps, a serious heart attack forestalled any further prosecution. Attended by French and American physicians, and nursed by his wife, Carrel died of heart failure in Paris on November 5, 1944. After his death, his body was buried in St. Yves chapel near his home on the island of Saint Gildas, Cotes-du-Nord.

Carrel's reputation remains that of a brilliant, yet temperamental man. His motivations for his involvement with the Nazi-dominated Vichy government remain the subject of debate. Yet there is no question that his achievements ushered in a new era in medical science. His pioneering techniques paved the way for successful organ transplants and modern heart surgery, including grafting procedures and bypasses.

SELECTED WRITINGS BY CARREL:

Books

Man, the Unknown, Harper & Brothers, 1935.
(With Charles A. Lindbergh) *The Culture of Organs,* Hoeber, 1938.
Prayer, Morehouse-Gorham, 1948.
Voyage to Lourdes, translated by Virgilia Peterson, Harper, 1950.
Reflections on Life, translated by Antonia White, H. Hamilton, 1952.

SOURCES:

Books

Durkin, Joseph T., *Hope for Our Times: Alexis Carrel on Man and Society,* Harper, 1965.
Edwards, William Sterling, *Alexis Carrel: Visionary Surgeon,* Thomas, 1974.
Malinin, Theodore I., *Surgery and Life: The Extraordinary Career of Alexis Carrel,* Harcourt, 1979.
Poole, Lynn, and Gray Poole, *Doctors Who Saved Lives,* Dodd, 1966, pp. 110–118.

—*Sketch by Liz Marshall*

Willis Carrier
1876-1950
American engineer and inventor

Willis Carrier is widely regarded as the father of modern refrigeration and air conditioning. Carrier received more than 80 patents over fifty years in the field of air conditioning. He was the founder and chief executive officer of the giant Carrier Corporation, one of the largest manufacturing companies in the United States, and his name has become almost synonymous with air conditioning.

Willis Haviland Carrier, an only child, was born on November 26, 1876, to Duane and Elizabeth Carrier, in Angola, a small town in upstate New York. He received his secondary education in the local school system and also attended the Buffalo General High School. Carrier won a competitive scholarship to study mechanical engineering at Cornel University in Ithaca, New York, where he was active in boxing, crew, and cross-country.

Begins a Career in Air Conditioning

Carrier graduated from Cornell in 1901, and accepted a position as an engineer with the Buffalo Forge Company in Buffalo, New York. From the beginning of his career, he was determined to put mechanical engineering on a more rational basis then what was the practice at that time. Because engineers did not really understand the reasons their machinery functioned the way they did, they were forced to build large "factors of safety" into their designs, which led to inefficiencies. To investigate the principals behind the functioning of the company's products, Carrier founded the world's first industrial laboratory at the Buffalo Forge Company. With the better understanding that he gave them, the Buffalo Forge designers were able to design better, safer, more efficient products. The laboratory more than paid for itself in its first year of existence.

Although the term air conditioning would not be coined for five years, Carrier's first design job as a young engineer was to develop an air conditioning system for the Sackett-Wilhelm lithographing company (lithography is a form of printing) in Brooklyn, New York. The problem faced by the Sackett-Wilhelm Company was not heat, but humidity. The paper in their printing plant would shrink or expand depending on the amount of water it absorbed from the air. Since color lithography requires separate printings for each color used, this variability in paper size made lining up the colors impossible. Carrier met this problem by designing a system for the company that cooled the air in its plant to a constant temperature and reduced the air's humidity. Work on the Sackett-Wilhelm problem with humidity, besides winning him a $20 a week raise, sparked Carrier's interest in the physical properties of air. His first major contribution to the field of air conditioning and refrigeration came in 1904 when he discovered that air could be dehumidified by spraying water through it. Carrier came to this conceptual breakthrough while waiting for a train on a fog-shrouded railroad platform. He realized that fog is nothing more than water vapor that has condensed out of air. From his research, Carrier knew that the amount of water vapor air can contain is dependent on the its temperature. As air's temperature drops, the amount of water vapor it can contain also drops. So, if humid air is cooled (by spraying cold water through it, for instance) the amount of water vapor it can contain drops. Eventually, despite the extra water being sprayed through it, the amount of water vapor in the air becomes greater than the maximum amount of water vapor the air can contain. When this happens, water vapor becomes water and fog or morning dew forms. The temperature where this occurs is called the air's "dew point." Within a few years the system was in use in industries as widespread as textiles and brewing. Interestingly, the fact that cool air was produced by Carrier's invention was only a side effect of the dehumidifying process. The original purchasers of his dehumidifier weren't interested in comfort, only in increasing the productivity of their facilities by getting rid of excess moisture in the air. Five years after joining the Buffalo Forge Company, Carrier had risen to become the company's chief engineer. In 1906 he convinced management that the promise of air conditioning was so great that they allowed him to found the Carrier Air Conditioning Corporation of America as a wholly-owned subsidiary of the Buffalo Forge Company. As Carrier had predicted, air conditioning soon became more important for the comfort it provided than for the industrial processes that it made possible. Air conditioning began to appear in theaters and concert halls and in the skyscrapers that were beginning to appear in New York City and Chicago. In 1911 Carrier was invited to give a lecture to the American Society of Mechanical Engineers, a high honor for someone so young. Carrier's lecture, published with the unpromising title of "Rational Psychometric Formulae," became the basis upon which the air conditioning industry was founded. Carrier's psychometric formulas describe the different combinations of temperature and humidity that are possible for air at a given pressure, and are still in use today. Using the formulas, an engineer can design an efficient air conditioner that is capable of converting air at one temperature and humidity into air at a second, presumably lower, temperature and humidity.

Founds the Carrier Corporation

Carrier and six of his subordinates left the Buffalo Forge Company in 1915 to found the Carrier Engineering Company. Started with $35,000, mainly the savings of its founders, the company prospered. The net worth of the company had risen to $4,000,000 in 1930 at the start of the Great Depression. Despite the Depression, air conditioning was an invention that's time had come. Carrier and his staff designed the first centrifugal compressor for use in air conditioners. The centrifugal compressor, besides being much smaller than its predecessors, was also much safer and efficient. Using it in combination with lightweight finned coils, he was able to design the portable air conditioners that became ubiquitous in the 1940s and 1950s. He had made air conditioning available for everyone. Carrier was also a pioneer in the refrigeration industry. He was elected president of the American Society of Refrigeration Engineers in 1927 in recognition of his work in that field. He also served as the president of the American Society of Heating and Ventilating Engineers in 1931. He received an honorary Doctor of Engineering degree

from Lehigh University and an honorary Doctor of Science from Alfred University. In 1949, the prestigious Newcomen Society of Great Britain honored him as the father of air conditioning. Carrier retired as chairman of the board of the Carrier Corporation in 1943. He devoted his retirement to spreading the benefits of air conditioning to the rest of the world. He died on October 10, 1950.

SOURCES:

Books

Ingels, Margaret, *Willis Haviland Carrier: Father of Air Conditioning,* [Garden City, New Jersey], 1952.
Wampler, Cloud, *Dr. Willis Carrier: Father of Air Conditioning,* Newcomen Society of England, American Branch, 1949.

—*Sketch by Jeff Raines*

George R. Carruthers
1939-
American astrophysicist

George R. Carruthers is best known for his invention of a camera and spectrograph—imaging devices—which uses ultraviolet light to capture images of both Earth and space from the surface of the moon. A team of engineers built a model according to his design for use during the Apollo 16 mission in 1972, and the resulting photographs provided startling new evidence about ways to control pollution in the Earth's atmosphere and about the presence of hydrogen in deep space.

Carruthers was born on October 1, 1939, in Cincinnati, Ohio. At an early age he developed an interest in physics, which his father, a civil engineer, encouraged. Carruthers was also an avid science fiction reader and enjoyed constructing model rockets. He grew up on the South Side of Chicago, graduated from Englewood High School in 1957, and entered the College of Engineering at the University of Illinois. He earned a B.S. in physics in 1961 and a M.S. in 1962; in 1964 he earned his Ph.D. in aeronautical and astronautical engineering, with a thesis written on atomic nitrogen recombination. In 1964 he was awarded a National Science Foundation fellowship in rocket astronomy at the Naval Research Laboratory in Washington, D.C.

In 1966, Carruthers became a research assistant at the Navy's E. O. Hulburt Center for Space Research, and here he began the work that would occupy him for much of the next several decades: the development of imaging devices to elucidate the make up of deep space. In particular, he concentrated on ultraviolet imaging mechanisms and spectroscopy—the use of the color spectrum of substances to detect their constituent parts. In 1969, he patented an image converter for detecting electromagnetic radiation. He then invented the Far Ultraviolet Camera/Spectrograph, a device which would examine both the Earth's atmosphere and deep space from a location that would avoid the distortions created by Earth.

Carruthers' imaging device was designed in effect to use the moon as a deep-space observatory. It took several years for the idea to become reality, but by 1972 Carruthers' camera/spectrograph was constructed—a gold-plated instrument mounted on a tripod. Commander John W. Young carried the device aboard the Apollo 16 mission and placed it on the surface of the moon. Over 200 pictures of the Earth's atmosphere and geocorona, as well as of the Milky Way and deep space, were taken from this lunar observatory. Much was learned about the Earth's atmosphere, including possible new ways to control air pollution. Most startling of all was the detection of hydrogen in deep space. This was evidence that plants are not the only source of Earth's oxygen, and the discovery also led to new thinking on the origins of stars. Carruthers' camera was also used on Skylab 4, when it observed Comet Kohoutek in 1974.

A private man, Carruthers devotes his life to his research and is characteristically low-key about his own contributions. Married in 1973, he has continued his work at the Naval Research Laboratory, developing a telescope to be used in space, as well as other photometric devices. A member of the American Astronomical Society and several other professional organizations, Carruthers won the Arthur S. Fleming Award in 1971, the Exceptional Achievement Scientific Award from NASA in 1972, the Warner Prize, and the National Civil Service League Exceptional Achievement Award.

SELECTED WRITINGS BY CARRUTHERS:

Periodicals

(With R. C. Henry) "Far-Ultraviolet Photography of Orion: Interstellar Dust," *Science,* October 30, 1970, pp. 527–531.
"Apollo 16 Far-Ultraviolet Camera/Spectrograph: Earth Observations," *Science,* September 1, 1972, pp. 788–791.

"Sounding Rockets in Space Astronomy," *Sky and Telescope,* October, 1972, pp. 218–221.
"Astronomy with the Space Shuttle," *Sky and Telescope,* September, 1974, pp. 152–156.
(With C. B. Opal) "Far-Ultraviolet Rocket Survey of Orion," *Sky and Telescope,* April, 1977, pp. 270–275.
(With others) "The Hydrogen Coma of Comet P-Halley Observed in Lyman Alpha Using Sounding Rockets," *Astronomy and Astrophysics,* May, 1992, pp. 555–565.

SOURCES:

Books

Blacks in Science: Ancient and Modern, Transaction Books, 1984, pp. 258–262.
Carwell, Hattie, *Blacks in Science: Astrophysicist to Zoologist,* Exposition Press, 1977, pp. 13–14.
Sammons, Vivian Ovelton, *Blacks in Science and Medicine,* Hemisphere Publishing Corporation, 1990, p. 49.

Periodicals

"Earth's Eye on the Moon," *Ebony,* October, 1973, pp. 61–63.
"Star Radiation Investigator," *Ebony,* October, 1970, p. 6.

—*Sketch by J. Sydney Jones*

Benjamin S. Carson
1951-
American pediatric neurosurgeon

Benjamin S. Carson is an internationally acclaimed neurosurgeon best known for leading a surgical team in a successful operation to separate Siamese twins. He is also recognized for his expertise in performing hemispherectomies, where half the brain is removed to stop seizures. He is the director of pediatric neurosurgery at Johns Hopkins University Hospital as well as assistant professor of neurosurgery, oncology, and pediatrics at the School of Medicine.

Born on September 18, 1951, Benjamin Solomon Carson came from a poor family in Detroit. He was the second son of Robert Solomon Carson, a Baptist minister, and Sonya Copeland Carson. His father was

Benjamin S. Carson

twenty-eight when he married, but his mother was only thirteen; she married in order to escape a difficult home situation. When Carson was only eight years old and his brother, Curtis, was ten, their parents divorced and his mother took them to live with relatives in a Boston tenement, while she rented out their house in Detroit. Working as many as three domestic jobs at a time, she earned enough money to move her family back to Detroit two years later.

Both Carson and his brother had a difficult time in school, and their low grades fanned the racial prejudice against them. But their mother took charge of their education, even though she herself had not gone past the third grade. By limiting the television they could watch and insisting they both read two books a week and report on them, she helped them raise their grades considerably. Carson discovered he enjoyed learning, and by the time he reached junior high school he had risen from the bottom to the top of his class.

But even then he continued to face racial prejudice; in the eighth grade, he listened to a teacher scold his class for allowing him, a black student, to win an achievement award. These early difficulties left Carson with a violent temper as a young man. He was often in fights: "I would fly off the handle," he told *People* contributors Linda Kramer and Joe Treen. Once he almost killed a friend in an argument. Carson tried to stab him in the stomach with a knife, but luckily the boy was wearing a heavy belt buckle, which

stopped the blade. Only fourteen at the time, Carson was shocked at what he had almost done, and he saw the direction his life could have taken. This experience drove him more deeply into his religion—he is still a Seventh-Day Adventist—and his faith in God helped him control his temper.

He studied hard and did so well during high school that he won a scholarship to Yale University. He received his bachelor's degree from Yale in 1973. He had always dreamed of becoming a doctor and was very interested in psychiatry, but once in medical school at the University of Michigan, he realized he was good with his hands and set his sights on neurosurgery. After completing medical school in 1977, he was one of the few graduates and the first black accepted into the residency program at Johns Hopkins Hospital in Baltimore. In 1983 because of a shortage of neurosurgeons in Australia, Carson was offered a chief neurosurgical residency at Queen Elizabeth II Medical Center in Perth, where he gained a great deal of operating experience. He returned to Johns Hopkins in 1984, and after a year he was promoted to director of pediatric neurosurgery, becoming one of the youngest doctors in the country to head such a division.

One of Carson's accomplishments was reviving the use of a procedure called hemispherectomy—an operation that removes half the patient's brain to cure diseases such as Rassmussen's encephalitis, which cause seizures. These operations had been stopped because of their high mortality rate, but with Carson's skills the procedure has been highly successful.

But Carson's best known accomplishment was the operation he performed in September 1987 to separate seven-month-old German Siamese twins, who were joined at the head. Carson was the lead surgeon on the team which performed "perhaps the most complex surgical feat in the history of mankind," as he described the operation to *Ebony*. There was a team of seventy medical staff members, including five neurosurgeons, seven pediatric anesthesiologists, five plastic surgeons, two cardiac surgeons, and dozens of nurses and technicians, and it took five months of preparation, including five three-hour dress rehearsals. A crowd of media people waited outside the operating room for Carson and his medical team to emerge, triumphant, at the end of the twenty-two-hour operation.

In 1988 Carson was awarded both the Certificate of Honor for Outstanding Achievement in the Field of Medicine by the National Medical Fellowship and the American Black Achievement Award. He has received honorary doctor of science degrees from several universities, and the Candle Award for Science and Technology from Morehouse College in 1989.

Carson married Lacena Rustin—whom he met at Yale—in 1975; she holds a M.B.A. degree and is an accomplished musician. They have three sons. Carson feels strongly about motivating young people to fulfill their potential, as he did, and he often lectures to students around the nation. He advises young people to "think big," and he has written a book by that title. Carson was also on the editorial advisory board of the Time-Life series *Voices of Triumph,* about the history and achievements of African Americans.

SELECTED WRITINGS BY CARSON:

Books

(With Cecil Murphey) *Gifted Hands, The Ben Carson Story,* Zondervan Publishing House, 1990.
Think Big: Unleashing Your Potential for Excellence, Zondervan Publishing House, 1992.

Periodicals

"Factors Affecting Minority Learning in Scientific Fields," *Journal of College Science Teaching,* March/April, 1988, pp. 340–341.

SOURCES:

Books

Blacks in Science and Medicine, Hemisphere Publishing Co., 1990.

Periodicals

Ebony, January, 1988, pp. 52–58.
People, Fall, 1991, p. 96.

—*Sketch by Linda Lewin*

Rachel Carson

Rachel Carson
1907-1964
American marine biologist

Rachel Carson is considered one of America's finest science and nature writers. She is best known for her 1962 book, *Silent Spring,* which is often credited with beginning the environmental movement in the United States. The book focussed on the uncontrolled and often indiscriminate use of pesticides, especially dichlorodiphenyltrichloroethane (commonly known as DDT), and the irreparable environmental damage caused by these chemicals. The public outcry Carson generated by the book motivated the U.S. Senate to form a committee to investigate pesticide use. Her eloquent testimony before the committee altered the views of many government officials and helped lead to the creation of the Environmental Protection Agency (EPA).

Rachel Louise Carson, the youngest of three children, was born on May 27, 1907, in Springdale, Pennsylvania, a small town twenty miles north of Pittsburgh. Her parents, Robert Warden and Maria McLean Carson, lived on sixty-five acres and kept cows, chickens, and horses. Although the land was not a true working farm, it had plenty of woods, animals, and streams, and here, near the shores of the Allegheny River, Carson learned about the interrelationship between the land and animals.

Carson's mother was the daughter of a Presbyterian minister, and she instilled in her a love of nature and taught her the intricacies of music, art, and literature. Carson's early life was one of isolation; she had few friends besides her cats, and she spent most of her time reading and pursuing the study of nature. She began writing poetry at age eight and published her first story, "A Battle in the Clouds," in *St. Nicholas* magazine at the age of ten. She later claimed that her professional writing career began at age eleven, when *St. Nicholas* paid her a little over three dollars for one of her essays.

Focuses on Career in the Sciences

Carson planned to pursue a career as a writer when she received a four-year scholarship in 1925 from the Pennsylvania College for Women (now Chatham College) in Pittsburgh. Here she fell under the influence of Mary Scott Skinker, whose freshman biology course altered her career plans. In the middle of her junior year, Carson switched her major from English to zoology, and in 1928 she graduated magnum cum laude. "Biology has given me something to write about," she wrote to a friend, as quoted in *Carnegie* magazine. "I will try in my writing to make animals in the woods or waters, where they live, as alive to others as they are to me."

With Skinker's help, Carson obtained first a summer fellowship at the Marine Biology Laboratory at Woods Hole in Massachusetts and then a one-year scholarship from the Johns Hopkins University in Baltimore. While at Woods Hole over the summer, she saw the ocean for the first time and encountered her first exotic sea creatures, including sea anemones and sea urchins. At Johns Hopkins, she studied zoology and genetics. Graduate school did not proceed smoothly; she encountered financial problems and experimental difficulties but eventually managed to finish her highly detailed master's dissertation, "The Development of the Pronephoros during the Embryonic and Early Larval Life of the Catfish (*Inctalurus punctaltus*)." In June 1932, she received her master's degree.

Begins Her Writing Career in Federal Government

Carson was entering the job market at the height of the Great Depression. Her parents sold their Pennsylvania home and moved to Maryland to ease some of her financial burdens. She taught zoology at Johns Hopkins during the summers and on a part-time basis at the University of Maryland during the regular school year. While she loved teaching, the meager salaries she earned were barely enough to sustain herself, and, in 1935, her financial situation became even more desperate when her father died unexpectedly, leaving her solely responsible for supporting her fragile mother.

Before beginning her graduate studies at Johns Hopkins, Carson had arranged an interview with Elmer Higgins, who was head of the Division of Scientific Inquiry at the U.S. Bureau of Fisheries. Carson wanted to discuss her job prospects in marine biology, and Higgins had been encouraging, though he then had little to offer. Carson contacted Higgins again at this time, and she discovered that he had an opening at the Bureau of Fisheries for a part-time science writer to work on radio scripts. The only obstacle was the civil service exam, which women were then discouraged from taking. Carson not only did well on the test, she outscored all other applicants.

She went on to become only the second woman ever hired by the bureau for a permanent professional post.

At the Bureau of Fisheries, Carson wrote and edited a variety of government publications—everything from pamphlets on how to cook fish to professional scientific journals. She earned a reputation as a ruthless editor who would not tolerate inconsistencies, weak prose, or ambiguity. One of her early radio scripts was rejected by Higgins because he found it too "literary." He suggested that she submit the script in essay form to the *Atlantic Monthly,* then one of the nation's premier literary magazines. To Carson's amazement, the article was accepted and published as "Undersea" in 1937. Her jubilation over the article was tempered by personal family tragedy. Her older sister, Marian, died at age forty that same year, and Carson had to assume responsibility for Marian's children, Marjorie and Virginia Williams.

The *Atlantic Monthly* article attracted the notice of an editor at the publishing house of Simon & Schuster, who urged Carson to expand the four-page essay into book form. Working diligently in the evenings, she was able to complete the book in a few years; it was published as *Under the Sea-Wind.* Unfortunately, the book appeared in print in 1941, just one month before the Japanese attacked Pearl Harbor. Despite favorable, even laudatory reviews, it sold fewer than 1,600 copies after six years in print. It did, however, bring Carson to the attention of a number of key people, including the influential science writer William Beebe. Beebe published an excerpt from *Under the Sea-Wind* in his 1944 compilation *The Book of Naturalists,* including Carson's work alongside the writings of Aristotle, Audubon, and Thoreau.

The poor sales of *Under the Sea-Wind* made Carson concentrate on her government job. The Bureau of Fisheries merged with the Biological Survey in 1940 and was reborn as the Fish and Wildlife Service. Carson quickly moved up the professional ranks, eventually reaching the position of biologist and chief editor after World War II. One of her postwar assignments, a booklet about National Wildlife Refuges called *Conservation in Action,* took her back into the field. As part of her research, she visited the Florida Everglades, Parker River in Massachusetts, and Chincoteague Island in the Chesapeake Bay.

Attracts National Notice with Science Writing

After the war, Carson began work on a new book that focussed on oceanography. She was now at liberty to use previously classified government research data on oceanography, which included a number of technical and scientific breakthroughs. As part of her research, she did some undersea diving off the Florida coast during the summer of 1949. She battled skeptical administrators to arrange a deep-sea cruise to Georges Bank near Nova Scotia aboard the Fish and Wildlife Service's research vessel, the *Albatross III.*

Entitled *The Sea around Us,* her book on oceanography was published on July 2, 1951. It was an unexpected success; abridged in *Reader's Digest,* it was a Book-of-the-Month Club alternative selection and it remained on the *New York Times* bestseller list for eighty-six weeks. The book brought Carson numerous awards, including the National Book Award and the John Burroughs Medal, as well as honorary doctorates from her alma mater and Oberlin College. Despite her inherent shyness, Carson became a regular on the lecture circuit. Money was no longer the overarching concern it had been; she retired from government service and devoted her time to writing.

Freed from financial burdens, Carson began work on another book, focussing this time on the intricacies of life along the shoreline. She took excursions to the mangrove coasts of Florida and returned to one of her favorite locations, the rocky shores of Maine. She fell in love with the Maine coast and in 1953 bought a summer home in West Southport on the shore of Sheepscot Bay. *The Edge of the Sea* appeared in 1955 and earned Carson two more prestigious awards, the Achievement Award of the American Association of University Women and a citation from the National Council of Women of the United States. The book remained on the bestseller list for twenty weeks, and RKO Studios bought the rights to it. In typical Hollywood fashion, the studio sensationalized the material and ignored scientific fact. Carson corrected some of the more egregious errors but still found the film embarrassing, even after it won an Oscar as the best full-length documentary of 1953.

From 1955 to 1957, Carson concentrated on smaller projects, including a telescript, "Something about the Sky," for the *Omnibus* series. She also contributed a number of articles to popular magazines. In July 1956, Carson published "Help Your Child to Wonder" in the *Woman's Home Companion.* The article was based on her own real-life experiences, something rare for Carson. She intended to expand the article into a book and retell the story of her early life on her parent's Pennsylvania farm. After her death, the essay reappeared in 1965 as the book *The Sense of Wonder.*

Investigates Pesticide Use

In 1956, one of the nieces Carson had raised died at age 36. Marjorie left her son Roger; Carson now had to care for him in addition to her arthritic mother, who was now eighty-eight. She legally adopted Roger that same year and began looking for a suitable place to rear the child. She built a new winter home in Silver Spring, Maryland, on an uncultivated

tract of land, and she began another project shortly after the home was finished. The luxuriant setting inspired her to turn her thoughts to nature once again. Carson's next book grew out of a long-held concern about the overuse of pesticides. She had received a letter from Olga Owens Huckins, who related how the aerial spraying of DDT had destroyed her Massachusetts bird sanctuary. Huckins asked her to petition federal authorities to investigate the widespread use of such pesticides, but Carson thought the most effective tactic would be to write an article for a popular magazine. When her initial queries were rejected, Carson attempted to interest the well-known essayist E. B. White in the subject. White suggested she write the article herself, in her own style, and he told her to contact William Shawn, an editor at the *New Yorker.* Eventually, after numerous discussions with Shawn and others, she decided to write a book instead.

The international reputation Carson now enjoyed enabled her to enlist the aid of an array of experts. She consulted with biologists, chemists, entomologists, and pathologists, spending four years gathering data for her book. When *Silent Spring* first appeared in serial form in the *New Yorker* in June 1962, it drew an aggressive response from the chemical industry. Carson argued that the environmental consequences of pesticide use underscored the futility of humanity's attempts to control nature, and she maintained that these efforts to assume control had upset nature's delicate balance. Although the message is now largely uncontroversial, the book caused near panic in some circles, challenging the long-held belief that humans could master nature. The chemical companies, in particular, attacked both the book and its author; they questioned the data, the interpretation of the data, and the author's scientific credentials. One early reviewer referred to Carson as a "hysterical woman," and others continued this sexist line of attack. Some chemical companies attempted to pressure Houghton Mifflin, the book's publisher, into suppressing the book, but these attempts failed.

The general reviews were much kinder and *Silent Spring* soon attracted a large, concerned audience, both in America and abroad. A special CBS television broadcast, "The Silent Spring of Rachel Carson," which aired on April 3, 1963, pitted Carson against a chemical company spokesman. Her cool-headed, commonsensical approach won her many fans and brought national attention to the problem of pesticide use. The book became a cultural icon and part of everyday household conversation. Carson received hundreds of invitations to speak, most of which she declined due to her deteriorating health. She did find the strength to appear before the Women's National Press Club, the National Parks Association, and the Ribicoff Committee—the U.S. Senate committee on environmental hazards.

In 1963 Carson received numerous honors and awards, including an award from the Izaak Walton League of America, the Audubon Medal, and the Cullen Medal of the American Geographical Society. That same year, she was elected to the prestigious American Academy of Arts and Sciences. She died of heart failure on April 14, 1964, at the age of fifty-six. In 1980, President Jimmy Carter posthumously awarded her the President's Medal of Freedom. A Rachel Carson stamp was issued by the U.S. Postal Service in 1981.

SELECTED WRITINGS BY CARSON:

Books

Under the Sea-Wind, Dutton, 1941.
The Sea around Us, Oxford University Press, 1951.
The Edge of the Sea, Houghton Mifflin, 1955.
Silent Spring, Houghton Mifflin, 1962.
A Sense of Wonder, Harper and Row, 1965.

Periodicals

"Undersea," *Atlantic Monthly,* September, 1937.
"The Bat Knew It First," *Colliers,* November 18, 1944.
"Help Your Child to Wonder," *Woman's Home Companion,* July, 1956.
"Rachel Carson Answers Her Critics," *Audubon Magazine,* September, 1963.

SOURCES:

Books

Brooks, Paul, *The House of Life: Rachel Carson at Work,* Houghton Mifflin, 1972.
Gartner, Carol B., *Rachel Carson,* Ungar, 1983.
McKay, Mary A., *Rachel Carson,* Twayne, 1993.

Periodicals

Brooks, Paul, "The Courage of Rachel Carson," *Audubon 89,* Volume 12, January, 1987, pp. 14–15.
McKibben, Bill, "The Mountain Hedonist," *New York Review of Books,* April 11, 1991, pp. 29–32.
Wareham, Wendy, "Rachel Carson's Early Years," *Carnegie,* November/December, 1986, pp. 20–34.

—*Sketch by Tom Crawford*

George Washington Carver
1865(?)-1943
American agricultural chemist

George Washington Carver, born in slavery and orphaned in infancy, rose to national and international fame as an agricultural scientist. Carver grew up and was educated in the northern states and later became a faculty member at the all-black Tuskegee Institute in Alabama, working in the forefront of the infant discipline of "scientific agriculture." Carver devised and promoted scores of uses for peanuts and sweet potatoes, and he had a significant effect on the diversification of southern agricultural practices. His testimony in 1921 before the House Ways and Means Committee achieved a tariff to protect the U.S. peanut industry and was the beginning of his identity as the peanut wizard. He also worked with hybrid cotton, conducted experiments in crop rotation and restoration of soil fertility, and developed useful products from Alabama red clay. Carver was a widely talented man who became an almost mythical American folk hero. He was deeply religious, explaining his wide-ranging interests as attempts to understand the work of the "Great Creator."

Carver was born near the end of the Civil War in Newton County, Missouri. His birth date is uncertain, although historian Linda O. McMurry suggests that he was likely born in the spring of 1865. His mother, Mary, was owned by Moses and Susan Carver, who were successful farmowners in the state. His father is believed to be a slave on a nearby plantation, and he was killed in an accident soon after Carver was born. His mother disappeared following a kidnapping by bushwhackers, and Carver and his brother were brought up by Moses and Susan. Carver was a frail and sickly child, and because of his weak health, he helped with the lighter tasks on the farm. He quickly mastered various household tasks, including cooking, laundering, canning, crocheting, needlework, as well as learning the alphabet and music. He also spent considerable time indulging his deep curiosity about nature, building a pond for his frog collection and keeping a little plant nursery in the woods. His talent with plants made him the neighborhood "plant doctor." At the nearby Locust Grove Church, Carver heard a variety of Methodist, Baptist, Campbellite, and Presbyterian circuit preachers, and acquired a nondenominational faith.

Pursues an Education

In 1877 Carver left home for the county seat of Neosho, to attend a school for blacks. This was the

George Washington Carver

small Methodist College in Indianola. Carver quickly made friends on campus. He had intended to pursue art, but his art teacher, Etta Budd, encouraged him to consider a career in botany and suggested he enroll at the agricultural college at Ames, where her own father was a faculty member. The idea appealed to Carver; agriculture would allow him to be of service, and in 1891 he left for Ames and the Iowa State College of Agriculture and Mechanic Arts.

At Iowa, Carver was a popular student and active in a variety of campus affairs. During this time his painting entitled *Yucca and Cactus* was exhibited in Cedar Rapids and selected as an Iowa representative for the World's Columbian Exposition in Chicago in 1893. For his wide-ranging abilities, Carver was affectionately called "doctor" by the other students. His academic record was excellent, and his skills in raising, cross-fertilizing, and grafting plants were recognized by his professors. His bachelor's degree thesis, "Plants as Modified by Man," described the positive aspects of hybridization. He stayed on at Iowa for graduate work and was appointed an assistant in botany. Freed at last from odd jobs, Carver could now devote himself to greenhouse studies and teaching.

The Tuskegee Years

Carver received his master's degree from Iowa in 1896 and accepted a position at Tuskegee Institute, Alabama, at the invitation of its president, Booker T. Washington. He was to spend forty-seven years at Tuskegee, living most of that time in Rockefeller Hall, a dormitory occupied by students. The early years were difficult for Carver as he had numerous responsibilities at the institute. Besides heading the agriculture department, Carver was also director of the newly established Agricultural Experiment Station. Additionally, he managed the school's two farms, taught classes, and served on committees and councils. Despite all this, in 1910, unhappy with the number of agriculture graduates, Washington removed Carver from his charge of the Agriculture Department. Carver submitted his resignation, following which, Washington made him director of a new research department and "consulting chemist."

Experimental work was more to Carver's liking. From the beginning Carver had worked on a number of projects to help improve the lot of poor southern farmers. He analyzed water, feed, and soil. He experimented with paints that could be made with clay. He worked with organic fertilizers. He demonstrated uses for cheap and locally available materials, such as swamp muck. He searched for new, cheap foodstuffs to supplement the farmers' diets. In addition to human food items, he developed stock feeds, cosmetics, dyes, stains, medicines and ink from peanuts and sweet potatoes. In his agricultural bulle-

beginning of a long journey through three states in pursuit of basic education. In these years he supported himself with odd jobs working for, and living with, various families along the way. In Neosho, he lived with a black couple, Andrew and Mariah Watkins, and helped with chores. He learned herbalism from Mariah, and he quickly recognized that his knowledge outstripped that of his teacher. In the late 1870s he hitched a ride to Fort Scott, Kansas, and moved in with the family of a blacksmith. Shortly thereafter he moved to Olathe, Kansas, where he made his home with another black couple, Ben and Lucy Seymour. He entered school, helped Lucy with her laundry business, and taught a class at the Methodist church. In the summer of 1880 he followed the Seymours to Minneapolis, where he established a laundry business and spent four years attending school. In 1884 he moved to Kansas City, acquired a typewriter, and took a job as a clerk at the Union Depot. His thirst for education continued, and he was accepted, by mail, into a small college in Highland, Kansas, only to be told when he arrived there that the college did not accept blacks. He stayed in Highland for a while, then moved to Ness County as a homesteader. On the frontier, Carver built a sod house, farmed, took his first art lessons, played accordion for local dances, and joined the literary society.

Around 1890 he sold his homestead and moved to Winterset, Iowa, where his talents and industry impressed a white couple, Dr. and Mrs. John Milholland. They persuaded him to enter Simpson College, a tins, he offered elementary information to uneducated farmers.

In 1916 Carver received two prestigious invitations: to serve on the advisory board of the National Agricultural Society and to become a fellow of the Royal Society for the Arts in London. In 1919, under Tuskegee president Robert Russa Moton, he received his first salary increase in twenty years. He had become increasingly popular as a lecturer and his testimony before the House Ways and Means Committee in 1921 thrust him into the national limelight. In 1923 he was awarded the Spingarn Medal from the NAACP (National Association for the Advancement of Colored People) for his contributions to agricultural chemistry and for his lectures to religious, educational, and farming audiences that had "increased inter-racial knowledge and respect." Other honors included an honorary doctorate from Simpson College in 1928.

Becomes a Spokesman for "Chemurgy"

In the mid–1930s, the word *chemurgy* was coined to mean putting chemistry to work in industry for the farmer. Carver became a spokesman for chemurgy, just as he had been for the peanut industry and the "New South." In 1937 Carver met the industrialist Henry Ford at a chemurgy conference Ford had sponsored. A long friendship developed between the two men and when, in 1940, Carver established a foundation to continue and preserve his work, the Carver Museum in Tuskegee was dedicated by Ford. The museum contained seventy-one of Carver's pictures as well as handicrafts, case studies, and results of his research.

Carver received numerous awards and honors for his contributions to the field of scientific agriculture. Noteworthy among these were the Roosevelt Medal, which he received in 1939, an honorary doctorate from the University of Rochester, and the first award for "outstanding service to the welfare of the South" from the Catholic Conference of the South. In 1942 Ford erected a Carver memorial cabin in Greenfield Village, Michigan, and established a nutritional laboratory in Carver's honor in Dearborn, Michigan. Carver also received an honorary doctorate from Selma University, a fellowship from the Thomas A. Edison Institute, and was a member of Kappa Delta Pi, an honorary education society.

Carver's health had begun to fail in the 1930s. When he died on January 5, 1943, Tuskegee Institute was flooded with letters of sympathy from many people. Carver was buried in the Tuskegee Institute cemetery near the grave of Booker T. Washington. On January 9, 1943, President Franklin D. Roosevelt paid tribute to Carver in an address before Congress, and on July 14, 1943, Roosevelt signed legislation making Carver's Missouri birthplace a national monument.

SOURCES:

Books

Elliott, Lawrence, *George Washington Carver: The Man Who Overcame,* Prentice Hall, 1966.

Graham, Shirley, and George D. Lipscomb, *Dr. George Washington Carver: Scientist,* Julian Messner, 1944.

Holt, Rackham, *George Washington Carver: An American Biography,* Doubleday, 1943.

Kremer, Gary R., editor, *George Washington Carver: In His Own Words,* University of Missouri Press, 1987.

McMurry, Linda O., *George Washington Carver: Scientist and Symbol,* Oxford University Press, 1981.

Periodicals

"Dr. Carver Is Dead: Negro Scientist," *New York Times,* January 6, 1943, p. 25.

Mackintosh, Barry, "George Washington Carver: The Making of a Myth," *Journal of Southern History,* November, 1976, pp. 507–28.

—*Sketch by Jill Carpenter*

George Castro
1939-
American physical chemist

George Castro's work in photoconductors and superconductors has led the way to new and improved electrophotographic copying machines as well as digital information storage systems. Additionally, he has worked for twenty-five years in civic activities on behalf of the Hispanic American community to ensure adequate education and employment opportunities.

Castro was born on February 23, 1939, in Los Angeles, California, the second of five children. His parents are both of Mexican descent. Castro grew up in Los Angeles, where he attended Roosevelt High School. Graduating in 1956, Castro won the Los Romanos Scholarship. Although it provided him with only a small amount of money, the scholarship was an important vote of confidence from the local Hispanic community. Castro was the first of his family ever to attend college. He went to UCLA, where he earned a B.S. in chemistry. He then became a research fellow in the chemistry department at Dartmouth College. Castro returned to Los Angeles in 1963 and married Beatrice Melendez, with whom he had attended both junior high and high schools. He finished his graduate studies at the University of California at Riverside, earning his Ph.D. in physical chemistry in 1965. For the next three years, Castro served as a postdoctoral fellow, first at the University of Pennsylvania, and then at Caltech.

In 1968, Castro joined the staff of IBM at its San Jose Research Lab. By 1971, he had become a project manager, and by 1973, a department manager. His early work was in photoconduction—the increased electrical conductivity of a substance when subjected to light waves. In particular, Castro discovered how organic photoconductors were generated by intrinsic charge carriers, an essential element in the technology of both electrophotographic copying machines and laser printers. His early work contributed to the understanding of the principles of the photogeneration process, which is essential to both copying and printing technology. Research teams he managed also discovered a mechanism called photochemical hole burning. By this mechanism, very high densities of digital information can be stored in solids at greater numbers than accomplished by other optical processes.

In 1975, Castro was made manager of the entire physical sciences division of the IBM San Jose Research Lab. Under his directorship the lab has made breakthrough discoveries in superconductors, high-resolution laser techniques, and new methods for investigating magnetic materials. From 1986 to 1992, Castro worked jointly with a team from Stanford University to develop a synchrotron X-ray facility—one which utilizes the mechanism of synchronized acceleration produced in atomic particles passing through an electrically energized magnetic field. Other research he has supervised includes the construction of a photoelectron microscope for high resolution spectroscopic studies.

Castro has consistently taken time from his busy work schedule to become involved in the education of Hispanic youth. He has taught math and science classes on a volunteer basis, served on the boards of numerous local associations and schools, and developed on-the-job training programs at IBM. Castro won the Outstanding Innovation Award from IBM in 1978, the Outstanding Hispanic Professional award from the San Jose Mexican-American Chamber of Commerce in 1984, and the Hispanic in Technology National Award from the Society of Hispanic Professional Engineers in 1986; he was elected a member of the American Physical Society in 1990. He and his wife have four children.

SELECTED WRITINGS BY CASTRO:

Periodicals

(With J. F. Henry) "Multiple-Charge Carrier Generation Processes in Anthracene," *Journal of Chemical Physics,* Volume 42, 1965, pp. 1459–1460.

"On Wannier Excitons in Anthracene," *Journal of Chemical Physics,* Volume 46, 1967, pp. 4997–4998.

"Photoconduction in Aromatic Hydrocarbons," *IBM Journal of Research and Development,* Volume 15, 1971, pp. 27–33.

(With D. Haarer) "Singlet Exciton Diffusion and Exciton Quenching in Phenanthrene Single Crystals," *Journal of Luminescence,* Volumes 12–13, 1976, pp. 233–238.

(With F. Cuellar) "Photochemical and Nonphotochemical Hole Burning in Dimethyl-s-tetrazine," *Journal of Chemical Physics,* Volume 54, 1981, pp. 217–225.

Other

Castro, George, interview with J. Sydney Jones conducted April 12, 1994.

—Sketch by J. Sydney Jones

Thomas R. Cech
1947-
American biochemist

The work of Thomas R. Cech has revolutionized the way in which scientists look at RNA and at proteins. Up to the time of Cech's discoveries in 1981 and 1982, it had been thought that genetic coding, stored in the DNA of the nucleus, was imprinted or transcribed onto RNA molecules. These RNA molecules, it was believed, helped transfer the coding onto proteins produced in the ribosomes. The DNA/RNA nexus was thus the information center of the cell, while protein molecules in the form of enzymes were the workhorses, catalyzing the thousands of vital chemical reactions that occur in the cell. Conventional wisdom held that the two functions were separate—that there was a delicate division of labor. Cech and his colleagues at the University of Colorado established, however, that this picture of how RNA functions was incorrect; they proved that in the absence of other enzymes RNA acts as its own catalyst. It was a discovery that reverberated throughout the scientific community, leading not only to new technologies in RNA engineering but also to a revised view of the evolution of life. Cech shared the 1989 Nobel Prize for Chemistry with **Sidney Altman** at Yale University for their work regarding the role of RNA in cell reactions.

Cech was born in Chicago on December 8, 1947, to Robert Franklin Cech, a physician, and Annette Marie Cerveny Cech. As he recalls in an autobiographical sketch for *Les Prix Nobel,* he grew up in "the safe streets and good schools" of Iowa City, Iowa. His father had a deep and abiding interest in physics as well as medicine, and from an early age Cech took an avid interest in science, collecting rocks and minerals and speculating about how they had been formed. In junior high school he was already conferring with geology professors from the nearby university. He went to Grinnell College in 1966; at first attracted to physical chemistry, he soon concentrated on biological chemistry, graduating with a chemistry degree in 1970.

It was at Grinnell that he met Carol Lynn Martinson, who was a fellow chemistry student. They married in 1970 and went together to the University of California at Berkeley for graduate studies. His thesis advisor there was John Hearst who, Cech recalled in *Les Prix Nobel,* "had an enthusiasm for chromosome structure and function that proved infectious." Both Cech and his wife were awarded their Ph.D. degrees in 1975, and they moved to the east coast for postdoctoral positions—Cech at the Massachusetts Institute of Technology (MIT) under **Mary Lou Pardue**, and his wife at Harvard. At MIT Cech focussed on the DNA structures of the mouse genome, strengthening his knowledge of biology at the same time.

Concentrates on Gene Expression

In 1978, both Cech and his wife were offered positions at the University of Colorado in Boulder; he was appointed assistant professor in chemistry. By this time, Cech had decided that he would like to investigate more specific genetic material. He was particularly interested in what enables the DNA molecule to instruct the body to produce the various parts of itself—a process known as gene expression. Cech set out to discover the proteins that govern the DNA transcription process onto RNA, and in order to do this he decided to use nucleic acids from a single-cell protozoa, *Tetrahymena thermophila.* He chose *Tetrahymena* because it rapidly reproduced genetic material and because it had a structure which allowed for the easy extraction of DNA.

By the late 1970s much research had already been done on DNA and its transcription partner, RNA. It had been determined that there were three types of RNA: messenger RNA, which relays the transcription of the DNA structure by attaching itself to the ribosome where protein synthesis occurs; ribosomal RNA, which imparts the messenger's structure within the ribosome; and transfer RNA, which helps to establish amino acids in the proper order in the protein chain as it is being built. Just prior to the time Cech began his work, it was discovered that DNA and final-product RNA (after copying or transcription) actually differed. In 1977 **Phillip A. Sharp** and others discovered that portions of seemingly noncoded DNA were snipped out of the RNA and the chain was spliced back together where these intervening segments had been removed. These noncoded sections of DNA were called introns.

Cech and his coworkers were not initially interested in such introns, but they soon became fascinated with their function and the splicing mechanism itself. In an effort to understand how these so-called nonsense sequences, or introns, were removed from the transcribed RNA, Cech and his colleague Arthur Zaug decided to investigate the pre-ribosomal RNA of the *Tetrahymena,* just as it underwent transcription. In order to do this, they first isolated unspliced RNA and then added some *Tetrahymena* nuclei extract. Their assumption was that the catalytic agent or enzyme would be present in such an extract. They also added small molecules of salts and nucleotides for energy, varying the amounts of each in subsequent experiments, even excluding one or more of the additives. But the experiment took a different turn than they expected.

Research on Catalytic RNA Wins Nobel Prize

What Cech and Zaug discovered was that RNA splicing would occur even without the nucleic material being present. This was a development they did not understand at first; it was a long-held scientific belief that proteins in the form of enzymes had to be present for catalysis to occur. But here was a situation in which RNA appeared to be its own catalytic motivator. At first they suspected that their experiment had been contaminated. Cech did further experiments involving recombinant DNA in which there could be no possibility of the presence of splicing enzymes, and these had the same result: the RNA spliced out its own intron. Further discoveries in Cech's laboratory into the nature of the intron led to his belief that the intron itself was the catalytic agent of RNA splicing, and he decided that this was a sort of RNA enzyme which they called the ribozyme.

Cech's findings of 1982 met with heated debate in the scientific community, for it upset many beliefs about the nature of enzymes. Cech's ribozyme was in fact not a true enzyme, for thus far he had shown it only to work upon itself and to be changed in the reaction; true enzymes catalyze repeatedly and come out of the reaction unchanged. Other critics argued that this was a freak bit of RNA on a strange microorganism and that it would not be found in other organisms. They were soon proved wrong, however, when scientists around the world began discovering other RNA enzymes. In 1984, **Sidney Altman** proved that RNA carries out enzyme-like activities on substances other than itself.

The discovery of catalytic RNA has had profound results. In the medical field alone RNA enzymology may lead to cures of viral infections. By using these rybozymes as gene scissors, the RNA molecule can be cut at certain points, destroying the RNA molecules that cause infections or genetic disorders. In life sciences, the discovery of catalytic RNA has also changed conventional wisdom. The old debate about whether proteins or nucleic acids were the first bit of life form seems to have been solved. If RNA can act as a catalyst and a genetic template to create proteins as well as itself, then it is rather certain that RNA was first in the chain of life.

Cech and Altman won the Nobel Prize for Chemistry in 1989 for their independent discoveries of catalytic RNA. Cech has also been awarded the Passano Foundation Young Scientist Award and the Harrison Howe Award in 1984; the Pfizer Award in Enzyme Chemistry in 1985; the U. S. Steel Award in Molecular Biology; and the V. D. Mattia Award in 1987. In 1988, he won the Newcombe-Cleveland Award, the Heineken Prize, the Gairdner Foundation International Award, the Louisa Gross Horwitz Prize, and the Albert Lasker Basic Medical Research Award; he was presented with the Bonfils-Stanton Award for Science in 1990.

Cech was made full professor in the department of chemistry at the University of Colorado in 1983. He and his wife have two daughters. In the midst of his busy career in research, Cech still finds time for skiing and backpacking.

SELECTED WRITINGS BY CECH:

Periodicals

"RNA As an Enzyme," *Scientific American*, November, 1986, pp. 64–74.
"The Chemistry of Self-Splicing RNA and RNA Enzymes," *Science*, Volume 236, June 19, 1987, pp. 1532–40.
"Ribozymes and Their Medical Implications," *Journal of the American Medical Association*, November 25, 1988, pp. 3030–35.
"Defining the Inside and the Outside of a Catalytic RNA Molecule," *Science*, Volume 245, July 21, 1989, pp. 276–83.
"Self-Splicing of Group-I Introns," *Annual Review of Biochemistry*, Volume 59, 1990, pp. 543–68.

"RNA Editing—World's Smallest Introns," *Cell*, Volume 64, February 22, 1991, pp. 667–69.
"Catalytic RNA—Structure and Mechanism," *Biochemical Society Transactions*, Volume 21, May 1993, pp. 229–34.
"RNA—Fishing for Fresh Catalysts," *Nature*, September 16, 1993, pp. 204–05.

SOURCES:

Books

Les Prix Nobel 1989, Almqvist & Wiksell International, 1989, pp. 162–88.
Nobel Prize Winners Supplement 1987–1991, H. W. Wilson, 1992, pp. 58–60.

Periodicals

Amato, I. "RNA Researchers Earn Chemistry Nobel," *Science News*, October 21, 1989, p. 262.
Horgan, John, "Nobel Prizes," *Scientific American*, December, 1989, p. 34.
Waldrop, M. Mitchell, "Catalytic RNA Wins Chemistry Nobel," *Science*, October 20, 1989, p. 325.
Wickelgren, I. "Laskers Highlight Addiction, RNA Work," *Science News*, November 19, 1988, p. 326.

—*Sketch by J. Sydney Jones*

James Chadwick
1891-1974
English physicist

James Chadwick, who is remembered principally for his work in nuclear physics, received the Nobel Prize in 1935 for his discovery of the neutron. That discovery gave rise to new approaches and techniques in the physical sciences, new developments in the biological sciences, and a new form of warfare. Chadwick himself was actively involved with the development of the atomic bomb. Although he was shy and did not have the public visibility of other physicists of his time, his work in science, diplomacy, and administration left permanent marks in twentieth-century history. Knighted in 1945, Chadwick received the Medal of Merit from the United States government in 1946, and the Copley Medal of the Royal Society in 1950.

James Chadwick

Chadwick was born in Bollington, not far from Manchester, England, on October 20, 1891, to John Joseph Chadwick and Ann Mary Knowles. Chadwick senior owned a laundry business in Manchester. At the age of sixteen, Chadwick won a scholarship to the University of Manchester, where he had intended to study mathematics. However, because he was mistakenly interviewed for admittance to the physics program and was too shy to explain the error, he decided to stay in physics.

Initially Chadwick was disappointed in the physics classes, finding them too large and noisy. But in his second year, he heard a lecture by experimental physicist **Ernest Rutherford** about his early New Zealand experiments. Chadwick established a close working relationship with Rutherford and graduated in 1911 with first honors. Chadwick stayed at Manchester to work on his master's degree. During this time he made the acquaintance of others in the physics department, including **Hans Geiger** and **Niels Bohr**. Chadwick completed his M.Sc. in 1913 and won a scholarship that required him to do his research away from the institution that granted his degree. At this time Geiger returned to Germany, and Chadwick decided to follow him.

Internment in Germany

Chadwick had not been in Germany long when World War I broke out. Unsure of his plans, he postponed leaving the country. Soon he was arrested and sat in a Berlin jail for ten days until Geiger's laboratory interceded for his release. Eventually Chadwick was interned for the duration of the war, as were all other Englishmen in Germany. Chadwick spent the war years confined at a race track, where he shared with five other men a stable intended for two horses. His four years there were quiet, cold, and hungry. To keep up his morale, he participated in a scientific society formed by a group of internees. He managed to maintain correspondence with Geiger, and he even persuaded his German captors to supply some basic scientific equipment. One such piece he obtained was a bunsen burner. However, it lacked a bellows, so Chadwick enlisted one of his fellow captives to blow air through a tube into the burner. Although the work he did under such harsh conditions was not very fruitful, Chadwick later believed that it helped greatly to keep up his spirits at the time. He also felt that the experience of internment contributed to his maturity. Moreover, when Chadwick returned to England, he found that no one else had made much progress in nuclear physics during his time away.

Discovery of the Neutron

In 1919 Ernest Rutherford was appointed director of Cambridge University's Cavendish Laboratory, the leading research center for nuclear physics at the time. Rutherford brought Chadwick with him, and the two began a partnership that lasted sixteen years. Chadwick earned his Ph.D. in physics from Cambridge in 1921 and was made a fellow at Gonville and Caius College, enabling him to continue working with Rutherford at the Cavendish lab. Rutherford had been working on atomic structure and had discovered many of the essential properties of the proton. One of Chadwick's first tasks was to help Rutherford establish a unit of measurement for radioactivity, to aid in experiments with the radiation of atomic nuclei. Chadwick then developed a method to measure radioactivity that required the observation of flashes, called scintillations, in zinc sulfide crystals under a microscope and in complete darkness. Although this method was difficult and prone to error, later experiments using newer detection techniques confirmed Chadwick's radiation measurements. In 1922 Chadwick became assistant director of research under Rutherford. In this post, Chadwick supervised all the research at the laboratory. Chadwick and Rutherford spent much time experimenting with the transmutation of elements, attempting to break up the nucleus of one element so that different elements would be formed. These experiments involved bombarding the nuclei of nitrogen and other elements with alpha particles (helium nuclei). This work eventually led to other experiments to gauge the size and map the structure of the atomic nucleus.

Throughout the years of work on the transmutation of elements, Chadwick and Rutherford struggled with an inconsistency. They saw that almost every element had an atomic number that was less than its atomic mass. In other words, an atom of any given element seemed to have more mass than could be accounted for by the number of protons in its nucleus. Rutherford initially thought that the extra mass was made up of proton-electron pairs, which would add mass but no additional charge to the nucleus. However, the nucleus did not seem to have room enough for such pairs. Rutherford then suggested the possibility of a particle with the mass of a proton and a neutral charge, but for a long time his and Chadwick's attempts to find such a particle were in vain.

For twelve years, Chadwick looked intermittently and unsuccessfully for the neutrally-charged particle that Rutherford proposed. In 1930 two German physicists, **Walther Bothe** and Hans Becker, found an unexpectedly penetrating radiation, thought to be gamma rays, when some elements were bombarded with alpha particles. However, the element beryllium showed an emission pattern that the gamma-ray hypothesis could not account for. Chadwick suspected that neutral particles were responsible for the emissions. Work done in France in 1922 by physicists **Frédéric Joliot-Curie** and **Irène Joliot-Curie** supplied the answer. Studying the hypothetical gamma-ray emissions from beryllium, they found that radiation increased when the emissions passed through the absorbing material paraffin. Although the Joliot-Curie team concluded that gamma rays emitted by beryllium knocked hydrogen protons out of the paraffin, Chadwick immediately saw that their experiments would confirm the presence of the neutron, since it would take a neutral particle of such mass to move a proton. He first set to work demonstrating that the gamma-ray hypothesis could not account for the observed phenomena, because gamma rays would not have enough energy to eject protons so rapidly. Then he showed that the beryllium nucleus, when combined with an alpha particle, could be transmuted to a carbon nucleus, releasing a particle with a mass comparable to that of a proton but with a neutral charge. The neutron had finally been tracked down. Other experiments showed that a boron nucleus plus an alpha particle results in a nitrogen nucleus plus a neutron. Chadwick's first public announcement of the discovery was in an article in the journal *Nature* with a title characteristic of his unassuming personality, "Possible Existence of a Neutron." In 1935 Chadwick was awarded the Nobel Prize in physics for this discovery. That same year, Chadwick took a position at the University of Liverpool to establish a new research center in nuclear physics and to build a particle accelerator.

The Race to Make the Bomb

Chadwick's discovery of the neutron made possible more precise examinations of the nucleus. It also led to speculations about uranium fission. Physicists found that bombarding uranium nuclei with neutrons caused the nuclei to split into two almost equal pieces and to release energy in the very large amounts predicted by Einstein's formula $E=mc^2$. This phenomenon, known as nuclear fission, was discovered and publicized on the eve of World War II, and many scientists immediately began to speculate about its application to warfare. Britain quickly assembled a group of scientists under the Ministry of Aircraft Production, called the Maud Committee, to pursue the practicality of an atomic bomb. Chadwick was put in charge of coordinating all the experimental efforts of the universities of Birmingham, Cambridge, Liverpool, London, and Oxford. Initially Chadwick's responsibilities were limited to the very difficult and purely experimental aspects of the research project. Gradually, he became more involved with other duties in the organization, particularly as spokesperson.

Chadwick's work in evaluating and presenting evidence convinced British government and military leaders to move ahead with the project. Chadwick's involvement was broad and deep, forcing him to deal with scientific details of uranium supplies and radiation effects as well as broader issues of scientific organization and policy. His correspondence during this time referred to issues ranging from Britain's relationship with the United States to the effects of cobalt on the health of sheep.

Diplomatic Engagements

As the pressures of war became greater, the British realized that even with their theoretical advances, they did not have the practical resources to develop a working atomic bomb. In 1943 Britain and the United States signed the Quebec Agreement, which created a partnership between the two countries for the development of an atomic bomb. Chadwick became the leader of the British contingent involved in the Manhattan Project in the United States. Although he was shy and used to the isolation of the laboratory, Chadwick became known for his tireless efforts at collaboration and his keen sense of diplomacy. He maintained friendly Anglo-American relations despite a great variety of scientific challenges, political struggles, and conflicting personalities. On July 16, 1945, he witnessed the first atomic test in the New Mexico desert.

After the war Chadwick's work continued to focus on nuclear weapons. He was an advisor for the British representatives to the United Nations regarding the control of atomic energy around the world. He believed that the British had to have their own atomic weapons, and he pushed hard for Britain's atomic independence. This issue was particularly evident to him when the United States and Britain argued over an earlier agreement for dividing up the uranium supplies they had jointly accumulated during the development of the atomic bomb. Chadwick used his diplomacy to effect a compromise that enabled the British to reclaim the uranium needed for their own atomic projects. Chadwick's postwar involvement with nuclear energy was not limited to weapons. He also was interested in medical applications of radioactive materials, and he worked to develop ways of regulating radioactive substances.

Chadwick was a dedicated and tireless scientist who balanced his commitments to science with a commitment to his family. He and his wife, Aileen Stewart-Brown, whom he married in 1925, had twin daughters. Though he was shy and serious, he did not lack a sense of humor: to celebrate the operation of a new cyclotron (particle accelerator) at Liverpool, Chadwick passed around laboratory beakers full of champagne.

Chadwick had an exacting sense of discipline and a tireless attention to detail. When he was at the Cavendish laboratory, all papers that went out for publication passed under his critical gaze. In an article in the *Bulletin of the Atomic Scientists*, Mark Oliphant, who had been a research student under Chadwick, remarked that "he was a severe critic of English usage and seemed to carry in his head the whole of Roget's *Thesaurus of English Words and Phrases*."

Much of Chadwick's early career went toward searching for the neutron. When he found it, the physics community quickly seized on the prospect of developing from it the atomic bomb. Much of the rest of Chadwick's career was spent in assisting that development. Although he pushed for atomic policy issues as much as he pushed for scientific solutions, Chadwick eventually saw the uselessness of the atomic bomb. Margaret Gowing, in her article, "James Chadwick and the Atomic Bomb," quoted Chadwick as saying of the bomb, "Its effect in causing suffering is out of all proportion to its military effect." James Chadwick died in Cambridge, England, on July 24, 1974.

SELECTED WRITINGS BY CHADWICK:

Books

Radioactivity and Radioactive Substances, Pitman, 1934.

SOURCES:

Books

Pais, Abraham, *Inward Bound,* Oxford University Press, 1986.

Rhodes, Richard, *The Making of the Bomb,* Simon & Schuster, 1986.

Periodicals

Gowing, Margaret, "James Chadwick and the Atomic Bomb," *Notes and Records of the Royal Society of London,* January, 1993, pp. 79–92.
Oliphant, Mark, "The Beginning: Chadwick and the Neutron," *The Bulletin of the Atomic Scientists,* December, 1982, pp. 14–18.
Pollard, Ernest, "Neutron Pioneer," *Physics World,* October, 1991, pp. 31–33.
Time, August 5, 1974.

—Sketch by Lawrence Souder

Ernst Boris Chain
1906-1979
German-born English biochemist

Ernst Boris Chain was instrumental in the creation of penicillin, the first antibiotic drug. Although the Scottish bacteriologist **Alexander Fleming** discovered the *penicillium notatum* mold in 1928, it was Chain who, together with **Howard Florey**, isolated the breakthrough substance that has saved countless victims of infections. For their work, Chain, Florey, and Fleming were awarded the Nobel Prize in physiology or medicine in 1945.

Chain was born in Berlin on June 19, 1906 to Michael Chain and Margarete Eisner Chain. His father was a Russian immigrant who became a chemical engineer and built a successful chemical plant. The death of Michael Chain in 1919, coupled with the collapse of the post-World War I German economy, depleted the family's income so much that Margarete Chain had to open up her home as a guesthouse.

One of Chain's primary interests during his youth was music, and for a while it seemed that he would embark on a career as a concert pianist. He gave a number of recitals and for a while served as music critic for a Berlin newspaper. A cousin, whose brother-in-law had been a failed conductor, gradually convinced Chain that a career in science would be more rewarding than one in music. Although he took lessons in conducting, Chain graduated from Friedrich-Wilhelm University in 1930 with a degree in chemistry and physiology.

Chain began work at the Charite Hospital in Berlin while also conducting research at the Kaiser Wilhelm Institute for Physical Chemistry and Electrochemistry. But the increasing pressures of life in Germany, including the growing strength of the Nazi party, convinced Chain that, as a Jew, he could not expect a notable professional future in Germany. Therefore, when Hitler came to power in January 1933, Chain decided to leave. Like many others, he mistakenly believed the Nazis would soon be ousted. His mother and sister chose not to leave, and both died in concentration camps.

Chain arrived in England in April 1933, and soon acquired a position at University College Hospital Medical School. He stayed there briefly and then went to Cambridge to work under the biochemist **Frederick Gowland Hopkins**. Chain spent much of his time at Cambridge conducting research on enzymes. In 1935, Howard Florey became head of the Sir William Dunn School of Pathology at Oxford. Florey, an Australian-born pathologist, wanted a top-notch biochemist to help him with his research, and asked Hopkins for advice. Without hesitation, Hopkins suggested Chain.

Intrigued By Fleming's Research

Florey was actively engaged in research on the bacteriolytic substance lysozyme, which had been identified by Fleming in his quest to eradicate infection. Chain came across Fleming's reports on the penicillin mold and was immediately intrigued. He and Florey both saw great potential in the further investigation of penicillin. With the help of a Rockefeller Foundation grant, the two scientists assembled a research team and set to work on isolating the active ingredient in *penicillium notatum*.

Fleming, who had been unable to identify the antibacterial agent in the mold, had used the mold broth itself in his experiments to kill infections. Assisted in their research by fellow scientist Norman Heatley, Chain and Florey began their work by growing large quantities of the mold in the Oxford laboratory. Once there were adequate supplies of the mold, Chain began the tedious process of isolating the "miracle" substance. Succeeding after several months in isolating small amounts of a powder which he obtained by freeze-drying the mold broth, Chain was ready for the first practical test. His experiments with laboratory mice were successful, and it was decided that more of the substance should be produced to try on humans. To do this, the scientists needed to ferment massive quantities of mold broth; it took 125 gallons of the broth to make enough penicillin powder for one tablet. By 1941 Chain and his colleagues had finally gathered enough penicillin to conduct experiments with patients. The first two of eight patients died from complications unrelated to their infections,

but the remaining six, who had been on the verge of death, were completely cured.

One potential use for penicillin was the treatment of wounded soldiers, an increasingly significant issue during the Second World War. However, for penicillin to be widely effective, the researchers needed to devise a way to mass-produce the substance. Florey and Heatley went to the United States in 1941 to enlist the aid of the government and of pharmaceutical houses. New ways were found to yield more and stronger penicillin from mold broth, and by 1943 the drug went into regular medical use for Allied troops. After the war, penicillin was made available for civilian use. The ethics of whether to make penicillin research universally available posed a particularly difficult problem for the scientific community during the war years. While some believed that the research should not be shared with the enemy, others felt that no one should be denied the benefits of penicillin. This added layers of political intrigue to the scientific pursuits of Chain and his colleagues. Even after the war, Chain experienced firsthand the results of this dilemma. As chairman of the World Health Organization in the late 1940s, Chain had gone to Czechoslovakia to supervise the operation of penicillin plants established there by the United Nations. He remained there until his work was done, even though the Communist coup occurred shortly after his arrival. When Chain applied for a visa to visit the United States in 1951, his request was denied by the State Department. Though no reason was given, many believed his stay in Czechoslovakia, however apolitical, was a major factor.

Heads New Institute in Rome

After the war, Chain tried to convince his colleagues that penicillin and other antibiotic research should be expanded, and he pushed for more state-of-the-art facilities at Oxford. Little came of his efforts, however, and when the Italian State Institute of Public Health in Rome offered him the opportunity to organize a biochemical and microbiological department along with a pilot plant, Chain decided to leave Oxford.

Under Chain's direction, the facilities at the State Institute became known internationally as a center for advanced research. While in Rome, Chain worked to develop new strains of penicillin and to find more efficient ways to produce the drug. Work done by a number of scientists, with Chain's guidance, yielded isolation of the basic penicillin molecule in 1958, and hundreds of new penicillin strains were soon synthesized.

In 1963 Chain was persuaded to return to England. The University of London had just established the Wolfson Laboratories at the Imperial College of Science and Technology, and Chain was asked to direct them. Through his hard work the Wolfson Laboratories earned a reputation as a first-rate research center.

In 1948, Chain had married Anne Beloff, a fellow biochemist, and in the following years she assisted him with his research. She had received her Ph.D. from Oxford and had worked at Harvard in the 1940s. The couple had three children.

Chain retired from Imperial College in 1973 but continued to lecture. He cautioned against allowing the then-new field of molecular biology to downplay the importance of biochemistry to medical research. He still played the piano, for which he had always found time even during his busiest research years. Over the years, Chain also became increasingly active in Jewish affairs. He served on the Board of Governors of the Weizmann Institute in Israel, and was an outspoken supporter of the importance of providing Jewish education for young Jewish children in England and abroad—all three of his children received part of their education in Israel.

In addition to the Nobel Prize, Chain received the Berzelius Medal in 1946 and was made a commander of the Legion d'Honneur in 1947. In 1954 he was awarded the Paul Ehrlich Centenary Prize. Chain was knighted by Queen Elizabeth II in 1969. Increasing ill health did not slow Chain down initially, but he finally died of heart failure on August 14, 1979.

SELECTED WRITINGS BY CHAIN:

Books

(With H. W. Florey, N. G. Heatley, and others) *Antibiotics,* Oxford University Press, 1949.

SOURCES:

Books

Clark, Ronald, *The Life of Ernst Chain,* St. Martin's, 1985.
Curtis, Robert H. *Great Lives: Medicine,* Scribner, 1993, pp. 77–90.

Periodicals

Chain, Benjamin, "Penicillin and Beyond," *Nature,* October 10, 1991, pp. 492–94.

—*Sketch by George A. Milite*

Owen Chamberlain
1920-
American physicist

Owen Chamberlain won the 1959 Nobel Prize in physics for confirming the existence of the antiproton. He shared this honor with his colleague of many years, **Emilio Segrè**. The antiproton was hypothesized as being a mirror image of the proton, a particle found in the nucleus of atoms. Proving the existence of the antiproton confirmed that idea of atomic symmetry; it was also an important breakthrough for particle physicists in their study of antimatter. Chamberlain and Segrè's work in high-energy physics at the University of California, Berkeley, was made possible by the development of the bevatron particle accelerator. This powerful accelerator, which was built at Berkeley, was able to fire protons of 6.2 billion electron volts, a nuclear force far stronger than the energy generated by the hydrogen bomb or by stars. Prior to his work at Berkeley, Chamberlain had done atomic research for the Manhattan Project (the U.S. secret program to build the atomic bomb), in addition to carrying out early studies on alpha particle decay, neutron diffraction, and high-energy nuclear reactions. After proving the existence of the antiproton, he went on to discover the antineutron.

Chamberlain was born in San Francisco, California, on July 10, 1920, to Edward and Genevieve Owen Chamberlain. His father was a radiologist at Stanford University Hospital. The Chamberlains moved to Philadelphia when their son was ten years old, and he entered the Germantown Friends School there. He received his undergraduate degree at Dartmouth College in 1941 and had begun graduate work at the University of California at Berkeley when the United States entered World War II. His education plans changed by the war, Chamberlain left school to join the Manhattan Project, researching uranium isotopes with **Ernest O. Lawrence**, inventor of the cyclotron, the first particle accelerator. Chamberlain was sent to Los Alamos in 1943 and took part in the testing of the first atom bomb. When the war ended, he continued his work in atomic physics at the Argonne National Laboratory in Chicago, studying with the atomic physicist **Enrico Fermi**. He received his Ph.D. from the University of Chicago in 1948 and returned to Berkeley that same year. Except for a brief period during the late 1950s when he was on leave for a Guggenheim fellowship in Rome and as Loeb lecturer at Harvard University, Chamberlain was to remain at Berkeley for his entire career, becoming professor emeritus in 1989.

The Search for Antiparticles

The existence of antiparticles had been predicted in 1928 by the English physicist **Paul Dirac**. He theorized that mirror images of known particles, such as the electron and the proton, must exist, although he could offer no experimental proof. But in the early 1930s his theory was given a thrust forward when **Carl D. Anderson** discovered the positron (so called because it has a positive electrical charge), a twin of the negative electron. Anderson's discovery of this antiparticle created great excitement among particle physicists and was to spur further research, particularly in the area of high-energy particle accelerators, because the present accelerators could not deliver the energy needed for heavy particle creation.

Chamberlain's work with the cyclotron at Berkeley established the groundwork for his later attempts to produce and detect antiprotons. His investigation of the scattering of high-energy protons and neutrons succeeded in producing the first triple-scattering of polarized protons. These investigations took Chamberlain, Segrè, and their research group into the next level of study, that of antiprotons. By the early 1950s, the Bevatron accelerator had been constructed at Berkeley. Its ability to propel particles to energy levels of a billion electron volts enabled the group to produce antiprotons. Finding the short-lived antiprotons amidst the collision debris generated by the atom smashing process was the next major hurdle to be overcome. Chamberlain and his group solved that problem by inventing a series of focusing and measuring devices that could isolate the antiprotons. Then a photographic process was developed to document protons and antiprotons colliding and destroying each other. The detection procedure was time-consuming. Only about one out of thirty thousand particles was identified as an antiproton, and on average it took about one hour to record four antiproton sightings. In 1955, after forty antiproton sightings had been recorded, the group felt confident enough to announce the results of their experiments.

In his Nobel address, Chamberlain looked ahead to new discoveries made possible by the work done on the antiproton: "Since the proton and neutron are close sisters, it was expected that the discovery of the antineutron [would] quickly follow that of the antiproton. In fact, it is natural to infer that antiparticles of all charged particles exist."

The author of many scientific papers regarding his discoveries, Chamberlain's work was published in journals at home and abroad. His professional affiliations include the American Physical Society, the National Academy of Sciences, and the American Association for the Advancement of Science. He has also been a Fellow of the American Academy of Arts and Sciences. Chamberlain married Beatrice Babette Cooper in 1943. They had three daughters and a son,

and were divorced in 1978. He married June Steingart in 1980.

SELECTED WRITINGS BY CHAMBERLAIN:

Periodicals

(With others) "Observation of Antiprotons," *Physical Review,* Volume 100, 1955, pp. 947–950.
(With others) "Antiproton Star Observed in Emulsion," *Physical Review,* Volume 101, 1956, pp. 909–910.
(With others) "Example of an Antiproton Nucleon Annihilation," *Physical Review,* Volume 102, 1956, pp. 921–923.

SOURCES:

Books

Wasson, Tyler, editor, *Nobel Prize Winners,* H. W. Wilson, 1987, pp. 197–199.

Periodicals

Nature, October 17, 1959, p. 1189.

—*Sketch by Jane Stewart Cook*

Thomas Chrowder Chamberlin
1843-1928
American geologist

Thomas Chrowder Chamberlin was one of the great scientific intellects in the United States in the period between 1875 and 1925. In his obituary in the December 21, 1928, issue of *Science,* H. L. Fairchild said that the nation had lost "her greatest geologist and the world one of its boldest thinkers." Chamberlin's scientific research fell into two large categories: glaciology and cosmology. For many years he was particularly interested in the study of glaciers and in the climate that may have made them possible. In the later 1890s, he also turned to a study of theories regarding the Earth's origin, becoming an outspoken proponent for the stellar collision theory of planetary formation. Chamberlin also held a number of important academic and professional positions, including the presidency of the University of Wisconsin from 1887 to 1892.

Chamberlin was born in Mattoon, Illinois, on September 25, 1843. His father was John Chamberlin, a farmer and itinerant Methodist preacher, and his mother was the former Cecilia Gill. The senior Chamberlin was described as a man of rare integrity who encouraged his sons to think critically.

When Chamberlin was three years old, his family moved to a farm near Beloit, Wisconsin. He later expressed the view that his new home, amid the rolling hills formed by glacial moraines, was to be an important influence on his choice of a scientific career. He recalled wondering about the fascinating geological phenomena around him, especially the fossil remains of sea animals. After completing his primary and secondary education in local schools, Chamberlin entered Beloit College, from which he received his bachelor of arts degree in 1866. He then took a job as principal of the high school in Delavan, Wisconsin, where he remained for two years. During this period he married Alma Isabel Wilson, of Beloit, on Christmas Eve, 1869. The Chamberlins later had one son, Rollin Thomas, who was later to become professor of geology at the University of Chicago.

Embarks on a Career in Geology

Dissatisfied with his situation at Delavan, Chamberlin decided to spend the 1868–69 academic year at the University of Michigan, pursuing graduate studies in geology. At the end of that year, he took a post as professor of natural sciences at the State Normal School at Whitewater, Wisconsin. The year of 1873 marked an important turning point in Chamberlin's life. He was appointed professor of geology, zoology, and botany at Beloit College, and simultaneously was named assistant geologist at the newly established Wisconsin Geological Survey. He was assigned responsibility for the southeastern part of the state, an area where glacial characteristics were obvious. As a result, his study of glaciation was not entirely voluntary.

For three years Chamberlin carried on his two careers, one at Beloit and the other at the Geological Survey. Then, in 1876, he took a leave of absence from the college in order to take on new responsibilities as chief geologist for the state of Wisconsin. Over the next six years, he supervised an extensive survey of the state's geological features, a study that was later summarized in four large volumes, *Geology of Wisconsin,* published between 1877 and 1883. The work has been described as a model of pioneer geological research.

Chamberlin's work focused, of course, on a description of the existing geological features of the Wisconsin countryside, features such as moraines (accumulations of earth and stones), glacial drift, fossilized coral reefs, and glacial deposits. But it also forced him to think about the climatic conditions from past history that might have made possible the giant ice sheets whose effects he now studied. He was one of the first scientists to recognize that varying concentrations of carbon dioxide in the Earth's atmosphere might result in the retention of greater or lesser amounts of heat in the atmosphere and, hence, in temperature changes that might make possible alternating periods of glaciation and warming. In this line of thinking, first presented in an 1897 paper, Chamberlin foreshadowed the modern-day debate regarding global warming and climate change.

Considers the Problem of Planetary Formation

Chamberlin's hypothesis that the Earth has gone through periods of warming and cooling in its history seemed to contradict the traditional view of Earth's history. According to that view, the Earth was thought to have formed out of a hot mass of material and then to have undergone a slow, but continuous, cooling throughout its history. Almost inevitably, given his questioning mind, Chamberlin began to think about this issue. He found it increasingly difficult to accept the nebular theory of planetary formation, originally suggested by Pierre-Simon Laplace in the early nineteenth century.

Instead Chamberlin revived an alternative hypothesis proposed by George Buffon in 1745. According to Buffon's theory the Earth was formed as the result of a near-collision between a mammoth comet and our own sun. In that near-collision, many tiny fragments (planetesimals) were formed and then coalesced to form the Earth and other planets. Although the question of planetary origin has still not been solved, Chamberlin's theory appears to have lost favor among modern cosmologists.

In 1881 Chamberlin was invited to become director of the newly formed glacial division of the U.S. Geological Survey. Over the next six years, he was responsible for a number of important memoirs that appeared in its official reports. Although he continued to hold his Geological Survey title until 1904, Chamberlin also went on to other jobs. In 1887 he was named president of the University of Wisconsin. During his five-year tenure in Madison, Chamberlin transformed the school from a small, somewhat parochial college into a nationally known first-rate university.

Yet another opportunity presented itself in 1891 when Chamberlin was offered the chairmanship of the department of geology at the newly established University of Chicago, a post he assumed a year later. He served simultaneously as director of the university's Walker Museum. Chamberlin remained at Chicago until his retirement in 1918, when he was named professor emeritus. He died in Chicago on November 15, 1928.

Chamberlin was active in many professional organizations. He served as president of the Wisconsin Academy of Science, Arts, and Letters from 1885 to 1986, of the Geological Society of America in 1895, of the Chicago Academy of Sciences from 1897 to 1914, of the Illinois Academy of Science in 1907, and of the American Association for the Advancement of Science from 1908 to 1909. Chamberlin founded the *Journal of Geology* in 1893 and served as editor in chief until 1922 and then as senior editor from 1922 to 1928.

Among his many awards were medals from the 1878 and 1893 Paris Expositions, the 1910 Culver Medal of the Geographical Society of Chicago, the 1920 Hayden Medal of the Philadelphia Academy of Natural Sciences, the 1924 Penrose Medal of the Society of Economic Geologists, and the 1927 Penrose Medal of the Geological Society of America. He also received honorary degrees from the Universities of Michigan, Wisconsin, Toronto, Illinois, and Columbia and from Beloit College.

SELECTED WRITINGS BY CHAMBERLIN:

Books

(With R. D. Salisbury) *The Geology of Wisconsin*, four volumes, Commissioners of Public Printing, 1873–82.

(With R. D. Salisbury) *College Geology*, three volumes, Holt, 1904–06.

The Origin of the Earth, University of Chicago Press, 1916.

The Two Solar Families: The Sun's Children, University of Chicago Press, 1928.`

Periodicals

"Glacial Phenomena of North America," *The Great Ice Age*, edited by James Geikie, third edition, D. Appleton, 1895.

"A Group of Hypotheses Bearing on Climatic Changes," *Journal of Geology*, Volume 5, 1897, pp. 653–683.

"The Method of Multiple Working Hypotheses," *Journal of Geology*, Volume 5, 1897, pp. 837–848. (With F. R. Moulton) "The Development of the Planetesimal Hypothesis," *Science*, Volume 30, 1909, pp. 643–645.

SOURCES:

Books

Chamberlin, Rollin T., "Thomas Chrowder Chamberlin, 1843–1928," in *Biographical Memoirs*, Volume 15, National Academy of Sciences, 1934, pp. 307–407.

Dictionary of American Biography, Volume 3, Scribner, 1929, pp. 600–601.

Dictionary of Scientific Biography, Volume 3, Scribner, 1975, pp. 189–191.

National Cyclopaedia of American Biography, Volume 19, James T. White, 1967, pp. 25–26.

Periodicals

Fairchild, H. L., "Thomas Chrowder, Chamberlin—Teacher, Administrator, Geologist, Philosopher," *Science*, December 21, 1928, pp. 610–612.

Mather, Kirtley, "Thomas Chrowder Chamberlin (1843–1928)," *Proceedings of the American Academy of Arts and Sciences*, Volume 70, 1936, pp. 505–508.

Willis, Bailey, "Memorial of Thomas Chrowder Chamberlin," *Bulletin of the Geological Society of America*, Volume 40, 1929, pp. 23–44.

—*Sketch by David E. Newton*

Britton Chance
1913-
American biochemist and biophysicist

Combining an interest in electronics with his specialties of chemistry and biology, Britton Chance developed new equipment and techniques for research in biochemistry and biophysics, including invention of the double-beam spectrophotometer and the reflectance fluorometer and application of computer methods to the study of enzyme action and metabolic control. Furthermore, the experimental results he has obtained using his own innovative procedures are of major importance in such areas as determining the actions of narcotics and poisons on living cells.

Born in Wilkes-Barre, Pennsylvania, on July 24, 1913, Chance was the son of Edwin M. Chance, a chemist who was honored for research in mine gases and who worked with the Chemical Warfare Service during World War I. His mother was Eleanor Kent Chance. Both parents were from Philadelphia, Pennsylvania, and the family returned there after Britton's birth, with the senior Chance becoming an engineer. Summers were spent at Barnegat Bay, New Jersey, where the family kept a 100-foot cruiser that they sailed as far as the Caribbean and Europe.

After graduating from the Haverford School, Chance studied at the University of Pennsylvania, where he earned a B.S. degree in chemistry in 1935, and an M.S. the following year. His experience with sailing led him to an interest in navigation and automatic steering, which he thought could be improved using electronics; he found room in his curriculum to study enough physics and electrical engineering to pursue that interest. Under the guidance of Martin Kilpatrick, his chemistry mentor at Pennsylvania, Chance investigated rapid chemical reaction techniques. Using his knowledge of electronics, he developed better instrumentation for observing the small, quick changes in optical density that accompany reactions involving enzymes—the protein produced by living cells that stimulates such important functions as food digestion and the release of energy.

An Excursion into Electronics

After receiving his master's degree, Chance traveled to England to supervise the installation of the marine electronic steering system he had invented, which was first used on a 12,000-ton ship. In 1938 he married his childhood sweetheart, Jane Earle, and they used the ship's trial cruise to Australia as their honeymoon. Upon returning to England, Chance enrolled as a research student at Cambridge University. He studied under F. J. W. Roughton, who had developed a fundamental procedure for observing rapid reactions, and G. A. Millikan, a physiologist. Millikan was using Roughton's technique to study muscle pigments, and Chance adapted the same procedure to reactions between small quantities of substances. Altering both the experimental technique and the equipment, Chance devised the "accelerated flow modification" procedure: reactants were simultaneously injected into a fine tube, where the changes in light absorption of the reacting material were continuously monitored with a highly sensitive oscilloscope. This important modification allowed experiments to be conducted more quickly, was more sensitive to reactions, and required less materials to complete experiments.

At the outbreak of World War II in 1939, Chance returned to the United States and joined the faculty at the University of Pennsylvania's Eldridge Reeves Johnson Foundation of Medical Physics. There, he finished developing his technique for measuring the reaction between hydrogen peroxide and the enzyme peroxidase. He was awarded a Ph.D. in physical chemistry in 1940 and became acting director of the Johnson Foundation. Two years later, he was awarded a Ph.D. in biology and physiology by Cambridge.

During World War II, Chance was invited to work on radar at the Massachusetts Institute of Technology's Radiation Laboratory. Between 1941 and 1946, he headed the Precision Components Group, served as associate head of the Receiver Components Division, and was one of the younger members of the laboratory's Steering Committee. Among the devices he helped develop were precision timing and computing circuits for bombing and navigation. In 1942, he applied advanced electronic circuits to measuring small changes in light absorption, and in 1943, he experimentally validated the Michaelis-Menton theory of enzyme action, which had first been proposed in 1913.

Postwar Studies in Biophysics and Biochemistry

When the war ended, Chance devoted himself to the study of the nature of enzymes and won a Guggenheim Fellowship to study at the Nobel Institute in Sweden and the Molteno Institute in Great Britain from 1946 to 1948. His interest in boating continued; while in Europe, he and his wife (a skilled helmsman) won numerous races for Class E scows that were held in the Baltic Sea.

In 1949, Chance returned to the University of Pennsylvania as a professor, chairperson of the department of biophysics and physical biochemistry, director of the Johnson Foundation, and faculty adviser for the university yacht club. His research on enzymatic reactions in living systems directed him to the creation of the double-beam or dual-wavelength spectrophotometer, an optical device that was used to study mitochondria—those elements of the cell nucleus that produce energy—as well as cell suspensions and other biological systems. Adapting the double-beam spectrophotometer to living materials, he developed the reflectance fluoromcter, an instrument that led, eventually, to a better understanding of the actions of narcotics, hormones and poisons on human cells.

In addition to his work with these ground-breaking devices, Chance began to apply analog and digital computers to his research in the 1940s, producing the first computer solution of the differential equations describing enzyme action. Beginning in 1955, Chance concentrated his studies on the control of metabolism, especially as it is related to mitochondria. Chance studied these energy-producing elements in the cell nucleus, attempting to determine their role as optical indicators of change within the cell. His work on the concentration of adenosinediphosphate (ADP) in tumor cells gave scientists a better understanding of the role of mitochondria in regulating the body's utilization of glucose.

During the next four decades, Chance developed increasingly sophisticated instruments for optical spectroscopy and imaging of tissues, particularly in living patients. In the area of tumor oxygenation, he found significant differences in hemoglobin oxygenation between the surface and deeper regions of solid tumors, which a 1992 article in *Proceedings of the IEEE* described as being "of great importance clinically, for example, in relation to the oxygen-dependent response to radiation therapy." In another study, he made time-resolved measurements of photon migration on the forehead of a patient with Alzheimer's disease, finding the scattering coefficient of the brain tissue in some regions to be one-half to one-third of normal values.

International Acclaim

Recognition of Chance's fundamental contributions to biomedical electronics and other fields came from all over the world. His pioneering work with rapid enzyme reactions was described in a 1949 issue of *Nature:* "The value and scope of this experimental technique in the field of reaction kinetics can scarcely be overestimated." His achievements were further acknowledged in 1954 with his election to the National Academy of Sciences, and he became a life fellow in the Institute of Electrical and Electronics Engineers (IEEE) in 1961. He holds several honorary medical degrees, including an honorary M.D. from the Karolinska Institute of the University of Stockholm. Chance has also been honored with the Dutch Chemical Society's Genootschaps-Medaille and the Franklin Medal of the Franklin Institute. President Gerald Ford presented him with the National Medal of Science in 1974, and in 1976, the University of Pennsylvania named him university professor, its highest academic appointment. He retired from the university in 1983.

In 1956, Chance married for the second time, wedding Lilian Streeter Lucas. He has served as father to twelve children, including the four from his first marriage and four stepchildren.

SELECTED WRITINGS BY CHANCE:

Books

Control of Energy Metabolism, Academic Press, 1965.
Tunneling in Biological Systems, Academic Press, 1979.
"Photon Migration in Muscle and Brain," *Photon Migration in Tissues,* Plenum, 1990, pp. 121–135.
Time-Resolved Spectroscopy and Imaging of Tissues, SPIE, 1991.

Periodicals

(With Brian C. Wilson and others) "Time-Dependent Optical Spectroscopy and Imaging for Biomedical Applications" *Proceedings of the IEEE,* June, 1992, pp. 918–930.

SOURCES:

Books

Modern Men of Science, McGraw-Hill, 1966, pp. 95–97.

Periodicals

"Britton Chance Wins Paul-Lewis Award in Enzyme Chemistry," *Chemical and Engineering News,* May 8, 1950.
"Medical Physics at the University of Pennsylvania: Dr. Britton Chance," *Nature,* April 9, 1949, pp. 558–559.

—*Sketch by Rodolfo A. Windhausen*

Subrahmanyan Chandrasekhar 1910-

Indian-born American astrophysicist and applied mathematician

Subrahmanyan Chandrasekhar is an Indian-born American astrophysicist and applied mathematician whose work on the origins, structure, and dynamics of stars has secured him a prominent place in the annals of science. His most celebrated work concerns the radiation of energy from stars, particularly white dwarf stars, which are the dying fragments of stars. Chandrasekhar demonstrated that the radius of a white dwarf star is related to its mass: the greater its mass, the smaller its radius. Chandrasekhar has made numerous other contributions to astrophysics. His expansive research and published papers and books include topics such as the system of energy transfer within stars, stellar evolution, stellar structure, and theories of planetary and stellar atmospheres. For nearly twenty years, he served as the editor-in-chief of the *Astrophysical Journal,* the leading publication of its kind in the world. For his immense contribution to science, Chandrasekhar has received numerous awards and distinctions, most notably, the 1983 Nobel Prize for Physics for his research into the depths of aged stars.

Chandrasekhar, better known as Chandra, was born on October 19, 1910, in Lahore, India (now part of Pakistan), the first son of C. Subrahmanyan Ayyar and Sitalakshmi nee (Divan Bahadur) Balakrishnan. Chandra came from a large family: he had two older sisters, four younger sisters, and three younger brothers. As the firstborn son, Chandra inherited his

Subrahmanyan Chandrasekhar

paternal grandfather's name, Chandrasekhar. His uncle was the Nobel Prize-winning Indian physicist, Sir C. V. Raman.

Chandra received his early education at home, beginning when he was five. From his mother he learned Tamil, from his father, English and arithmetic. He set his sights upon becoming a scientist at an early age, and to this end, undertook at his own initiative some independent study of calculus and physics. The family moved north to Lucknow in Uttar Pradesh when Chandra was six. In 1918, the family moved again, this time south to Madras. Chandrasekhar was taught by private tutors until 1921, when he enrolled in the Hindu High School in Triplicane. With typical drive and motivation, he studied on his own and steamed ahead of the class, completing school by the age of fifteen.

After high school, Chandra attended Presidency College in Madras. For the first two years, he studied physics, chemistry, English, and Sanskrit. For his B.A. honors degree he wished to take pure mathematics but his father insisted that he take physics. Chandra resolved this conflict by registering as an honors physics student but attending mathematics lectures. Recognizing his brilliance, his lecturers went out of their way to accommodate Chandra. Chandra also took part in sporting activities and joined the debating team. A highlight of his college years was the publication of his paper, "The Compton Scattering and the New Statistics." These and other early

successes while he was still an eighteen-year-old undergraduate only strengthened Chandra's resolve to pursue a career in scientific research, despite his father's wish that he join the Indian civil service. A meeting the following year with the German physicist **Werner Heisenberg**, whom Chandra, as the secretary of the student science association, had the honor of showing around Madras, and Chandra's attendance at the Indian Science Congress Association Meeting in early 1930, where his work was hailed, doubled his determination.

Leaves India for Cambridge, England

Upon graduating with a M.A. in 1930, Chandra set off for Trinity College, Cambridge, as a research student, courtesy of an Indian government scholarship created especially for him (with the stipulation that upon his return to India, he would serve for five years in the Madras government service). At Cambridge, Chandra turned to astrophysics, inspired by a theory of stellar evolution that had occurred to him as he made the long boat journey from India to Cambridge. It would preoccupy him for the next ten years. He also worked on other aspects of astrophysics and published many papers.

In the summer of 1931, he worked with physicist **Max Born** at the Institut für Theoretische Physik at Göttingen in Germany. There, he studied group theory and quantum mechanics (the mathematical theory that relates matter and radiation) and produced work on the theory of stellar atmospheres. During this period, Chandra was often tempted to leave astrophysics for pure mathematics, his first love, or at least for physics. He was worried, though, that with less than a year to go before his thesis exam, a change might cost him his degree. Other factors influenced his decision to stay with astrophysics, most importantly, the encouragement shown him by astrophysicist **Edward Arthur Milne**. In August 1932, Chandra left Cambridge to continue his studies in Denmark under physicist **Niels Bohr**. In Copenhagen, he was able to devote more of his energies to pure physics. A series of Chandra's lectures on astrophysics given at the University of Liège, in Belgium, in February 1933 received a warm reception. Before returning to Cambridge in May 1933 to sit his doctorate exams, he went back to Copenhagen to work on his thesis.

Chandrasekhar's uncertainty about his future was assuaged when he was awarded a fellowship at Trinity College, Cambridge. During a four-week trip to Russia in 1934, where he met physicists **Lev Davidovich Landau**, B. P. Geraismovic, and Viktor Ambartsumian, he returned to the work that had led him into astrophysics to begin with, white dwarfs. Upon returning to Cambridge, he took up research of white dwarfs again in earnest.

As a member of the Royal Astronomical Society since 1932, Chandra was entitled to present papers at its twice monthly meetings. It was at one of these that Chandra, in 1935, announced the results of the work that would later make his name. As stars evolve, he told the assembled audience, they emit energy generated by their conversion of hydrogen into helium and even heavier elements. As they reach the end of their life, stars have progressively less hydrogen left to convert and emit less energy in the form of radiation. They eventually reach a stage when they are no longer able to generate the pressure needed to sustain their size against their own gravitational pull and they begin to contract. As their density increases during the contraction process, stars build up sufficient internal energy to collapse their atomic structure into a degenerate state. They begin to collapse into themselves. Their electrons become so tightly packed that their normal activity is suppressed and they become white dwarfs, tiny objects of enormous density. The greater the mass of a white dwarf, the smaller its radius, according to Chandrasekhar. However, not all stars end their lives as stable white dwarfs. If the mass of evolving stars increases beyond a certain limit, eventually named the *Chandrasekhar limit* and calculated as 1.4 times the mass of the sun, evolving stars cannot become stable white dwarfs. A star with a mass above the limit has to either lose mass to become a white dwarf or take an alternative evolutionary path and become a supernova, which releases its excess energy in the form of an explosion. What mass remains after this spectacular event may become a white dwarf but more likely will form a neutron star. The neutron star has even greater density than a white dwarf and an average radius of about .15 km. It has since been independently proven that all white dwarf stars fall within Chandrasekhar's predicted limit, which has been revised to equal 1.2 solar masses.

Theory of Stellar Evolution Unexpectedly Ridiculed

Unfortunately, although his theory would later be vindicated, Chandra's ideas were unexpectedly undermined and ridiculed by no less a scientific figure than astronomer and physicist **Sir Arthur Stanley Eddington**, who dismissed as absurd Chandra's notion that stars can evolve into anything other than white dwarfs. Eddington's status and authority in the community of astronomers carried the day, and Chandra, as the junior, was not given the benefit of the doubt. Twenty years passed before his theory gained general acceptance among astrophysicists, although it was quickly recognized as valid by physicists as noteworthy as **Wolfgang Pauli**, Niels Bohr, Ralph H. Fowler, and **Paul Dirac**. Rather than continue sparring with Eddington at scientific meeting after meeting, Chandra collected his thoughts on the matter into his first book, *An Introduction to the Study of Stellar Structure*, and departed the fray to take up new research around

stellar dynamics. An unfortunate result of the scientific quarrel, however, was to postpone the discovery of black holes and neutron stars by at least twenty years and Chandra's receipt of a Nobel Prize for his white dwarf work by fifty years. Surprisingly, despite their scientific differences, he retained a close personal relationship with Eddington.

Chandra spent from December 1935 until March 1936 at Harvard University as a visiting lecturer in cosmic physics. While in the United States, he was offered a research associate position at Yerkes Observatory at Williams Bay, Wisconsin, staring in January 1937. Before taking up this post, Chandra returned home to India to marry the woman who had waited for him patiently for six years. He had known Lalitha Doraiswamy, daughter of Captain and Mrs. Savitri Doraiswamy, since they had been students together at Madras University. After graduation, she had undertaken a masters degree. At the time of their marriage, she was a headmistress. Although their marriage of love was unusual, as both came from fairly progressive families and were both of the Brahman caste, neither of their families had any real objections. After a whirlwind courtship and wedding, the young bride and groom set out for the United States. They intended to stay no more than a few years, but, as luck would have it, it became their permanent home.

Joins Staff of Yerkes Observatory in the United States

At the Yerkes Observatory, Chandra was charged with developing a graduate program in astronomy and astrophysics and with teaching some of the courses. His reputation as a teacher soon attracted top students to the observatory's graduate school. He also continued researching stellar evolution, stellar structure, and the transfer of energy within stars. In 1938, he was promoted to assistant professor of astrophysics. During this time Chandra revealed his conclusions regarding the life paths of stars.

During the Second World War, Chandra was employed at the Aberdeen Proving Grounds in Maryland, working on ballistic tests, the theory of shock waves, the Mach effect, and transport problems related to neutron diffusion. In 1942, he was promoted to associate professor of astrophysics at the University of Chicago and in 1943, to professor. Around 1944, he switched his research from stellar dynamics to radiative transfer. Of all his research, the latter gave him, he recalled later, more fulfillment. That year, he also achieved a lifelong ambition when he was elected to the Royal Society of London. In 1946, he was elevated to Distinguished Service Professor. In 1952, he became Morton D. Hull Distinguished Service Professor of Astrophysics in the departments of astronomy and physics, as well as at the Institute for Nuclear Physics at the University of

Chicago's Yerkes Observatory. Later the same year, he was appointed managing editor of the *Astrophysical Journal,* a position he held until 1971. He transformed the journal from a private publication of the University of Chicago to the national journal of the American Astronomical Society. The price he paid for his editorial impartiality, however, was isolation from the astrophysical community.

Chandra became a United States citizen in 1953. Despite receiving numerous offers from other universities, in the United States and overseas, Chandra never left the University of Chicago, although, owing to a disagreement with Bengt Strömgren, the head of Yerkes, he stopped teaching astrophysics and astronomy and began lecturing in mathematical physics at the University of Chicago campus. Chandra voluntarily retired from the University of Chicago in 1980, although he remained on as a post-retirement researcher. In 1983, he published a classic work on the mathematical theory of black holes. Since then, he has studied colliding waves and the Newtonian two-center problem in the framework of the general theory of relativity. His semi-retirement has also left him with more time to pursue his hobbies and interests: literature and music, particularly orchestral, chamber, and South Indian.

Receives Numerous Honors and Awards

During his long career, Chandrasekhar has received many awards. In 1947, Cambridge University awarded him its Adams Prize. In 1952, he received the Bruce Medal of the Astronomical Society of the Pacific, and the following year, the Gold Medal of the Royal Astronomical Society. In 1955, Chandrasekhar became a Member of the National Academy of Sciences. The Royal Society of London bestowed upon him its Royal Medal seven years later. In 1962, he was also presented with the Srinivasa Ramanujan Medal of the Indian National Science Academy. The National Medal of Science of the United States was conferred upon Chandra in 1966; and the Padma Vibhushan Medal of India in 1968. Chandra received the Henry Draper Medal of the National Academy of Sciences in 1971 and the Smoluchowski Medal of the Polish Physical Society in 1973. The American Physical Society gave him its Dannie Heineman Prize in 1974. The crowning glory of his career came nine years later when the Royal Swedish Academy awarded Chandrasekhar the Nobel Prize for Physics. ETH of Zurich gave the Indian astrophysicist its Dr. Tomalla Prize in 1984, while the Royal Society of London presented him with its Copley Prize later that year. Chandra also received the R. D. Birla Memorial Award of the Indian Physics Association in 1984. In 1985, the Vainu Bappu Memorial Award of the Indian National Science Academy was conferred upon Chandrasekhar. In May 1993, Chandra received

the state of Illinois's highest honor, Lincoln Academy Award, for his outstanding contributions to science.

While his contribution to astrophysics has been immense, Chandra has always preferred to remain outside the mainstream of research. He described himself to his biographer, Kameshar C. Wali, as "a lonely wanderer in the byways of science." Throughout his life, Chandra has striven to acquire knowledge and understanding, according to an autobiographical essay published with his Nobel lecture, motivated "principally by a quest after perspectives."

SELECTED WRITINGS BY CHANDRASEKHAR:

Books

An Introduction to the Study of Stellar Evolution, University of Chicago Press, 1939, reprinted, Dover Publications, 1967.

Principles of Stellar Dynamics, University of Chicago Press, 1943, reprinted, Dover Publications, 1960.

Radiative Transfer, Clarendon Press, 1950, reprinted, Dover Publications, 1960.

Plasma Physics, Chicago University Press, 1960.

Hydrodynamic and Hydromagnetic Stability, Clarendon Press, 1961, reprinted, Dover Publications, 1987.

Ellipsoidal Figures of Equilibrium, Yale University Press, 1968, reprinted, Dover Publications, 1987.

The Mathematical Theory of Black Holes, Clarendon Press, 1983.

Eddington: The Most Distinguished Astrophysicist of His Time, Cambridge University Press, 1983.

Truth and Beauty: Aesthetics and Motivations in Science, University of Chicago Press, 1987.

Selected Papers (6 volumes), University of Chicago Press, 1989–90.

Periodicals

"The Compton Scattering and the New Statistics," in *Proceedings of the Royal Society,* Volume 125, 1929.

"Stochastic Problems in Physics and Astronomy," *Review of Modern Physics,* Volume 15 1943, pp. 1–89, reprinted in *Selected Papers on Noise and Stochastic Processes,* edited by Nelson Wax, Dover Publications, 1954.

SOURCES:

Books

The Biographical Dictionary of Scientists, Astronomers, Blond Educational Company (London), 1984, pp. 36.

Chambers Biographical Encyclopedia of Scientists, Facts-on-File, 1981.

Goldsmith, Donald, *The Astronomers,* St. Martin's Press, 1991.

Great American Scientists, Prentice-Hall, 1960.

Land, Kenneth R. and Owen Gingerich, editors, *A Sourcebook in Astronomy and Astrophysics,* Harvard University Press, 1979.

Modern Men of Science, McGraw-Hill, 1966, p. 97.

Wali, Kameshwar C., *Chandra: A Biography of S. Chandrasekhar,* Chicago University Press, 1991.

—*Sketch by Avril McDonald*

Min-Chueh Chang

Min-Chueh Chang
1908-1991
Chinese-born American biologist

Reproductive biologist Min-Chueh Chang was best known for his role in developing an oral contraceptive, along with **Gregory Goodwin Pincus** and **John Rock**. Chang also did pathbreaking work on in vitro fertilization, which led to the first "test-tube babies," as they are often called—pregnancies begun by the fertilization of a female egg outside the body.

Chang was born on October 10, 1908, in T'ai-yüan, China, to Gen Shu and Shih (Laing) Chang. In 1933, he received a B.Sc. degree in animal psychology from Tsing Hua University in Beijing. Shortly after, he moved to England, where he studied animal breeding at Cambridge University. He earned his Ph.D. in 1941 and subsequently completed four years of postdoctoral work as a member of a research group headed by John Hammond at the Cambridge University School of Agriculture. In 1945, he moved to Massachusetts, where he became a research associate with the Worcester Foundation for Experimental Biology in Shrewsbury; in 1954, he was named senior and principal scientist there. He also joined the staff of Boston University in 1951, obtaining a full professorship in reproductive biology in 1961.

Develops Birth-Control Pill

Soon after Chang's arrival at the Worcester Foundation, he and Pincus, an expert in mammalian reproduction, began to study progesterone, the female hormone whose secretion begins with ovulation. In 1951, Chang and Pincus began research into oral contraceptives for humans. Progesterone is a hormone that regulates menstruation, and its secretion usually ceases with pregnancy and lactation. It prepares the walls of the fallopian tubes and uterus for the implantation of a fertilized egg, and it is also the hormone that prevents women from ovulating during pregnancy. In the menstrual cycle, the ovum matures as directed by the action of the follicle-stimulating hormone, the luteinizing hormone, and the female hormone estrogen. After the cycle begins, estrogen starts the process of preparing the uterus for pregnancy by increasing vascularity and blood flow there and thickening the uterine lining. Ovulation occurs soon after estrogen levels reach their highest point. Then, progesterone is secreted at increased levels, the levels of other hormones decrease, and the maturation of other ova is temporarily suppressed.

Chang and Pincus realized that increasing blood levels of progesterone could suppress ovulation. They experimented with more than two hundred substances in order to find natural steroids that imitated the combined actions of estrogen and progesterone. At that point, they began a collaboration with John Rock of the Rock Reproduction Clinic in Brookline, Massachusetts. The team developed a pill made of three steroid compounds, including estrogen and progesterone derived from a wild Mexican yam. They began human trials on groups of women in Brookline, as well as in Haiti and Puerto Rico. Their trials were successful, but the researchers decided to try eliminating estrogen from the pill because they considered it an impurity. Subsequent trials, however, had seriously negative results, including pregnancies and break-through bleeding. They restored estrogen to the pill and in so doing developed a form of contraception that was over ninety-nine percent effective and relatively safe. The combined estrogen-progesterone pill was approved by the U.S. Food and Drug Administration in 1960.

Chang, Pincus, and Rock's research permanently changed reproductive rates as well as sexual behavior in many of the world's societies. Chang believed, according to the London *Times,* "that the pill made possible two sociological changes: the liberation of women and the separation of sex from child-bearing."

Besides oral contraceptives, Chang's work had a profound impact on two other areas of fertility research—embryo transfer and in vitro fertilization. His fundamental research on embryo transfer in rabbits with Cyril Adams in the 1950s created the opportunity for new methods of fertilizing farm animals. Their research also led to the development of in vitro fertilization in humans, a method of fertilizing an ovum with sperm outside the human body. Using in vitro fertilization, an infertile woman could have a fertilized egg implanted in her uterus and give birth to what have become known as "test-tube babies." In 1983, Chang was awarded the Pioneer Award by the International Embryo Transfer Society, and in 1987, he was honored for his career contributions to the field at the Fifth World Congress of the In Vitro Fertilization and Embryo Transfer.

Chang married Isabelle C. Chin on May 28, 1948, and they had three children. Chang was naturalized as an American citizen in 1952. Throughout his career he contributed to over 350 scientific studies. He received the Ortho Award in 1950, the Lasker Foundation Award in 1954, and the Ortho Medal in 1961. He was honored with the Marshall Medal by the British Society for the Study of Fertility in 1971 and was elected to the U.S. National Academy of Sciences in 1990. Chang died of heart failure on June 5, 1991 in Worcester, at the age of eight-two.

SOURCES:

Periodicals

Lamming, Eric, "Dr. Min-Chueh Chang," *Journal of Reproduction and Fertility,* January, 1992.
"M.C. Chang; Obituary," *London Times,* June 14, 1991.
"M.C. Chang, Scientist, Dies at 82: A Developer of the Birth-Control Pill," *New York Times,* June 7, 1991.

—*Sketch by John Henry Dreyfuss*

Erwin Chargaff
1905-
Austrian-born American biochemist

In his own eyes he was a natural philosopher, part of an extinct species of researcher. But in the world of science, Erwin Chargaff was a pioneer in biochemistry whose demonstration that genes were comprised of deoxyribonucleic acid (DNA), was one of the most fundamental discoveries in the study of heredity. His accomplishments ranged over much of the field of biochemistry, including the study of lipids of microorganisms, blood coagulation, and the use of radioactive isotopes in the study of metabolism.

Chargaff was born on August 11, 1905 in Czernowiz, Austria, which at the time was the provincial capital of the Austrian monarchy. Although he considered his education at Vienna's Maximilians Gymnasium excellent in quality, he found it limited in scope. While his parents were not wealthy, having lost their money to an inflated economy, Chargaff successfully earned his doctoral degree in chemistry at the University of Vienna's Spath's Institute in 1928, working under the direction of Fritz Feigl.

His family's dire financial problems made a strong impression on Chargaff, who chose the field of chemistry because he believed it would be the most likely to offer employment. In fact, because students had to pay for their own chemicals and equipment, he chose to do his research with a particular chemistry professor whose work did not require much time or money.

Chargaff began his long, productive career in biochemistry at Yale University, where he worked under Rudolph J. Anderson from 1928 to 1930. From 1930 to 1933, he was an assistant at the University of Berlin before moving to Paris to work for nearly two years at the Pasteur Institute. In 1935 he settled into a permanent home at Columbia University, assuming the position of assistant professor of biochemistry. He became full professor in 1952 and was chairman of the department from 1970 until 1974, when be became professor emeritus. Chargaff was presented Columbia's Distinguished Service Award in 1982.

Chargaff's early work included studies of the complex lipids, the fats or fatty acids that occur in microorganisms. He helped to discover the unusual fatty acids and waxes in so-called acid-fast mycobacteria. This initial work led him to study the metabolism and biological role of lipids in the body, especially the lipoproteins, which are lipids attached to proteins.

Chargaff was a pioneer in the use of radioactive isotopes of phosphorus as a tool to study the synthesis and breakdown of phosphorus-containing lipid molecules (phospholipids) in living cells. As a result, he published the first paper on the synthesis of a radioactive organic compound called alpha-glycerophosphoric acid. Blood coagulation also caught his interest, and Chargaff studied the biochemistry of this important phenomenon, including the control of blood clotting by enzymes.

In 1944, while at Columbia, Chargaff's path veered sharply away from lipid metabolism and blood coagulation to the study of nucleic acids. Until then, most scientists believed that amino acids—the building blocks of proteins—carried genetic information. This seemed reasonable, since it was thought that the twenty amino acids that occur in cells could create enough combinations to form the complex code needed to make many thousands of different genes. DNA was also believed to be an unspecific aggregate of "tetranucleotides" made up of adenine, guanine, cytosine and thymine, that served as an attachment site for the amino acids that made up genes. But in 1944, **Oswald T. Avery** and his collaborators determined that DNA was a key element in property transfer between certain bacteria, and recognized that DNA could be the principle constituent of genes.

It was already known that a cell's nucleus is comprised in part by DNA, which is itself composed of sugar, phosphate and two types of complex molecules called purine bases (adenine and guanine) and pyrimidine bases (cytosine and thymine). Using two newly developed experimental techniques, Chargaff isolated DNA from cell nuclei and broke the giant, parent molecules down into constituent purines and pyrimidines. He first separated the bases from each other using a technique called paper chromatography. By then exposing these to ultraviolet light he identified the individual bases. Since different bases absorb ultraviolet light of specific wavelengths, he was able to determine how much of which bases were present by measuring the amount of light each quantity of base absorbed.

The results of this work represented a major contribution to the understanding of the structure of DNA. Chargaff and his colleagues showed that adenine and thymine occur in DNA in equal proportions in all organisms; likewise, cytosine and guanine are also found in equal quantities. However, the proportions of each pair of these nucleic acids differs among organisms. In other words, the presence of each pair of nucleotides is linked to the presence of the other.

Chargaff concluded that DNA, rather than protein, carries genetic information, and while there are only four different nucleic acids, the number of different combinations in which they can appear in DNA provides enough complexity to form the basis of heredity. In addition, he concluded that the identity

of combinations differs from species to species; thus DNA strands differ from species to species.

These conclusions helped trigger a rush of new insights into DNA, the most important of which led **James Watson** and **Francis Crick** of the Cavendish Laboratory in Cambridge, England, to determine the exact structure of DNA. The Cavendish team showed that DNA consisted of two strands of sugar and phosphate connected by crosslinks of purines and pyrimidines. They concluded that the nucleic acids that make up each pair always occur in the same proportion because they always bond together, adenine to thymine, cytosine to guanine—known as the base-pairing rules. The entire molecule is stabilized by being twisted into a double helix structure. For their success in clarifying the structure of DNA, the Cavendish team won the Nobel Prize in 1962.

Chargaff continued to contribute to the understanding of how DNA and RNA (ribonucleic acid) work during the years after the double helix model was proposed. In 1962, Chargaff attended a symposium at Columbia University at which the nature of the genetic code was debated. He challenged a current concept of how the DNA code is translated into a precise sequence of amino acids. The theory held that each amino acid within a protein was coded by a specific series of three nucleic acids in the gene. But Chargaff's investigation of the genes for the protein bovine ribonuclease showed that the code, as then understood, could not be responsible for the specific amino acid sequences in this protein. Either the code was wrong, he suggested, or some amino acids may be coded by more than one sequence of nucleic acids. This theory, supported by the Spanish-American biochemist **Severo Ochoa**, turned out to be correct.

Despite his important contributions to the understanding of the biochemistry of nucleic acids, Chargaff was also very concerned with the state of the world at large. In his book, *Heraclitean Fire: Sketches From a Life Before Nature,* he wrote that society in general—manners, literature, music, and even science—had declined during his lifetime. He was particularly disillusioned with both his adopted country and the scientific community after the atom bomb was unleashed upon Hiroshima and Nagasaki at the close of World War II.

Chargaff also wrote longingly of the simpler days of science when research was not as influenced by money and politics. He summed up his disappointment with the way the world had turned out by saying that he had been "searching for a destiny that did not exist." His destiny, however, lead to important contributions in the field of biochemistry, including the addition of a key piece in the puzzle of the structure of DNA. In turn, this knowledge led to major developments in the field of medical genetics, and, ultimately helped pave the way for gene therapy and the birth of the biotechnology industry.

A visiting professor at Cornell University in 1967, Chargaff served that function in many countries around the world, including Sweden (1949), Japan (1958), and Brazil (1959). He also held the Einstein Chair at the College de France, Paris, in 1965. Among the many awards conferred upon him throughout his career, Chargaff received the Charles Leopold Mayer Prize in 1963, one of the highest awards granted by the French Academy of Sciences. The following year, he became the first recipient of the Heineken Prize in biochemistry from the Royal Netherlands Academy of Sciences. He received honorary degrees from both Columbia University and the University of Basel in 1976.

SELECTED WRITINGS BY CHARGAFF:

Books

Heraclitean Fire: Sketches From a Life Before Nature, Rockefeller University Press, 1979.

Periodicals

(With R. Lipschitz, C. Green, and M. E. Hodes) "The Composition of the Deoxyribonucleic Acid of Salmon Sperm," *Journal of Biological Chemistry,* Volume 192, 1951, pp. 223–30.

SOURCES:

Books

Singer, Maxine and Paul Berg, *Genes and Genomes,* University Science Books, 1991.
Watson, James D., *The Double Helix,* New American Library, 1968.

Periodicals

New York Times, March 13, 1962, p. A23; March 8, 1964, p. A35.
New York Times Book Review, January 7, 1979, pp. 15–16.

Other

Pines, Maya, *Inside the Cell,* U.S. Department of Health, Education and Welfare, 1975.

—*Sketch by Marc Kusinitz*

Georges Charpak
1924-
Polish-born French physicist

Georges Charpak received the Nobel Prize in physics in 1992 for his invention and development of particle detectors, most notably the multiwire proportional chamber. A number of his colleagues, who received the Nobel Prize before him, had used his invention to make important discoveries in physics. Charpak is credited with creating instrumentation that is used by thousands of other scientists at CERN, the European laboratory for particle physics located in Geneva, Switzerland, as well as by researchers in other prominent laboratories involved in the study of the nature of matter.

Born on August 1, 1924, in Dabrovica, Poland, to Maurice Charpak and Anna Szapiro, Charpak moved to France with his family in 1929. In 1943 the French Vichy government accused the young Charpak of being a terrorist and sentenced him to the concentration camp in Dachau, West Germany (now Germany). Charpak remained in the camp until its liberation in 1945. Upon his return to France, he completed a degree in civil engineering from the Ecole des Mines in Paris, and in 1946 he became a French citizen.

Two years later, as a graduate student in nuclear physics at the Collège de France in Paris, Charpak went to work in the laboratory of physicist Frédéric Joliot-Curie. It was in this laboratory that Charpak began building the equipment he needed to perform his experiments (he constructed his own equipment out of necessity, as the laboratory had none). Charpak contends that he was not good at invention but had to learn in order to perform his experiments. In 1955 he received his Ph.D. from the Collège de France.

Develops the Multiwire Proportional Chamber

In awarding the Nobel Prize to Charpak, the Swedish Academy of Sciences traced the history of the development of detector devices in physics. The cloud chamber and the bubble chamber were two earlier inventions that had received recognition from the academy. Both relied on photographic techniques to capture particle events. In 1958 Charpak was invited by experimental physicist **Leon Lederman**, who had heard Charpak lecture in Padua, to come to CERN to work on sparking devices to detect particles. Though these devices were an improvement over existing techniques, they, too, relied on photographic recording, which was slow and cumbersome to analyze. Charpak turned to the problem of a spark chamber reading without photographic film, and built his first multiwire proportional tracking chamber in 1968.

Georges Charpak

The multiwire proportional chamber extended the technology of the Geiger-Muller tube, bubble chamber, and cloud chamber in two ways. The multiwire proportional chamber replaced the single positively charged wire of the Geiger-Muller tube, which attracts electrons in a chamber of ionized gas, with a multiwire device; it also replaced photographic analysis of a trail of bubbles with computerized electronic analysis of current produced in the wires as they attract electrons. Charpak credited his background in nuclear physics with the success of his invention.

Since liberating physics from dependence on film readings, Charpak has turned his interests to medicine and aerospace problems. Work he has done in the latter area makes it possible to produce an X-ray radiograph of turbine blades as they spin. In the field of medicine, his chamber is able to analyze the structure of a protein with X rays a thousand times faster than was previously possible. He also is working on imaging problems to identify receptors in the brain.

Charpak's particle work mimics the state of the universe as it was a fraction of a second after the Big Bang. It is believed that some of the particles have not existed in nature since that time, and the ability of physicists to study them will reveal and increase the understanding of the relationships among the forces of nature. Whereas Charpak built on the work of his predecessors with the bubble and spark chambers, others have used his invention to make their own

contributions to the field of physics. A group led by **Samuel Ting** discovered the first manifestation of charmed quarks at Brookhaven in 1974, and **Carlo Rubbia** led a group to discover the W and Z particles. (Charmed quarks and W and Z particles are subatomic particles.)

Works on Behalf of Soviet Dissidents

Charpak has worked on behalf of other scientists imprisoned by repressive governments. He is the founder of the SOS committee at CERN. This association worked diligently on the part of Soviet dissidents, such as **Andrei Sakharov**, Yuri Orlov, and Anatoly Sharansky, when they were deprived of their civil rights under the former Soviet Union.

Charpak married Dominique Vidal in 1953; they have two sons and one daughter. Some of Charpak's leisure interests include skiing, music, and hiking. He has been a member of the French Academy of Sciences since 1985. In addition to his continued association with CERN, Charpak is also the Joliot-Curie Professor at the Ecole Supérieure de Physique et Chimie in Paris, a position he has held since 1984. In 1989 he received the High Energy and Particle Physics Prize from the European Physical Society. He has published numerous papers in scientific journals.

SOURCES:

Books

Close, Frank, *The Particle Explosion,* Oxford, 1987.

Fernow, Richard C., *Introduction to Experimental Particle Physics,* Cambridge, 1986.

Sutton, Christine, *The Particle Connection: The Discovery of the Missing Links of Nuclear Physics,* Hutchinson, 1984.

Periodicals

Appenzeller, Tim, "Physics: Applause for a High Wire Act," *Science,* October 23, 1992, p. 543–544.

Browne, Malcolm W., "Science Nobels Given for Work on Nature of Matter," *New York Times,* October 15, 1992, p. B14.

Chown, Marcus, "Detector That Opened Up the Subatomic World," *New Scientist,* October 24, 1992, p. 6.

Garwin, Laura, and Robert Finn, "Nobel Prizes Go to Caltech Chemist, CERN Physicist," *Nature,* October 22, 1992, p. 664.

Schwarzschild, Bertram, "Nobel Physics Prize to Charpak for Inventing Particle Detectors," *Physics Today,* January, 1993, pp. 17–20.

—Sketch by Vita Richman

Praveen Chaudhari
1937-

Indian-born American metallurgist and physicist

Praveen Chaudhari has conducted and directed important research on materials basic to modern science and technology and has played a significant role in the development of United States science policy. He was born in Ludhiana, India, on November 30, 1937, the son of Hans Raj and Ved Palta Chaudhari. He received his degree in metallurgy in 1961 from the Indian Institute of Technology in Kharagpur. Seeking to continue his studies, Chaudhari applied to the Massachusetts Institute of Technology (MIT) and Cambridge; both universities accepted him, but MIT also offered a fellowship, so Chaudhari came to the United States. He earned his S.M. in physical metallurgy in 1963 and his Sc.D., also in physical metallurgy and with a minor in physics, in 1966, both from MIT.

After receiving his doctoral degree, Chaudhari joined IBM, where he has remained throughout his career. He was a member of the research staff at IBM's Thomas J. Watson Research Center in Yorktown Heights, New York, from 1966 to 1980. He became director of the physical science department of the center in 1981 and vice president of the science division in 1982. In the latter capacity, he was responsible for IBM's science programs at Almaden, Yorktown, and Zurich. During these years, the research programs at IBM's laboratories grew significantly, and IBM scientists won two Nobel Prizes. In 1989 Chaudhari joined IBM's Corporate Technical Committee in Armonk, New York, and in 1990 he returned to the Research Division as a research staff member.

During his years at IBM, Chaudhari has researched the structure and properties of amorphous (shapeless) solids, the mechanical properties of thin films, defects in solids, quantum transport in disordered systems, and superconductivity (disappearance of electrical resistance in a material, especially at low temperatures). He has conducted magnetic monopole (hypothetical north or south magnetic pole existing alone) and neutrino mass experiments (uncharged particles with little or no mass), establishing bounds within which the magnetic monopole would exist. His work on the magnetic properties of thin films led to the discovery of the amorphous magneto-optic material used in erasable compact discs. Chaudhari was the first to demonstrate that superconducting materials could carry very large currents, and he demonstrated the problem of grain boundaries—the lowering of current at the interface between two superconducting surfaces. He also found that grain boundaries can be useful in making easily built and operated SQUIDs—superconducting quantum interference devices—that are used for looking at currents generated by the brain and heart and that also have applications to geology and the search for natural resources such as petroleum. His subsequent work with superconductivity has focused on developing an understanding of why and how it exists at high temperatures.

Chaudhari has served on numerous visiting committees to universities and on many professional committees. He cochaired the National Research Council's Study on Materials Science and Engineering. The study's report was the basis of a presidential initiative on advanced materials and processing programs announced in January 1992. Chaudhari was also executive secretary of President Reagan's Advisory Council on Superconductivity in 1988, a member of the National Commission on Superconductivity that reported its findings to President Bush in 1989, and a member of the New York State Institute on Superconductivity. He served on the U.S. National Critical Technologies Panel from 1992 to 1993. At the request of the government of India, Chaudhari reported in 1990 on science and technology to the prime minister and led an IBM group to evaluate Indian computer science in 1993.

Chaudhari holds over a dozen patents, primarily in electronics, magneto-optics, and superconductivity, including one on erasable materials used in optical storage devices such as CDs. He has published over 150 technical papers and edited two books. His awards include many from IBM; the first Leadership Award, in 1986, of the Metallurgical Society of AIME for his contributions to advancing the science and technology of electronic materials; the Pake Award of the American Physical Society (of which he is a fellow), in 1987, for his personal contributions to and management of science; and the 1992 Liebmann Memorial Award of the Institute of Electrical and Electronics Engineers for the discovery of amorphous magnetic films in magneto-optic data storage systems. Chaudhari married Karin Romhild in 1964; they had two children—a son, Ashok, and a daughter, Pia. He became a naturalized United States citizen in 1987.

SELECTED WRITINGS BY CHAUDHARI:

Periodicals

"Metallic Glasses," *Scientific American,* April 1980, pp. 98–117.

"Needed: More Materials Research at Universities" (editorial), *Physics Today,* October 1984, p. 160.

"Electronic and Magnetic Materials," *Scientific American,* October 1986, pp. 136–44.

"Complexity in Materials Research," *Physics Today,* October, 1992. 'Corporate R & D in the United States," *Physics Today,* December, 1993.

SOURCES:

Periodicals

"Academies Say Advances in Materials Will Recreate Industries in 1990s," *Physics Today,* February 1990, pp. 70–71.
"Depressed by Lack of Grants and Jobs, Materials Scientists Warm to OSTP Plan," *Physics Today,* June 1991, pp. 89–91.

Other

Chaudhari, Praveen, biographical sketch furnished to Kathy Sammis, January 1994.
Chaudhari, Praveen, interview with Kathy Sammis, conducted on January 28, 1994.

—*Sketch by Kathy Sammis*

Pavel A. Cherenkov
1904-1990
Russian physicist

Pavel A. Cherenkov was a physicist whose work helped build the foundation for modern nuclear physics. He is best known for his discovery in 1934 of Cherenkov radiation, which he first noticed as a faint blue light in water that was absorbing radiation. In 1937, **Ilya Frank** and **Igor Tamm** established that this light was caused by radioactive particles that move faster through water than the speed of light does, and for their work the three men shared the 1958 Nobel Prize in physics. Cherenkov radiation has been used to design and build a sensitive tool for measuring high-energy particles, known as the Cherenkov counter, which has important uses in experimental physics.

Cherenkov was born to peasant parents in the Voronezh region of Russia on July 28, 1904. He went to Voronezh University, where he graduated in 1928 with a degree in physics and mathematics. From there he taught in a high school, then moved to Leningrad in 1930, where he began graduate studies in physics. He studied at the Institute of Physics and Mathematics under Sergei I. Vavilov; soon after he began his affiliation there, the institute was transferred to

Moscow and renamed the P. N. Lebedev Institute of Physics. Cherenkov would remain there for the rest of his life.

It had long been observed that irradiated liquids produced certain kinds of luminescence, and Cherenkov was still a graduate student when he began researching the causes of this phenomenon. He was quickly able to establish that in most cases this light was the result of atomic and molecular activity in the fluids themselves, a phenomenon known as fluorescence. But he discovered that high-energy gamma rays, when passed through liquid, produced a light that was not so easily explained. It was Cherenkov's assumption that this light was caused by the radiation itself and not the liquid, and he set out to prove this theory in a series of taxing experiments. He used little more than a weak source of gamma radiation and a variety of liquids and measured the light with only his eyes. In an obituary for Cherenkov in *Physics Today,* Alexander E. Chudakov writes: "I imagine a young and enthusiastic fellow who for several years started his working day by spending an hour in a totally dark room to prepare his eyes to observe faint light, and who scrupulously repeated the observations again and again, varying the liquids and the geometry of the experiment, trying to find the clue to the nature of the puzzling radiation that now bears his name."

Cherenkov was first able to show that the gamma rays produced the same light in a number of different liquids, thus establishing that the light was not affected by the medium through which the high-energy particles passed. After verifying that the effect was not the result of the medium, he proved that this light lacked a characteristic which fluorescence had: The light was not dimmed or "quenched" by the introduction of additives. The light produced by gamma rays was also not polarized in the same way fluorescent light was, and the results of this last experiment established definitively that what Cherenkov had been observing was a new and distinct phenomenon.

Cherenkov was only able to explain the radiation he had discovered with the theoretical assistance of Ilya Frank and Igor Tamm. Frank and Tamm developed a mathematical theory which explained the phenomenon as the result of high-energy particles moving faster than the speed of light within the liquid. Light travels more slowly in a transparent medium than it does in a vacuum, and gamma rays have enough energy to pass it, creating a visible cone or wave of light, analogous to a supersonic boom when an airplane exceeds the speed of sound. Cherenkov, Frank, and Tamm were able to prove these theories after an additional series of experiments. Though the majority of their scientific colleagues initially showed little interest in their work, the growth of nuclear physics during and after World War II made the importance of their discovery increasingly apparent, and they were awarded the State Prize from the Soviet Government in 1946 and the Nobel Prize in 1958.

Cherenkov was always modest about his role in the identification and explanation of Cherenkov radiation. As Chudakov notes in his obituary: "Limiting his own contribution to the period of the 1930s, Cherenkov always emphasized the crucial role of Sergei Vavilov, Frank and Tamm in the discovery." Tamm went on to work with **Andrei Sakharov** and others on the development of the first Soviet hydrogen bomb in 1953; he also helped formulate the theoretical basis for controlled thermonuclear fusion—the use of thermonuclear power for generating electricity. The Cherenkov effect has been used by others to develop counters to identify the velocity of high-energy particles. Cherenkov detectors are used in instruments sent up in satellites or balloons to study primary cosmic rays, exploring the effect of some particles that reach Earth's atmosphere from further out in the galaxy. The detectors have also been used in studies of Cherenkov radiation under the Antarctic ice cap.

Cherenkov earned his doctorate in 1940. He became a professor of experimental physics in 1959, then a senior scientific officer at the institute. Cherenkov was elected a member of the U.S.S.R. Academy of Sciences in 1970, and he headed the department of high-energy physics of the Lebedev Institute until he died January 6, 1990.

SELECTED WRITINGS BY CHERENKOV:

Periodicals

"Visible Radiation Produced by Electrons Moving in Mediums with Velocity Exceeding That of Light," *Physical Review,* Volume 52, 1937, pp. 378–379.

SOURCES:

Books

McGraw-Hill Modern Scientists and Engineers, Volume 1, McGraw-Hill, 1980.
Snell, A. H., editor, *Nuclear Instruments and Their Uses,* Volume 1, John Wiley, 1962.

Periodicals

Chudakov, Alexander E., "Obituaries: Pavel Alexeyevich Cherenkov," *Physics Today,* December, 1992, pp. 106–107.

"Eyes Down: South Pole Ice Is Used for Study of Neutrinos," *The Economist,* Volume 322, February 29, 1992, p. 92.

—*Sketch by Melinda Jardon Thach*

Harold Chestnut
1917-
American electrical engineer

Harold Chestnut is a retired American engineer who, during a career with General Electric that spanned more than forty years, was active in systems engineering and analysis, a field that focuses on establishing the most efficient means for a system to accomplish a given task. His research into systems includes investigations of adaptive (self-regulatory) control, system modeling and simulation, and the control of industrial businesses. Chestnut is also recognized as an expert in control systems analysis, especially as it applies to regulation of industrial, electric utility, and military systems. Since his retirement from General Electric, Chestnut has served as president of the SWIIS Foundation, Inc., a body he founded in 1983 whose task is to identify and implement ways for improving international political stability.

Harold Chestnut was born on November 25, 1917, in Albany, New York. He took his B.S. degree in Electrical Engineering at the Massachusetts Institute of Technology, graduating in 1939. He remained at MIT to pursue an M.S. in Electrical Engineering, which he received in 1940. Following his graduation, Chestnut went to work for General Electric (GE) in Schenectady, New York, where he would remain for the rest of his career. Before being given any work assignments, Chestnut was obliged to continue his education. He became a student in General Electric's Advanced Engineering Program's Electrical Engineering Course, a three year commitment. During the latter part of the course, he gave tutorials to more junior students.

After finishing the program in 1943, Chestnut joined General Electric's Aeronautics and Ordnance Department. He was given responsibility for systems engineering and project work for a number of military aircraft, including the Mark 56 GFCS and the F–104, as well as some missile applications. Soon after beginning this post, Chestnut married Erma Ruth Callaway of Colorado Springs on August 24, 1944.

The couple had three children—Peter Callaway, Harold Thomas, and Andrew Trammell.

Chestnut remained in the Aeronautics and Ordnance Department until 1956. That year, he became manager of the Systems Engineering and Analysis Branch of GE's Advanced Technology Lab. He was put in charge of working groups which investigated automatic control and information systems for various applications, such as rapid transit and the reliability systems for the space program's Apollo mission to the moon.

In 1961, Chestnut, in addition to working for GE, became editor of the Pergamon Press journal *Automatica;* he retained the post for the following six years. In 1965, he was appointed editor of a series by the John Wiley publishing company on systems engineering and analysis, a position he maintained until 1985. In 1972, he became a consultant to GE on systems engineering. One of his main responsibilities became the automation of electrical distribution systems, which regulate the flow and voltage of electricity. He continued in this role until 1983.

That year, Chestnut retired from General Electric. He did not remain idle for long, however. He quickly busied himself helping to establish the SWIIS Foundation Inc., a body whose mission is to identify and implement "supplemental ways to improve international stability." As the organization's president, Chestnut has been at the forefront of its efforts to set up a Cooperative Security System, whose purpose is to develop and lobby for a cooperative system of international security. By creating a security system that would protect nations equally, individual countries could feel safer, thereby increasing their political stability. Also in 1983, Chestnut became coeditor of the International Federation of Automatic Control Proceedings on International Conflict Resolution. He held the same position again in 1986 and in 1989. Throughout his career, Chestnut has been active in the affairs of various professional engineering bodies. In 1957, he served on the founding committee for the International Federation of Automatic Control, and was named its first president, from 1957 to 1958. He was elected a fellow of the Institute of Electrical and Electronics Engineers (IEEE) in 1962 for his "contribution to the theory and design of control systems." That same year, he was made chairman of the American Institute of Electrical Engineering's (AIEE) Schenectady branch. He was president of the American Automatic Control Council between 1962 and 1964. He served as IEEE's treasurer from 1968 to 1969, and as vice-president of its Technical Activities Board and Regional Activities Board. He became IEEE's president in 1973. In these various capacities, he has been active in promoting continuing education and cooperation amongst engineers. Chestnut was elected a member of the National Academy of Engineering in 1974 and a fellow of the Instrument Society of America. He is also a member of the National Society of Professional Engineers, and a fellow of the American Association for the Advancement of Science. In 1980, he was made a Case Centennial Scholar.

In addition to holding many important offices, Chestnut has served on many technical committees, including as chairman of AIEE's technical committees on Automatic Control and Systems, Man, and Cybernetics. He has been a member of IEEE's board of directors and executive committee, and has chaired many of its committees on feedback control. Between 1975 and 1978, Chestnut served as a member of the Commission on Sociotechnical Systems of the National Research Council. Chestnut received honorary doctorates of Engineering from Case Western Reserve University in 1966, and Villanova University in 1972. He was awarded the Honda Prize for ecotechnology in 1981, the Centennial Medal of the Institute of Electrical and Electronics Engineers in 1984, and the American Automatic Control Council's Bellman Control Heritage Award in 1985. Active in his church and community, Chestnut continues to live in Schenectady, New York, with his wife.

SELECTED WRITINGS BY CHESTNUT:

Books

(With Robert W. Mayer) *Servomechanisms and Regulating Systems Design,* Wiley, Volume 1, 1951, Volume 2, 1955, 2nd edition, 1959.
Systems Engineering Tools, Wiley, 1965.
Systems Engineering Methods, Wiley, 1967.

—Sketch by Avril McDonald

Geoffrey Foucar Chew
1924-
American theoretical physicist

Geoffrey Foucar Chew works in the areas of elementary particle physics, scattering matrix (S-matrix) theory, topological bootstrap theory, and strong interactions. His most important contribution to particle physics is his "bootstrap hypothesis," which postulates that elementary particles' physical properties and interactions have an internal consistency that results from S-matrix theory. S-matrix theory is a table of probabilities that describes the possible outcomes of subatomic particle collisions.

According to S-matrix theory, subatomic particles are intermediate states in a network of interactions.

Chew was born in Washington, DC, on June 5, 1924. His father, Arthur Percy Chew, was a journalist, and his mother, Pauline Lisette Foucar, was a teacher. Chew was educated at George Washington University and received his B.S. degree in 1944, the same year he became a junior theoretical physicist at Los Alamos Science Laboratory in New Mexico. In 1945, he married Ruth Elva Wright, with whom he had two children, Beverly and Berkeley.

From 1946 to 1948, Chew was a National Research Fellow at the University of Chicago, where he worked on his doctoral thesis under the supervision of American physicist **Enrico Fermi**. After receiving his Ph.D. in 1948, he worked as an assistant professor of physics at the Theoretical Physics Research Laboratory at the University of California, Berkeley, becoming an assistant professor of physics in 1949. He left Berkeley to take up a position as professor of physics at the University of Illinois in 1950, but returned to Berkeley as professor of physics in 1957. He is also a senior research physicist at the Lawrence Berkeley Laboratory and occasionally heads the Laboratory's Theoretical Group.

After the death of his wife in 1971, Chew remarried later that year. He and his second wife, Denyse Mettel, have three children: Pierre-Yves, Jean-François, and Pauline. From 1981 to 1982, Chew was Miller Professor of Physics at Berkeley. He was a visiting professor of physics at the University of Paris between 1983 and 1984. In 1986, he became Dean of Physical Sciences at Berkeley.

Chew has received a number of honors, including the Hughes Medal of the American Physical Society in 1962, the Ernest O. Lawrence Award in 1969, and an Alumni Achievement Award from George Washington University in 1973. He is a member of the National Academy of Science and a Fellow of the American Physical Society and the American Academy of Arts and Sciences.

SELECTED WRITINGS BY CHEW:

Books

The S-matrix Theory of Strong Interactions, W. A. Benjamin, 1961.
The Analytic S-matrix: A Basis for Nuclear Democracy, W. A. Benjamin, 1966.

SOURCES:

Books

A Passion for Physics: Essays in Honor of Geoffrey Chew, World Scientific, 1985.

—*Sketch by Avril McDonald*

Charles Manning Child
1869-1954
American zoologist

Charles Manning Child was a nationally recognized zoologist who became a leader in the study of morphogenesis, which is the formation and differentiation of tissues and organs. His most important contribution to the field of zoology was the gradient theory, the concept that an organism's regenerative ability takes place in physiological stages along an axis, with each physiological stage being connected to and affecting those areas surrounding it. "In this gradient Child believed he had found the mechanism of correlation by which the mass of cells that constitutes an animal is maintained as a unified whole of definite form and construction. The chief factor in correlation is . . . each level dominates the region behind and is dominated by that in front," Libbie H. Hyman explained in *Biographical Memoirs of the National Academy of Sciences.* Child received many honors in his lifetime and was highly respected in his field. While he was an able lecturer, Child was happiest and most proficient in the area of research. He preferred to spend his time in the laboratory, where he trained many graduate students.

Child, the fifth and only survivor of five sons, was born to Mary Elizabeth Manning and Charles Chauncey Child on February 2, 1869, in Ypsilanti, Michigan. Although both families were of long-standing New England lineage, Mary Elizabeth traveled to Ypsilanti to be under the care of her father, a physician, at the time of Charles's birth. Mrs. Child and the infant returned to the family home in Higganum, Connecticut, shortly thereafter. Child's father was a fourth-generation descendant of Higganum shipbuilders who were forced to close their shipyard when the mechanization of shipping vessels appeared on the scene. The Childs lived in one of the family's three homes facing the Connecticut river on the grounds where the shipyard had been. His father also retained a small family-owned farm to be used primarily as a source of food.

Influenced by his parents' love of reading, Child became a fervent reader at a very early age. His interest in the natural sciences began at age ten when he became an avid collector of minerals from the granite hills around his boyhood home. Taught by his mother at home until he was nine, Child entered the formalized district school system in Higganum in 1878. From 1882 to 1886, Child attended high school in Middletown, Connecticut, graduating first in his class. Child then entered Wesleyan University in 1886 where his interest in both chemistry and zoology made choosing a major field of study difficult, but he finally decided on zoology. He was awarded the Seney scholarship for high academic achievement in all but his freshman year and was elected to the esteemed Phi Beta Kappa honor society. He graduated from Wesleyan University in 1890 with a Ph.D. and continued his studies there, receiving an M.S. in biology in 1892.

With his parents gone, Child sold the family home and went to the University of Leipzig in Germany. For a short time he studied psychology under Wilhelm Wundt and published his first original work in the *American Naturalist.* In 1894 he completed his Ph.D. in zoology under Rudolf Leuckart. His doctoral dissertation on the insect sense organ was published in a leading German zoological journal and is still considered a standard in the field of entomology (a branch of zoology dealing with insects). Immediately following the completion of his Ph.D., Child conducted independent research at the Naples Zoological Station.

In 1895 Child returned to the United States and joined the staff of the University of Chicago, where he remained for his entire academic career. He achieved full professorship in 1916 and maintained that position until retirement in 1934. When he reached retirement age, Child was asked to stay on at the University of Chicago as chairman of the zoology department, which he accepted and maintained until 1937. During his summers at the University of Chicago, he conducted research at the Marine Biological Laboratory at Woods Hole, Massachusetts, at the Naples Zoological Station, and at various marine stations on the Pacific coast. In 1899 Child married Lydia Van Meter, daughter of John Van Meter, the longtime dean and acting president of Goucher College in Baltimore. They had one daughter, Jeannette Manning Child. As a zoologist, Child's research and experimentation centered on animal organisms' reactivity and sensitivity as well as their developmental and reproductive problems. Child's colleagues criticized his controversial concept of the gradient theory, suggesting that his findings were too general since they were based on experiments with simple animals. Still, his contribution to the field of morphogenesis was significant. In conjunction with the University of Chicago Press, Child founded the journal *Physiological Zoology* in 1928 and became its first editor. As his reputation grew, Child drew national and international attention. He was frequently asked to teach and lecture at colleges and universities around the world. In 1930 he was a visiting professor at Duke University, and from 1930 to 1931 he traveled to Japan, where he was invited as a visiting professor of the Rockefeller Foundation at Tohoku University, Sendai, Japan.

Child retired from his post at the University of Chicago in 1937 and, with his wife Lydia, moved to California. As impassioned about nature as he was about his work, Child frequently went hiking and mountain climbing. He had a special fascination for the beautiful Sierras. He also became a frequent visitor in the zoology department on the campus of Stanford University, where he often participated as a guest speaker and lecturer. Due to his reserved nature, Child was not an easy person to get to know. But when friendships did develop, they generally lasted a lifetime. Child died of cancer on December 19, 1954. He established very high standards for himself, standards he maintained throughout his personal life and professional career. He remained a committed scientist to the very end. Just prior to his death, Child was in the process of writing a book called *Physiological Factors in Organization and Reorganization,* which was a summation of his most important works as well as a synopsis of a previous volume, *Patterns and Problems of Development.* At the time of his death, the book remained unfinished, with only the placement of captions yet to be done.

SELECTED WRITINGS BY CHILD:

Books

Individuality in Organisms, University of Chicago Press, 1915.
The Origin and Development of the Nervous System from a Physiological Viewpoint, University of Chicago Press, 1921.
Patterns and Problems of Development, University of Chicago Press, 1941.

SOURCES:

Books

Hyman, Libbie H., "Charles Manning Child, 1869–1954," in *Biographical Memoirs of the National Academy of Sciences,* Volume 30, 1957, pp. 73–103.

—*Sketch by Paula M. Morin*

May Edward Chinn
1896-1980
American physician

May Edward Chinn is best remembered for the racial barriers she confronted as one of the first black women physicians in New York City. Denied hospital privileges and research opportunities at New

York City hospitals early in her career, she became a family doctor in Harlem, where she was the only practicing black woman physician for several years. For her determination to provide medical care to the disadvantaged and for her work in cancer detection, she received honorary doctor of science degrees from New York University and Columbia University, and a distinguished alumnus award from Columbia Teachers College.

May Edward Chinn was born on April 15, 1896, in Great Barrington, Massachusetts. Her mother, Lulu Ann, was the daughter of a Chickahominy Native American and a slave. Her father, William Lafayette, was the son of a slave and a plantation owner. Chinn went to the Bordentown Manual and Training Industrial School, a boarding school in New Jersey, and spent one year of her childhood on the estate of Charles Tiffany, the jewelry magnate, where her mother was a live-in cook. The Tiffanys treated Chinn like family and took her to classical music concerts in New York City. She later learned to play the piano and became an accompanist to popular singer Paul Robeson in the early 1920s. Chinn played classical music and church music throughout her life and performed for black soldiers during World War I. Although she never completed high school, she was admitted to Columbia Teachers College on the basis of her entrance examination. Originally intending to pursue a degree in music, Chinn quickly abandoned music for science because a music professor who believed that blacks were unsuited for classical music ridiculed her, but another professor praised her for a paper she had written on sewage disposal. In 1921 she received a bachelor's degree in science from Columbia Teachers College, and in 1926 she became the first black woman to graduate from Bellevue Hospital Medical College.

Faces Repeated Barriers to Practice

Upon graduation Chinn found that no hospital would allow her practicing privileges. The Rockefeller Institute had seriously considered her for a research fellowship until they discovered that she was black. With her fair skin and last name, many assumed that she was white or Chinese. She later told Muriel Petioni, former president of the Society of Black Women Physicians, that black workers often snubbed her because they assumed she was passing as white, and they did not want to jeopardize her position.

Though she was the first African American woman intern at Harlem Hospital, racial and gender discrimination kept her from obtaining hospital privileges there. Chinn described her early practice in Harlem as akin to an old-fashioned family practice in the rural South a century earlier. She performed major medical procedures in patient's homes, while minor procedures were done in her office. She told

May Edward Chinn

George Davis of the *New York Times Magazine* "that conditions were so bad that it seemed that you were not making any headway." To get at the roots of poverty, she earned a master's degree in public health from Columbia University in 1933.

In the 1940s Chinn became very interested in cancer but was still prohibited from establishing formal affiliations with New York hospitals. Instead, she had her patients' biopsies read secretly for her at Memorial Hospital. In 1944 she was invited to join the staff of the Strang Clinic, a premier cancer detection facility affiliated with Memorial and New York Infirmary hospitals. She worked there for twenty-nine years and became a member of the Society of Surgical Oncology.

1930s Mayoral Health Committee Pivotal in Integrating Medicine

In her autobiographical paper written in 1977, Chinn noted that the committees established by Mayor LaGuardia after the Harlem riots of 1935 were pivotal in integrating blacks into medicine in New York City. As committee findings were reported in the newspapers, conditions began to change. Chinn saw this firsthand when she became the first black woman granted admitting privileges at Harlem Hospital in 1940.

African American male doctors were another source of discrimination. In a *New York Times* interview with Charlayne Hunter-Gault in 1977, she described three types: "those who acted as if I wasn't there; another who took the attitude 'what does she think that she can do that I can't do?' and the group that called themselves support[ive] by sending me their night calls after midnight." Like other black women physicians of her era, Chinn worked long hours but never got rich from her practice. By 1978 Chinn had given up her practice and begun examining African American students as a consultant to the Phelps-Stokes Fund. In late 1980 she collapsed and died at age eighty-four at a Columbia University reception honoring a friend.

SOURCES:

Periodicals

Brozan, Nadine, "For a Doctor at 84, A Day to Remember," *New York Times,* May 17, 1980, p. 12.

Davis, George, "A Healing Hand in Harlem," *New York Times Magazine,* Apr. 22, 1979, pp. 40+.

Ennis, Thomas W., "Obituary: Dr. May Edward Chinn, 84, Long a Harlem Physician," *New York Times,* Sect. II, Dec. 3, 1980, p.11.

Hunter-Gault, Charlayne, "Black Women M.D.'s: Spirit and Endurance," *New York Times,* Nov. 16, 1977, pp. C1+.

Other

Petioni, Muriel, interview with Laura Newman conducted on March 11, 1994.

—Sketch by Laura Newman

Alfred Y. Cho
1937-

Chinese-born American electrical engineer

Alfred Y. Cho is an electrical engineer specializing in microwave and optoelectronics (a branch of electronics dealing with devices that emit, modulate, transmit, or sense light). He has contributed significantly to the fields of electronics and quantum physics through his work in the development of molecular beam epitaxy. For this work he has received numerous patents and awards, including the National Medal of Sciences presented in 1993 by President Clinton and the Institute of Electrical and Electronics Engineers (IEEE) Medal of Honor in 1994. He is a member of the American Academy of Art and Sciences, the National Academy of Engineering, and the National Academy of Sciences.

The third child of Edward I-Lai, a professor of economics, and Mildred (Chen) Cho, Alfred Y. Cho was born on July 10, 1937, in Beijing, China. He attended Pui Ching high school in Hong Kong before coming to the United States in 1955. His college education began at Oklahoma Baptist University, where he studied general science. Desiring to study electrical engineering, Cho transferred to the University of Illinois in 1956. There he attained his Bachelors degree in 1960 and his Masters degree in 1961. He then joined the Ion Physics Corporation of Burlington, Massachusetts, as a research physicist. Cho became a naturalized U.S. citizen in Boston in 1962. Later that year he moved to TRW's Space Technology Laboratory in Redondo Beach, California. Cho worked for TRW until 1965, when he returned to the University of Illinois to pursue a doctorate in electrical engineering.

In 1968, after receiving his Ph.D and joining the technical staff of AT&T Bell Labs in Murray Hill, New Jersey, Cho briefly returned to Illinois to marry Mona Lee Willoughby in June. The have four children. At AT&T Cho progressed from the research staff to department head (1984) and to director of the Materials Processing Research Lab (1987). In 1990, Cho moved to a parallel position as director of semiconductor research.

Cho's greatest contribution in the field of solid state electronics has been in the development of a semiconductor preparation process called molecular beam epitaxy (MBE). This process is used to prepare semiconductor components for microwave and optoelectronic devices. It allows engineers and scientists to prepare crystalline structures that do not exist in nature one atomic layer at a time. These preparations, which have unique electrical and optical properties, have many scientific and industrial uses. Most compact disc players, for instance, use semiconductor lasers made with MBE materials. Cho has received over forty patents related to this process and has authored over four hundred publications, primarily in the fields of solid state electronics and materials.

Cho is a fellow of the IEEE and of the American Physical Society. In addition to the awards previously mentioned, he has also won awards from the Electrochemical Society, the American Physical Society, and the Chinese Institute of Engineers, among others. He holds an adjunct professorship at the University of Illinois and serves on the board of directors of Instruments SA in Edison, New Jersey.

Besides his technical interests, Cho enjoys painting, photography, table tennis, and golf. In his biography in *Who's Who in America,* Cho commented that his secret for success as a research scientist is "that I combine Oriental patience with Western technology."

SELECTED WRITINGS BY CHO:

Books

(With J. R. Arthur) "Molecular Beam Epitaxy," *Progress in Solid State Chemistry,* Volume 10, edited by G. Somorjai and J. McCaldin, Pergamon, 1975, p. 157.
"Molecular Beam Epitaxy," *Technology of Physics of Molecular Beam Epitaxy,* edited by H. C. Parker and M. B. Dowsett, Plenum, New York, 1985.

Periodicals

"Epitaxy by Periodic Annealing," *Surface Science,* Volume 17, 1969, p. 494.
"Film Deposition by Molecular Beam Techniques," *Journal of Vacuum Science and Technology,* Volume 8, 1971, S31–38.
"Growth of Periodic Structures by the Molecular Beam Method," *Applied Physics Letters,* Volume 19, 1971, p. 467.
"Growth of III-V Semiconductors by Molecular Beam Epitaxy and Their Properties," *Thin Solid Films,* Volume 100, 1983, p. 291.

SOURCES:

Other

Cho, Alfred Y., personal correspondence with G. A. Ferrance, January 24, 1994.
Cho, Alfred Y., interview with G. A. Ferrance conducted February 8, 1994.

—*Sketch by George A. Ferrance*

Paul Ching-Wu Chu

Paul Ching-Wu Chu
1941-
Chinese American physicist

Paul Ching-Wu Chu is one of the best-known superconductivity scientists in the world. In 1987, Chu and a team of physicists discovered materials capable of conducting electricity at temperatures significantly higher than had ever previously been recorded. Certain metals experience a total loss of electrical resistance, turning them into superconductors capable of carrying currents without any loss of energy, as well as in some cases creating massive, powerful magnetic fields. Scientists have been competing for decades to find a practical superconductor—one that performs at or near room temperature rather than at extremely cold temperatures (often reaching four hundred degrees below zero) which are too expensive to produce for commercial use. James Gleick describing the importance of this discovery in a *New York Times* article, predicted that practical-use superconductors would initiate "a turning point in scientific history ... a new age of electricity—a world of absurdly cheap power and trains floating in the grips of magnets."

Chu was born in the Hunan Province of China on December 2, 1941, and was raised in Taiwan. Graduating from Cheng Kung University in 1962, with a baccalaureate of science, he came to the United States the following year to pursue graduate studies at Fordham University, in the Bronx, New York. With his Master of Science degree, Chu moved on to the University of California at San Diego in 1965. There he completed, in 1968, his Ph.D. in physics, working as a research assistant under the superconducting expert Bernd T. Matthias. That same year, Chu married May P. Chern, with whom he has two children, Claire and Albert.

In 1970 Chu moved to Cleveland State University in Ohio, where he had been promoted from assistant professor to professor of physics, by 1979. That same year he became professor of physics at the University of Houston, Texas, and later accepted a position as director of the Texas Center for Superconductivity. He has held numerous concurrent positions since 1968, including positions at Bell Labs in Murray Hill, New Jersey; the Marshall Space Flight Center, NASA, Huntsville, Alabama; the Los Alamos Science Lab, Los Alamos, New Mexico; and the National Academy of Science's Panel on High Temperature Superconductivity. In 1988, Chu received a National Medal of Science and the Comstock Award from the National Academy of Science.

Becomes the Heir of the Grand Old Man of Superconductivity

Chu's career has been influenced by Matthias, who was dubbed "the grand old man of superconductivity" by James Gleick in the *New York Times.* The German-born Matthias was considered to be directly or indirectly responsible for almost every temperature increase at which materials became superconductors, and Chu's study under the master reflects the discipline and revolutionary thinking of Matthias's laboratory. Indeed, many of Chu's scientific researches—from scouring the world's scientific journals for clues on new superconducting materials, to putting his faith in the possibility that some of the best scientific ideas can literally be found in dreams—were acknowledged as a legacy from Matthias while Chu was his student at the University of California.

In one notable breakthrough, Chu, routinely reading through a little-known scientific journal late in 1986, discovered a report from Nobel prize-winning researchers **K. Alex Müller** and **Johannes Georg Bednorz**, concerning the construction of a complex ceramic material at IBM's Zurich research laboratory that was proven to superconduct up to temperatures of 35 Kelvin (a temperature of 0 Kelvin is equivalent to minus 460 degrees Fahrenheit or minus 273 degrees Celsius). The article, published in *Zeitschrift für Physik,* sparked Chu and his colleagues to an inspired rush to break that new barrier and make scientific history. Chu worked with a group of scientists at the University of Houston, in collaboration with a team from the University of Alabama in Huntsville, which was headed by his former graduate student Mau-Kwen Wu. By 1987 the team had discovered that a mixture of metals and rare earth oxides was capable of superconducting electricity at temperatures as warm as 93K—a measurement far surpassing temperatures reached by Müller and Bednorz only a year earlier. The key ingredients, yttrium, barium and copper, were later patented by Chu as compound 1–2–3.

On March 18, 1987, the world's top physicists gathered in New York City for the annual meeting of the American Physical Society. Chu's experiments, and those of his peers confirming that rare earth-based oxide ceramics could superconduct at extremely high temperatures, suddenly became front page news—the meeting became known in the media as "the Woodstock of physics," reported Arthur L. Robinson in *Science.* Uses envisioned for a practical superconductor include fast, quiet, and cheap transportation, improved computer technology, and smaller, less expensive medical diagnostic imaging machines.

The Importance of High-Temperature Superconductivity

Superconductivity occurs in many metals and organic materials when they are cooled to temperatures close to 0 K (known as absolute zero). In 1911, Dutch scientist Heike Kammerlingh Onnes, observed superconductivity with mercury which had been cooled to near absolute zero with the use of liquid helium, a rare and costly substance. Since then, the quest has intensified to find cheaper materials which perform the same feats of magnetism and conductivity at higher temperatures. Materials superconducting at temperatures above 77 K meant that nitrogen, which boils at 77 K, could become the new coolant for superconductivity, replacing helium, which is rare. The possibility of using liquid nitrogen, which can be carried in a styrofoam cup, meant the transformation of superconductivity from a costly means to a potentially cheap means of generating, transmitting, storing, and using electrical power efficiently. And because nitrogen makes up 78 percent of air, it has been called "as plentiful as air" and "cheaper than beer."

The discoveries made by Chu, and confirmed by other scientists in early 1987, were also considered a breakthrough toward the achievement of room temperature superconductivity, which has become a kind of holy grail of science. Some predict that its attainment will be as transforming to human life as the invention of the transistor or the lightbulb, envisioning an inexpensive means of generating power that has led some to theorize the invention of high-speed trains that would float on magnetic fields and others to anticipate the solution to practical nuclear fusion. Chu's discovery, which involved the element yttrium, was the first to show practical superconductivity at temperatures well above 77 K. Arthur L. Robinson in *Science* wrote that "physicists describe the finding to be with no exaggeration revolutionary, both scientifically and technologically."

When Chu's findings were published in *Physical Review Letters* on March 2, 1987, it set off a chain reaction of experiments, as scientists around the world duplicated the results, many of them over a weekend. High-temperature superconductivity had been achieved, and it meant the possibility of constructing efficient, cost-effective superconducting devices for the first time in the history of the field. Although subsequent experiments have suggested that the behavior of oxide superconductors such as compound 1–2–3 may, in fact, be problematic, and fundamentally different from "conventional" materials, there is no question that Chu's breakthrough was a turning point in the history of superconductivity.

SELECTED WRITINGS BY CHU:

Periodicals

(With P.H. Hor, R.L. Meng, L. Gao, Z.J. Huang and Y.Q. Wang) "Evidence for Superconductivity Above 40 K in the La-Ba-Cu-O Compound System," *Physical Review Letters,* Volume 58, January, 1987, p. 405.

"Superconductivity at 93 K in a New Mixed-Phase Y-Ba-Cu-O Compound System at Ambient Pressure," *Physical Review Letters,* Volume 58, March 2, 1987, p. 908.

SOURCES:

Books

Dahl, Per Fridtjof, *Superconductivity: Its Historical Roots and Development from Mercury to the Ceramic Oxides,* American Institute of Physics, 1992.

High-Temperature Superconductivity, reprints from *Physical Review Letters* and *Physical Review B,* January-June, 1987.

Mayo, Jonathan L., *Superconductivity: The Threshold of a New Technology,* Tab Books Inc., 1988.

Periodicals

Business Week, April 6, 1987, pp. 94–100.
Newsweek, December 19, 1988, p. 63.
New York Times, August 16, 1987, pp. 29–77.
Physics Today, April, 1987, pp. 17–23.
Popular Science, July, 1987, pp. 54–58, 97.
Science, March 27, 1987, p. 1571.
Science News, January 10, 1987, p. 23; August 15, 1987, pp. 106–109.
Time, May 11, 1987, pp. 64–75.

—*Sketch by Mindi Dickstein*

Alonzo Church
1903-
American mathematician and logician

Alonzo Church is an American mathematician and logician who provided significant innovations in number theory and in the decision theory that is the foundation of computer programming. His most important contributions focus on the degrees of decidability and solvability in logic and mathematics.

Church was born in Washington, D.C., on June 14, 1903, to Samuel Robbins Church and Mildred Hannah Letterman Church. He took his undergraduate degree from Princeton University in 1924. On August 25, 1925, he married Mary Julia Kuczinski. They had three children: Alonzo, Mary Ann, and Mildred Warner. Church completed his Ph.D. in mathematics at Princeton in 1927. After receiving his doctorate, he was a fellow at Harvard from 1927 to 1928. He studied in Europe from 1928 to 1929 at the University of Göttingen, a prestigious center for the study of mathematics and physics. He taught mathematics and philosophy at Princeton from 1929 to 1967. Among his Ph.D. students at Princeton was the British mathematician **Alan Turing**, who was to crack the German's World War II secret code, called Enigma, which played a key role in allowing the Western Allies to defeat Nazi Germany. Church was a professor of mathematics and philosophy at the University of California at Los Angeles from 1967 until his retirement in 1990. He also edited the *Journal of Symbolic Logic* from 1936 to 1979. His wife died in February, 1976.

Church's private life is very quiet and unremarkable. As Andrew Hodges said in his biography of Alan Turing (Church's famed student who killed himself in 1954 after being arrested on homosexual charges), Church "[is] a retiring man himself, not given to a great deal of discussion."

Cracking the Decidability Problem

One of the key problems in the foundations of mathematics was stated by the German mathematician **David Hilbert** (1862–1943): Is mathematics decidable? That is, as Andrew Hodges explains in his biography of Alan Turing, "did there exist a definite method which could, in principle, be applied to any assertion, and which was guaranteed to produce a correct decision as to whether that assertion was true"? Although Hilbert thought the answer would be yes, Church's answer was no. Church's theorem says in effect that there is no method to guarantee in advance that a mathematical assertion will be correct or incorrect. Specific mathematical assertions may be found to be correct or incorrect, but there is no general method that will work in advance for all mathematical assertions.

What Church's proof—and the proofs of other mathematicians such as **Kurt Friedrich Gödel**—showed was that mathematics in general was not as tidy, logical, and airtight as people had always thought it was. And, to make matters worse, mathematics could *never* be perfectly tidy, logical, or airtight. There would always be some statements that were undecidable, inconsistent, and incomplete. Church and other mathematicians of his time showed that like everything else, mathematics was fallible.

Laying the Foundation of Computer Programming

For computer programs to run, programmers have to be able to reduce all problems to the kinds of simple binary logical (or on/off) statements that can be processed by the electronic circuits inside the computer. For a problem to be solvable by a computer, it must be possible to break it down into an operational set of rules and terms. Next it must be possible to apply these rules recursively—that is repeatedly—to the problem until it is solved in terms of the existing set of rules. In short, a computer's binary circuits can only solve a problem under three conditions: (1) if the problem can be expressed as a meaningful set of rules (i.e., meaningful to the computer); (2) if the result of each step is also meaningful in terms of the computer's predefined set of rules; (3) if the computer's set of rules can be applied repeatedly to the problem. For example, in a simple addition or subtraction computer program, it must be possible for a small number (e.g., 1) to be repeatedly added to or subtracted from a larger number (e.g., 100) to get some result, say 10 or 10,000. If any of these three conditions mentioned above is absent, then a computer program cannot solve the problem.

Church's contribution to the foundation of computer programming is that he discovered—as did Alan Turing and Emil Post simultaneously and independently—the importance of recursiveness in solving logical problems. That is, for calculations to take place, some actions (e.g., adding or subtracting) have to be repeated a certain number of times. Church's deceptively simple thesis (which is often called the Church-Turing thesis) is that a function is computable or calculable if it is recursive. That is, the idea of recursiveness (repeatability) is tightly bound up with computability. Church's thesis is important because the repetition of a simple action can result in significant changes. It also means that one simple action can be useful over a broad range of problems, and at different levels of a problem.

Church's contributions to decidability theory have led to many honors, including induction into the National Academy of Science and the American

Academy of Arts and Sciences. He has received honorary doctorates from Case Western Reserve University in 1969, Princeton University in 1985, and the State University of New York at Buffalo in 1990.

SELECTED WRITINGS BY CHURCH:

Books

Introduction to Mathematical Logic, Volume 1, Princeton University Press, 1956.

Periodicals

"An Unsolvable Problem of Elementary Number Theory," *American Journal of Mathematics,* Volume 58, 1936, pp. 345–363.

SOURCES:

Books

Hodges, Andrew, *Alan Turing: The Enigma,* Simon & Schuster, 1983.
Hofstadter, Douglas R., *Gödel, Escher, and Bach: An Eternal Golden Braid,* Basic Books, 1979.

—*Sketch by Patrick Moore*

Edith Clarke
1883-1959
American engineer

Edith Clarke is chiefly recognized for her contributions to simplifying and mechanizing the calculations required in power systems analysis. A pioneering female engineer, Clarke was the first woman granted an M.S. in electrical engineering from the Massachusetts Institute of Technology (MIT) and later became the first woman to deliver a technical paper before the American Institute of Electrical Engineers (AIEE).

Clarke was born on a farm near Ellicott City, Maryland, one of nine children of Susan Dorsey (Owings) and John Ridgely Clarke, a lawyer. She attended a nearby school until 1897, when she entered boarding school after the deaths of her parents. She returned home two years later with no ambition for a career. Clarke decided to study languages with a tutor, however, and entered Vassar College in 1904. There she studied mathematics and astronomy, graduating with an A.B. in 1908.

Clarke taught math and science in San Francisco and later in Huntington, West Virginia, before renewing her studies in 1911 at the University of Wisconsin. After one year of course work in civil engineering, she joined the American Telephone and Telegraph company (AT&T) in New York as a computing assistant to research engineer George A. Campbell. At the time, computing mathematical problems for engineers was considered an appropriate profession for women with advanced training in mathematics. During World War I, Clarke led a group of women who made calculations for the Transmission Department at AT&T. Concurrently, she studied radio at Hunter College and electrical engineering at Columbia University in the evenings.

Awarded Landmark Degree from MIT

In 1919 Clarke became the first woman to graduate from the Massachusetts Institute of Technology (MIT) with an M.S. degree in electrical engineering. Even with such credentials, however, she was unsuccessful in acquiring a position as an engineer. She worked briefly as a computor for General Electric (GE) before accepting a post teaching physics at Constantinople Women's College (now Istanbul American College) in 1921. The following year, Clarke returned to GE—this time as an engineer. She analyzed electric power systems and researched special problems related to power-system operations.

Clarke remained with GE for twenty-six years. Chief among her contributions there were innovations in long-distance power transmission and the development of the theory of symmetrical component and circuit analysis. Her method of regulating the voltage on power transmission lines was patented in 1927. In 1932 she became the first woman to present a paper before the AIEE and garnered recognition for her work as the best paper of the year in the northern district. Her paper explored the use of multiple conductor transmission lines to increase power line capacity. While at GE, Clarke also published a textbook which covered circuit analysis of alternating-current power systems. Prior to World War II, Clarke devised calculating charts which greatly streamlined the computation process.

Clarke retired to Maryland in 1945 but was drawn back to engineering within a year, this time accepting an associate professorship in electrical engineering at the University of Texas. Gaining full professorship in 1947, Clarke also served on numerous committees and was a graduate student advisor, providing special assistance to foreign students. Clarke was elected a fellow of the AIEE (now the Institute for Electrical and Electronics Engineers,

known as the IEEE) in 1948, the first woman to be so named. In 1957, at age 74, Clarke retired a second time. She died two years later in Baltimore.

SELECTED WRITINGS BY CLARKE:

Books

Circuit Analysis of A-C Power Systems, Volume 1, 1943.

SOURCES:

Books

Goff, Alice C., *Women Can Be Engineers,* Edwards Brothers, 1946, pp. 50–65.

Periodicals

Brittain, James E., "From Computor to Electrical Engineer: The Remarkable Career of Edith Clarke," *IEEE Transactions on Education,* November, 1985, pp. 184–89.
"Edith Clarke Dies, 1954 SWE Award Winner," *Society of Women Engineers Newsletter,* December, 1959, p. 3.

—Sketch by Karen Withem

Albert Claude
1898-1983
Belgian American cell biologist

Biologist Albert Claude received the Nobel Prize in 1974 for his discoveries concerning the fine structure of the cell. His early work described the nature of mitochondria as the powerhouse of the cell, paving the way for much groundbreaking research by others. In addition, he demonstrated that the interior of cells were not merely an arbitrary mass of substances, but rather a highly organized space delineated by the net-like endoplasmic reticulum, a formation that he was the first to recognize.

Born in Longlier, Belgium (now Luxembourg), on August 24, 1898, Albert Claude chose to become a U.S. citizen at age 43. Though he maintained dual citizenship, his decision was the logical outcome of a growing research career in the United States, a place of opportunity for an individual who began life with what seemed like limited prospects. Claude's father, Florentin Joseph Claude, was a baker and unable to provide the kind of upbringing one might expect a Nobel Prize winner to have had. His mother, Marie-Glaudicine Wautriquant, and his father evidently provided the right attitude for young Claude, for he overcame the constraints of a limited education and poverty to gain acceptance into the University of Liege. This was possible because of his service in World War I, in which he won the Interallied Medal along with veteran status. The university admitted him under a special program designed for war veterans.

Claude earned an M.D. degree in 1928 under his continuing government scholarship and attended the Kaiser Wilhelm Institute in Berlin for further study. He relocated to the United States in 1929 to join the staff of the Rockefeller Institute in New York City, home to much of the great biomedical research and discoveries of the early twentieth century. There Claude studied the tumor agent of Rous sarcoma, a virus of chickens. Though Claude had not been invited to join the Institute, the director, **Simon Flexner**, one of the country's leading medical educators, approved his hiring.

In the laboratory of James B. Murphy, Claude began earnest work on isolating the originating factor of the sarcoma, a malignant plasma, first discovered in 1911 at Rockefeller Institute by **Peyton Rous**, that was a type of soft-tissue cancer in chickens. Only recently had microbiologists first suggested that cancers might be caused by newly discovered agents known as viruses. But it was not until 1932 that Rous' work was vindicated by the discovery of transmissible wild rabbit cancers that were proven to be viral in nature.

Diligently pursuing the new field of virology, Claude developed a technique using a high-speed centrifuge to spin fractionated (broken-up) cells infected with viruses in an attempt to isolate their agents. Though his primitive machine was constructed from meat grinders and sieves, Claude was able to fractionate various components of cells that had never been separated before, paving the way for new understanding of their varying functions. Though he never succeeded in fully isolating the virus within the cell mixture (a development that came years later by other investigators), his discoveries nevertheless became crucial to the study of cell biology.

The Rous virus is among those now known as a ribonucleic acid (RNA) virus, that is, its genetic material is derived from RNA rather than the more common deoxyribonucleic acid (DNA). Claude was surprised to find that it was not only virus-infected cells that showed a high RNA content, but also healthy cells. By the early 1940s Claude joined forces with biochemists George Hogeboom and Rollin

Hotchkiss in an attempt to determine the origins of this cellular RNA.

Determines Role of Mitochondria

Claude, Hogeboom, and Hotchkiss found a variety of different "granules" in the cells that they determined were mitochondria, which were first discovered in 1897. However, the purpose of these often abundant cell components, especially in the liver cells, still remained unknown. Claude found that the mitochondria were not the source of the cells' RNA, but they did harbor certain enzymes that seemed to be involved in the cells' energy metabolism, a process dimly understood at the time. Claude and his colleagues, in fact, proved in 1945 that mitochondria are the "powerhouses" of all cells, from bacteria to liver, from plants to fungi to animals. The RNA, it turned out, was concentrated in other cell particles that fellow researcher **George Palade** discovered and called microsomes. Later renamed ribosomes, these particles were shown to be the centers of protein production in all cells of every type of living thing. In 1974 Claude, Palade, and a third researcher, **Christian R. de Duvé**, shared the Nobel Prize for physiology or medicine.

By the early 1940s, Claude had significantly perfected ultracentrifugation (the process of separating cell particles) and was seeking other new technologies with which to probe the cell. In 1942 he became convinced that the newly developed electron microscope would be useful in furthering his studies and secured the use of the device at the Interchemical Corporation, home to the only electron microscope in New York City which was used primarily for metallurgical purposes.

The cells that Claude and his associate, Keith Porter, observed under the microscope showed the presence of a "lace-work" structure that was eventually proven to be the major structural feature of the interior of all but bacterial cells. This lace-work structure was also responsible in part for providing the shape of cells as well as the location for many granular cell components, including ribosomes. The discovery of this endoplasmic reticulum (derived from the Latin word for "fishnet") altered biologists' view of cells as simply bags of "stuff" to highly organized biological units.

In 1948 Claude returned to his native Belgium and for a time gave up active research to become an administrator at the Université Libre de Bruxelles, where he spent the next twenty years developing a significant cancer research center. During the same period he headed the Institut Jules Bordet, where he resumed research on the fine structure of cells.

In 1972 the Rockefeller University (formerly Institute) awarded Claude emeritus standing. Other honors accrued over the span of his career include the Medal of the Belgian Academy of Medicine, the Louisa G. Horowitz Prize of Columbia University, and the Paul Ehrlich and Ludwig Darmstaedter Prize of Frankfurt. In addition, Claude was a full member of the Belgian and French academies of science and an honorary member of the American Academy of Arts and Sciences. Other honors included the Order of the Palmes Académiques of France, the Grand Cordon of the Order of Léopold II, and the Prix Fonds National de la Recherche Scientifique from Belgium.

SELECTED WRITINGS BY CLAUDE:

Periodicals

"Fractionation of Chicken Tumor Extracts by High Speed Centrifugation," *American Journal of Cancer,* Volume 30, 1937, pp. 742–745.
"Distribution of Nucleic Acids in the Cell and Morphological Constitution of the Cytoplasm," *Biological Symposia,* Volume 10, 1943, pp. 111–129.

SOURCES:

Periodicals

Hicks, Nancy, "Albert Claude," *New York Times,* October 12, 1974.
Rensberger, Boyce, "Three Cell Biologists Get Nobel Prize," *New York Times,* October 12, 1974.

—*Sketch by Donald J. McGraw*

Georges Claude
1870-1960
French chemist and inventor

Trained as a chemist, Georges Claude was a prolific inventor who was responsible for technological developments ranging from innovations in the use of acetylene to the invention of neon lights. His inventions made him wealthy, but he spent much of this money during the 1920s and 1930s on experiments that his contemporaries considered unconventional. Claude was an eccentric man, with strong, right-wing political views. Having collaborated with the Nazis during the occupation of France in

World War II, he was imprisoned after the war's end. Claude was born in Paris, France, on September 24, 1870, and was educated at the École de Physique et Chimie, a municipal school for physics and chemistry. Graduating in 1886, he was employed in the engineering department of an electricity company, and then as an engineer in several different industrial plants. He married in 1893 and subsequently had three children.

It was while working in industry that Claude started upon his long career of inventions and discoveries. He determined in 1897 that acetylene, a highly combustible gas, could be safely transported if dissolved in acetone. Acetylene was—and still is—highly valued in industry because of its use in the cutting and welding of metals, and Claude's innovation greatly increased its demand in industry. By 1927, the production of acetylene was valued at ten million dollars per year in the United States alone.

In 1902, Claude developed a method for liquefying air, which was used by other scientists to identify the inert gases. Once these gases had been identified, Claude found a way to separate nitrogen and oxygen from liquefied air and then developed methods to produce these gases in large quantities. He proposed the use of liquid oxygen in iron smelting in 1910, and although he proved the technique could be successful, it was not widely adopted until after World War II. During World War I, however, Claude adapted the procedures he had developed during these experiments to manufacture liquid chlorine, which was employed for poisonous gas attacks.

Claude's work with inert gases also led to more peaceful inventions. In 1910, he discovered that the electrification of neon (a mostly inert gas) produced a bright, red light. He then produced specially coated tubes—which could be bent and twisted into any shape—to keep the light active. Such was the beginning of neon lights, a major transformation in the lighting and advertising industries. He introduced his invention to the United States at a conference in 1913, but World War I put off the general use of neon lights until close to 1920. The invention eventually brought Claude fame and a substantial sum of money. In the 1930s, the potential for neon lighting increased with yet another innovation: the coating of the interior of the tubes with fluorescent material, which created the white lights still in use today. Fluorescent bulbs soon replaced American inventor **Thomas Edison**'s incandescent lighting in businesses and factories, earning Claude the nickname "Edison of France".

In 1917, Claude invented a method to produce synthetic ammonia, a procedure which was similar to the Haber Process developed in Germany at around the same time. Claude used the Haber principles, but he applied them with four times greater pressure, thus producing an ammonia with greater efficiency (among the most important practical applications of ammonia is as an element in fertilizer). Claude's thinking was scorned by many contemporary scientists, but his idea was successful, producing ammonia and earning him election to the French Academy of Sciences in 1924.

After 1926, Claude concentrated on developing new sources of energy. He was particularly interested in the temperature differences in ocean waters—which in some regions can be quite extreme—and he theorized that there was a way to exploit them. Water under lower than normal pressure boils at temperatures below one hundred degrees centigrade, and Claude believed that he could create a turbine-type system using the upper ocean water for steam production and the lower, cooler water for condensation. The steam, caught in transit between the boiler and the condenser, could easily be harnessed to power a turbine. With the scientific knowledge of the day indicating that Claude was at least theoretically correct, he set out to build a small model. Although the model was successful, prominent scientists still gave Claude a great deal of opposition. Determined to prove his theory, Claude used his own money to build a plant in Belgium in which a turbine was, indeed, successfully operated by harnessing differences in ocean temperature.

After building a successful plant in Belgium, Claude received financial backing and moved his operations to Cuba, where he believed his ideas would be better received. His project, however, suffered large-scale problems. To reach water that was deep enough—and therefore cold enough—special tubing had to be developed. A tube six thousand feet long and over six feet in diameter was designed to reach over a third of a mile into the ocean. The first of these tubes was set out in 1930 but was lost when they attempted to put it in place. A second tube was also lost; Claude reported that it had been sabotaged. A third tube was finally put in place, but it was soon ruined because of waves and currents, though not before sucking up a previously unknown species of fish subsequently named after Claude by the Havana Academy of Science. After the destruction of the third tube, Claude permanently abandoned the project. Later, however, Claude's plans were reviewed by a French bureaucrat, improvements in the tubing were made, and experimentation with the theory continued. By this time Claude himself was involved in the activities which would eventually lead to his prison sentence.

Claude had joined the political organization *Action Francaise* in 1919. During World War II, he lectured at his own expense on the benefits of National Socialism and encouraged the Vichy government—which ruled as a Nazi puppet state following the fall of France—to take stronger action against the resistance movement. Following the Allied army landing in North Africa, Claude is reported to have attempted suicide with an overdose of strychnine. At the end of the war, he was put on trial for his lecturing activities, found to be a Vichy sympathizer, and sentenced to life imprisonment. Claude also lost his membership in the French Academy of Sciences.

Imprisoned at the age of seventy-four, Claude still conducted experiments during his confinement. He attempted to develop a deep-water tube for fishing, which would suck fish directly from the water into boats; the fish would then be immediately frozen with liquid air. Through the efforts of friends, Claude was released from prison in 1950 after serving four and a half years of his sentence. He passed away in Saint-Cloude, France, on May 23, 1960, actively working and writing his memoirs up until his death.

Claude's innovative methods often met with strong criticism, and if he was at all successful in having his inventions adopted, it was because of years of salesmanship. Claude realized that timing played a key role in invention. In an interview with *Scientific American* in 1929, he said: "The difficulty of an inventor is not to make an invention, but to choose from among the multitude of inventive ideas which strike his mind the one which is really worth while." In a different interview with *Scientific American* the following year, he observed that his strict rule concerning inventing was that "only simple solutions are worth considering."

SELECTED WRITINGS BY CLAUDE:

Books

L'air liquide, sa production, ses proprietes, ses applications, par Georges Claude, preface by M. d'Arsonval, Dunod, 1903, translation by Henry E. P. Cotrell, published as *Liquid Air, Oxygen, Nitrogen, by Georges Claude,* Blakiston's Sons, 1913.
Souvenirs et enseignements d'une experience electorale, Nouvelle Librairie Francaise, 1931.
Ma vie et mes inventions, Plon, 1957.

SOURCES:

Books

Williams, Trevor I., editor, *A Biographical Dictionary of Scientists,* Third Edition, Adam & Charles Black, 1982.

Periodicals

"Commercial Property Notes," *Scientific American,* June, 1929, pp. 568–569.

"Foreign News," *Time,* July 9, 1945, p. 22.

"Science," *Time,* January 5, 1948, p. 29.

"Science News," *Science—Supplement,* July 11, 1930, pp. X-XII.

Wright, Milton, "Inventors Who Have Achieved Commercial Success," *Scientific American,* June, 1927, p. 396.

—*Sketch by Kimberly McGrail*

Jacob Clay
1882-1955
Dutch physicist

Jacob Clay made important contributions to our knowledge of low-temperature physics and cosmic rays. He was also a distinguished philosopher of science. Some of his most important research was done in Indonesia, where, from 1920 to 1929, he was the first director of the physics laboratory at the Bandung Institute of Technology, located on Java. His research catapulted the new institute to the front ranks of the scientific world. Among his pupils at Bandung was one of the architects of Indonesian independence, Sukarno. Clay ended his career as professor of experimental physics at the University of Amsterdam.

Clay, the son of farmer Pieter Claij and Neeltje Molenaar, was born in Berkhout, near Hoorn, in the Netherlands. He had one sister, Anna, two years his junior. Early talent in school at Spierdijk, in Alkmaar, led his family to send him to the Erasmiaans Gymnasium in Rotterdam, a secondary school offering Greek and Latin, which was unusual in being coeducational. In 1900 he entered the University of Leiden. There, in 1908, he completed a doctoral dissertation on galvanic properties of metals and alloys at low temperatures. His doctoral adviser was **Heike Kamerlingh Onnes**, the early twentieth-century pioneer of low-temperature physics. In the same year, he married physicist Tettje Clasina Jolles, who was also a student with Kamerlingh Onnes.

From 1909 to 1920 Clay continued to work with Kamerlingh Onnes, and he published on low-temperature phenomena. However, his principal source of income derived from a position as a secondary-school teacher in Delft. Well into the twentieth century it was common for Dutch scientists to begin their career as schoolteachers (some of the most distinguished, including **Hendrik Lorentz**, had done so). Professor-

ships were few and junior university positions provided less-than-adequate salaries for raising a family.

Takes Leading Role in Philosophy of Science

While conducting low-temperature research and teaching school, Clay continued an early interest in philosophy, which had been awakened at Leiden under the Neohegelian Gerardus Johannes Petrus Josephus Bolland. By 1915 Clay's knowledge of modern quantum physics and relativity persuaded him that Neohegelian doctrine was inadequate, and he published well-received epistemological works over the next five years. Clay also took his pedagogical charge seriously. From 1916 onwards, he belonged to a circle of educators who eventually opened an international school of philosophy at Amersfoort. By 1920 he was the most prominent philosopher of science in the Netherlands. In his view, philosophers had to learn from practicing scientists, not the reverse. During spare moments, Clay taught his brand of philosophy as a lecturer at the Delft Institute of Technology. In 1922 the Faculty of Letters at the University of Leiden named Clay as its first choice of a successor to Bolland, but the university curators reversed this decision and chose a theologically-inclined philosopher, Arthur Joseph de Sopper, instead.

Research on Cosmic Rays

Clay's philosophical, pedagogical, and scientific qualifications propelled him into the position of first professor of physics at a new institute of technology at Bandung, in central Java, which was then at the center of the Dutch colonial empire in the Malay archipelago. The institute, offering university-level education, arose from donations by traders, industrialists, and agriculturists in the East Indies and in the Netherlands. Clay, his wife, and their three children were present for the opening in 1920. Clay's physics laboratory, a splendid structure of stone, timber, and sweeping Javan roofs, came courtesy of Karel Albert Rudolf Bosscha, the principal scientific philanthropist of the East Indies. The laboratory was well-appointed and came complete with an instrument-maker and glass-blower. Clay's mandate went far beyond apprising Indonesians of Newton's laws. He was expected to carry out original research in pure science.

In anticipation of going to Bandung, Clay had studied radioactivity with physicist **Ernest Rutherford** at Manchester, England. He decided to begin a new line of research on Java by investigating the atmosphere, the source of radiation that was then attracting many researchers who could not afford a laboratory emitter. He focused on the so-called penetrating radiation discovered in 1912 by physicist **Victor Hess** and later known as cosmic rays. During their years at Bandung, **Tettje Clasina Clay-Jolles** served as Clay's laboratory assistant and collaborated with him on the radiation research (besides working on a private interest in vacuum pump technology). From 1920 to 1925, the team designed and constructed electrometers launched in high-altitude balloons. They also measured the effect of cosmic rays in deep subterranean mines and under the ocean. Then, in 1927, Clay measured the intensity of atmospheric radiation during the course of an ocean voyage from Java to the Netherlands. He discovered that the intensity varied with latitude. The discovery also provided compelling evidence that cosmic rays consisted of charged particles rather than photons.

Clay's latitude effect was for many years denied particularly by United States physicists, who, along with **Robert A. Millikan**, imagined that cosmic rays were electromagnetic radiation. Nobel laureate **Arthur Holly Compton** proposed Clay (along with Victor Hess and Millikan's student **Carl David Anderson**) for the 1936 Nobel prize, but to have credited Clay in this way would have meant discrediting Millikan—a step the Nobel committee was loathe to take. The Royal Netherlands Academy of Science, however, was glad to recognize Clay's work and elected him as a fellow in that year.

Clay, who had become professor of experimental physics at the University of Amsterdam in 1929, found little to admire in Millikan's behavior. Clay noted (in English) in 1939 in the draft of a review of a book by Millikan, "From the beginning of his work on cosmic rays up to 1933, he [Millikan] has unfortunately been on the wrong side with nearly all his own experiments and conclusions. This fact would be of no importance, if Millikan had not afterwards tried to turn the facts in such a way that they prove that he has been right; and partly he tries to attain his end by distorting the results of others and depreciating their work." Clay became a leading authority on cosmic rays and one of Netherlands' finest original thinkers. He died in 1955.

SELECTED WRITINGS BY CLAY:

Books

De drieledigheid der natuurkennis, [Haarlem], 1912.

Schets eener kritische geschiedenis van het begrip Natuurwet in de nieuwere wijsbegeerte, [Leiden], 1915.

De dialektiek en de leer van de tegenstrijdigheid bij Hegel en Bolland, [Santpoort-Bloemendaal], 1919.

De ontwikkeling van het denken, Van Loghum Slaterus & Visser, 1920, reprinted W. de Haan, 1949.

(Editor) *Zeven artikelen over Grieksche kultuur,* [Bandung], 1923.

Kosmische stralen, [The Hague], 1948.

Atmosferische electriciteit, [The Hague], 1951.

SOURCES:

Books

Berkel, Klaas van, *In het voetspoor van Stevin: Geschiedenis van de natuurwetenschap in Nederland 1580–1940,* Boom, 1985, pp. 218–19.

Heijerman, A. F., and M. J. van den Hoven, editors, *Filosofie in Nederland: De Internationale School voor Wijsbegeerte als ontmoetingsplaats 1916–1986,* [Amsterdam], 1986, pp. 65–92.

Kargon, Robert H., *The Rise of Robert Millikan,* Cornell University Press, 1982, pp. 158–61.

Pyenson, Lewis, *Empire of Reason: Exact Sciences in Indonesia, 1840–1940,* E.J. Brill, 1989, pp. 133–56.

Veldkamp, J., *History of Geophysical Research in the Netherlands and Its Former Overseas Territories,* [North-Holland], 1984, pp. 27–29.

Periodicals

Beth, E. W., "In memoriam Jacob Clay," *Algemeen Nederlands Tijdschrift voor wijsbegeerte en psychologie,* Volume 47, 1955, pp. 233–35.

Boasson, J. J., "Jacob Clay," *Jaarboek van de Maatschappij der Nederlandse Letterkunde te Leiden,* 1955–56, pp. 55–58.

Jongen, H. F., "The Physicist Jacob Clay," *Synthese,* Volume 9, 1955, pp. 428–32.

Rathenau, G. W., "Levensbericht van Jacob Clay," Amsterdam, Koninklijke Akademie van Wetenschappen, *Jaarboek, s. v.,* 1955–56.

—*Sketch by Lewis Pyenson*

Tettje Clasina Clay-Jolles
1881-1972
Dutch physicist

Tettje Clasina Jolles was one of the first Dutch women scientists. Although she abandoned her doctoral research under the pressure of family duties, she collaborated with her husband, **Jacob Clay**, in his research on cosmic rays and ultraviolet radiation. She also made contributions to the technology of vacuum pumps.

Jolles was born in Assen, the Netherlands, to Maurits Aernout Diederik Jolles and Eva Dina Halbertsma. She had two older sisters, Hester and Leida. After her primary schooling (which she began at age five), she attended the *gymnasium,* or classical secondary school, at Assen, where she was the first and only girl for the six-year course of study. Jolles took and passed both Dutch secondary-school leaving examinations (the so-called alpha and beta series, with concentrations in the humanities and exact sciences, respectively) at one time—a rare feat.

Upon graduating from the *gymnasium* at age eighteen, Jolles began university in nearby Groningen, commuting daily by train from Assen. In 1903 she decided to continue her studies in the physical sciences at the University of Leiden. There she became one of the few women students of physics. For a number of years she worked toward a doctorate in low-temperature physics under the direction of **Heike Kamerlingh Onnes.** She continued her research after marrying Jacob Clay—another of Kamerlingh Onnes's students—in June 1908, although she finally abandoned the thesis work in December of that year. (The first woman to receive a doctorate in physics at a Dutch university was H. B. van Bilderbeek-van Meurs, in 1909, under Pieter Zeeman at Amsterdam.) Over the next dozen years Clay-Jolles devoted herself to raising her children.

Research on Ultraviolet Radiation

In 1920 Clay-Jolles and her children (a daughter and two sons) accompanied Jacob Clay to Bandung, Java, where he was appointed professor of physics at the new Institute of Technology. She worked as an assistant in the handsome physics laboratory, continuing her interest from student days in the technology of vacuum pumps. In 1921 she edited a volume of lectures by Nobel laureate **Hendrik Lorentz,** an exacting and prestigious task usually undertaken by only the best of younger scientists. According to her daugher, she also typed and edited all of her husband's publications.

From 1920 to 1929, Clay-Jolles worked with her husband on measuring the intensity of atmospheric radiation. They made major advances in the understanding of the nature of cosmic rays. Another area of investigation was radiation in the ultraviolet solar spectrum. Jacob Clay discovered that radiation varies with latitude, and he and Clay-Jolles continued research into the causes of the variation. They concluded that ultraviolet penetration at various latitudes relates directly to the physics of the upper atmosphere and the ozone layer.

Clay-Jolles and Clay disputed the findings of Jan Boerema and Maarten Pieter Vrij, who had proclaimed the existence of tropical ultraviolet penetration. Both Boerema and Vrij were based in Batavia (now Jakarta) at the Magnetical and Meteorological Observatory and at the Medical Faculty. The hus-band-and-wife team used a cadmium electrocell to show the relatively weak penetration of ultraviolet light in the tropics—a finding supported by the work of their old friend from student years at Leiden, Cornelis Braak, who had previously directed the Batavia Observatory. Clay and Clay-Jolles concluded that the ozone layer above Switzerland was substantially thinner than above Bandung.

In 1929 the family returned to the Netherlands, where Jacob became professor of experimental physics at the University of Amsterdam. Clay-Jolles and Maarten Vrij defended their different points of view on ultraviolet penetration in an exchange published in the *Natuurkundig tijdschrift voor Nederlandsch-Indië,* the principal scientific journal of the East Indies. This publication marked the end of Clay-Jolles's research. She died in Amsterdam in 1972.

SELECTED WRITINGS BY CLAY-JOLLES:

Books

(Editor) Hendrik Antoon Lorentz, *Lessen over theoretische natuurkunde, Volume 4: Thermodynamica,* Leiden, 1921.

Periodicals

(With husband, Jacob Clay) "Measurements of Ultraviolet Sunlight in the Tropics," *Proceedings of the Amsterdam Academy of Sciences,* Volume 35, 1933, pp. 69–82, 172–85.
"Vergelijking van het ultraviolet zonlicht op Java en in Europa," *Natuurkundig Tijdsschrift voor Nederlandsch-Indië,* Volume 93, 1933, pp. 126–38.

SOURCES:

Books

Een eeuw natuurwetenschap in Indonesië 1850–1950, [Jakarta], 1950, p. 38.
Mulder, Denis, *Malaria,* [The Hague/Bandung], 1931, pp. 85–6.
Pyenson, Lewis, *Empire of Reason: Exact Sciences in Indonesia, 1840–1940,* E.J. Brill, 1989, pp. 120–24, 133–59.

—*Sketch by Lewis Pyenson*

Preston Cloud
1912-1991
American geologist

Geologist Preston Cloud was known as the founder of biogeology—the integrated study of life formation and geology. From that holistic discipline he developed several facets of early evolutionary theory which have become widely accepted. Cloud combined inquiries in the fields of invertebrate paleontology, geochemistry, and marine ecology to give rise to biogeology. He was the author of several books, including *Oasis in Space: Earth History from the Beginning.*

Preston Ercelle Cloud was born in West Upton, Massachusetts, on September 26, 1912, the son of Preston E. Cloud and Pauline L. Wiedemann Cloud. After several years in the U.S. Navy he attended college, graduating from George Washington University with a bachelor of science in 1938. He went on to obtain a Ph.D. from Yale University in 1940. Cloud taught at the Missouri School of Mines briefly before joining the United States Geological Survey (USGS) during World War II, at which time he worked on geologic mapping. In 1946 he left the USGS to teach at Harvard University, but he returned in 1948. During this second stint with the USGS Cloud studied Pacific tropical reefs. He served as chief of the branch of paleontology and stratigraphy for a decade, receiving several distinguished service awards for his work, which included marine geology expeditions to the Bahamas and a petroleum survey of northeastern Spain. He then began studies of coastal areas and the continental shelves.

Once again, in 1961, Cloud left the USGS, this time to chair the University of Minnesota's department of geology and geophysics. That same year he was elected to the National Academy of Sciences. He also headed the university's School of Earth Science for some time. It was during his tenure at Minnesota that Cloud turned his attention to the prehistoric evolution of life. He continued his studies in this area while teaching at the University of California—first in Los Angeles and later in Santa Barbara—for nine years. While teaching in Santa Barbara, in 1972, he married Janice Gibson, bringing to the union three children from a previous marriage. In 1974 Cloud again joined the USGS. By this time he had become a member of the American Academy of Arts and Sciences and the American Philosophical Society and received the Paleontological Society Medal.

Developed Interactive Theory of Life and Crust Formation

Cloud's innovations in geology and his development of the field of biogeology grew out of his inquiries into the successive formation of older rocks and the life they documented. Prior to his studies, geologists had trouble accurately interpreting the record of life contained in the oldest rocks. They could determine the relative ages of rocks by measuring their radioactivity, but more specific details on the development of life and the earth's history eluded them. Cloud developed the theory, later widely supported by geologists, that the appearance of early life and the formation of earth's atmosphere and crust were highly interactive. This meant that in addition to determining age, scientists could piece together information about atmospheric conditions and the development of life at the time a rock was formed, based on its composition and characteristics. An iron-rich rock of known age that lacked the rusty color of iron exposed to oxygen, for example, identified an era when the earth's atmosphere contained relatively little oxygen and when oxygen-producing life forms were few or nonexistent.

Within the framework of this multidisciplinary study, Cloud illuminated the development of single-cell life and of metazoans—multicellular animals possessing specialized cells that form tissues and organs—which followed single-cell life. Cloud was the first to assert that metazoans developed rapidly, arising from different ancestors toward the start of Paleozoic time (about 680 million years ago) when the atmosphere had sufficient oxygen to support such life. He detailed the long-standing existence of microbial life forms and used knowledge of those life forms to postulate early changes in the earth's chemistry and sediment.

Documented Origin of Planet and Its Life

In his 1988 book, *Oasis in Space: Earth History from the Beginning,* Cloud culminated his life's research with a comprehensive account of the earth's history. True to his integrated approach to geology, he described plant and animal life which flourished within the early biosphere. Geologist Euan Nisbet described the book as "a biography of the planet" in his review in *Science.* "*Oasis in Space* is a paean to the glory of the earth," wrote Nisbet. "It is a fine exposition of the history of our planet, written in a chatty style that hides deep learning and wise judgment." Cloud's narrative begins at the beginning, with the origin of the planet. From there the book takes the reader through an exploration of the three billion years to follow, discussing the formation of the earth's crust and later continental and mountain formation, atmosphere and climate, evolution and extinction, and the more familiar accounting of metazoans. According to a *Scientific American* reviewer, *Oasis in Space* is a "closely argued and beautifully written book, the first introductory geology to devote central attention to . . . decisive ancient events" such as the formation of continents and the joint development of life and atmosphere.

Cloud's synthesis of scientific disciplines, which became the field of biogeology, distinguished his career from that of other geologists. His comprehensive theory of early earth history and life formation, though controversial at first, gained widespread acceptance among the scientific community before his death. Cloud died in Santa Barbara on January 16, 1991, of amyotrophic lateral sclerosis, popularly known as Lou Gehrig's disease.

SELECTED WRITINGS BY CLOUD:

Books

Cosmos, Earth, and Man: A Short History of the Universe, Yale University Press, 1978.
Oasis in Space: Earth History from the Beginning, Norton, 1988.

SOURCES:

Books

McGraw-Hill Modern Scientists and Engineers, Volume 1, McGraw, 1980, pp. 210–11.

Periodicals

Los Angeles Times, January 31, 1991.
New York Times, January 29, 1991.
Nisbet, Euan, "Biography of Our Planet," *Science,* May 20, 1988, p. 1072.
Scientific American, November, 1988, pp. 147–48.

—*Sketch by Karen Withem*

Jewel Plummer Cobb
1924-
American cell biologist

Jewel Plummer Cobb is known for her contributions to the field of cell biology and for promoting minority involvement in the sciences. She has focused much of her research on melanin, a brown or black skin pigment, and the factors that affect the causes and growth of normal and cancerous pigment cells. Her research into the effects of drugs on cancer cells was important to future work in the field of chemo-

therapy. As an educator, Cobb initiated a number of programs to encourage ethnic minorities and women in the sciences.

Born in Chicago on January 17, 1924, Cobb was the only child of Frank V. Plummer, a doctor and graduate of Cornell University, and Carriebel (Cole) Plummer, who taught dance in public schools and participated in the Works Projects Administration (WPA) efforts. Cobb's family had a history in the sciences: not only was her father a doctor, but her paternal grandfather was a pharmacist who had graduated from Howard University in 1898.

As an upper-middle-class African American, Cobb was exposed to a variety of African American professionals through her parents, all accomplished in their fields. She also socialized with well-off peers during her summers at a northern Michigan resort. Although the schools in Chicago were largely segregated, Cobb received a solid public school education, bolstered by her exposure to her father's library at home. Her interest in biology was sparked in her sophomore year by her first look through the lens of a microscope.

A member of her high school's honor society, Cobb attended the University of Michigan after graduation. She was drawn there partly by the knowledge that some of her summer friends would be there and by the university's nationally known football team. The segregation she had experienced in public schools continued in college, however: all the African American students had to live in one house. After three semesters at Michigan, Cobb transferred to Alabama's Talladega College, and in 1944 she graduated with a bachelor of arts degree in biology. She then accepted a teaching fellowship at New York University, which had at first turned her down. Her poise and credentials finally tipped the scales in her favor. She maintained her fellowship for five years and undertook graduate studies in cell physiology.

Pursues Career as Cell Biologist

By 1950 Cobb had completed her master's degree and doctorate. Because she enjoyed research and a theoretical approach to biology, Cobb decided to become a cell biologist. As a cell biologist, her focus was the action and interaction of living cells. She was particularly interested in tissue culture, in which cells are grown outside of the body and studied under microscopes. Among her most important work was her study with Dorothy Walker Jones of how new cancer-fighting drugs affected human cancer cells.

As a researcher, Cobb has held a series of positions at various colleges and research facilities throughout the United States. She was a fellow at the National Cancer Institute for two years after receiving her doctorate, and from 1952 to 1954 she was the director of the Tissue Culture Laboratory at the University of Illinois. At the end of this period Cobb married, and in 1957 she and her husband had a son, Roy Jonathan Cobb. After leaving Illinois, Cobb worked at several universities, including New York University and Hunter College in New York, and in 1960 she was appointed professor of biology at Sarah Lawrence College. There Cobb taught and continued her research into skin pigment. She was particularly interested in melanoma, or skin cancer, and melanin's ability to protect skin from damage caused by ultraviolet light.

Establishes Programs for Minority Students

In 1969, two years after she and her husband divorced, Cobb was appointed dean of Connecticut College and professor of zoology. In addition to teaching and continuing her research, she established a privately funded premedical graduate program and a pre-dental program for minority students. Numerous other colleges used these programs as models for their own, but after she left in 1976, the programs at Connecticut were discontinued. From 1976 to 1981 Cobb served as dean and professor of biological sciences at Douglass College. Although she had to give up her research in order to fulfill her administrative and teaching obligations, she continued to press for the advancement of minorities and women in the sciences.

Cobb wrote about the difficulties women face in scientific fields in a 1979 paper, "Filters for Women in Science," published in the book *Expanding the Role of Women in the Sciences,* which was edited by Anne M. Briscoe and Sheila M. Pfafflin. In this piece, Cobb argued that various pressures, particularly in the educational system, act as filters that prevent many women from choosing science careers. The socialization of girls has tended to discourage them from pursuing math and the sciences from a very early age, and even those women who got past such obstacles have struggled to get university tenure and the same jobs (at equal pay) as men.

In 1981 Cobb was named president at California State University (CSU) in Fullerton. She was extremely active in initiating improvements for the campus, notably in obtaining state funding for a new engineering and computer science building and a new science building. In addition, she built an apartment complex for students (later named in her honor), ending the university's years as a commuter campus, and established the president's opportunity program for ethnic students. Her work also extended to the community, for which she founded a privately funded gerontology center.

Cobb became a trustee professor at California State College in Los Angeles in 1990, and in 1991 she was made principal investigator for Southern Califor-

nia Science and Engineering ACCESS Center and Network. A trustee of several colleges, with numerous honorary degrees, Cobb worked with a consortium of six colleges to raise private funds to replace diminishing government grants and fellowships for minorities in science and engineering. The group worked to motivate minorities in the sciences, to bring more of them into the field. Over the years, Cobb had become increasingly aware of the disparity between the number of black men in sports and those in the lab, for instance. As part of her group's effort, faculty members tutored students on an individual basis in order to solidify their math skills, which Cobb felt were a crucial foundation for a career in the sciences. President emeritus of CSU since 1990, Cobb continues to use her skill as an educator, administrator, and scientist to promote the educational needs and careers of minorities in the sciences.

SELECTED WRITINGS BY COBB:

Periodicals

(With D. G. Walker) "Studies on Human Melanoma Cells in Tissue Cultures. I. Growth Characteristics and Cytology," *Cancer Research,* Volume 20, 1960, pp. 858–67.
(With Walker) "Cytologic Studies on Human Melanoma Cells in Tissue Culture after Exposure to Five Chemotherapeutic Agents," *Cancer Chemotherapy Reports,* Volume 51, 1968, pp. 543–52.
"I Am Woman, Black, Educated," *Hartford Courant Sunday Supplement,* February 4, 1973.
"Filters for Women in Science," *Expanding the Role of Women in the Sciences,* edited by Anne M. Briscoe and Sheila M. Pfafflin, New York Academy of Sciences, 1979, pp. 236–48.
"The Role of Women Presidents/Chancellors in Intercollegiate Athletics," *Women at the Helm,* edited by J. A. Sturnick, J. E. Milley, and C. A. Tisinger, AASCU Press, 1991, pp. 42–50.

SOURCES:

Books

Hine, Darlene Clark, editor, *Black Women in America: An Historical Encyclopedia,* Carlson Publishing Inc., 1993, pp. 257–58.
Notable Black American Women, Gale, 1992, pp. 195–98.

—*Sketch by Geeta Kothari*

William Montague Cobb
1904-1990
American anatomist

As an educator, scientist, and civic activist, William Montague Cobb devoted his career to the advancement of African Americans. He taught anatomy to medical and dental students at Howard University over the course of more than forty years, and he fought for the integration of hospitals and medical societies to provide opportunities for his students when they graduated. He is also considered an important historian of African Americans in medicine, and he often used his scientific knowledge to argue against racist characterizations. Active in many professional societies and civil rights organizations, Cobb was recognized both as a scholar and an aggressive proponent of justice. He is quoted in *New Directions* as saying, "I'm a seasoned fighter and the battle never bothered me."

Cobb was a lifelong resident of Washington, D.C., except for a few years spent in college and graduate school. He was born there October 12, 1904, the son of William Elmer and Alexzine Montague Cobb. His father was a printer who had moved to Washington from Selma, Alabama, in 1899 to work for the Government Printing Office; he later opened his own printing shop. Cobb attended segregated Patterson Elementary School and Dunbar High School in Washington. Dunbar was famous for the high quality of its teaching staff and curriculum, and its many notable alumni. He graduated from Dunbar in 1921 and enrolled in Amherst College in Massachusetts. At Amherst, Cobb distinguished himself in scholarship and athletics. He won the Blodgett Scholarship as the outstanding biology student in his class, which allowed him to study embryology the summer after graduation at the Marine Biological Laboratory at Woods Hole, Massachusetts. He was also a successful athlete, winning the intramural cross-country championships three times and boxing championships twice.

Cobb's career in medical science began in 1925, after he graduated from Amherst and enrolled in the College of Medicine at Howard University in Washington. When he was a senior, he was invited to teach a course in embryology, as a result of his summer at Woods Hole, and it was because of this experience that he decided that he would prefer to teach medical science than to practice medicine. After graduation in 1929, he completed his internship at Freedmen's Hospital (now Howard University Hospital), and left to study anatomy and physical anthropology at Western Reserve (now Case Western) University in Cleveland. His dissertation advisor at Western Reserve was

Thomas Wingate Todd, who had collected a large number of human and mammalian skeletons for the university's Hamann Museum of Comparative Anthropology and Anatomy, which inspired Cobb's own collections later at Howard University. Cobb's investigations of skeletons of different races convinced him of the erroneous and worthless arguments of white supremacists who contended that African Americans were mentally inferior, supposedly based on anatomical studies. He published his observations and conclusions in a number of professional journals and in popular magazines. He later analyzed X-ray photographs of Olympic champions of 1936 to show that there were no fundamental differences in bone structure between black and white runners.

Cobb received his Ph.D. in 1932 and returned to Howard as an assistant professor of anatomy in the medical school; he was promoted to associate professor in 1934 and professor in 1942. In 1947 he was appointed head of the anatomy department, a position which he held for twenty-two years. As an educator, Cobb was innovative and inspiring. His unique personality made his anatomy classes memorable: He interjected quotations from the Bible, William Shakespeare, and classic literature into his lectures. He imitated the movements of the embryo in the womb and occasionally played his violin during dissections in the anatomy laboratory in order to help the students relax. He assembled a varied collection of more than 600 human skeletons, used slides and motion pictures which he produced himself in his courses, and developed a graphic method of teaching anatomy through student drawings. Although 6000 students received anatomy instruction from Cobb, in 1969 many complained that his course was outdated and did not cover the material on licensing examinations. A struggle ensued, with the students demanding that Cobb relinquish the chair, and the university administration eventually removed Cobb from his post. However, he was immediately appointed the university's first Distinguished Professor, a position in which he remained until retiring in 1973.

Cobb served in a variety of scientific, medical, and civic organizations, and made distinguished contributions to all of them. He was president of the Anthropological Society of Washington and the American Association of Physical Anthropologists, and was council member, vice-president, and chair of Anthropology of the American Association for the Advancement of Science (AAAS). Cobb vigorously opposed the AAAS convention site of Atlanta in 1955, because of the segregated facilities in that city. He refused to attend the meeting when it was held there, and his pressure led to the adoption in 1956 of an antisegregation policy for future meetings. Cobb was able to obtain the same kind of policy for the American Association of Anatomists in 1958.

Cobb was prominent in several medical associations, particularly those whose members were African American. As president of the Medico-Chirurgical Society of the District of Columbia, he successfully fought for the admission of black physicians to the present D.C. General Hospital in 1948, and to the Medical Society of the District of Columbia in 1952. He served the National Medical Association as editor of its journal from 1949 to 1977 and as its president in 1964. He is credited with changing the *Journal of the National Medical Association* from a modest house organ to an influential medical periodical. He published numerous editorials and articles in this journal, many about the history of medicine, especially biographies of black physicians. He is quoted in *Modern Medicine* as saying, "Negro physicians ... have contributed to the health care of the American populace under handicaps which no other segment of the population has had to suffer." When he was president of the National Medical Association, he testified in Congress in support of Medicare, the only representative of a medical association who actually endorsed the proposed legislation. He was a guest of President Lyndon B. Johnson's the signing of the bill.

For many years, Cobb was active in the National Association for the Advancement of Colored People (NAACP). In 1946, on behalf of the NAACP, he wrote "Medical Care and the Plight of the Negro" and "Progress and Portents for the Negro in Medicine" in support of government financed health care. He served on the board of directors for many years, and was national president from 1976 to 1982. The latter position gave Cobb the opportunity to speak on contemporary issues to a wide audience.

In 1929, Cobb married Hilda B. Smith, who taught in the Washington schools for over forty years. They had two daughters and four grandchildren. Cobb had a wide circle of friends in the medical community and at Howard University, with whom he spent many pleasant hours. He enjoyed playing the violin and reading. When he was seventy-seven years old, he made his debut as an actor at the Kennedy Center, playing the role of W. E. B. Du Bois in a production directed by his daughter. Near the end of his active and rewarding life, Cobb was quoted in *New Directions* as saying, "When I go down, I hope I'll go down still pushing for something in the forward direction." He died in Washington on November 20, 1990, at the age of eighty-six.

SELECTED WRITINGS BY COBB:

Periodicals

"Physical Anthropology of the American Negro," *American Journal of Physical Anthropology,* 1942, Volume 29, pp. 113–223.

"The Skeleton," in *Problems of Ageing,* edited by A. I. Lansing, Williams & Wilkins, 1952, pp. 791–856.

SOURCES:

Periodicals

Lawlah, John W., "The President-Elect," *Journal of the National Medical Association,* November, 1963, Volume 55, pp. 551–554.
Scarupa, Harriet Jackson, "W. Montague Cobb," *New Directions,* April, 1988, pp. 6–17.
"W. Montague Cobb," *Modern Medicine,* December 28, 1970, pp. 16–25.

—*Sketch by Martin R. Feldman*

John D. Cockcroft
1897-1967
English atomic physicist

John Cockcroft was an English atomic physicist who is noted, with physicist **Ernest Walton**, for their breakthrough achievement in artificially splitting the nucleus of an atom, thus paving the way for the development of nuclear energy. Cockcroft himself played an integral role in its later development, as an advisor on atomic power to the British government and as the director of various nuclear research projects. In the course of his career he served as a scientist, engineer, administrator, and policy maker.

Born in Todmorden, Yorkshire, England, on May 27, 1897, John Douglas Cockcroft was the first of John Arthur and A. Maude (Fielden) Cockcroft's five sons. His father's family had been established in and around the West Pennines since the sixteenth century, originally as farmers and, beginning in the eighteenth century, in the textile business. Maude Fielden had abandoned a teaching career when her mother was widowed and they were obliged to open a hat shop in Todmorden. At the age of eleven, Cockcroft was transferred from the nearby Church of England school to Roomfield Grammar School in Todmorden, where he distinguished himself in sports and as a student. There he also struck an immediate friendship with Eunice Elizabeth Crabtree, who would later become his wife.

Encouraged by his headmaster, Cockcroft won a three-year West Riding Country Major Scholarship to

John Cockcroft

Manchester University. He entered the university to study pure mathematics. His real interest, though, was atomic physics, and he attended first year physics lectures. These classes first brought him into contact with **Ernest Rutherford**, the New Zealander "father of radioactivity" who had taken over the university's physics department in 1907. Cockcroft pursued his studies until 1915, when he left to serve in the Royal Field Artillery. Demobilized in January 1919, Cockcroft decided not to return to math, but to take a degree in electrical engineering, the better, he wrote to his sweetheart, Elizabeth, that he could get a decent job and enable them to marry. The following year, he became a college apprentice at the engineering company of Metropolitan Vickers, while simultaneously working on his M.Sc. thesis. Cockcroft spent the next three years there, before advancing to Cambridge University in 1922 to read mathematics. In his second year, he also started attending lectures at Cambridge's Cavendish Physical Laboratory, which, under the current leadership of Rutherford, was occupied primarily with the emerging science of radioactivity.

At the Cavendish, Cockcroft became an assistant to the Russian scientist and electrical engineer **Pyotr Kapitsa**, whom he helped construct a machine that generated the most powerful magnetic fields hitherto produced. They used it to disturb the outer shells of atoms, and thus learn more about atomic structure. Cockcroft also helped to design another magnet, with an adjustable field, useful for beta ray spectroscopy. In late 1924, Cockcroft, with the aid of grants from

Metropolitan Vickers and St. John's College, Cambridge, elected to undertake a doctorate at the Cavendish. The following year, he and Elizabeth married at last and settled in Cambridge. Cockcroft continued to work on his Ph.D. until 1928, when he became a fellow of St. John's College, Cambridge, his alma mater. He was also busy supervising the rewiring of the college and continuing to help Kapitsa in the magnetic lab. His heavy workload helped to distract him from a personal tragedy that had clouded his otherwise contented life: the unexpected death from asthma of his son, Timothy, the first of Cockcroft's two sons and four daughters.

Splits the Atom

After the completion of his thesis in the fall of 1928, Cockcroft began working with a young Irish physicist, Ernest Walton. Together they set about designing an apparatus that would permit them to accelerate atomic particles sufficiently to enable the particles to penetrate the nucleus of a light element, causing it to disintegrate. The apparatus they created was essentially a vacuum discharge tube to which up to 500 kilovolts of energy were added. Cockcroft and Walton worked for almost four years without success. Finally, in 1932, they achieved a breakthrough. When they placed hydrogen nuclei, which consist of just one proton, into the accelerator, and used them to bombard the nuclei of lithium atoms, an emission of alpha particles (helium–4 particles) was observed. The presence of these positively charged nuclear particles was proof that the lithium atom, with a mass of seven, had captured a hydrogen proton, and that their combined mass of eight had, indeed, split into two helium atoms, each with a mass of four. The collision resulted in the release of energy.

Cockcroft and Walton's achievement was immediately hailed within the scientific community as an important step forward in the understanding of the physical universe. Its full practical implications were not, however, immediately appreciated. Indeed, Rutherford himself believed that the energy released by splitting a nucleus was too small, compared with that needed to produce it, to render atomic disintegration of much practical use. It was only several years later that an experiment in Berlin, involving the bombardment of the uranium nucleus, demonstrated the vast potential of nuclear fission. When the uranium nucleus, bombarded by a neutron, split into two approximately equal halves, their loss of mass yielded a huge energy release. This discovery heralded the birth of the nuclear age.

After their successful experiment, Cockcroft worked with Walton on accelerating heavy particles. When they bombarded carbon with isotopes of hydrogen known as deuterons or diplons, they were able to detect radioactive emissions. They concluded that diplons were far more effective at penetrating and splitting atomic nuclei than high speed protons. In recognition of his pioneering research, Cockcroft was elected a fellow of the Royal Society in 1933. In 1935, he was appointed assistant director of the Society's Mond Laboratory, a position which he used to develop his interest in low temperature physics, and in 1938 Cockcroft and Walton were jointly awarded the Society's Hughes Medal for their work on atomic disintegration.

Advises Churchill During War

With a war brewing, Cockcroft found himself preparing for the role he and other scientists would play. In the months preceding its outbreak, he thoroughly acquainted himself with various aspects of defense research. In 1940, he joined the Ministry of Supply's Advisory Council for Scientific Research and Technical Development. In 1941, he was appointed Chief Superintendent of the Air Defence, Research and Development Establishment, and was responsible for the development of shortwave radar equipment for controlling anti-aircraft guns and searchlights, acoustical equipment for artillery ranging, and radio-operated proximity fuses. Frequently, Prime Minister Winston Churchill sought out his advice, and together they often toured England's bombed cities. For the duration of the war, Cockcroft served, also, as Jacksonian Professor of Natural Philosophy at Cambridge. In 1944, Cockcroft left England for Montreal to take up an appointment of director of the Atomic Energy division of the National Research Council of Canada. Here, important work on nuclear energy had been ongoing since the early 1940s. Cockcroft, who had often expressed interest in the development of a uranium bomb and in the peaceful applications of nuclear energy, was given the opportunity to finally realize some of the potential of his earlier experiment. In Montreal, he reorganized the laboratory's staff and set to work developing a nuclear reactor plant at Chalk River on the Upper Ottawa River. The laboratory eventually produced the first two heavy-water reactors in Canada.

In 1945, Cockcroft was appointed director of the British government's Atomic Energy Research Establishment at Harwell, England, which he established as an international center for nuclear research and applied technology. It was a position which allowed Cockcroft to influence government atomic policy. Cockcroft played a key role in promoting research undertaken for the production of fissionable material used at a reactor site and of radioisotopes in the two experimental reactors at Harwell. Most important was his contribution to a research program for nuclear power reactors used to generate electricity. Cockcroft used his position as Britain's unofficial "atom chief" to expound upon the possibilities and the dangers of nuclear energy—its capacity for both good and evil—

to both scientific and lay audiences. He took part in the BBC series, *The Problem of Nuclear Energy*, which did much to demystify atomic energy for the general public, and was particularly vocal about the necessity of bringing nuclear weapons under international control.

Belatedly Awarded Nobel Prize

Cockcroft received numerous honors in recognition of his contribution to the development of atomic energy. In 1948, he was made a Knight Bachelor for his work in establishing Harwell as a center for basic and applied research in nuclear physics. Three years later, he and his former physics partner, Ernest Walton, at long last received full recognition for their pioneering work in the artificial disintegration of atoms, when they were awarded the 1951 Nobel Prize for physics. In 1953, Cockcroft was appointed Knight Commander of the Bath in the Queen's Coronation and Birthday Honours List. Cockcroft also received numerous international awards, including the Medal of Freedom with golden palms from the United States, for his work with American scientists during World War II, and the Military Order of Christ from the Portuguese government.

With Harwell complete, Cockcroft became part-time chair of the government's Defence Research Policy Committee. As a member of the government's Advisory Council on Scientific Policy, he helped advise Churchill on ways to prevent a "brain drain" of British scientists, by establishing equivalent research opportunities at home. Cockcroft became a member of the Atomic Energy Board when it was established in 1952. This body's recommendation that the government set up an independent atomic energy authority was accepted, and Cockcroft was appointed head of the Authority's research branch. Throughout the 1950s, he was instrumental in the development of a controlled thermonuclear fusion project, which involved the fusion of two deuterons to release an enormous amount of energy. This process held the potential of tapping an unlimited energy supply without any serious waste disposal problems. However, it has since transpired that fusion is far more troublesome and difficult to accomplish than was first imagined.

1956 brought Cockcroft a welcome return to the academic sphere as vice-president of the Manchester College of Science and Technology. Now in his sixties, Cockcroft continued to sustain an enormous workload. He was active in the founding of the National Institute for Research in Nuclear Science and served as a member of its governing board and as chair of its physics committee. He was also active on the Medical Research Council Committee, dealing with the medical and biological applications of nuclear physics, and spoke widely on the dangers of radiation. Beyond his professional interests, Cockcroft was president of the Harwell Angling Club, and enjoyed tennis, gardening, music, and literature. Throughout his life, Cockcroft endeavored to promote cooperation between international scientists, traveling the world and meeting world leaders and scientists. He was especially successful in forging closer ties between British and American scientists. In 1958, he became a member of the Scientific Advisory Committee of the International Atomic Energy Agency, a position he used to promote the international exchange of information about thermonuclear and plasma physics. For his work in promoting peaceful applications of nuclear and thermonuclear energy, Cockcroft was awarded the Order of Merit by the Queen in 1957. His other awards included the Niels Bohr Gold Medal in 1958 and the Atoms for Peace Award, an American honor, in 1961.

With the 1959 establishment of Churchill College, Cambridge—a college dedicated to science and technology for which Cockroft had fiercely lobbied—Cockcroft returned to the academic world as its first master. Although he continued to serve as a part-time member of the Atomic Energy Authority, Cockcroft devoted most of his efforts to raising money for the new college. In the last years of his life, he also served as honorary chancellor of the Australian National University in Canberra. At the same time, he took a marked interest in scientific education opportunities in developing countries, and played an active role in Liberal Party politics. Despite his close association with the development of nuclear weapons, Cockcroft was ultimately a man of peace, pressing for test bans, bilateral disarmament, and an end to nuclear proliferation. He died of a heart attack at the age of seventy, on September 18, 1967.

SELECTED WRITINGS BY COCKCROFT:

Books

The Development and Future of Nuclear Energy, Clarendon Press, 1950.
The Development of Radiation Chemistry and Radiochemistry, Royal Institute of Chemistry, 1954.
The Organization of Research Establishments, Cambridge University Press, 1965.

Periodicals

"Disintegration of light elements by fast neutrons" (with Ernest Walton), *Nature,* Volume 131, 1933, p. 703.

SOURCES:

Books

Allibone, T. E. and Hartcup, Guy, *Cockcroft and the Atom,* Adam Hilger (Bristol), 1984.
Clark, R., *Sir John Cockcroft,* Phoenix, 1965.
Crowther, J. G., *History of the Cavendish Laboratory,* Macmillan, 1974.
Hendry, J. H., editor, *Cambridge Physics in the Thirties,* Adam Hilger, 1984.

—Sketch by Avril McDonald

Paul Cohen
1934-
American mathematician

Paul Cohen's reputation as a mathematician has been earned at least partly because of his ability to work successfully in a number of very different fields of mathematics. He received the highly regarded Bôcher Prize of the American Mathematical Society, for example, in 1964 for his research on the Littlewood problem. Two years later he was awarded perhaps the most prestigious prize in mathematics, the Fields Medal, for his research on one of **David Hilbert**'s "twenty-three most important problems" in mathematics, proving the independence of the continuum hypothesis.

Paul Joseph Cohen was born in Long Branch, New Jersey, on April 2, 1934, but his childhood and adolescence were spent in Brooklyn, New York. His parents were Abraham Cohen and the former Minnie Kaplan. Both parents had immigrated to the United States from western Russia (now part of Poland) while they were still teenagers. Cohen's father became a successful grocery jobber in Brooklyn.

Cohen appears to have had a natural and precocious interest in mathematics from an early age. To a large extent, he was self-educated, depending on books that he could find in the public library or that his elder sister Sylvia was able to borrow for him from Brooklyn College. He told interviewers Donald J. Albers and Constance Reid for their book *More Mathematical People* that "by the time I was in the sixth grade I understood algebra and geometry fairly well. I knew the rudiments of calculus and a smattering of number theory."

For his secondary education, Cohen attended the Stuyvesant High School in lower Manhattan, widely regarded as one of the two (along with the Bronx High School of Science) best mathematics and science high schools in the United States. In 1950, having skipped "a few grades," as he told Albers and Reid, he graduated from Stuyvesant at the age of sixteen. He ranked sixth in his class and received one of the forty national Westinghouse Science Talent Search awards given that year. He then enrolled at Brooklyn College, where he remained for two years. In 1952 he was offered a scholarship at the University of Chicago, from which he received his M.S. in mathematics in 1954 and his Ph.D. in 1958.

Solves the Littlewood Problem of Harmonic Analysis

Until he reached Chicago, Cohen had a relatively unstructured and diverse background in mathematics. He was fairly knowledgeable in some areas that interested him especially and that he had been able to teach himself. But he was still naive about some important areas of mathematics, such as logic, in which he had never had a formal course or even any informal training. Partly through the influence of one of his professors at Chicago, Antoni Zygmund, Cohen became interested in a classical problem in harmonic analysis commonly known as the Littlewood problem, named for the English mathematician John Edensor Littlewood. Cohen's solution to this problem won him the American Mathematical Society's Bôcher Prize in 1964.

On receiving his degree from Chicago, Cohen accepted a position as instructor of mathematics at the Massachusetts Institute of Technology (MIT). A year later he moved to the Institute for Advanced Studies at Princeton, New Jersey, where he was a fellow from 1959 to 1961. At MIT and Princeton Cohen continued to work on problems of analysis and seemed to have found a field to which he could devote his career. That illusion soon evaporated, however. As Cohen later told Albers and Reid, he has a restless mind and is constantly looking for new fields to conquer. "I [have been] told by many people that I should stick to one thing," he said, "but I have always been too restless."

Solution of the Consistency Proof Problem Brings the Fields Medal

An occasion for shifting gears presented itself to Cohen soon after he was appointed assistant professor at Stanford in 1961. At a departmental lunch, Cohen's colleagues were discussing the problems of developing a "consistency proof" in logic, first suggested by Georg Cantor in the late nineteenth century. The term *consistency* in mathematics refers to the condition that any mathematical theorem be free from contradiction. Developing a consistency proof had been listed as number one on David Hilbert's 1900 list of the twenty-three most important problems in mathematics for the twentieth century. Although he had no specific background in the field of logic, in which the consistency proof is particularly relevant, Cohen was intrigued by the challenge. He saw it as a way of providing convincing evidence "that set theory is based on some kind of truth," as he told Albers and Reid.

Cohen's work on the consistency proof went forward in fits and starts over the next two years. During one period he became so discouraged that he set the work aside and concentrated on other problems. He seems to have had a glimpse of the general approach for solving his problem during a vacation with his future wife to the Grand Canyon in late 1962. Still, it was another four months before the details of that approach were worked out and a solution produced. Two years later, Cohen received his second major award in mathematics, the International Mathematics Union's Field Prize, for his work on the consistency proof.

In 1964 Cohen was promoted to the post of professor of mathematics at Stanford, a position he has held since. He continues to work on a variety of problems, including those in the fields of analysis and logic. Cohen was married to Christina Karls, a native of Sweden, in 1963. They have three sons, Steven, Charles, and Eric. In addition to the Bôcher Prize and the Fields Medal, Cohen was awarded the Research Corporation of America Award in 1964 and the National Medal of Science in 1967.

SELECTED WRITINGS BY COHEN:

Books

Set Theory and the Continuum Hypothesis, W. A. Benjamin, 1966.

SOURCES:

Books

Albers, Donald J., Gerald L. Alexanderson, and Constance Reid, *More Mathematical People,* Harcourt, 1991, pp. 43–58.

—*Sketch by David E. Newton*

Stanley Cohen
1922-
American biochemist

A pioneer in the study of growth factors—the nutrients that differentiate the development of cells—Stanley Cohen is best known for isolating nerve growth factor (NGF), the first known growth factor, and for subsequently discovering and fully identifying the epidermal growth factor (EGF). Cohen shared the 1986 Nobel Prize for physiology or medicine with his colleague, Italian American neurobiologist **Rita Levi-Montalcini**, who first discovered NGF. Research on NGF has led to better understanding of such degenerative disorders as cancer and Alzheimer's disease, while studies concerning EGF have proved useful in exploring alternative burn treatments and skin transplants.

Cohen was born in Brooklyn, New York, in 1922 to Russian immigrant parents. Though his father earned only a modest living as a tailor, both parents, Louis and Fannie (Feitel) Cohen, ensured that their four children received quality educations. As a child, Cohen was stricken with polio, imparting him with a permanent limp. His illness, however, influenced him to pursue intellectual interests. While a student at James Madison High School he earnestly studied science as well as classical music, learning to play the clarinet. Cohen entered Brooklyn College to study chemistry and zoology, graduating in 1943 with a B.A. Following his undergraduate studies, Cohen received a scholarship to Oberlin college in Ohio, where he earned an M.A. in zoology in 1945. He then attended the University of Michigan on a teaching fellowship in biochemistry, earning his Ph.D. in 1948.

From 1948 until 1952, Cohen worked at the University of Colorado School of Medicine in Denver, holding a research and teaching position in the Department of Biochemistry and Pediatrics. There Cohen earned the respect of his peers for his collaborative studies with pediatrician Harry H. Gordon on the metabolic functions of creatinine (a chemical found in blood, muscle tissue, and urine) in newborn infants. Cohen moved to St. Louis, Missouri, in 1952 to work as a postdoctoral fellow in the radiology department at Washington University. The following year, he was asked to become a research associate in the laboratory of renowned zoologist **Viktor Hamburger**, who was conducting studies on growth processes. Levi-Montalcini, who had been researching nerve cell growth in chicken embryos that had been injected with the tumor cells of male mice, had just returned from Rio de Janeiro, where she had conducted successful tissue-culture experiments that definitively proved the existence of NGF. Working at the

Stanley Cohen

lab in St. Louis, Levi-Montalcini relied on Cohen's expertise in biochemistry to isolate and analyze NGF.

Productive Collaboration Spans Six Years

The collaboration between Levi-Montalcini and Cohen combined two similar personalities. Both scientists have been characterized by their unassuming manners despite their obvious intellectual abilities and perceptive intuitions. Describing her early recollections of Cohen, Levi-Montalcini wrote in her autobiography *In Praise of Imperfection,* "I had been immediately struck by Stan's absorbed expression, total disregard for appearances—as evidenced by his motley attire—and modesty. . . . He never mentioned his competence and extraordinary intuition which always guided him with infallible precision in the right direction." Between the years 1953 and 1959, Cohen and Levi-Montalcini conducted intense research, both enthusiastically pursuing thier findings concerning NGF.

By 1956 Cohen had succeeded in extracting NGF from a mouse tumor; however, this proved to be a difficult substance to work with. Upon the suggestion of biochemist **Arthur Kornberg**, Cohen added snake venom to the extract, hoping to break down the nucleic acids that made the extract too gelatinous. Fortuitously, the snake venom produced more nerve growth activity than the tumor extract itself, and Cohen was able to proceed more rapidly with his studies. In 1958 he discovered that an abundant source of NGF could be found in the salivary glands of male mice—glands not unlike the venom sacs of snakes. Cohen's biochemical advances enabled Levi-Montalcini to study the neurological effects of NGF in rodents.

At a time when Levi-Montalcini and Cohen were advancing rapidly in their collaborative research, funding for Hamburger's laboratory could no longer support Cohen. Before leaving Washington University, Cohen was able to purify NGF as well as produce an antibody for it; however, its complete chemical structure was not fully determined until 1970 when researchers at Washington University completed analysis of NGF's two identical chains of amino acids. Before departing St. Louis, Cohen also observed an unusual occurrence in newborn rodents that had been injected with unpurified salivary NGF. Unlike control mice, whose eyes opened on the thirteenth or fourteenth day, those injected with the unpurified NGF opened their eyes on the seventh day; they also sprouted teeth earlier than did the control group.

Cohen left Washington University in 1959 to join a research group at Vanderbilt University in Nashville, Tennessee; there he continued his work with growth factors, focusing on identifying the unknown factor in unpurified NGF that had caused the mice to open their eyes earlier than normal. By 1962, Cohen had extracted the contaminant in these samples of NGF and was able to purify a second substance, a protein that promoted skin cell and cornea growth which he called epidermal growth factor, or EGF. This protein has found widespread use in treating severe burns; a solution rich in EGF can promote the speedy healing of burned skin, while a skin graft soaked in EGF will quickly bond with damaged tissue. Cohen also isolated the protein which acted as a receptor for EGF—an important step toward understanding the transmission of signals that stimulate normal and abnormal cell growth—that has been particularly crucial in studying cancer development. Cohen was successful in fully identifying the amino acid sequence of EGF by 1972.

Despite his significant contributions, Cohen has never managed a large laboratory, and for many years his work went unacknowledged. He remarked in *Science* that while the scientific community took little notice of his early studies on growth factors, this anonymity proved beneficial. "People left you alone and you weren't competing with the world," he recalled. "The disadvantage was that you had to convince people that what you were working with was real." Cohen's work has subsequently gained wide recognition, and he has received numerous awards in addition to the Nobel, including the Alfred P. Sloan Award in 1982, as well as both the National Medal of Science and the Albert Lasker Award in 1986.

SELECTED WRITINGS BY COHEN:

Periodicals

"Nerve Growth-Stimulating Factor Isolated from Sarcomas 37 and 180," *Proceedings of the National Academy of Science: United States,* Volume 40, 1954, pp. 1014–18.
"A Nerve Growth-Stimulating Factor Isolated from Snake Venom," *Proceedings of the National Academy of Science: United States,* Volume 42, 1956, pp. 571–74.
"Isolation and Biological Effects of an Epidermal Growth-Stimulating Protein," *National Cancer Institute Monograph,* Volume 13, 1964, pp. 13–27.

SOURCES:

Books

Levi-Montalcini, Rita, *In Praise of Imperfection: My Life and Work,* Basic Books, 1988, pp. 161–68.
Mount, Ellis, and Barbara A. List, editors, *Milestones in Science and Technology: The Ready Reference Guide to Discoveries, Inventions, and Facts,* Oryx Press, 1987, pp. 36, 56.
Nobel Prize Winners, H. W. Wilson, 1987, pp. 210–12.

Periodicals

Gleick, James, "Holdout on Big Science," *New York Times,* October 14, 1986, p. C3.
Levine, Joe, "Lives of Spirit and Dedication," *Time,* October 27, 1986, pp. 66–68.
Marx, Jean L., "The 1986 Nobel Prize for Physiology or Medicine," *Science,* October 31, 1986, pp. 543–44.
Schmeck, Harold M., Jr., "Two Pioneers in Growth of Cells Win Nobel Prize," *New York Times,* October 14, 1986, pp. A1, C3.

—Sketch by Elizabeth Henry

Stanley N. Cohen
1935-
American geneticist

Modern biology, biochemistry, and genetics were fundamentally changed in 1973 when Stanley N. Cohen, **Herbert W. Boyer**, Annie C. Y. Chang, and Robert B. Helling developed a technique for

Stanley N. Cohen

transferring deoxyribonucleic acid (DNA), the molecular basis of heredity, between unrelated species. Not only was DNA propagation made possible among different bacterial species, but successful gene insertion from animal cells into bacterial cells was also accomplished. Their discovery, called recombinant DNA or genetic engineering, introduced the world to the age of biotechnology.

As with any revolutionary discovery, the benefits of this new technology were both immediate and projected. Immediate gains were made in the advancement of fundamental biology by increasing scientists' knowledge of gene structure and function. This knowledge promised new ways to overcome disease, increase food production, and preserve renewable resources. For example, the use of recombinant DNA methodology to overcome antibiotic resistance on the part of bacteria anticipated the development of better vaccines. A new source for producing insulin and other life sustaining drugs had the potential to be realized. And, by creating new, nitrogen-fixing organisms, it was thought that food production could be increased, and the use of expensive, environmentally harmful nitrogen fertilizers eliminated. Genetic engineering also offered the promise of nonpolluting energy sources, such as hydrogen-producing algae. In the decades following the discovery of the means for propagating DNA, many assumptions regarding the benefits of genetic engineering have proved to be viable, and the inventions and technology that were by-products of genetic engineering re-

search became marketable commodities, propelling biotechnology into a dynamic new industry.

Stanley N. Cohen was born on February 17, 1935, in Perth Amboy, New Jersey, to Bernard and Ida Stolz Cohen. He received his undergraduate education at Rutgers University, and his doctoral degree from the University of Pennsylvania in 1960. Then followed medical positions at Mt. Sinai Hospital in New York City, University Hospital in Ann Arbor, Michigan, the National Institute for Arthritis and Metabolic Diseases in Bethesda, Maryland, and Duke University Hospital in Durham, North Carolina. Cohen completed postdoctoral research in 1967 at the Albert Einstein College of Medicine in the Bronx, New York. He joined the faculty at Stanford University in 1968, was appointed professor of medicine in 1975, professor of genetics in 1977, and became Kwoh-Ting Li professor of genetics in 1993.

DNA Discoveries Have Scientific and Practical Applications

At Stanford Cohen began the study of plasmids —bits of DNA that exist apart from the genetic information-carrying chromosomes—to determine the structure and function of plasmid genes. Unlike species ordinarily do not exchange genetic information. But Cohen found that the independent plasmids had the ability to transfer DNA to a related-species cell, though the phenomenon was not a commonplace occurrence. In 1973 Cohen and his colleagues successfully achieved a DNA transfer between two different sources. These functional molecules were made by joining two different plasmid segments taken from *Escherichia coli,* a bacteria found in the colon, and inserting the combined plasmid DNA back into *E. coli* cells. They found that the DNA would replicate itself and express the genetic information contained in each original plasmid segment. Next, the group tried this experiment with an unrelated bacteria, *staphylococcus.* This, too, showed that the original *staphylococcus* plasmid genes would transfer their biological properties into the *E. coli* host. With this experiment, the DNA barrier between species was broken. The second attempt at DNA replication between unlike species was that of animal to bacteria. This was successfully undertaken with the insertion into *E. coli* of genes taken from a frog. This experiment had great significance for human application; bacteria containing human genetic information could now be used to create the body's own means for fighting disease and birth disorders. The biological cloning methods used by Cohen and other scientists came to be popularly known as genetic engineering. The cloning process consisted of four steps: separating and joining DNA molecules acquired from unlike species; using a gene carrier that could replicate itself, as well as the unlike DNA segment joined to it; introducing the combined DNA molecule into another bacterial host; and selecting out the clone that carries the combined DNA.

DNA research not only added to the store of scientific knowledge about how genes function, but also had practical applications for medicine, agriculture, and industry. By 1974 there was already speculation in the media about the benefits that could accrue from gene transplant techniques. The creation of bacteria "factories" that could turn out large amounts of life-saving medicines was just one possibility. In fact, insulin made from bacteria was just seven years from becoming a reality. Still in the future at that time, but proved possible within two decades, were supermarket tomatoes hardy enough to survive cross-country trucking that taste as good as those grown in one's own garden. Using DNA technology, other plants were also bred for disease and pollution resistance. Scientists also projected that nitrogen-fixing microbes, such as those that appear in the soil near the roots of soybeans and other protein-rich plants, could be duplicated and introduced into corn and wheat fields to reduce the need for petroleum-based nitrogen fertilizer. Cohen himself said, in an article written for the July 1975 issue of *Scientific American:* "Gene manipulation opens the prospect of constructing bacterial cells, which can be grown easily and inexpensively, that will synthesize a variety of biologically produced substances such as antibiotics and hormones, or enzymes that can convert sunlight directly into food substances or usable energy."

Concerns Voiced over Safety of DNA Experiments

When news of this remarkable research became widespread throughout the general population during the 1970s and 1980s, questions were raised about the dangers that might be inherent in genetic engineering technology. Some people were concerned that the potential existed for organisms altered by recombinant DNA to become hazardous and uncontrollable. Although safety guidelines had long been in place to protect both scientists and the public from disease-causing bacteria, toxic chemicals, and radioactive substances, genetic engineering seemed, to those outside the laboratory, to require measures much more restrictive. Even though, as responsible scientists, Cohen and others who were directly involved with DNA research had already placed limitations on the types of DNA experiments that could be performed, the National Academy of Sciences established a group to study these concerns and decide what restrictions should be imposed. In 1975 there was an international conference on this complicated issue, which was attended by scientists, lawyers, legislators, and journalists from seventeen countries. Throughout this period, Cohen spent much time speaking to the public and testifying to government agencies regarding DNA technology, trying to persuade them that their concerns regarding biohazar-

dous experiments were magnified out of proportion. He explained that even though no evidence existed that certain DNA experiments could be hazardous, there was also no way to prove that a hazard did not exist. Cohen was concerned that the "scare tactics" used by the media served only to exaggerate the hypothetical risk in the public's mind and obscure the fact that very stringent protections against such risks were already in place.

Cohen contended that public outcry over the safety of DNA experiments resulted in an overly cautious approach that slowed the progress of DNA research and reinforced the public's belief that real, not conjectural, hazards existed in the field of biotechnology. In an article on this subject published in 1977 for *Science* he pointed out that during the initial recombinant DNA experiments, billions of bacteria played host to DNA molecules from many sources; these DNA molecules were grown and propagated "without hazardous consequences so far as I am aware. And the majority of these experiments were carried out prior to the strict containment procedures specified in the current federal guidelines."

The controversy over the safety of DNA technology absorbed much of Cohen's time and threatened to obscure the importance of other plasmid research with which he was involved during those years. For instance, his work with bacterial transposons, the "jumping genes" that carry antibiotic resistance, has yielded valuable information about how this process functions. He also developed a method of using "reporter genes" to study the behavior of genes in bacteria and eukaryotic cells. In addition, he has searched for the mechanism that triggers plasmid inheritance and evolution. Increased knowledge in this area offers the medical community more effective tools for fighting antibiotic resistance and better understanding of genetic controls.

Cohen has made the study of plasmid biology his life's work. An introspective, modest man, he is most at home in the laboratory and the classroom. He has been at Stanford University for more than twenty-five years, serving as chair of the Department of Genetics from 1978 to 1986. He is the author of more than two hundred papers, and has received many awards for his scientific contributions, among them the Albert Lasker Basic Medical Research Award in 1980, the Wolf Prize in Medicine in 1981, both the National Medal of Science and the LVMH Prize of the Institut de la Vie in 1988, the National Medal of Technology in 1989, the American Chemical Society Award in 1992, and the Helmut Horten Research Award in 1993. Cohen has held memberships in numerous professional societies, including the National Academy of Sciences (chairing the genetics section from 1988 to 1991), the Institute of Medicine of the National Academy, and the Genetics Society of America. In addition, he served on the board of the

Journal of Bacteriology in the 1970s, and was associate editor of *Plasmid* from 1977 to 1986. Since 1977 he has been a member of the Committee on Genetic Experimentation for the International Council of Scientific Unions. Married in 1961 to Joanna Lucy Wolter, and the father of two children, Anne and Geoffrey, Cohen has lived near the university in a small, rural community. Free time away from his laboratory and his students has been spent skiing, playing five-string banjo, and sailing his aptly named boat, *Genesis.*

SELECTED WRITINGS BY COHEN:

Periodicals

"The Manipulation of Genes," *Scientific American,* Volume 233, July 12, 1975, pp. 25–33.
"Recombinant DNA: Fact and Fiction," *Science,* Volume 195, February 18, 1977, pp. 654–657.

SOURCES:

Periodicals

Bain, Lisa J., "First Cloner," *Penn Medicine,* winter, 1990–91, pp. 28–33.
McElheny, Victor K., "Gene Transplants Seen Helping Farmers and Doctors," *New York Times,* May 20, 1974, p. 61.

Other

Biographical Press Release, Stanford University School of Medicine, October, 1992.

—*Sketch by Jane Stewart Cook*

Mildred Cohn
1913-
American biochemist and biophysicist

Mildred Cohn overcame both gender and religious prejudice to have a profound impact on biochemistry and biophysics. Her research contributed to the scientific understanding of the mechanisms of enzymatic reactions and the methods of studying them. Cohn authored numerous papers that are considered classics and received many honors, including the 1982 National Medal of Science presented by President Ronald Reagan. She was a member of the National Academy of Sciences, the American Academy of Arts and Sciences, and the American Philosophical Society.

Cohn was born on July 12, 1913, to Isidore M. and Bertha (Klein) Cohn, the second of their two children. Her parents were both immigrants from Sharshiv, a small town in Russia. Her father was a businessman who did linotype work for the printing trade and published a journal on printing. Cohn attended public schools in New York City, demonstrating an interest in mathematics and chemistry by the time she reached high school. In 1928, at age fourteen, she enrolled at Hunter College in New York to study chemistry and physics. She received her B.A. *cum laude* little more than three years later, at age seventeen. Cohn was determined to pursue a graduate education in the physical sciences in spite of the many barriers raised against her.

Overcomes Obstacles to Attain Career

Cohn entered the doctoral program at Columbia University but was not accepted as a teaching assistant, because the positions were awarded only to men. She worked as a babysitter to help pay for her first year of education in thermodynamics, classical mechanics, molecular spectroscopy, and physical chemistry. In 1932, after being awarded an M.A., she accepted a job in the laboratory at the National Advisory Committee for Aeronautics at Langley Field, Virginia. She was initially assigned computational work and later a research position in the engine division. The project was to develop a fuel-injection, spark-ignition airplane engine that operated on the diesel cycle. Cohn believed that her positions at Langley impressed upon her the importance of attacking problems on many levels, including the practical and theoretical.

In 1934, Cohn decided that her opportunities for scientific advancement had declined at Langley and she returned to Columbia to seek a Ph.D. She worked under **Harold Clayton Urey**, separating stable isotopes. She was not successful in trying to separate the isotopes but learned experimental and theoretical methods from which she benefited throughout her career. Cohn wrote her Ph.D. dissertation in 1937 and published it with Urey under the title "Oxygen Exchange Reactions of Organic Compounds and Water." Upon graduation, she considered applying for an industrial position, as many of the other graduates did. Due to her sex and Jewishness, however, she was not even granted interviews with large corporations, including Du Pont and Standard Oil.

Cohn was eventually offered and accepted a postdoctoral position with **Vincent du Vigneaud**, professor of biochemistry at George Washington University Medical School. He wanted to introduce isotopic tracers into his research on sulfur-amino acid metabolism. Isotopic tracers are forms of chemical elements; because of their difference in nuclear structure, either mass or radioactivity, they can be observed as they progress through a metabolic pathway. By following an isotope, Cohn was able to understand more clearly the mechanisms of chemical reactions in animals. For example, one study, which Cohn told contributor John Henry Dreyfuss was "the most elegant tracer experiment done in du Vigneaud's lab," involved what she called "doubly labeled" methionine. The researchers used the labeled methionine—a large, complicated molecule to which two isotopes had been added—to observe the mechanism by which methionine was converted to the amino acid cystine in a rat.

Contributes Advances in Medicine

Cohn married Henry Primakoff, a physicist, on May 31, 1938. During World War II, Cohn and the draft-exempt men in du Vigneaud's lab continued their research, while du Vigneaud and the others supported the war effort. In 1946, her husband accepted a position in the physics department at Washington University in St. Louis. Cohn took a position in the biochemistry department, where she worked with the Nobel Prize-winning husband and wife team of **Gerty T. Cori** and **Carl Ferdinand Cori**. One of her major objectives at Washington University was to study the mechanisms of enzyme-catalyzed reactions. Cohn used an isotope of oxygen to gain insight into the enzyme-catalyzed reactions of organic phosphates and in 1958 initiated work with nuclear magnetic resonance (NMR) toward the same goal.

Two years later, her husband was named Donner Professor of Physics at the University of Pennsylvania, and Cohn joined the biophysics department there. At Pennsylvania, Cohn pursued her research on energy transduction within cells and cellular reactions in which adenosinetriphosphate (ATP) is utilized using NMR. Cohn told Dreyfuss that she began to look more deeply into the structure and function of enzymes by studying manganese-enzyme-substrate complexes, utilizing "every technically feasible aspect of magnetic resonance." Cohn performed other important collaborative studies, including NMR of transfer ribonucleic acid (RNA), a key chemical in cellular protein synthesis. Cohn's work with nuclear magnetic resonance of various types of molecules, structures, and reactions was probably her most important contribution to science and medicine.

Cohn and Primakoff had three children. Besides her scientific work, she enjoyed the theater, hiking, writing, and reading. In 1958, after nearly twenty-one years as a research associate, she was promoted to associate professor; she was a Career Investigator of the American Heart Association for fourteen years

after 1964. In 1982, she was named Benjamin Bush Professor in Biochemistry and Biophysics at the University of Pennsylvania. From 1982 to 1985, she was a senior scientist at the Fox Chase Cancer Center. In 1982, she was awarded the National Medal of Science and in 1987 the Distinguished Award of the College of Physicians. From 1978 to 1979, she was president of the American Society of Biological Chemistry. Cohn was also elected to the American Academy of Arts and Sciences and American Philosophical Society.

SELECTED WRITINGS BY COHN:

Periodicals

(With Harold Clayton Urey) "Oxygen Exchange Reactions of Organic Compounds and Water," *Journal of the American Chemical Society,* Volume 60, 1938, pp. 679–87.
"Atomic and Nuclear Probes of Enzyme Systems," in *Annual Review of Biophysics and Biomolecular Structure,* Volume 21, 1992, pp. 1–24.

SOURCES:

Cohn, Mildred, interview with John Henry Dreyfuss.

—*Sketch by John Henry Dreyfuss*

Zanvil Cohn
1926-1993
American biologist

A physician and scientist who spent most of his career at Rockefeller University, Zanvil Cohn is known as the father of the modern study of macrophages. First discovered by Russian biologist **Élie Metchnikoff** in 1884, macrophages are white blood cells that play an important role in the immune system. They were still little understood when Cohn arrived at Rockefeller in 1958, and he developed laboratory techniques to explore their physiological function, eventually establishing how they identify and destroy infectious microbes. He later applied the techniques he had developed for macrophages to clinical studies of leprosy, tuberculosis, and acquired immunodeficiency syndrome (AIDS).

Zanvil A. Cohn was born in Forest Hills in New York City on November 16, 1926. His father, David Cohn, had emigrated from Germany as a teenager, rising quickly from working as a delivery boy in his uncle's butcher shop on Manhattan's Lower East Side to owning the Kansas Meat Packing Company. His mother, Esther Schwartz, was a women's clothing buyer. Cohn spoke only German until the age of six and required tutoring in English before enrolling in public grade school. After his parents bought a second house in Amityville, Long Island, he and his younger brother Donald became devoted to salt-water fishing, as well as hunting, birding, and boating on the Great South Bay. Cohn was senior class president at Manhattan's private Columbia Grammar School, where he preferred baseball and football to scholarship.

Cohn spent two years at Bates College before joining the Merchant Marine during World War II as a corpsman. At age eighteen, he sailed as purser and pharmacist on Liberty Ships in the Atlantic and Pacific. He was the only medically trained person on board, and he once had sole medical responsibility for 1,500 soldiers for eleven days. He returned to Bates after the war and received his B.S. degree in 1948. In December of that year, he married his chemistry classmate, Fern Dworkin.

Cohn entered Harvard Medical School in 1948, where he first became interested in solving medical problems involving host-parasite relationships. He did independent research and published his first paper on the interaction of viruses and chicken eggs while still in medical school. After receiving his M.D. *summa cum laude* in 1953, he interned at Massachusetts General Hospital and then entered the Army Medical Corps at Walter Reed Army Institute for Research. With Joseph Smadel, Cohn explored respiratory enzymes and cell walls of the intracellular parasite *Rickettsia*.

Begins Research on Immunology

In 1958, microbiologist **René Dubos**, who discovered the antibiotic gramicidin, invited Cohn to join his laboratory at The Rockefeller Institute for Medical Research. Antibiotics were then so successful that many scientists were predicting an end to infectious diseases. Cohn, however, was drawn to Dubos's emphasis on understanding the microenvironment of inflammation and finding therapies to enhance the body's own defense mechanisms. Research on these questions was being actively pursued in Dubos's laboratory, where James Hirsch was studying phagocytes—a class of white blood cells that eats or scavenges microbes in the bloodstream. Hirsch's goal was to determine what antibiotics these white blood cells used to destroy invading microorganisms.

Cohn began working with Hirsch, and within three years they were the first to isolate and describe how granules in the polymorphonuclear leucocyte, or granulocyte, digest microbes. They identified the granules as lysosomes that discharge their digestive enzymes into vacuoles containing phagocytosed microbes. This research was part of a formative era in cell biology when recently developed techniques in centrifugation, cell fractionation, autoradiography, and electron microscopy gave scientists new ways to sort and visualize individual cells.

Focuses Work in Phagocytes on Macrophages

Cohn decided to explore a type of white blood cell which he suspected was a more potent scavenger than leukocytes and more critical in resolving inflammation: the mononuclear phagocyte that matures into a macrophage. Macrophages are produced in the bone marrow and they migrate through the bloodstream to almost every part of the body. They multiply rapidly during inflammation, functioning as what Lois Wingerson in *Mosaic* calls "sanitation engineers," consuming bacteria and other potentially harmful cells. Cohn was the first to characterize these cells. He began his research with peritoneal macrophages in mice, and he and his colleagues were able to discover the intricate process by which macrophages eat (phagocytosis) and drink (pinocytosis). His research also did much to increase the general understanding of how cells function.

Cohn conducted other studies on biochemical and morphological features of the macrophage's maturation, work which traced the cell from its origin in bone marrow, to its entrance into the circulatory system and its differentiation into various types upon entering body tissues. These experiments led, in 1972, to the redefinition of the reticuloendothelial system. Now known as the mononuclear phagocyte system, it is based on processing of materials in the endocytic pathway.

Cohn subsequently shifted emphasis from the substances being metabolized to the structures digesting them. His laboratory observed that a macrophage takes in and recycles its plasma membrane every thirty minutes while engulfing its prey. During the 1970s, Cohn and his colleagues learned macrophages do much more than eat and digest. They secrete some fifty hormone-like substances, among them lysozyme, proteases, prostaglandins, leukotrienes, and oxygen metabolites. His team discovered that these products take active roles in responding to tissue injury. Depending on the amount secreted, some responses are beneficial and can lead to wound healing, tissue remodeling, or the destruction of microbes and tumors. In excess, other secretions are harmful and can intensify diseases such as rheumatoid arthritis and multiple sclerosis. Because macrophages emigrate into many tissues and respond to local demands to protect the host, Cohn identified them as the "versatile element of inflammation." Many questions about these secretions remain unsolved and are still being studied.

Cohn's knowledge of macrophages has generated insights into other immune cells. In 1974, he and Ralph Steinman discovered a new white blood cell, the dendritic cell. They isolated and characterized this cell as distinct in structure, appearance, and function. They demonstrated its role as the potent stimulator and initiator of the immune response. These findings changed one aspect of the initial understanding of the macrophage: Dendritic cells, not macrophages, are the antigen presenters that spur cell division of lymphocytes to make more antibodies. Studies have continued on the role of dendritic cells in transplantation and graft rejection. In 1992, Cohn's lab reported that when dendritic cells carrying the human immunodeficiency virus (HIV) stimulate the T lymphocytes, this sensitization may account for their depletion and lead to the collapse of the human immune system in AIDS.

The Cohn laboratory also proved that products called lymphokines from another immune cell, the T lymphocyte, stimulate macrophages to kill parasites and tumor cells. He and physician Nadia Nogueira first demonstrated this acquired killing capacity with *Trypanosoma cruzi,* the protozoa of Chagas' disease. They showed that an activated macrophage rapidly kills and degrades this intracellular parasite in the cytoplasm. With Carl Nathan and Samuel Silverstein, Cohn showed how activated macrophages also achieve extracellular killing of tumor cells. This work is expected to lead to a better understanding of host defense mechanisms against cancer.

Conducts Clinical Research on Leprosy

Early in the 1980s, in order to explore macrophage defenses in human diseases, Cohn and his colleagues initiated clinical research on lepromatous leprosy at Rockefeller University, as well as in Asia and Latin America where the disease is endemic. This chronic and disfiguring form of leprosy presented a model where cell-mediated immunity is suppressed. Cohn and his team found a defect in lymphokine production that allowed bacilli of *Mycobacterium leprae* to parasitize macrophages in skin lesions, preventing them from killing and even from being activated to kill. They injected two genetically engineered lymphokines in the skin: interferon gamma, which causes macrophages to produce toxic oxygen intermediates and to kill parasites, and interleukin-2, which expands cell populations that produce other healing lymphokines. As Cohn expected, both lymphokines mobilized local cell-mediated responses and decreased the number of leprosy bacilli in the lesions. These trials gave Cohn hope that lymphokines and other agents interacting with macrophages could someday be used by physicians to fight disease. At his

death, Cohn was extending these studies to patients with tuberculosis and AIDS—two diseases in which macrophages also play a major role.

At Rockefeller, Cohn became professor and senior physician in 1966; he was named the first Henry G. Kunkel Professor in 1986, and Vice-President for Medical Affairs in 1992. He mentored scores of young scientists, many of whom have become leaders in universities worldwide. Eighty of his 370 publications were coauthored with his students. He was deeply committed to scientific medicine, and his belief in the unique role of the physician-scientist is reflected in the M.D.-Ph.D. program that he helped establish at Rockefeller in the early 1970s. He was an editor of the *Journal of Experimental Medicine* and served on its board for twenty years. His many awards include election to the National Academy of Sciences in 1975 and honorary degrees from Bates College (1986), Oxford University (1988), and Rijksuniversiteit, Leiden, The Netherlands (1990).

Cohn was planning more years of research when he died suddenly at home from an aortic dissection on June 28, 1993. He was sixty-six years old. With his wife, his son, and his daughter, he had shared both his love of fishing and many reflective hours at the edge of the sea in Montauk.

SELECTED WRITINGS BY COHN:

Periodicals

(With J. G. Hirsch) "The Isolation and Properties of the Specific Cytoplasmic Granules of Rabbit Polymorphonuclear Leucocytes," *Journal of Experimental Medicine,* Volume 112, 1960, pp. 983–1004.

"The Structure and Function of Monocytes and Macrophages," *Advances in Immunology,* Volume 9, 1968, pp. 163–214.

(With S. Gordon) "The Macrophage," *International Review of Cytology,* Volume 36, 1973, pp. 171–214.

(With R. M. Steinman) "Identification of a Novel Cell Type in Peripheral Lymphoid Organs of Mice" (A series of five reports), *Journal of Experimental Medicine,* Volume 137, 1973, pp. 1142–1162; Volume 139, 1974, pp. 380–397 and 1431–1445; Volume 141, 1975, pp. 804–820; Volume 149, 1979, pp. 1–16.

(With S. C. Silverstein and R. M. Steinman) "Endocytosis," *Annual Review of Biochemistry,* Volume 46, 1977, pp. 669–722.

"The Macrophage: Versatile Element of Inflammation," *The Harvey Lectures,* Series 77, 1983, pp. 63–80.

(With G. Kaplan) "Leprosy and Cell-Mediated Immunity," *Current Opinion in Immunology,* Volume 3, 1991, pp. 91–96.

SOURCES:

Periodicals

Bardossi, B., and J. N. Schwartz, "Stalking the Macrophage," *Research Profiles,* number 12, Spring 1983, pp. 1–6.

Steinman, R. M., and C. L. Moberg, "Zanvil Alexander Cohn, 1926–1993. An Appreciation of the Physician-Scientist," *Journal of Experimental Medicine,* Volume 179, 1994, pp. 1–30.

Wingerson, L., "Killers on Call," *Mosaic,* Volume 15, 1984, pp. 2–9.

Other

Cohn, Donald, interview with Carol Moberg conducted February 7, 1994.

—Sketch by Carol L. Moberg

Margarita Colmenares
1957-

American environmental engineer

Margarita Colmenares was the first Hispanic engineer to be selected for a White House fellowship, and she was also the first woman to be elected national president of the Society of Hispanic Professional Engineers (SHPE). Employed by Chevron USA since 1981 and presently an air-quality specialist in its office for environmental affairs, she has in her short career established herself as a national leader in the fields of both education and engineering.

Margarita Hortensia Colmenares was born in Sacramento, California, on July 20, 1957, the eldest of five children. Her parents, Luis S. Colmenares and Hortensia O. Colmenares, had emigrated from Oaxaca, Mexico, and her childhood world was bicultural and bilingual. Her parents believed strongly in the importance of a good education and sacrificed to send their children to private Catholic schools. In high school, Colmenares founded an organization for Mexican-American students in her all-girls school. She began her college career at California State University in Sacramento studying business, but she realized in her freshman year that engineering was the field she really wanted to pursue. She returned to junior college for more chemistry, physics, and calculus courses, and she also accepted a part-time engineering job with the California Department of Water Resources. Funded by five different scholarships, she entered Stanford University and graduated with a B.S. in civil engineering in 1981.

Begins Association with Chevron Corporation

Between her junior and senior years at Stanford, Colmenares entered the Chevron Corporation's Co-Op Education Program, and after graduation she joined that company as a field construction engineer. By 1982 she had founded the San Francisco chapter of SHPE. After serving Chevron as a recruiting coordinator, she took on a field construction position whose duties led her to Colorado, Utah, Idaho, and Nevada. Her upward path at Chevron continued as she became a foreign trade representative in 1983 and subsequently won promotion to compliance specialist. It was in this position that she first became involved with environmental issues. In 1986, she was the lead engineer for an eighteen million dollar environmental cleanup project at the Chevron refinery in El Segundo, near Los Angeles. Following this experience with environmental engineering, Colmenares was promoted in 1989 to air-quality specialist at the El Segundo plant.

In that same year, she was elected SHPE's first woman president. As president of this national society, Colmenares achieved a platform from which she could address many of the issues facing the engineering community in general and Hispanics in particular. Her agenda was based on the importance of education, and she stressed to the society's members that they should seek election to positions that could have an impact on education, engineering, or policy making. Following her term as society president, she applied for a White House fellowship and was chosen as one of the sixteen members of the class of 1991–1992. Colmenares became the first Hispanic engineer selected since the program was established in 1964. As part of this program, she chose to work at the Department of Education and became special assistant to David T. Kearns, the department's deputy secretary.

Colmenares has received many honors and awards during her career. In 1989 she was named Outstanding Hispanic Woman of the Year by *Hispanic* magazine, as well as Hispanic Role Model of the Year by SHPE. That same year she also received *Hispanic Engineer* magazine's Community Service Award. In 1990 and 1992, *Hispanic Business* magazine named her one of the one hundred most influential Hispanics in the United States, and in 1991 she was the youngest recipient ever to receive the California Community College League's Outstanding Alumni Award. Her career was also profiled on the Public Broadcasting Service (PBS) series "Choice for Youth."

Colmenares plans to continue her education, possibly in the area of public policy, and she would like to continue working for the betterment of the educational system in the United States. One of her many avocations is an interest in Mexican folk dance and during college she taught, directed, and performed with the Stanford Ballet Folklorico.

SOURCES:

Books

Telgen, Diane and Jim Kamp, editors, *Notable Hispanic American Women,* Gale, 1993, pp. 104–07.

Periodicals

"The 1989 Hispanic Engineer National Achievement Awards," *Hispanic Engineer,* Conference Issue, 1989, pp. 43–46.

—*Sketch by Leonard C. Bruno*

Rita R. Colwell

Rita R. Colwell
1934-
American marine microbiologist

Rita R. Colwell is a leader in marine biotechnology, the application of molecular techniques to marine biology for the harvesting of medical, industrial and aquaculture products from the sea. As a scientist and professor, Colwell has investigated the ecology, physiology, and evolutionary relationships of marine bacteria. As a founder and president of the University of Maryland Biotechnology Institute, she has nurtured a vision to improve the environment and human health by linking molecular biology and genetics to basic knowledge scientists had gleaned from life and chemistry in the oceans.

Rita Rossi was born in Beverly, Massachusetts, November 23, 1934, the seventh of eight children to parents Louis and Louise Di Palma Rossi. Her father was an Italian immigrant who established his own construction company, and her mother was an artistic woman who worked to help ensure her children would have a good education. She died when her daughter was just thirteen years old, but she had been proud of her success in school. In the sixth grade, after Rossi had scored higher on the IQ exam than anyone in her school's history, the principal asked sternly whether

she understood that she had the responsibility to go to college. Rossi had answered, "Yes, ma'am," and eventually received a full scholarship from Purdue University. She earned her bachelor of science degree with distinction in bacteriology in 1956. Although she had been accepted to medical school, Rossi chose instead to earn a master's degree so that she could remain at the same institution as graduate student Jack Colwell, whom she married on May 31, 1956. Colwell would have continued her studies in bacteriology, but the department chairman at Purdue informed her that giving fellowship money to women would have been a waste. She instead earned her master's degree in the department of genetics. The University of Washington, Seattle, granted her a Ph.D. in 1961 for work on bacteria commensal to marine animals, which is the practivce of an organism obtaining food or other benefits from another without either harming or helping it. Colwell's contributions included establishing the basis for the systematics of marine bacteria.

In 1964, Georgetown University hired Colwell as an assistant professor, and gave her tenure in 1966. Colwell and her research team were the first to recognize that the bacterium that caused cholera occurred naturally in estuaries. They isolated the bacterium from Chesapeake Bay and in ensuing years sought to explain how outbreaks in human populations might be tied to the seasonal abundance of the host organisms in the sea, particularly plankton. In 1972, Colwell took a tenured professorship at the

University of Maryland. Her studies expanded to include investigations on the impact of marine pollution at the microbial level. Among her findings was that the presence of oil in estuarine and open ocean water was associated with the numbers of bacteria able to break down oil. She studied whether some types of bacteria might be used to treat oil spills. Colwell and her colleagues also made a discovery that held promise for improving oyster yields in aquaculture—a bacterial film formed on surfaces under water attracted oyster larvae to settle and grow.

In the spirit of using knowledge gained from the sea to benefit humans and the environment, Colwell prepared a seminal paper on marine biotechnology published in the journal *Science* in 1983. It brought attention to the rich resources of the ocean that might be tapped for food, disease-curing drugs, and environmental clean-up by the applications of genetic engineering and cloning. In order to realize the potential of marine biotechnology as originally outlined in her 1983 paper, Colwell helped foster the concept and growth of the University of Maryland Biotechnology Institute, established in 1987. As president of the U.M.B.I., she has formed alliances between researchers and industry and has succeeded in raising funds to develop the center as a prestigious biotech research complex.

In addition, Colwell has held numerous professional and academic leadership positions throughout her career and is a widely published researcher. At the University of Maryland, Colwell was director of the Sea Grant College from 1977 to 1983. She served as president of Sigma Xi, the American Society for Microbiology, and the International Congress of Systematic and Evolutionary Biology, and was president-elect of the American Association for the Advancement of Science. Colwell has written and edited more than sixteen books and over four hundred papers and articles; she also produced an award-winning film, *Invisible Seas*. Her honors included the 1985 Fisher Award of the American Society for Microbiology, the 1990 Gold Medal Award of the International Institute of Biotechnology, and the 1993 Phi Kappa Phi National Scholar Award.

Colwell is the mother of two daughters who pursued careers in science. She is an advocate for equal rights for women, and one of her long-standing aspirations is to write a novel about a woman scientist. Her hobbies include jogging and competitive sailing.

SELECTED WRITINGS BY COLWELL:

Books

(With L. H. Stevenson) *Estuarine Microbial Ecology,* University of South Carolina Press, 1973.

(Editor) *Biomolecular Data: A Resource in Transition,* Oxford University Press, 1989.

(Editor, with others) *Biotechnology of Marine Polysaccharides,* Hemisphere, 1985.

Periodicals

"Biotechnology in the Marine Sciences," *Science,* October 7, 1983, pp. 19–24.

SOURCES:

Periodicals

Andrews, Joan Kostick, "Lady With A Mission," *Natural Science,* May, 1991, pp. 304–310.

Henderson, Randi, "Scientist Plays Many Roles," *The Baltimore Sun,* October 13, 1991.

Sherman, Scott L., "The Long Road From the Laboratory," *Warfield's,* August, 1990.

—*Sketch by Miyoko Chu*

Barry Commoner
1917-
American biologist and environmental scientist

Barry Commoner is widely known as a writer and lecturer on the relationships between environmental, energy, and resource problems and their economic and political implications. Long before ecology became a national concern, Commoner was convinced that scientists had a moral obligation to inform the public about the potentially disastrous effects of some technological developments. Frequently referred to as "the granddaddy of environmentalists," Commoner has led the science information movement in his longstanding efforts to alert the public about the effects of the "technosphere" on the biosphere. Two of his early concerns were nuclear fallout and disarmament, and in the 1950s he worked with fellow biologist **Linus Pauling** in drafting a document, signed by 11,000 scientists, that called on the United States and the then Union of Soviet Socialist Republics to end atmospheric testing of atomic weapons. Later Commoner moved his focus to energy and broad environmental issues.

Besides working as an environmentalist, Commoner has had a long and distinguished career as a research scientist. His early work was on viral replica-

Barry Commoner

tion, and he made basic discoveries regarding the roles of free radicals (molecules with unpaired electrons) in living things. Known as an innovator, he applied developments in various other fields to the study of biology. He founded and is director of the Center for the Biology of Natural Systems (CBNS), now located at the Flushing campus of Queens College of the City University of New York. CBNS research topics include the occurrence of carcinogens in the environment; agricultural sources of pollution; organic farming; energy conservation systems for urban housing; solar energy; waste reduction and alternative methods of municipal waste disposal; and the origin of dioxin in incinerators. In 1992 Commoner became distinguished professor of industrial policy at the University of Massachusetts. He has been recognized with thirteen honorary degrees.

Commoner was born in New York City on May 28, 1917, to Isidore Commoner, a tailor who imigrated from Russia, and Goldie Yarmolinsky Commoner. Despite his city upbringing in East New York and Flatbush, as a youth Commoner showed a strong interest in nature, and he frequently roamed trhough Brooklyn parks collecting specimens to study. In 1933 he graduated from the James Madison High School in Brooklyn. At Columbia College, he majored in zoology, was elected to Phi Beta Kappa, and graduated with honors in 1937. He then spent three years at Harvard University, earning a master's degree in biology and completing most of the requirements for his Ph.D. He left Harvard to teach in the biology department of

Queens College while he finished his dissertation. His Ph.D. in biology was awarded in 1941. When the United States entered World War II, Commoner was called to active duty as a lieutenant with the Naval Reserve and assigned as a science officer to the Naval Tactical Air Squadron at Patuxent, Maryland.

Navy Experiences Deal with Social Impacts of Science

During Commoner's naval service, navy and marine commanders were worried that the troops landing on beaches in the Pacific would contract insect-vectored diseases. Therefore, they planned to have the beaches sprayed with an insecticide, DDT, before the troops landed. It fell to Commoner to devise a makeshift sprayer for the pesticide, and to test it on mosquitoes on the New Jersey shore. An unforeseen result of the spraying was that millions of fish living along the New Jersey shore were killed. This experience led Commoner to realize the serious social and ecological consequences of technology. From the end of the war until his 1946 discharge, Commoner worked in Washington, D.C., as naval liaison to the Senate Military Affairs Committee, where he helped set up the first hearings on the Manhattan Project and the atomic bomb. He also helped draft early versions of legislation that led to the creation of the National Science Foundation and the Atomic Energy Commission, now the Nuclear Regulatory Commission.

As a civilian, Commoner worked, from 1946 to 1947, as associate editor of *Science Illustrated* magazine. He then became associate professor of plant physiology at the Henry Shaw School of Botany at Washington University in St. Louis, MO. He had turned down the idea of working at Yale University with Joshua Lederberg and Edward Tatum, winners of the Nobel Prize in 1958 for their discoveries in bacterial genetics, to work on his own. At Washington University, Commoner quickly established himself as a witty and articulate lecturer and a creative researcher. He advanced to full professor in 1953 and became chairman of the botany department in 1965. In January 1966, with a $4.25 million grant from the U.S. Public Health Service, he organized the Center for the Biology of Natural Systems for the purpose of researching environmental and energy problems and training graduate students in those areas. In 1976 Commoner was made university professor of environmental science at Washington University.

Commoner's early research work involved the tobacco mosaic virus (TMV). Although TMV is a plant virus, Commoner's findings suggested that knowledge about its structure, replication and activity could have practical applications in the treatment of a number of viral diseases affecting humans. The work developed into long-range studies of basic biochemical processes in cells, and was funded by grants from the American Cancer Society, Lederle Laboratories, the National Foundation for Infantile Paralysis, and the Rockefeller Foundation. In 1953, for his TMV work, Commoner received the Newcomb Cleveland prize of the American Association for the Advancement of Science (AAAS); the award is given to the young scientist who delivers the most noteworthy report at the association's annual meeting.

In 1950 Commoner had also begun pioneering research into free radicals. He joined with physicist George E. Pake, also at Washington University, to test a hypothesis set forth in 1930 by the biochemist Leonor Michaelis. Commoner and Pake invited another physicist, Jonathan Townsend, to build an electron spin resonance (ESR) spectrometer that would detect small amounts of free radicals in cells. As the biophysical experiments became more complicated, Commoner's research team expanded to include biologists, zoologists, physicists and medical scientists. The first experiments involved testing dried organic materials; in 1954, the group detected free radicals in living tissue and confirmed that these molecules played a significant role in energy transfer in both plant and animal cells. In 1965, they found that abnormal free radicals were associated with cancer in laboratory rats. Later, the group built more sensitive detection devices and found free radicals in tissues; this was considered an important development in early cancer detection applications. Commoner also challenged the Watson-Crick dogma of deoxyribonucleic acid (DNA)—that DNA was as solely responsible for inheritance in the cell—as being overly simplistic. Commoner suggested that the whole cell, and not just its DNA, is responsible for inheritance. In 1966 Commoner dropped his TMV work and changed the focus of his research and political interest to the environment. "I tend very strongly to do idiosyncratic work," Commoner told writer Rae Goodell. "I have a strong feeling that there is not much point in doing something that someone else can do."

Characterized as a "Visible" Scientist

Commoner has published scores of technical and popular articles. In 1963, he published his first book, *Science and Survival.* The book was seen as an "urgent warning" about the consequences of post-World War II technological developments, including widespread use of nitrogen fertilizers, the rise of the vast petrochemical industry, and the manufacture of larger, more polluting automobiles. It was followed with *The Closing Circle* in 1971, *The Poverty of Power: Energy and the Economic Crisis* in 1976, and *The Politics of Energy* in 1979. *The Closing Circle* received the Phi Beta Kappa Award in 1972, and it also gained Commoner the International Prize for Safeguarding the Environment from the City of Cervia, Italy, where

he had served as president of the scientific committee of the Cervia Environmental Foundation. Commoner's books are highly readable treatments of aspects of the same theme, and many of them have been bestsellers. In his writings, Commoner often points out that science and politics, the private sector and public policy, the right to consume and the price of that right, are issues that must be dealt with collectively, not separately.

In 1954, Commoner became involved in the AAAS as secretary of the botanical section, and in 1960, as chairman of the section, he introduced social responsibility problems into the agenda. With Margaret Mead, in 1958 he persuaded the AAAS to create a Committee on Science in the Promotion of Human Welfare, which held a symposium on nuclear fallout. The St. Louis Committee for Nuclear Information (later known as the Committee for Environmental Information) was formed that year. It evolved into the Scientists' Institute for Public Information (SIPI) in 1963, the year the nuclear test-ban treaty was adopted. Commoner served on the SIPI board of directors from 1963 through 1980, and ten of those years were as chairman. SIPI has worked to provide reliable scientific information to the public, and through its media resource service has made more scientists "visible."

In 1981, Commoner moved the Center for the Biology of Natural Systems (CBNS) to Queens College of the City University of New York, where he also became professor in the college's department of earth and environmental science, as well as visiting professor of community health at Albert Einstein College of Medicine. He held the latter two posts through 1987. He continues to direct CBNS, whose projects are funded from a variety of sources, including the New York City Department of Sanitation, the Pew Charitable Trusts, the J. P. Morgan Charitable Trust, the North Shore Unitarian Universalist Veatch Program, the Public Welfare Foundation, and Greenpeace U.S.A.

Commoner received the First International Humanist Award from the International Humanist and Ethical Union in 1970. In 1979, he received the American Institute of Architects Medal. He has been honored by the Italian government as a Commander in the Order of Merit for his environmental efforts in Italy. Commoner began accumulating honorary degrees in 1963 with a D.Sc. from Hahnemann Medical College. His honorary doctorate from Connecticut College in 1992 brought the total to thirteen. Commoner serves on the Scientific Advisory Board of the Vietnam Veterans of America Foundation Council on Dioxin, and the Committee for Responsible Genetics. He is president of the Scientific Committee of the Cervia Environmental Foundation, Cervia, Italy. Commoner married Lisa Feiner in 1980. His children, Lucy Alison and Fredric Gordon, are from his 1946 marriage to Gloria C. Gordon, a psychologist.

SELECTED WRITINGS BY COMMONER:

Books

Science and Survival, Viking, 1963.
The Closing Circle, Knopf, 1971.
The Poverty of Power: Energy and the Economic Crisis, Knopf, 1976.
The Politics of Energy, Knopf, 1979.
Making Peace With the Planet, Pantheon, 1990.

SOURCES:

Books

Goodell, Rae, *The Visible Scientists,* Little, Brown, 1975, pp. 51, 60–69, 140.

Periodicals

Sheridan, Dick, "Report from the War Zone," *Daily News Magazine,* April 22, 1990, pp. 3943.

—*Sketch by Jill Carpenter*

Arthur Holly Compton
1892-1962
American physicist

Arthur Holly Compton's research on the scattering of X rays, which he explained by assuming that the rays consist of tiny, discrete particles now called photons, earned him a share of the 1927 Nobel Prize for physics. Compton also was a member of the Manhattan Project team of scientists convened during World War II, serving as director of the Metallurgical Laboratory at the University of Chicago.

Compton was born on September 10, 1892, in Wooster, Ohio. His father, Elias Compton, was a Presbyterian minister and professor of philosophy and dean at the University (later the College) of Wooster. Arthur's oldest brother, Karl, was to become professor of physics and later president of the Massachusetts Institute of Technology. His mother was the former Otelia Catherine Augspurger, who received an honorary LL.D. degree by Western College in Oxford,

Arthur Holly Compton

Ohio; in all, the six members of the Compton family eventually received more than seventy earned and honorary degrees.

Family and Education Influence Life Views

Compton completed his early education at the Wooster Elementary and Grammar School, and at the Wooster Preparatory School. He entered the College of Wooster in the fall of 1909, and, under the advice of his father and brother Karl, chose science over religion as his major. He graduated from Wooster with a B.S. degree in 1913. Compton's biographers have commented on the strong religious influences exerted on him by family and his early education. Robert S. Shankland, in the *Dictionary of Scientific Biography,* for example, claims that Compton's years at the College of Wooster "had a decisive influence on [him] throughout his career. His attitudes towards life, science, and the world in general were almost completely determined as he grew to manhood and received his basic education there."

For his graduate studies, Compton chose to follow his older brothers, Karl and Wilson, to Princeton University. He had originally planned on majoring in engineering, since that field held more promise as a way of solving human problems. But he became fascinated with the challenges of pure physics and abandoned his plans for an engineering career. Working first under Nobel laureate **Owen W. Richardson** and later under H. L. Cooke, Compton earned his

M.A. degree at Princeton in 1914 and his Ph.D. two years later. Shortly after graduation Compton married a former Wooster classmate, Betty Charity McCloskey, on June 28, 1916. They had two sons, Arthur Alan, who later served as an officer in the U.S. State Department, and John Joseph, who became professor and head of the philosophy department at Vanderbilt University.

The three years following Compton's graduation from Princeton were marked by some uncertainty about the future direction of his career. He taught physics for one year at the University of Minnesota before accepting a job as research engineer at the Westinghouse Lamp Company in East Pittsburgh, Pennsylvania. At Westinghouse, he was active in the early development of sodium vapor and fluorescent lamps and, during the war years of 1917 and 1918, worked on aircraft instruments for the U.S. Signal Corps.

Returns to Academia and Begins X-Ray Research

The work at Westinghouse convinced Compton that his interests lay with questions of basic research rather than with applied research or development. Consequently, he applied for and received a National Research Fellowship for 1919 to 1920 which allowed him to spend a year working at the Cavendish Laboratories at Cambridge University. There, at one of the busiest and most exciting research centers in the world at the time, Compton was able to work closely with **J. J. Thomson** and **Ernest Rutherford** in their pioneering research on the structure of atoms.

Upon his return to the United States in 1920, Compton was appointed professor of physics and head of the department at Washington University in St. Louis, Missouri. He focused his full attention on the scattering of X rays, making use of techniques originally developed by the father-and-son team of **William Henry Bragg** and **William Lawrence Bragg**. Compton studied the changes in wavelengths of X rays by light elements, especially carbon (in the form of graphite). He found, contrary to the laws of classical physics, that some of the scattered X rays had wavelengths greater than those of the incident radiation. In order to explain this phenomenon—later named the Compton effect in his honor—Compton adopted the principles of quantum theory. Suppose, he argued, that one conceives of an X ray as a beam of discrete particles, similar to **Max Planck**'s "quanta." When one of these particles collides with an electron in a carbon atom, it yields some of its energy to the electron; the resulting lower levels of energy in the particle reflect a lower frequency of radiation (longer wavelength). Going one step further, Compton was able to derive an equation that could be used to predict the wavelength of a scattered wave under various conditions. Later research confirmed the

accuracy of that equation. These results were especially important because they provided strong support for the argument that electromagnetic waves have a dual character. Apart from validating **Albert Einstein**'s light quantum theory proposed in 1905, Compton's discovery of wave-particle signatures inspired the development of quantum theory during the years of 1924 to 1927.

The timing of Compton's finding was also significant because it came at nearly the same moment in history when Prince **Louis Victor de Broglie** demonstrated the wave character of electrons. By the 1930s, therefore, it had become apparent that both matter and energy can be interpreted in terms of particles or as wave phenomena. In recognition of his discovery and explanation of the Compton effect, Compton was awarded a share (with **C. T. R. Wilson**) of the 1927 Nobel Prize for physics.

Shortly after presenting conclusive proof of the wave-particle behavior of X rays, Compton accepted an appointment as professor of physics at the University of Chicago. During his first decade at Chicago, he extended his research on the scattering of X rays while carrying a full teaching load. He was well liked and widely respected by both colleagues and students. Biographer Shankland says that "his contagious enthusiasm, friendliness, and great mental powers made his classes and laboratory meetings memorable experiences for all who were privileged to attend them."

Cosmic Radiation Dominates New Research

Early in the 1930s, Compton became interested in a new research topic, the nature of cosmic radiation. Cosmic rays strike all parts of the earth's atmosphere and appear to originate from deep space. Though first discovered by **Victor Hess** in 1912, their true nature remained ambiguous even by the 1930s. Some scientists argued that they were a highly energetic form of electromagnetic radiation, while others believed them to be rapidly moving charged particles.

One approach to the resolution of this debate was to study the distribution of cosmic rays at various points on the earth's surface. If cosmic rays are a form of energy, they will not be deflected by the earth's magnetic field but detectable at equal intensities anywhere on the earth. If they are charged particles, they will be deflected by the earth's magnetic field and will be found in greater concentrations in some latitudes than in others.

Throughout the mid–1930s, Compton recorded measurements of cosmic ray intensities at many points on the earth's surface. Fortunately, Compton and his wife loved to travel, and he was in great demand as a speaker and consultant. By 1938, Compton had collected enough data to show without question that the intensity of cosmic rays is greatest at the poles, decreasing to a minimum at the equator. It was clear that at least some cosmic radiation consists of charged particles. A similar conclusion had been obtained ten years earlier by the Dutch physicist **Jacob Clay**, although his results were not well known to other scientists, including Compton.

Joins the Manhattan Project

At the conclusion of his cosmic ray research, Compton began to feel the need to withdraw from active research. He had become involved in the administration of higher education and of science and had told a friend and colleague, Samuel K. Allison, that he was ready to turn over his experimental work "to younger men who could do it better." But the onset of World War II justified Compton's decision to remain in the laboratory.

As news of the discovery of nuclear fission reached the United States in the early 1940s, physicists began to lobby politicians and government officials about its potential application for weapons development. In 1941, President Franklin D. Roosevelt appointed a committee to explore the possibility of developing a fission bomb. The president asked Compton to serve as chairman of that committee.

The decision reached by the committee culminated in the birth of the Manhattan Project, through which the world's first atomic bombs were designed and built. As part of that effort, Compton created a facility at the University of Chicago known as the Metallurgical Laboratory, and became its director. It was at the Metallurgical Laboratory that the world's first nuclear reactor was constructed and put into operation in December 1942.

At the war's conclusion, Compton was offered the post of chancellor of Washington University. He served in that position from 1945 to 1954 when he retired, but continued at Washington as Distinguished Service Professor of Natural Philosophy until resigning in 1961. For the last year of his life, Compton divided his time among St. Louis, the College of Wooster, and the University of California at Berkeley. He died of a cerebral hemorrhage in Berkeley on March 15, 1962.

SELECTED WRITINGS BY COMPTON:

Books

X-Rays and Electrons, Van Nostrand, 1926.
(With S. K. Allison) *X-Rays in Theory and Experiment,* Van Nostrand, 1935.
The Freedom of Man, Yale University Press, 1935.

The Human Meaning of Science, University of North Carolina Press, 1947.
Atomic Quest: A Personal Narrative, Oxford University Press, 1956.

SOURCES:

Books

Allison, Samuel K., *Arthur Holly Compton,* Columbia University Press, 1965.
Heathcote, Niels H. de V., *Nobel Prize Winners in Physics, 1901–1950,* Henry Schuman, 1953, pp. 259–268.
Johnston, M., editor, *The Cosmos of Arthur Holly Compton,* Knopf, 1967.
Shankland, Robert S., essay in *Dictionary of Scientific Biography,* Volume 3, Scribner, 1975, pp. 366–372.
Weber, Robert L., *Pioneers of Science: Nobel Prize Winners in Physics,* American Institute of Physics, 1980, pp. 82–83.

Periodicals

Allison, Samuel K., "Arthur Holly Compton, Research Physicist," *Science,* November 16, 1962, pp. 794–797.

—Sketch by David E. Newton

Lynn Ann Conway
1938-
American engineer

Lynn Ann Conway has been recognized for her pioneering work in very large scale integrated (VLSI) circuit and system design methodology. She helped simplify the way integrated computer circuit chips are designed, and then went on to develop a rapid means of prototype fabrication that fundamentally changed computer design methodology and contributed to an explosion of new hardware and software. A professor of electrical engineering and computer sciences and associate dean of the College of Engineering at the University of Michigan, Conway includes computer architecture, artificial intelligence, and collaboration technology among her research interests.

Born in Mount Vernon, New York, on January 2, 1938, Conway received an M.S. degree in electrical engineering from Columbia University in 1963 and worked as a staff researcher at IBM Corporation from 1964 to 1969. Conway then served as senior staff engineer at Memorex Corporation from 1969 to 1973, when she accepted a research position with Xerox Corporation at its Palo Alto Research Center in California. She founded the VLSI systems and Knowledge Systems research departments at Xerox and remained resident fellow and manager there until 1983, when she began two years of service as chief scientist and assistant director of Strategic Computing at the Defense Advisory Research Projects Agency (DARPA). In 1985 Conway accepted her current position at the University of Michigan's College of Engineering.

Helps Develop New Approach to Chip Design and Fabrication

Conway is renowned for two major developments in circuitry. Her first, a joint effort with several colleagues, was the invention of a new approach to the design of integrated computer circuit chips. Previously, many designers, each with specialized skills, were needed in the laborious process of circuitry development. Conway helped create a unified structural methodology which allowed computer engineers with general backgrounds to design chips—demystifying the design process.

Her second major achievement, which was published in the textbook *Introduction to VLSI Systems*, was a new method of chip fabrication, whereby designers could very rapidly obtain prototypes with which to test their hardware and software inventions. Both this quick turnaround fabrication facility and Conway's earlier contribution to the design of integrated circuitry have added to the increased democratization of information in the computer field.

Conway has received extensive recognition for her work, including the John Price Wetherill Medal from the Franklin Institute in 1985; the Meritorious Civilian Service Award, given by the Secretary of Defense in 1985; and the Harold Pender Award, bestowed by the University of Pennsylvania in 1984. She was honored in 1990 with an achievement award of the Society of Women Engineers (SWE), presented for "essential contributions to very large scale integrated (VLSI) circuit and system design methodology, and for rapid propagation of the new innovations throughout the engineering community." She also received the Major Educational Innovation Award from the Institute of Electrical and Electronics Engineers (IEEE), and the Electronics Magazine Achievement Award.

Conway has held numerous consulting positions and was visiting associate professor of electrical engineering and computer sciences at the Massachusetts Institute of Technology from 1978–79. She has served on such advisory panels as the United States Air Force Scientific Advisory Board, the Executive Council of the American Association for Artificial Intelligence, and the Technical Council Society for Machine Intelligence. Her love of adventure has led her to the hobby of motocross racing.

SELECTED WRITINGS BY CONWAY:

Books

Introduction to VLSI Systems, Addison Wesley Publishing, 1980.

SOURCES:

Books

Society of Women Engineers Achievement Awards, 1993.

Other

Conway, Lynn Ann, interview with Karen Withem.

—*Sketch by Karen Withem*

Esther Marly Conwell
1922-
American physicist

A research fellow at Xerox Corporation, Esther Marly Conwell is chiefly recognized for her work in the field of solid state physics, for which she received the Society of Women Engineers (SWE) Achievement Award in 1960.

A native of New York City, Conwell was born May 23, 1922. She earned a bachelor's degree from Brooklyn College in 1942, a master's degree from the University of Rochester in 1945, and a Ph.D. in physics from the University of Chicago in 1948. While studying, she taught physics at Brooklyn College, where she remained until 1951. In that year Conwell joined the technical staff of Bell Telephone Laboratories. She accepted a post as engineering specialist at GTE Laboratories the following year.

From 1962 to 1963 Conwell was a visiting professor at the University of Paris and was appointed manager of the physics department at GTE in 1963. Remaining there for seven years, she directed the solid state physics group. Conwell left GTE to become a principal scientist at Xerox in 1970. A decade later, she was awarded her current appointment as research fellow. Conwell also held the Abby Rockefeller Mauze Chair at Massachusetts Institute of Technology in 1972.

As explained in the *Society of Women Engineers Achievement Awards,* Conwell's 1960 SWE award resulted from her collaboration on the theory "behind conduction of electricity in semi-conductor materials used in transistors." She has also studied theoretical aspects of xerography, or the functioning of copy machines, including how photoconductors work using the transport of electrical charge, and how the development system reproduces a copied image. Additional honors include a fellowship with the American Physical Society and membership in American Men of Science, the National Academy of Sciences, and the National Academy of Engineering.

SOURCES:

Books

Society of Women Engineers Achievement Awards, 1993 edition.

Other

Conwell, Esther Marly, interview with Karen Withem conducted March 24, 1994.

—*Sketch by Karen Withem*

Lloyd M. Cooke
1916-
American industrial chemist

Lloyd M. Cooke spent thirty years working in chemical, technical, and market research in cellulose and carbohydrate chemistry for companies. Although he worked in industry throughout his career, he developed a respected reputation in the scientific community and was instrumental in preparing a publication on chemistry and the environment that was widely adopted as a university textbook. He is a member of a number of scientific boards and societies, and has received many awards and honors, including the Proctor Prize in Science from the Science Research Association in 1970. Cooke transferred to the area of urban affairs (a community relations position) for Union Carbide in 1970, a position which made him responsible for areas such as equal opportunity employment and education.

Lloyd Miller Cooke was born in La Salle, Illinois, on June 7, 1916, the son of William Wilson and Anna (Miller) Cooke. His father, an engineer and architect for the U.S. government, advised him against his first choice for a career, aeronautical engineering, because he said a black wouldn't be able to find work in the field. Hoping for more opportunity, Cooke elected to major in chemistry instead. Although he graduated first in his class in 1937 with a bachelor of science from the University of Wisconsin, he could not get a job. Cooke went on to McGill University in Canada and received his doctorate in organic chemistry in 1941.

Cellulose Research Leads to Employment

Cooke's studies in the chemistry of cellulose (a polysaccharide found in plant cell walls and used in the manufacture of goods such as rayon, paper, and cellophane) led to a job as researcher and section leader in starch chemistry at the Corn Products Refining Company in Argo, Illinois. In 1946, Cooke moved to the Visking Corporation in Chicago to do research in carbohydrate chemistry. Cooke advanced steadily within the films and packaging division of Visking, whose products included hot dog casings. He was manager of the cellulose and casing research department from 1950 to 1954, then assistant manager of a technical division from 1954 to 1957. Cooke's areas of chemical research, on which he has published in professional journals, include the structure of lignin (a polymer related to cellulose), starch modification and derivatives, cellulose derivatives, the chemistry of viscose (a solution of cellulose treated with caustic alkali and carbon disulfide, used in the manufacture of rayon and films), and carbohydrate and polymer chemistry.

When Visking was taken over by Union Carbide, a leading chemical company, in 1957, Cooke volunteered for challenging assignments. "I decided I was happiest when I was on a problem with a time limit where, come a date, I had to make a decision," he told the *New York Times.* At Union Carbide in Chicago, Cooke served as assistant director of research from 1957 to 1965, manager of market research from 1965 to 1967, and manager of planning from 1967 to 1970. It was as manager of planning that he was responsible for the preparation of the book *Cleaning our Environment—The Chemical Basis for Action,* which was published by the American Chemical Society in 1969. Although the book was written for the lay person, especially for politicians and environmental leaders, it was also adopted as a college text by twenty universities, and sold more than fifty thousand copies.

Shifts Focus to Urban Affairs

In 1970, Cooke accepted a new challenge as director of urban affairs for Union Carbide in New York, where he became responsible for issues of equal employment and education access for minorities. Cooke explained his shift in direction to the *New York Times:* "I had decided to make a career change anyway before this offer came.... My real interest was in problem solving and I'd had fun getting involved in the environmental problem." In this new position, which Cooke held until 1978, he fostered an innovative partnership between Union Carbide and the New York City public school system and focussed on secondary science and mathematics education. Between 1978 and his retirement, Cooke served as a senior consultant to Union Carbide.

Cooke was awarded both the Proctor Prize in Science and the Honor Scroll Award of the Chicago Chapter of the American Institute of Chemists in 1970. He is a member of the National Academy of Sciences, the American Institute of Chemists, the American Chemical Society, and the American Marketing Association, among other scientific and professional organizations. Cooke served as a member of the National Science Board from 1970 to 1982, a trustee for the Carver Research Foundation of the Tuskegee Institute from 1971 to 1978, president of the National Action Council on Minorities in Engineering from 1981 1983, and as a senior advisor to the chancellor of the New York public schools from 1984 to 1987. In 1957, Cooke married Vera E. Schlegel, a biochemist he met at Visking. He acknowledged in the *New York Times* in 1971, "Every single thing I've written she's approved." Cooke and his wife have two children, Barbara and William.

SELECTED WRITINGS BY COOKE:

Books

Cleaning Our Environment: The Chemical Basis for Action, American Chemical Society, 1969.

SOURCES:

Books

Scientists in the Black Perspective, Lincoln Foundation, 1974, pp. 142–143.

Periodicals

New York Times, April 25, 1971, section III, p. 7.

—*Sketch by M. C. Nagel*

William D. Coolidge
1873-1975
American physical chemist

William D. Coolidge was an American physical chemist and inventor who made important contributions to three areas of twentieth-century technical development. He developed a pliable filament that improved the electric light, making it possible to mass produce the electric light bulb for commercial, industrial, and personal use. He developed X-ray technology so that it was possible to adapt X-ray techniques to many areas of medicine and technology. He also played a role in the development of the atomic bomb used by the United States at the end of World War II.

William David Coolidge was born on a farm in Hudson, Massachusetts, on October 23, 1873, to Albert Edward Coolidge, a shoe factory worker, and Martha Alice Shattuck. As a young boy, Coolidge showed an ability for electrical and mechanical projects. This ability was evident from the fact that he spent much of his spare time in a local machine shop. To help ease his family's economic difficulties, he temporarily left high school during his junior year to take a job in a rubber factory. He graduated from Hudson High School in 1891 after a six month delay.

A state scholarship and a loan from a friend's father made it possible for Coolidge to enter the Massachusetts Institute of Technology in 1891 to study electrical engineering. On account of illness, his graduation was delayed until 1896, when he also was appointed to the position of assistant in physics at M.I.T. His debts at the time amounted to $4,000, a large sum at that time, and he was not able to pay off the debt until he was in his early thirties.

Begins Long Affiliation With General Electric

In 1897, Coolidge received a graduate fellowship from the University of Leipzig, where he earned his Ph.D. in 1899. On his return to the United States, Coolidge did research in physical chemistry at M.I.T. for five years. He was an instructor from 1901 to 1903, and from 1904 to 1905 he was an assistant professor. In 1905, his former professor of chemistry at M.I.T., Willis R. Whitney, invited Coolidge to become a researcher in physico-chemistry at the General Electric Company in Schenectady, New York, where Whitney had become director of the General Electric laboratory in 1900.

Although the General Electric laboratory was expanding with the company's growth after the 1892 merger of the Edison General Electric Company with the Thomson-Houston Electric Company, Coolidge hesitated to accept the position offered to him because of doubts he had about the nature of the problems on which he would be working in industry. A promise was made to him that he could devote as much time as he wanted to conductivity measurement research (which had engaged his interests at M.I.T.) and Coolidge accepted the job. His early association with General Electric proved to be fruitful both in terms of the research he was able to do and in terms of his career status. He was appointed assistant director in 1908, associate director in 1928, director in 1932, and became vice president and director of research in 1940 before retiring as director emeritus in 1944.

During his long association with the General Electric Company, Coolidge developed a pliable form of tungsten called ductile tungsten, which could be drawn into fine wires only a sixth of the diameter of a human hair. Earlier, Thomas Edison had used carbon fibers, but they had proved too brittle to handle. Coolidge patented his technique in 1909. This technique is still used today in the production of incandescent light bulbs, and it has also proven useful in the development of radio tubes, electron tubes, contacts, and high-power water-cooled transmitting tubes.

Uses Tungsten to Produce X-ray Tubes

Coolidge's work with the electric light was successful by 1911, and by 1913, he began work on the X-ray tube. He was able to utilize the ductile tungsten he had developed for light bulbs to produce X-ray tubes that were accurate and stable. His version of the X-ray tube became known as the "Coolidge tube," and these tubes found wide use in the industrial and medical communities. By 1917, during World War I, he produced a portable X-ray generating outfit and a C-Tube that could be used as a listening device for submarines and for underwater signaling purposes.

In 1924, Coolidge developed an oil-immersed self-contained X ray that could be handled safely by technicians, dentists, and others. Significant applications of Coolidge's X-ray tube are found in cancer treatments and in the industrial application of gauging the thickness of metal as it is being processed. In 1928, Coolidge added to his contributions by explaining the cold-cathode effect that limits how much voltage can be used on a given tube. The Coolidge cathode-ray tube beam is also able to cause some chemicals to undergo changes and to destroy germs and insects rapidly.

From 1932 until his retirement in 1944, Coolidge served mainly in an advisory capacity at General Electric. During World War II, he was enlisted to help study the value of uranium for military use and was involved in the development of the atomic bomb. Shortly after the war, he was engaged in nuclear research at the Hanford Engineer Works in Richland, Washington. His work was considered important in so far as he could bring expert an engineering sense to the project.

During his lifetime, Coolidge held eighty-three patents and wrote numerous articles, beginning with "Ductile Tungsten" and "A Powerful X-Ray Tube with a Pure Electron Discharge," and going on to such titles as, "Measurement of the Dielectric Constant of Liquids," "Development of Modern X-Ray Generating Apparatus," and "The Production of X-Rays of Very Short Wave-Length." His many awards included the Rumford Medal, the Edison Medal, the John Scott Award, the Faraday Medal of the Institution of Electrical Engineers of England, and the Duddell Medal of the Physical Society of England.

Coolidge was married to Ethel Westcott Woodard in 1908. They had two children: a daughter, Elizabeth, and a son, Lawrence David. Ethel Coolidge died in 1915, and Coolidge married Dorothy Elizabeth MacHaffie in 1916. He died in Schenectady on February 3, 1975, at the age of 101.

SOURCES:

Books

Rhodes, Richard, *Making of the Atomic Bomb*, Simon and Schuster, 1988, pp. 363, 367, 373–74.

—*Sketch by Vita Richman*

Leon Cooper
1930-
American physicist and neural scientist

Leon N. Cooper began his scientific career while in his early twenties with pioneering work on the theory of superconductivity, a specialized field of physics that studies the resistanceless flow of electric-

Leon Cooper

ity through certain metals at very low temperatures. For his contributions to the discipline, Cooper was awarded the Nobel Prize in physics in 1972. In more recent years, he has directed his attention towards the neural and cognitive sciences, working toward an understanding of memory and other brain functions.

Cooper's interest in biology reflects his early pursuit of the study of science while living in New York City. He was born in 1930, the son of Irving and Anna (Zola) Cooper. Like many other students at the specialized Bronx High School of Science, which he attended, young Cooper entered the prestigious Westinghouse Science Talent Search as a senior. His independent research project for this competition analyzed how bacteria can become resistant to penicillin. He was selected one of the forty national winners in the Westinghouse competition which has produced five Nobel laureates over its half-century duration.

Cooper then entered Columbia University where he spent seven years, earning his A.B. degree in 1951, his A.M. degree in 1953, and his Ph.D. degree in 1954 with a dissertation on the mu-mesonic atom. This latter work was done under the direction of Robert Serber, who was a friend of **J. Robert Oppenheimer**, a scientist instrumental in the creation of the atom bomb. Through this association, the young Cooper obtained a position as a National Science Foundation Postdoctoral Fellow at the Institute for Advanced Study in Princeton, New Jersey.

Moves to Superconductivity Research at Illinois

During a year-long stay at the institute, Cooper continued to investigate mu-mesonic atoms. His growing reputation in quantum field theory drew the attention of scientist **John Bardeen**, who was working on the phenomenon of superconductivity at the University of Illinois. Superconductivity had first been described by the Dutch physicist **Heike Kamerlingh Onnes** in 1911. Kamerlingh Onnes had reported that some metals lose all resistance to the flow of electrical current, becoming "superconductive," as they are cooled to temperatures close to absolute zero. The heightened conductivity derives from a free flow of electrons in the metal. Scientists were intrigued by this phenomenon for both theoretical and practical reasons. An understanding of superconductivity could potentially revolutionize the electronics industry. Every device that operates by means of an electric current wastes a huge amount of energy in overcoming electrical resistance. If superconducting materials could be used in those devices, virtually no energy would be lost to resistance. The practical problem posed by Kamerlingh Onnes's discovery was the low temperature required for superconductivity. In the intervening half century, scientists had been singularly unsuccessful in improving on his work. By the 1950s, the highest temperature at which superconductivity had been observed was still only about 20K, 20 degrees above absolute zero.

Bardeen needed a young physicist skilled in the latest theoretical techniques, and he invited Cooper to join him. Cooper served as a research associate at Illinois from 1955 to 1957. It was during those two years that Cooper, Bardeen and a third scientist, **J. Robert Schrieffer**, developed their Nobel Prize-winning theory of superconductivity. Cooper's notable contribution to superconductivity theory was the discovery of what became known as "Cooper pairs."

Cooper's own readings led to his conviction that research in the field needed to concentrate on the interaction between two electrons which normally repel each other but, when located among positive ions in a metal lattice, develop a small net attraction for each other. These "Cooper pairs" of electrons accumulate and sweep through the lattice all in the same direction, resulting in the resistanceless flow of electricity in the metal. The "Cooper pair" concept formed the heart of the BCS theory of superconductivity, named for its three originators: Bardeen, Cooper, and Schrieffer. The details of this theory were disclosed in a letter to the editor of *Physical Review,* and it was printed in the November 15, 1956 issue; another letter signed by the three collaborators was sent to the *Physical Review* editor early in 1957, followed by their comprehensive paper titled "The Theory of Superconductivity." It was this paper, printed in *Physical Review*'s December 1, 1957 issue, that earned Cooper and his two colleagues their claim to the Nobel Prize awarded to them fifteen years later.

In 1957 Cooper left Illinois to join the physics faculty at Ohio State University as an assistant professor. Here, he researched the properties of liquid Helium 3 (He 3) with Andrew Sessler and Robert Mills. Cooper was the first one to suggest that Helium 3 might be a superfluid, and his work drew favorable attention. However, Cooper's own preference for the East Coast made him accept an offer as associate professor at Brown University in 1958, where he became a full professor in 1962. He was appointed Thomas J. Watson, Sr. Professor of Science in 1974 and has served as co-chair of Brown's Center for Neural Sciences since 1973. Cooper is also director of the university's Institute for Brain and Neural Systems.

Shifts Career Emphasis at Brown

While at Brown, Cooper continued his interest in theoretical physics. He even developed a physics course for liberal arts students and wrote a remarkable textbook in 1968 titled *An Introduction to the Meaning and Structure of Physics*. However, his breadth of interest and curiosity also led him into the study of history, philosophy and the classics, and he published papers on such varying subjects as the place of science in human experience; the role of values in scientific inquiry; how science can serve mankind; the source and limits of human intellect, faith and science; and the relationships between history, science and American culture.

Cooper was also very intrigued by learning and memory, and in 1973 he and his colleagues founded the Center for Neural Studies at Brown. The center's objective was to study animal nervous systems and the human brain, especially to determine how the brain's neural network modifies itself through experience. As co-chair of the center, Cooper served with an interdisciplinary staff drawn from the departments of applied mathematics, biomedical sciences, linguistics and physics. Drawing on the nearly twenty years of research by the Center for Neural Studies, Cooper founded the Institute for Brain and Neural Systems in 1922. This organization has brought together an international group of scientists, and its objective is to pave the way for the next generation of cognitive pharmaceutical and intelligent systems for use in electronics, automobiles and communications. Its research aims to traverse the boundaries of the traditional sciences, drawing on the fields of biology, psychology, mathematics, engineering, physics, linguistics and computer science. Cooper also is co-founder and co-chair of Nestor, Inc. an industry leader in applying neural network systems to commercial and military applications.

Cooper's work has been widely recognized, and he has earned numerous awards besides his Nobel Prize. He was also recipient of the Comtock Prize (with Schrieffer) from the National Academy of Sciences in 1968; the Award of Excellence from the Graduate Faculties Alumni of Columbia University in 1974; the Descartes Medal Academie de Paris, from Universite René Descartes in 1977; and the John Jay Award of Columbia College in 1985. Cooper holds seven honorary degrees from universities in the United States and abroad as well as being a member of various scientific organizations, including the American Physical Society, American Academy of Arts and Sciences, American Philosophical Society, the National Academy of Sciences, the Sponsor Federation of American Scientists, the Society of Neuroscience, and the American Association for Advancement of Science. Cooper is married and the father of two children.

SELECTED WRITINGS BY COOPER:

Books

An Introduction to the Meaning and Structure of Physics, Harper, 1968, short edition, 1970.

Periodicals

(With E. M. Henley) "Mu-Mesonic Atoms and the Electromagnetic Radius of the Nucleus," *Physical Review,* Volume 92, 1953, p. 801.

"Bound Electron Pairs in a Degenerate Fermi Gas," *Physical Review,* Volume 104, 1956, p. 1189.

(With John Bardeen and John R. Schrieffer) "Theory of Superconductivity," *Physical Review,* Volume 106, 1957, p. 162.

"Superconductivity in the Neighborhood of Metallic Contacts," *Physical Review Letters,* Volume 6, 1961, p. 589.

"Something Deeply Hidden," *New York Times Review of the Week,* May 4, 1969.

"The Humble Cathedral," *Physics Today,* July, 1971, p. 62.

"Can Science Serve Mankind?" *Conference Proceedings; Science in the Service of Mankind,* July, 1979.

"Source and Limits of Human Intellect" *Daedalus,* spring, 1980, pp. 1–17.

(With Christopher L. Scofield) "Recent Developments in Neural Models," *Contemporary Physics,* Volume 26, no. 2, 1985, pp. 125–145.

"Future of Brain Research," *Naval Research Reviews,* Volume 39, 1987.

SOURCES:

Books

Magill, Frank N., editor, *The Nobel Prize Winners: Physics,* Volume 3, 1968–1988, Salem Press, 1989.

Phares, Tom K., *Seeking and Finding Science Talent: A 50-Year History of the Westinghouse Science Talent Search,* Westinghouse Electric Corporation, 1990.

Weber, Robert L., *Pioneers of Science: Nobel Prize Winners in Physics,* second edition, Adam Hilger, 1988.

—*Sketch by Tom K. Phares*

Elias James Corey
1928-

American chemist

Elias James Corey, a specialist in the synthesis of organic chemicals, developed many of the theories and methods that now define his field. Since his research career began in the 1950s, one of his goals has been to make the synthesis of chemicals more systematic, and he is best known for his logical approach to the creation of new substances, which he has named "retrosynthetic analysis." Corey's achievements in research, which resulted in far-reaching benefits for medicine and human health, were recognized in 1990 when he was awarded the Nobel Prize for Chemistry.

Corey was born July 12, 1928, to Fatina (Hasham) and Elias Corey in Methuen, Massachusetts. His father died eighteen months later. Corey had been named William at birth, but after his father's death his mother renamed him in his memory. Corey had three siblings, a brother and two sisters, and they were all raised by their mother, with the help of her sister and brother-in-law. His aunt and uncle actually moved in with them, and Corey still credits his mother's sister with being an important influence on his life. Corey enjoyed football and baseball as a child; he was also a good student, graduating from high school in 1945 and entering the Massachusetts Institute of Technology at the age of sixteen. He intended to study engineering but quickly developed an interest in chemistry. It was here that Corey began his research on organic synthesis, the manual formation of chemicals. He worked under John Sheehan on the organic synthesis of penicillin and received his Ph.D. in 1951.

After earning his doctorate, Corey accepted a position as instructor in chemistry at the University of Illinois at Champaign-Urbana. He continued his research on organic synthesis; in 1954 he became an assistant professor, and in 1955 he was named full professor of chemistry. In 1957, Corey received a Guggenheim fellowship. He left Illinois on sabbatical, and during this time he did research that laid the foundation for the rest of his career. He spent a portion of his sabbatical working on chemical synthesis with **Robert B. Woodward** at Harvard. The rest of the time he devoted solely to research in Europe, examining the problems of synthesizing prostaglandins (hormone-like substances with many different effects, found in the tissue of the body).

Develops Retrosynthetic Analysis

During the time Corey was a Guggenheim fellow, chemical synthesis was widely considered an intuitive process and often called an "art form." In a 1990 article in *Science,* Corey recalled his field as he found it in the 1950s: "Chemists approached each problem in an ad hoc way. Synthesis was taught by the presentation of a series of illustrative—and generally unrelated—examples of actual synthesis." It was while working with Woodward that Corey began his effort to systematize this intuitive process. Success in organic synthesis was often personal and difficult for the individual scientist to explain in full; Corey wanted the methods, as well as the results, to be both reproducible and teachable.

In 1959, Corey was offered a professorship of chemistry at Harvard, which he accepted. In his new position, he continued to search for what he has called the "deep logic" of chemical synthesis. His central innovation was to reverse the usual order of procedure by adding a planning process that began with the desired result, instead of the initial chemicals. Corey planned the process backwards from the molecule he wanted to synthesize, creating a chart or "tree" that included many possible compounds and reactions. This was retrosynthetic analysis, a formal system which eliminated much of the guesswork, as well as making it easier to use chemicals that were readily available or easy to synthesize. The system also made it possible to use computers for chemical synthesis, and Corey has been a pioneer in this application of artificial intelligence.

The actual results of Corey's work in chemical synthesis have been almost as important as his methodological innovations. In 1968, Corey and his colleagues were able to synthesize five different prostaglandins, which are involved in regulating many functions in the body including blood pressure, blood coagulation, and reproduction. Before this time only a small quantity of these substances was available, as they had to be extracted from the testes of Icelandic sheep. With scientists able to synthetically produce prostaglandins, their applications in medicine have increased profoundly. Eventually Corey's work on prostaglandins led to the development of what is now commonly known as the Corey lactone aldehyde. From this, prostaglandins of all three familial types can be derived.

Another result of Corey's work was the 1988 synthesis of ginkgolide B, a chemical naturally extracted from the ginkgo tree. This chemical is used for the treatment of asthma and circulatory problems in the elderly, and has grown to a market of over 500 million dollars a year. Besides these accomplishments, Corey also has improved or started over fifty new reactions. This has broadened the application of organic synthesis by increasing the tools available to the scientist.

Corey was awarded the 1990 Nobel Prize not for any specific scientific achievement but for his career as a whole. In conferring the award, the Nobel Prize committee said of him: "No other chemist has developed such a comprehensive and varied assortment of methods, often showing the simplicity of genius, which have become commonplace in organic synthesis laboratories." Corey continues his association with Harvard as head of an organic synthesis laboratory which operates with the help of graduate students. The "Corey research family" has contributed to the training of over one hundred-fifty university professors and an even greater number of scientists working in industry.

Corey has received eleven honorary degrees including doctorates from the University of Chicago in 1968 and Oxford University in 1982. He has received more than three dozen other awards from universities and scientific societies, including a 1971 Award for Creative Work in Synthetic Organic Chemistry, the Linus Pauling Award in 1973, and in 1988 the Robert Robinson Medal from the Royal Society of Chemistry. Corey was a member of the American Academy of Arts and Sciences from 1960 to 1968. He has been a member of the American Association for the Advancement of Science since 1966. He has served on the editorial board of several scientific journals and contributed over seven hundred articles for publication. He is co-author of a 1989 book, *The Logic of Chemical Synthesis*.

Corey was married in September 1961 to Claire Higham. He and his wife have three children (two sons and a daughter), and they reside in Cambridge, Massachusetts.

SELECTED WRITINGS BY COREY:

Books

(With Xue-min Cheng) *The Logic of Chemical Synthesis*, John Wiley & Sons, 1989.

SOURCES:

Books

McGuire, Paula, editor, *Nobel Prize Winners Supplement 1987–1991*, H. W. Wilson, 1992.

Periodicals

Amato, I., "Nobel Prize Goes to Molecule Maker," *Science News*, October 27, 1990, p. 262.
"Nobel Prize Winners," *New York Times*, October 18, 1990, p. A20.
Pool, Robert, "Chemistry 'Grand Master' Garners a Nobel Prize," *Science*, October 26, 1990, pp. 250–251.

—*Sketch by Kimberly McGrail*

Carl Ferdinand Cori
1896-1984
Austro-Hungarian-born American biochemist

Carl Ferdinand Cori and his wife, biochemist **Gerty T. Cori**, were prominent researchers in physiology, pharmacology, and biology. Their most important work involved carbohydrate metabolism (especially in tumors), phosphate processes in the muscles, the process of glucose-glycogen interconversion, and the action of insulin. The Coris shared the 1947 Nobel Prize for physiology or medicine (along with the Argentine physiologist **Bernardo Houssay**) "for their discovery of the course of the catalytic conversion of glycogen."

Cori was born on December 5, 1896, in Prague, which was then part of the Austro-Hungarian empire. His parents were Carl Isidor Cori, a professor of zoology at the German University of Prague, and Maria Lippich Cori. When Cori was still young, the family moved to Trieste, Italy, where his father had been appointed director of the Marine Biology Station. Cori studied at the Gymnasium in Trieste from 1906 to 1914, and then returned to Prague and began medical studies at the German University. His studies, however, were interrupted by World War I; serving in the Austrian army, he worked in hospitals for infectious diseases on the Italian front.

It was during his first term at the University of Prague that Cori met his wife, who was also a medical student. Described as redheaded and vivacious, Gerty Theresa Radnitz was the daughter of a Prague businessman and a lifelong resident of that city. As

Carl Ferdinand Cori

medical students, the Coris coauthored their first scientific publication; ultimately, they would publish over two hundred research articles together. They were married on August 5, 1920, shortly after receiving their medical doctorates.

From 1920 to 1922, Cori served first as a researcher at the First Medical Clinic in Vienna, Austria, and then in the same capacity at Austria's University of Graz. During this time, his wife worked as an assistant at a children's hospital in Vienna. In 1922, Cori accepted a position at the New York State Institute for the Study of Malignant Diseases in Buffalo. Gerty Cori joined him soon thereafter, and they continued their research together. During this period, the Coris were studying carbohydrate metabolism, particularly in tumor cells. They also researched the effects of the surgical removal of the ovaries on the incidence of tumors.

Researches Glucose Conversion

The Coris became American citizens in 1928, and in 1931 they accepted positions at the medical school of Washington University in St. Louis, Missouri, where Cori was to remain until 1966. Their research on carbohydrate metabolism now centered on glucose, or "blood sugar," the energy source for animal life. They developed methods to analyze the relationship of glucose to glycogen, the starchlike form in which glucose is stored in the liver and muscles. In the 1930s, the Coris performed ground-breaking research on the biochemical processes involved in the interconversion of glucose to glycogen, a process now called the Cori cycle. This interconversion is responsible for maintaining the blood sugar at a constant level.

In 1936, the Coris isolated glucose–1-phosphate, now known as the Cori ester, which is involved in the formation and breakdown of glycogen. The Coris also analyzed the function of insulin, a hormone in the pancreas that is vital to the body's processing of glucose. In 1938, the Coris analyzed the conversion of glucose–1-phosphate to glucose–6-phosphate. Then, in 1943, they isolated phosphorylase, an enzyme important to the glucose-glycogen interconversion, in crystalline form. The Coris were able in 1944 to synthesize glycogen in a test tube, the first such synthesis of a high molecular substance.

Cori was appointed professor of biochemistry at Washington University in 1944, and two years later he became chairman of the department. In 1947, he and his wife were awarded the Nobel Prize for physiology or medicine for their research on the relationship between glucose and glycogen. This led to many comparisons in the press between the Coris and the first husband-and-wife team to win the Nobel Prize, **Pierre** and **Marie Curie**.

In addition to sharing the Nobel Prize in 1947, Cori received numerous awards and honors, including the Isaac Adler Prize from Harvard University in 1944, the Midwest Award of the American Chemical Society in 1945, and the Harry M. Lasker Award of the American Society for the Control of Cancer in 1946. He also received the Squibb Award of the Society of Endocrinologists, which was bestowed on him along with his wife in 1947, and the Willard Gibbs Medal of the American Chemical Society in 1948. Cori received honorary degrees from Cambridge, Yale, and other universities, and was a member of various scientific societies.

In the same year they won the Nobel Prize, his wife was diagnosed with myelosclerosis, a disease of the blood. She died ten years later, on October 26, 1957, of complications from the disease, and Cori suffered the loss of both wife and scientific partner. They had one child, a son, Carl Thomas Cori. Cori subsequently remarried, wedding Anne Fitzgerald Jones on March 23, 1960. In 1966, after retiring from Washington University, Cori served as a visiting professor at the Harvard University School of Medicine. Cori died on October 20, 1984, in Cambridge, Massachusetts.

SELECTED WRITINGS BY CORI:

Periodicals

"Mammalian Carbohydrate Metabolism," *Physiological Reviews,* Volume 11, 1931, pp. 143–275.

(With Gerty T. Cori) "The Formation of Hexose-phosphate Esters in Frog Muscle," *Journal of Biological Chemistry,* Volume 116, 1936, pp. 119–128.

(With Cori and A. A. Green), "Crystalline Muscle Phosphorylase. III. Kinetics," *Journal of Biological Chemistry,* Volume 151, 1943, pp. 39–55.

(With Cori), "The Enzymatic Conversion of Phosphorylase a to b," *Journal of Biological Chemistry,* Volume 158, 1945, pp. 321–32.

(With Cori), "Glucose–6-Phosphatase of the Liver in Glycogen Storage Disease," *Journal of Biological Chemistry,* Volume 199, 1952, pp. 661–67.

SOURCES:

Books

Nobel Prize Winners, H. W. Wilson, 1987, pp. 216–220.

Opfell, Olga S., *The Lady Laureates,* Scarecrow, 1986, pp. 213–23.

Periodicals

McCue, George, "Cori + Cori = Nobel Prize," *Science Illustrated,* February, 1948, pp. 19–23, 70.

—*Sketch by David Sprinkle*

Gerty T. Cori
1896-1957
Austro Hungarian-born American biochemist

Gerty T. Cori made significant contributions in two major areas of biochemistry, which increased understanding of how the body stores and uses sugars and other carbohydrates. For much of her early scientific career, Cori performed pioneering work on sugar metabolism (how sugars supply energy to the body), in collaboration with her husband, **Carl Ferdinand Cori**. For this work they shared the 1947 Nobel Prize in physiology or medicine with **Bernardo A. Houssay**, who had also carried out fundamental studies in the same field. Cori's later work focused on a class of diseases called glycogen storage disorders. She demonstrated that these illnesses are caused by

Gerty T. Cori

disruptions in sugar metabolism. Both phases of Gerty Cori's work illustrated for other scientists the importance of studying enzymes (special proteins that permit specific biochemical reactions to take place) for understanding normal metabolism and disease processes.

Gerty Theresa Radnitz was the first of three girls born to Otto and Martha Neustadt Radnitz. She was born in Prague, then part of the Austro-Hungarian Empire, on August 15, 1896. Otto was a manager of sugar refineries. It is not known if his work helped shape his eldest daughter's early interest in chemistry and later choice of scientific focus. However, her maternal uncle, a professor of pediatrics, did encourage her to pursue her interests in science. Gerty was first taught by tutors at home, then enrolled in a private girls' school. At that time, girls were not expected to attend a university. In order to follow her dream of becoming a chemist, Gerty first studied at the Tetschen *Realgymnasium.* She then had to pass a special entrance exam (*matura*) that tested her knowledge of Latin, literature, history, mathematics, physics, and chemistry.

In 1914 Gerty Radnitz entered the medical school of the German University of Prague (Ferdinand University). There she met a fellow classmate, Carl Ferdinand Cori, who shared her interest in doing scientific research. Together they studied human complement, a substance in blood that plays a key role in immune responses by combining with antibodies. This was the first of a lifelong series of collaborations. In 1920 they both graduated and received their M.D. degrees.

Shortly after graduating, they moved to Vienna and married. Carl worked at the University of Vienna's clinic and the University of Graz's pharmacology department, while Gerty took a position as an assistant at the Karolinen Children's Hospital. Some of her young patients suffered from a disease called congenital myxedema, in which deposits form under the skin and cause swelling, thickening, and paleness in the face. The disease is associated with severe dysfunction of the thyroid gland, located at the base of the neck, which helps to control many body processes, including growth. Gerty's particular research interest was in how the thyroid influenced body temperature regulation.

Immigrates to United States

In the early 1920s, Europe was in the midst of great social and economic unrest in the wake of World War I, and in some regions, food was scarce; Gerty suffered briefly from malnourishment while working in Vienna. Faced with these conditions, the Coris saw little hope there for advancing their scientific careers. In 1922 Carl moved to the United States to take a position as biochemist at the New York State Institute for the Study of Malignant Diseases (later the Roswell Park Memorial Institute). Gerty joined him in Buffalo a few months later, becoming an assistant pathologist at the institute.

Life continued to be difficult for Gerty Cori. She was pressured to investigate malignant diseases, specifically cancers, which were the focus of the institute. Both she and Carl did publish studies related to malignancies, but studying cancer was not to be the focus of either Gerty's or Carl's work. During these early years in the United States, the Coris' publications covered topics from the biological effects of X rays to the effects of restricted diets on metabolism. Following up on her earlier work on the thyroid, Gerty published a report on the influence of thyroid extract on paramecium population growth, her first publication in English.

Colleagues cautioned Gerty and Carl against working together, arguing that collaboration would hurt Carl's career. However, Gerty's duties as an assistant pathologist allowed her some free time, which she used to begin studies of carbohydrate metabolism jointly with her husband. This work, studying how the body burns and stores sugars, was to become the mainstream of their collaborative research. During their years in Buffalo, the Coris jointly published a number of papers on sugar metabolism that reshaped the thinking of other scientists about this topic. In 1928 Gerty and Carl Cori became naturalized citizens of the United States.

In 1931 the Coris moved to St. Louis, Missouri, where Gerty took a position as research associate at Washington University School of Medicine; Carl was a professor there, first of pharmacology and later of biochemistry. The Coris' son, Carl Thomas, was born in 1936. Gerty become a research associate professor of biochemistry in 1943 and in 1947 a full professor of biochemistry. During the 1930s and 1940s the Coris continued their work on sugar metabolism. Their laboratory gained an international reputation as an important center of biochemical breakthroughs. No less than five Nobel laureates spent parts of their careers in the Coris' lab working with them on various problems.

For their pivotal studies in elucidating the nature of sugar metabolism, the Cori's were awarded the Nobel Prize for physiology or medicine in 1947. They shared this honor with Argentine physiologist Bernardo A. Houssay, who discovered how the pituitary gland functions in carbohydrate metabolism. Gerty Cori was only the third woman to receive a Nobel Prize in science. Previously, only Marie Curie and Iréne Joloit-Curie had been awarded such an honor. As with the previous two women winners, Cori was a co-recipient of the prize with her husband.

Significance of the Coris' Research

In the 1920s, when the Coris began to study carbohydrate metabolism, it was generally believed that the sugar called glucose (a type of carbohydrate) was formed from another carbohydrate, glycogen, by the addition of water molecules (a process known as hydrolysis). Glucose circulates in the blood and is used by the body's cells in virtually all cellular processes that require energy. Glycogen is a natural polymer (a large molecule made up of many similar smaller molecules) formed by joining together large numbers of individual sugar molecules for storage in the body. Glycogen allows the body to function normally on a continual basis, by providing a store from which glucose can be broken down and released as needed.

Hydrolysis is a chemical process that does not require enzymes. If, as was believed to be the case in the 1920s, glycogen were broken down to glucose by simple hydrolysis, carbohydrate metabolism would be a very simple, straightforward process. However, in the course of their work, the Coris discovered a chemical compound, glucose–1-phosphate, made up of glucose and a phosphate group (one phosphorus atom combined with three oxygen atoms—sometimes known as the Cori ester) that is derived from glycogen by the action of an enzyme, phosphorylase. Their finding of this intermediate compound, and of the enzymatic conversion of glycogen to glucose, was the basis for the later understanding of sugar metabolism and storage in the body. The Coris' studies opened up research on how carbohydrates are used, stored, and converted in the body.

Cori had been interested in hormones (chemicals released by one tissue or organ and acting on another) since her early thyroid research in Vienna. The discovery of the hormone insulin in 1921 stimulated her to examine its role on sugar metabolism. Insulin's capacity to control diabetes lent great clinical importance to these investigations. In 1924 Gerty and Carl wrote about their comparison of sugar levels in the blood of both arteries and veins under the influence of insulin. At the same time, inspired by earlier work by other scientists (and in an attempt to appease their employer), the Coris examined why tumors used large amounts of glucose.

Their studies on glucose use in tumors convinced the Coris that much basic research on carbohydrate metabolism remained to be done. They began this task by examining the rate of absorption of various sugars from the intestine. They also measured levels of several products of sugar metabolism, particularly lactic acid and glycogen. The former compound results when sugar combines with oxygen in the body.

The Coris measured how insulin affects the conversion of sugar into lactic acid and glycogen in both the muscles and liver. From these studies, they proposed a cycle (called the Cori cycle in their honor) that linked glucose with glycogen and lactic acid. Their proposed cycle had four major steps: (1) blood glucose becomes muscle glycogen, (2) muscle glycogen becomes blood lactic acid, (3) blood lactic acid becomes liver glycogen, and (4) liver glycogen becomes blood glucose. Their original proposed cycle has had to be modified in the face of subsequent research, a good deal of which was carried out by the Coris themselves. For example, scientists learned that glucose and lactic acid can be directly inter-converted, without having to be made into glycogen. Nonetheless, the Coris' suggestion generated much excitement among carbohydrate metabolism researchers. As the Coris' work continued, they unraveled more steps of the complex process of carbohydrate metabolism. They found a second intermediate compound, glucose–6-phosphate, that is formed from glucose–1-phosphate. (The two compounds differ in where the phosphate group is attached to the sugar.) They also found the enzyme that accomplishes this conversion, phosphoglucomutase.

By the early 1940s the Coris had a fairly complete picture of carbohydrate metabolism. They knew how glycogen became glucose. Rather than the simple non-enzymatic hydrolysis reaction that, twenty years earlier, had been believed to be responsible, the Coris' studies painted a more elegant, if more complicated picture. Glycogen becomes glucose–1-phosphate through the action of one enzyme (phosphorylase).

Glucose–1-phosphate becomes glucose–6-phosphate through the action of another enzyme (phosphoglucomutase). Glucose–6-phosphate becomes glucose, and glucose becomes lactic acid, each step in turn mediated by one specific enzyme. The Coris' work changed the way scientists thought about reactions in the human body, and it suggested that there existed specific, enzyme-driven reactions for many of the biochemical conversions that constitute life.

Resumes Early Interest in Pediatric Medicine

In her later years, Cori turned her attention to a group of inherited childhood diseases known collectively as glycogen storage disorders. She determined the structure of the highly branched glycogen molecule in 1952. Building on her earlier work on glycogen and its biological conversions via enzymes, she found that diseases of glycogen storage fell into two general groups, one involving too much glycogen, the other, abnormal glycogen. She showed that both types of diseases originated in the enzymes that control glycogen metabolism. This work alerted other workers in biomedicine that understanding the structure and roles of enzymes could be critical to understanding diseases. Here again, Cori's studies opened up new fields of study to other scientists. In the course of her later studies, Cori was instrumental in the discovery of a number of other chemical intermediate compounds and enzymes that play key roles in biological processes.

At the time of her death, on October 26, 1957, Cori's influence on the field of biochemistry was enormous. She had made important discoveries and prompted a wealth of new research, receiving for her contributions, in addition to the Nobel Prize, the prestigious Garvan Medal for women chemists of the American Chemical Society as well as membership in the National Academy of Sciences. As the approaches and methods that she helped pioneer continue to result in increased scientific understanding, the importance of her work only grows greater.

SELECTED WRITINGS BY CORI:

Periodicals

(With Carl F. Cori) "Glycogen Formation in the Liver from d- and l-Lactic Acid," *Journal of Biological Chemistry,* Volume 81, 1929, pp. 389–403.

(With C. F. Cori and S. P. Colowick) "The Enzymatic Conversion of Glucose–1-Phosphoric Ester to 6-Ester in Tissue Extracts," *Journal of Biological Chemistry,* Volume 124, 1938, pp. 543–55.

"Glycogen Structure and Enzyme Deficiencies in Glycogen Storage Disease," *Harvey Lectures,* Volume 48, 1952–53, pp. 145–71.

SOURCES:

Books

Cori, Carl F., "Gerty Theresa Cori," in *American Chemists and Chemical Engineers*, American Chemical Society, 1976, pp. 94-5.

Dictionary of Scientific Biography, Volume 3, Scribner, 1971, pp. 415-16.

Magill, F. N., editor, *The Nobel Prize Winners, Physiology or Medicine*, Volume 2, 1944-1969 Salem Press, 1991, pp. 550-59.

—*Sketch by Ethan E. Allen*

Allan M. Cormack
1924-
South African-born American physicist

Allan M. Cormack is a physicist whose theoretical analysis and experiments in the fields of nuclear and particle physics, computer tomography and math led to his invention of a mathematical technique for computer-assisted X-ray tomography. Computerized axial tomography, otherwise known as the CAT scan, is a process by which X rays can be concentrated on specific sections of the human body at a variety of angles. Once this information is analyzed by a computer, it is combined to reproduce images of internal structures previously unviewable by medical technology. It is considered the most revolutionary development in the field of radiography since the discovery of the X ray by **Wilhelm Conrad Röntgen** in 1895. Cormack was the first to analyze the possibility of such an examination of a biological system, in 1963 and 1964, and to develop the equations needed for computer-assisted X-ray reconstruction of pictures of the human brain and body. In 1979 Cormack was awarded the Nobel Prize for physiology or medicine, along with **Godfrey Hounsfield**, a British engineer who, independently of Cormack, developed the first commercially successful CAT scanning devices.

Allan MacLeod Cormack was born in Johannesburg, South Africa, on February 23, 1924, the son of George and Amelia (MacLeod) Cormack, a civil service engineer and a teacher respectively, who had emigrated from Scotland to South Africa prior to World War I. Cormack's father died in 1936. Young Cormack attended the Rondebosch Boys High School, where he showed a keen interest in astronomy, physics, mathematics, tennis, debating and acting. Indeed, his first love was astronomy. But at the University of Cape Town, South Africa, Cormack chose the field of engineering, intending to obtain a degree that would allow him a good living. Nevertheless, his interest shifted once more before two years had passed, and he changed his major to physics, completing a baccalaureate of science in 1944.

He remained at the University of Cape Town, completing a Master of Science degree in the field of crystallography in 1945. During the years that followed, Cormack became a lecturer in physics at the University of Cape Town and pursued graduate studies in the field of theoretical physics for two years at Cambridge University in England. Working as a research student in the university's Cavendish Laboratory, he studied radioactive helium under the tutelage of **Otto Robert Frisch**. He also attended lectures on quantum physics given by Nobel Prize winner **Paul Dirac**. While his study of physics did not lead him to a career in astronomy, as he had anticipated, he remained avidly interested in that field.

In 1950 Cormack returned to South Africa from Cambridge to resume his position as a lecturer in physics at the University of Cape Town, where he would remain until 1956. It was during this period that he was asked to serve a six-month service as resident medical physicist in the radiology department at the Groote Schuur Hospital in Cape Town, where he supervised the use of radioisotopes as well as the calibration of film badges used to measure hospital workers' exposure to radiation.

The Seed Of A Nobel Prize-winning Idea

At Groote Schuur, Cormack witnessed first hand how radiation was being used in the diagnosis and treatment of cancer patients. Baffled by deficiencies in the technology used for such procedures, the experience helped plant the seeds of theoretical analysis that would lead Cormack to develop the CAT scan equations and techniques that would earn him the Nobel Prize in 1979. "I asked myself," he told the *New York Times* following the announcement of the prize, "how can you give a dose of radiation if you don't know the material through which it has to pass?"

This simple question led Cormack to a series of experiments and analyses, the results of which were two papers published separately between 1963 and 1964 in the *Journal of Applied Physics.* By this time, Cormack was also conducting theoretical physics research in Boston on subatomic particles, following a

1956 Harvard University sabbatical as a Research Fellow, where he worked in the cyclotron laboratory under director Andreas Koehler.

Following a brief return to Cape Town in 1957, Cormack returned to the United States, accepting a post as assistant professor of physics at Tufts University in Medford, Massachusetts. Between 1956 and 1964, most of his research in connection with the development of computerized axial tomography was conducted on his own time. Indeed, neither of his two *Journal of Applied Physics* papers met with significant response, despite the fact that they proved the feasibility of his method for producing images of heretofore unviewable or barely viewable cross sections of the human body.

Cormak was naturalized as a citizen of the United States in 1966, and continued his academic career and his research in particle physics at Tufts. He was eventually promoted to associate and then full professor of physics, serving as chairman of the physics department from 1968 to 1976. He and his wife, Barbara Jeanne Seavey, an American whom he married on January 6, 1950, raised their three children, Margaret Jean, Jean Barbara, and Robert Allan Seavey. Meanwhile, Hounsfield was independently coming to conclusions similar to Cormack's, and developed the first CAT scanner as early as 1972.

In 1979 Cormack and Hounsfield were awarded the Nobel Prize for physiology or medicine for their joint, though independent, development of CAT scan theory and technology. At the time, their selection as recipients of the prize was considered highly unusual. Unlike previous Nobel recipients, neither Cormack nor Hounsfield held a doctorate in medicine or science; further, their discovery was awarded the prize only after the Nobel Assembly vetoed the first choice of the selection committee, reportedly due to a split between factions, with one side favoring discoveries in basic science and the other, those in applied science; and, finally, it was highly unusual that the two men had never met or worked together, yet had worked on the same invention concurrently.

In 1980, Tufts appointed Cormack to university professor, its highest professorial rank, and awarded him with an honorary doctoral degree. In 1990, as one of several scientists receiving the National Medal of Science, Cormack was recognized by President George Bush. Bush was quoted in the *New York Times,* lauding the group of scientists as "real life pioneers who press the very limits of their fields." Cormack is a member of the National Academy of Science and the American Academy of Arts and Sciences, and is a fellow of the American Physical Society.

Cormack is described by his friends as a man with a pungent sense of humor. His many hobbies and outside interests have included tennis, swimming, sailing, rock climbing, and music, and he remains avidly interested in astronomy.

SELECTED WRITINGS BY CORMACK:

Books

"The Development of Computerized Axial Tomography," anthologized in *Technology of Our Times: Technology and Innovation in Optics and Optoelectronics,* S.P.I.E., Washington, 1990.

Periodicals

"Representation of a Function by its Line Integrals with Some Radiological Applications," *Journal of Applied Physics,* Number 34, September, 1963, pp. 2722–2727.
"Representation of Function by its Line Integrals with Some Radiological Applications, Part 2," *Journal of Applied Physics,* Number 35, October, 1964, pp. 2908–2913.
(With J. N. Palmiere and D. J. Steinberg) "Small-Angle Scattering of 143-mev Polarized Protons," *Nuclear Physics,* Number 56, 1964, pp. 46–64.
(With M. W. Shapiro and A. M. Coehler) "Measurement of Cross Sections with Neutrons as Targets," *Physical Review,* Number 138, 1965, pp. 823–830.

SOURCES:

Periodicals

New Scientist, October 18, 1979, pp. 164–65.
The New York Times, October 12, 1979, p. 1; November 14, 1990, p. 22.
Physics Today, December, 1979, pp. 17–20.
Science, November 30, 1979, pp. 1060–1062.

—*Sketch by Mindi Dickstein*

John Cornforth
1917-
Australian-born English organic chemist

John Warcup Cornforth received the Nobel Prize for chemistry in 1975 for his research on the stereochemistry of enzyme-catalyzed reactions. The prize was shared with **Vladimir Prelog** for his work on the stereochemistry of organic molecules and reactions. Stereochemistry is a branch of chemistry that deals with the shapes, or architecture, of molecules and the way their three-dimensional structure affects chemical properties.

The study of stereochemistry is considered vital to understanding the organic world at its most basic biochemical level. It has been called a "point of view" in chemistry, which shows how things fit together at the molecular level and how they affect such fundamental aspects of life as taste and smell. It has been specifically in this area of chemistry that Cornforth has made his contributions.

Cornforth was born in Sydney, Australia, on September 7, 1917, to J. W. Cornforth and Hilda Eipper Cornforth. His undergraduate work was completed at Sydney University in 1938, and he took his doctoral degree at Oxford University in England, receiving a Ph.D. in 1941. At Oxford, he studied with Sir **Robert Robinson**, a 1947 Nobel Prize winner. During World War II, Cornforth worked with Robinson on the structure of penicillin as well as the problem of chemical synthesis in steroids, compounds that are principal to the structure of cells in plants and animals.

From 1946 until 1962, Cornforth worked for the National Institute of Medical Research at the Mill Hill Research Laboratories in London. During this association, he developed his technique for studying the stereochemical processes of enzymes, whereby he was able to show the pathways of biochemical processes. In 1962, he became the director of the Milstead Laboratory of Chemical Enzymology of Shell Research at Sittingbourne in Kent, an association that continued until 1975. By this time, besides winning the Nobel Prize, he had also received numerous other awards for his contributions to stereochemistry.

Cornforth also held some academic positions. He first served as an associate professor at the school of molecular science at the University of Warwick between 1965 and 1971. In 1971, he accepted the position of visiting professor at the University of Sussex, and in 1974, he became a permanent faculty member of the Royal Society as a research professor, remaining with the university until 1982.

Studies Biosynthesis of Steroids

Cornforth's early contributions were related to the synthesis and description of the structure of many natural products (including plant hormones) and olefins (which are synthetic and used in textiles). He continued his work with the biosynthesis of steroids, such as cholesterol, and was able to trace more than a dozen stereochemical steps in the biosynthesis of squalene, a precursor of cholesterol that is widely distributed in nature.

Cornforth's key contribution to stereochemistry was his development of a technique to label hydrogen isotopes to show how a molecule becomes synthesized within a cell. Cornforth was able to detail all the chemical steps that a cell goes through before it takes its final form. He accomplished this by tracing the steps taken by acetic acid to form cholesterol.

In addition to his early collaboration with Sir Robert Robinson, Cornforth collaborated with George Popják (for twenty years) and with Professor H. Eggerer of Munich. His most notable collaboration, however, was with his wife, Rita H. (Harradence) Cornforth, who also holds a doctorate from Oxford. She worked with Cornforth for decades, coauthoring with him an important article on squalene. Rita Cornforth was an invaluable link between Cornforth and his colleagues because he suffered from deafness (he had begun to lose his hearing when he was fourteen years old). By 1945, he depended completely on lip reading and on written communication. The Cornforths married in 1941, and they have three children: a son, John, and two daughters, Brenda and Philippa. Cornforth received numerous awards for his contributions to chemistry, including the Corday-Morgan and Flintoff Medals of the Chemical Society of London, the CIBA Medal, the Davy Medal of the Royal Society, and the Guenther Award of the American Chemical Society, and in 1977 he was knighted. He has held memberships in scientific academies in Australia, the United States, the Netherlands, Germany, and England throughout his scientific career. Cornforth detailed his work in a number of publications.

Cornforth excelled in numerous leisure activities, notably chess, which he played in a manner comparable to his method of solving a stereochemical process. He also played tennis well and enjoyed gardening.

SELECTED WRITINGS BY CORNFORTH:

Books

(With others) *The Chemistry of Penicillin,* Princeton University Press, 1949.

Periodicals

(With I. Youhotsky and G. Popják) "Absolute Configuration of Cholesterol," *Nature* 173, 1954, p. 536.

"Total Synthesis of Steroids," *Progress in Organic Chemistry* 3, 1955, pp. 1–43.

(With R. H. Cornforth and K. K. Mathew) "Stereoselective Synthesis of Squalene," *Journal of the Chemical Society,* 1959, pp. 2539–47.

"Absolute Stereochemistry of Some Enzymic Processes," *Biochemical Journal* 86, 1963, p. 7.

SOURCES:

Periodicals

Science 190, November 21, 1975, pp. 772–74.

—*Sketch by Jordan Richman*

Jean Coulomb
1904-
Algerian French geophysicist

Jean Coulomb, the most illustrious North African physicist of modern times, made important contributions to many scientific fields as a researcher, a teacher, and an administrator. His primary research focus was in seismology, and he made significant advances in the knowledge of earthquake propagation along the surface of the earth besides conducting research on microseismic disturbances, deep-focus earthquakes, and seismometry. Coulomb's work in meteorology and climatology led to the establishment of meteorological networks in North Africa. He was also an early investigator of terrestrial magnetism and became a pioneer in magneto-hydrodynamics.

Coulomb was born in Blida, Algeria, some 50 kilometers from Algiers. His father, Charles Coulomb, was a teacher of Greek and Latin at the local *collège* (secondary school), and his mother, Blanche d'Izalguier, was a teacher at a modernist middle school for girls. Coulomb attended his father's school and then the *lycée* (classical secondary school) at Algiers, when his parents were tranfered there. At the time Algeria was an integral political unit of France, and the Coulombs were servants of the French state educational authorities. They lived in a French cocoon, insulated from Algerians and Algerian concerns.

Coulomb completed secondary school at Marseilles, where his parents had once more been transfered. He took the national examinations for entering the most prestigious institutions of higher learning, succeeding brilliantly by gaining entry to both the Ecole normale supérieure and the Ecole polytechnique. Coulomb chose the Ecole normale. He graduated in 1926 (having also completed a university *licence,* or undergraduate diploma, in 1925). He then satisfied the national French military requirement by teaching in a military school at Metz. He obtained a scholarship from the Faculty of Sciences at the Sorbonne (the University of Paris) and began work toward a doctorate, which in France involves independent study leading to a dissertation. His material needs provided for by an independent source of funds, Coulomb looked about Paris for a congenial mentor. He settled on Marcel Brillouin, professor at the Collège de France (the old independent national institution that, because it required so few duties of its highly paid professors, stood at the pinnacle of French academia). In 1931 Coulomb defended his doctoral thesis on the propagation of seismic waves under Brillouin's tutelage.

Early Career

Upon graduation, the state educational authorities appointed Coulomb as an assistant physicist at the geophysical institute of the University of Clermont-Ferrand, which also administered an observatory on top of Puy-de-Dôme, a nearby mountain. The move was congenial, as Coulomb's wife (Alice Gaydier, whom he married in 1928, and with whom he had two sons and two daughters) had roots in the surrounding Auvergne. There Coulomb contributed to diverse geophysical projects, while at the same time completing individual, theoretical work in seismology. In 1938, his collaboration with the institute director Gaston Grenet netted them both the Victor Raulin Prize of the Paris Academy of Sciences. During his time at Clermont, Coulomb also collaborated with old schoolmates from the Ecole normale in founding the mathematical group known as Bourbaki. Coulomb's contribution concerned mathematical physics, and he withdrew from the group when the other members finally decided to devote themselves exclusively to pure mathematics.

In 1937 the directorship of the Algiers geophysical institute fell vacant, and Coulomb received the position. Coulomb's predecessor Albert Lasserre had established the institute—a part of the University of Algiers—as an important center for meteorology, and he had created a branch-observatory 2000 kilometers south of Algiers in the Sahara, at Tamanrasset. Coulomb greatly expanded the institute's geophysical programs. He also had the presence of mind to employ Albert Camus, another native-born Algerian of French descent who would win a Nobel Prize in literature, as a meteorological assistant. Coulomb's organizational activities bore increasingly meagre fruit as Europe prepared for a conflagration. By the summer of 1939 his staff had been drafted, and then he himself was also mobilized. The institute came under a caretaker administrator. With the fall of France, Coulomb returned to the institute briefly, also teaching at the Algiers agricultural institute.

Leadership Role in Research

In 1941 Coulomb became director of the Institute of Geophysics in Paris, replacing Charles Maurain who had watched over his career for a decade. During the German occupation, he saved the institute from probable dissolution. Coulomb continued to direct the institute until 1958, when he began four years as director general of the Centre National de la Recherche Scientifique, France's string of national research laboratories in the sciences and the humanities. Elected a member of the Paris Academy of Sciences in 1960 (he served as president in 1977 and 1978), he then presided over a number of organizations in the exact sciences, including the French Space Agency, the French Bureau of Longitudes (1966) and the International Union of Geodesy and Geophysics (1967). In 1972 he became vice-president of the International Council of Scientific Unions.

The honors and administrative responsibilities derived from Coulomb's magisterial command of geophysics—a unique mastery of the practial and the theoretical side of the discipline. His doctoral work on the theory of seismic surface waves (so-called Rayleigh waves) continued through his career, making him a world authority on earthquake propagation; to this he added research into microseismic disturbances, deep-focus earthquakes, and seismometry. General responsibilities for meteorology also resulted into research leading to general climatologies for Algeria, published by Coulomb's collaborators Paul Seltzer and Jean Dubief. His long years devoted to terrestrial magnetism made him a pioneer of magneto-hydrodynamics. Coulomb's sensitivity to the integrity of diverse cultures led him to organize a geophysical institute in Turkey during the middle 1950s.

SELECTED WRITINGS BY COULOMB:

Books

(With Julien Loisel) *La physique des nuages,* Albin Michel, 1940.

Titres et travaux scientifiques, Impriméries "La Typo-litho" et Jules Carbonel, 1941.

La constitution physique de la terre, Albin Michel, 1952.

A Course in Geophysics (translated into Turkish by Ihsan Ozdogan), Sirketi Murettibiye Basimevi [Istanbul], 1956.

(With G. Jobert) *Physical Constitution of the Earth,* Oliver and Boyd, 1963.

SOURCES:

Books

Pyenson, Lewis, *Civilizing Mission: Exact Sciences and French Overseas Expansion, 1830–1940,* Johns Hopkins University Press, 1993, pp. 114–126.

—Sketch by Lewis Pyenson

Richard Courant
1888-1972
German American mathematician

Richard Courant received worldwide recognition as one of the foremost organizers of mathematical research and teaching in the twentieth century. Most of Courant's work was in variational calculus and its applications to physics, computer science, and other fields. He contributed significantly to the resurgence of applied mathematics in the twentieth century. While the Mathematics Institute in Göttingen, Germany, and the Courant Institute of Mathematical Sciences at New York University stand as monuments to his organizing and fund-raising abilities, his numerous honorary degrees and awards, as well as the achievements of his students, testify to his noteworthy contributions to mathematics and other sciences.

Courant, the first of three sons, was born on January 8, 1888, in Lublinitz, a small town in Upper Silesia that was then German but later Polish. The family moved to Glatz when he was three; when he was nine they moved to the Silesian capital, Breslau (now Wroclaw). He was enrolled in Breslau's König Wilhelm Gymnasium, preparing to attend a university. At the age of fourteen, Courant felt a need to become self-supporting and started tutoring students for the high-school math finals, which he himself had not yet taken. He was asked to leave the school for this reason in 1905, and he began attending lectures in mathematics and physics at the local university. He passed the high-school finals later that year and became a full-time student at the University of Breslau. Unhappy with the lecture methods of his physics instructors, he began to concentrate on mathematics.

In 1907 Courant enrolled at the University of Göttingen to take courses with mathematician **David Hilbert**, a professor there. Soon Courant became an assistant to Hilbert, working principally on subjects in analysis, an area of mathematics with a close relationship to physics. Under Hilbert, Courant obtained his Ph.D. in 1910 for a dissertation in variational calculus.

Military Service

In the fall of 1910, Courant was called up for a year of compulsory military service, during which he became a noncommissioned officer. After Courant completed his tour of duty, Hilbert encouraged him to come back to Göttingen for the *Habilitation,* an examination that qualified him for a license as a *privatdozent,* an unsalaried university lecturer or teacher remunerated directly by students' fees. In 1912 Courant received his license to teach at Göttingen.

Two years of teaching and other mathematical work in Göttingen came to an abrupt halt when Courant received his orders to serve in the Army on July 30, 1914. The Kaiser declared war the next day. Courant, like many others, thought the war would be over quickly and was eager to serve. He believed that Germany's cause was right and that his country would be victorious. After about a year of fighting in the trenches, Courant was wounded and was subsequently deployed in the wireless communications department. Courant proposed that the use of mirrors to obtain visibility of what was going on above ground would help save lives. He also proposed the use of earth telegraphy, a means of communication that would use the earth as a conduit. Both ideas were utilized by the army.

Between the Wars

About two weeks after the Armistice, which was signed November 11, 1918, in the midst of tremendous political turmoil, Courant managed to sign a contract with Ferdinand Springer to serve as editor for a series of mathematics books. Courant had made the original proposal for this series to Springer a year earlier. He envisioned timely mathematical treatises that would be especially pertinent to physics. These yellow-jacketed books became known worldwide as the *Yellow Series,* and their publication continued after Courant resigned as editor.

Courant returned to Göttingen in December of 1918 and resumed teaching as *Privatdozent* in the spring of 1919. During the summer of 1919, he completed a lengthy paper on the theory of eigenvalues of partial differential equations (of importance in quantum mechanics). After teaching at the University of Münster for a year, he returned as a professor to Göttingen in 1920; in addition to teaching, he was expected to take care of the informal administrative duties of the mathematics department. During the period from 1920 to 1925, Courant succeeded in making Göttingen an international center of theoretical and applied mathematics. Courant's emphasis on applied mathematics attracted physicists from all over the world, making the university a hub of research in quantum mechanics. His tireless efforts as a researcher, teacher, and organizer finally resulted in

the creation of the Mathematics Institute of the University of Göttingen. Defining his vision of the future of mathematics, Courant said, "The ultimate justification of our institute rests in our belief in the indestructible vitality of mathematical scholarship. Everywhere there are signs to indicate that mathematics is on the threshold of a new breakthrough which may deepen its relationship with the other sciences and demand their mathematical penetration in a manner quite beyond our present understanding."

In the 1920s and 1930s, Courant worked with Hilbert on his most important publication, *Methoden der mathematischen Physik,* later translated into English as *Methods of Mathematical Physics.* The text was tremendously successful because it laid out the basic mathematical techniques that would play a role in the new quantum theory and nuclear physics. The Great Depression of the early 1930s created a need for university faculties to cut expenses, and there was an order to discharge most of the younger assistants. Courant successfully helped lead the fight of members of the mathematics and natural science faculty to pass a proposal that professors themselves pay the salaries of the assistants who were to be dismissed. He also helped students get scholarships and arranged for some to become part of his household to assist them financially. Those from wealthy families were encouraged to work without pay so that stipends could be available for needy students.

Courant took a leave of absence from Göttingen during the spring and summer of 1932 to lecture in the United States. His positions as professor and director of the Göttingen Mathematics Institute ended on May 5, 1933, when he and five other Göttingen professors received official word that they were on leave until further notice. The move reflected the National Socialist government's escalating campaign against German Jews as well as its displeasure with the university, which had become a locus of independent liberal thought. As Americans and other foreigners were leaving Göttingen at this time, Courant observed that the spirit of the institute had already been destroyed. During the 1933–1934 academic year he became a visiting lecturer at Cambridge in England. In January of 1934, he accepted an offer of a two-year contract with New York University.

New York Years

In 1936, when his temporary position ended, he was appointed professor and head of New York University's mathematics department. In that position, he did for New York University what he had done for Göttingen by creating a center of mathematics and science of international importance. In recognition of his work, Courant was made director of the new mathematics institute at New York University, later named the Courant Institute of Mathematical

Sciences. Courant's success as an organizer was largely due to his ability to attract promising young mathematicians. He was always available to them as a teacher, helped them to publish their work, and organized financial support for them if they needed it. His students often remained loyal to him for the rest of their lives and tended to stay in his orbit.

During World War II, Courant was a member of the Applied Mathematics Panel, which assisted scientists involved with military projects and contracted for specific research with universities throughout the country. While the group at New York University under contract with the panel made important contributions to the war effort, the contract in turn played a vital role in setting up a scientific center at New York University. Courant's mathematical work in numerical analysis and partial difference equations played a vital role in the development of computer applications to scientific work. Courant was also instrumental in getting the Atomic Energy Commission to place its experimental computer UNIVAC at New York University in 1953. Courant retired in 1958, the same year he was honored with the Navy Distinguished Public Service Award and the Knight-Commander's Cross and Star of the Order of Merit of the Federal Republic of Germany. In 1965, he received an award for distinguished service to mathematics from the Mathematical Association of America.

Married in 1912 to a woman he had tutored as an adolescent, Courant was divorced in 1916. In 1919 he married Nerina (Nina) Runge, and they had two sons and two daughters. He enjoyed skiing and hiking, and played the piano. In November of 1971, Courant suffered a stroke. He died on January 27, 1972, a few weeks after his eighty-fourth birthday. According to a *New York Times* obituary by Harry Schwartz, Nobel laureate in physics **Niels Bohr** once remarked that "every physicist is in Dr. Courant's debt for the vast insight he has given us into mathematical methods for comprehending nature and the physical world." At a memorial in Courant's honor, the mathematician Kurt O. Friedrichs said of him: "One cannot appreciate Courant's scientific achievements simply by enumerating his published work. To be sure, this work was original, significant, beautiful; but it had a very particular flavor: it never stood alone; it was always connected with problems and methods of other fields of science, drawing inspiration from them, and in turn inspiring them."

SELECTED WRITINGS BY COURANT:

Books

(With Herbert Robbins) *What Is Mathematics?,* Oxford University Press, 1941.

(With Kurt O. Friedrichs) *Supersonic Flow and Shock Waves,* Interscience Publishers, 1948.

Dirichlet's Principle, Conformal Mapping, and Minimal Surfaces, Interscience Publishers, 1950.

(With David Hilbert) *Methods of Mathematical Physics* (translation of *Methoden der mathematischen Physik*), 2 volumes, Interscience Publishers, 1953, 1962.

Differential and Integral Calculus, 2 volumes, Interscience Publishers, 1965, 1974.

(With Fritz John) *Introduction to Calculus and Analysis,* 2 volumes, Interscience Publishers, 1965, 1974.

Periodicals

"Objectives of Applied Mathematics Education," *Society for Industrial and Applied Mathematics (SIAM) Review,* Volume 9, 1967, pp. 303–05.

(With Friedrichs and Hans Lewy) "On the Partial Difference Equations of Mathematical Physics," *IBM Journal of Research and Development,* March, 1967, pp. 215–34.

SOURCES:

Books

Albers, Donald J., and G. L. Alexanderson, editors, *Mathematical People: Profiles and Interviews,* Birkhäuser, 1985.

Beyerschen, Alan D., *Scientists under Hitler: In Politics and the Physics Community in the Third Reich,* Yale University Press, 1977.

Courant Anniversary Volume: Studies and Essays Presented to Richard Courant on his 60th Birthday, Interscience Publishers, 1948.

Reid, Constance, *Courant in Göttingen and New York: The Story of an Improbable Mathematician,* Springer-Verlag, 1976.

Struik, Dirk, J., *A Concise History of Mathematics,* Dover Publications, fourth revised edition, 1987.

Periodicals

Journal of Mathematical and Physical Sciences, a Journal of the Indian Institute of Madras, March, 1973, pp. i-iv.

Schwartz, Harry, *New York Times,* January 29, 1972, p. 32.

Other

Friedrichs, Peter D. Lax, K. Müller, Karl-Friedrich Still, Richard Emery, Jerome Berkowitz, and James M. Hester, "Richard Courant,

1888–1972: Remarks Delivered at the Memorial, February 18, 1972, and at the Meeting of the Graduate Faculty, March 15, 1972," New York University.

Richard Courant in Göttingen and New York (video), The Mathematical Association of America, MAA Video Classics No. 4, 1966.

—*Sketch by Jeanne Spriter James*

André F. Cournand
1895-1988
French-born American physician

André F. Cournand shared the 1956 Nobel Prize in physiology or medicine with German surgeon **Werner Forssmann** and American physiologist **Dickinson Woodruff Richards, Jr.** for pioneering work in the field of cardiac and pulmonary physiology. Cournand helped develop the technique of cardiac catheterization, which permits blood samples to be obtained from the heart for determining cardiac abnormalities.

Cournand was born in Paris on September 24, 1895. His father, Jules Cournand, and his grandfather were both dentists. Cournand writes in his autobiography, *From Roots to Late Budding: The Intellectual Adventures of a Medical Scientist,* that his decision to study the sciences and medicine stemmed from his father's regrets of his own choice of dentistry over medicine. At age 15, young André began to accompany his parents to the salon of a physician friend where many internationally known scientists met and discussed issues of their day. Cournand's mother, Marguerite Weber Cournand, loved literature and learning and encouraged in her son a deep interest in philosophy and art, which Cournand maintained even while pursuing his medical studies and research.

In 1913, Cournand received his bachelor's degree from the University of Paris-Sorbonne, where he also began his medical studies in 1914. But in that year the first World War broke out, and many medical professors enlisted in the army. In the spring of 1915, Cournand decided to postpone his studies. In July of that year he joined a surgical unit that provided emergency care on the front lines. By 1916 he was trained as an auxiliary battalion surgeon and was serving in the trenches. He didn't return to medical school until 1919. After serving as an intern, he received his M.D. in 1930.

Begins Investigative Work in the United States

Cournand had decided to specialize in upper respiratory diseases and, delaying his entry into private practice, pursued further training in the United States. He joined a residency program at the Tuberculosis Service of the Columbia University College of Physicians and Surgeons at Bellevue Hospital in New York City. He stayed at Columbia for the remainder of his career, rising from his initial position as investigator to a full professor in 1951. He became a naturalized citizen of the United States in 1941.

At Bellevue Cournand began what would become a long collaboration with Dickinson W. Richards. Together, they investigated the theories of a Harvard physiologist, Lawrence J. Henderson, who had postulated that the heart, lungs, and circulatory system are a functional unit designed to transport respiratory gases from the atmosphere to the tissues in the body and back out again.

In order to study respiratory gases and their concentrations in the blood as it passed through the heart, samples of blood from the heart had to be obtained. At this time, there was no established technique for this task. Catheters—flexible tubes intended to introduce and remove fluids from organs—had been used for the past 100 years, but only in animal experiments. The safety of catheter use in humans was doubtful. But Cournand was aware that in 1929 a German scientist, Werner Forssmann, had dramatically demonstrated the safety of cardiac catheterization by performing it on himself. He had inserted a catheter into one of his arm veins and then threaded it into his right atrium. Cournand became convinced of the safety of catheterization after speaking with one of his professors in Paris who had also performed a type of catheterization on himself, and subsequently scores of others, without any problems.

The Bellevue team experimented on animals for four years, working to standardize the procedure and perfect the equipment they were convinced was necessary for their studies of the cardiac system. When at last cardiac catheterization was used to obtain a sample of mixed venous blood in humans, what could previously be only vaguely determined by clinical observation could be physiologically described. Cardiac catheterization not only allows for samples of mixed venous blood to be collected, but it also measures blood pressure in various parts of the cardiac circulatory system—the right atrium, the ventricles, and the arteries—and measures total blood flow and gas concentrations. In short, the functions of the heart and lungs can be fully specified through cardiac catheterization.

During World War II, Cournand led a team of physicians investigating the use of cardiac catheterization on patients suffering from severe circulatory shock resulting from traumatic injury. Obtaining physiological measurements of cardiac output in these patients helped identify the cause of shock—a fall in cardiac output and return. As a result of these findings, it was determined that the best treatment for shock was a total blood transfusion rather than simply replacing plasma, which had previously been used and was found to cause anemia.

After the war, Cournand applied the technique of cardiac catheterization to patients with heart and pulmonary diseases. The team continually worked to improve the technique and was able, at this time, to obtain simultaneous readings of blood pressure in the right ventricle and the pulmonary artery. This allowed for greater diagnostic accuracy of congenital defects as well as evaluations of treatment. Eventually these investigations led to increased understanding of acquired heart diseases and the relation between diseases of the lungs and cardiac function, thus opening up the field of pulmonary heart diseases.

Career Recognized

Cournand began to be recognized for his research in the mid–1940s, when he was invited to speak at and lead various conferences. In 1949 he won the Lasker Award, and in 1952 he was invited by the National Institutes of Health to screen grant applications for the Lung, Heart and Kidney Study Section. Cournand's increasing recognition culminated in the fall of 1956 when he was awarded the Nobel Prize. In 1958 he was elected to the National Academy of Science.

During his years of research, Cournand remained interested and involved in the arts. While still in Paris, he had become a follower of the modern art movement and was friends with such painters as Jacques Lipschitz and Robert Delaunay and such writers as Andre Breton. In 1924 he married Sibylle Blumer, a daughter of Jeanne Bucher, who was a prominent gallery owner in Paris. They were married until her death in 1959. In 1963 Cournand married Ruth Fabian, who died in 1973. He was married again, to Beatrice Bishop Berle, in 1975. He had four children, three daughters and an adopted son.

Cournand retired in 1964 and devoted the years until his death to the study of the social and ethical implications of modern science. He died on February 19, 1988, in Great Barrington, Massachusetts.

SELECTED WRITINGS BY COURNAND:

Books

From Roots to Late Budding: The Intellectual Adventures of a Medical Scientist, Gardner Press, 1986.

SOURCES:

Books

McGraw-Hill Modern Men of Science, McGraw-Hill, 1966, pp. 117–118.
Sourkes, Theodore L., *Nobel Prize Winners in Medicine and Physiology: 1901–1965,* revised edition, Abelard-Schuman, 1966.

—*Sketch by Dorothy Barnhouse*

Jacques Cousteau
1910-
French oceanographer

Jacques Cousteau is known worldwide through his television programs, feature-length films, and books, all of which have focused on the wonders and tragedies of the marine world. Through these films and publications, Cousteau has helped demystify undersea life, documenting its remarkable variety, its interdependence, and its fragility. Through the Cousteau Society, which he founded in the 1970s, he is still leading efforts to call attention to environmental problems, to reduce marine pollution, and perhaps most importantly, to bring lasting peace to the world.

Jacques-Yves Cousteau was born in St. André-de-Cubzac, France, on June 11, 1910, to Elizabeth Duranthon and Daniel Cousteau. At the time, the elder Cousteau worked as a legal adviser to American entrepreneur James Hyde, founder of the Equitable Life Assurance Society. In 1917, after a heated argument, Hyde fired Daniel and the family briefly fell on hard times, their problems compounded by the poor health of Jacques, who for the first seven years of his life suffered from chronic enteritis, a painful intestinal condition. In 1918, after the Treaty of Versailles, Daniel found work as legal adviser to Eugene Higgins, a wealthy New York expatriate. Higgins traveled extensively throughout Europe, with the Cousteau family in tow. Cousteau recorded few memories from his childhood; his earliest impressions, however, involve water and ships. His health greatly improved around this time, thanks in part to Higgins, who encouraged young Cousteau to learn how to swim.

In 1920 the Cousteaus accompanied Higgins to New York City. Here, Jacques attended Holy Name School in Manhattan, learning the intricacies of stickball and roller skating. He spent his summers at a camp on Vermont's Lake Harvey, where he first

Jacques Cousteau

learned to dive underwater. At age thirteen, after a trip south of the American border, he authored a hand-bound book he called "An Adventure in Mexico." That same year, he purchased a Pathé movie camera, filmed his cousin's marriage, and began making short melodramatic films.

During his teens, Cousteau was expelled from a French high school for "experimenting" on the school's windows with different-sized stones. As punishment, he was sent to a military-style academy near the French-German border, where he became a dedicated student. He graduated in 1929, unsure of which career path to follow. The military won out over filmmaking simply because it offered the opportunity for extended travel. After passing a rigorous entrance examination, he was accepted by the Ecole Navale, the French naval academy. His class embarked on a one-year world cruise, which he documented, filming everything and everyone—from Douglas Fairbanks, the famous actor, to the Sultan of Oman. After graduating second in his class in 1933, he was promoted to second lieutenant and sent to a naval base in Shanghai, China. His assigned duty was to survey and map the countryside, but in his free time he filmed the locals in China and Siberia.

In the mid–1930s, Cousteau returned to France and entered the aviation academy. Shortly before graduation, in 1936, he was involved in a near-fatal automobile accident that mangled his left forearm. His doctors recommended amputation but he stead-

fastly refused. Instead, he chose rehabilitation, using a regimen of his own design. He began taking daily swims around Le Mourillon Bay to rehabilitate his injured arm. He fell in love with goggle diving, marveling at the variety and beauty of undersea life. He later wrote in his book *The Silent World:* "One Sunday morning . . . I waded into the Mediterranean and looked into it through Fernez goggles. . . . I was astonished by what I saw in the shallow shingle at Le Mourillon, rocks covered with green, brown and silver forests of algae and fishes unknown to me, swimming in crystalline water. . . . Sometimes we are lucky enough to know that our lives have been changed, to discard the old, embrace the new, and run headlong down an immutable course. It happened to me at Le Mourillon on that summer's day, when my eyes were opened on the sea."

During his convalescence he met seventeen-year-old Simone Melchior, a wealthy high-school student who was living in Paris. After a one-year courtship, the couple married on July 12, 1937, and moved into a house near Le Mourillon Bay. The Cousteaus' first son, Jean-Michel, was born in March of 1938. A second son, Philippe, was born in December of 1939. Around this time, the new family's tranquil life on the edge of the sea was threatened by world events. In 1939 France began preparing for war, and Cousteau was promoted to gunnery officer aboard the *Dupleix.* The war was largely limited to ground action, however, and Germany quickly overran the ill-prepared French Army. Living in the unoccupied section of France enabled Cousteau to continue his experiments and allowed him to spend many hours with his family. In his free time, he experimented with underwater photography devices and tried to develop improved diving apparatuses. German patrols often questioned Cousteau about his use of diving and photographic equipment. Although he was able to convince authorities that the equipment was harmless, Cousteau was, in fact, using these devices on behalf of the French resistance movement. For his efforts, he was later awarded the Croix de Guerre with palm.

Undersea Work Leads to Development of the Aqualung

Although he loved diving, Cousteau regretted the limitations of goggle diving; he simply could not spend enough time under water. The standard helmet and heavy suit apparatus had similar limitations; the diver was helplessly tethered to the ship, and the heavy suit and helmet made Cousteau feel like "a cripple in an alien land," as cited in *Contemporary Authors New Revision Series.* A number of experiments with other diving equipment followed, but all the existing systems proved unsatisfactory. He designed his own "oxygen re-breathing outfit," which was less physically constrictive but which ultimately proved ineffective and dangerous. Also during this period he began his initial experiments with underwater filmmaking. Working with two colleagues, Philippe Taillez, a naval officer, and Frédéric Dumas, a renowned spearfisherman, Cousteau filmed his first underwater movie, *Sixty Feet Down,* in 1942. The eighteen-minute film reflects the technical limitations of underwater photography but was quite advanced for its time. Cousteau entered the film in the Cannes Film Festival, where it received critical praise and was purchased by a film distributor.

As pleased as he was with his initial efforts at underwater photography, Cousteau realized that he needed to spend more time underwater to accurately portray the ocean's mysteries. In 1937 he had begun a collaboration with Emile Gagnan, an engineer with a talent for solving technical problems. In 1942 Cousteau again turned to Gagnan for answers. The two spent approximately three weeks developing an automatic regulator that supplied compressed air on demand. This regulator, along with two tanks of compressed air, a mouthpiece, and hoses, was the prototype Aqualung, which Gagnan and Cousteau patented in 1943.

That summer, Cousteau, Talliez, and Dumas tested the Aqualung off the French Riveria, making as many as five hundred separate dives. This device was put to use on the group's next project, an exploration of the *Dalton,* a sunken British steamer. This expedition provided material for Cousteau's second movie, *Wreck.* The film deeply impressed French naval authorities, who recruited Cousteau to assist with the dangerous task of clearing mines from French harbors. When the war ended, Cousteau received a commission to continue his research as part of the Underwater Research Group, which included both Talliez and Dumas. With increased funding and ready access to scientists and engineers, the group expanded its research and developed a number of innovations, including an underwater sled.

In 1947 Cousteau, using the Aqualung, set a world's record for free diving, reaching a depth of 300 feet. The following year, Dumas broke the record with a 306-foot dive. The team developed and perfected many of the techniques of deep-sea diving, working out rigorous decompression schedules that enabled the body to adjust to pressure changes. This physically demanding, dangerous work took its toll; one member of the research team was killed during underwater testing.

Begins World Adventures Aboard *Calypso*

On July 19, 1950, Cousteau bought *Calypso,* a converted U.S. minesweeper. On November 24, 1951, after undergoing significant renovations, *Calypso* sailed for the Red Sea. The *Calypso* Red Sea Expedition (1951–52) yielded numerous discoveries, including the identification of previously unknown plant and animal species and the discovery of volcanic basins beneath the Red Sea. In February of 1952, *Calypso* sailed toward Toulon. On the way home, the crew investigated an uncharted wreck near the southern coast of Grand Congloué and discovered a large Roman ship filled with treasures. The discovery helped spread Cousteau's fame in France. In 1953, with the publication of *The Silent World,* Cousteau achieved international notice. The book, drawn from Cousteau's daily logs, was written originally in English with the help of U.S. journalist James Dugan and later translated into French. Released in more than twenty languages, *The Silent World* eventually sold more than five million copies worldwide.

In 1953 Cousteau began collaborating with **Harold Edgerton**, a pioneer in high-speed photography who had invented the strobe light and other photographic devices. Edgerton and his son, William, spent several summers aboard *Calypso,* outfitting the ship with an innovative camera that skimmed along the ocean floor, sending back blurry but intriguing photos of deep-sea creatures. The death of William Edgerton in an unrelated diving accident effectively ended the experiments, but Cousteau had already realized the limitations of such a method of exploring the ocean depths. Instead, he and his team began work on a small, easily maneuverable submarine, which he called the diving saucer, or DS–2. The sub has made more than one thousand dives and has been part of countless undersea discoveries.

In 1955 *Calypso* embarked on a 13,800-mile journey that was recorded by Cousteau for a film version of *The Silent World.* The ninety-minute film premiered at the 1956 Cannes International Film Festival, where it received the coveted Palme d'Or. The following year, the film won an Oscar from the American Academy of Motion Picture Arts and Sciences. In 1957, in part due to his film's success, Cousteau was named director of the Oceanographic Institute and Museum of Monaco. He filled the museum's aquariums with rare and unusual species garnered from his ocean expeditions.

Cousteau addressed the first World Oceanic Congress in 1959, an event that received widespread coverage and led to his appearance on the cover of *Time* magazine on March 28, 1960. The highly favorable story painted Cousteau as a poet of the deep. In April of 1961 he received the National Geographic Society's Gold Medal at a White house ceremony hosted by President John F. Kennedy. The medal's inscription reads: "To earthbound man he gave the key to the silent world."

Television Programs Bring Worldwide Recognition

After the White House ceremony, Cousteau appeared to be at the pinnacle of his career, but bigger things were still to come. During the early 1960s he and his crew participated in the Conshelf Saturation Dive program, which was intended to prove the feasibility of extended underwater living. The success of the first mission led to Conshelf II, a month-long project involving five divers. The Conshelf program and the DS–2 project provided material for the fifty-three-minute film *World without Sun,* which debuted in the United States in December of 1964.

Cousteau's first hour-long television special, "The World of Jacques-Yves Cousteau," was broadcast in April of 1966, with Orson Welles providing the narration. The program's high ratings and critical acclaim helped Cousteau land a lucrative contract with the American Broadcasting Company (ABC). The *Undersea World of Jacques Cousteau* premiered in 1968 and has since been rebroadcast in hundreds of countries. The program starred Cousteau and his sons, Philippe and Jean-Michel, and sea creatures from around the globe. The show ran for eight seasons, with the last episode airing in May of 1976. In 1977 the *Cousteau Odyssey* series premiered on the Public Broadcasting System. The new show reflected Cousteau's growing concern about environmental destruction and tended not to focus on specific animal species.

In the 1970s the Cousteau Society, a nonprofit environmental group that also focuses on peace issues, opened its doors in Bridgeport, Connecticut. By 1975 the society had more than 120,000 members and had opened branch offices in Los Angeles, New York, and Norfolk, Virginia. Eventually, Cousteau decided to make Norfolk the homebase for *Calypso.*

On June 28, 1979, Philippe Cousteau was killed when the seaplane he was piloting crashed on the Tagus River near Lisbon, Portugal. Philippe's death deeply affected Cousteau, who remains unable to talk about the accident or the loss of his son. Philippe was expected to eventually take command of his father's empire; instead, Jean-Michel was given increased responsibility for overseeing the Cousteau Society and his father's other ventures.

Finds New Outlet on Cable TV

In 1980 Cousteau signed a one-million-dollar contract with the National Office of Canadian Film to produce two programs on the greater St. Lawrence waterway. In 1984 the *Cousteau Amazon* series premiered on the Turner Broadcasting System. The four shows were enthusiastically reviewed, and called attention to the threatened native South American cultures, Amazon rain forest, and creatures who lived in one of the world's great rivers. The final show of the series, "Snowstorm in the Jungle," explored the frightening world of cocaine trafficking. In the mid–1980s "Cousteau/Mississippi: The Reluctant Ally" received an Emmy for outstanding information-

al special. In all, Cousteau's television programs have earned more than forty Emmy nominations.

In addition to his television programs, Cousteau continued to produce new inventions. The Sea Spider, a many-armed diagnostic device, was developed to analyze the biochemistry of the ocean's surface. In 1980 Cousteau and his team began work on the Turbosail, which uses high-tech wind sails to cut fuel consumption in large, ocean-going vessels. In spring of 1985 he launched a new wind ship, the *Alcyone,* which was outfitted with two 33-foot-high Turbosails.

In honor of his achievements, Cousteau received the Grand Croix dans l'Ordre National du Mérite from the French government in 1985. That same year, he also received the U.S. Presidential Medal of Freedom. In November of 1987 he was inducted into the Television Academy's Hall of Fame and later received the founder's award from the International Council of the National Academy of Television Arts and Sciences. In 1988 the National Geographic Society honored him with its Centennial Award for "special contributions to mankind throughout the years."

While some critics have challenged his scientific credentials, Cousteau has never claimed "expert" status in any discipline. His talents seem to be more poetic than scientific; his films and books—which include the eight-volume "Undersea Discovery" series and the twenty-one-volume "Ocean World" encyclopedia series—have a lyrical quality that conveys the captain's great love of nature. This optimism is tempered by his concerns about the environment. He has emphatically demonstrated, perhaps to a greater degree than any of his contemporaries, how the quality of both the land and sea is deteriorating and how such environmental destruction is irreversible.

SELECTED WRITINGS BY COUSTEAU:

Books

The Silent World, Harper, 1953.
(With James Dugan) *The Living Sea,* Harper, 1963.
Le Monde sans soleil, Hachette, 1964, English-language version edited by James Dugan, published as *World without Sun,* Harper, 1965.

SOURCES:

Books

Contemporary Authors New Revision Series, Volume 15, Gale, 1985, pp. 90–93.
Cousteau, Jean-Michel, *Cousteau's Papua New Guinea Journey,* Abrams, 1989.

Munson, Richard, *Cousteau: The Captain and His World,* Morrow, 1989.

—*Sketch by Tom Crawford*

Patricia S. Cowings
1948-
American research psycho-physiologist

Patricia S. Cowings

Patricia S. Cowings pioneered the use of biofeedback techniques to help astronauts cope with and avoid symptoms of motion sickness. Her career-long focus on the relatively new field of biological feedback enabled her to devise innovative techniques for teaching subjects how to suppress this illness. As an African American female working in a scientific field, Cowings has had to deal with and overcome multiple gender and racial barriers which have challenged her belief in herself and her determination. Her success to date, and her position at the National Aeronautics and Space Administration (NASA) Ames Research Center in California, indicate how much she has achieved.

Patricia Suzanne Cowings was born in New York City on December 15, 1948. Her father, Albert S. Cowings, owned a neighborhood grocery store, and her mother, Sadie B. Cowings, obtained an A.A. degree at the age of sixty-five, becoming an assistant teacher for the New York Board of Education. Cowings has three brothers, the oldest is a two-star general in the U.S. Army, another is a professional jazz vocalist, and the youngest is a professional disc jockey and musician.

By the age of eleven, Cowings had become interested in science and particularly in space. After high school, she pursued her interest in science and attended the State University of New York at Stony Brook and studied psychology. After receiving her B.A. in 1970 and graduating Cum Laude (while winning psychology honors), Cowings continued her graduate education in psychology at the University of California at Davis. In 1971 the university gave her its Distinguished Scholarship Award, and in 1973 she was awarded both her M.A. and Ph.D. degrees in psychology. That same year she received a National Research Council Post-Doctoral Associateship which enabled her to conduct research at NASA's Ames Research Center at Moffett Field, California, for two years.

Begins Career with NASA

Cowings's teaching career began at Stony Brook in 1968, where she was a Research Assistant in the Department of Psychology. She continued in the same position upon entering the University of California, Davis. From 1972 to 1975, she was a Graduate Research Assistant in its Department of Psychology. In 1987 she returned to teaching, accepting the position of Adjunct Associate Professor of Psychology at the University of Nevada at Reno. Since 1977 however, her full-time position has been at the Ames Research Center. It was during her graduate school years that Cowings first made contact with the National Aeronautics and Space Administration, serving in its NASA-Summer Student Program in both 1971 and 1972, and then working at Ames Research Center (1973–1975) after graduate school. After a two-year hiatus as a Research Specialist at the San José State University Foundation, Cowings returned to NASA in 1977 as a Research Psychologist and Principal Investigator in Ames' Psychophysiological Research Laboratory.

Cowings then began in earnest her research on what was called the "zero-gravity sickness syndrome." Once NASA had decided to fly a space shuttle and keep its astronaut crews in space for increasingly longer periods, this syndrome—similar to the more common motion sickness—became a real concern. Cowings was asked to devise a program that might help astronauts minimize these symptoms without drugs. She then designed twelve half-hour sessions in which astronauts were taught biofeedback techniques to prevent this sickness. Her program used fifty volunteers who were instructed how to monitor themselves and how to mentally raise their body temperature and to relax certain muscles at the onset of motion sickness. Sixty-five percent of those trained were able to suppress the symptoms completely, and eighty-five percent were at least able to improve their ability to withstand motion sickness. None of Cowings' control group of sixty volunteers (those who received no biofeedback training) could show any improvement over time.

Cowings' work was finally put to use in space during a September, 1992 Spacelab-J mission. During this eight-day flight of the space shuttle *Endeavour* which took aloft Japan's first astronaut, members of the crew wore a harness apparatus to monitor their ability to suppress the onset of motion sickness. Cowings is currently researching exercises to enable astronauts to maintain muscle strength while in zero gravity for extended periods of time. Cowings's research has been the subject of several Public Broadcasting System television programs. A member of the Aerospace Medical Association, the Society for Psychophysiological Research, the AAAS, the New York Academy of Sciences, and several other major organizations, she is also the recipient of several awards: the NASA Individual Achievement Award (1993), the Black United Fund of Texas Award (1991), and the Innovative Research Award of the Biofeedback Society of California (1990), among many others. She is married to William B. Toscano, a colleague at Ames with whom she has collaborated on many scientific papers, and they have a son, Christopher Michael Cowings Toscano.

SELECTED WRITINGS BY COWINGS:

Periodicals

(With W.B. Toscano) "The Relationship of Motion Sickness Susceptibility to Learned Autonomic Control for Symptom Suppression," *Aviation, Space and Environmental Medicine,* Volume 53, 1982, pp. 570–575.

(With Toscano, J. Kamiya, N. E. Miller, and J. C. Sharp) "Autogenic-Feedback Training as a Preventive Method for Space Adaptation Syndrome," *NASA Conference Publication #2429, Spacelab 3 Mission Science Review,* 1985, pp. 84–89.

"Autogenic-Feedback Training: A Preventive Method for Motion and Space Sickness," *Motion and Space Sickness,* CRC Press, 1990, pp. 354–372.

SOURCES:

Periodicals

Air Progress, December, 1980, p. 30.
Aviation Week and Space Technology, September 21, 1992, pp. 24-25.
Savvy, January, 1985, p. 16.
SciQuest, July/August, 1980, p. 4.

—*Sketch by Leonard C. Bruno*

Elbert Frank Cox
1895-1969
American mathematician

Elbert Frank Cox was the first African American to earn a Ph.D. in pure mathematics. Cox entered the teaching profession as a high school instructor and eventually rose to become the head of Howard University's mathematics department. In addition to his contributions to abstract mathematics, he made his mark as an educator by helping to craft Howard's grading system in 1947 and guiding scores of successful masters degree candidates in mathematics.

Cox was born in Evansville, Indiana, on December 5, 1895. He was the oldest of three boys born to Johnson D. Cox, an elementary school principal, and his wife, Eugenia D. Cox. Close knit and highly religious, the Cox family had a respect for learning that reflected Johnson's educational occupation. When young Elbert demonstrated unusual ability in high school mathematics and physics, he was directed toward Indiana University. While at Indiana, he was elected to undergraduate offices and joined the Kappa Alpha Psi fraternity. After graduation in 1917, Cox entered the U.S. Army as a private during World War I and was promoted to staff sergeant in six months. Upon discharge, he became an instructor of math at a high school in Henderson, Kentucky.

In 1920 or 1921 (sources vary) Cox joined the faculty of Shaw University in Raleigh, North Carolina, and left there two years later to attend Cornell University with a full scholarship. In the summer of 1925, when Cox graduated from Cornell with his Ph.D., he became the first black to earn such a degree in pure mathematics. This abstract and highly difficult field is largely concerned with mathematical theory rather than with practice or application. The title of Cox's dissertation demonstrates this point very well: "The Polynomial Solutions of Difference Equations of $(X-1)$ $6F(X)$ = Phi (x)."

In the fall of 1925, Cox became the head of the mathematics and physics department at West Virginia State College and remained there until 1929 when he joined the faculty of Howard University in Washington, DC. Cox became chair of the university's department of mathematics in 1947 and held that position until 1961 when a university rule mandated that all department heads resign at the age of 65. He remained as a full professor in the department until his retirement in 1966.

During his career Cox specialized in difference equations, interpolation theory, and differential equations. Among his professional accolades were memberships in such educational societies as Beta Kappa Chi, Pi Mu Epsilon, and Sigma Pi Sigma, and he was also active in the American Mathematical Society, the American Physical Society, and the American Physics Institute. He married Beulah P. Kaufman, an elementary school teacher, on September 14, 1927. They had three sons, James, Eugene, and Elbert. Cox died at Cafritz Memorial Hospital on November 28, 1969, after a brief illness.

SOURCES:

Periodicals *The Washington Post,* December 2, 1969, p. C6.

Other

Cox, James D., written biographical information provided to Leonard C. Bruno.

—Sketch by Leonard C. Bruno

Geraldine V. Cox
1944-

American biologist

Geraldine V. Cox, a biologist whose specialty is environmental science, is currently Vice President of Fluor Daniel, a subsidiary of Fluor Corporation. Her professional career has involved developing policy for the chemical industry in the fields of health and safety, water pollution, and hazardous waste management. She was granted a White House Fellowship in 1976, serving as Special Assistant to the Secretary of Labor.

Geraldine Anne Vang Cox is a native of Philadelphia, Pennsylvania, where she was born January 10, 1944. In 1970, she earned her doctorate degree in environmental sciences at Drexel University, where she had also completed her undergraduate studies and earned a master of science degree. She began her professional career at the Raytheon Company in 1970, where she served as Technical Coordinator of Environmental Programs until 1976. She then served as Special Assistant to the Secretary of the U.S. Department of Labor for one year.

Responds to Bhopal, India Disaster

In 1977, Cox joined the American Petroleum Institute as Environmental Scientist, a post she held until 1979, when she was named Vice President and Technical Director of Chemical Manufacturing Association. She held that position until 1991, when she joined Fluor Daniel as Vice President. Her contributions have reflected such specialties as marine and fresh water pollution, environmental health, and ecological damage assessment. Cox was responsible for establishing the chemical industry's guidelines for community emergencies following the explosion of a plant in Bhopal, India. The result in 1985 was the establishment of CAER (Community Awareness and Emergency Response), which led to the adoption of a federal law, and later an international standard drafted by the United Nations—both based on Cox's model. She also developed guidelines for epidemiology studies and other community and worker health and safety standards.

Cox has held various posts concurrently. She was a member of the Program Committee of the Water Pollution Control Federation from 1974 to 1979; she founded the Marine Water Quality Committee and chaired it from 1975 to 1980; she was a member of the National Academy of Sciences Environmental Measurement Panel of the National Bureau of Standards from 1977 to 1980.

During the 1980s, Cox chaired the U.S. Coast Guard's Marine Occupational Safety and Health Committee and was a member of the Transportation Advisory Committee, for which she received the Coast Guard Meritorious Public Service Award in 1991. She served on the American Chemical Society's Committee on Science, and was President of the Federation of Organizations for Professional Women from 1982 to 1984. Cox has received numerous other honors, including the Society of Women Engineers Achievement Award in 1984, "for her contributions in the field of environmental management, in particular water pollution." In addition, Cox has been a member of the American Society for Testing and Materials, the Water Pollution Control Federation, and the American National Standards Institute.

SELECTED WRITINGS BY COX:

Books

(Editor) *Oil Spill Studies: Strategies and Techniques,* American Petroleum Institute, 1977.

SOURCES:

Cox, Geraldine Ann Vang, interview with Karen Withem conducted March 24, 1994.

—Sketch by Karen Withem

Gertrude Mary Cox
1900-1978
American statistician

Gertrude Mary Cox organized and directed several agencies dedicated to research and teaching in statistics. "By her missionary zeal, her organizational ability and her appreciation of the need for a practical approach to the statistical needs of agricultural, biological and medical research workers she did much to counter the confused mass of theory emanating from mathematical statisticians, particularly in the United States, who had little contact with scientific research," eulogized Frank Yates in the *Journal of the Royal Statistical Society.*

Cox was born in Dayton, Iowa, on January 13, 1900, to John William Allen and Emmaline (Maddy) Cox. After graduating from Perry (Iowa) High School in 1918, she devoted several years to social service and training for the role of deaconess in the Methodist Episcopal Church. She spent part of that time caring for children in a Montana orphanage. By 1925, however, she had decided on different career goals. She entered Iowa State College in Ames, earning a B.S. in mathematics in 1929, and registered for graduate work under the direction of George Snedecor, a proponent of the research methods of British statistician and geneticist **Ronald A. Fisher**. Cox and Fisher became friends when he worked at Iowa State during the summers of 1931 and 1936. In 1931, Cox earned Iowa State's first M.S. degree in statistics. For the next two years, she worked as a graduate assistant at the University of California at Berkeley, studying psychological statistics.

Snedecor asked Cox to return in 1933 to work at Iowa State's new statistical laboratory, where she gained a reputation for expertise in experimental design. By 1939, she had become an assistant professor at Iowa State, although her teaching and consulting activities did not allow her time to write a doctoral dissertation. Eventually, in 1958, she was awarded an honorary doctor of science degree by Iowa State.

When Snedecor was asked to recommend nominees to head the new department of experimental statistics being formed at the North Carolina State College School of Agriculture, he showed his list to Cox, who asked why her name was not included. So he added a footnote to his letter: "'Of course if you would consider a woman for this position I would recommend Gertrude Cox of my staff,'" as quoted by R. L. Anderson in *Biometrics*. Cox was hired in 1940, becoming the first woman to head a department at North Carolina State.

In 1944, Cox assumed additional duties as director of the North Carolina State Institute of Statistics, which she had organized. By 1946, the University of North Carolina joined the institute, taking responsibility for teaching statistical theory while North Carolina State provided courses in methodology. Cox saw the institute's mission as developing strong statistical programs throughout the South.

Cox helped create the Biometrics Society in 1947 and edited *Biometrics Bulletin* and *Biometrics* from 1945 to 1955. In 1949, she became the first female member of the International Statistical Institute. Seven years later, she was elected president of the American Statistical Association. In 1950, Cox and her colleague William G. Cochran published *Experimental Designs,* which was intended to be a reference book for research workers with little technical knowledge; in fact, the work became a widely used textbook, which Yates described nearly thirty years later as "still the best practical book on the design and analysis of replicated experiments," as cited in the *Journal of the Royal Statistical Society*. In her own experimental design classes, Cox taught by focusing on specific examples gleaned from her years of consulting experience.

Cox played an integral role in planning what would become the Research Triangle Institute for consulting and research, uniting the resources of the University of North Carolina, North Carolina State, and Duke University. In 1960, she retired from North Carolina State and became the first director of Research Triangle Institute's statistics section. After retiring a second time in 1964, Cox spent a year in Egypt establishing the University of Cairo's Institute of Statistics. She had always loved world travel, making twenty-three trips to various international destinations. On five different occasions she worked on statistical assistance programs in Thailand. At age seventy-six, she toured Alaska and the Yukon Territory by bus, train, and boat.

Although she received numerous honors, including her 1975 election to the National Academy of Sciences, Cox was particularly pleased with the dedication of the statistics building at North Carolina State University as "Cox Hall" in 1970, and the establishment by her former students of the $200,000 Gertrude M. Cox Fellowship Fund for outstanding students in statistics at North Carolina State in 1977.

Cox died of leukemia on October 17, 1978, at Duke University Medical Center in Durham. During the preceding year, she had kept meticulous records of her treatment and response, making herself the subject of her final experiment.

SELECTED WRITINGS BY COX:

Books

(With William G. Cochran) *Experimental Designs,* Wiley, 1950, 2nd edition, 1957.

Periodicals

"The Multiple Factor Theory in Terms of Common Elements," *Psychometrika,* Volume 4, 1939, pp. 59–68.
"Enumeration and Construction of Balanced Incomplete Block Configurations," *Annals of Mathematical Statistics,* Volume 11, 1940, pp. 72–85.
(With William G. Cochran) "Designs of Greenhouse Experiments for Statistical Analysis," *Soil Science,* Volume 62, 1946, pp. 87–98.
(With W. S. Connor) "Methodology for Estimating Reliability," *Annals of the Institute of Statistical Mathematics,* Volume 16, 1964, pp. 55–67.

SOURCES:

Books

Grinstein, Louise S., and Paul J. Campbell, editors, *Women of Mathematics,* Greenwood Press, 1987, pp. 26–29.

Periodicals

Anderson, R. L., R. J. Monroe, and L. A. Nelson, "Gertrude M. Cox—A Modern Pioneer in Statistics," *Biometrics,* March, 1979, pp. 3–7.
Cochran, William G., "Gertrude Mary Cox, 1900–1978," *International Statistical Review,* April, 1979, pp. 97–98.
Cochran, William G., "Some Reflections," *Biometrics,* March, 1979, pp. 1–2.

Monroe, Robert J., and Francis E. McVay, "Gertrude Mary Cox, 1900–1978," *American Statistician,* February, 1980, p. 48.
Yates, Frank, "Gertrude Mary Cox, 1900–1978," *Journal of the Royal Statistical Society,* Volume 142, Part 4, 1979, pp. 516–517.

—*Sketch by Loretta Hall*

Donald J. Cram
1919-
American organic chemist

Organic chemistry underwent profound changes in the second half of the twentieth century, and one of the scientists responsible for these advances is Donald J. Cram. When he entered the profession in the 1940s, organic chemistry was primarily concerned with elucidating molecular structure and with synthesizing new molecules by mixing reagents with organic compounds by a method that was more or less ad hoc. The mechanisms of reactions were infrequently exploited in directing reactions towards a desired product. In the years after World War II reaction mechanisms attracted new attention; the exact three-dimensional details of how molecules combine to form products became known, and chemists realized that compounds of very specific shapes could be constructed. This was called stereochemistry, and it had valuable applications for the discipline of making molecules that make other molecules—that is, building compounds that can hold other compounds in a specific configuration, which in turn can lead to a specific reaction that would not otherwise have taken place. It was for his studies in this area, specifically his work in host-guest molecules, that Cram shared the Nobel Prize in 1987.

Donald James Cram was born April 22, 1919, in Chester, Vermont, the fourth child and only son of William and Joanna Shelley Cram, who had recently come from Ontario. The family moved to Brattleboro, Vermont, in 1921, and Cram's father died of pneumonia in 1923. Many years later, Cram recalled that this loss "forced me to construct a model for my own character that was composed of pieces taken from many different individuals; some being people I studied and others I lifted from books." He spent his childhood in Brattleboro, a curious, mischievous, bookish teenager who read through most of the standard classics but also played varsity sports. He supported himself and the family with a succession of odd jobs paid by barter, including dental work in exchange for lawn mowing; these taught him self-discipline, but convinced him that he did not want to spend his life in a job that was repetitive and uninspiring. In 1935, when he was sixteen, his family dispersed and he entered Winwood, a small, private school on Long Island, where he finished his high school studies in 1937.

Cram received a scholarship to Rollins College in Florida, where he earned his B.S. in 1941. The chemistry department at Rollins was small and underfunded, but it was here that Cram realized research could provide the ever new experience he had hoped to find in a career. He went on to receive an M.S. in chemistry at the University of Nebraska in 1942, and then spent the war years with Merck and Company, a pharmaceutical firm, in their penicillin program. Three years later, with a research fellowship and a strong recommendation from Merck's Max Tishler, he moved to Harvard University, where he received his Ph.D. under **Louis Fieser** in 1947. After a three-month postdoctoral stint with John D. Roberts at the Massachusetts Institute of Technology, Cram accepted an assistant professorship at the University of California at Los Angeles. He would remain here for the rest of his career, becoming a full professor in 1956 and Saul Winstein Professor of Chemistry in 1985.

Concentrates First Half of Career on Reaction Mechanisms

Cram's research divides chronologically into two sections. In the first phase, from 1948 to about 1970, he concentrated on reaction mechanisms. He conducted his first mechanistic study on the substitution reaction of a compound with two adjacent asymmetric carbon atoms (carbons with four different groups attached, arranged in a specific order in space). As the asymmetry was preserved during the reaction, it was clear that something prevented rotation of the carbon atoms on their common bond in the transition state. Cram proposed that they were held in place by what he named a phenonium ion, formed by a phenyl (benzene-ring) group on one of the carbons; he believed this acted as a bridge between them in the transition state. Cram adduced other evidence to support the existence of this new ion, and he carried this kind of study to other organic molecules. The implications of such studies were particularly important in biological systems, where the greater number of large molecules contain asymmetric carbons.

Cram then turned to elimination reactions with the same sort of compound, containing two adjacent asymmetric carbon atoms. In an elimination reaction, an atom or group is removed from each carbon, creating a double bond between them, and the adjacent asymmetric carbon atoms show how the remaining groups will be arranged on the resulting

double-bonded compound. He formulated his findings in what came to be called "Cram's rule." He went on to study many more molecules that formed a negative carbon atom in the transition state, and he showed that the associated positive ion could do many previously unsuspected things—including migrating to an adjacent carbon atom, or skating around a double-bond system and ending up on the other side of the carbon to which it was originally attached. At the same time that he performed his work on reaction mechanisms, Cram created and studied a new class of compounds, called the cyclophanes, in which two benzene rings are fastened together at each end by bridges of two or more carbon atoms. This brings the rings into close juxtaposition and also creates considerable angular strain.

Wins Nobel Prize for Investigations of Host-Guest Molecules

Eventually, Cram decided that his research was becoming repetitive—precisely the situation he had resolved to avoid many years before. At age fifty he turned to a new field, the investigation of host-guest molecules. For his first host molecules he chose the "crown ethers" that had been synthesized by **Charles John Pedersen** of DuPont Chemical's research laboratories. Crown ethers are cyclic compounds in which oxygen atoms recur regularly around the ring, spaced apart by two or more carbons. In some conformations the oxygen atoms stick up like the points of a crown; hence the name. These atoms, which are polar and possess unbonded electron pairs, can form complexes with a variety of positive or incipiently positive atoms or molecules.

The simplest of these crown-ether structures was already known to form complexes with potassium ions by turning its oxygen atoms into the center to form what Cram called a corand. He discovered that a corand can be used to separate potassium from other ions. By constructing other corands and basket-shaped molecules he called cavitands, with interiors of carefully controlled size, Cram was able to select out each of the alkali metal ions (lithium, sodium, potassium, rubidium, cesium) from solution with a high degree of specificity. This had important applications in analytical chemistry, particularly in medical and biological systems. Other cavitands were synthesized that looked less and less like crown ethers, except that they had oxygen or nitrogen atoms in their interiors for complexation. Cram extended these studies to organic molecules. A special asymmetric compound was devised that could form complexes with either right- or left-handed amino acids; this was worked into a continuous mechanical separator for these asymmetric molecules.

The ultimate goal of those working with artificial enzymes has long been to produce large molecules.

This has not yet been attained, but Cram's work has made great strides in this direction. For his research on host-guest molecules, he shared the 1987 Nobel Prize in chemistry with Pedersen and **Jean-Marie Lehn** of Strasbourg University. Cram delivered a lecture at the awards ceremony entitled "The Design of Molecular Hosts, Guests, and Their Complexes." Newspaper accounts emphasized the ramifications of his discoveries for both medical and industrial research, and it was observed that Cram had taught many of the chemists working on molecular recognition around the world.

Cram has co-authored an undergraduate textbook on organic chemistry, organized not by types of compounds (like nearly all other such works) but by types of reaction mechanism; it has gone through four editions and has been translated into thirteen languages. He also wrote another lower-level text, *Essence of Organic Chemistry,* with his second wife, Jane Maxwell Cram. These publications attest to his ongoing interest in undergraduate teaching. Cram's *Fundamentals of Carbanion Chemistry,* published in 1965, summarizes work in the field. In 1990, he produced the autobiographical *From Design to Discovery,* which contains relatively little personal information but is of great interest to chemists who want a review, with bibliography, of his research over four decades.

Other awards and honorary degrees have been presented to Cram in addition to the Nobel Prize. In 1974, he received the California Scientist of the Year award and the American Chemical Society's Arthur C. Cope Award. He was presented with the Richard Tolman Medal, the Willard Gibbs Award, and the Roger Adams Award, all in 1985. He also has received honorary doctorates from six institutions, including his undergraduate alma mater.

Cram has been married twice, first to Jean Turner from 1940 to 1968, and then in 1969 to Jane Maxwell, who is also a chemist. Both marriages have been childless. A man of abundant drive and energy, Cram spends his leisure time surfing and downhill skiing; he also sings folksongs and plays the guitar.

SELECTED WRITINGS BY CRAM:

Books

(With George Hammond) *Organic Chemistry,* McGraw-Hill, 1960.
Fundamentals of Carbanion Chemistry, Academic Press, 1965.
(With Jane Maxwell Cram) *Essence of Organic Chemistry,* Addison-Wesley, 1978.
From Design to Discovery, American Chemical Society, 1990.

Periodicals

"Molecular Cells, Their Guests, Portals, and Behavior," *CHEMTECH,* 1987, pp. 120–125.
"The Design of Molecular Hosts, Guests, and Their Complexes," *Angewandte Chemie, International Edition in English,* Volume 27, 1988, pp. 1009–1112.

SOURCES:

Books

James, Laylin K., editor, *Nobel Laureates in Chemistry, 1901–1992,* American Chemical Society, 1993, pp. 708–714.
Magill, Frank N., editor, *The Nobel Prize Winners: Chemistry,* Volume 3, Salem Press, 1990, pp. 1165–1176.

Periodicals

Peterson, Ivars, "Cages, Cavities and Clefts," *Science News,* August 8, 1987, pp. 90–93.

—*Sketch by Robert M. Hawthorne, Jr.*

Seymour Cray
1925-
American computer engineer

Seymour Cray is an electronics engineer and one of the founding fathers of the computer industry. His seminal work in computer design features the semiconductor as a component to store and process information. Cray's dense packing of hundreds of thousands of semiconductor chips, which reduced the distance between signals, enabled him to pioneer very large and powerful "supercomputers." Among his accomplishments was the first computer to employ a freon cooling system to prevent chips from overheating. However, Cray's most significant contribution was the supercomputer itself. Seeking to process vast amounts of mathematical data needed to simulate physical phenomena, Cray built what many consider the first supercomputer, the CDC 6600 (with 350,000 transistors). To such fields as engineering, meteorology, and eventually biology and medicine, the supercomputer represented a technological revolution, akin to replacing a wagon with a sports car in terms of accelerating research.

Seymour Cray

A maverick in both his scientific and business pursuits, Cray eventually started his own company devoted entirely to the development of supercomputers. For many years Cray computers dominated the supercomputer industry. A devoted fan of "Star Trek," a 1960s television show about space travel, Cray included aesthetically pleasing touches in his computers, such as transparent blue glass that revealed their inner workings.

Early Computer Innovations

Cray was born on September 28, 1925, in Chippewa Falls, Wisconsin, a small town situated in the heart of Wisconsin's dairy farm country. The eldest of two children, Cray revealed his talent for engineering while still a young boy, tinkering with radios in the basement and building an automatic telegraph machine by the time he was ten years old. Cray's father, a city engineer, and his mother fully supported his scientific interests, providing him with a basement laboratory equipped with chemistry sets and radio gear. Cray's early aptitude for electronics was evident when he wired his laboratory to his bedroom, and included an electric alarm that sounded whenever anyone tried to enter his inner sanctum. While attending Chippewa Falls High School, Cray sometimes taught the physics class in his teacher's absence. During his senior year, he received the Bausch & Lomb Science Award for meritorious achievement in science.

While serving in the U.S. Army during the final years of World War II, Cray utilized his natural gifts in electronics as a radio operator and decipherer of enemy codes. After the war, he enrolled in the University of Wisconsin, but later transferred to the University of Minnesota in Minneapolis, where he received his bachelor's degree in electrical engineering in 1950 and a master's degree in applied mathematics the next year. Cray began his corporate electronics career when he was hired to work for Engineering Research Associates (ERA). When Cray joined the company, it was among a small group of firms on the cutting edge of the commercial computer industry. One of his first assignments with ERA was to build computer pulse transformers for Navy use. Cray credited his success on the project to a top-of-the-line circular slide rule that enabled him to make a multitude of calculations needed to build the transformers. In a speech before his colleagues at a 1988 supercomputer conference, Cray recalled feeling "quite smug" about his accomplishment until he encountered a more experienced engineer working at the firm who told Cray that he did not use complicated slide rules or many of the other standard engineering approaches in his work, preferring to rely on intuition. Intrigued, Cray put away his slide rule and decided that he would do likewise.

For his next computer project, Cray and his colleagues developed a binary programming system. With the addition of magnetic core memory, which allowed Cray and his coworkers to program 4,096 words, the age of the supercomputer dawned. Although devoted to his laboratory work, Cray was also interested in the business side of the industry; his efforts to market ERA's new technology resulted in the Remington Rand typewriter company buying out ERA. With a formidable knowledge of circuits, logic, and computer software design, Cray designed the UNIVAC 1103, the first electronically digital computer to become commercially available.

Despite his growing success, Cray became dissatisfied with the large corporate atmosphere of ERA, which had been renamed the Sperry Rand Corporation. A friend and colleague, William Norris, who also worked at Sperry Rand, decided to start his own company, Control Data Corporation (CDC), and recruited Cray to work for him. Lacking the financial resources of larger companies, Cray and Control Data set out to make affordable computers. Towards this end, Cray built computers out of transistors, which he purchased at an electronics outlet store for 37 cents each. Although the chips were of diverse circuitry, Cray successfully replaced the cumbersome and expensive tubes and radio "valves" which were then standard in the industry.

Control Data began developing a line of computers like the CDC 1604, which was immensely successful as a tool for scientific research. Cray went on to develop the CDC 6600, the most powerful computer of its day and the first to employ freon to cool its 350,000 transistors. In 1969, the corporation introduced the CDC 7600, which many considered to be the world's first supercomputer. Capable of 15 million computations per second, the 7600 placed CDC as the leader in the supercomputer industry to the chagrin of the IBM corporation, CDC's primary competitor. Even with a legion of researchers, IBM was unable to match CDC's productivity, and eventually resorted to questionable tactics to overtake CDC, which eventually filed and won an antitrust suit against IBM. But as Control Data grew, so did its bureaucracy. As Russell Mitchell recounted in *Business Week,* Norris once asked Cray to develop a five-year plan. What Norris received in return was a short note that said Cray's five-year plan was "to build the biggest computer in the world," and his one-year plan was "to achieve one-fifth of the above." After developing the CDC 8600, which the company refused to market, Cray, in 1972, decided to leave CDC and set up his own company, Cray Research Corporation. Norris and CDC graciously invested $500,000 to assist Cray in his fledgling business effort.

The Supercomputer Emerges

Cray Research immediately set out to build the fastest supercomputer. In 1976 the CRAY–1 was introduced. Incorporating a revolutionary vector processing approach, which allowed the computer to solve various parts of a problem at once, the CRAY–1 was capable of performing 32 calculations simultaneously, outpacing even the best CDC computer. When the National Center for Atmospheric Research met the computer's $8.8 million price tag, Cray Research finally had solid financial footing to continue building faster and more affordable computers. For Cray, this meant manufacturing one product at a time, a radical approach in the computer industry. The first CRAY–2 was marketed in 1985 and featured a phenomenal 2-billion byte memory that could perform 1.2 billion computer operations per second, a tenfold performance increase over the Cray–1. Capable of providing computerized models of physical phenomena described mathematically, the CRAY computers were essential catalysts in accelerating research. For example, in such areas as pharmaceutical development, supercomputer modeling of a drug's molecules and its biological components eliminated much trial and error, reducing the time necessary to solve complicated mathematical equations.

In 1983, Cray turned his attention to developing gallium arsenide (GaA) circuits. Although the CRAY–2 was based on silicon chips, Cray continued to develop GaA chips in the spinoff Cray Computers Corporation. Although extremely difficult to work with because of their fragility, gallium arsenide computer chips marked a major advance in computer circuitry with their ability to conduct electrical impulses with less resistance than silicon. Adding even more speed to the computer, the GaA chip also effectively reduced both heat and energy loss.

While Cray's advances in computer technology enabled him to corner the market on the supercomputer industry for many years, the advent of parallel processing allowed others in the industry to make inroads into the same market. Utilizing hundreds of mini-computers to work on individual aspects of a problem, parallel processing is a less expensive approach to solving huge mathematical problems. Although Cray for many years denounced parallel processing as impractical, he eventually accepted this approach and made plans with other companies to incorporate it into his computer research and business.

Cray's first wife, Verene, was a minister's daughter. Married shortly after World War II, they had two daughters and two sons, who have characterized their father as a man intensely dedicated to his work; in fact, Cray demanded their absolute silence while traveling in the car so that he could think about the next advance in supercomputers. In 1975, Cray and Verene divorced, and he wed Geri M. Harrand five years later. Although he engaged in outdoor pursuits with his new wife, such as windsurfing and skiing, Cray remained devoted to his research. In 1972, he was awarded the Harry Goode Memorial Award for "outstanding achievement in the field of information processing." As Cray looked forward to the future of supercomputers, especially to the use of GaA computer chips, many experts in the field characterized his vision as impractical. Nonetheless, Cray's numerous conceptual breakthroughs in computer and information science have firmly established him as an innovator in computer technology.

SOURCES:

Books

Slater, R, *Portraits in Silicon,* MIT Press, 1989, pp. 195–204
Spenser, Donald, *Macmillan Encyclopedia of Computers,* Macmillan Publishing Company, 1992, pp.

Periodicals

Anthes, Gary H, "Seymour Cray: Reclusive Genius," *Computerworld,* June 22, 1992, p. 38.
Elmer-Dewitt, Philip, "Computer Chip Off the Old Block: Genius Seymour Cray and the Company He Founded Split Up," *Time,* May 29, 1989, p. 70.

Krepchin, Ira, "Datamation 100 North American Profiles," *Datamation,* June 15, 1993, p. 81.
Mitchell, Russell, "The Genius," *Business Week,* April 30, 1990, pp. 80–88.

—*Sketch by David Petechuk*

Francis Crick
1916-
English molecular biologist

Francis Crick

Francis Crick is one half of the famous pair of molecular biologists who unraveled the mystery of the structure of deoxyribonucleic acid (DNA), carrier of genetic information, thus ushering in the modern era of molecular biology. Since this fundamental discovery, Crick has made significant contributions to the understanding of the genetic code and gene action, as well as of molecular neurobiology. In Horace Judson's book *The Eighth Day of Creation,* the Nobel laureate **Jacques Lucien Monod** is quoted as saying, "No one man created molecular biology. But Francis Crick dominates intellectually the whole field. He knows the most and understands the most." Crick shared the Nobel Prize in medicine in 1962 with **James Watson** and **Maurice Wilkins** for the elucidation of the structure of DNA.

Before the Double Helix

The eldest of two sons, Francis Harry Compton Crick was born to Harry Crick and Anne Elizabeth Wilkins on June 8, 1916, in Northampton, England. His father and uncle ran a shoe and boot factory. He attended grammar school in Northampton, and was an enthusiastic experimental scientist at an early age, producing the customary number of youthful chemical explosions. As a schoolboy, he won a prize for collecting wildflowers. In his autobiography, *What Mad Pursuit,* Crick describes how, along with his brother, he "was mad about tennis," but not much interested in other sports and games. At the age of fourteen, he obtained a scholarship to Mill Hill School in North London. Four years later, at eighteen, he entered University College, London. At the time of his matriculation, his parents had moved from Northampton to Mill Hill, and this allowed Crick to live at home while attending university. He obtained a second-class honours degree in physics, with additional work in mathematics, in three years. In his autobiography, Crick writes of his education in a rather light-hearted way. He feels that his background

in physics and mathematics was sound, but quite classical, while he says that he learned and understood very little in the field of chemistry. Like many of the physicists who became the first molecular biologists and who began their careers around the end of World War II, Crick read and was impressed by **Erwin Schrödinger**'s book *What Is Life?,* but later recognized its limitations in its neglect of chemistry. Nonetheless, it is clear that Crick read widely and grasped the essence of the argument and logic of what he read.

Following his undergraduate studies, Crick conducted research on the viscosity of water under pressure at high temperatures, under the direction of Edward Neville da Costa Andrade, at University College. It was during this period that he was helped financially by his uncle, Arthur Crick. In 1940, Crick was given a civilian job at the Admiralty, eventually working on the design of mines used to destroy shipping. Early in the year, Crick married Ruth Doreen Dodd. Their son Michael was born during an air raid on London on November 25, 1940. By the end of the war, Crick was assigned to scientific intelligence at the British Admiralty Headquarters in Whitehall to design weapons.

Realizing that he would need additional education to satisfy his desire to do fundamental research, Crick decided to work toward an advanced degree. Surprisingly, he found himself fascinated with two areas of biology, particularly, as he describes it in his autobiography, by "the borderline between the living and the nonliving, and the workings of the brain." He chose the former area as his field of study, despite the fact that he knew little about either subject. After preliminary inquiries at University College, Crick settled on a program at the Strangeways Laboratory in Cambridge under the direction of Arthur Hughes in 1947, to work on the physical properties of cytoplasm in cultured chick fibroblast cells. Two years later, he joined the Medical Research Council Unit at the Cavendish Laboratory, ostensibly to work on protein structure with British chemists **Max Perutz** and **John Kendrew** (both future Nobel Prize laureates), but eventually to work on the structure of DNA with Watson.

The Double Helix

In 1947, Crick divorced Doreen, and in 1949 married Odile Speed, an art student whom he had met during the war, when she was a naval officer and Crick was working for the admiralty. Their marriage coincided with the start of Crick's Ph.D. thesis work on the x-ray diffraction of proteins. X-ray diffraction is a technique for studying the crystalline structure of molecules, permitting investigators to determine elements of three-dimensional structure. In this technique, x rays are directed at a compound, and the subsequent scattering of the x-ray beam reflects the molecule's configuration on a photographic plate.

In 1941 the Cavendish Laboratory where Crick worked was under the direction of physicist Sir **William Lawrence Bragg**, who had originated the x-ray diffraction technique forty years before. Perutz had come to the Cavendish to apply Bragg's methods to large molecules, particularly proteins. In 1951, Crick was joined at the Cavendish by James Watson, a visiting American who had been trained by Italian physician **Salvador Edward Luria** and was a member of the Phage Group, a group of physicists who studied bacterial viruses (known as bacteriophages, or simply phages). Like his phage colleagues, Watson was interested in discovering the fundamental substance of genes and thought that unraveling the structure of DNA was the most promising solution. The informal partnership between Crick and Watson developed, according to Crick, because of their similar "youthful arrogance" and similar thought processes. It was also clear that their experiences complemented one another. By the time of their first meeting, Crick had taught himself a great deal about x-ray diffraction and protein structure, while Watson had become well informed about phage and bacterial genetics.

Both Crick and Watson were aware of the work of biochemists Maurice Wilkins and **Rosalind Franklin** at King's College, London, who were using x-ray diffraction to study the structure of DNA. Crick, in particular, urged the London group to build models,

much as American chemist **Linus Pauling** had done to solve the problem of the alpha helix of proteins. Pauling, the father of the concept of the chemical bond, had demonstrated that proteins had a three-dimensional structure and were not simply linear strings of amino acids. Wilkins and Franklin, working independently, preferred a more deliberate experimental approach over the theoretical, model-building scheme used by Pauling and advocated by Crick. Thus, finding the King's College group unresponsive to their suggestions, Crick and Watson devoted portions of a two-year period discussing and arguing about the problem. In early 1953, they began to build models of DNA.

Using Franklin's x-ray diffraction data and a great deal of trial and error, they produced a model of the DNA molecule that conformed both to the London group's findings and to the data of Austrian-born American biochemist **Erwin Chargaff**. In 1950 Chargaff had demonstrated that the relative amounts of the four nucleotides (or "bases") that make up DNA conformed to certain rules, one of which was that the amount of adenine (A) was always equal to the amount of thymine (T), and the amount of guanine (G) was always equal to the amount of cytosine (C). Such a relationship suggests pairings of A and T, and G and C, and refutes the idea that DNA is nothing more than a "tetranucleotide," that is, a simple molecule consisting of all four bases.

During the spring and summer of 1953, Crick and Watson wrote four papers about the structure and the supposed function of DNA, the first of which appeared in the journal *Nature* on April 25. This paper was accompanied by papers by Wilkins, Franklin, and their colleagues, presenting experimental evidence that supported the Watson-Crick model. Watson won the coin toss that placed his name first in the authorship, thus forever institutionalizing this fundamental scientific accomplishment as "Watson-Crick."

The first paper contains one of the most remarkable sentences in scientific writing: "It has not escaped our notice that the specific pairing we have postulated immediately suggests a possible copying mechanism for the genetic material." This conservative statement (it has been described as "coy" by some observers) was followed by a more speculative paper in *Nature* about a month later that more clearly argued for the fundamental biological importance of DNA. Both papers were discussed at the 1953 Cold Spring Harbor Symposium, and the reaction of the developing community of molecular biologists was enthusiastic. Within a year, the Watson-Crick model began to generate a broad spectrum of important research in genetics.

The Genetic Code

Over the next several years, Crick began to examine the relationship between DNA and the genetic code. One of his first efforts was a collaboration with Vernon Ingram, which led to Ingram's 1956 demonstration that sickle cell hemoglobin differed from normal hemoglobin by a single amino acid. Ingram's research presented evidence that a "molecular genetic disease," caused by a Mendelian mutation, could be connected to a DNA-protein relationship. The importance of this work to Crick's thinking about the function of DNA cannot be underestimated. It established the first function of "the genetic substance" in determining the specificity of proteins.

About this time, South African-born English geneticist and molecular biologist **Sydney Brenner** joined Crick at the Cavendish Laboratory. They began to work on "the coding problem," that is, how the sequence of DNA bases would specify the amino acid sequence in a protein. This work was first presented in 1957, in a paper given by Crick to the Symposium of the Society for Experimental Biology and entitled "On Protein Synthesis." Judson states in *The Eighth Day of Creation* that "the paper permanently altered the logic of biology." While the events of the transcription of DNA and the synthesis of protein were not clearly understood, this paper succinctly states "The Sequence Hypothesis . . . assumes that the specificity of a piece of nucleic acid is expressed solely by the sequence of its bases, and that this sequence is a (simple) code for the amino acid sequence of a particular protein." Further, Crick articulated what he termed "The Central Dogma" of molecular biology, "that once 'information' has passed into protein, it cannot get out again. In more detail, the transfer of information from nucleic acid to nucleic acid, or from nucleic acid to protein may be possible, but transfer from protein to protein, or from protein to nucleic acid is impossible." In this important theoretical paper, Crick establishes not only the basis of the genetic code but predicts the mechanism for protein synthesis. The first step, transcription, would be the transfer of information in DNA to ribonucleic acid (RNA), and the second step, translation, would be the transfer of information from RNA to protein. Hence, to use the language of the molecular biologists, the genetic message is "transcribed" to a messenger, and that message is eventually "translated" into action in the synthesis of a protein.

A few years later, American geneticist **Marshall Warren Nirenberg** and others discovered that the nucleic acid sequence U-U-U (polyuracil) encodes for the amino acid phenylalanine, and thus began the construction of the DNA/RNA dictionary. By 1966, the DNA triplet code for twenty amino acids had been worked out by Nirenberg and others, along with details of protein synthesis and an elegant example of the control of protein synthesis by French geneticist **François Jacob**, Arthur Pardée, and French biochemist Jacques Lucien Monod. Brenner and Crick themselves turned to problems in developmental biology in the 1960s, eventually studying the structure and possible function of histones, the class of proteins associated with chromosomes.

The Salk Institute

In 1976, while on sabbatical from the Cavendish, Crick was offered a permanent position at the Salk Institute for Biological Studies in La Jolla, California. He accepted an endowed chair as Kieckhefer Professor and has been at the Salk Institute ever since. At the Salk Institute, Crick began to study the workings of the brain, a subject that he had been interested in from the beginning of his scientific career. While his primary interest was consciousness, he attempted to approach this subject through the study of vision. He published several speculative papers on the mechanisms of dreams and of attention, but, as he stated in his autobiography, "I have yet to produce any theory that is both novel and also explains many disconnected experimental facts in a convincing way."

An interesting footnote to Crick's career at the Salk Institute was his proposal of the idea of "directed panspermia." Along with Leslie Orgel, he published a book, *Life Itself,* which suggested that microbes drifted through space, eventually reaching Earth and "seeding" it, and that this dispersal event has been caused by the action of "someone." Crick himself was ambivalent about the theory, but he and Orgel proposed it as an example of how a speculative theory might be presented.

During his career as an energetic theorist of modern biology, Francis Crick has accumulated, refined, and synthesized the experimental work of others, and has brought his unusual insights to fundamental problems in science. There is probably no better description of Crick's intellectual gifts than that of François Jacob, who, in his book *The Statue Within,* describes Crick's famous paper "On Protein Synthesis" by noting, "On this difficult subject, Crick was dazzling. He had the gift of going straight to the crux of the matter and ignoring the rest. Of extracting from the hodge-podge of the literature, the solid and the relevant, while rejecting the soft and the vague."

SELECTED WRITINGS BY CRICK:

Books

Of Molecules and Men, University of Washington Press, 1966.
(With Leslie Orgel) *Life Itself,* Simon & Schuster, 1981.
What Mad Pursuit: A Personal View of Scientific Discovery, Basic Books, 1988.
The Astonishing Hypothesis: The Scientific Search for the Soul, Scribner, 1994.

Periodicals

(With James D. Watson) "A Structure for Deoxyribonucleic Acid," *Nature,* Volume 171, 1953, pp. 737–738.

(With James D. Watson) "Genetical Implications of the Structure of Deoxyribonucleic Acid," *Nature,* Volume 171, 1953, pp. 964–967.

"On Protein Synthesis," *Symposium of the Society for Experimental Biology,* Volume 12, 1957, pp. 138–163.

"The Genetic Code—-Yesterday, Today, and Tomorrow," *Cold Spring Harbor Symposium of Quantitative Biology,* Volume 31, 1966, pp. 3–9.

SOURCES:

Books

Jacob, François, *The Statue Within,* Basic Books, 1988.

Judson, Horace Freeland, *The Eighth Day of Creation,* Simon & Schuster, 1979.

Olby, Robert, *The Path to the Double Helix,* Macmillan, 1974.

Sayre, Anne, *Rosalind Franklin & DNA,* Norton, 1978.

Stent, Gunther, *Paradoxes of Progress,* Freeman, 1978.

Watson, James D., *The Double Helix: A Personal Account of the Discovery of the Structure of DNA,* Atheneum, 1978.

—Sketch by **Russell Aiuto**

James W. Cronin
1931-
American physicist

Once regarded as inviolate and a fundamental part of physical laws, symmetry and conservation laws—ideas stating that the amount of such qualities as charge, energy, or matter of a substance are not altered by internal changes or reactions—first came into question as a result of theoretical suggestions made by physicists **Tsung-Dao Lee** and **Chen Ning Yang** in the mid–1950s. Through the analysis of certain reactions that violate basic symmetry rules involving elementary particles, physicist James W. Cronin and his colleague, **Val Logsdon Fitch**, in 1964

showed the violation of symmetry and conservation laws to be more far-reaching than even Lee and Yang had suspected. Cronin interpreted his observations of CP (charge conjugation and parity) violations as "a cryptic message from nature that will be deciphered." For their discovery, Cronin and Fitch were jointly awarded the 1980 Nobel Prize in physics.

James Watson Cronin was born in Chicago, Illinois, on September 29, 1931, to James Farley Cronin, a graduate student in classical languages at the University of Chicago, and the former Dorothy Watson. After receiving his degree, the senior Cronin moved his family briefly to Alabama before settling in Dallas, Texas, where he taught Greek and Latin at Southern Methodist University (SMU). The younger Cronin attended local public elementary and high schools before enrolling as a physics major at SMU in 1947. He received his B.S. four years later, then began graduate studies at the University of Chicago, earning a master's degree in 1953. The completion of his doctoral studies led to a Ph.D. in 1955. At Chicago, Cronin was especially influenced by the work of **Murray Gell-Mann**, Nobel Prize winner in 1969 for his development of a classification system of elementary particles according to a quality called strangeness.

After graduating from Chicago, Cronin accepted a job as a research physicist at the Brookhaven National Laboratory on Long Island. His work at Brookhaven made use of one of the world's most powerful accelerators, the 3-billion electron volt cosmotron. During his three years at Brookhaven, Cronin also made the acquaintance of Val Fitch, who eventually invited Cronin to join him at Princeton University. Cronin accepted the offer and was appointed assistant professor of physics at Princeton in the fall of 1958.

Attacks the Question of CP Symmetry

At Princeton, Cronin became involved in the research that was to win him and Fitch the 1980 Nobel Prize in physics. The roots of that research go back to a classic experiment suggested in 1956 by Tsung-Dao Lee and Chen Ning Yang on the conservation of parity during certain nuclear reactions. One of the most fundamental laws in which physicists believed in the mid-twentieth century was the principle of conservation. Students of high school physics are familiar with laws dealing with the conservation of mass, energy, conservation, charge, momentum, and other qualities. Such laws state that there is a symmetry between the amount of each property prior to and following any change in a system. In 1956, Lee and Yang found reason to believe that a property known as parity (P)—a kind of "left-handedness" versus "right-handedness"—is not conserved in some types of nuclear changes. Reactions might be possible, they said, in which an excess of left-handed or right-handed particles might be observed. Shortly after this theory was announced, another researcher, **Chien-Shiung Wu**, found the precise violation of parity anticipated.

This revolutionary discovery raised a number of new issues for theoretical physicists. Was it possible, they asked, that other types of symmetry could also be violated? Were there ways of "explaining away" the failure of parity symmetry in the Wu experiment? Lee and Yang themselves suggested one such system. Perhaps it is possible, they said, that the combination of parity and another property, charge conjugation (C), is conserved even if each alone is not. The term charge conjugation refers to the balance between positively- and negatively-charged particles in a reaction. Specifically, the combination CP might remain symmetrical, Lee and Yang said, even if neither C nor P did in a particular reaction.

In June and July of 1963, Cronin and Fitch began a series of experiments that eventually found evidence for the concept of CP violation. The original purpose of these experiments was somewhat more modest, namely to investigate the behavior of elementary particles known as neutral K-mesons. The investigators were interested in knowing more about the process by which a beam of neutral K-mesons can be separated into two parts, one consisting of short-lived neutral K-mesons that decay into two pi-mesons and another consisting of long-lived neutral K-mesons that decay into three pi-mesons.

Chance and Hard Work Lead to Nobel Prize

The kind of experiments conducted by Cronin and Fitch in 1964 would in later decades be able to be analyzed at lightning speed by computers. At the time, however, the process was much more laborious, involving the careful, frame-by-frame study of dozens of rolls of film taken in spark chambers. Only six months after the process had begun and the primary focus of the research on neutral K-meson decay had been completed did Cronin and Fitch suddenly realize that they also had evidence for violation of CP conservation. Ultimately they found 45 examples of CP violation in more than 23,000 frames studied. Yet to assure they were correct, Cronin and Fitch spent another six months looking for alternative explanations of their findings. Discovering none, they announced their results in *Physical Review Letters* on July 27, 1964. For their work, they were jointly awarded the 1980 Nobel Prize in physics. The significance of the Cronin-Fitch research has been explained by a theorist quoted in the November 7, 1980, *Science* report of the 1980 Nobel Prize winners. "The old [prejudice in favor of symmetry] is dying out," he said. "You used to have to explain why when if fails. Now you have to explain why it is respected."

Cronin remained at Princeton after his award-winning work, having become associate professor in 1962 and then full professor in 1964. In 1971, he left Princeton to accept an appointment as professor of physics at the University of Chicago. In addition to his Nobel Prize, Cronin has been awarded the Research Corporation Award in 1968, the John Price Wetherill Medal of the Franklin Institute in 1975, and the Ernest O. Lawrence Award in 1977. Cronin was married to the former Annette Martin, a classmate at the University of Chicago, on September 11, 1954. They have a son, David, and two daughters, Emily and Cathryn.

SELECTED WRITINGS BY CRONIN:

Periodicals

"Experimental Status of CP Violation," *AEC Accession Number 19428, Report Number ANL–7130*, 1965, pp. 17–28.
"Weak Interactions and CP Violation-Experimental," *Proceedings of the 14th International Conference on High Energy Physics*, 1968, pp. 281–303.

SOURCES:

Books

Nobel Prize Winners, H. W. Wilson, 1987, pp. 232–234.
Weber, Robert L., *Pioneers of Science: Nobel Prize Winners in Physics*, American Institute of Physics, 1980, pp. 267–268.

Periodicals

"Fitch and Cronin Share Nobel Prize for CP Violation," *Physics Today*, December 1980, pp. 17–19.
Robinson, Arthur L., "1980 Nobel Prize in Physics to Cronin and Fitch," *Science*, November 7, 1980, pp. 619–621.

—Sketch by David E. Newton

Elizabeth Caroline Crosby
1888-1983
American neuroanatomist

Elizabeth Caroline Crosby was the first woman to be appointed a full professor at the University of Michigan's medical school. Her descriptive studies of reptilian and other vertebrate brains provided insight into their evolutionary history and helped lay the foundation for the science of comparative neuroanatomy. During a career spanning more than six decades, Crosby made important contributions to the male-dominated areas of science and medicine. Between 1920 and 1958 she taught neuroanatomy to an estimated 8,500 students and became known as the "angel of the medical school." Following her official retirement, Crosby continued her energetic pace, applying her comprehensive knowledge of the human brain to help neurosurgeons map brain surgery.

Crosby was born in Petersburg, Michigan, on October 25, 1888, the only child of Lewis Frederick and Frances Kreps Crosby. In the log house on their homestead, Crosby read adult books before she went to school. When she graduated from high school, her father promised her four years of college as a graduation present. Majoring in mathematics at nearby Adrian College, she completed the four-year program in three years, graduating in 1910. With one year left of her father's gift, she applied to C. Judson Herrick's anatomy program at the University of Chicago. At that time her only background for the course was one undergraduate course in zoology. Crosby was a diligent student. She stayed so late in the laboratory studying that, at one point, Herrick took away her key to force her to get some rest. When he saw her making her way home with her heavy reference books, microscope, and box of slides in her arms, however, he returned the key.

She received a master's degree in 1912 and was given a fellowship in the anatomy department. Her Ph.D. degree followed in 1915, and her dissertation, *The Forebrain of Alligator mississippiensis,* became an influential work. Prior to Crosby's study, little was known about reptilian brains. In 1918, Crosby and Herrick published *A Laboratory Outline of Neurology* with detailed instructions for brain dissection. Throughout her career, she received ten honorary doctorates, and her honorary M.D. from the University of Groningen in The Netherlands allowed her to add that designation behind her name.

With her parents' health failing, Crosby returned home to Petersburg, where she taught zoology, mathematics, and Latin in the high school, and coached the local boys' basketball team. She became principal of the school in 1916 and superintendent of schools in 1918. Her mother died that year, and in 1920, Crosby secured a job as junior instructor at the University of Michigan in Ann Arbor, thirty miles from Petersburg. There she taught histology and assisted G. Carl Huber, head of the anatomy department, with the neuroanatomy course. Crosby and Huber developed a close personal and working relationship. They continued her work on the alligator brain, then turned to descriptive studies of the brains of birds. After her father died in 1923, Crosby took several leaves to study at the University of London and the Central Institute for Brain Research in Amsterdam, The Netherlands.

Publishes Comparative Anatomy Text

C. U. Ariens Kappers, Crosby's colleague in Amsterdam, had published a comparative neurology textbook in German, and Huber and Crosby agreed to join him in preparing an English translation that incorporated more recent material. But because so much new descriptive information had accumulated, the book was almost a new effort; it ultimately became a ten-year project. Huber died of leukemia in 1934, and Crosby produced the book with little assistance. Although the two volumes of *The Comparative Anatomy of the Nervous System of Vertebrates, Including Man* list Crosby as the third author after Ariens Kappers and Huber, it is essentially her work. The book was published in 1936, the same year that Crosby achieved the rank of full professor.

Spending the school year of 1939 to 1940 at Marischal College of the University of Aberdeen, Scotland, Crosby helped to organize the school's first course in histology and neuroanatomy. There she met a young girl, Kathleen, whom she later sent for and legally adopted.

The graduate research program at Michigan grew rapidly, and Crosby determined to continue the programs that she and Huber had begun. When she retired in 1958, thirty-eight students had received Ph.D. degrees under her direction, and many visiting scientists had come to Ann Arbor to work with her. Crosby often published with students and colleagues, and often deferred first authorship to them even when her contribution was great. Each year, the University of Michigan presents the Elizabeth C. Crosby Award to an outstanding medical student in the basic sciences.

Her work in comparative anatomy was fundamental. Prior to the intense descriptive period in which she worked, scientists had only crude knowledge of the interior of the brain. By the time Crosby had retired, she had gathered, according to *Time* magazine, "the largest collection of sub-mammalian and mammalian brains in the world." In addition to her research she had also taught an estimated 8,500 students; she was well-loved and known as an excellent teacher. In 1957, the Galens Society of the medical school established the Elizabeth C. Crosby Award for outstanding teaching in the basic sciences. According to a University of Michigan press release, Crosby believed that teachers "must do research. Teaching keeps you alert to the unanswered questions and by doing research you get your students interested. I learned a great deal from what my students needed to know."

Turns to Clinical Work, Assisting Surgeons

As practicing physicians and neurologists brought their patients' problems to her, Crosby became more clinically oriented. She conferred on the wards, discussed cases at bedside, and consulted in operating rooms. In 1955 she collaborated with Edgar A. Kahn, Richard C. Schneider, and James A. Taren on *Correlative Neurosurgery*. In 1962, she published *Correlative Anatomy of the Nervous System* with Tryphena Humphrey and Edward Lauer.

In 1963 Humphrey, one of Crosby's first graduate students, took a position in the department of anatomy at the University of Alabama in Birmingham. As they continued their friendship and collaboration, Crosby became a frequent visitor to Alabama, sharing her talents with that school's faculty and students. The relationship was formalized with Crosby's appointment as professor emeritus of anatomy at Alabama's medical school. For eighteen years she commuted between Alabama and her consultantship at the University of Michigan, whose neurosurgery section named its research laboratories after her in 1982, the same year *Comparative Correlative Neuroanatomy of the Vertebrate Telencephalon* was published, co-edited with H. N. Schnitzlein of the University of South Florida. Crosby was inducted into both the Alabama and Michigan Women's Hall of Fame.

Over the years, numerous other honors were bestowed upon Crosby. In 1950, she received the Achievement Award of the American Association of University Women. She was the first non-neurosurgeon to be named an honorary member of the American Association of Neurological Surgeons, and was named the first woman non-clinician to become an honorary member of the Harvey Cushing Society. The University of Michigan honored her in 1946 with its Henry Russel Lectureship, and in 1956 with its Distinguished Faculty Achievement Award; in both cases she was the first woman to receive the award. In 1980, she received from President Jimmy Carter the federal government's highest honor for scientists, the National Medal of Science.

Although Crosby never married, she took pleasure in her adopted daughter's five children, whom she called her "pseudograndchildren," and to whom she was "auntie-grandma." She also considered her

students her family, and former students passing through often contacted "Ma Crosby." She died on July 28, 1983, at age ninety-four.

SELECTED WRITINGS BY CROSBY:

Books

The Forebrain of Alligator mississippiensis, [Philadelphia], 1917.
(With C. U. Ariens Kappers and G. Carl Huber) *The Comparative Anatomy of the Nervous System of Vertebrates, Including Man,* Volume I and II, Macmillan, 1936.
(Editor with H. N. Schnitzlein) *Comparative Correlative Neuroanatomy of the Vertebrate Telencephalon,* Macmillan, 1982.

SOURCES:

Books

Rossiter, Margaret W., *Women Scientists in America: Struggles and Strategies to 1940,* The Johns Hopkins University Press, 1982, pp. 185, 188–89.

Periodicals

"Elizabeth Crosby: Laying the Foundations of Neuroscience," *The Research News,* University of Michigan, August/September, 1983, pp. 3-13, 16–17.
"Goodbye, Messrs. Chips," *Time,* July 21, 1958, p. 64.
Ryan, Virginia, "Dr. Elizabeth Crosby Champions Good Teaching," *The Ann Arbor News,* September 11, 1964.
"The Strange Case of the Whodunit She Didn't Do," *The Michigan Alumnus,* May, 1966, pp. 14–15.
Woodburne, Russell T., "Elizabeth Caroline Crosby, 1888–1983," *The Anatomical Record,* September, 1984, pp. 175–77.

Other

University of Michigan press release, August 17, 1978.

—*Sketch by Jill Carpenter*

David Nelson Crosthwait, Jr.
1892(?)-1976
American engineer

David Nelson Crosthwait Jr. was a mechanical engineer who specialized in heating, ventilation, and air conditioning (HVAC). During his long career with the C. A. Dunham Company, his research led to innovations in the field, and he received over thirty U.S. patents for HVAC apparatus. Crosthwait was also a National Technological Association (NTA) Medalist in 1936 and the first African American honored by the American Society of Heating, Refrigeration, and Air Conditioning Engineers (ASHRAE). Among his many accomplishments is the design for the heating system of New York's Radio City Music Hall.

Crosthwait was born in Nashville, Tennessee, on May 27, 1892 (some sources lists 1890, 1891, or 1898), to Dr. David Nelson and Minnie (Harris) Crosthwait. He attended elementary and high school in Kansas City, Missouri, and studied mechanical engineering at Purdue University. In 1913, after receiving his bachelor of science degree, he began his long association with the C. A. Dunham Company. At Dunham, Crosthwait progressed from engineer to engineering checker in 1915 to research engineer in 1919. During this time he continued his education, earning his M.S. degree from Purdue in 1920 while also contributing to technical magazines, including *Power* and *Industrial Management*. In 1925 Crosthwait was named director of research, and five years later he was promoted to technical advisor. As research director Crosthwait was responsible for heat transfer research, steam transport research, and application of the resistance thermometer principle to thermostats.

On May 3, 1930, Crosthwait married E. Madolyne Towels in Chicago, Illinois. They had one child, David Nelson III, who died before the age of six. Madolyne died in August of 1939, and two years later Crosthwait married Blanche Ford.

From 1930 until he retired in 1969, Crosthwait remained a technical consultant and advisor at C. A. Dunham, which later became Dunham-Bush. He continued to conduct research on heating systems, including devising and applying techniques for reducing noise caused by steam and non-condensible gases in heating systems. Additionally, he was responsible for product and process development applications and the policies regarding these developments. Crosthwait continued contributing to the HVAC field as an author, rewriting chapters of the *American Society of Heating and Ventilation Engineers Guide* for the 1939, 1959, and 1967 editions. He also wrote articles for *Heating and Ventilation* magazine.

Crosthwait was active in technical societies, including ASHRAE, the American Chemical Society, the National Society of Professional Engineers, and the American Association for the Advancement of Science. Crosthwait was involved in community affairs as well, serving on the North West Comprehensive Health Planning Executive Committee, and as president of the Michigan City Redevelopment Commission in his home town of Michigan City, Indiana. He was also active in the Masons, having held the positions of Grand Junior Warden and Grand Senior Warden.

In addition to receiving the NTA medal, Crosthwait became the first African American to be honored for excellence in engineering when he was made a fellow of ASHRAE in 1971. In the spring of 1975 Crosthwait was honored by Purdue University with an honorary doctorate in technology. He enjoyed studying history, reading biographies, and listening to classical music. Crosthwait died on February 25, 1976, after a brief hospital stay.

SELECTED WRITINGS BY CROSTHWAIT:

Books

(Contributor) *American Society of Heating and Ventilation Engineers Guide,* 1939.
(Contributor) *American Society of Heating, Refrigeration and Air Conditioning Engineers Guide,* 1959.

Periodicals

"Making Up the Labor Shortage," *Industrial Management,* May, 1918, pp. 412–413.
"Heating System Vacuum," *Power,* October 21, 1919, pp. 614–616.

SOURCES:

Periodicals

"Retired Michigan City Inventor David Crosthwait Jr. Dies," *Michigan City News Dispatch,* February 25, 1976, p. 1.

—Sketch by George A. Ferrance

Marie Curie
1867-1934
Polish-born French physicist and radiation chemist

Marie Curie

Marie Curie was the first woman to win a Nobel Prize, and one of very few scientists ever to win that award twice. In collaboration with her physicist-husband **Pierre Curie**, Marie Curie developed and introduced the concept of radioactivity to the world. Working in very primitive laboratory conditions, Curie investigated the nature of high energy rays spontaneously produced by certain elements, and isolated two new radioactive elements, polonium and radium. Her scientific efforts also included the application of X rays and radioactivity to medical treatments.

Curie was born to two schoolteachers on November 7, 1867, in Warsaw, Poland. Christened Maria Sklodowska, she was the fourth daughter and fifth child in the family. By the age of five, she had already begun to suffer deprivation. Her mother Bronislawa had contracted tuberculosis and assiduously avoided kissing or even touching her children. By the time Curie was eleven, both her mother and her eldest sister Zosia had passed away, leaving her an avowed atheist. Curie was also an avowed nationalist (like the other members in her family), and when she completed her elementary schooling, she entered Warsaw's "Floating University," an underground, revolutionary Polish school that prepared young Polish students to become teachers.

Curie left Warsaw at the age of seventeen, not for her own sake but for that of her older sister Bronya. Both sisters desired to acquire additional education abroad, but the family could not afford to send either of them, so Marie took a job as a governess to fund her sister's medical education in Paris. At first, she accepted a post near her home in Warsaw, then signed on with the Zorawskis, a family who lived some distance from Warsaw. Curie supplemented her formal teaching duties there with the organization of a free school for the local peasant children. Casimir Zorawski, the family's eldest son, eventually fell in love with Curie and she agreed to marry him, but his parents objected vehemently. Marie was a fine governess, they argued, but Casimir could marry much richer. Stunned by her employers' rejection, Curie finished her term with the Zorawskis and sought another position. She spent a year in a third governess job before her sister Bronya finished medical school and summoned her to Paris.

In 1891, at the age of twenty-four, Curie enrolled at the Sorbonne and became one of the few women in attendance at the university. Although Bronya and her family back home were helping Curie pay for her studies, living in Paris was quite expensive. Too proud to ask for additional assistance, she subsisted on a diet of buttered bread and tea, which she augmented sometimes with fruit or an egg. Because she often went without heat, she would study at a nearby library until it closed. Not surprisingly, on this regimen she became anemic and on at least one occasion fainted during class.

In 1893, Curie received a degree in physics, finishing first in her class. The following year, she received a master's degree, this time graduating second in her class. Shortly thereafter, she discovered she had received the Alexandrovitch Scholarship, which enabled her to continue her education free of monetary worries. Many years later, Curie became the first recipient ever to pay back the prize. She reasoned that with that money, yet another student might be given the same opportunities she had.

Marries Pierre Curie and Two Begin Radiation Research

Friends introduced Marie to Pierre Curie in 1894. The son and grandson of doctors, Pierre had studied physics at the Sorbonne; at the time he met Marie, he was the director of the École Municipale de Physique et Chimie Industrielles. The two became friends, and eventually she accepted Pierre's proposal of marriage. Their Paris home was scantily furnished, as neither had much interest in housekeeping. Rather, they concentrated on their work. Pierre Curie accepted a job at the School of Industrial Physics and Chemistry of the City of Paris, known as the EPCI. Given lab space there, Marie Curie spent eight hours a day on her investigations into the magnetic qualities of steel until she became pregnant with her first child, Irene, who was born in 1897.

Curie then began work in earnest on her doctorate. Like many scientists, she was fascinated by French physicist **Antoine-Henri Becquerel**'s discovery that the element uranium emitted rays that contained vast amounts of energy. Unlike **Wilhelm Röntgen**'s X rays, which resulted from the excitation of atoms from an outside energy source, the "Becquerel rays" seemed to be a naturally occurring part of the uranium ore. Using the piezoelectric quartz electrometer developed by Pierre and his brother Jacques, Marie tested all the elements then known to see if any of them, like uranium, caused the nearby air to conduct electricity. In the first year of her research, Curie coined the term "radioactivity" to describe this mysterious force. She later concluded that only thorium and uranium and their compounds were radioactive.

While other scientists had also investigated the radioactive properties of uranium and thorium, Curie noted that the minerals pitchblende and chalcolite emitted more rays than could be accounted for by either element. Curie concluded that some other radioactive element must be causing the greater radioactivity. To separate this element, however, would require a great deal of effort, progressively separating pitchblende by chemical analysis and then measuring the radioactivity of the separate components. In July, 1898, she and Pierre successfully extracted an element from this ore that was even more radioactive than uranium; they called it polonium in honor of Marie's homeland. Six months later, the pair discovered another radioactive substance—radium—embedded in the pitchblende.

Although the Curies had speculated that these elements existed, to prove their existence they still needed to describe them fully and calculate their atomic weight. In order to do so, Curie needed an abundant supply of pitchblende and a better laboratory. She arranged to get hundreds of kilograms of waste scraps from a pitchblende mining firm in her native Poland, and Pierre Curie's EPCI supervisor offered the couple the use of a laboratory space. The couple worked together, with Marie performing the physically arduous job of chemically separating the pitchblende and Pierre analyzing the physical properties of the substances that Marie's separations produced. In 1902 the Curies announced that they had succeeded in preparing a decigram of pure radium chloride and had made an initial determination of radium's atomic

weight. They had proven the chemical individuality of radium.

Pierre Curie's father had moved in with the family and assumed the care of their daughter, Irene, so the couple could devote more than eight hours a day to their beloved work. Pierre Curie's salary, however, was not enough to support the family, so Marie took a position as a lecturer in physics at the École Normal Supérieure; she was the first woman to teach there. In the years between 1900 and 1903, Curie published more than she had or would in any other three-year period, with much of this work being coauthored by Pierre Curie. In 1903 Curie became the first woman to complete her doctorate in France, summa cum laude.

Receives Her First Nobel

The year Curie received her doctorate was also the year she and her husband began to achieve international recognition for their research. In November the couple received England's prestigious Humphry Davy Medal, and the following month Marie and Pierre Curie—along with Becquerel—received the Nobel Prize in physics for their efforts in expanding scientific knowledge about radioactivity. Although Curie was the first woman ever to receive the prize, she and Pierre declined to attend the award ceremonies, pleading they were too tired to travel to Stockholm. The prize money from the Nobel, combined with that of the Daniel Osiris Prize—which she received soon after—allowed the couple to expand their research efforts. In addition, the Nobel bestowed upon the couple an international reputation that furthered their academic success. The year after he received the Nobel, Pierre Curie was named professor of physics of the Faculty of Sciences at the Sorbonne. Along with his post came funds for three paid workers, two laboratory assistants and a laboratory chief, stipulated to be Marie. This was Marie's first paid research job.

In December, 1904, Marie gave birth to another daughter, Eve Denise, having miscarried a few years earlier. Despite the fact that both Pierre and Marie frequently suffered adverse effects from the radioactive materials with which they were in constant contact, Eve Denise was born healthy. The Curies continued their work regimen, taking sporadic vacations in the French countryside with their two children. They had just returned from one such vacation when on April 19, 1906, tragedy struck; while walking in the congested street traffic of Paris, Pierre was run over by a heavy wagon and killed.

A month after the accident, the University of Paris invited Curie to take over her husband's teaching position. Upon acceptance she became the first woman to ever receive a post in higher education in France, although she was not named to a full professorship for two more years. During this time, Curie came to accept the theory of English physicists **Ernest Rutherford** and **Frederick Soddy** that radioactivity was caused by atomic nuclei losing particles, and that these disintegrations caused the transmutation of an atomic nucleus into a different element. It was Curie, in fact, who coined the terms disintegration and transmutation.

In 1909, Curie received an academic reward that she had greatly desired: the University of Paris drew up plans for an Institut du Radium that would consist of two branches, a laboratory to study radioactivity—which Curie would run—and a laboratory for biological research on radium therapy, to be overseen by a physician. It took five years for the plans to come to fruition. In 1910, however, with her assistant André Debierne, Curie finally achieved the isolation of pure radium metal, and later prepared the first international standard of that element.

The First Scientist to Win a Second Nobel

Curie was awarded the Nobel Prize again in 1911, this time "for her services to the advancement of chemistry by the discovery of the elements radium and polonium," according to the award committee. The first scientist to win the Nobel twice, Curie devoted most of the money to her scientific studies. During World War I, Curie volunteered at the National Aid Society, then brought her technology to the war front and instructed army medical personnel in the practical applications of radiology. With the installation of radiological equipment in ambulances, for instance, wounded soldiers would not have to be transported far to be x-rayed. When the war ended, Curie returned to research and devoted much of her time to her work.

By the 1920s, Curie was an international figure; the Curie Foundation had been established in 1920 to accept private donations for research, and two years later the scientist was invited to participate on the League of Nations International Commission for Intellectual Cooperation. Her health was failing, however, and she was troubled by fatigue and cataracts. Despite her discomfort, Curie made a highly publicized tour of the United States in 1921. The previous year, she had met Missy Meloney, editor of the *Delineator,* a woman's magazine. Horrified at the conditions in which Curie lived and worked (the Curies had made no money from their process for producing radium, having refused to patent it), Meloney proposed that a national subscription be held to finance a gram of radium for the institute to use in research. The tour proved grueling for Curie; by the end of her stay in New York, she had her right arm in a sling, the result of too many too strong handshakes. However, with Meloney's assistance, Curie left America with a valuable gram of radium.

Curie continued her work in the laboratory throughout the decade, joined by her daughter, **Irene Joliot-Curie**, who was pursuing a doctoral degree just as her mother had done. In 1925, Irene successfully defended her doctoral thesis on alpha rays of polonium, although Curie did not attend the defense lest her presence detract from her daughter's performance. Meanwhile, Curie's health still continued to fail and she was forced to spend more time away from her work in the laboratory. The result of prolonged exposure to radium, Curie contracted leukemia and died on July 4, 1934, in a nursing home in the French Alps. She was buried next to Pierre Curie in Sceaux, France.

SELECTED WRITINGS BY CURIE:

Books

Recherches sur les substances radioactives, 2nd edition, [Paris], 1904.
La Radiologie et la Guerre, Librarie Felix Alcan, 1921.
Pierre Curie, Macmillan, 1923.
Radioactivite, Herman, 1935.
Oeuvres de Marie Sklodowska-Curie, edited by Irene Joliot-Curie, [Warsaw], 1954.

Periodicals

"Les mesures en radioactivitéet l'étalon du radium," *Journal de physique,* Volume 2, 1912, p. 715.

SOURCES:

Books

Curie, Eve, *Madame Curie: A Biography by Eve Curie,* translated by Vincent Sheean, Doubleday, 1937.
Pflaum, Rosalynd, *Grand Obsession: Madame Curie and Her World,* Doubleday, 1989.
Reid, Robert William, *Marie Curie,* Dutton, 1974.
Rossiter, Margaret W., *Women Scientists in America: Struggles and Strategies to 1940,* Johns Hopkins University Press, 1982.

—*Sketch by Shari Rudavsky*

Pierre Curie
1859-1906
French physicist

Pierre Curie

Pierre Curie was a noted physicist who became famous for his collaboration with his wife **Marie Curie** in the study of radioactivity. Before joining his wife in her research, Pierre Curie was already widely known and respected in the world of physics. He discovered (with his brother Jacques) the phenomenon of piezoelectricity—in which a crystal can become electrically polarized—and invented the quartz balance. His papers on crystal symmetry, and his findings on the relation between magnetism and temperature also earned praise in the scientific community. Curie died in a street accident in 1906, a physicist acclaimed the world over but who had never had a decent laboratory in which to work.

Pierre Curie was born in Paris on May 15, 1859, the son of Sophie-Claire Depouilly, daughter of a formerly prominent manufacturer, and Eugène Curie, a free-thinking physician who was also a physician's son. Dr. Curie supported the family with his modest medical practice while pursuing his love for the natural sciences on the side. He was also an idealist and an ardent republican who set up a hospital for the wounded during the Commune of 1871. Pierre was a dreamer whose style of learning was not well adapted to formal schooling. He received his pre-university education entirely at home, taught first by his mother and then by his father as well as his older brother, Jacques. He especially enjoyed excursions into the countryside to observe and study plants and animals, developing a love of nature that endured throughout his life and that provided his only recreation and relief from work during his later scientific career. At the age of 14, Curie studied with a mathematics professor who helped him develop his gift in the subject, especially spatial concepts. Curie's knowledge of physics and mathematics earned him his bachelor of science degree in 1875 at the age of sixteen. He then enrolled in the Faculty of Sciences at the Sorbonne in Paris and earned his *licence* (the equivalent of a master's degree) in physical sciences in 1877.

Shares Discoveries with Brother

Curie became a laboratory assistant to Paul Desains at the Sorbonne in 1878, in charge of the physics students' lab work. His brother Jacques was working in the mineralogy laboratory at the Sorbonne at that time, and the two began a productive five-year scientific collaboration. They investigated pyroelectricity, the acquisition of electric charges by different faces of certain types of crystals when heated. Led by

their knowledge of symmetry in crystals, the brothers experimentally discovered the previously unknown phenomenon of piezoelectricity, an electric polarization caused by force applied to the crystal. In 1880 the Curies published the first in a series of papers about their discovery. They then studied the opposite effect—the compression of a piezoelectric crystal by an electric field. In order to measure the very small amounts of electricity involved, the brothers invented a new laboratory instrument: a piezoelectric quartz electrometer, or balance. This device became very useful for electrical researchers and would prove highly valuable to Marie Curie in her studies of radioactivity. Much later, piezoelectricity had important practical applications. **Paul Langevin**, a student of Pierre Curie's, found that inverse piezoelectricity causes piezoelectric quartz in alternating fields to emit high-frequency sound waves, which were used to detect submarines and explore the ocean's floor. Piezoelectric crystals were also used in radio broadcasting and stereo equipment.

In 1882 Pierre Curie was appointed head of the laboratory at Paris' new Municipal School of Industrial Physics and Chemistry, a poorly paid position; he remained at the school for 22 years, until 1904. In 1883 Jacques Curie left Paris to become a lecturer in mineralogy at the University of Montpelier, and the brothers' collaboration ended. After Jacques's departure, Pierre delved into theoretical and experimental research on crystal symmetry, although the time available to him for such work was limited by the demands of organizing the school's laboratory from scratch and directing the laboratory work of up to 30 students, with only one assistant. He began publishing works on crystal symmetry in 1884, including in 1885 a theory on the formation of crystals and in 1894 an enunciation of the general principle of symmetry. Curie's writings on symmetry were of fundamental importance to later crystallographers, and, as Marie Curie later wrote in *Pierre Curie,* "he always retained a passionate interest in the physics of crystals" even though he turned his attention to other areas.

From 1890 to 1895 Pierre Curie performed a series of investigations that formed the basis of his doctoral thesis: a study of the magnetic properties of substances at different temperatures. He was, as always, hampered in his work by his obligations to his students, by the lack of funds to support his experiments, and by the lack of a laboratory or even a room for his own personal use. His magnetism research was conducted mostly in a corridor. In spite of these limitations, Curie's work on magnetism, like his papers on symmetry, was of fundamental importance. His expression of the results of his findings about the relation between temperature and magnetization became known as Curie's law, and the temperature above which magnetic properties disappear is called the Curie point. Curie successfully defended his thesis before the Faculty of Sciences at the University of Paris (the Sorbonne) in March 1895, thus earning his doctorate. Also during this period, he constructed a periodic precision balance, with direct reading, that was a great advance over older balance systems and was especially valuable for chemical analysis. Curie was now becoming well-known among physicists; he attracted the attention and esteem of, among others, the noted Scottish mathematician and physicist William Thomson (Lord Kelvin). It was partly due to Kelvin's influence that Curie was named to a newly created chair of physics at the School of Physics and Chemistry, which improved his status somewhat but still did not bring him a laboratory.

Begins Great Scientific Partnership with Marie Curie

In the spring of 1894, at the age of 35, Curie met Maria (later Marie) Sklodowska, a poor young Polish student who had received her *licence* in physics from the Sorbonne and was then studying for her *licence* in mathematics. They immediately formed a rapport, and Curie soon proposed marriage. Sklodowska returned to Poland that summer, not certain that she would be willing to separate herself permanently from her family and her country. Curie's persuasive correspondence convinced her to return to Paris that autumn, and the couple married in July, 1895, in a simple civil ceremony. Marie used a cash wedding gift to purchase two bicycles, which took the newlyweds on their honeymoon in the French countryside and

provided their main source of recreation for years to come. Their daughter Irene was born in 1897, and a few days later Pierre's mother died; Dr. Curie then came to live with the young couple and helped care for his granddaughter.

The Curies' attention was caught by **Henri Becquerel**'s discovery in 1896 that uranium compounds emit rays. Marie decided to make a study of this phenomenon the subject of her doctor's thesis, and Pierre secured the use of a ground-floor storeroom/machine shop at the School for her laboratory work. Using the Curie brothers' piezoelectric quartz electrometer, Marie tested all the elements then known to see if any of them, like uranium, emitted "Becquerel rays," which she christened "radioactivity". Only thorium and uranium and their compounds, she found, were radioactive. She was startled to discover that the ores pitchblende and chalcolite had much greater levels of radioactivity than the amounts of uranium and thorium they contained could account for. She guessed that a new, highly radioactive element must be responsible and, as she wrote in *Pierre Curie,* was seized with "a passionate desire to verify this hypothesis as rapidly as possible."

Pierre Curie too saw the significance of his wife's findings and set aside his much-loved work on crystals (only for the time being, he thought) to join Marie in the search for the new element. They devised a new method of chemical research, progressively separating pitchblende by chemical analysis and then measuring the radioactivity of the separate constituents. In July 1898, in a joint paper, they announced their discovery of a new element they named polonium, in honor of Marie Curie's native country. In December 1898, they announced, in a paper issued with their collaborator G. Bémont, the discovery of another new element, radium. Both elements were much more radioactive than uranium or thorium.

Confirms Discovery of Two "New" Elements

The Curies had discovered radium and polonium, but in order to prove the existence of these new substances chemically, they had to isolate the elements so the atomic weight of each could be determined. This was a daunting task, as they would have to process two tons of pitchblende ore to obtain a few centigrams of pure radium. Their laboratory facilities were woefully inadequate: an abandoned wooden shed in the School's yard, with no hoods to carry off the poisonous gases their work produced. They found the pitchblende at a reasonable price in the form of waste from a uranium mine run by the Austrian government. The Curies now divided their labor. Marie acted as the chemist, performing the physically arduous job of chemically separating the pitchblende; the bulkiest part of this work she did in the yard adjoining the shed/laboratory. Pierre was the physicist, analyzing the physical properties of the substances that Marie's separations produced. In 1902 the Curies announced that they had succeeded in preparing a decigram of pure radium chloride and had made an initial determination of radium's atomic weight. They had proven the chemical individuality of radium.

The Curies' research also yielded a wealth of information about radioactivity, which they shared with the world in a series of papers published between 1898 and 1904. They announced their discovery of induced radioactivity in 1899. They wrote about the luminous and chemical effects of radioactive rays and their electric charge. Pierre studied the action of a magnetic field on radium rays, he investigated the persistence of induced radioactivity, and he developed a standard for measuring time on the basis of radioactivity, an important basis for geologic and archaeological dating techniques. Pierre Curie also used himself as a human guinea pig, deliberately exposing his arm to radium for several hours and recording the progressive, slowly healing burn that resulted. He collaborated with physicians in animal experiments that led to the use of radium therapy—often called "Curie-therapie" then—to treat cancer and lupus. In 1904 he published a paper on the liberation of heat by radium salts.

Struggles and Disappointment, Recognition, and Tragedy

Through all this intensive research, the Curies struggled to keep up with their teaching, household, and financial obligations. Pierre Curie was a kind, gentle, and reserved man, entirely devoted to his work—science conducted purely for the sake of science. He rejected honorary distinctions; in 1903 he declined the prestigious decoration of the Legion of Honor. He also, with his wife's agreement, refused to patent their radium-preparation process, which formed the basis of the lucrative radium industry; instead, they shared all their information about the process with whoever asked for it. Curie found it almost impossible to advance professionally within the French university system; seeking a position was an "ugly necessity" and "demoralizing" for him (*Pierre Curie*), so posts he might have been considered for went instead to others. He was turned down for the Chair of Physical Chemistry at the Sorbonne in 1898; instead, he was appointed assistant professor at the Polytechnic School in March 1900, a much inferior position.

Appreciated outside France, Curie received an excellent offer of a professorship at the University of Geneva in the spring of 1900, but he turned it down so as not to interrupt his research on radium. Shortly afterward, Curie was appointed to a physics chair at the Sorbonne, thanks to the efforts of **Jules Henri Poincaré**. Still, he did not have a laboratory, and his teaching load was now doubled, as he still held his post at the School of Physics and Chemistry. He began to suffer from extreme fatigue and sharp pains through his body, which he and his wife attributed to overwork, although the symptoms were almost certainly a sign of radiation poisoning, an unrecognized illness at that time. In 1902, Curie's candidacy for election to the French Academy of Sciences failed, and in 1903 his application for the chair of mineralogy at the Sorbonne was rejected, both of which added to his bitterness toward the French academic establishment.

Recognition at home finally came for Curie because of international awards. In 1903 London's Royal Society conferred the Davy medal on the Curies, and shortly thereafter they were awarded the 1903 Nobel Prize in physics—along with Becquerel—for their work on radioactivity. Curie presciently concluded his Nobel lecture (delivered in 1905 because the Curies had been too ill to attend the 1903 award ceremony) by wondering whether the knowledge of radium and radioactivity would be harmful for humanity; he added that he himself felt that more good than harm would result from the new discoveries. The Nobel award shattered the Curies' reclusive work-absorbed life. They were inundated by journalists, photographers, curiosity-seekers, eminent and little-known visitors, correspondence, and requests for articles and lectures. Still, the cash from the award was a godsend, and the award's prestige finally prompted the French parliament to create a new professorship for Curie at the Sorbonne in 1904. Curie declared he would remain at the School of Physics unless the new chair included a fully funded laboratory, complete with assistants. His demand was met, and Marie was named his laboratory chief. Late in 1904 the Curies' second daughter, Eve, was born. By early 1906, Pierre Curie was poised to begin work—at last and for the first time—in an adequate laboratory, although he was increasingly ill and tired. On April 19, 1906, leaving a lunchtime meeting in Paris with colleagues from the Sorbonne, Curie slipped in front of a horse-drawn cart while crossing a rain-slicked rue Dauphine. He was killed instantly when the rear wheel of the cart crushed his skull. The world mourned the untimely loss of this great physicist. True to the way he had conducted his life, he was interred in a small suburban cemetery in a simple, private ceremony attended only by his family and a few close friends. In his memory, the Faculty of Sciences at the Sorbonne appointed Curie's widow Marie to his chair.

SELECTED WRITINGS BY CURIE:

Books

Oeuvres de Pierre Curie, [Paris], 1908.

Periodicals

(With Jacques Curie) "Développement, par pression, de l'électricité polaire dans les cristaux hémièdres à faces inclinées," *Comptes rendus hebdomadaires des séances de l'Académie des sciences,* Volume 91, 1880.

"Symétrie dans les phénomènes physiques, symétrie d'un champ électrique et d'un champ magnétique," *Journal de physique,* Volume 3, 1894.

(With Marie Curie and G. Bémont) "Nouvelle substance fortement radioactive, contenu dans la pechblende," *Comptes rendus hebdomadaires des séances de l'Académie des sciences,* Volume 127, 1898.

"Conductibilité des diélectriques liquides sous l'influence des rayons du radium et des rayons de Röntgen," *Comptes rendus hebdomadaires des séances de l'Académie des sciences,* Volume 134, 1902.

(With Charles Bouchard and Victor Balthazard) "Action physiologique de l'émanation du radium," *Comptes rendus hebdomadaires des séances de l'Académie des sciences,* Volume 138, 1904.

SOURCES:

Books

Curie, Eve, *Madame Curie: A Biography by Eve Curie,* translated by Vincent Sheean, Doubleday, 1937.

Curie, Marie, *Pierre Curie,* Macmillan, 1923.

Giroud, Françoise, *Marie Curie: A Life,* Holmes & Meier, 1986.

Heathcote, Niels H. de V., *Nobel Prize Winners in Physics 1901–1950,* Henry Schuman, 1953.

Magill, Frank N., *The Nobel Prize Winners: Physics,* Volume 1: *(1901–1937),* Salem Press, 1989.

Reid, Robert, *Marie Curie,* Dutton, 1974.

Romer, Alfred, editor, *The Discovery of Radioactivity and Transmutation,* Dover, 1964.

Segre, Emilio, *From X-Rays to Quarks: Modern Physicists and Their Discoveries,* University of California Press, 1980.

Weaver, Jefferson Hane, *The World of Physics,* Simon & Schuster, 1987.

—*Sketch by Kathy Sammis*

D

Henry Hallett Dale
1875-1968
English physiologist

Henry Hallett Dale was a British physiologist who devoted his scientific career to the study of how chemicals in the body regulate physiological functions. Although his work had many facets, the most significant was his collaborative effort with German pharmacologist **Otto Loewi**. In 1936 Dale and Loewi were jointly awarded the Nobel Prize in physiology or medicine for research demonstrating that nerve cells communicate with one another primarily by the exchange of chemical transmitters. In addition to his scientific work, Dale was a prominent figure in science and medicine in England at critical junctures in that nation's history. He was knighted in 1932.

Born June 9, 1875, in London, Henry Hallett Dale was the second son of seven children born to Charles Dale, a London businessman, and his wife, Frances Hallett Dale. After graduating from Tollington Park College, London, and the Leys School, Cambridge, Dale entered Trinity College at Cambridge University in 1894. His academic skills gained him first honors in the natural sciences and the Coutts-Trotter studentship at Trinity College. Dale's predecessor in the studentship was **Ernest Rutherford**, the physicist and chemist who would go on to win the Nobel Prize in chemistry in 1908.

Dale left Cambridge in 1900 to finish his clinical work in medicine at St. Bartholomew's Hospital in London. He received his bachelor's degree in 1903, and his medical doctorate in 1909. During this time, he also was awarded the George Henry Lewes studentship, which allowed him to pursue further physiological research. Later, Dale also received the Sharpey studentship in physiology at University College, London. Dale used these opportunities for research from 1902 to 1904, studying with **Ernest Henry Starling** and **William Maddock Bayliss** at University College. Starling and Bayliss identified secretin—a substance secreted by the small intestine—as the first hormone, and Dale collaborated with the pair in further studies on the impact of secretin on cells in the pancreas. Dale's work with Starling and Bayliss instilled in him the idea that physiological functions could be affected by such chemicals as hormones. It was also in this

Henry Hallett Dale

laboratory that Dale first met Otto Loewi, who at the time was visiting University College from Germany. Dale and Loewi would go on to become lifelong friends, collaborators, and co-recipients of the 1936 Nobel Prize.

Begins Professional Career with Wellcome Laboratories

In 1904 Dale spent three months working in the laboratory of the chemist **Paul Ehrlich** in Germany. Members of Ehrlich's laboratory were studying the relationship between the chemical structure of biological molecules and their effect on immunological responses, research that would garner for Ehrlich the 1908 Nobel Prize in physiology or medicine. As did the experience at Starling's laboratory in London, Ehrlich's research introduced Dale to the potential impact that chemicals can have on mediating biological and physiological processes.

After Dale returned to Starling's London laboratory, he was recommended to chemical manufacturer Henry Wellcome for a position with London's Wellcome Physiological Research Laboratories, a commercial laboratory. Established in the 1890s to produce an antitoxin for diphtheria, the laboratories, by the first decade of the 1900s, had begun to promote and pursue basic scientific research. Against the advice of colleagues who distrusted the commercial nature of the laboratory, Dale accepted the post. He reasoned that it would provide him the stability that would allow him to marry Ellen Harriett Hallett, his first cousin. (This marriage in 1904 would produce a son and two daughters; the older daughter, Alison, would go on to marry **Alexander Todd**, who would win the 1957 Nobel Prize in chemistry.) The post also provided a well-equipped laboratory, freedom from teaching and administrative duties, and the intellectual freedom to pursue his own course of research.

Embarks on Studies of Ergot

Once Dale had settled at Wellcome, the company suggested that he consider examining the therapeutic properties of ergot, a fungus being used by obstetricians to induce and promote labor. For the next decade, Dale devoted his research efforts to studying the properties of the drug. Although he failed at the stated purpose of his research—articulating the properties of ergot—accidental findings turned out to be of great significance, leading, for instance, to his discovery of the phenomenon of adrenaline (or epinephrine) reversal, in which the normally excitatory effects of these drugs are neutralized.

Dale's research on the effects of ergot also introduced him to ongoing efforts to study the central nervous system. T. R. Elliott, Dale's friend and colleague at Cambridge, postulated that epinephrine (a neurotransmitter, or substance that transmits nerve impulses) when applied by itself could produce an effect similar to stimulating the sympathetic branch of the autonomic nervous system. The autonomic nervous system is responsible for involuntary physiological functions, such as breathing and digestion. This system's sympathetic branch affects such functions as increasing heart rate in response to fear and opening arteries to increased blood flow during exercise. Dale built on Elliott's research and showed, with the chemist George Barger, that epinephrine is one chemical in a class of such chemicals that has "sympathomimetic" properties.

Dale's serendipitous accomplishments drew the attention of Henry Wellcome, and Dale was promoted in 1906 to the directorship of the Wellcome Laboratories. After this promotion, Dale began to apply what he had learned while a student in the laboratories of Starling and Ehrlich. Dale understood that there are a number of active components in ergot. Wanting to understand the chemical mechanisms that underlie physiological functions, Dale began studies of the chemicals that operate in the posterior pituitary lobe of the brain. It is this area of the brain where ergot has its effects, since this area is responsible for inducing contractions of the uterine muscles.

Dale resigned from the Wellcome Laboratories in 1914, and joined the scientific staff of the Medical Research Committee; after 1920 this group came to be known as the Medical Research Council. The onset of World War I placed new demands on Dale's administrative and scientific skills. He joined the war effort by engaging in physiological studies of shock, dysentery, gangrene, and the effects of inadequate diet.

After the war, the Medical Research Council evolved to become the National Institute for Medical Research, and Dale served as the organization's first director from 1928 until 1942. Although he continued to perform physiological research, administrative and public duties for the Medical Research Council and the National Institute for Medical Research limited the time and energy that he could devote to the laboratory. His research efforts during the 1920s continued the work he began during the war—studying how histamine contributes to the swelling of tissue after traumatic shock. Dale demonstrated that histamine leads to the loss of plasma fluid into the tissues and produces swelling. This could lead to more serious problems, including decreased blood circulation, shock, and ultimately death.

Dale's study of histamine also contributed to his subsequent work on the nervous system. Histamine, like the neurotransmitter acetylcholine, dilates vascular tissue in the human body. Dale had long known from his work in Starling's laboratory that acetylcholine increases the diameter of vascular tissue. The question remaining for Dale was how this chemical produces the physiological effect.

Receives Nobel Prize

In 1927 Dale collaborated with H. W. Dudley to isolate acetylcholine from the spleen of an ox and a horse. Having isolated the crucial compound, Dale sought to understand how and where acetylcholine plays its role in vasodilatation, or the widening of the cavities of blood vessels. Over the next decade, Dale worked with colleagues at the National Institute for Medical Research and concluded that acetylcholine serves as a neurotransmitter and that this is the chemical mediator involved in the transmission of nerve impulses. Dale's findings disproved the proposition of **John Carew Eccles** and other neurophysiologists who maintained that nerve cells communicate with one another via an electrical mechanism. Dale demonstrated that a chemical process and not an electrical one was the underlying mechanism for nerve transmission. A similar conclusion had been reached by Otto Loewi: As early as 1921 Loewi suggested that a chemical mediator was responsible for the conduction of nerve impulses; it would be Dale who would identify the mediator.

For their work, Dale and Loewi were jointly awarded the 1936 Nobel Prize in physiology or medicine. During the 1930s, Dale continued collaborative research with G. L. Brown, W. Feldberg, J. H. Gaddum, and M. Vogt at the National Institute for Medical Research. Their efforts produced more evidence that acetylcholine is a neurotransmitter involved in nerve impulses.

By the 1940s Dale was devoting much of his time to administrative duties in various organizations. During World War II, he served as chair of the Scientific Advisory Committee to the War Cabinet. Having been elected a fellow of the Royal Society in 1914, he served as secretary from 1925 to 1935, and as president from 1940 to 1945. His many other public affiliations included serving as president of various organizations, such as the Royal Institution of Great Britain during the mid–1940s, the British Association for the Advancement of Science in 1947, the Royal Society of Medicine from 1948 to 1950, and the British Council during the 1950s.

Other distinctions bestowed upon Dale include receiving the Copley Medal from the Royal Society in 1937 and being knighted with the Grand Cross Order of the British Empire in 1943. He also garnered the Order of Merit in 1944. Since 1959 the Society for Endocrinology has awarded the Dale Medal for the kind of excellence in research exemplified by Dale; and since 1961 the Wellcome Trust he chaired from 1938 until 1960 has endowed the Henry Dale professorship with the Royal Society.

In later years Dale worked with Thorvald Madsen of Copenhagen directing an international campaign to standardize drugs and vaccines. The 1925 conference of the Health Organization of the League of Nations adopted such standards for insulin and pituitary products largely because of Dale's efforts. He repeated these efforts to see into law the Therapeutic Substances Act in England. His other political activities included promoting both the peaceful use of nuclear energy and the value of scientific research. He died on July 23, 1968, after a brief illness.

SELECTED WRITINGS BY DALE:

Books

An Autumn Gleaning: Occasional Lectures and Addresses, Pergamon, 1954.
Adventures in Physiology, with Excursions into Autopharmacology, Wellcome Trust, 1965.

Periodicals

"Pharmacology and Nerve Endings," *Proceedings of the Royal Society of Medicine,* Volume 28, 1935, pp. 310–332.

"Acetylcholine as a Chemical Transmitter of the Effects of Nerve Impulses," *Journal of the Mount Sinai Hospital,* Volume 4, 1937, pp. 401–429.
"Autobiographical Sketch," *Perspectives in Biology and Medicine,* Volume 1, 1958, pp. 125–137.

SOURCES:

Books

Biographical Memoirs of Fellows of the Royal Society, Volume 16, Royal Society (London), 1970, pp. 77–174.
Feldberg, William, "The Early History of Synaptic and Neuromuscular Transmission by Acetylcholine: Reminiscences of an Eye Witness," *Pursuit of Nature,* edited by A. L. Hodgkin and others, Cambridge University Press, 1977, pp. 65–83.
Gillispie, Charles C., editor, *Dictionary of Scientific Biography,* Scribner's 1978, pp. 104–107.

Periodicals

Gasser, Herbert S., "Sir Henry Dale: His Influence on Science," *British Medical Journal,* June 4, 1955, pp. 1359–1361.

—*Sketch by D. George Joseph*

Nils Dalén
1869-1937
Swedish engineer and inventor

Nils Dalén is sometimes referred to as "the benefactor of sailors" because of the improved navigational aids that he invented. Before his work, all lighthouses and marine beacons had to be operated manually, greatly restricting the areas in which they could be utilized. Dalén's inventions made it possible to store and burn acetylene gas under controlled conditions, allowing the automated use of acetylene beacons in virtually any area. He was awarded the 1912 Nobel Prize in physics for his inventions. At the age of forty-three, Dalén was blinded while conducting a demonstration of his acetylene storage system. He continued with his inventing, however, almost until his death in 1937.

Nils Gustav Dalén was born on November 30, 1869, in Stenstorp, Sweden. His parents, Anders

Johannson and Lovisa Andersdotter Dalén, owned a small farm that they expected to pass on to their son. For some time, Dalén attended courses in agriculture, horticulture, and dairy-farming, but he was very much interested in and skilled at working with mechanical devices. In his book *Lives That Moved the World*, Horace Shipp describes a mechanism that Dalén invented as a young boy that would turn on lights, start a coffee maker, and sound a bell to awaken him in the morning. Shipp quotes an anonymous friend who described Dalén's mental skills by saying, "Ideas! Dalén in that mind of his had twenty ideas a second."

Turns from Farming to Invention

Torn for some time between his commitment to the family farm and a possible career in science, Dalén finally chose the latter at the age of twenty-three. He enrolled in the Chalmers Technical Institute in Göteborg, receiving his degree in mechanical engineering in 1896. He then traveled to Zürich, Switzerland, where he spent a year studying at the famous Swiss Federal Institute of Technology.

Upon his return to Sweden, Dalén was employed briefly at the de Laval Steam Turbine Company in Stockholm, where he worked on the development of hot air turbines, compressors, and air pumps. In 1900, he and a friend formed the engineering firm of Dalén and Alsing (one source cites Dalén's engineering partner as Celsing) to develop and market their own inventions. On July 13, 1901, he married his childhood sweetheart, Elma Axelia Persson, with whom he had two sons, Gunnar and Anders, and two daughters. That same year, Dalén was appointed works chief at the Swedish Carbide and Acetylene Company in Stockholm. It was at this company, which became the Swedish Gas Accumulator Company in 1909, that Dalén produced his most important work.

Creates Automated Acetylene Lighting Device

Engineers had long been aware of the value of acetylene as a source of light in lamps, but the gas is extremely dangerous to work with and most devices in which it was used had a tendency to explode under stress. Dalén produced a porous material that significantly reduced the dangers involved in handling acetylene-filled containers. Contained within a steel cylinder, the highly porous material he called *aga* was half filled with acetone. The acetylene was then forced into the container under ten atmospheres of pressure and kept at a temperature of fifteen degrees Celsius. In this state, the acetylene could be stored and transported with virtually no danger.

Dalén improved upon the gas accumulator through the invention of a mechanism for releasing, igniting, and burning the stored acetylene so as to produce very precise signals. The device could open and close a vent almost instantaneously, allowing for the very rapid release of acetylene gas. In this way, a single tank of gas could produce several thousand brief, but very bright, flashes of light. The mechanism made it possible for each lighthouse or beacon to be assigned a specific pattern of light flashes (such as in Morse code) by which it could be uniquely identified.

In 1907, Dalén struck upon a means by which to turn a signaling beacon on at night and off during the day. His so-called "sunshine valve" made use of the differential absorption of heat by dark and light surfaces. One of a set of four metal bars within a glass tube is blackened, while the other three are left gilded and bright. As sunlight increases, its heat is reflected by the polished bars and absorbed by the black bar, causing it to expand and thus close the acetylene gas valve. As the sun set or was blotted by fog, the black bar contracted and opened the valve, which was then lit by a bypass jet. Dalén's inventions made it possible to install signaling beams on reefs, inaccessible islands, and other locations that had previously been without warning lights. In addition, the aga system eventually found a number of other applications, as in the lighting of railway cars, in railway signals, and in the use of acetylene for welding and cutting tools.

In recognition of his development of automatic regulators for acetylene lighting systems, Dalén was awarded the 1912 Nobel Prize for physics. He was unable to attend the Nobel Prize ceremonies in Stockholm, however, because of an accident that had occurred only a few months earlier. While Dalén was demonstrating the safety of his gas accumulating device, a valve failed and an acetylene tank exploded. Dalén was blinded in the accident and fell briefly into despair at the thought that his career was over. He soon recovered his good spirits, although not his eyesight, and went on to make a number of other useful inventions in the last three decades of his life. Among these was a particularly efficient cooking stove. Dalén was awarded the Morehead Medal of the International Acetylene Association in 1933, and was elected to the Royal Swedish Academy of Sciences in 1913 and the Swedish Academy of Science and Engineering in 1919. He died of cancer in Lidingö, Sweden, on December 9, 1937.

SELECTED WRITINGS BY DALÉN:

Books

Chemische Technologie des Papiers, J. A. Barth, 1911.

SOURCES:

Books

A Biographical Encyclopedia of Scientists, Volume 1, Facts on File, 1981, p. 179.

Nobel Prize Winners, H. W. Wilson, 1987, pp. 242–43.

Nobel Prize Winners in Physics, 1901–1950, Henry Schuman, 1953, pp. 102–07.

Shipp, Horace, *Lives That Moved the World,* Evans Brothers, Ltd., 1948, pp. 41–47.

Weber, Robert L., *Pioneers of Science: Nobel Prize Winners in Physics,* American Institute of Physics, 1980, pp. 45–46.

—*Sketch by David E. Newton*

Francisco Dallmeier

Francisco Dallmeier
1953-

Venezuelan-born American biologist

Francisco Dallmeier is a leading wildlife biologist who specializes in biodiversity issues. His work in developing countries, particularly in Latin America, helped form strategies for sustainable exploitation of their natural resources. He also refined the use of long-term research plots to evaluate and monitor changes in the ecological balance of tropical forests.

Francisco Gómez-Dallmeier was born on February 15, 1953, in Caracas, Venezuela. He began his professional career while still a student, becoming the Curator of Mammals at the LaSalle Museum of Natural History in Caracas at the age of eighteen. He was the museum's director from 1973 until 1977, when he received his licentiate in biology from the Central University of Venezuela. During this period, Dallmeier served as a research assistant with Central University's Institute of Tropical Zoology, studying the flora and fauna of Southern Venezuela; his work in this field led to the banding of more than 3,000 birds. While at the institute, he collaborated in a number of ecological efforts with Polish scientists Kazimierz Dobrolowski and Jan Pinowski. After earning his licentiate, Dallmeier worked in private until 1981, coordinating the ecological program for INELMECA, a Venezuelan environmental engineering company. He also helped prepare Venezuela's first environmental impact statement for the Morón Power Plant.

Dallmeier earned his master's degree in 1984 and his doctorate in 1986 from Colorado State University in Fort Collins, Colorado, specializing in wildlife ecology. He then joined the staff of the Smithsonian Institution, becoming program manager of its Man and the Biosphere (SI/MAB) Biological Diversity Program, a joint project with UNESCO.

Dallmeier was concerned about the profound effects of human economic development on tropical ecosystems. In the late 1980s, biologists estimated that more than a million species of plants and animals would become extinct before the middle of the twenty-first century. In an effort to encourage sustainable development, Dallmeier began an intensive research and education program to train ecologists from developing countries in methods of assessing the biodiversity status of their natural resources. By 1989 the SI/MAB program had conducted field research and training workshops in nine Latin American countries as well as China and four sites in the United States. During the early 1990s, Dallmeier coordinated long-term biodiversity research in more than ten countries.

Long-term biodiversity research is accomplished primarily by establishing forest inventory plots which can be observed in great detail and monitored for changes over time. Dallmeier helped develop a plot research technique that would provide standardized information so that research from many different sites could be compared accurately. A research plot is laid out in a grid and a census taken of every species (usually trees) within the plot. The density, variety, and dominance of each species is recorded. Standard methods of measuring tree and branch size are used, both for living stands of trees, snags, and fallen trees. Researchers note geological, topographical, and climatic factors as well as the area's land use history. Over time, shifts in the survival rate and health of each species can be noted. Dallmeier helped establish a research methodology that enabled ecologists to accumulate large amounts of data and make it widely available for the first time. This method emphasized the use of personal computers to record data in the field and to apply new analytic techniques to the resulting databases.

Dallmeier is especially interested in tropical birds, holding memberships in the Audubon Society of Venezuela, the Wildfowl Trust, the American Ornithologists Union, and many other ecological organizations. As author, editor, or co-author, he has published more than seventy scholarly reports. In addition to his formal scientific training, Dallmeier studied management communication, including neuro-linguistic programming and transactional analysis. He also took training in computer programming and database management and became a certified open water diver and private pilot. Dallmeier married Nancy Joy Parton, with whom he has two children.

SELECTED WRITINGS BY DALLMEIER:

Books

(With A. T. Cringan) *Biology, Conservation and Management of Waterfowl in Venezuela,* Editorial Ex Libris, 1990.

Periodicals

(With M. H. Rylander) "Observations on the Feeding Ecology and Bioenergetics of the White-Faced Whistling Suck in Venezuela," *Wildfowl,* Volume 33, 1982, pp. 17–21.

"Forest Biodiversity in Latin America: Reversing the Losses?" *Journal of Tropical Forest Science,* Volume 5, number 2, 1992, pp. 232–70.

"Tracking Biodiversity for Practical Applications, "*Global Biodiversity,* Volume 3, number 1, 1993, pp. 24–27.

SOURCES:

Books

Hispanic-American Almanac, Gale, 1993, p. 684.

Periodicals

Biodiversity, winter, 1992, p. 2.
BioScience, Volume 43, number 11, p. 762.

—*Sketch by Valerie Brown*

G. Brent Dalrymple
1937-
American geologist

G. Brent Dalrymple, a research geologist with the U.S. Geological Survey, holds the distinction of being a principal investigator for the moon rocks collected during the Apollo 11 and Apollo 12 lunar voyages, and later, the Apollo 15 and 17 lunar voyages. His research clocking geologic time through isotopic dating methods—then applying these findings to a range of geophysical problems—has led to his reputation as one of the leading experts on the age of our planet. He described the history of magnetic field reversals, which led directly to the theory of Plate Tectonics, and he demonstrated the hot spot origin of the Hawaiian-Emperor volcanic chain. He is currently researching lunar basin history. In 1990, he was elected to the presidency of the American Geophysical Union, a position he held for two years, and in 1993, he was elected to the National Academy of Sciences.

Gary Brent Dalrymple, the son of Donald I. and Wynona E. Pierce Dalrymple, was born in Alhambra, California, on May 9, 1937. He married Sharon Tramel in 1959, and the couple have three daughters—Stacie, Robynne, and Melinda. Dalrymple attended Occidental College, in his home state of California, where he earned a B.A. in geology in 1959. He then moved to the University of California, Berkeley, to do his graduate work. He earned his Ph.D. in geology in 1963.

After graduation, Dalrymple began his career as a research geologist with the U.S. Geological Survey (USGS) in Menlo Park, California, in the Branch of Theoretical Geophysics. He remained there until the early 1970s, when he moved to the Branch of Isotope Geology. Between 1981 and 1984, he was assistant chief geologist for the Western Region of the USGS, during which time he was the principal contact within the USGS for the state geologists of the western states. Since 1984 he has served as a research geologist for the USGS.

Dalrymple's Role in the Theory of Plate Tectonics

One of Dalrymple's most significant investigations centers on his work in the 1960s, which proved that the earth's magnetic field reverses polarity. He and his colleagues Allan Cox and Richard Doell ascertained the time scale of these reversals over the past 3.5 million years. This work resulted in the theory of Plate Tectonics. Science historian William Glen writes of this work and its importance in his book *The Road to Jaramillo.* Another of Dalrymple's investigations confirmed the hypothesis that the volcanoes in the Hawaiian-Emperor volcanic chain—which extends from Hawaii to the Aleutian Trench near Siberia—were formed by the Pacific Plate's motion over a fixed source of lava in the earth's mantle.

Clocking Geologic Time

Throughout his career Dalrymple has been involved in developing new methodology and instrumentation for determining the ages of rocks and minerals. His contributions include the development and refinement of potassium-argon dating methods and instruments. His interest in radiometric dating led to the publication of *Potassium-Argon Dating,* a guide to understanding the principles and techniques involved, which he co-authored with Marvin A. Lanphere in 1969. The book began as an abbreviated pamphlet, but was later expanded into a book by popular request. As the authors note in their preface, the book is not meant to be "a scholarly or comprehensive review" of the topic, but is instead intended to answer "practical questions of what the method can and cannot do." The authors begin with the basics, explaining about atoms, elements, and isotopes, before defining radioactivity. Then they explain how one form of potassium (K) decays, transforming into a form of argon (Ar), and how time measurements can be made by quantifying such changes. Although the book was published over 20 years ago, the potassium-argon method continues to be the primary means of radiometric dating, and the book remains the definitive work on this method of dating.

Another book, *The Age of the Earth,* published in 1991, resulted from Dalrymple's involvement in science education. Dalrymple's reputation as a leading authority on the age of the earth and radiometric dating has led to his involvement as an expert witness in court cases. He has served in cases involving creation "science" at both the state and federal levels. Dalrymple has also lectured and written several papers on the inappropriateness of including creation science in the science curriculum of public schools.

Moon Rocks

Dalrymple has been involved in two phases of research with moon rocks. "In our early investigations with the Apollo lunar rocks, we tried to understand how the stored energy from the trapped electrons in the rock, which can be released by heating to give off light, might be used to determine the rates and frequency of lunar surface processes," Dalrymple told contributor Patricia M. McAdams in an interview. "We eventually gave up because the results seemed to be reflecting small-scale impact phenomena that could not be correlated with the broader aspect of lunar history."

"We started working on moon rocks again a few years ago," Dalrymple explained. "Now we're using [Argon] methods to see if we can determine the history of lunar basin formation." Lunar basins, he notes, are the very big craters that form the face of the "man in the moon." Dalrymple and his colleagues have developed new methods of precisely measuring the age of tiny (sub-milligram) fragments of melt rocks that are created by basin-forming impacts of asteroid-sized objects into the lunar surface. "We are testing the hypothesis that the lunar basins were formed during a brief interval between 3.8 and 3.9 billion years ago, instead of over a prolonged interval between 4.5 and 3.8 billion years ago, as is the conventional wisdom," he said. "So far we have found no evidence for older basin-forming impacts in the rocks from the Apollo 15 or Apollo 17 missions."

In addition to his primary research at the U.S. Geological Survey, Dalrymple has served in various roles at Stanford University, including visiting professor, lecturer, research associate, and consulting professor in the school of earth sciences. His affiliation with Stanford was intermittent during the 1970s and 1980s, but has been continuous since 1990. He has also authored more than 150 journal articles, and dozens of other publications. In 1993 he was elected to the National Academy of Sciences, and received an honorary Doctor of Science degree from his undergraduate Alma Mater, Occidental College. He was elected to the American Academy of Arts and Sciences in 1992, and was the Distinguished Alumni Centennial Speaker at Occidental College in the 1980s. Other awards include the Meritorious Service Award of the Department of the Interior in 1984. In addition to his role as president of the American Geophysical Union—a society 30,000 strong—Dalrymple serves on the board of governors of the American Institute of Physics, and was elected to the executive committee of that institute in 1993. He served on the Council of Scientific Society Presidents between 1990 and 1992.

When he is not working, Dalrymple relaxes by downhill skiing or sailing with his family. He is also an instructor in celestial navigation.

SELECTED WRITINGS BY DALRYMPLE:

Books

(With Marvin A. Lanphere) *Potassium-Argon Dating: Principles, Techniques, and Applications to Geochronology,* W. H. Freeman and Co. (San Francisco), 1969.
The Age of the Earth, Stanford University Press, 1991.

Periodicals

"How Old Is the Earth?: A Reply to 'Scientific Creationism,'" *Proceedings of the 63rd Annual Meeting, American Association for the Advancement of Science, Pacific Division,* Volume 1, No. 3, 1984, pp. 66–131.

(With G. Ryder) "40Ar/39Ar Age Spectra of Apollo 15 Impact Melt Rocks by Laser Step-Heating and Their Bearing on the History of Lunar Basin Formation," *Journal of Geophysical Research—Planets,* Volume 98, 1993, pp. 13,085–13,095.

SOURCES:

Books

Glen, William, *The Road to Jaramillo,* Stanford University Press, 1982.

Other

Dalrymple, G. Brent, interview with Patricia M. McAdams, conducted September 24, 1993.

—*Sketch by Patricia M. McAdams*

Marie M. Daly
1921-

American biochemist

Marie M. Daly was the first African American woman to earn a Ph.D. in chemistry. Throughout her career, her research interests focused on areas of health, particularly the effects on the heart and arteries of such factors as aging, cigarette smoking, hypertension, and cholesterol. In addition to research, she taught for fifteen years at Yeshiva University's Albert Einstein College of Medicine.

Marie Maynard Daly was born in Corona, Queens, a neighborhood of New York City, on April 16, 1921. Her parents, Ivan C. Daly and Helen (Page) Daly, both valued learning and education and steadily encouraged her. Her father had wanted to become a chemist and had attended Cornell University, but was unable to complete his education for financial reasons and became a postal clerk. Daly attended the local public schools in Queens and graduated from Hunter College High School in Manhattan. She credits her interest in science to both her father's scientific

background and to influential books such as Paul DeKruif's *The Microbe Hunters.*

Daly enrolled in Queens College as a chemistry major, graduating with a B.S. degree in 1942. The following year she received her M.S. from New York University and then went to Columbia University where she entered the doctoral program in biochemistry. In 1948 she made history at that university, becoming the first African American woman to earn a Ph.D. in chemistry.

Daly began teaching during her college days as a tutor at Queens College. She began her professional career a year before receiving her doctorate, when she accepted a position at Howard University in Washington, D.C., as an instructor in physical sciences. In 1951 she returned to New York first as a visiting investigator and then as an assistant in general physiology at the Rockefeller Institute. By 1955 she had become an associate in biochemistry at the Columbia University Research Service at the Goldwater Memorial Hospital. She taught there until 1971 when she left Columbia as an assistant professor of biochemistry to become associate professor of biochemistry and medicine at the Albert Einstein College of Medicine at Yeshiva University in New York.

Daly conducted most of her research in areas related to the biochemical aspects of human metabolism (how the body processes the energy it takes in) and the role of the kidneys in that process. She also focused on hypertension (high blood pressure) and atherosclerosis (accumulation of lipids or fats in the arteries). Her later work focused on the study of aortic (heart) smooth muscle cells in culture.

During her career, she held several positions concurrently with her teaching obligations, such as investigator for the American Heart Association from 1958 to 1963 and career scientist for the Health Research Council of New York from 1962 to 1972. She was also a fellow of the Council on Arteriosclerosis and the American Association for the Advancement of Science, a member of the American Chemical Society, a member of the board of governors of the New York Academy of Science from 1974 to 1976, and a member of the Harvey Society, the American Society of Biological Chemists, the National Association for the Advancement of Colored People, the National Association of Negro Business and Professional Women, and Phi Beta Kappa and Sigma Xi. In 1988 Daly contributed to a scholarship fund set up at Queens College to aid African American students interested in the sciences. Daly, who married Vincent Clark in 1961, retired from teaching in 1986.

SELECTED WRITINGS BY DALY:

Books

(With Q. B. Deming and H. Wolinsky) "Hypertension: A Precursor of Arteriosclerosis," in

Hypertension: Mechanisms and Management, edited by Gaddo Onesti, Kwan Eun Kim, and John H. Moyer, Grune & Stratton (New York), 1973.

SOURCES:

Books

Women in Chemistry and Physics, edited by Louise S. Grinstein, Rose K. Rose, and Miriam H. Rafailovich, Greenwood Press, 1993, pp. 145–149.

Periodicals

Prestwidge, K. J., "Scientifically Speaking ...!", *New York Voice,* February 4, 1984.

—*Sketch by Leonard C. Bruno*

Reginald Aldworth Daly
1871-1957
Canadian-born American geologist

Reginald Aldworth Daly was a renowned geologist whose extensive field research laid the groundwork for numerous theories. His observations at Mt. Ascutney, Vermont, led him to develop the concept of magmatic stoping, while his work in the Pacific islands stimulated ideas about glacial control over the creation of coral reefs. He was recognized as a gifted lecturer and a thorough author, and his 150 papers, books, and numerous lectures reached a wide audience. In addition, his influence on the research of other geologists was vast.

Daly was born on a farm near Napanee, Ontario, Canada, on May 19, 1871. He was the youngest of nine children of Edward Daly, a tea merchant, and Jane Maria Jeffers Daly. In 1876, the family moved into the town of Napanee, where Daly attended public schools. Later he entered Victoria College, from which he earned an A.B. degree in 1891 and an S.B. in 1892, and where he also served as a mathematics instructor for a year. It was during this period that Daly's interest in geology was first awakened, when a professor held up a piece of granite and remarked that the formation was comprised of crystals.

Theorizes about the Origin of Igneous Rocks

His curiosity aroused, Daly began graduate work in geology at Harvard, where he received an M.A. degree in 1893 and a Ph.D. in 1896. Awarded a traveling fellowship, he spent the next two years studying in Heidelberg and Paris and vacationing throughout Europe. From 1898 to 1901, Daly returned to Harvard as an instructor of physical geography. During this time, he accompanied a party of undergraduates on a cruise along the Labrador coast of Canada, which may have inspired his long-lasting fascination with shoreline geography and marine geology. He also undertook the mapping of complex geological configurations at Mt. Ascutney, which, he eventually concluded, were formed during the region's volcanic birth by the sinking of detached blocks of overlying rock into liquid magma below. This is the essence of the influential idea known as magmatic stoping.

Yet Daly was restless, and, in 1901, he began an arduous survey of 2,500 square miles along the 49th Parallel for the Canadian International Boundary Commission. The task gave Daly an opportunity to master many research techniques and gain significant data; he collected 1,500 rock specimens, took 1,300 photographs, studied 960 thin sections, and ordered 60 chemical analyses. His exhaustive final report on the project filled three large volumes when it was finally published in 1912.

By that time, Daly had been in his new post as professor of physical geology at the Massachusetts Institute of Technology for five years. In 1912, he returned once again to Harvard, this time as Sturgis-Hooper Professor of Geology—a position he held until his retirement in 1942. Daly's early lectures at Harvard primarily dealt with his theories about igneous rocks, which form from the cooling and crystallization of molten magma. These ideas also served as the basis for his 1914 textbook, *Igneous Rocks and Their Origin.* Although some of his notions are now obsolete, they make up the framework upon which much of modern petrology is built. For example, Daly recognized that, when chunks of original rock were dissolved into underlying magma, they would change the molten rock's composition, giving rise to different varieties of igneous formations. He later revised his belief that this differentiation was due to the separation of liquid magma into parts.

Daly was reputed to be a superb lecturer, whose classes in elementary geology often drew applause from his students. His papers and books were similarly clear and concise. Yet despite his writing and teaching duties, Daly managed to travel widely. He observed volcanoes in Hawaii; investigated the risk of landslides at Turtle Mountain, Alberta; and studied the Kiruna ore body in Sweden. Other summers were spent visiting Butte, Montana; Crater Lake; the

Grand Canyon; Duluth, Minnesota; the Adirondacks; and the New England Mountains in Australia. Even World War I did not break the pattern, as Daly journeyed to France as chief librarian for the Young Men's Christian Association (YMCA).

Proposes Ideas on the Formation of Reefs

In 1910, after his trip to Hawaii, Daly formulated and proposed his well-known glacial-control theory of coral reefs, which he continued to elaborate and defend for the next quarter-century. Looking at charts of shorelines, Daly noted a remarkable similarity in the depths of lagoons for dozens of atolls and continental banks. Interestingly, the depth of these bodies of water were very close to the depth the sea would have been lowered during the height of the Ice Age glaciers. Daly inferred that the flattened platforms upon which living reefs now grow had first been planed off during this glacial period and that present corals then grew upward as the sea rose and covered the planed area. Daly's theory has since been criticized for inadequately noting the role of subsidence—the alternate forming and subsiding that makes up the growth cycle of reefs—but it is still considered partially correct. More expeditions followed. Between the end of World War I and 1922, Daly traveled to Saint Helena and the Ascension islands in the southern Atlantic, Samoa, and South Africa as part of a team effort to study the Transvaal region; this South African trip was Daly's last field investigation. By this point, he had crossed North America twenty-four times and the Atlantic Ocean fourteen times. He had visited every American state except South Dakota and every Canadian province except Prince Edward Island.

After 1922, Daly concentrated most of his prodigious energy on lecturing and publishing. Typically, the two pursuits were closely intertwined. A series of talks at the Lowell Institute in Boston became the book *Our Mobile Earth,* while lectures at Yale became *The Changing World of the Ice Age.* Similar orations at Northwestern University, Harvard, and the University of Virginia became, respectively, the books *Architecture of the Earth, Strength and Structure of the Earth,* and *The Floor of the Ocean.* In addition, Daly served as an associate editor of the *American Journal of Science.* He also accumulated numerous honors during this phase of his career, including the 1935 Penrose Medal of the Geological Society of America, the Wollaston Medal of the Geological Society of London, and the Bowie Medal of the American Geophysical Union. He became a U.S. citizen in 1920.

Daly married Louise Porter Haskell on June 3, 1903, in Columbia, South Carolina. Their only child, a son also named Reginald Aldworth, died at the age of three. Daly's wife not only shared his home life but

also accompanied him on his travels and critiqued his manuscripts. Her death in 1947 was a severe blow to the geologist. Daly's own robust health deteriorated until he was virtually confined to his home in Cambridge, Massachusetts. He died there on September 19, 1957.

SELECTED WRITINGS BY DALY:

Books

Geology of the North American Cordillera at the 49th Parallel, 3 volumes, Department of the Interior (Canada), 1912.
Igneous Rocks and Their Origin, McGraw-Hill, 1914.
Our Mobile Earth, Scribner's, 1926.
The Changing World of the Ice Age, Yale University Press, 1934.
Architecture of the Earth, D. Appleton-Century, 1938.
Strength and Structure of the Earth, Prentice-Hall, 1940.
The Floor of the Ocean, University of North Carolina Press, 1942.

SOURCES:

Books

Birch, Francis, "Reginald Aldworth Daly," *Biographical Memoirs,* Volume 34, Columbia University Press, 1960, pp. 31–64.
Dictionary of Scientific Biography, Volume 3, Scribner's, 1971, pp. 547–48.

Periodicals

Billings, Marland P., "Memorial to Reginald Aldworth Daly," *Proceedings, Geological Society of America, 1958,* September, 1959, pp. 115–21.
Billings, "Reginald A. Daly, Geologist," *Science,* January 3, 1958, pp. 19–20.

Other

Harvard University Archives, miscellaneous materials.

—Sketch by Linda Wasmer Smith

Henrik Dam
1895-1976
Danish biochemist

Henrik Dam is best known for his discovery of vitamin K, which gives blood the ability to clot, or coagulate. The discovery of vitamin K dramatically reduced the number of deaths by bleeding during surgery, and for the discovery Dam received the 1943 Nobel Prize in medicine and physiology. (**Edward A. Doisy**, the American biochemist who isolated and synthetically produced vitamin K, shared this prize with Dam.)

Carl Peter Henrik Dam was born in Copenhagen, Denmark, on February 21, 1895. His interest in science was shaped at least in part by his background. His father, Emil Dam, was a pharmaceutical chemist who wrote a history of pharmacies in Denmark. His mother, Emilie Peterson Dam, was a schoolteacher. He attended the Polytechnic Institute in Copenhagen, from which he received his master of science degree in 1920. He was associated with the Royal School of Agriculture and Veterinary Medicine in Copenhagen for the next three years, after which he spent five years as an assistant at the University of Copenhagen's physiological laboratory. He became assistant professor of biochemistry in 1928 and associate professor in 1929 (a post he held until 1941).

During these years Dam studied microchemistry under **Fritz Pregl** in Austria (1925) at the University of Graz, and collaborated with biochemist Rudolf Schoenheimer in Freiburg, Germany (on a Rockefeller Fellowship) from 1932 to 1933. He was awarded a doctorate in biochemistry by the University of Copenhagen in 1934. Afterwards, he worked with the Swiss chemist Paul Xarrer at the University of Zurich in 1935. Dam specialized in nutrition, which became his area of expertise.

Experiments with the Diet of Hens

It was while Dam was studying in Copenhagen that he became interested in what would become the vitamin K factor. In the late 1920s he began experimenting with hens in an attempt to discover how the animals synthesized cholesterol. Providing them with a synthetic diet, Dam discovered that they developed internal bleeding in the form of hemorrhages under the skin—lesions similar to those found in the disease scurvy. He added lemon juice to the diet (citrus fruits, high in vitamin C, had been found by the eighteenth century Scottish physician James Lind to cure scurvy in sailors), but the supplement did little to reverse the hens' condition.

After experimenting with a variety of food additives, Dam came to the conclusion that some vitamin must exist to give blood the ability to clot—and that this vitamin was what was missing from his synthetic hen diet. He made his findings known in 1934, naming the vitamin "K" from the German word *Koagulation*. Dam's continued research, along with the work of Doisy and other biochemists, led to the isolation of vitamin K and its synthetic production.

Dam's discovery proved vitally important in two areas: in surgical procedures and in treatment of newborn babies. Prior to surgery, patients are given vitamin K to assist in clotting the blood and reduce the risk of death by hemorrhage. Newborns are born deficient in vitamin K. Normally, beneficial bacteria that exist in the environment enter the intestinal tracts of infants and induce production of vitamin K. Modern hospitals are disinfected to such an extreme, however, that they kill these good bacteria along with the harmful ones. Mothers are injected with vitamin K shortly before giving birth to ensure that adequate amounts of the vitamin will be in the newborn's system.

Accepts Nobel Prize in New York

Dam's discovery led not only to the Nobel Prize but also the Christian Bohr Award in Denmark in 1939. Dam came to the United States in 1940 for a series of lectures in the U.S. and Canada under the auspices of the American-Scandinavian Foundation. During his visit Nazi Germany invaded Denmark. Dam chose not to return to his native country and accepted a position as senior research associate at the University of Rochester's Strong Memorial Hospital. Because of the war, the Nobel Prize Committee decided to present the awards in New York in 1943. The Nobel recipients of that year, including Dam, were the first to be awarded their prize in the United States. In 1945, Dam became an associate member of the Rockefeller Institute for Medical Research.

After Denmark was liberated, Dam returned in 1946 to accept the position of head of the biology department at the Polytechnic Institute (the position had been awarded to him in absentia in 1941). He returned to the U.S. in 1949 for a three-month lecture tour, this time to discuss vitamin E. In 1956, he was named head of the Danish Public Research Institute. He was a member of numerous organizations including the American Institute of Nutrition, the Society for Experimental Biology and Medicine, the Royal Danish Academy of Science, the Société Chimique of Zurich, and the American Botanical Society. During his career he published more than one hundred articles in scientific journals on vitamin K, vitamin E, cholesterol, and a variety of other topics. Dam married Inger Olsen in 1925. His primary form of recreation was travel. After he returned to Denmark, he pointedly criticized the American hospital system, saying it was hurt by too much emphasis on the business of running hospitals. He died in Copenhagen at the age of eighty-one on April 17, 1976. At his request, news of his death was delayed by one week to allow for private services.

SOURCES:

Books

Current Biography, H. W. Wilson, 1949, p. 136.

Periodicals

New York Times, April 25, 1976.
Science, November 10, 1944.

—*Sketch by George A. Milite*

Walter T. Daniels
1908-1991
American structural engineer

Walter T. Daniels was the first African American to earn a Ph.D. in engineering. During his long career as an educator and administrator at Howard University, he realized his professional goal of developing a renowned engineering program for black students.

Walter Thomas Daniels (some sources cite the surname as "Daniel") was born in Fort Ring Gold, Texas, on April 26, 1908, and was raised in Arizona. Daniels enrolled in Prairie View A&M College in 1925, intent on pursuing a career in engineering. The following year he was accepted into the engineering program at the University of Arizona. Due to the racial barriers then enforced at the university, Daniels was not permitted to associate with his classmates and was therefore prevented from taking laboratory classes, which required interaction with a lab partner. Furthermore, he was made to sit physically apart from the other students in the classroom. Despite these obstacles, he graduated with a bachelor of science degree in 1929.

Daniels returned to Prairie View College and taught there for two years. During that time, his goal of creating professional engineering opportunities for African Americans was crystallized. Energized by this ambition, Daniels first sought advanced education for himself and entered the civil engineering graduate program at Iowa State University. He received a master of science degree in 1932, and, following several years of teaching at North Carolina A&T College, he returned to Iowa State to take a Ph.D. in civil engineering in 1941. In doing so, Daniels became the first African American to earn a doctoral degree in the field. After graduating he taught for one year at Southern University. Upon receiving his professional license in 1943, he also became the first African American engineer to be licensed in the state of Louisiana.

Daniels became a member of the civil engineering faculty at Howard University in Washington, DC, in 1943. He eventually became chair of the civil engineering department and was dean of the School of Engineering for a short time. During his years as professor of structural engineering he was able to realize his dream, developing a curriculum that comprised an outstanding engineering program for African American students. Although he resigned his position as department chair in 1971, he continued to teach at Howard until 1976 when he retired due to health problems

Daniels made significant contributions not only in engineering education, but also in the real world of the practicing engineer. He designed structures that were constructed in Washington, DC, Baltimore, Maryland, and West Africa. On the Howard campus, he designed the L. K. Downing Engineering Building and helped develop the University Physical Plant, including designing its water loop system. Daniels also served as a curriculum consultant in science and mathematics to the District of Columbia public school system. He was a member of the American Society of Civil Engineers, the American Concrete Institute, the American Society for Engineering Education, the Prestressed Concrete Institute, Tau Beta Pi, and Sigma Xi. He was married and had two children.

SOURCES:

Periodicals

"Walter Daniels: A Special Tribute to an Engineering Giant," *The Black Collegian,* January/February 1979, pp. 136, 138.

—*Sketch by Leonard C. Bruno*

George Bernard Dantzig
1914-
American mathematician

George Bernard Dantzig is a mathematician and the father of linear programming, a mathematical technique that has had extensive scientific and technical applications in such areas as computer programming, logistics, and scheduling. Applicable to such endeavors as military research, industrial engineering, and business and managerial studies, linear programming is a method for formulating solutions to problems of how to optimally allocate resources among competitive activities. For example, linear programming could be used to develop a diet that contains all the necessary minimal quantities of dietary elements at a minimum cost by factoring in such variables as calories, protein, vitamins, and the prices of food. Dantzig also discovered the simplex method, an algorithm that was remarkably efficient for use in the linear programming of computers. It has been largely through Dantzig's vision that mathematical programming has become a field in which deep interactions between mathematics, computation, and application models are probed and developed. Dantzig is also coauthor of the book *Compact City,* which suggests improved approaches to urban development, including the use of computer programming that takes into account the "socioeconomic as well as physical aspects of complex urban systems."

Dantzig was born on November 8, 1914, in Portland, Oregon, to Tobias and Anja (Ourisson) Dantzig. Dantzig's father was born in Russia and participated in a failed revolution in 1905. After spending nine months in a Russian prison, Tobias Dantzig went to Paris and studied mathematics at the Sorbonne before immigrating to the United States in 1909. A well-known mathematician in his own right, Tobias Dantzig wrote the influential book, *Number, the Language of Science,* which focused on the concept of the evolution of numbers as related to the growth of the human mind.

Following in his father's footsteps, Dantzig attended the University of Maryland to study mathematics and physics. Upon graduation in 1936, Dantzig was appointed a Horace Rackham Scholar at the University of Michigan, where he earned his M.A. in mathematics in 1938. For the next two years, Dantzig worked as a junior statistician for the U.S. Bureau of Labor Statistics before enrolling in the mathematics doctoral program at the University of California, Berkeley; his studies were interrupted, however, when the United States entered World War II. Dantzig left Berkeley in 1941 to become chief of the combat analysis branch of the U.S. Air Force's statistical control headquarters. In 1944, he received the War Department Exceptional Civilian Service Medal for his efforts. In the meantime, Dantzig had returned to his doctoral studies at Berkeley, studying under Jerzy Neyman, a major contributor to modern mathematical statistics. He received his Ph.D. in mathematics in 1946.

Makes Groundbreaking Discovery in Linear Programming

Rapid advances in technology combined with the effects of World War II and urban development brought on a new era of large-scale planning tasks. With his valuable war-time military experience, Dantzig was asked to continue working for the Air Force and, in 1946, was appointed chief mathematical adviser on the staff of the Air Force Comptroller. At this time, the Air Force had begun Project SCOOP (Scientific Computation of Optimum Programs), which was designed to increase the mechanization and speed for planning and deploying military forces. Focusing primarily on the planning segment of the project, Dantzig discovered that linear programs could be used to solve a wide range of planning problems. Conceptually, this discovery was an important step toward a mathematical approach to many planning and management difficulties, but it was Dantzig's simultaneous discovery of the simplex method—an algorithm that could be efficiently used to solve programming problems—that revealed the enormous power of linear programming. Dantzig's discovery was facilitated by the fact that the modern era of computer research was also getting underway. The development of technology that could rapidly solve complicated equations—equations that otherwise could take years to complete—made linear computing programming a practical resource for use in such areas as industry and economics, which could now quickly compare the many factors involved in interdependent courses of action.

The key to linear programming and the simplex method is the use of a "best value" or set of best values for many variables involved in a certain problem. Linear programming works most efficiently when a quantity can be optimized, or made as perfect and functional as possible. This quantity, called the objective function, for example, could be the most economical way to produce and distribute a product taking into account various "system" factors, such as product composition, production scheduling, and distribution. A key to the programming's success is to develop proportional values for these factors, such as their linear interdependency, in which at least one linear combination of an element equals zero when the coefficients are taken from another given set and at least one of its coefficients is not equal to zero.

In 1952, Dantzig went to work with the RAND Corporation, one of the first private industries to use computer technology. As a research mathematician at RAND, Dantzig played a major role in developing the new discipline of operations research using linear programming, and became a pioneer in identifying its exhaustive uses. In Michael Olinick's book *An Introduction to Mathematical Models in the Social and Life Sciences,* Dantzig notes: "Industrial production, the flow of resources in the economy, the exertion of military effort in a war theater—all are complexes of numerous interrelated activities. Differences may exist in the goals to be achieved, the particular processes involved and the magnitude of effort. Nevertheless, it is possible to abstract the underlying similarities in the management of these seemingly disparate systems."

Helps Establish the Field of Linear Programming

Over the years, Dantzig helped refine linear programming and contributed to establishing the field in both industry and academia. By the 1970s, decision-making software based on the principles of linear programming was being marketed for both technical and nontechnical users. As the growing importance of this field became apparent, universities began developing academic studies of operations research, also referred to as mathematical decision making, in such areas as business science, industrial engineering, and mathematical computing. In 1960, Dantzig left private industry and joined the University of California, Berkeley, as chairman of the Operations Research Center. Located in the heart of the "silicon valley," home of the computer programming and software industry, Dantzig was ideally situated to continue his studies. In 1963, he published the highly influential book *Linear Programming and Extensions,* which includes discussions of the origins of linear programming; according to Dantzig, the theories of linear programming date back to Jean Baptiste Joseph Fourier, a French mathematician known for his research into numerical equations and the conduction of heat. In the book, Dantzig also delves into how the field was developed both on a theoretical basis and by real-life problems presented in the military and economics. His book has become a classic in the field.

In 1966, Dantzig became a professor of operations research and computer science at Stanford and served as acting chairman of the Operations Research Department from 1969 to 1970. He contributed to the development of such major areas of mathematical programming and operations research as quadratic programming, complementary pivot theory, nonlinear equations, convex programming, integer programming, stochastic programming, dynamic programming, game theory, and optimal control theory. With the mathematician Philip Wolfe, he also originated the decomposition principle, a method for solving large systems by exploiting the special characteristics of their block-diagonal structure. This procedure was successfully used in 1971 to solve an equation containing 282,468 variables and 50,215 equations in just 2.5 hours; such an equation would have otherwise required 37 years to complete. Throughout his career, Dantzig consulted on the development of large-scale management planning models and created mathematical models of chemical and biological processes. He also utilized computers as a fundamental aspect of mathematical programming—for example, he participated in the development of a computer language and compiler which was designed to facilitate experimentation on mathematical programming algorithms.

Co-develops Plans for High-Tech Urban Development

One of Dantzig's primary interests was in the development of analytical models of transportation systems; in 1974, he was the recipient of an endowed chair at Stanford, the C. A. Criley Chair of Transportation. Dantzig's interest in transportation and the efficient and most economical use of resources through mathematical programming led him to write *Compact City, A Plan for a Livable Urban Environment* with Thomas L. Saaty. Dantzig and Saaty set out to learn more about city planning by consulting with a range of experts, including engineers, economists, social workers, sociologists, seismologists, waste-removal engineers, and environmentalists. Concerned with such urban crises as the shortage of energy, growth of slums, congestion, and pollution, the book focuses on finding more advanced ways of developing urban areas while increasing the standard of living and minimizing the consumption of nonrenewable resources.

Compact City describes a new concept of living in which as many as two million people could live in ideal weather in spacious homes and gardens and walk to work within a few minutes. An integral part of the planning process was to transform urban development from "flat, predominantly two-dimensional cities to four-dimensional cities in which vertical space and time are exploited." In addition to simplifying transportation systems and alleviating the burden on energy consumption, Dantzig and Saaty were also concerned with "bringing the community together" and offering new opportunities for the underprivileged. Computers and linear programming played an integral part in the planning by taking into account not only the physical aspects but also the socioeconomic aspects of urban development.

As the conceptual developer of linear programming, Dantzig was invited to lecture around the world. He went on a one-year sabbatical in 1974 as head of the methodology group at the International Institute for Applied Systems Analysis, in Laxenburg,

Austria, and received an honorary degree of doctor of science from the Israel Institute of Technology in 1973. During his career, Dantzig also received honorary degrees from the University of Linköping in Sweden, the University of Maryland, and Yale University. In 1975, U.S. President Gerald Ford awarded him the National Medal of Science in recognition of his inventing linear programming, developing methods that allowed it to be applied widely in industry and science, and using computers to incorporate mathematical theory. On November 1, 1976, California passed State Resolution No. 1748, honoring Dantzig's contributions to applied science.

In addition to his many honors, including being elected to the National Academy of Sciences in 1971, Dantzig served in many scientific societies and was the founder of the Mathematical Programming Society. Dantzig married Anne S. Shmumer on August 23, 1936. They have three children, David Franklin, Jessica Rose, and Paul Michael.

SELECTED WRITINGS BY DANTZIG:

Books

Linear Programming and Extensions, Princeton University Press, 1963.
(With Thomas L. Saaty) *Compact City, A Plan for a Livable Urban Environment,* W. H. Freeman, 1973.

SOURCES:

Books

Biographical Dictionary of Scientists: Mathematicians, Peter Bedrick Books, 1986, pp. 36–37.
Cortada, James W., *Historical Dictionary of Data Processing,* Greenwood Press, 1987, pp. 68–70.
McGraw-Hill Modern Engineers and Scientists, McGraw, 1980, pp. 262–263.
Olinick, Michael, *An Introduction to Mathematical Models in the Social and Life Sciences,* Addison-Wesley, 1978, pp. 164–167.

—Sketch by David Petechuk

Christine Darden
1942-
American aeronautical engineer

Christine Darden conducts research for the National Aeronautics and Space Administration (NASA) aimed at reducing sonic booms from supersonic aircraft. This is an important environmental and commercial problem; the federal government would like the country to be able to make greater use of supersonic aircraft, but the disruptions, as well as the damage caused by sonic booms have effectively prevented this so far.

Darden was born Christine Voncile Mann to Noah Horace and Desma Chaney Mann on September 10, 1942, in Monroe, North Carolina. Her father was an insurance agent for North Carolina Mutual Life, and her mother was an elementary school teacher. She attended the Winchester Avenue School in Monroe for most of her early schooling and then transferred to Allen High School, a Methodist boarding school in Asheville, where she received her diploma. She earned a B.S. in mathematics from the Hampton Institute in 1962 and an M.S. from Virginia State College in 1967. It was not until well into her career that she switched to engineering, eventually obtaining a Ph.D. in that field from George Washington University in 1983.

Begins Association with NASA

After graduating from college, Darden taught mathematics at a series of high schools before becoming a research assistant in aerosol physics at Virginia State College in 1965 and then an instructor in mathematics there in 1966. In 1967, she accepted a position with NASA at the Langley Research Center. Initially a data analyst, Darden was promoted first to aerospace engineer in 1973 and then, in 1989, to leader of the Sonic Boom Group, a research team working on methods of reducing the sonic boom impact from supersonic aircraft.

When an airplane accelerates beyond the speed of sound it creates what is known as a sonic boom—a loud, crashing sound that results from the turbulent air flow passing around such a fast-moving object. Sonic booms can be so loud that they break windows and cause structural damage to buildings. Currently, the only supersonic aircraft permitted in the United States are military in nature—and they are restricted to high altitudes so that the effect of their sonic boom is minimized. The Concorde, a supersonic commercial transport plane operated by companies in Britain and France, cannot fly over the continental United States, although it has permission to land in restricted

Christine Darden

coastal areas. Commercial supersonic flight is desirable due to its time-saving nature, but its inherent noise problem has effectively prevented a widespread development. In her efforts to reduce such noise problems, Darden has developed several mathematical algorithms, and her research group designs and tests new wing and nose-cone shapes for their aerodynamic and sonic properties. It is most likely that sonic booms will not be entirely eliminated, but it may be possible, through aerodynamic engineering, to soften, redirect, or dilute the sound. Additionally, Darden is looking into the other environmental impacts of supersonic flight, including the effects on the ozone layer that shields the earth from the sun's harmful ultraviolet light.

When asked how and why she became interested in science, Darden told contributor Gail B. C. Marsella: "The 'power' of mathematics and physical principles in understanding why things work has always fascinated me. I've had parents, teachers, and some supervisors who have encouraged me to pursue what I enjoyed. People often ask me if I have had a 'mentor.' While I have never formally been in a mentor program, there have been many adults along the way who have offered words of advice [that] have helped me in my career. We must somehow get our students to accept mentorship whenever and however offered."

Darden is married to Walter L. Darden, Jr., a middle school science teacher, and they have two children. She has been active in local school systems, the Presbyterian Church, the National Technical Association, and the American Institute of Aeronautics and Astronautics. Among her many awards and recognitions are the Dr. A. T. Weathers Technical Achievement Award from the National Technical Association in 1985 and the Certificate of Outstanding Performance from the Langley Research Center in 1989, 1991, and 1992. She is the author or coauthor of over forty publications, and she frequently gives both community and technical presentations.

SELECTED WRITINGS BY DARDEN:

Periodicals

"The Importance of Sonic Boom Research in the Development of Future High Speed Aircraft," *Journal of the National Technical Association,* winter, 1992, pp. 54–62.
"Study of the Limitations of Linear Theory Methods As Applied to Sonic Boom Pressure Signatures," *Journal of Aircraft,* November-December, 1993, pp. 911–17.

SOURCES:

Books

'Sonic Boom," *McGraw-Hill Encyclopedia of Science and Technology,* Volume 16, McGraw-Hill, 1990, p. 680.
"Supersonic Flight," *McGraw-Hill Encyclopedia of Science and Technology,* Volume 17, McGraw-Hill, 1990, p. 674.
Van Sertima, Ivan, editor, *Blacks in Science: Ancient and Modern,* Transaction Books, 1985.

Other

Darden, Christine Mann, interview with Gail B. C. Marsella conducted April, 1994.

—*Sketch by Gail B. C. Marsella*

Raymond A. Dart
1893-1988
Australian anatomist and anthropologist

A doctor and surgeon by training, Raymond A. Dart was drawn into the field of anthropology early in his career, abandoning plans to become a medical missionary in China. Shortly after beginning his academic career in South Africa, and partly out of necessity, Dart was to discover the first fossils of *Australopithecus africanus*, or "southern ape of Africa," forging the modern era of paleoanthropology.

Raymond Arthur Dart was born to Samuel Dart, a general store operator, and the former Eliza Anne Brimblecombe, on February 4, 1893, the fifth of nine children. Devout Baptists and pioneers in the settlement of Queensland, Australia, Dart's parents raised him in the Brisbane suburb of Toowong, later moving the family to a bush farm in Blenheim, where the future scientist spent his youth milking cows and hiking to school. In 1911, scholarship in hand, he entered Brisbane's newly founded University of Queensland, where he earned both bachelor's and master's degrees in biology. Another scholarship sent him in 1914 to St. Andrew's College at the University of Sydney, where, before the completion of his second year of medical studies, he was appointed as a tutor in biology and granted membership on the college staff. The year 1914 also saw the outbreak of World War I in Europe as well as the British Association's meeting in Sydney. Dart attended the gathering, which brought in noted scientists such as Grafton Elliot Smith and W. J. Sollas. The conference signalled a turning point in Dart's career as he became intrigued by the announcement of the discovery of Australia's first human fossil find, the Talgai Skull from Queensland, unearthed by Antarctic geologic explorer T. Edgeworth David. The description was presented by James T. Wilson, head of the university's department of anatomy. Soon thereafter Dart became an assistant to Wilson on neurological research and came to regard him as a mentor.

Dart's intentions to conduct more in-depth neurological research were hampered by his own schoolwork and administrative roles as demonstrator in anatomy and acting vice principal of St. Andrew's College. After receiving his bachelor's degree in medicine and a master's degree in surgery in August of 1917, he enlisted in the Australian Army Medical Corps, finishing his service in France as a captain. Upon his release from the military in 1919, he was immediately appointed to the post of senior demonstrator in anatomy at University College, London, by Grafton Elliot Smith. In 1920, at Elliot Smith's recommendation, the Rockefeller Foundation awarded Dart one of its first two foreign fellowships, allowing him the opportunity to teach at Washington University in St. Louis, and study at the Wood's Hole marine research station in Massachusetts.

By 1922, Dart had rejoined the University's faculty as a lecturer in histology and embryology. At the insistence of Elliot Smith, however, Dart applied for the vacant anatomy chair at the newly established School of Medicine at the University of Witwatersrand in Johannesburg, South Africa, a place of which he had never heard. "The very idea revolted me; I

turned it down flat instantly," he wrote in recollections for the *Journal of Human Evolution.*

Acquires Rare Fossil

After some reflection, Dart changed his mind and arrived in South Africa in January of 1923. Dart found the School of Medicine in dire need of equipment, facilities, and a collection of bones with which to create a proper anatomy museum. To acquire the latter, Dart encouraged his students to search for fossil bones during holidays. In the summer of 1924, a fossilized baboon skull was brought to Dart's attention by Josephine Salmons, one of his student demonstrators, who had secured the skull from E. G. Izod of Rand Mines Limited. The fossil had been detected while mining a sheet of limestone at Taungs (now Taung) in the Bechuanaland Protectorate, where other fossil baboon skulls had been discovered as early as 1920. His interest piqued, Dart asked his colleague, geology professor R. B. Young, to look for similar specimens since Young was going to investigate the lime deposit at Taungs. By November 28, 1924, Dart had in his hands a fossil skull that would change the face of paleoanthropology.

Young sent back two crates full of bones, one of which held a face and skull still embedded in matrix, along with the internal cast of a cranium found by one of the quarry workers. A quick examination of this endocast brought to light a startling revelation, derived from Dart's earlier neurological studies with Elliot Smith. He had learned that convolutions toward the back of the primate brain cause two fissures which are farther apart in humans than in apes. This, Elliot Smith attributed to the evolutionary expansion of the cerebrum. Yet, the cast Dart then held in his hand exhibited fissures that were farther apart than those displayed by any primate he had ever seen.

Dart freed the face and skull from its rock casing shortly before Christmas of 1924. The face was nearly complete, exhibiting cranial and mandibular features of humanoid rather than anthropoid characteristics. The shape of the jaw and alignment of the teeth also resembled those of humans, as did the set of emerging molars which Dart likened to those of a six-year old child or slightly younger ape. Because of the near completeness of the specimen, Dart was able to measure the position of the foramen magnum—the opening at the base of the skull through which the spinal cord enters the cranial cavity. In his preliminary account of the specimen, published in *Nature* on February 7, 1925, he noted that the foramen magnum's "relatively forward situation" suggested "an attitude appreciably more erect than that of the modern anthropoids. . . . The specimen is of importance because it exhibits an extinct race of apes intermediate between living anthropoids and man."

Dart believed he had found the "missing link," and that his discovery might bare out English naturalist Charles Darwin's earlier revelation that man's origins were linked to Africa. He named the creature *Australopithecus africanus*, the "southern ape of Africa."

Findings Are Subject of Controversy

Dart's views were immediately met with derision by the general public and adamant disagreement by many of his own colleagues, including Elliot Smith and **Arthur Keith**, who immediately categorized the find within the fossil family of modern gorillas and chimps. His opponents proposed a lack of evidence in morphology and geologic age, and were appalled that the discovery was made in Africa. During that era, Asia was seen as the cradle of humankind. Yet, Dart did have his defenders, particularly in the person of Scottish anthropologist Robert Broom, whose defense of Dart has been compared to English biologist Thomas Henry Huxley's staunch support of Darwin. Broom's successive series of Taung-like fossil discoveries in Sterkfontein in 1936, and Kromdraii in 1938, would turn the tide of evidence in favor of Dart's South African ape-man.

Despite the controversy that surrounded him, Dart was elected president of the Anthropological Section of the South African Association for the Advancement of Science in 1925, became dean of Witwatersand's School of Medicine in 1926, and was appointed vice president of the Anthropology Section of the British Association in 1929. The following year, with a growing belief in man's African origins, he set out on a series of archeological and anthropological expeditions. His joint venture with the Italian African Scientific Expedition of 1930 gave him his first glimpse of the gorilla in its natural habitat, precluding his sponsorship of the University of Witwatersrand's Gorilla Research Unit in the late 1950s. Dart's investigation of the Auni-Khomani groups of Southern Bushmen in 1936 was considered the most complete physical study conducted up to that time.

The year 1945 proved another turning point in Dart's scientific career. Again, baboon fossils had been found in South Africa, this time at Makapansgat in the northern Transvaal. Just as the baboons had foreshadowed the appearance of *Australopithecus africanus* at Taung, as well as Broom's Sterkfontein, so did they at Makapansgat. The subsequent excavation of the site during April of 1947, turned up some three dozen australopithecine fossils, a number of fossilized baboon skulls, and thousands of animal bone fragments. Fractures in many of the baboon skulls found at Makapansgat, Sterkfontein, and Taungs, as well as those found in six australopithecine skulls, led Dart to the conclusion that his ape men had inflicted these mortal blows using bone weapons such as an antelope's upper arm bone, evident in abundance around the Makapansgat site. He further concluded that theirs was a culture adept in the manufacturing of tools and weapons from bones, teeth, and horns, and thus named it the *osteodontokeratic culture*. While this theory was ultimately rejected by the scientific community, Dart's observations helped create a new field of science called taphonomy, concerning the environmental circumstances that act upon bones after death.

Divorced from his first wife, Dora Tyree, in 1934, Dart married again on November 28, 1936. His second wife, Marjorie Gordon Frew, was chief librarian of the Witwatersrand Medical Library. They had two children, Diana Elizabeth and Galen Alexander. Dart retired from the chair of anatomy in 1958. From 1966 to 1986, he spent half of each year in Johannesburg and the other half in Philadelphia, where he had been appointed United Steelworkers of America Professor of Anthropology in the Avery Postgraduate Institute of the Institutes for the Achievement of Human Potential.

On the advent of his eightieth birthday, Dart remarked upon his achievements in the *Journal of Human Evolution*. "To open closed doors, to find lost things, or to shed light where gloom enshrouded understanding, these are but types of the privileges common to all intelligent individuals." Dart died on November 22, 1988.

SELECTED WRITINGS BY DART:

Books

(Editor) *Africa's Place in the Human Story,* South African Broadcasting Corp., 1954.
The Osteodontokeratic Culture of Australopithecus Prometheus, Transvaal Museum, 1957.
(With Dennis Craig) *Adventures with the Missing Link,* Harper, 1959.
Beyond Antiquity, South African Broadcasting Corp., 1965.

Periodicals

"*Australopithecus africanus:* The Man-Ape of South Africa," *Nature,* February 7, 1925, pp. 195–99.
"Recollections of a Reluctant Anthropologist," *Journal of Human Evolution,* 1973, pp. 417–27.

SOURCES:

Books

Broom, Robert, and G. W. H. Schepers, *The South African Fossil Ape-Men: The Australopithecinae,* AMS Press, 1978, pp. 11–43.

Broom, Robert, *Finding the Missing Link,* Watts, 1951.

Johanson, Donald, and James Shreeve, *Lucy's Child: The Discovery of a Human Ancestor,* Avon Books, 1989, pp. 53–58.

Periodicals

"Homage to Emeritus Professor Raymond Arthur Dart on His 75th Birthday," *South African Journal of Science,* February, 1968, pp. 42–50.

—*Sketch by John Spizzirri*

Jean Dausset
1916-
French immunologist

As a researcher who made important discoveries about the human immune system, Jean Dausset fostered the breakthroughs that led to successful organ transplantation. A specialist in blood diseases, he discovered the existence of a human biological system that determines whether a body will accept or reject foreign substances called antigens. This made it possible for surgeons to "type" cells to determine whether a prospective donor and patient are a compatible match. His research earned Dausset the Nobel Prize for medicine or physiology in 1980.

Jean Baptiste Gabriel Dausset was born October 19, 1916, in Toulouse, France, to Henri Dausset and the former Elizabeth Brullard. Dausset followed in the footsteps of his father, a physician and radiologist, by embarking upon a medical career. His studies at the University of Paris were interrupted by the onset of World War II, when he was drafted into military service. Following the fall of France to Germany in 1940, he left his occupied country to fight with the Free French forces in North Africa. Before he left Paris, Dausset gave his identification papers to a Jewish colleague at the Pasteur Institute, who thus survived Nazi persecution by impersonating Dausset.

While in North Africa, Dausset served in the blood transfusion unit of the Free French Army, where he developed his interest in transfusion reactions. Participating in his country's liberation in 1944, Dausset attained the rank of second lieutenant before leaving the service in 1945. After receiving his medical degree from the University of Paris, he was appointed administrator of the National Blood Transfusion Center, a post he held until 1963. In 1948 Dausset became a graduate student at Harvard Medical School, studying hematology and immunology. His studies paid off in 1951, when he discovered that the type-O blood group, which had been assumed safe for transfusions with all other blood types, was in some cases hazardous to the recipients with blood types other than O. Dausset found that persons with type-O blood who had received vaccines against diphtheria or tetanus often developed strong antibodies in their blood system. Since this blood had been conditioned to fight foreign substances, it often reacted with the properties of other blood types—in essence attacking the antigens in the recipient's blood. Often when this fortified type-O blood was transfused into other blood types, the reaction would cause dangerous clotting.

Discovers Key to Human Immune System

Dausset's work at this time also involved research on the disease agranulocytosis, an illness characterized by acute fevers that was often triggered by drug hypersensitivity. He found that those suffering agranulocytosis had an unusually low white blood cell (leukocyte) count. Dausset also found similarly low leukocyte counts in patients who had numerous transfusions. In a 1952 paper titled "Presence of a Leucoagglutinate in the Serum of a Case of Agranulocytosis," he theorized that the patients' systems had created antibodies which reacted against the antigens in foreign white blood cells while simultaneously distinguishing—and not attacking—its own white blood cells. Dausset called these developed antibodies human leukocyte antigens (HLA), and found them to be crucial in determining whether or not blood, tissue, or an organ could be transferred from one person to another. The paper built upon work done with the immune systems of mice and, in particular, the discovery of an antigen similar to human HLA called H–2. H–2 had been discovered by American scientist **George Snell** in the 1940s, following research on skin grafts with the animals.

From his knowledge of HLA, Dausset established the existence of a histocompatibility system in humans, known as the major histocompatibility complex (MHC). This genetically controlled system is the human body's method for keeping out material that it deems harmful. It could be used to determine whether a body would accept or reject the tissue of donor. Through typing for HLA, doctors would be able to classify tissue systems as they had blood. It also enabled doctors to determine whether a transplant would be successful by the use of blood tests, instead of the previous system (which was time-consuming and difficult) of taking skin grafts. Both heart and kidney transplantation were thus considered far less risky to perform. As a means of persuading surgeons of the importance of screening donors for their HLA prior to transplantation, Dausset helped found the

Transplantation Society in 1966 and served as secretary for the organization's first four years.

To obtain greater understanding of the MHC, more research had to be done on human histocompatibility. Dausset, who became professor of hematology at the University of Paris in 1958, and professor of immunohematology ten years later, helped organize a series of conferences at which scientists compared their techniques and discoveries regarding the genetic complex. At a 1965 conference held in Prague, Czechoslovakia, Dausset contributed to a report which revealed that HLA are related to one another and that a genetic system exists which controls what specific antigens appear in human cells.

In order to find out if the genetic laws which had been discovered were valid for the entire human race, and not just certain groups, Dausset and his colleagues, in the late–1960s, conducted anthropological research on fifty-four widely dispersed racial and ethnic populations. Obtaining blood samples from these groups, the scientists found the genetic laws regarding the MHC were valid for all peoples. The investigation also had the benefit of, as Dausset stated in *Current Biography,* "drawing a biological map of humanity before the modern mixture of population obscures their differences."

Link Found between HLA and Diseases

After becoming chief biologist for the Paris General Hospital System and cochair of the Institute for Research into Blood Diseases during the early 1960s, Dausset began to investigate the relationship between certain HLAs and diseases. Other scientists followed his lead and found that particular types of histocompatibility antigens are linked to some kinds of arthritis, juvenile diabetes, multiple sclerosis, and perhaps a great many other diseases as well. He theorized that people prone to these diseases could be identified by the presence of these HLAs in their systems. Further study of the HLA factors could result in treatment or prevention of certain diseases in people whose immune systems are identified as susceptible to these types of illnesses.

After teaching at the University of Paris for many years, Dausset was appointed as head of the facility's immunology department in 1977. The same year, he was selected as professor of experimental medicine at the College de France. He also was elected to the Academy of Science at the Institute of France and to the French Academy of Medicine. Dausset's extensive research on HLA and the human immune system earned him the 1980 Nobel Prize for medicine or physiology. He shared the prize with Snell, whose work pioneered antigen study in the 1940s, and with **Baruj Benacerraf**, who had built upon Dausset's work.

Dausset married his wife, Rosita Lopez, in March of 1963. The couple have two children—a son, Henri, and a daughter, Irene. A man with a strong interest in modern art, Dausset was once co-owner of a Parisian art gallery, La Galerie du Dragon, which specialized in Impressionist paintings. Well-known to colleagues for his industriousness and devotion to his work, Dausset lives up to his motto, quoted in the *New York Times,* "Vouloir pour valoir ... to achieve any worthwhile goal, you must work at it hard enough."

SELECTED WRITINGS BY DAUSSET:

Books

Immuno-Hematologie Biologicque et Clinique, Flammarion, 1956.
Tissue Typing, S. Karger, 1966.
Advances in Transplantation, Williams and Wilkins, 1968.
(With Felix T. Rapaport) *Human Transplantation,* Grune and Stratton, 1968.
Histocompatibility Testing, Williams and Wilkins, 1973.
(With George Snell and Stanley Nathanson) *Histocompatibility,* Academic Press, 1976.
(With M. Gorereau) *Immunology,* Academic Press, 1980.
(With Rapaport) *A Modern Illustration of Experimental Medicine in Action,* Elsevier (North Holland), 1980.

SOURCES:

Books

Current Biography, H. W. Wilson, 1981, pp. 108–12.
Dowie, Mark, *"We Have A Donor": The Brave New World of Organs Transplants,* St. Martin's Press, 1988.
Kittridge, Mary, *Organ Transplants,* Chelsea House, 1989.

Periodicals

Altman, Lawrence, "Antigens May Prove Key to Organ Transplantations," *New York Times,* October 11, 1980, p. 7.
Borders, William, "Three Cell Researchers Win Medicine Nobel," *New York Times,* October 11, 1980, p. 1.
Clark, Matt, "A Nobel Piece of Research," *Newsweek,* October 20, 1980, p.66.

Marx, Jean, "1980 Noble Prize in Physiology or Medicine," *Science,* November 7, 1980, pp. 621–23.

New York Times Biographical Service, October, 1980.

—*Sketch by Francis Rogers*

Margaret B. Davis
1931-
American paleoecologist

Margaret B. Davis is a distinguished paleoecologist noted for her analysis of ancient pollen to determine trends in plant growth and migration. Her work challenged the prevailing scientific idea that plant and animal communities tend to be stable, moving intact to new locations as the climate changes. By studying pollen from ancient plants (in a discipline known as palynology), she reconstructed past plant communities and showed how they change in response to variations in climate or other environmental influences. She found that associations between plant and animal communities are more fluid than once believed and that change is the order of the day for ecosystems.

Born in Boston, Massachusetts, on October 23, 1931, Margaret Bryan Davis grew up in the Boston area and graduated from Radcliffe College in 1953 with an A.B. degree in biology. While at Radcliffe, she took courses from noted paleobotanist Elso Borghoorn and was intrigued by the vegetational history of the late-Quaternary period, some ten thousand years ago. She believed that to best understand and interpret the history of ancient plant life it was more important to understand the physiology and ecology of flora, rather than just the stratigraphic interpretation of pollen records.

Davis was awarded a Fulbright fellowship and studied from 1953 to 1954 at the University of Copenhagen with palynologist Johannes Iversen of the Danish Geological Survey. Her work took her to Greenland where she recorded plant pollen deposited during the interglacial period. In 1954 she published her first paper, "Interglacial Pollen Spectra from Greenland," in a Danish geological journal. Combining both field work and paleoecology in Denmark, she returned to Boston and obtained a Ph.D. in biology from Harvard University in 1957. Davis was convinced that the growing new field of palynology was the best path to follow in tracing the history of ancient

vegetation. Over the following four years, Davis continued her studies as a National Science Foundation postdoctoral fellow, first at Harvard, then at the California Institute of Technology where she concentrated in geology. In 1960, she became a research fellow at Yale University; her objective there was to clarify the relationship between pollen in lake sediments and vegetation composition, as a means to enhance the precision of pollen records for describing past vegetation.

In 1961, Davis accepted a position as a research associate in the University of Michigan's department of botany. She remained in Ann Arbor, Michigan, for the next twelve years and concluded her stay as professor of zoology before returning to Yale to serve as professor of biology. She remained at Yale for three years, then moved in 1976 to the University of Minnesota where she is Regents' Professor in the department of ecology, evolution and biology.

During Davis's stay at Michigan, she attracted international attention with a paper on the theory of pollen analysis, published in 1963 in the *American Journal of Science.* For years scientists had assumed that fossil pollen produced by trees tens of thousands of years ago could provide a clear picture of plant life during the period. However, since some species of trees produce more pollen than others, they had suggested that a correction factor ranging from 4:1 to 35:1 be used to equalize the difference. Davis' research on lake bed sediments showed that these correction factors were erroneous, and these factors could range as much as 24,000:1.

Davis' findings, cast doubt on many theories of ancient plant life, and opened the door to a new scientific method of understanding the history and ecology of plants that lived on earth thousands of years ago. "These methods allow us a new approach to some long-standing environmental questions," Davis said in a University of Minnesota press release. "We can begin to distinguish between the impacts of humans and the natural process of change that has always occurred. For example, we can examine the response of ecosystems to past climatic change and use our findings to predict responses to future climatic warming." Davis has warned that the climatic changes predicted in response to the build-up of greenhouse gases will be at least one order of magnitude more rapid than climatic changes in the past, and will tax the ability of biotic systems to change and disperse from one area to another.

Davis also compiled maps for eastern North America depicting the migration of various species of trees during the past fourteen thousand years. Her maps indicate that the temperate forest trees moved at different rates and from different directions.

In 1982, Davis was elected to the National Academy of Sciences. She has also served as president of the American Quaternary Association and the Ecological Society of America. Davis is the author of more than sixty-five scientific publications and the recipient of numerous honors, including the Eminent Ecologist Award, bestowed by the Ecological Society of America. In 1993, she was also awarded the Nevada Medal and a cash prize of five thousand dollars in recognition for her work in "unlocking the history of environmental change and using it to understand present and future shifts in plant and animal communities."

SELECTED WRITINGS BY DAVIS:

Periodicals

"On the Theory of Pollen Analysis," *American Journal of Science,* Volume 261, 1963, pp. 897–912.

(With E. S. Deevey, Jr.) "Pollen Accumulation Rates: Estimates from the Late-Glacial Sediment of Roger Lake," *Science,* Volume 145, 1964, pp. 1293–1295.

(With L. E. Frelich, R. R. Calcote, and J. Pastor) "Patch Formation and Maintenance in an Oldgrowth Hemlock-Hardwood Forest," *Ecology,* Volume 74, 1993, pp. 513–527.

SOURCES:

Periodicals

Bulletin of the British Ecological Society, December, 1991, pp. 103–104.
Bulletin of the Ecological Society of America, September, 1987, pp. 490–491.

—*Sketch by Benedict A. Leerburger*

Marguerite Davis
1887-1967
American chemist

Marguerite Davis is best known as co-discoverer of vitamins A and B. Her research at the University of Wisconsin in Madison with biochemist **Elmer Verner McCollum** led to definitive identification of both vitamins and paved the way for later research in nutrition.

Davis was born on September 16, 1887, in Racine, Wisconsin. Her father, Jefferson J. Davis, was a physician and botanist who taught at the University of Wisconsin. Her grandmother, Amy Davis Winship, was a social worker and an early champion of women's rights. Her background, coupled with her own interest in science, led her to enroll at the University of Wisconsin in 1906. She transferred to the University of California at Berkeley in 1908 and received her bachelor of science degree there in 1910. Upon graduation, she returned to the University of Wisconsin and pursued graduate studies, although she never completed the master's program. She worked briefly for the Squibbs Pharmaceutical Company in New Brunswick, New Jersey, but returned to Wisconsin.

It was during her time at the University of Wisconsin that she began her work with McCollum, who had been studying nutrition for several years. The Dutch physician **Christiaan Eijkman** and the British biochemist Sir **Frederick Gowland Hopkins** had determined that traces of as-yet unidentified elements in foods were essential for adequate nutrition. The Polish-American biochemist Casimir Funk, believing the substances were amines, proposed the name "vitamine"—literally, "life-giving amine" (when it later became clear that not all the substances were amines the "e" was dropped). McCollum was trying to create simple mixtures that could replace natural food in animal diets. Although his efforts were unsuccessful, he wanted to find out whether natural food contained some special substance like that proposed by Eijkman and Hopkins.

Discovers Vitamin A

Davis and McCollum worked with various food components and in 1913 discovered a factor in some fats that apparently was essential to life. Because the substance differed chemically from one described earlier by Eijkman, Davis and McCollum named theirs fat-soluble A and Eijkman's water-soluble B. These were later called vitamins A and B. The identification of A and B led later to the discovery of the other vitamins and their specific roles in nutrition, as well as which foods contain them.

Davis joined the University of Wisconsin's chemical research staff and founded its nutrition laboratory. She later went on to Rutgers University in New Jersey and organized a similar lab for its school of pharmacy. She retired and moved back to Racine in 1940 but continued to serve as a chemistry consultant for many years. She became active in Racine civic affairs and pursued other interests, including history and gardening. In 1958 Racine's Women's Civic Council recognized Davis for her contributions as a civic leader. Davis died in Racine in September 19, 1967, three days after her eightieth birthday.

SOURCES:

Periodicals

Racine Journal-Times, September 19, 1967, p. 1A.

—*Sketch by George A. Milite*

Raymond Davis, Jr.
1914-
American astrochemist

Raymond Davis, Jr. has devoted much of his scientific career to pursuing one of the universe's great phantoms, the neutrino (low-mass grains of matter from the sun that travel at the speed of light). Davis created the first working neutrino detector while at Brookhaven National Laboratory, and the results he and his collaborator John Bahcall obtained have led physicists to reevaluate the assumptions made concerning the relationship between the internal fires of stars to the internal workings of the atom.

Davis was born October 14, 1914, in Washington, D.C., the older of two brothers. His father, Raymond, worked in the photographic division of the National Bureau of Standards. His mother was Ida Rogers Younger Davis. He attended Washington, DC public schools. Although an indifferent student, Davis loved learning and early on became enamored of chemistry; he would frequently visit the library and read the *Smithsonian Technical Reports.* He received his bachelor's degree in chemistry from the University of Maryland in 1937, and then worked for a year for Dow Chemical Company in Midland, Michigan. In 1939, he earned his master's degree in physical chemistry from the University of Maryland. He then went on to Yale University, receiving his Ph.D. in 1942.

Davis served in the U.S. Army Air Corps from 1942 to 1946. After the war, he worked as a research chemist for Monsanto Chemical Company's Mound Laboratory in Dayton, OH, from 1946 to 1948. In that year he moved to the Brookhaven National Laboratory on Long Island, NY, where he worked as a research chemist from 1948 to 1984. In 1984 he was named a research professor in the astronomy department at the University of Pennsylvania, concurrently

serving as a consultant to the Los Alamos National Laboratory in New Mexico.

Neutrinos, named by Italian physicist Enrico Fermi, who believed they could never be detected, are particles of extremely low mass. During the 1950s astrophysicists theorized that these particles formed during fusion reactions within the sun's internal furnace, and as a result, the sun threw off neutrinos by the trillion.

Davis was fascinated by the new theory that depicted the sun as a gigantic nuclear furnace. If neutrinos could be found, he thought, they could provide a clue to the sun's internal workings. But the question was, How to detect something smaller than an electron with almost no mass at all? Neutrinos pass unnoticed—and unimpeded—through the sun's matter, through space, through stone, and through our bodies. Besides having little mass, some neutrinos (called pp neutrinos) have very little energy and interact weakly with atomic nuclei and with each other.

Builds First Neutrino Detector

In 1955, Davis built his first neutrino detector. Located twenty feet underground at the Brookhaven National Laboratory (the underground location would keep cosmic rays from interfering with the results), it was filled with 1,000 gallons of chlorine compound. "I didn't really expect to see anything," Davis told *Discover* magazine. "There was still too much background radiation, and the pp neutrino energies were too low."

The Brookhaven detector failed to find even a single pp neutrino. But in 1958, other researchers discovered there were more energetic neutrinos—thirty times more energetic than the pp neutrinos Davis had been seeking—shooting out of the sun. These energetic neutrinos resulted from a different reaction, and were called boron-8 neutrinos. In 1962, Davis contacted astrophysicist John Bahcall, who calculated that about eight of these neutrinos might be detected each day. Davis built another neutrino detector in an abandoned gold mine a mile beneath the Black Hills of South Dakota. Completed in 1967, the forty-eight-foot long metal tank is filled with 100,000 gallons of perchlorothylene, a kind of dry cleaning fluid.

The detector worked when neutrinos, passing through rock and metal, would travel through the fluid in the tank. Occasionally, one of them would strike a chlorine atom, splitting a neutron into a proton and an electron, and changing the chlorine into radioactive argon. Every couple of months, the argon would be drawn off and its atoms counted by measuring the rate of radioactive decay; the result would indicate how many neutrinos had passed through the tank and reacted with the chlorine. The results were surprising. The tank detected not eight neutrinos a day as calculations had predicted, but one neutrino every two days. These figures remained consistent for over a quarter of a century, and have been confirmed by another neutrino detector deep within the Kamioka Mine in Japan.

Davis's work has created a worldwide effort by researchers to probe the secret of the neutrino. Astrophysicists and particle physicists, due in part to Davis's research, have developed a closer working relationship as they try to learn the neutrino's secrets. Davis, for his part, is planning a new detector using iodine, thought to be even more sensitive to neutrino bombardment than chlorine.

In addition to his work with neutrinos, Davis also took part in the analysis of lunar samples gathered by the Apollo moon missions of the 1970s, and measured the radioactivity of material from the moon's surface. Davis has also written more than sixty scientific papers, primarily in nuclear chemistry, geochemistry, and astrochemistry, and contributed articles to a number of books. He is a member of the National Academy of Sciences, the American Academy of Science, the Geochemical Society, Meteorite Society, the American Geophysical Union, the American Physical Society and the American Astronomical Society.

Among the honors he has received are the W.H.K. Panofsky Prize from the American Physical Society, 1992; the Bonner Prize for Nuclear Physics from the American Physical Society, 1988; the American Chemical Society Award for Nuclear Chemistry, 1979; the Comstock Award from the National Academy of Sciences, 1978; and the Boris Pregel Prize from the New York Academy of Sciences, 1957. In 1948, Davis married Anna Marsh Torrey, whom he met while working at Brookhaven, where she was a biology technician. They have five children: Andrew M. Davis, Martha S. Kumler, Nancy E. Klemm, Roger W. Davis, and Alan P. Davis.

SELECTED WRITINGS BY DAVIS:

Books

"Neutrino Astronomy," in *The Encyclopedia of Physical Science and Technology,* Academic Press, 1987.

Periodicals

(With D. S. Harmer and K. C. Hoffman) "A Search for Neutrinos from the Sun," in *Physical Review of Letters,* Volume 20, 1968, pp. 1205–1209.
(With John N. Bahcall) "Solar Neutrinos: A Scientific Puzzle," *Science,* Volume 191, 1976, pp. 264–67.

SOURCES:

Periodicals

Freedman, David H., "The Ghost Particle Mystery," *Discover,* May, 1991, pp. 66–72.

—*Sketch by F. C. Nicholson*

Clinton Davisson
1881-1958
American physicist

A major focus of Clinton Davisson's research at Bell Telephone Laboratories (formerly Western Electric Company) was the scattering of electrons by crystals. In 1927, while working with a colleague named Lester Germer, Davisson accidentally discovered evidence to support the earlier hypothesis of Prince **Louis Victor de Broglie** that a beam of electrons has wave properties. For this discovery, Davisson was awarded a share of the 1937 Nobel Prize in physics. He remained at Bell until his retirement in 1946.

Clinton Joseph Davisson was born in Bloomington, Illinois, on October 22, 1881. His father, Joseph Davisson, was a veteran of the Union Army who worked as a contract painter; his mother was the former Mary Calvert, a school teacher before her marriage. The Davissons also had one daughter, Carrie. Young Clinton attended local schools and graduated from Bloomington High School in 1902. He entered the University of Chicago on a scholarship, as a physics major.

Davisson's intellectual promise soon became apparent. At the end of his sophomore year, one of his professors, Nobel laureate **Robert A. Millikan**, recommended Davisson as a replacement for a physics instructor at nearby Purdue University who had recently died. Davisson took that post and spent the last half of the 1903–04 academic year at Purdue. He returned to Chicago in the fall of 1904, but was there only a year when he was offered a position as instructor in physics at Princeton University the following autumn. At Princeton he also worked as a research assistant under another Nobel winner, **Owen W. Richardson**. Over the next six years, Davisson worked on both his B.S. at Chicago by attending summer sessions and his Ph.D. at Princeton during the regular academic year. He received the former in 1908 and the latter in 1911.

Shortly after graduation from Princeton, on August 4, 1911, Davisson was married to the former Charlotte Sara Richardson, his mentor's sister. Davisson had met Richardson while she was staying with her brother at Princeton on a visit from England. The Davissons had four children, Clinton Owen Calvert, James Willans, Richard Joseph, and Elizabeth Mary. A few weeks after his marriage, Davisson began his new job as assistant professor of physics at Carnegie Institute of Technology in Pittsburgh.

Davisson's experience at Carnegie over the next six years was largely unsatisfactory. His teaching load was so heavy that he had virtually no time to spend on research. Indeed, as Mervin J. Kelly writes in his obituary of Davisson in the National Academy of Sciences' *Biographical Memoirs,* "he had been able to carry only one research to the point where, with his lifelong high standards, he would publish it." As a result, Davisson was not at all disappointed in May 1917 to receive a leave of absence from Carnegie to take on war-related research in the Engineering Department of the Western Electric Company (later, the Bell Telephone Laboratories). When the war ended, Davisson chose to continue on at Western Electric rather than to return to academic life. He remained with the company for another 29 years, retiring in 1946 at the age of 65.

Laboratory Accident Leads to Discovery of Electron Diffraction

Davisson's first research assignment at Western Electric was carried out in connection with a patent suit in which the company was involved regarding rights on vacuum tubes. That research concerned a study of electron emission patterns produced when a metal filament is bombarded by positive ions. When that research was completed, Davisson moved on to a variation of that topic, the characteristics of electron emission when metals are bombarded by electrons rather than by positive ions. For about six years, Davisson and a colleague, C. H. Kunsman, bombarded a variety of metals with electrons and measured the angles at which secondary electrons were emitted from the metal surface. Throughout this period, however, they were unable to develop a theoretical model that explained their results.

Finally, in April 1925, a laboratory accident provided some key new information. A vacuum tube being used by Davisson and L. H. Germer (who had replaced Kunsman) exploded, resulting in the rapid oxidation of the nickel target inside the tube. Intending to restore the target for re-use in another vacuum tube, Davisson was forced to re-heat the nickel for an extended period of time. When new experiments were begun using a vacuum tube containing the rejuvenated nickel target, some remarkable results were obtained. Specifically, electrons were not just reflected from the nickel target, but diffracted as well. Later studies revealed that the heating process had converted many tiny nickel crystals in the original sample to a few much larger crystals in the restored sample.

The new findings were significant because diffraction is a characteristic of waves. Although the Davisson-Germer results suggested that electron beams reflected from the nickel target behaved as if they were traveling in waves, Davisson did not fully appreciate the meaning of his results until the summer of 1926. While attending a meeting of the British Association for the Advancement of Science, he learned for the first time about Prince Louis de Broglie's recently announced hypothesis of the wave nature of electrons. Using de Broglie's theory, Davisson was able to calculate the wavelength of the electrons diffracted in his experiment. His results matched de Broglie's predictions so closely that they could be regarded as confirmation of the French physicist's theory.

Davisson continued his research on electron scattering over the next two decades of his tenure, first at Western Electric, and then at Bell Laboratories. After his retirement in 1946 he accepted an appointment as visiting professor of physics at the University of Virginia. He resigned from that post in 1954 and died in Charlottesville, Virginia, on February 1, 1958. In addition to the 1937 Nobel Prize, Davisson received a number of other honors and awards, including the Comstock Prize of the National Academy of Sciences in 1928, the Elliot Cresson Medal of the Franklin Institute in 1935, the Hughes Medal of the Royal Society in 1935, and the University of Chicago Alumni Medal in 1941.

SELECTED WRITINGS BY DAVISSON:

Periodicals

(With L. H. Germer) "Diffraction of Electrons," *Physical Review,* Series 1, Volume 30, 1927, pp. 705–740.
(With L. H. Germer) "Scattering of Electrons by a Single Crystal of Nickel," *Nature,* Volume 119, 1927, pp. 558–560.
"Wave Properties of Electrons," *Science,* Volume 71, 1930, pp. 651–654.

SOURCES:

Books

Biographical Memoirs, Volume 36, National Academy of Sciences, 1962, pp. 51–84.
Dictionary of Scientific Biography, Volume 3, Scribner's, 1975, pp. 597–598.

Heathcote, Niels H. de V., *Nobel Prize Winners in Physics, 1901–1950,* Henry Schuman, 1953, pp. 353–362.

Nobel Prize Winners, H. W. Wilson, 1987, pp. 247–249.

Weber, Robert L., *Pioneers of Science: Nobel Prize Winners in Physics,* American Institute of Physics, 1980, pp. 109–111.

—*Sketch by David E. Newton*

Michael Ellis DeBakey

Michael Ellis DeBakey
1908-
American surgeon and inventor

Michael Ellis DeBakey is a world renowned cardiovascular surgeon, medical inventor, medical statesperson, and teacher who is chancellor of the Baylor College of Medicine in Houston, chair and Olga Keith Weiss Professor of its department of surgery, and director of the DeBakey Heart Center. He is the recipient of the America's highest civilian honor, the Medal of Honor with Distinction (awarded in 1969), and of the country's highest scientific award, the National Medal of Science (1987). DeBakey is best known for his landmark cardiovascular surgeries, including the first successful implantation of an artificial heart in 1966. He also pioneered the use of artificial arteries and coronary bypass, invented new equipment and instruments, and conducted important research on the causes of arteriosclerosis.

Born on September 7, 1908, in Lake Charles, Louisiana, to Shaker Morris and Raheega (Zorba) DeBakey, Michael DeBakey was the oldest of five children. His father was a successful pharmacist and businessperson, his mother "a compassionate person who was always trying to help someone," according to DeBakey in the *Tulanian.* His keen intellect was obvious at an early age: as a reward for doing well in his schoolwork, DeBakey's parents would let him read the *Encyclopedia Britannica;* he had completed the whole set before entering high school. His ingenuity, however, was not limited to academics; he played several musical instruments, participated in sports, sewed, and maintained a garden with his brother.

Invented First Medical Device at Age Twenty-three

The variety in DeBakey's life did not change when he entered Tulane University in 1926. In college, he became an accomplished billiards player and played saxophone in the Tulane University band and orchestra. DeBakey had earned enough credits to enter medical school by the time he was a sophomore, but he also wanted a baccalaureate degree. He therefore persuaded the university to let him complete his degree while concurrently attending medical school. While still a medical student, DeBakey created his first invention: a modified roller pump for blood transfusions which did not damage the blood during the procedure. Twenty years later, this device became a major component of John H. Gibbon's heart-lung machine, used in the first open-heart surgery. While at Tulane, DeBakey met his mentor, the surgeon Alton Ochsner.

With his medical degree in hand in 1932, DeBakey completed two years of surgical residency training at Charity Hospital in New Orleans. He then went to Europe to study under two prominent surgeons: Rene Leriche of the University of Strasbourg, France, and Martin Kirschner of the University of Heidelberg, Germany. Upon his return to the United States, DeBakey completed his master's of science degree at Tulane.

Changed Outlook for Returning Wounded Soldiers

In 1937, DeBakey returned to Tulane to serve on its faculty until, at the beginning of World War II, he volunteered for military service; after serving four years in the U.S. Surgeon General's office, he was appointed director of the Surgical Consultants' Division there. His work led to the establishment of the mobile army surgical hospitals (MASH units). He also helped organize a specialized medical center system to treat soldiers returning from the war; that system later became the Veterans' Administration (VA) Medical Center System. DeBakey also proposed a systematic follow-up of veterans with certain medical problems, which eventually became the VA's Medical Research Program. He received the Legion of Merit Award in 1945 for his wartime achievements.

In 1946, DeBakey again returned to Tulane as an associate professor of surgery. Two years later, he was named chair of the department of surgery at Baylor University College of Medicine. He remained at Baylor for the rest of his academic career, becoming first the president of the College of Medicine in 1969 and, a decade later, its chancellor.

New Hope for Patients with Heart Disease

DeBakey's record is filled with many firsts, all targeting the diagnosis and treatment of arteriosclerosis (hardening of the arteries). When Debakey began his research, the prognosis for patients with arteriosclerosis was poor—individuals with the disease usually died by age fifty. Now, in large part due to DeBakey's work, such patients can live well into their eighties. During the 1950s, DeBakey was the first to classify arterial disease by location, characteristic, and pattern, making diagnosis much easier. The cause, however, was still unknown.

Between 1950 and 1953, DeBakey developed the Dacron and Dacron-velour artificial grafts to replace diseased arteries—a process which is now commonly practiced worldwide. Though DeBakey sewed his first Dacron graft on his wife's sewing machine, subsequent Dacron artificial arteries were created using a special knitting machine developed by the Philadelphia College of Textiles. In 1953, DeBakey performed the first successful removal and graft replacement of an aneurysm (a swelling caused by a weakness in a vessel wall) of the thoracic aorta; this procedure, too, is now widely used around the world. Also in 1953, DeBakey performed the first successful removal of a blockage of the main (carotid) artery of the neck, a procedure known as an endarterectomy. This procedure has become the standard method for treating stroke.

Beginning in 1953, DeBakey pioneered four different kinds of operations for the treatment of aneurysms in different areas of the aorta: the removal (resection) and graft replacement of an aneurysm in the downward section of the aortic arch, which curves like a cane handle over the top of the heart; the resection of an aneurysm in the muscle layer of the aorta; the resection and graft replacement of an aneurysm of the upper part of the aorta; and the resection of an aneurysm of the portion of the aorta between the chest and the abdomen. In 1958, DeBakey also performed the first successful patch-graft angioplasty to reverse the narrowing of an artery caused by an endarterectomy.

By the early 1960s DeBakey had established the standard procedure of therapy in arterial disease, for which he received the Albert Lasker Clinical Research Award in 1963. A year later, DeBakey was the first to successfully perform an aortocoronary artery bypass, now commonly referred to as "bypass surgery." Using a large vein removed from the patient's leg, he rerouted blood around any damaged area between the aorta and coronary arteries, leaving healthy areas intact. Since the 1960s, DeBakey has also tested different artificial- and partial-artificial heart devices, and in 1966 conducted the landmark operation in which the first partial-artificial heart was successfully transplanted. In 1968, DeBakey was one of the first surgeons to perform heart transplantations; however, rejection problems led him to suspend this practice until 1984, when better anti-rejection drugs (such as cyclosporine) and other technological advances became available.

Epidemiological Research Leads to New Findings

From 1983 to 1987, DeBakey teamed with Dr. Joseph Melnick and other colleagues to study more closely the causes of arteriosclerosis. They found that the cytomegalovirus (known as CMV), a common virus which causes arterial lesions when first contracted early in life, could lay dormant for years after initial infection. Those individuals with arteriosclerosis were found to have high levels of antibodies to the virus, and it was suggested that CMV might play a role in the development of arteriosclerosis. In 1987, DeBakey and his research team announced that high cholesterol levels, long thought to be one of the major causes of heart disease, were in fact not related to how quickly arteries became blocked. In another study, they also showed that while smoking, a high fat diet, and high blood pressure may put an individual at high risk, they do not themselves cause arteriosclerosis.

In order to apply the specialized medical center system to the civilian sector, DeBakey (with the help of federal funding) founded the Cardiovascular Research and Training Center at the Texas Medical Center in the early 1970s. Later, in 1985, Baylor established the DeBakey Heart Center for research and public education in the prevention and treatment of heart disease.

More Accomplishments Outside the Operating Room

While his reputation as a surgeon grew, DeBakey continued teaching, writing research papers, attending medical symposia and consulting governments on different aspects of health care. As a member of the

Medical Task Force of the Hoover Commission on Organization of the Executive Branch, DeBakey helped establish the National Library of Medicine in Washington, DC, in the early 1950s. It is now the world's largest and most prestigious repository of medical archives. He has served as an advisor to almost every president over the past 50 years, works to improve international health standards, and consults for European, Eastern block, and Middle and Far East countries to establish better health care systems. DeBakey has performed almost 50,000 cardiovascular procedures, trained almost 1,000 surgeons, and has written 1,200 medical articles, chapters, books, research papers on surgery, medicine, health, medical research and education, ethics and social issues. He corresponds regularly with many of his patients, from princes to paupers, is the editor of many professional publications, and holds the rank of colonel in the United States Army Reserves. He has received numerous awards, honorary degrees and appointments.

By 1976, DeBakey had trained so many surgeons and physicians that they decided to form the Michael E. DeBakey International Surgical Society, which offers medical symposia biennially. His former students describe him as a workaholic, single-minded, focused, and expecting the highest standards of excellence from everyone with whom he deals. "He didn't ask more of anyone else than he asked of himself," recalled pulmonary and vascular surgeon Daniel Mahaffey in the *Tulanian*. Ochsner, DeBakey's mentor, told the *Tulanian*, "I've never known anyone who works harder and with less apparent strain. His capacity for work is almost unlimited."

In 1936, DeBakey married Diane Cooper, a Texas native, with whom he had four sons; two became businessmen, one a restaurateur and one an attorney. His wife died of a massive heart attack in 1972; DeBakey, who had been performing cardiac surgery at the time, rushed to his wife's bedside, but was unable to keep her alive. Two years later, he married Katrin Fehlhaber, a German artist and actor. In 1977, they had a daughter.

SELECTED WRITINGS BY DEBAKEY:

Books

(With Gilbert Wheeler Beebe) *Battle Casualties: Incidence, Mortality and Logistic Considerations,* Thomas, 1952.
(With John Boyd Coates) *General Surgery,* Office of the Surgeon General, 1955.
(With Daniel C. Elkin) *Vascular Surgery,* Office of the Surgeon General, 1955.
(With Tom French Whayne) *Cold Injury, Ground Type,* Office of the Surgeon General, 1958.

(With Christopher Frederick and Alton Ochsner) *Christopher's Minor Surgery,* Saunders, 1959.
(With Antonio Gotto) *The Living Heart,* McKay, 1977.
Advances in Cardiac Valves: Clinical Perspectives, Yorke Medical Books, 1983.
The Living Heart Diet, Raven Press, 1984.

SOURCES:

Books

Contemporary Authors, Volume 73–76, Gale, 1978.
Modern Scientists and Engineers, Volume 1, pp. 273–274, McGraw-Hill, 1980.

Periodicals

Griffin, Susannah Moore, "One for the Heart," *Tulanian,* fall, 1987.

—*Sketch by Denise Adams Arnold*

Louis Victor de Broglie
1892-1987
French theoretical physicist

Louis Victor de Broglie, a theoretical physicist and member of the French nobility, is best known as the father of wave mechanics, a far-reaching achievement that significantly changed modern physics. Wave mechanics describes the behavior of matter, including subatomic particles such as electrons, with respect to their wave characteristics. For this groundbreaking work, de Broglie was awarded the 1929 Nobel Prize for physics.

Louis Victor Pierre Raymond de Broglie was born on August 15, 1892, in Dieppe, France, to Duc Victor and Pauline d'Armaille Broglie. His father's family was of noble Piedmontese origin and had served French monarchs for centuries, for which it was awarded the hereditary title *Duc* from King Louis XIV in 1740, a title that could be held only by the head of the family. A later de Broglie assisted the Austrian side during the Seven Years War and was awarded the title *Prinz* for his contribution. This title was subsequently borne by all members of the family. Another of de Broglie's famous ancestors was his great-great-grandmother, the writer Madame de Stael.

Louis Victor de Broglie

The youngest of five children, de Broglie inherited a familial distinction for formidable scholarship. His early education was obtained at home, as befitted a great French family of the time. After the death of his father when de Broglie was fourteen, his eldest brother Maurice arranged for him to obtain his secondary education at the Lycée Janson de Sailly in Paris.

After graduating from the Sorbonne in 1909 with baccalaureates in philosophy and mathematics, de Broglie entered the University of Paris. He studied ancient history, paleography, and law before finding his niche in science, influenced by the writings of French theoretical physicist **Jules Henri Poincaré**. The work of his brother Maurice, who was then engaged in important, independent experimental research in X rays and radioactivity, also helped to spark de Broglie's interest in theoretical physics, particularly in basic atomic theory. In 1913, he obtained his Licencié ès Sciences from the University of Paris's Faculté des Sciences.

De Broglie's studies were interrupted by the outbreak of World War I, during which he served in the French army. Yet even the war did not take the young scientist away from the country where he would spend his entire life; for its duration, de Broglie served with the French Engineers at the wireless station under the Eiffel Tower. In 1919, after what he considered to be six wasted years in uniform, de Broglie returned to his scientific studies at his brother's laboratory. Here he began his investigations into the nature of matter, inspired by a conundrum that had long been troubling the scientific community: the apparent physical irreconcilability of the experimentally proven dual nature of light. Radiant energy or light had been demonstrated to exhibit properties associated with particles as well as their well-documented wave-like characteristics. De Broglie was inspired to consider whether matter might not also exhibit dual properties. In his brother's laboratory, where the study of very high frequency radiation using spectroscopes was underway, de Broglie was able to bring the problem into sharper focus. In 1924, de Broglie, with over two dozen research papers on electrons, atomic structure, and X rays already to his credit, presented his conclusions in his doctoral thesis at the Sorbonne. Entitled "Investigations into the Quantum Theory," it consolidated three shorter papers he had published the previous year.

Thesis Revolutionizes Physics

In his thesis, de Broglie postulated that all matter—including electrons, the negatively charged particles that orbit an atom's nucleus—behaves as both a particle and a wave. Wave characteristics, however, are detectable only at the atomic level, whereas the classical, ballistic properties of matter are apparent at larger scales. Therefore, rather than the wave and particle characteristics of light and matter being at odds with one another, de Broglie postulated that they were essentially the same behavior observed from different perspectives. Wave mechanics could then explain the behavior of all matter, even at the atomic scale, whereas classical Newtonian mechanics, which continued to accurately account for the behavior of observable matter, merely described a special, general case. Although, according to de Broglie, all objects have "matter waves," these waves are so small in relation to large objects that their effects are not observable and no departure from classical physics is detected. At the atomic level, however, matter waves are relatively larger and their effects become more obvious. De Broglie devised a mathematical formula, the matter wave relation, to summarize his findings.

American physicist **Albert Einstein** appreciated the significant of de Broglie's theory; de Broglie sent Einstein a copy of his thesis on the advice of his professors at the Sorbonne, who believed themselves not fully qualified to judge it. Einstein immediately pronounced that de Broglie had illuminated one of the secrets of the universe. Austrian physicist **Erwin Schrödinger** also grasped the implications of de Broglie's work and used it to develop his own theory of wave mechanics, which has since become the foundation of modern physics. Still, many physicists could not make the intellectual leap required to understand what de Broglie was describing.

De Broglie's wave matter theory remained unproven until two separate experiments conclusively demonstrated the wave properties of electrons—their ability to diffract or bend, for example. American physicists **Clinton Davisson** and Lester Germer and English physicist **George Paget Thomson** all proved that de Broglie had been correct. Later experiments would demonstrate that de Broglie's theory also explained the behavior of protons, atoms, and even molecules. These properties later found practical applications in the development of magnetic lenses, the basis for the electron microscope.

Disagreements over Implications of Wave Mechanics

De Broglie devoted the rest of his career to teaching and to developing his theory of wave mechanics. In 1927, he attended the seventh Solvay Conference, a gathering of the most eminent minds in physics, where wave mechanics was further debated. Theorists such as German physicist **Werner Karl Heisenberg**, Danish physicist **Niels Bohr**, and English physicist **Max Born** favored the uncertainty or probabilistic interpretation, which proposed that the wave associated with a particle of matter provides merely statistical information on the position of that particle and does not describe its exact position. This interpretation was too radical for Schrödinger, Einstein, and de Broglie; the latter postulated the "double solution," claiming that particles of matter are transported and guided by continuous "pilot waves" and that their movement is essentially deterministic. De Broglie could not reconcile his pilot wave theory with some basic objections raised at the conference, however, and he abandoned it.

The disagreement about the manner in which matter behaves described two profoundly different ways of looking at the world. Part of the reason that de Broglie, Einstein, and others did not concur with the probabilistic view was that they could not philosophically accept that matter, and thus the world, behaves in a random way. De Broglie wished to believe in a deterministic atomic physics, where matter behaves according to certain identifiable patterns. Nonetheless, he reluctantly accepted that his pilot wave theory was flawed and throughout his teaching career instructed his students in probabilistic theory, though he never quite abandoned his belief that "God does not play dice," as Einstein had suggested.

In 1928, de Broglie was appointed professor of theoretical physics at the University of Paris's Faculty of Science. De Broglie was a thorough lecturer who addressed all aspects of wave mechanics. Perhaps because he was not inclined to encourage an interactive atmosphere in his lectures, he had no noted record of guiding young research students.

Wins Nobel Prize

In 1929, at the age of thirty-seven, de Broglie was awarded the Nobel Prize for physics in recognition of his contribution to wave mechanics. In 1933, he accepted the specially created chair of theoretical physics at the Henri Poincaré Institute—a position he would hold for the next twenty-nine years—where he established a center for the study of modern physical theories. That same year, he was elected to the Académie des Sciences, becoming its Life Secretary in 1942; he used his influence to urge the Académie to consider the harmful effects of nuclear explosions as well as to explore the philosophical implications of his and other modern theories.

In 1943, anxious to forge stronger links between industry and science and to put modern physics, especially quantum mechanics, to practical use, de Broglie established a center within the Henri Poincaré Institute dedicated to applied mechanics. He was elected to the prestigious Academie Francaise in 1944 and, in the following year, was appointed a counsellor to the French High Commission of Atomic Energy with his brother Maurice in recognition of their work promoting the peaceful development of nuclear energy and their efforts to bridge the gap between science and industry. Three years later, de Broglie was elected to the National Academy of the United States as a foreign member.

During his long career, de Broglie published over twenty books and numerous research papers. His preoccupation with the practical side of physics is demonstrated in his works dealing with cybernetics, atomic energy, particle accelerators, and wave-guides. His writings also include works on X rays, gamma rays, atomic particles, optics, and a history of the development of contemporary physics. He served as honorary president of the French Association of Science Writers and, in 1952, was awarded first prize for excellence in science writing by the Kalinga Foundation. In 1953, Broglie was elected to London's Royal Society as a foreign member and, in 1958, to the French Academy of Arts and Sciences in recognition of his formidable output. With the death of his older brother Maurice two years later, de Broglie inherited the joint titles of French duke and German prince. De Broglie died of natural causes on March 19, 1987, at the age of ninety-five, having never fully resolved the controversy surrounding his theories of wave mechanics.

SELECTED WRITINGS BY DE BROGLIE:

Books

Matter and Light: The New Physics, Norton, 1937.
Continu et discontinu en physique moderne, [Paris], 1941.

Optique electonique et corpusculaire, [Paris], 1947.

De la Mecanique ondulatoire a la theorie du noyau, [Paris], 1947.

Physique et microphysique, [Paris], 1947.

The Revolution in Physics: A Non-Mathematical Survey of Quanta, Noonday Press, 1953.

New Perspectives in Physics, translated by A. J. Pomerans, Basic Books, 1962.

The Current Interpretation of Wave Mechanics: A Critical Study, Elsevier, 1964.

SOURCES:

Books

Cline, Barbara Lovett, *Men Who Made a New Physics,* University of Chicago Press, 1987.

Guillemin, Victor, *The Story of Quantum Mechanics,* Scribner, 1968.

Heathcote, Niels H., *Nobel Prize Winners in Physics, 1901–1950,* Books for Libraries Press, 1953.

Modern Men of Science, Volume II, McGraw-Hill, 1968.

Weber, Robert L., *Pioneers of Science: Nobel Prize Winners in Physics,* Institute of Physics, 1980.

Periodicals

Proceedings of the Royal Society, Volume 34, 1988.

—Sketch by Avril McDonald

Peter Debye
1884-1966
Dutch–born American chemical physicist

Most of Peter Debye's professional work involved the application of physical laws to the structure and behavior of molecules. In the 1910s, for example, he determined the dipole moments of many molecules, obtaining results that allowed him to calculate the polarity of such molecules. In recognition of this work, the unit of dipole moment, the debye, was named in his honor. Debye was also awarded the 1936 Nobel Prize in chemistry for this research, although he is perhaps best known for his contribution to the theory of electrolytic dissociation, the Debye-Hückel theory, announced in 1923. Driven out of Germany and the Netherlands during World War II, Debye immigrated to the United States and became professor of chemistry at Cornell University.

Debye was born Petrus Josephus Wilhelmus Debije on March 28, 1884, in Maastrict, the Netherlands. He is better known by the Anglicized form of his name, Peter Joseph William (or Wilhelm) Debye. His father, Joannes Wilhelmus Debije, was a foreman at a metalware manufacturer, while his mother was the former Maria Anna Barbara Ruemkens, a theater cashier prior to her marriage. The Debije's had one other child, a daughter four years younger than Peter.

Debye attended the Hoogere Burger School in Maastricht from 1896 to 1901. He then enrolled at the Technische Hochschule in Aachen, thirty kilometers from his home across the Dutch-German border. The cost of an advanced education placed a severe strain on the modest budget of the Debije family. But, as Mansel Davies writes in the *Biographical Memoirs of Fellows of the Royal Society,* Peter's father vowed that he "would work night and day" to keep his son in school. As a result, Debye eventually completed his studies at Aachen and received his degree in electrical engineering in 1905.

Education and Research Lead to University Posts

By a stroke of good fortune, one of Debye's teachers at Aachen had been the great German physicist **Arnold Sommerfeld**. When Sommerfeld was called to the chair of theoretical physics at the University of Münich in 1906, he asked Debye to join him as an assistant. Debye remained at Münich for five years, earning his doctorate in physics in 1908. The subject of his thesis was the effect of radiation on spherical particles with a variety of refractive properties. After earning his degree, Debye continued his research at Münich, serving as lecturer in physics during his last year there.

In 1911, Debye was offered the prestigious chair of theoretical physics at the University of Zürich, a post most recently held by **Albert Einstein**. Debye remained only a year at Zürich, but it appears to have been an important one. During this time he seems to have made his first serious attack on the question of the physical properties of molecules.

By the early 1900s, a fair amount of information was known about the chemical properties of molecules, but relatively little was known about their physical structure and behavior. Debye chose to deal with one aspect of this topic, the dipole moment of molecules, during his year at Zürich. The dipole moment of a molecule is its tendency to rotate in an external magnetic field, a property that is a function of the distribution of electric charge in (the polarity of) the molecule.

Hoping to do more experimental work than was expected at Zürich, Debye moved to the University of

Utrecht in 1912, but stayed in this post only two years. He completed some exploratory research on the dipole of molecules there, but published relatively little on the subject. It was not until nearly a decade later that this research would be brought to fruition, with spectacular success.

In the meanwhile, Debye moved on again, this time to the University of Göttingen in 1914 as professor of theoretical and experimental physics. During his stay at Utrecht, Debye had married Matilde Alberer on April 10, 1913. Matilde was one of three daughters at the boarding house where Debye lived. The Debyes eventually had two children, Peter Paul Ruprecht and Mathilde Maria Gabiele. The younger Peter Debye became a physicist and collaborated with his father on a number of occasions.

Makes Important Discoveries

Debye's most important work at Göttingen involved X-ray diffraction studies. The use of X rays to determine the structure of materials had been developed only a few years earlier by **Max von Laue** and by **William Henry Bragg** and **William Lawrence Bragg**. The most serious problem with the Laue-Bragg discoveries was that they required the preparation of relatively large crystals. Debye, working with a colleague named Paul Scherrer, found that X-ray diffraction could also be used with powders. They developed this technique and eventually reported on the structure of a number of materials examined by this method.

In 1920, Debye returned to the University of Zürich where he served as professor of experimental physics and director of the physics laboratory at the Federal Institute of Technology. It was during his stay at Zürich that Debye developed the concept for which he is probably best known, the Debye-Hückel theory of electrolytic dissociation. Pioneering work on the behavior of electrolytes, substances that conduct electricity through the movement of ions, had been conducted by the Swedish chemist **Svante Arrhenius** in the late 1880s. Arrhenius had argued that molecules break up spontaneously in solution, with the liberated ions becoming electrolytic agents.

Debye took a different approach to the problem by way of redefining the mathematical application to physicochemical data, instead of to each possible configuration of ions. Electrolytes *must* dissociate almost completely in solution, he proposed, because they are already completely ionic in the solid state. The reason they do not behave that way in solution, he said, is that each ion has become surrounded by other ions of opposite charge. The movement of ions through a solution, then, is disturbed by the dragging effect of the surrounding ions. Working with a colleague, Erich Hückel, Debye generated a mathematical theory that precisely described the behavior of electrolytes in solution.

Flees Europe for the United States

After his success with solution theory, Debye returned to his research on X-ray diffraction. In 1923, he also developed a theory that mathematically explained the Compton effect—the way the wavelengths of X rays change when they collide with electrons—and provided additional support for the wave-particle theory of electromagnetic radiation. He continued those studies when he moved to the University of Leipzig from 1927 to 1934 and then to the University of Berlin in 1934. The Nobel Prize in chemistry he received in 1936 was given in recognition of his contributions in many fields, including "his contributions to our knowledge of molecular structure through the investigations of dipole moments and on the diffraction of X rays and electrons in gases."

The rise of National Socialism resulted in an increase of political issues in German research, and Debye was soon required to become a German citizen in order to retain his post in Berlin. He chose instead to accept an appointment as professor of chemistry and head of the department at Cornell University in Ithaca, New York, in 1940. He became a U.S. citizen in 1946. Debye officially retired from his Cornell post in 1952, but continued his research in the field of polymer chemistry for another decade.

During this time, Debye was much in demand as a lecturer, both in the United Sates and Europe and remained active in the scientific community until the age of 81. He suffered a heart attack at Kennedy International Airport in April 1966 while awaiting a flight to Europe and then a fatal attack, on November 2, 1966, at his home in Ithaca. During his lifetime, Debye collected a host of honors and awards, including the Rumford Medal of the Royal Society (1930), the Lorentz Medal of the Royal Netherlands Academy of Sciences (1935), the Franklin Medal of the Franklin Institute (1937), the Faraday Medal (1949), as well as the Gibbs Medal (1949), the Kendall Award (1957), the Nichols Medal (1963), and the Priestley Medal (1963) of the American Chemical Society.

SELECTED WRITINGS BY DEBYE:

Books

Polar Molecules, Chemical Catalog Company, 1929.
The Dipole Moment and Chemical Structure, Blackie and Sons, 1931.
The Structure of Matter, University of New Mexico Press, 1934.

SOURCES:

Books

Biographical Memoirs, Volume 46, National Academy of Sciences, 1975, pp. 23–68.

Biographical Memoirs of Fellows of the Royal Society, Volume 16, Royal Society (London), 1970, pp. 175–232.

Nobel Prize Winners, H. W. Wilson, 1987, pp. 232–235.

The Way of the Scientist, Simon & Schuster, 1966, pp. 77–84.

—*Sketch by David E. Newton*

Christian de Duvé
1917-
English-born Belgian biochemist and cell biologist

Christian René de Duvé's ground-breaking studies of cellular structure and function earned him the 1974 Nobel Prize in physiology or medicine (shared with **Albert Claude** and **George Palade**). However, he did much more than discover the two key cellular organelles—lysosomes and peroxisomes—for which the Swedish Academy honored him. His work, along with that of his fellow recipients, established an entirely new field, cell biology. De Duvé introduced techniques that have enabled other scientists to better study cellular anatomy and physiology. De Duvé's research has also been of great value in helping clarify the causes of and treatments for a number of diseases.

De Duvé's parents, Alphonse and Madeleine (Pungs) de Duvé, had fled Belgium after its invasion by the German army in World War I, escaping to safety in England. There, in Thames-Ditton, Christian René de Duvé was born on October 2, 1917. De Duvé returned with his parents to Belgium in 1920, where they settled in Antwerp. (De Duvé later became a Belgian citizen.) As a child, de Duvé journeyed throughout Europe, picking up three foreign languages in the process, and in 1934 enrolled in the Catholic University of Louvain, where he received an education in the "ancient humanities." Deciding to become a physician, he entered the medical school of the university.

Finding the pace of medical training relaxed, and realizing that the better students gravitated to research labs, de Duvé joined J. P. Bouckaert's group. Here he studied physiology, concentrating on the hormone insulin and its effects on uptake of the sugar glucose. De Duvé's experiences in Bouckaert's laboratory convinced him to pursue a research career when he graduated with an M.D. in 1941. World War II disrupted his plans, and de Duvé ended up in a prison camp. He managed to escape and subsequently returned to Louvain to resume his investigations of insulin. Although his access to experimental supplies and equipment was limited, he was able to read extensively from the early literature on the subject. On September 30, 1943, he married Janine Herman, and eventually had four children with her: Thierry, Anne, Francoise, and Alain. Even before obtaining his Ph.D. from the Catholic University of Louvain in 1945, de Duvé published several works, including a four-hundred page book on glucose, insulin, and diabetes. The dissertation topic for his *Agrégé de l'Enseignement Supérieur* was also insulin. De Duvé then obtained an M.Sc. degree in chemistry in 1946.

After graduation, de Duvé decided that he needed a thorough grounding in biochemical approaches to pursue his research interests. He studied with **Hugo Theorell** at the Medical Nobel Institute in Stockholm for eighteen months, then spent six months with **Carl Ferdinand Cori**, **Gerty Cori**, and **Earl Sutherland** at Washington University School of Medicine in St. Louis. Thus, in his early postdoctoral years he worked closely with no less than four future Nobel Prize winners. It is not surprising that, after this hectic period, de Duvé was happy to return to Louvain in 1947 to take up a faculty post at his alma mater teaching physiological chemistry at the medical school. In 1951, de Duvé was appointed full professor of biochemistry. As he began his faculty career, de Duvé's research was still targeted at unraveling the mechanism of action of the anti-diabetic hormone, insulin. While he was not successful at his primary effort (indeed the answer to de Duvé's first research question was to elude investigators for more than thirty years), his early experiments opened new avenues of research.

Develops New Techniques to Search for Enzymes

As a consequence of investigating how insulin works in the human body, de Duvé and his students also studied the enzymes involved in carbohydrate metabolism in the liver. It was these studies that proved pivotal for de Duvé's eventual rise to scientific fame. In his first efforts, he had tried to purify a particular liver enzyme, glucose–6-phosphatase, that he believed blocked the effect of insulin on liver cells. Many enzymes would solidify and precipitate out of solution when exposed to an electric field. Most could then be redissolved in a relatively pure form given the right set of conditions, but glucose–6-phosphate stubbornly remained a solid precipitate. The failure of this electrical separation method led de Duvé to try a different technique, separating components of the cell by spinning them in a centrifuge, a machine that rotates at high speed. De Duvé assumed that particular enzymes are associated with particular parts of the cell. These parts, called cellular organelles (little organs) can be seen in the microscope as variously shaped and sized grains and particles within the body of cells. It had long been recognized that there existed several discrete types of these organelles, though little was known about their structures or functions at the time.

The basic principles of centrifugation for separating cell parts had been known for many years. First cells are ground up (homogenized) and the resultant slurry placed in a narrow tube. The tube is placed in a centrifuge, and the artificial gravity that is set up by rotation will separate material by weight. Heavier fragments and particles will be driven to the bottom of the tube while lighter materials will layer out on top. At the time de Duvé began his work, centrifugation could be used to gather roughly four different fractions of cellular debris. This division proved to be too crude for his research, because he needed to separate out various cellular organelles more selectively.

For this reason, de Duvé turned to a technique developed some years earlier by fellow-Belgian Albert Claude while working at the Rockefeller Institute for Medical Research. In the more common centrifugation technique, the cells of interest were first vigorously homogenized in a blender before being centrifuged. In Claude's technique of differential centrifugation, however, cells were treated much more gently, being merely ground up slightly by hand prior to being spun to separate various components.

When de Duvé used this differential centrifugal fractionation technique on liver cells, he did indeed get better separation of cell organelles, and was able to isolate certain enzymes to certain cell fractions. One of his first findings was that his target enzyme, glucose–6-phosphatase, was associated with microsomes, cellular organelles which had been, until that time, considered by cell biologists to be quite uninteresting. De Duvé's work showed that they were the site of key cellular metabolic events. Further, this was the first time a particular enzyme had been clearly associated with a particular organelle.

Results Raise Questions, Lead to Discoveries

De Duvé was also studying an enzyme called acid phosphatase that acts in cells to remove phosphate groups (chemical clusters made up of one phosphorus and three oxygen atoms) from sugar molecules under acidic conditions. The differential centrifugation technique isolated acid phosphatase to a particular cellular fraction, but measurements of enzyme activi-

ty showed much lower levels than expected. De Duvé was puzzled. What had happened to the enzyme? He and his students observed that if the cell fraction that initially showed this low level of enzyme were allowed to sit in the refrigerator for several days, the enzyme activity increased to expected levels. This phenomenon became known as enzyme latency.

De Duvé believed he had a solution to the latency mystery. He reasoned that perhaps the early, gentle hand-grinding of differential centrifugation did not damage the cellular organelles as much as did the more traditional mechanical grinding. What if, he wondered, some enzymes were not freely exposed in the cells' interiors, but instead were enclosed *within* protective membranes of organelles. If these organelles were not then broken apart by the gentle grinding, the enzyme might still lie trapped within the organelles in the particular cell fraction after centrifugation. If so, it would be isolated from the chemicals used to measure enzyme activity. This would explain the low initial enzyme activity, and why over time, as the organelles' membranes gradually deteriorated, enzyme activity would increase.

De Duvé realized that his ideas had powerful implications for cellular research. By carefully observing what enzymes were expressed in what fractions and under what conditions, de Duvé's students were able to separate various enzymes and associate them with particular cellular organelles. By performing successive grinding and fractionations, and by using compounds such as detergents to break up membranes, de Duvé's group began making sense out of the complex world that exists within cells.

De Duvé's research built on the work of other scientists. Previous research had clarified some of the roles of various enzymes. But de Duvé came to realize that there existed a group of several enzymes, in addition to acid phosphatase, whose primary functions all related to breaking down certain classes of molecules. These enzymes were always expressed in the same cellular fraction, and showed the same latency. Putting this information together, de Duvé realized that he had found an organelle devoted to cellular digestion. It made sense, he reasoned, that these enzymes should be sequestered away from other cell components. They functioned best in a different environment, expressing their activity fully only under acidic conditions (the main cell interior is neutral). Moreover, these enzymes could damage many other cellular components if set loose in the cells' interiors. With this research, de Duvé identified lysosomes and elucidated their pivotal role in cellular digestive and metabolic processes. Later research in de Duvé's laboratory showed that lysosomes play critical roles in a number of disease processes as well.

De Duvé eventually uncovered more associations between enzymes and organelles. The enzyme monoamine oxidase, for example, behaved very similarly to the enzymes of the lysosome, but de Duvé's careful and meticulous investigations revealed minor differences in when and where it appeared. He eventually showed that monoamine oxidase was associated with a separate cellular organelle, the peroxisome. Further investigation led to more discoveries about this previously unknown organelle. It was discovered that peroxisomes contain enzymes that use oxygen to break up certain types of molecules. They are vital to neutralizing many toxic substances, such as alcohol, and play key roles in sugar metabolism.

Research Widens, Wins Acclaim from Fellow Scientists

Recognizing the power of the technique that he had used in these early experiments, de Duvé pioneered its use to answer questions of both basic biological interest and immense medical application. His group discovered that certain diseases result from cells' inability to properly digest their own waste products. For example, a group of illnesses known collectively as disorders of glycogen storage result from malfunctioning lysosomal enzymes. Tay Sachs disease, a congenital neurological disorder that kills its victims by age five, results from the accumulation of a component of the cell membrane that is not adequately metabolized due to a defective lysosomal enzyme.

In 1962 de Duvé joined the Rockefeller Institute (now Rockefeller University) while keeping his appointment at Louvain. In subsequent years, working with numerous research groups at both institutions, he has studied inflammatory diseases such as arthritis and arteriosclerosis, genetic diseases, immune dysfunctions, tropical maladies, and cancers. This work has led, in some cases, to the creation of new drugs used in combatting some of these conditions. In 1971 de Duvé formed the International Institute of Cellular and Molecular Pathology, affiliated with the University at Louvain. Research at the institute focuses on incorporating the findings from basic cellular research into practical applications.

De Duvé's work has won him the respect of his colleagues. Workers throughout the broad field of cellular biology recognize their debt to his pioneering studies. He helped found the American Society for Cell Biology. He has received awards and honors from many countries, including more than a dozen honorary degrees. In 1974, de Duvé, along with Albert Claude and George Palade, both also of the Rockefeller Institute, received the Nobel Prize in physiology or medicine, and were credited with creating the discipline of scientific investigation that became known as cell biology. De Duvé was elected a foreign associate of the United States National Academy of Sciences in 1975, and has been acclaimed by Belgian, French, and British biochemical societies. He has also served as a member of numerous prestigious biomedical and health-related organizations around the globe.

SELECTED WRITINGS BY DE DUVÉ:

Books

Glucose, Insuline, et Diabéte, [Paris], 1945.
A Guided Tour of the Living Cell, W. H. Freeman, 1985.

Periodicals

"The Use of Differential Centrifugation in the Study of Tissue Enzymes," *International Review of Cytology,* Volume 3, 1954, pp. 225–275.
"The Lysosome," *Scientific American,* May, 1963, pp. 64–72.
"The Peroxisome: A New Cytoplasmic Organelle," *Proceedings of the Royal Society: Biological Sciences B,* Volume 173, 1969, pp. 71–83.
(With H. Beaufray) "A Short History of Tissue Fractionation," *Journal of Cell Biology,* Volume 91, 1981, pp. 293–299.
"Microbodies of the Living Cell," *Scientific American,* May, 1983, pp. 74–84.

SOURCES:

Books

Magill, F. N., editor, *The Nobel Prize Winners: Physiology or Medicine,* Volume 3: *1970–1990,* Salem Press, 1991, pp. 1177–1187.

Periodicals

Bainton, Dorothy F., "The Discovery of Lysosomes," *Journal of Cell Biology,* Volume 91, 1981, pp. 66–76.

—Sketch by Ethan E. Allen

Lee de Forest
1873-1961
American engineer and inventor

Lee de Forest was one of several scientists who contributed to the development of radio. A controversial and litigious man who seemed nearly as much concerned with fame as with science, de Forest

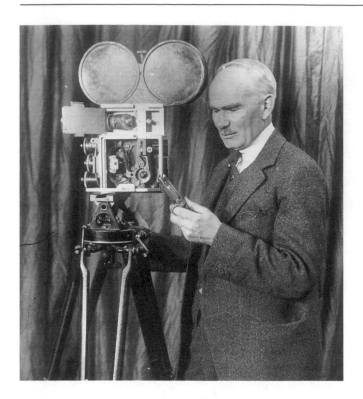

Lee de Forest

is generally credited with the invention of the triode, or three-electrode vacuum tube, which he called the Audion. This tube made possible the amplification of electrical energy by introducing a third element into the existing two-electrode vacuum tube, allowing control over the flow of electrons, or ions, through ionized gas in the tube. De Forest's invention paved the way for radio signals to be received through the airwaves, without wires.

De Forest was born August 26, 1873, the son of the Reverend Henry Swift De Forest (he retained the capital D in his name, while his son preferred the lowercase) and the former Anna Robbins. His father, president of Talladega College in Alabama, had hoped that his son would also become a minister, but early in life Lee had shown an intense interest in inventing. As preparation for what his father hoped would be a religious career, de Forest was enrolled at Mount Hermon school in Massachusetts. The school's emphasis on hard work (students did most of the chores in order to defray the expenses) left de Forest little time for inventing, and he was unhappy there. Nevertheless, after graduation he was able to convince his parents to allow him to attend the Sheffield Scientific School at Yale University.

An unpopular and unsociable youth (he was voted the "homeliest boy in school"), de Forest was deeply concerned, perhaps even obsessed, with receiving recognition from his peers. Unlike many of his classmates, de Forest had to work to supplement his scholarship money, and still was often in debt. In an attempt to raise his status, de Forest sought money and fame by inventing several devices which he hoped to sell to companies or enter in contests with large prizes. Although none of his inventions were accepted, de Forest was certain of future success; he wrote in his diary that "I must be brilliant, win fame, show the greatness of genius and to no small degree," as Tom Lewis related in *Empire of the Air.*

De Forest received his bachelor's degree in 1896 and went on to receive a Ph.D. in physics from Yale in 1899; his dissertation, "Reflection of Hertzian Waves from the Ends of Parallel Wires," was a pioneering study of a phenomenon of radio waves. By 1902 he had founded the De Forest Wireless Telegraph Company, based on his invention of an improved wireless receiver. The company was the first of a series of businesses that were to fail, largely because of questionable practices by de Forest's business partners.

De Forest's Breakthrough: The Audion

Despite his creativity, de Forest seemed to be weak in theoretical understanding; he frequently did not see the potential in his inventions and often misunderstood why they worked. De Forest's triode was based on the Fleming valve, which was itself a variation on inventor **Thomas Edison**'s incandescent lamp. Edison had noticed that the insides of his incandescent lamps tended to blacken, as if particles were being emitted from the carbon filament. When he inserted a metal plate into the lamp and connected it to the "positive" side of the filament, he found that current somehow flowed to the positively charged plate. At this time nothing was known of the existence of electrons, the negatively charged particles of electricity, and Edison did not pursue this line of research, although he did receive a patent for the two-element lamp in 1883.

The emission of particles to the plate, known as the "Edison effect," became the focus of experiments by **J. Ambrose Fleming**, an engineer who recognized that current flowed in only one direction, from the filament to the plate, and could therefore convert an input of alternating current (AC), or current continuously switching polarity, to an output of direct current (DC). The Fleming valve, invented in 1903, was physically no different from Edison's two-element lamp, but unlike Edison, Fleming understood both its operation and its potential.

In the meantime, de Forest was working on an improved detector for wireless telegraph signals. Existing detectors used a gas flame to ionize gas; by employing a filament in a partially evacuated vacuum tube instead of an open flame, he found that he could create a more stable detector. His tube differed from Fleming's chiefly in that it retained some gas in the tube, on the theory that this residual gas was necessary for ionization. This tube, the first of two to which he gave the name Audion, became the subject of litigation by Fleming, although de Forest claimed that his source was the gas-flame detector, not Fleming's valve.

De Forest's further modification of this tube, however, was his own work, and it was to be his most significant development; this was the triode, created by the addition of a third element, the grid, between the two existing components of the vacuum tube, the filament and the plate. When current was applied to this grid, the current received by the plate was strengthened, or amplified, allowing weak telegraph signals—and, after engineer **Ernst F. W. Alexanderson**'s development of Reginald Fessenden's high-frequency alternator, radio signals—to be heard more easily. De Forest did not fully understand how this tube worked; he believed, mistakenly, that the operation of the triode was dependent on the presence of gas (ions) within the tube. He failed to realize that the presence of gas limited the tube's life, weakened its signal, and generated noise, making it only marginally useful as an amplifier. It was not until 1912 that other scientists showed that the total evacuation of the tube produced a stronger, less noisy tube that had potential not only as an amplifier of weak radio signals but as an oscillator—a necessary component in the construction of a radio transmitter. By this time it was too late for de Forest to take full advantage of his invention; others with a clearer understanding of the technology had left him behind.

A Pioneer in the Broadcasting Industry

De Forest clearly had foresight, however, in his understanding of the potential of radio broadcasting as a public service—an opportunity to bring educational, cultural, and informational material to a wide spectrum of people. Once it was demonstrated (by 1906) that high-frequency radio signals could carry sound—of music and of the human voice—the possibilities of radio as a tool for communication unfolded. De Forest's vision for the medium frequently exceeded its existing technical capabilities, but he created a compelling popular image of what radio could achieve. On January 13, 1910, he attempted the first live broadcast from the stage of the Metropolitan Opera House in New York City, a performance of Mascagni's *Cavalleria rusticana* featuring Emmy Destinn and Enrico Caruso. The medium was still primitive—employing an antenna strung across the roof of the opera house, an arc generator to provide the radio-frequency signal, and a telephone transmitter to send the signal out over the airwaves—and the broadcast could be heard only at a few locations in the city, its sound quality compromised by heavy background noise. Nevertheless, it represented an attempt to use radio to raise the cultural level of Americans.

De Forest also made what may have been the first news broadcast, an inaccurate announcement of the outcome of the 1916 presidential election.

De Forest continued producing inventions related to radio, but none had the importance of the triode. In 1912 he developed a method for transmitting two signals over a single line—a diplex system. That same year he developed a cascade amplifier circuit, which fed the output of one triode into the input of another. It increased the amplification by a factor of three; a series of three tubes thus produced twenty-seven times the original signal.

A more significant outcome of this research was the feedback, or regenerative, circuit. In this circuit, the output of one triode was fed back to become its own input. This not only increased the output even further, but it allowed the tube to produce oscillations, that is, alternating current (AC). This enabled the tube to be used as a transmitter. But de Forest did not realize the true potential of this discovery; by the time he applied for a patent on the feedback circuit in 1915, the device had been patented by inventor **E. Howard Armstrong**. Litigation over the patent dragged on until 1934; although the courts found in de Forest's favor, the industry did not; it viewed the feedback circuit as Armstrong's invention and credited de Forest only with the invention of the triode.

Even the Audion triode, de Forest's most successful invention, did not produce the financial rewards he sought. Although American Telephone and Telegraph showed interest in the tube, the firm feared legal action by the giant Marconi companies, which owned the rights to the Fleming valve, of which the Audion was still seen as a possible patent infringement. De Forest did eventually sell the rights to the Audion to AT&T, but for a low sum; he had been advised to do so by one of his partners who, unknown to de Forest, was associated with AT&T.

Expanding Horizons: Sound Recording, The Phonofilm, and Television

During the early 1920s, de Forest turned his attention to sound recording, intending to develop a method for recording sound using electricity—based on his Audion—as opposed to the purely mechanical methods then in use. He succeeded in recording sound on magnetic wire, which had been done by engineer **Valdemar Poulsen** in 1898, but without the advantage of de Forest's Audion. He later succeeded in recording sound on film using what were, in effect, photographed sound waves read by a photoelectric cell; this, too, was derivative of an earlier inventor's work—Eugen Lauste had made recordings using light as early as 1903—but again, the Audion provided the amplification lacking in the earlier device.

It was a small conceptual step from this idea to that of recording sound directly on motion picture film—avoiding the synchronization problems of the existing sound films using disk recordings—a goal he achieved by 1921, which he called "Phonofilm." A series of sound films followed, and theaters began to be equipped with Phonofilm equipment by 1924, a full three years before Warner's Vitaphone sound-on-disk method produced *The Jazz Singer,* the first full-length film using sound and the one usually credited with launching the sound film era. Inadequate interest by Hollywood studios, de Forest's lack of expertise as a producer, his decision to make only short films, and legal troubles with the inventor of the photoelectric cell used in the process all contributed to the demise of the De Forest Phonofilm Corporation by 1925. Ironically, this light-on-film soundtrack method was eventually adopted by the motion picture industry.

After 1925 de Forest developed a television system. This was a mechanical (rather than purely electronic) device for transmitting and receiving pictures over the airwaves. Later, in 1946, he developed a color television system; this was also a mechanical system, and it could not compete with the all-electronic color television developed by RCA in the early 1950s. As with radio, de Forest believed that television had the potential to raise the level of civilization. He became severely critical of the radio and television programming of his time, however, feeling that it perpetuated the lowest forms of entertainment.

De Forest's life was punctuated with business reverses and long-running litigation that gave him as much notoriety in the radio industry as fame. In his private life as well, de Forest encountered considerable difficulty. There was a series of failed marriages. The first, to Lucile Sheardown, lasted barely a month before they separated; they were divorced in 1907. His second wife was Nora Stanton Blatch, a civil engineer at Cornell University who was the granddaughter of Elizabeth Cady Stanton and daughter of suffragist Harriot Stanton Blatch. Nora had a strong interest in electrical engineering—she had studied under the inventor Michael Pupin—and she worked alongside her husband in his laboratory. This did not conform with de Forest's idea of a woman's place, however, and relations between them became strained. A daughter, Harriot Stanton de Forest, was born in 1909, but by this time her parents had separated, their divorce becoming final in 1911. De Forest married his third wife, singer Mary Mayo, in December 1912. Apparently depressed about giving up her stage career, and suffering from severe rheumatism, she became an alcoholic. After three difficult pregnancies—two daughters survived, but the third child, the son for whom de Forest had long hoped, died after two days—Mayo left her husband; they were divorced in 1929. His fourth and final marriage,

to Marie Mosquini, a motion picture actress, took place in 1930.

Throughout his life, de Forest held to the belief that he was the "father of radio"—in fact, this was the title of his autobiography, published in 1950. He could not understand why he did not receive this recognition, and he saw his life as a series of hurdles placed in his path by business partners and other scientists in an effort to rob him of the glory he felt was his due. Others in the industry, however, found engineer **Guglielmo Marconi** or Fleming as more deserving of the appellation "father of radio," pointing out that de Forest's inventions were adaptations of others' and, in any case, that he did not completely understand how they worked. Radio was not the invention of a single person; rather, it evolved from the separate, sometimes overlapping, inventions of several people, including Edison's incandescent lamp, Marconi's wireless telegraph, Fleming's valve, and Fessenden's electrolytic detector. Lee de Forest died of heart failure on June 30, 1961, and is remembered not as the "father of radio," as he intended, but as one of several contributors to its development.

SELECTED WRITINGS BY DE FOREST:

Books

Television Today and Tomorrow, Dial, 1942.
Father of Radio, Wilcox & Follett, 1950.

SOURCES:

Books

Hijiya, James A., *Lee de Forest and the Fatherhood of Radio,* Lehigh University Press, 1992.
Lewis, Tom, *Empire of the Air: The Men Who Made Radio,* Edward Burlingame, 1991.
Maclaurin, W. Rupert, *Invention and Innovation in the Radio Industry,* Macmillan, 1949.
Read, Oliver, and Walter L. Welch, *From Tin Foil to Stereo,* Howard W. Sams, 1976.

Periodicals

Wynne, Peter, "Wireless Wonders," *Opera News,* November, 1993, pp. 30–36, 61.

—*Sketch by Michael Sims*

Pierre-Gilles de Gennes
1932-
French physicist

The winner of the 1991 Nobel Prize for physics, Pierre-Gilles de Gennes has been called the "Isaac Newton of our time." He succeeded in marrying chemistry and physics by means of mathematics and has a rare talent for recognizing unlikely relationships between problems. De Gennes concentrated on liquid crystals and polymers, areas most physicists avoided as intractable. He was able to untangle the physics of polymers by comparing them to simpler systems. During his career, he brought together several groups of scientists from different disciplines and was able to successfully explain a number of important phenomenon with extraordinary simplicity.

Explores Unusual Areas of Physics

De Gennes was born in Paris, France, in 1932 to Robert de Gennes and Yvonne Morin-Pons. His early education was in the École Normale Supérieure, and he received his Ph.D. as a research scientist from the Centre d'Études Nucléaires de Saclay, which he attended from 1955 to 1959. His association with academic institutions included his professorship of solid-state physics at the University of Paris, Orsay, for a decade from 1961 to 1971.

His early research was in the areas of magnetism and superconductivity, the disappearance of electrical resistance in a substance, especially at very low temperatures. By the 1960s, de Gennes turned to a neglected subject that had been discovered in the 1920s—liquid crystals. They have been called "nature's delicate phase of matter" because their molecules can be arranged in many ways, and the arrangements can be easily disturbed by weak magnetic or electrical fields. A familiar use of liquid crystals is in pocket calculators and digital watches.

Another description of liquid crystals is that they are soaplike. In this phase, the molecules flow only in two dimensions and in parallel layers. An industrial interest in this property of liquid crystals has come about with the development of "flat" television screens. By the end of the 1960s, de Gennes had formed the liquid crystal group at Orsay. His team comprised both theoreticians and experimenters. His book, *The Physics of Liquid Crystals,* was published in 1974 and became the standard work in the field.

De Gennes's shift into liquid crystals came after he had completed substantial work in the area of superconductivity. In 1966 he had published *Super-conductivity of Metals and Alloys.* He had also organized a group of scientists in the 1960s at Orsay, and they became widely known and respected throughout the worldwide scientific community for their experiments. As the field became more technically sophisticated, de Gennes began working with liquid crystals, a field in which he was able to work on simpler experiments. De Gennes earned the Nobel Prize for his interest in studying order in simple systems and generalizing the findings to more complex forms of matter.

Untangling Polymers

The general problem in physics of trying to explain how systems behave in their transition from order to disorder is one that de Gennes addressed in his work with polymers. Work on polymers has been described by physicists as "messy" and called "dirt physics, dirt chemistry." The ordinary rules of physics were difficult to apply to the complexities posed by a beaker of molten plastic. Made up of long chains of repeating units, polymers have been compared on the molecular level to clumps of spaghetti.

While their properties and behavior had been described by chemical laws, it was de Gennes who analyzed polymers using the laws of physics. He was able to compare polymers to systems that were simpler, like magnets, liquid crystals, and superconductors, whose mysteries he already understood. De Gennes discovered mathematical relationships that were shared by all these systems and was able to demonstrate that the thickness of the polymer chain was a function of its length. He was also able to calculate the length of the polymer chain using the same mathematics that defines the size of bubbles when liquid is boiled.

De Gennes's work on polymers is considered invaluable because the knowledge he brought to the understanding of their nature makes it possible to control the important properties of the material when it is being used. William Graessley, a chemical engineer, remarking on de Gennes's work in a *Science* interview said that he "[has] brought a lot of fresh insights. His work has had dramatic effects in chemistry, materials science, and chemical engineering."

Others have commented on de Gennes's willingness to veer off into unconventional areas and to learn new fields. He has been praised for his insatiable curiosity and his desire to see unifying principles. De Gennes won the American Chemical Society's Award in Polymer Chemistry in 1988, one of many honrs that he has received during his career. His work on polymers has led him to investigations into some fields that had been considered engineering disciplines. One such field is tribology, the study of the design, friction, wear, and lubrication of interacting surfaces in motion, such as gears or bearings.

In 1976 de Gennes became the director of the École de Physique et Chimie in Paris and in 1988 he became the science director for chemical physics at Rhône-Poulenc. The STRASACOL was a joint project with physicists and chemists from Strasbourg, Saclay, and the Collège de France that de Gennes formed for polymer studies. He describes this period of his work in his book, *Scaling Concepts in Polymer Physics,* published in 1979. The Royal Swedish Academy of Sciences noted in its announcement of the Nobel Prize to de Gennes that he "has shown that even 'untidy' physical systems can be described in general terms."

De Gennes married Anne-Marie Rouet in 1954. He enjoys the outdoor sports of kayaking and windsurfing and the indoor hobby of drawing in his leisure time. In 1990 de Gennes was one of two recipients of the Wolf Prize in Physics, cited for his pioneering contributions to the understanding of complex systems.

SELECTED WRITINGS BY DE GENNES:

Books

Superconductivity of Metals and Alloys, translated by P. A. Pincus, W. A. Benjamin, 1966.
The Physics of Liquid Crystals, Clarendon, 1974.
Scaling Concepts in Polymer Physics, Cornell, 1979.
Introduction to Polymer Dynamics, Cambridge, 1990.

Periodicals

"Soft Matter," *Science,* April 24, 1992, pp. 495–497.

SOURCES:

Periodicals

Ball, Philip, "A Gift for Unraveling Complexity," *Nature,* October 24, 1991, p. 689.
Coghlan, Andy, "High-flier Wins Chemistry Nobel," *New Scientist,* October 26, 1991, pp. 14–15.
Dagani, Ron, "Materials Theorist Wins Nobel in Physics," *Chemical and Engineering News,* October 21, 1991, p. 5.
Flam, Faye, "Nobel Prizes '91," *Science,* October 25, 1991, p. 518.
Levi, Barbara Goss, "De Gennes Wins Nobel Physics Prize for Work on Complex Systems," *Physics Today,* December, 1991, pp. 17–19.

"Wolf Prize Goes to Condensed-Matter Theorists de Gennes and Thouless," *Physics Today,* June, 1990, p. 91.

Other

Royal Swedish Academy of Sciences, announcement of Nobel Prize award to Pierre-Gilles de Gennes, October 16, 1991.

—*Sketch by Jordan Richman*

Hans Dehmelt
1922-
German-born American physicist

Hans Dehmelt has devoted his career as a physicist to developing means of performing highly precise, accurate atomic measurements. In pursuit of this goal, Dehmelt devised a trap that for the first time isolated a single electron, which in turn made possible the precise experimental measurements that verified the theory of quantum electrodynamics. For his work, Dehmelt was honored with a share in the 1989 Nobel Prize in physics.

The son of Georg Karl and Asta Ella Klemmt Dehmelt, Hans Georg Dehmelt was born on September 9, 1922, in Görlitz, Germany. An early interest in the workings of radios led Dehmelt to the study of physics, which was interrupted by service in the German army and a period as a prisoner of war in France during World War II. After the war, Dehmelt continued his studies in physics at the University of Göttingen, financing himself in part by repairing broken radios. During one college course, Dehmelt became interested in the possibility of isolating the electron, something theorists said couldn't be done. "From then on," Dehmelt told *Discover* contributor David H. Freedman, "I never forgot my electron."

Dehmelt earned his Ph.D. from Göttingen in 1950 and stayed on for postdoctoral work until 1952, concentrating on nuclear magnetic resonance, and using his skill in electronics to make up for a postwar lack of conventional experimental equipment. He continued these studies from 1952 to 1955 at Duke University in the United States, and became a professor at the University of Washington in 1955, remaining in that position into the 1990s. While at Washington, Dehmelt returned to his original interest in isolating the electron in order to accurately measure it. Although the electron's mass and charge could be measured precisely with existing methods, its spin

Hans Dehmelt

and magnetism could not be. Quantum electrodynamics (QED) did predict the electron's spin and magnetism, as part of QED's explanation of all interactions between electrically charged particles, but until spin and magnetism were actually measured on existing electrons, QED remained an unproven theory.

Develops Penning Trap

In 1959, Dehmelt's electronics background once again came into play. He used an electronic component called a Penning discharge tube to build what he called a Penning trap: a vacuum tube with a strong magnetic field and a weak electric field that trapped and held electrons. Throughout the 1960s Dehmelt and his colleagues tried to devise ways of measuring the gyromagnetic ratio, or *g*-factor, of an electron, which had been calculated theoretically via quantum mechanics. Dehmelt pursued this goal with great intensity and drive. Finally, he and his hard-worked team found that by manipulating voltage, they could drive electrons out of the trap until only a single one remained. This breakthrough was accomplished in 1973, and soon the team was able to capture and hold single electrons for extended periods of time. Two years later, Dehmelt worked out a way to cool the trapped electron, which slowed its motion and made accurate measurement easier. In 1976 Dehmelt and his coworkers used their trap to observe the quantum jump of a single ion, again confirming a prediction of quantum mechanics.

Soon Dehmelt and his team were able to measure the *g*-factor to ten times its previously calculated value. Driven by his passion for ever more accurate atomic measurements, Dehmelt applied a number of refinements to his trap so the *g*-factor could be measured to twelve decimal places by 1991. Dehmelt and his colleagues have also trapped positrons (antielectrons). One of these positrons, which he named Priscilla, was held for three months, performing its quantum jumps and thus allowing the first experimental measurement of the *g*-factor for antimatter. Dehmelt named the positron because, he said in an article he wrote for *Science,* its "well-defined identity . . . deserves to be recognized by being given a name, just as pets are given names of persons." Dehmelt also initiated and guided an experiment at the University of Heidelberg in 1974 to trap and observe a single barium ion. This eventually produced the first photograph, in black and white, of a charged atom. With his long-time collaborator Robert Van Dyck, Dehmelt later was able to take a color photograph of a blue barium ion they named Astrid.

Earns Nobel Prize for Electron Work

For his particle-trapping work, Dehmelt shared half of the 1989 Nobel Prize in physics with **Wolfgang Paul** of the University of Bonn, who also devised an ion trap. The work of **Norman Foster Ramsey** of Harvard University, the other 1989 Nobel physics laureate, led to the development of the atomic clock. The precise measurement methods made possible by the work of these three men, said the Nobel committee, made it possible "to conduct experiments that might force us to reconsider some basic physical laws."

Late in his career, Dehmelt noted the discrepancies between the theoretical *g*-factor predicted by QED and the actual *g*-factor he had measured. Although the discrepancy was minuscule, Dehmelt speculated that it might indicate that the electron could be broken down into smaller and smaller particles, or subquarks, finally ending in the "cosmon." A linked cosmon and anticosmon, Dehmelt theorized, spontaneously came into being out of nothingness in a quantum jump and then instantly decayed, creating the Big Bang that began the universe.

Dehmelt became a naturalized U.S. citizen in 1962. He had one son from his first marriage and then wed Diana Elaine Dundore in 1989. He acted as a consultant to Varian Associates of Palo Alto, California, from 1956 through 1976, and has contributed numerous articles to professional journals. He was elected to the National Academy of Sciences in 1978 and has won several prestigious scientific awards. In his speeches and published works, he is fond of quoting Albert Einstein's pronouncement, "You know, it would be sufficient to really understand the electron."

SELECTED WRITINGS BY DEHMELT:

Periodicals

"Less Is More: Experiments with an Individual Atomic Particle at Rest in Free Space," *American Journal of Physics,* January, 1990, p. 17.
"Experiments on the Structure of an Individual Elementary Particle," *Science,* February 2, 1990, pp. 539–545.

SOURCES:

Books

Chester, Marvin, *Primer of Quantum Mechanics,* Wiley, 1987.
"Quantum Theory," *Encyclopedia of Physical Science & Technology,* Volume 11, 1987.

Periodicals

Freedman, David H., "Moby Electron," *Discover,* February, 1991, pp. 51–56.
New York Times, October 13, 1989, p. A10.
Physics Today, December 1989, pp. 17–19.
Science, October 20, 1989, pp. 327–328.
Science News, June 21, 1986, p. 388; January 21, 1989, p. 38; October 21, 1989, p. 262.
Time, October 23, 1989, p. 74.

—*Sketch by Kathy Sammis*

Johann Deisenhofer
1943-
German biochemist and biophysicist

Johann Deisenhofer is a biochemist and biophysicist whose career has been devoted to analyzing the composition of molecular structures. An expert in the use of X-ray technology to analyze the structure of crystals, he became part of a team of scientists in the 1980s who were studying photosynthesis—the process by which plants convert sunlight into chemical energy. In 1988, he shared the Nobel Prize for Chemistry with **Robert Huber** and **Hartmut Michel**, awarded

for their work in mapping the chemical reaction at the center of photosynthesis.

Deisenhofer was born September 30, 1943, in Zusamaltheim, Bavaria, approximately fifty miles from Munich, Germany. He was the only son of Johann and Thekla Magg Deisenhofer; his parents were both farmers and they expected him to take over the family farm, as was the tradition. It was clear from an early age, however, that Deisenhofer was not interested in agriculture, and his parents sent him away to school in 1956. Over the next seven years, Deisenhofer attended three different schools, graduating from the Holbein Gymnasium in 1963. He then took the *Abitur,* an examination German students must take in order to qualify for university. He passed the exam and was awarded a scholarship. He then spent eighteen months in the military, as was required for young German men, before enrolling at the Technical University of Munich to study physics. His interest in physics had been developed through reading popular works on the subject, and he had an early passion for astronomy. Deisenhofer soon found himself doing an increasing amount of work in solid-state physics, which concerns the structures of condensed matter or solids. He secured a position in the laboratory of Klaus Dransfeld, and there he narrowed his interests further to biophysics, the application of the principles of the physical sciences to the study of biological occurrences. In 1971, Deisenhofer published his first scientific paper and received his diploma, roughly equal to a master's degree. He then began work on his Ph.D. in biochemistry at the Max Planck Institute in Munich under the direction of Robert Huber. Here, Deisenhofer began using a technique known as X-ray crystallography, which had first been demonstrated by **Max von Laue** in 1912.

A crystal is a solid characterized by a very ordered internal atomic structure. The structural base of any crystal is called a lattice, which is defined by M.F.C. Ladd and R.A. Palmer in *Structure Determination by X-ray Crystallography* as "a regular, infinite arrangement of points in which every point has the same environment as any other point." Crystallography, the study of crystals, is considered a field of the physical sciences, and X-ray crystallography is the study of crystals using radiation of known length. When X rays hit crystals, they are scattered by electrons. Knowing the wavelength of the X rays used, and measuring the intensities of the scattered X rays, the crystallographer is able to determine first the specific electron structure of the crystal and then its atomic structure.

Deisenhofer finished work for his Ph.D. in 1974. He chose to remain in Huber's laboratory and continue his work with X-ray crystallography, first on a postdoctoral basis, and later as a staff scientist. At the same time, he was developing computer software to be used in the mapping of crystals. While working on his doctorate, Deisenhofer had embarked on a collaborative effort with Wolfgang Steigemann; they studied crystallographic refinement of the structure of Bovine Pancreatic Trypsin Inhibitor, and their findings were published in *Acta Crystallographica* in 1975.

Collaboration Leads to Nobel

In 1979, Hartmut Michel joined Huber's laboratory. He had been studying photosynthesis for several years and was trying to develop a method for a detailed analysis of the molecules essential to this reaction. Photosynthesis is a very complicated process, about which much is still not known. The photosynthetic reaction center, which is a membrane protein, is considered a key to understanding the process, since it is here the electron receives the energy which drives the reaction. In 1981, Michel discovered a way to crystallize the photosynthetic reaction center from the purple bacterium *Rhodopseudomonas viridis.* Once Michel had developed this technique, he turned to Huber for help in analyzing it. Huber directed Michel to Deisenhofer, and a four-year collaboration began.

Deisenhofer, with Kunio Miki and Otto Epp, used his X-ray crystallography techniques to determine the position of over 10,000 atoms in the molecule. They produced the first three-dimensional analysis of a membrane protein. *New Scientist* magazine, as quoted in *Nobel Prize Winners Supplement 1987–1991,* called the combined efforts "the most important advance in the understanding of photosynthesis for twenty years." The Royal Swedish Academy of Sciences awarded the 1988 Nobel Prize for Chemistry jointly to Huber, Michel, and Deisenhofer for this work. Their findings opened the possibility of creating artificial reaction centers, but the scientists were credited with more than an increase in knowledge of photosynthesis. Their findings will aid efforts to increase the scientific understanding of other functions, such as respiration, nerve impulses, hormone action, and the introduction of nutrients to cells. Deisenhofer and Michel were also recipients of the 1986 Biological Physics Prize of the American Physical Society and the 1988 Otto-Bayer Prize.

In 1987, Deisenhofer accepted the Virginia and Edward Linthicum Distinguished Chair in Biomolecular Science at the University of Texas Southwestern Medical Center at Dallas; his goal there is to establish a major center for X-ray crystallography. He has continued his research interests in the areas of protein crystallography, macromolecules, and crystallographic software. Deisenhofer has been awarded the Knight Commander's Cross of the Order of Merit of the Federal Republic of Germany, as well as the Bavarian Order of Merit. He is a fellow of the American Association for the Advancement of Science and a member of the American Crystallographic Association, the German Biophysical Society, and Academia Europa. In 1993, Deisenhofer, with James R. Norris of the Argonne National Laboratory, published a two-volume book called *The Photosynthetic Reaction Center,* based on work that grew out of Diesenhofer's collaboration with Michel.

Deisenhofer was married in 1989 to a fellow scientist, Kirsten Fischer Lindahl. He enjoys music, history, skiing, swimming, and chess in his free time. After Diesenhofer won the Nobel Prize, Dr. Kern Wildenthal, president of the Southwestern Medical School, described him to the *New York Times* as "very shy" and a man whose "life was his work." Wildenthal further observed that the scientist is "quiet, peaceful and calm. But beneath that exterior, he is scientifically fearless."

SELECTED WRITINGS BY DEISENHOFER:

Books

(With James P. Norris) *The Photosynthetic Reaction Center,* Academic Press, 1993.

Periodicals

(With H. Michel) "Nobel Lecture: The photosynthetic reaction center from the purple bacterium Rhodopseudomonas viridis," *Embo j,* August, 1989, pp. 2149–2170.

SOURCES:

Books

Ladd, M.F.C., and Palmer, R.A., *Structure Determination by X-Ray Crystallography,* Plenum Press, 1977.
McGuire, Paula, editor, *Nobel Prize Winners Supplement 1987–1991,* H. W. Wilson, 1992.

Periodicals

Dagani, Ron, and Stephen Stinson, "Nobel Prizes: Photosynthesis, Drug Studies Honored," *Chemical and Engineering News,* October 24, 1988, pp. 4–5.
Levi, Barbara Goss, "Nobel Chemists Shed Light on Key Structure in Photosynthesis," *Physics Today,* February, 1989, pp. 17–18.
Lewin, Roger, "Membrane Protein Holds Photosynthetic Secrets," *Science,* November 4, 1988, pp. 672–673.
"Stories of Patience and Triumph," *Time,* October 31, 1988, p. 65.

"Winners of Nobel Prizes," *The New York Times,* October 20, 1988, p. B13.

—*Sketch by Kimberlyn McGrail*

Max Delbrück
1906-1981
German-born American molecular biologist

Max Delbrück

Max Delbrück has often been called the founder of molecular biology. Although educated as a physicist, Delbrück quickly became interested in bacteriophages, a type of virus that infects bacterial cells. He perfected a method of culturing bacteriophages and found that they could infect a bacterial cell and, within twenty minutes, erupt out of the cell in a hundredfold their original number. Each of these offspring bacteriophages was then ready to infect another bacterial cell. Among his many contributions to the field, Delbrück and another researcher together discovered that bacterial cells could spontaneously mutate to become immune to the bacteriophages. He also found that two different types of bacteriophages could combine to create a new type of bacteriophage. Perhaps as much or more than his discoveries, he forged the field of molecular biology through his involvement in the work of so many other scientists . While he was highly critical and not easily convinced of a new discovery, Delbrück also inspired many scientists to new heights. His work paved the way for an explosion of new findings in the field of molecular biology, including the discoveries that viruses contain the genetic material deoxyribonucleic acid (DNA), along with the eventual unveiling of the structure of DNA itself. In 1969, Delbrück won the Nobel Prize for physiology or medicine, which he shared with **Alfred Day Hershey** and **Salvador Edward Luria**, for their work in molecular genetics.

Delbrück was born on September 4, 1906, in Berlin as the youngest of seven children to Hans and Lina Thiersch Delbrück. Many of his relatives were prominent academicians, including his father, who was a professor of history at the University of Berlin and editor of the journal *Prussian Yearbook;* his maternal great–grandfather, Justus von Liebig, is considered the originator of organic chemistry. Throughout his youth in the middle-class suburb of Grünewald, Delbrück developed his interests in mathematics and astronomy, and carried those interests into college.

In 1924 he enrolled in the University of Tübingen, but switched colleges several times before enrolling at the University of Göttingen, where he obtained his Ph.D. in physics in 1930. Delbrück began writing a dissertation about the origin of a type of star, but abandoned it because of his lack of understanding of both the necessary math and English, the language in which most of the pertinent literature was written. He took up a new topic, and completed his dissertation by explaining the chemical bonding of two lithium atoms, and why this bonding is much weaker than the bond between two hydrogen atoms.

Switches from Quantum Mechanics to Biology

For the next year and a half, through a research grant, he did postgraduate studies in quantum mechanics at the University of Bristol in England There, he became friends with other researchers, several of whom went on to make major contributions in the fields of physics and chemistry. In the early 1930s, he continued his research as a Rockefeller Foundation postdoctoral fellow under **Neils Bohr** at the University of Copenhagen, one of the major intellectual centers in the world. Bohr's beliefs had a strong impact on Delbrück. Bohr had developed a theory of complementarity, stating that electromagnetic radiation could be described by either waves or particles, but not both at the same time. He followed that by a now-famous lecture in 1932 called "Light and Life."

In it, Bohr suggested that a similar paradox existed in living things: they could be either described as whole organisms or as groups of molecules. Delbrück was hooked. He began to study biology. In 1932, Delbrück returned to Berlin and the Kaiser Wilhelm Institute. He remained at the institute for five years, and continued his shift from physics to biology. From 1932 to 1937, while an assistant to Professor **Lise Meitner** in Berlin, Delbrück was part of a small group of theoretical physicists which held informal private meetings; he was devoted at first to theoretical physics, but soon turned to biology. In his acceptance speech for the Nobel Prize, Delbrück recalled that "Discussions of (new findings) within our little group strengthened the notion that genes had a kind of stability similar to that of the molecules of chemistry. From the hindsight of our present knowledge," he said, "one might consider this a trivial statement: what else could genes be but molecules? However, in the mid-'30s, this was not a trivial statement."

In 1937, by virtue of his second Rockefeller Foundation fellowship, Delbrück immigrated to the United States, where he began to study biology and genetics and the reproduction of bacteriophages, in particular, at the California Institute of Technology in Pasadena. A year later, he met Emory Ellis, a biologist also working on these viruses, and together they designed experiments to study bacteriophages and the mathematical system to analyze the results.

Publishes Milestone Paper on Bacterial Mutation

By 1940, Delbrück had joined the faculty of Vanderbilt University in Tennessee and during the following summers continued his phage research intensively at the Cold Spring Harbor Laboratory on Long Island in New York. Also in 1940 he met Italian physician Salvador Luria, with whom he would eventually share the Nobel Prize. Luria was conducting bacteriophage research at the College of Physicians and Surgeons of Columbia University in New York City. Their collaborative work began, and in 1943 Delbrück and Luria became famous in the scientific community with the publication of their landmark paper, "Mutations of Bacteria from Virus Sensitivity to Virus Resistance." The paper confirmed that phage-resistant bacterial strains developed through natural selection: once infected with a bacteriophage, the bacterium spontaneously changes so that it becomes immune to the invading virus. Their work also outlined the experimental technique, which became a standard analytical tool for measuring mutation rates. The publication of this paper is now regarded as the beginning of bacterial genetics.

Also in 1943, the so-called Phage Group held its first informal meeting, with Delbrück, Luria and microbiologist Alfred Hershey in attendance. At group meetings, members discussed research and ideas involving bacteriophages. The number of members grew along with the excitement over the possibilities presented by this area of research. The meetings were much like those Delbrück had so enjoyed while he was working in Meitner's lab in Berlin. In the following year, the Phage Group drafted guidelines—called the Phage Treaty of 1944—to ensure that results gained from different laboratories could be compared easily and accurately. The treaty urged all bacteriophage investigators to conduct their studies on a specific set of seven bacteriophages that infect *Escherichia coli* strain B and its mutants. It also spelled out the standard experimental conditions to be used.

While on the faculty at Vanderbilt University, Delbrück organized the first of his summer phage courses at Cold Spring Harbor in 1945, the year he also became a U.S. citizen. The course became an annual event and drew biologists, geneticists and physicists who traveled from laboratories all over the world to learn not only about the experimental and analytical methods of phage research but also about its potential.

In 1946, Delbrück's and Hershey's labs separately discovered that different bacteriophage strains that both invade the same bacterial cell could randomly exchange genetic material to form new and unique viral strains. They called the phenomenon genetic recombination. According to *Biographical Memoirs of Fellows of the Royal Society,* this finding "led, about 10 years later, to the ultimate genetic analysis of gene structure by **Seymour Benzer**."

Describes Cell as "Magic Puzzle Box"

The following year, Delbrück returned to the California Institute of Technology as a professor in the biology department. In 1949, he delivered an address, "A Physicist Looks at Biology," that recalled his scientific journey. "A mature physicist, acquainting himself for the first time with the problems of biology, is puzzled by the circumstance that there are no 'absolute phenomena' in biology. Everything is time bound and space bound. The animal or plant or microorganism he is working with is but a link in an evolutionary chain of changing forms, none of which has any permanent validity. . . . If it be true that the essence of life is the accumulation of experience through the generations, then one may perhaps suspect that the key problem of biology, from the physicist's point of view, is how living matter manages to record and perpetuate its experiences." He described the cell as a "magic puzzle box full of elaborate and changing molecules (that) carries with it the experiences of a billion years of experimentation by its ancestors."

In the late 1940s and early 1950s, Delbrück expanded his interests to include sensory perception, eventually studying how the fungus *Phycomyces* uses light and how light affects its growth. As he did with the phage research, Delbrück formed a *Phycomyces* Group to gather and discuss ideas. Despite his shift, he and his work continued to have an influence in bacteriophage research. In 1952 Hershey, one of the original three members of the Phage Group, and Martha Chase confirmed that genes consist of DNA and demonstrated how phages infect bacteria. The following year molecular biologist **Francis Crick** and physicist **James Watson**, once a graduate student of Luria's, determined the three-dimensional, double-helix structure of DNA. While their work was in progress, Watson would frequently write Delbrück to discuss ideas and to tell him about their results, including the first details of the double-helix structure.

Delbrück remained busy throughout the 1950s and 1960s as investigators and students sought his knowledge and advice, despite his reputation for being a tough critic with a brusque manner. Following an investigator's explanation of his research and results, Delbrück would often respond, "I don't believe a word of it," or if it was a more formal presentation, "That was the worst seminar I have ever heard." Once, according to Seymour Benzer in *Phage and the Origins of Molecular Biology,* Delbrück wrote to Benzer's wife, "Dear Dotty, please tell Seymour to stop writing so many papers. If I gave them the attention his papers *used* to deserve, they would take all my time. If he *must* continue, tell him to do what **Ernst Mayr** asked his mother to do in her long daily letters, namely, *underline what is important.*" Yet, many scientists persisted in bringing their research to Delbrück. In his essay in *Phage and the Origins of Molecular Biology,* molecular biologist Thomas Anderson recalled Delbrück: "At each phase in our groping toward discovery, Max Delbrück seemed to be present not so much as a guide, perhaps, but as a critic. To the lecturer he was an enquiring, and sometimes merciless, logician. If one persevered, he would be fortunate to have Max as conscience, goad and sage."

Delbrück also had a lighter side. As reported in *Thinking About Science,* Delbrück remembered pitting his wits against those of his college professors. He wouldn't take notes during the lectures, but would try to follow and understand the professor's mathematical argument. "When the professor made a little mistake, with a plus or minus sign or a factor of 2, I did not point that out directly but waited 10 minutes until he got entangled and then pointed out, to his great relief, how he could disentangle himself—a great game." When Delbrück joined the faculty ranks, he developed a rather unusual tradition with his students and peers. He often invited them along on camping trips with his family, including his wife and eventually their four children. Delbrück married Mary Adeline

Bruce in 1941. They had two sons, Jonathan and Tobias, and two daughters, Nicola and Ludina.

Wins Nobel Prize and Peers' Accolades

In 1961, while still a professor at the California Institute of Technology, Delbrück took a two-year leave of absence to help the University of Cologne in Germany establish its Institute of Genetics. In 1966 back in California, the former Phage Group members celebrated Delbrück's sixtieth birthday with a book in his honor, *Phage and the Origins of Molecular Biology.* The book is a collection of essays by the group members, many of whom had gone on to make important discoveries in bacterial genetics. The larger scientific community also recognized Delbrück's contributions with a variety of awards. In December of 1969, Delbrück, Luria and Hershey accepted the Nobel Prize in physiology or medicine for their work in molecular biology, particularly the mechanism of replication in viruses and their genetic structure.

Delbrück continued his sensory perception research into the next decade. He retired from the California Institute of Technology in 1977, and died of cancer four years later in Pasadena on March 10, 1981. In *Phage and the Origin of Molecular Biology,* phage course alumnus N. Visconti recalled a conversation he had with Delbrück. "I remember he once said to me, 'You don't have the inspiration or the talent to be an artist; then what else do you want to do in life besides be a scientist?' For Max Delbrück it was as simple as that."

SELECTED WRITINGS BY DELBRÜCK:

Books

"A Physicist Looks at Biology," *Phage and the Origins of Molecular Biology,* edited by John Cairns, Gunther S. Stent, and James Watson, Cold Spring Harbor Laboratory of Quantitative Biology, 1966.
Mind From Matter? An Essay on Evolutionary Epistemology, Blackwell Scientific Publications, 1986.

Periodicals

"Mutations of Bacteria from Virus Sensitivity to Virus Resistance," *Genetics,* Volume 28, 1943, pp. 491–511.
"A Physicist's Renewed Look at Biology: Twenty Years Later," *Science,* June 12, 1970, pp. 1312–1315.

SOURCES:

Books

Biographical Memoirs of Fellows of the Royal Society, Volume 28, Royal Society (London), 1982.

Fischer, Ernst P., and Carol Lipson, editors, *Thinking about Science: Max Delbrück and the Origins of Molecular Biology,* W. W. Norton, 1988.

Periodicals

Hayes, William, "Max Delbrück and the Birth of Molecular Biology," *Social Research,* autumn, 1984, pp. 641–673.

Kay, Lily, "Conceptual Models and Analytical Tools: The Biology of Physicist Max Delbrück," *Journal of the History of Biology,* summer, 1985, pp. 207–246.

Physics Today, June, 1981, pp. 71–74.

—*Sketch by Leslie Mertz*

Pierre Deligné
1944-
Belgian mathematician

Pierre Deligné is a research mathematician who has excelled at making connections between various fields of mathematics. His research has led to several important discoveries, the most critical of which is the proof of a conjecture made by the mathematician **André Weil**. For this work, he received both the Fields Medal, the highest available honor in mathematics, and the Crafoord Prize.

Pierre R. Deligné was born in Brussels, Belgium, on October 3, 1944. His parents, Albert and Renee Bodart Deligné, raised their son in the Belgian capital. The young Deligné showed an early affinity for mathematics, and his interest was encouraged by M. J. Nijs, his high school teacher. Nijs lent Deligné mathematics texts, including one by N. Bourbaki which introduced concepts of modern mathematics, such as topology, long before discussing the topics traditionally studied first. Despite the unfamiliar and complicated terminology, Deligné's understanding of mathematics flourished, and after completing high school he went to the University of Brussels. He obtained his degree in mathematics there in 1966 and remained for graduate study.

Deligné's adviser at the University of Brussels was group theorist Jacques Tits, and in 1965 he suggested that Deligné travel to Paris. Since Deligné was most interested in algebraic geometry, Tits felt that he should study where some of the most important algebraic geometrists, such as **Jean-Pierre Serre** and **Alexander Grothendieck**, were teaching and researching. Deligné went, and met both Serre and Grothendieck; his association with them would strongly influence his career. He attended seminars and lectures by these mathematicians and others before returning to Brussels to complete work on his dissertation. He received his Ph.D. in 1968.

In 1968, Deligné took up residence in Bures-Sur-Yvette, a small community south of Paris, where the Institut des Hautes Etudes Scientifiques (Institute for Advanced Scientific Study-IHES) is located. He had been appointed a visiting member of this organization so that he could continue his research with Grothendieck; he became a permanent member of the IHES in 1970. For several years, Grothendieck had been working to generalize and update the field of algebraic geometry by making it more compatible with recent abstract mathematical theories. Deligné admired and learned from Grothendieck's work, although he followed a different approach. Whereas Grothendieck tried to connect algebraic geometry with all other fields by creating new theories or rules, Deligné instead worked to uncover connections already implied by previous work in these fields. He looked for simple solutions; as David Mumford and John Tate observe in their article in *Science:* "He preferred to find an elegant fundamental new idea suddenly clarifying a whole area or old problem."

Research on Weil Conjectures

A prime example of Deligné's methods is his work on the Weil conjectures. Proposed by the mathematician André Weil, these conjectures state that it should be possible to determine the number of solutions for certain systems of equations by predicting the shape the solutions will make when graphed. In other words, by using certain topological concepts, algebraic results can be obtained. Weil felt sure that he was correct, but he was never able to prove the conjectures. Over a period of several years, Deligné combined a new theory of cohomology (a branch of topology) called *étale cohomology,* which had been initially developed by Grothendieck, and a related conjecture by the Indian number theorist **S. I. Ramanujan**, to determine the final proof in 1974. His work has been valued not only because he solved an important problem in mathematics, but also because he proved that many seemingly disparate subjects can be connected. For this latter reason as much as for the work itself, the International Mathematics Union in 1978 awarded Deligné their highest honor, the Fields Medal.

Deligné continued to study the Weil conjectures even after his first success, attempting to use automorphic forms (equations involving multiple functions) and prime numbers to determine more and more exact solutions. He worked on several problems proposed by the American mathematician Robert Langlands. Langlands was leading a major research program in the area of automorphic forms at Princeton's Institute for Advanced Studies (IAS). He invited Deligné to America, asking him to help organize a conference at Oregon State University in 1977.

Also in the late seventies, Deligné gave a series of lectures in étale cohomology with the help of Grothendieck and others in the field of algebraic geometry. These lectures were considered definitive in describing this relatively new field, but Deligné's contributions were not limited to lecturing. He added to the field by his work with Shimura varieties and by proving some conjectures of the mathematician William Vallance Douglas Hodge.

In 1980, Deligné married Elena Vladimirovna Alexeeva, with whom he had two children. He brought his young family to the United States in 1984 to continue his mathematical research at the IAS. He has remained at the IAS, and in 1988 he received the Crafoord Prize for Mathematics, given by the Royal Swedish Academy of Sciences. Grothendieck was the co-recipient; the award was given for their work in defining étale cohomology and their applications of it to algebraic geometry.

SELECTED WRITINGS BY DELIGNÉ:

Books

Cohomologie Etale, Springer-Verlag, 1977.
(With J. Milne, A. Ogus, and S. Kuang-yen) *Hodge Cycles, Motives, and Shimura Varieties,* Springer-Verlag, 1982.

SOURCES:

Books

Tarwater, D., editor, *The Bicentennial Tribute to American Mathematics 1776-1976,* Mathematical Association of America, 1977.

Periodicals

Katz, N. M., "The Work of Pierre Deligné," *Proceedings of the International Congress of Mathematicians,* Volume 1, Academia Scientarium Fennica, 1980, pp. 47–52.

Mumford, David and John Tate, "Fields Medals (IV): An Instinct for the Key Idea," *Science,* November 17, 1978, pp. 737–739.

—*Sketch by Karen Sands*

Jack B. Dennis
1931-
American computer scientist

Jack B. Dennis is a computer science educator and researcher who is best known for his pioneering work in computer timesharing and dataflow technology. His early mechanical and electrical engineering interests led him to study computer technology at a time when it was just emerging as a field that would revolutionize the world. In addition to his computer research, Dennis has had a major role in shaping the computer science curriculum at the Massachusetts Institute of Technology (MIT).

Jack Bonnell Dennis was born on October 13, 1931, in Elizabeth, New Jersey, to Wolcott Dennis and Nereide Bonnell. His father was from Seattle and was employed at the Air Reduction Company in New Jersey. His duties included "boiling air," an oxygen extraction process where air is cooled to a liquid form, then gradually heated to "boil off" the nitrogen, leaving pure liquid oxygen. Dennis's mother grew up in Elizabeth, New Jersey, and became a teacher. Dennis has an older brother, Robert, who served for several years as the harbormaster of Darien, Connecticut, and owned an auto service center. When Jack was one year old, the Dennis family moved to Darien, Connecticut.

Dennis was educated in the Darien public schools and graduated from high school in 1949. Throughout his childhood, the family always kept a supply of the most recent *Popular Science* magazines, which Dennis and his brother read without fail. *Popular Science* was characterized by good explanations of how things worked—particularly mechanical equipment. Dennis supplemented this material by taking mechanical household items apart, like the sewing machine and the family clocks. He remembered fondly in an interview with contributor Roger Jaffe how he and his brother came into possession of an Underwood typewriter, which they took apart and reassembled many times.

As a teenager Dennis read other scientific materials, including *Elements of Electricity, The RCA Receiving Tube Manual,* and *The Radio Amateur's*

Jack B. Dennis

Handbook. Reading these publications sparked an interest in electrical design. On the advice of his high school guidance counselor, he completed an enrollment application to the Massachusetts Institute of Technology. His knowledge of electrical and mechanical design and his work in school gave him the necessary qualifications for acceptance into MIT in 1949.

MIT Years Mark Time of Discovery

The year that Dennis began his studies at MIT also marked a milestone in the computer age. In Cambridge and Manchester, England, the first stored-program computer was tested. This computer was unique in that the software, or set of instructions the computer is to carry out, was stored in memory within the computer. While Dennis was at MIT, the university obtained its first stored-program computer, called the "Whirlwind." During his junior and senior years, Dennis and other students experimented and studied the computer, its characteristics and limitations.

At the same time, Dennis put his mechanical and electrical design skills to use by creating a new automatic cab selection for a local model railroad club. Prior to reworking the system, the club had a primitive control system for allowing more than one train to run on the layout at the same time. Using surplus relays and other electrical equipment donated

from the local telephone company, Dennis modernized the railroad control system.

Dennis received bachelor's and master's degrees together from MIT in 1954. To qualify for the dual degree program, Dennis signed up for a cooperative work program in 1951, giving him an opportunity to work outside the school in a real-world environment. Dennis found a position with the Air Force Cambridge Research Laboratory (AFCRL) doing work in speech processing. He also worked on projects involving experimental radar systems using the lab's home-made computer. It was with the AFCRL that Dennis had his first hands-on practical problem-solving experience with computer equipment. The summer after receiving his degrees, Dennis designed, built and evaluated equipment for the Bell Telephone Laboratories. His technology was used by Bell in the first electronic switching installation for the phone company in Illinois.

Dennis elected to pursue a doctorate at MIT and joined the university as a research and teaching assistant. Under the guidance of Professor Robert Saunders, Dennis designed and wrote optimization software for aircraft alternators. He also used computer science techniques and linear programming to solve the classic "transportation problem." In its simplest form, this problem assumes a given number of factories and a given number of warehouses, which are all assigned positions on a map. One needs to transport goods from the factories to the warehouses at a minimum cost. Dennis's solution to this problem was later put to good use by a major oil company.

While in the doctorate program, Dennis also explored queueing theory, at that time a brand-new branch of computer science theory dealing with the sequence in which computer information is processed. His doctoral dissertation used the close relationship between mathematical programming problems to solve electrical networks. Dennis received his doctor of science degree in electrical engineering from MIT in 1958, although much of his work had been with the burgeoning field of computer technology. He joined the MIT faculty as an instructor and started experiments with the university's newly acquired TX–0 computer system. In the late 1950s there were no high-level programming languages other than FORTRAN, so most of Dennis's work on the TX–0 was done with primitive machine and assembly languages.

Develops Computer Time Sharing Concept

In the early 1960s, Dennis developed his "time sharing" concept for computers. His idea was to allow a large number of users access to a computer by giving the first user a short amount of processing time, then switching to the next user, and so on. The switching was done very quickly so it appeared that each user had sole access to the computer. Dennis designed software for the TX–0 to implement the time sharing technology. His concept was later used by the PDP–1, Digital Equipment Corporation's first multi-user computer. In 1963 Dennis served with the "Multics" project, dedicated to make timesharing an effective way of computing for a large group of computer users. He served on this committee until 1964, then decided to pursue individual research. Today, timeshare systems form the heart of many university computing systems. For his pioneering work on the timesharing concept, he was made a fellow of the Institute of Electrical and Electronics Engineers (IEEE).

Dennis formed the Computation Structures research group within the MIT Laboratory for Computer Science. The work of his group on dataflow models for computation, or how information is routed and processed by a system, and their use in guiding novel concepts of computer architecture, or hardware systems, has influenced work in industry and in research institutions around the world. This work led to the Eckert-Mauchly award for 1984 from the IEEE and the Association for Computing Machinery (ACM), and in 1994 he was made a fellow of the ACM.

During his tenure at MIT, Dennis developed six course subjects in new areas of computer theory. Some of these have become part of the core curriculum at the university and others have become classic subjects in computer science. In 1987 Dennis became professor emeritus at MIT, and began his tenure as president of Dataflow Computer Corporation, a firm specializing in the practical and commercial development of dataflow technology. The computer scientist also holds several patents in the field of parallel computing technology.

Dennis is married to Therese Smith, a systems engineer, with whom he has two children, Randall and Jessica; he also has a son, David, from a previous marriage. Dennis enjoys music, plays the piano and cello and is an accomplished choral singer. He has sung in many groups and, for a time, was a tenor in the Tanglewood Festival Chorus, which performs regularly with the Boston Symphony Orchestra.

SELECTED WRITINGS BY DENNIS:

Books

Mathematical Programming and Electrical Networks, Wiley, 1959.
(With P. J. Denning and J. E. Qualitz) *Machines, Languages, and Computation,* Prentice-Hall, 1979.
The Nuclear Almanac: Confronting the Atom in War and Peace, Addison-Wesley, 1984.

Periodicals

"A High-Speed Computer Technique for the Transportation Problem," *Journal of the ACM,* April, 1958.
"A Multi-user Computer Facility for Education and Research," *Communications of the ACM,* September, 1964.
"Segmentation and the Design of Multiprogrammed Computer Systems," *Communications of the ACM,* October, 1965.
"Dataflow Supercomputers," *IEEE Computer,* November, 1980.
"Machines and Models for Parallel Computing," *International Journal of Parallel Programming,* February, 1994.

SOURCES:

Dennis, Jack B., interview with Roger Jaffe conducted March 15, 1994.

—*Sketch by Roger Jaffe*

Willem de Sitter
1872-1934
Dutch astronomer and mathematician

Willem de Sitter, one of the first astronomers to realize the cosmic implications of physicist **Albert Einstein**'s theories of relativity, helped refine these theories and introduce them to English-speaking countries. Consequently, he is considered one of the fathers of cosmology, the study of the origin and central structure of the universe. He made other significant contributions to the field of astronomy, particularly in celestial mechanics, earth rotation, and computation of astronomical constants.

De Sitter was born on May 6, 1872, in the northern Netherlands town of Sneek. His mother was T. W. S. Bertling and his father was L. U. de Sitter, a judge who became president of the court in the city of Arnhem, where young de Sitter attended secondary school at the gymnasium.

De Sitter entered the University of Groningen to study mathematics and physics. While there, he worked in the university's astronomical laboratory, where he became interested in the research being conducted by astronomer Jacobus Kapteyn. Upon graduation, de Sitter was invited to study under Sir

David Gill at the Royal Observatory in Cape Town, South Africa. The location and facilities in Cape Town provided excellent conditions for astronomical observations. De Sitter stayed there from August, 1897, until December, 1899, gathering data for his doctoral dissertation. During his stay in Cape Town, de Sitter met Eleonora Suermondt, whom he married and helped to raise two sons and two daughters; in 1948, de Sitter's widow wrote his biography, which was published in Dutch. At Gill's suggestion, de Sitter undertook an analysis of Jupiter's moons, a study he would pursue throughout his career. Taking his own measurements of brightness and angular distances, he investigated the motion of Jupiter's known moons relative to the planet and to each other. His results included sizable corrections to existing values for each satellite's orbital inclination and the point at which their orbital paths cross the plane of Jupiter's equator. He returned to Groningen to work as an assistant to Kapteyn and complete work on his doctoral dissertation, "Discussion of Heliometer Observations of Jupiter's Satellites." He received his Ph.D. in 1901 and continued to work at Groningen for seven more years.

In 1908, de Sitter accepted a professorship in theoretical astronomy at the University of Leiden (about twenty miles north of Rotterdam). Eleven years later, he took on additional responsibilities as director of the Leiden Observatory. He reorganized the facility, adding a department of astrophysics, updating the equipment, and instigating an equipment-sharing agreement with the Union Observatory in Johannesburg. Under his leadership, the Leiden institution rose to prominence among European observatories. The Royal Astronomical Society elected him an associate in 1909 and awarded him its Gold Medal in 1931; in 1929, the National Academy of Sciences in the United States presented him with its Watson Gold Medal.

Develops Astronomical Theory

De Sitter arranged for observatories in Cape Town, Greenwich, Johannesburg, Leiden, and Pulkovo (near St. Petersburg, later Leningrad) to take a series of photographic observations of Jupiter's moons. He incorporated this information with data from the Royal Observatory in Cape Town—which maintained records dating from 1668— describing eclipses of these satellites by their parent planet. From this wealth of information, de Sitter was able to derive significant results, including a calculation of Jupiter's mass. In 1925, he published a paper proposing a new mathematical theory of Jupiter's satellites; four years later he published tables accurately describing the orbital elements and masses of the four largest moons.

In an attempt to apply astronomical theories to the Earth, de Sitter undertook a study relating gravity measurements and geodetic data (information on the Earth's size and shape) to celestial observations. He concluded that the rotation of the Earth varies; among the causes he proposed was tidal friction, which he suggested might also affect the moon.

Another of de Sitter's goals was to update the values of astronomical constants, such as angles of parallax, the constant of aberration, and the constant of nutation, or the oscillation of a rotating body on its axis. Existing values had been published in 1895, and large amounts of data had been collected at various observatories since then. Over the course of his career, de Sitter recalculated every known astronomical constant. He presented the results in papers published in 1915 (focusing on the Earth), 1927 (including precession, solar and lunar parallax, and mass of the Earth's moon), and, posthumously, in 1938.

Refines the Theories of Relativity

When Einstein published his special theory of relativity in 1905, few astronomers realized its implications to their field. De Sitter, however, wrote a paper in 1911 which applied the new theory to the Earth's moon and the planets in this solar system. Einstein published key elements of his general theory of relativity in 1915 and 1916 in the German journal *Annalen der Physik* and sent copies to de Sitter, who was residing in the Netherlands (a neutral country during World War I). De Sitter immediately began to analyze the material. He also sent copies to Sir **Arthur Eddington**, a British astronomer, thus disseminating the information to the English-speaking world despite wartime barriers to communication.

De Sitter presented three related papers to the Royal Astronomical Society during 1916 and 1917. The first two were largely reviews of Einstein's work, while the third contained a mathematical analysis that departed from Einstein's. In the general theory, Einstein presented a system of equations, which he solved to produce a mathematical model of the universe. Initially, his solution described an expanding universe, but since that did not seem to agree with astronomical observations, he modified the theory so it would describe a static, or fixed, universe.

De Sitter took a fresh look at the equations and found that there was not a single, unique solution. In fact, he presented additional solutions that described an oscillating universe and two versions of an expanding universe. He suggested it would be interesting to analyze light from distant galaxies in search of a shift toward the red end of the spectrum (the Doppler effect implies a red shift for receding motion). He also described what is known as the de Sitter universe—a static universe containing no matter. While de Sitter knew his model of an empty, static universe was a theoretical phenomenon that did not describe reality, he hoped it would inspire further investigations. Other researchers soon found that adding small amounts of matter to the de Sitter universe introduced motion, which caused the points of matter to fly away from each other—in other words, it produced an expanding universe. Intrigued by these results, Eddington and other British colleagues looked with interest at red-shift data being generated in the early 1920s. They, in turn, conducted a joint experiment in Brazil and on Principe Island, in the Gulf of Guinea. During a solar eclipse, they observed light from distant stars as it passed near the sun; the measurements showed that the light bent as predicted by the general theory of relativity.

In 1932, de Sitter and Einstein collaborated on the development of another model of the universe. Known as the Einstein-de Sitter model, it represented the simplest solution to the basic equations of general relativity. The model describes an expanding universe (as the American astronomer **Edwin P. Hubble** had established from his 1929 experiment), and it features flat space consistent with the special theory of relativity. Looking backward through time, it implies a moment of beginning, which is now described as the Big Bang.

De Sitter was recognized as a prominent scientist during his lifetime. He received numerous awards, including honorary degrees from Cape Town, Cambridge, Oxford, and Wesleyan universities. In addition to his direct contributions to science, de Sitter promoted cooperation among his fellow researchers. As president of the International Astronomical Union from 1925 to 1928, for example, he worked to reconstruct cooperation between scientists from nations opposed to each other during World War I.

De Sitter faced repeated episodes of illness throughout his life. Nevertheless, his steady output of important scholarly papers continued until his death from pneumonia in Leiden, on November 19, 1934.

SELECTED WRITINGS BY DE SITTER:

Books

Kosmos, A Course of Six Lectures on the Development of Our Insight into the Structure of the Universe, Harvard University Press, 1932.

SOURCES:

Books

Abbott, David, editor, *The Biographical Dictionary of Scientists: Astronomers,* Peter Bedrick Books, 1984, pp. 41–42.

Gribbin, John R., *In Search of the Big Bang: Quantum Physics and Cosmology,* Bantam, 1986, pp. 122–26.
Magill, Frank N., editor, *Great Events from History II,* Volume 2, Salem Press, 1991, pp. 684–88.

Periodicals

Jones, H. Spencer, *Monthly Notices of the Royal Astronomical Society,* February, 1935, pp. 343–47.

—*Sketch by Loretta Hall*

Félix d'Hérelle
1873-1949
Canadian microbiologist

Félix d'Hérelle's major contribution to science was the discovery of bacteriophage, a microscopic agent that appears in conjunction with and destroys disease-producing bacteria in a living organism. Like many researchers, d'Hérelle spent much of his life exploring the effects of his major discovery. He was also well-traveled: in the course of his life he lived for long or short periods of time in Canada, France, the Netherlands, Guatemala, Mexico, Indochina, Egypt, India, the United States, and the Soviet Union.

D'Hérelle was born in Montreal, Quebec, Canada, on April 25, 1873. His father, Félix d'Hérelle—a member of a well-established French Canadian family, died when the young Félix was six years old. After his father's death, he moved with his mother, Augustine Meert d'Hérelle—a Dutch woman—to Paris, France. In Paris, d'Hérelle received his secondary education at the Lycée Louis-le-Grand and began his medical studies. He completed his medical program at the University of Leiden in the Netherlands. He married Mary Kerr, of France, on July 11, 1893; the couple had two daughters, Marcelle and Huberte. In 1901 d'Hérelle moved to Guatemala City, Guatemala, to become the director of the bacteriology laboratory at the general hospital and to teach microbiology at the local medical school. In 1907 he moved to Merida, Yucatan, Mexico, to study the fermentation of sisal hemp, and in 1908 the Mexican government sent him back to Paris to further his microbiological studies. D'Hérelle became an assistant at Paris's Pasteur Institute in 1909, became chief of its laboratory in 1914, and remained at the Institute until 1921.

Discovery of Bacteriophage

During his time at the Pasteur Institute, d'Hérelle studied a bacterium called *Coccobacillus acridiorum*, which caused enteritis (inflammation of the intestines) in locusts and grasshoppers of the acrididae family of insects, with a view toward using the microbe to destroy locusts. In growing the bacteria on culture plates, d'Hérelle observed empty spots on the plates and theorized that these spots resulted from a virus that grew along with and killed the bacteria. He surmised that this phenomenon might have great medical significance as an example of an organism fighting diseases of the digestive tract. In 1916 he extended his investigation to cultures of the bacillus which caused dysentery and again observed spots free of the microbe on the surface of the cultures. He was able to filter out a substance from the feces of dysentery victims which totally destroyed in a few hours a culture broth of the bacillus. On September 10, 1917, he presented to the French Academy of Sciences a paper announcing his discovery entitled "Sur un microbe invisible, antagoniste du bacille dysentérique." He named the bacteria–rather than—destroying substance bacteriophage (literally, "eater of bacteria"). He devoted most of his research and writing for the rest of his life to the various types of bacteriophage which appeared in conjunction with specific types of bacteria. He published several books dealing with his findings.

From 1920 to the late 1930s, d'Hérelle traveled and lived in many parts of the world. In 1920 he went to French Indochina under the auspices of the Pasteur Institute to study human dysentery and septic pleuropneumonia in buffaloes. It was during the course of this expedition that he perfected his techniques for isolating bacteriophage. From 1922 to 1923 he served as an assistant professor at the University of Leiden. In 1924 he moved to Alexandria, Egypt, to direct the Bacteriological Service of the Egyptian Council on Health and Quarantine. In 1927 he went to India at the invitation of the Indian Medical Service to attempt to cure cholera through the use of the bacteriophage associated with that disease. D'Hérelle served as professor of bacteriology at Yale University from 1928 to 1933, and in 1935 the government of the Soviet Socialist Republic of Georgia requested that d'Hérelle establish institutes dedicated to the study of bacteriophage in Tiflis, Kiev, and Kharkov. However, unstable civil conditions forced d'Hérelle's departure from the Soviet Union in 1937, and he returned to Paris, where he lived, continuing his study of bacteriophage, for the remainder of his life.

D'Hérelle attempted to make use of bacteriophage in the treatment of many human and animal diseases, including dysentery, cholera, plague, and staphylococcus and streptococcus infections. Such treatment was widespread for a time, especially in the Soviet Union. However, use of bacteriophage for this purpose was superseded by the use of chemical drugs and antibiotics even within d'Hérelle's lifetime. Today bacteriophage is employed primarily as a diagnostic ultravirus. Of the many honors d'Hérelle received, his perhaps most notable is the Leeuwenhoek Medal given to him by the Amsterdam Academy of Science in 1925; before d'Hérelle, Louis Pasteur had been the only other French scientist to receive the award. D'Hérelle was presented with honorary degrees from the University of Leiden and from Yale, Montreal, and Laval Universities. He died after surgery in Paris on February 22, 1949.

SELECTED WRITINGS BY D'HÉRELLE:

Books

Le bactériophage: son rôle dans l'immunite, 1921, translation by George H. Smith published as *The Bacteriophage: Its Role in Immunity,* Williams & Wilkins Company, 1922.
Les défenses de l'organisme, 1923, translation by George H. Smith published and enlarged as *Immunity in Natural Infectious Disease,* Williams & Wilkins Company, 1924.
Le bactériophage et son comportement, 1926, translations by George H. Smith published as *The Bacteriophage and its Behavior,* Williams & Wilkins Company, 1926, and *The Bacteriophage and its Clinical Applications,* C. C. Thomas, 1930.

Periodicals

"Sur un microbe invisible, antagoniste du bacille dysentérique," *Comptes rendus hebdomadaires des séances de l'Academie des sciences,* 1917, pp. 373–375.

SOURCES:

Books

Dictionary of Scientific Biography, Volume 6, Scribner, 1972, pp. 297–299.
Historical Register of Yale University, 1701–1937, Yale University Press, 1939, p. 234.

Periodicals

Compton, A., "Prof. Félix d'Hérelle," *Nature,* June 25, 1949, pp. 984–985.
"Death of Félix d'Hérelle," *Journal of the American Medical Association,* July 9, 1949, p. 907.
Lépine, Pierre, "Félix d'Hérelle (1873–1949)," *Annales de l'Institut Pasteur,* 1949, pp. 457–460.

—Sketch by John E. Little

Henry F. Diaz
1948-
Cuban meteorologist

A distinguished atmospheric scientist, Henry F. Diaz has written extensively on climatic variability and global and regional climate analysis. He has also co-edited a book on the phenomenon of El niño, a periodic warming of Pacific ocean currents that has the potential to affect weather conditions worldwide.

Born in Santiago de Cuba on July 15, 1948, Diaz is the son of Francisco Diaz, an attorney of Spanish and French descent, and Maria Vias. He became interested in geography and tropical weather after moving to Havana in 1959. During the early 1960s, Diaz immigrated to the United States, attending high school in Miami and later college at Florida State University in Tallahassee. After earning an undergraduate degree in meteorology, he matriculated at the University of Miami and received a master's degree in atmospheric science in 1974.

Begins Work with NOAA

Following graduation, Diaz found employment as a meteorologist with the National Oceanic and Atmospheric Administration (NOAA) in Washington, D.C. A year later, he moved with his wife, Marla Cremin, and his son to Asheville, North Carolina, where he had accepted a position in the Climate Analysis Division of NOAA's National Climatic Data Center. In 1980, intrigued by the phenomenon of climatic variability, Diaz enrolled at the University of Colorado in Boulder on a NOAA scholarship. He received his doctorate in geography with a specialization in climatology five years later.

During his twenty-year career with NOAA, Diaz has published numerous articles, atlases, and technical reports on climatic fluctuation; he is best known, however, for his 1992 study *El Niño: Historical and Paleoclimatic Aspects of the Southern Oscillation.* Diaz presently works for NOAA in Boulder and has received several awards for his work. His professional associations include membership in the Cooperative Institute for Research in Environmental Sciences (CIRES) of the University of Colorado, where he also teaches geography. An avid outdoorsman, Diaz has been honored as a visiting scientist by the Scripps Institution of Oceanography (summer, 1982) and the University of Massachusetts (1988–89).

SELECTED WRITINGS BY DIAZ:

Books

"Some Characteristics of Wet and Dry Regimes in the Contiguous United States: Implications for Climate Change Detection Efforts," in *Greenhouse-Gas-Induced Climatic Change,* edited by M. E. Schlesinger, Elsevier, 1991, pp. 269–296.

El Niño: Historical and Paleoclimatic Aspects of the Southern Oscillation, Cambridge University Press, 1992.

"Documenting Natural Climatic Variations: How Different Is the Climate of the 20th Century from that of Previous Centuries?," in *Climate Variability on Decade to Century Time Scale,* National Academy of Sciences, 1994.

Periodicals

"The Climate of the United States Since 1895: Spatial and Temporal Changes," *Monthly Weather Review,* Volume 108, 1980, pp. 249–266.

"Some Aspects of Major Dry and Wet Periods in the Contiguous United States, 1895–1981," *Journal of Climate and Applied Meteorology,* Volume 22, 1983, pp. 3–16.

"Northern Hemisphere Surface Air Temperature Variations: 1851–1984," *Journal of Climate and Applied Meteorology,* Volume 25, 1986, pp. 161–179.

"An Analysis of Twentieth Century Climate Fluctuations in Northern North America," *Journal of Climate and Applied Meteorology,* Volume 25, 1986, pp. 1625–1657.

"Urbanization: Its Detection and Effects in the U.S. Climate Record," *Journal of Climate,* Volume 1, 1988, pp. 1099–1123.

"Global Climatic Anomalies Associated with Extremes in the Southern Oscillation," *Journal of Climate,* Volume 2, 1989, pp. 1069–1090.

"Precipitation Fluctuations Over Global Land Areas Since the Late 1800s," *Journal of Geophysical Research,* Volume 94, 1989, pp. 1195–1210.

"Utility of Satellite-Derived Sea Surface Temperature Data for Seasonal and Interannual Climate Monitoring," *Journal of Geophysical Research,* Volume 96, 1991, pp. 20613–20622.

"Recent Changes in the North American Arctic Boundary Layer in Winter," *Journal of Geophysical Research,* Volume 98, 1993, pp. 8851–8858.

—*Sketch by Margaret DiCanio*

Nance K. Dicciani
1947-
American chemical engineer

Nance K. Dicciani

Nance K. Dicciani has made important contributions in the pure sciences, in the practical applications of new technologies in industry, and in the management of major industrial corporations. Dicciani was born in Philadelphia in 1947. Her father, an industrial engineer, and her mother, a homemaker, encouraged Dicciani's love of the sciences from an early age. As early as the fifth grade, Dicciani never doubted that she could have a career in the sciences or that she would be successful competing with male scientists.

Dicciani received her undergraduate education in chemical engineering at Villanova University in Philadelphia. She became interested in chemical engineering because it allowed her to combine her love for mathematics with a deep interest in the hard sciences, especially physics and chemistry. Chemical engineering is also a practical science, which Dicciani relished because it gave her a chance to work in a field where the results of her endeavors would be tangible.

After graduating from Villanova in 1969, Dicciani attended the University of Virginia, where she received her master's degree in chemical engineering in 1970. After she spent four years with the Philadelphia Department of Public Works, which included three years as the city's superintendent of reservoirs, Dicciani's love of scientific research and the academic life brought her back to the University of Pennsylvania, where she pursued doctoral research in chemical engineering.

Dicciani received her Ph.D. in chemical engineering from Penn after two years of advanced studies. Her area of research was the application of chemical engineering to medical imaging. Her dissertation, titled "Ultrasonically-Enhanced Diffusion of Macro Molecules in Gels," was the result of a joint research project between the University of Pennsylvania, the National Science Foundation, and the government of the Soviet Union. Dicciani's work was one of the pioneering efforts in the development of ultrasonic scanning devices that are now used routinely to examine women during pregnancy.

Dicciani's first position in industry was with Air Products and Chemicals, Inc., as a process chemical engineer. Dicciani rose rapidly at Air Products, being promoted first to Senior Research Engineer and then to Research Section Manager in less than two years. In 1981, four years after receiving her Ph.D., Dicciani was appointed as the Director of Research for the process systems group. Three years later she was appointed Director of Research and Development for her division, and in 1988 she assumed the position of General Manager of the Chemicals Commercial Development and Technology group of her company. Dicciani is currently a Vice President and the Business Director of the Petroleum Chemicals Division of Rohm and Haas, one of the world's largest chemical companies.

Dicciani attributes her rapid rise to hard work, self-confidence and successful research. Since leaving academia, Dicciani has made contributions in the areas of petrochemicals, energy, chemical processes, waste water treatment, and catalysis of the production of commercially important petrochemicals. She also attended the Wharton Business School, one of the five top business schools in the United States, where she received her M.B.A. in 1986.

Dicciani is active in the Society of Women Engineers, the Chemical Engineering Advisory Board at the University of Virginia and the University of Pennsylvania, and is a past board member of the Bethlehem Women's Health Center Advisory Board. In addition to her duties at Rohm and Haas, Dicciani serves on the Board of Directors of the Pennsylvania Power and Light Company and the World Affairs Council of Philadelphia.

Dicciani firmly believes that anyone with a love of science, or for that matter any field, can succeed with hard work, determination, and self-confidence.

SOURCES:

Dicciani, Nance K., interview with Jeff Raines, conducted February 25, 1994.

—*Sketch by Jeff Raines*

Otto Diels

Otto Diels
1876-1954
German chemist

A skillful organic chemist, Otto Diels is known primarily for the Diels-Alder reaction, which he and his student **Kurt Alder** developed in 1928, and for which they received the Nobel Prize for chemistry in 1950. This reaction involves a synthesis between a molecule containing a double bond and a second molecule containing two adjacent double bonds. Diels's work in determining the structure of compounds led to the discovery of carbon suboxide, and helped other scientists determine the structure of cholesterol. As a professor, he was a masterful lecturer and produced a popular organic chemistry textbook.

Otto Paul Hermann Diels was born to Hermann and Bertha (née Dübell) Diels on January 23, 1876, in Hamburg, Germany. The second of three sons, he grew up in an atmosphere of learning and culture. His father was a noted classical philologist and professor at the Friedrich Wilhelm University in Berlin. In later life, Diels commented on the amount of time that his father was able to spend with his sons, despite a heavy commitment to teaching and research. His mother, the daughter of a district judge, was an unpretentious and forthright woman, though nervous and rather melancholy. Diels believed he had inherited his tendencies toward pessimism and plain speaking from her. In addition to their regular schooling, the boys were taught book binding, fret work, chess, cards, and sketching, at which Otto was especially proficient. Diels's older brother, Ludwig, became a professor of botany, a subject in which Diels himself held a lifelong interest. His younger brother, Paul, became a professor of Slavic philology. Diels also had an abiding love of theater and music, favoring the composers Wagner and Verdi.

Experiment and Accidents Lead to Interest in Chemistry

Diels was fascinated by the chemical demonstrations performed by one of his teachers in the sixth grade. However, it was not until several years later, when he was thirteen or fourteen years old, that he made the decision to become a chemist as a result of carrying out chemical experiments at home. Initially acting only as his older brother's assistant, Diels soon became the leader in the activity as Ludwig's attention turned more and more to botany. The experiments were halted by his mother after he spilled sulfuric acid on his father's desk, and turned some window curtains red by spraying them with a powdered dye.

Diels received his early education in a classical gymnasium. He only went to school, he said, because his father insisted, and told him a diploma was essential for a worthwhile career. In 1895, still determined to study chemistry, he entered Friedrich Wilhelm University, where his father was a professor. He had wished to go somewhere else, but his parents decreed otherwise. With time out for his year of military service in 1896, he received a doctorate in 1899 for his work on cyanuric compounds under the direction of the eminent German chemist **Emil Fischer**. Upon graduation, he accepted an offer to become Fischer's assistant at the university's Institute of Chemistry. In 1904, he became a lecturer in organic chemistry and began overseeing a display of chemical apparatus that was part of Germany's chemistry exhibit at the Louisiana Purchase Exposition in St. Louis, Missouri. An international jury awarded it a gold medal.

First Major Discovery

At Fischer's suggestion, Diels's first independent research was an investigation of certain compounds that could be extracted in large quantities from coal tar, but for which there was no commercial demand. From one of these, fluorene, he was able to synthesize a number of dyes. Unfortunately, their cost was too high for commercial success. Disappointed by this failure, he sought a more fruitful area of research and turned his attention to a class of compounds called diacetyls. In 1906, in connection with this work, he dehydrated diethyl malonate with phosphorus pentoxide, producing an evil-smelling gas instead of the products he'd expected. On examination, the gaseous material turned out to be a new oxide of carbon made up of three carbon atoms and two oxygen atoms. The existence of this compound, which Diels named carbon suboxide, had never been suspected. Diels is said to have prized this discovery above any of the others that he had made.

On Fischer's recommendation, Diels was appointed assistant professor at Friedrich Wilhelm University in 1906, and assumed the post of division head in 1913. In 1916, he was called to Christian Albrecht University in Kiel as full professor and director of its Chemical Institute. Like Fischer, Diels constantly tried to improve his lectures. Simplicity, exactness, and clarity were the hallmarks of his numerous lectures and of his textbook, *Einführung in die Organische Chemie.* First published in 1907, it proved very popular and remained in print through 1966, having gone through twenty-two editions. He also wrote a lab manual for elementary inorganic chemistry, which appeared in 1922. His graduate students numbered more than one hundred, and went on to play important roles in the academic and industrial worlds.

Develops Successful Dehydrogenating Process

Cholesterol was first isolated from gall stones in 1775, and its composition established in 1894. Found to occur in a large variety of animal tissues, its molecular structure was not known when, in 1903, Diels began a study of the compound at the suggestion of Swiss chemist and physiologist Emil Abderhalden, who had obtained a quantity of gall stones from a Berlin hospital. Diels isolated pure cholesterol from these in an attempt to establish the structure of the compound. Although unsuccessful, his work did supply an essential step in the final determination of the structure by fellow German chemists **Heinrich Wieland** and **Adolf Windaus**. The demands of supervising a growing number of doctoral students caused Diels to abandon work on cholesterol for a time, but he returned to it in the early 1920s to make his second major discovery, a new method for dehydrogenating compounds.

In attempting to work out the structure of a compound, chemists would dehydrogenate it, i.e. carry out a reaction to remove hydrogen atoms from the molecule in order to produce a simpler molecule from which, perhaps, some features of the unknown structure could be inferred. Although none of the standard dehydrogenation procedures worked satisfactorily with cholesterol, Diels thought that one of them, a reaction commonly produced by sulfur, might be suitable if the sulfur were replaced with selenium, an element just below sulfur in the periodic table, and less active. The process of dehydrogenation with selenium, which he and his co-workers developed, was published in 1927. When Diels applied it to cholesterol, he obtained a hydrocarbon, 3'methyl–1,2 cyclopentenophenanthrene, sometimes called the "Diels hydrocarbon." This compound is the basic structural unit not only of cholesterol, but also of many other important natural products, such as the steroids (including the sex and adrenocortical hormones), bile acids, and the active components of digitalis, which are used medically as a heart stimulant. It was this work that Diels chose to talk about in his Nobel Prize address, perhaps to avoid duplicating what Alder might say, but also because of the importance he attached to it.

Discovers Nobel Prize-winning Reaction

The work for which Diels is best known is the Diels-Alder reaction, the union of a dienophile, a molecule containing a double bond, with a second molecule containing two adjacent double bonds, called a conjugated diene. This versatile synthesis, which produces a six-membered ring compound, is one of the most useful processes in organic chemistry. It takes place under quite mild conditions, room temperature often sufficing, and without the need of catalysts or condensing agents. As a result, the formation of by-products is minimized, and yields of the desired product are maximized. Furthermore, the two reactants join together in a very specific way, so that the structure of the product is known with certainty. The structure of camphor, for example, was confirmed when it was synthesized by means of a Diels-Alder reaction. During World War II, both the Allies and Germany used the reaction of butadiene (the diene) with styrene (the dienophile) to make a synthetic rubber. Since suitable dienes occur widely in nature and the reaction conditions are so mild, Diels thought that many natural products were synthesized in nature through a Diels-Alder reaction. The resultant paper appeared in 1928, and Diels continued to work on diene reactions for the next sixteen years, publishing thirty-three papers on the subject. The last experimental work he published, in 1944, was on this topic. Because of the theoretical and practical developments that the reaction made possible, the Nobel

Foundation recognized Diels and Alder with the 1950 Nobel Prize in chemistry.

In the turmoil that accompanied the end of World War I in Germany, Diels played an important role in reviving the university. There, he carried out his own laboratory research, lectured, and oversaw the research of his graduate students until 1944, when the bombing raids on Kiel destroyed the institute (as well as Diels's home). This brought a halt to his research activity, and he was unable to resume it after the war's end. His request for retirement was granted early in 1945, but he remained on staff from 1946 to 1948, when his successor was named. He continued to lecture until 1950, when, at the age of seventy-four, his deteriorating physical and mental condition forced him to stop. He was able, nevertheless, to summon enough energy to go to Stockholm in December of that year to receive the Nobel Prize in person.

In spite of his professional success, Diels's personal life was marked by loss. In 1909, after a six-year acquaintance, Diels married Paula Geyer, the daughter of a government official, with whom he had five children, Volker, Hans Otto, Klaus, Joachim, Renate, and Marianne. As to so many others, World War II brought a great deal of sorrow to the Diels family. In the winter of 1943–44, Hans and Klaus were killed within three months of each other on the Russian front. The death of Diels's wife in 1945 was another severe blow. As if this marked the end of his own life, he ceased making diary entries. Invited by the Norwegian Chemical Society in 1950 to speak at the University of Oslo in connection with his Nobel Prize, Diels withdrew at the last minute so that he could return to Germany to visit his wife's grave on her seventieth birthday. In addition to the emotional pain occasioned by these losses, his last years were burdened with arthritis, which limited his beloved nature walks and eventually left him housebound. Diels regretted that ten years of war and its aftermath had prevented him from contributing as much to chemistry as he was capable. Still, a bibliography of his research papers appended to Sigurd Olsen's biographical sketch of Diels in *Chemische Berichte* lists 180 papers over forty-six years. On March 7, 1954, at the age of seventy-eight, Diels died of a heart attack.

SELECTED WRITINGS BY DIELS:

Books

Einführung in die Organische Chemie, Leipzig, 1907.

Periodicals

(With B. Wolf) "Über das Kohlensuboxyd I," *Berichte der Deutschen Chemischen Gesellschaft,* No. 39, 1906, pp. 689–97.

(With W. Gädke and P. Körding) "Über die Dehydrierung des Cholesterins III," *Justus Liebigs Annalen der Chemie,* No. 459, 1927, pp. 1–26.

(With K. Alder) "Synthesen in der hydroaromatischen Reihe, I. Mitteilung Anlagerungen von 'Di-en'-kohlenwasserstoffen," *Justus Liebigs Annalen der Chemie,* No. 460, 1928, pp. 98–122.

SOURCES:

Books

Gillespie, C. C., editor, *Dictionary of Scientific Biography,* Scribner, 1971, pp. 90–92.
Leicester, H. M., editor, *A Source Book in Chemistry 1900–1950,* Harvard University Press, 1968, pp. 256–59.
Nobel Lectures Including Presentation Speeches and Laureate's Biographies—Chemistry, 1942–1962, Elsevier, 1964, pp. 255–67.

Periodicals

"Diels-Alder Reaction Proves Potent Chemical Ally," *Chemical & Engineering News,* Volume 28, 1950, p. 4266.
Olsen, Sigurd, "Otto Diels," *Chemische Berichte,* Volume 95, No. 2, 1962.

—*Sketch by R. F. Trimble*

Theodor Otto Diener
1921-
Swiss-born American plant pathologist

Theodor Otto Diener has achieved international recognition as the discoverer of viroids, the smallest known agents of infectious disease. The identification of these tiny RNA molecules, which are only about one-thousandth the size of the smallest virus, sparked new interest in pathogens other than microorganisms and viruses. For this accomplishment, which has been compared with the discovery of bacteria, Diener received the National Medal of Science in 1987.

Diener was born on February 28, 1921, in Zurich, Switzerland, the son of Theodor Emanuel Diener, a postal employee, and Hedwig Rosa Baumann Diener, an accountant. From an early age, Diener was fascinated by nature. As he related to contributor Linda Wasmer Smith, "As a boy, I always

Theodor Otto Diener

kept animals at home: turtles, salamanders, frogs, white mice, hamsters, etc. Whereas my parents exhibited a large dose of tolerance to this, neighbors often did not. . . . Later, my interests fortunately gravitated toward smaller and smaller animals, particularly after I had invested money earned by sorting mail at the Christmas/New Year holiday in an old Leitz microscope."

When Diener eventually entered the Swiss Federal Institute of Technology in Zurich, it was with the intention of studying science. He was awarded a diploma in natural sciences—equivalent to a master's degree—by that institution in 1946. Two years later, he earned a doctoral degree in biology. During this time, Diener first came under the influence of Ernst Gäumann, a pioneer in the emerging specialty of plant pathology. Diener credits his choice of career field to Gäumann's inspirational teaching style.

During his last three years of college, Diener gained valuable experience as a research assistant in the botany department. After completing his studies, he first took a post as a plant pathologist at the Swiss Federal Experimental Station in Waedenswil. Then in 1950 he came to the United States to accept a short-term position as an assistant professor at the University of Rhode Island. In that same year he moved on to Washington State University, where he worked at the Irrigation Experiment Station in Prosser for a decade. Diener became an American citizen in 1955. Finally, in 1959, he began what proved to be a long

and highly productive career in experimental plant pathology for the Agricultural Research Service of the U.S. Department of Agriculture in Beltsville, Maryland. This association lasted even beyond Diener's formal retirement in 1988; he continues to collaborate with USDA scientists in ongoing investigations.

Discovers a New Class of Plant Pathogens

It was not until Diener was fifty years old that he made his greatest contribution to science. At the time, he was studying spindle tuber disease in potatoes, an infection that causes the tubers to grow gnarled, elongated, and cracked. While it was known that the disease spread easily from plant to plant, no bacteria or other microorganisms were consistently associated with it, and attempts to isolate a viral cause had also ended in failure. Yet Diener noted that infected tissues did contain very small molecules of an unusual form of RNA, or genetic ribonucleic acid. Healthy plants of the same species did not exhibit these molecules, but if they were introduced, the plants soon developed symptoms. Diener concluded that these tiny particles were the causative agent. In 1971 he coined the term viroids for this novel class of plant pathogens.

In later work Diener further explored the nature and role of viroids. Before their physical and chemical properties could be studied, however, it was necessary to separate viroids from the nucleic acids of cells they infected. The low concentration of viroid RNA, as compared with host RNA, made this challenging. But using the leaves of tomato plants Diener and his colleagues eventually developed new separation and purification techniques for the purpose. Once purified viroid preparations were available, it became possible to study the molecule's structure. Scientists elsewhere soon identified two viroid forms: long, threadlike molecules and circular ones. Diener and his associates were able to show that both types are infectious and present in diseased plants.

Viroids have thus far been found only in higher plants, including potatoes, tomatoes, cucumbers, avocados, coconuts, and chrysanthemums. But Diener reasoned that they might also be responsible for some diseases in human beings and other animals for which no other cause had been identified. Among the most promising candidates seemed to be a group of degenerative brain diseases including kuru and Creutzfeldt-Jakob disease in man and scrapie in sheep and goats.

Although these conditions were commonly attributed to slow viruses, no causative agent had yet been found. Furthermore, the pathogens apparently had several characteristics, such as extreme insensitivity to ultraviolet rays, that are either unknown or unusual in conventional viruses. Diener's 1972 proposal that viroids might be involved prompted a flurry of activity in labs around the world. Diener himself ultimately rejected this hypothesis after it was demonstrated that the responsible pathogens, unlike viroids, contained protein. Nevertheless, his suggestion had opened other avenues of important research, including work on small protein particles called prions. In addition, a viroidlike RNA has since been discovered that is a component of hepatitis delta virus, which does infect humans. Diener has participated in a number of conferences on this topic.

In 1988 Diener moved to the University of Maryland, where he soon assumed concurrent posts as distinguished professor in the department of botany and acting director at the Center for Agricultural Biotechnology. Not surprisingly, he has been honored on several occasions by his former employer, the USDA, including induction into that organization's Science Hall of Fame in 1988. In addition, he received the Campbell Award of the American Institute of Biological Sciences in 1968, the Ruth Allen Award of the American Phytopathological Society in 1976, and the Wolf Award in Agriculture in 1987. The latter, presented before Israel's Knesset, carried a stipend of $100,000. Among other Wolf honorees that year was violinist Isaac Stern. As Diener recalled to Linda Wasmer Smith, "I still vividly remember the animated conversations we had relating to the similarity of the sciences and the arts as different expressions of the human spirit."

Diener has been elected a fellow or member of such organizations as the New York Academy of Sciences; the U.S. National Academy of Sciences; the American Academy of Arts and Sciences; and the German Academy of Natural Scientists, Leopoldina. For several years, he also served as an editor of the journal *Virology,* where many of his most influential papers appeared. A popular lecturer, he has presented approximately two hundred talks and seminars at leading universities around the United States, as well as at numerous institutions around the world.

In his leisure time Diener is an avid private pilot who has had a lifelong interest in aviation. Diener's first marriage in 1950 to Shirley Baumann produced three sons: Theodor, Robert, and Michael. That union ended in divorce in 1966, and Diener was married to Sybil Mary Fox on May 11, 1968, in Winchester, Virginia. The pair make their home in Beltsville, Maryland, the site of Diener's greatest scientific triumphs.

SELECTED WRITINGS BY DIENER:

Books

Viroids and Viroid Diseases, Wiley, 1979.
(Editor) *The Viroids,* Plenum, 1987.

Periodicals

"Potato Spindle Tuber 'Virus': IV. A Replicating, Low Molecular Weight RNA," *Virology,* 1971, Volume 45, pp. 411–428.
"Viroids," *Scientific American,* January, 1981, pp. 66–73.

SOURCES:

Books

Berberich, Stephen M., *The Naked Intruder: USDA and the Discovery of the Viroid* (booklet), U.S. Department of Agriculture, April, 1989.

Periodicals

Coy, Ruth, "Tracking the Elusive Viroid," *Agricultural Research,* May, 1989, pp. 4–7.
"Science Medals Presented at White House," *Science,* June 26, 1987, p. 1621.

Other

Diener, Theodor Otto, interview with Linda Wasmer Smith conducted on January 6, 1994.
Diener, Theodor Otto, letters to Linda Wasmer Smith written on January 3 and 14, 1994.

—Sketch by Linda Wasmer Smith

Edsger W. Dijkstra
1930-
Dutch computer scientist

Edsger W. Dijkstra has highly influenced the manner in which computer programs, the sets of instructions that tell computers what to do, are constructed. His persuasive support for the concept and practice of *structured programming* permanently changed the way computer programs are written. It was once assumed that bugs or program errors were inevitably introduced into programs during their development and that, as a consequence, programs had to be debugged in order to work properly. Dijkstra argued that this was not necessarily so; he convinced the scientific community that computer programs could be correctly constructed from the initial stages of design.

Edsger W. Dijkstra

Dijkstra was born in Rotterdam, The Netherlands, on May 11, 1930. He was the third of four children. His father, Douwe W. Dijkstra, was a chemist and inventor who had been president of the Dutch Chemical Society, and his mother, Brechtje Cornelia Kluyver, was a mathematician. Dijkstra originally intended to study law, but his scientific talents came to light following his final exams at the gymnasium in 1948. His exam grades were better than most of his teachers had ever seen, and he was convinced, as he recalled in a written interview with contributor Frank Hertle, "that it would be a pity if I did not devote myself to science." Dijkstra enrolled at Leyden University to study mathematics and physics. It was during his early years at Leyden that Dijkstra was introduced to computers. As a reward for his academic performance, in 1951 his father offered him the opportunity to attend a three-week computer programming course (for the Electronic Delay Storage Automatic Calculator, or EDSAC) in Cambridge, England. Dijkstra, who then had plans to become a theoretical physicist, thought it would be a good idea to learn more about computers. When A. van Wijngaarden, the director of the computation department at the Mathematical Centre in Amsterdam, heard by chance of Dijkstra's plans to attend this course, he interviewed him and offered him a job. Dijkstra began working part-time at the Mathematical Centre in 1952 and took a full-time position there in 1956. In 1957, Dijkstra married Maria Cornelia Debets; they would eventually have three children together.

While at the Mathematical Centre, Dijkstra worked with Bram J. Loopstra and Carel S. Scholten on the design and construction of a computer, known as the ARMAC. He was primarily responsible for the software, and they for the hardware, and his involvement included writing the programming manual that was to contain a complete functional description of the machine. The document served as a "contract" between Dijkstra and the two other men: they knew what they had to build and Dijkstra knew what he would build upon. This project had an important influence on the course of his career. Dijkstra already sensed that computers would be a permanent and important part of the modern world and had become convinced of the need to program them accurately. From this point forward, he felt personally challenged to develop a methodology for constructing programs that could be proven correct before being run on a computer.

During this period, Dijkstra designed some of his first computer algorithms—sequences of instructions designed to perform specific mathematical tasks. Dijkstra developed one of his most famous algorithms—the Shortest Path (to find the shortest distance between two cities on a map)—over coffee on a cafe terrace in Amsterdam, and without paper and pencil.

When Loopstra and Scholten set out to design their next machine, they wanted it to be able to respond to what is known as a real-time interrupt. A real-time interrupt is a spontaneous event originating outside the computer that influences the action that the program running in the computer will take. Dijkstra devised a solution to this problem; he called it a real-time interrupt handler, and it became his doctoral thesis. In 1959 he received a Ph.D. from the University of Amsterdam, but he remained at the Mathematical Centre, where he worked with J. A. Zonneveld designing an ALGOL 60 compiler. The project frequently took him outside of The Netherlands and gave him the opportunity to begin polishing his English. The ALGOL implementation took eight months to complete and was done in August of 1960, more than a year before their nearest competitor. This work helped establish Dijkstra's reputation among computer scientists in America.

Challenges a Common Programming Technique

In 1962, Dijkstra became professor of mathematics at the Technical University in Eindhoven, The Netherlands. His work there included a collaboration that produced a multiprogramming operating system (called "THE Multiprogramming System") for the university's computer, an Electrologica X8. THE Multiprogramming System was to influence the design of nearly all later operating systems. It was while at Eindhoven that Dijkstra challenged one of the most basic techniques of programming at that time: the abrupt transfer of control from one point in a flow of computer instructions to some other point in the program. This technique was called a GOTO statement, and programmers were using them to interrupt sequences of computer instructions in order to perform a different instruction or set of instructions. GOTO is a generic term for an instruction that causes a program to "go to" some location within itself for its next instruction. GOTO statements, also called "branches" or "transfers," were commonly used in early computer program designs.

In a famous 1968 letter to the editor of *Communications of the ACM,* Dijkstra argued that the ability of programmers to read and understand programs written in high-level languages was severely compromised by the number of GOTO statements in these programs. High-level languages (meant to resemble written English or mathematical statements) are to a certain degree self-documenting; this means that the reader should be able to understand the flow of operations simply by reading the programming statements. The use of GOTO statements interrupts the logical flow, and the composition and interpretation of a program (especially a large one) becomes more difficult as the number of GOTO statements increases. In his letter, entitled by the ACM editors "Go To Statement Considered Harmful," Dijkstra termed the statements as "primitive" in high-level programming languages, calling them "too much an invitation to make a mess of one's program."

The alternative Dijkstra offered he called structured programming. It is a style, or methodology, of programming in which a program is put together by connecting a number of smaller structured programs or program segments. It is easiest to understand structured programming if one thinks of an English sentence containing several difficult words; these words are like GOTO statements. The reader must look up these words in order to understand the sentence, but taking the time to find a word in the dictionary is an interruption, and one tends to lose track of the meaning of the original sentence. If the same sentence were written in a structured fashion, each difficult word would be replaced by an expression that defined it, thus ending the need to look elsewhere for clarification. While it is generally agreed that the idea of structuring programs had supporters before Dijkstra's letter, there is no question that his arguments brought everyone's attention to the issue and led the way to the wide implementation of structured programming.

In 1972 Dijkstra contributed to the book *Notes on Structured Programming,* in which he wrote that "program testing can be used to show the presence of bugs, but never to show their absence!" He advanced the idea that "it is not only the programmer's task to produce a correct program but also to demonstrate its correctness in a convincing manner." In order to provide the proof, the program must be "usefully structured." In Dijkstra's view, every effort must always be made to design programs to be as error-free as possible from the beginning; he believed that this method of design made programs easier to construct and understand. The easier it was to write and comprehend a program, he argued, the easier it was to avoid introducing errors or bugs into it.

Dijkstra left Eindhoven in August of 1973 to accept a position as a research fellow with the Burroughs Corporation. Even though the company was headquartered in Detroit, Michigan, Dijkstra's position allowed him to continue to work and live in his home in Nuenen, a village near Eindhoven in The Netherlands. Burroughs gave Dijkstra great latitude in the use of his time, and he traveled widely during his years with the company, lecturing all over the world and frequently visiting the United States.

In the early 1980s, the intellectual climate at Burroughs changed: the company became more concerned with short-term profits and Dijkstra's colleagues became disenchanted and began to leave. Additionally, Dijkstra's interests were shifting from computers and programming to mathematical methodology in general. He felt it appropriate to return to a university environment, and the University of Texas offered him the Schlumberger Centennial chair in Computer Science.

The vocabulary of computer programmers is far richer for the influence of Dijkstra. He introduced and popularized a number of terms including *go-to-less programming, structured programming, semaphore, guarded command,* and *deadly embrace.* Semaphores are elements used to coordinate the activities of two or more simultaneously running programs that share data. Guarded commands are those that execute conditionally, that is, only when some condition that can be tested for is satisfied. A deadly embrace (also called a deadlock) occurs when a program cannot continue because it is waiting for some event that will never happen.

Dijkstra's philosophy can perhaps best be summarized by a passage from *Notes on Structured Programming:* "My point is that a program is never a goal in itself; the purpose of a program is to evoke computations and the purpose of the computations is to establish a desired effect." He goes on to say that "although the program is the final product made by the programmer, the possible computations evoked by it . . . are the true subject matter of his trade." Programs, in other words, are not ends in themselves but rather means to ends, those ends being correct computations and outcomes. The elegance of a program should increase the ease with which the program can be comprehended and maintained.

In 1972 Dijkstra was presented with the Turing Award. This award is made each year by the Association for Computing Machinery (ACM) as a memorial to **A. M. Turing**. The award recognized Dijkstra's tremendous influence on programming methodology. In 1974, Dijkstra received the Harry Goode Memorial Award as recognition of his achievements in the field of information processing.

SELECTED WRITINGS BY DIJKSTRA:

Books

(With O. J. Dahl, and C. A. R. Hoare), *Notes on Structured Programming,* Academic Press, 1972.
A Discipline of Programming, Prentice Hall, 1976.
Selected Writings on Computing: A Personal Perspective, Springer-Verlag, 1982.
Development of Programs and Proofs, Addison-Wesley, 1990.

Periodicals

"Go To Statements Considered Harmful," *Communications of the ACM,* Volume 11, 1968, pp. 147–148.

SOURCES:

Books

Encyclopedia of Computer Science and Engineering, Van Nostrand Reinhold, 1983, pp. 508, 877–878, 1311, 1348.
Macmillan Encyclopedia of Computers, Macmillan, 1992, pp. 100–101.

Other

Dijkstra, E. W., written response to interview questions from Frank Hertle on December 7, 1993.

—*Sketch by Frank Hertle*

Paul Dirac
1902-1984
English physicist

Paul Adrien Maurice Dirac was one of the twentieth century's leading theoretical physicists. Instrumental in developing quantum mechanics, the theoretical study of atomic structure and properties,

Paul Dirac

and quantum electrodynamics, the study of the electrical interactions between atomic particles, Dirac also postulated the existence of the positron, a positive-charge electron, which led to later discoveries concerning antimatter. For his work on the development of quantum mechanics, Dirac shared the 1933 Nobel Prize in physics with Austrian physicist **Erwin Schrödinger**.

Dirac was born in Bristol, England, on August 8, 1902. His father, Charles Adrien Ladislas Dirac, was a Swiss immigrant, and his mother, Florence Hannah (Holten) Dirac, was British. Charles Dirac took a position as a teacher of French at the Merchant Venturer's Technical College, where young Dirac enrolled for his early schooling. After graduating in 1918, Dirac entered Bristol University, where he majored in electrical engineering and received his bachelor's degree in 1921. His hopes for employment after graduation were postponed, however, by Great Britain's postwar depression, and he decided instead to return to school, accepting a two-year scholarship from the department of mathematics at Bristol.

When Dirac's scholarship at Bristol came to an end, he was accepted at St. John's College, Cambridge, as a research student in mathematics. He soon became familiar with the latest developments in atomic theory, partly through his class work and partly by reading the works of Danish physicist **Niels Henrik David Bohr**, German physicist **Max Born**, German physicist **Arnold Sommerfeld**, English astronomer **Arthur Stanley Eddington**, and other leaders in the field. In addition, he had the opportunity to hear lectures by Bohr, German physicist **Werner Karl Heisenberg**, and others during their visits to Cambridge. Dirac's first research papers were published in 1925, while he was still a student. He received his Ph.D. in physics from Cambridge in 1926. His thesis involved an elaboration of quantum mechanical concepts that had originally been developed by Heisenberg.

In the fall of 1926, Dirac traveled to Copenhagen, where he spent much time talking with Bohr. In February, 1927, he moved on to Göttingen, where he came into contact with Born, American physicist **J. Robert Oppenheimer**, American physicist **James Franck,** and Russian physicist **Igor E. Tamm**, among others. In late 1927, Dirac returned to England where he was elected a fellow at St. John's College, Cambridge. It was there during the winter of 1927–1928 that he made an improvement on Schrödinger's wave equation.

Develops Wave Equation

Schrödinger's wave equation sought to explain the behavior of an electron in an atom, but Schrödinger chose to ignore relativistic effects in his calculations. Dirac's approach was to begin with only the simplest information known about the electron—its mass and charge—and devise a mathematical theory that would describe the electron's properties more fully than Schrödinger's equation did. He was successful in this effort, producing equations that accurately predicted the electron's spin, magnetic charge, and other properties, as measured in experimental work. In recognition of their work on the wave equation, Dirac and Schrödinger shared the 1933 Nobel Prize in physics.

One consequence of Dirac's mathematical analysis led to his hypothesis of the positive electron. In working with his equations for the electron, Dirac discovered that two solutions were possible, suggesting that the electron could either have positive or negative kinetic energy. Dirac's theory also suggested experiments a researcher might use to look for the positive electron, examining situations in which positively-charged electrons would be produced (always in connection with negatively-charged electrons and always in such a way that the two would annihilate each other). Exactly these conditions were noted in 1932 when American physicist **Carl David Anderson** first observed the positive electron or, as it was later named, the positron.

By extension, Dirac's theory also suggested the existence of other forms of antimatter, including the antiproton and antineutron. Those predictions took much longer to be fulfilled, but were eventually confirmed. Today, considerable speculation exists as to the possibility of a whole universe of matter made out of antiprotons, positrons, and antineutrons, as well as to the ultimate consequences of the collision of such a universe with our own.

Appointments at Cambridge and Worldwide Travel after 1929

In 1929, Dirac was appointed to the post of university lecturer and praelector in mathematical physics at St. John's. The appointment carried with it very few specific duties, allowing him to spend as much time as he liked on research, writing, and travel, the latter of which had become a great passion for him. In fact, he spent five months abroad in 1929, during which time he taught briefly at the University of Michigan and the University of Wisconsin. At the end of this trip, he returned to England in 1930 by way of Japan and Siberia. Upon his return, he was elected to the Royal Society and, two years later, was chosen for the post of Lucasian Professor of Mathematics at Cambridge, a position once held by the seventeenth-century English physicist and mathematician Isaac Newton.

In 1934, Dirac returned to the United States, spending most of the 1934–1935 academic year at the Institute for Advanced Studies at Princeton University. While there, he met his future wife, Margit ("Manci") Wigner, sister of the physicist Eugene Wigner. Dirac and Margit returned to Cambridge and were eventually married in London in January, 1937. They had two daughters, Mary Elizabeth, born in 1940, and Florence Monica, born in 1942. Dirac remained at Cambridge during World War II, but became involved in a number of government projects related to the development of atomic energy. He was especially interested in techniques for the separation of uranium isotopes, although none of his suggestions was specifically incorporated into later weapons development programs.

During the last half century of his life, Dirac became increasingly interested in problems of cosmology, a branch of astronomy that is concerned with the origins of the universe. One of the first topics in this field to capture his attention was that of "large numbers." During the 1920s, Eddington had become intrigued by the realization that certain fundamental physical constants had relationships to each other that fall in the range of 10^{39-40}. For example, the ratio of the gravitational attraction between an electron and proton to their electrostatic attraction is about $10^{40}:1$, as is the ratio of the radius of the universe to the radius of the electron. Dirac argued that this recurring ratio was variable over time, a hypothesis not yet proven by experiment.

In 1969, Dirac retired from his post at Cambridge and moved to the United States. He stayed briefly at the Center for Theoretical Studies of the

University of Miami before accepting an appointment as professor of physics at Florida State University in Tallahassee in 1972. He continued to travel, write, and speak during the next decade. After 1982, however, his health began to deteriorate, and he died in Tallahassee on October 20, 1984.

SELECTED WRITINGS BY DIRAC:

Books

The Principles of Quantum Mechanics, Clarendon Press, 1930.
Spinors in Hilbert Space, University of Miami Center for Theoretical Studies, 1974.
General Theory of Relativity, Wiley, 1975.

Periodicals

"The Evolution of the Physicist's Picture of Nature," *Scientific American,* May, 1963, pp. 45–53.

SOURCES:

Books

Kursunoglu, Behram N., and Eugene P. Wigner, editors, *Reminiscences about a Great Physicist: Paul Adrien Maurice Dirac,* Cambridge University Press, 1987.
Salaam, A., and Eugene P. Wigner, editors, *Aspects of Quantum Theory,* Cambridge University Press, 1972.
Taylor, J. G., editor, *Tribute to Paul Dirac,* [Bristol], 1987.
Weber, Robert L., *Pioneers of Science: Nobel Prize Winners in Physics,* American Institute of Physics, 1980, pp. 97–98.

Periodicals

Moyer, Donald F., "Origins of Dirac's Electron," *American Journal of Physics,* 1986, pp. 944–949.

—*Sketch by David E. Newton*

Carl Djerassi
1923-
Austrian-born American chemist

Carl Djerassi has been called the "father of the birth-control pill." As a youth in his twenties Djerassi headed a research team of young scientists in a small, obscure Mexican laboratory where, using a locally grown yam, he first was able to synthesize cortisone, a drug used to treat rheumatoid arthritis. Within twelve months, he also created the first steroid that effectively blocked fertillization. The resulting use of the contraceptive, commonly called the Pill, has raised controversy around the world.

Djerassi was born in Vienna on October 29, 1923. His parents, Samuel and Anna Friedmann, both physicians, were Austrian Jews. Djerassi had his early schooling in Vienna, but when the German army invaded Poland in 1938, Djerassi's mother—separated from Djerassi's father in 1929—moved with her son to Bulgaria. After a year in Sofia, mother and son left for the United States, arriving penniless in America in the winter of 1939.

Djerassi attended Newark Junior College before enrolling in Kenyon College in Ohio in 1941 with a major in chemistry. He received his A.B. the next year. Following graduation, Djerassi returned to his home in New Jersey and accepted a position as junior chemist with the Swiss pharmaceutical firm CIBA, where he worked as an assistant to another Austrian emigre, Charles Huttrer. Within a year, the pair discovered one of the first antihistamines, pyribenzamine, used to combat allergy and cold symptoms. They received their first patent for the discovery. After a year at CIBA, Djerassi took leave to study for his doctorate in chemistry at the University of Wisconsin, Madison. Within three years, he received his degree, became a U.S. citizen, and married Norma Lundholm. (He divorced in 1976, and in 1985 married Diane Middlebrook.)

Djerassi returned to CIBA in 1945 where he remained for another four years before being invited to head a research group working in the field of steroid chemistry at Syntex, Inc., a small drug company in Mexico City. While at Syntex, Djerassi was involved in synthesizing cortisone on a commercial basis from chemicals found in yams. In the process of developing a method to derive steroids from plants, Djerassi also produced the hormone progesterone, the first synthesis of a steroid oral contraceptive. To test the effectiveness of the ovulation-inhibiting properties of the steroid on humans, Djerassi worked with Harvard Medical School gynecologist **John Rock** to undertake the long period of clinical studies.

Over the next several decades, Djerassi was involved in trying to influence public policy regarding birth control. He has advocated, for example, that the government develop a global contraceptive policy for developing countries. Djerassi also believes that too often governmental agencies, such as the Food and Drug Administration, are more concerned with the possible side effects of the Pill, rather than in promoting the Pill's benefits.

In 1952, Djerassi left Mexico to accept the position of associate professor of chemistry at Detroit's Wayne University (now Wayne State University). He continued his work on steroids at Wayne State, developing the spectropolarimeter (a device to conduct measurements on steroids), as well as various projects in the field of antibiotics. In 1959, he left Michigan with most of his research staff to become professor of chemistry at Stanford University—a position he currently holds. His research at Stanford has ranged from studying chemical structures obtained by satellite spectrography to developing methods to detect lead poisoning in urine.

In 1989, Djerassi was named to the board of Monoclonal Antibodies, a biotechnology company in California. He is working with the company trying to develop a home test for progesterone. His goal is to provide a "red light, green-light" test that will tell a woman exactly when she is fertile, and when she is not.

For his synthesis of an oral contraceptive, Djerassi was awarded the National Science Medal in 1973. In 1978, he was named to the Inventor's Hall of Fame. Djerassi is the recipient of many other honors, including the Perkin Medal, 1975; the Wolf Prize in chemistry, 1978; the John and Samuel Bard Award in science and medicine, 1983; the Esselen Award, 1989; the National Medal of Technology, 1991; and the Nevada Medal, 1992. In 1992, he was also awarded the American Chemical Society's prestigious Priestley Medal for his life's work. In addition to his scientific research and professional writing, Djerassi has written more than a dozen works of fiction, non-fiction, and poetry, including his autobiography, *The Pill, Pygmy Chimps, and Degas' Horse,* published in 1992.

SELECTED WRITINGS BY DJERASSI:

Books

Steroids Made It Possible, American Chemical Society, 1990.
Cantor's Dilemma, Doubleday, 1991.
Clock Runs Backwards: A Chapbook of Poetry, Story Line, 1991.
The Pill, Pygmy Chimps, and Degas' Horse: The Remarkable Autobiography of the Award-Winning Scientist Who Synthesized The Pill, Basic Books, 1992.

SOURCES:

Periodicals

Grouse, Lawrence, review of *The Pill, Pygmy Chimps, and Degas' Horse, JAMA: Journal of the American Medical Association,* August 26, 1992, p. 1033.
"Keeping the Beat," *Economist,* March 23, 1991, p. 92.
McQuade, Molly, review of *The Pill, Pygmy Chimps, and Degas' Horse, American Health: Fitness of Body and Mind,* May, 1992, p. 90.

—*Sketch by Benedict A. Leerburger*

Theodosius Dobzhansky
1900-1975
Russian-born American biologist

Theodosius Dobzhansky's work in genetics and evolutionary biology ensures his recognition as an influential scientist of the twentieth century. The recipient of the 1964 Medal of Science, his most significant contributions were in the development of the modern theory of evolution. His first book on evolutionary theory, *Genetics and the Origin of Species,* is considered by many scientists to be the most important book on the subject to be written in the twentieth century. In it, Dobzhansky was able to link the work of Austrian botanist Gregor Mendel and English naturalist Charles Darwin. He accomplished this by gathering empirical evidence that supported Mendel's mathematical theories of inherited traits, while extending critical evolutionary issues far beyond the mathematical model.

A common thread of biological evolution runs through his enormous output of written work—nearly six hundred publications, including twelve books—spanning biological, philosophical, and humanistic disciplines. Dobzhansky's gifts as an original thinker and theoretical synthesizer, combined with his research skills in the field and laboratory, were central to the rapid advances that were made in the study of population genetics during his time, and pivotal to his evolutionary concepts.

Dobzhansky was born on January 25, 1900, in Nemirov, Russia. He was the only child of Sophia Voinarsky and Grigory Dobrzhansky (surname transliteration), a high school mathematics teacher. Until he was nine years old, Dobzhansky was educated at home by his mother and a German governess. In

Theodosius Dobzhansky

1910, the family moved to Kiev, where he entered the second year of an eight-year Russian gymnasium (high school) program. His interest in the natural sciences surfaced at this time, and he spent considerable time collecting butterflies. However, when he was fifteen, he was persuaded by a young entomologist, Victor Luchnik, that to be a success, he would have to specialize. Dobzhansky chose to study the genus *Coccinella,* or ladybird beetles. (He was to continue this study throughout his early career; they were the subject of his first published work in 1918.) As a young man, he read Charles Darwin's *On the Origin of Species,* which also had a great influence on his decision to become a biologist.

He was graduated from the University of Kiev in 1921, and took a position as an instructor of zoology at the Polytechnic Institute in Kiev. His friendship with a young professor of botany, Gregory Levitsky, was the stimulus to a beginning interest in genetics. Literature on new genetic discoveries in Germany, England, and the United States was just beginning to be disseminated in Russia, and Dobzhansky was able to study these works. He remained at Kiev until 1924, when he became an instructor in genetics at the University of Leningrad. It was during this time that he began to study the genetics of *Drosophila* fruit flies.

In 1927, on a two-year fellowship from the International Board of the Rockefeller Foundation, he came to Columbia University to work with geneticist Thomas Hunt Morgan. When Morgan left Columbia

for the California Institute of Technology in 1928, Dobzhansky went with him. He remained there as professor of genetics until he returned to Columbia University in 1940 as professor of zoology. He was to stay at Columbia until 1962, when he became professor at the Rockefeller Institute in New York City. In 1971, he returned to California to become adjunct professor in the department of genetics at the University of California at Davis. He remained at Davis until his death.

Early Years of Genetic Research

Dobzhansky brought his skills as an anatomist and field naturalist to Morgan's laboratory at Columbia, but what he needed to learn was *Drosophila* genetics. Even though he had conducted research at Leningrad on the pleiotropic effects (the observation that each gene acts on each part of the body) of mutant *Drosophila* genes, he believed that current research had surpassed his knowledge. It was at this point that he came under the guidance of American geneticist Alfred H. Sturtevant. Their collaboration, at first one of student and teacher, and later one of equals, was to continue for many years, although their association was later marked by professional disagreement, and, at the end, personal bitterness. Dobzhansky's research on population genetics of *Drosophila* in the early thirties involved the physiological, developmental, and genetic causes of hybrid sterility in this genus. This led him, in 1935, to formulate the genetic concept that what sets species apart is reproductive isolation. It also defines speciation as a slowly changing evolutionary process. Dobzhansky coined the term "isolating mechanisms" to describe events that interfere with gene exchange between species.

Beginning in 1932, Dobzhansky began to extrapolate his genetic studies toward a theory of natural evolution. In 1933, he published a major study in the *American Naturalist* on geographical variation and evolution in ladybird beetles. Although important because it could be understood by both geneticists and systematists, it pointed to a major problem that remained to be solved before evolution could be studied by means of modern genetics: genetic analysis of species differences in ladybird beetles and fruit flies was next to impossible; therefore, no genetic experiments could be conducted. The study of evolution would have to wait for a more cooperative organism.

It was during this period that *Drosophila pseudoobscura* entered the picture. It was this fruit fly, determined to be a separate species of the American form found in the Pacific Northwest, that would be the basis of Dobzhansky's evolutionary research for the rest of his scientific career. The study and reconstruction of geographical chromosome arrangements in *D. pseudoobscura* was crucial, because this research gave him the tools to reconstruct the evolutionary history of many species. His study of chromosomal variability led to a series of writings on hybrid sterility in *D. pseudoobscura* that began in 1933. Through his research, Dobzhansky was able to determine that the sterility factor was connected in some way with the autosomes, or non-sex chromosomes. This discovery was of great importance toward the development of a theory of evolution in wild populations.

Toward A Modern Evolutionary Theory

Although previous groundwork on *D. pseudoobscura* had been done by other geneticists in the United States and Europe, it was Dobzhansky's published accounts of his experiments that led to widespread *D. pseudoobscura* collection and subsequent development of detailed chromosome maps by many other groups. The group headed by Dobzhansky and Sturtevant at the California Institute of Technology was now recognized as the center of *D. pseudoobscura* research. From 1936 through 1976, Dobzhansky, in collaboration with Sturtevant and others, produced a body of work that was eventually published under the title "Genetics of Natural Populations." This series of forty-three papers—a synthesis of genetic theory backed up with empirical evidence—is a major contribution to modern evolutionary genetics. In 1937, Dobzhansky wrote the seminal *Genetics and the Origin of Species,* building on the outcome of thirty-five years of genetic laboratory research; the theoretical framework of English geneticists Ronald A. Fisher and John Burdon Sanderson Haldane and American geneticist Sewall Wright; and his own experimental work.

In the early 1940s, Dobzhansky's experiments on speciation with *D. willistoni* augmented his studies of *D. pseudoobscura.* Collection of this group of fruit flies took him to Colombia, South America. His work with this species involved the relationships between ecological and genetic diversity, as well as a study of physiological adaptation. He published papers on his conclusions in 1957 and 1959.

Ecological and Philosophical Contributions

Dobzhansky's work in South America extended to other areas of biological inquiry, such as ecology and systematics. In 1943, he made the first of many visits to Brazil, where he compared population structure and evolutionary process in the constant environment of a tropical rain forest to the changing seasons of a temperate climate. His study of the diversity of species in tropical forests led him to develop a hypothesis accounting for the causes of this diversity. In the early 1960s, he also published several papers discussing the innate reproductive capacity of fruit fly populations. Although Dobzhansky conducted only brief research into human genetics, he had a strong interest in human evolution and wrote several books on the subject. His *Mankind Evolving,* published in 1962, used the integration of Mendelism, or mathematical theory of inherited traits, and Darwinism, the theory of evolution by natural selection, as a basis of understanding human nature. Through a synthesis of anthropology, evolutionary theory, genetics, and sociology, Dobzhansky discusses the two-dimensional aspects of human nature—the biological and the cultural—and their interrelatedness as a force in human diversity and race.

His concern for humanity led him to speak out against racial bigotry. After World War II, he wrote several publications criticizing the eugenic movement, which was concerned with improving the hereditary qualities of the population. His first major book about race was *Heredity, Race, and Society,* published in 1946. This was followed that same year by an exposé of Soviet biologist Trofim Denisovich Lysenko's suppression of genetics in the Soviet Union. Dobzhansky also explored the evolutionary roots of religion in articles published in the 1960s and 1970s, and published *The Biology of Ultimate Concern* in 1967. Also during that time, in an effort to show how evolutionary biology raises new philosophical problems and enlightens old ones, he wrote several essays on various philosophical subjects.

The Rewards of a Distinguished Career

Dobzhansky was a man possessed with tremendous energy and discipline. He was a world traveler and fluent in six languages. He enjoyed the outdoors and was always eager to get out in the field, whether for work or for relaxation. His enthusiastic personality made him a successful teacher, and under his tutelage more than thirty students obtained their Ph.D. degrees.

He received numerous honors and awards throughout his academic and scientific career. He was elected to the U. S. National Academy of Sciences, the American Academy of Arts and Sciences, and the American Philosophical Society, as well as many scientific societies in other countries. He served as president of six professional societies, and was a member or honorary member of many more, both in the United States and abroad. He received, among others, the Daniel Giraud Elliot Medal in 1946, the Kimber Genetics Award in 1958, the Darwin Medal in 1959, the Pierre Lecomte du Nouy Award in 1963, the National Medal of Science in 1964, and capped off his honors with the Gold Medal Award for Distinguished Achievement in Science, given by the American Museum of Natural History in 1969.

Dobzhansky married Natalia (Natasha) Petrovna Sivertzev, also a geneticist, on August 8, 1924. She died in 1969. Their only child, Sophia, became an anthropologist. Dobzhansky was diagnosed as suffering from chronic lymphatic leukemia in 1968. Surprisingly, the disease did not affect his productivity during the remaining years of his life, and he continued to work until the day before his death. He died of heart failure on December 18, 1975.

SELECTED WRITINGS BY DOBZHANSKY:

Books

Genetics and the Origin of Species, Columbia University Press, 1937.
(With L. C. Dunn) *Heredity, Race and Society,* New American Library, 1946.
Mankind Evolving: The Evolution of the Human Species, Yale University Press, 1962.
The Biology of Ultimate Concern, New American Library, 1967.
Genetics of the Evolutionary Process, Columbia University Press, 1970.

SOURCES:

Books

Hecht, Max K., and William C. Steere, editors, *Essays in Evolution and Genetics in Honor of Theodosius Dobzhansky,* Appleton, 1970.
Holmes, Frederick L., editor, *Dictionary of Scientific Biography,* Volume 17, Supplement II, Scribner, 1990, pp. 233–241.
Lewontin, R. C., John A. Moore, William B. Provine, and Bruce Wallace, editors, *Dobzhansky's Genetics of Natural Populations I-XLIII,* Columbia University Press, 1981.

Periodicals

New York Times, December 19, 1975.
Washington Post, December 20, 1975.
Time, December 29, 1975.

—*Sketch by Jane Stewart Cook*

Edward A. Doisy
1893-1986
American biochemist

Edward Adelbert Doisy was an acclaimed biochemist whose contributions to research involved studying how chemical substances affected the body. In addition to research on antibiotics, insulin, and female hormones, he is remembered for his successful isolation of vitamin K, a substance that encourages blood clotting. Because he was able to synthesize this substance, many thousands of lives are saved each year. For this research, Doisy shared the 1943 Nobel Prize in medicine or physiology with Danish scientist **Henrik Dam**.

Doisy, one of two children, was born November 13, 1893, in Hume, Illinois, to Edward Perez Doisy, a traveling salesman, and Ada (Alley) Doisy. His parents, while themselves having little in the way of higher education, encouraged him to attend college. Doisy received his baccalaureate degree in 1914 from the University of Illinois at Champaign and then obtained his master's in 1916. The advent of World War I interrupted his schooling for two years, during which time he served in the Army. After the war, Doisy received his Ph.D. from Harvard University Medical School in 1920. Beginning in 1919 he rapidly rose through the academic ranks, achieving the position of associate professor of biochemistry in the Washington University School of Medicine, St. Louis. He left this position in 1923 to go to the St. Louis University School of Medicine, and a year later he was appointed to the chair of biochemistry, where he engaged in research and teaching. He also was named the biochemist for St. Mary's Hospital. Doisy held these positions until his retirement in 1965.

For 12 years—from 1922 until 1934—Doisy worked with biologist Edgar Allen to study the ovarian systems of rats and mice. During this time he participated in research that isolated the first crystalline of a female steroidal hormone, now called oestrone. He later isolated two other related products, oestriol and oestradiol-17β. When Doisy administered these in tiny quantities to female mice or rats whose ovaries had been removed, the creatures acted as if they still had ovaries. Many women have benefitted from this research, as these compounds and their derivatives have been used to treat several hormonally-related problems, including menopausal symptoms.

Vitamin K Research Leads to Nobel Prize

Doisy, in 1936, turned from this line of research to trying to isolate an antihemorrhagic factor that had been identified by Danish researcher Henrik Dam. Dam had discovered a chemical in the blood of chicks that decreased hemorrhaging; he called this substance *Koagulations Vitamine,* or vitamin K. Using Dam's work as a springboard, Doisy and his co-workers spent three years researching this new vitamin. They discovered that the vitamin had two distinct forms, called K1 and K2, and successfully isolated each—K1 from alfalfa, K2 (which differs in a side chain) from rotten fish. After Doisy had isolated these two compounds he successfully determined their structures, and was able to synthesize the extremely delicate vitamin K1.

Synthesizing vitamin K enabled large quantities of it to be produced relatively inexpensively. It has since been used to treat hemorrhages that would previously have been fatal, especially in newborns and other individuals who lack natural defenses; it is estimated that the use of vitamin K saves almost five thousand lives each year in the United States alone. For these research advances, Doisy shared the 1943 Nobel Prize for medicine or physiology with Dam. Some of this research was funded by the University of St. Louis and some of the funds were contributed by the pharmaceutical manufacturer Parke-Davis and Co.—a financial arrangement that Doisy saw as a model for future industry-university research relations.

Over the course of his career, most of Doisy's research focused on how various chemical substances worked in the human body. In addition to vitamin K, his team studying the effects of certain antibiotics, sodium, potassium, chloride, and phosphorus. He also developed a high-potency form of insulin, for use in treating diabetes.

Honored by Memberships and Awards

Doisy was made St. Louis University's distinguished service professor in 1951, and later was named emeritus professor of biochemistry. As a sign of his contributions, the university's department of biochemistry was named in his honor in 1965, and he was made its emeritus director. Because of his prominence and his loyalties to the University, there are numerous plaques and buildings bearing his name.

Doisy's contributions to the field of biochemistry are recognized by the numerous honorary awards he held and the scientific societies to which he belonged. He was member of the League of Nations Committee on the Standardization of Sex Hormones from 1932 to 1935, and in 1938 was elected to the National Academy of Sciences. In 1941 he was honored with the Willard Gibbs Medal of the American Chemical Society, which is perhaps the highest distinction in chemical science. He served as both the vice president and then president, from 1943 to 1945, of the American Society of Biological Chemists, and was the 29th president of the Endocrine Society in 1949.

Doisy married Alice Ackert on July 20, 1918, and they had four children: Edward Adelbert, Robert, Philip, and Richard. His second marriage, after his first wife died, was to Margaret McCormick, on April 19, 1965. He died October 23, 1986.

SELECTED WRITINGS BY DOISY:

Books

(With Edgar Allen and C. H. Danforth) *Sex and Internal Secretions: A Survey of Recent Research,* Williams and Wilkins, 1939.

Periodicals

"An Autobiography," *Annual Review of Biochemistry,* 1976, pp. 1–9.

SOURCES:

Books

Jaffe, Bernard, *Men of Science,* Simon and Schuster, 1958, pp. 453–456.
McGraw-Hill Modern Scientists and Engineers, McGraw-Hill, 1980, pp. 298–299.

Periodicals

Newsweek, November 6, 1944, p. 84.
New York Times, May 24, 1941, p. 34; October 27, 1944, p. 15.
Science, January 19, 1940, p. 58; November 10, 1944, p. 10.
Time, November 6, 1944, p. 88.

—*Sketch by Barbara J. Proujan*

Vincent P. Dole
1913-
American biologist

In the 1960s Vincent P. Dole pioneered human studies on the biological basis of heroin addiction. He discovered that methadone can quell an addict's craving and that maintenance doses can return narcotics users to productive lives. Dole's innovative approach to studying addiction as a medical problem was conducted at The Rockefeller University Hospital in New York, a unique clinical research center where a scientific approach to this problem was possible. Dole has spent fifty years in biomedical research at Rockefeller and opened several areas of scientific medicine. His early contributions to understanding metabolic disturbances in patients with kidney disease, high blood pressure, and obesity provided the

Vincent P. Dole

underpinnings of his seminal work in the biology and pharmacology of addiction.

Vincent Paul Dole, Jr., born in Chicago, Illinois on May 8, 1913, was named after his father, an importer of olive oil and olives. His mother, Anne Dowling, once taught school in the rural Wisconsin village where she grew up. Dole's only brother died in childhood. Young Vincent often went on long trips with his parents to visit his father's business interests. He spent the first two years of secondary school at Loyola Academy in Chicago and the final two years at Culver Military Academy in Indiana.

In 1934, he received a bachelor's degree in mathematics from Stanford University. While fascinated by math, Dole really wanted to explore the interplay of living systems. His aunt, a physician, introduced him to the dean of the University of Wisconsin's medical school, and Dole mastered seven semesters of biology that summer in time to enroll. Two years later, he decided to complete a more research-oriented program and transferred to Harvard Medical School. His M.D. from Harvard in 1939 included both clinical research in psychiatry and rheumatoid arthritis as well as laboratory studies in anatomy. His first scientific publication was on the regeneration of nerves.

Generates New Knowledge of Disease in Patient Studies

Following an internship at Massachusetts General Hospital, Dole was invited to join The Rockefeller Institute for Medical Research in 1941. In the laboratory of Donald D. Van Slyke, a founder of clinical chemistry, Dole participated in hundreds of patient investigations. The clinical scientists in this group observed the effects of various diets on levels of albumin and lipids in the blood, measured the metabolism of proteins, amino acids and fats, and monitored the balance of salts in the body and its effects on edema. The team's work established the standard knowledge about nephrosis (kidney disease) for medical students and physicians.

When the institute's hospital became a naval research unit during World War II, Dole helped develop the copper sulfate method, a test that measures blood density in shock victims, and indicates how much fluid they need to have replaced. Blood banks continue to use this test to determine whether potential donors have sufficient hemoglobin to give blood.

After the war, Dole spent one year at the Massachusetts General Hospital arthritis clinic and another year in Europe studying kidney diseases. He returned to Rockefeller in 1947 to establish his own laboratory devoted to the study of hypertension. Using the hospital's resources to study selected patients, he monitored their metabolic state with many elaborate analyses. He tested the low-salt, low-protein diet recommended for kidney disease on these patients, and discovered that sodium was the salt ion contributing to elevated blood pressure. He also found that the diet's low-protein element contributed to diminished appetite and weight loss. Other studies related to hypertension led to Dole's characterization of human sweat gland physiology. Dole became curious about whether the experimental diet he used for hypertension could also treat obesity. In further studies of patients, he discovered that obese people are not consistent overeaters and that their metabolism is abnormal when they lose weight. Dole's work pointed to obesity as a symptom of an underlying metabolic disease.

As he studied obese patients, Dole began to wonder about the function of their fat, whether it was needed, and how it moves from tissues to muscles where it is burned. In the mid–1950s, he made a significant contribution when he isolated free fatty acids from blood plasma. Despite their low concentration, he found their exceptionally rapid turnover was due to their role as the major carrier of energy in the blood stream. He traced their origin to triglyceride molecules in fat cells and showed how they interact with insulin and carbohydrates, findings that are basic to understanding mechanisms of arteriosclerosis (hardening of the arteries).

Discovers New Method to Treat Heroin Addiction

In 1963, Dole turned his attention to the epidemic of drug addiction he saw growing around him in

New York City. At the time addiction had no place in organized medicine, and was assumed to be a sign of moral weakness that was often relegated to practitioners of psychopathology.

However, Dole persuaded Rockefeller president **Detlev Bronk** to establish the world's first research program on addiction at the university's hospital. This involved getting permission to treat addicts with long criminal records, administering illegal drugs to them without legal interference, and performing medical studies with an unprecedented degree of thoroughness.

Dole approached this novel problem as a physician and as a scientist. He was profoundly influenced by psychiatrist Marie Nyswander and her book *The Drug Addict as Patient* (1956). Her twenty years of working with addicts suggested that conventional psychotherapy, detoxification, or lock-up programs for chronic narcotic users failed, not through lack of motivation by the addict but for want of effective medical treatment. Physicians Dole and Nyswander (who were married in 1965) admitted tough, hard-core addicts to The Rockefeller Hospital and studied them as sick people. They learned from these patients that they suffered from an organic disease, one needing a medicine that would abolish the pathological craving for narcotics. They needed to restore the addict's neurochemical imbalance before social rehabilitation could even be addressed.

As clinical scientists, Dole, Nyswander, and Mary Jeanne Kreek traced metabolic factors and mechanisms of heroin's action to learn about the body's chemical appetite, tolerance, and physical dependence. They tested many drugs and discovered that a synthetic opiate called methadone—a narcotic in limited use as an analgesic and cough suppressant—had a normalizing effect and eliminated the compulsive narcotic hunger without producing euphoria. They later established that methadone acts as a buffer, and that its stabilizing effect is due to its slow elimination from the body.

Dole's initial studies were successful in treating addicts with daily doses of methadone. Like insulin for diabetes, methadone maintenance only corrects, but does not cure, and must be taken for life. More than two-thirds of those who discontinue methadone treatment return to illegal drugs. However, methadone is life saving, as it makes patients alert, healthy, and helps them resume fulfilling and socially productive lives, free of heroin use.

Within a year, Dole expanded his small clinical study, first to Beth Israel Hospital in New York City and then to the city's municipal hospitals. Methadone maintenance programs continue to have a major impact on reducing both crime and the spread of such epidemic infectious diseases as tuberculosis, hepatitis, and Acquired Immunodeficiency Syndrome (AIDS).

"The simple fact is that it works," Dole told contributor Carol Moberg in an interview, and that this "treatment has survived challenge by professional skeptics, by ideologically hostile agencies, and by competitive modalities." Three decades after its beginning, 115,000 heroin addicts are being treated with methadone in 750 clinics in the United States, as well as thousands more in clinics worldwide.

In 1983, Dole broadened his research to study alcoholism, often a complicating factor in narcotic addiction, that afflicts an even greater segment of the population. Until Dole retired from lab work in 1991, he searched for a model of alcoholism in mice so that potential medicines could be tested that would benefit human alcoholics. However, his detailed report in 1986 discusses why he believes mouse metabolic data cannot be correlated with human alcoholism. He discovered that mice burn alcohol eight times faster than humans, so they cannot reproduce the high blood levels and symptoms of intoxication found in humans; also, mice prefer fats or sugars to alcohol when all are offered in their diets.

Dole's family includes three children from his first marriage in 1942 to Elizabeth Ann Strange: the oldest, Vincent, continues to run the family's olive oil business, Susan heads the Vermont Bar Association, and Bruce manages an electronics business. Marie Nyswander, his second wife and research collaborator, died in 1986. He married Margaret MacMillan Cool in 1992.

Dole was appointed a member of The Rockefeller Institute in 1951 and professor in 1954 when the institute became a graduate university. He has published nearly 200 scientific papers during his career and served as editor of *The Journal of Experimental Medicine* from 1953 to 1965. Dole has received many awards for his work on methadone and for his earlier lipid studies. He was elected a member of the National Academy of Sciences in 1972 and received an Albert Lasker Medical Research Award in 1988. Research into the biology of addictive diseases continues at Rockefeller, where Dole remains active in lecturing and writing.

SELECTED WRITINGS BY DOLE:

Periodicals

(With L. K. Dahl, George C. Cotzias, D. D. Dziewiatkowski, and C. Harris) "Dietary treatment of hypertension. II. Sodium depletion as related to the therapeutic effect," *Journal of Clinical Investigation,* Volume 30, 1951, pp. 584–595.
"The significance of nonesterified fatty acids in plasma," *Archives of Internal Medicine,* Volume 101, 1958, pp. 1005–1008.

(With M. E. Nyswander) "A medical treatment for diacetylmorphine (heroin) addiction," *JAMA: Journal of the American Medical Association,* Volume 193, 1965, pp. 646–650.

"Addictive Behavior," *Scientific American,* Volume 243, 1980, pp. 138–154.

"On the relevance of animals models to alcoholism in humans," *Alcoholism: Clinical and Experimental Research,* Volume 10, 1986, pp. 361–363.

"Implications of methadone maintenance for theories of narcotic addiction. The Albert Lasker Award," *JAMA: The Journal of the American Medical Association,* Volume 260, 1988, pp. 3025–3029.

"Addiction as a public health problem," *Alcoholism: Clinical and Experimental Research,* Volume 15, 1991, pp. 749–752.

SOURCES:

Books

Corner, George W., *A History of the Rockefeller Institute, 1901–1953: Origins and Growth,* The Rockefeller Institute Press, 1964, pp. 488–491.

Periodicals

Bardossi, B., and J. N. Schwartz, "Busy in the Meadow," *The Rockefeller University Research Profiles,* Number 13, Summer 1983, pp. 1–6.

Other

Dole, Vincent P., interviews with Carol Moberg conducted September 17 and 20, 1993.

—*Sketch by Carol L. Moberg*

Gerhard Domagk
1895-1964
German biochemist

Gerhard Domagk was a biochemist who discovered sulfonamide therapy for bacterial infections. Prior to his work, only a few chemical compounds had been found effective against these infections, and most of these had serious side effects. Domagk was awarded the Nobel Prize in physiology or medicine in 1939 for this discovery, but the

Gerhard Domagk

German government forced him to decline it. In 1947, he was awarded the Nobel Prize Medal. In presenting this award, Nanna Svartz of the Royal Caroline Institute said that Domagk's discovery "meant nothing less than a revolution in medicine." The introduction of sulfonamide therapy prior to World War II undoubtedly saved many thousands of lives.

Domagk was born October 30, 1895, in Lagow, Brandenburg, Germany, to Paul and Martha Reiner Domagk. His father was assistant headmaster of a school, and he sent his son to a grade school that specialized in the sciences. Domagk enrolled in the University of Kiel as a medical student in 1914. His studies, however, were almost immediately interrupted by World War I. He enlisted in the German Army, fought at Flanders, and was transferred to the eastern front in December of 1914, where he was wounded. He was then transferred to the medical corps. He served in several hospitals, and his experience attempting to treat wounds and infectious diseases with the inadequate tools of the time undoubtedly influenced the direction of his later research.

Domagk resumed his studies at the University of Kiel following the war and earned his medical degree in 1921. In 1924 he took up the post of lecturer of pathological anatomy at the University at Greifswald, and in 1925 he moved on to a similar post at the University at Münster. In 1927, Domagk took a leave of absence from the university, which reshaped his career. He left to work in the laboratories of a company called I. G. Farbenindustrie, where he would remain for the rest of his professional life.

Revolutionizes Bacterial Chemotherapy

Domagk's career was profoundly influenced by the work of **Paul Ehrlich**. In 1907, Ehrlich had discovered arsphenamine, a compound specifically developed to be toxic to trypanosomes, and in 1909 this drug had been found to be quite effective against the bacterium that causes syphilis. Ehrlich's work had stimulated a number of searches for other antibacterials, and Domagk systematically continued this work at I. G. Farbenindustrie.

Domagk investigated thousands of chemicals for their potential as antibacterials. He would first test them against bacterial cultures in the test tube, then find the doses tolerated by animals such as mice, and lastly determine if compounds that worked in the test tube also worked against bacteria in living animals. For five years Domagk searched in vain for a "magic bullet" that would be toxic to bacteria and not to animals. His success illustrates Pasteur's dictum that chance favors the prepared mind. Methodically checking thousands of compounds for antibacterial activity, Domagk found in 1932 that a red leather dye showed a small effect on bacteria in the test tube. Developed by others at the company, the compound was called Prontosil Rubrum, and it proved quite non-toxic to mice.

Domagk's original experiment to determine the effectiveness of Prontosil Rubrum was straightforward. He injected twenty-six mice with a culture of hemolytic streptococcal bacteria. Fourteen mice served as controls, receiving no therapy, and all died within four days, as expected from previous experiments with untreated animals. The remaining twelve mice were injected with a single dose of Prontosil Rubrum an hour and a half after being infected with the bacteria. All twelve survived in good condition. In 1932, I. G. Farbenindustries began clinical testing of Prontosil Rubrum. For reasons that are unknown, however, Domagk delayed publishing the results of his experiment for three years. But it is clear that he understood its implications. During this time his daughter contracted a streptococcal infection from a needle prick and failed to respond to traditional therapies. As she lay near death, Domagk injected her with Prontosil Rubrum, and she subsequently recovered.

There was some initial skepticism when Domagk first published his experimental results, but rapid replication of his findings led to widespread acceptance of the value of Prontosil Rubrum therapy. Throughout Europe, hospitals treated a variety of illnesses—including pneumonia, meningitis, blood poisoning, and gonorrhea—with Prontosil Rubrum

and closely allied compounds. Subsequent laboratory studies have shown that it is only a part of the Prontosil Rubrum molecule, the sulfonamide group itself, that is responsible for its effect on bacteria. Moreover, the compound does not kill bacteria but interferes with their metabolism and therefore with their ability to reproduce.

Nazi Government Forces Him to Reject Nobel Prize

Although the importance of his work was widely recognized by physicians and fellow scientists, the world of politics obstructed formal acknowledgement of his discovery. Carl von Ossietzky, a German pacifist incarcerated in a prison camp, had been awarded the Nobel Peace Prize in 1936, and Hitler had declared that no German citizen could accept a Nobel Prize. When he was awarded the prize in 1939, Domagk notified the German government and was promptly arrested. He was soon released but was forced to decline the prize. He was awarded the Nobel Medal after the war, but the prize money had reverted to the foundation.

During the late 1930s and throughout World War II, Domagk continued to investigate other compounds for their antibacterial effects. He concentrated considerable effort on anti-tubercular drugs, recognizing the problem of increasing resistance to streptomycin. His work resulted in some drugs of limited use against tuberculosis, though the class of compounds he studied proved to be somewhat toxic. Domagk retired in 1958 but remained active in research. He spent the last few years of his career attempting without success to find an anti-cancer drug.

In addition to the Nobel Prize, Domagk received numerous other accolades. In 1959, he was elected to the Royal Society of London. He was awarded medals by both Spain and Japan, and several German universities conferred honorary doctorates upon him.

Domagk married Gertrude Strube in 1925. They had four children, three sons and a daughter. Domagk died of a heart attack on April 24, 1964.

SELECTED WRITINGS BY DOMAGK:

Periodicals

"Ein Beitrag zur Chemotherapie der bakteriellen Infektionen," *Deutsche medizinische Wochenschrift,* Volume 61, 1935, pp. 250–253.

"Investigations on the Anti-tuberculous Activity of the Thiosemicarbazones *in vitro* and *in vivo,*" *American Review of Tuberculosis and Pulmonary Diseases,* Volume 61, 1950, pp. 8–19.

SOURCES:

Books

Magill, Frank N., editor, *The Nobel Prize Winners: Physiology or Medicine,* Volume 1, Salem Press, 1991, pp. 455–464.
McGraw-Hill Modern Scientists and Engineers, Volume 1, McGraw-Hill, 1980, pp. 299–300.

—*Sketch by Ethan E. Allen*

Simon Donaldson
1957-
English mathematician

Throughout history, physicists have routinely used the findings of mathematicians to explain natural phenomena. Simon Donaldson, however, reversed this trend by applying his knowledge of theoretical physicists to the field of mathematics instead. In doing so, he returned to the tradition of using phenomena present in the physical world as a source of inspiration for mathematics, although at a new level of complexity.

Donaldson was born on August 20, 1957, in Cambridge, England. He attended Pembroke College in Cambridge University and received his B.A. degree in 1979. During his second year of graduate studies at Worcester College in Oxford University, Donaldson made the spectacular discovery of "exotic" or non-standard differential structures on four-dimensional Euclidean space. In other words, he found that there were different ways of orienting a mathematical structure in ordinary space with the addition of a fourth dimension. Because the standard differential structure is the only one possible in all other dimensions, the mathematical community was amazed at the exceptions created by the addition of the fourth dimension. After receiving his Ph.D. in 1983, Donaldson spent a year at the Institute for Advanced Study in Princeton. He was a visiting scholar at Harvard University during the spring of 1985. He then returned to England where he holds an appointment at the Mathematics Institute in Oxford.

Since the pioneering work begun in 1954 by **Chen Ning Yang** and Robert Mills, mathematicians and physicists have benefitted from cross-fertilization. In that year, the two scientists collaborated on derivations of mathematical formulae which combined the branch of mathematics known as topology —studying the ways in which coordinate structures

attach at a point—and the branch of physics called quantum electrodynamics—the study of electromagnetic phenomena under the rules of quantum mechanics. In doing so, they built upon the work of James Clerk Maxwell who had introduced equations in the nineteenth century to describe the behavior of electromagnetic waves. The Yang-Mills equations generalize Maxwell's equations to more complex spaces. Certain outcomes of the Yang-Mills equations yield instantons, a colorful term for highly abstract objects.

One of the difficulties in treating physics by mathematical means has been the discrepancy between the intuitive definitions in physics and the more rigorous definitions in mathematics. What made Donaldson's work so remarkable was his ability to borrow from the less mathematically familiar ideas of Yang and Mills elements that he needed for strictly mathematical problems. The solutions to the Yang-Mills equations depended on a finite number of parameters, and Donaldson exploited this collection of parameters as a tool in geometry. What had been a theoretical difficulty became in Donaldson's hands the key to translate between the parameter space of instantons and the mathematical structure of four-dimensional space.

Donaldson further developed the use of instantons to obtain deeper understanding of the differential structure on four-dimensional spaces. He also discovered an algebraic description of instantons that permits calculation of some of the invariants used to tell these differential structures from one another.

At the 1986 International Congress of Mathematicians, Donaldson received the Fields Medal, the equivalent in mathematics of the Nobel Prize. In summarizing the work of Donaldson in connection with the presentation of this award, **Michael Francis Atiyah** concluded, "It is remarkable and encouraging that such a young mathematician can understand and harness such a wide range of ideas and techniques in so short a time and put them to such brilliant use. It is an indication that mathematics has not lost its unity, or its vitality."

SELECTED WRITINGS BY DONALDSON:

Periodicals

"Self-dual Connections and the Topology of Smooth 4-Manifolds," *Bulletin of the American Mathematical Society,* Volume 8, 1983, pp. 81–83.
"The Geometry of 4-Manifolds," *Proceedings of the International Congress of Mathematicians,* [Berkeley, CA], 1986, pp. 43–54.

SOURCES:

Periodicals

Atiyah, Michael, "On the Work of Simon Donaldson," *Proceedings of the International Congress of Mathematicians,* [Berkeley, CA], 1986, pp. 3–6.

Atiyah, Michael, "The Work of Simon Donaldson," *Notices of the American Mathematical Society,* Volume 33, number 6, November, 1986, pp. 900–901.

"Fields Medals," *Notices of the American Mathematical Society,* Volume 33, number 5, October, 1986, pp. 736–737.

—*Sketch by Robert Messer*

Donald W. Douglas

Donald W. Douglas
1892-1981
American aircraft engineer

Donald W. Douglas, the founder of Douglas Aircraft, was a designer and entrepreneur who contributed immeasurably to the growth of civil and military aviation. The aircraft developed under his leadership included the legendary DC–3, which opened up vast areas of the globe to air transportation and remained in worldwide service sixty years after its conception.

Donald Wills Douglas, Sr., was born in Brooklyn, New York, on April 6, 1892. He was the second son of William Douglas, a bank cashier of Scottish descent, and Dorothy Hagenlocker, a German immigrant. Douglas was an energetic and precocious child who was once sent home by a grade school teacher for correcting her pronunciation. He liked to write, and when he was only fourteen, he published a book of his own poems on his home printing press. In the summers his family vacationed on Long Island Sound, where Douglas learned to sail and acquired a great affection for the sea. In 1908, at Fort Meyer, Virginia, the young man saw the Army Signal Corps perform initial tests of the **Wright brothers**' *Flyer.* This crude flying machine made a lasting impression on Douglas' imagination.

From Naval Cadet to Airplane Builder

Despite his burgeoning fascination with aircraft, Douglas followed his brother Harold into the U.S. Naval Academy. Chafing at the restrictions of mili-

tary life and the lack of enthusiasm for aviation he found at Annapolis, Douglas left the school in 1912 to enroll at the Massachusetts Institute of Technology. There he studied mechanical engineering while learning all he could about airplanes. Graduating from MIT's four-year program in just two years, Douglas stayed on campus another year as a research assistant. He also worked briefly for the Connecticut Aircraft Company, building the U.S. Navy's first dirigible, or airship. In 1915, aviation pioneer Glenn Martin invited Douglas to join his company in California. The "boy engineer," as Martin called him, soon showed his talent by designing the Martin Model S, a two-place hydroplane the company sold to the Signal Corps. In 1916, on his then-handsome salary of 50 dollars a week, Douglas married Charlotte Ogg, an Iowa-born nursing student whom he met on a blind date.

Douglas became Martin's chief engineer, but left in December, 1916, for a civilian position with the Signal Corps. The Corps purchased several British and French planes to study as a basis for designing American planes, but the Aircraft Production Board, which wanted the well-established automobile industry to handle plane-building, ordered that no American airplane builder be allowed access to the aircraft. An enraged Douglas secretly copied all documentation on the planes and sent the information to American designers. When he quit the Signal Corps at the end of 1917, a grateful Martin hired him again. At Martin's Cleveland plant he designed the MB–1, purchased as a fighter-bomber by the U.S. military and as a mail plane by the U.S. Post Office.

In 1920, Douglas returned to California to go into business for himself. He and wealthy sportsman David Davis formed the Davis-Douglas Company, which began operations in the back room of a Los Angeles barbershop. Davis financed development of a high-performance biplane, the Cloudster, but then dropped out of the company. Douglas sold a Cloudster derivative to the navy, obtaining the money to start production with the help of *Los Angeles Times* publisher Harry Chandler. Another modification of this plane was devised to meet an army request for a plane capable of a flight around the world. The Douglas World Cruisers did circle the globe in 1924, an aviation first which made the company famous and brought military orders pouring in. As the Douglas Company grew, Douglas himself began to focus on management, bringing his father in as treasurer and turning most of the day-to-day design work over to such talented engineers as Edward Heinemann, Jack Northrop, and James "Dutch" Kindelberger. Both Northrop and Kindelberger went on to head other major aircraft manufacturing companies.

Douglas never lost his love for the sea, and sailing remained his chief pleasure all his life. In 1932, he competed in the Los Angeles Olympics as a member of the U.S. yachting crew. This interest also influenced his fascination with amphibian designs. These never were great commercial successes, although the Douglas Dolphin, an innovative and luxurious aircraft, drew a sizeable military order and brought Douglas much satisfaction when rival planemaker William Boeing purchased one for his personal use. Douglas was to misjudge the market more than once during his career, but every one of his planes earned a reputation as a solid and reliable machine.

A company reorganization in 1928 created the Douglas Aircraft Company, Inc., which survived the Depression mainly by filling military requirements. In 1932, a request from TWA inspired Douglas' development of the world's most advanced airliner, the DC-2. This was a great success, leading to Donald Douglas' receipt of the prestigious Collier Trophy in 1936. As superior as this twin-engined, all-metal monoplane was for the time, it was completely eclipsed by its follow-on, the renowned DC-3, which first flew in 1935. The company built over ten thousand DC-3s, which became the backbone of military and civil air transport service around the world. The four-engined DC-4, a much larger transport, followed in 1938. By the time the war began, Douglas planes were flying no less than 95 percent of America's domestic passenger traffic.

Helps Win a War, Leads a Difficult Conversion in Peace

As war loomed close, Douglas built the DB-7 fighter-bomber, ordered by France and other friendly nations. Once the war started, the company redesigned the DB-7 into the widely used A20 attack plane, one of several Douglas types which made important contributions to the war effort. Douglas SBD dive bombers were credited with the sinking of four Japanese carriers at the Battle of Midway in 1942, an event which turned the tide of war in the Pacific. Douglas himself organized the Aircraft War Production Council and served as its president.

After the war, Douglas brought out the DC-6 and DC-7 airliners, but focused too long on propeller-driven transports before scrambling to join the jet age with the 1958 launch of the DC-8. The company never entirely recovered from this misstep, even though Douglas went on to build a variety of research, combat, and transport aircraft, including the popular DC-9 airliner. The company also branched out into guided missiles. One Douglas product was the Thor missile, which first flew in 1957 and, modified into the Delta launch vehicle, was still putting satellites into orbit a quarter-century later.

In contrast to his earlier disdain for the strict military life, Douglas as an executive was a meticulous man who kept to an unvarying personal routine. He spent free time reading or sailing, and took up the bagpipes as well. He and Charlotte divorced in 1953. Their marriage had produced four sons, Donald W., Jr., William E., Malcolm M., and James S., and one daughter, Barbara Jean. Shortly after the divorce, Douglas married his personal assistant, Peggy Tucker. In 1957, Douglas handed the presidency of Douglas Aircraft over to his eldest son. The company, however, did not survive the costly DC-8 program and the loss of several competitions for military contracts. Creditors forced a merger with the McDonnell Company in 1967. Douglas remained a member of the new McDonnell Douglas Corporation's board, but did not play an active role. He designed a new yacht, the *Ladyfair,* and retired from business. The honors for his contributions continued. Douglas received the Wings Club Distinguished Achievement Award in 1979, adding it to the Guggenheim Gold Medal in 1939, the Wright Brothers Trophy, and many other tributes.

Now the revered elder statesman of aviation, Douglas died of cancer in Palm Springs, California, on February 1, 1981. Peggy passed away in 1989. In 1990, James Douglas, the last of Douglas' sons to be involved with the company, was laid off. That marked the end of the Douglas family's work in aircraft manufacturing, but the legacy of Donald Douglas was secure. A decade after his death, an estimated two thousand of his beloved DC-3s were still in service.

SELECTED WRITINGS BY DOUGLAS:

Books

Wings for the World!: The DC Family in Global Service, Newcomen, 1955.

Periodicals

"Of Men and Planes," *Flying,* September, 1959, pp. 40–47.

SOURCES:

Books

Biddle, Wayne, *Barons of the Sky,* Simon & Schuster, 1991.

Cunningham, Frank, *Sky Master: The Story of Donald Douglas,* Dorrance & Company, 1943.

Francillon, Rene J., *McDonnell Douglas Aircraft since 1920: Volume I,* Naval Institute Press, 1988.

Holden, Henry M., *The Douglas DC-3,* Tab Books, 1991.

Maynard, Crosby, editor, *Flight Plan for Tomorrow: The Douglas Story—A Condensed History,* Douglas Aircraft Company, 1966.

Periodicals

Buckley, William F., "Donald W. Douglas, R I P," *National Review,* March 6, 1981, p. 208.

"The Passionate Engineer," *Time,* November 22, 1943, pp. 77–84.

—*Sketch by Matthew A. Bille*

Charles Stark Draper

Charles Stark Draper
1901-1987
American aeronautical engineer

Charles Stark Draper was a pioneering engineer who developed advanced weapons technologies and sophisticated navigational and guidance systems. His most important scientific contribution was in the field of automatic control systems for piloting, specifically his inertial guidance system. This system successfully implemented completely automatic navigation, with applications that reached from the depths of the oceans in the Polaris submarine to the Apollo moon mission. An avid private pilot, Draper was first drawn to engineering by his navigator's interest in flight instrumentation. During World War II, Draper and colleagues in his lab at the Massachusetts Institute of Technology (MIT) developed the Mark 14 gun sight for use on U.S. battleships. Using gyroscopes to correct for target motion in flight, the gun sight is credited with successfully thwarting attacks of Japanese Kamikaze pilots. Draper spent almost his entire career at MIT and took great pride in his role as an educator who spurred his students on to significant scientific research efforts. Despite his stolid appearance as a bespectacled engineer, Draper was, at least academically, a free thinker. His interests in a variety of subjects gave rise to an MIT legend that he had taken more courses for credit than anyone else in the school's history.

Draper was born on October 2, 1901, in Windsor, Missouri, a small town near Kansas City. His father, Arthur Draper, was a dentist; his mother, Martha Washington (Stark) Draper, was a former schoolteacher. After graduating from the Windsor public school system, Draper enrolled in the University of Missouri in Columbia in 1917 with intentions of studying medicine. When Draper's parents moved to California, Draper transferred to Stanford University, where he obtained his bachelor of arts degree in psychology. But instead of enrolling in medical school, Draper decided to become a ship's radio operator and enrolled in Herald's Radio College. After finishing at Herald's, he traveled back East with a friend who was going to Harvard University. Draper liked Cambridge, Massachusetts, and decided to enroll at MIT.

In 1926, Draper earned his bachelor of science degree in electrochemical engineering at MIT. Still, he hesitated to commit himself to one field of study. His wide-ranging interests included mathematics, chemistry, physics, metallurgy, and aeronautical engineering. In 1928, despite not having earned enough credits in any one field for a master's degree, the university awarded him a master of science degree without departmental specification. The following year the university appointed him as a research assistant in aeronautical engineering. As he became more focused, Draper's superior intellect began to shine. Continuing his studies in pursuit of a doctorate, Draper took a new course in hydro- and aerodynamics conducted by Julius A. Stratton. "It would be difficult to say whether it was teacher or student in the course of that winter who learned most from the other," said Stratton in *Air, Space, and Instruments,* a volume of essays that celebrated Draper's sixtieth birthday.

Draper continued to pursue a wide range of interests and gained renown at MIT as the person to take the most credits ever at the school without receiving a doctorate. Eventually, MIT insisted that Draper finish his doctoral studies. In 1938, he received his doctor of science degree, twenty-one years after he first enrolled at a college.

In addition to his studies at MIT, Draper had gained his private pilot's license through the Army Air Corps reserve flight school in 1926. Draper's early interest in flying combined with his diligence and "bulldog" tenacity in thinking a problem through led him to make many inroads into aeronautical engineering. In *Air, Space, and Instruments,* Stratton recalled one particularly harrowing demonstration in which Draper finally convinced his instructor to fly with him in an open cockpit as he demonstrated how more sophisticated airplane instrumentation could prevent stalling and spinning in blind flying. To prove his point, Draper nosed the plane up to make it stall and then took it on a nose dive. "It occurred to me that I had left a good many things undone and that the Department would be hard put to find someone to teach mechanics," Stratton recalled. Fortunately for both men, Draper's "practical demonstration" was a success as the plane leveled out and the two safely concluded their flight.

Navigational Invention Finds Practical Application

The year after he received his doctorate, Draper was appointed a professor and given the helm of MIT's Instrumentation Laboratory. Working with Jimmy Doolittle, Elmer Sperry, and the Sperry Gyroscope Company, which provided support for his research, Draper completed a project to develop a new gyroscopic rate of turn indicator for navigational purposes. Despite the project's success, the indicator did not seem to have immediate practical applications. However, when the United States entered World War II, Draper's rate-of-turn indicator proved to be the stepping stone for a high-tech gyroscopic gun sight. In *The Eagle Has Returned,* Brigadier General

Robert Duffy wrote that Draper's "gun sight would correct for 'Kentucky Windage,' or target motion in flight, and became the basis for the new technological field of aided tracking fire control."

Based on high-precision rate-measuring gyros, Draper used "damping," or rotors immersed in viscous fluid, to develop the Mark 14 gun sight, which semiautomatically adjusted for range, wind, and ballistics relying on deck coordinates as reference axes rather than complicated gyro-stabilized references. Draper's "black box" gun sight with moving crosshairs proved to be an effective antiaircraft gun sight for ships and was used on a wide variety of antiaircraft weaponry. Draper's Instrumentation Laboratory was staffed by several hundred people at the height of World War II. For his engineering efforts during the war, Draper was awarded the Sylvanus Albert Reed Award in 1945. After the war, Draper continued to work on control systems for military purposes, including a sight control system for U.S. Air Force F–86 fighter planes during the Korean War in the early 1950s; he later also worked on missile fire control systems.

Develops Automatic Navigation System

As Draper systematically improved upon his control systems, primarily through advances in gyroscopic instrumentation, he began to pursue his long-held belief that these gyroscopic-based systems could be used to develop a revolutionary guidance system. Working with the Air Force Armament laboratory, Draper and his colleagues at the Instrumentation Laboratory began work on an inertial guidance system. This ultimate navigational system would require no outside reference points, such as radio signals or celestial guides. In addition to increasing safety by effectively eliminating many aeronautical guidance problems due to such circumstances as bad weather conditions, the system would become a vital development for space exploration.

Draper's diverse background at MIT served him well as he oversaw a group of researchers and doctoral students in interdisciplinary research that combined geometry, kinematics, and dynamics with aerodynamics, electronics, and mechanics. Based on his gun sight systems of World War II, which used the single-degree-of-freedom integrating gyro floating in a viscous fluid, Draper developed an improved gyro accelerometer that could accurately measure acceleration and velocity, as well as distance, or position. Essentially, the inertial guidance system used three friction-free gyros that responded to motion on one axis only to develop a computerized system that could measure and "remember" a plotted course, taking into account such factors as the earth's rotation. Draper's device, sometimes referred to as "astronomy in a closet" was ultimately connected to instruments that recorded the plane's altitude and direction, thus effectively creating a self-contained system for guidance.

Draper's inertial guidance system could be applied both to naval and aeronautical craft. Despite Draper's engineering credentials, many engineers and others doubted whether his invention would really work; after all, it represented a virtual revolution in the ancient art of navigation. With a flair for the dramatic, to which Draper's early teacher Stratton could attest, Draper set out on a flight from Bedford, Massachusetts, to Los Angeles, California, using only his inertial navigation system to guide the plane on its journey. With an Air Force piloting crew and seven other MIT engineers, Draper took off on February 8, 1953, in a B–29 for a twelve-hour flight that amazed all those aboard. Without anyone touching the controls, the plane flew across the continental United States, adjusting for altitude and direction as it sped across the Midwest, over the Rocky Mountains, and to within ten miles of the Los Angeles International Airport, where the crew took over.

Draper's System Guides Apollo Moon Mission

Because of the significant military applications of his system, the general public did not learn of the historic flight until 1957. But during those intervening years, the military supported Draper as he developed more sophisticated inertial guidance systems for submarines, missiles, and manned aircraft. The submarine inertial navigation system (SINS) was unveiled in 1954 and was eventually used to guide the Navy's Polaris submarines as well as the Polaris missiles. Further development of SINS and SPIRE (Space Inertial Reference Equipment) brought about even more sophisticated inertial guidance systems for use in military craft, including bombers, jet fighters, and submarines. By the 1970s commercial aircraft were also being equipped with inertial guidance systems.

The most dramatic use of Draper's guidance system, however, was initiated in 1961 when Draper and colleagues in his laboratory at MIT began designing a guidance and control systems for the Apollo spacecraft missions to the moon. Despite his success with the system so far, many doubted Draper's ability to devise such a system for space flight. Despite his advancing years, Draper proposed that he would be the logical choice to go on an Apollo mission, since he had the most intimate knowledge of the system. Although NASA turned down his offer to go along on the flight (reportedly arousing Draper's anger), the entire world was witness to Draper's engineering genius as millions watched the televised landing of a man on the moon and the safe splashdown of the capsule that returned the astronauts to earth.

In honor of Draper, the MIT Instrumentation Laboratory was renamed the Charles Stark Draper Laboratory, and the National Academy of Engineering created the Charles Stark Draper Prize in 1988. Draper's career in MIT included an appointment as chairman of the aeronautical engineering department from 1951 to 1966. He was appointed a senior scientist at the laboratory in 1973. Among his many honors were the Holley Medal of the American Society of Mechanical Engineers in 1971, the National Medal of Science in 1964, and the Foundation Medal of the National Academy of Engineering in 1970.

Draper married Ivy Willard on September 7, 1938, and had four children: James, Martha, Michael, and John. He died on July 25, 1987, in Cambridge, Massachusetts.

SELECTED WRITINGS BY DRAPER:

Books

(With Sidney Lees and Walter McKay) *Instrument Engineering,* McGraw-Hill, 1952.
(With Walter Wrigley and John Hovorka) *Inertial Guidance,* Pergamon, 1960.

SOURCES:

Books

Current Biography, H. W. Wilson, 1965, pp. 130–132.
Duffy, Robert, *The Eagle Has Returned,* American Astronautical Society, 1976.
Lees, Sidney, editor, *Air Space, and Instruments,* McGraw-Hill, 1963.
McGraw-Hill Modern Engineers and Scientists, McGraw-Hill, 1980, pp. 307–308.
Wolko, Howard S., *In the Cause of Flight: Technologists of Aeronautics and Astronautics,* Smithsonian Institution, 1981, pp. 112–113.

Periodicals

Murray, Don, "'Doc' Draper's Wonderful Tops," *Reader's Digest,* 1957, Volume 73, pp. 63–67.

—Sketch by David Petechuk

Mildred S. Dresselhaus
1930-
American physicist

Mildred S. Dresselhaus

Born during the Depression to a poor immigrant family, Mildred S. Dresselhaus possessed a natural intelligence and love of science that brought her recognition in the field of solid state physics. She has contributed a great deal of new knowledge about the electronic properties of many materials, particularly semimetals such as graphite, and was the recipient of the National Medal of Science in 1990. Dresselhaus is currently Institute Professor of Electrical Engineering and Physics at Massachusetts Institute of Technology, as well as consultant to Lawrence Livermore National Laboratory in California and Treasurer of the National Academy of Sciences. Her public service includes work on behalf of the National Research Council and the National Science Foundation.

Mildred Spiewak Dresselhaus was born on November 11, 1930, in Brooklyn, New York; her father was a journalist. As a child, she worked in sweatshops and factories to help with family expenses. At age eleven, she spent one year teaching a mentally retarded child how to read and write. In helping the child, she found her first insight into her future—in education. Dresselhaus' ambition then was to become an elementary school teacher. Her other love was music, and she and her talented brother received free violin lessons from philanthropic organizations which served as an introduction to the world of education.

Dresselhaus' parents encouraged her natural love of learning, and she studied diligently for an entrance exam for Hunter College High School—a girls' preparatory school associated with Hunter College in New York. She not only passed the exam, she did so with a perfect score in mathematics. Dresselhaus struggled at the school initially because her prior education was meager. She also had a difficult time socially among upper-middle-class schoolmates and their families. But her drive, intelligence and wit carried her through these early challenges. She excelled in high school and, with the help of a state scholarship, entered Hunter College, where she was graduated with highest honors in 1951. By that time, she was preparing for a career in physics.

Earns Scholarship to Cambridge

Dresselhaus then accepted a Fulbright Fellowship and performed graduate studies at Newnham, the women's college of Cambridge University. After returning from England, where she had benefited from her studies as well as the new friendships she formed, she earned a master of science degree in physics from Radcliffe College in Massachusetts. Upon her graduation from Radcliffe in 1953, Dresselhaus entered the prestigious doctoral program in physics at the University of Chicago. Solid state physics, the specialty which addresses matter in a condensed state, was in its infancy. The transistor had just been developed, and pioneers in the field were researching practical applications of semiconductors. In her graduate research, Dresselhaus explored the activities of superconductors. She found that some materials are excellent conductors of current at extremely low temperatures. She wrote two papers, "Magnetic Field Dependence of High-Frequency Penetration into a Super-Conductor" and "Magnetic Field Dependence of the Surface Impedance of Superconducting Tin," in 1958 and 1959, respectively, which were significant contributions to an area that few had begun to investigate.

Soon after receiving her doctorate degree, she married a colleague, solid state physicist Gene Dresselhaus. In 1958, she accepted a postdoctoral appointment as a National Science Foundation Fellow at Cornell University, while he became a junior faculty member there. Two years later, following the birth of her first child, Dresselhaus accepted a staff position at Lincoln Laboratory, a part of Massachusetts Institute of Technology that at that time specialized in semiconductors. Her husband also obtained a position there. Around that same time, a revolutionary development occurred in physics: the invention of integrated circuits, which would later be used in computers, automobile electronics, and entertainment systems. Dresselhaus began focusing on this area, examining the transport of electrons in high magnetic fields.

Studies Superconductors and Semimetals

While at Lincoln Laboratory, where she remained until 1967, Dresselhaus resumed her study of low temperature superconductors. She researched the behavior of various materials at temperatures as low as negative 250 degrees Celsius—the point at which hydrogen gas liquifies. She inquired into why semiconductors carry electrical current at room temperature, and applied what she discovered to further study. Dresselhaus also embarked on a study of semimetals—materials such as arsenic and graphite. These semimetals were shown to have properties in common with semiconductors and even superconductors. Dresselhaus' work on the structure of graphite (a form of pure carbon) was extremely original and earned her the respect of her colleagues. Apart from her academic life, Dresselhaus had three more children during the 1960s.

Dresselhaus was named Abby Rockefeller Mauze Visiting Professor in 1967, and the following year received a full professorship at M.I.T. She served as Associate Department Head of Electrical Science and Engineering from 1972 to 1974, and Director of the Center of Material Science and Engineering from 1977 to 1983. In 1973, she became permanent holder of the Abby Rockefeller Mauze Chair, and in 1983, she was named Professor of Physics. Two years later, she was named Institute Professor, a lifetime honor conferred on no more than twelve active professors at M.I.T. Beginning in the 1980s she and her associates investigated the properties of carbon, finding it to harbor hollow clusters, each containing sixty atoms. Today scientists are experimenting with these clusters—known as Buckminster Fullerenes, or "Buckyballs," on account of their shape—for their potential use as a delivery system for drugs, and as an extremely strong form of wire tubing.

Champions Women in Science

The challenges Dresselhaus faced as a prominent physicist and mother of four children caused her to become an advocate of women scientists. When her children were small, she had met with a lack of support from her male colleagues, and as a result she worked with other female colleagues at M.I.T. to expand the admission opportunities for women at the Institute. She also began a Women's Forum to explore solutions for difficulties faced by working women. Her initiative in this forum led to her appointment to the Committee on the Education and Employment of Women in Science and Engineering, part of the National Research Council's Commission on Human Resources.

Concurrent with her work at M.I.T., Dresselhaus has held numerous advisory and service positions. She was a member of the National Academy of Sciences' Executive Committee of Physics and Math Sciences from 1975 to 1978. She chaired the Steering Committee Evaluation Panels of the National Bureau of Standards from 1978 to 1983. She served as President of the American Physical Society in 1984. She chaired the English Section of the National Academy of Sciences from 1987 to 1990, and is a member of the National Academy of Engineering, as well as a senior member of the Society of Women Engineers.

Dresselhaus has received many honors. In 1977, she received the Society of Women Engineers Annual Achievement Award "for significant contributions in teaching and research in solid state electronics and materials engineering." In addition, she was a visiting Professor at the University of Campinas in Brazil in 1971, and at the Technion Israel Institute of Technology in Haifa. She also was Hund-Klemm Lecturer at the Max Planck Institute in Stuttgart, Germany, and received the Ann Achievement Award from the English Societies of New England, both in 1988. In 1990, Dresselhaus was awarded the prestigious National Medal of Science.

Her lifetime of achievements in the field of solid state physics might have surprised some who knew of her early circumstances, but Dresselhaus has no regrets. "All the hardships I encountered," she has said, as quoted in Iris Noble's *Contemporary Women Scientists of America,* "provided me with the determination, capacity for hard work, efficiency, and a positive outlook on life that have been so helpful to me in realizing my professional career."

SELECTED WRITINGS BY DRESSELHAUS:

Books

(With Gene Dresselhaus, K. Sugihara, I. L. Spain, and H. A. Goldberg) *Graphite Fibers and Filaments,* Springer-Verlag (Berlin), 1988.
(With G. Dresselhaus and P. C. Eklund) *Physical Properties of Fullerenes,* Academic Press, 1993.

SOURCES:

Books

Noble, Iris, *Contemporary Women Scientists of America,* Julian Messner, pp. 138–51.

Periodicals

Lear's, March, 1994, pp. 56–61, 82–83.

—Sketch by Karen Withem

Charles R. Drew
1904-1950
American surgeon and blood researcher

Charles R. Drew

Charles R. Drew was a renowned surgeon, teacher, and researcher. He was responsible for founding two of the world's largest blood banks. Because of his research into the storage and shipment of blood plasma—blood without cells—he is credited with saving the lives of hundreds of Britains during World War II. He was director of the first American Red Cross effort to collect and bank blood on a large scale. In 1942 a year after he was made a diplomat of surgery by the American Board of Surgery at Johns Hopkins University, he became the first African American surgeon to serve as an examiner on the board.

Charles Richard Drew was the eldest of five children. He was born on June 3, 1904, in Washington, DC, to Richard T. Drew, a carpet layer, and Nora (Burrell) Drew, a school teacher and graduate of Miner Teachers College. As a student, Drew excelled in academics and sports, winning four swimming medals by the age of eight. In 1922 he graduated from Paul Laurence Dunbar High School, where he received the James E. Walker Memorial Medal in his junior and senior years for his athletic performance in several sports, including football, basketball, baseball, and track.

Drew attended Amherst College in Western Massachusetts on an athletic scholarship. He would be one of sixteen black students to graduate from Amherst during the years 1920 to 1929. He served as captain of the track team; he was enormously popular and was awarded several honors, including the Thomas W. Ashley Memorial Trophy for being the football team's most valuable player.

Although Drew was a gifted athlete, he worked hard in school to keep high grades. By the time he graduated in 1926, he had decided to apply to medical school. However, his funds were severely limited. Before he could go to medical school, he had to work for a couple of years. He accepted a job at Morgan State College in Baltimore, Maryland, as a professor of chemistry and biology, as well as director of the college's sports program. During the next two years, he paid off his undergraduate loans and put some money aside for medical school.

In 1928 he was finally able to apply to medical school. However, African Americans who wished to become doctors at that time did not have many opportunities. There were two colleges open to them. Drew applied to Howard University and was rejected because he did not have enough credits in English.

Harvard University accepted him for the following year, but he did not want to wait so he applied to and was immediately accepted to McGill University in Montreal, Canada.

Embarks on Research in Blood

At McGill, Drew continued to excel in sports and academics. In 1930 he won the annual prize in neuroanatomy and was elected to Alpha Phi Omega, the school's honorary medical society. During this time, under the influence of Dr. John Beattie, a visiting professor from England, Drew began his research in blood transfusions. The four different types of blood—A, B, AB, and O—had recently been discovered. Subsequently, doctors knew what type of blood they were giving to patients and were avoiding the negative effects of mixing incompatible blood types. However, because whole blood was highly perishable, the problem of having the appropriate blood type readily available still existed. In 1930 when Drew and Beattie began their research, blood could only be stored for seven days before it began to spoil.

In 1933 Drew graduated from McGill with his Medical Degree and Master of Surgery degree. He interned at the Royal Victoria Hospital and finished his residency at Montreal General. During this time, he continued researching with Beattie. Because of his father's death in 1934, Drew decided to return to Washington, DC, to take care of his family. In 1935 he accepted a position to teach pathology at Howard University Medical School. The next year he obtained a one-year residency at Freedmen's Hospital in Washington, DC.

Develops Process to Preserve Plasma

In 1938 having accepted a two-year Rockefeller Fellowship, Drew continued his work in blood at Columbia University-Presbyterian Hospital in New York. Under the auspices of the Department of Surgery, he worked with Dr. John Scudder and Dr. E. H. L. Corwin on the problem of blood storage. Drew began to study the use of plasma as a substitute for whole blood. Because red blood cells contain the substance that determines blood type, their absence in plasma means that a match between donor and recipient is not necessary, which makes it ideal for emergencies. In 1939, while supervising a blood bank at Columbia Medical Center, Drew developed a method to process and preserve blood plasma so that it could be stored and shipped to great distances. (Dehydrated plasma could be reconstituted by adding water just before the transfusion.)

Drew graduated from Columbia University in 1940, with a Doctor of Science degree; he was the first African American to receive this degree. In his dissertation, "Banked Blood: A Study in Blood Preservation," Drew showed that liquid plasma lasted longer than whole blood. He was asked to be the medical supervisor on the "Blood for Britain" campaign, launched by the Blood Transfusion Betterment Association. At the height of World War II, Nazi warplanes were bombing British cities regularly and there was a desperate shortage of blood to treat the wounded. In order to meet the huge demand for plasma, Drew initiated the use of "bloodmobiles"—trucks equipped with refrigerators. The Red Cross has continued to use them during blood drives. In 1941 after the success of "Blood for Britain," Drew became director of the American Red Cross Blood Bank in New York. He was asked to organize a massive blood drive for the U.S. Army and Navy, consisting of 100,000 donors. However, when the military issued a directive to the Red Cross that blood be typed according to the race of the donor, and that African American donors be refused, Drew was incensed. He denounced the policy as unscientific, stating that there was no evidence to support the claim that blood type differed according to race. His statements were later confirmed by other scientists, and the government eventually allowed African American volunteers to donate blood, although it was still segregated. Ironically, in 1977 the American Red Cross headquarters in Washington, DC, was renamed the Charles R. Drew Blood Center.

Drew was asked to resign from the project. He returned to Washington, DC, and resumed teaching.

In 1941 he was made professor of surgery at Howard University, where he had been rejected 13 years earlier, and chief surgeon at Freedmen's Hospital. In 1943 he became the first black surgeon to serve as an examiner on the American Board of Surgery. He was an inspiration and role model to his students and received numerous honorary degrees and awards during this period of his life, including the National Association for the Advancement of Colored People (NAACP) Spingarn Medal in 1944. He wrote numerous articles on blood for various scientific journals, and in 1946 was elected Fellow to the International College of Surgeons.

In 1939 Drew married (Minnie) Lenore Robbins, and they had four children. Drew continued teaching in Washington, DC; and, during the summer of 1949, as a consultant to the Surgeon General, he travelled with a team of four physicians, assessing hospital facilities throughout Occupied Europe. On March 31, 1950, after performing several operations, Drew allowed his colleagues and some of his students to talk him into attending a medical meeting being held at Tuskegee Institute as part of its Founder's Day celebrations. When Drew dozed off while driving near Burlington, North Carolina, his car overturned, and he was killed.

Despite his untimely death at the age of 45, Drew left behind a legacy of life-saving techniques. Additionally, many of his students rose to prominence in the medical field. In 1976 Drew's portrait was unveiled at the Clinical Center of the National Institutes of Health, making him the first African American to join its gallery of scientists. Four years later, his life was honored with a postage stamp, issued as part of the U.S. Postal Service's "Great Americans" series.

SOURCES:

Books

Haber, Louis, *Black Pioneers of Science and Invention,* Harcourt, 1970, pp. 151–167.

Hardwick, Richard, *Charles Richard Drew: Pioneer in Blood Research,* Scribners, 1967.

Lichello, Robert, *Pioneer in Blood Plasma: Dr. Charles Richard Drew,* Simon & Schuster, 1968.

Sammons, Vivian Ovelton, *Blacks in Science and Medicine,* Hemisphere Publishing, 1990, pp. 78–79.

Wynes, Charles, *Charles Richard Drew: The Man and the Myth,* University of Illinois Press, 1988.

Periodicals

Bims, Hamilton, "Charles Drew's 'Other' Medical Revolution," *Ebony,* February 1974, pp. 88–96.

Journal of the National Medical Association, March, 1971, pp. 156–57; July 1950, pp. 239–45.

　　　　　　　　　—Sketch by Geeta Kothari

Daniel Charles Drucker
1918-
American mechanical engineer

Daniel Charles Drucker is an American engineer and researcher in applied mechanics whose ingenuity has discovered important new ways of determining stress. His field of expertise is materials engineering and stress analysis. His best known work concerns photoelasticity—the change in light-transmitting properties of solids (such as glass) caused by stress—in particular, photoelastic analysis of the interior of complex bodies which are under a stress load. He has also carried out important research in soil mechanics, plasticity, and the mechanics of metal cutting and deformation processing. He pioneered a method of classifying materials according to their degree of stability, now known as "Drucker's postulate." In the latter part of his career, he turned his attention to materials research, including research at the level of the optical and electron microscopes.

Drucker was born in New York City on June 3, 1918, the son of a civil engineer. From an early age, he realized his ambition was to be a design engineer. He was educated at New York's Columbia University, and received his B.S. degree in 1937. He remained at the University to pursue further studies in engineering, and received his C.E. degree in Engineering in 1938. He then went on for doctoral studies, and was awarded his Ph.D. in 1940. The previous August, he had married Ann Bodin. The couple has two children, R. David Drucker and Mady Upham.

After completing his education, Drucker was offered a position as instructor in Engineering at Cornell University in Ithaca, New York. He then served as supervisor of mechanics of solids at the Armour Research Foundation. Drucker spent a short while in the U.S. Army Air Corps, then returned to academic life to become assistant professor at the Illinois Institute of Technology. In 1947, Drucker transferred to Brown University in Rhode Island, where he spent the next 21 years; he became a full professor in 1950, and served as the L. Herbert Ballou University Professor from 1964 to 1968. In 1953 he became chairman of the department of Engineering, and he was chair of the university's Physical Sciences Council between 1961 and 1963.

Drucker moved to the University of Illinois at Urbana-Champaign as Dean of the College of Engineering in 1968. He remained in that position until 1984, when he accepted a post as Graduate Research Professor of Aerospace at the University of Florida in Gainesville. That same year, 1984, he retired the technical editorship of the *Journal of Applied Mechanics* of the American Society of Mechanical Engineers, which he had held since 1956.

During his career, Drucker has developed many innovative engineering techniques. In collaboration with engineer H. Tachau, he designed a simple wire rope that is protected against fatigue failure. The development of "Drucker's postulate," a means of classifying materials according to their stability, gave rise to a general method for dealing with varying classes of stress-strain relations for metals and alloys. In addition, the postulate led to a general theorem for the analysis and design of engineering structures in the important range of relatively small displacement. Finally, using optical and electron microscopes, Drucker hypothesized—correctly, it turned out—that tiny precipitates, rather than grain size, determine the flow strength of steel and aluminum alloys. He also outlined some of the properties of various iron-alloy steels and of sintered carbides, carbides that have been formed by heating without melting.

Drucker is a member of many learned societies, including the American Academy of Arts and Sciences, to which he was elected in 1955; the National Academy of Engineering, of which he became a member in 1967; and the American Society of Mechanics. In addition, he served as chairman of the U.S. National Committee on Theoretical and Applied Mechanics, was a member of the General Committee of the International Council of Scientific Unions between 1976 and 1986; was the first vice-president and chairman of the Engineering College Council of the American Society for Engineering Education, and was a member of the National Science Board beginning in 1988. Drucker has also held some honorary lectureships, including the Marburg Lectureship of the American Society for Testing and Materials in 1966, the W. M. Murray Lectureship of the Society for Experimental Stress Analysis in 1967, and Washington University's Raymond R. Tucker Memorial Lectureship in 1967.

Drucker's career has been saluted many times. He served as a Guggenheim Fellow from 1960 to 1961. He has been awarded an honorary Doctorate of Engineering by Lehigh University in 1976 and an

Honorary Doctorate of Science in Technology by the Israel Institute of Technology. He won the Max M. Frocht Award of the Society for Experimental Stress Analysis in 1967 and the Lamme Award of the American Society for Engineering Education the same year. In 1978, he was presented with the Egleston Medal of the Engineering Alumni Association of Columbia University. Drucker remains active in engineering research and in stress analysis. He also devotes a good deal of his time to teaching at the University of Florida in Gainesville.

SELECTED WRITINGS BY DRUCKER:

Books

(Editor with J. J. Gilman) *Fractures of Solids; Proceedings of an International Conference Sponsored by the Institute of Metals Division, American Institute of Mining, Metallurgical, and Petroleum Engineers,* Gordon & Breach, 1963.
Introduction to the Mechanics of Deformable Bodies, McGraw-Hill, 1967.

SOURCES:

Books

McGraw-Hill Modern Scientists and Engineers, Volume 1, McGraw-Hill, 1980, pp. 310.

—*Sketch by Avril McDonald*

Eugène Dubois
1858-1940
Dutch anatomist and paleoanthropologist

An anatomy assistant under the Dutch morphologist Max Furbringer, Eugène Dubois knew little of the science of paleoanthropology—the study of the fossil remains of humankind's ancestors—when, in 1887, he decided flatly that he would devote his scientific efforts to the search for Charles Darwin's proposed "missing link". His unearthing of Java man, near the village of Trinil on Java, was the first fossil discovery of *Homo erectus,* a direct ancestor of modern man, and the first deliberate search for man's fossil ancestors. Despite the controversy surrounding his discovery, Dubois worked at his research on the

growth relationship between brain and body size and conducted investigations into the climate of the geologic past.

On January 28, 1858, Marie Eugène Francoise Thomas Dubois was born into the family of Jean Joseph Balthasar Dubois and Maria Catharina Floriberta Agnes Roebroeck at Eijsden in the province of Limburg, Netherlands. He was cast into a world that teetered on the brink of enormous scientific enlightenment and heresy. His birth had been preceded two years earlier by the discovery of primitive human fossils in Germany's Neander Valley, the bones of which were still confounding scientists up to the time of Dubois's own discovery. Then, on October 26, 1859, several months before Dubois's second birthday, Darwin's *On the Origins of Species* was released upon an unsuspecting public.

Dubois proved to be something of a naturalist from an early age, learning the names of local flora and collecting herbs for his father's pharmacy. His father encouraged the younger Dubois, lending Eugène his equipment with which to perform chemistry experiments. Dubois's path toward a career in the natural sciences was further plotted while attending the state high school in Roermond, where his interest in human origins began. In 1877, Dubois attended the University of Amsterdam. Initially a medical student, his interest in the natural sciences proved too strong a force to ignore and Dubois devoted himself to their study.

As his talents became recognized among the faculty, he was appointed assistant to Furbringer in 1881, thus guiding his career, somewhat reluctantly, into anatomy. According to Bert Theunissen in *Eugène Dubois and the Ape-Man from Java,* "Dubois's main achievement in this study was to establish that the thyroid cartilage, part of the larynx, was homologous to the fourth and fifth branchial arches." In 1886, Dubois became a lecturer in anatomy at Amsterdam University, but he was never really content with his work. After a falling–out with Furbringer over his work on the larynx, Dubois decided on an alternative route.

On the Path That Leads to Java

Dubois was certainly familiar with the discovery of Neanderthal man shortly before his birth, and his growing interest in human ancestry was further incited by his talks on the subject with the Dutch botanist **Hugo De Vries**. Dubois studied Darwin, Charles Lyell and Ernst Haeckel, who had proposed the name *Pithecanthropus alalus* for Darwin's so-called "missing link". In 1876 and 1877, Dubois tried his hand at excavation near previously discovered Neolithic flint mines in his own country, but found nothing of prehistoric value.

The Neanderthal fossils remained the subject of scientific scrutiny decades after their discovery, and while Dubois acknowledged their primitiveness, he believed they were closely related to modern man and not deserving of a new taxon. He determined that still older forms would be found but not in prehistoric Europe, where the cold climate could not have supported the evolutionary progress of humankind's forebears. Therefore, the tropics of the Old World, inhabited by man's closest primate relative, the ape, must have been the jumping off point for transitionary man. And while Darwin had suggested Africa as the birthplace of humankind based on humans' close anatomical relationship to chimpanzees and gorillas, Lyell and Alfred Russel Wallace had opted in part for the East Indies on zoogeographical grounds. Dubois's determination to find the intermediate species between man and ape sent him packing for the Dutch East Indies on October 29, 1887.

Because the Dutch government refused his request to financially support such a venture, Dubois secured passage to the East Indies by enlisting in the Royal Dutch East Indies Army as a surgeon. He was assigned to a post on Sumatra, but his medical duties interfered with his plans to search out fossil man. A transfer to the Sumatran village of Pajakombo in May 1888 led to the discovery of animal fossils in the Lida Adjer Cave. This proved noteworthy for Dubois, as he had earlier posited the theory that, since human fossil remains up to that point had been discovered in caves, he would then have his greatest chance of success searching there. While later excavations in Sumatra turned up little, his finds at Lida Adjer secured a government subsidy for further research on Java, where a fossil human skull had recently been discovered in Wadjak Cave. This discovery excited in Dubois the notion that yet older fossils could be found there.

In June 1890, Dubois began his work on Java near the Wadjak discovery site. By September, his crew had unearthed a skull similar to the first Wadjak find, followed by fragments of the skeleton. A year later, Dubois's crew was concentrating much of its efforts near Trinil, a site along the Solo River that proved rich in mammal fossils. By August of that year they had uncovered the fossilized molar of a primate, followed in October by a skullcap that appeared not quite human, yet not quite ape. These, Dubois believed, belonged to a chimpanzee with decidedly human traits. In May of 1892, more proof of the apes' human-like tendencies came to light when a nearly complete left thigh bone was discovered at Trinil. By Dubois's estimate, the femur had been found approximately twelve meters from where the earlier fossil had been found, suggesting to him that all three fossils belonged to the same individual. More than that, the structure of the thigh bone bore a striking resemblance to a human femur, testifying to the fact that his "chimpanzee" had walked erect. The thigh bone and later recalculation of the skull capacity left no doubt in Dubois's mind that he had discovered the "missing link". He named the specimen *Pithecanthropus erectus,* the "ape-man who walked upright."

Faces Criticism Over *Pithecanthropus* Interpretation

The discovery also confirmed for Dubois two theories popular in the scientific circles of the time. One, that upright posture was "the first step on the road to becoming human," and that the East Indies, not Africa, was the cradle of humankind. From the study of the fossils, estimated at roughly half a million years old, Dubois also began to develop a saltationist theory concerning man's evolutionary progress, which emphasized a more rapid, punctuated rate of evolution than Darwin's gradualist theory presumed. In August 1894, Dubois's findings along with his theories were published in the thirty-nine page treatise *Pithecanthropus erectus, eine menschenaehnliche Uebergangsform.* The publication met with immediate criticism, mainly in Dubois's assertion that the molar, skull cap and thigh bone belonged to the same individual. There seemed no argument, even from his fiercest opponents, that the femur was human-like if not altogether human, but the structure of the skull cap, according to the French and Germans, was too decidedly gibbon-like for any serious discussion of its relationship to the femur. While he was derided for his ape-man theory, he was applauded both for his discovery of a new species of gibbon and for further dating man's existence to the Pliocene epoch some five million years earlier.

British criticism was altogether different, regarding as a mistake Dubois's neglect of modern human and the earlier Neanderthal skulls in the initial anatomical comparisons of his ape-man. The British anatomist Daniel J. Cunningham concluded that the skull was unquestionably human and furthermore the skull capacity fit a gradualist interpretation, wherein *Pithecanthropus* formed the bottom rung of man's climb to humanity, followed by the intermediate Neanderthals. Dubois and his Java man returned to the Netherlands in August of 1895 to confront the critics. On September 21, the remains of *Pithecanthropus erectus* were displayed before attendants of the Third International Congress of Zoology held in Leiden. Included among the group of prominent scientists were Dubois's American defender, Othniel C. Marsh, and the German pathologist, Rudolf Virchow, who felt that Dubois's arguments were wildly speculative at best and attributed the femur to a specialized species of gibbon. Dubois stood his ground on the interpretations, adding to them more comprehensive information than had been published in his treatise a year earlier, including his comparative analysis of *Pithecanthropus* and Neanderthal crania.

Filling the Evolutionary Gaps

Dubois spent the next several years traveling with his ape-man, defending his interpretations of the remains, and studying those of other fossil primates and men. In 1897, he and his wife, Anna Geertruida Lojenga, whom he married in 1886, settled in Haarlem, west of Amsterdam. There he became curator of the Teylers Museum, a position he would hold until his death, and was awarded an honorary doctorate in botany and zoology from the University of Amsterdam. As the 1890s came to a close, some of Dubois's more influential critics had begun to shift their opinions of *Pithecanthropus* in Dubois's favor. Even the prominent British anatomist **Arthur Keith**, who had at once been skeptical of Dubois's interpretations, came to agree with Dubois's assigned age for the creature and its genealogical position on the human family tree. But after 1900, regardless of this acceptance, Dubois would have no further word on the subject for nearly 25 years.

From 1900, Dubois kept himself busy on a series of studies that examined in mammals the evolution of brain size relative to body size. His earlier calculations concluded that brain size doubled with every evolutionary progression, but since these calculations did not work with his assignment of *Pithecanthropus erectus* to an intermediate form between man and ape, he had to revise his methods. This method proved self-serving, in that Dubois augmented *Pithecanthropus'* body weight to fit the scheme and support his saltationist theory of evolution. Dubois's theory later led to the misconception that he had consigned his ape-man to the lower status of gibbon, just as Virchow had suggested in 1895. But Dubois never doubted or intended to change its stature in the annals of evolutionary history. As he wrote in 1932, as quoted in *Natural History,* his reinterpretation suggested that *Pithecanthropus* was "a gigantic genus allied to the gibbons, however superior to the gibbons on account of its exceedingly large brain volume and ... its faculty of assuming an erect attitude and gait.... I still believe, now more firmly than ever, that the *Pithecanthropus* of Trinil is the real 'missing link.'"

Throughout the 1920s and 1930s, fossils similar to those of *Pithecanthropus erectus* were coming to light in the East, beginning in 1929 with the partial skull of Peking (Beijing) man in China. The continuing acceptance of Dubois's claims for Java man led the Dutch anatomist Ralph von Koenigswald to Java, where he eventually unearthed the fossil remnants of nearly 40 *Pithecanthropus*-like individuals. This new evidence proved that Dubois's ape-man was not an intermediate species between man and ape, but rather a direct ancestor to modern man. These fossils, including Dubois's original *Pithecanthropus erectus,* were later reclassified as *Homo erectus.* Having never changed his mind on the matter, Dubois died at his estate in central Limburg on December 16, 1940.

SELECTED WRITINGS BY DUBOIS:

Periodicals

"The Place of Pithecanthropus in the Genealogical Tree," *Nature,* 1895–1896, pp. 245, 247.
"Remarks upon the Brain-Cast of Pithecanthropus erectus," *Proceedings of the Fourth International Congress of Zoology, Cambridge,* 1899, pp. 78–95.
"The Distinct Organization of Pithecanthropus of Which the Femur Bears Evidence, Now Confirmed from Other Individuals of the Described Species," *Proceedings,* 1932, pp. 716–722.

SOURCES:

Books

International Dictionary of Anthropologists, Garland Publishing, 1991, pp. 163–64.
Johanson, Donald, and Edey Maitland, *Lucy: The Beginnings of Human Kind,* Simon and Schuster, 1981, pp. 30–37.
Leakey, Richard, and Roger Lewin, *Origins Reconsidered: In Search of What Makes Us Human,* Doubleday, 1992, pp. 47–54.
Milner, Richard, *The Encyclopedia of Evolution: Humanity's Search for Its Origins,* Facts On File, 1990, pp. 146–148.
Theunissen, Bert, *Eugène Dubois and the Ape-Man from Java: The History of the First Missing Link and Its Discoverer,* Kluwer Academic Publishers, 1989.

Periodicals

Gould, Stephen Jay, "Men of the Thirty-third Division," *Natural History,* April, 1990, pp. 12–24.

—*Sketch by John Spizzirri*

René Dubos
1901-1982
French-born American microbiologist and ecologist

René Dubos was a distinguished microbiologist whose pioneering work with soil-dwelling bacteria paved the way for the development of life-saving antibiotic drugs. Widely acclaimed for his discovery

René Dubos

of tyrothricin—a chemical substance capable of destroying dangerous *staphylococcus, pneumococcus,* and *streptococcus* bacteria in both humans and animals—Dubos later turned to the study of tuberculosis and the role of physiological, social, and environmental factors in an individual's susceptibility to infection. In the 1960s, Dubos's interest in the effects of the total environment on human health and well-being prompted him to give up his laboratory work at New York's Rockefeller Institute for Medical Research to concentrate on writing and lecturing on ecological and humanitarian issues.

Over the years, Dubos produced a number of popular books on scientific subjects, including *So Human an Animal,* the 1968 Pulitzer-Prize winner for general nonfiction, and *Only One Earth: The Care and Maintenance of a Small Planet,* which formed the basis for the United Nations Conference on the Human Environment in 1992. Dubos's greatest concern was not man's inability to adapt to pollution, noise, overcrowding, and the other problems of highly industrialized societies, but rather the ease with which this adaptation could occur and its ensuing cost to humanity. "It is not man the ecological crisis threatens to destroy, but the quality of human life," Dubos wrote in *Life* magazine. "What we call humanness is the expression of the interplay between man's nature and the environment, an interplay which is as old as life itself and which is the mechanism for creation on earth."

Dubos was born on February 20, 1901, in Saint-Brice-sous-Foret, France, the only child of Georges Alexandre and Adeline Madeleine de Bloedt Dubos. Young Dubos spent his early years in the farming villages of Ile-de-France, north of Paris. Amongst the rolling hills and agricultural fields, Dubos developed a keen appreciation for the influence of landscape on the human spirit—a subject which would come to dominate his thoughts in later years. A bout with rheumatic fever at the age of ten both restricted Dubos's physical activity and enhanced his contemplative nature. When Dubos was thirteen, his father moved the family to Paris to open a butcher shop; a few months later, Georges Dubos was called to military service in World War I, leaving his wife and young son in charge of the business. Despite the best efforts of mother and son, the shop did poorly and the family had a difficult time getting by. Upon completing high school at the College Chaptal in 1919, Dubos had hoped to study history at the university, but the death of his father from head injuries suffered at the front forced him to stay closer to home to look after his mother. Dubos was granted a scholarship to study agricultural science at the Institut National Agronomique in Paris, receiving his bachelor of science degree in 1921. He spent part of the next year as an officer trainee in the French Army, but was soon discharged because of heart problems.

Launches Career in Bacteriology

In 1922, Dubos was offered the job of assistant editor at a scholarly journal called *International Agriculture Intelligence,* published by the International Institute of Agriculture—then part of the League of Nations—in Rome. Not long after he arrived in Italy, Dubos came across an article on soil microbes written by the Russian bacteriologist Sergei Winogradsky, who was then associated with the Pasteur Institute in Paris. Winogradsky's contention that microbes should be studied in their own environment rather than in pure, laboratory-grown cultures so intrigued Dubos that he resolved to become a bacteriologist. "This is really where my scholarly life began," he told John Culhane in an interview for the *New York Times Magazine.* "I have been restating that idea in all forms ever since." Soon after, Dubos happened to meet the American delegate to the International Institute of Agriculture, who convinced him to pursue graduate studies in the United States.

In order to finance his trip, Dubos translated books on forestry and agriculture and gave guided tours of Rome to foreign visitors. He eventually set sail for New York in 1924. During the crossing, Dubos ran into **Selman Waksman**, head of the soil microbiology division of the State Agricultural Experiment Station at Rutgers University in New Jersey (a man the aspiring scientist had guided around Rome some months before). After the ship docked in New

York, Waksman introduced Dubos to his colleagues at Rutgers, helping the young man secure a research assistantship in soil microbiology. While serving as an instructor in bacteriology over the next three years, Dubos completed work on his doctorate. His thesis, published in 1927, focused on the ways in which various soil microorganisms work to decompose cellulose in paper.

Upon completing his work at Rutgers, Dubos left for the University of North Dakota at Fargo to accept a teaching position in the department of microbiology. Soon after he arrived, however, Dubos received a telegram from the Rockefeller Institute for Medical Research in New York City offering him a fellowship in the department of pathology and bacteriology. Dubos immediately packed his bags, in part because the offer involved work on a project begun by Rockefeller bacteriologist **Oswald T. Avery**. Avery and his colleagues had been searching for a substance that could break down the semi-cellulose envelope which protects pneumococci bacteria—the microorganisms responsible for lobar pneumonia in human beings—from attack by the body's defense mechanisms. Dubos's bold assertion that he could identify an enzyme capable of decomposing this complex polysaccharide capsule with minimal damage to the host had evidently impressed Avery. With the exception of a two-year period in the early 1940s when he served on the faculty at Harvard Medical School, Dubos remained at the Rockefeller Institute—renamed Rockefeller University in 1965—for the next forty-four years.

Identifies Important Disease-Fighting Microbes

Guided by the studies of renowned bacteriologist Louis Pasteur, who maintained that any organic substance that accumulated could be broken down by natural energy, Dubos spent his first two years at the Institute searching fields, bogs, and swamps for a bacterium or fungus that could attack and decompose the tough polysaccharide coat surrounding pneumococci bacteria. Unlike other scientific investigators, who used enriched laboratory solutions to cultivate bacteria and force them to produce enzymes, Dubos concocted a solution rich in capsular polysaccharide which he spread over a variety of soils. In 1929, he succeeded in isolating a swamp-dwelling bacillus which, because of its need for nourishment in an energy-starved environment, had been compelled to produce an enzyme capable of decomposing the polysaccharide capsule and digesting the pneumococci within. The following year Dubos was able to demonstrate the value of this particular enzyme in fighting pneumococcal infections in both animals and humans. The discovery confirmed Dubos's belief that soil bacteria were an important source of anti-infectious agents, inspiring him to search for other disease-fighting microbes.

In 1939, Dubos announced the discovery of a substance called tyrothricin, which had proved effective in fighting staphylococcus, pneumococcus, and streptococcus infections. Produced by the soil microorganism Bacillus brevis, tyrothricin was later found to contain two powerful chemicals, gramicidin and tyrocidine, which, though too toxic for ingestion, found widespread application in the treatment of external conditions, such as boils in humans and udder infections in cows. Dubos's groundbreaking work prompted scientists from around the world to conduct a wide-ranging search for antibiotic substances in natural environments. This ultimately resulted in a reexamination of the therapeutic properties of penicillin—first discovered in a bread mold ten years earlier by **Alexander Fleming**—and led to the isolation of a variety of new antibiotics, including streptomycin and the tetracyclines.

The death of Dubos's first wife, Marie Louise Bonnet, from tuberculosis in 1942 had a profound effect upon the scientist's career. "There seemed no reason," he recalled for Culhane. "Why should she get [tuberculosis] in this environment?" After spending two years as a professor of tropical medicine at Harvard Medical School, Dubos returned to the Rockefeller Institute to begin a full-scale investigation of tuberculosis and its causes. Until that time, scientists attempting to study tuberculosis bacilli had been hindered by the fact that laboratory methods of cultivation often modified the organisms to such an extent that they no longer resembled or behaved like the strains that infected humans. By 1947, however, Dubos had discovered that by adding a common detergent called "Tween" to the culture medium, he could raise bacilli so quickly and in such large quantities that they had little chance to mutate. This enabled researchers to study the microorganism more closely and develop the highly effective Bacillus Calmette-Guérin, or BCG, vaccine.

Uncovers Environmental Causes of Tuberculosis

During the course of his research with tuberculosis, Dubos focused on the importance of heredity, nutrition, physiology, and social and emotional trauma on an individual's vulnerability to infection. He used his wife's case as his first example. A careful examination of her early health records revealed that she had suffered from tuberculosis as a child. Although his wife recovered from the acute attack, Dubos became convinced that the emotional upheaval of World War II and her concern for her family's safety in France had served to weaken her and reawaken the dormant germ. Some years later, Dubos's second wife's battle with tuberculosis and her subsequent recovery prompted the couple to collaborate on *The White Plague: Tuberculosis, Man, and Society,* a non-technical account of the disease. Published in 1952, the book provided additional evidence linking tuberculosis with certain environmental conditions, such as inadequate nourishment and sudden economic or social disturbances.

As time went on, Dubos's interest in the effects of the total environment on human health encouraged him to become involved with the sociomedical problems of poor communities and to speak out on the dangers of pollution, as well as social, economic, and spiritual deprivation. By 1964, he had become a leading spokesman for the fledgling environmental movement and an outspoken critic of what he viewed as the narrow, short-range approach used by most biologists. Dubos maintained that the modern scientific perspective ignored the study of man's true nature as well as the biological characteristics that influence both human development and human behavior. It was his belief, for example, that giving medical aid to people in underdeveloped countries was of little use, since most health problems were the result of deprivation during infancy and could not be rectified in later life.

Writings Focus on Man's Spiritual Survival

According to Dubos, the problems of technologically advanced societies posed an equal—if not greater—threat to human survival. Two of Dubos's most popular books, *Man Adapting* and *So Human an Animal,* examine the close relationship between environmental conditions and man's physical, mental, and spiritual development, emphasizing the dangers inherent in adapting to a polluted, highly mechanized, highly stressful environment. "Wild animals can survive in zoos, but only at the cost of losing the physical and behavioral splendor they possess in their natural habitat," he wrote in *Life.* "Similarly, human beings can survive in the polluted cage of technological civilization, but in adapting to such conditions, we may sacrifice much of our humanness." Dubos also warned against introducing new substances, such as laundry detergents containing potentially dangerous enzymes, into the American marketplace without thorough testing. Unlike many environmentalists, however, Dubos maintained an enormous faith in both the ability of nature to recover from man's abuses and man's own capacity to recognize and learn from mistakes.

After retiring from his teaching and research position at Rockefeller University in 1971, Dubos was named professor and director of environmental studies at the State University of New York College at Purchase. He also served as an adviser at Richmond College on Staten Island, and continued to lecture and write on environmental issues. In this same period, Dubos became intrigued by the efforts of ordinary citizens to create a bird sanctuary on a garbage dump in New York's Jamaica Bay. He viewed this and other examples of grassroots environmental action as important symbols of man's willingness to improve the quality of his surroundings. In 1980, the René Dubos Center for Human Environments was established to encourage and promote similar activities in the New York area.

Dubos became a naturalized American citizen in 1938. Although he maintained a laboratory and an apartment in New York City, Dubos spent most weekends at his large estate in Garrison, New York. There, he and his wife planted trees, raised vegetables, and enjoyed long walks in the scenic Hudson River Valley. Over the years, Dubos earned numerous awards for his work, including the Modern Medicine Award, 1961, the Phi Beta Kappa Award, 1963, for *The Unseen World,* and the Tyler Ecology Award, 1976; he also received more than thirty honorary degrees from various colleges and universities. A member of professional organizations such the National Academy of Sciences, Dubos was also appointed by President Richard M. Nixon in 1970 to serve on the Citizens' Advisory Committee on Environmental Quality. Always eager to make his scientific and philosophical ideas accessible to people from all walks of life, Dubos continued to write and lecture until shortly before his death from heart failure on February 20, 1982, in New York City.

SELECTED WRITINGS BY DUBOS:

Books

The Bacterial Cell in its Relation to Problems of Virulence, Immunity and Chemotherapy, Harvard University Press, 1945.
(With Jean Porter Dubos) *The White Plague: Tuberculosis, Man, and Society,* Little, Brown, 1952.
Mirage of Health: Utopias, Progress and Biological Change, Harper, 1959.
The Dreams of Reason: Science and Utopias, Columbia University Press, 1961.
The Unseen World, Rockefeller University Press, 1962.
Man Adapting, Yale University Press, 1965.
So Human an Animal, Scribner's, 1968.
Man, Medicine, and Environment, Praeger, 1968.
Reason Awake: Science for Man, Columbia University Press, 1970.
(With Barbara Ward) *Only One Earth: The Care and Maintenance of a Small Planet,* Norton, 1972.
Celebrations of Life, 1981.

Periodicals

"Why Survival Is Not Enough," *Life,* July 24, 1970.

SOURCES:

Books

Corner, George Washington, *A History of the Rockefeller Institute, 1901–1953: Origins and Growth,* Rockefeller University Press, 1965.

Current Biography, H. W. Wilson, 1973, pp. 105–108.

Lechevalier, Herbert A., and Solotorovsky, Morris, editors, *Three Centuries of Microbiology,* McGraw-Hill, 1965.

Modern Scientists and Engineers, Volume 1, McGraw-Hill, 1980, pp. 313–314.

Periodicals

Anderson, Alan, "Prophet of Optimism," *Time,* May 31, 1971, p. 51.

Culhane, John, "En Garde, Pessimists! Enter René Dubos," *New York Times Magazine,* October 17, 1971, p. 44.

Montgomery, Paul L., "René Dubos, Scientist and Writer, Dead," *New York Times,* February 21, 1982, p. 32.

Sanoff, Alvin P., "A Conversation With René Dubos," *U.S. News & World Report,* February 23, 1981, pp. 72–73.

Waksman, Selman A., "Dr. René J. Dubos—A Tribute," *Journal of the American Medical Association,* Volume 174, number 5, October 1, 1960.

—*Sketch by Caroline B. D. Smith*

Renato Dulbecco
1914-
Italian-born American virologist

Renato Dulbecco was a pioneer in the field of virology, the study of viruses. He began as a practicing physician in the military service of his native Italy during World War II and continued to practice as physician with partisan units fighting the German occupation of that country near the end of the war. It was only with his immigration to the United States in 1947 that he began his lengthy and highly distinguished second career in scientific research. Dulbecco developed the plaque assay technique which allowed scientists to quantify the number of viral units in a laboratory culture, thus making possible most of the later major discoveries in virology. He then went on to devote most of his life to the study of viruses that could cause cancer in animals and human beings. For his work in this field, Dulbecco shared the Nobel Prize in medicine or physiology for 1975 with microbiologist **David Baltimore** and oncologist **Howard Temin**.

Dulbecco was born in Catanzaro, a town in the southernmost part of Italy, on February 22, 1914, the son of Leonardo Dulbecco, a civil engineer, and Maria Virdia Dulbecco. His father was called into military service during World War I, and his mother moved the children to northern Italy, where they lived in Turin and Cuneo. After the war, the family relocated to Imperia, where Dulbecco received his primary and secondary education. He developed an interest in physics and built an electronic seismograph, one of the earliest of its kind. He considered going into physics, but his mother persuaded him to study medicine when he entered the University of Turin in 1930 at the age of sixteen. By the end of his first year of study, he realized that he was more interested in biology than in medicine per se, so he went to work as an assistant in the laboratory of Giuseppe Levi, a professor of anatomy and an expert on nerve tissue, where he learned histology (the study of plant and animal tissue structure at the microscopic level) and the techniques of cell culture. His fellow students included microbiologist **Salvador Edward Luria** and neurologist **Rita Levi-Montalcini**, both of whom were to be Nobel Prize winners and were to influence Dulbecco's scientific career.

Dulbecco received his doctorate of medicine in 1936 and was soon drafted into the Italian army as a physician. He was discharged in 1938 but was recalled in 1939 at the outset of World War II. He married Giuseppina Salvo in 1940; they eventually had a son, Peter Leonard Dulbecco, and a daughter, Maria Vittoria Dulbecco. After Italy, led by dictator Benito Mussolini, became a belligerent in 1940, Dulbecco served in France and then in Russia. A serious wound in Russia in 1942 hospitalized him for several months, after which he went home. Following the fall of Mussolini's government, Dulbecco went into hiding in a small village near Turin and became a physician to the local partisan units resisting the German occupation. After the end of the war in 1945, he was elected a city councilor of Turin but soon gave up the position to return to scientific study and research at the University of Turin. In 1946 Luria invited Dulbecco to join his research group at the University of Indiana at Bloomington. Dulbecco and Levi-Montalcini both immigrated to the United States the following year. He became an American citizen in 1953.

Scientific Career in the United States

At Indiana, Dulbecco experimented with bacteriophage, viruses that invade and kill bacteria cells.

His principal discovery at this time was that bacteriophage previously rendered inactive by exposure to ultraviolet light could be reactivated by exposure to white light of short wavelength. This work attracted the attention of **Max Delbrück**, a German-born physicist-turned-microbiologist. Delbrück invited Dulbecco to join him at the California Institute of Technology (Caltech) in Pasadena. Dulbecco and his family traveled from Indiana to California in an old car with a trailer in the summer of 1949. The beauty and size of the country and the kindness of its people made a strong impression on him, and he was especially attracted to the climate and life of southern California. Dulbecco became a research fellow and later a professor of biology at Caltech, where he remained until 1963.

In his first years at Caltech, Dulbecco continued his studies of bacteriophage. In the early 1950s, however, Delbrück suggested to him that animal virology, that is, the study of the viruses that invade animal cells, might be a fruitful field for investigation. Dulbecco plunged into the new subject with enthusiasm. His first important contribution in the field was his development of a method for determining the number of units of a given virus in a culture of animal cell tissue. This method, called the plaque assay technique, enabled the researcher to count the viral units in a culture by examining the number of plaques, or clear spots, in the culture, where the viruses had killed the host cells. This method was the basis for many of the later important advances made in animal virology. One spectacular practical result of the use of the plaque assay technique was the development of physician **Albert Sabin**'s polio vaccine, developed from a living virus, used to prevent poliomyelitis, a paralyzing and sometimes lethal disease. This vaccine eventually superseded the vaccine produced earlier by physician **Jonas Salk**, which was made with a virus killed by formaldehyde.

Research on Tumor Viruses

In the late 1950s Dulbecco's interest shifted to the study of animal viruses that could cause cancerous tumors. His research over the next twenty years was devoted to an investigation of the precise manner in which particular viruses could transform host cells in such ways that the cell was either killed or multiplied indefinitely (that is, became cancerous). After working for a while with a virus that causes tumors in chickens, he and his colleagues concentrated primarily on the polyoma virus, which causes tumors in mice. They eventually discovered that the virus's DNA (deoxyribonucleic acid) combined with the DNA of the host cell and remained there as a provirus (a virus that is integrated with a cell's genetic material and that can be transmitted without causing disintegration when the cell reproduces) which controlled the genetic mechanism of the cell. In a process called cell transformation, the virus could induce a cancer-like state, causing the cell to multiply endlessly in a tissue culture environment in the laboratory. In an animal body, the same process of cell transformation and subsequent cell multiplication led to the growth of cancerous tumors.

In 1963 several important changes occurred in Dulbecco's life. During that year, he was divorced from his first wife and married Maureen Muir; Renato and Maureen later had one daughter, Fiona Linsey Dulbecco. In 1963 he also left Caltech to become one of the original fellows of the Salk Institute, a research organization founded by Salk in La Jolla, California. There Dulbecco continued his research on animal tumor viruses.

In 1972 Dulbecco moved to London to become assistant (later deputy) director of research at the Imperial Cancer Research Fund. He was by then involved in the study of cancer in human beings, concentrating on breast cancer. It was while he was in London that he, Baltimore, and Temin were jointly awarded the Nobel Prize in medicine or physiology for their work on tumor virology. In his Nobel Prize lecture Dulbecco, after first outlining the research that had led to his award, made a strong plea for the governments of the world to ban or otherwise remove cancer-causing substances from the environment. He especially called upon them to prevent the use of tobacco. While scientists spent their lives asking questions about the nature of cancer and finding ways to prevent or cure it, he said, "society merrily produces oncogenic [tumor-causing] substances and permeates the environment with them."

Dulbecco returned to his beloved southern California in 1977 to become a distinguished research professor at the Salk Institute. He became president of the institute in 1982 and held that position until his retirement in 1992. In addition, during the late 1970s Dulbecco taught at the University of California in San Diego.

SELECTED WRITINGS BY DULBECCO:

Books

The Design of Life, Yale University Press, 1987.
(With Harold S. Ginsberg) *Virology,* 2nd edition, Lippincott, 1988.

SOURCES:

Books

McGraw-Hill Modern Scientists and Engineers, McGraw, 1980, p. 315.

*Nobel Lectures: Physiology or Medicine,
    1971–1980,* World Scientific Publishing, 1992,
    pp. 229–40.

Periodicals

Science, November 14, 1975, pp. 650, 712, 714.

—*Sketch by John E. Little*

William F. Durand
1859-1958
American aeronautical engineer

William F. Durand was an internationally known teacher and researcher in aeronautical propulsion during the first half of the twentieth century. He made enormous contributions to the development of flight, fired the enthusiasm of the first generation of aeronautical engineers involved in aviation research, and virtually created the aeronautical engineering program at Stanford University. During a career spanning more than five decades of aircraft research and development, he helped establish the principles of propulsion used on aircraft reciprocating engines and later on jet aircraft.

William Frederick Durand was born on March 5, 1859, in Bethany, Connecticut, the son of William L. and Ruth Coe Durand, local business people. Educated in the public schools, Durand entered the U.S. Naval Academy at Annapolis in 1876, long before aviation became a technological possibility. He did well at Annapolis, graduating second in his class in 1880. He immediately entered the Naval Engineering Corps, where he worked on the problems of marine engineering. Adept in his duties, he was sent by the Navy to work on a Ph.D. in engineering. Durand graduated from Lafayette College in 1888, though he had resigned his naval commission a year earlier to accept a post as professor of mechanical engineering at the Agricultural and Mechanical College of Michigan. He remained there until 1891, when he moved to Cornell University to teach marine engineering.

Becomes a Leader in Aeronautical Engineering

In 1904, Durand moved to Stanford University on the West Coast, ostensibly to teach mechanical engineering. He soon became involved in the new technology of airplanes—the Wright brothers had made their historical flight the previous year—and began studying the problems of flight. Over the next several years, Durand created an aeronautical engineering curriculum at Stanford that became one of the best in the nation. By 1915, both Durand personally and his department at Stanford collectively had been recognized as leaders in solving the problems of flight.

The United States government recognized the importance of fostering aeronautical development by establishing the National Advisory Committee for Aeronautics (NACA) in 1915. Its purpose, as set forth in the Naval Appropriations Act of 1915, was "to supervise and direct the scientific study of the problems of flight, with a view to their practical solution." Governed by a committee of largely non-government experts, the NACA became an enormously important government research and development organization for the next half century, materially enhancing the development of aeronautics. Durand served as a member of the committee from 1915 until 1933, and again between 1941 and 1945. He also chaired the committee in 1917–1918, during World War I. Over the years, most of the research conducted under NACA auspices was done in its own facilities, but until the first of those facilities was constructed in 1918, the committee let contracts to educational institutions. Durand's research team at Stanford led all other contractors with its NACA-funded experimentation with propellers. This would have been considered a conflict of interest at a different time, but in the midst of World War I, and given the lax regulatory environment of the era, no one questioned it. This and other contracts paid off; the NACA's research on aircraft engines was the first major success of the organization and helped develop the Liberty Engine, the major contribution the United States made to aeronautics during World War I.

Plays Role in Development of Modern Air Force

On September 12, 1925, President Calvin Coolidge established the Morrow Board to study the use of aircraft in national defense. Among its members was William Durand, who lent considerable experience and expertise in aeronautics to its deliberations. The board held hearings and found that there was little agreement as to how many usable aircraft the Army Air Service had. While it rejected the most strident claims for air power, its report of November 30, 1925, recommended the appointment of two additional airmen as brigadier generals, one to head procurement and the other to command the flying schools. The board also recommended increased appropriations for the training of airmen and the development of modern airplanes, and suggested changing the name of the Army Air Service to Air Corps. In response, Congress passed the Air Corps Bill of 1926 to formalize many of these recommendations, setting the stage for the creation of the modern military air arm that would emerge during World War II.

In addition to serving on the Morrow Board, Durand participated in numerous other technical committees and advisory boards employed by a wide range of government entities. For instance, in 1929 he was a member of the advisory board of engineers for the Boulder Dam project, a significant effort that brought greatly increased supplies of water and electricity to the American southwest. He was also a member of the National Research Council between 1915 and 1945, and chair of the Navy Department's Special Committee on Airship Design and Construction in 1935.

Leads Special Committee on Jet Propulsion

Perhaps no technological innovation has been more significant in the development of aviation than the turbojet engine. Although it is relatively simple in its principles, its development required a unique combination of metallurgical capability, cooling and velocity control, and an unconventional understanding of Newton's third law of motion. By the 1930s and 1940s, no American researchers had solved the jet propulsion problem, leaving the nation far behind Great Britain and Germany in jet development during those crucial years. The United States had to make an enormous effort in the 1940s and get help from the British in order to catch up with developments elsewhere.

In March 1941, at the request of Hap Arnold, chief of staff of the Army Air Forces, the NACA created a special committee to study jet propulsion. Under Durand's leadership, this special committee met seven times in five months, finally recommending that the military award industrial firms contracts to study jet propulsion. Allis Chalmers, Westinghouse, and General Electric were chosen for their promising ideas on the subject. Durand's efforts as both engineer and advisor were important for the development of the jet engine and its application to military aircraft near the end of World War II.

While Durand had been recognized as a leading authority in aeronautics since the early 1900s, he was especially revered as the sage of the discipline in the postwar era. Durand received numerous awards from government, industry, and foundations for his contributions to the development of aviation in America, including the Presidential Award of Merit in 1946. He died at age ninety-nine on August 9, 1958, just as the space age was dawning.

SELECTED WRITINGS BY DURAND:

Books

The Resistance and Propulsion of Ships, Wiley, 1898.

Practical Marine Engineering, Marine Engineering, Inc., 1901.
Motor Boats, International Marine Engineering, 1907.
Hydraulics of Pipe Lines, Van Nostrand, 1921.
Robert Henry Thurston, American Society of Mechanical Engineers, 1929.
(Editor) *Aerodynamic Theory,* six volumes, J. Springer, 1934–36.
Selected Papers, California Institute of Technology, 1944.

SOURCES:

Books

Constant, Edward W. II, *The Origins of the Turbojet Revolution,* Johns Hopkins University Press, 1980.
Maurer, Maurer, *Aviation in the U.S. Army,* Office of Air Force History, 1987.
Nicolson, Harold, *Dwight Morrow,* Harcourt, 1935.
Rae, John B., *Climb to Greatness: The American Aircraft Industry, 1920–1960,* MIT Press, 1968.
Roland, Alex, *Model Research: The National Advisory Committee for Aeronautics, 1915–1958,* two volumes, NASA SP–4301, 1985.

Periodicals

Launius, Roger D., "'Never Was Life More Interesting': The National Advisory Committee for Aeronautics, 1936–1945," *Prologue: The Journal of the National Archives,* Winter, 1992, pp. 361–73.

—Sketch by Roger D. Launius

Gerald Durrell
1925-
English naturalist and conservationist

Gerald Durrell's lifelong commitment to the care and preservation of animals led to his 1958 creation of a scientific zoo and wildlife trust on the Channel Island of Jersey, aimed at promoting conservation and protecting endangered species through breeding and research. The first of its kind, the zoo is still widely visited today, and Durrell's travels throughout the world to collect and protect endangered species are the fodder for a number of his successful books and television documentaries.

Gerald Malcolm Durrell was born January 7, 1925, in Jamshedpur, India. His mother was Louisa Florence Dixie. His father, Lawrence Samuel, was an Anglo-Irish civil engineer working on the construction of India's fledgling system of railroads and bridges. Durrell was the youngest of four children, all individualists in their own right. One older brother, Lawrence, was a celebrated poet and novelist, remembered for *The Alexandria Quartet*. Another brother, Leslie, is a talented painter, while his sister, Margot, is a designer.

When Durrell was two, his father died. The family left India for England in 1928 and, for more than a decade, lived in a variety of cities and towns in England and on the continent. From his earliest days, Durrell enjoyed the company of animals. In fact, the first understandable word he spoke was "zoo." As he writes in his book, *A Bevy of Beasts*, "I am an exceptionally lucky person, for at the age of two I made up my mind quite firmly and unequivocally that the only thing I wanted to do was study animals. Nothing else interested me."

Durrell's education was anything but typical. He didn't attend a formal school system, rather, he gained his schooling from private tutors in Greece, France, Italy and Switzerland. The period of his life most impressed upon his memory were the five years he spent on the Greek island of Corfu in the late 1930s. He recounts in a trio of books (*My Family and Other Animals; Birds, Beasts, and Relatives;* and *The Garden of the Gods*) his enjoyable years there, describing his youthful adventures with local flora and fauna, and how his family reacted to his life as a budding naturalist. Fortunately, Durrell had the tutelage of the Greek scientist Theodore Stephanides during his Corfu days.

A Bevy of Beasts

It was not uncommon for the young Durrell to spend twelve hours a day wandering the hills and beaches of Corfu, filling his collection bottles with samples of the local wildlife. He recounts in *My Family and Other Animals* how his brother Larry would recoil in horror upon discovering a scorpion and her infant brood nesting in his match box, or finding snakes coiled in the bathtub. In *A Bevy of Beasts,* Gerald tells how "my marmoset had tried to climb in bed with Larry in the early morning and, on being repulsed, had bitten him in the ear." Despite the rather humorous portrait Gerald paints of his brother, it was Larry who exerted a father-like influence over his younger brother. Lawrence Durrell, thirteen years older than Gerald, constantly urged his brother to spend time reading and, later, to write of his animal exploits.

When the tides of World War II encroached upon the small Greek island, the Durrells returned to England, where for a while, they took up residence in London. Durrell obtained a job in a local pet store and, when not engaged there, made constant visits to the London zoo. In 1945, the twenty-year old Durrell was offered the position of student keeper at Whipsnade, the Zoological Society of London's zoo for the breeding and preservation of animals in the country community of Bedfordshire. Here he did more than the routine tasks of feeding, grooming and cage-cleaning; he initiated a systematic approach to recording animal behavior, comparing his findings with those expounded in the current literature. Durrell was aware that many of the zoo's species were extremely rare and that much of the world's wildlife faced extinction.

Becomes a Writer to Support His Calling

On his twenty-first birthday, Durrell came into an inheritance of three thousand pounds. He left the zoo and used the money to finance the first of many animal-collecting trips. On his trip to the rain forests of the British Cameroons, he collected over a hundred crates of mammals, reptiles, and birds for zoos throughout England. Between 1947 and 1949, Durrell made two expeditions to the Cameroons and one to British Guiana in search of rare animal species for local zoos. While the zoos profited from his adventures, Durrell was left with wonderful memories and a drained bank account. At a loss for a way to fund additional expeditions, Durrell took his brother Larry's advice and decided to write about his expeditions to pay for future trips. His first book, *The Overloaded Ark,* published in 1953, described his first trip to the Cameroons. It was an immediate success. The following year he published *The Bafut Beagles,* describing his second Cameroon expedition, and *Three Tickets to Adventure,* which covered his adventures in British Guiana. All three books were extremely successful financially; Durrell had finally found a way to finance his prime interest, the gathering of and caring for animals. In his search throughout England for a place to create his own zoo, he found the local bureaucracy so difficult that he decided to look elsewhere.

In 1958, Durrell established a thirty-five-acre site on Jersey, one of the Channel Islands that lie between England and France, on which he established his own nonprofit zoo. He intended to create a wildlife preserve devoted to animal conservation, scientific research and specialized training programs. Despite its island location, more than 200,000 people visit his zoo annually. In 1963, Durrell founded the Jersey Wildlife Preservation Trust to operate the zoo, and serves as the group's honorary chairman. A decade later, he established an affiliate of his Jersey trust, a worldwide conservation group called the Wildlife

Preservation Trust International, which has headquarters in Philadelphia.

Durrell's first marriage to Jacqueline Sonia Rasen in 1951 ended in a divorce in 1979. He married American zoologist Lee Wilson McGeorge the same year, and in the late 1980s, the two went on an animal-gathering expedition to Madagascar that led to a series of television shows for BBC and a book entitled *The Aye-Aye and I.* Durrell is a member of the Royal Geographical Society, the Fauna Preservation Society, the American Zoo-parks Association, and the Zoological Society of London. He holds an honorary degree from the University of Durham, and has been made an Officer of the Order of the British Empire.

The author of more than a dozen books, including several novels and a half-dozen children's books, Durrell continues to finance his various zoological and conservation activities with income from his writings. He makes it clear that he only writes to finance his true love—working with animals. In an interview for the *Christian Science Monitor,* he stated that "I try to get it over with as quickly as possible. Larry writes for posterity, but I write for money—it provides me with the wherewithal to do the things I really like doing, which is rushing off to Mexico to catch volcano rabbits."

SELECTED WRITINGS BY DURRELL:

Books

My Family and Other Animals, Hart-Davis, 1956.
Birds, Beasts and Relatives, Viking, 1969.
Beasts in My Belfry, Collins, 1973, published in the U.S. as *A Bevy of Beasts,* Simon & Schuster, 1973.
The Garden of the Gods, Collins, 1978, published in the U.S. as *Fauna and Family,* Simon and Schuster, 1979.
(With Lee Durrell) *The Amateur Naturalist: A Practical Guide to the Natural World,* Knopf, 1983.
The Aye-Aye and I, Arcade Publishing, 1993.

SOURCES:

Periodicals

Christian Science Monitor, November 28, 1979.
Discover, December, 1984, p. 42.
People, March 15, 1982, p. 119.

—*Sketch by Benedict A. Leerburger*

Vincent du Vigneaud
1901-1978
American biochemist

Vincent du Vigneaud, an American biochemist, received the 1955 Nobel Prize for Chemistry for his breakthrough achievement of synthesizing oxytocin—a hormone released by the posterior pituitary gland used to induce labor and lactation in pregnant women, and for his work with sulfur. Throughout his career, du Vigneaud was recognized for isolating and synthesizing penicillin and the hormone vasopressin, which is used to suppress urine flow, identifying the chemical composition of insulin, discovering the structure of vitamin H, otherwise known as biotin, and his pioneering work with methyl groups.

Du Vigneaud was born in Chicago, Illinois, on May 18, 1901, to Alfred, an inventor and designer of machines, and Mary Theresa (O'Leary) du Vigneaud. Early in his high school education in Chicago's public school system, du Vigneaud demonstrated an aptitude for chemistry and physiology. He constructed a laboratory in his parents' basement, where he carried out his first experiments. Du Vigneaud enrolled in the University of Illinois as an organic chemistry major and graduated in 1923. He stayed on to earn a masters degree in 1924, studying under C. S. Marvel. Also in 1924, du Vigneaud married Zella Zon Ford. Both of their children went on to become doctors. Their son, Vincent du Vigneaud, Jr., became an obstetrician and gynecologist, and their daughter, Marilyn Renee Brown, became a pediatric gastroenterologist.

From 1924 to 1925, du Vigneaud was an assistant biochemist at the University of Pennsylvania's Graduate School of Medicine and also worked in Philadelphia General Hospital's clinical chemistry laboratory. He then moved to the University of Rochester in New York to study for his Ph.D. under John R. Murlin at the School of Medicine. For his doctoral research, he undertook an examination of the chemical makeup of insulin, the protein hormone and sulfur compound that is secreted by the islets of Langerhans located in the pancreas. Du Vigneaud's investigations, which were inspired by a lecture given by renowned biochemist W. C. Rose at the University of Illinois, sparked a lifelong interest in the range of sulfur compounds, but especially the sulfur-containing amino acids methionine, homocystine, cystine, cysteine, and cystathionine.

After receiving his doctorate in 1927, du Vigneaud became a National Research Council fellow. He worked first at Johns Hopkins Medical School's Department of Pharmacology under John J. Abel, where he continued his research into the structure of insulin. His suspicion that insulin was a derivative of the amino acid cystine was justified when he succeeded in isolating cystine from insulin crystals. He was thereby able to prove that insulin consists only of amino acids and an ammonia by-product.

Du Vigneaud left the United States for Germany in 1928 on a brief overseas tour. He first stopped at the Kaiser Wilhelm Institute in Dresden, where he worked under Max Bergman, an expert on the chemistry of amino acids and peptides (chains of amino acids). Du Vigneaud later turned down an assistantship position with Bergman to proceed to the University of Edinburgh's Medical School, where he worked with biologist George Barger. He also spent time at the University College Hospital Medical School at the University of London, where he worked with Charles Harrington.

Upon returning to the United States, du Vigneaud joined the University of Illinois's physiological chemistry staff under his mentor, W. C. Rose. In 1932, he left his alma mater to take up a position as head of the Department of Biochemistry at the George Washington University School of Medicine in Washington, DC. One of his innovations there was to add a course in biochemistry to the medical school curriculum. His own research lead him to investigate his hypothesis that insulin's blood sugar-lowering effects were related to disulfide bonds of cystine.

In 1936 he and his staff succeeded in artificially creating glutathione, a tripeptide containing the amino acids cysteine, glycine, and glutamic acid, that is widely occurring in plant and animal tissues and which plays a vital part in biological oxidation-reduction processes and the activation of some enzymes. He also continued to pursue his research into insulin. By the following year, he was in a position to prove that the amino acid cystine comprises insulin's entire complement of sulfur, and that insulin can be deactivated by the reduction of its bonds of insulin by cystine or glutathione. Also in the late 1930s, du Vigneaud's work with methionine revealed how the body shifts a methyl group (CH_3) from one compound to another.

In 1938 du Vigneaud was appointed head of Cornell University Medical College's biochemistry department. Within two years, he had succeeded in isolating biotin (vitamin H). He spent the next few years carefully studying the substance and by 1942, had figured out its structure. He next turned to the human posterior pituitary gland, especially the study of the hormones oxytocin and vasopressin that it produces. Oxytocin is known to stimulate the contraction of uterine muscles and the secretion of milk in women during labor. Vasopressin, also known as the antidiuretic hormone, is a polypeptide hormone responsible for causing increased blood pressure and decreased urine flow. Du Vigneaud and his colleagues managed to isolate a highly purified form of these hormones from the pituitary gland and set about discovering their chemical nature.

To his surprise, du Vigneaud discovered that oxytocin is made up of only eight amino acids. Most proteins are comprised of several hundred amino acids. It took du Vigneaud another ten years to determine their sequence in an oxytocin molecule. Once he had cracked this puzzle, he was finally able to synthesize oxytocin. The importance of du Vigneaud's achievement lay not only in its making available an unlimited supply of the protein, but also in the light it shed on the relationship between molecular structure and biological function. The synthetic protein was tested on pregnant women at the Lying-in Hospital of the New York Hospital-Cornell Medical Center, where it was found to be as effective in inducing labor and milk flow as pure oxytocin. In 1946 the journal *Science* announced another du Vigneaud breakthrough: his synthesis of penicillin. Although du Vigneaud carried out the decisive experiments at Cornell University, it was one of the greatest international efforts of its kind, said *Science,* the culmination of five years of concerted effort by thirty-eight teams of scientists in the U.S. and Britain.

Du Vigneaud's illustrious scientific career was widely recognized. In 1955, he was awarded the Nobel Prize for Chemistry for "his work on biochemically important sulfur compounds and especially for the first synthesis of a polypeptide hormone." Du Vigneaud's other awards include the Nichols Medal of the American Chemical Society in 1945, the Association of Medical Colleges' Borden Award in the Medical Sciences in 1947, the Public Health Association's Lasker Award in 1948, the Osborne and Mendal Award of the American Institute of Nutrition in 1953, Columbia University's Charles Frederick Chandler Medal, and the Willard Gibbs Medal of the American Chemical Society. In addition, he was a member of the American Philosophical Society, the National Academy of Sciences, and the New York Academy of the Arts and Sciences. Du Vigneaud's leisure interests included bridge and horse riding.

From 1967 to 1975, du Vigneaud served as Cornell University's professor of chemistry. In 1975 he advanced to the level of emeritus professor of biochemistry at Cornell. Du Vigneaud died at St. Agnes Hospital in White Plains, New York, on December 11, 1978.

SELECTED WRITINGS BY DU VIGNEAUD:

Books

A Trail of Research in Sulfur Chemistry and Metabolism, and Related Fields, Cornell University Press, 1952.

SOURCES:

Books

McGraw-Hill Modern Men of Science, Volume 1, McGraw-Hill, 1966, pp. 147.
Nobel Prize Winners, H.W. Wilson, 1987.
World of Scientific Discovery, Gale, 1994.

Periodicals

New York Times, December 12, 1978, p. C12.

—*Sketch by Avril McDonald*

Freeman J. Dyson
1923-
English-born American physicist

Freeman J. Dyson

Freeman J. Dyson developed a general theory of quantum electrodynamics that integrates a number of specific concepts previously developed by **Richard P. Feynman**, **Julian Schwinger**, and **Sin-Itiro Tomonaga**, among others. As a result of his work with **Edward Teller** on nuclear power plants and the fusion bomb, he became active in the debate over the nuclear test ban treaty, arguing first one side of the issue and then, at a later date, the opposite side. Since the late 1950s, Dyson has also been interested in space travel and in research on the possible existence of intelligent life elsewhere in the universe.

Freeman John Dyson was born on December 15, 1923 in Crowthorne, a village in the south of England. His father, George Dyson, was a music teacher at Winchester College, and later became director of the Royal College of Music in London. His mother, Mildred Atkey Dyson, was a lawyer. He has one sister, Alice. From an early age, Dyson had a passionate interest in mathematics, so much so that his mother expressed concern about his becoming too asocial if he followed that career. He was not deterred by her warnings, however, and, on one occasion when he was 15, taught himself calculus over the Christmas holidays from a mail-order textbook. After completing primary school, he enrolled at Winchester College and then, in 1941, entered Cambridge to major in mathematics. His schooling was interrupted after two years by World War II, however, when he was assigned to work in the operational research section of the Royal Air Force Bomber Command. His experience in trying to make bombing runs more effective revealed to him the horrible loss of human life that was taking place and left a life-long impression on him. He was particularly upset by his own role in promoting the war effort and later said that the only difference he could see between his own wartime work and that of Nazis who were tried and convicted at Nuremburg was that "they were sent to jail or hanged as war criminals and I went free."

Begins Research into Quantum Electrodynamics

At the war's completion, Dyson returned to Cambridge and received his bachelor of arts degree in mathematics in 1945. He then stayed on at Trinity College, Cambridge, for two years before winning a Commonwealth Fund Fellowship that allowed him to study physics at Cornell. The next three years were especially significant in his life since he had nearly daily contact at Cornell with **Hans Albrecht Bethe**, Feynman, and Schwinger, three physicists who were at the forefront of research on quantum electrodynamics.

Quantum electrodynamics (QED) is a field of physics that attempts to understand the interaction between electromagnetic fields and atoms. The origins of QED go back to the research of **Paul Dirac**, **Werner Karl Heisenberg**, **Wolfgang Pauli**, and other physicists during the early 1930s. As successful as early theories of QED were, many unsolved questions and problems remained nearly two decades later. By the late 1940s, however, many of these problems had begun to yield to the analysis of Bethe, Feynman, Schwinger, and Tomonaga.

Dyson's contribution to this effort was primarily that of a synthesizer. He showed how the independent theories of his colleagues could be brought together into a single unified theory of QED. The solution that he discovered occurred to him on a bus ride from California to the East Coast in the summer of 1948. He has explained that after working on the problems for many months, he had decided to take a vacation and to stop thinking about QED. But then, returning from his vacation, the solution for which he had been looking "suddenly became, somehow, transcendentally clear. It was one of those moments of illumination . . . which every scientist hopes for. It only happens once in a lifetime, but, anyway, it did happen."

In 1951, Dyson was invited to become professor of physics at Cornell, but he remained there for only two years. He had become more interested in the philosophy of physics and spent some time with **J. Robert Oppenheimer** discussing this topic. When he had the opportunity in 1953 to move to the Institute for Advanced Studies at Princeton University, where Oppenheimer was director, he did so eagerly. He has remained at the Institute ever since; he became a naturalized United States citizen in 1957.

Works on Commercial Applications of Nuclear Power

During the 1950s, Dyson became particularly interested in the possibilities of nuclear power as a commercial source of energy. He began spending his summers at the General Atomic Company, a division of General Dynamics. This work brought him into contact with, among others, Edward Teller, father of the hydrogen bomb and another fervent advocate of the use of nuclear power. Together, the two developed a nuclear reactor called the High Temperature Graphite Reactor that they regarded as "safe even in the hands of an idiot." The model was never put into use in the United States, however, because the nuclear power industry judged the initial construction costs to be too high.

The launch of the first artificial satellite by the Soviet Union in 1957 brought an immediate and concerned response from U.S. political and scientific leaders, Dyson among them. To help keep the U.S. from falling behind the Soviets in space technology, Dyson took a leave of absence from Princeton to join a research and development effort, the Orion Project in La Jolla, California, to construct a nuclear-powered satellite. The project experienced some exciting successes early on, and Dyson later referred to his first year at La Jolla as "the most exciting and in many ways the happiest of my scientific life." The U.S. government eventually decided not to use nuclear power for its satellite systems, however, and in 1965, the Orion Project was officially terminated.

Interest in Space Exploration

One of the programs with which Dyson's name is often connected is the search for the existence of intelligent life elsewhere in the universe. He points out that, as a young boy, the books of Jules Verne and H. G. Wells were among his favorite reading material. He even tells of finding among his mother's papers, after her death, an incomplete science fiction story about travel to the moon that he had started while still a teenager, and then forgotten about. His imaginative writings about possible extraterrestrial contact include the book *Disturbing the Universe,* published in 1979. Dyson has advocated the exploration and colonization of deep space and remains a fervent backer of attempts to communicate with alien civilizations.

Dyson was elected to the National Academy of Sciences in 1964 and continues to accumulate honors and prizes, including the Lorentz Medal of the Royal Netherlands Society (1966), the Hughes Medal of the Royal Society (1968), the Max Planck Medal of the German Physical Society (1969), the Harvey Prize of the Israeli Institute of Technology (1977), and Israel's Wolf Prize (1981). Dyson married the former Verene Haefeli-Huber in 1950, and the couple had two children, Esther and George. They were divorced in 1958. Dyson then married Imme Jung, with whom he had four more children, Dorothy, Emily, Miriam, and Rebecca. Although he never earned a degree higher than the B.A., Dyson has been awarded honorary doctorates by a number of institutions, including Yeshiva University, Princeton University, and the University of Glasgow.

SELECTED WRITINGS BY DYSON:

Books

Symmetry Groups in Nuclear and Particle Physics, W. A. Benjamin, 1966.
Neutron Stars and Pulsars, Academia Naxionale dei Lincei, 1971.
Disturbing the Universe, Harper, 1979.
Values at War, University of Utah Press, 1983.
Weapons and Hope, Harper, 1984.
Origins of Life, Cambridge University Press, 1986.
Infinite in All Directions, Harper, 1988.
From Eros to Gaia, Pantheon, 1992.

SOURCES:

Books

Contemporary Authors, New Revision Series, Volume 17, Gale, 1986, pp. 126–129.
Swift, David, *SETI Pioneers,* University of Arizona Press, 1990, pp. 311–326.

—Sketch by David E. Newton

Sylvia A. Earle
1935-
American marine biologist and oceanographer

Sylvia A. Earle is a former chief scientist of the National Oceanic and Atmospheric Administration (NOAA) and a leading American oceanographer. She was among the first underwater explorers to make use of modern self-contained underwater breathing apparatus (SCUBA) gear, and identified many new species of marine life. With her former husband, Graham Hawkes, Earle designed and built a submersible craft that could dive to unprecedented depths of 3,000 feet.

Sylvia Alice (Reade) Earle was born in Gibbstown, New Jersey on August 30, 1935, the daughter of Lewis Reade and Alice Freas (Richie) Earle. Both parents had an affinity for the outdoors and encouraged her love of nature after the family moved to the west coast of Florida. As Earle explained to *Scientific American,* "I wasn't shown frogs with the attitude 'yuk,' but rather my mother would show my brothers and me how beautiful they are and how fascinating it was to look at their gorgeous golden eyes." However, Earle pointed out, while her parents totally supported her interest in biology, they also wanted her to get her teaching credentials and learn to type, "just in case."

She enrolled at Florida State University and received her Bachelor of Science degree in the spring of 1955. That fall she entered the graduate program at Duke University and obtained her master's degree in botany the following year. The Gulf of Mexico became a natural laboratory for Earle's work. Her master's dissertation, a detailed study of algae in the Gulf, is a project she still follows. She has collected more than 20,000 samples. "When I began making collections in the Gulf, it was a very different body of water than it is now—the habitats have changed. So I have a very interesting baseline," she noted in *Scientific American.*

In 1966, Earle received her Ph.D. from Duke University and immediately accepted a position as resident director of the Cape Haze Marine Laboratories in Sarasota, Florida. The following year, she moved to Massachusetts to accept dual roles as research scholar at the Radcliffe Institute and research fellow at the Farlow Herbarium, Harvard University, where she was named researcher in 1975.

Sylvia A. Earle

Earle moved to San Francisco in 1976 to become a research biologist at and curator of the California Academy of Sciences. That same year, she also was named a fellow in botany at the Natural History Museum, University of California, Berkeley.

Although her academic career could have kept her totally involved, her first love was the sea and the life within it. In 1970, Earle and four other oceanographers lived in an underwater chamber for fourteen days as part of the government-funded Tektite II Project, designed to study undersea habitats. Fortunately, technology played a major role in Earle's future. A self-contained underwater breathing apparatus had been developed in part by **Jacques Cousteau** as recently as 1943, and refined during the time Earle was involved in her scholarly research. SCUBA equipment was not only a boon to recreational divers, but it also dramatically changed the study of marine biology. Earle was one of the first researchers to don a mask and oxygen tank and observe the various forms of plant and animal habitats beneath the sea, identifying many new species of each. She called her discovery of undersea dunes off the Bahama Islands "a simple Lewis and Clark kind of observation." But, she said in *Scientific American,* "the presence of dunes was a significant insight into the formation of the area."

Creates Deep-Sea Technology

Though Earle set the unbelievable record of freely diving to a depth of 1,250 feet, there were serious depth limitations to SCUBA diving. To study deep-sea marine life would require the assistance of a submersible craft that could dive far deeper. Earle and her former husband, British-born engineer Graham Hawkes, founded Deep Ocean Technology, Inc., and Deep Ocean Engineering, Inc., in 1981, to design and build submersibles. Using a paper napkin, Earle and Hawkes rough-sketched the design for a submersible they called *Deep Rover,* which would serve as a viable tool for biologists. "In those days we were dreaming of going to thirty-five thousand feet," she told *Discover* magazine. "The idea has always been that scientists couldn't be trusted to drive a submersible by themselves because they'd get so involved in their work they'd run into things." *Deep Rover* was built and continues to operate as a mid-water machine in ocean depths ranging 3,000 feet.

In 1990, Earle was named the first woman to serve as chief scientist at the National Oceanic and Atmospheric Administration (NOAA), the agency that conducts underwater research, manages fisheries, and monitors marine spills. She left the position after eighteen months because she felt that she could accomplish more working independently of the government.

Earle, who has logged more than 6,000 hours under water, is the first to decry America's lack of research money being spent on deep-sea studies, noting that of the world's five deep-sea manned submersibles (those capable of diving to 20,000 feet or more), the U.S. has only one, the *Sea Cliff.* "That's like having one jeep for all of North America," she said in *Scientific American.* In 1993, Earle worked with a team of Japanese scientists to develop the equipment to send first a remote, then a manned submersible to 36,000 feet. "They have money from their government," she told *Scientific American.* "They do what we do not: they really make a substantial commitment to ocean technology and science." Earle also plans to lead the $10 million deep ocean engineering project, Ocean Everest, that would take her to a similar depth.

In addition to publishing numerous scientific papers on marine life, Earle is a devout advocate of public education regarding the importance of the oceans as an essential environmental habitat. She is currently the president and chief executive officer of Deep Ocean Technology and Deep Ocean Engineering in Oakland, California, as well as the coauthor of

Exploring the Deep Frontier: The Adventure of Man in the Sea.

SELECTED WRITINGS BY EARLE:

Books

(With Al Giddings) *Exploring the Deep Frontier: The Adventure of Man in the Sea,* National Geographic Press, 1980.

SOURCES:

Periodicals

Brownlee, Shannon, "Explorers of the Dark Frontiers," *Discover,* February, 1986, pp. 60–67.
Holloway, Marguerite, "Fire in Water," *Scientific American,* April, 1992, pp. 37–40.

—*Sketch by Benedict A. Leerburger*

John C. Eccles
1903-
Australian neurophysiologist

John Carew Eccles is a neurophysiologist whose research has explained how nerve cells communicate with one another. He demonstrated that when a nerve cell is stimulated it releases a chemical that binds to the membrane of neighboring cells and activates them in turn. He further demonstrated that by the same mechanism a nerve cell can also inhibit the electrical activity of nearby nerve cells. For this research, Eccles shared the 1963 Nobel Prize for Physiology or Medicine with **Alan Lloyd Hodgkin** and **Andrew Huxley**.

Born January 27, 1903 in Melbourne, Australia, Eccles was the son of William James and Mary Carew Eccles. Both of his parents were teachers, and they taught him at home until he entered Melbourne High School in 1915. In 1919, Eccles began medical studies at Melbourne University, where he participated in athletics and graduated in 1925 with the highest academic honors. Eccles's academic excellence was rewarded with a Rhodes Scholarship, which allowed him to pursue a graduate degree in England at Oxford University. In September 1925, Eccles began studies at Magdalen College, Oxford. As he had done at Melbourne, Eccles excelled academically, receiving high honors for science and being named a Christopher Welch Scholar. In 1927, he received appointment as a junior research fellow at Exeter College, Oxford.

Embarks on Neurological Research

Even before leaving Melbourne for Oxford, Eccles had decided that he wanted to study the brain and the nervous system, and he was determined to work on these subjects with **Charles Scott Sherrington**. Sherrington, who would win the Nobel Prize in 1932, was then the world's leading neurophysiologist; his research had virtually founded the field of cellular neurophysiology. The following year, after becoming a junior fellow, Eccles realized his goal and became one of Sherrington's research assistants. Although Sherrington was then nearly seventy years old, Eccles collaborated with him on some of his most important research. Together, they studied the factors responsible for inhibiting a neuron, or a nerve cell. They also explored what they termed the "motor unit"—a nerve cell which coordinates the actions of many muscle fibers. Sherrington and Eccles conducted their research without the benefit of the electronic devices that would later be developed to measure a nerve cell's electrical activity. For this work on neural excitation and inhibition, Eccles was awarded his doctorate in 1929.

Eccles remained at Exeter after receiving his doctorate, serving as a Staines Medical Fellow from 1932 to 1934. During this period, he also held posts at Magdalen College as tutor and demonstrator in physiology. The research that Eccles had begun in Sherrington's laboratory continued, but instead of describing the process of neural inhibition, Eccles became increasingly interested in explaining the process that underlies inhibition. He and other neurophysiologists believed that the transmission of electrical impulses was responsible for neural inhibition. **Bernhard Katz** and Paul Fatt would eventually demonstrate, however, that it was a chemical mechanism and not a wholly electrical phenomena which was primarily responsible for inhibiting nerve cells.

Returns to Australia

In 1937, Eccles returned to Australia to assume the directorship of the Kanematsu Memorial Institute for Pathology in Sydney. During the late 1930s and early 1940s, the Kanematsu Institute, under his guidance, became an important center for the study of neurophysiology. With Katz, Stephen Kuffler, and others, he undertook research on the activity of nerve and muscle cells in cats and frogs, studying how nerve cells communicate with muscle or motor cells. His team proposed that the binding of a chemical (now known to be the neurotransmitter acetylcholine) by the muscle cell led to a depolarization, or a loss of

electrical charge, by the muscle cell. This depolarization, Eccles believed, occurred because charged ions in the muscle cell were released into the exterior of the cell when the chemical substance released by the nerve cell was bound to the muscle cell.

During World War II, Eccles served as a medical consultant to the Australian army, where he studied vision, hearing, and other medical problems faced by pilots. Returning to full-time research and teaching in 1944, Eccles became professor of physiology at the University of Otago in Dunedin, New Zealand. At Otago, Eccles continued the research that had been interrupted by the war, but now he attempted to describe in greater detail the neural transmission event, using very fine electrodes made of glass. This research continued into the early 1950s, and it convinced Eccles that transmission from nerve cell to nerve cell or nerve cell to muscle cell occurred by a chemical mechanism, not an electrical mechanism as he had thought earlier.

In 1952, Eccles left Otago for the Australian National University in Canberra. Here, along with Fatt and J. S. Coombs, he studied the inhibitory process in postsynaptic cells, which are the nerve or muscle cells that are affected by nerve cells. They were able to establish that whether nerve and muscle cells were excited or inhibited was controlled by pores in the membrane of the cells, through which ions could enter or leave. By the late 1950s and early 1960s, Eccles had turned his attention to higher neural processes, pursuing research on neural pathways and the cellular organization of the brain.

Begins a Second Career in the United States

In 1966 Eccles turned sixty-three and university policy at the Australian National University required him to retire. Wanting to continue his research career, he accepted an invitation from the American Medical Association to become the director of its Institute for Biomedical Research in Chicago. He left that institution in 1968 to become professor of physiology and medicine and the Buswell Research Fellow at the State University of New York in Buffalo. The university constructed a laboratory for him where he could continue his research on transmission in nerves. Even at this late stage in his career, Eccles's work suggested important relationships between the excitation and inhibition of nerves and the storing and processing of information by the brain.

At age seventy-two, Eccles reluctantly reduced his heavy research schedule, but by then he had already amassed a number of scientific distinctions. He had been elected to the Royal Society of London, the Royal Society of New Zealand, and the American Academy of Arts and Sciences. In addition to the Nobel Prize, he was awarded the Gotch Memorial Prize in 1927, and the Rolleston Memorial Prize in

1932. The Royal College of Physicians presented him with their Baly Medal in 1961, the Royal Society gave him their Royal Medal in 1962, and the German Academy awarded him the Cothenius Medal in 1963. He was knighted in 1958.

In 1928, Eccles married Irene Frances Miller of New Zealand. Their marriage ended in divorce in 1968, but their union produced four sons and five daughters. One of their daughters, Rosamond, earned her doctorate and participated with her father in his research. After his divorce from Irene Eccles, Eccles married Czechoslovakian neurophysiologist Helena Tabarikova in 1968. Tabarikova also served as Eccles's collaborator in his scientific research after their marriage.

SELECTED WRITINGS BY ECCLES:

Books

Reflex Activity of the Spinal Cord, Oxford University Press, 1938.
The Neurophysiological Basis of Mind, Clarendon, 1965.
The Cerebellum as a Neuronal Machine, Springer-Verlag, 1967.
The Physiology of Nerve Cells, Johns Hopkins University Press, 1968.
The Inhibitory Pathways of the Central Nervous System, Liverpool University Press, 1969.

SOURCES:

Books

Fox, D., and M. Meldrum, editors, *Nobel Laureates in Medicine or Physiology,* Garland, 1990, pp. 145–147.
One Hundred Most Important People in the World Today, Putnam, 1970, pp. 237–40.

—-*Sketch by D. George Joseph*

J. Presper Eckert
1919-1995
American computer engineer

Electrical engineer J. Presper Eckert invented the first general-purpose electronic digital computer, called the ENIAC, with **John William Mauchly**. Further collaboration between the two engineers led

J. Presper Eckert

to the development of the first commercial digital electronic computer, the UNIVAC. Their combined efforts ushered in the commercial computer revolution in America, a revolution that continues to change the world in profound ways.

John Presper Eckert, Jr., was born on April 9, 1919, in Philadelphia, to John Presper Eckert and Ethel Hallowell Eckert. His father was a self-made millionaire businessman, whose business interests would strongly influence his son's future. Eckert was an only child and spent much of his youth building radios and other mechanical and electronic gadgets. He wanted to attend the Massachusetts Institute of Technology (MIT), but his mother, who was devoted to him, did not want him so far away from home. His father even made up a story that he could not afford MIT's tuition. So Eckert settled instead on the Moore Engineering School at the University of Pennsylvania, where, upon discovering his father's lie during his freshman year, he became very angry, which had a negative effect on his grades. But Eckert persisted at Moore, eventually earning his undergraduate degree in electrical engineering in 1941, and his master's degree in 1943. On October 28, 1944, he married Hester Caldwell, with whom he had two sons, John Presper III and Christopher. Hester died in 1952. Eckert married Judith A. Rewalt on October 13, 1962, and they had two children, Laura and Gregory.

Eckert was widely regarded as a superb engineer while at the Moore School, but he could be stubborn and his work habits were interpreted as being odd. As Robert Slater wrote in *Portraits in Silicon,* "Eckert liked to work things out orally in the presence of someone; it didn't matter whether it was a technician or a night watchman. He was highly nervous and would rarely sit in a chair or stand still while thinking. Often he would crouch on top of a desk or pace back and forth."

Invents the First General-Purpose Electronic Computer

The first of the four computers that Eckert built with Mauchly was the ENIAC (Electronic Numerical Integrator and Computer). The ENIAC was comprised of over 10,000 capacitors, 70,000 resistors, and 500,000 soldered connections. Separate wire panels defined each of its programs, which meant that operators had to change its wiring manually by turning dials, changing switches, and moving cables every time they changed to a new program. Adding to its complexity were nearly 18,000 vacuum tubes, any one of which could burn out at any time and stopped a calculation. An expert on electric organs, Eckert thought about this problem carefully. He knew that organs contained many vacuum tubes that could be used over long periods of time without burning out, and found that if he ran the computer's tubes at a low rate of power, they too would last a long time. Eckert also instituted careful standards for the computer's circuits. He designed each one individually and insisted, for the sake of simplicity, that only his circuits be used in all areas of the computer. This enabled everyone who worked on the computer to understand exactly how it worked very quickly, which minimized confusion.

At eighty feet long, eight feet high, and three feet deep, the ENIAC occupied a total of 1,800 square feet and weighed thirty tons. Although it was enormous, power hungry, and slow compared to the average personal computer of the 1990s, its calculating speed was one thousand times faster than any mechanical calculator built up to that time. ENIAC could calculate a trajectory for an artillery shell in thirty seconds, while it took a person using a mechanical desk calculator twenty hours to perform the same calculation, with the possibility of error. The ENIAC was a general-purpose computer that could add, subtract, multiply, divide, compare quantities, and extract square roots. The ENIAC did not become operational until after World War II. It passed its first full operational test on December 10, 1945, and was dedicated on February 16, 1946. In August of 1947, it was used to solve trajectory problems and compute ballistics tables at the U.S. Army's Aberdeen Proving Ground, and was later engaged in the development of the hydrogen bomb. In 1944, while working as a research associate at the Moore School, Eckert began work with Mauchly on the EDVAC (Electronic Dis-

crete Variable Automatic Computer), greatly advancing the functions of its predecessor. Completed in 1952, EDVAC had an internal memory for storing programs, used only 3,600 vacuum tubes, and took up a mere 490 square feet.

Developing the First Commercial Computer

Shortly before the end of World War II, Eckert and Mauchly, with the grudging permission of the Moore School of Engineering, began the long process of patenting the ENIAC. However, subsequent administrators at the Moore School did not like the idea of their employees applying for patents on equipment developed for U.S. government projects. In early 1946, one administrator decided that the Moore School would retain future patents on all projects developed by employees of the school. When asked to sign a form consenting to this, Eckert and Mauchly refused, and resigned in March of 1946.

Though IBM had offered Eckert a job and his own lab for developing computers, Mauchly talked him into jointly starting the Electronic Control Company. Their first work in 1946 and 1947 was with the National Bureau of Standards and the Census Bureau. They developed the specifications for a computer eventually known as the UNIVAC (Universal Automatic Computer)—the Electronic Control Co. took this as their name in 1948. Like most start-up companies developing complex hardware, Eckert and Mauchly ran into their share of financial problems, consistently underestimating the development costs for their computers. To raise money, they signed a contract in the fall of 1947 with the Northrop Aircraft Company to create a small computer for navigating airplanes—the BINAC (Binary Automatic Computer). The BINAC, completed in August, 1949, and the UNIVAC were the first computers to employ magnetic tape drives for data storage. Smaller in size and comprised of fewer parts than the ENIAC, both machines had internal memories for storing programs and could be accessed by typewriter keyboards.

Eckert and Mauchly had been kept from bankruptcy by the support of Henry Straus, an executive for the American Totalisator Company, which manufactured the odds-making machines used at race tracks. When Straus was killed in a plane crash in October, 1949, Eckert and Mauchly knew they had to sell UNIVAC. The Remington Rand Corporation acquired their company on February 1, 1950. Eckert remained in research to develop the hardware for UNIVAC, while Mauchly devoted his time to developing software applications. The first UNIVAC, delivered to the Census Bureau in March of 1951, proved its value in the 1952 presidential election between Dwight Eisenhower and Adlai Stevenson, when, less than an hour after the polls closed, it accurately predicted that Eisenhower would be the next president of the United States. Eckert and Mauchly's patent on the ENIAC was eventually challenged during an infringement suit between Sperry-Rand (formerly Remington), who now owned the rights to the computer, and Honeywell. On October 19, 1973, the court invalidated the ENIAC patent and asserted that Iowa State University professor **John Vincent Atanasoff** was the true inventor of the digital electronic computer.

Eckert received his doctorate from the University of Pennsylvania in 1964. Eckert has received 87 patents and numerous awards for his innovations, including the Howard N. Potts and John Scott Medals, both of which he shared with Mauchly, and the National Medal of Science, given to him by President Lyndon B. Johnson in 1969. He was elected to the National Academy of Engineering in 1967. Eckert remained with the Remington Rand Corporation through a number of mergers, retiring in 1989 from what eventually became UNISYS. He and his wife manage a family trust from their home in Gladwyne, Pennsylvania, and he continues to serve as a consultant to the UNISYS Corporation and to the Eckert Scientific International Corporation, based in Tokyo, Japan. Eckert died in June 1995 at age 76.

Arthur Stanley Eddington

SOURCES:

Books

Metropolis, N., and others, editors, "The ENIAC," *A History of Computing in the Twentieth Century,* Academic Press, 1980, pp. 525–39.

Shurkin, Joel, *Engines of the Mind,* Pocket Books, 1984.

Slater, Robert, *Portraits in Silicon,* MIT Press, 1987.

Stern, Nancy, *From ENIAC to UNIVAC: An Appraisal of the Eckert-Mauchly Computers,* Digital Press, 1981.

—*Sketch by Patrick Moore*

Arthur Stanley Eddington
1882-1944
English astronomer

Arthur Stanley Eddington is considered to be one of the greatest astronomers of his age. During his career he led theoretical investigations into the structure of stars and the formation of the solar system and established the mass-luminosity law, which relates a star's brightness to its mass. He explained how Cepheid variable stars, which are at the edge of stability, could exist and was one of the first to understand the importance—and implications—of Einstein's theories of relativity.

Born on December 28, 1882, at Kendal, Westmorland, England, Arthur Stanley Eddington was the son of Arthur Henry Eddington and Sarah Ann (Shout) Eddington. From 1878 to 1884, the elder Eddington was the proprietor and headmaster of Stramongate School in Kendal. Upon his death, Mrs. Eddington took young Arthur, who was just two years old, and his six-year-old sister, Winifred, to Weston-super-Mare, Somerset. Mrs. Eddington's ancestors had been north-country Quakers for seven generations, and she raised her children as Quakers.

Eddington received a first-rate education. During the day he attended Brynmelyn School, where three exceptionally gifted teachers gave him a love for natural history, fine literature, and mathematics—all of which he would use during his life to make his impact on the world. (His great knowledge of science and mathematics, mixed with the lively ability to write, would make him one of the first "popularizers" of astronomy.) In the evening he received additional instruction at home.

Enters Cambridge

Before he was sixteen years old, he won an entrance scholarship to Owen's College (now the

University of Manchester), where he had the good fortune to receive instruction from Horace Lamb in mathematics and Arthur Schuster in physics. Eddington graduated with a degree in physics in 1902 and won an entrance scholarship to Trinity College in Cambridge, where he distinguished himself in mathematics. (Mathematician **Alfred North Whitehead** was one of his teachers.) He was at the head of his class in 1904, became the first second-year student to achieve the coveted position of "First Wrangler," and graduated in only three years, receiving his degree in 1905.

Following his graduation, Eddington was appointed chief assistant at the Royal Observatory at Greenwich. During the next seven years, from 1906 to 1913, he received extensive training in practical astronomy. He also made two long voyages; the first, in 1906, was to Malta, where he determined the latitude of the geodetic station there; the second was to Brazil, in 1912, where he was the leader of an expedition to observe a total solar eclipse. Returning to Cambridge after the eclipse expedition, Eddington became Plumian Professor of Astronomy and the director of the observatory. He remained there for the next thirty-one years.

During his career at Greenwich, his investigations into theoretical astronomy made Eddington the leader in astronomical research. His first topic of investigation was the proper (actual) motion of the stars through the sky. He also examined the distribution of stars of different spectral classes, observed planetary and gaseous nebulae, and studied open star clusters and globular clusters.

Eddington's first book, *Stellar Movements and the Structure of the Universe* (1914), a collection of fifteen papers, is considered to be a paradigm of clear scientific discourse. In it he summarized the celestial knowledge of his era, defined the most pressing problems facing astronomy, and stated his personal preference that the spiral nebulae were not a part of the Milky Way, but located far outside our galaxy. (Time proved this belief correct.) In the final chapter, called "Dynamics of the Stellar System," Eddington set the stage for the founding of a very important branch of research.

The Investigation into Stars

Eddington's major contribution to astronomy began in 1916, when he chose to penetrate deep into stars and attempt to determine what kept them from collapsing under their own force of gravity. He also hoped to establish how stellar energy was transported to the surface of celestial bodies. Astronomers had been plagued for years over the question of how a star could be a stable object. Since it was nothing more than a big ball of gas, why didn't all stars collapse and become white dwarf stars?

Eddington determined that three forces had to be taken into account: gravitation, gas pressure, and the pressure of radiation. He hypothesized that the inward crush of gravitation is offset by the pressure of the gases within the star and the force of stellar energy radiating outward. The concept of radiation force was very controversial: Scientists had believed that convection forces were responsible for stellar energy, but Eddington, using his radiation theory, established his own equation showing how stars maintained stability.

Eddington suggested that gravitational pull increases as one moves further toward the center of a star; hence, he hypothesized, radiation pressure moving outward must increase in order for a star to maintain stability. The only way for an increase in radiation pressure to occur would be if the star's temperature was greater toward the center of the star. Therefore, the hottest region of the star had to be closest to its core, where the temperature would reach into the millions of degrees. As **Hans Bethe** would show later, temperatures of great magnitude were required to initiate the nuclear fusion that powered the stars. As the pressure, radiation and temperature increased, so did the star's luminosity (brightness). From this, Eddington determined his mass-luminosity law in 1924. The relation between these two factors makes it possible to estimate the mass of a star based on its luminosity.

For stars with more mass than the sun, the increase in radiation pressure was remarkable. Eddington concluded that very few stars could exist if they were more than ten times the mass of the sun, and it would be *very* rare for a star with fifty times the sun's mass to exist; it would have so much radiation pressure, the star would be blown apart. Although there are extremely large stars, as far as *volume* goes, they are comprised of rarefied gasses which do not exceed Eddington's limit for *mass*. Cepheid variable stars (stars which pulse, physically changing their diameter), are at the very limit of stability, and Eddington devised a theoretical explanation for their behavior that is still accepted at present.

After applying his calculations to Sirius B, a companion star of Sirius (*Canis majoris*), Eddington, in the summer of 1920, calculated the diameters of several red giant stars. That December he received a letter from **George Ellery Hale**, one of the founders of astrophysics. The correspondence, part of which is reprinted in the *Dictionary of Scientific Biography,* conveyed that a measurement of the red supergiant star Betelgeuse, in Orion (Orionis), was "in close agreement with your theoretical value and probably correct within about ten percent." This was confirmation that Eddington's calculations were more than just "theory."

A Side Effect Affects the Solar System

An unexpected side effect to Eddington's work was how it affected the two main theories regarding the origin of the solar system. On one side of the question was **Thomas C. Chamberlin**, who held that, following the collapse of the rotating cloud which formed the sun, the material that remained behind accumulated into planets. On the other side was Sir James Jeans, who believed that a star had passed close to the sun eons ago. The gravitational pull of this star had drawn material out of the sun which condensed into planets.

Eddington's theory suggested that the material within the sun was under such great pressure, that had it been drawn out it would have exploded violently, not condensed. Jeans was not pleased to have his theory debunked, especially by such an illustrious man as Eddington, and a strong professional enmity developed between the two.

When World War I broke out, Eddington received an exemption as a conscientious objector because of his Quaker beliefs. While the war raged, he single-handedly finished transit observations to complete the zodiacal catalogue. In the meantime, another uproar had been unleashed; this one was the result of the work of **Albert Einstein**, who had published his general theory of relativity in 1915. (The special theory of relativity had been issued in 1905.)

Eddington and Einstein

Einstein's theories have been listed among the greatest intellectual achievements of the twentieth century. When first proposed, there were very few practical applications for them. More recently, however, the theories have become paramount in understanding such phenomena as quasars, pulsars and black holes. Eddington was one of the few people who could not only understand Einstein's theories but also realize their implications. He immersed himself in the study of the "new" mathematics, learned absolute differential calculus, became an expert in the use of tensors, and proceeded to develop his own concepts of relativity. His "Report on the Theory of Gravitation," issued in 1918, was the first comprehensive account of general relativity written in English. (Eddington would introduce an entire generation of adults and children to Einstein, making the difficult concepts comprehensible. Einstein considered Eddington's 1923 book, *Mathematical Theory of Relativity,* the finest presentation of relativity in any language.)

The theories of relativity went far beyond Isaac Newton's laws of gravitation, and there was considerable controversy surrounding them. Einstein himself suggested three, and only three, observational tests to verify his theories—all of which had to do with astronomical phenomena. These included two gravitational effects on starlight, involving both a stretching of starlight waves called the redshift effect and a bending of the waves as they traveled through space. The third proof involved the hypothesis that Mercu-

ry's perihelion—the point where the planet would be closest to the sun—would continually advance.

According to Einstein, relativity would cause Mercury's perihelion to advance a tiny bit more than what Newton's law of gravity expected. Since the predicted amount was a minuscule 43 arc-seconds, it would take about 30,000 years for the axis of Mercury's orbit to make a complete rotation. With that kind of time frame, it seemed unlikely that such a tiny measurement could be made, yet discrepancies in Mercury's orbit had been noticed, and Einstein's prediction accounted for what was observed.

The investigation was on to verify Einstein's two other tests. In a paper smuggled out of Germany during World War I, Einstein suggested an excellent, and rare, opportunity for an experiment; a total eclipse of the sun on May 29, 1919, would permit a test for the bending of starlight by gravity. During the brief period of totality, stars would be visible near the sun's position. As the starlight passed the sun, the sun's gravitational attraction should cause the light to bend. Unfortunately, the eclipse would not be visible from Europe or North America. As is often the case, the observers would have to travel a considerable distance to observe it, and travel conditions in 1919 were only for the adventurous.

Realizing that local weather conditions at the eclipse site would be a major concern, Eddington organized not one, but two expeditions to observe the eclipse—one on the island of Principe, off the coast of West Africa, and the second across the Atlantic Ocean at Sobral, in North Brazil. The weather at both sites was frustratingly troublesome, but each expedition was able to take some photographs of the sky. These were compared with photographs of the same area of the sky which had been made at another time of the year, obviously when the sun was nowhere near.

Starlight near the sun during the eclipse was, indeed, displaced, and the shift agreed with the theory of relativity's prediction. This resulted in making Einstein a celebrity around the globe, although Eddington, in a second edition of his book, warned the theory still had not met the test of the gravitational redshift.

To understand the redshift of light, consider sound waves: When an automobile drives by, sounding its horn, a noticeable change in pitch is heard because the sound waves are stretched out. Einstein predicted that gravity would stretch out light waves. As the waves were lengthened, a shift in color, toward the low (red) end of the spectrum, would be observed.

In order to provide the third proof for Einstein's theory, Eddington observed Sirius B, which had qualities which would made it a likely candidate for redshifting. Eddington wrote to W. A. Adams at the Mount Wilson Observatory and asked him to make a measurement of the spectrum of Sirius B. Adams immediately set to work and eventually was able to obtain a measurement in 1924 that closely matched prediction. The test of gravitational redshift was not only the third confirmation of Einstein's theories, it also verified density measures which Eddington had determined for Sirius B.

During the years, Eddington published extensively. His works include *The Nature of the Physical World* (1928), *The Expanding Universe* (1933), *New Pathways in Science* (1935), and *The Philosophy of Physical Science* (1939). Although some of these books had ponderous titles, all were written in an extremely lively, imaginative, and humorous manner, introducing new ideas and new ways of thinking. During his last years he threw all his energy into realizing his dream: calling it "Bottom's dream," it was nothing less than the unification of quantum physics and relativity. This is a topic that has yet to be resolved.

In the autumn of 1944, Eddington underwent a major surgical procedure from which he did not recover. He was only 61 years old when he died on November 22. Devoting his life to the advancement of knowledge, he had never married. (When he moved into the Cambridge Observatory House in 1913, be brought his mother and sister along.) His genius had been honored the world over; he had been elected to the Royal Astronomical Society in 1906 and the Royal Society in 1914. He received honoraria from many universities and was knighted in 1930, but his greatest honor was receiving the Order of Merit in 1938. In the same year he became president of the International Astronomical Union. Following his death an annual Eddington Memorial Lectureship was created, and the Eddington Medal was struck for annual presentation.

In 1945 astrophysicist **Edward Arthur Milne** wrote, as noted in the *Dictionary of Scientific Biography,* that Eddington brought the understanding of the structure of stars "all to life, infusing it with his sense of real physics and endowing it with aspects of splendid beauty.... Eddington will always be our incomparable pioneer." Judged in today's light, many of Eddington's great advances in understanding the structure of stars may seem very elementary. But for his day they were revolutionary.

SELECTED WRITINGS BY EDDINGTON:

Books

Stellar Movements and the Structure of the Universe, Macmillan, 1914.
Report on the Relativity Theory of Gravitation, Fleetway Press, 1918.
Space, Time, and Gravitation, Cambridge University Press, 1920.

The Mathematical Theory of Relativity, Cambridge University Press, 1923.
The Internal Constitution of the Stars, Cambridge University Press, 1926.
Stars and Atoms, Yale University Press, 1927.
The Nature of the Physical World, Macmillan, 1928.
Science and the Unseen World, Macmillan, 1929.
The Expanding Universe, Macmillan, 1933.
New Pathways in Science, Cambridge University Press, 1935.
Relativity Theory of Protons and Electrons, Macmillan, 1936.
The Philosophy of Physical Science, Macmillan, 1939.
Fundamental Theory, Edmund T. Whittaker, editor, Cambridge University Press, 1946.

SOURCES:

Books

Abbott, David, *Biographical Dictionary of Scientists, Astronomers,* Peter Bedrick, 1984.
Abell, George, et al, *Exploration of the Universe,* 6th Edition, Saunders College Press, 1991.
Gillispie, Charles Coulston, editor, *Dictionary of Scientific Biography,* Scribner, 1971.

—Sketch by Raymond E. Bullock

Gerald M. Edelman
1929-
American biochemist

For his "discoveries concerning the chemical structure of antibodies," Gerald M. Edelman and his associate **Rodney Porter** received the 1972 Nobel Prize in physiology or medicine. During a lecture Edelman gave upon acceptance of the prize, he stated that immunology "provokes unusual ideas, some of which are not easily come upon through other fields of study.... For this reason, immunology will have a great impact on other branches of biology and medicine." He was to prove his own prediction correct by using his discoveries to draw conclusions not only about the immune system but about the nature of consciousness as well.

Born in New York City on July 1, 1929, to Edward Edelman, a physician, and Anna Freedman

Gerald M. Edelman

Edelman, Gerald Maurice Edelman attended New York City public schools through high school. After graduating, he entered Ursinus College, in Collegeville, Pennsylvania, where he received his B.S. in chemistry in 1950. Four years later, he earned an M.D. degree from the University of Pennsylvania's Medical School, spending a year as medical house officer at Massachusetts General Hospital.

In 1955 Edelman joined the United States Army Medical Corps, practicing general medicine while stationed at a hospital in Paris. There, Edelman benefited from the heady atmosphere surrounding the Sorbonne, where future Nobel laureates **Jacques Lucien Monod** and **François Jacob** were originating a new study, molecular biology. Following his 1957 discharge from the Army, Edelman returned to New York City to take a position at Rockefeller University studying under Henry Kunkel. Kunkel, with whom Edelman would conduct his Ph.D. research, was examining the unique flexibility of antibodies at the time.

Performs Studies on Immunoglobulins

Antibodies are produced in response to infection in order to work against diseases in diverse ways. They form a class of large blood proteins called globulins—more specifically, immunoglobulins—made in the body's lymph tissues. Each immunoglobulin is specifically directed to recognize and incapaci-tate one antigen, the chemical signal of an infection. Yet they all share a very similar structure.

Through the 1960s and 1970s, a debate raged between two schools of scientists to explain the situation whereby antibodies share so many characteristics yet are able to perform many different functions. In one camp, **George Wells Beadle** and **Edward Lawrie Tatum** argued that despite the remarkable diversity displayed by each antibody, each immunoglobulin must be coded for by a single gene. This has been referred to as the "one gene, one protein" theory. But, argued the opposing camp, led by the Australian physician, Sir **Frank Macfarlane Burnet**, if each antibody required its own code within the deoxyribonucleic acid (DNA)), the body's master plan of protein structure, the immune system alone would take up all the possible codes offered by the human DNA.

Both camps generated theories, but Edelman eventually disagreed with both sides of the debate, offering a third possibility for antibody synthesis in 1967. Though not recognized at the time because of its radical nature, the theory he and his associate, Joseph Gally, proposed would later be confirmed as essentially correct. It depended on the vast diversity that can come from chance in a system as complex as the living organism. Each time a cell divided, they theorized, tiny errors in the transcription—or reading of the code—could occur, yielding slightly different proteins upon each misreading. Edelman and Gally proposed that the human body turns the advantage of this variability in immunoglobulins to its own ends. Many strains of antigens when introduced into the body modify the shape of the various immunoglobulins in order to prevent the recurrence of disease. This is why many illnesses provide for their own cure—why humans can only get chicken pox once, for instance.

But the proof of their theory would require advances in the state of biochemical techniques. Research in the 1950s and 1960s was hampered by the difficulty in isolating immunoglobulins. The molecules themselves are comparatively large, too large to be investigated by the chemical means then available. Edelman and Rodney Porter, with whom Edelman was to be honored with the Nobel Prize, sought methods of breaking immunoglobulins into smaller units that could more profitably be studied. Their hope was that these fragments would retain enough of their properties to provide insight into the functioning of the whole.

Porter became the first to split an immunoglobulin, obtaining an "active fragment" from rabbit blood as early as 1950. Porter believed the immunoglobulin to be one long continuous molecule made up of 1,300 amino acids—the building blocks of proteins. But Edelman could not accept this conclusion, noting that even insulin, with its 51 amino acids, was made up of two shorter strings of amino acid chains working as a unit. His doctoral thesis investigated several methods of splitting immunoglobulin molecules, and, after receiving his Ph.D. in 1960 he remained at Rockefeller as a faculty member, continuing his research.

Porter's method of splitting the molecules used enzymes that acted as chemical knives, breaking apart amino acids. In 1961 Edelman and his colleague, M. D. Poulik succeeded in splitting IgG—one of the most studied varieties of immunoglobulin in the blood—into two components by using a method known as "reductive cleavage." The technique allowed them to divide IgG into what are known as light and heavy chains. Data from their experiments and from those of the Czech researcher, Frantisek Franek, established the intricate nature of the antibody's "active sight." The sight occurs at the folding of the two chains which forms a unique pocket to trap the antigen. Porter combined these findings with his, and, in 1962, announced that the basic structure of IgG had been determined. Their experiments set off a flurry of research into the nature of antibodies in the 1960s. Information was shared throughout the scientific community in a series of informal meetings referred to as "Antibody Workshops," taking place across the globe. Edelman and Porter dominated the discussions, and their work led the way to a wave of discoveries.

Still, a key drawback to research remained. In any naturally obtained immunoglobulin sample a mixture of ever so slightly different molecules would reduce the overall purity. Based on a crucial finding by Kunkel in the 1950s, Porter and Edelman concentrated their study on myelomas, cancers of the immunoglobulin-producing cells, exploiting the unique nature of these cancers. Kunkel had determined that since all the cells produced by these cancerous myelomas were descended from a common ancestor they would produce a homogeneous series of antibodies. A pure sample could be isolated for experimentation. Porter and Edelman studied the amino acid sequence in subsections of different myelomas, and in 1965, as Edelman would later describe it: "Mad as we were, [we] started on the whole molecule." The project, completed in 1969, determined the order of all 1,300 amino acids present in the protein, the longest sequence determined at that time.

Knowledge of Immune System Shapes Research into Brain Activity

Throughout the 1970s, Edelman continued his research, expanding it to include other substances that stimulate the immune system, but by the end of the decade the principle he and Poulik uncovered led him to conceive a radical theory of how the brain works.

Just as the structurally limited immune system must deal with myriad invading organisms, the brain must process vastly complex sensory data with a theoretically limited number of switches, or neurons.

Rather than an incoming sensory signal triggering a predetermined pathway through the nervous system, Edelman theorized that it leads to a selection from among several choices. That is, rather than seeing the nervous system as a relatively fixed biological structure, Edelman envisioned it as a fluid system based on three interrelated stages of functioning.

In the formation of the nervous system, cells receiving signals from others surrounding them fan out like spreading ivy—not to predetermined locations, but rather to regions determined by the concert of these local signals. The signals regulate the ultimate position of each cell by controlling the production of a cellular glue in the form of cell-adhesion molecules. They anchor neighboring groups of cells together. Once established, these cellular connections are fixed, but the exact pattern is different for each individual.

The second feature of Edelman's theory allows for an individual response to any incoming signal. A specific pattern of neurons must be made to recognize the face of one's grandmother, for instance, but the pattern is different in every brain. While the vast complexity of these connections allows for some of the variability in the brain, it is in the third feature of the theory that Edelman made the connection to immunology. The neural networks are linked to each other in layers. An incoming signal passes through and between these sheets in a specific pathway. The pathway, in this theory, ultimately determines what the brain experiences, but just as the immune system modifies itself with each new incoming virus, Edelman theorized that the brain modifies itself in response to each new incoming signal. In this way, Edelman sees all the systems of the body being guided in one unified process, a process that depends on organization but that accommodates the world's natural randomness.

Dr. Edelman has received honorary degrees from a number of universities, including the University of Pennsylvania, Ursinus College, Williams College, and others. Besides his Nobel Prize, his other academic awards include the Spenser Morris Award, the Eli Lilly Prize of the American Chemical Society, Albert Einstein Commemorative Award, California Institute of Technology's Buchman Memorial Award, and the Rabbi Shai Schaknai Memorial Prize.

A member of many academic organizations, including New York and National Academy of Sciences, American Society of Cell Biologists, Genetics Society, American Academy of Arts and Sciences, and the American Philosophical Society, Dr. Edelman is also one of the few international members of the Academy of Sciences, Institute of France. In 1974 he became a Vincent Astor Distinguished Professor, serving on the board of governors of the Weizmann Institute of Science and is also a trustee of the Salk Institute for Biological Studies. Dr. Edelman married Maxine Morrison on June 11, 1950. They have two sons, Eric and David, and a daughter, Judith.

SELECTED WRITINGS BY EDELMAN:

Books

Cellular Selection and Regulation in the Immune Response, Raven Press, 1974.
Molecular Machinery of the Membrane, Massachusetts Institute of Technology Press, 1975.
(With V. B. Mountcastle) *The Mindful Brain: Cortical Organization and the Group-Selective Theory of Higher Brain Function,* Massachusetts Institute of Technology Press, 1978.
(With E. Gall and W. Cowan) *Dynamic Aspects of Neocortical Function,* Wiley, 1985.
(With Gall and Cowan) *Molecular Basis of Neural Development,* Wiley, 1985.
Neural Darwinism: The Theory of Neuronal Group Selection, Basic Books, 1987.

Periodicals

"The Structure and Function of Antibodies," *Scientific American,* August, 1970, pp. 34–42.
"Cell Adhesion Molecules," *Science,* February 4, 1983, pp. 450–57.
"Cell-Adhesion Molecules: A Molecular Basis for Animal Form," *Scientific American,* April, 1984, pp. 118–129.

SOURCES:

Books

Biographical Encyclopedia of Scientists, Facts on File, 1981.
Nobel Prize Winners, H. W. Wilson, 1987.

Periodicals

New Yorker, January 10, 1983.
Science, October 27, 1972, pp. 384–86.

—*Sketch by Nicholas Williamson*

Harold Edgerton
1903-1990
American inventor and electrical engineer

Harold Edgerton, an inventor who developed the strobe light and multiflash photography, was responsible for revolutionizing the art of picture taking in the twentieth century. He held over forty patents for inventions related to seeing the unseen, including high-speed camera equipment, sonar probes, and underwater lighting devices. While his inventions earned him the respect and admiration of his engineering colleagues, he is perhaps best known by the public for his photographs. The high-speed filming techniques he developed made it possible for him to freeze the action of such things as a bullet passing through an apple and a drop of milk as it splashes and forms a coronet.

Harold Eugene Edgerton was born on April 6, 1903, in Fremont, Nebraska, to Frank Eugene and Mary Nettie Coe Edgerton. One of his early childhood memories, recounted in his personal foreword to *Stopping Time: The Photographs of Harold Edgerton* by Estelle Jussim, is of designing and building a searchlight on the porch of his house. He was only ten, and already he had begun to experiment with the way in which optics control beams of light. As a child Edgerton moved several times during his first twelve years before settling in Aurora, Nebraska. There, while he was in junior high school, he bought his first camera, a postcard-folding Kodak. An uncle from Iowa had kindled his enthusiasm for photography and Edgerton had even set up a darkroom in his mother's kitchen. With his first camera, he had hoped to photograph a ham radio station he had assembled, but expectations were soon tempered by the reality of lighting problems. Most of his early photographs were badly underexposed. He began at this time to explore existing methods for illuminating photographic subjects. By the mid–1920s he would combine his knowledge about illumination with another keen interest, electric engines.

During his summers Edgerton worked for the Nebraska Power and Light Company in his hometown. In 1925 he completed his bachelor of science degree at the University of Nebraska, in the field of electrical engineering. He took a job with the General Electric Company in Schenectady, New York, analyzing the performance of large rotating motors. A year later he enrolled in the graduate program in electrical engineering at the Massachusetts Institute of Technology (MIT). As a young graduate student he wanted to study the action of rotors inside electrical engines, but because they whirled around so quickly they were seemingly impossible to observe. Edgerton determined that if he could control a light that flashed at a speed matching that of the engine's rotation, he could make the rotors appear to stand still.

Pioneers Flash Photography and Strobe Lighting

In 1926 Edgerton began experimenting with his first flashing light machine or "stroboscope," to capture the action of rotor blades. The stroboscope contained gas discharge tubes that emitted light when subjected to high voltage pulses. The tube in his first machines contained mercury vapor, but eventually Edgerton discovered that xenon and other rare gases were the most effective at producing bright light. The stroboscope was safe and reliable, a welcome replacement for the explosive and difficult-to-control flash powders and chemical flashbulbs used by early twentieth-century photographers to produce rapid bursts of light.

In 1927 Edgerton completed his M.S. in electrical engineering and in 1928 he accepted a position as instructor at MIT. He was to remain affiliated with MIT academically for the rest of his career. Edgerton's research with strobe lights and engines continued, and in 1931 he received his D.Sc. from MIT. By then his strobe was capable of producing an intermittent light that flashed repeatedly, on the command of the operator, at one-millionth of a second. Introduced for industrial use in the early 1930s, the strobe soon became an essential analytical tool. It was employed in factories to analyze the revolution rate of high-speed revolving machinery and had especially important textile and automotive industry applications. By 1932 Edgerton began seeking a patent on the invention. Litigation prevented him from receiving the patent until 1949. Meanwhile, he had accepted a position at MIT as assistant professor in 1932. By 1948 he became a full professor and in 1966 he was awarded the prestigious title of Institute Professor.

Following the invention of the stroboscope, Edgerton went on to develop high-speed cameras. He collaborated with two colleagues, Kenneth Germeshausen and Herbert E. Grier. Together they produced an electrical contactor that made it possible to synchronize a flashing light with film as it moved through a motion picture camera. By 1934 it was possible with their technology to photograph six thousand frames per second. The normal speed with which film travels through a camera is twenty-four frames per second. Their invention revolutionized cinematography. In 1940 Edgerton went to Hollywood to demonstrate high speed cinematography to Metro-Goldwyn-Mayer (MGM) Studios. There he collaborated on an Academy Award-winning short, *Quicker Than a Wink.*

A year before Edgerton's Hollywood debut, the U.S. Army Air Force commissioned him to design a strobe lamp for use in nighttime aerial photography.

During World War II Edgerton's lamp was employed on reconnaissance missions, including those that preceded the Normandy invasion by the Allied forces. In 1944 Edgerton served in Europe as a technical representative for the air force, and in 1946 he was awarded the Medal of Freedom from the War Department. After the war, in 1947, he and his two engineering partners formed a company called Edgerton, Germeshausen and Grier. In 1950 the company designed a camera shutter that had no moving mechanical parts, opening the way for high-speed still photography at exposure times as short as one ten-millionth of a second.

Achieves Recognition As Artist and Explorer

In the early 1930s Edgerton began to take photographs of things that move faster than the human eye can follow. The thirties and forties saw his first exhibits in art galleries and museums. Over the years his high-speed, freeze-action photos have appeared in magazines such as *Life* and *National Geographic,* and in many of the most prominent photography and art galleries and science institutions around the world. During his photographic career Edgerton captured subjects as diverse as athletes and dancers in motion, birds in flight, liquids splashing, dynamite, and even atomic bombs at their first moment of explosion. He also froze for the camera images of bullets piercing such targets as light bulbs, fruit, and Plexiglas.

In 1953 the National Geographic Society sponsored research by Edgerton on underwater electronic flashtubes and camera equipment. That year Edgerton began what was to be a lifelong association with the French undersea explorer **Jacques Cousteau**. The two men traveled together aboard the *Calypso,* Cousteau's research vessel, on expeditions that explored the Mediterranean, Lake Titicaca in the Andes Mountains, and the Caribbean. Edgerton developed underwater lighting equipment and sonar scanners for Cousteau, as well as for the Woods Hole Oceanographic Institution and other exploration teams. In 1961 he created a sonar device that could generate a continuous seismic profile of the ocean floor. In 1968 with the aid of his sonar technology, explorers located the *Mary Rose,* a sunken English warship from the time of Henry VIII. In 1973 Edgerton joined an expedition to locate the USS *Monitor,* a Civil War battleship sunk in 1862 off Cape Hatteras, North Carolina. Together Edgerton and Cousteau located the HMS *Britannic,* the twin ship to the *Titanic,* in 1975. In 1976 Edgerton accompanied a team on an unsuccessful search for the Loch Ness monster in Scotland. His Edgerton-Benthos camera was used in 1986 to photograph the sunken *Titanic,* found off the shore of Nova Scotia.

Edgerton was highly decorated for his technological and artistic achievements by engineering and industrial societies, museums and aquariums, photographic organizations, and explorer groups. In 1973 President Nixon awarded him the National Medal of Science. He was inducted into the National Inventors Hall of Fame in 1986.

Edgerton married Esther May Garrett in 1928. Together they had three children, Mary, born in 1931; William, born in 1933; and Robert, born in 1935. In 1968 Edgerton retired from teaching and became Institute Professor emeritus at MIT. He remained active in research and exploration until the last few months of his life. He died in Cambridge, Massachusetts, on January 4, 1990, at the age of eighty-seven.

SELECTED WRITINGS BY EDGERTON:

Books

(With James Killian, Jr.) *Flash! Seeing the Unseen by Ultra High-Speed Photography,* 2nd edition, Charles T. Branford, 1954.
Electronic Flash, Strobe, 2nd edition, MIT Press, 1979.
(With Killian) *Moments of Vision: The Stroboscopic Revolution in Photography,* MIT Press, 1979.
Sonar Images, Prentice Hall, 1986.

Periodicals

"Hummingbird in Action," *National Geographic,* 1948.

SOURCES:

Books

Dalton, Stephen, *Split Second: The World of High-Speed Photography,* J. M. Dent, 1983.
Jussim, Estelle, *Stopping Time: The Photographs of Harold Edgerton,* Harry N. Abrams, 1987.

Periodicals

Torrey, Lee, "Harold Edgerton: Inventor and Photographic Wizard," *New Scientist,* Volume 25, October, 1979, 264–67.
Trupp, Phil, "Profile: Dr. Harold Edgerton," *Sport Diver,* May-June, 1981.

Other

"Edgerton and His Incredible Seeing Machines," PBS *Nova* series, 1985.

—*Sketch by Leslie Reinherz*

Tilly Edinger
1897-1967
German-born American paleontologist

Tilly Edinger is credited as one of the originators of the field of paleoneurology, the study of the brain through fossil remains. She conducted the first systematic studies of the brain in fossil vertebrates, which led her to challenge the then popular conception of evolution as a unilinear process modeled upon the eighteenth- and nineteenth-century concept of a chain of being. Edinger made an important contribution to the notion of a branching process of evolution that is generally accepted today.

Tilly Edinger was born Johanna Gabrielle Ottelie in Frankfurt am Main, Germany, November 13, 1897, to independently wealthy parents, Ludwig E. and Anna Goldschmidt Edinger. She was the youngest of three children. Her parents were both prominent citizens of Frankfurt. Her father was a respected medical researcher who was key in developing the field of comparative neurology, and had a street, Edingerstrasse, named in his honor. Her mother, from a line of bankers, was active in social welfare groups, and was honored by the town with a bust in the town park. Edinger grew up with a respect for geology and comparative neurology, both of which were to influence her own career in the sciences.

Edinger attended the Universities of Heidelberg and Munich from 1916 to 1918. In 1921, she received her doctorate in natural philosophy from University of Frankfurt, for studies in geology, zoology, and psychology, with her dissertation on the cranium (brain) of the fossil reptile Nothosaurus. She then worked as a research assistant in paleontology there, from the year she earned her degree until 1927.

Edinger's remaining years in Germany—1927 to 1938—were spent as the curator of fossil vertebrates at the Senckenberg Museum in Frankfurt. Edinger received no pay for this work. She published the groundbreaking study, *Die fossilen Gehirne* ("Fossil Brains") in 1929. Because of the increasingly hostile climate in Germany with the rise of the Nazis, Edinger, who was Jewish, left Germany in May of 1939 to go to London, where she worked as a translator.

Re-examines Evolution

Edinger came to the United States in 1940 and became a naturalized citizen in 1945. At that time, Harvard University had set aside funds to provide employment for displaced European scholars. Edinger took advantage of this opportunity; she settled in

Massachusetts and joined the staff of Harvard's Museum of Comparative Zoology as a research associate. She continued her studies of the fossil brain, and began to challenge the commonly held notion that evolution consisted of a linear progression from "lower" animals, such as rats and mice, up to the "highest" creatures, human beings. Edinger instead developed and advanced the idea of evolution as a complex branching process. She left Harvard to serve as an instructor in zoology at Wellesley College from 1944 to 1945. Then she resumed her work at Harvard, producing the major work, *Evolution of the Horse Brain,* and becoming a full-fledged research paleontologist, both in 1948. She would remain at the Museum for the rest of her life.

Edinger established the need for direct study of fossil brains by using casts made from the cranial cavities of mammals, since brain tissue cannot fossilize. Casts of the inside of the skull allow experts to reconstruct a reasonable facsimile of the brain, which ultimately impacted the study of the evolution of intelligence. Edinger's studies of the enlargement of the forebrain in the horse established that the rate of evolution varies for different lineages, and that as mammals adapt to different environments, the parts of the brain interact differently. Edinger's was the first strong voice in favor of a branching model of evolution, and the prototype she advanced is generally accepted today.

Both the Guggenheim Foundation and the American Association of University Women assisted Edinger in her work through fellowships. She received many honorary degrees, including doctorates from Wellesley College in 1950, the University of Giessen in 1957, and the University of Frankfurt in 1964. From 1963 to 1964 she also served as president of the Society of Vertebrate Paleontology.

Edinger died on May 27, 1967, after being struck by an automobile near her home in Cambridge the day before.

SELECTED WRITINGS BY EDINGER:

Books

Die fossilen Gehirne, Verlag, 1929.
Evolution of the Horse Brain, Geological Society of America, Memoir 25, 1948.
(With A. S. Romer, N. E. Wright, and R. Frank) *Bibliography of Fossil Vertebrates, Exclusive of North America, 1509–1927,* two volumes, Geological Society of America, Memoir 87, 1962.

Periodicals

"Paleoneurology, 1804–1966: An Annotated Bibliography," *Advances in Anatomy, Embryology and Cell Biology,* 49, parts 1–6, 1975.

SOURCES:

Books

Gould, S. J., *Notable American Women: The Modern Period,* edited by B. Sicherman and C. H. Green, Harvard University Press, 1980, pp. 218–219.
Kass-Simon, G., and P. Farnes, *Women of Science: Righting the Record,* Indiana University Press, 1990, p. 60.

Periodicals

Romer, A. S., "Tilly Edinger," *Society of Vertebrate Paleontology News Bulletin,* no. 81, 1967, pp. 51–53.

　　　　　　　　　　　—Sketch by Sharon F. Suer

Thomas Alva Edison
1847-1931
American inventor

Thomas Alva Edison's nickname, "The Wizard of Menlo Park," reflects his amazing inventive talent. Over his lifetime, more than 1300 patents were issued in his name, far more than have been credited to any other individual in American history. Among the best known of his inventions are a stock-ticker machine, the incandescent light bulb, an automatic telegraphy machine, the phonograph, and the motion picture machine. Edison's one major accomplishment in scientific research was the discovery of the emission of electrons from a heated cathode, a phenomenon now known as the Edison effect.

Thomas Alva Edison was born in Milan, Ohio, on February 11, 1847. He was the seventh and youngest child of Samuel Ogden Edison, Jr., and the former Nancy Elliott. Edison's parents had met in Canada, where the family had moved after the Revolutionary War. Sam Edison, in turn, had fled Canada in 1837 when an insurrection against the government in which he was involved failed. He established a successful grain and lumber business in Milan that allowed him to bring his wife and four children to the United States in 1839. Eight years later, Thomas Alva was born.

Disaster struck Milan in 1854 when a new railroad line bypassed the city and isolated it from commercial traffic. Before long, eight percent of the city's population had left the area, including the

Thomas Alva Edison

Edison family. Samuel Edison relocated his family to Port Huron, Michigan, began again, and established a grain and lumber business that was soon very successful. In Port Huron, young Thomas began his education in a one-room school taught by the Reverend G. B. Engle and his wife. That schooling was to last only a few months, however, because young Tom heard Mrs. Engle refer to him as "addled." She had apparently become convinced that Tom's impatience with formal schooling was a sign of mental inferiority. Furious at her son's report of this remark, Nancy Edison withdrew him from school and from that point on, provided for his education at home.

Carries Out Chemical Experiments at Home

Nancy Edison introduced her son to natural philosophy, a mixture of physics, chemistry, and other sciences, among other subjects. Before long, Tom became fascinated with chemistry in particular and built a chemical laboratory in a corner of the cellar. By the age of ten, he was conducting various original experiments in his home.

Edison's entrepreneurial spirit became apparent while he was still quite young. He obtained permission to ride the train that ran between Port Huron and Detroit, selling newspapers and magazines, candy, apples, sandwiches, molasses, peanuts, tobacco, and other materials along the way. During the layover in Detroit, Edison spent his time at the city's public library. Writing about these experiences later, he said,

"I didn't read a few books. I read the library." Over time, Edison expanded his activities on the train, receiving permission to use an empty part of the baggage car to set up first a small chemistry laboratory and later a printing press on which he printed a small newspaper.

Begins to Lose His Hearing

It was on one of the early train runs that a famous event occurred that affected Edison's future life. While Edison was running to catch the train, one of the conductors reached down, grabbed him by the ears, and pulled him aboard. Edison later reported that he felt something snap inside his head and that shortly thereafter he began to lose his hearing until he was almost completely deaf. Some have theorized, however, that Edison's deafness may have had an organic basis, since his son later also became deaf, or that it may have been caused by a childhood bout with Scarlet fever.

His loss of hearing marked a critical turning point in Edison's life. Matthew Josephson in *Edison: A Biography* pointed out that his deafness not only caused him to become "more solitary and shy," but also changed his viewpoint on the reading and study to which he had devoted so much time. "He had been only 'playing,' hitherto, with his books and his 'experiments,'" Josephson writes. "Now he put forth tremendous efforts at self-education, for he had absolutely to learn everything for himself." One of the lifelong habits he developed during this period was to work long hours with only short naps to keep him going. Later in life, it was not unusual for Edison to spend twenty out of every twenty-four hours at work.

Learns about Telegraphy

One of the subjects in which Edison became interested during his railroad days was telegraphy, a means of communicating over a great distance by using coded signals transmitted by wire. In 1862, J. U. MacKenzie, whose three-year-old son Edison had saved from being run over by a rail car, offered Edison the chance to learn telegraphy. Within a year, Edison had become skilled enough as a telegrapher to hold jobs in a variety of cities and towns in the Midwest, including Adrian, Michigan; Fort Wayne, Indiana; Cincinnati, Ohio; Nashville, Tennessee; and Louisville, Kentucky. At each location, he not only performed his assigned duties but also worked on ways of improving the telegraphy apparatus itself.

Edison's Midwest travels finally ended in the fall of 1867 when he returned to Port Huron. He found his family home in a shambles, his mother ill and his father distraught and remote. Thomas decided to strike out on his own again and headed to Boston, where he found a job with the Western Union

Telegraph Company. Although the job itself was boring, Edison found enough time to continue his practice of studying and inventing on his own. An important breakthrough came when he came across a copy of Michael Faraday's *Experimental Researches in Electricity,* read the two-volume work through in one sitting, and concluded that he could repeat such experiments himself. Edison was about to begin a new era in his life.

Receives First Patent in 1869

The first invention that resulted from his experimentation was a device for electronically recording the voice votes taken in a legislative assembly. For that invention, Edison was awarded patent number 90,646 on June 1, 1869, the first patent of his career. Unfortunately, he discovered that legislators were not interested in speeding up the process of vote recording and thus concluded that in the future, he would investigate the necessity of a product before inventing it.

June of 1869 may have been a milestone in Edison's career as an inventor, but he was still desperately poor, trying to survive day-to-day on very low wages. He decided that nothing was to be lost by making yet another move, this time down the coast to New York City. He arrived in the city without a cent in his pockets and was saved by a remarkable stroke of good fortune. While Edison was waiting to interview for a job in the offices of Law's Gold Indicator Company, the central transmitting machine broke down. Edison quickly found the problem and fixed the machine. The next day, the owner of the company, Dr. S. S. Laws, offered Edison a job as general manager of the firm, with the princely salary of $300 a month.

The job Laws offered Edison allowed him to think more seriously about a career in invention. Only four months after accepting the job, therefore, Edison joined with two other men, Franklin L. Pope and James N. Ashland to form a new company. Pope, Edison and Company was to be, they announced, a firm of "electrical engineers" and "constructors of various types of electric devices and apparatus." They were prepared, according to Burlingame, to "design telegraphic instruments, test materials, build telegraph lines, design fire alarms, construct experimental apparatus, and render other services." Within a year, the company was bought by the Gold and Stock Telegraphic Company, who also paid Edison $40,000 for a device that kept stock tickers working in unison. This was quite a fortune for a twenty-three-year-old man from Port Huron with essentially no formal education.

Opens First "Invention Factory"

The profit from the Gold and Stock deal allowed Edison to put into practice a scheme about which he had been thinking for some time. He opened a firm consisting of about fifty consulting engineers in Newark, New Jersey, which was to be, as he described it, an "invention factory." The Newark plant operated for six years, turning out a variety of inventions primarily related to improvements in stock tickers and telegraphy equipment, but also dozens of minor products. In all, Edison was granted about two hundred new patents for work completed in the Newark laboratories. Those laboratories are generally regarded as the first formally organized non-academic research center in the United States.

In 1876, Edison had outgrown his Newark facilities and arranged for the construction of a new plant at Menlo Park, New Jersey. His most productive work was accomplished at this location over the next decade. Three inventions in particular stand out among the dozens produced by Edison and his coworkers: a telephone, the phonograph, and the incandescent light bulb. Although Alexander Graham Bell invented the telephone, Edison developed a carbon-resistance transmitter that great improved the quality of Bell's invention that same year.

Invents the Phonograph and Improves the Light Bulb

In 1877, Edison produced what he himself named his favorite invention: the phonograph. The first model, in which sound vibrations were transferred by means of a steel stylus to a cylinder wrapped in tin foil, produced recognizable sounds, but of poor quality. Edison originally saw no application for the phonograph and in a newspaper interview called it "a mere toy, which has no commercial value." He then set it aside and did not return to work on it again for a decade. Josephson has described this decision to abandon research on the phonograph as "one of the inventor's greatest blunders, one that in the end was to cost him dearly."

A year later, in 1878, Edison began work on yet another invention, one that was not original with him but that he made commercially feasible: the incandescent light bulb. As early as 1848, the English physicist Sir Joseph Swan had investigated the possibility of converting an electrical current into light. The concept was simple enough: when an electrical current passes through a thin wire, it encounters resistance that causes the wire to become warmer. At some point, the wire becomes hot enough to glow, that is, to reach incandescence.

The problem that Swan encountered was that, as wire gets hot, it tends to oxidize, or burn up. In theory, the solution to this problem is to encase the wire in a vacuum. In Swan's time, however, it was not possible to make vacuums good enough to prevent wires from oxidizing. As a result, a wire might be brought to incandescence and to produce light for a short time, but it quickly burned up and the light went out.

Swan continued to work on the incandescent light bulb for the next two decades and finally solved the problem at about the same time that Edison did. An important key to Edison's success was that much better vacuums were available in 1878 than had been obtainable in 1848. In addition, Edison discovered an ideal material for use as the "wire" in a light bulb, a charred length of cotton thread. On October 21, 1879, Edison first demonstrated in public an incandescent light bulb, made with his charred cotton thread, that burned continuously for forty hours.

The incandescent light bulb was, of course, a remarkable success, and Edison spent the next few years adapting it for large-scale use. He found it necessary, for example, to invent the generating, switching, and transmitting devices needed to supply electricity to a large number of light bulbs at the same time. Within three years he had solved many of these problems and was operating the world's first power station on Pearl Street in New York City. When the plant began operation on September 4, 1882, it supplied power to four hundred incandescent light bulbs owned by eighty-five customers.

During his work on the incandescent light bulb, Edison made his one and only important scientific discovery. In attempting to modify the construction of the bulb, he introduced a wire into the bulb adjacent to the filament. When the lamp was turned on, Edison observed that electrical current flowed from the filament to the wire. He saw no practical application of this discovery and so did no further work on it. The Edison effect, as the discovery is now called, later had important applications as a way of rectifying DC current.

Invents Early Motion Picture Machine

By 1887, the laboratories at Menlo Park had become too small for Edison's many products, and he moved to a new site in West Orange, New Jersey. There he constructed a new building ten times larger than the Menlo Park facility. At that point, the Edison laboratories were practically an invention mill where, at peak production, Edison was receiving an average of one new patent every five days.

Probably the best known invention to come out of this period was the kinetograph, a primitive form of the moving picture. Edison developed a method for arranging a series of photographs on a strip of celluloid film and then running the film through a projector. He used this technique to produce *The Great Train Robbery* in 1903, one of the first moving pictures, and then lost interest in the technology.

A tendency to go from subject to subject was characteristic of Edison's personality. In some cases

he stayed with a project long enough to see it to commercial production. In other cases, he spent time developing the early stages of an idea and then moved on to something new. Among the inventions to which he made at least some contribution were the lead storage battery, the mimeograph machine, the dictaphone, and the fluoroscope. He also developed an interest in iron mining and processing and in cement production. As he went from project to project and interest to interest, he made and lost a fortune many times over.

Edison was married twice, the first time on Christmas day, 1871, to Mary Stilwell, whom he had met in Newark. They had three children, Marion Estell, Thomas Alva, and William Leslie. Mary Edison died on August 8, 1884, and two years later, on February 24, 1886, Edison was married a second time, to Mina Miller. Three children, Charles, Madeleine, and Theodore, were born to this marriage. Edison died in West Orange, New Jersey, on October 18, 1931. In recognition of his accomplishments he had been elected to the National Academy of Sciences in 1927, and he was elected to the Hall of Fame for Great Americans in 1960. In addition he was awarded the Albert Medal of the British Society of Arts in 1892, the John Fritz Medal of the American Engineering Societies in 1908, and the Rumford Medal of the American Academy of Arts and Sciences. In 1920 the Department of the Navy awarded Edison the Distinguished Service Medal for his wartime service. The inventor declined the honor, however, because of his disappointment with the way in which he thought he had been treated by the military. Eight years later Edison did accept a special gold medal awarded to him by the U.S. Congress in recognition of his life's work.

SELECTED WRITINGS BY EDISON:

Books

The Diary and Sundry Observations of Thomas A. Edison, edited by Dagobert D. Runes, Philosophical Library, 1948, Greenwood Press, 1968.

Periodicals

"The Phonograph and Its Future," *North American Review,* June, 1878.
"Dangers of Electric Lighting," *North American Review,* November, 1889.

SOURCES:

Books

Dickson, William Kennedy-Laurie, and Antonia Dickson, *The Life and Inventions of Thomas A. Edison,* Crowell, 1894.

Dyer, F. L., T. C. Martin, and W. H. Meadow-croft, *Edison, His Life and Inventions* Harper, 1929.

Ford, Henry, and Samuel Crowther, *Edison As I Know Him,* Cosmopolitan Book Corp., 1930.

Gillispie, Charles Coulson, editor, *Dictionary of Scientific Biography,* Volume 4, Scribner, 1975, pp. 283–284.

Jehl, Francis, *Menlo Park Reminisces,* Edison Institute, 1937.

Jones, Francis A., *Life Story of Thomas A. Edison,* Grosset & Dunlop, 1931.

Josephson, Matthew, *Edison: A Biography,* McGraw-Hill, 1959.

McClure, J. B., editor, *Edison and His Inventions,* Rhodes & McClure, 1879.

Nerney, Mary C., *Edison, Modern Olympian,* H. Smith & R. Haas, 1934.

Simonds, William, *Edison, His Life, His Work, His Genius,* Bobbs-Merrill, 1934.

Tate, Alfred O., *Edison's Open Door,* Dutton, 1938.

—*Sketch by David E. Newton*

Cecile Hoover Edwards

Cecile Hoover Edwards
1926-

American nutritional researcher

Cecile Hoover Edwards, a nutritional researcher and educator, devoted her career to improving the nutrition and well-being of disadvantaged people. In recognition of her achievements, she was cited by the National Council of Negro Women for outstanding contributions to science and by the Illinois House of Representatives for "determined devotion to the cause of eliminating poverty through the creation of a quality environment."

Edwards was born in East St. Louis, Illinois, on October 26, 1926. Her mother, Annie Jordan, was a former schoolteacher and her father, Ernest Hoover, was an insurance manager. Edwards enrolled at Tuskegee Institute, the college made famous by Booker T. Washington and **George Washington Carver**, at age fifteen, and entered a home economics program with minors in nutrition and chemistry. "I knew from the first day that I had no interest in dietetics," Edwards told Laura Newman in an interview. "My real interest was in improving nutrition through research." Edwards was awarded a bachelor of science degree with honors from Tuskegee in 1946. With a fellowship from Swift and Co. she conducted chemical analyses of an animal source of protein. In 1947, she earned a master's degree in chemistry from Tuskegee. Edwards received a Ph.D. in nutrition from Iowa State University in 1950. Edwards's doctoral dissertation was a study of methionine, an essential amino acid that she said has "not only the good things needed to synthesize protein, but also has sulfur, which can be given to other compounds and be easily released." Edwards wrote at least twenty papers on methionine.

Appointed Head of Tuskegee's Food and Nutrition Department

After completing her doctorate, Edwards returned to Tuskegee as a faculty member and a research associate of the Carver Foundation, remaining there for six years. "Staying in nutrition at Tuskegee seemed like an opportunity," said Edwards. "I felt obligated to pay back the opportunity Tuskegee had given me." In 1952 she became head of Tuskegee's department of foods and nutrition. Edwards's nutritional research later expanded to studies of the amino acid composition of food, the utilization of protein from vegetarian diets, and the planning of well-balanced and nutritious diets, especially for low-income and disadvantaged populations in the United States and developing countries.

Develops Human Ecology Curriculum at Howard University

Designing a new curriculum for the School of Human Ecology at Howard University, Washington, D.C., in the 1970s was a high point of Edwards's career. Just before she came to Howard, in 1969, Arthur Jensen had argued in his paper, "How Much Can We Boost IQ," that blacks were inherently inferior, and that providing education, nutrition, and other resources could not bring them equality. Disproving the Jensen hypothesis became a major goal for Edwards. Howard's School of Human Ecology conducted research and evaluated work in providing resources for low-income people so that they could help themselves. It taught parenting, childcare, nutrition, budgeting, job skills, and other skills useful in overcoming obstacles. In 1974, Edwards was appointed Dean of the School of Human Ecology, a position she held until 1987.

In 1985 Edwards became director of a five-year project sponsored by the National Institute of Child Health and Human Development to study the nutritional, medical, psychological, socioeconomic, and lifestyle factors which influence pregnancy outcomes in low-income women. In 1994 she served as editor of the *Journal of Nutrition* May supplement on "African American Women and Their Pregnancies." A humanitarian and prolific writer who published numerous scientific papers, Edwards helped to establish a family resource development program in her birthplace, East St. Louis, Illinois.

SELECTED WRITINGS BY EDWARDS:

Books

(Editor) *Current Knowledge of the Relationships of Selected Nutrients, Alcohol, Tobacco, and Drug Use, and Other Factors to Pregnancy Outcomes,* School of Human Ecology, Howard University, 1988.
(Editor with others) *Human Ecology: Interactions of Man with His Environments,* Kendall-Hunt, 1991.

Periodicals

"Utilization of Methionine by the Adult Rat, Distribution of the alpha-carbon of DL-methionine–2-C^{14} in Tissues, Tissue Fractions, Expired Carbon Dioxide, Blood and Excreta," *Journal of Nutrition,* Volume 72, 1960, p. 185.
(With L. K. Booker, C. H. Rumph, and S. N. Ganapathy) "Utilization of Wheat by Adult Man: Vitamins and Minerals," *American Journal of Clinical Nutrition,* Volume 24, 1971, p. 547.

"Low Income Black Families: Strategies for Survival in the 1980s," *Journal of Negro Education,* Volume 51, 1982, pp. 85–89.
"Quality of Life: Black Families," *Human Ecology Monograph,* School of Human Ecology, Howard University, 1991.

SOURCES:

Edwards, Cecile Hoover, interview with Laura Newman conducted March 12, 1994.

—Sketch by Laura Newman

Helen T. Edwards
1936-
American physicist

Helen T. Edwards is an accelerator physicist, who has helped to design and build the Tevatron accelerator at Fermilab in Batavia, Illinois, and headed up the accelerator systems division for the U.S. Superconducting Super Collider until the project was canceled in 1993. Her work on accelerators, particularly the systems that produce collisions between protons and antiprotons at Fermilab, have led to major advances in particle physics.

Helen Thom Edwards was born in Detroit, Michigan, on May 27, 1936. She received her B.A. from Cornell University in Ithaca, New York, in 1957. A master's degree and Ph.D. in physics from the same university followed in 1963 and 1966. Edwards stayed on at Cornell as a research associate until 1970, when she moved on to Fermi National Accelerator Laboratory to become Associate Head of the Booster Group. She stayed at Fermilab until 1989, eventually becoming head of the Accelerator Division.

Builds Tevatron Accelerator

In 1978 Fermilab began work on building a superconducting proton accelerator. Protons are positively charged elementary particles. Edwards was put in charge of the design of the new accelerator, called the Tevatron. When the design phase was completed, she became responsible for directing the technical aspects of building the Tevatron, which became the first successful superconducting proton accelerator and is the most powerful accelerator presently in

Helen T. Edwards

operation. The Tevatron accelerates particles to about 1 TeV, or 1 trillion electron volts (whence the name of the accelerator), so that collisions occur in the Tevatron's detectors at about 2 TeV. These are energy levels similar to those that reigned in the universe a fraction of a second after the big bang, the explosion thought to have created the universe we live in. As a consequence, particles are thought to replicate early atomic behavior.

Not long after the Tevatron was completed, the accelerator was fitted out with the equipment to produce and store antiprotons for use in collisions with protons. Antiprotons are the antimatter equivalents of protons; that is to say, they are identical to protons except for a negative charge. Antiprotons are produced by collisions between electrons, negatively charged elementary particles, and their antimatter equivalents, positrons. High-energy collisions of protons and antiprotons, it was hoped, would yield the first observations of the hypothetical particles called top quarks. Quarks are the basic building-blocks of which particles such as protons and electrons are thought to be composed. Although a facility for producing and storing antiprotons was in operation in Geneva, Switzerland, Fermilab's capacity to generate antiprotons was to exceed that of the Swiss facility by far. Again, Edwards was in charge of design and construction. She is particularly notable for her design of a system that transfers protons and antiprotons from different sources into the Tevatron detectors almost simultaneously, so that very high energy

collisions can be obtained. So far the top quark has not been detected, leading scientists to speculate that it has much greater mass than previously suspected.

In 1986 Edwards received one of the Ernest O. Lawrence Awards from the U.S. Department of Energy in recognition of her work in accelerator design and construction. She also received a MacArthur Foundation Fellowship for outstanding contributions in particle physics in 1988. The following year she was awarded the National Medal of Technology and accepted a position as Head of the Accelerator Division of the Superconducting Super Collider (SSC) to be built at Waxahachie, Texas. The SSC was designed to produce collisions at 40 TeV (40 trillion electron volts) and was hoped to yield more data on quarks and a hypothetical particle called the Higgs boson. Budget cutting in Congress, however, led to the cancellation of the SSC in 1993.

SOURCES:

Books

Lederman, Leon and Dick Teresi, *The God Particle,* Houghton Mifflin, 1993.

Periodicals

"Five Physicists Receive Lawrence Awards," *Physics Today,* October, 1986, p. 137.
"MacArthur Foundation Confers Five Physics-Related Fellowships," *Physics Today,* March, 1989, p. 123.

—Sketch by Olga K. Anderson

Paul Ehrenfest
1880-1933
Austrian-born Dutch physicist

Paul Ehrenfest is best known as a profound, yet engaging teacher who popularized and explained many new ideas in physics, particularly in the categories of quantum theory and relativity. His own research and collaborations with his wife served to solidify existing concepts in physics, while his personal devotion to science forged bonds between himself and the likes of physicists **Max Planck** and **Albert Einstein**. Ehrenfest succeeded **Hendrik Lorentz** as professor of theoretical physics at the University of Leiden, where he remained until his death in 1933.

Paul Ehrenfest was born in Vienna (in what was then Austria-Hungary), on January 18, 1880. His parents—Sigmund Ehrenfest and the former Johanna Jellinek—had moved to Vienna in the 1860s from the small village of Loschwitz in Moravia. Although very poor at the time of this move, the Ehrenfests had used Johanna's dowry to establish a grocery store in Vienna. By the time Paul (the youngest of five sons) was born, the business had become a successful enterprise and the family was living comfortably. Ehrenfest's interest in science was the result of his elder brother Arthur's encouragement and instruction, and it was a pursuit that offset an adolescence impaired by consistently poor health and the persistent and powerful anti-Semitic atmosphere that prevailed in Vienna at the time. The loss of Ehrenfest's mother, when he was ten, and his father, when he was sixteen, contributed to his sense of depression and a lack of confidence which would plague him throughout his life.

Ehrenfest Studies at Vienna and Göttingen

After completing his primary education in 1890, Ehrenfest entered the Akademisches Gymnasium, graduating nine years later. Throughout this period, his formal schooling was supplemented by the education he received at home from his four older brothers. In the fall of 1899, Ehrenfest enrolled at the Vienna Technische Hochschule, where he was at first interested in majoring in chemistry. He soon changed his mind, however, after attending lectures on the mechanical theory of heat given by the famous Ludwig Boltzmann. Eventually taking a close personal interest in Ehrenfest, Boltzmann later supervised the thesis that earned his student a doctoral degree in 1904.

Two years after entering the Technische Hochschule, Ehrenfest decided to spend a year at the University of Göttingen, where he was exposed to some of the most brilliant minds in science and mathematics. He also met his future wife, Tatyana Alexeyevna Afanassjewa, a mathematics student from Russia. The two soon fell in love and were married on December 21, 1904. They eventually had four children together, Tatyana Pavlovna, Anna, Paul Jr., and Vassily. The husband-and-wife team of Paul and Tatyana Ehrenfest would later produce a number of scholarly papers, primarily in the field of statistical mechanics. They lived at first in Vienna, then in Göttingen, and finally in St. Petersburg, moves necessitated by the fact that between 1904 and 1911, Ehrenfest was unable to obtain a permanent teaching appointment.

Ehrenfest Is Appointed Professor of Theoretical Physics at Leiden

Ehrenfest's fortunes took a turn for the better in May, 1912, when he received a letter from Lorentz, the prominent Dutch physicist. Retiring as professor of theoretical physics at the University of Leiden, Lorentz offered to suggest Ehrenfest as his successor. Delighted with the offer, Ehrenfest moved to Leiden in October, 1912, where he remained for the next two decades. During his tenure at Leiden, Ehrenfest became one of the most highly respected members of the world scientific community. His fame came not from any great contribution, but primarily because of his skills as a teacher and through his role in disseminating coherently the new developments in physics. In a memorial to Ehrenfest, published in *Out of My Later Years,* Einstein wrote of the Dutch physicist: "He was not merely the best teacher in our profession whom I have ever known; he was also passionately preoccupied with the development and destiny of men, especially his students." **George Uhlenbeck**, discoverer of electron spin and one of Ehrenfest's students, called him "one of the really great teachers," in a 1956 article in the *American Journal of Physics.*

Ehrenfest contributed greatly in clarifying the modern concepts of physics. Throughout the early 1900s, many tenets of classical physics were being overthrown and replaced by new concepts governing quantum mechanics, relativity, and other fields. However, technical expositions of "the new physics" were often internally inconsistent and difficult to understand—in many cases, to both scientists and nonscientists. Ehrenfest had the remarkable ability to sort out what was going on at the frontiers of research and summarize it in a way that could be more easily understood. Unfortunately, the accolades of his students and colleagues were not enough to overcome his deep-rooted sense of inferiority and insecurity. Those feelings were compounded in the early 1930s by both personal and professional problems. He was partially estranged from his wife, whom he loved with a passion the likes of which, Einstein observed, "I have not often witnessed in my life." In addition, Ehrenfest took very personally the growing threat posed to his fellow scientists by the rise of the Nazi party in Germany. Finally, he seems to have felt overwhelmed and inadequate to deal with the continuing changes taking place in physics during the early 1930s. All of these factors appear to have contributed to his decision to end his own life in Amsterdam, The Netherlands, on September 25, 1933.

SELECTED WRITINGS BY EHRENFEST:

Books

(With wife, Tatiana Ehrenfest) *The Conceptual Foundations of the Statistical Approach in Mechanics,* Cornell University Press, 1959.
Collected Scientific Papers, Interscience, 1959.

SOURCES:

Books

Einstein, Albert, *Out of My Later Years,* Philosophical Library, 1950, pp. 236–39.
Gillispie, Charles Coulson, editor, *Dictionary of Scientific Biography,* Volume 4, Scribner, 1975, pp. 292–94.
Klein, Martin J., *Paul Ehrenfest,* Volume 1: *The Making of a Theoretical Physicist,* North-Holland Publishing, 1970.

Periodicals

Uhlenbeck, G. E., "Reminiscences of Professor Paul Ehrenfest," *American Journal of Physics,* Volume 24, 1956, pp. 431–33.

—*Sketch by David E. Newton*

Tatiana Ehrenfest-Afanaseva
1876-1964
Russian Dutch theoretical physicist

Tatiana Ehrenfest-Afanaseva was one of the most accomplished theoretical physicists of the twentieth century. Together with her husband, **Paul Ehrenfest**, Ehrenfest-Afanaseva authored a critique of statistical thermodynamics which centered on a newer, statistical treatment of the behavior of gas molecules. Their work in articulating the ergodic hypothesis helped illuminate how microscopic particles in an unbalanced state could explain the overall macroscopic balance of matter.

Tatiana Alexeyevna Ehrenfest-Afanaseva (sometimes spelled Afanassjewa) was born in Kiev, Ukraine, on November 19, 1876. Her father, a civil engineer of Russian-Orthodox faith, died when she was a child, and she went to live with a childless uncle, who was a professor at the Polytechnical Institute in St. Petersburg. During the generation leading up to World War I, St. Petersburg offered special university-level institutions for women, notably in engineering, medicine, and teaching. The institution that shadowed the imperial university (reserved for men) was the Women's Curriculum, which offered courses in arts, sciences, and law. Afanaseva attended the women's pedagogical (teaching) school and then the Women's Curriculum, among whose physics professors was Orest D. Chvolson,

author of an introductory text used widely in Europe. She excelled in mathematics.

In 1902 Afanaseva, accompanied by her aunt Sonya, travelled to the University of Göttingen in Germany, then renowned for mathematics and physics. There she met and fell in love with Paul Ehrenfest, a Jewish physics student from Vienna. The couple married in 1904, shortly after Paul Ehrenfest completed his doctorate under Ludwig Boltzmann at the University of Vienna. They lived in Vienna at first, then moved to Göttingen, and in 1907 settled in St. Petersburg, Russia, living on inherited income. As Russian law prohibited marriages between Jews and Christians, they were allowed to live as husband and wife only by declaring themselves to be without religion—a risky step in view of the power of the Russian theocracy. In St. Petersburg, Ehrenfest-Afanaseva raised two daughters and also took care of her mother and her aunt. The household was vegetarian, teetotal, and non-smoking.

Ehrenfest-Afanaseva published her first paper in theoretical physics in 1905, and she continued issuing published work during her Russian years, both in Russian and in German. Paul Ehrenfest also published theoretical papers—rather more frenetically than his wife. Paul's most important work, a magisterial critique of statistical thermodynamics written for a mathematical encyclopedia edited by Felix Klein, was written jointly with his wife. The monograph centered on the so-called H-theorem—by which Boltzmann had provided a statistical proof of the second law of thermodynamics, which concerns the conservation of entropy, or available energy within a system. In the monograph, the Ehrenfests brought out the newer, statistical treatment of gas molecules, and they emphasized the importance of the ergodic hypothesis (in which a portion of a process represents the whole) for understanding how the disequilibrium, or imbalance, of microscopic particle dynamics may account for the macroscopic equilibrium of matter—how, for example, a cup of hot tea slowly cools to room temperature.

Following the work of the Ehrenfests, the ergodic problem occupied the attention of a number of mathematicians. Ehrenfest-Afanaseva's role in writing the monograph, she recalled, was a critical one: While Paul collected the literature and organized the structure, she discussed all the problems with her husband, a number of which she clarified. She was the critical logician, while he provided physical intuition. This type of collaboration, familiar to those who have studied **Albert Einstein**'s interaction with his mathematician-physicist wife Mileva Marić, contributed to Paul Ehrenfest's call, in 1912, to succeed **Hendrik Antoon Lorentz** in the chair of theoretical physics at the University of Leiden in the Netherlands.

At Leiden, Ehrenfest-Afanaseva expanded her horizons by publishing in Dutch and English. She designed a new house for the family which was completed in July 1914. Her family grew—sons were born in 1915 and 1918. The Ehrenfests had firm ideas about training young minds, and they educated their children at home. Ehrenfest-Afanaseva took a professional interest in questions of education, publishing a number of monographs and articles in German, Russian, and Dutch that discussed such issues as axiomatization, randomness and entropy, geometrical intuition and physical reality, and teaching method. Her output slowed after the suicide of her husband in 1933, but it resumed in the 1950s, when she wrote two major monographs. Her last work, published at age 84 in 1960, was a 164-page treatise on the teaching of mathematics. Although Ehrenfest-Afanaseva neither completed a doctorate nor held a regular university teaching position, her writings substantially enriched physics in the Netherlands. She died on April 14, 1964, in Leiden.

SELECTED WRITINGS BY EHRENFEST-AFANASEVA:

Books

Die Grundlagen der Thermodynamik, [Leiden], 1956. (With Paul Ehrenfest) *The Conceptual Foundations of the Statistical Approach in Mechanics,* translated by Michael J. Moravcsik, Cornell University Press, 1959.
Wiskunde: Didactische opstellen, [Zutphen], 1960.

Periodicals

"On the Use of the Notion 'Probability' in Physics," *American Journal of Physics,* Volume 26, 1958, pp. 388–392.

SOURCES:

Books

Frankfurt, Yu. I., *P. Ehrenfest* (in Russian), Nauka (Moscow), 1972.
Klein, Martin, *Paul Ehrenfest: The Making of a Theoretical Physicist,* North Holland, 1970.
Tropp, Eduard A., Viktor Ya. Frenkel, and Artur D. Chernin, *Alexander A. Friedmann: The Man Who Made the Universe Expand,* translated by Alexander Dron and Michael Burov, Cambridge University Press, 1993.

Periodicals

Sviridonov, M. N., "Razvitiye ponyatiya entropii v rabotakh T. A. Afanas'yevoy-Erenfest," *Istoriya i metodologiya yestestnevvykh nauk: Fizika,* Volume 10, 1971, p. 77–111.

Visser, C., "In memoriam T. Ehrenfest-Afanassjewa," *Viernieuwing van opvoeding en onderwijs,* Volume 22, 1964, p. 217.

—*Sketch by Lewis Pyenson*

Paul Ehrlich
1854-1915
German bacteriologist and immunologist

Paul Ehrlich's pioneering experiments with cells and body tissue revealed the fundamental principles of the immune system and established the legitimacy of chemotherapy—the use of chemical drugs to treat disease. His discovery of a drug which cured syphilis saved many lives and demonstrated the potential of systematic drug research. His studies of dye reactions in blood cells helped establish hematology—the scientific field concerned with blood and blood-forming organs—as a recognized discipline. Many of the new terms he coined as a way to describe his innovative research, including "chemotherapy," are still in use. From 1877 to 1914, Ehrlich published 232 papers and books, won numerous awards, and received 5 honorary degrees. In 1908, Ehrlich received the Nobel Prize in medicine or physiology. Along with **Robert Koch**, Nobel Prize winner in 1905, and **Emil von Behring**, Nobel Prize winner in 1901, he is considered one of the "Big Three" in medicine. Ehrlich, Koch, and von Behring were contemporaries and frequent collaborators.

Ehrlich was born on March 14, 1854, in Strehlen, Silesia, once a part of Germany, but now a part of Poland known as Strzelin. He was the fourth child after three sisters in a Jewish family. His father, Ismar Ehrlich, and mother, Rosa Weigert, were both innkeepers. As a boy, Ehrlich was influenced by several relatives who studied science. His paternal grandfather, Heimann Ehrlich, made a living as a liquor merchant but kept a private laboratory and gave lectures on science to the citizens of Strehlen. Karl Weigert, cousin of Ehrlich's mother, became a well-known pathologist. Ehrlich, who was close friends with Weigert, often joined his cousin in his lab, where he learned how to stain cells with dye in order to see them better under the microscope. Ehrlich's research into the dye reactions of cells continued during his time as a university student. He studied science and medicine at the universities of Breslau, Strasbourg, Freiburg, and Leipzig. Although Ehrlich conducted most of his course work at Breslau, he submitted his

Paul Ehrlich

final dissertation to the University of Leipzig, which awarded him a medical degree in 1878.

Ehrlich's 1878 doctoral thesis, "Contributions to the Theory and Practice of Histological Staining," suggests that even at this early stage in his career he recognized the depth of possibility and discovery in his chosen research field. In his experiments with many dyes, Ehrlich had learned how to manipulate chemicals in order to obtain specific effects: Methylene blue dye, for example, stained nerve cells without discoloring the tissue around them. These experiments with dye reactions formed the backbone of Ehrlich's career and led to two important contributions to science. First, improvements in staining permitted scientists to examine cells—healthy or unhealthy—and microorganisms, including those that caused disease. Ehrlich's work ushered in a new era of medical diagnosis and histology (the study of cells), which alone would have guaranteed Ehrlich a place in scientific history. Secondly, and more significantly from a scientific standpoint, Ehrlich's early experiments revealed that certain cells have an affinity to certain dyes. To Ehrlich, it was clear that chemical and physical reactions were taking place in the stained tissue. He theorized that chemical reactions governed all biological life processes. If this were true, Ehrlich reasoned, then chemicals could perhaps be used to heal diseased cells and to attack harmful microorganisms. Ehrlich began studying the chemical structure of the dyes he used and postulated theories for what chemical reactions might be taking place in the body

in the presence of dyes and other chemical agents. These efforts would eventually lead Ehrlich to study the immune system.

Upon Ehrlich's graduation, medical clinic director Friedrich von Frerichs immediately offered the young scientist a position as head physician at the Charite Hospital in Berlin. Von Frerichs recognized that Ehrlich, with his penchant for strong cigars and mineral water, was a unique talent, one that should be excused from clinical work and be allowed to pursue his research uninterrupted. The late nineteenth century was a time when infectious diseases like cholera and typhoid fever were incurable and fatal. Syphilis, a sexually transmitted disease caused by a then unidentified microorganism, was an epidemic, as was tuberculosis, another disease whose cause had yet to be named. To treat human disease, medical scientists knew they needed a better understanding of harmful microorganisms.

At the Charite Hospital, Ehrlich studied blood cells under the microscope. Although blood cells can be found in a perplexing multiplicity of forms, Ehrlich was with his dyes able to begin identifying them. His systematic cataloging of the cells laid the groundwork for what would become the field of hematology. Ehrlich also furthered his understanding of chemistry by meeting with professionals from the chemical industry. These contacts gave him information about the structure and preparation of new chemicals and kept him supplied with new dyes and chemicals.

Improves Test for Tuberculosis

Ehrlich's slow and steady work with stains resulted in a sudden and spectacular achievement. On March 24, 1882, Ehrlich had heard Robert Koch announce to the Berlin Physiological Society that he had identified the bacillus causing tuberculosis under the microscope. Koch's method of staining the bacillus for study, however, was less than ideal. Ehrlich immediately began experimenting and was soon able to show Koch an improved method of staining the tubercle bacillus. The technique has since remained in use.

On April 14, 1883, Ehrlich married 19-year-old Hedwig Pinkus in the Neustadt Synagogue. Ehrlich had met Pinkus, the daughter of an affluent textile manufacturer of Neustadt, while visiting relatives in Berlin. The marriage brought two daughters, Steffa and Marianne. In March, 1885, von Frerichs committed suicide and Ehrlich suddenly found himself without a mentor. Von Frerichs's successor as director of Charite Hospital, Karl Gerhardt, was far less impressed with Ehrlich and forced him to focus on clinical work rather than research. Though complying, Ehrlich was highly dissatisfied with the change. Two years later, Ehrlich resigned from the Charite Hospital, ostensibly because he wished to relocate to a dry climate to cure himself of tuberculosis. The mild case of the disease, which Ehrlich had diagnosed using his staining techniques, was almost certainly contracted from cultures in his lab. In September of 1888, Ehrlich and his wife embarked on an extended journey to southern Europe and Egypt and returned to Berlin in the spring of 1889 with Ehrlich cured.

In Berlin, Ehrlich set up a small private laboratory with financial help from his father-in-law, and in 1890 he was honored with an appointment as Extraordinary Professor at the University of Berlin. In 1891, Ehrlich accepted Robert Koch's invitation to join him at the Institute for Infectious Diseases, newly created for Koch by the Prussian government. At the institute, Koch began his immunological research by demonstrating that mice fed or injected with the toxins ricin and abrin developed antitoxins. He also proved that antibodies were passed from mother to offspring through breast milk. Ehrlich joined forces with Koch and von Behring to find a cure for diphtheria, a deadly childhood disease. Although von Behring had identified the antibodies to diphtheria, he still faced great difficulties transforming the discovery into a potent yet safe cure for humans. Using blood drawn from horses and goats infected with the disease, the scientists worked together to concentrate and purify an effective antitoxin. Ehrlich's particular contribution to the cure was his method of measuring an effective dose.

Diphtheria Cure Creates Rift with von Behring

The commercialization of a diphtheria antitoxin began in 1892 and was manufactured by Höchst Chemical Works. Royalties from the drug profits promised to make Ehrlich and von Behring wealthy men. But Ehrlich—possibly at von Behring's urging—accepted a government position in 1885 to monitor the production of the diphtheria serum. Conflict-of-interest clauses obligated Ehrlich to withdraw from his profit-sharing agreement. Forced to stand by as the diphtheria antitoxin made von Behring a wealthy man, he and von Behring quarreled and eventually parted. Although it is unclear whether or not bitterness over the royalty agreement sparked the quarrel, it certainly couldn't have helped a relationship that was often tumultuous. Although the two scientists continued to exchange news in letters, both scientific and personal, the two scientists never met again.

In June of 1896, the Prussian government invited Ehrlich to direct its newly created Royal Institute for Serum Research and Testing in Steglitz, a suburb of Berlin. For the first time, Ehrlich had his own institute. In 1896 Ehrlich was invited by Franz Adickes, the mayor of Frankfurt, and by Friedrich Althoff, the Prussian Minister of Educational and Medical Affairs, to move his research to Frankfurt.

Ehrlich accepted and the Royal Institute for Experimental Therapy opened on November 8, 1899. Ehrlich was to remain as its director until his death sixteen years later. The years in Frankfurt would prove to be among Ehrlich's most productive.

In his speech at the opening of the Institute for Experimental Therapy, Ehrlich seized the opportunity to describe in detail his "side-chain theory" of how antibodies worked. "Side-chain" is the name given to the appendages on benzene molecules that allow it to react with other chemicals. Ehrlich believed all molecules had similar side-chains that allowed them to link with molecules, nutrients, infectious toxins and other substances. Although Ehrlich's theory is false, his efforts to prove it led to a host of new discoveries and guided much of his future research.

The move to Frankfurt marked the dawn of chemotherapy as Ehrlich erected various chemical agents against a host of dangerous microorganisms. In 1903, scientists had discovered that the cause of sleeping sickness, a deadly disease prevalent in Africa, was a species of trypanosomes (parasitic protozoans). With help from Japanese scientist Kiyoshi Shiga, Ehrlich worked to find a dye that destroyed trypanosomes in infected mice. In 1904, he discovered such a dye, which was dubbed "trypan red".

Disregards Conventions as Laboratory Director

Success with trypan red spurred Ehrlich to begin testing other chemicals against disease. To conduct his methodical and painstaking experiments with an enormous range of chemicals, Ehrlich relied heavily on his assistants. To direct their work, he made up a series of instructions on colored cards in the evening and handed them out each morning. Although such a management strategy did not endear him to his lab associates—and did not allow them opportunity for their own research—Ehrlich's approach was often successful. In one famous instance, Ehrlich ordered his staff to disregard the accepted notion of the chemical structure of atoxyl and to instead proceed in their work based on his specifications of the chemical. Two of the three medical scientists working with Ehrlich were appalled at his scientific heresy and ended their employment at the laboratory. Ehrlich's hypothesis concerning atoxyl turned out to have been correct and would eventually lead to the discovery of a chemical cure for syphilis.

In September of 1906, Ehrlich's laboratory became a division of the new Georg Speyer Haus for Chemotherapeutical Research. The research institute, endowed by the wealthy widow of Georg Speyer for the exclusive purpose of continuing Ehrlich's work in chemotherapy, was built next to Ehrlich's existing laboratory. In a speech at the opening of the new institute, Ehrlich used the phrase "magic bullets" to illustrate his hope of finding chemical compounds that would enter the body, attack only the offending microorganisms or malignant cells, and leave healthy tissue untouched. In 1908, Ehrlich's work on immunity, particularly his contribution to the diphtheria antitoxin, was honored with the Nobel Prize in medicine or physiology. He shared the prize with Russian bacteriologist **Élie Metchnikoff**.

Discovers a Cure for Syphillis

By the time Ehrlich's lab formally joined the Speyer Haus, he had already tested over 300 chemical compounds against trypanosomes and the syphilis spirochete (distinguished as slender and spirally undulating bacteria). With each test given a laboratory number, Ehrlich was testing compounds numbering in the nine hundreds before realizing that "compound 606" was a highly potent drug effective against relapsing fever and syphilis. Due to an assistant's error, the potential of compound 606 had been overlooked for nearly two years until Ehrlich's associate, Sahashiro Hata, experimented with it again. On June 10, 1909, Ehrlich and Hata filed a patent for 606 for its use against relapsing fever.

The first favorable results of 606 against syphilis were announced at the Congress for Internal Medicine held at Wiesbaden in April 1910. Although Ehrlich emphasized he was reporting only preliminary results, news of a cure for the devastating and widespread disease swept through the European and American medical communities and Ehrlich was besieged with requests for the drug. Physicians and victims of the disease clamored at his doors. Ehrlich, painfully aware that mishandled dosages could blind or even kill patients, begged physicians to wait until he could test 606 on ten or twenty thousand more patients. But there was no halting the demand and the Georg Speyer Haus ultimately manufactured and distributed 65,000 units of 606 to physicians all over the globe free of charge. Eventually, the large-scale production of 606, under the commercial name "Salvarsan," was taken over by Höchst Chemical Works. The next four years, although largely triumphant, were also filled with reports of patients' deaths and maiming at the hands of doctors who failed to administer Salvarsan properly.

In 1913, in an address to the International Medical Congress in London, Ehrlich cited trypan red and Salvarsan as examples of the power of chemotherapy and described his vision of chemotherapy's future. The City of Frankfurt honored Ehrlich by renaming the street in front of the Georg Speyer Haus "Paul Ehrlichstrasse." Yet in 1914, Ehrlich was forced to defend himself against claims made by a Frankfurt newspaper, *Die Wahrheit* (The Truth), that Ehrlich was testing Salvarsan on prostitutes against their will, that the drug was a fraud, and that Ehrlich's motivation for promoting it was personal monetary gain. In June 1914, Frankfurt city authorities took action against the newspaper and Ehrlich testified in court as an expert witness. Ehrlich's name was finally cleared and the newspaper's publisher sentenced to a year in jail, but the trial left Ehrlich deeply depressed. In December, 1914, he suffered a mild stroke.

Ehrlich's health failed to improve and the start of World War I had further discouraged him. Afflicted with arteriosclerosis, a disease of the arteries, his health deteriorated rapidly. He died in Bad Homburg, Prussia (now Germany), on August 20, 1915, after a second stroke. Ehrlich was buried in Frankfurt. Following the German Nazi era—during which time Ehrlich's widow and daughters were persecuted as Jews before fleeing the country and the sign marking Paul Ehrlichstrasse was torn down—Frankfurt once again honored its famous resident. The Institute for Experimental Therapy changed its name to the Paul Ehrlich Institute and began offering the biennial Paul Ehrlich Prize in one of Ehrlich's fields of research as a memorial to its founder.

SELECTED WRITINGS BY EHRLICH:

Books

The Collected Papers of Paul Ehrlich, four volumes, edited by F. Himmelweit, Pergamon, 1957–58.

SOURCES:

Books

Baumler, Ernst, *Paul Ehrlich,* Holmes & Meier, 1984.

Farber, Eduard, *Great Chemists,* Interscience Publishers, 1961, pp. 1041–1063.

Magner, Lois N., *A History of the Life Sciences,* Dekker, 1979, pp. 276–79.

Marquardt, Martha, *Paul Ehrlich,* Henry Schuman, 1951.

Poole, Lynn and Gray Poole, *Doctors Who Saved Lives,* Dodd, 1966, pp. 88–100.

Reid, Robert, *Microbes and Men,* Saturday Review Press, 1975, pp. 125–133.

—Sketch by Liz Marshall

Paul R. Ehrlich
1932-
American population biologist

Paul R. Ehrlich

Paul R. Ehrlich, Bing Professor of Population Studies at Stanford University, has long been an advocate of population control and ecological awareness. Originally trained as an entomologist, he has published widely in fields of ecology, evolution, and behavior, and he offers a plan for survival and a program for action to make the world environmentally secure. According to Ehrlich, humans must stop exploiting the earth and learn to see it as a limited resource.

Paul Ralph Ehrlich was born on May 29, 1932, in Philadelphia, Pennsylvania, to William and Ruth Rosenberg Ehrlich. His father worked in sales; his mother taught Latin in the public schools. Ehrlich spent most of his childhood in Maplewood, New Jersey, where he first became interested in the natural sciences and ecology. After high school, from which he graduated in 1949, Ehrlich attended the University of Pennsylvania, graduating in 1953 with a B.A. in zoology. The following year he married Anne Fitzhugh Howland, an educator and writer, with whom he later had one daughter, Lisa Marie. He received his M.A. from the University of Kansas in 1955 and his Ph.D. in 1957. While at the University of Kansas, Ehrlich acted as an associate investigator for a U.S. Air Force research project. His field work took him to the Bering Sea to survey biting flies and to the Canadian Arctic and subarctic to investigate insect genetics and behavior. Between 1957 and 1959 Ehrlich did brief stints as a research associate of the Chicago Academy of Sciences and the University of Kansas department of entomology. In 1959 he joined the faculty at Stanford University in California as an assistant professor of biology. He became an associate professor in 1962, was promoted to professor of biology in 1966, and became the Bing Professor of Population Studies in 1976.

Much of Ehrlich's writing has dealt with such matters as crowding in human populations, the relation of population pressure to sociopolitical events, and the results of policy research on human population as it relates to specific resources and to the environment in general. But he has also written on subjects such as butterflies, biology, immigration, extinction, and race. Ehrlich's first book was the handbook *How to Know the Butterflies,* illustrated by his wife, Anne, who has collaborated on a number of his writings and is a senior research associate in biological sciences at Stanford University. Ehrlich's interest in butterflies also resulted in a project in which he used ants to control butterfly caterpillars. In

a 1988 article for *Sierra,* Ehrlich wrote about the ecological significance of birds. According to the article, migratory birds reveal much about the environment because of their sensitivity to toxins and their vulnerability to the destruction of more than one habitat.

Overpopulation and Zero Population Growth

The topic with which Ehrlich has become most strongly associated, however, is overpopulation. Since 1958, Ehrlich argues, the human population has been increasing faster than the food supply—a formula for disaster. Overpopulation threatens to destroy the environment, as the planet's resources are depleted by high consumption and crowding. And although richer nations, which often have lower birth rates than poorer ones, are not generally thought of as overpopulated, Ehrlich calls the impact of people on the environment a truer measure of overpopulation than mere numbers. He maintains that the populations of rich countries are harming the environment more than the rapidly growing populations in poor countries. Thus the population of the United States, which consumes a disproportionate amount of the earth's resources, is a greater threat to the environment than are the larger populations of India or China.

With overpopulation, people survive by using up and destroying natural resources—fossil fuels, the soil, fresh water, and wildlife. According to Ehrlich, mankind must begin at once to husband resources, with particular attention to those classified as nonrenewable. Human overpopulation has already had a significant effect on the ecosystem; in addition to the depletion of mineral, soil, and other resources, a number of organisms are becoming or have become extinct as well. Ehrlich fears that entire species and communities will soon be lost, and that this loss of biodiversity will impair many vital functions performed by the environment. Ecosystems (communities of plants and animals and the physical environments with which they interact) regulate the climate, create supplies of fresh water, generate and regenerate agricultural and forest soils, and facilitate crop pollination, among other things. If overpopulation does destroy biodiversity, the habitability of the planet will be threatened.

The first and most important step toward solving the planet's problems, says Ehrlich, is to bring overpopulation to a halt, and, if possible, to reverse the trend. To this end, Ehrlich helped found Zero Population Growth, a political organization that supports strategies such as abortion, government involvement in birth control, and a two-child limit for families. Putting his views into practice on a personal level, Ehrlich was himself sterilized by a vasectomy after the birth of his only child. He sees zero population growth, when the number of people being born equals the number dying, as a way of buying time to solve the serious environmental issues facing the planet.

Suggestions for World Survival

Ehrlich's many books and articles offer readers a guide to the environment, information on crucial environmental issues, and suggestions for immediate action, both at a governmental level and at a personal, individual level. He provides suggestions for changes that will sustain the life of the planet. Humans must become more conscious of the environment, he is convinced, and must learn to consider the long-term environmental threats posed by the problems that already exist. For example, Ehrlich contends that if the destruction of tropical rain forests continues at its current rate, the result, within the next fifty years, will be the extinction of twenty-five percent or more of all the species presently alive on Earth. One of Ehrlich's primary aims is to increase the awareness of human beings about themselves, their planet, and the way in which they are affecting their environment. Humans require some understanding of basic science, he feels, and one of their most important tools for long-term species survival is a basic global ecological education.

Ehrlich contends that the American agenda must be to do everything possible to lessen the impact of the United States on the environment and to encourage other nations to follow suit. In addition to curbing population growth, he believes all government bodies should strive to preserve the integrity of extensive natural ecosystems. Ehrlich suggests that the United States move immediately to establish and implement a policy for population reduction, averting a threat he deems greater than that of nuclear war—especially since the end of the Cold War brought with it a lessening of international concern about the possibility of a nuclear war. Ehrlich also targets energy use, waste, debt in developing countries, and the need to preserve tropical forests.

Ehrlich's research and writings have won him a number of awards, including the Sierra Club's John Muir Award in 1980 and the World Wildlife Foundation medal in 1987. In 1990 he shared the Crafoord prize in Population Biology and Conservation of Biodiversity. His professional career, in addition to teaching, includes memberships in many academic and professional organizations, such as the American Academy of Arts and Sciences, the National Academy of Sciences, and the Entomological Society of America, and he is an honorary life member of the American Museum of Natural History. Ehrlich, a trustee of the Rocky Mountain Biological Laboratory, has also served as president of the Conservation Society. His leisure activities include running, which he does daily, and flying—he is a licensed pilot.

SELECTED WRITINGS BY EHRLICH:

Books

(With wife, Anne H. Ehrlich, and others) *How to Know the Butterflies,* William C. Brown, 1961.

(With Richard W. Holm) *The Process of Evolution,* McGraw, 1963, second edition, also with Dennis R. Parnell, 1974.

The Population Bomb, Ballantine Books, 1968, revised and expanded edition, 1971.

(With S. Shirley Feldman) *The Race Bomb: Skin Color, Prejudice, and Intelligence,* New York Times Co., 1977.

(With A. H. Ehrlich) *Extinction: The Causes and Consequences of the Disappearance of Species,* Random House, 1981.

The Machinery of Nature, Simon & Schuster, 1986.

(Editor with John P. Holdren) *The Cassandra Conference: Resources and the Human Predicament,* Texas A&M University Press, 1988.

(With A. H. Ehrlich) *The Population Explosion,* Simon & Schuster, 1990.

(With A. H. Ehrlich) *Healing the Planet,* Addison-Wesley, 1991.

Periodicals

"Winged Warning," *Sierra,* September/October, 1988, pp. 56–61.

"Population, Plenty, and Poverty," *National Geographic,* December, 1988, pp. 914–45.
(With Gretchen C. Daily) "Population, Sustainability, and Earth's Carrying Capacity," *BioScience,* November, 1992, pp. 761–72.

SOURCES:

Books

Contemporary Authors New Revision Series, Volume 28, Gale, 1990, pp. 151–52.

—*Sketch by Jessica Jahiel*

Manfred Eigen
1927-
German physical chemist

Manfred Eigen shared the Nobel Prize for chemistry in 1967 with **George Porter** and **Ronald G. W. Norrish** for their combined work on fast chemical reactions. Whereas previously scientists had no means of calculating the rates of these reactions, Eigen discovered that high-frequency sound waves could be used to create pulses of energy in a chemical system. Observing the change as the system returned to a state of equilibrium enabled him to measure rates of reactions that lasted only a billionth of a second. Most of his long career has been spent at the Max Planck Institute for Physical Chemistry in Göttingen. Eigen was born in the town of Bochum in the Ruhr region of Germany on May 9, 1927, to Ernst Eigen and Hedwig Feld Eigen. His father was an accomplished chamber musician, and Eigen was a talented pianist. He served briefly with an army anti-aircraft artillery unit at the end of World War II. He then returned to the University of Göttingen (where he had begun his education), earning his doctorate in 1951.

For several years Eigen worked as a research assistant at the University of Göttingen, and then he joined the staff at the Max Planck Institute for Physical Chemistry. In 1958 he was appointed a research fellow at the institute, and in 1962 he became head of the department of biochemical kinetics. In 1964 he was made the director.

Works With High-Frequency Sound Waves

Eigen discovered in his early research that the reason sound waves are absorbed by seawater more quickly than by water is that they disrupt the charged particles of magnesium sulfate, small amounts of which are dissolved in seawater. The sound wave causes the loss of a small amount of energy. This discovery led Eigen to use high-frequency sound waves to produce disturbances in a chemical system in order to measure rates of chemical processes that had not been measured before. He was able to study chemical reactions measuring from a thousandth to a billionth of a second. This technique is called a relaxation technique because it measures a new state of equilibrium in a chemical system.

The Origins of Life

Eigen's interest in fast chemical reactions is related to his interest in biology. He concentrated his research on extremely rapid biochemical body reactions in an effort to discover how molecules formed and evolved into the first forms of life. Basically, his theory is built on the premise that the first organisms evolved from a chance set of circumstances coming together. In *Laws of the Game,* a book that he coauthored with his associate Ruthild Winkler, Eigen explores how the principles of nature govern chance. The authors believe that chance and necessity cause all events. They develop their models from general science, philosophy, sociology, and aesthetics, as well as from biology. The models are used to explore complex scientific concepts. The authors see the play of games as being basic to both the organization of the physical world and to human behavior.

Applications of Relaxation Techniques

Eigen's relaxation techniques have been used to study enzyme-catalyzed reactions and the coding of biological information. During the 1970s he worked on hypercycles (the self-organization of nucleic acids into complex structures and their interaction with proteins). Eigen's work has been extremely valuable in many other areas of scientific investigation; it has been used in areas such as radiation chemistry and enzyme kinetics, where the sequence of processes becomes converted into products.

Much of Eigen's research is considered by his colleagues to be groundbreaking, since he opened new areas of application for relaxation techniques. He has received wide recognition for his work, winning a number of important awards, including the Otto Hahn Prize from the German Physical Society in 1962, the Linus Pauling Medal of the American Chemical Society in 1967, and the Faraday Medal of the British Chemical Society in 1977, and receiving honorary doctorates from universities in Europe and the U.S. He has written more than 100 papers and several books, and has traveled and lectured widely.

Eigen married Elfriede Mueller in 1952. The Eigens have two children, Gerald and Angela. Hobbies that Eigen enjoys are hiking and wild mushroom collecting (in which he is considered an expert).

SELECTED WRITINGS BY EIGEN:

Books

(With Peter Schuster) *The Hypercycle, a Principle of Natural Self-Organization,* Springer-Verlag, 1979.
(With Ruthild Winkler) *Laws of the Game: How the Principles of Nature Govern Chance,* Knopf, 1981.

Periodicals

"Methods for Investigation of Ionic Reactions in Aqueous Solutions with Half Times as Short as 10–9 Sec.: Application to Neutralization and Hydrolysis Reactions," *Discussions of the Faraday Society* 17, 1954, pp. 194–205.
(With G. Czerlinski) "A Temperature-Jump Method for the Examination of Chemical Relaxation," *Zeitschrift für Elektrochemie* 63, 1959, 652–61.

SOURCES:

Books

Wasson, Tyler, editor, *Nobel Prize Winners,* H. W. Wilson, 1987, pp. 286–87.

Periodicals

New Yorker, August 24, 1981, p. 102.
New York Times, October 31, 1967.
Science, November 10, 1967, pp. 746–747.

—*Sketch by Jordan Richman*

Christiaan Eijkman
1858-1930
Dutch physician

Christiaan Eijkman was a pioneer in the study of diseases that result from deficiencies in a patient's diet. His major contribution was the discovery that the lack of some vital substance in food caused a disease in chickens similar to beriberi in man. For this work, which helped lead to the concept of vitamins, he received the Nobel Prize in physiology or medicine in 1929.

Eijkman was born on August 11, 1858, in Nijkerk, Netherlands. He was the seventh child of a schoolmaster father, also named Christiaan Eijkman, and Johanna Alida Pool Eijkman. Theirs was a family of academically gifted sons whose professional careers would encompass the fields of chemistry, linguistics, and radiology. Soon after Eijkman's birth, the family moved to Zaandam, where he received his early education. In 1875, he began training as a military medical officer at the University of Amsterdam. There, his own ability quickly made itself apparent; he received a medical degree with high honors in 1883.

Studies Beriberi in the Dutch East Indies

That same year, Eijkman was dispatched by the army to the Dutch East Indies (now Indonesia), where he served on the islands of Java and Sumatra until a severe case of malaria forced him to return home in 1885. This proved to be a blessing in disguise, however, for Eijkman used his recuperation time to study the new science of bacteriology under one of the field's founders, Robert Koch, in Berlin. A year later, Eijkman was strong enough to return to the East Indies as part of a Dutch government mission to investigate the disease beriberi. He owed his spot on the research team to personal contacts he had made while working in Koch's laboratory.

The name beriberi comes from the Sinhalese word for "extreme weakness." The disease, characterized by impairment of the nerves, heart, and digestive system, can cause such symptoms as paralysis, numbness, swelling, and difficulty breathing. At the time, the illness was spreading rapidly in Asia, and many European doctors were convinced that the epidemic was bacterial in origin. Eijkman, too, erroneously believed that his search for the source of beriberi would ultimately lead to a microorganism.

In 1888, Eijkman was appointed head of the Javanese Medical School and director of a bacteriological laboratory in Batavia (now Djakarta), where he made a chance observation that would change the course of medicine. An illness, very much like beriberi, suddenly broke out among the laboratory chickens, then just as mysteriously went away. Eijkman learned that an attendant had, for a short time, been feeding the birds cooked white rice from the hospital kitchen. The disappearance of the birds' symptoms coincided with the arrival of a new cook, who refused to allow hospital rice to be used for this purpose. Eijkman soon found that he could produce the disease at will by feeding the chickens hulled and polished rice, and he could just as readily cure it with a diet of whole rice. Eijkman's observations were the starting point for a line of inquiry that led others to an understanding of and treatment for beriberi. Later researchers traced the disease to a lack of thiamine (vitamin B1), a vitamin found in the hulls of unpolished rice. Ironically, Eijkman failed to grasp the true meaning of his findings. He hypothesized that the rice hulls contained a substance that neutralized a toxin carried in or produced by the rice grains. Nevertheless, Eijkman had shown that not every illness could be explained by the then-revolutionary germ theory of disease, and it is for this achievement that he is primarily remembered today.

Conducts Research in Physiology and Hygiene

Eijkman's other important work in the Dutch East Indies was his study of the physiology of people living in the region. He disproved many widely held notions about the effects of tropical life on Europeans, which in the past had led to several unnecessary precautions. For example, he demonstrated that expected differences in metabolism, respiration, perspiration, and temperature regulation between Europeans and natives of the tropics did not, in fact, exist. In 1896, Eijkman once again returned to the Netherlands on sick leave. Two years later, he assumed the post of professor of public health and forensic medicine at the University of Utrecht, where he conducted fermentation tests by examining water for signs of bacterial pollution produced by human and animal defecation. As a lecturer, Eijkman was known for his clear demonstrations, perhaps the result of decades of hands-on experience in the lab.

Eijkman did not confine his interests to the university, however. He was actively involved in such issues as the public water supply, housing, school hygiene, and physical education. As a member of his nation's Health Council and Health Commission, he fought against alcoholism and tuberculosis. In recognition of Eijkman's many contributions to society, the Dutch government conferred several orders of knighthood upon him. He was also made a member of the Netherlands' Royal Academy of Sciences in 1907. But the 1929 Nobel Prize, which he shared with Sir Frederick Gowland Hopkins of Great Britain, the discoverer of growth-stimulating vitamins, was his crowning honor. Sadly, though, the seventy-one-year-old Eijkman, who had retired a year earlier, was by this time too sick to travel to Stockholm to receive his prize in person.

Eijkman's first wife, the former Aaltje Wigeri van Edema, had died in 1886, soon after his initial return from the East Indies, and just three years after their marriage. Eijkman subsequently married Bertha Julie Louise van der Kemp in 1888, in Batavia. Their son, Pieter Hendrik, who was born in 1890, went on to become a physician. Eijkman himself died on November 5, 1930, in Utrecht, Netherlands, after a protracted illness. Yet, insights gleaned from writings he left behind, primarily in Dutch reports and periodicals, insure that his legacy will long remain alive.

SELECTED WRITINGS BY EIJKMAN:

Books

"Antineuritic Vitamin and Beriberi," in *Nobel Lectures Including Presentation Speeches and Laureates' Biographies: Physiology or Medicine 1922–1941,* Elsevier, 1965, pp. 199–210.

SOURCES:

Books

Dictionary of Scientific Biography, Scribner, 1971, pp. 310–12.

Periodicals

Carter, K Codell, "The Germ Theory, Beriberi, and the Deficiency Theory of Disease," *Medical History,* April, 1977, pp. 119–36.

—*Sketch by Linda Wasmer Smith*

Albert Einstein
1879-1955
German-born American physicist

Albert Einstein ranks as one of the most remarkable theoreticians in the history of science. During a single year, 1905, he produced three papers that are among the most important in twentieth-century physics, and perhaps in all of the recorded history of science, for they revolutionized the way scientists looked at the nature of space, time, and matter. These papers dealt with the nature of particle movement known as Brownian motion, the quantum nature of electromagnetic radiation as demonstrated by the photoelectric effect, and the special theory of relativity. Although Einstein is probably best known for the last of these works, it was for his quantum explanation of the photoelectric effect that he was awarded the 1921 Nobel Prize in physics. In 1915, Einstein extended his special theory of relativity to

Albert Einstein

include certain cases of accelerated motion, resulting in the more general theory of relativity.

Einstein was born in Ulm, Germany, on March 14, 1879, the only son of Hermann and Pauline Koch Einstein. Both sides of his family had long-established roots in southern Germany, and, at the time of Einstein's birth, his father and uncle Jakob owned a small electrical equipment plant. When that business failed around 1880, Hermann Einstein moved his family to Munich to make a new beginning. A year after their arrival in Munich, Einstein's only sister, Maja, was born.

Although his family was Jewish, Einstein was sent to a Catholic elementary school from 1884 to 1889. He was then enrolled at the Luitpold Gymnasium in Munich. During these years, Einstein began to develop some of his earliest interests in science and mathematics, but he gave little outward indication of any special aptitude in these fields. Indeed, he did not begin to talk until the age of three and, by the age of nine, was still not fluent in his native language. His parents were actually concerned that he might be somewhat mentally retarded.

Leaves School Early and Moves to Italy

In 1894, Hermann Einstein's business failed again, and the family moved once more, this time to Pavia, near Milan, Italy. Einstein was left behind in Munich to allow him to finish school. Such was not to be the case, however, since he left the *gymnasium*

after only six more months. Einstein's biographer, Philipp Frank, explains that Einstein so thoroughly despised formal schooling that he devised a scheme by which he received a medical excuse from school on the basis of a potential nervous breakdown. He then convinced a mathematics teacher to certify that he was adequately prepared to begin his college studies without a high school diploma. Other biographies, however, say that Einstein was expelled from the *gymnasium* on the grounds that he was a disruptive influence at the school.

In any case, Einstein then rejoined his family in Italy. One of his first acts upon reaching Pavia was to give up his German citizenship. He was so unhappy with his native land that he wanted to sever all formal connections with it; in addition, by renouncing his citizenship, he could later return to Germany without being arrested as a draft dodger. As a result, Einstein remained without an official citizenship until he became a Swiss citizen at the age of 21. For most of his first year in Italy, Einstein spent his time traveling, relaxing, and teaching himself calculus and higher mathematics. In 1895, he thought himself ready to take the entrance examination for the Eidgenössiche Technische Hochschule (the ETH, Swiss Federal Polytechnic School, or Swiss Federal Institute of Technology), where he planned to major in electrical engineering. When he failed that examination, Einstein enrolled at a Swiss cantonal high school in Aarau. He found the more democratic style of instruction at Aarau much more enjoyable than his experience in Munich and soon began to make rapid progress. He took the entrance examination for the ETH a second time in 1896, passed, and was admitted to the school. (In *Einstein,* however, Jeremy Bernstein writes that Einstein was admitted without examination on the basis of his diploma from Aarau.)

The program at ETH had nearly as little appeal for Einstein as had his schooling in Munich, however. He apparently hated studying for examinations and was not especially interested in attending classes on a regular basis. He devoted much of this time to reading on his own, specializing in the works of Gustav Kirchhoff, Heinrich Hertz, James Clerk Maxwell, Ernst Mach, and other classical physicists. When Einstein graduated with a teaching degree in 1900, he was unable to find a regular teaching job. Instead, he supported himself as a tutor in a private school in Schaffhausen. In 1901, Einstein also published his first scientific paper, "Consequences of Capillary Phenomena."

In February, 1902, Einstein moved to Bern and applied for a job with the Swiss Patent Office. He was given a probationary appointment to begin in June of that year and was promoted to the position of technical expert, third class, a few months later. The seven years Einstein spent at the Patent Office were the most productive years of his life. The demands of his work were relatively modest and he was able to devote a great deal of time to his own research.

The promise of a steady income at the Patent Office also made it possible for Einstein to marry. Mileva Marić (also given as Maritsch) was a fellow student in physics at ETH, and Einstein had fallen in love with her even though his parents strongly objected to the match. Marić had originally come from Hungary and was of Serbian and Greek Orthodox heritage. The couple married on January 6, 1903, and later had two sons, Hans Albert and Edward. A previous child, Liserl, was born in 1902 at the home of Marić's parents in Hungary, but there is no further mention or trace of her after 1903 since she was given up for adoption.

Explains Brownian Movement and the Photoelectric Effect

In 1905, Einstein published a series of papers, any one of which would have assured his fame in history. One, "On the Movement of Small Particles Suspended in a Stationary Liquid Demanded by the Molecular-Kinetic Theory of Heat," dealt with a phenomenon first observed by the Scottish botanist Robert Brown in 1827. Brown had reported that tiny particles, such as dust particles, move about with a rapid and random zigzag motion when suspended in a liquid.

Einstein hypothesized that the visible motion of particles was caused by the random movement of molecules that make up the liquid. He derived a mathematical formula that predicted the distance traveled by particles and their relative speed. This formula was confirmed experimentally by the French physicist **Jean Baptiste Perrin** in 1908. Einstein's work on the Brownian movement is generally regarded as the first direct experimental evidence of the existence of molecules.

A second paper, "On a Heuristic Viewpoint concerning the Production and Transformation of Light," dealt with another puzzle in physics, the photoelectric effect. First observed by Heinrich Hertz in 1888, the photoelectric effect involves the release of electrons from a metal that occurs when light is shined on the metal. The puzzling aspect of the photoelectric effect was that the number of electrons released is not a function of the light's intensity, but of the color (that is, the wavelength) of the light.

To solve this problem, Einstein made use of a concept developed only a few years before, in 1900, by the German physicist **Max Planck**, the quantum hypothesis. Einstein assumed that light travels in tiny discrete bundles, or "quanta," of energy. The energy of any given light quantum (later renamed the photon), Einstein said, is a function of its wavelength. Thus, when light falls on a metal, electrons in the metal absorb specific quanta of energy, giving them enough energy to escape from the surface of the metal. But the number of electrons released will be determined not by the number of quanta (that is, the intensity) of the light, but by its energy (that is, its wavelength). Einstein's hypothesis was confirmed by several experiments and laid the foundation for the fields of quantitative photoelectric chemistry and quantum mechanics. As recognition for this work, Einstein was awarded the 1921 Nobel Prize in physics.

Refines the Theory of Relativity

A third 1905 paper by Einstein, almost certainly the one for which he became best known, details his special theory of relativity. In essence, "On the Electrodynamics of Moving Bodies" discusses the relationship between measurements made by observers in two separate systems moving at constant velocity with respect to each other.

Einstein's work on relativity was by no means the first in the field. The French physicist **Jules Henri Poincaré**, the Irish physicist George Francis FitzGerald, and the Dutch physicist **Hendrik Lorentz** had already analyzed in some detail the problem attacked by Einstein in his 1905 paper. Each had developed mathematical formulas that described the effect of motion on various types of measurement. Indeed, the record of pre-Einsteinian thought on relativity is so extensive that one historian of science once wrote a two-volume work on the subject that devoted only a single sentence to Einstein's work. Still, there is little question that Einstein provided the most complete analysis of this subject. He began by making two assumptions. First, he said that the laws of physics are the same in all frames of reference. Second, he declared that the velocity of light is always the same, regardless of the conditions under which it is measured.

Using only these two assumptions, Einstein proceeded to uncover an unexpectedly extensive description of the properties of bodies that are in uniform motion. For example, he showed that the length and mass of an object are dependent upon their movement relative to an observer. He derived a mathematical relationship between the length of an object and its velocity that had previously been suggested by both FitzGerald and Lorentz. Einstein's theory was revolutionary, for previously scientists had believed that basic quantities of measurement such as time, mass, and length were absolute and unchanging. Einstein's work established the opposite—that these measurements could change, depending on the relative motion of the observer.

In addition to his masterpieces on the photoelectric effect, Brownian movement, and relativity, Einstein wrote two more papers in 1905. One, "Does the

Inertia of a Body Depend on Its Energy Content?," dealt with an extension of his earlier work on relativity. He came to the conclusion in this paper that the energy and mass of a body are closely interrelated. Two years later he specifically stated that relationship in a formula, $E=mc^2$ (energy equals mass times the speed of light squared), that is now familiar to both scientists and non-scientists alike. His final paper, the most modest of the five, was "A New Determination of Molecular Dimensions." It was this paper that Einstein submitted as his doctoral dissertation, for which the University of Zurich awarded him a Ph.D. in 1905.

Fame did not come to Einstein immediately as a result of his five 1905 papers. Indeed, he submitted his paper on relativity to the University of Bern in support of his application to become a *privatdozent*, or unsalaried instructor, but the paper and application were rejected. His work was too important to be long ignored, however, and a second application three years later was accepted. Einstein spent only a year at Bern, however, before taking a job as professor of physics at the University of Zurich in 1909. He then went on to the German University of Prague for a year and a half before returning to Zurich and a position at ETH in 1912. A year later Einstein was made director of scientific research at the Kaiser Wilhelm Institute for Physics in Berlin, a post he held from 1914 to 1933.

Debate Centers on the Role of Einstein's Wife in His Work

In recent years, the role of Mileva Einstein-Marić in her husband's early work has been the subject of some controversy. The more traditional view among Einstein's biographers is that of A. P. French in his "Condensed Biography" in *Einstein: A Centenary Volume*. French argues that although "little is recorded about his [Einstein's] domestic life, it certainly did not inhibit his scientific activity." In perhaps the most substantial of all Einstein biographies, Philipp Frank writes that "For Einstein life with her was not always a source of peace and happiness. When he wanted to discuss with her his ideas, which came to him in great abundance, her response was so slight that he was often unable to decide whether or not she was interested."

A quite different view of the relationship between Einstein and Marić is presented in a 1990 paper by Senta Troemel-Ploetz in *Women's Studies International Forum*. Based on a biography of Marić originally published in Yugoslavia, Troemel-Ploetz argues that Marić gave to her husband "her companionship, her diligence, her endurance, her mathematical genius, and her mathematical devotion." Indeed, Troemel-Ploetz builds a case that it was Marić who did a significant portion of the mathematical calcula-

tions involved in much of Einstein's early work. She begins by repeating a famous remark by Einstein himself to the effect that "My wife solves all my mathematical problems." In addition, Troemel-Ploetz cites many of Einstein's own letters of 1900 and 1901 (available in *Collected Papers*) that allude to Marić's role in the development of "our papers," including one letter to Marić in which Einstein noted: "How happy and proud I will be when both of us together will have brought our work on relative motion to a successful end." The author also points out the somewhat unexpected fact that Einstein gave the money he received from the 1921 Nobel Prize to Marić, although the two had been divorced two years earlier. Nevertheless, Einstein never publicly acknowledged any contributions by his wife to his work.

Any mathematical efforts Mileva Einstein-Marić may have contributed to Einstein's work greatly decreased after the birth of their second son in 1910. Einstein was increasingly occupied with his career and his wife with managing their household; upon moving to Berlin in 1914, the couple grew even more distant. With the outbreak of World War I, Einstein's wife and two children returned to Zurich. The two were never reconciled; in 1919, they were formally divorced. Towards the end of the war, Einstein became very ill and was nursed back to health by his cousin Elsa. Not long after Einstein's divorce from Marić, he was married to Elsa, a widow. The two had no children of their own, although Elsa brought two daughters, Ilse and Margot, to the marriage.

Announces the General Theory of Relativity

The war years also marked the culmination of Einstein's attempt to extend his 1905 theory of relativity to a broader context, specifically to systems with non-zero acceleration. Under the general theory of relativity, motions no longer had to be uniform and relative velocities no longer constant. Einstein was able to write mathematical expressions that describe the relationships between measurements made in *any* two systems in motion relative to each other, even if the motion is accelerated in one or both. One of the fundamental features of the general theory is the concept of a space-time continuum in which space is curved. That concept means that a body affects the shape of the space that surrounds it so that a second body moving near the first body will travel in a curved path.

Einstein's new theory was too radical to be immediately accepted, for not only were the mathematics behind it extremely complex, it replaced Newton's theory of gravitation that had been accepted for two centuries. So, Einstein offered three proofs for his theory that could be tested: first, that relativity would cause Mercury's perihelion, or point of orbit closest to the sun, to advance slightly more than was predicted by Newton's laws. Second, Einstein predicted that light from a star will be bent as it passes close to a massive body, such as the sun. Last, the physicist suggested that relativity would also affect light by changing its wavelength, a phenomenon known as the redshift effect. Observations of the planet Mercury bore out Einstein's hypothesis and calculations, but astronomers and physicists had yet to test the other two proofs.

Einstein had calculated that the amount of light bent by the sun would amount to 1.7 seconds of an arc, a small but detectable effect. In 1919, during an eclipse of the sun, English astronomer **Arthur Eddington** measured the deflection of starlight and found it to be 1.61 seconds of an arc, well within experimental error. The publication of this proof made Einstein an instant celebrity and made "relativity" a household word, although it was not until 1924 that Eddington proved the final hypothesis concerning redshift with a spectral analysis of the star Sirius B. This phenomenon, that light would be shifted to a longer wavelength in the presence of a strong gravitational field, became known as the "Einstein shift."

Einstein's publication of his general theory in 1916, the *Foundation of the General Theory of Relativity,* essentially brought to a close the revolutionary period of his scientific career. In many ways, Einstein had begun to fall out of phase with the rapid changes taking place in physics during the 1920s. Even though Einstein's own work on the photoelectric effect helped set the stage for the development of quantum theory, he was never able to accept some of its concepts, particularly the uncertainty principle. In one of the most-quoted comments in the history of science, he claimed that quantum mechanics, which could only calculate the probabilities of physical events, could not be correct because "God does not play dice." Instead, Einstein devoted his efforts for the remaining years of his life to the search for a unified field theory, a single theory that would encompass all physical fields, particularly gravitation and electromagnetism.

Becomes Involved in Political Issues

Since the outbreak of World War I, Einstein had been opposed to war, and used his notoriety to lecture against it during the 1920s and 1930s. With the rise of National Socialism in Germany in the early 1930s, Einstein's position became difficult. Although he had renewed his German citizenship, he was suspect as both a Jew and a pacifist. In addition, his writings about relativity were in conflict with the absolutist teachings of German leader Adolf Hitler's party. Fortunately, by 1930, Einstein had become internationally famous and had traveled widely throughout the world. A number of institutions were eager to add his name to their faculties.

In early 1933, Einstein made a decision. He was out of Germany when Hitler rose to power, and he decided not to return. Instead he accepted an appointment at the Institute for Advanced Studies in Princeton, New Jersey, where he spent the rest of his life. In addition to his continued work on unified field theory, Einstein was in demand as a speaker and wrote extensively on many topics, especially peace. The growing fascism and anti-Semitism of Hitler's regime, however, convinced him in 1939 to sign his name to a letter written by American physicist **Leo Szilard** informing President Franklin D. Roosevelt of the possibility of an atomic bomb. This letter led to the formation of the Manhattan Project for the construction of the world's first nuclear weapons. Although Einstein's work on relativity, particularly his formulation of the equation $E=mc^2$, was essential to the development of the atomic bomb, Einstein himself did not participate in the project. He was considered a security risk, although he had renounced his German citizenship and become a U.S. citizen in 1940.

After World War II and the bombing of Japan, Einstein became an ardent supporter of nuclear disarmament. He also lent his support to the efforts to establish a world government and to the Zionist movement to establish a Jewish state. In 1952, after the death of Israel's first president, Chaim Weizmann, Einstein was invited to succeed him as president; he declined the offer. Among the many other honors given to Einstein were the Barnard Medal of Columbia University in 1920, the Copley Medal of the Royal Society in 1925, the Gold Medal of the Royal Astronomical Society in 1926, the Max Planck Medal of the German Physical Society in 1929, and the Franklin Medal of the Franklin Institute in 1935. Einstein died at his home in Princeton on April 18, 1955, after suffering an aortic aneurysm. At the time of his death, he was the world's most widely admired scientist and his name was synonymous with genius. Yet Einstein declined to become enamored of the admiration of others. He wrote in his book *The World as I See It:* "Let every man be respected as an individual and no man idolized. It is an irony of fate that I myself have been the recipient of excessive admiration and respect from my fellows through no fault, and no merit, of my own. The cause of this may well be the desire, unattainable for many, to understand the one or two ideas to which I have with my feeble powers attained through ceaseless struggle."

SELECTED WRITINGS BY EINSTEIN:

Books

On the Method of Theoretical Physics, Oxford University Press, 1933.
Essays on Science, Philosophical Library, 1934.

The World as I See It, John Lane, 1935.

(With L. Infeld) *The Evolution of Physics: The Growth of Ideas from Early Concepts to Relativity and Quanta,* Simon and Schuster, 1938.

The Meaning of Relativity, Princeton University Press, 1950.

Out of My Later Years, Philosophical Library, 1950.

(With others) *The Principle of Relativity,* Dover, 1952.

Ideas and Opinions, Crown, 1954.

Investigations on the Theory of the Brownian Movement, edited by R. Fürth, Dover, 1956.

Einstein on Peace, edited by Otto Nathan and Heinz Norden, Schocken Books, 1960.

Relativity: The Special and General Theory, Crown, 1961.

The Collected Papers of Albert Einstein, Princeton University Press, Volume 1, 1987, Volume 2, 1989, Volume 3, 1993.

Periodicals

"On the Movement of Small Particles Suspended in a Stationary Liquid Demanded by the Molecular-Kinetic Theory of Heat," *Annalen der Physik,* 1905.

"On a Heuristic Viewpoint concerning the Production and Transformation of Light," *Annalen der Physik,* 1905.

"On the Electrodynamics of Moving Bodies," *Annalen der Physik,* 1905.

"Does the Inertia of a Body Depend on Its Energy Content?," *Annalen der Physik,* 1905.

"A New Determination of Molecular Dimensions," 1905.

SOURCES:

Books

Bernstein, Jeremy, *Einstein,* Fontana, 1973.

Clark, Ronald W., *Einstein: The Life and Times,* World Publishing, 1971.

Feldman, Anthony, and Peter Ford, *Scientists & Inventors,* Facts on File, 1979, pp. 264–265.

Frank, Philipp, *Einstein: His Life and Times,* Knopf, 1947.

French, A. P., *Einstein: A Centenary Volume,* Harvard University Press, 1979.

Highfield, Roger, and Paul Carter, *The Private Lives of Albert Einstein,* Faber, 1993.

Hoffmann, Banesh, *Albert Einstein: Creator and Rebel,* Viking, 1972.

Infeld, Leopold, *Quest,* Doubleday, Doran, 1941.

Pais, Abraham, *Subtle Is the Lord,* Oxford University Press, 1982.

Seelig, Carl, *Albert Einstein: A Documentary Biography,* Staples Press, 1956.

Will, Clifford M., *Was Einstein Right?: Putting General Relativity to the Test,* Basic Books, 1986.

Periodicals

Shankland, Robert S., "Conversations with Albert Einstein," *American Journal of Physics,* Volume 31, 1963, pp. 37–47.

Troemel-Ploetz, Senta, "Mileva Einstein-Marić: The Woman Who Did Einstein's Math," *Women's Studies International Forum,* Volume 13, number 5, 1990, pp. 415–432.

—*Sketch by David E. Newton*

Willem Einthoven
1860-1927
Dutch physiologist

Although trained in medicine, Willem Einthoven was always very much interested in physics, and his greatest contributions to science involve the application of physical principles to the development of new instruments and techniques in physiological studies. One such instrument, the string galvanometer, made possible the first valid and reliable electrocardiogram, thereby providing physicians with one of their most valuable tools for the study of cardiovascular disorders. For his invention of the string galvanometer, Einthoven was awarded the Nobel Prize for Physiology or Medicine in 1924.

Einthoven was born on May 21, 1860, in Semarang, Java, in what was then the Dutch East Indies and is now Indonesia. His father, Jacob Einthoven, was a physician in Semarang. When Jacob died in 1866, his wife, Louise M. M. C. de Vogel, returned to her native Holland with her six children, Willem included. The family settled in Utrecht, where young Willem attended local grammar and high schools. Upon graduation from high school in 1879, he enrolled in the medical program at the University of Utrecht. Six years later, Einthoven received his Ph.D. in medicine, having written his doctoral thesis on the use of color differentiation techniques in spectroscopic analysis. He was immediately offered an appointment as professor of physiology at the University of Leiden, a job he actually began after passing his final state medical examinations on February 24, 1886. Einthoven would remain at his post at the University of Leiden for the next forty-two years until his death in 1927. Also in 1886, Einthoven was married to Frédérique Jeanne Louise de Vogel, a cousin, with whom he would father four children: a son and three daughters. Perhaps the most significant feature of Einthoven's career is the way he made use of his interest in—and knowledge of—physics in his study of physiological problems. The research for which he is best known involved the detection of the association between electrical currents and the beating human heart. Physiologists in the 1880s knew that each contraction of the heart muscle is accompanied by electrical changes in the body, but no precise quantitative data existed for this phenomenon. At that time, the only equipment available to measure electrical charges in the body was not sensitive enough to detect the minute changes in potential difference—the amount of energy released—associated with a heartbeat. The most commonly used device, a capillary electrometer, made use of the rise and fall of a thin column of mercury in a glass tube. Unfortunately, the measurement process of such an instrument took place too slowly to determine actual changes in potential difference resulting from muscular contractions.

Around 1903, Einthoven invented an improved method for measuring such changes: the string galvanometer. Einthoven's new instrument consisted of a very thin quartz wire suspended in a magnetic field. An electric current, even one as small as those associated with muscular contraction, caused a deflection of the wire. By focusing a moving picture camera on the wire, Einthoven could obtain a visual record of the movement of the wire as it was displaced by electrical currents from the heart.

As a result of his research, Einthoven was able to detect and identify a number of different kinds of electrical waves associated with a beating heart, waves that he originally labeled as P, Q, R, S, and T waves. He was eventually able to show that some of these waves result from contractions and electrical changes in the atria and others from contractions and electrical changes in the ventricles of the heart.

Einthoven published a complete description of his string galvanometer in 1909 as *Die Konstruktion des Sitengalvanometers*. In this work, he outlined a method for using the galvanometer to record heart action using three combinations of electrode placement: right hand to left hand, right hand to left foot, and left hand to left foot. Such arrangements of the electrodes could be used, he showed, to locate the position of the heart and to detect any abnormalities in its function.

In *Nobel Prize Winners*, Einthoven's biographer points out that the invention of the string electrode "revolutionized the study of heart disease." For his accomplishment, Einthoven was awarded the Nobel Prize for Physiology or Medicine in 1924. Interesting-

ly enough, the basic principles of electrocardiography, while first developed by Einthoven, were also derived independently a short time later by the English physicians Sir Thomas Lewis, Sir William Ogler, and James Herrick.

Einthoven continued to refine, develop, and extend the applications of his string galvanometer throughout the rest of his career. For example, later in his life he modified the device so that it could be used to receive long-distance radio telegraph signals and to measure changes in electric potential in nerves. He was also very popular as a lecturer and made a number of trips to Europe and the United States to talk about his work. Among the many honors Einthoven received was his election as an honorary member of the Physiological Society in 1924, and his induction into England's prestigious Royal Society two years later in 1926.

Einthoven died in Leiden, Netherlands, on September 28, 1927. His obituary in the periodical *Nature* spoke of the "grace, beauty, and simplicity of his character." Although he left few students or disciples behind, Einthoven's impact on the development of electrocardiography was profound.

SELECTED WRITINGS BY EINTHOVEN:

Periodicals

"The Relation of Mechanical and Electrical Phenomena of Muscular Contraction with Special Reference to the Cardiac Muscle," in *Harvey Society Lectures,* [Philadelphia], 1924.
"Das Saitengalvanometer und die Messung der Aktionsströme des Herzens," in *Les Prix Nobel 1924–1925,* [Stockholm], 1926.

SOURCES:

Books

A Biographical Dictionary of Scientists, Wiley, 1974, pp. 163–64.
Dictionary of Scientific Biography, Volume 4, Scribner, 1975, pp. 333–35.
Nobel Prize Winners, H. W. Wilson, 1987, pp. 294–95.

Periodicals

Hill, A. V., "Obituary: Prof. W. Einthoven," *Nature,* October 22, 1927, pp. 591–92.
Hill, Leonard, "Willem Einthoven," *British Medical Journal,* Volume 2, 1927, p. 665.

Lewis, T., "Willem Einthoven," *British Medical Journal,* Volume 2, 1927, pp. 664–65.

—*Sketch by David E. Newton*

Thomas Eisner
1929-
German-born American entomologist

Thomas Eisner is one of the world's foremost authorities on the role of chemicals in the behavior and survival of insects. He has also played an active role in the crusade to preserve the world's endangered rain forests and other threatened lands. Eisner was born in Berlin, Germany, on June 25, 1929, the second of two children. His father, Hans E. Eisner, was a chemist, and as a hobby made perfumes, lotions, and home remedies. The intriguing odors that filled their home caused Eisner to develop an early interest in both chemistry and the art of "sniffing." His mother, Margarete Heil Eisner, a painter, instilled in him an appreciation for nature's beauty.

Eisner's father was Jewish and in 1933, when Eisner was only four years old, the family fled Nazi Germany. They settled for a few years in Barcelona, Spain, and there the young Eisner began to develop a fascination with insects. One day, while sitting in a sand box playing with pill bugs (wood lice), a violent explosion shook the neighborhood. Eisner's recollection, according to a *Scientific American* profile in 1991, was that he was annoyed rather than frightened. The commotion had interrupted the fun he was having with his insects. The explosion was a harbinger of the Spanish Civil War. Its violence caused the Eisners to flee again, this time for France, aboard a freighter carrying diseased cattle and hordes of refugees. They settled in Paris for half a year, and there the family rented a piano. It was Eisner's first introduction to the instrument on which he would eventually become accomplished. In 1937, with the threat of World War II looming, the Eisner family left Europe altogether and set off for South America, eventually finding a home in Uruguay. There was much insect life in his new environment, and as a young boy Eisner made collections of the beetles, tropical moths, and ants he encountered. His fascination with insects was rivaled only by his enjoyment of music. He considered becoming a professional pianist, but eventually chose the sciences.

In 1947 Eisner's family moved again, this time to New York City. He enrolled in Champlain College in Plattsburg, New York, but two years later transferred to Harvard University, where he received the B.A. degree in 1951. In 1952 he became a naturalized U.S. citizen, and that same year he married Maria Lobell. Originally trained in social work, she went on to become an entomologist and occasional research collaborator with Eisner. Together they had three daughters, Yvonne Maria in 1954, Vivian Martha in 1957, and Christina Margaret in 1959.

During Eisner's senior year at Harvard he had taken a course in entomology, an experience that led him to realize it was possible to make a career out of studying insects. He went on to enroll in the entomology department at Harvard and received his Ph.D. in 1955. While a graduate student he discovered, by performing delicate microscopic surgery, an unusual valve in the digestive tract of certain ants. The valve enables the ants to ingest enormous amounts of food that they later regurgitate and feed to other ants. During the two years following his graduate work, Eisner did postdoctoral research at Harvard on insect physiology. In 1957 he accepted an appointment as an assistant professor at Cornell University, in Ithaca, New York.

Develops Field of Chemical Ecology

Eisner has remained on the faculty at Cornell University since 1957, rising through the ranks to full professorship in 1966. Since 1976 he has held the title of Jacob Gould Schurman Professor of Biology. At Cornell Eisner's research interests shifted from insect physiology to the chemical aspects of insect behavior. Since then his scientific work has focused on the intricate and unusual ways in which insects use chemistry to court, communicate, defend themselves, and remain healthy. A pioneer in his field, he is considered the father of chemical ecology, the study of chemical relationships among living things.

Using high-speed photography and microscopic lenses, he has detected previously unknown insect strategies for capturing prey and repelling enemies. Many of these strategies involve the use of chemicals. Eisner is perhaps best known for his discovery of the unusual defensive behavior of the bombardier beetle. At the tip of the beetle's abdomen is a gland that operates like a gun turret, firing rounds of scalding hot poison at a rate of five hundred pulses per second. Eisner has helped decipher the flash code of "femme-fatale fireflies" and documented the use of disguise by green lacewing larvae to gain access to their prey, woolly alder aphids. He is intrigued by the chemical odors that insects give off, and employs the olfactory skills he developed in his youth to detect chemical communication among his research subjects. Many of Eisner's practical discoveries have been the result of collaborative efforts with his colleague, Cornell University chemist Jerrold Meinwald. Together they have discovered nerve drugs in millipedes, cardiac stimulants in fireflies, and cockroach repellents in an endangered mint plant.

Leads Conservationist Movement

Eisner's interest in insect life has led naturally to a broader concern for preservation of natural habitats. He has taken a leadership role in the conservation movement, testifying before United States Senate subcommittees on the Endangered Species Act, helping to publicize the effects of overpopulation on the environment, and serving on the advisory council of the World Resources Institute. He was responsible for convincing the pharmaceutical firm of Merck & Company to strike a deal with the Costa Rican government that preserves their rain forest and provides chemical prospecting rights to Merck. Eisner's research and activism have increased public awareness about the benefits of biodiversity.

Eisner has received numerous awards for his conservation efforts and other achievements, including the Karl Ritter von Frisch Medal from the Deutsche Zoologische Gesellschaft and the Tyler Prize for Environmental Achievement. He has held two Guggenheim fellowships. He became a member of the National Academy of Sciences in 1969. He has been awarded honorary doctorate degrees from colleges and universities in the United States, Germany, Switzerland, and Sweden.

In his spare time, Eisner continues to pursue his love of music, conducting an amateur Cornell University orchestra called BRAHMS, an acronym for Biweekly Rehearsal Association of Honorary Musicians. His insect laboratory at the university is equipped with an upright piano.

SELECTED WRITINGS BY EISNER:

Books

(Editor with E. O. Wilson) *Animal Behavior: Readings from Scientific American,* W. H. Freeman, 1975.
(Editor with E. O. Wilson) *The Insects: Readings from Scientific American,* W. H. Freeman, 1977.

Periodicals

(With E. O. Wilson) "Quantitative Studies of Liquid Food Transmission in Ants," *Insectes sociaux,* Volume 4, 1957, pp. 147–166.
"How Moths Escape from Spider Webs," *Nature and Science,* Volume 4, 1967, pp. 6–7.

(With D. J. Aneshansley, J. M. Widom, and B. Widom) "Biochemistry at 100°C: Explosive Secretory Discharge of Bombardier Beetles (*Brachinus*)," *Science,* Volume 165, 1969, pp. 61–63.
(With J. Eppinger) "Nature's chemists," *GEO,* January, 1979, pp. 64–82.
"Insect Spray: Only Some Do It Hot," *Science News,* 1979, p. 83.
"Prospecting for Nature's Chemical Riches," *Issues in Science and Technology,* June, 1990, pp. 31–34.

SOURCES:

Periodicals

Ackerman, Diane, "A Reporter at Large: Insect Love," *New Yorker,* August 17, 1992, pp. 34–54.
Horgan, John, "The Man Who Loves Insects," *Scientific American,* December, 1991, pp. 60–64.

—*Sketch by Leslie Reinherz*

Niles Eldredge
1943-
American paleontologist

Niles Eldredge is a paleontologist best known for a theory he developed with fellow paleontologist **Stephen Jay Gould** called punctuated equilibrium—an evolutionary theory that challenged Darwinian gradualism and changed the way scientists interpret the fossil record. A curator of invertebrate paleontology at the American Museum of Natural History in New York, Eldredge has used the fossil record to improve current theories of evolution, and he has applied some of these theories to better understanding the problems faced by living species. He has been a staunch opponent of the so-called "scientific creationism" movement, and he remains a prolific author.

Eldredge was born in Brooklyn, New York, on August 25, 1943, to Robert and Eleanor Eldredge. His father was an accountant and his mother a homemaker. As a young boy growing up in the northern suburbs of New York City, he would sometimes venture into the city and visit the American Museum of Natural History. "That was definitely formative, no question about it," he told John Spizzirri in an interview. Having done well in Latin in high school, Eldredge planned to study classics when he entered Columbia University in 1961; he intended to become a lawyer but discovered himself increasingly fascinated with academic research.

Eldredge met his future wife, Michelle J. Wycoff, at Columbia University; she introduced Eldredge to various members of the anthropology department and he began taking courses in this subject. His participation in an ethnographic study turned his attention toward evolution. In the summer of 1963, he served as a trainee with anthropologists studying in a Brazilian fishing village, and he began collecting invertebrate (having no spinal column) fossils from the surrounding reef. After taking courses in paleontology and geology the following semester, Eldredge recalled in his book *Fossils: The Evolution and Extinction of Species,* "embarked on a lifetime career of trying to make some sense of the fossil record of the history of life." On June 6, 1964, he married Wycoff, with whom he would have two sons. He received his bachelor's degree in anthropology in 1965, graduating *summa cum laude.*

While still an undergraduate, Eldredge met Stephen Jay Gould, who was then a graduate student two years his senior. They both shared an interest in scrutinizing the fossil record of invertebrates at the species level. By the time Eldredge began graduate studies at Columbia University, his interest in invertebrate paleontology had turned to the Paleozoic era, and it was from this era that he chose the subject for his Ph.D. thesis, trilobites. Trilobites lived between 530 and 245 million years ago and they represent one of the earliest groups of arthropods—invertebrate animals with jointed limbs. Fossil evidence has been collected from all over the world which establishes that they existed in a diverse range of environments over an extremely long period of time.

Finds Abrupt Changes in Descendant Lines

After receiving his Ph.D. in geology from Columbia University in October of 1969, Eldredge assumed the post of adjunct assistant professor in Columbia's geology department, while simultaneously holding a position as an assistant curator in the American Museum of Natural History's department of invertebrate paleontology. By 1971, his work on Paleozoic invertebrates had led to a rethinking of the evolutionary process; he published his theory in the journal *Evolution.* Frustrated that he could find no evolutionary changes in his trilobites despite their wide distribution over time and space, Eldredge conducted a more detailed examination of his specimens. "Then I started noticing these very slight patterns of differences between the eyes in different populations," he

told Spizzirri. "I looked at these in terms of where they were distributed on a map, and how they were distributed in time, and saw that there were these great periods of stability that were interrupted at varying intervals by small, but definitive change, and the change seemed to be concentrated at these short intervals." The following year, Gould contributed to Eldredge's hypothesis. Republished in the collection, *Models in Paleobiology,* their theory of "punctuated equilibrium" seemed to contradict certain fundamental elements of Darwinian evolution.

Darwin argued that evolution was gradual and continuous, but his concept of a gradual progression of species over time was often marred by gaps in the fossil record, although he believed these would eventually be filled by later research. In the early 1940s, the American paleontologist **George Gaylord Simpson** suggested that these gaps were not necessarily the result of a poor fossil record and speculated that evidence of continuous evolution might never be found. He went on to delineate the circumstances in which abrupt changes could occur, but he limited the scope of his research to the larger groups, like whales and bats, because he believed that specific species, the individual constituents of groups, were not important to this process. Eldredge and Gould redefined Simpson's theories by concentrating on species, where they were able to incorporate aspects of speciation theories that suggested that the branching off, or budding, of lineages served as the primary mechanism for abrupt change. In the theory proposed by Eldredge and Gould, change is only abrupt relative to geological time and the long history of evolution. "Most anatomical change in the fossil record," Eldredge told Neil A. Campbell in the *American Biology Teacher,* "seems to be concentrated in relatively brief bursts punctuating longer periods of relative stability." The theory of punctuated equilibria initially met with mixed reviews and still has its opponents, though leading evolutionary biologists tend to agree that stasis plays an integral role in the process of evolution.

In 1972, Eldredge became adjunct professor of biology at the City University of New York; in 1974, he advanced to associate positions at Columbia University and the American Museum of Natural History, where he was named curator of the department of invertebrate paleontology in 1979. As an extension of his work on species, Eldredge began to look at the hierarchical relationships of living systems, working to define the interactive nature of organisms and their environments within successively larger systems. "Large scale entities—ecosystems, species, social systems—are real entities in and of themselves composed of parts," Eldredge explained to Spizzirri. "Just like organisms are composed of parts and organisms are parts of populations, populations are parts of these larger scale systems."

In the early 1980s, Eldredge unwillingly became the subject of controversy over scientific creationism. Creationist leader Luther Sunderland co-opted the theory of punctuated equilibria and, using the ideas of stasis and gaps in the fossil record, he claimed it could disprove evolution. After conducting an interview with Eldredge under the guise of being a consultant for the New York State Board of Regents, Sunderland apparently referred to Eldredge as an advocate for the simultaneous teaching of evolution and creationism in the classroom. Embarrassed and angry, Eldredge wrote an article for the *New Republic,* denouncing claims of scientific creationism as bad science, if even science at all. He later expanded the article into the book *The Monkey Business: A Scientist Looks at Creationism,* and he has written other critical pieces against the movement.

Eldredge has continued to study events of the geologic past, with a particular interest in the connections between environmental change and speciation and extinction, as well as the role these events play within living systems. Looking at the mass extinctions of the past, Eldredge has tried to derive from them answers that might help solve modern concerns about biodiversity. Examples from the past have shown that when habitats are radically and abruptly altered and organisms are unable to find similar or suitable habitats elsewhere, they will become extinct. He believes extinction has played a critical role in the emergence of new species, particularly humans, as he told Neil A. Campbell in the *American Biology Teacher:* "There is nothing inevitable in the system that human beings would emerge. And that is where the importance of extinction really is—it reshuffles the deck." But he argues that evolution is not necessarily good, and he believes that our survival depends on the survival of other species in the complex global ecosystem.

Eldredge co-edited the publication *Systematic Zoology* from 1973 to 1976, and has written over 160 articles, books, and reviews. The recipient of the Schuchert Award from the Paleontological Society in 1979, he is a lecturer on issues concerning evolutionary theory and biodiversity. Besides his hobby as a bird-watcher, which he says "has real implications for my professional career," he plays and collects trumpets and cornets.

SELECTED WRITINGS BY ELDREDGE:

Books

(With Stephen Jay Gould) "Punctuated Equilibria: An Alternative to Phyletic Gradualism," *Models in Paleobiology,* edited by T. J. M. Schopfy, Freeman, Cooper, 1972, pp. 82–115.

(With J. Cracraft) *Phylogenetic Patterns and the Evolutionary Process: Method and Theory in Comparative Biology,* Columbia University Press, 1980.

The Monkey Business: A Scientist Looks at Creationism, Pocket Books, 1982.

Time Frames, Simon & Schuster, 1985.

Life Pulse: Episodes from the Story of the Fossil Record, Facts on File, 1987.

Fossils: The Evolution and Extinction of Species, Abrams, 1991.

Periodicals

"The Allopatric Model and Phylogeny in Paleozoic Invertebrates," *Evolution,* Volume 25, 1971, pp. 156–67.

"Creationism Isn't Science," *New Republic,* April 4, 1981, pp. 15–17.

(With Gould) "Punctuated Equilibrium Comes of Age," *Nature,* November 18, 1993, pp. 223–27.

SOURCES:

Books

Hen's Teeth and Horse's Toes, Norton, 1983, pp. 253–62.

The Panda's Thumb, Norton, 1983, pp. 179–85.

Periodicals

Campbell, Neil A., "A Conservation with . . . Niles Eldredge," *American Biology Teacher,* May, 1990, pp. 264–67.

Other

Eldredge, Niles, interview with John Spizzirri conducted February 18, 1994.

—*Sketch by John Spizzirri*

Gertrude Belle Elion
1918-
American biochemist

Gertrude Belle Elion's innovative approach to drug discovery furthered the understanding of cellular metabolism and led to the development of medications for leukemia, gout, herpes, malaria, and

Gertrude Belle Elion

the rejection of transplanted organs. Azidothymidine (AZT), the first drug approved for the treatment of AIDS, came out of her laboratory shortly after her 1983 retirement. One of the few women who has held a top post at a major pharmaceutical company, Elion worked at Wellcome Research Laboratories for nearly five decades. Her work, with colleague **George H. Hitchings**, was recognized with the Nobel Prize for physiology or medicine in 1988. Her Nobel award was notable for several reasons: few winners have been women, few have lacked the Ph.D., and few have been industrial researchers.

Elion was born on January 23, 1918, in New York City, the first of two children, a daughter and a son, of Robert Elion and Bertha Cohen. Robert, a dentist, immigrated to the United States from Lithuania as a small boy. Bertha came to the United States from Russia at the age of 14. Elion, an excellent student who was accelerated two years by her teachers, graduated from high school at the height of the Great Depression. As a senior in high school, she had witnessed the painful death of her grandfather from stomach cancer and vowed to become a cancer researcher. She was able to attend college only because several New York City schools, including Hunter College, offered free tuition to students with good grades. In college, she majored in chemistry because that seemed the best route to her goal.

In 1937 Elion graduated Phi Beta Kappa from Hunter College with a B.A. at the age of 19. Despite her outstanding academic record, Elion's early efforts

to find a job as a chemist failed. One laboratory after another told her that they had never employed a woman chemist. Her self-confidence shaken, Elion began secretarial school. That lasted only six weeks, until she landed a one-semester stint teaching biochemistry to nurses and then took a position in a friend's laboratory. With the money she earned from these jobs, Elion began graduate school. To afford tuition, she continued to live with her parents and to work as a substitute science teacher in the public schools. In 1941, she graduated summa cum laude from New York University with a M.S. degree in chemistry.

Upon her graduation, Elion again faced difficulties finding work appropriate to her experience and abilities. The only job available to her was as a quality control chemist in a food laboratory, checking the color of mayonnaise and the acidity of pickles for the Quaker Maid Company. After a year and a half, she was finally offered a job as a research chemist at Johnson & Johnson. Unfortunately, her division closed six months after she arrived. The company offered Elion a new job testing the tensile strength of sutures, but she declined.

Seeks Opportunity at Wellcome Research Laboratories

As it did for many women of her generation, the start of World War II ushered in a new era of opportunity for Elion. As men left their jobs to fight the war, women were encouraged to join the workforce. "It was only when men weren't available that women were invited into the lab," Elion told the *Washington Post*.

For Elion, the war created an opening in the research lab of biochemist George Herbert Hitchings at Wellcome Research Laboratories in Tuckahoe, NY, a subsidiary of Burroughs Wellcome Company, a British firm. When they met, Elion was 26 years old and Hitchings was 39. Their working relationship began on June 14, 1944, and lasted for the rest of their careers. Each time Hitchings was promoted, Elion filled the spot he had just vacated, until she became head of the Department of Experimental Therapy in 1967, where she was to remain until her retirement 16 years later. Hitchings became vice president for research. Over the years, they have written many scientific papers together.

Settled in her job and thrilled by the breakthroughs occurring in the field of biochemistry, Elion took steps to earn a Ph.D., the so-called "union card" that all serious scientists are expected to have as evidence that they are capable of doing independent research. Only one school offered night classes in chemistry, the Brooklyn Polytechnic Institute (now Polytechnic University), so that's where Elion enrolled. Attending classes meant taking the train from

Tuckahoe into Grand Central Station and transferring to the subway to Brooklyn. Although the hour-and-a-half commute each way was exhausting, Elion persevered for two years, until the school accused her of not being a serious student and pressed her to attend full-time. Forced to choose between school and her job, Elion had no choice but to continue working. Her relinquishment of the Ph.D. haunted her, until her lab developed its first successful drug, 6-mercaptopurine (6MP).

In the 1940s, Elion and Hitchings employed a novel approach to fighting the agents of disease. By studying the biochemistry of cancer cells, and of harmful bacteria and viruses, they hoped to understand the differences between the metabolism of those cells and normal cells. In particular, they wondered whether there were differences in how the disease-causing cells used nucleic acids, the chemicals involved in the replication of DNA, to stay alive and to grow. Any dissimilarities discovered might serve as a target point for a drug that could destroy the abnormal cells without harming healthy, normal cells. By disrupting one crucial link in a cell's biochemistry, the cell itself would be damaged. In this manner, cancers and harmful bacteria might be eradicated.

Elion's work focused on purines, one of two main categories of nucleic acids. Their strategy, for which Elion and Hitchings would be honored by the Nobel Prize 40 years later, steered a radical middle course between chemists who randomly screened compounds to find effective drugs and scientists who engaged in basic cellular research without a thought of drug therapy. The difficulties of such an approach were immense. Very little was known about nucleic acid biosynthesis. Discovery of the double helical structure of DNA still lay ahead, and many of the instruments and methods that make molecular biology possible had not yet been invented. But Elion and her colleagues persisted with the tools at hand and their own ingenuity. By observing the microbiological results of various experiments, they could make knowledgeable deductions about the biochemistry involved. To the same ends, they worked with various species of lab animals and examined varying responses. Still, the lack of advanced instrumentation and computerization made for slow and tedious work. Elion told *Scientific American,* "if we were starting now, we would probably do what we did in 10 years."

Discovers Drug That Fights Leukemia

By 1951, as a senior research chemist, Elion discovered the first effective compound against childhood leukemia. The compound, 6-mercaptopurine (6MP) (trade name Purinethol), interfered with the synthesis of leukemia cells. In clinical trials run by the Sloan-Kettering Institute (now the Memorial Sloan-Kettering Cancer Center), it increased life expectancy

from a few months to a year. The compound was approved by the Food and Drug Administration (F.D.A.) in 1953. Eventually 6MP, used in combination with other drugs and radiation treatment, made leukemia one of the most curable of cancers.

In the next two decades, the potency of 6MP prompted Elion and other scientists to look for more uses for the drug. Robert Schwartz, at Tufts Medical School in Boston, and Roy Calne, at Harvard Medical School, successfully used 6MP to suppress the immune systems in dogs with transplanted kidneys. Motivated by Schwartz and Calne's work, Elion and Hitchings began searching for other immunosuppressants. They carefully studied the drug's course of action in the body, an endeavor known as pharmacokinetics. This additional work with 6MP led to the discovery of the derivative azathioprine (Imuran), that prevents rejection of transplanted human kidneys and treats rheumatoid arthritis. Other experiments in Elion's lab intended to improve 6MP's effectiveness led to the discovery of allopurinol (Zyloprim) for gout, a disease in which excess uric acid builds up in the joints. Allopurinol was approved by the F.D.A. in 1966. In the 1950s, Elion and Hitchings's lab also discovered pyrimethamine (Daraprim and Fansidar) a treatment for malaria, and trimethoprim (Bactrim and Septra) for urinary and respiratory tract infections. Trimethoprim is also used to treat Pneumocystis carinii pneumonia, the leading killer of people with AIDS.

Launches Antiviral Program

In 1968, Elion heard that a compound called adenine arabinoside appeared to have an effect against DNA viruses. This compound was similar in structure to a chemical in her own lab, 2,6-diaminopurine. Although her own lab was not equipped to screen antiviral compounds, she immediately began synthesizing new compounds to send to a Wellcome Research lab in Britain for testing. In 1969, she received notice by telegram that one of the compounds was effective against herpes simplex viruses. Further derivatives of that compound yielded acyclovir (Zovirax), an effective drug against herpes, shingles, and chicken pox. An exhibit of the success of acyclovir, presented in 1978 at the Interscience Conference on Microbial Agents and Chemotherapy, demonstrated to other scientists that it was possible to find drugs that exploited the differences between viral and cellular enzymes. Acyclovir (Zovirax), approved by the F.D.A. in 1982, became one of Burroughs Wellcome's most profitable drugs. In 1984 at Wellcome Research Laboratories, researchers trained by Elion and Hitchings developed azidothymidine (AZT), the first drug used to treat AIDS.

Although Elion retired in 1983, she continued at Wellcome Research Laboratories as scientist emeritus and keeps an office there as a consultant. She also accepted a position as a research professor of medicine and pharmacology at Duke University, where she works with a third-year medical student each year on a research project. Since her retirement, Elion has served as president of the American Association for Cancer Research and as a member of the National Cancer Advisory Board, among other positions. Hitchings, who retired in 1975, also remains active at Wellcome Research Laboratories.

In 1988, Elion and Hitchings shared the Nobel Prize for physiology or medicine with Sir James Black, a British biochemist. Although Elion had been honored for her work before, beginning with the prestigious Garvan Medal of the American Chemical Society in 1968, a host of tributes followed the Nobel Prize. She received a number of honorary doctorates and was elected to the National Inventors' Hall of Fame, the National Academy of Sciences, and the National Women's Hall of Fame. Elion maintained that it was important to keep such awards in perspective. "The Nobel Prize is fine, but the drugs I've developed are rewards in themselves," she told the *New York Times Magazine.*

Elion never married although she was engaged once. Sadly, her fiance died of an illness. After that, Elion dismissed thoughts of marriage. She is close to her brother's children and grandchildren, however, and on the trip to Stockholm to receive the Nobel Prize, she brought with her 11 family members. Elion has said that she never found it necessary to have women role models. "I never considered that I was a woman and then a scientist," Elion told the *Washington Post.* "My role models didn't have to be women—they could be scientists." Her interests are photography, travel, and music, especially opera. Although her home is in North Carolina, she still keeps her subscription to the Metropolitan Opera in New York.

SELECTED WRITINGS BY ELION:

Periodicals

"The Quest for a Cure," *Annual Review of Pharmacology and Toxicology,* Volume 33, 1993, pp. 1–23.

SOURCES:

Books

Bertsch, Sharon McGrayne, *Nobel Prize Women in Science: Their Lives, Struggles, and Momentous Discoveries,* Carol Publishing Group, 1992.

McGuire, Paula, editor, *Nobel Prize Winners: 1987–1991 Supplement,* H. W. Wilson, 1992, pp. 77–78.

Periodicals

Altman, Lawrence K., "3 Drug Pioneers Win Nobel in Medicine," *New York Times,* October 18, 1988, p. 1.
Bouton, Katherine, "The Nobel Pair," *New York Times Magazine,* January 29, 1989.
Colburn, Don, "Pathway to the Prize," *Washington Post,* October 25, 1988.
"Drug Pioneers Win Nobel Laureate," *New Scientist,* October 22, 1988, pp. 26–27.
Holloway, Marguerite, "The Satisfaction of Delayed Gratification," *Scientific American,* October, 1991, pp. 40–44.
Marx, Jean L., "The 1988 Nobel Prize for Physiology or Medicine," *Science,* Volume 242, October 28, 1988, pp. 516–517.
"Tales of Patience and Triumph," *Time,* October 31, 1988, p. 71.

—Sketch by Liz Marshall

Mostafa Amr El-Sayed
1933-
Egyptian-born American physical chemist

Mostafa Amr El-Sayed is a physical chemist who has used lasers to study changing energy states in molecules; he is the Julius Brown Professor of Chemistry at the Georgia Institute of Technology. El-Sayed was one of the first to employ two-color lasers and ionization direction, and he has used laser technology to study the mechanism of photosynthetic systems. El-Sayed was born on May 8, 1933, in Zifta, a small town on the western branch of the Nile River in Egypt. He was the youngest of seven children born to Amr and Zakia (Ahmed) El-Sayed. His father was a high school mathematics teacher, and two of El-Sayed's strongest dreams were to become a university professor and to travel to the United States. In 1953, when El-Sayed completed his undergraduate studies at Ein Shams University in Cairo, he was offered his first teaching job. He began work as a chemistry instructor in the fall, but the job was only to last a few months. He had applied for a doctoral fellowship at Florida State University, and late in December of that year he received word that he had been accepted. By February he was headed for Florida; he recalls

Tallahassee as "a delightful town which I consider my birthplace in this country."

While in graduate school, El-Sayed developed an interest in molecular spectroscopy, the study of a molecule's response to light waves. This was to become his primary field of research. He received his Ph.D. in physical chemistry from Florida State in 1958. El-Sayed did postdoctoral work at Harvard in 1959 in the area of molecular spectroscopy and continued his research on another postdoctorate degree at the California Institute of Technology from 1960 to 1961. In 1961 he was offered a position in the chemistry and biochemistry department at the University of California, Los Angeles (UCLA). He became full professor there in 1967 and remained affiliated with that institution until 1994.

Throughout his career El-Sayed's research has been aimed at understanding how atoms within molecules respond to light. In some molecules light can be absorbed and transformed into useful chemical energy. When this transformation occurs, it is because an atom absorbs a photon and lifts some of its electrons into a higher energy state. This change of the energy state of electrons is what makes possible such molecular functions as photosynthesis in plants and vision in animals. Using sophisticated laser techniques that he developed, El-Sayed has been able to explore the minute details of this energy transfer. His molecular subjects have varied from isolated gases to the photosynthetic system of a microbe called bacteriorhodopsin.

El-Sayed received the Fresenius National Award in Pure and Applied Chemistry in 1967, the McCoy Award in 1969, and the Gold Medal Award of the American Chemical Society in 1971. He was elected to the National Academy of Science in 1980. In 1988 he received the Egyptian American Outstanding Achievement Award, and in 1990 he won both the King Faisal International Prize in the Sciences and the Tolman Award. He has published over 300 professional articles about spectroscopy and molecular dynamics, and since 1980 he has served as the chief editor of the *Journal of Physical Chemistry* and the United States editor of the *International Reviews in Physical Chemistry*. El-Sayed and his wife, Janice, have five children.

SELECTED WRITINGS BY EL-SAYED:

Periodicals

"Laser Applications in Chemistry and Biophysics," *Proceedings of the International Society for Optical Engineering,* January 23–24, 1986, pp. 1–136.

SOURCES:

El-Sayed, Mostafa Amr, autobiographical statement furnished to Leslie Reinherz on March 22, 1994.

—Sketch by Leslie Reinherz

Charles Elton
1900-
English ecologist

Charles Elton was a well known and highly respected biologist in the field of animal ecology, an area in which he wielded extraordinary influence. Elton's entire life was dedicated to furthering the understanding of the environment's effects on animal populations. His most significant contribution to the field of science, however, was not a noted discovery, but the establishment of the Bureau of Animal Population (BAP), which became an internationally acclaimed research center on the dynamics of animal population and ecology.

Charles Sutherland Elton was born on March 29, 1900, in Manchester, England, to Professor and Mrs. Oliver Elton. Professor Elton was chair of the English Literature department at the university there at the time of the younger Elton's birth. Charles Elton was very proud of his maternal heritage. His mother, it is said, was a descendent of crofters (farmers) from the Isle of Coll in Scotland. Shortly after Charles' birth, the Eltons moved to the east coast of England, where his father joined the staff of Liverpool University. It was there, at about age nine, that the naturalist traits began to develop in Elton under the watchful eye of his older brother, Geoffrey Yorke Elton. Geoffrey had a tremendous impact on his younger brother's life and, consequently, Elton was devastated when Geoffrey died suddenly at age thirty-three. Elton was indebted to his brother for fostering his appreciation of the beauty of the world around him. Geoffrey taught him to carefully observe all living things and to watch for the principles that regulate their lives. That is the vocation to which Charles Elton dedicated his life.

In 1918, Elton entered Oxford, where he studied zoology under the tutelage of **Julian Sorell Huxley**, grandson of Thomas Henry Huxley, who boldly defended the theory of evolution as put forth in Charles Darwin's epochal 1859 work, *On the Origin of Species*. As an undergraduate, Elton was invited to assist Huxley on Oxford's first Arctic expedition to

Spitsbergen in 1921. This study proved less successful than was expected due to extreme weather conditions. Elton was invited to go along on the second Spitsbergen expedition in 1923, in which he found only nine dry-land invertebrates out of a possible sixty or more known species for that locale. On the third expedition in 1924, Elton was placed in charge of all scientific work. He spent most of his time working from the base camp, conducting a general survey of animal life in that region. It was during this trip that Elton almost lost his life when he fell through the ice. It is thought that this accident may have actually aided Elton's scientific endeavors by increasing his consciousness of the impact of accidental occurrences in the population dynamics of animal life. All together, these expeditions resulted in numerous publications in the fields of botany, geology and zoology.

After graduating from Oxford in 1922 with high honors, Elton accepted a part-time position there as departmental demonstrator in zoology. This position enabled him to continue his research and documentation of animal population fluctuations and the reasons behind them. Offering a modest salary, the position eventually became full-time in 1929, and Elton held the post until 1945. He had also been appointed biological consultant to the Hudson Bay Company in 1925. During the five years he held this post, Elton conducted studies on the fluctuation of fur-bearing animals and their prey. With the help of George Binney of the Hudson Bay Company, Elton established a simple yet sophisticated recording system that provided input from hundreds of observers from a wide geographic area. Combined with the company's archives, this data eventually enabled Elton to trace the population fluctuation of the Canadian lynx back to 1736.

Establishes the Bureau of Animal Population (BAP)

The Bureau of Animal Population (BAP) was created on January 25, 1932. Establishing its own library and providing an atmosphere conducive to the study of population dynamics with a minimum of distraction, it acted as a world-class research center for the next thirty-five years. Throughout the BAP's existence, Elton worked tirelessly to obtain funding that would secure its future. The Bureau of Animal Population worked on a budget that was inconceivably small by research standards at that time, yet the quality and depth of research conducted by its members was never compromised, due in large part to Elton's strict adherence to the goals and objectives set forth by the BAP. On December 10, 1934, almost three years after its establishment, the Bureau of Animal Population became an official unit of Oxford University with a three-year grant to continue operations. While this alleviated some of the financial concerns for the foreseeable future, Elton continued

his search for additional funding that would provide for materials and instrumentation not covered by the grant.

Faced with the possibility of a war with Germany, the British government notified all scientists that they would be exempted from military service in order to carry out applicable research. Elton did not wait for the inevitable to happen. He notified the Agricultural Research Council (ARC) that the Bureau was ready to offer its services in investigating the loss of food due to rodents in the field and in storage areas. Elton's staff was already experienced in this area, because they'd faced the same problem during the First World War. Elton's plan was approved by the ARC in August 1939, and by the university shortly after the outbreak of the war. Elton's team proved to be highly successful in controlling the rodent problem and much of the Bureau's research during this period was published by the ARC after the war.

Witnesses the Demise of the BAP

The BAP's reputation grew under the powerful, but low-key leadership of Charles Elton, as did the number of those who came to the Bureau to study and conduct research. Elton made many friends within the national and international ecological network, but he tended to stay out of the university's political arena. This, in the end, contributed to the dissolution of the Bureau as a separate research institute within the university. Elton did not have a political base of support when it became apparent that the current administration was out to dismantle the BAP.

Based on a report by the committee appointed to determine the status of the BAP, it was decided that Bureau personnel would be absorbed into Oxford's zoology department without any independent status. This was announced in the *University Gazette* on August 7, 1964, and would take effect upon Elton's retirement on September 30, 1967. Once that decision was made, the university treated the BAP as a nonentity, never acknowledging its existence in any report beyond September 1965. Scientists from around the world who had ever worked with the BAP or with Charles Elton were astounded that it would cease to exist. Peter Crowcroft, in his book *Elton's Ecologists,* wrote, "For twenty years, the Bureau had sought to function as an international institute, and the presence of its alumni in important jobs worldwide was evidence that it succeeded." Elton fought and won to keep the BAP library intact after the Bureau closed, as well as for space to continue the Wytham Biological Survey.

It has been said that the Bureau of Animal Population, unlike any other ecological institution, has influenced the lives of so many people that it will continue to live on through their work and research.

Charles Elton, the quiet yet resourceful founder of the BAP and its staunchest supporter, always sought to stay out of the spotlight. He told Peter Crowcroft in 1978, "I would only object to your book if it overemphasized me in the BAP picture, or tried to be biographical in a larger or more general sense." Elton went on to say, "The whole nature of the BAP performance was its mixture of team-work and freedom." Crowcroft summed up Elton's involvement with the Bureau of Animal Population very adequately, when he said, "One cannot produce *Hamlet* without the Prince of Denmark."

SELECTED WRITINGS BY ELTON:

Books

Animal Ecology, [London], 1927.
Animal Ecology and Evolution, [London], 1930.
The Pattern of Animal Communities, [London], 1966.

SOURCES:

Books

Crowcroft, Peter, *Elton's Ecologists: A History of the Bureau of Animal Population,* University of Chicago Press, 1991.
Vernoff, Edward, *The International Dictionary of 20th Century Biography,* New American Library, 1987.

—*Sketch by Paula M. Morin*

Gladys Anderson Emerson
1903-
American biochemist and nutritionist

Gladys Anderson Emerson was a landmark biochemist who conducted valuable research on vitamin E, amino acids, and the B vitamin complex. She later studied the biochemical bases of nutrition and the relationship between disease and nutrition. An author and lecturer, Emerson helped establish dietary allowances for the United States Department of Agriculture.

Emerson was born in Caldwell, Kansas, on July 1, 1903, the only child of Otis and Louise (Williams) Anderson. When the family moved to Texas, Emerson attended elementary school in Fort Worth. She later graduated from high school at El Reno, Oklahoma, where she excelled in debate, music, languages, and mathematics. In 1925 she received a B.S. degree in chemistry and an A.B. in English from the Oklahoma College for Women.

Following graduation, Emerson was offered assistantships in both chemistry and history at Stanford University and earned an M.A. degree in history in 1926. She eventually became head of the history, geography, and citizenship department at an Oklahoma City junior high school, then a short time later accepted a fellowship in biochemistry and nutrition at the University of California at Berkeley, where she received her Ph.D. in animal nutrition and biochemistry in 1932. That same year Emerson was accepted as a postdoctoral fellow at Germany's University of Gottingen, where she studied chemistry with the Nobel Prize-winning chemist **Adolf Windaus** and **Adolf Butenandt**, a prominent researcher who specialized in the study of hormones.

In 1933 Emerson returned to the United States and began work as a research associate in the Institute of Experimental Biology at the University of California at Berkeley. She remained there until 1942, conducting pioneering research on vitamin E; using wheat germ oil as a source, Emerson was first to isolate vitamin E. In 1942 she joined the staff of Merck and Company, a pharmaceutical firm, eventually heading its department of animal nutrition. Staying with Merck for fourteen years, Emerson directed research in nutrition and pharmaceuticals. In particular, she studied the structure of the B vitamin complex and the effects of B vitamin deprivation on lab animals; she found that when vitamin B6 was withheld from rhesus monkeys, they developed arteriosclerosis, or hardening of the arteries.

During World War II Emerson served in the Office of Scientific Research and Development. From 1950 to 1953 she worked at the Sloan Kettering Institute, researching the link between diet and cancer. From 1962 to her retirement in 1970, she was professor of nutrition and vice-chairman of the department of public health at the University of California at Los Angeles.

In 1969 President Richard M. Nixon appointed Emerson vice president of the Panel on the Provision of Food as It Affects the Consumer (the White House Conference on Food, Nutrition, and Health). In 1970 she served as an expert witness before the Food and Drug Administration's hearing on vitamins and mineral supplements and additives to food. A photography enthusiast who won numerous awards for her work, Emerson was also a distinguished board member of the Southern California Committee of the World Health Organization and was active on the California State Nutrition Council.

SELECTED WRITINGS BY EMERSON:

Periodicals

"Agnes Fay Morgan and Early Nutrition Discoveries in California," *Federation Proceedings,* Volume 36, pp. 1911–1914.

SOURCES:

Books

Haber, Louis, *Women Pioneers of Science,* Harcourt, 1979.
Siegel, J. P., and R. T. Finley, *Women in the Scientific Search,* Scarecrow, 1985.
Vare, E. V., and G. Ptacek, *Mothers of Invention,* Morrow, 1988.

—*Sketch by John Henry Dreyfuss*

John F. Enders
1897-1985
American virologist

John F. Enders' research on viruses and his advances in tissue culture enabled microbiologists **Albert Sabin** and **Jonas Salk** to develop their vaccines against polio, a major crippler of children in the first half of the twentieth century. His work also served as a catalyst in the development of vaccines against measles, mumps and chicken pox. As a result of this work, Enders was awarded the 1954 Nobel Prize in medicine or physiology.

John Franklin Enders was born February 10, 1897, in West Hartford, Connecticut. His parents were John Enders, a wealthy banker, and Harriet Whitmore Enders. Entering Yale in 1914, Enders left during his junior year to enlist in the U.S. Naval Reserve Flying Corp following America's entry into World War I in 1917. After serving as a flight instructor and rising to the rank of lieutenant, he returned to Yale, graduating in 1920. After a brief venture as a real estate agent, Enders entered Harvard in 1922 as a graduate student in English literature. His plans were sidetracked in his second year when, after seeing a roommate perform scientific experiments, he changed his major to medicine. He enrolled in Harvard Medical School, where he studied under the noted microbiologist and author **Hans Zinsser**. Zinsser's influence led Enders to the study of micro-

biology, the field in which he received his Ph.D. in 1930. His dissertation was on anaphylaxis, an allergic condition that can develop after a foreign protein enters the body. Enders became an assistant at Harvard's Department of Bacteriology in 1929, eventually rising to assistant professor in 1935, and associate professor in 1942.

Following the Japanese attack on Pearl Harbor, Enders came to the service of his country again, this time as a member of the Armed Forces Epidemiology Board. Serving as a consultant to the Department of War, he helped develop diagnostic tests and immunizations for a variety of diseases. Enders continued to work with the military after the war, offering his counsel to the U.S. Army's Civilian Commission on Virus and Rickettsial Disease, and the Secretary of Defense's Research and Development Board. Enders left his position at Harvard in 1946 to set up the Infectious Diseases Laboratory at Boston Children's Hospital, believing this would give him greater freedom to conduct his research. Once at the hospital, he began to concentrate on studying those viruses affecting his young patients. By 1948 he had two assistants, **Frederick Robbins** and **Thomas Weller**, who, like him, were graduates of Harvard Medical School. Although Enders and his colleagues did their research primarily on measles, mumps, and chicken pox, their lab was partially funded by the National Foundation for Infantile Paralysis, an organization set up to help the victims of polio and find a vaccine or cure for the disease. Infantile paralysis, a virus affecting the brain and nervous system was, at that time, a much-feared disease with no known prevention or cure. Although it could strike anyone, children were its primary victims during the periodic epidemics which swept through communities. The disease often crippled and, in severe cases, killed those afflicted.

Discovers Breakthrough for Polio Vaccine

During an experiment on chicken pox, Weller produced too many cultures of human embryonic tissue. So as not to let them go to waste, Enders suggested putting polio viruses in the cultures. To their surprise, the virus began growing in the test tubes. The publication of these results in a 1949 *Science* magazine article caused major excitement in the medical community. Previous experiments in the 1930s had indicated that the polio virus could only grow in nervous system tissues. As a result, researchers had to import monkeys in large numbers from India, infect them with polio, then kill the animals and remove the virus from their nervous system. This was extremely expensive and time-consuming, as a single monkey could provide only two or three virus samples, and it was difficult to keep the animals alive and in good health during transport to the laboratories.

The use of nervous system tissue created another problem for those working on a vaccine. Tissue from that system often stimulate allergic reactions in the brain—sometimes fatally—when injected into another body, and there was always the danger some tissue might remain in the vaccine serum after the virus had been harvested from the culture. The discovery that the polio virus could grow outside the nervous system provided a revolutionary breakthrough in the search for a vaccine. As many as 20 specimens could be taken from a single monkey, enabling the virus to be cultivated in far larger quantities. Since no nervous system tissue had to be used, there was no danger of an allergic reaction through inadvertent transmission of the tissue. In addition, the technique of cultivating the virus and studying its effects also represented a new development in viral research. Enders and his assistants placed parts of the tissues around the inside walls of the test tubes, then closed the tubes and placed the cultures in a horizontal position within a revolving drum. Because this method made it easier to observe reaction within the culture, Enders was able to discover a means of distinguishing between the different viruses in human cells. In the case of polio, the virus killed the cell, whereas the measles virus made the cells fuse together and grow larger.

Although Enders had as good an opportunity as anyone to develop a vaccine against polio, he refused suggestions by Robbins and Weller to take that road. The exact reason for his refusal is unclear, although it may have been that Enders was reluctant to submit himself to the restrictions which the National Foundation might have placed on his research. But because his breakthrough made it possible to develop a vaccine against polio, Enders, Robbins and Weller were awarded the Nobel Prize for medicine or physiology in 1954. Interestingly enough, Enders originally opposed Salk's proposal to vaccinate against polio by injecting killed viruses into an uninfected person to produce immunity. He feared that this would actually weaken the immunity of the general population by interfering with the way the disease developed. In spite of their disagreements, Salk expressed gratitude to Enders by stating that he could not have developed his vaccine without the help of Enders' discoveries.

Continues Battle Against Disease

Enders' work in the field of immunology did not stop with his polio research. Even before he won the Nobel Prize, he was working on a vaccine against measles, again winning the acclaim of the medical world when he announced the creation of a successful vaccine against this disease in 1957. Utilizing the same techniques he had developed researching polio, he created a weakened measles virus which produced the necessary antibodies to prevent infection. Other researchers used Enders' methodology to develop vaccines against German measles and chicken pox.

In spite of his accomplishments and hard work, Enders' progress in academia was slow for many years. Still an assistant professor when he won the Nobel Prize, he did not become a full professor until two years later. This may have resulted in his dislike for university life—he once said that he preferred practical research to the "arid scholarship" of academia. But by the mid-fifties, Enders began receiving his due recognition. He was given the Kyle Award from the U.S. Public Health Service in 1955 and, in 1962, became a university professor at Harvard, the highest honor the school could grant. Enders received the Presidential Medal of Freedom in 1963, the same year he was awarded the American Medical Association's Science Achievement Award, making him one of the few non-physicians to receive this honor.

Enders married his first wife, Sarah Bennett, in 1927, and in 1943 she passed away. They had two children, John Enders II and Sarah Steffian. He married again in 1951 to Carolyn Keane. Affectionately known as "The Chief" to students and colleagues, Enders took a special interest in those he taught, keeping on the walls of his lab portraits of those who became scientists. When speaking to visitors, he was able to identify each student's philosophy and personality. Enders wrote some 190 published papers between 1929 and 1970. Towards the end of his life, he sought to apply his knowledge of immunology to the fight against AIDS, especially in trying to halt the progress of the disease during its incubation period in the human body. Enders died September 8, 1985, of heart failure, while at his summer home in Waterford, Connecticut.

SELECTED WRITINGS BY ENDERS:

Books

(With Hans Zinsser and Leroy Fothergill), *Immunity, Principles and Application in Medicine and Public Health,* Macmillian, 1939.

Periodicals

"Cultivation of the Lansing Strain of Poliomyelitis Virus in Cultures of Various Human Embryonic Tissue," *Science,* January 28, 1949, pp. 85–87.

SOURCES:

Books

Current Biography Yearbook, H. W. Wilson, 1955, pp. 182–184.

Klein, Aaron, *Trial By Fury: The Polio Vaccine Controversy,* Scribner, 1972.

Smith, Jane, *Patenting the Sun: Polio and the Salk Vaccine,* Morrow, 1990.

Periodicals

New York Times, October 19, 1954, p. 1; September, 10, 1985, p. 6.
Time, March 10, 1957, p. 71.

—*Sketch by Francis Rogers*

Adolph Gustav Heinrich Engler
1844-1930
German botanist

Adolph Gustav Heinrich Engler was a botanist who made outstanding contributions to plant classification and plant geography. He served as a college professor, journal editor and botanic garden director, and traveled throughout much of the world, making studies of plants in most of the European countries, Africa, Asia and the United States. In recognition of his prolific botanical contributions, the Linnean Society of London elected him a foreign member in 1888, and honored him with the Linnean Gold Medal in 1913. Typically, he accepted that medal in absentia, being on an expedition to Africa at the time.

Engler was born on March 25, 1844, in Sargans, Lower Silesia (now Sagan, Poland) to August Engler, a shopkeeper of modest means and Pauline (Scholtz). When his father died at an early age, the family moved to Breslau (now Wrocław, Poland). His career in botany started while he was still a pupil at the Magdalenen-Gymnasium there, when he developed an extraordinary knowledge of the area's plants. He continued with the study of botany at the University of Breslau, which he entered in 1863, and earned a Ph.D. in 1866 based on his thesis "De Genere Saxifraga."

Early Research and Fieldwork

By this time, Engler's interest in plant classification and distribution from an evolutionary point of view was established. The publication of Charles Darwin's *The Origin of Species* seven years earlier influenced Engler's own observations about the evolution of plant species and their classification. At first, his research papers dealt with the classification and evolution of the floras of Europe, with special attention to those of the Alps, all based on his extensive fieldwork during his early travels. Later, he continued with numerous contributions on the phytogeography —or plant geography—of Africa and other regions of the world, summarizing his personal research there in numerous papers.

After obtaining his doctorate in 1866, Engler returned to his old school, Magdalenen-Gymnasium, as a teacher of natural history. In 1872, he became curator of the Herbarium Botanical Collection in Munich and a lecturer at the University of Munich. Two years later, he married Marie Firle, who bore him a son and two daughters. In 1878, he accepted an appointment as professor of botany at the University of Kiel. While there, he founded the journal *Botanishche Yarbucher* (*Botanical Yearbook*), which he edited for the next 50 years. In 1884, he succeeded his former teacher, H. R. Goeppert, in the chair of botany at his old college, the University of Breslau. There, also as director, he brought about the reorganization of the Royal Botanic Garden, based on his own system of plant classification.

Leader in Plant Classification and Phytogeography

Engler's interest in plant classification extended beyond mere categorizing of plants according to their characteristics. He organized them in a new phyletic system by which plants were ranked according to their evolutionary development. Under this mode of classification, plants were arranged in a garden or herbarium according to whether they were primitive in their floral structure or more advanced. Although more modern interpretations of Engler's idea were later proposed, it retains its importance as a dominant example of classification according to the evolutionary relationships among families of plants. Engler first used his new system for the arrangement of plants in the Royal Botanic Garden when he became its director in 1889. When he expanded the system more fully in his 23-volume *Die natürlichen Pflanzenfamilien* with Karl Prantl, the book became the authoritative reference in the field, and continued to be the basis of most of the world's plant collections even after more modern phyletic systems were developed.

After the unification of Germany in 1870, Engler found himself a beneficiary of the expanding opportunities for intellectual advancement and freedom of research that placed his country in the forefront of scientific advancement. His personal attributes of wide-ranging studies and physical vigor earned for him an international reputation as a leader in the field of botany. A book by the American botanist, Asa Grey, *The Elements of Botany,* published in 1887, included his name among a list of botanists mentioned in the classification of plant species.

Engler started the publication of an encyclopedia of the plant kingdom *Die natürlichen Pflanzenfamilien* (*The Natural Plant Families*) in 1887, a project that was to continue for the next twenty-one years. The encyclopedia was considered one of the greatest plant taxonomic (classification) works, and it became a standard reference in the field of botanical taxonomy. Two years later, Engler was appointed Professor of Botany at the University of Berlin. He held this prestigious position—the most important position in botany in all of Germany—until 1921, a total of 32 years. One of his major responsibilities was the transfer of the Botanic Garden at Schoneberg to Dahlem. Under his guidance, the new Botanic Garden became world-renowned. In this endeavor, Engler received the support of the expanding German government, which had set up new colonies on the continent of Africa. He led botanical expeditions to these sites and incorporated their flora into a major exhibit, called the "Botanische Zentrallstelle fur die Kolonien," at the new Botanic Garden. His firsthand knowledge of these plants also led him to write a continuing series of research papers on African floras.

When he died on October 10, 1930, at the age of 87, Engler was buried under the trees of the Botanic Gardens at Dahlem. The Linnean Society of London observed his passing with a seven-page obituary in its *Proceedings*. During his lifetime, he had dominated and left his mark on a half-century of plant taxonomy and phytogeography, while his *Botanishche Yarbucher*, or "Engler's Yarbucher" as it came to be known, was recognized as the leading journal of plant systematics and phytogeography in the world.

SELECTED WRITINGS BY ENGLER:

Books

(Editor with Karl A. E. Prantl) *Die natürlichen Pflanzenfamilien,* 23 volumes, [Leipzig], 1887–1915; 2nd edition, [Leipzig], 1924–1960.
(With O. Drude) *Die Vegetation der Erde,* 15 volumes, [Leipzig], 1896–1923.

SOURCES:

Books

Stuessy, Tod F., *Plant Taxonomy,* Columbia University Press, 1990, p. 55.

Periodicals

Diels, Ludwig, "Zum Gedachtnis von Adolf Engler," in *Botanische Jarbucher fur Systematik, Pflanzengeschichte und Pflanzengeographie,* Volume 64, 1931, pp. i–lvi.

Proceedings of the Linnean Society of London, Sessions 121–125, November, 1908-June, 1913, pp. 45–48; Session 143, October, 1930-May, 1931, pp. 171–176.

—*Sketch by Maurice Bleifeld*

David Enskog
1884-1947
Swedish mathematician and physicist

David Enskog's research addressed the subject of the kinetic theory of gases, which involved the behavior of gas molecules in nonequilibrium conditions. Much of his work, however, was unknown or neglected until late in his life when its applications to modern technological problems became more apparent. After spending much of his life teaching at high schools and small colleges in his native Sweden, in 1930 he received a major appointment as professor of mathematics and physics at the Royal Institute of Technology in Stockholm.

David Enskog was born in Västra Ämtervik, Värmland, Sweden, on April 22, 1884, the son of Nils Olsson, a minister, and Karolina (Jonasdotter) Enskog. Enskog attended the Karlstad Läroverk for his secondary education and then enrolled at the University of Uppsala, where he received his licentiate in philosophy (similar to a master's degree) in 1911.

While still a student, Enskog carried out important research on the kinetic theory of gases which he published the year of his graduation. That paper appears to have contained the first mention of the phenomenon now known as thermal diffusion, or the process of a substance moving from an area of higher to lower concentration when heated. A year later he published a second paper containing the first accurate calculation of the thermal diffusion coefficient of a gas.

After earning his degree, Enskog attempted to obtain a scholarship that would allow him to continue his studies overseas. Failing in that effort, he accepted a high school teaching position in Stockholm; he later taught at small colleges in Skövde from 1913 to 1918 and Gävle from 1918 to 1929. During his first year at Skövde, he was also married to Anna Aurora Jönsson, The Enskogs eventually had three children, a son and two daughters.

Enskog's health was apparently never robust, a factor which excused him from military service during World War I. During that period, he began his doctoral studies at the University of Uppsala while continuing his teaching at Gävle. He was granted a Ph.D. in 1917 for his dissertation on the Maxwell-Boltzmann equation, a problem that went back nearly half a century.

Solves the Maxwell-Boltzmann Equation

In 1867, James Clerk Maxwell had conducted a study of the way internal and external factors affect the movement of a gas. Although Maxwell laid out a general theory for this phenomenon, he was not able to solve all of the specific problems involved. For example, he was unable to find a way of calculating the distribution of molecular velocities in a nonequilibrium gas. Five years later, Ludwig Boltzmann had found a complex integral equation that described this distribution; however, solving the equation eluded him as well.

In his doctoral dissertation, Enskog developed a mathematical series that could be used to solve the Maxwell-Boltzmann equation. His good friend and colleague, Sydney Chapman, later wrote in the February 7, 1948 issue of *Nature* that Enskog's solution was "not easy, but his work had great mathematical elegance." That work was eventually incorporated into Chapman's own book (written with T. G. Cowling), *The Mathematical Theory of Non-Uniform Gases,* long considered the standard reference in the field. Working in cooperation with each other, Enskog and Chapman continued to refine the kinetic theory of nonequilibrium gases. Their work was not adopted by most scientists for more than two decades, however, because of the quantum revolution then taking place in physics.

In 1922, Enskog finally obtained a "traveling scholarship" from the Swedish Academy of Sciences that allowed him to spend nine months at the universities of Göttingen and Münich. Upon his return to Sweden, Enskog's interests expanded to include a number of other topics in addition to kinetic theory. He later published papers on nuclear structure, radioactivity, and integral equations.

Largely as a result of Chapman's influence, Enskog at age 46 was finally appointed to a major university post in 1930 at the Kungliga Tekniska Högskolan (Royal Institute of Technology) in Stockholm, where he was named professor of mathematics and mechanics. Apparently Chapman hoped that the new position would bring Enskog more leisure time but, in fact, it only increased his work load. His physical condition began to deteriorate and he remained in poor health for the rest of his life. He died in Stockholm on June 1, 1947. In recognition of his accomplishments, Enskog had been awarded the Thalens prize in 1923, the Wallmarks prize in 1928, and the Svante Arrhenius Medal of the Royal Swedish Academy of Science in 1946.

SELECTED WRITINGS BY ENSKOG:

Books

"The Chapman-Enskog solution of the transport equation for moderately dense gases," monograph in *Kinetic Theory,* edited by Stephen G. Brush, 3 volumes, Pergamon, 1965–72.

SOURCES:

Books

Chapman, Sydney, and T. G. Cowling, *The Mathematical Theory of Non-Uniform Gases,* Cambridge, 1939, 2nd edition, 1952.
Dictionary of Scientific Biography, Volume 4, Scribner, 1975, pp. 375–376.

Periodicals

Chapman, S., obituary of Prof. David Enskog, *Nature,* February 7, 1948, pp. 193–194.

—*Sketch by David E. Newton*

Joseph Erlanger
1874-1965
American physiologist

Joseph Erlanger was an American physiologist whose pioneering work with his collaborator, **Herbert Spencer Gasser**, helped to advance the field of neurophysiology. For their work, Erlanger and Gasser shared the 1944 Nobel Prize in medicine or physiology. The prize committee cited their work on "the highly differentiated functions of single nerve fibers." Although unstated, the awarding of the Nobel Prize to Erlanger and Gasser also recognized their roles in developing the most basic tool in modern neurophysiology, the amplifier with cathode-ray oscilloscope. The prize culminated for Erlanger a distinguished career in medical education and physiological research.

Erlanger was born on January 5, 1874 in San Francisco, California. His father, Herman Erlanger, had immigrated to the United States in 1842 at the age of sixteen from his home in Würtemberg, in Southern Germany. After struggling as a peddler in the Mississippi Valley, he went to California during the Gold Rush. Unsuccessful at mining, Erlanger turned to business and became a moderately successful merchant. In 1849, he married Sarah Galinger, also an immigrant from Southern Germany and the sister of his business partner. Joseph was the sixth of seven children, five sons and two daughters.

From an early age, Erlanger showed an interest in the natural world, a fact that led his older sister to give him the nickname "Doc." In 1889, he entered the classical Latin curriculum at the San Francisco Boys' High School. After graduating in 1891, he began studies in the College of Chemistry at the University of California at Berkeley, receiving a bachelor's degree in 1895. It was at Berkeley that Erlanger performed his first research—studying the development of newt eggs. He then enrolled at the Johns Hopkins University School of Medicine in Baltimore and earned a medical degree in 1899, fulfilling his childhood aspirations of becoming a doctor. Erlanger excelled as a student while at Johns Hopkins, graduating second in his class. This distinction allowed him to work as an intern in internal medicine for William Osler, the renowned physician and teacher.

Begins Academic Career at Johns Hopkins

After arriving in Baltimore, Erlanger decided that medical research and not medical practice would be his life's pursuit. In the summer of 1896, he worked in the histology laboratory of Lewellys Barker, demonstrating his zeal for research by studying the location of horn cells in the spinal cord of rabbits. The following summer, he undertook a different project—determining how much of a dog's small intestine could be surgically removed without interfering with its digestive processes. This study led to Erlanger's first published paper in 1901, and to his appointment as assistant professor of physiology at Johns Hopkins by William H. Howell, one of America's most important physiologists and head of the department. He was later promoted to associate professor of physiology.

Erlanger spent the next several years exclusively at Johns Hopkins except for a six week trip in the summer of 1902 to study biochemistry at the University of Strassburg in Germany. His career to that point was exceptional for two reasons. Unlike the generation of scientists that preceded him, Erlanger did not migrate to Europe to study. This decision reflected the improving standards of medical education and scientific research in the United States at the close of the nineteenth century. Second, Erlanger, although he was a trained physician, chose to pursue a full-time career in research instead of medical practice. Physician-scientists before Erlanger could devote only part of their time to research, as the rest was spent on patient care.

During his career at Johns Hopkins, Erlanger studied a number of problems that were important in medicine. In 1904, he designed and constructed a sphygmomanometer—a device that measures blood pressure. Erlanger improved on previous designs by making it sturdier and easier to use. Later that year, he used the device to find a correlation between blood pressure and orthostatic albuminuria, wherein proteins appear in the urine when a patient stands. His last few years at Johns Hopkins were spent studying electrical conduction in the heart, particularly the activity between the auricles and the ventricles that is responsible for the consistent beating of the heart. Using a clamp of his own design, he was able to determine that a conduction blockage, or heart block, in the bundle of His, a connection between the auricles and ventricles, was responsible for the reduced pulse and fainting spells associated with Stokes-Adams syndrome.

On June 21, 1906, Erlanger married Aimée Hirstel, a fellow San Franciscan. Their marriage of more than fifty years was a strong and vibrant one, and produced three children, Margaret, Ruth Josephine, and Hermann. The personalities of Joseph and Aimée Erlanger complemented one another. He was reserved, quiet, and introverted; she was effusive, active, and extroverted. Their mutual love of walking, camping, and the outdoors stayed with them throughout Erlanger's lengthy professional career.

In 1906, Erlanger left Johns Hopkins and moved to the University of Wisconsin, where he became the first professor of physiology at the university's medical school. Though the university's administration recruited Erlanger to build and equip a physiological laboratory, his efforts were continually hampered by a lack of funds. This situation contributed to his decision to leave Wisconsin in 1910 for the Washington University School of Medicine, in Saint Louis. The medical school at Washington had been newly reorganized and had sufficient funds to meet Erlanger's needs. He worked at Washington for the remainder of his career, serving as professor of physiology and department chairman. Even after his retirement in 1946, Erlanger continued to work part-time performing research and helping graduate students in their work.

Continues a Distinguished Career at Washington University

After arriving at Washington University, Erlanger devoted much of his time and energy to the formidable task of helping to reorganize the medical school. Erlanger and the other department heads constituted the new school's executive faculty which oversaw administration and offered significant input into the construction and design of the new medical school buildings. In 1917, the United States' entry into World War I drew Erlanger's attention away from his administrative duties, presenting him with the opportunity to return to the laboratory and to his research on cardiovascular physiology. He participated with other physiologists in the study of wound shock and helped to develop therapeutic solutions that were used by the United States Army in Europe. He also continued the work that he had begun at Johns Hopkins, studying the sounds of Korotkoff, the sound one hears in an artery when measuring blood pressure with a stethoscope.

Although Erlanger would remain interested in cardiovascular physiology throughout his career, he experienced an intellectual transition in the early 1920s, when he took up questions of neurophysiology. The arrival at Washington University of Herbert Spencer Gasser, a student of Erlanger's from Wisconsin and a fellow Johns Hopkins graduate, spurred this change. Erlanger and Gasser would collaborate at Washington University until Gasser's departure in 1931 for the Cornell Medical College. Understanding how nerves transmit electrical impulses preoccupied Erlanger and Gasser during the 1920s. The difficulty in studying nerves was that the electrical impulses were too weak and too brief to measure them accurately. In 1920, one of Gasser's former classmates, H. Sidney Newcomer, developed a device that would amplify nerve impulses by some 100,000 times, allowing physiologists to measure and study the subtle changes that occur during nerve transmission. A year later, Erlanger and Gasser, based on advances made at the Western Electric Company, constructed a cathode-ray oscilloscope that could record the nerve impulse. The cathode-ray oscilloscope with amplifier was a technological breakthrough that permitted neurophysiologists to overcome the barrier posed by the subtlety and brevity of nerve activity. Erlanger and Gasser went on to study the details of nerve transmission. Their most significant contribution derived from these researches was their conclusion that larger nerve fibers conducted electrical impulses faster than smaller ones. Also, they demonstrated that different nerve fibers can have different functions.

Nobel Prize Culminates Career

Erlanger and Gasser's work on nerve physiology increased Erlanger's already important role in American physiology. Not only had he made significant contributions to the science of physiology, but his career—based on a wholly American education and consisting of a full-time research effort—represented a new generation of American physiologists. For his scientific efforts, Erlanger was elected a member of the National Academy of Sciences, the Association of American Physicians, the American Philosophical Society, and the American Physiological Society. He also received honorary degrees from universities of California, Michigan, Pennsylvania, Wisconsin, and Johns Hopkins University, Washington University, and the Free University of Brussels. His highest honor came when he shared, with Gasser, the 1944 Nobel

Prize for physiology or medicine. Erlanger died of heart failure on December 5, 1965, one month before his ninety-second birthday.

SELECTED WRITINGS BY ERLANGER:

Books

(With Herbert S. Gasser), *Electrical Signs of Nervous Activity,* University of Pennsylvania Press, 1937.

Periodicals

"A New Instrument for Determining the Minimum and Maximum Blood-pressures in Man," *Johns Hopkins Hospital Reports,* Volume 12, 1904, pp. 53–100.
(With H. S. Gasser), "A Study of the Action Currents of Nerve with the Cathode Ray Oscillograph," *American Journal of Physiology,* Volume 62, 1922, pp. 496–524.
(With H. S. Gasser), "The Compound Nature of the Action Current of Nerve as Disclosed by the Cathode Ray Oscillograph," *American Journal of Physiology,* Volume 70, 1924, pp. 624–66.
"A Physiologist Reminisces," *Annual Review of Physiology,* Volume 26, 1964, pp. 1–14.

SOURCES:

Books

Frank, Robert G., Louise H. Marshall, and H. W. Magoun, "The Neurosciences," *Advances in American Medicine: Essays at the Bicentennial,* edited by John Z. Bowers and Elizabeth F. Purcell, Port City Press, 1976, pp. 552–613.

Periodicals

Davis, Hallowell, "Joseph Erlanger, January 5, 1874-December 5, 1965," *National Academy of Sciences Biographical Memoirs,* Volume 41, 1970, pp. 111–39.
Marshall, Louise H., "The Fecundity of Aggregates: The Axonologists at Washington University 1922–1942," *Perspectives on Biology and Medicine,* Volume 26, 1983, pp. 613–36.

—*Sketch by D. George Joseph*

Richard R. Ernst
1933-
Swiss chemist

Richard R. Ernst was congratulated by the president of Switzerland and friends in Zurich, who organized a party to celebrate his award of the 1991 Nobel Prize in chemistry, while he was in flight to receive another award from Columbia University. The pilot of the aircraft called Ernst into the cockpit to give him the news. The Royal Swedish Academy of Sciences noted in its citation of the award that Ernst's development of the methodology of high-resolution nuclear magnetic resonance (NMR) spectroscopy is the most important instrumental measuring technique within chemistry. Ernst's contributions in this field led to the development of magnetic resonance imaging (MRI), the biomedical instrument widely used today to perform noninvasive diagnosis of the human body.

Born on August 14, 1933, to Robert Ernst and Irma Brunner in Winterthur, Switzerland, Richard Robert Ernst was educated at the Eidgenössische Technische Hochschule (ETH) in Zurich, where he received his doctorate in 1962. In 1976 he became a full professor at the ETH. After receiving his Ph.D., Ernst moved to Palo Alto, California, to become a research scientist at Varian Associates. There he worked with Weston A. Anderson on efforts to make NMR spectroscopy more sensitive.

Builds on Early Work

Ernst's contribution built on the NMR experiments reported in 1945 by **Felix Bloch** at Stanford University and **Edward Mills Purcell** at Harvard. Bloch and Purcell shared the Nobel Prize in physics for this work. They demonstrated that some atomic nuclei can be knocked out of alignment in a strong magnetic field when exposed to a slow sweep of radio frequencies. The nuclei realign in response to "resonant" frequencies, emitting signals that are like a chemical signature. When he received his prize, Purcell predicted NMR would become a tool for chemical analysis. For that to happen, however, it was necessary to overcome limited sensitivity of the early NMR method to the chemical signature of the substance being analyzed. Only a few substances—hydrogen, fluorine, and phosphorus—had spectra strong enough to identify reliably.

In 1966 Ernst and Anderson were able to enhance NMR spectra by replacing the slow sweep of radio frequencies with short, intense pulses. Spectra too weak to identify previously became discernable. The spectra resulting from exposure to the pulse of radio frequencies were complex, and to analyze them, Ernst made use of a Fourier transformation, which computers of the mid–1960s could use to interpret the small fluctuations in brightness of the NMR spectra. NMR equipment became widely available to the chemical research community by the early 1970s.

Ernst later developed an even more sophisticated variant, two-dimensional NMR spectroscopy, which replaced single pulses of radio frequencies with a sequence of pulses, just as the pulse had replaced a sweep of radio frequencies. Building further on the concept underlying this advance, subsequent multidimensional techniques (COSY, for example, which stands for correlation spectroscopy; others are SECSY, NOESY, and ROESY) made it possible to analyze the three-dimensional structures of proteins and other large biological molecules. They were the basis for the development of magnetic resonance imaging or MRI, which is used in medical diagnosis. The methods also enable researchers to gather information about the chemical environment of the molecules under study. Ernst's contribution to this multidimensional study of molecules is admired by his colleagues for its elegance.

Simultaneous Recognition

The award that Ernst was on his way to accept when he heard the airborne news about the Nobel Prize was the 1991 Louisa Gross Horwitz Prize at Columbia University. This was a joint award to Ernst and his colleague Kurt Wüthrich for their work in developing NMR methods that could show both the behavior and structure of complex biological molecules. The scientific community was not surprised with Ernst's awards since his MRI method is so widely used in clinical studies. He also received the Wolf Prize in Chemistry for 1991.

Commenting in an interview with *Physics Today* on his work with NMR spectroscopy and MRI, Ernst said, "I did not expect that it would become as useful and practical as it has." He and his group are engaged in studying how molecules interact with one another over time and how they change shape. His work is considered cross-disciplinary since it falls between chemistry and physics and also involves problems in quantum mechanics (a theory that assumes that energy exists in discrete units). His book on NMR is considered a classic in the field, invaluable for its cross-references to related literature.

On October 9, 1963, Ernst married Magdalena Kielholz; they had two daughters, Anna Magdalena and Katharina Elisabeth, and a son, Hans-Martin Walter. Ernst holds a number of patents for his inventions and has received recognition from many scientific societies for his work. He serves on the editorial boards of several journals dealing with magnetic resonance. He enjoys music for relaxation and pursues an interest in Tibetan art.

SELECTED WRITINGS BY ERNST:

Books

Principles of Nuclear Magnetic Resonance in One and Two Dimensions, Oxford, 1987.

SOURCES:

Periodicals

Aldhous, Peter, "Bringing NMR to the Masses," *Nature,* October 24, 1991, p. 689.

Amato, Ivan, "Chemistry: A Certain Resonance," *Science,* October 25, 1991, pp. 518–19.

Browne, Malcolm W., "European Scientists Win Physics and Chemistry Nobel Prizes," *New York Times,* October 17, 1991, p. A16.

Coghlan, Andy, "High-Flier Wins Chemistry Nobel," *New Scientist,* October 26, 1991, p. 14.

Collins, Graham P., "Nobel Chemistry Prize Recognizes the Importance of Ernst's NMR Work," *Physics Today,* December, 1991, pp. 19–21.

Stinson, Stephen, "Nobel Chemistry Prize: Ernst Honored for NMR Achievements," *Chemical and Engineering News,* October 21, 1991, p. 4.

—*Sketch by Vita Richman*

Leo Esaki

Leo Esaki
1925-
Japanese physicist

Leo Esaki was awarded a share of the 1973 Nobel Prize in physics, along with physicists **Ivar Giaever** and **Brian D. Josephson**. All three researchers were honored for their work on the quantum mechanical phenomenon known as "tunneling" in semiconductors. Esaki made his historic discovery in quantum physics—which led to a whole new field of study in physics—while still a graduate student at the University of Tokyo. His discovery of the tunnel or Esaki diode is also an important component in electronic equipment, including computers.

Esaki was born in Osaka, Japan, on March 12, 1925. His father was Soichiro Esaki, an architect, and his mother, Niyoko Ito Esaki. After completing his primary and secondary education in Osaka, Esaki entered the University of Tokyo, where he majored in physics. His original plan had been to specialize in nuclear physics, but World War II had essentially negated that possibility. The Japanese had neither the will nor the facilities with which to pursue research in a field that had become so heinous to them. Instead, Esaki selected the new and rapidly developing field of solid-state physics as his specialty.

Appointed Research Team Leader at Sony

After receiving his master's degree in physics in 1947, Esaki continued into a doctoral program at Tokyo. While working on his doctorate, Esaki also took outside employment, first at the Kobe Kogyo Corporation and then, in 1956, at the Sony Corporation. At Sony, he was made leader of a small research team working on semiconductors. It was at Sony that Esaki made his momentous discovery of a device that has since become known as a "tunnel diode" or "Esaki diode".

The Esaki diode makes use of a phenomenon that can be explained by quantum physics, but not by classical physics. According to the laws of classical physics, an electric current can not flow in a circuit across an insulator, that is, a region with a high resistance. The insulator acts as a barrier or a "wall" across which electrons can not travel.

That situation is more complex in quantum physics because of the uncertainty principle. According to that principle, it is impossible to specify precisely where an electron is located at any given time. That means that the possibility exists that an electron can be anywhere within a system, even within an energy barrier of the type described above. It follows, then, that a probability exists that an electric current will flow across an insulating barrier. In order to contrast this possibility with the laws of classical physics, that process is known as "tunneling," as in "tunneling under or through a supposed barrier."

The theory of tunneling had first been proposed in the early 1930s, but two decades later, there was still no experimental evidence to support the theory. That evidence was to come, however, as a result of Esaki's work at Sony. Esaki found that the critical factor in producing a tunneling effect was to greatly increase the concentration of impurities in (the "doping" of) a semiconductor. When he did so, he discovered a backward diode which has a polarity opposite of an ordinary diode.

Esaki was eventually able to produce diodes with very thin junctions. These devices have proved to be extremely efficient for the generation and detection of high-frequency signals. As a result of this research, he received not only his Ph.D. in physics from the University of Tokyo in 1959, but also a share of the Nobel Prize for physics in 1973.

Begins Long Career with IBM

A year after receiving his degree, Esaki left Japan to take a research position at IBM's Thomas J. Watson Research Center. He originally planned to stay in the United States for only one year, but that one year eventually stretched to thirty-three years. In 1965, he was made an IBM Fellow at the Center. He has also held concurrent appointments at the University of Pennsylvania and the University of Tokyo. Over the past three decades, his research has continued to concentrate on the search for quantum mechanical effects in semiconductors that have been predicted but not yet observed.

For his work on solid-state phenomena, Esaki has received a host of honors and awards including the Morris N. Liebman Memorial Prize of the Institute of Radio Engineers in 1961, the Stuart Ballantine Medal of the Franklin Institute in 1961, the Medal of Honor of the Institute of Electrical and Electronic Engineers in 1991, and Japanese Nishina Memorial Award. He is also a member of many honorary societies including the National Academy of Sciences, the National Academy of Engineers, the American Academy of Arts and Sciences, and the Japan Academy.

In 1993, Esaki retired from IBM and accepted an appointment as president of Japan's Tsukuba University. The university had been established in 1973 to be the nation's premier institution of higher education in science and technology although it had never reached that lofty goal. Largely to help the university move more efficiently toward that objective, its board of trustees elected Esaki, its first academic scientist, as its new president.

Esaki married the former Masako Araki in 1959. They have three children, Nina, Anna, and Eugene. They retained their Japanese citizenship while living in the United States.

SELECTED WRITINGS BY ESAKI:

Periodicals

"New Horizons in Semimetal Alloys," *IEEE Spectrum,* Volume 3, 1966, pp. 74–80.
"Tunneling Studies on the Group 5 Semimetals and the 4–6 Semiconductors," *Journal of the Physical Society of Japan,* Supplement 21, 1966, pp. 589–97.

SOURCES:

Books

McGraw-Hill Modern Men of Science, Volume 1, McGraw-Hill, 1984, pp. 156–157.
McGraw-Hill Modern Scientists and Engineers, Volume 1, McGraw-Hill, 1980, pp. 343–344
Nobel Prize Winners, H. W. Wilson, 1987, pp. 304–306.
Weber, Robert L., *Pioneers of Science: Nobel Prize Winners in Physics,* American Institute of Physics, 1980, pp. 229–230.

Periodicals

Kumagai, Jean, "Esaki Leaves IBM to Become President of Japan's Tsukuba University," *Physics Today,* October 1992, pp. 111–112.
Pollack, Andrew, "Making a Difference: A Prize Winner in Research," *New York Times,* June 30, 1991, p. C12.

—*Sketch by David E. Newton*

Katherine Esau
1898-
Russian-born American botanist

Botanist Katherine Esau is best known for her research into the effects of viruses upon plant tissues, and her studies of plant tissue structures and physiology. Esau's definitive work, *Plant Anatomy,* was published in 1953 and revised in 1965. She received the National Medal of Science in 1989.

Esau was born in Ekaterinoslav, Russia, on April 3, 1898, and spent her formative years in that industrial city. She completed her first year of college before political events within the country led her parents to emigrate. Escaping from the Russian Revolution and the ensuing civil war, the Esaus left Russia in 1919 to take up residence in Germany. Katherine was able to complete her baccalaureate degree in Germany in 1922 before European political events following the first World War led her parents to move again. The family arrived in America in 1922 and settled in California. Esau obtained work with the Spreckels Sugar Company in the agricultural Salinas Valley, where she became a member of the experiment station staff trying to develop a strain of sugar beet resistant to a virus called "curly top." The disease caused the leafy bloom of the sugar beet plant to wilt, diminishing the size of the valuable white root. She worked in Salinas for six years before the company's experiment station staff was transferred to the campus of the University of California in Davis. Esau moved to Davis and continued her experimental work at the station, now under the aegis of the university's School of Agriculture. In 1928, she enrolled in the graduate department of botany at the university and three years later was awarded her doctorate degree.

In 1931 Esau became an instructor of botany and junior botanist at the University of California, Davis. She became a full professor of botany in 1949. In 1963, Esau transferred to the University of California's Santa Barbara campus, where she was named emeritus professor in 1965. She was a special lecturer at the Botanical and Plant Research Institute of the University of Texas in 1956, the Prather Lecturer at Harvard University in 1960, a national lecturer for Sigma Xi in 1965 and 1966, a lecturer at the J. C. Walker Conference on Plant Pathology at the University of Wisconsin, Madison, in 1968, and the John Wesley Powell Lecturer at the American Academy of Art and Science in 1973. Esau was a Guggenheim fellow in 1940.

Esau's research into plant viruses focused on how viruses effect the structure and development of a plant's food-conducting tissue known as the phloem. This research enabled her to distinguish between primary and secondary viral symptoms, allowing studies of viral damage to specific plant tissues to be conducted. In addition, Esau clarified the development phases of plant tissues, particularly the sieve tubes which serve to move solutes throughout a plant. Her research provided an impetus to phloem study in America.

Esau has published more than 160 papers and five books. She was elected to the National Academy of Sciences in 1971 and the Swedish Royal Academy in 1971. She is a member of the American Philosophical Society, American Academy of Art and Science, International Society of Plant Morphologists and the Botanical Society of America (she served as the organization's president in 1951).

SELECTED WRITINGS BY ESAU:

Books

Plant Anatomy, Wiley, 1953, 2nd edition, 1965.
Anatomy of Seed Plants, Wiley, 1960.
Plants, Viruses and Insects, Harvard University Press, 1961.

—Sketch by Benedict A. Leerburger

Thelma Estrin
1924-
American engineer

Thelma Estrin has contributed to science through her endeavors in the application of computer technology to neurophysiological research. She is currently Professor Emerita at the University of California at Los Angeles (UCLA), having retired in 1991 as Assistant Dean of the School of Engineering and Applied Sciences. Until 1990, she also served as Director of the Department of Engineering and Science at the UCLA School of Continuing Education. Estrin developed methods of utilizing the brain's electrical signals, as measured by computers, to study information processing in humans and animals. Her innovations have been further developed by medical researchers, and are widely used in the delivery of health care. Applications include the creation of internal brain maps of patients based on external imaging prior to surgery, and the identification of epileptic foci in the brain. For this work she received the 1981 Society of Women Engineers Achievement Award, which cited her "outstanding contributions to the field of biomedical engineering, in particular neurophysiological research through application of computer science."

Estrin was born in New York City on February 21, 1924. She received all of her higher education at the University of Wisconsin, earning a bachelor of science degree in 1948, a master of science the following year, and her doctorate degree in electrical engineering in 1951. Her association with UCLA began in 1960, when she accepted a position as Resident Engineer with the Health Sciences Center at the University. She held this position for a decade. In 1970, she was named Director of the Data Processing Laboratory of the Brain Research Institute. Ten years later, Estrin received a full professorship at UCLA's Computer Sciences Department.

In 1982, Estrin was appointed Director of the Division of Electronics, Computer and Systems Engineering at the National Science Foundation, a position she held for two years. She then was named Assistant Dean of the School of Engineering and Applied Sciences, and Director of the Department of Engineering and Sciences. Both of these appointments occurred in 1984. Estrin was a Fulbright Fellow with the Weizmann Institute of Science in Rehovot, Israel in 1963.

She was also a member of the Board of Trustees for the Aerospace Corporation from 1979 to 1982 (the first woman to hold that position), and served on the Army Sciences Board from 1980 to 1982; the National Institutes of Health Biotechnology Resources Review Committee from 1981 to 1986; the National Research Council (NRC) Board of Telecommunications and Computer Applications in 1982; and the NRC Energy Engineering Board from 1984 to 1989.

Promotes Advancement of Women Scientists

In addition, Estrin has served as President of the Biomedical Engineering Society and Executive Vice President of the Institute for Electrical and Electronics Engineers. She was the first woman to be certified as a Clinical Engineer. Estrin has been a leader in the application of engineering to neurophysiology. She also helped build the first computer in the Middle East in 1954. She continues to actively promote the inclusion and advancement of women in scientific and technological fields. "Most of the decisions we make today are based on technology. Women have to be able to contribute to technology and be leaders in the field," Estrin said in an interview. She also believes women generally approach and solve problems differently than men. "Women take more of a system view. They are more concerned with how their work is related to that of others, and how their work affects society."

SOURCES:

Estrin, Thelma, interview with Karen Withem conducted March 23, 1994.

—Sketch by Karen Withem

Ulf von Euler
1905-1983
Swedish physiologist

Ulf von Euler devoted his life to searching for the chemical signals that control physiological processes. In a career spanning six decades and during which he published four hundred and sixty-five scientific papers, von Euler achieved remarkable success. While still in his twenties, he discovered both substance P and prostaglandin, two important compounds that have since been studied extensively. Prostaglandins have become valuable to doctors for the treatment of many disorders, and may be used to treat blood pressure problems, infertility, peptic ulcers, and asthma. Martin A. Wasserman, in *American Pharmacy,* wrote on the significance of prostaglandins to modern medicine, stating that "'Prostaglandin' signifies more to scientists today than any medical term since cortisone. For millions of people around the world, prostaglandins hold the promise of relief from an extraordinary range of physical discomforts and life-threatening illnesses." In addition, von Euler became the first person to isolate and identify noradrenaline, a key transmitter of nerve impulses which control such involuntary functions as the heartbeat. For the later accomplishment, he was awarded the 1970 Nobel Prize in physiology or medicine.

Ulf Svante von Euler was born on February 7, 1905, in Stockholm, Sweden. From the beginning, he seemed destined for scientific greatness. His father, **Hans von Euler-Chelpin**, was a chemist who received the 1929 Nobel Prize for research into the role of enzymes in sugar fermentation. Von Euler's mother, Astrid Cleve von Euler, was a professor of botany, and his grandfather, Per Teodor Cleve, was a chemist who discovered the elements holmium and thulium. Moreover, von Euler was also a distant relative of the famous eighteenth-century mathematician, Leonhard Euler.

Discovers Substance P and Prostaglandins

With the help of his father, von Euler coauthored his first scientific paper when he was just seventeen years old. He went on to receive a medical degree from the Karolinska Institute in Stockholm in 1930. That same year, with the aid of a Rockefeller Fellowship, von Euler traveled to London to work in the laboratory of **Henry Hallett Dale**, who would himself win a Nobel Prize in 1936 for discoveries relating to the chemical transmission of nerve impulses. At the time von Euler arrived, one particular compound—acetylcholine—was the focus of most of the study in Dale's laboratory.

It was while von Euler was conducting an experiment involving acetylcholine that he made his first significant observation. He noticed that a section of rabbit intestine would contract whenever it was exposed to an intestinal extract. Surprisingly, though, the addition of atropine to the extract fluid did not suppress the contraction, as was expected. Young von Euler exuberantly declared that he had discovered a new biologically active substance—a bold claim that was soon borne out.

Along with John H. Gaddum, a senior assistant at the lab, von Euler spent the next few months systematically studying the effects of this newly identified compound. The two men demonstrated that extracts of brain would also contract the rabbit gut, and that the extracts that accomplished this result also had the effect of lowering the blood pressure as well. In order to carry out their investigations, the men used a purified preparation, abbreviated "P." Thus, quite unintentionally, the chemical agent causing these effects became known as Substance P. Back in Sweden, von Euler established that this substance had the properties of a polypeptide, a molecular chain of amino acids (the building blocks of proteins).

Von Euler returned to the Karolinska Institute, where he was made an assistant professor of pharmacology and physiology. In 1939, he was named professor and chairman of the physiology department there, a position in which he remained until his retirement in 1971.

In 1934, von Euler made the second most important discovery of his career. While continuing his tests on different kinds of tissue extracts, he found that extracts of sheep vesicular gland dramatically lowered blood pressure when injected into animals. He realized that some unknown factor in the extracts was exerting a powerful physiological effect. Human seminal fluid also seemed to contain this unidentified substance. Soon it became clear that the factor was a fatty acid. Von Euler dubbed it prostaglandin, in the mistaken belief that it originated in the prostate gland.

During the 1930s, von Euler followed up this finding, describing methods for extracting the compound, as well as defining its basic properties. However, it was not until the late 1950s that von Euler's protegé at the Karolinska Institute, **Sune Karl Bergs-**

tröm, used newly developed technology to achieve the first purification of a prostaglandin. Von Euler later wrote in the scientific journal *Progress in Lipid Research,* that "a discovery is in principle like an invention, or even a piece of art, in the sense that the result is greater than the sum of its parts. . . . It is sometimes said that the prostaglandins lay dormant for some 20 years after their discovery. This is not exactly true, since Sune Bergström took over in 1945 where I left it, and with consummate skill and perseverance conducted the chemical work to isolation and identification, thus starting the second stage of the prostaglandin history." Subsequent research revealed that prostaglandins are not a single substance, but a group of chemical compounds that perform a variety of jobs throughout the body, including playing a major role in reproduction. For his contributions to the field, Bergström was one of the recipients of the 1982 Nobel Prize in medicine or physiology.

Isolates and Identifies Noradrenaline

Meanwhile, von Euler continued the search for chemical transmitters that allow nerve cells to communicate. The idea that such neurotransmitters might exist had been proposed as early as 1905, but it was not until forty-one years later that von Euler succeeded in detecting a critical one in the sympathetic nervous system, which controls such automatic actions as the body's response to stress. He had already observed that certain biological extracts seemed to contain a substance that was similar to adrenaline, yet different in some of its actions. Von Euler set about pinpointing this substance, which he soon established to be noradrenaline (also called norepinephrine).

Later, von Euler investigated the way certain nerve endings store and release noradrenaline. Other of his studies dealt with the role of chemical agents in regulating respiration, circulation, and blood pressure. It was for his ground-breaking experiments involving noradrenaline that von Euler shared the 1970 Nobel Prize with **Julius Axelrod** of the United States and **Bernard Katz** of Great Britain, two other prominent figures in the study of chemical transmitters.

Von Euler was not only an eminent researcher, however; he was also known as a fine teacher who nurtured the curiosity of his pupils. An editorial which he wrote for the American journal *Circulation* sums up his approach to teaching and to science: "There are few things as rewarding for a scientist as having young students starting their research work and finding that they have . . . made an original observation. . . . the pleasure of witnessing the progress of the young starting fresh is one, which [the scientist] has every reason to feel happy about and where he can assist by means of his experience. . . .

We must always guard the liberties of the mind and remember that some degree of heresy is often a sign of health in spiritual life."

Von Euler was a member of the Swedish Academy of Sciences, as well as chief editor of the journal *Acta Physiologica Scandinavica* for many years. His international reputation was solidified by numerous awards, including the Order of the North Star in Sweden, the Cruzeiro do Sul in Brazil, the Pahnes Academiques in France, and the Grand Cross Al Merito Civil in Spain, as well as the Nobel Prize. Few scientists have been as closely identified with the Nobel Prize as von Euler; not only did he win one himself but so did his father, his mentor, and his protegé. Von Euler served as president of the Nobel Foundation from 1966 until 1975.

Von Euler married his first wife, the former Jane Sodenstierna, on April 12, 1930. They were divorced in 1957, and he subsequently married Dagmar Cronstedt on August 20, 1958. He was the father of four children: two sons, Leo and Christopher, and two daughters, Ursula and Marie. Von Euler died of complications following open heart surgery on March 10, 1983, in Stockholm.

SELECTED WRITINGS BY VON EULER:

Books

"Neurotransmission in the Adrenergic Nervous System," in *The Harvey Lectures,* Academic Press, 1961, pp. 43–65.
(With Rune Eliasson) *Prostaglandins,* Academic Press, 1967.
(With Bengt Pernow) *Substance P,* Raven Press, 1977.
"Pieces in the Puzzle," in *The Excitement and Fascination of Science,* Volume 2, Annual Reviews, 1978, pp. 674–86.

Periodicals

Editorial, *Circulation,* December, 1962, pp. 1233–34.
"Prostaglandin Historical Remarks," in *Journal of Progress in Lipid Research,* edited by Ralph T. Holman, Volume 20, 1981.

SOURCES:

Books

A Biographical Encyclopedia of Scientists, Volume 2, Facts on File, 1981, p. 815.
Modern Scientists and Engineers, Volume 1, McGraw-Hill, 1980, pp. 349–51.

Periodicals

American Pharmacy, June, 1979.
Stjärne, L., "Ulf von Euler," *The Physiologist,* October, 1983, pp. 282–3.

—*Sketch by Linda Wasmer Smith*

Hans von Euler-Chelpin
1873-1964
German-born Swedish biochemist

Hans von Euler-Chelpin described the role of enzymes in the process of fermentation and also researched vitamins, tumors, enzymes, and coenzymes. He was an important contributor in the discovery of the structure of certain vitamins. In 1929, he shared the Nobel Prize in chemistry with **Arthur Harden** for their research on the fermentation of sugar and enzymes. Euler-Chelpin's research has far-reaching implications in the fields of nutrition and medicine.

Hans Karl Simon August von Euler-Chelpin was born in Augsburg in the Bavarian region of Germany on February 15, 1873, to Rigas, a captain in the Royal Bavarian Regiment, and Gabrielle (Furtner) von Euler-Chelpin. His mother was related to the Swiss mathematician Leonhard Euler. Shortly after his birth, Euler-Chelpin's father was transferred to Munich and Euler-Chelpin lived with his grandmother in Wasserburg for a time. After his early education in Munich, Würzburg, and Ulm, he entered the Munich Academy of Painting in 1891 intending to become a artist. The problems of pigmentation led him to change his professional interest to science.

In 1893, Euler-Chelpin enrolled at the University of Munich to study physics with **Max Planck** and Emil Warburg. He also studied organic chemistry with **Emil Fischer** and A. Rosenheim, after which he worked with **Walther Nernst** at the University of Göttingen on problems in physical chemistry. This post-doctoral work in the years 1896 to 1897 was undertaken after Euler-Chelpin received his doctorate in 1895 from the University of Berlin.

The summer of 1897 was the first of several that Euler-Chelpin spent in apprentice roles in Stockholm and in Berlin. He served as an assistant to **Svante Arrhenius** in his laboratory at the University of Stockholm, becoming a privatdocent (unpaid tutor) there in 1899. Returning to Germany that summer, he studied with **Eduard Buchner** and Jacobus Van't Hoff in Berlin until 1900. His studies during this period centered on physical chemistry, which was receiving a great deal of attention at that time in both Germany and Sweden. Recognition came early to Euler-Chelpin for his work. He received the Lindblom Prize from Germany in 1898.

Interest Continues in Organic Chemistry

It was evident that there were new opportunities in organic chemistry. The new equipment used to measure properties could be applied to the complexities of chemical changes that took place in organisms. Euler-Chelpin's interests, therefore, shifted to organic chemistry. He visited the laboratories of others working in the field, such as Arthur Hantzsch and Johannes Thiele in Germany and G. Bertrand in Paris. These contacts contributed to his developing interest in fermentation.

In 1902, Euler-Chelpin became a Swedish citizen and in 1906 he was appointed professor of general and organic chemistry at the University of Stockholm, where he remained until his retirement in 1941. By 1910, Euler-Chelpin was able to present the fermentation process and enzyme chemistry into a systematic relationship with existing chemical knowledge. His book, *The Chemistry of Enzymes,* was first published in 1910 and again in several later editions.

In spite of being a Swedish citizen, Euler-Chelpin served in the German army during World War I, fulfilling his teaching obligations for six months of the year and military service for the remaining six. In the winter of 1916–1917 he took part in a mission to Turkey, a German ally during World War I, to accelerate the production of munitions and alcohol. He also commanded a bomber squadron at the end of the war.

Focuses on the Role of Enzymes in Fermentation

After the war, Euler-Chelpin began his research into the chemistry of enzymes, particularly in the role they played in the fermentation process. This study was important because enzymes are the catalysts for biochemical reactions in plant and animal organisms. An integral aspect of Euler-Chelpin's work with enzymes was to identify each substrate (the molecule upon which an enzyme acted) in the reaction. He succeeded in demonstrating that two fragments (hexose) that split from the sugar molecule were disparate in energy. He further illustrated that the less energetic fragment, which is attached to the phosphate, is destroyed in the process. Apart from tracing the phosphate through the fermentation sequence, Euler-Chelpin detailed the chemical makeup of cozymase, a non-protein constituent involved in cellular respiration.

In 1929, Euler-Chelpin was awarded the Nobel Prize in chemistry, which he shared with Arthur Harden "for their investigations on the fermentation of sugar and of fermentative enzymes." The presenter of the award noted that fermentation was "one of the most complicated and difficult problems of chemical research." The solution to the problem made it possible, the presenter continued, "to draw important conclusions concerning carbohydrate metabolism in general in both the vegetable and the animal organism."

In 1929, Euler-Chelpin became the director of the Vitamin Institute and Institute of Biochemistry at the University of Stockholm, which was founded jointly by the Wallenburg Foundation and the Rockefeller Foundation. Although he retired from teaching in 1941, he continued research for the remainder of his life. In 1935 he had turned his attention to the biochemistry of tumors and developed, through his collaboration with George de Hevesy, a technique for labeling the nucleic acids present in tumors which subsequently made it possible to trace their behavior. He also helped elucidate the function of nicotinamide and thiamine in compounds which are metabolically active.

Euler-Chelpin was twice married, each time to a woman who assisted him in his research. His first wife, Astrid Cleve, was the daughter of P. T. Cleve, a professor of chemistry at the University of Uppsala. She helped him in his early research in fermentation. They married in 1902, had five children, and divorced in 1912. Euler-Chelpin married Elisabeth, Baroness Ugglas in 1913, with whom he had four children. This marriage lasted for fifty-one years. A son by his first wife, **Ulf von Euler**, later also won a Nobel Prize. His award was made in 1970 in the field of medicine or physiology for his work on neurotransmitters and the nervous system.

Euler-Chelpin was awarded the Grand Cross for Federal Services with Star from Germany in 1959. He also received numerous honorary degrees from universities in Europe and America. He held memberships in Swedish science associations, as well as many foreign professional societies. He is the author of more than eleven hundred research papers and over half a dozen books. Euler-Chelpin died on November 6, 1964, in Stockholm, Sweden.

SELECTED WRITINGS BY EULER-CHELPIN:

Books

(With Paul Lindner) *Chemie der Hefe und der Alkoholischen Gärung,* Akademische Verlagsgesellschaft, 1915.
Chemie der Enzyme, J. F. Bergman, 1920–1927.
Biokatalysatoren, Enke, 1930.

(With Bol Skarzynski) *Biochemie der Tumoren,* Enke, 1942.

(With Leo Heller) *Studies on Experimental Rheumatism,* 1951.

SOURCES:

Books

Gillispie, Charles Coulston, editor, *Dictionary of Scientific Biography,* Volume 4, Scribner, 1972.

—*Sketch by Vita Richman*

Alice Evans
1881-1975
American microbiologist

The eminent bacteriologist Alice Evans was a pioneer both as a scientist and as a woman. She discovered that brucellae bacteria, contracted from farm animals and their milk, was the cause of undulant fever in humans, and responded by fighting persistently for the pasteurization of milk, eventually achieving success. She was the first woman president of the Society of American Bacteriologists (now American Society of Microbiology). Although marginalized early in her career, Evans overcame many obstacles and lived to see her discoveries repeatedly confirmed. She had a major impact on microbiology in the United States and the world and received belated honors for her numerous achievements in the field.

Alice Catherine Evans was born on January 29, 1881, in the predominantly Welsh town of Neath, Pennsylvania, the second of William Howell and Anne Evans' two children. William Howell, the son of a Welshman, was a surveyor, teacher, farmer, and Civil War veteran. Anne Evans, also Welsh, emigrated from Wales at the age of 14. Evans received her primary education at the local district school. She went on to study at the Susquehanna Institute at Towanda, Pennsylvania. She wished to go to college but, unable to afford tuition, took a post as a grade school teacher. After teaching for four years she enrolled in a tuition-free, two year course in nature study at the Cornell University College of Agriculture. The course was designed to help teachers in rural areas inspire an appreciation of nature in their students, but it changed the path of Evans' life and she never returned to the schoolroom.

Begins Research on Bacteria

At Cornell Evans discovered her love of science and received a B.S. degree in agriculture. She chose to pursue an advanced degree in bacteriology and was recommended by her professor at Cornell for a scholarship at the University of Wisconsin. She was the first woman to receive the scholarship, and under the supervision of E. G. Hastings she studied bacteriology with a focus on chemistry. In 1910 she received a Master of Science degree in bacteriology from Wisconsin. Although encouraged to pursue a Ph.D., Evans accepted a research position with the University of Wisconsin Agriculture Department's Dairy Division and began researching cheese-making methods in 1911. In 1913 she moved with the division to Washington, DC, and served as bacteriological technician in a team effort to isolate the sources of contamination of raw cow's milk which were then believed to be external.

On her own, Evans began to focus on the intrinsic bacteria in raw cow's milk. By 1917 she had found that the bacterium responsible for undulant or "Malta" fever was similar in important respects to one associated with spontaneous abortions in cows, and that the two bacteria produced similar clinical effects in guinea pigs. Prevailing wisdom at the time held that many bovine diseases could not be transmitted to humans. That year she presented her findings to the Society of American Bacteriologists; her ideas were received with skepticism that seems to have been more due to her gender and level of education than her data.

In 1918 Evans was asked to join the staff of the U.S. Public Health Service by director George McCoy. There she was absorbed in the study of meningitis. Although she was unable to continue her milk studies during this time, support for Evans' findings was trickling in from all over the world. By the early 1920s it was recognized that undulant fever and Malta fever were due to the same bacteria, but there was still resistance to the idea that humans could contract brucellosis by drinking the milk of infected cows. Because the symptoms of brucellosis were so similar to those of influenza, typhoid fever, tuberculosis, malaria, and rheumatism, it was not often correctly diagnosed. Evans began documenting cases of the disease among humans in the U.S. and South Africa, but it was not until 1930, after brucellosis had claimed the lives of a number of farmers' children in the U.S., that public health officials began to recognize the need for pasteurization.

In 1922, Evans herself, like many others who researched these organisms, became ill with brucellosis. Her condition was chronic, plaguing her on and off for almost 23 years, and perhaps providing her with new insight into the disease. As the problem of chronic illness became widespread, Evans began surveying different parts of the U.S. to determine the numbers of infected cows from whom raw milk was sold, and the numbers of chronic cases resulting from the milk.

Argues for Pasteurization

In 1925 Evans was asked to serve on the National Research Council's Committee on Infectious Abortion. In this capacity Evans argued for the pasteurization of milk, a practice that later became an industry standard. In recognition of her achievements, Evans was in 1928 elected the first woman president of the American Society of Bacteriologists. In 1930 she was chosen, along with Robert E. Buchanan of Iowa State University, as an American delegate to the First International Congress of Bacteriology in Paris. She attended the second Congress in London in 1936 and was again able to travel widely in Europe. She returned to the United States and eventually was promoted to senior bacteriologist at the Public Health Service, by then called the National Institute of Health. By 1939 she had changed her focus to immunity to streptococcal infections and in 1945 she retired. Evans, who never married, died at the age of 94 on September 5, 1975, in Alexandria, Virginia, following a stroke.

SOURCES:

Books

Kass-Simon, G., and P. Farnes, *Women of Science,* Indiana University Press, 1990, p. 278.

O'Hern, Elizabeth M., *Profiles of Pioneer Women Scientists,* Acropolis, 1985, pp. 127–138.

Siegel, J. P., and R. T. Finley, *Women in the Scientific Search,* Scarecrow, 1985, pp. 67–70.

Periodicals

"Alice Evans, 94, Bacteriologist, Dies," *Washington Post,* September 8, 1975, p. B4.

MacKaye, Milton, "Undulant Fever," *Ladies Home Journal,* December, 1944, pp. 23, 69–70.

O'Hern, Elizabeth M., "Alice Evans, Pioneer Microbiologist," *American Society for Microbiology News,* September, 1973.

—*Sketch by John Henry Dreyfuss*

James C. Evans
1900-
American engineer and government official

James C. Evans is one of America's first outstanding African American engineers. After taking his college and postgraduate degrees at Massachusetts Institute of Technology, Evans became an award-winning researcher in electronics as well as an inventor and patent-holder. He came to prominence during World War II as a high-ranking civilian aide to the U.S. Secretary of War, after which he taught electrical engineering at Howard University.

James Carmichael Evans was born in Gallatin, Tennessee, on July 1, 1900. When he was eighteen years old, he enlisted in the U.S. Army and served as an instructor in the Student Army Training Corps. After receiving his B.A. from Roger Williams University in Memphis, Tennessee, in 1921, he realized that he was not fully prepared to go on to graduate school and pursue a professional technical career. He then re-enrolled at the undergraduate level at the Massachusetts Institute of Technology in Cambridge. Four years later, in 1925, he graduated with a B.S., and in 1926 he received his master's degree. He took a job in electrical and construction engineering upon graduating and also taught for a year at the Booker T. Washington High School in Miami, Florida. In 1928 Evans accepted a position he would hold until 1937. He was named professor of technical industries at West Virginia State College as well as its director of the trade and technical division. The year he joined West Virginia State College was also the year he married his wife, Roselline, with whom he later had two children, James and Rose. In 1937 he became administrative assistant to that university's president, and he remained there until 1942. With the outbreak of World War II in Europe, Evans took on the responsibility of coordinating pilot training programs for civilians and military personnel, and in 1941 he became a technical training specialist with the War Production Board. In 1943, however, he moved from the technical side of things when he accepted a position as a civilian aide to the U.S. Secretary of War. After war's end he remained connected with the federal government through 1949, serving Secretary of Defense Louis Johnson as his highest adviser on racial relations at a time when the Army, Navy, and Air Force were studying their personnel policies to assure equal treatment and opportunity for all their members. It was during these postwar years that he became affiliated with Howard University. He joined that university in 1946 as a professor of electrical engineering and remained there until his retirement in 1970.

Early in his career, Evans did research in pre-radar electronics, and in 1926 he received the Harmon Award for scientific research in electronics. He was also interested in aeronautical problems, and he held a patent on a method of using airplane exhaust gases to prevent ice from forming on aircraft. In 1953 Evans was given the Dorie Miller Foundation Award, and he also received the Career Service Award in 1959 from the National Civil Service League. He was a member of various professional organizations, including the National Institute of Science and the National Education Association, as well as several honor societies. He was also a widely known member of the National Technical Association and served as its national executive secretary for twenty consecutive years, from 1932 to 1952.

SOURCES:

Books

Christmas, Walter, editor, *Negroes in Public Affairs and Government,* Educational Heritage Inc., 1966, p. 334.

—*Sketch by Leonard C. Bruno*